ALMANACS OF AMERICAN WARS

WORLD WAR II
ALMANAC

VOLUME I

Keith D. Dickson

Facts On File
An imprint of Infobase Publishing

World War II Almanac

Copyright © 2008 Keith D. Dickson

Facts On File, Inc.
An imprint of Infobase Publishing
132 West 31st Street
New York NY 10001

Library of Congress Cataloging-in-Publication Data

Dickson, Keith D.
    World War II almanac / Keith D. Dickson.
       p. cm. — (Almanacs of American wars)
    Includes bibliographical references and index.
    ISBN 13: 978-0-8160-6297-3 (hc : alk. paper)
    1. World War, 1939–1945—Almanacs. 2. World War, 1939–1945—Chronology. 3. Almanacs, American. I. Title. II. Title: World War Two almanac. III. Title: World War 2 almanac.
    D731.D53 2008
    940.540973'03—dc22   2007011207

Text design by Erika K. Arroyo
Cover design by Pehrsson Design/Salvatore Luongo

Printed in the United States of America

VB Hermitage 10 9 8 7 6 5 4 3 2 1

 CONTENTS

VOLUME I

Dedication   v

Preface   vii

How the Almanac Is Organized   xi

Keep the Following in Mind   xii

History   1

Chronology of Key Events
October 28, 1922–August 7, 1944   38

VOLUME II

Chronology of Key Events
August 8, 1944–November 19, 1945   659

American Servicemen Awarded the
Medal of Honor in World War II   1156

Biographies of Key Leaders 1193

Glossary of Terms 1212

Glossary of Abbreviations 1221

Weapons 1223

Appendixes
I. Ship and Landing Craft Classifications 1232
II. Commands 1233
III. Composition of Divisions 1238
IV. U.S. Ground Combat Units by Division
and Regiment 1240
V. Losses: The Battle of the Atlantic 1244
VI. Enemy Aircraft Destroyed by the Army
Air Force during World War II 1245
VII. Casualties 1246
VIII. Maps 1247

Bibliography 1267

Index 1283

DEDICATION

This book is dedicated to Captain Edward J. Irving, 77th Bomber Squadron, Tenth Air Force. During a diversionary bombing mission against Araito Island in the Kuriles on June 9, 1945, Irving's B-25 bomber came under attack from both Japanese fighter aircraft and Soviet antiaircraft fire and crashed near Cape Lopatka on the Kamchatka Peninsula in the Soviet Union. War is filled with tragic ironies that often make the losses bitterer still. Captain Irving and his crew were downed when they came under attack by a military unit of the Soviet Union—neutral in the Pacific war but an active partner in the war in Europe. The bomber was lost just a few days before Tenth Air Force halted all combat missions.

Captain Irving was an only child. He lies at rest next to his mother and father in his family cemetery in Appomattox County, Virginia, on the farm where he was raised. Captain Irving, like so many other young men who went to war and never came back, left behind an enormous number of unfulfilled hopes and promises; his parents, who spent the rest of their lives on the farm, undoubtedly often pondered what might have been.

I have the 1945 Esso Oil Company map of the Pacific his parents used to track their son's progress in the war and I used it as a reference while working on this project. Their wishes for his safe return undoubtedly pressed on their hearts every time they took out the map to follow the war news. Each time I took out the map to locate specific places, Captain Irving was on my mind as well.

May this American's sense of duty in serving his country inspire others to do the same, both today and in the years to come.

PREFACE

This is a time when we hear a great deal about the Greatest Generation, the Americans who came of age in the Great Depression and then went on to serve in the fields, the factories, and the Armed Forces to defeat a mortal threat. World War II is on everyone's mind through films, books, and a grand monument on the Mall in Washington, D.C. Part of this belated recognition and adulation is natural as the years pass. But there is a sense of urgency to honor this group of Americans, especially those who faced the enemy in combat. There is a feeling that when the World War II generation passes, something will also pass from America, because within these men and women exist certain qualities and ideals that have been bled from the consciousness of most Americans.

The victory achieved in World War II is one of America's proudest memories and a touchstone of national identity. This Almanac is an attempt to tell the story of arms and men in a different form. It is a chronicle of the daily events that represented the collective experience of tens of thousands of Americans in different parts of the world who participated in combat operations against the enemy. By examining these daily events, the reader can gain an appreciation for the scope and complexity of that experience. There are great battles included, to be sure—Midway, Wake, Guadalcanal, Tarawa, the Bulge, D-day, Okinawa, Savo Islands, Leyte and Luzon, Okinawa, Saipan, Leyte Gulf, and the Coral Sea. But in between the great battles there are the dangerous daily tasks that have to be done. Day after day, as this Almanac recounts, young men climbed into a tank, a fighter, or a bomber, or took watch on ship, or rolled upright from the protective ground with bodies that felt like lead to face another day of uncertainty.

In some portions of the chronology, there is a repetitive sameness about the missions, especially some air and naval missions. But in reality these missions were never routine. Danger was a constant companion, not just from the enemy, but from the weather, mechanical failure, fatigue, fear, and a host of other uncertainties that constantly weighed on the mind. Yet as the chronology shows, the same men, the same crews, and the same support organizations pursued the mission day after day. The entries in the chronology, then, represent men both collectively and individually facing fears, gathering their courage, and doing what was required of them. More often than not, they did the impossible.

Although struggling futilely and mightily to stay out of war, the United States, once involved, sought to win the war as quickly as possible and return to peacetime pursuits. All wartime decisions were made with this goal in mind. Americans were then, and remain today, impatient for results and insistent on a rapid resolution of the crisis. But Americans in 1941 were amateurs at warfare, lacking both expertise in large-scale operations and an appreciation for the complexities of combat fought simultaneously on land, air, and sea. Their tanks and weapons were inferior and their ships and aircraft outdated. What usually took a generation to accomplish, Americans accomplished in a matter of years, applying the country's vast human and material resources to produce the most modern and dominant military force ever created. But this capability was paid for through bitter experience. National guardsmen fought the Japanese on New Guinea while Old Breed marines battled for Guadalcanal. The navy, with little more than raw courage and instinct, fought outnumbered and challenged the enemy for supremacy of the seas in the South Pacific. The U.S. Coast Guard and the merchant marine faced the U-boat menace on the east coast of the United States with little more than prayers. The tiny regular army formed the nucleus of the troops that landed on the beaches of North Africa. The chronology reveals this period of weakness as the limited military resources of the nation are expended at a fearful rate between late 1941 and throughout 1942. But as time passes, the days show a growing capability as vast, air, naval, and ground forces are assembled and employed against the enemy's defenses in Europe and the Pacific starting in late 1943 and growing ever stronger every month after that.

The story of the United States at war from 1941 to 1945 is one of blood and bone and will pitted against a determined enemy—pure attrition warfare. The enemy, believing superior military skill would eventually win out over the application of mass numbers, is willing to fight a prolonged battle of attrition. But it is a battle that cannot be won; inexorably, American superiority in resources proves decisive. This is the American way of war that brought victory, but also the agony of the Hürtgen Forest, Okinawa, Metz, Cassino, Peleliu, and Anzio. But success was undeniable and the battlefields of World War II were the training ground for the generals who would lead new generations of soldiers onto new battlefields in Korea and Vietnam. They would seek the same approach to victory, but with far different results.

The war in the air in Europe and the Pacific followed a similar attritional approach. Air power advocates believed a nation could be brought to its knees through air bombardment alone. The United States was the only nation with the industrial capacity to put this theory into action. As a result, vast numbers of American bombers attacked the cities and industrial areas of Germany, Austria, and Japan. Despite this intense and continuous bombing, growing in intensity and effectiveness each year, Germany and Japan were unbowed. The bomber crews were subjected to fearful losses until American military production capacity and technology could develop fighter escorts capable of protecting the bombers throughout their entire mission. The role of air power was undeniable in establishing the air supremacy in 1944 that was essential for the ground war in Europe to succeed. Japanese garrisons were neutralized from the air and, after 1943, few Japanese aircraft ever threatened American ground forces. However, air power alone could not stop the major Japanese ground offensive in China in 1944, as the American commander of the Fourteenth Air Force had promised.

The emergence of the aircraft carrier as both the dominant combat ship and the most versatile operational platform is seen in the role carriers played in antisubmarine warfare in the Atlantic as well as their role in overcoming Japan's early advantage in deploying carrier aircraft against fleet forces. Carriers not only played a decisive role in eliminating enemy fleets but also were essential for supporting ground operations in later stages of the war in the Pacific.

Undersea warfare was also telling. U.S. unrestricted submarine warfare in the Pacific combined with the antisubmarine warfare in the Atlantic secured the means to victory. Without secure sea lines of communication in the Atlantic, the invasion of the continent of Europe was impossible; and without the destruction of Japan's sea lines of communication in the Pacific, no decisive advance into the inner defensive ring protecting the Japanese home islands was possible.

The role of the Marine Corps in the Pacific war was invaluable. Amphibious warfare techniques were perfected, but at a high cost. Nevertheless, marines fought with unsurpassed courage and tenacity in every battle against the Japanese. From the commanding general down to the marine rifleman, every man had a sense of responsibility for achieving victory. Well trained and superbly led, marines made the difference in numerous battles whose names are now spoken with a mixture of awe and reverence: Tarawa, Iwo Jima, Guadalcanal.

Airborne warfare also proved its worth, establishing a new capability of mobility and versatility in warfare. No soldiers were more aggressive or capable than the paratroopers who descended from the sky and, after landing, fought for days and often weeks with minimum support as infantrymen. Fighting on the rocky hills of Sicily, the bocage of Normandy, the frozen fields of Bastogne, in the jungles of Leyte, or amid the rubble of Corregidor, the American paratrooper proved to be an indomitable force, acting with initiative and courage in the most difficult situations. It is not surprising that the first American units to take on occupation duties were the 82nd Airborne Division in Germany and the 17th Airborne Division in Japan.

Army-Navy rivalry had a hand in crippling the war effort (the air force at the time was a part of the army). Neither service would accept working under the orders and overall direction of the other service. Therefore in the Pacific, an army theater of war existed under an army general (Southwest Pacific Area under General MacArthur) and a navy theater of war existed under a navy admiral (Pacific Ocean Areas under Admiral Nimitz). Although each commander had other service components under his direct command, the coordination between theaters was limited and far less effective than if the entire fore had been employed as a coherent whole. Only when the war was nearly over was a single commander (General MacArthur) appointed to control ground, air, and sea operations in the Pacific. The duplication of effort often led to the misapplication of forces and a lack of coordination as each theater pursued a different operational approach to achieve the same strategic goal.

The animosity between Great Britain and the United States over the strategic direction of the war and the employment of forces was also a problem. Acutely aware of their amateurism early in the war, Americans were stung by the British air of superiority and confidence. But as the preponderance of forces and capabilities shifted to the Americans after 1943, the mood changed and Americans came to dominate the partnership. The struggle over the direction of the main effort (whether British- or American-dominated) and the rivalry between British and American commanders created less and less cohesiveness and coordination. By 1945, the British and Americans were fighting two separate wars in Europe.

American general Joseph J. Stilwell's dislike of the British and his tumultuous relationship with Generalissimo Chiang Kai-shek of China hindered overall coordination of efforts in the China-India-Burma Theater. China demanded an ever larger share of resources from an already limited capability (supplies had to be flown by cargo aircraft over the Himalaya Mountains), and it was clear that British strategic goals in the theater were quite different from American goals for China. As in Europe, by 1945 the United States and Great Britain were fighting two separate wars in Burma and China.

At the strategic level, the partnership between American president Franklin D. Roosevelt and British prime minister Winston Churchill was essential for Allied victory. Churchill, undoubtedly the greatest man of the 20th century, had saved Britain from defeat in the dark days of 1940 when American neutrality appeared unassailable, but he needed American power to save the day and rescue Europe. The partnership that was born kept the alliance together even as their commanders argued over strategy. The Anglo-American partnership began to fray as the emerging power of the Soviet Union clearly indicated the eclipse of the old order in Europe. Even as President Roosevelt sought to find accord with the Soviet leader Joseph Stalin, Churchill never abandoned his role as the conscience of the free world, warning the Americans in 1945 that political objectives to forestall Soviet dominance in Europe were far more crucial than military objectives.

With Roosevelt's death in April 1945, the new president, Harry S. Truman, took a far more practical approach to international affairs and came to see Churchill's point of view. Events by that time had moved far too fast; Churchill was voted out of power in July and the Soviets had firm control of Eastern Europe. Truman was left to deal with the Soviets alone, recasting the relationship later in 1945 in terms of give and take, with the underlying power of the atomic bomb always in the forefront.

The American experience in World War II validated the faith Americans had placed in their ideals, exemplified in the Four Freedoms articulated by President Roosevelt (freedom of speech, freedom of worship, freedom from fear, freedom from want). American confidence, justification, and optimism were at their height. But the aftermath of the war created new dynamics within the United States and placed the world on a new plane of action. Trouble loomed on the horizon in devastated Europe and China. Ahead were new and unforeseen crises that would challenge America's satisfaction with the victory it had obtained at such cost.

How the Almanac Is Organized

The vast size and scope of military operations create a need to show several events happening at the same time in the same general geographic area but without combining them all under one general heading. Therefore, the following organizational system has been set up to assist the reader.

The entries entitled **Atlantic** and **Pacific** deal largely with strategic decisions, plans, and meetings, as well as actions of major units (deployments or redeployments of forces intended for a strategic purpose) or strategic activities related to the region (the bombing of Japan or the German U-boat campaign). After each strategic entry are the subordinate theaters, such as the **Aleutians, Southwest Pacific Area (SWPA), European Theater of Operations (ETO), Mediterranean, China-Burma-India (CBI).** These entries usually describe the activities of fleets, numbered air forces, and land forces at the corps, army, and army group level. Below each theater are subordinate geographic regions: **New Guinea, Southern Pacific, Central Pacific, Italy, North Africa.** These entries address deployments and operations conducted in the region, and focus on specific combat actions of ships, aircraft, divisions, regiments, battalions, and companies and occasionally will even reach down to the individual soldier, sailor, or marine.

The chronology can create an impression of detachment from the reality of warfare. The events become sterile and monotonous, giving the impression that nothing much was happening. For most combat actions, however mundane they may appear, there is a cost in killed and wounded. I have shown these costs throughout the text where appropriate. It is often a grim and sometimes shocking tally, but essential to appreciating the level of danger and sacrifice that these Americans were willing to bear every day. I have also, wherever appropriate, moved from the impersonal operational picture of fleets, divisions, and air forces to the personal and immediate—people facing great danger or impossible circumstances and taking extraordinary action. These stories are drawn from the citations awarding individuals the highest American medal for valor—the

Medal of Honor. These men, often at the cost of their lives, experienced both the devastation and the exhilaration of combat. These portraits of American heroes, it is hoped, will keep the reader aware of the human dimension of warfare and acquaint the reader with men who have gained a measure of immortality for their deeds.

KEEP THE FOLLOWING IN MIND

The inclusion of specific events or actions is based on an intent to provide a representative overview of land, sea, and air operations and provide a comprehensive overview of events as they unfold each day across the globe. The decisions made for including items or summarizing events is a subjective decision and have been mine alone. Therefore any mistakes, omissions, or inaccuracies are mine alone.

Dates for certain events can vary in a global war. What is happening in the Pacific is hours ahead of what is happening in the Atlantic. The dates correspond to daylight operations. To cover periods of darkness where events carry into the early hours of the next day, the earlier date on which the action or activity began is always used. To alert the reader that events are occurring past midnight of the date cited, a sentence prefaced by the phrase "during the night" is used.

All U.S. Army and Navy aircraft are identified by name and type throughout the text (B-25 Mitchell, P-51 Mustang, SBD Dauntless, A-26 Invader). There are several exceptions, however. The B-17 Flying Fortress, the main heavy American bomber of the war, is simply identified as the B-17, mostly because the bomber was and is universally known by its type and not its name. The P-40 Warhawk fighter also is identified only by its type in the text for the same reason. The B-29 Superfortress is best known by its type, but in the text the name and type are not always included together.

There are discrepancies in sources concerning numbers of aircraft involved in some missions, reports of numbers of enemy aircraft shot down, and level of destruction of targets. Wherever possible an accurate determination of numbers was verified, but this was not always possible. Aircrews and pilots often made claims on enemy aircraft destroyed that, when compared to actual combat loss numbers discovered after the war, are far removed from reality. This reflects the fear and excitement of combat and is certainly understandable. To indicate where sources have been used that do not verify the numbers of enemy aircraft shot down or level of destruction of targets attacked, the entry is prefaced with "pilots report" or "aircrews report." This reflects the immediacy of the events rather than the absolute, historically accurate account.

The names of locations used in the chronology are from the original reports and therefore may not correspond to modern transliterations. This is especially true of China and southern Europe.

HISTORY

THE UNITED STATES AND EUROPE, 1936–1941

The United States emerged from the Great War in 1918 as a major world power, but the results failed to bring about the idealistic goals that Americans had wished for when the nation intervened in Europe in 1917. Observing the peace conference at Versailles, Americans had become disillusioned by the vengeful treatment of Germany and the establishment of a new European order dominated by Britain and France. The League of Nations, established by the Versailles Treaty, was intended to be an international body dedicated to preserving peace and settling disputes between nations without war. But this plan to mitigate the problems arising from the postwar settlement was rendered almost immediately impotent when in March 1920 the U.S. Senate rejected the Versailles Treaty. Although desiring peace in the aftermath of the War to End All Wars, America showed no interest in supporting any international actions to preserve the peace through the League of Nations. As a compromise, American foreign policy in the 1920s sought to take a leading role in fostering collective security through diplomacy and treaties.

Unfortunately, conditions for an enduring peace did not exist. Europe itself was a patchwork of new states, all weak and suspicious of each other. The two dominant post-war powers, France and Britain, were uncertain and cautious. France was fearful of a resurgent Germany and looked to Britain for security guarantees. Britain was unwilling to make any commitments that would lead to fighting another war on the continent. Germany, although a fledgling democracy, had not abandoned either nationalism or its long-standing tradition of the military playing a substantial role in government policy. The new Soviet Union had isolated itself from Europe, but its proclaimed goal of fostering worldwide socialist revolution caused fear and added to the general political turmoil.

The 1920s were a period of peace and prosperity for the United States. The problems of Europe and Asia seemed far away beyond protective oceans. Defense issues were unimportant and a general public hostility to military expenditures led successive Republican administrations to gain security guarantees through diplomacy. During this decade, a flurry of U.S.-sponsored treaties to reduce international tensions and promote peaceful relations dominated the foreign policy agenda. In November 1921, at the invitation of the United States, eight nations met in Washington to hear an extraordinary proposal. The nations would initiate an immediate program of disarmament, starting with a 10-year pledge not to build any major combat ships (battleships and heavy cruisers) and a drive to scrap combat ships to a total of 1.9 million tons until the ratio of all types of warships maintained in the fleets of the United States, Britain, and Japan reached a balance of 5:5:3, respectively. This proposal was ratified in the Five Power Treaty in 1922, with France and Italy joining the original three and each pledging to disarm to a lower ratio of 1:75. The signatories agreed to a 10-year holiday during which no major combat ships would be built. The treaty was to remain in effect until 1936, when signatories could give a two-year notice before leaving the agreement. The Japanese agreed to the treaty, but asked for additional security guarantees to accommodate their inferior status in major warships. Both the United States and Britain agreed not to fortify their possessions in the Pacific. For the United States, this meant that, with the exception of the Hawaiian Islands, the islands of Wake, Guam, the Philippines, and the Aleutians would have no further defensive improvements.

The Four Power Treaty, signed in 1921 between Britain, France, the United States, and Japan, was essentially a small League of Nations for Asia, in which each nation pledged to respect each signatory's rights in Asia, and to hold a joint conference in case of a dispute. If an outside power threatened the status quo in Asia, then the four nations would consult to find a mutually agreeable response. This led to the Nine Power Treaty in 1922, which bound the participating nations to respect the territorial integrity, sovereignty, and independence of China. The United States gained what it had sought: Japanese recognition of America's commitment to China and a reaffirmation of its Open Door policy, ensuring equal access of all nations to the China market.

These treaties eased tensions, but did not guarantee security for the United States. Although the Five Power Treaty limited large warships, it put no limits on destroyers, submarines, or light cruisers, which Japan, France, and Britain began to build at rapid rates between 1922 and 1930. During this period, for example, the United States built 11 warships while the Japanese built 125. The Nine Power Treaty had no provisions for actually protecting China in case of a violation of the treaty, so it was nothing more than an empty promise. The Four Power Treaty simply acknowledged the status quo in Asia, again with only vague references to consultations and meetings in case of threat or dispute.

A conference in Geneva in 1927 to seek further limits on smaller warships failed to achieve any agreements, but another diplomatic breakthrough was in the making. France and the United States announced that they were willing to enter into a mutual agreement to outlaw war and invited other nations to join. The August 1928 Pact of Paris (or the Kellogg-Briand Pact), signed by the United States and France along with 15 other nations, pledged to outlaw war as an instrument of national policy. Defensive war was still allowed—and exactly what constituted defensive war was not defined. Other nations eagerly joined the pact over the next few months, leading to a feeling of great satisfaction among Americans.

A disarmament conference in London in 1929 led to a treaty the following year, signed by Britain, France, Japan, the United States, and Italy, that imposed limits on certain categories of smaller warships. It also scrapped a number of existing large warships, and maintained the balance of major warships that existed under the original Five Power Treaty. Although on paper the United States had maintained its credibility, the reality was that other nations were already eclipsing America's naval power. The pursuit of security through international agreements was faltering. The following year, the Japanese campaign in Manchuria illustrated how little the treaties of the 1920s meant. At the 1932 World Disarmament Conference in Geneva, President Herbert Hoover attempted to reduce land armaments by one-third and the destruction of all offensive weapons (although what marked an offensive weapon from a defensive weapon was never clarified). Hoover's noble gesture failed in the light of events in Europe and in China. While the conference was going on, Japan attacked Shanghai; its indiscriminate bombing of civilians in the city shocked the world. Given these events, disarmament lost its cachet. On December 29, 1934, Japan gave its two-year notice that it would no longer be bound by the limits of the 1922 Five Power Treaty. Another naval conference in 1935 accomplished nothing. When the United States refused to meet Japanese demands for absolute parity in warships, the Japanese delegation walked out of the meeting. This ominous warning was compounded by an unsettling economic downturn and a series of troubling events in Europe.

The worldwide depression that began to take hold in the first years of the 1930s only aggravated existing social and political problems in Europe. As the depression worsened and popular discontent grew, it appeared that democratic governments were particularly helpless. Desperate, angry people began to turn to communism and authoritarian models for solutions. In Germany, Adolf Hitler was attacking the Versailles Treaty and receiving an enthusiastic response from sullen Germans eager to hear his words. Hitler focused on the frustrations and fears of the nation and promised to return Germany to its destined greatness as the dominant power in Europe. His dreams for the future, though, were tinged with hatred for inferior peoples who would not exist in the new order. Germany's path to its destiny lay to the east, in Russia; the Jews and the Slavs, who blocked that path, would have to be destroyed.

In 1933 Hitler became chancellor of Germany and immediately embarked on a program to end the nation's subservient position in Europe, withdrawing from the League of Nations in October. On March 16, 1935, Hitler announced that Germany had an air force and that he would reinstate conscription and build an army of 550,000 men, both actions in direct violation of the Versailles Treaty restrictions. The League Council condemned Germany, but took no action. In effect, the league had given Germany the approval to become a major power in Europe again. Faced with problems at home and uncertain of Hitler's motives, France and Britain could not mount an effective counter. Neither France nor Britain had the means to use military force without significant political and economic cost, and neither nation was willing to consider war unless it suffered a direct attack. These conditions gave Hitler the opportunity to take greater and greater risks.

Fearing that war in Europe was an absolute certainty in the near future, Congress took the initiative to avoid American involvement and establish the rights of a neutral nation. The Neutrality Act of 1935 authorized the president to declare nations at war belligerents and thereby forbid the sale or transportation of armaments or munitions to them. The president could declare that American citizens traveling on belligerent ships did so at their own risk. These measures were intended to prevent the United States from becoming entangled in the conflict.

Benito Mussolini, the Fascist dictator of Italy since 1922, saw his opportunity to defy the league and pursue his ambitions to restore Italian imperial power in the Horn of Africa. A clash between Italian and Ethiopian troops on December 5, 1934, led to a full-scale invasion on October 3, 1935. The United States enacted the Neutrality Act provisions and awaited further action from the League of Nations. The league declared Italy an aggressor, but hesitated to impose sanctions on commodities, such as oil, that would truly affect Italian actions. The United States decided to impose a moral embargo on Italy and asked for U.S. oil companies to restrict shipments to Italy voluntarily. On February 29, 1936, President Roosevelt received another neutrality bill from Congress and signed it into law. The Neutrality Act of 1936 extended the provisions of the previous act and added a provision that prevented the president from authorizing loans to belligerents.

Meanwhile, on March 7, 1936, Hitler seized the French-occupied Rhineland area that bordered France and Belgium. Again the league met and condemned Germany for violating the Versailles Treaty but, outside of talk, nothing happened. Undeterred by the weak international response, Italy completed its conquest in May of 1936. Withdrawing from the league, Italy signed a pact with Germany in October 1936. Hitler had been willing to go to war over the Rhineland, but now, having taken the measure of his opponents, Hitler decided to press his demands even more stridently.

The United States believed that as long as neutrality was maintained and the nation avoided any political commitments, events in Europe would have no effect on its interests. This belief held when the Spanish civil war began on July 18, 1936. General Francisco Franco led a revolt against the republican government. Germany and Italy sent advisers and equipment to support Franco's pro-fascist forces. The USSR provided the bulk of the aid to the republican Loyalist forces. France and Britain declared an embargo on both sides, and the United States followed by initiating a moral embargo in August, followed by a formal embargo in January 1937. Isolated by the major democracies, which refused to embroil themselves in the conflict, the Loyalists were defeated by 1939.

Shaken by events in Europe and Asia, Congress again put new neutrality legislation on President Roosevelt's desk. On May 1, Roosevelt signed the Neutrality Act of 1937, which authorized him to declare embargoes on arms shipments to belligerents, a ban on loans to belligerents, and dictated that travel on belligerent ships was unlawful for U.S. citizens. The president was authorized to specify certain commodities that could be sold to belligerents for a period of two years, but only on a "cash and carry" basis. The buyer was required to come to the United States to purchase these goods and had to use its own ships to transport the goods to the home country. Although widely viewed as a major step in keeping the United States out of war, it also reflected the ambivalent attitude Americans had about neutrality. They wanted to avoid war, but still find a way to make a profit and, while desiring to declare neutral rights, did not want to assert those rights or take action to defend them.

In 1937, Adolf Hitler accelerated his timetable for war in Europe. He took personal control of both military policy and the German armed forces and then began to take control of events as he exploited opportunities presented to him. One such opportunity was Austria. Hitler's intent had been to bring Austria into the Greater Germany, and internal political conditions in Austria allowed him first to manipulate and then to overwhelm the opposition. German military forces moved into Austria without opposition on March 12, 1938. Europeans were angry at Germany's aggression, but desired peace more than anything. Hitler's conquest of Austria stood.

Hitler turned to his goal of wiping Czechoslovakia, with its multiethnic population (including about three million Germans), off the map. The German population must be returned to its native land or Germany would fight. He ordered his military staff to develop war plans to attack by October 1, 1938. Czechoslovakia, emboldened by an alliance with France and the USSR, decided to hold firm. President Roosevelt made direct appeals for peace to both Hitler and Mussolini. What effect Roosevelt had is unknown, but Italy and Germany decided to hold discussions with France and Britain in Munich between September 29 and 30. The USSR was not invited. The meeting pushed the Czechs to accept Hitler's demands and France decided not to honor the treaty of alliance. Czechoslovakia was at the mercy of Germany.

President Roosevelt sought to test U.S. public opinion in January 1939 by criticizing the aggressor governments that threatened the peace. On March 15, German forces occupied the remainder of Czechoslovakia. As Hitler rejoiced over another easy victory, the reality of the danger Hitler's Germany represented seemed to take hold in Europe. Britain and France offered security guarantees to both Romania and Poland if attacked by Germany. Roosevelt sought to make it clear that the United States would support the cause of democracy. He asked Congress to modify the 1937 Neutrality Act to allow the sale of war materiel to belligerents on a permanent cash and carry basis, to ensure that unfriendly nations would not be guaranteed an easy victory. Although the American people were willing to see a repeal of the Neutrality Act, Congress was not willing to listen.

Hitler shocked the world when, on August 23, 1939, Germany signed a pact with its sworn enemy, the Soviet Union. Each country pledged not to attack the other and would remain neutral if either country became involved in a war. A secret provision divided Poland between the two dictators. This cynical act put Poland in Hitler's sights. All that was needed was a suitable pretext to create the crisis necessary for war. Roosevelt's appeals for peace were fruitless. Hitler made his demands for the return of German territory now owned by Poland. Poland's steadfast refusal led to the invasion of Poland on September 1, 1939. With declarations of war by Britain and France, Europe was again at war.

Poland's rapid defeat and Americans' support for the democracies shaped American public opinion to favor changes in neutrality legislation to deal with the realities of war, even as Roosevelt dutifully invoked American neutrality.

Under current legislation, no belligerent could purchase arms. The cash and carry provisions had expired in May 1939. On September 21, the president addressed a special session of Congress to ask for repeal of the embargo on weapons to belligerents. He sought to return to the cash and carry provisions while keeping the strict ban on American ships or travelers entering a war zone. By November, Congress had responded to the president with a new Neutrality Act that allowed Americans to sell arms to belligerents but did not allow travel into declared war zones. The United States could still not provide loans to belligerents, nor could U.S. citizens travel on belligerent ships. The Western Hemisphere became a neutral zone in September with the Declaration of Panama. Nations of the Western Hemisphere below Canada established a neutral zone that stretched hundreds of miles into the ocean. This neutral zone was forbidden to belligerent warships. The zones would be patrolled by the navies of the signatories. Off the Atlantic coast of the United States, the zone stretched out for 300 miles and was patrolled by the U.S. Navy.

The illusion that America had solved its neutrality problem was shattered in April of 1940 when the German army struck north and westward. Denmark and Norway fell to the Germans, followed in rapid succession by Belgium, the Netherlands, and Luxembourg. By June 4, France had been decisively defeated and the British army had barely survived annihilation by an evacuation out of Dunkirk. The psychological effect of mechanized forces teamed with aircraft providing close support shattered armies expecting to fight another "Great War," in trenches year after dreary year. By June 22, France had signed an armistice, and Germany stood as the dominant power on the European continent. In the midst of Germany's lightning campaign in Europe, Congress appropriated $1.5 billion for defense; by September total defense appropriations reached $10.5 billion as the news from Europe became bleaker. Britain was fighting for its life—a German victory would put Hitler's full power against the United States, especially if the British fleet fell into German hands. The United States began to take action to assure Britain's survival.

Because Britain was dependent for its survival on ship convoys to sustain its war effort, protecting those convoys from German U-boats was essential. In June 1940 alone, nearly 300,000 tons of shipping had been lost to submarine attack. On September 3, Roosevelt responded to an earlier appeal from Prime Minister Winston Churchill for assistance in replacing destroyers lost in the war. By executive order he transferred 50 World War I–era destroyers in exchange for a 99-year lease on specific British bases stretching from Placentia Bay, Newfoundland to Georgetown, British Guiana. The destroyer deal, for all intents and purposes an act of war if the Germans had desired to see it so, ended any pretense of American neutrality. Germany was the enemy and Britain's survival was essential to America's survival.

In early December 1940, Churchill made Britain's position clear to Roosevelt. Britain was on the verge of economic collapse. Without U.S. loans or other means, Britain's future was bleak. Roosevelt created Lend-Lease, a means to support Britain without involving money. The United States, he proposed, would lend arms,

The USS *Black Hawk* tends destroyers at Chefoo, China, a few years before World War II. Destroyers such as these World War I–vintage ships were transferred to the British in the destroyers-for-bases program that preceded the Lend-Lease Act. *(National Archives and Records Administration)*

equipment, and matériel to Britain for a period of time until it was no longer needed, then it would be returned. After extensive debate, Congress passed the bill and the president signed it into law on March 11. Although sold as a measure to aid a democratic nation while keeping out of war, in essence the Lend-Lease bill committed the United States to a de facto alliance with Great Britain. In fact, while Congress was involved with the Lend-Lease bill, U.S. and British military staffs met in Washington, D.C., from January 29 to March 27 to discuss strategic options if the United States entered into the war against Germany at some future date. A general plan was developed called ABC-1, which served as the military basis of the Anglo-American alliance.

To stem the increasing number of ships lost to German submarines in the summer of 1941 and ensure that Lend-Lease supplies got through to Britain, and because as Germany extended its war zone farther west, allowing its submarines to operate more freely, the United States responded by extending its own neutral zone farther east and extending naval patrols. In April, Roosevelt signed an executive agreement with the Danish minister in exile to give the United States control of Greenland with the authorization to establish naval and air bases on the island. On May 21, 1941, the *Robin Moor,* a U.S. merchant ship, was torpedoed and sunk.

Although no lives were lost, the United States retaliated by freezing German and Italian assets and closing all consulates. A few days later Roosevelt publicly declared that supplying Britain was imperative and announced a state of "unlimited national emergency"; he was unwilling to take any further steps in the summer of 1941 than what he had already done.

Germany's June 22 attack on the Soviet Union created new challenges for the United States. Along with Great Britain, the United States pledged to support the Soviet Union in order to stop Nazi Germany. President Roosevelt announced that the Neutrality Act would not be invoked, allowing U.S. ships to carry war materiel to the USSR. Americans were uneasy supporting a communist government that only a short time ago had been a partner with the Germans in dismembering Poland, had invaded Finland, and occupied the Baltic States. But at the same time they saw the importance of making a common cause with any enemy of Hitler.

As German submarines continued to take a heavy toll on British merchant shipping in the Atlantic, Roosevelt moved the United States closer to co-belligerency with Great Britain when he announced on July 1, and with the agreement of Icelandic authorities, that U.S. Marines would be stationed in Iceland to protect the island and forestall any threat to the Western Hemisphere from Germany. Shortly thereafter, Roosevelt met with Churchill off the coast of Newfoundland to discuss a broad range of issues from aid to the USSR, to convoy security, to the situation in Asia, to postwar arrangements. Out of this meeting came the Atlantic Charter, a statement of common aims and principles. Churchill's assessment of the meeting was that the president intended to wage war without declaring it.

September 1941 saw a rise in British shipping losses to U-boats. Great Britain could not escort convoys across the Atlantic as well as escort convoys to the USSR without some assistance from the United States. The U.S. destroyer *Greer* had been attacked by a German submarine on September 4 in the North Atlantic. Even though the U.S. warship had been actively participating in antisubmarine operations with a British seaplane and had been justifiably attacked in self-defense, Roosevelt saw the incident as an opportunity to take aggressive action. He declared in a nationwide radio address on September 11 that U.S. warships could shoot Axis vessels on sight in the defensive zone and announced that U.S. warships would begin escorting multinational convoys from the shores of North America to Iceland. American support was immediate and enthusiastically in favor of the president's decision. By October, U.S. ships were attacking German submarines— but not without cost. Eleven sailors were killed when the destroyer USS *Kearney* was hit by a German torpedo. Over 100 sailors were killed when the destroyer USS *Ruben James* was torpedoed and sunk. The attack on the *Kearney* and *Ruben James* led to Congress modifying the Neutrality Act of 1939 in November to allow U.S. merchant ships to travel anywhere with any type of cargo; merchant ships were also allowed to be armed. Although Americans were still banned from travel on belligerent ships and no direct loans could be issued to belligerents (a restriction that Lend-Lease had made meaningless), the United States had abandoned neutrality in favor of active assistance to Great Britain and the USSR and was engaged in a quasi-war with Germany in the Atlantic. To get to this point, President Roosevelt had followed a cautious path, keeping one eye on Congress and one eye on public opinion as he made each decision. By late 1941, diplomacy had failed in Asia and Hitler was a clear threat to the United States. Roosevelt had committed the nation to a point-blank confrontation with the Axis. It was now only a question of when and where real war would start.

THE ROAD TO WAR IN THE PACIFIC, 1936–1941

The strategic interests of the United States and Japan had been at odds since the beginning of the 20th century. Japan's military prowess, demonstrated most effectively in the Russo-Japanese War of 1905, and its involvement in China during World War I led the United States to follow a policy of watchful concern. Japan had long viewed Manchuria and China proper as its rightful sphere of influence and had resented international actions that had made it back down from its territorial demands on China immediately after World War I. As a major power in Asia, the United States had built a sizable fleet. Its possessions in Hawaii, Guam, Wake, and the Philippines required protection and served as stepping stones to the Chinese market. The United States also championed the territorial integrity of China and equal access to trade for all foreign nations through its Open Door policy.

The postwar period marked an accommodation between Japan and the Western powers. Japan maintained its current position in Asia without major concessions. The 1921 Washington Naval Treaty reduced warships in the Pacific in an attempt to reduce the threat of war, but the Japanese were assigned a lower ratio of battleships than were maintained by either the United States or Great Britain. In exchange for Japanese acceptance of a smaller fleet of warships, the United States and Great Britain agreed not to fortify any of their Pacific island bases. Japan's participation in the Nine Power Treaty of 1922 committed the signatories (United States, Great Britain, Italy, China, Belgium, Japan, Portugal, France, and the Netherlands) to respect the sovereignty, independence, and territorial integrity of China. Although no enforcement provisions were contained in the treaty, the agreement seemed to solidify U.S. strategic goals in the Pacific. Americans, satisfied with their diplomatic efforts, turned their attention away from the Pacific. By the 1930s isolationism and the economic effects of the Great Depression combined to focus attention inward.

During this lull in tensions, Japan began fortifying and integrating economically its Pacific island mandates, the former German possessions transferred to Japan by the League of Nations. World economic conditions pressed the need for Japan to have both capital and raw materials for national survival. The Japanese believed that control of the natural resources in Manchuria and exporting its products abroad were the keys to their future. The Japanese had gained certain access rights in southern Manchuria and controlled the vital South Manchurian Railway.

But control was contested. Nationalist China had fought a short war with the USSR over control of northern Manchuria in 1929, and certainly desired to assert its control of southern Manchuria, despite Japanese claims.

In the 1930s, Japan had moved toward a strident patriotism based on worship of the emperor as a god. Military success bred a sense of invincibility and destiny that drove Japanese ambitions for the next decade. Whatever group claimed to speak and act for the emperor would immediately have the loyalty of the nation. Japanese politics moved in an increasingly authoritarian direction between 1928 and 1936. The voice of the military leadership, especially the army, began to have greater influence in politics. The Japanese government, under an increasingly powerful nationalist-militarist element, began efforts to expand Japanese control into China. In their view, Japan's survival relied upon access to critical raw materials in both Manchuria and the Southwest Pacific that would allow Japan's industrialized economy to be self-sufficient. Japan increasingly came to see the United States as an obstacle to its ambitions on the Asian mainland.

On September 18, 1931, using a bomb explosion on the tracks of the South Manchurian Railway as a pretext, Japanese forces in Korea attacked Chinese troops in Manchuria. From the speed and coordination of the attacks it was obvious that everything had been planned in advance and rehearsed. Although the military had acted without government approval, it soon became clear that Japan's government would no longer function without direct control by military officers. In January 1932, Japanese air and ground forces attacked Chinese forces defending Shanghai and caused thousands of civilian deaths before withdrawing in May. The world was horrified by the scenes of destruction and brutality that modern war visited upon the population. By February 1932, the Japanese had overrun Manchuria and established a puppet state called Manchukuo, declaring that it was no longer sovereign territory of China.

The United States's response to the aggression against Manchuria was to seek a way to support the international peace system, embodied in the League of Nations. Although the United States was not a member of the league, it was essential that the league demonstrate its ability to maintain order in this first great test of its authority. In an unprecedented move, a representative of the United States attended the meeting of the League Council. But the league, led by Britain and France, wanted no part of a possible war or sanctions that would hurt them economically. Although the league did send a commission to investigate the incident in Manchuria, its condemnation of Japan in February 1933 had no effect except to drive Japan out of the league. With neither President Herbert Hoover nor American public opinion willing to go further, the United States had to rely on moral force. Therefore, the United States announced on January 7, 1932 that it would refuse to recognize Japan's occupation of Manchuria because it violated the Nine Power Treaty. Although the United States gained some satisfaction when the league adopted the U.S. position in a formal resolution against Japan, the West had failed its first test to halt aggression.

Spurred by the success of the army's action in Manchuria, patriotic fever swept aside all moderation. The Japanese army continued to expand its control into northern China, annexing the province of Jehol. In November 1936, Japan joined

Nazi Germany in the Anti-Comintern Pact. Although touted as international resistance to communist influence, it was clearly intended to threaten the Soviet Union so that Japan could pursue its interests in China. By 1937, Japan was under military domination and certain that it had no need to accept an inferior position to the great powers of the West. In July 1937, Japanese troops clashed with Chinese soldiers near Peking (Beijing) at the Marco Polo Bridge. When the Nationalist Chinese refused to back down, Japan entered into an all-out war of conquest against China. Japan never declared war, choosing instead to refer to its invasion as the "China Incident." In August, Shanghai again was attacked, and by the end of the year, the Nationalist capital of Nanking had fallen and the population was subjected to savage violence. Japan had 700,000 troops engaged in combat operations. During this time the gunboat USS *Panay* was attacked and sunk. Although public opinion in the United States was aroused, Japan's quick apologies and reparation payment of over $2 million quieted things down quickly.

By 1938, Japanese troop strength in China had increased to one million. The capture of Hankow and Canton in late 1938 gave the Japanese control of China's richest and most populous areas. Nationalist leader Chiang Kai-shek moved his capital to Chungking. Although the Japanese were unsettled by the fierceness of Chinese resistance, the government announced it would establish a new order in Greater East Asia, a military-economic-cultural collaboration dominated by Japan. Thus, control of the Netherlands East Indies, French Indochina, Malaya, Borneo, Burma, and Thailand were important not only for oil, cotton, coal, rubber, and other natural resources, but also for achieving Japan's goal to replace European influence with Japanese influence and direction.

In 1939, Japan attempted to isolate China from outside assistance and force it into surrender. As China's seaports were closed one by one, there were only two routes of supply left. One was the railroad from Haiphong in French Indochina to Kunuwo in Chinese Yunnan. The other was the overland route from British Burma to Kunming. If China was to fall, it became clear that the Western colonial powers of France, Britain, the Netherlands, and the United States, which resisted Japanese ambitions, had to be dealt with. Of these, the United States was the most dangerous potential adversary. With 60 percent of Japan's oil, as well as billions of dollars in raw materials and machine tools coming from the United States, Japan sought to mollify its primary trading partner through a combination of negotiation and intimidation. Thus, while offering a variety of political and economic inducements for the United States to accept the fait accompli Japan had established in China, the Japanese government continued to declare that the "China Incident" would be resolved and peace would come to Asia as soon as third parties stopped interfering.

The United States was unmoved by the Japanese approach, and since 1939 had been slowly and cautiously pressuring Japan diplomatically. American opinion and the Congress saw no need to become involved in China. Believing the events in the Pacific were too far away for their concern and absorbed by a continuing economic crisis at home, Americans showed little interest. Japan had for all intents and purposes declared the Open Door invalid, and ignored the stream of official protests from the U.S. State Department, which refused to recognize territorial changes made by force, maintaining support of the Open Door policy, and protested Japanese treatment of American citizens and property. In 1938, the United States had enacted a moral embargo against Japan by refusing to sell aircraft. It supported loans to China, and in July 1939 the United States notified Japan that in six months it would terminate the 1911 trade treaty. This step was clearly intended to warn the Japanese government—loss of this lucrative and essential treaty marked a major threat to the Japanese economy. It meant that, once the treaty expired, the moral embargoes could be replaced with real economic embargoes.

Meanwhile, war had broken out in Europe and German victories in Europe between September 1939 and July 1940 created a new strategic situation for the United States. Neutrality was no longer a guarantee of security. With the fall of France, the focus of America was on Europe, not Asia. Britain was alone against the might of Hitler and under threat of invasion. If Britain fell, the entire continent of Europe would become an impregnable fortress of Nazism with dire consequences for the world. The Roosevelt administration began to move away from neutrality to open support of Britain. In the meantime, Japan had to be deterred from further expansion and China had to be supported. Roosevelt desired to maintain peace for as long as possible, but not on Japanese terms. The only weapon available to halt Japan was a powerful one—economic embargo. By cutting off Japan's access to oil and raw materials, the United States could at any time force Japan into economic ruin and cause the army and navy to grind to a halt. Such drastic action had dangers as well. Economic sanctions could actually bring on war rather than prevent it. There was no way to know what embargoes would deter and what would incite. On July 25, 1940, the president ordered export restrictions on petroleum products for use as aviation fuel, lubricants, and high-grade scrap metal, and less than a week later, he restricted the sale of all aviation fuel to the Western Hemisphere. The Japanese protested vigorously, and the United States responded that it was willing to continue to negotiate.

The Japanese continued their efforts to isolate China. In July, the Japanese pressured the British to close the Burma Road. Fearing for its colonial possessions and fighting for its very survival, Britain complied. The newly established French government in Vichy came under pressure to allow Japanese forces access to Indochina. In September, Japanese ground and air forces were operating in the country and the rail line into China was cut off. China was now isolated. Without China's resistance, Japan's ambitions to expand the "Greater East Asia Co-Prosperity Sphere" beyond French Indochina to the Netherlands East Indies, Thailand, Malaya, Burma, India, and the Philippines would be made a reality and Japan's power in Asia would be unchallengeable. American diplomatic protests were sharpened by the announcement that the United States would provide a $25 million loan to keep China in the war. On September 26, President Roosevelt declared an embargo on all iron and steel scrap sales outside of the Western Hemisphere (except for Great Britain). The next day, Japan announced that it had joined the Axis of Germany and Italy. The pact pledged mutual support if attacked by a power not currently involved in either the European or Asian war, a thinly veiled notice to the United States. Germany and

Italy also recognized Japan's leadership in establishing a new order in Asia. The Axis powers hoped the pact would deter the United States from threatening Japan. Nevertheless, Japan made it clear through diplomatic channels that a war between the United States and Germany would not obligate Japan to attack the United States. For its part, the American leadership viewed the Axis as an alliance aimed at world domination and a clear threat to democracy and freedom throughout the world. Attitudes toward Japan began to harden. The State Department warned American citizens to leave the Far East.

Negotiations between Japanese ambassador Nomura Kichisaburo and Secretary of State Cordell Hull opened in the spring of 1941. Nomura continued to stress that the United States accept the new status quo in Asia, while Hull laid out the U.S. position that Japanese aggression in Asia was immoral. Hull outlined the U.S. position: Japan must respect the territorial integrity of states in Asia and must not interfere with their internal affairs; accept equality of economic opportunity; and it must accept a return to the situation in the Far East that existed in the 1920s. As the days drifted by in negotiations, Japan's interpretation of the American position made it vital that the oil, rubber, and tin of the Netherlands East Indies had to come under Japanese control sooner rather than later. Thus, to secure its vital northern flank for a future thrust into the south, Japan signed a neutrality pact with the USSR on April 13. If either nation became engaged in a war, the other would remain neutral. Diplomatically, Japan would try to convince the United States and Britain that expansion was a matter of survival. It did not seek war, but if Japan had to fight, it would not be a two-front war.

By the summer of 1941, the United States was actively supporting China and the USSR, which had been attacked by Germany on June 22. Carefully gauging public opinion, Roosevelt was still seeking a way to bring the United States into a more direct role of supporting Britain without actually entering the war and at the same time keeping Japan at bay. Japan, however, had already made important strategic decisions that would affect the president's plans. On July 2, the Japanese government decided to commit itself to the realization of the Co-Prosperity Sphere by forcing Vichy France to allow Japanese forces to gain access to southern Indochina, building airfields, occupying harbors, and stationing troops. This decision would risk war with Britain and the United States, but the economic noose America had placed around Japan could not be drawn much tighter.

The Japanese decision was known in Washington almost as soon as it was made. Navy cryptologists had broken the Japanese diplomatic code. Known as "Magic," this code allowed the United States a number of options to counter Japanese moves in Indochina. After the Japanese invaded Indochina on July 24, Roosevelt took action. On July 25, the president ordered all Japanese assets in the United States frozen, which eliminated Japan's access to key technology, financial assets, and raw materials, most importantly, oil. The United States had also begun to build ground and air forces in a hasty effort to protect the Philippines and moved the bulk of its fleet to Pearl Harbor. Both the British and the Netherlands were supporting the American economic embargo and reinforcing bases in the Far East. Despite all these provocative actions, Roosevelt still believed that the Japanese could be held off long enough for the "show-down," as he called it, to be more advantageous to the United States. He presented this view to Prime Minister Churchill during their secret meeting off the coast of Newfoundland in August 1941. The British leader, doubtful of this approach, desired a much more decisive approach to Japan, but Roosevelt had faith in his approach of ambiguity and delay.

With its military forces consuming 12,000 tons of fuel per day, Japan had about an 18-month supply of oil without further imports. Faced with economic collapse or war, it became clear that the United States had to be forced to accept the Japanese new order in Asia. Japanese military leaders decided that war preparations would have to be initiated in October if the Netherlands East Indies were to be captured by the end of the year. Negotiations would continue with the United States, but if no progress was made, war was inevitable. A September proposal for a high-level conference between President Roosevelt and the Japanese premier failed to materialize, and a new government under General Tojo Hideki took power in October—a clear indication of Japan's intent to pursue its declared goals in Asia. On November 20, 1941, Japan presented its final terms: It would withdraw Japanese troops from southern Indochina to northern Indochina. In return, the United States would restore full trade to Japan, allowing oil and other strategic materials to flow freely, and allow Japan to settle the situation in China without interference. Once trade was restored, Japan would withdraw all troops from Indochina and make no further armed advances into Southeast Asia or the Pacific. Secretary of State Cordell Hull's response on November 26 was unequivocal: Japan must withdraw its forces from both China and Indochina and sign a nonaggression pact with the United States that pledged both countries to support the territorial sovereignty of the states of East Asia. In response, the United States would reopen trade and unfreeze Japanese assets. By November 25, the carrier force that would carry out the first strike had already left port, awaiting a recall message that never came. On December 1, the Japanese government rejected the American position and made the final decision for war.

Japanese military planners had formulated a bold offensive. A surprise attack on Pearl Harbor would cripple the U.S. fleet. Rapid and simultaneous attacks to seize the British possessions of Hong Kong and Singapore, the Netherlands East Indies, and the American possessions of the Philippines, Guam, and Wake would accomplish all of Japan's strategic goals. It would provide the Japanese economic self-sufficiency, a free hand to deal with China, and create a formidable defensive barrier that would force the Americans, Dutch, and British to face a long, exhausting struggle or make peace. As part of this strategy, the Japanese intended to draw the main strength of the U.S. Navy toward Japan so that it could be destroyed in a decisive battle. For Japan to succeed, hostilities had to end as early as possible. The main concern for the Japanese planners was this: After a swift early victory, could the nation sustain a protracted war?

As reports arrived that Japan was massing forces in Indochina, Roosevelt made a personal appeal to Emperor Hirohito for a withdrawal of these forces to prevent "further death and destruction in the world." The message was dispatched to Tokyo on December 6, 1941. Roosevelt's answer would come the next morning.

AMERICAN PREWAR STRATEGIC CHOICES: 1938–1941

Events in the world posed a unique problem for American military strategists in the last years of peace. Without a doubt, events pointed toward the worst-case scenario: The United States would fight a two-ocean war, either alone or as part of a coalition, opposed by the Axis powers, acting either separately or in concert. The strategic assessment, completed in April and May of 1939, concluded that the Western Hemisphere was safe from attack, but Germany and Italy could threaten the United States directly if Great Britain and France either remained neutral or were defeated in a European war. In the Far East, the assessment was that Japan would continue to expand into China and outlying areas of Asia peacefully, but would use force against Great Britain and the United States to achieve stated goals. The Axis was capable of acting together to support mutual interests, and would be willing to go to war if the United States or other nations opposed them.

For American military strategists, the problem of the two-ocean war required holding in the Pacific, while protecting vital areas such as the Panama Canal. Using the Caribbean as a strategic base of operations, the U.S. Fleet could operate on interior lines to block any direct threat to the homeland. The Atlantic had always been America's strategic lifeline and the approaches to the Western Hemisphere had to be secured as a priority.

In case of war with Germany and Italy, the United States would build combat strength sufficient to defeat unilaterally an Axis threat from the Atlantic. If Japan began a war in the Pacific first, then the United States, by still maintaining a defensive approach in the Pacific, would deter Germany and Italy from threatening the Western Hemisphere. A war in the Pacific would require U.S. forces to defeat Japan by a series of naval battles and amphibious assaults. The planners identified four major avenues of advance to the Japanese homeland originating from four bases: the Aleutians, Pearl Harbor, the Marshalls, and Samoa. The Aleutians offered a direct path to the Japanese islands. The Pearl Harbor avenue of advance included Midway Island and the main island of Luzon in the Philippines, then to Japan. The Marshalls avenue of advance led through the Carolines, the Marianas, and Yap and Peleliu to Japan. The final avenue of advance used Samoa as a base, then through New Guinea and thence to Mindanao in the Philippines. The planners believed that two avenues were necessary. The strategic approach had a common perspective—the Philippines could not be held. Reinforcing and protecting U.S. bases in Hawaii, Alaska, and Panama—but not the Philippines—were essential to the strategy.

By June 1939, American planners were examining five separate scenarios that the United States could face in the near future. Each of these was to have a plan associated with it. These came to be known as the Rainbow series of plans. Version 1 was a unilateral defense plan. The army and navy would act jointly to protect the homeland, U.S. possessions, and strategic lines of sea commerce. In the Pacific, the United States would hold Japan behind a line stretching from Alaska to Hawaii to Panama until strength could be built up for a counteroffensive. Version 2 was a multilateral defense plan involving Great Britain and France. With the Allies holding Germany and Italy at bay in Europe and the Atlantic, the United States could take the offensive to defeat Japan in the Pacific, supporting mutual interests and objectives in the region. Version 3 was a unilateral plan that assumed no threat to the homeland from Germany and Italy, allowing the United States to initiate offensive operations against Japan. Version 4 was also a unilateral plan that focused on reinforcing the Western Hemisphere's weak southern flank, while being prepared to conduct joint operations in the eastern Atlantic. This plan required that the United States remain on the defensive in the Pacific until victory was assured in the Atlantic, then forces would be moved to conduct offensive operations against Japan. Version 5 was a multilateral plan that included Great Britain and France as allies of the United States. The defense of the Western Hemisphere would be the U.S. priority, but joint and combined operations in the eastern Atlantic, Europe, and Africa were expected to defeat Germany and Italy. Again, the United States would hold in the Pacific until Germany and Italy were defeated, then forces would shift to the Pacific for a counteroffensive against Japan.

As Hitler's armies swept over Poland on September 1, 1939, American planners focused on Rainbow's version 2. As America maintained its neutrality, it took initial actions both diplomatically and militarily to protect the homeland. Hemispheric defense and military preparedness were the main efforts. By the spring and summer of 1940, American planners found themselves overwhelmed by events in Europe and the Pacific. By June, Germany had complete mastery of western Europe. France had collapsed and the British Expeditionary Force had been driven off the continent. Britain braced for invasion, and suddenly the prospect of a threat to the homeland from the European Axis powers appeared very possible. If the Axis took control of the British and French fleets, the U.S. Navy would be unable to stop an offensive aimed at the Western Hemisphere. In the Far East, the situation was not much better. The "China Incident," as the Japanese called their aggression, had put China close to collapse. Japan had not been swayed by diplomacy and appeared intent on creating its Greater East Asia Co-Prosperity Sphere at the expense of the Western powers. American planners now began to look at Version 4 of the Rainbow plans.

As Britain withstood the onslaught of German bombers, it became clear to President Roosevelt that America's survival depended on Britain remaining in the war. The fate of the British fleet was critical—it must not fall under Hitler's control. Thus, by necessity, British and American planners began a close cooperation. British and American strategies had to complement each other. The British had two strategic objectives: Secure the United Kingdom and the Empire from attack and control the water around the islands; maintain access to the Mediterranean and its lifeline through the Suez to British possessions in the Far East. Although Italy was a threat, Germany was the main enemy and had to be defeated first. Through a strategic bombing offensive combined with economic pressure, German morale and war-making capabilities would be weakened sufficiently to conduct an invasion of the continent by land forces. The offensive operations that followed would ensure the defeat of the Axis. In the Far East, the British had few resources to offer, and viewed the U.S. fleet as the main deterrent against Japan.

The growing belief that Britain's survival was a priority for America's own defense planning reinforced Rainbow versions 1 and 4, which put the United States on the defensive in the Pacific until the Atlantic was secure. This approach also supported the primary security concern for the United States, namely the security of the Western Hemisphere. The difficult task the United States had to pursue in the Far East was asserting American interests in the Pacific while avoiding a confrontation with Japan that would lead to war.

The initial British-American staff talks, known as the ABC meetings (American-British Conversations), were held in Washington from January 29 through March 29, 1941. The meetings were kept secret to avoid influencing American public opinion against the Lend-Lease bill, which was being debated in Congress. The British staff representatives intended to outline in broad terms a combined strategy in the event that the United States entered the war against the Axis powers. While the U.S. planners desired to focus on Europe and the Pacific, the British desired to broaden the discussion to include a combined strategy for the Mediterranean and the Middle East. This divergence of strategic perspective would haunt the British-American relationship for many months to come.

The final report was called ABC-1 and laid out several key decisions. The most important was that the priority of effort would be directed against the European theater. Germany and Italy would be defeated first, followed by Japan. The details of this strategy were include in the ABC-1 report, and later incorporated into the American strategic plan, called Rainbow 5. Both contained specific strategic tasks. These included the use of military, economic, and diplomatic measures to put pressure on Germany and Italy; a sustained regional air offensive to cripple German military strength; breaking the Axis by eliminating Italy early in the war; raids and small offensives aimed at weakening Axis strength; actively supporting resistance movements in occupied Europe; and building the necessary forces for an eventual decisive offensive against Germany.

Within this approach, the United States intended to protect the vital sea lanes of communications, as well as important outlying military bases or islands of strategic importance, and prevent any Axis incursions into the Western Hemisphere. At the same time, the primary effort of the United States would be directed toward building sufficient land, air, and naval power for decisive offensive operations against the Axis powers.

In the Far East, the army would defend the Philippines but would receive no reinforcements. The commander in chief, United States Asiatic Fleet, would support the U.S. Army, as well as the land and air forces of Britain, the Commonwealth, and other associated nations.

One of the problems for the United States in supporting this strategy was the weakness of the U.S. Army. It would take months before any trained force would be ready for combat operations. This left nearly all of the strategic tasks to the navy. In February German troops were fighting British and Commonwealth troops in North Africa; in April German forces overwhelmed the Balkans, supporting an ineffectual Italian offensive, and drove the British from Greece and Crete. As the summer of 1941 began, American planners were increasingly concerned about whether Great Britain could stand alone much longer. Britain's defeat would place the entire burden of the war on the United States. When Germany invaded the Soviet Union in June of 1941, it became clear that both Great Britain and the USSR had to be supported with military equipment and supplies until the United States had built its military capabilities sufficiently to enter the war. Britain desired to bring the United States into the war as soon as possible.

The August 9–12, 1941, Atlantic Conference between President Roosevelt and Prime Minister Churchill, on warships off the coast of Newfoundland, allowed the Anglo-American military staffs to update their earlier strategic discussions. Given the difficult situation the British were facing in the Mediterranean, the British proposed a combined operation against Axis forces by invading French North Africa and supporting operations in the Middle East. The rapid introduction of American forces into the Mediterranean would potentially reverse the current military situation.

The Americans rejected this proposal as far too optimistic. Outside of naval forces, the United States had neither land nor air forces capable of conducting such an operation. Thus, the United States believed it would be of greatest assistance to Great Britain and the USSR as a neutral rather than a belligerent. Although American planners believed that the time of entering the war would be at their choosing, events on the other side of the world would dictate a different timeline.

ALLIED STRATEGY 1941–1942: ARCADIA AND THE PACIFIC

At the Arcadia conference in Washington, held between December 24, 1941 and January 14, 1942, President Franklin Roosevelt, Prime Minister Winston Churchill, and the British and American chiefs of staff met to determine basic strategic goals for the war against the Axis. At this meeting, the Anglo-American Combined Chiefs of Staff was created to support the strategic conduct of the war. The agreement that Germany was the primary enemy and would be defeated first while holding Japan in Asia was an outgrowth of American prewar strategic planning. The ways to reach this strategic end reflected a decidedly British view that an indirect approach, attacking the periphery of the Axis-controlled areas of Europe, would form a ring that would be steadily squeezed as British-American military capability grew. The means decided upon were blockades, strategic bombing to weaken Axis war production capability, supporting resistance movements in Europe, and limited offensive operations against exposed Axis force concentrations. These efforts were intended to steadily weaken the Axis until a final decisive attack could be launched that would bring about its defeat. The buildup of the combat power necessary to conduct this decisive attack would be a concurrent effort to the peripheral approach.

But Japanese advances in the Far East forced the Allies to commit forces to protect and maintain the lines of communication and supply to Australia by securing a string of fortified island bases stretching from the New Hebrides to Hawaii.

In addition the Japanese threat to Australia itself, from New Guinea and the Solomons, had to be halted. By August 1942, the United States and Australia were involved in a brutal battle of survival to turn the Japanese tide. By February 1943, the Japanese had been halted, but not before consuming much of the initial land, air, and sea resources of U.S. forces. This first effort in the Pacific had an effect on the ABC-1 and Rainbow 5 planning that had focused on a Germany first strategy.

The Americans were impatient to undertake a decisive attack on Germany; uncomfortable with the peripheral strategy, they proposed a rapid buildup of British and American forces in Britain, followed by a cross-Channel invasion in 1943 to drive into Germany. The plan for the buildup of over one million men formed into 48 maneuver divisions was called Bolero; the invasion plan to include six divisions initially landing somewhere between Le Havre and Boulogne was called Roundup. An alternate plan was called Sledgehammer, intended as a contingency using just over three divisions, with two U.S. divisions making the initial assault. This invasion of Europe would be launched as a diversionary attack if the USSR was in danger of collapse, to draw German strength away from the eastern front. Or it could be conducted in the unlikely event of a rapid Axis collapse. These plans were completed and George C. Marshall visited London in April of 1942 to present them to the British. Although accepted in principle, the British soon began to backtrack, especially about Sledgehammer, which they viewed as exceptionally perilous. The British had been pushed off the Continent in 1940; they were in no mood to return so quickly unless Germany had been sufficiently weakened to guarantee success. On April 3, 1942, the Combined Planning Staff estimated that predicted force strengths in September would be insufficient to conduct Sledgehammer. On April 9 General Marshall in London insisted on a decision on the timing of a cross-Channel invasion. The debate between the American and British chiefs of staff came close to ending any Anglo-American operations at all, with the Americans chiefs of staff recommending to the president in July 1942 that the United States abandon the Germany-first strategy altogether and apply all resources available to fighting the Japanese.

But President Roosevelt, as commander in chief, ordered Admiral King and General Marshall to London to find a compromise and insisted that U.S. forces be involved in combat in Europe as soon as possible. If Sledgehammer was not a feasible plan, then they had to find a compromise for operations in the Middle East or North Africa. On July 24, the plans for Sledgehammer were set aside and replaced with the basic outline of a British plan to invade North Africa, originally named Gymnast, but now retitled Torch. Torch met the president's requirements, but the commitment of resources would delay any cross-Channel attack for at least a year. Thus, the Americans found themselves supporting the peripheral strategy of the British, and to American strategists, following the British lead in the Mediterranean was folly; no decisive result could be obtained there, and the British were seen as pursuing their own imperial interests in securing the Mediterranean.

The Combined Chiefs issued a directive on August 13 for planning for Torch. General Dwight Eisenhower was designated as commander of Allied Force Headquarters responsible for the operation. Torch was the largest amphibious operation conducted up to that time, and the first Anglo-American operation. The North Africa landings and the subsequent campaign in Tunisia eventually did succeed in achieving the strategic objectives outlined by the Combined Chiefs of Staff. Axis forces were driven from North Africa, and the Mediterranean lines of communication were again opened from Gibraltar to Suez. The British and Americans learned many important lessons on cooperation. But the campaign ended all chances of launching Roundup in 1943. With an offensive in the Pacific underway and with U.S. and British forces occupying Tunisia, the question now was what would be the next step for the Allies?

In March of 1942, the Combined Chiefs of Staff agreed to give the strategic direction of the war in the Pacific to the U.S. Joint Chiefs of Staff (JCS). The strategy of winning in Europe while holding the Japanese, then winning in the Pacific, was reflected in the agreement that the buildup in Britain for a cross-Channel invasion would take priority, while the Japanese would be contained with the Allied forces available or allocated to the theater.

The Pacific Theater was divided on March 30 into the Southwest Pacific Area (SWPA), under Commander in Chief General Douglas MacArthur (CINCSWPA), which included the South China Sea, the Gulf of Siam, the Philippines, and the Netherlands East Indies minus Sumatra, the Solomons, Australia, and waters to the south. The Pacific Ocean Area (POA), under command of Admiral Chester Nimitz, included the land and water area outside of SWPA, from the west coast of North America to China and south to New Zealand. Nimitz as both commander in chief, U.S. Pacific Fleet (CINCPAC), and as commander in chief of the Pacific Ocean Area (CINCPOA), personally commanded two sub-regions, the North and Central Pacific, but had a subordinate commander for the South Pacific. Both MacArthur and Nimitz reported to the U.S. Joint Chiefs—MacArthur dealing with General George C. Marshall, army chief of staff, and Nimitz dealing with Admiral Ernest J. King, commander in chief, U.S. Fleet.

By the summer of 1942, the United States was facing a strategic dilemma. Its dedication to the priority of Germany as the main enemy was unchanged, and the U.S. Chiefs were sending air and ground forces to Britain in support of a buildup of forces for an eventual offensive against the European Axis powers. But Japanese advances in the Solomons and New Guinea threatened the vital lines of communication from the United States to Australia and New Zealand that had to be protected if the United States was ever to mount a counteroffensive against Japan in the future. Resources to support a two-front war and the win-hold-win strategy were stretched very thin, especially transportation assets and trained ground forces capable of functioning on the battlefield against tough, combat-experienced German and Japanese soldiers.

Nevertheless, the Japanese seaplane base at Tulagi and their new airfield under construction at Guadalcanal presented a threat against the Australia-Midway-Hawaii-U.S. line of communication in the Pacific. With the battles of the Coral Sea and Midway creating a short pause in the previously unstemmed Japanese advance across the Pacific, the U.S. Joint Chiefs of Staff issued a directive for a limited offensive in the Pacific on July 6, 1942—the ultimate objective being the Japanese base at Rabaul, via the Solomons, New Guinea, New Britain, and New Ireland. Ironically this directive came out just days before Japanese Imperial Headquarters cancelled its orders for an advance against New Caledonia, Samoa, and the Fiji Islands. It was a signal that the strategic initiative was shifting, but in which direction it would ultimately turn was completely unknown and would depend, as always, on a few courageous and resolute men.

ALLIED STRATEGY 1943: FROM CASABLANCA TO EUREKA

By the end of 1942, it was obvious that the Allies would need to clear Tunisia of Axis forces in order to achieve the strategic goal of acquiring complete control of North Africa, established by the Combined Chiefs of Staff in August of 1942. In the meantime, the British and American staffs had to agree on the next step after Torch.

Since Arcadia, Winston Churchill had maintained that the Mediterranean offered the best opportunities for the Allies. During his August 12–15 meeting with Stalin in Moscow, Churchill had stressed how Torch would expose "the underbelly of the Axis." He subsequently coordinated with Roosevelt in examining possibilities for offensive operations in the Mediterranean.

On December 10, 1942, Roosevelt discussed future actions with the JCS. General Marshall believed the Mediterranean approach was wasteful and that, once the objectives of Torch were accomplished, the main effort should return to the buildup of forces in Britain in preparation for a cross-Channel invasion of Europe (essentially the Roundup plan) in March or April of 1943. General Henry Arnold, chief of Army Air Forces, believed that employing an integrated air offensive from both Britain and North Africa could maintain the pressure on Germany regardless of where Allied forces were concentrated. He asserted that precision bombing raids against German targets would in six months cripple the enemy sufficiently so that a cross-Channel invasion would be possible.

American military planners understood the enormous logistical burdens that a cross-Channel invasion would impose. Attempting to land a minimum number of divisions capable of being supported with a limited supply line would have significant risks. With the failure of the Dieppe raid in August 1942 fresh in their minds, the planners were cautious about taking such risks without the sufficient logistical support needed to bring in as many divisions as possible in the initial landing force. Thus, Roundup appeared to be less of a possibility than some offensive action in the Mediterranean in 1943. While not the second front that Churchill and Roosevelt had promised to Stalin, the Mediterranean did offer the Soviets some relief. Italy was vulnerable, and U.S. and British forces were already concentrated at one location in North Africa, making logistics easier. Germany still would be under attack by British and American bombers the entire time.

Roosevelt decided to keep his options open, looking at a buildup in both North Africa and in Britain in order to take advantage of whatever strategic opportunities presented themselves, such as the participation of Turkey in the war or the further weakening of German air and land forces in France.

The Pacific was a different issue entirely. In October 1942, President Roosevelt pressed General Marshall to have General MacArthur secure the northeast coast of New Guinea quickly as a prelude to further land, air, and sea operations against the main Japanese base in Rabaul. On December 1, 1942, with the initiative at both Guadalcanal and New Guinea passing to American forces, General Marshall proposed to Admiral King what amounted to a continuation of the concept of operations laid out in the JCS July 2, 1942, directive. Offensive operations for 1943 would be directed at seizing and occupying the remainder of the Solomon Islands, northeast New Guinea, and the islands of New Britain and New Ireland with the objective of capturing Rabaul. General MacArthur, as the commander responsible for the Southwest Pacific Area, would provide the overall strategic direction of the campaign. Admiral Nimitz would provide the necessary task forces under the direct command of a naval officer, who would control all naval and amphibious operations. But Admiral King balked at the proposal, not wishing the Pacific Fleet to be divided between Nimitz and MacArthur, and nothing was resolved. By the time of the Casablanca Conference, the army and navy had reached no agreement on the details of the strategy and command arrangements for continuing operations against Rabaul.

From January 14 to 23, 1943, Roosevelt, Churchill, and the Combined Chiefs of Staff met in Casablanca to map out strategy for 1943. Because the U.S. Joint Chiefs of Staff had not defined a strategic plan by the time of Casablanca, the Americans found themselves tied to a British peripheral strategy that they had never liked, and they chafed at the British hesitation to commit to a definitive time for a cross-Channel invasion. Churchill and the Imperial General Staff had a well-prepared plan and simply outmatched the Americans during the debates over the strategic direction of the war in early 1943.

The major decisions were arrived at with limited debate. The Atlantic sea lanes had to be secured from the U-boat threat to ensure not only support to Allied efforts worldwide, but also supply convoys vital to sustaining the USSR war effort. Sicily would be the next target of the Allies. The goal was to secure the Mediterranean line of communications, provide a limited second front to draw German forces away from the USSR, and increase pressure on the weakest Axis power, Italy. A combined air offensive from Britain would strike at German submarine bases and key industrial production sites. The British chief of air staff would direct the offensive, but the American commander would maintain tactical control. This compromise allowed for the British to continue the night area attacks they preferred, while the Americans would conduct daylight precision bombing. The buildup for Bolero would continue, with a goal of 938,000 men and 15 divisions. Raids and support to resistance movements would also continue.

The decision that delayed a cross-Channel invasion until 1944 had been the major point of discussion. Despite American arguments for a cross-Channel invasion as the Allied priority, the British were not convinced that Germany had been sufficiently weakened to warrant an invasion in 1943. Essentially, the British idea that southern Europe, not northern France, offered the best approach to rapid victory won out. To the Americans, this hesitation to address a cross-Channel invasion appeared to be foot-dragging and a waste of resources directed against an ambiguous target.

Faced with a delay in launching the cross-Channel invasion, the United States stressed it would continue to pressure the Japanese as fully as possible, taking advantage of successes in the Pacific and moving over to the offensive. The United States would continue its offensive to capture the Japanese base at Rabaul, and advance toward Truk and Guam via the Marshalls and Carolines. An American proposal to launch an offensive into Burma to reopen the Burma Road lifeline to China was shelved. Although only about 15 percent of U.S. resources were committed to the Pacific at this time, the Casablanca decision to keep pressure on the Japanese gave the United States essentially a free hand to pursue the offensive and take advantage of opportunities.

In the aftermath of Casablanca, therefore, the United States moved deliberately toward a more balanced strategic approach of fighting a two-front war than the initial win-hold-win approach agreed upon at the Arcadia conference in 1941.

At the Trident conference, held in Washington, D.C., from May 12 to 25, 1943, the British continued to press for the peripheral strategy, advocating continuing offensives in the Mediterranean, especially concentrating on defeating Italy to avoid an operational pause that could have disastrous consequences for the USSR. It was best to continue the attack onto the Italian mainland, even if Bolero had to be delayed, the British planners argued. The Americans, seeking relief from what they believed to be an improper strategic focus, pressed for a cross-Channel invasion at the earliest possible date—or, if Bolero was delayed, the United States desired an increased emphasis on operations in the Pacific. The compromise was presented to Roosevelt and Churchill on May 25. The combined bomber offensive would attempt to cripple and demoralize the Germans sufficiently by April 1, 1944, so that a cross-Channel invasion was feasible. The target buildup was 29 divisions in Britain ready by the target date, which was set for May 1, 1944. A lodgement would be established with nine divisions, followed by a rapid buildup of three to five divisions per month, then a breakout and advance to the east supported by Allied air power. Meanwhile, support to the USSR and China would continue, as would the effort to eliminate the U-boat threat in the Atlantic. The Allies would continue the offensive in the Mediterranean to defeat Italy. As a trade-off for the agreement to continue operations in the Mediterranean, the Combined Chiefs of Staff approved "The Strategic Plan for the Defeat of Japan" on May 19. The main effort was designated in the Central Pacific. The objectives were the Philippines and the recapture of Hong Kong. Once bases in China were occupied, a strategic bombing campaign would be conducted against the Japanese home islands, followed by an amphibious offensive. No specific timelines were established, nor were additional forces allocated in the plan. Southwest and Central Pacific theaters were to work together, but operations would be sequential rather than simultaneous, due to limits on the availability of shipping and trained amphibious divisions.

Much of the discussion over feasibility of a cross-Channel invasion hung on the availability of heavy transports, the LST (Landing Ship Tank). There was enough landing craft of this size and capability in theater to carry only three divisions. The addition of two airborne divisions gave the Allies a five-division force, but it was considered to be the minimum force necessary to attack the fortified coast of Europe. To speed planning along, the Combined Chiefs established a headquarters on April 23, 1943, under General Sir Frederick Morgan to act as COSSAC—Chief of Staff of the Supreme Allied Commander. Morgan was to form the nucleus of an Anglo-American headquarters that would oversee the invasion and subsequent campaign to defeat Germany. His staff was ordered to begin planning for a cross-Channel invasion, scheduled for May 1, 1944. But the problem continued to be landing craft availability; although U.S. shipyards were producing 20 LSTs a month, nearly all of them were being sent to the Pacific, where Admiral King was overseeing a major campaign against the Japanese-held islands in the Central Pacific. It was not until the last three months of 1943 that LSTs were supplied to the ETO.

Even with all the LSTs produced and currently in theater, General Morgan found that there were not enough landing craft to support the invasion force. For the British, the invasion was their nation's last supreme effort; it had to succeed because there would be no second chance. Thus, Germany had to be sufficiently weakened and near collapse before an invasion should be launched. To the British the invasion marked the end of the war, so they continued to insist that the invasion be adequately resourced in terms of both combat divisions committed in the assault, and in the transport assets necessary to bring those divisions to the beaches of France. To the Americans, the invasion was only a first step in a long campaign. What was needed was a foothold from which a subsequent rapid buildup would allow for offensive operations designed to battle the Germans to ultimate defeat.

The Quadrant Conference was held in Quebec August 14—24, 1943. The Combined Chiefs of Staff accepted COSSAC's concept plan for Overlord and authorized detailed planning. The British advocated a major campaign in Italy to keep German forces occupied in order to support a cross-Channel invasion. An advance into northwest Italy would allow the Allies to establish airbases to support the strategic bomber offensive. The Americans were unwilling to commit too many resources to Italy, as their view was that Overlord was the priority effort. Quadrant reaffirmed a cross-Channel invasion for May of 1944, along with a simultaneous 10-division invasion of southern France. German U-boats had been sufficiently suppressed in the Atlantic and the U.S. war economy was fully mobilized, allowing for both the movement of forces across the Atlantic, and sufficient availability of support and sustainment for operations in Europe. In the Mediterranean, Rome and its surrounding air bases were designated as the objectives. After the fall of Rome, the Allies would advance as far as practicable.

The Sextant Conference in Cairo, held November 22–26 and December 3–7, 1943, gave the British an opportunity to question the invasion of southern France and push instead for support of an advance deeper into the Mediterranean with a goal of bringing Turkey into the war, moving into the Aegean to further stretch German defenses, and aiding partisans in Yugoslavia and Greece. If the resources necessary to conduct these operations delayed Overlord, the British saw no significant difficulties. To the Americans, Overlord was the most direct means to a rapid victory and the transfer of resources to the Pacific to finish Japan. Another delay would push the cross-Channel invasion into 1945. The situation was further complicated by a Roosevelt promise to Chiang Kai-shek and endorsed by Churchill to conduct an amphibious attack against the Japanese in the Bay of Bengal in 1944. The leaders' promise took American planners by surprise; there were not enough landing craft to conduct amphibious operations in the Mediterranean, the Bay of Bengal, and Europe. Something had to give.

At the Eureka Conference in Tehran (Teheran) November 28–30, 1943, the Combined Chiefs of Staff agreed to a compromise. Allied forces in Italy would advance as far north as the Pisa-Rimini Line and the partisans in Yugoslavia would receive additional aid. Turkey would be brought into the war, and Allied operations in the Aegean would support maintaining access to the Dardanelles. Overlord would be delayed to support the Bay of Bengal landing. On November 28, first day of the Eureka Conference, Roosevelt asked Stalin which operation would best support the Soviet war effort: the British offensive plan for the Mediterranean or the northwestern Europe invasion. Stalin promised to enter the war against Japan as soon as Germany was defeated. Barring Turkey entering the war, Stalin believed that a cross-Channel invasion by British and American forces in May of 1944 would best support the Soviet Union, still struggling to contain German counterattacks. The British continued to argue that operations in the Mediterranean would distract the Germans and prevent any reinforcements from the south being sent against the invasion force. On November 30, the Combined Chiefs of Staff agree to launch Overlord in May of 1944 in conjunction with an invasion of southern France. On December 5, the Bay of Bengal invasion would be limited in order that sufficient landing craft were available for Overlord and the landings in southern France, now called Anvil. Overlord and Anvil were designated as the priorities for 1944. The Italian campaign would continue, but the Bay of Bengal invasion would be cancelled. Overlord and Anvil finally gave the Americans free reign to do what they had wished since the beginning of the war—take the fight to the heart of Germany. The American strategic approach had finally won out, but only after the intervention of Stalin. The British, still clinging to an advance into Germany and Austria through Italy, were rebuffed at every turn, as more and more resources were diverted from the Mediterranean to the invasion of Europe.

OPERATIONS IN THE PACIFIC, 1943: THE SEARCH FOR A STRATEGY

A Pacific military conference was held in mid-March 1943 to determine the focus of operations. MacArthur proposed a single command for SWPA and South Pacific with efforts focused on Rabaul, using an indirect approach by seizing bases in New Georgia and New Guinea, followed by assaults on New Britain and Bougainville. The plan called for a total of nearly 13 divisions, 10 of which would be amphibious-capable.

Two carriers and several battleships would reinforce naval forces; air forces would include a total of 45 air groups and 14 independent squadrons. The JCS, faced with a buildup of air forces in Europe to support the strategic bombing campaign and hesitation from the navy in providing carriers to MacArthur to command, led to a modification of the strategy. MacArthur would be reinforced with two additional divisions and aircraft, but nothing near the proposed forces.

On March 28, 1943, a new strategic directive was issued to replace the July 1942 strategic plan. Rabaul would no longer be the objective of SWPA or SOPAC. Instead Rabaul would be isolated through Allied control of the Bismarck Sea with air and naval forces in New Guinea, Bougainville, and the Solomons. MacArthur was to command operations in the theater, with Admiral Halsey; SOPAC commander would operate quasi-independently, with MacArthur having general supervision. Commander POA, Admiral Nimitz, remained in control of naval and air assets in theater, but the JCS could direct naval assets to support operations. U.S. strategy in the Pacific, appearing as a mirror image of the 1941 Japanese strategy, would advance only as far as land-based aircraft could fly. The SWPA and SOPAC staffs coordinated on a plan called Cartwheel, which was completed on April 26, 1943. MacArthur's forces would move along the northwest coast of New Guinea, while Halsey's SOPAC forces moved into the Solomons. The campaign would end with landings on New Britain, Bougainville, and Buka Island, near Bougainville. A total of eight army and two marine divisions, plus a New Zealand and an Australian division, supported by a total of 686 fighters, 879 bombers, and 275 transport aircraft were involved. The operation began on June 30.

For the Central Pacific, the JCS planners submitted a concept of operations for an offensive against the Japanese in the Marshall Islands. Kusaire and Eniwetok were the targets of the combined amphibious invasion. These islands would be used as airbases for an attack on Truk, the key Japanese naval base. But Nimitz was hesitant to move into the Marshalls without having some support from airbases in the

U.S. carrier pilots get a pre-mission briefing below decks. *(National Archives and Records Administration)*

Gilbert Islands first. On July 10, the JCS planners revised their concept, focusing on Tarawa, Makin, and Nauru in the Gilbert Islands. To make this attack, significant support would have to come from the Southwest Pacific Theater, thus delaying any further operations there until 1944. Protests from MacArthur's staff led to modifications of Cartwheel. The coast of New Guinea would be cleared, and Manus Island would be seized. Subsequent operations would be directed to capture air bases at Wewak, New Guinea, followed by an invasion of New Ireland and the Admiralty Islands. Capturing these objectives would effectively neutralize Rabaul and consequently free additional land forces for the Central Pacific. An August 6 version of the plan saw MacArthur continuing west to capture the Vogelkop Peninsula in western New Guinea. The British would begin an attack into Burma to open the land supply routes into China. In the Central Pacific, Nimitz would seize objectives in the Gilberts and the Marshalls, aiming for the Japanese base at Truk in the Carolines. A follow-up offensive would capture bases in the Palau Islands. At the completion of Cartwheel, JCS planners envisioned an American ring stretching from New Guinea to the Palau Islands, all pointing to the Philippines and China.

MacArthur viewed the JCS plan as placing SWPA in a supporting role to the Central Pacific offensives. His staff devised an alternative concept of operations called Reno II, which had as its objective the Philippine Islands. Instead of attacks directed at the fringes of Japanese defenses, MacArthur looked at one combined attack directed to separate the Japanese home islands from their resources in the southeast, thereby crippling Japan's ability to continue the war. Mindanao would serve as the best airbase from which to launch air attacks against the Japanese sea lines of communication and supply. From Mindanao, U.S. forces would invade Luzon, which would put American air, land, and naval forces within striking distance of China, Indochina, and the home islands themselves. MacArthur viewed the capture of Rabaul as essential, along with seizure of the Vogelkop Peninsula, all supported by the Pacific fleet. But in the Central Pacific, MacArthur saw only the Palau Islands as significant, because they could serve as a base of operation for an attack on Mindanao. Nimitz argued that the Bismarck Sea was too constrictive for a large fleet, and the Central Pacific allowed for the U.S. fleet to be ready to engage the remainder of the Japanese fleet in open water. Also, an offensive in the Gilberts and Carolines would force the Japanese to divide their forces between the two theaters.

On August 24, 1943, the JCS issued instructions for offensive operations in the Pacific for 1943–44. Central Pacific Theater tasks were to seize the Gilbert Islands and to prepare to attack the Marshalls and the Carolines. Truk would be captured and used as an airbase. The Palau Island assault would follow, with a move to capture bases in the Mariana Islands. These islands would be used to support the strategic bomber offensive against the Japanese home islands. Southwest Pacific Theater objectives were New Guinea and the Admiralty Islands. Rabaul would be isolated, not captured. The Central Pacific Theater had the priority of effort primarily because capture of bases in the islands would support extended air operations, and most likely force the Japanese navy into a major battle to protect the home islands. Thus, the June initial plan was hardly changed.

The Combined Chiefs of Staff approved the American strategic concept for the defeat of Japan, essentially the same as laid out in the August 24 instructions. SWPA and Central Pacific Theater objectives would place U.S. forces in early 1945 in an area to support attacks against the Philippines, China, or Formosa. MacArthur submitted a plan for the recapture of the Philippines, called Reno III. Nimitz offered a Granite plan that would focus his offensive on the Palau Islands more quickly, bypassing Truk, in order to support MacArthur's advance toward the Philippines.

The division of the Pacific into two theaters of war caused significant problems for the U.S. Joint Chiefs of Staff planners throughout the war. Not only were commanders jealous of their prerogatives, but service biases also limited what each commander was willing to do in support of the other. Arguments over objectives reflected a lack of strategic clarity within the JCS concerning how the Japanese were to be defeated and what the appropriate sequence of events should be to bring about that result. As a result, commanders offered alternatives that arose from opportunities created through unexpected events of the campaigns in both theaters. Events in the two theaters, and not any JCS plan of operation, more often than not dictated the strategic direction of the war in the Pacific.

ALLIED STRATEGY 1944: FROM EUREKA THROUGH OCTAGON

By the end of 1943, the United States military planners had made important progress in planning future direction of the war against Germany and Japan. The battles of attrition in the Solomons, the Gilberts, and New Guinea, the brutal fighting in North Africa and Italy, the losses of men and aircraft in the skies over Europe, and the navy's hard-won triumphs in the North Atlantic and South Pacific had resulted in progress, but at a great cost. The danger for the Allies as they moved into 1944 was culmination and stalemate. Even though the Allies were superior in resources, the Germans and Japanese could through a skillful and stubborn defense, stretch the conflict out and progressively wear down the morale of the people of the United States and Great Britain. The Allied political and military leadership recognized that the tempo of operations must increase and the enemy must be pressed hard on all fronts if the war was to be brought to a satisfactory end. As the strategic initiative passed to the Allies in 1944, the most important problem to solve was how to take advantage of the opportunities presented.

STRATEGIC IMPERATIVES

The emphasis on timelines and schedules in strategic plans in late 1943 reflected an urgency to make identifiable progress. The declared goal for the rapid defeat of Germany in 1944 followed by the defeat of Japan one year later, as well as a desire to initiate an offensive to open the Burma Road and support China, reflected the views among American planners that enough time had already been wasted and decisive operations had to take place. The strategic direction of the European theater had finally been settled, but only by submitting the divergent British and American strategic options to Stalin for his resolution. Overlord, the cross-Channel invasion of Europe, would be the Allied supreme effort in the west. An amphibious landing in southern France, named Anvil, would support Overlord. The American strategy of a rapid and direct attack into the continent by a cross-Channel invasion in order to bring about the defeat of Germany in the shortest amount of time won out over the British desire to continue to wear the enemy down over time through limited operations in the Mediterranean. The agreement to limit operations in the Mediterranean, expand the Combined Bomber Offensive against Germany to include bases in the Mediterranean as well as in Britain, and commit the preponderance of resources to launch and support Overlord and Anvil initially brought a strategic clarity and unity of effort that had been lacking since 1942.

The basic planning for the cross-Channel invasion had been underway since March 5, 1943, with the creation of COSSAC (Chief of Staff to the Supreme Allied Commander). Logistics and transport were the critical factors that shaped planning. Because the Allies had put priority on the construction of antisubmarine assets, especially destroyers and escort carriers in 1943, landing craft and other transportation assets were not available in sufficient quantity to meet operational requirements in both the European and the Mediterranean theaters. Because there were not enough landing craft available to conduct both Overlord and Anvil, the Anvil operation was delayed until August 15.

THE BRITISH-AMERICAN STRATEGIC DEBATE IS RENEWED

Rapidly changing events in Europe by mid-1944 renewed the debates between British and American planners over the proper employment of forces in Europe and the Mediterranean to meet strategic goals. The British began to doubt the value of Anvil, especially after the fall of Rome just days before the Normandy landings. The British began to argue for keeping the Anvil forces in Italy to exploit success. But General Eisenhower, the Allied commander responsible for operations in Europe, was relying on an invasion of southern France. Anvil was to use the U.S. Seventh Army and General de Lattre de Tassigny's French First Army to secure two major ports and move north to join the rest of Allied forces in northern France in an advance into Germany.

While in agreement that the Italian campaign had kept German divisions out of France and the eastern front, American and British planners diverged on the value of any future operations in the Mediterranean theater. To the British, Italy offered additional strategic opportunities, especially in throwing the Germans off-balance in the Balkans. By landing forces in Trieste and advancing into the Ljubljana Gap, not only would additional German forces be occupied, but also there were political-strategic advantages in having British and American forces in Budapest and Vienna instead of Soviet forces. But the Americans were adamant that no diversion of forces from the main effort in France could be tolerated.

The United States grew suspicious of British motives, especially as military decisions took on postwar implications after the fall of 1944. To the Americans it appeared that the British were more interested in obtaining postwar strategic advantages in Europe than defeating Germany as quickly as possible. For the Americans, nothing mattered more than to end the war quickly and turn to the defeat of Japan. Any strategic maneuvering should come at the end of the war, when, after a short time of occupation, U.S. forces would leave Europe to its own devices.

The growing Soviet-American relationship became a driving factor in many decisions made in mid-1944. To the Americans, collaboration with the Soviets was essential not only for winning the war in Europe and Asia, but also for maintaining the peace and security of the world when the war ended. Without such cooperation, the Soviets would have to be confronted militarily and the United States was the only nation capable of doing so. A confrontation would most likely lead to yet another major war, but with U.S. power in Europe limited and the American people unwilling to make such a commitment, the only real recourse was cooperation. Therefore, the United States sought to build a strong relationship with the Soviet Union in order to create a sense of trust. This trust would be built largely by following through on promises made at the Eureka conference in Tehran in November 1943. Thus, long-term strategic interests for postwar Europe were subordinated to the immediate military requirement of defeating Germany as rapidly as possible once the cross-Channel attack had begun.

This rather narrow approach began to change, especially in the light of Soviet conduct in the fall of 1944. The Red Army's pause along the banks of the Vistula River in August while the Poles were battling the Germans in the city of Warsaw clearly indicated that Stalin was willing to let the Germans destroy any Polish armed resistance before Soviet forces advanced. Suspicions of Stalin's intent were confirmed when the Soviets refused to allow British or American aircraft to airdrop supplies to the Polish fighters. This event raised doubts about the optimistic American assessment of postwar conditions. Even as the Americans continued to cooperate in good faith with the Soviets, believing that the ground forces of the USSR were essential to victory both in Europe and the Pacific, concerns about the future grew ever larger in the months ahead.

ALLIED STRATEGY IN EUROPE

After gaining a secure beachhead in Normandy, the Allies planned to build sufficient combat power to defeat German forces in northern France, link up with Allied forces advancing from southern France along the way, and advance to the German border on a broad front. In the land campaign to defeat Germany, the Ruhr was the major objective. The Ruhr, located in the northwest part of Germany, was the industrial heart of the nation; to survive, Germany would have to commit significant ground and air forces to defend it.

Eisenhower envisioned an approach with two axes of advance, one following the northern route to the Ruhr through Belgium and Holland, and one following south of the Ardennes toward Metz, then turning northward to the Ruhr. The final advance through Germany would follow the destruction of German forces. The plan depended on opening enough port facilities to bring in supplies and reinforcements to sustain the advance. In July of 1944 Eisenhower had 18 Allied divisions in Normandy. On July 25, the Normandy breakout began at St-Lô, continued at Avranches, and culminated at the Falaise Gap on 19 August. In the aftermath of that series of battles, the German Fifth Panzer Army and Seventh Army had been destroyed. On August 25 Paris was liberated and, with the Germans in full retreat across northern France, the Allies were soon crossing the Seine River unopposed and months ahead of schedule. After the breakout from Normandy, which ended the Overlord plan, General Eisenhower directed strategy and took broad direction from the Combined Chiefs of Staff.

By September of 1944, logistics problems were crippling the speed of the Allied advance. Supplies of food, fuel, and ammunition could not be brought to the front line units in sufficient quantities from the beaches in Normandy and the port of Cherbourg. Other ports, particularly Antwerp, had not been captured. Motor transport was unavailable and the major road and rail routes in northern France had been destroyed in the bombing campaign prior to the landing. Faced with a difficult strategic decision, Eisenhower chose to give General Bernard Montgomery's 21st Army Group priority of support in order to cross the Rhine River, while General Omar Bradley's U.S. 12th Army Group made limited advances. Eisenhower would maintain both the broad front approach and the original strategic design of two simultaneous thrusts toward the Ruhr, but instead of an equal rate of advance, the priority of support would go to the 21st Army Group.

Montgomery's plan was to make an all-out rapid thrust by armored divisions deep into Germany, supported by a carpet of airborne forces securing key bridges in Holland on the line of advance, protected by overwhelming airpower. His plan, called Operation Market Garden, which began on September 17 with great confidence and collapsed in frustration and stalemate on September 26, ended any hope of outflanking the German armies and engaging in decisive operations by the fall of 1944. Between October and December of 1944, the Allies became involved in a battle of attrition against regrouped German forces defending the border along the Siegfried Line. It became very clear that there would be no victory in Europe in 1944.

General Eisenhower consolidated his forces in preparation for renewing the broad-front advance to the Rhine River in the spring. In December, the Germans launched a surprise offensive against the weakly held Allied line in the Ardennes forest with the intent to split the Allied armies and capture the port of Antwerp. The famous Battle of the Bulge was desperately fought, but the outcome was never in doubt. The preponderance of American land and airpower destroyed the last significant combat forces available to the German high command in the west. Although the Germans had been decisively defeated, the offensive was a deep shock to the Allies.

OPTIONS IN THE PACIFIC

As the fortunes of war shifted in Europe, strategic decisions in the Pacific were forced to shift as well. The United States was heartened by pledges from both Stalin and Churchill at the Eureka conference that they would participate in the final campaign to defeat Japan. Soviet manpower, the British and U.S. fleets, and U.S. strategic airpower appeared to be the keys to ending the war in the Pacific. The U.S. Joint Chiefs of Staff (JCS) had almost total control of the plan of operations for the Pacific, with the Combined Chiefs of Staff providing the British stamp of approval on the American plans. The desire was to press the Japanese throughout the Pacific and achieve significant results.

Despite this pressure to move forward, the goals for the Pacific theaters for most of 1944 remained purposely unclear. It was not yet decided how Japan was to be defeated. The divergence of views between the army and the navy over whether Formosa and China or the Philippines offered the best intermediate step toward the final assault on the Japanese home islands led to disruptions in the theaters of war as well as within the JCS planning staff as different options were submitted, modified, or rejected. With only broad direction, General Douglas MacArthur (Southwest Pacific Area—SWPA) and Admiral Chester Nimitz (Pacific Ocean Areas—POA) would have to pursue their campaign objectives in their theaters without a clear strategic focus to their operations. Meanwhile, in Southeast Asia Command (SEAC), General Stilwell, the American commander under Admiral Mountbatten, struggled to bring Chinese military power to bear in Burma against the Japanese.

During 1944, the two-pronged offensive plan remained the basis for offensive operations. But the JCS, with all the resources now being gathered for Overlord, had to decide how best to maintain the initiative and achieve the most advantageous results with the resources available. For General MacArthur, commanding the SWPA, this meant advancing through New Guinea to Mindanao and, later, Leyte in the Philippines. For Admiral Nimitz and the POA, it meant an advance in the Central Pacific through the Gilberts and the Marshalls to Formosa and ultimately to China. Pursuing a two-pronged offensive allowed for operational flexibility and prevented the Japanese from concentrating all of their strength at one point, but there was no clear direction or purpose to these operations, creating challenges for planners to decide who would do what, where, and for what purpose.

MacArthur's approach through New Guinea depended on speed of execution for success. Although not considered an objective by the JCS, MacArthur argued that the capture of the main island of Luzon in the Philippines was not only key to the defeat of Japan, but also a matter of national honor. Nimitz's approach was more deliberate, but offered the advantage of air and submarine bases in the Marshall and Mariana Islands that would allow the United States to strike the Japanese home islands quickly and would most likely lead to a decisive battle with the Japanese fleet. MacArthur pursued operations to isolate Rabaul and Kavieng and by August had advanced to the Vogelkop Peninsula in New Guinea, covering a distance of 1,000 miles and conducting 14 amphibious landings. Nimitz's forces cleared Kwajalein, Eniwetok, and isolated the Truk Atolls. In June, the battle for Saipan in the Marianas was underway and the Battle of the Philippine Sea ended Japanese naval airpower and crippled the Japanese carrier fleet. Guam and Tinian were captured in August. Meanwhile, the Japanese offensive in Burma had been halted at Imphal and Kohima and British forces were pursuing the remnants of the enemy. By June of 1944, SWPA had advanced along the northern coast of New Guinea as far as Biak Island. The Central Pacific offensive had begun in the Marianas. In the CBI, the Japanese offensive toward India had been stopped at Imphal. The reduction of the Japanese fleet and the growing weakness of Japanese air power gave the United States increasing freedom of action in the Pacific. It became clear to planners that Japan would not be subdued by a naval blockade or air attack. The Japanese home islands would have to be invaded.

General Stilwell's forces had reached Myitkyina in Burma, and the Japanese were pressing Chiang's armies in eastern China. It became apparent that China was not going to become a major contributor to the war. In the China-Burma-India theater, therefore, priority shifted toward keeping Chinese armies in the field and occupying Japanese forces so that those forces could not be shifted to the outer defense of other parts of the Pacific. China also could serve as a base for Allied aircraft to support other offensive operations.

DECISIONS ARE MADE

For months Formosa had been the key objective in preparation for the attack on the Japanese home islands. Luzon would be bypassed, but Leyte would be seized to serve as an airbase to support the attack on Formosa. The Palau Islands were to be captured to also provide sea and air bases. The reason for the decision to capture Formosa was related to the anticipated release of significant air and ground forces after Germany's defeat in late 1944. With these additional forces, attack on Formosa would be possible in 1944 and an attack on the Japanese home islands would be possible in early 1945.

But with the realization that Germany could not be defeated by the end of 1944, it became clear that an invasion of Formosa was unsupportable with the current resources available in theater. JCS planners then turned to Luzon as an alternative, because an invasion of Leyte and Luzon could be done with current forces and transportation available in theater. Both Nimitz and MacArthur were poised to converge their forces for a coordinated attack to capture the Philippines. MacArthur had played a key role in this decision, winning President Roosevelt to his side in a July Pacific strategy conference at Pearl Harbor by arguing passionately and eloquently for the liberation of the Philippines as a sacred American obligation.

As events in the Pacific took on a quicker tempo, the Allied planning staffs at the Octagon conference in Quebec in September established a schedule for the invasion of the Japanese home islands, starting with Kyushu in October 1945 (Operation Olympic) and the decisive assault on Honshu to capture Tokyo in December 1945 (Operation Coronet). The British would provide air and naval forces to support these operations once the war in Europe was over. Admiral Mountbatten was to recapture Burma as quickly as possible and an amphibious landing to capture Rangoon (Operation Dracula) was scheduled for March of 1945.

By October, the U.S. Navy had destroyed much of the Japanese air fleet on Formosa and marines were still fighting on Peleliu in the Palaus while MacArthur made preparations for an invasion of Leyte with 200,000 men of the Sixth Army under Lieutenant General Walter Krueger. The Battle of Leyte Gulf ended the Japanese navy as a threat, despite the near success of the Japanese plan. The successful landing at Leyte sealed the fate of Japan. Nevertheless, for the remainder of 1944, the Japanese and American forces would fight a series of pitiless battle on Leyte often in atrocious weather. By the end of the year, Krueger was preparing for the invasion of Luzon even as the fighting on Leyte continued. Increasingly desperate, the Japanese fought back, adding the suicide plane, the kamikaze, to their arsenal in the hope that these human-directed bombs would eliminate the American fleets. In the meantime, Marianas air bases had been established and the new B-29 Superfortress strategic bombers were arriving. On November 24, the B-29s flew their first bombing mission over Tokyo.

The Allies had been overly optimistic in early 1944 in both Europe and the Pacific. Both enemy resistance, which was much stronger than expected, and logistics constraints prevented the Allies from moving too far beyond plans developed in late 1943. In Europe, U.S. strategic interests continued to clash with British interests. While the Americans took a short-term view, concentrating on building trust with the Soviet Union and winning the war as quickly as possible, the British were far more concerned about the long-term consequences of Soviet power in Europe and believed military operations should be directed to broader political-strategic ends. The British viewpoint after late 1943 was increasingly discarded as American planners took control of the war.

In the Pacific, the desire to maintain the strategic initiative often made the objectives less clear as debate continued throughout most of 1944 over what the intermediate objectives were in preparation for an eventual invasion of Japan. High hopes for early and rapid advances were dashed, as were estimates that forces would be transferred from Europe to the Pacific with the rapid collapse of Germany. As the tempo of operations increased in the fall of 1944, strategic objectives became clearer and the Philippines became the intermediate objective while the strategic bombing of Japan continued.

THE ALLIES APPROACH VICTORY: 1945

The Allies were closing in on central Europe, but there was little movement when the new year began. The Italian front had stalled; reduced in manpower and faced with the formidable defenses of the Apennines, the Allies would make no major advances. The Battle of the Bulge still raged in the Ardennes as soldiers fought in temperatures colder than anyone alive in Europe could remember. The German surprise offensive had reached its limit, and the Bulge, 60 miles long and 40 miles wide and containing 24 German divisions, was slowly being pushed back.

German weapons such as the V-2 and the Me-262 jet fighter were significant additions to German capabilities, but came far too late in the war to have an effect. The Allied strategic bombing campaign reached its apogee. The German air force could no longer put up any significant resistance. The German fuel industry and transportation systems were attacked without pause for the last few months of the war, denying many German units both tactical and strategic mobility. Additional U.S. air force assets were diverted to supporting ground forces in order to isolate the Ruhr and deny Germany its economic base.

After the Battle of the Bulge, Eisenhower sought to employ his combat power to destroy as many German forces west of the Rhine River as possible. In keeping with his broad-front strategy, Eisenhower wanted a continuous and simultaneous effort from each army group so that the Allies all reached the Rhine at the same time. Stung by the German surprise attack in the Ardennes, he was more determined than ever to maintain a strong front to deal with any German counteroffensive. Once the Allies reached the Rhine River, Eisenhower believed it would serve as a strong line of defense from which the Allies could then concentrate forces and launch deep thrusts into the heart of Germany.

A German Me-262, photographed just before delivery to the Luftwaffe *(National Archives and Records Administration)*

The advance to the Rhine River, the last physical barrier into Germany, would occupy the Allies for most of the spring. The British disliked General Eisenhower's broad-front strategy, the approach that kept equal pressure on the German defenses throughout Germany. Instead, the British wanted to continue with a major offensive in northern Germany to gain access to the north German plain, seize the North Sea ports, and advance to Berlin.

In March 1945 the Allies crossed the Rhine in several places. Montgomery now hoped to lead his 21st Army Group in a thrust toward Berlin but was instead ordered to encircle the Ruhr while the American 12th Army Group advanced into central Germany and Austria and entered Czechoslovakia. Montgomery's forces advanced onto the north German plain and on May 4, at Luneberg Heath, he received the surrender of the German forces opposed to him. The official German surrender came on May 8, but the war had ended for all intents and purposes four days earlier. Instead of the United States and Britain occupying Berlin and most of central Europe, those spoils fell to the Soviets. The stage was set for the Cold War.

POLITICAL ISSUES DOMINATE

Throughout 1945, Great Britain was increasingly concerned about the encroaching Soviet power in eastern Europe, led by the advance of the Soviet armies. Churchill for years had sought both through military operations in the ETO and the Mediterranean theater and by direct political negotiations with Stalin to limit that advance.

For Roosevelt, America's larger political-strategic goals were simple: total military victory and the establishment of a lasting and secure peace in the shortest time possible with the fewest losses. To achieve these goals, cooperation with the Soviet Union was essential as long as the war against Germany continued. Roosevelt believed that he could deal with Stalin honestly and openly and the Soviet leader would respond in kind.

For both Great Britain and the USSR, Poland was the key issue. Great Britain had declared war in 1939 to defend Poland and had pledged to maintain a free and independent Poland. For the Soviets, half of Poland had been Soviet territory since 1939 (a result of the Nazi-Soviet nonaggression pact) and they had no intention of giving up this important buffer between the USSR and Germany. A pro-Soviet government in Poland was essential to Stalin's postwar security objectives. The United States was in the middle—largely uninterested in postwar arrangements and firm in the belief that all people, whether liberated by the Soviet, American, or British forces, had the right to free elections. Roosevelt had suspicions of Great Britain's true intentions, believing that Britain sought to reassert its prewar imperial dominance.

The strategic dilemma for the United States throughout the first half of 1945 was to maintain Stalin's cooperation and goodwill to ensure the USSR would contribute ground forces to the defeat of Japan even as the United States and the Soviet Union were growing further apart as each pursued separate postwar goals in Europe. The United States sought long-term peace and security in Europe through the promotion of liberty and democracy for the newly freed nations of Europe, while the Soviet Union increasingly displayed its interests to be the pursuit of long-term security through occupation and domination of the states of eastern Europe under the totalitarian control of pro-Soviet leaders. Great Britain, now the minor power, sought to keep the Soviets out of Europe as much as possible and to use the power and influence of the United States as leverage.

With the death of President Roosevelt in April of 1945 and the subsequent defeat and occupation of Germany, a new president and secretary of state now felt less sensitive to accommodating the Soviet Union. There were growing concerns within the military leadership that the Soviet Union intended to expand its influence and control at every opportunity in the postwar period. How much expansion should the United States accept became one of the most important military policy questions in mid-1945.

THE UNCERTAIN ROLE OF ALLIED FORCES IN THE PACIFIC

In the Pacific, the Allies still faced formidable Japanese land forces in China and Southeast Asia, even as the enemy was being worn down in the Philippines and Burma. The Japanese navy was powerless after the Battle of Leyte Gulf in October 1944 to change the strategic situation. For the Japanese, fighting decisive battles in China and the Philippines would grind down the Americans as they bought time to solidify the homeland defenses for a final battle of attrition that they believed they could win and from which they would still emerge victorious.

In January 1945 there were 27 U.S. combat divisions in the Pacific, six of those marine divisions. General MacArthur commanded 1.5 million men in the Allied air, land, and sea forces. Admiral Nimitz commanded the largest navy in the history of the world. The U.S. Navy in January 1945 consisted of 1,167 combat ships, nearly 55,000 landing craft and assault ships, and 37,000 aircraft.

For the Americans there were two strategic approaches to defeating Japan. One was the air bombardment and naval blockade of Japan to force the Japanese to surrender through starvation and massive destruction of their industrial base and cities. The other was the direct invasion of Japan and the direct conquest of the home islands. Like most of the major strategic issues for the Pacific during the war, no final decision was made until the press of events largely dictated the choice. The atomic bomb arrived almost as a deus ex machina, solving the immediate problem of direct invasion of the Japanese home islands.

By July 1945 the Joint Chiefs of Staff were against allowing any more concessions to the Soviet Union, especially in its demands for access to strategic waterways in northern and southern Europe. Only the need for Soviet manpower to deal with Japanese forces on the Asian mainland required the United States to maintain the spirit of cooperation that had marked the war years. With the successful detonation in the New Mexico desert of the first atomic weapon on July 16, the military leadership was even less willing to continue cooperating with the Soviets. They argued that the Red Army would not be necessary to end the war with Japan. However, the strategic goals of speeding the surrender of Japan and minimizing American casualties had always been the paramount reasons for keeping the Soviets in the planning for the Pacific. No one could be sure that the atomic bombs alone would have the decisive effect on Japan that would end the war. Therefore, the Soviets had to be involved as part of achieving the overall strategic purpose.

The surrender of Japan ended all pretenses for continuing good relations with the Soviet Union. Any hopes for a postwar cooperative effort with the USSR to maintain peace had been abandoned as the Soviets reneged on their pledges made at Yalta and Potsdam. The United States had realized too late its strategic interest in keeping Europe from being dominated by a hostile power. This concern now expanded to areas of the Pacific and Asia as well.

The atomic bomb opened a new chapter in strategy and deterrence, leaving a powerful and prosperous United States standing astride a shocked and uncertain world that struggled to adapt to the tumultuous new circumstances that had emerged from the most terrible war ever fought.

CHRONOLOGY OF KEY EVENTS

1922

October 28
ITALY: The Italian Fascist Party under the leadership of Benito Mussolini conducts its famous "March on Rome." Mussolini is appointed premier two days later and will dissolve Parliament in 1926. He establishes an authoritarian dictatorship, gaining power through appeals to nationalism and by using a clever combination of bluff and intimidation.

1931

September 18
CHINA: Japan invades Manchuria.

1932

January 29
CHINA: Japanese land, air, and naval forces attack Shanghai.

February 18
CHINA: Japan establishes the puppet state of Manchukuo, formerly Manchuria.

1933

January 30
GERMANY: Adolf Hitler is appointed chancellor of Germany.

February 24
JAPAN: Japan withdraws from the League of Nations.

October 14
GERMANY: Germany withdraws from the League of Nations and initiates peacetime military conscription.

1935

October 3
ITALY: Italy invades Ethiopia without a declaration of war.

October 5
ATLANTIC: Under the Neutrality Act of 1935, the United States declares Italy and Ethiopia belligerents and embargoes arms to both countries. Americans are warned not to travel on ships of either belligerent. President Roosevelt issues a warning that Americans who engage in trade with ether Italy or Ethiopia do so at their own risk. This last warning is a diplomatic slap to Italy, since Ethiopia is a landlocked country anyway.

1936

October 25
GERMANY: Rome-Berlin Axis is formed

November 25
GERMANY: Japan signs an Anti-Comintern Pact with Germany.

1937

July 7
CHINA: Incident at the Marco Polo Bridge between Japanese and Chinese troops leads to full-scale war.

July 29
CHINA: Japanese forces occupy Beijing (Peking).

August 8
CHINA: Japanese naval forces land in Shanghai after two Japanese marines are killed by Chinese forces.

August 12
CHINA: The U.S. 4th Marines at Shanghai are reinforced by over 100 marines and sailors from the USS *Augusta*. Elements of the 4th Marines provide support to municipal police in accordance with an international agreement.

August 17
CHINA: Evacuations of American citizens from Shanghai begin.

September 19
CHINA: A brigade headquarters and the 6th Marines from San Diego arrive in Shanghai, bringing the entire marine detachment to over 2,500 men.

November 8
CHINA: Chinese forces are driven out of Shanghai.

November 9

ATLANTIC: The United States Joint Board directs its planners to examine how simultaneous threats from German and Italian aggression in Europe and from Japanese expansion in the Far East might threaten American security and interests.

December 11

ITALY: Italy withdraws from the League of Nations. Spanish civil war begins. Both Italy and Germany provide advisers and weapons to Spanish fascists.

December 12

CHINA: U.S. gunboat *Panay* on Yangtze River, assisting the evacuation of foreigners from the fighting near Nanking, is sunk by Japanese air attack. Three Americans are killed. Japan apologizes and pays a $2.2 million indemnity, while promising to control its forces around Nanking.

December 13

CHINA: Japanese forces occupy Nanking. More than 370,000 Chinese men, women, and children are brutally murdered in a series of atrocities that shocks the world.

1938

January 30

GERMANY: Germany announces it no longer is bound by the Versailles Treaty.

February 17

PACIFIC: The 6th Marines and the brigade headquarters redeploy to San Diego from Shanghai.

March 11

AUSTRIA: German troops cross the Austrian frontier.

March 12

AUSTRIA: Germany occupies Austria.

March 13

AUSTRIA: The Austro-German Union proclaimed at Vienna. Austria is part of the German Reich (empire).

April 16

BRITAIN: A British-Italian agreement signed. Great Britain recognizes the conquest of Ethiopia in exchange for a promise from Italy to withdraw all troops from Spain at the conclusion of the civil war.

April 27

BRITAIN: A three-day Anglo-French military conference begins in London. The British and French general staffs agree to collaborate more closely for mutual defense.

September 15
GERMANY: British prime minister Neville Chamberlain and Adolf Hitler hold talks in Berchtesgaden, Germany, over Hitler's demands to protect the German population in the Sudetenland of Czechoslovakia. Czechoslovakia is willing to go to war to defend itself against German aggression.

September 26
ATLANTIC: President Franklin Roosevelt appeals for peace directly to Hitler and President Eduard Beneš of Czechoslovakia.

September 29
GERMANY: Neville Chamberlain, Edouard Daladier, Adolf Hitler, and Benito Mussolini sign the Munich Pact. Germany wins control of the Sudetenland in Czechoslovakia.

September 30
GERMANY: Chamberlain and Hitler sign a declaration of peace.

October 1
GERMANY: German forces begin occupation of the Sudetenland.

November 9
ATLANTIC: The Joint Board begins reviewing U.S. national readiness for war. The board orders the Joint Planning Committee to "make exploratory studies and estimates" to examine the courses of action available to the United States in case of a violation of the Monroe Doctrine by Italy or Germany or an attack by Japan on the Philippines.

The Joint Board exists to coordinate on issues of mutual interest for the army and the navy and to make recommendations to the civilian service secretaries. The Joint Board is made up of the army chief of staff, his deputy, the head of the army's War Plans Division, the chief of naval operations, his assistant chief, and the director of naval war plans. It is not intended to be a higher staff or to provide unified direction of commanders in wartime.

November 13
PACIFIC: Japan closes the Yangtze River to all foreign ships.

December 6
GERMANY: A Franco-German peace declaration is signed.

1939

March 6
PACIFIC: Japan announces a full-scale naval building program to reach parity with United States and Great Britain.

March 15
CZECHOSLOVAKIA: Czechoslovakia is invaded and incorporated into Germany.

March 31
BRITAIN: Prime Minister Neville Chamberlain in the House of Commons announces that Great Britain and France pledge to come to the assistance of Poland in the event of any action that threatens Poland's independence.

April 1
SPAIN: General Francisco Franco declares the end of the civil war in Spain.

April 6
BRITAIN: Prime Minister Chamberlain announces in the House of Commons that Poland and Britain have joined with France in an alliance.

April 7
ITALY: Italy attacks Albania.

April 13
BRITAIN: Prime Minister Chamberlain announces in the House of Commons that Britain and France will guarantee the borders of Romania and Greece and will lend all support possible where there are clear threats to the independence of either Romania or Greece.

April 14
ATLANTIC: President Roosevelt appeals to both Hitler and Mussolini for a 10-year guaranty of peace.

April 28
GERMANY: The German government abrogates the 10-year nonaggression treaty with Poland signed in 1934 and demands the return of the free city Danzig and the Polish Corridor, taken from Germany in the Versailles Treaty after World War I to provide Poland access to the Baltic Sea.

May 22
ITALY: Italy signs a 10-year military pact with Germany, called the "Pact of Steel."

July 5
ATLANTIC: President Roosevelt orders that the Joint Board and other boards under control of the secretaries of the army and navy will now operate under the direction and supervision of the commander in chief. As world tensions mount, Roosevelt wants more direct approval authority for actions taken by the military departments.

July 26
PACIFIC: The United States informs Japan that it will not renew the 1911 trade agreement, leaving the United States free after six months to initiate economic sanctions against Japan.

August 1
ATLANTIC: Admiral Harold R. Stark becomes U.S. chief of naval operations. He presses for a coordinated effort by all representatives of government to address issues of national security.

August 23
SOVIET UNION: Germany and the Soviet Union sign a nonaggression pact.

August 24
ATLANTIC: President Roosevelt sends appeals for peace to European leaders.

August 25
BRITAIN: Great Britain and Poland sign a formal treaty of mutual assistance.

September 1
GERMANY: Germany invades Poland, beginning the Second World War.
    General George C. Marshall becomes army chief of staff.

September 3
BRITAIN: Britain and France declare war, honoring their pledge to protect Poland.
Australia and New Zealand follow suit.

September 5
ATLANTIC: President Franklin D. Roosevelt declares America neutral. U.S. Navy
begins offshore patrolling along the East Coast and in the Caribbean to monitor
foreign warships.

September 8
ATLANTIC: Roosevelt declares a limited national emergency and orders the increase
of the authorized strength of the navy and Marine Corps.

September 10
ATLANTIC: Canada declares war on Germany.

September 16
ATLANTIC: Soviet troops invade Poland.
    British begin convoy operations for merchant ships from Halifax to Great Brit-
ain to protect the vital flow of supplies from North America. German submarines
begin attacks on convoys.

September 21
ATLANTIC: Roosevelt requests that the Neutrality Act of 1937 be changed to allow
for sale of arms to belligerents.

September 27
POLAND: Poland surrenders.

September 28
SOVIET UNION: German-Soviet border and friendship treaty is signed, resulting in
the partition of Poland.

October 5
PACIFIC: Hawaiian Detachment, U.S. Fleet, led by the carrier USS *Enterprise* along
with other warships and auxiliary vessels, moves to Pearl Harbor under command
of Vice Admiral Adolphus Andrews.

October 15
TURKEY: The Anglo-French-Turkish 15-year mutual-assistance pact signed in Ankara.

November 4
ATLANTIC: Neutrality Act of 1939 allows for a policy of "cash and carry" for belligerents to replace a total arms embargo. The act prohibits U.S. ships from entering combat zones. Roosevelt declares the waters around Great Britain to be a combat zone.

November 30
SOVIET UNION: Soviet troops invade Finland.

1940

January 20
ATLANTIC: U.S. government issues an official protest to the British government concerning the boarding and inspection of neutral American ships in the Mediterranean.

March 8
PACIFIC: United States authorizes $20 million loan to China. Japan declares it an unfriendly act.

March 12
SOVIET UNION: Soviet-Finnish peace treaty and protocol is signed in Moscow.

April 2
PACIFIC: U.S. Fleet departs the West Coast for a major fleet exercise off Hawaii.

April 8
BRITAIN: Great Britain and France announce that three areas off the coast of Norway have been mined to prevent shipments of Scandinavian ore to Germany.

April 9
DENMARK: German troops invade Denmark. Germany attacks Norway.
ATLANTIC: U.S. planners begin to modify existing war plans to reflect a simultaneous threat in Europe and the Pacific.

April 10
ATLANTIC: Roosevelt extends the war zone in the waters northeast to the USSR.

April 17
ATLANTIC: Secretary of State Cordell Hull issues a formal statement declaring any change in status quo in the Pacific "would be prejudicial to the cause of stability, peace and security."

April 25
ATLANTIC: Roosevelt declares neutrality in war between Germany and Norway.

May 7

PACIFIC: Roosevelt orders the U.S. Fleet to remain in the Pacific as a deterrent to the Japanese.

May 9

ATLANTIC: British forces occupy Iceland.

May 10

WESTERN EUROPE: Germany invades Netherlands, Belgium, and Luxembourg. British prime minister Neville Chamberlain resigns. He is replaced by the first lord of the Admiralty, Winston S. Churchill.

May 11

ATLANTIC: Roosevelt declares America neutral in the conflict between Germany, Belgium, Luxembourg, and the Netherlands. The United States declares it will not allow any other nation to control the Netherlands (Dutch) East Indies, a pointed warning to Japan.

May 14

NETHERLANDS: Netherlands surrenders to Germany; German ground and air forces conduct a breakthrough of French defenses in the Ardennes area.

May 15

NETHERLANDS: The army of the Netherlands surrenders.

May 16

ATLANTIC: Roosevelt asks Congress to appropriate almost $900 million for defense and national security.

May 26

FRANCE: British and French troops begin evacuation at Dunkirk, crossing the English Channel to Britain and safety.

May 28

BELGIUM: Belgium surrenders to Germany.

June 9

NORWAY: The Norwegian high command orders the army to cease hostilities at midnight.

June 10

ITALY: Italy declares war on France and Great Britain. Norway surrenders to Germany.

June 11

ATLANTIC: Australia, New Zealand, and South Africa declare war on Italy. President Roosevelt declares the Mediterranean and the Red Sea a war zone.

June 14

ATLANTIC: President Roosevelt signs the Naval Expansion Act. The navy's carrier, cruiser, and submarine tonnage will expand to 167,000 tons. Auxiliary shipping will also increase by 75,000 tons. Naval aviation will grow by 4,500 aircraft.

June 14
FRANCE: German troops enter Paris.

June 15
ATLANTIC: Naval aviation strength increased to 10,000 aircraft.

June 15
SOVIET UNION: Soviet troops occupy Lithuania.

June 17
SOVIET UNION: The Soviet Union declares that Estonia and Latvia have agreed to the free passage of Soviet forces through their territory and will form new pro-Soviet governments.

June 19
ATLANTIC: President Roosevelt signs the Two Ocean Navy Act, expanding the size of the U.S. Fleet by 70 percent.

June 22
FRANCE: Armistice declared. France is divided into a German occupied area and a quasi-independent area with a government body led by Marshal Henri Pétain located in Vichy. A Free French government-in-exile is established in Britain under the nominal leadership of Charles de Gaulle.

June 24
FRANCE: Franco-Italian armistice signed.

June 26
PACIFIC: Roosevelt orders that no aviation gasoline, or steel, or iron scrap will be sold to Japan.

June 27
ROMANIA: Romania cedes Bessarabia to the Soviet Union.

June 28
BRITAIN: The British government recognizes General Charles de Gaulle as the leader of Frenchmen who continue to pledge resistance to the Nazis.

July 3
MEDITERRANEAN: The British sink or seize a major part of the French fleet in Oran, Algeria, to prevent combat ships from falling into German hands.

July 5
FRANCE: Vichy French government of Marshal Pétain breaks off diplomatic relations with Great Britain as result of British attack on the French fleet at Oran.

July 18
BRITAIN: Under pressure from the Japanese, Prime Minister Winston Churchill announces terms of a temporary agreement for stoppage of war supplies to China through Burma and Hong Kong.

August 10
PACIFIC: The Japanese extend their naval blockade of China southward.

August 17
ATLANTIC: Germany declares a total blockade of the British Isles. All ships in the area will be sunk without warning.

August 25
SOVIET UNION: Estonia, Latvia, and Lithuania are formally incorporated into the Soviet Union. The United States refuses to recognize the incorporation.

August 31
ATLANTIC: Roosevelt calls to active service 60,000 members of the National Guard.

September 1
PACIFIC: Fleet Marine Force establishes a detachment of nine officers and 168 enlisted men on Midway Island.

September 3
ATLANTIC: Roosevelt announces that the United States will provide Britain 50 World War I–era destroyers in exchange for use of air and naval bases in Newfoundland, Bermuda, Bahamas, Jamaica, St. Lucia, Trinidad, and British Guiana. Bases at these locations will be obtained by a 99-year lease.

September 4
ATLANTIC: Secretary of State Cordell Hull warns the Japanese not to attempt to change the status of French Indochina.

September 16
ATLANTIC: The Selective Training and Service Act is signed, creating the first peacetime draft in American history.

September 22
PACIFIC: Vichy France allows Japanese forces to access three airfields in French Indochina and maintain a 6,000-man garrison.

September 27
GERMANY: Germany, Italy, and Japan sign the Tripartite Pact. The Berlin-Rome-Tokyo Axis is formed.

October 5
PACIFIC: Japan offers recognition of U.S. dominance in the Western Hemisphere in return for U.S. recognition of Japanese dominance of East Asia.

October 28
ITALY: Italy attacks Greece prior to the expiration of its ultimatum.

November 5
ATLANTIC: Roosevelt wins his third consecutive term as president.

November 10
ATLANTIC: Marine Corps Reserve units are integrated into the regular Marine Corps.

November 12
ATLANTIC: Admiral Harold R. Stark, chief of naval operations, recommends that the U.S. Army and Navy begin secret talks with British, Canadian, and Dutch military leaders to reach agreements on cooperation in case the United States enters the war.

November 20
HUNGARY: Hungary signs a protocol of adherence to the Axis tripartite pact.

November 23
ROMANIA: Romania signs a protocol of adherence to the Axis tripartite pact.

November 24
SLOVAKIA: Slovakia signs a protocol of adherence to the Axis tripartite pact.

November 30
PACIFIC: U.S. loans $100 million to China for wartime needs.

December 6
PACIFIC: Japanese-Thai pact of amity is signed.

December 9
PACIFIC: Japan's foreign minister denies that its alliance with Germany is intended to threaten the United States. Japan pledges that it will not fight the United States unless the United States acts as an aggressor.

December 19
ATLANTIC: President Roosevelt approves $25 million in military aid to China. This will allow China to purchase 100 U.S. P-40 fighter planes.

December 20
ATLANTIC: President Roosevelt appoints William Knudsen to head a four-man defense board to plan for national defense and coordinating aid to Great Britain.

December 29
ATLANTIC: President Roosevelt, in a radio address to the nation, warns Americans of impending danger and appeals to citizens to support rearmament. "The people of Europe who are defending themselves do not ask where to do their fighting. They ask us for the implements of war, the planes, the tanks, the guns, the freighters which will enable them to fight for their liberty and for our security. Emphatically we must get these weapons to them, get them to them in sufficient volume and quickly enough so that we and our children will be saved the agony and suffering of war which others have had to endure. . . . We must be the great arsenal of democracy."

December 31
ATLANTIC: U-boats have sunk 2.6 million tons of Allied and neutral shipping, amounting to 55 percent of all shipping losses.

1941

January 6
ATLANTIC: In an address to Congress, President Roosevelt outlines a desire for a world not based on a "new order of tyranny" but on "four essential human freedoms." He describes these as freedom of speech and expression, freedom to worship God, freedom from want, and freedom from fear. "Freedom means the supremacy of human rights everywhere. Our support goes to those who struggle to gain those rights or keep them. Our strength is our unity of purpose. To that high concept there can be no end save victory."

January 9
PACIFIC: U.S. State Department advises American citizens to leave Japan.

January 29
ATLANTIC: Secret initial talks begin in Washington between U.S. and British planners to discuss options to determine the best way to defeat the Axis powers if the United States enters the war.

January 30
PACIFIC: French Indochina-Thailand armistice is signed in Saigon.

January 31
ATLANTIC: At the end of January, a total of 21 ships (over 126,000 tons) have been lost to U-boats in the Atlantic.

February 3
ATLANTIC: The Navy Department creates three independent fleets: U.S. Pacific Fleet, U.S. Atlantic Fleet, and U.S. Asiatic Fleet. Admiral Husband Kimmel is the commander in chief, Pacific Fleet, Admiral Ernest J. King is the commander in chief, Atlantic Fleet, and Admiral Thomas C. Hart is the commander in chief, Asiatic Fleet.

February 6
GERMANY: Hitler orders that all German sea and air assets be employed against Allied supply ships.

February 10
BRITAIN: Great Britain severs diplomatic relations with Romania.

February 28
ATLANTIC: At the end of February, a total of 39 ships (over 196,000 tons) have been lost to U-boats in the Atlantic.

March 1
BULGARIA: Bulgaria signs a protocol of adherence to the Axis tripartite pact.

March 5

BRITAIN: Great Britain severs diplomatic relations with Bulgaria.

March 11

ATLANTIC: Congress passes Lend-Lease Act. Aimed primarily at Great Britain, it allows the president to provide food aid, monetary loans, and war materiél to any country friendly to the United States as a means to keep out of the war in Europe and Asia.

March 12

SOVIET UNION: The Soviet Union establishes diplomatic relations with Thailand.

March 18

PACIFIC: The Marine 7th Defense Battalion arrives in Samoa.

March 24

TURKEY: Turkish-Soviet communiqué promises neutrality if either should be attacked.

March 25

YUGOSLAVIA: Yugoslavia signs a protocol of adherence to the Axis tripartite pact. The German war zone is extended beyond Iceland.

March 27

ATLANTIC: Military representatives of the United States, Canada, and Great Britain meet in Washington, D.C., to map out strategy in case of America entering the war against Germany. The U.S. Navy would support convoy operations to Britain, and the U.S. Pacific Fleet would be used offensively against Japanese economic power.

Anti-Axis coup d'etat is underway in Yugoslavia.

March 29

ATLANTIC: Meetings are completed and a report is produced known as ABC-1. The report addresses not only strategic policy but also command organization and strategic direction and planning. The emphasis is on collaboration in planning and execution of military operations, reflecting the unease of Americans in allowing the British to have too much influence on U.S. military affairs. The report sets the stage for a U.S.-Great Britain strategic partnership.

March 31

ATLANTIC: At the end of the month of March, a total of 41 ships (about 243,000 tons) have been lost to U-boats in the Atlantic. Five U-boats have been sunk.

April 3

IRAQ: Pro-Nazi coup d'etat is under way in Iraq.

April 5

YUGOSLAVIA: Yugoslav-Soviet treaty of friendship and nonaggression is signed.

April 6

YUGOSLAVIA: Germany invades Yugoslavia and Greece. Italy declares war on Yugoslavia.

April 7
BRITAIN: Great Britain severs diplomatic relations with Hungary.

April 9
ATLANTIC: The United States signs an agreement with Denmark, agreeing to defend Greenland against invasion in return for basing rights.

April 10
ATLANTIC: President Roosevelt under the provisions of Lend-Lease transfers Coast Guard cutters to Great Britain. Roosevelt issues a proclamation modifying the Red Sea combat zone.

April 12
ATLANTIC: Japanese ambassador to the United States Nomura presents Secretary of State Cordell Hull with a proposal for peace in the Pacific.

April 13
SOVIET UNION: Japan and the Soviet Union sign a five-year nonaggression pact with a joint declaration regarding the frontiers of the Japanese protectorate of Manchukuo. This agreement allows Japan to pursue the conquest of China without fear of Soviet interference.

April 17
YUGOSLAVIA: Yugoslavia surrenders to Germany.

April 18
PACIFIC: Admiral Husband E. Kimmel, commander in chief of the Pacific Fleet (CINCPAC), identifies Wake Island as a priority defense requirement to Admiral Harold R. Stark, chief of naval operations.

April 22
ATLANTIC: The regular army enlisted strength is authorized to increase to 232,000.

April 27
GREECE: German forces occupy Athens.

May 2
IRAQ: British begin fighting Iraqi troops in Iraq.

May 6
SOVIET UNION: Joseph Stalin is announced as Soviet premier.

May 6
PACIFIC: Japan and Vichy France sign an agreement for economic collaboration in French Indochina.

May 9
PACIFIC: A French Indochina-Thailand peace treaty is signed. Japan will guarantee the borders.

May 14
ATLANTIC: Germany declares a Red Sea danger zone.

The Joint Board approves the basic joint war plan and incorporates U.S. and British strategic and operational direction.

May 15
FRANCE: Marshal Pétain at Vichy announces the replacement of the armistice agreement with a new collaboration agreement.

May 16
SOVIET UNION: Iraq and the Soviet Union establish diplomatic relations.

May 21
ATLANTIC: Unarmed U.S. merchant ship *Robin Moor* is torpedoed and sunk off the coast of Africa by a German submarine. No American casualties.

May 27
ATLANTIC: Roosevelt announces the Atlantic neutrality patrols will be extended to prevent German warships from threatening the Western Hemisphere. He also announces that the United States will give all aid and support necessary to Great Britain and any other country resisting Hitler's Germany.

The American Liaison Committee, a group of military representatives, meets with British staff officers in London to receive information on current military operations and future plans.

May 31
IRAQ: British-Iraqi armistice is signed in Baghdad.

June 8
MIDDLE EAST: British and Free French troops enter French Syria and Lebanon.

June 18
TURKEY: German-Turkish 10-year friendship pact is signed in Ankara.

June 21
ATLANTIC: The War Department creates the Army Air Forces with its own general staff. General Arnold is the chief, on equal footing with Admiral King and General Marshall.

June 22
SOVIET UNION: Nazi Germany attacks the Soviet Union. Italy declares war on the Soviet Union. The Romanians occupy Bessarabia.

June 23
PACIFIC: Admiral Stark orders elements of the 1st Marine Defense Battalion to be established on Wake Island.

June 27
HUNGARY: Hungary declares war on the Soviet Union.

June 28

ATLANTIC: Albania declares war on the Soviet Union.

President Roosevelt creates the Office of Scientific Research. Dr. Vannevar Bush, the chairman of the new group, will coordinate war-related scientific research.

June 30

ATLANTIC: Vichy France severs diplomatic relations with the Soviet Union.

The active duty strength of the U.S. Marine Corps is 54,359.

July 1

ATLANTIC: Admiral King establishes task forces to escort convoys between the United States and Iceland.

July 2

ATLANTIC: The Joint Board approves the addition of two new members: Major General Henry H. Arnold, deputy chief of staff for air, and the chief of the Bureau of Aeronautics, Rear Admiral J. H. Towers.

July 3

CHINA: Army Chief of Staff General George C. Marshall establishes the American Military Mission to China (AMMISCA), and appoints Brigadier General John Magruder to lead the group, which will advise the Chinese on identifying military items needed to equip the Chinese military so that these can then be matched to U.S. defense production requirements.

July 7

ATLANTIC: Iceland authorizes U.S. forces to be stationed on the island. The 1st Marine Brigade lands at Reykjavik to prevent any possibility that German forces will occupy the island.

July 9

ATLANTIC: The British Joint Staff Mission is established in Washington, D.C. These officers arrive with the intention to act as counterparts to the U.S. Army chief of staff and the navy chief of naval operations.

July 12

ATLANTIC: A force of 5,000 marines relieves British troops at Reykjavik, Iceland, as the United States takes responsibility for the defense of Iceland.

British-Soviet mutual-assistance agreement is signed in Moscow.

July 25

PACIFIC: Japan announces a protectorate over French Indochina; United States freezes Japanese assets totaling $130 million and ends the export of oil to Japan; Canada freezes both Japanese and Chinese funds.

July 26

ATLANTIC: Great Britain freezes Japanese assets and announces its intention to end its commercial treaty. President Roosevelt orders the formation of the U.S. Army

Forces Far East (USAFFE) under the command of Lieutenant General Douglas MacArthur in the Philippines. The 150,000-man Philippine army is combined with U.S. Army forces.

July 27
PACIFIC: New Zealand freezes Japanese assets.

July 28
PACIFIC: Netherlands East Indies freezes Japanese assets and refuses to provide any further oil shipments to Japan. Australia freezes all Japanese assets.

July 30
ATLANTIC: The United States recognizes the Czechoslovak government-in-exile in London.

July 31
PACIFIC: Strength of the Philippine Division is reported at 10,473—over 2,000 are U.S. Army regulars, the rest are U.S.-led and trained Philippine Scouts. Total U.S. strength in the Philippines, including the Philippine Division, the air corps, harbor defenses, and service detachments, is 22,532.

August 1
ATLANTIC: President Roosevelt orders the end of shipment of oils and motor fuels to Japan. Japan and Thailand sign an economic trade agreement. Thailand will extend $3.6 million in credits. A naval air station is established on Midway Island.

August 9
ATLANTIC: President Roosevelt, on the cruiser USS *Augusta,* arrives in Placentia Bay off Newfoundland after a three-day secret trip and meets with Prime Minister Winston Churchill, who arrives on the battleship HMS *Prince of Wales.* The two leaders discuss strategy and war aims, producing the Atlantic Charter, a document outlining common democratic principles of free peoples. Roosevelt assures Churchill that America will fight against Germany first, and that the United States would protect British convoys from America to Britain.

August 12
ATLANTIC: The Roosevelt-Churchill meeting ends.

August 14
ATLANTIC: The Atlantic Charter is issued.

> The President and the Prime Minister have had several conferences. They have considered the dangers to world civilization arising from the policies of military domination by conquest upon which the Hitlerite government of Germany and other governments associated therewith have embarked, and have made clear the stress which their countries are respectively taking for their safety in the face of these dangers. . . . They have agreed upon the following joint declaration:

> Joint declaration of the President of the United States of America and the Prime Minister, Mr. Churchill, representing His Majesty's Government in the United Kingdom, being met together, deem it right to make known certain common principles

in the national policies of their respective countries on which they base their hopes for a better future for the world.

First, their countries seek no aggrandizement, territorial or other;

Second, they desire to see no territorial changes that do not accord with the freely expressed wishes of the peoples concerned;

Third, they respect the right of all peoples to choose the form of government under which they will live; and they wish to see sovereign rights and self-government restored to those who have been forcibly deprived of them;

Fourth, they will endeavor, with due respect for their existing obligations, to further the enjoyment by all States, great or small, victor or vanquished, of access, on equal terms, to the trade and to the raw materials of the world which are needed for their economic prosperity;

Fifth, they desire to bring about the fullest collaboration between all nations in the economic field with the objector securing, for all, improved labor standards, economic advancement and social security;

Sixth, after the final destruction of the Nazi tyranny, they hope to see established a peace which will afford to all nations the means of dwelling in safety within their own boundaries, and which will afford assurance that all the men in all the lands may live out their lives in freedom from fear and want;

Seventh, such a peace should enable all men to traverse the high seas and oceans without hindrance;

Eighth, they believe that all of the nations of the world, for realistic as well as spiritual reasons must come to the abandonment of the use of force. Since no future peace can be maintained if land, sea or air armaments continue to be employed by nations which threaten, or may threaten, aggression outside of their frontiers, they believe, pending the establishment of a wider and permanent system of general security, that the disarmament of such nations is essential. They will likewise aid and encourage all other practicable measures which will lighten for peace-loving peoples the crushing burden of armaments.

August 19
PACIFIC: Work begins on defenses at Wake Island.

September 1
ATLANTIC: U.S. Navy begins to escort convoys to Britain starting at Newfoundland and ending at Iceland. The Iceland-Greenland strait is patrolled by U.S. warships.

September 4
ATLANTIC: U.S. destroyer *Greer* is attacked by a German submarine southwest of Iceland; it responds with depth charges, damaging the sub.

September 8
ATLANTIC: President Roosevelt asks that recommendations of the Joint Board be presented to him by both the chief of naval operations and the army chief of staff. This increases the importance of these military leaders in providing advice directly to the president.

September 11
ATLANTIC: Roosevelt issues a "shoot on sight" order to the navy to protect both U.S.-flagged ships and those ships escorted by U.S. ships. Roosevelt warns that if

any German or Italian warship enters the American neutrality zone, it does so at its own risk.

September 14–28
ATLANTIC: Large-scale army maneuvers are conducted in Louisiana.

September 19
ATLANTIC: The Joint Board approves the addition of a Joint Intelligence Committee to provide daily intelligence summaries to the president and the leaders of the War Department as well as special intelligence studies, when requested by the Joint Board.

September 27
ATLANTIC: The first Liberty Ship (EC-2 type freighter), *Patrick Henry,* is launched at Baltimore, Maryland.

October 16
ATLANTIC: U.S. destroyers assist in fighting off German submarines from a British convoy, but the Germans succeed in sinking six merchant ships. The destroyer *Kearney* is attacked and damaged southwest of Iceland. Eleven crewmen are killed and 22 wounded. A British destroyer (a former U.S. destroyer given to Great Britain in the destroyer for bases deal) is also sunk.

October 18
PACIFIC: General Tojo Hideki takes control of Japanese cabinet as premier, war minister, and home minister.

October 31
ATLANTIC: U.S. destroyer *Reuben James* is torpedoed and sunk escorting a convoy off Iceland. It is the first American warship lost in action in World War II. There are 36 survivors; 115 sailors are killed.

November 2
PACIFIC: Total marine strength on Wake Island is increased to 15 officers and 373 enlisted men.

November 3
PACIFIC: Major General Lewis H. Brereton takes command of the new Far East Air Force (FEAF) in the Philippines. The chief of the Japanese Naval General Staff approves the draft plan for the attack on the U.S. Pacific Fleet at Pearl Harbor.

November 10
ATLANTIC: Prime Minister Winston Churchill, speaking in London about the situation in Asia, makes the following statement: "The United States' time-honored interests in the Far East are well known. They are doing their utmost to find a way of preserving peace in the Pacific. We do not know whether their efforts will be successful, but if they fail, I take this occasion to say—and it is my duty to say—that should the United States become involved in war with Japan the British declaration will follow within the hour."

November 10
PACIFIC: The commander of the Asiatic Fleet is given permission to withdraw marines and gunboats from China.

November 15–30
ATLANTIC: Army conducts a second set of large-scale maneuvers in North and South Carolina.

November 17
ATLANTIC: Congress authorizes arming of U.S. merchant ships and allows them to enter war zones.

November 20
PACIFIC: Japan submits its final proposal for peace in the Pacific. The United States must give Japan a free hand in China. Therefore, the United States must discontinue aid to the Chinese Nationalist government, recognize Manchukuo, recognize the Greater East Asia Co-Prosperity Sphere, restore the U.S.-Japanese trade treaties, and unfreeze Japanese assets.

November 26
ATLANTIC: Secretary of State Cordell Hull passes to the Japanese the final proposal of the United States for peace in the Pacific: Japan has to respect the territorial integrity of China, accept change in the Pacific through peaceful means, and respect open markets in China. Japan is to withdraw from the Axis and withdraw all military and police forces from Indochina and China before the United States will resume trade with Japan. A six-carrier task force departs Japan headed for Hawaii. If negotiations fail, the task force commander, Admiral Nagumo Chuichi, is to attack the U.S. Pacific Fleet at Pearl Harbor.

November 27
ATLANTIC: Admiral Harold R. Stark, chief of naval operations, and General George C. Marshall, army chief of staff both send out war warning messages to their respective commanders in Hawaii.

November 28
PACIFIC: Reports are received of transports sailing south toward Indochina carrying a sizable number of Japanese troops. A naval air station is established at Wake Island.

November 30
PACIFIC: The Japanese foreign minister rejects the U.S. final proposal. U.S. strength in the Philippines stands at 31,095. The arrival of the 200th Coast Artillery Regiment and the 192nd and 194th Tank Battalions from the National Guard, represent a part of a 40 percent increase in combat strength. The tank battalions bring 108 of the newest American tank, M3. The Far East Air Force (FEAF) has the largest concentration of air power outside of the continental United States, with 107 P-40 fighters and 35 B-17 Flying Fortress bombers. The Philippine army has mobilized 10

divisions for national defense, which have been integrated into MacArthur's defensive plan. The 4th Marines deploy from Shanghai to the Philippines.

December 4

PACIFIC: The carrier *Enterprise* takes on 12 Marine F4F-3 Wildcat fighters for transport to Wake Island.

December 5

PACIFIC: Dawn to dusk air patrols begin on Wake Island.

December 6

ATLANTIC: Great Britain declares war against Finland, Hungary, and Romania.

December 7

ATLANTIC: The U.S. Army as of this day has 1.6 million men available, including 29 infantry divisions, five armored divisions, two cavalry divisions, and an air corps of 270,000 men.

PACIFIC: Japanese naval task force launches air attack on Oahu at the U.S. naval base at Pearl Harbor with the intent to cripple the American Pacific Fleet. Coming in two waves, 353 Japanese carrier-based aircraft attack the fleet and the combat aircraft at Hickam and Wheeler airfields. The attack achieves near-total surprise and succeeds in sinking four battleships (USS *Oklahoma,* USS *West Virginia,* USS *Arizona,* and USS *California*), seriously crippling the battleship USS *Nevada,* and inflicting damage on 19 other ships. The Army Air Force loses all but 79 of its 239 aircraft. Almost half of the navy's 169 aircraft are destroyed. Nearly 3,400 Americans are killed or wounded. The Japanese lose less than 30 aircraft. A Japanese midget sub tries to enter Pearl Harbor before the morning attack, but is spotted and sunk by the destroyer USS *Ward* on channel entrance patrol. The captain's report of hostile contact appears to have no effect on the chain of command. During the attack, the destroyer USS *Monaghan* sinks another midget sub inside the harbor. Vice Admiral Nagumo Chuichi, commander of the task force, ends the attack without finding the American carriers. USS *Enterprise* and USS *Lexington* are deployed to support Wake and Midway Islands; *Saratoga* is in port in San Diego. Nagumo also misses the ship repair facilities, fuel storage tanks, and submarine base, all of which will prove invaluable to future operations. During the attack, Ensign Francis C. Flaherty is in a turret on the USS *Oklahoma.* The order is given to abandon ship when it becomes clear that the battleship is going to capsize. Ensign Flaherty orders the turret crew to escape, holding a flashlight so they can see their way out. Flaherty sacrifices his own life to save his men. For his gallantry, Ensign Flaherty will receive the Medal of Honor.

Hours after the attack, Chief of Naval Operations Admiral Harold R. Stark issues the following order: "Execute unrestricted air and submarine warfare against Japan."

December 8

PACIFIC: United States and Great Britain declare war on Japan. The Netherlands East Indies and Canada also declare war on Japan.

Japanese bombard Midway and Guam. At Guam, the Japanese sink a U.S. mine-sweeper and cause serious damage. Japanese bombers attack Wake Island, destroying seven of the eight fighter aircraft on the island. Japanese aircraft attack Clark and Iba airfields in the Philippines—half of the American aircraft are destroyed or heavily damaged. Rear Admiral William A. Glassford orders the Asiatic Fleet to seek safety in the waters off the Philippines. Japanese amphibious forces move into position to begin landings on Luzon, the main island of the Philippines. The marine garrison in Beijing (Peking) surrenders to the Japanese.

Thailand and Malaysia are invaded. Thailand surrenders.

December 9
PACIFIC: Australia, South Africa, and New Zealand declare war on Japan. China declares war on the Axis powers.

December 9
PACIFIC: Japanese forces invade the Gilbert Islands; Japanese bombers attack Nichols Field on Luzon, near Manila. China declares war on the Axis powers. Wake Island and Guam undergo another heavy air attack.

MacArthur intends to defend Luzon, dividing his command into four elements. The North Luzon Force is to defend against the most dangerous Japanese approach from the landing beaches at Lingayen Gulf. Major General Jonathan M. Wainwright commands the 26th Cavalry Regiment, Philippine Scouts, an infantry battalion of the Philippine Scouts, four Philippine army divisions, and three artillery batteries. The South Luzon Force, commanded by Brigadier General George M. Parker, Jr., protects the area south and east of Manila with two Philippine army divisions and two Philippine Scout artillery batteries. The Reserve Force under MacArthur's direct command has the FEAF and the U.S. Army Philippine Division of 10,233 officers and men located north and west of Manila. Major General George F. Moore commands the Harbor Defense Forces, which protect Manila Bay. The Visayan-Mindanao Force, commanded by Brigadier General William F. Sharp, has three Philippine infantry divisions and is responsible for the islands south of Luzon.

December 10
PACIFIC: About 6,000 Japanese troops capture an unfortified Guam from a garrison force of about 500 marines and sailors; Wake Island comes under air attack. A 4,000-man Japanese assault force makes two landings in north Luzon in the vicinity of Aparri and Vigan and begins to move inland to control major roads and seize a key airstrip. Japanese aircraft provide air cover for the initial invasion, attacking U.S. airfields. Cavite naval base and Nichols airfield are heavily damaged. Japanese gain air supremacy—the remaining U.S. aircraft of the Far East Air Force are able to fly only limited missions.

Captain Colin P. Kelly becomes the first hero of the war when it is reported that his B-17 bomber has crashed into the Japanese battleship *Haruna* and sunk it. In actuality, he has attacked the heavy cruiser *Ashigara*, but missed the target. Kelly ordered his crew to bail out over Luzon and tried to bring his badly damaged plane back to Clark airfield, but the intrepid pilot died in the crash. Awarded the

Distinguished Service Cross posthumously, the truth about Kelly's mission will not be revealed until later in the war.

Japanese landing forces seize Makin Atoll in the Gilberts. Tarawa is declared occupied.

December 11
ATLANTIC: Germany and Italy declare war on the United States. The United States in turn declares war on Germany and Italy.

December 11
PACIFIC: The Wake Island garrison, composed of 522 soldiers, marines, and sailors (assisted by a number of civilian contractors), repels the initial Japanese landing attempt, sinking two destroyers and damaging two other ships. Japanese casualties are estimated at between seven and eight hundred. A radio message from Wake is decoded in Hawaii and unwittingly reformed into the message "Send us more Japs." Although a great morale boost for Americans at home when publicized, the message itself is false and has nothing to do with the real attitude of the defenders.

December 12
PACIFIC: Task Force South Pacific is organized under Brigadier General Julian F. Barnes and heads for Australia, escorted by the cruiser USS *Pensacola*. A 2,500-man Japanese assault force from the Palau Islands lands in southern Luzon at Legaspi and captures the airfield. The initial Japanese landing force in northern Luzon continues to advance, supported by heavy air strikes on American airfields throughout Luzon. The 11th Division of the Philippine army offers little or no resistance.

December 12
BURMA: Japanese ground forces from Thailand enter Burma. General Sir Archibald Wavell is given responsibility for the defense of Burma and India. The American Volunteer Group (AVG) fighter aircraft from China arrive at Mingaladon to support the British.

December 13
ATLANTIC: Hungary and Bulgaria declare war with the United States and Great Britain.

Admiral Karl Dönitz initiates the U-boat campaign against American shipping on the Atlantic coast.

December 14
PACIFIC: Japanese air strikes virtually eliminate American airpower in Luzon; Major General Lewis H. Brereton, FEAF commander and General Douglas MacArthur's Air Corps commander, begins evacuating the remainder of his B-17s to Mindanao, then to Darwin, Australia. Admiral Thomas C. Hart, commander of U.S. Asiatic Fleet, withdraws naval air support as well. Encountering little opposition, the Japanese Luzon force moves toward Lingayen Gulf. Japanese air attacks on Wake Island leave the marines with only one operational aircraft.

December 15
PACIFIC: The Wake Island relief force, designated Task Force 14, leaves Hawaii under command of Rear Admiral Frank J. Fletcher. TF 14 has the carrier USS *Saratoga* with 117 aircraft, and grows to 13 destroyers, three cruisers, a seaplane tender, and an oiler.

December 17
PACIFIC: The fallout from the Pearl Harbor disaster leads to wholesale changes in American senior commanders. Admiral Chester W. Nimitz replaces Admiral Husband E. Kimmel as commander in chief, Pacific Fleet; Vice Admiral William S. Pye will be the acting commander until Nimitz arrives. The new commanding general of the Hawaiian Department is Lieutenant General D. C. Emmons, replacing Lieutenant General Walter C. Short. The Hawaiian Air Force Department's new commander is Major General Clarence L. Tinker, replacing Major General Frederick L. Martin. The U.S. Navy reinforces Midway with marine aircraft.

December 18
ATLANTIC: President Roosevelt issues an executive order that gives the commander in chief, United States Fleet (CominCh), command of operating fleets and coastal commands. The CominCh is immediately responsible to the president under the general direction of the secretary of the navy.

PHILIPPINES: The Japanese Legaspi landing force reaches Naga after pushing past Filipino defenders.

December 19
ATLANTIC: President Roosevelt signs an executive order establishing the Office of Censorship under Byron Price, a former Associated Press editor. Price is given absolute discretion to censor all international communications. Price seeks voluntary compliance by military and civilian supervisors to prevent information of potential benefit to the enemy from being published. By 1942, 10,000 federal employees in 18 censorship stations across the country will be examining mail going overseas.

PHILIPPINES: The Legaspi force advances toward Daet. A Japanese force of 5,000 troops from Palau lands at Davao on Mindanao, supported by heavy air attacks.

BURMA: The SS *Tulsa* issue quickly develops into an incident. The American Military Mission to China (AMMISCA) under Brigadier General John Magruder is authorized by the War Department to transfer Lend-Lease matériel awaiting transportation in the port of Rangoon from Chinese to British control, subject to Generalissimo Chiang Kai-shek's approval. An American officer in Rangoon requests that the government of Burma impound the Lend-Lease matériel, most of which is on board the SS *Tulsa* in Rangoon harbor and destined for China. The Chinese representative in Burma, objecting to the transfer of material to the British, suggests a committee be formed to determine the disposition of the supplies.

December 20
ATLANTIC: Admiral Ernest J. King is appointed commander in chief, United States Fleet (CominCh). Admiral Stark's position as chief of naval operations is reduced to mainly administrative duties within the Department of the Navy.

PACIFIC: Wake Island receives news of Task Force 14's approach from a navy PBY patrol plane.

PHILIPPINES: On Mindanao, the Japanese capture Davao and seize the nearby airfield. In Luzon, Japanese forces begin a movement from Vigan toward Lingayen Gulf. The 4th Marines are transferred to General MacArthur's operational control.

CHINA: Colonel Claire Chennault's American Volunteer Croup (AVG), under control of the Chinese Air Force, attacks enemy aircraft headed to Kunming, reportedly downing nine bombers. The AVG, based at Kunming, is responsible for protecting the Burma Road and contesting Japanese air operations along the southwest border region. The popular press of China calls them *Fei Wing*, or flying tigers.

December 21

PACIFIC: Largest attack yet on Wake Island begins. Japanese send 49 aircraft, both dive bombers and fighters to hit American defenses. Task Force 14 is about 600 miles from Wake.

PHILIPPINES: The Japanese Fourteenth Army with 60,000 men under command of Lieutenant General Homma Masaharu arrives at Lingayen Gulf, supported by the Japanese Third Fleet. At Bacnotan, Philippine army units encounter the Japanese Vigan force as it advances.

December 22

PACIFIC: Wake Island loses the last of its F4F-3 Wildcats. Task Force 14 halts for refueling at sea, which consumes most of the day and evening.

PHILIPPINES: The Japanese land at Aringay, Agoo, and Bauang in Lingayen Gulf and advance inland, linking up with the Vigan force. The Philippine Scouts (26th Cavalry) and elements of the Philippine Army 71st Division offer resistance. U.S. submarines attack Japanese ships in the gulf, while a few American planes harass the enemy fleet. American B-17s from Darwin, Australia, bomb Japanese transports at Davao, land at Del Monte field, then proceed to attack Japanese forces in Lingayen Gulf.

CHINA: Generalissimo Chiang Kai-shek releases the Chinese Fifth and Sixth armies to support the British defense of Burma. Wavell takes control of the Sixth Army's 93rd Division as it moves into Burma.

SOUTHWEST PACIFIC: U.S. Forces in Australia (USFIA) established in Brisbane under Brigadier General Julian F. Barnes.

December 23

PACIFIC: Task Force 14 is 425 miles from Wake, but has no information on the defenders' situation. Fletcher hesitates, then receives orders from Vice Admiral Pye, acting commander in chief of the Pacific Fleet, to move to Midway. The Japanese launch two attack waves of 1,000 men each to storm the beaches. Captain Henry T. Elrod, a Wildcat pilot from VMF-211 who sank a Japanese destroyer on December 11, is killed in furious fighting on the beach. Elrod defends his position with such tenacious courage that he will receive the Medal of Honor. After about 11 hours of resistance, the commander of Wake, Winfield S. Cunningham, orders American forces to surrender. About 1,600 Americans—both military and civilian—begin a long and brutal captivity.

Philippines: General Douglas MacArthur abandons Manila and orders a with-drawal of U.S. and Filipino forces to Bataan. USAAF B-17s attack Japanese ships in Lingayen Gulf and Davao; other American planes attack the Japanese landing force on Luzon.

Southwest Pacific: A convoy disembarks 4,600 soldiers of the U.S. Army Air Corps and artillery at Brisbane, Australia. The convoy has been diverted from its original destination, the Philippines.

December 24

Atlantic: The Arcadia Conference. The Anglo-American Arcadia conference begins in Washington, D.C. Prime Minister Winston Churchill, President Franklin Roosevelt, and the British and American chiefs of staff begin to determine a com-bined war strategy. Conference will end on January 14, 1942.

Pacific: Brigadier General Henry B. Claggett takes temporary command of the USFIA.

Midway receives reinforcements from the 4th Defense Battalion.

Philippines: A Japanese force of 7,000 men from the Ryukyu Islands lands at Lamon Bay, attacking Mauban and Siain, then moving in two directions with the intent of cutting off Manila to the north and linking with the Legaspi invasion force to the south. Major General Jonathan M. Wainwright, commanding the North Luzon Force, is unable to stop Homma's advance. With the Philippine Scouts con-ducting a brilliant defense, Wainwright falls back to the Agno River. The South Luzon Force, now under command of Brigadier General Albert M. Jones, begins a retreat past Manila and heading north to reach Bataan. The Bataan Defense Force, commanded by Brigadier General George M. Parker, Jr., begins preparations to establish two defensive lines for the arriving troops. The 4th Marines are ordered to Corregidor.

December 25

Atlantic: At the Arcadia conference, Chief of Staff of the Army General George C. Marshall suggests that all Allied forces in the Far East be placed under a single commander. This is the origin of the Australia-British-Dutch-American (ABDA) Command.

Pacific: Midway receives additional marine fighter aircraft, originally intended for Wake Island, from the carrier USS *Saratoga*.

Philippines: MacArthur establishes his headquarters on Corregidor, an island in the mouth of Manila Bay. Japanese breach Wainwright's Agno River line. The South Luzon Force continues to move north under heavy pressure from Japanese ground and air forces. Rear Admiral F. W. Rockwell takes command of all naval forces in the Philippines from Admiral Thomas C. Hart, who leaves by submarine for Java to establish a new Asiatic Fleet headquarters.

China: Chiang Kai-shek announces through a military representative that he will recall Chinese troops from Burma after determining that the British seized the *Tulsa*'s Lend-Lease cargo with American assistance. He declares that the Chinese will no longer work with the British.

December 26

PACIFIC: Midway receives ground elements of the intended Wake Island relief force. Manila is declared an open city.

PHILIPPINES: The North Luzon Force retreats from the Agno River, defending from Santa Ignacia to San Jose. The Southern Luzon Force establishes a defensive line in the vicinity of Sariaya.

CHINA: Chiang is mollified over the *Tulsa* issue with promises of support from the U.S. representative of the American Military Mission to China. Although Chiang eventually will allow the transfer of the Lend-Lease shipment to Britain, it quickly becomes clear to the Americans that the Chinese leader will be a difficult ally.

December 27

PHILIPPINES: Wainwright withdraws to his final defensive position along the Tarlac-Cabanatuan line. Japanese forces, pressing the South Luzon Force, capture Candelaria.

December 28

ATLANTIC: U.S. Navy authorizes construction battalions (SEABEES).

PHILIPPINES: South Luzon Force is ordered to move to Bataan.

December 29

PHILIPPINES: Japanese aircraft begin bombardment of Corregidor. Japanese begin to crack the North Luzon defenses.

CHINA: The China theater established under command of Chiang Kai-shek, supported by an Allied staff. The theater boundaries include portions of China, Thailand, and Indochina not occupied by enemy forces.

December 30

PHILIPPINES: As the North Luzon Force's defense begins to crack under Japanese assaults, South Luzon Force rapidly moves to cross Calumpit Bridge over the Pampanga River to safety. Philippine president Manuel Quezon is inaugurated on Corregidor.

December 31

ATLANTIC: At the Arcadia conference, General Wavell is appointed commander of the Australian-British-Dutch-American Command (ABDA), with responsibility to coordinate Allied operations in the Far East.

PHILIPPINES: The North Luzon Force reaches its final defensive position along the Bamban-Arayat line. Commander of the South Luzon Force, Brigadier General Albert Jones conducts a desperate counterattack and North and South Luzon Forces are able to link at San Fernando. All forces east of the Pampanga River come under command of General Jones.

December 31

ATLANTIC: With 86 operational U-boats (36 in the Atlantic, 12 on the U.S. east coast) the German navy has sunk over 2.1 million tons of shipping in 1941, representing about 50 percent of all Allied and neutral shipping losses.

PACIFIC: Major General George H. Brett takes command of AFIA (American Forces in Australia). Admiral Chester W. Nimitz assumes duties as CINCPAC (commander in chief, Pacific).

CHINA: A Joint Military Council is established in Chungking.

1942

January 1

ATLANTIC: Declaration of the United Nations is signed in Washington, D.C.

PHILIPPINES: South Luzon Force disbanded and integrated into other units. Main defense line is established in southern Luzon between Porac and Guagua.

CHINA: Chinese request assistance from Lend-Lease to build an overland supply route from Ledo, India, through north Burma and on to Lungling, China.

January 2

PHILIPPINES: Japanese attack at Porac; Japanese forces cross Pampanga River and advance toward San Fernando, joining forces with Japanese troops advancing south. Manila is occupied and daily air attacks begin on Corregidor, but little damage results over the next week.

January 3

PACIFIC: General Archibald Wavell, as commander of all allied forces available in the Pacific under the title of ABDACOM (Australian-British-Dutch-American Command), is ordered by the CCS to hold Burma and Australia and defend as far forward as possible of the line stretching from Burma and the Malay Peninsula, through Sumatra and Java, across to the Philippines and Okinawa, North Australia, the Netherlands East Indies, New Guinea, to the Solomons, and as far south as New Zealand. Wavell is to maintain contact with all Allied forces in theater and block the Japanese advance by holding key areas. He is ordered to take the offensive at the earliest possible opportunity.

PHILIPPINES: The Japanese continue pressure on the Porac and Guagua defensive line in Luzon.

January 4

PHILIPPINES: Japanese outflank defenses at Guagua, forcing the defenders to retreat south and form another hasty line of defense between Lubao and Santa Cruz.

January 5

ATLANTIC: The U.S. government orders the rationing of tires to preserve limited rubber supplies for military vehicles.

PHILIPPINES: Troop rations for American and Philippine units are cut in half to save food. Brigadier General Richard J. Marshall establishes his headquarters in Bataan. Defenders establish a shorter defensive line at the base of the Bataan peninsula.

January 6

CHINA: As supreme Allied commander of the China theater, Chiang Kai-shek requests an American officer to serve as his chief of staff.

January 7

PHILIPPINES: The main Bataan defensive line stretching 20 miles from Mauban to Mabatang is established. Defenders are reorganized into I and II Philippine Corps. I Philippine Corps has 22,500 men and is responsible for the western half of the line. II Philippine Corps has 25,000 men and is responsible for the eastern half. A provisional unit is organized from navy, marine, and air force units to protect the main supply base at Mariveles.

January 8

ATLANTIC: The headquarters of U.S. Armed Forces in the British Isles is established to oversee the arrival of troops and supplies in Britain.

January 9

PHILIPPINES: Initial Japanese assault on Bataan advance defenses is repulsed. U.S. submarine *Pollack* sinks a Japanese merchant ship in the waters southwest of Inubozaki, Japan.

January 10

PHILIPPINES: General MacArthur inspects Bataan defenses.

January 11

ATLANTIC: Operation *Paukenschlag* ("roll of the kettledrums") begins. Five German submarines (*U-66, U-109, U-123, U-125,* and *U-130*) begin patrolling the east coast of the United States. Within the next month, over 26 Allied ships will be sunk by this group.

PHILIPPINES: Japanese attack Bataan's main defenses, achieve temporary success, but are driven back. Japanese forces pulled from Philippines land in Netherlands East Indies at Tarakan, Dutch Borneo, and Mendano on Celebes. Paratroops land near Mendano to support an attack to capture the main airfield.

PACIFIC: General Wavell, commander of ABDACOM, moves the U.S. 2nd Battalion, 131st Field Artillery to Surabaya in Java.

January 12

ATLANTIC: President Roosevelt establishes the War Labor Board by executive order. The 11-member board is to mediate and arbitrate labor and management disputes affecting war production.

PHILIPPINES: Japanese attacks on the Bataan defensive line continue.

January 14

ATLANTIC: Arcadia Conference Ends. The Allies decide to defeat Germany first and engage in discussions for possible offensive action. Prominently offered by the British is Gymnast, an invasion of North Africa. Japanese begin infiltration actions along the west coast of Bataan and through the center of the peninsula. The Combined chiefs of staff (CCS) is formed. The British Chiefs of Staff and their American counterparts will meet to make recommendations regarding U.S.-British strategic direction. In addition, the Combined Chiefs of Staff will provide recommendations on program requirements needed to support strategic decisions, submit general directives on policy for distribution of war matériel, and establish priorities for overseas military movements.

CHINA: Major General Joseph W. Stilwell is nominated to serve as Chiang Kai-shek's chief of staff.

January 15

ATLANTIC: U.S. government bans the production of new automobiles. Manufacturing plants will produce military vehicles.

PHILIPPINES: Japanese attacks threaten to split the Bataan defensive line in two at Mt. Natib. Reserves are committed to assist in holding the line. General Wavell establishes ABDA headquarters in Batavia, Java. Lieutenant General George H. Brett, USAAF, is the deputy commander and Admiral Thomas C. Hart U.S. Navy is the naval forces commander.

January 16

ATLANTIC: The War Production Board is established under Donald M. Nelson. Its function is to convert the civilian peacetime economy of the United States into full-scale war production. The War Production Board will take control of scarce resources and eliminate any manufacturing or production it deems nonessential to the war effort.

PHILIPPINES: When a gun position is knocked out of action during heavy fighting in the II Corps area on Bataan, Sgt. Jose Calugas, a mess sergeant of another battery, runs 1,000 yards to the gun position. Despite heavy enemy artillery fire, Calugas takes charge of a group of volunteers and puts the gun back in action. For his courage and daring, Sgt. Calugas later receives the Medal of Honor.

PACIFIC: Japanese forces from Thailand invade Burma.

January 17

PHILIPPINES: I Corps defenders pushed out of Morong on west flank of Bataan defensive line; reserves plugging gaps in center as Japanese exploit success. II Corps attempts to protect its open western flank.

PACIFIC: General Brereton is appointed commander of tactical forces in ABDA command.

January 18

ATLANTIC: Germany, Italy, and Japan renew the Axis Pact in Berlin. Japan will have complete freedom of action in all areas east of 70 degrees East Longitude.

A U.S. freighter is sunk by German submarine *U-552* off Newfoundland. Two U.S. tankers are attacked by submarines *U-66* and *U-123* off Cape Hatteras, North Carolina. One tanker sinks, the other is damaged.

January 19

ATLANTIC: A U.S. steamship is torpedoed and sunk off North Carolina by German submarine *U-123*.

January 20

PACIFIC: The 2nd Marine Brigade, commanded by Brigadier General Henry L. Larson, arrives at Samoa to support the protection of the U.S. line of communication to Australia. Two naval task forces, Task Force 8, formed around carrier USS *Enterprise* and commanded by Vice Admiral William F. Halsey, Jr., and Task Force 17, commanded by Rear Admiral Frank Jack Fletcher and formed around carrier USS *Yorktown,* escort the marines.

January 21
PACIFIC: Japanese air attacks on Rabaul (New Britain) and New Guinea near Lae and Salamaua.
CHINA: Chinese accept Stilwell as chief of staff and allow Stilwell to have executive authority over Allied forces.

January 22
ATLANTIC: A U.S. freighter is torpedoed and sunk by German submarine *U-123* south of Cape Hatteras, North Carolina.
PHILIPPINES: General MacArthur orders withdrawal to the second Bataan defensive line from Pilar to Bagac, just south of Orion on the east coast of the peninsula. A Japanese attempt to make an amphibious landing near Bagac is intercepted by U.S. PT boats and two enemy transports are sunk.

January 23
ATLANTIC: The Combined Chiefs of Staff conducts its first meeting in Washington, D.C. Admiral Harold R. Stark, chief of naval operations, Admiral Ernest J. King, commander in chief, United States Fleet, Lieutenant General Henry H. Arnold, chief of Army Air forces, and General George C. Marshall, army chief of staff, represent the United States. The first order of business is to attempt to deal with the disintegrating situation in the Far East.

A U.S. collier is sunk by German submarine *U-66* off Cape Hatteras, North Carolina.
PHILIPPINES: Bataan defenders begin a withdrawal to the second defensive line under pressure from Japanese attacks. An amphibious landing near Mariveles makes limited progress when scraped-together U.S. and Philippine troops counterattack.
PACIFIC: Japanese land troops at Rabaul and Kavieng, New Ireland, and land at Kieta, Bougainville, in the Solomons. U.S. submarine *Seadragon* damages a Japanese merchant ship off the northern coast of French Indochina.

January 24
PACIFIC: The Battle of Makassar Strait. A Japanese invasion force moving through the Makassar Strait to land at Balikpapan, Borneo, is intercepted by four U.S. destroyers. Three convoy ships, a cargo ship, and a patrol boat are sunk. A Japanese cruiser and two destroyers pursue, but the Americans escape. This is the first surface engagement of the war between American and Japanese ships. American P-40 fighters arrive in Java from Australia. Lae and Salamaua are evacuated in New Guinea.

January 25
ATLANTIC: A U.S. freighter is attacked and sunk by German submarine *U-125* off the North Carolina coast.

PACIFIC: Thailand declares war on the United States. Midway is shelled by Japanese submarine *I-73*.

January 26
ATLANTIC: German submarine *U-125* attacks and sinks a second U.S. freighter off the North Carolina coast.
PHILIPPINES: The second Bataan defensive line is established from Orion on the east to Bagac on the west. Heavy Japanese pressure continues all along the line. The Japanese continue to build a beachhead in the south in what is now called the Battle of the Points.

January 27
ATLANTIC: German submarines *U-66* and *U-130* sink a steamer, a freighter, and two tankers off the North Carolina coast.
PHILIPPINES: General Wainwright sends reinforcements south to try and dislodge enemy forces threatening the rear area, but the attacks are unsuccessful in dislodging the Japanese. Other Japanese attacks are made against the main defensive line.
PACIFIC: Near Borneo, U.S. B-17 bombers damage a Japanese seaplane carrier.

January 28
ATLANTIC: The Eighth Air Force is activated in Savannah, Georgia, commanded by Brigadier General Asa N. Duncan. The Eighth Air Force is initially designated the air component for Gymnast.

January 29
ATLANTIC: U.S. Coast Guard cutter *Alexander Hamilton* is torpedoed by German submarine *U-132* off Reykjavik, Iceland, and has to be scuttled.

January 30
ATLANTIC: A U.S. tanker is sunk by German submarine *U-106* off Chesapeake Bay.
PHILIPPINES: General MacArthur assumes command of all naval forces in the Philippines. The I Corps defensive line is broken, but the Japanese are contained in small pockets and are slowly eliminated in hard fighting.

February 1
PHILIPPINES: American fighter aircraft, PT boats, and artillery attack another Japanese amphibious movement near Quinauan Point on the west side of Bataan, but fail to prevent troops from landing. Philippine Scouts take heavy casualties attempting to control the beach.
PACIFIC: After departing from Samoa on 20 January, two American naval task forces conduct raids on Japanese bases. Halsey's Task Force 8, with the carrier USS *Enterprise,* attacks Kwajalein in the Marshal Islands, sinking a transport ship, a submarine chaser, and a gunboat, and damaging a cruiser, a submarine, and seven other auxiliary and support ships. Rear Admiral Yatsushiro Sukeyoshi is killed when his headquarters is bombed. Fletcher's Task Force 17, with the carrier USS *Yorktown,* attacks the Gilberts, but finds few targets. These are the first U.S. carrier strikes of the war.

February 2

ATLANTIC: An unarmed U.S. tanker is sunk by German submarine *U-103* near the mouth of the Delaware River.

Lieutenant General Joseph Stilwell is appointed to serve as Generalissimo Chiang Kai-shek's chief of staff and principal military adviser. His mission is to improve the combat capability of the Chinese army and maintain a supply line to keep China in the war. Stilwell and the Joint Chiefs of Staff agree that the overland route to China through Burma is the most important priority. Stilwell is to work toward improving the training of Chinese forces in India and overseeing the effort to equip the units properly for combat in Burma. Additional Chinese divisions will be trained and equipped in China to support future operations in Burma.

February 3

PHILIPPINES: First Lieutenant Willibald C. Bianchi of the 45th Infantry Regiment, Philippine Scouts, leads an attack on enemy machine gun positions. Wounded in the hand and unable to fire his rifle, he continues to lead, firing his pistol. Destroying one position with grenades, he is wounded again. Ignoring his injuries, Bianchi climbs on top of an American tank to fire its machine gun at the enemy until he is hit again and falls from the tank, unable to fight any longer. For his gallantry, Bianchi will receive the Medal of Honor.

February 4

ATLANTIC: An unarmed U.S. tanker is torpedoed and sunk by German submarine *U-103* off Cape May, New Jersey.

PACIFIC: A U.S.-Dutch ABDA naval force of four cruisers and 10 destroyers attempts to disrupt a Japanese landing on the coast of Borneo, but is driven off at Madoera Strait by enemy aircraft. Units of the Asiatic Fleet under Admiral Thomas C. Hart are reorganized into Naval Forces, Southwest Pacific Area, under Vice Admiral William A. Glassford.

February 5

ATLANTIC: Far East, Caribbean, Hawaiian, and Alaskan Air Forces are redesignated as Fifth, Sixth, Seventh, and Eleventh Air Forces, respectively.

February 6

ATLANTIC: The United States and Great Britain establish the Combined Chiefs of Staff in Washington to direct a combined war strategy.

February 7

ATLANTIC: President Roosevelt establishes the War Shipping Administration (WSA) by executive order. The WSA's mission is to provide overall control and operation of all U.S. merchant shipping. Rear Admiral Emory S. Land is appointed as director and reports directly to the president.

PHILIPPINES: I Corps conducts counterattack to eliminate Japanese pockets; enemy force trapped on Quinauan Point on the southwest coast of Bataan is eliminated; an attempt to rescue the trapped defenders is driven off by U.S. P-40 fighters and artillery.

February 8
PHILIPPINES: The Japanese commander, Lieutenant General Homma Masaharu, orders a withdrawal to rest and refit his weary units and receive reinforcements. Midway is shelled by Japanese submarine *I-69*.
PACIFIC: U.S. submarine *S-37* attacks a Japanese destroyer in the Makassar Strait.

February 9
ATLANTIC: The Joint Board meeting, now with Admiral King in attendance, shifts to the Joint Chiefs of Staff. A newly formed Joint Secretariat under Brigadier General Walter Bedell Smith serves both the JCS and the Joint Board. As time progresses, the JCS will subsume most of the activities of the Joint Board. The functions and duties of the JCS are never formally defined. Because the JCS evolves out of the Joint Board, the organization is able to adapt to meet the unprecedented requirements of a global war. Eventually Joint Staff Planners, a Joint Strategic Survey Committee, and a Joint Logistics Committee will be established to support JCS decisions.

The first formal meeting of the U.S. Joint Chiefs of Staff (JCS) is held in Washington. The JCS is composed of General George C. Marshall, army chief of staff, Lieutenant General Henry H. Arnold, chief of the Army Air Corps, Admiral Harold R. Stark, chief of naval operations, and Admiral Ernest J. King, COMINCH.
PACIFIC: U.S. submarine *Trout* sinks a Japanese gunboat off Formosa (Taiwan). A Japanese destroyer, torpedoed the previous day, sinks.

February 10
PACIFIC: While shelling Midway, Japanese submarine *I-69* is attacked and damaged by Marine F2A Buffalo fighters.

February 11
PACIFIC: Submarine USS *Shark* is sunk in the Celebes by a Japanese destroyer.

February 12
ATLANTIC: Tenth Air Force is activated at Patterson Field, Ohio, and assigned to General Stilwell for operations in China. In Bataan, I Corps continues to eliminate Japanese defenders trapped in pockets within the corps' main defensive line.

February 14
PACIFIC: Japanese paratroopers land on Sumatra near Palembang in the Netherlands East Indies to capture oil refineries. Vice Admiral Conrad E. L. Helfrich, Royal Navy, replaces Admiral Thomas C. Hart as Commander in Chief Allied Naval Forces in Southwest Pacific. U.S. submarine *Swordfish* sinks a Japanese transport off Davao in the Philippines.

February 15
PACIFIC: Singapore, the main bastion of British power in the Far East, with a garrison of 64,000 men, surrenders unconditionally to the Japanese.

February 18
ATLANTIC: Admiral Ernest J. King, commander in chief of the U.S. Fleet and chief of naval operations, proposes to Chief of Staff George C. Marshall that army troops

occupy islands in the south and southwest Pacific in preparation for using marine forces against the Japanese.

February 19

ATLANTIC: President Roosevelt signs an executive order authorizing the military to relocate and intern over 120,000 Japanese Americans living in California, Oregon, Washington, and Arizona. Within a month these people will move or be sent to internment camps throughout the United States.

A U.S. tanker is torpedoed and sunk by German submarine *U-128* off Cape Canaveral, Florida.

PACIFIC: As the Japanese begin landing forces on Bali, an ABDA naval force of Dutch and American ships launches an attack. Three Japanese destroyers are damaged, one Dutch destroyer is sunk, and an American destroyer is damaged. This night action is called the Battle of Badung Strait. Japanese carrier striking force under command of Vice Admiral Nagumo Chuichi attacks Darwin, Australia, sinking a U.S. destroyer, a transport ship, and a freighter. Airfields and depots are also damaged in the attack.

February 20

ATLANTIC: An unarmed U.S. freighter is torpedoed and sunk by German submarine *U-432* near Ocean City, Maryland.

PACIFIC: Japanese invade Timor Island in the Netherlands East Indies. A U.S. naval task force with the carrier USS *Lexington,* four heavy cruisers, and 10 destroyers under command of Vice Admiral Wilson Brown intends to conduct an air and surface attack on the Japanese base at Rabaul. Discovered by enemy patrol aircraft, a major air battle develops as Japanese bombers are sent to attack the carriers. Nine Japanese bombers are headed to attack the *Lexington* when Lieutenant Edward H. "Butch" O'Hare, piloting an F4F Wildcat, singlehandedly attacks the formation. Disregarding enemy fire, he fights alone until he runs out of ammunition. When he flies away six minutes later, he has downed five bombers and in all likelihood saved the *Lexington* from destruction. O'Hare becomes the first navy ace of the war and for his exceptional courage he will receive the Medal of Honor. The task force escapes damage and loses one pilot.

February 21

ATLANTIC: A U.S. freighter is attacked by German submarine *U-504* off the Florida coast.

PACIFIC: Fifth Air Force and U.S. troops are evacuated from Java.

February 22

ATLANTIC: A U.S. freighter is torpedoed and sunk by German submarine *U-504* and a U.S. tanker is sunk by German submarine *U-128* off the Florida coast. A U.S. freighter is sunk by German submarine *U-129* southeast of the island of Trinidad.

February 23

ATLANTIC: A U.S. freighter is torpedoed and later sinks after an attack by German submarine *U-161* near Martinique.

PACIFIC: B-17s attempt to bomb Rabaul with little success. General Brereton terminates Fifth Air Force Headquarters and leaves for India.

Japanese submarine *I-17* fires 13 shells at an oil refinery near Santa Barbara, California.

February 24
PACIFIC: Admiral William F. Halsey's *Enterprise* task force conducts air strikes on Wake Island.

February 25
ATLANTIC: U.S. Coast Guard assumes responsibility for coastal defense.
PACIFIC: ABDA command is dissolved.
BURMA: U.S. P-40s of the American Volunteer Group (AVG—also known as the Flying Tigers) and British Royal Air Force (RAF) fighters attack 40 Japanese fighters and 12 bombers over Burma. It is the AVG's best day in combat, recording 19 confirmed kills and eight probables.

February 26
ATLANTIC: A U.S. bulk carrier is torpedoed and sunk by German submarine *U-432* off the North Carolina coast; a U.S. tanker is torpedoed by German submarine *U-578* off Sea Girt, Delaware.

February 27
PACIFIC: The Battle of the Java Sea. A naval force of Dutch, American, British, and Australian cruisers and destroyers attempts to prevent a Japanese landing on Java. It encounters a 17-ship Japanese cruiser-destroyer force. In the ensuing fight lasting over seven hours, the ABDA force loses two cruisers and three destroyers; two Japanese destroyers are damaged. This Allied defeat allows the Japanese free access to the Java Sea from Malaya to Borneo. The U.S. Navy's first aircraft carrier, the USS *Langley,* now serving as an aircraft transport and carrying 32 P-40 fighters, is sunk by Japanese aircraft en route to Java.

February 28
ATLANTIC: U.S. destroyer *Jacob Jones* is sunk by a German submarine off the Delaware Capes.
PACIFIC: The Battle of Sunda Strait. A U.S. and a British cruiser, survivors of the Battle of the Java Sea, encounter a Japanese landing force at Banten Bay on the west end of Java in the Sunda Strait. The cruisers wreak havoc on the transports, sinking three and damaging three others, but they themselves are sunk by an overwhelming force of three cruisers and nine destroyers.

March 1
ATLANTIC: U.S. patrol aircraft sink the German submarine *U-565* off Newfoundland, marking the navy's first successful U-boat attack.
PACIFIC: Japanese air attacks sink the remainder of the ABDA Java Sea fleet. Two U.S. destroyers, one British destroyer, and a British cruiser are lost. Another U.S. destroyer and a gunboat are lost to enemy surface attack off Java. Of the origi-

nal combined naval force of five cruisers and 10 destroyers organized to defend the Netherlands East Indies, only four U.S. destroyers eventually escape to Australia. ABDA command is formally dissolved. Japanese units land on Java. They are opposed by an ad hoc ground force of two regiments and a brigade acting as a mobile reserve. This force contains one American army unit, the 2nd Battalion, 131st Artillery, a Texas National Guard unit.

March 3

ATLANTIC: President Roosevelt by executive order designates the Army Air Forces and the Army Ground Forces as the two major combat commands of the U.S. Army.

PACIFIC: U.S. submarine *Perch* is attacked by Japanese destroyers in the Java Sea. The boat is scuttled and the entire 59-man crew is taken prisoner.

The Java defenders, supported by the U.S. 2nd Battalion, 131st Artillery, hold the Japanese long enough for Allied forces to withdraw from Batavia.

The Western Pacific is reorganized. Responsibility for the area including Burma and all Southeast Asia west of Java and Sumatra is given to the British, commanded by Sir Archibald P. Wavell and under the strategic direction of the British Chiefs of Staff. The area eastward is controlled by the U.S. Joint Chiefs of Staff.

March 4

PACIFIC: Admiral Halsey's *Enterprise* task force aircraft attack Marcus Island, about 800 miles northwest of Wake Island. General MacArthur begins a reorganization of the command and control structure of the Philippine defense. Brigadier General William F. Sharp maintains command of forces on Mindanao, but the defense of Visayan is transferred to Brigadier General Bradford G. Chynoweth. MacArthur contemplates a Luzon-Bataan force under General Wainwright and harbor defenses under General Moore. His idea is to establish an indirect command headquarters at Corregidor under a deputy chief of staff of USAFFE, Colonel (on March 17, Brigadier General) Lewis C. Beebe, through which he can maintain command and control from Australia. MacArthur does not inform the War Department of his reorganization.

CHINA: At Chungking, Lieutenant General Stilwell establishes Headquarters, American Army Forces, China, Burma, and India (CBI). American Military Mission to China (AMMISCA) personnel are assigned to the new headquarters.

March 5

ATLANTIC: A U.S. freighter from convoy HX 178 (New York to Liverpool) is torpedoed and sunk by German submarine *U-404* off the coast of Nova Scotia.

March 7

PACIFIC: Major General Alexander M. Patch arrives in New Caledonia as the commander of the U.S. Army's New Caledonia task force.

March 8

ATLANTIC: The War Production Board regulates the production of clothing in the United States, specifying certain styles to conserve cloth.

March 8

ATLANTIC: U.S. Army forces relieve the 1st Marine Brigade on Iceland.

PACIFIC: Japanese forces land at Lae and Salamaua on New Guinea. Tenth Air Force begins movement from United States to India.

Allied forces on Java surrender to the Japanese. The men of the U.S. 2nd Battalion, 131st Artillery, essentially disappear once they fall into enemy hands. The prisoners endure a brutal captivity, eventually serving on railway labor gangs in Thailand. No news will be heard of the unit until the end of the war.

March 9

ATLANTIC: The Department of the Army is reorganized into three commands: Army Ground Forces, under Lieutenant General Lesley J. McNair; Army Air Forces (AAF), under Lieutenant General Henry H. "Hap" Arnold; and Services of Supply (later to become Army Service Forces), under Major General Brehon B. Somervell. This reorganization frees the chief of staff, General George C. Marshall, to focus on higher strategic issues dictated by his membership in the Joint Chiefs of Staff and the Combined Chiefs of Staff. The president, as commander in chief, exercises his duties directly through the army chief of staff.

Admiral Harold R. Stark is relieved as chief of naval operations and takes command of U.S. naval forces in Europe. Admiral Ernest J. King assumes his duties. The role of CNO and CominCh are thus combined. Admiral King is now the principal naval adviser to the president and responsible for the coordination and direction of the Navy Department. General Marshall and Admiral King are now the president's military advisers and provide the strategic direction for the war.

March 10

ATLANTIC: A U.S. tanker is torpedoed and sunk by submarine *U-588* near Barnegat, New Jersey.

PACIFIC: The Netherlands East Indies surrenders to the Japanese. Admiral Brown's Task Force 11 launches a 100-plane raid on New Guinea, attacking the Japanese invasion fleet of Rear Admiral Kajioka Sadamichi. Three enemy ships are sunk and several others, including a cruiser and five destroyers, are damaged. U.S. and Australian B-17 and Hudson bombers also strike targets on New Guinea but cause no damage. At Midway, marine fighters intercept a Japanese Kawanishi 97 flying boat, leading CINCPAC intelligence analysts to believe that the Japanese are planning an attack in the direction of Hawaii.

March 11

ATLANTIC: A U.S. freighter is torpedoed and sunk by German submarine *U-158* near Cape Lookout, North Carolina. German submarine *U-126* sinks a U.S. freighter in the waters off Cuba.

PACIFIC: Lieutenant General Douglas MacArthur, under direct orders of President Roosevelt, leaves Corregidor with his wife and son. Rear Admiral Francis W. Rockwell and selected staff officers accompany MacArthur. The group is on board four PT boats headed for Mindanao. Aircraft are waiting there to take them to Australia. General Jonathan M. Wainwright takes command of the forces in Luzon. General

Albert M. Jones takes command of I Corps. U.S. submarine *Pollack* sinks two Japanese cargo ships in the East China Sea.

BURMA: General Stilwell takes command of the Chinese Fifth and Sixth armies in Burma, a force of about 100,000 men. Stilwell's command is mostly ceremonial; Chiang Kai-shek retains primary control.

March 12

ATLANTIC: A U.S. tanker is damaged off the coast of North Carolina by German submarine *U-158*. German submarine *U-126* sinks a U.S. freighter and damages another off the coast of Cuba.

PACIFIC: Major General Alexander M. Patch's 17,500-man task force arrives in Nouméa, New Caledonia.

By executive order of the president, the duties of commander in chief U.S. Fleet and chief of naval operations are combined.

March 13

ATLANTIC: German submarine *U-332* sinks a U.S. schooner off the coast of Florida; a Chilean freighter is sunk by German submarine *U-404* off the New Jersey coast.

PACIFIC: U.S. submarine *Gar* sinks a Japanese cargo ship south of Tokyo Bay. Two U.S. prisoners of war who are on the ship are killed. The men were from an SBD Dauntless dive-bomber from USS *Enterprise,* shot down and captured on a 24 February raid on Wake Island.

American cryptanalysts break the Japanese navy's general-purpose code and identify the codeword for Midway Island. Two American naval intelligence centers are in operation in the Pacific providing communications intelligence on the Japanese navy. One is in Melbourne, Australia, and the other at Pearl Harbor, led by Commander Joseph J. Rochefort. The Navy Radio Intelligence Section in Hawaii, identified as OP-20-G, has the responsibility to intercept enemy radio communications, decode and translate the information, then pass it to the Pacific Fleet commander.

March 14

ATLANTIC: German submarine *U-404* torpedoes and sinks a U.S. collier off Atlantic City, New Jersey.

The U.S. Joint Chiefs of Staff commit to a buildup of U.S. forces in Great Britain to support the strategy of defeating Germany first.

PHILIPPINES: General MacArthur reaches Mindanao.

March 15

ATLANTIC: German submarine *U-158* sinks two U.S. tankers off Cape Lookout, North Carolina. A U.S. Navy PBO Hudson providing convoy security attacks and sinks German submarine *U-503* off the coast of Newfoundland. German submarine *U-161* sinks a U.S. Coast Guard lighthouse tender off Haiti.

March 16

ATLANTIC: German submarine *U-332* damages a U.S. tanker off the coast of North Carolina. The ship is later scuttled.

March 17

ATLANTIC: German submarine *U-124* off Diamond Shoals, North Carolina, damages two U.S. tankers in two days. One later sinks, the other is towed to Norfolk, Virginia. German submarine *U-332* sinks another tanker and a freighter in the same location.

PACIFIC: MacArthur arrives in Darwin, Australia, and is appointed supreme commander of the Southwest Pacific. Upon his arrival, MacArthur makes the following statement: "The President of the United States ordered me to break through the Japanese lines and proceed from Corregidor to Australia for the purpose, as I understand it, of organizing the American offensive against Japan, a primary objective of which is the relief of the Philippines. I came through and I shall return."

The United States agrees to accept responsibility for the defense of the Pacific Ocean.

U.S. submarine *Grayback* sinks a Japanese collier off the coast of Chichi Jima in the Bonin Islands.

March 19

PHILIPPINES: A message from President Roosevelt to General Wainwright pledges "every possible means and method" to assist the beleaguered defenders of Bataan and Corregidor and notifies him that he has been nominated for the rank of lieutenant general "because of the confidence I have in your leadership and in the superb gallantry of the devoted band of American and Filipino soldiers under your command."

March 20

ATLANTIC: Army Air Force (AAF) planners lay out a concept for a strategic bombing campaign against Germany launched from bases in Britain. The United States will emphasize precision daylight attacks against critical industrial targets, complementing the British emphasis on night area bombing.

March 21

ATLANTIC: German submarine *U-124* damages one U.S. tanker and sinks another off the North Carolina coast. Two U.S. tankers will be sunk by *U-124* the following day in the same area. Another U.S. tanker is sunk by *U-123*.

PHILIPPINES: Wainwright officially becomes a lieutenant general and moves to Corregidor to take command of U.S. forces in the Philippines. Major General Edward P. King takes command of the Luzon Force.

BURMA: General Stilwell's Chinese divisions support the British defenses, covering the area from Toungoo to Prome, defending along the Sittang and Salween Rivers. British and Indian forces under General William J. Slim will defend the area from the Irrawaddy River to Prome.

March 24

ATLANTIC: The Combined Chiefs of Staff designate the Pacific theater and assign to the United States primary responsibility for military operations.

March 25

ATLANTIC: Task Force 39, consisting of a battleship, two cruisers, the carrier USS *Wasp*, and a destroyer squadron, leaves for Britain to support the British Home Fleet.

March 26

ATLANTIC: The U.S. Navy is given operational control over U.S. Army Air Forces in conducting antisubmarine patrols. A U.S. Navy "Q ship," a warship disguised as a merchant vessel, is sunk by German submarine *U-123* in an engagement off the North Carolina coast. *U-123* is damaged in the fight, but the American crew is lost. A U.S. tanker is sunk by German submarine *U-71* off Diamond Shoals, North Carolina. *U-160* sinks a Panamanian freighter off the Virginia Capes.

PHILIPPINES: U.S. B-17s evacuate Philippine president Quezon and his family to Australia.

March 27

ATLANTIC: U.S. War Plans Division develops three options for Europe. Sledgehammer is the name for the contingency plan for a small-scale cross-Channel attack in 1942 as a raid or to establish a permanent foothold on the continent. It is intended as an emergency measure to divert German forces from the USSR if the USSR appears to be in danger of imminent collapse and defeat. The plan for the full-scale invasion of Europe in 1943 is called Roundup. The U.S.-British forces in the United Kingdom are considered to be the first phase of the buildup of additional U.S. forces for Roundup. This plan is called Bolero.

PACIFIC: U.S. submarine *Gudgeon* sinks a Japanese freighter off Kumun Island.

March 29

ATLANTIC: U.S. steamship is torpedoed and sunk by German submarine *U-160* off Cape Hatteras, North Carolina.

PACIFIC: The U.S. Marine 4th Defense Battalion and Fighter Squadron 212 arrive at Efate, New Hebrides, joining 500 army troops. Work begins on an airstrip.

March 30

ATLANTIC: A U.S. freighter, part of a convoy to Murmansk, USSR, is sunk by German submarine *U-435*.

PACIFIC: The Pacific theater is divided into two areas, each with its own commander. MacArthur has the Southwest Pacific area (Philippines, Australia, New Guinea, Solomons, Netherlands East Indies, and the Bismarck Archipelago). MacArthur is to protect lines of communication within his area and guard the approaches into his area, defend Australia, and support operations in the Pacific Ocean area. Admiral Nimitz has the Pacific Ocean area (North, Central, and South Pacific Ocean). His mission is to protect lines of communication in his area and support operations in the Southwest Pacific. Nimitz commands all naval forces in the Pacific, including those forces provided to MacArthur. Both commanders are ordered to prepare for offensive action. Nimitz's command has three subdivisions: North, South, and Central Pacific. Vice Admiral Robert L. Ghormley will command the South Pacific, while Nimitz has command of the North and Central Pacific. The Pacific War Council is established in Washington, D.C., to develop war policy. Nations represented are China, the Netherlands, Great Britain, Canada, New Zealand, Australia, and the United States. U.S. submarine *Tambor* damages a Japanese transport off Eniwetok Atoll. U.S. submarine *Sturgeon* sinks a Japanese transport off Makassar City in the Java Sea.

March 31

ATLANTIC: German submarine *U-754* attacks and sinks a tugboat and two barges at the mouth of Chesapeake Bay and will later sink a U.S. tanker in the same area. Italian submarine *Pietro Calvi* sinks a U.S. tanker in the Caribbean bound for Venezuela.
BURMA: Stilwell's Chinese division is driven out of Toungoo.

April 1

PACIFIC: Japanese forces begin landings on Dutch New Guinea.

    U.S. submarine *Seawolf* torpedoes a Japanese light cruiser off Christmas Island.

April 2

BURMA: General Brereton, commander of the Tenth Air Force, leads a bombing raid on Japanese shipping targets, claiming damage to a cruiser and a transport.

April 2

ATLANTIC: German submarine *U-123* torpedoes and damages a U.S. tanker off the North Carolina coast. *U-552* shells and sinks a U.S. freighter off the Eastern Shore of Virginia.

April 3

ATLANTIC: A U.S. freighter is torpedoed and sunk by German submarine *U-754* off Cape Henry, Virginia. A U.S. freighter is torpedoed and sunk off the west coast of Africa by German submarine *U-505*.
PACIFIC: Admiral Nimitz is named commander in chief Pacific Ocean area (CINCPOA) in addition to his position as commander in chief Pacific Fleet (CINCPAC).
PHILIPPINES: A five-hour air and artillery bombardment of the Bataan defensive line precedes a Japanese ground assault. Major General Albert Jones's I Corps holds, but the left flank of Major General George Parker's II Corps gives way and the 41st Division of the Philippine Army collapses. Attempts to block the Japanese advance with infantry and tanks from the reserve force are only partially successful.
BURMA: General Stilwell deploys the Chinese 96th Division in the Sittang Valley to support the withdrawal of the Chinese 22nd Division to Pyinmana.

April 4

ATLANTIC: A U.S. tanker is sunk off Puerto Rico by German submarine *U-552*.
PHILIPPINES: Japanese air and artillery bombardments open a second day of attacks to exploit the collapse of II Corp's left flank. Japanese tanks and infantry press remnants of the Philippine 41st and 21st Divisions back, opening a wide gap between I and II Corps.

April 5

ATLANTIC: A U.S. tanker is sunk by German submarine *U-154* off the shores of the Dominican Republic.

April 5

PHILIPPINES: Japanese forces seize Mount Samat, the key terrain feature in II Corps zone.

April 6
ATLANTIC: A U.S. tanker is damaged by a torpedo attack from German submarine *U-160* off Cape Lookout, North Carolina.
PACIFIC: Advance elements of the U.S. Army's 41st Infantry Division arrive in Melbourne, Australia.
PHILIPPINES: II Corps counterattacks to recapture Mount Samat, but poor coordination among units, including an inability of some units even to conduct an attack, combined with an effective Japanese defense supported by effective air and artillery support, cause the effort to fail. Two divisions and a regiment are lost and two other regiments are surrounded and cut off. Having committed its reserve to the counterattack, II Corps is forced into a small defensive line on the San Vicente River.

April 7
ATLANTIC: Eighth Air Force is ordered to Britain.
PHILIPPINES: The Japanese press their attack on II Corps, forcing the remnants to retreat to the Mamala River, but are unable to hold. Sensing victory, General Homma orders his forces to attack south to seize Cabcaben, on the southeast tip of the peninsula. Both the Luzon force reserve and I Corps reserve are committed, but fail to stop the Japanese advance.

April 8
ATLANTIC: Two U.S. tankers are sunk in shallow water by German submarine *U-123* off the Georgia coast. The two tankers are later salvaged and returned to service.
PHILIPPINES: A defensive line is established on the Alagan River, but the exhausted and starved men have become disorganized and command and control has broken down. Supported by artillery and air attacks, the Japanese easily locate gaps in the defenses and push south. "It is with deep regret," Wainwright reports to MacArthur, "that I am forced to report that the troops on Bataan are fast folding up." I Corps, untouched for the most part, is ordered to withdraw to the Binuangan River, and then receives an order originating from MacArthur to attack northward. Major General Jones, committed to a withdrawal, reports his troops are physically incapable of conducting an attack. Food stocks on Bataan are used up, and the rear area is in chaos.

U.S. submarine *Seadragon* arrives at Corregidor and takes off navy communications intercept and intelligence personnel.

April 9
ATLANTIC: German submarine *U-123* sinks a U.S. freighter off the coast of Georgia. German submarine *U-160* sinks a U.S. freighter and *U-552* sinks two U.S. tankers off Cape Hatteras, North Carolina. Italian submarine *Pietro Calvi* conducts a surface attack on a U.S. tanker off the coast of Brazil, forcing the crew to abandon ship.
PHILIPPINES: Despite direct orders from General Wainwright (which came from General MacArthur and President Roosevelt) to continue the fight and under no circumstances surrender, Major General Edward King, commander of Luzon Force, meets with Major General Nagano Kameichiro to arrange terms for surrender. Believing further resistance would lead only to the slaughter of his men, General King takes action without notifying Wainwright. About 2,000 American and Fili-

American prisoners on the Bataan Death March *(Library of Congress)*

pino troops escape to Corregidor. King unconditionally surrenders 78,000 soldiers to the Japanese. The Bataan Death March begins—a 65-mile march from Mariveles at the base of the Bataan peninsula to the railhead at San Fernando. Lacking food and water, and already exhausted and ill, the prisoners are treated with barbaric cruelty. An estimated 7,000 to 10,000 captives will die, including 2,330 Americans.

April 10
ATLANTIC: German submarine *U-123* conducts a surface attack on a U.S. tanker, which is silhouetted by the lights of Jacksonville, Florida.
PHILIPPINES: U.S. submarine *Snapper* evacuates personnel from Corregidor. Japanese forces land on Cebu Island at Cebu City. Philippine units on the island conduct a delaying action. The headquarters of the Visayan Force, under command of Brigadier General Bradford Chynoweth, is located on the island. U.S. submarine *Thresher* sinks a Japanese freighter near the mouth of Tokyo Bay.

April 11
ATLANTIC: A U.S. tanker is damaged by German submarine *U-203* south of Cape Lookout, North Carolina. A British steamship is sunk by *U-160* off the Virginia Capes.

PACIFIC: U.S. submarine *Trout* sinks a Japanese fleet tanker off the island of Honshu west of the air and naval base of Shiono Mikasi. Fifth Air Force aircraft attack Japanese cargo ships off Lae, New Guinea, damaging one ship.

April 12

ATLANTIC: A U.S. freighter is sunk by German submarine *U-123* off the coast of Florida. A Panamanian tanker is sunk off the North Carolina coast by German submarine *U-203*.

General Arnold, chief of Army Air Forces, provides General Marshall in London with the air plan for Bolero, calling for the establishment of the Eighth Air Force in Britain.

CARIBBEAN: A U.S. freighter is torpedoed and sunk near Haiti by German submarine *U-154*. A U.S. tanker is attacked by German submarine *U-130* near Puerto Rico.

PHILIPPINES: General Chynoweth retreats with elements of his force into the mountains of north Cebu to begin a guerrilla campaign. Fifth Air Force B-25 Mitchells from Australia bomb targets on Cebu, while B-17s from Mindanao also strike Cebu. Japanese artillery and aircraft from Bataan begin intensive attacks on Corregidor.

April 13

PACIFIC: Vice Admiral Robert L. Ghormley is designated as commander, South Pacific Area (COMSOPAC). Ghormley is responsible for all Allied base defense forces and local defense forces in the South Pacific, except New Zealand.

April 14

ATLANTIC: U.S. destroyer *Roper* sinks German submarine *U-58* off the Virginia Capes. A British freighter is sunk by German submarine *U-203* off Diamond Shoals, North Carolina.

The British accept the U.S. plan for Bolero, the buildup of Allied forces in Britain for a cross-Channel invasion.

Detachment 101 of the Office of Coordination of Information is activated. It is an American unit tasked with conducting guerrilla warfare, sabotage, and espionage in the Far East.

April 15

ATLANTIC: A U.S. freighter is torpedoed and sunk off the coast of Massachusetts by German submarine *U-575*.

Headquarters, U.S. Bomber Command, is established in England. Eighth Air Force is reassigned to Britain and no longer attached to Gymnast.

BURMA: British forces destroy the oilfields at Yenangyaung as General Slim begins to withdraw northward. The Chinese 38th Division fights well in covering the British retreat. With his flank exposed, Stilwell orders the Chinese to hold. One entire Chinese division deserts and disappears into the hills of Burma.

April 16

ATLANTIC: German submarine *U-123*, having used up all its torpedoes on this patrol, conducts a surface attack on a U.S. freighter. The submarine evades a ramming attempt and then allows the freighter's crew to abandon ship safely before destroying the ship with gunfire.

PACIFIC: U.S. submarine *Tambor* sinks a Japanese stores ship off Kavieng, New Ireland.

PHILIPPINES: Japanese forces land on Panay Island; Colonel Albert Christie's 7,000-man Panay Force retreats into the mountains to conduct guerrilla operations. General Wainwright designates Brigadier General William F. Sharp as the commander of the Visayan garrisons and orders him to organize his Visayan-Mindanao Force for a defense of Mindanao.

April 17

BURMA: General Stilwell, outflanked by rapidly advancing Japanese forces, abandons his plans to defend at Pyinmana. Stilwell continues to have trouble in getting the Chinese division commanders to respond to his orders. Chinese generals insist on getting guidance from Chiang Kai-shek. The Chinese 55th Division is destroyed south of Loikaw, leaving the road to Lashio and the Burma Road open.

April 18

ATLANTIC: A U.S. tanker is torpedoed off Cape Hatteras by German submarine *U-136,* but is able to make port in Norfolk, Virginia.

PACIFIC: The Doolittle Raid on Japan. Task Force 16 under command of Admiral William F. Halsey, with the carriers USS *Enterprise* and USS *Hornet,* approaches the coast of Japan. On board the *Hornet* are 16 B-25 Mitchell bombers of the Eighth Air Force's XVII Bomber Group. The pilots have been trained to take off from the carrier's small deck but are too large to land on the deck. The plan is a strike on the Jap homeland. The intent is to launch the bombers from the carrier, bomb targets, then fly to airfields in China. But on April 18, at 650 miles off, a Japanese patrol ship discovers the task force. Halsey decides to launch the B-25s, led by Lieutenant Colonel James H. Doolittle. Although launched at the maximum limit of their range, Doolittle's bombers still achieve surprise and hit targets in Tokyo, Yokohama, Kobe, Yakosuka, and Nagoya. After dropping their bombs, the planes head for China, but, unable to land at the planned airfields, the crews will either crash-land their planes or parachute out and attempt to escape to Chinese lines. One plane will land in Vladivostok and its crew will be interned by the Soviets. Of the 80 airmen who make the attack, 71 will survive. Doolittle and 62 others reach safety in China. Five are killed and eight others are captured.

Meanwhile, Halsey's carrier aircraft from USS *Enterprise* attack Japanese picket boats, damaging eight as well as an armed merchant cruiser. The cruiser USS *Nashville* sinks two picket boats with direct gunfire. Halsey's task force then withdraws safely. The attack will have little effect in terms of damage, but will be a deep psychological blow to the Japanese (one of Doolittle's bombers flies directly over the emperor's palace), demonstrating that the Japanese homeland is not secure. Most importantly, American morale receives a sorely needed boost. Doolittle will later receive the Medal of Honor for his daring act.

B-25 Mitchells are ready to take off from the deck of the USS *Hornet* to bomb Tokyo, April 18, 1942. Sixteen bombers were launched for this highly secret mission under the command of Lieutenant Colonel James H. Doolittle.

April 19

ATLANTIC: U.S. freighter is torpedoed and sunk by German submarine *U-136* west of Bermuda.

April 20

ATLANTIC: A U.S. freighter is torpedoed and sunk by German submarine *U-752* off Nantucket.

U.S. carrier *Wasp* is moved into the Mediterranean to deliver British fighter aircraft to Malta.

SOUTHWEST PACIFIC AREA: General George H. Brett assumes command of Allied Air Forces, subordinate to MacArthur's Southwest Pacific Area (SWPA) command. It includes the U.S. Fifth Air Force, as well as Australian and Dutch air forces. Also within SWPA, General Sir Thomas Blamey is appointed commander, Allied Land Forces, and Admiral Herbert F. Leary commands Allied Naval Forces.

April 21

ATLANTIC: U.S. freighter is torpedoed and sunk by German submarine *U-576* off the east coast. *U-201* sinks a U.S. freighter off the east coast.

April 23
ATLANTIC: A U.S. freighter is torpedoed and sunk by German submarine *U-125* off the east coast.
BURMA: Chinese Sixth Army retreats into China. Other units under Stilwell take up defensive positions in the Sittang Valley. The Chinese 200th Division moves to halt the Japanese advance near Loikaw.

April 24
PACIFIC: U.S. submarine *Trout* sinks Japanese merchant ship near Kii Strait.

April 25
PACIFIC: U.S. submarine *Spearfish* sinks Japanese military transport off Luzon.

April 26
ATLANTIC: U.S. freighter is torpedoed and sunk by German submarine *U-66* near the Netherlands West Indies.
PACIFIC: U.S. submarine *Pickerel* damages a Japanese hospital ship in Manipa Strait.

April 28
ATLANTIC: A joint U.S.-British naval task force sails from Scapa Flow to escort convoy PQ 15, heading for the USSR.

April 29
ATLANTIC: German submarine *U-108* torpedoes and sinks a U.S. tanker off the east coast; *U-507* torpedoes and sinks a U.S. tanker off Cuba.
PACIFIC: The Japanese Imperial General Staff Headquarters designates Port Moresby as a priority objective to assist in controlling New Guinea and the Solomons. The MO Plan is developed to establish a base in Tulagi while a major landing takes place at Port Moresby, New Guinea. The plan involves five elements, including a landing force element, a support group, a carrier striking force with the two fleet carriers, the *Shokaku* and *Zuikaku,* a patrol group, and a covering group, with the light carrier *Shoho.*
PHILIPPINES: Japanese forces begin offensive on Mindanao, landing nearly 5,000 men from Cebu on the island. Philippine army units are unable to halt the attackers and begin to withdraw.

The Japanese continue to intensify the bombardment of Corregidor. Rations and water are in short supply, and power to the Malinta tunnel, where the bulk of the garrison is located, is failing. Bombs and artillery shells have demolished most of the fixed defensive positions. A Japanese landing force occupies the abandoned Australian seaplane base at Tulagi in the Solomons.
BURMA: Japanese forces capture Lashio, cutting the Burma Road. British forces begin a retreat to India. Chinese Fifth Army retreats into China.

April 30
PACIFIC: Fifth Air Force aircraft attack Japanese bases on Lae and Salamaua in New Guinea. U.S. Navy PBY Catalinas take civilians and military personnel off

Corregidor. U.S. submarine *Greenling* sinks a Japanese ammunition ship in the Caroline Islands.

May 1
PACIFIC: U.S. submarine *Triton* sinks a Japanese cargo ship off Formosa.
BURMA: The Japanese capture Mandalay after the withdrawal of the Chinese 22nd Division from the city. Stilwell initiates plans for the withdrawal of his forces from Burma via Myitkyina.

May 2
ATLANTIC: General Carl A. Spaatz is designated commander of Eighth Air Force.
PACIFIC: Japanese force from Tulagi lands on Florida Island in the Solomons. U.S. submarine *Drum* sinks a Japanese seaplane carrier off the coast of Japan's Honshu Island; U.S. submarine *Trout* sinks a Japanese freighter off Honshu.

May 3
PHILIPPINES: A Japanese amphibious force from Panay lands on Mindanao; Corregidor faces steady air and artillery attacks. Japanese forces establish a seaplane base on Tulagi in the Solomon Islands. The U.S. submarine *Spearfish* arrives at Corregidor and takes 25 passengers along with vital records and mail to Australia.

May 4
ATLANTIC: Commander in Chief U.S. Fleet Admiral King orders the Coast Guard Auxiliary to use civilian small craft as coastal pickets in response to the German U-boat threat. U.S. freighter is sunk by German submarine *U-162* off the coast of British Guiana. Three U.S. tankers are sunk by *U-507* in the waters off Cuba. *U-564* torpedoes a U.S. freighter off the coast of Florida. *U-123* sinks a U.S. freighter in the southern Caribbean. The submarine rescues 34 survivors; the captain questions the group, then gives them directions to land and casts them off. The survivors will be picked up later by a steamship and brought to Cartagena, Colombia.

The War Production Board rations sugar to save scarce sources.
PACIFIC: Aircraft from Rear Admiral Frank Jack Fletcher's Task Force 17 with the carrier *Yorktown,* three cruisers, six destroyers, and the oiler USS *Neosho,* attack the Japanese at Tulagi, sinking a destroyer, a minesweeper, two auxiliary minesweepers, and damaging several other enemy ships. Japanese transports leave Rabaul for Port Moresby, New Guinea. The Japanese carrier striking force with the *Zuikaku* and *Shokaku* reaches San Cristobal Island at the southernmost end of the Solomon Island group to protect the Port Moresby invasion force coming from Rabaul. Meanwhile, Rear Admiral Aubrey Fitch with the carrier USS *Lexington,* five U.S. destroyers, and five Australian cruisers awaits a linkup at a predesignated area in the Coral Sea.

U.S. submarine *Trout* sinks a Japanese gunboat off the coast of Honshu, Japan. U.S. submarine *Greenling* sinks a Japanese gunboat near Truk.
PHILIPPINES: Philippine defenders on Mindanao establish a new defensive line. Corregidor undergoes greatest bombardment to date. A total of 16,000 artillery shells fall on the island in a 24-hour period. The garrison has suffered 600 casualties since

April 9 and the water supply is down to four days. Wainwright reports to General Marshall that "we have something less than even chance to beat off an assault."

May 5

ATLANTIC: U.S. freighter is torpedoed and sunk by German submarine *U-108* off Haiti. *U-133* torpedoes and damages a U.S. tanker off the coast of Florida.

PACIFIC: Japanese Imperial General Staff Headquarters sends orders to prepare for the invasion of Midway Island, called the MI Plan. A supporting operation to attack the Aleutians is named the AL Plan.

PHILIPPINES: The Japanese make a night landing on the north shore of Corregidor. Beach defenses have been thoroughly obliterated, and information can be sent only by messenger. Although American defenders cause heavy casualties to the initial landing force, the Japanese gain a foothold and advance rapidly using tanks and light artillery. American counterattacks are disrupted and the defenders begin to suffer heavy casualties. Between 600 and 800 men are killed and nearly 1,000 wounded by the middle of the day. Wainwright decides to surrender. In a message to President Roosevelt and General MacArthur notifying them of his decision, Wainwright writes: "Please say to the nation that my troops and I have accomplished all that is humanly possible and that we have upheld the best traditions of the United States. . . ."

May 6

ATLANTIC: German submarine *U-333* torpedoes and sinks a U.S. tanker off the coast of Florida. *U-507* and *U-125* each attack and sink a U.S. freighter in the Gulf of Mexico.

PACIFIC: U.S. submarine *Skipjack* torpedoes and sinks a Japanese cargo ship off Indochina. U.S. submarine *Triton* sinks two Japanese cargo ships off Formosa.

PHILIPPINES: Lieutenant General Jonathan Wainwright surrenders unconditionally to the Japanese. All U.S. and Filipino forces are ordered to end resistance throughout the Philippines. About 11,000 on Corregidor become prisoners. Japanese forces continue their attack on Mindanao, moving toward Dalirig, above the Del Monte airfields in northern Mindanao.

May 7

CBI: Japanese forces capture Myitkyina. Stilwell decides to walk to India with 80 handpicked staff members and a handful of other followers. The Chinese 22nd and 38th Divisions move in good order from upper Burma into India. Other Chinese units, including the 200th Division and part of the 55th Division, escape to China.

PACIFIC: The Battle of the Coral Sea. As the Japanese Port Moresby invasion force approaches New Guinea, Admiral Fletcher moves his united task force to intercept. The support group of the Port Moresby operation is attacked by 93 aircraft from the carriers USS *Lexington* and USS *Yorktown*, sinking the light carrier *Shoho*. Meanwhile, the U.S. destroyer *Sims* and the oiler *Neosho* are attacked by Japanese aircraft, which mistake them for a carrier and a cruiser. The *Sims* is sunk and the *Neosho* is heavily damaged and is later scuttled. Aircraft from the Japanese carrier striking force also attack three Australian cruisers and two destroyers sent by Fletcher to locate the Port Moresby landing force. Later, B-26 Marauders from Fifth Air Force mistakenly bomb the Allied ships. That night 27 planes are dispatched to locate the American carriers. Only six return, which will limit the strikes that the Japanese can later launch against the American carriers. Not knowing where the U.S. carriers are located, the Port Moresby landing is postponed for two days. The Japanese occupy Hollandia, New Guinea.

May 8

CBI: P-40s of the American Volunteer Group (Flying Tigers) attack Japanese forces on the banks of the Salween River in an attempt to prevent an advance to Kunming, China.

SOUTHWEST PACIFIC AREA: General Douglas MacArthur, commander of SWPA, offers to General George C. Marshall a plan to attack the Japanese base at Rabaul. He requests significant naval and air support, including aircraft carriers, along with additional army reinforcements.

U.S. submarine *Skipjack* torpedoes and sinks an army cargo ship off Indochina.

PACIFIC: The Battle of the Coral Sea. Aircraft from the USS *Lexington* locate the Japanese carrier striking force. Dive bombers and torpedo bombers from the carriers USS *Lexington* and USS *Yorktown* attack and damage the *Shokaku*. A 70-plane counterstrike from the Japanese carriers damages both the *Yorktown* and the *Lexington*. The *Lexington* is hit by two torpedoes and two bombs, lists badly and is unable to receive aircraft. A fuel explosion later in the day leaves the ship too badly damaged to survive, and she is sunk by a torpedo from an American destroyer. The Japanese lose 43 aircraft and American losses are 33 aircraft. Nimitz orders Fletcher to withdraw, while the Japanese, thinking both U.S. carriers are sunk, return to Truk. Although that order will be countermanded in Tokyo, the American fleet is gone.

Lieutenant John Powers on both May 7 and 8 plays a critical role in the outcome of the Battle of the Coral Sea. Leading a section of three Douglas SBD Dauntless dive-bombers, he ignores heavy antiaircraft fire to drop his bomb directly on the *Shoho* at an altitude that seems to guarantee his own destruction. The following day, Powers tells his fellow pilots, "Remember the folks back home are counting on us. I am going to get a hit if I have to lay it on their flight deck." Leading his section of dive-bombers to attack the *Shokaku* from an altitude of 18,000 feet, Powers again dives through antiaircraft fire and enemy fighter planes to drop his bomb on the deck of the carrier, scoring a direct hit. He disappears in smoke and flame attempting to recover from his harrowing dive. For his acts of skill and courage Lieutenant Powers will receive the Medal of Honor.

Lieutenant Milton E. Ricketts is in charge of a damage control party on the carrier USS *Yorktown* when a bomb explosion causes heavy casualties and a major fire. Although mortally wounded, Lieutenant Ricketts uses a fire hose to contain the blaze until his last breath. For his selfless sacrifice in saving his ship, Lieutenant Ricketts will receive the Medal of Honor.

The Battle of the Coral Sea is a tactical victory for the Japanese, but a strategic victory for the United States. It is the first naval battle in history where ships do not fire at each other; aircraft conduct all engagements; and carrier aircraft inflict all the damage on the ships. The Japanese for the first time have been stopped in naval combat. The Port Moresby landings are cancelled. More importantly, the damage to *Shokaku* prevents it from being added to the Midway MI Plan. The Japanese also lose irreplaceable skilled pilots.

U.S. submarine *Grenadier* sinks an army transport ship off the coast of Kyushu, Japan.

May 9

ATLANTIC: U.S. freighter is damaged by German submarine *U-588* off Nova Scotia; *U-564* sinks a U.S. freighter off Florida. U.S. Coast Guard cutter sinks German submarine *U-352* off the coast of North Carolina. U.S. carrier *Wasp* continues operations in the Mediterranean to deliver British aircraft to Malta.

PACIFIC: Japanese take Dalirig at Mindanao and pursue the scattered defenders.

May 10

ATLANTIC: U.S. freighter is torpedoed and sunk by German submarine *U-506* off the coast of Louisiana.

PHILIPPINES: General Sharp orders his Visayan-Mindanao force to surrender. Some units, still resisting, do so reluctantly.

U.S. submarine *Silversides* conducts a surface attack and damages a Japanese guardboat near Marcus Island.

May 11

PACIFIC: U.S. submarine *S-42* damages a Japanese minelaying ship in the Solomons. B-17 bombers attack Japanese ships in the northern Solomons.

May 12

CBI: Tenth Air Force B-17s attack Myitkyina in Burma to disrupt Japanese fighters from interfering with the aerial supply route to China.

ATLANTIC: U.S. tanker is sunk by German submarine *U-507* off the coast of Louisiana; *U-162* torpedoes and sinks a U.S. tanker off Barbados.

PACIFIC: U.S. submarine *S-44* sinks Japanese repair ship in the Solomons.

May 13

CARIBBEAN: A U.S. freighter is torpedoed and sunk by German submarine *U-169*.

SOUTHWEST PACIFIC AREA: B-17s and B-26 Marauders from Fifth Air Force bomb Rabaul.

PACIFIC: U.S. submarine *Drum* torpedoes and sinks a Japanese cargo ship off the coast of Honshu, Japan.

May 14

BURMA: Tenth Air Force B-17 bombers attack Myitkyina.

ATLANTIC: German submarine *U-213* lays mines off St. Johns, Newfoundland.

Congress enacts legislation establishing the Women's Army Auxiliary Corps (WAAC). These women, designated as neither military nor civilian, will provide support to the war effort through their knowledge, skills, and special training.

PACIFIC: Fifth Air Force B-17s and B-26 Marauders attack Rabaul and Lae.

May 15

ATLANTIC: U.S. freighter is torpedoed and sunk by German submarine *U-751* near the Bahamas. German aircraft attack the port of Murmansk in an attempt to damage U.S. cargo ships delivering supplies.

May 16

CBI: Tenth Air Force B-17 bombers attack Japanese positions at Myitkyina.
CARIBBEAN: *U-103* torpedoes and sinks a U.S. freighter.
ATLANTIC: Two U.S. tankers are damaged and one tanker is sunk by torpedoes from German submarine *U-506* off the coast of Louisiana.
SOUTHWEST PACIFIC AREA: Fifth Air Force B-25 Mitchells, B-17s, and B-26 Marauders attack Lae and Deboyne Island in New Guinea.
PACIFIC: U.S. submarine *Tautog* sinks Japanese tanker near Truk.

May 17

CARIBBEAN: U.S. freighter and a British tanker are torpedoed and sunk by German submarine *U-155*.
PACIFIC: U.S. submarine *Silversides* damages a Japanese transport off Honshu, Japan. U.S. submarine *Skipjack* sinks a Japanese army transport in the Gulf of Siam. U.S. submarine *Tautog* sinks Japanese submarine *I-28* near Rabaul. U.S. submarine *Triton* sinks Japanese submarine *I-64* off Kyushu, Japan.

May 18

ATLANTIC: German bombers attack the port of Murmansk, but cause little damage to American merchant ships. U.S. freighter is sunk by German submarine *U-156* in the Caribbean. *U-125* sinks two U.S. freighters in the Gulf of Mexico.
PACIFIC: The Japanese Imperial General Headquarters designates New Caledonia, Fiji, and Samoa as objectives for the Seventeenth Army and the Combined Fleet.

May 19

ATLANTIC: General Ira C. Eaker takes command of all U.S. Army air forces in Britain. U.S. freighter is torpedoed and sunk by German submarine *U-506* off the coast of Louisiana; *U-103* sinks a U.S. freighter off the coast of Mexico; *U-751* sinks a U.S. freighter off the coast of Haiti.

May 20

CBI: General Stilwell emerges from the jungles of Burma after a march of 150 miles through formidable terrain and reports to the British garrison at Imphal, India. No one in the group has been lost. Three days later, in Delhi for a strategy conference, Stilwell will face a group of reporters who are eager to label him a hero for his vaunted walkout of Burma. Stilwell will tell them plainly: "No military commander in history ever made a voluntary retreat. All retreats are ignominious as hell. I claim we got a hell of a beating. We got run out of Burma—and it is humiliating as hell. I think we ought to find out what caused it, go back, and retake it."

CARIBBEAN: A U.S. freighter is torpedoed and sunk by German submarine *U-752* off the coast of Mexico. German submarine *U-103* torpedoes and sinks two U.S. freighters off the coast of Cuba.

ATLANTIC: *U-506* torpedoes and sinks a U.S. tanker off the coast of Louisiana.

SOUTHWEST PACIFIC AREA: Fifth Air Force B-17s attack Japanese airfields on Timor Island.

PACIFIC: Rear Admiral John S. McCain takes command of naval air forces in the South Pacific.

May 21
ATLANTIC: A U.S. freighter is torpedoed and sunk by German submarine *U-588* off the East Coast.

SOUTHWEST PACIFIC AREA: Fifth Air Force B-17s bomb Lae in New Guinea.

May 22
ATLANTIC: A U.S. freighter is torpedoed and sunk by German submarine *U-588* off the East Coast.

SOUTHWEST PACIFIC AREA: Fifth Air Force B-17s attack shipping and airfields at Rabaul, while B-26 Marauders attack the harbor and airfields at Lae.

May 23
ALEUTIANS: U.S. fighter reinforcements arrive on Umnak Island in the Aleutians as part of the effort to counter the Japanese Midway attack plan.

CARIBBEAN: A U.S. tanker is torpedoed and sunk by German submarine *U-103* off the coast of Mexico.

SOUTHWEST PACIFIC AREA: Fifth Air Force B-25 Mitchells attack facilities at Lae.

May 24
CARIBBEAN: A U.S. freighter is torpedoed and sunk by German submarine *U-558* near Jamaica.

SOUTHWEST PACIFIC AREA: Fifth Air Force B-26 Marauders attacking Lae come under heavy attack by Japanese fighters. Several bombers are lost.

PACIFIC: U.S. submarine *Pompano* sinks a Japanese fishing boat off Formosa.

May 25
CBI: Tenth Air Force B-17s bomb Japanese logistics facilities at Rangoon, Burma.

CARIBBEAN: U.S. destroyer is torpedoed by German submarine *U-156* off the island of Martinique. U.S. freighter is sunk by German submarine *U-103* in the Gulf of Mexico.

SOUTHWEST PACIFIC AREA: Fifth Air Force B-17s bomb Rabaul.

U.S. submarine *Permit* damages a Japanese transport in the Makassar Strait.

PACIFIC: U.S. submarine *Tautog* sinks Japanese transport off the Caroline Islands; U.S. submarine *Pompano* sinks Japanese tanker off Okinawa; U.S. submarine *Drum* sinks a Japanese cargo ship off Honshu, Japan.

May 26
CARIBBEAN: German submarine *U-106* torpedoes and sinks one U.S. freighter and conducts an unsuccessful surface attack on another freighter in the Gulf of Mexico. The *U-106*'s commander is reported to purposely kill survivors attempting to escape in a lifeboat.

ATLANTIC: U.S. and British air commanders meet to decide on allocation of assets against targets in Germany. Convoy PQ 16 on its way to Murmansk is attacked by German submarine *U-703*, which sinks a U.S. freighter.

PACIFIC: Reinforcements arrive at Midway, delivered by USS *Kittyhawk*. U.S. submarine *Salmon* sinks a Japanese repair ship off the coast of Indochina.

May 27
CARIBBEAN: A U.S. freighter is torpedoed and sunk by German submarine *U-502*.

ATLANTIC: German bombers attack convoy PQ 16 on its way to Murmansk, sinking three U.S. freighters and damaging one.

SOUTHWEST PACIFIC AREA: Fifth Air Force B-17s attack Rabaul.

PACIFIC: The Japanese carrier strike group leaves Japan for Midway. The Americal Division under General Alexander M. Patch is activated in New Caledonia. (Americal is an amalgamation of the words "America" and "Caledonia.") Under orders from Admiral Nimitz, Rear Admiral Robert A. Theobald organizes Task Force 8 to defend the Aleutians. It is composed of surface and air strike groups. Theobald believes Dutch Harbor is the Japanese objective, despite information from Nimitz's headquarters that the islands of Attu and Kiska are the targets of the Japanese invasion fleet.

May 28
CARIBBEAN: A U.S. tanker is torpedoed and sunk by German submarine *U-103*.

SOUTHWEST PACIFIC AREA: U.S. submarine *Salmon* sinks a Japanese freighter off the coast of Indochina; U.S. submarine *Seal* damages a Japanese cargo ship near Balbac Strait. Fifth Air Force B-26 Marauders attack Lae.

PACIFIC: The main body of the Japanese strike force leaves Japan for Midway. Rear Admiral Raymond A. Spruance's Task Force 16, with the carriers USS *Enterprise* and USS *Hornet,* leaves for Midway from Pearl Harbor. About 500 army soldiers are moved from Efate to occupy Espiritu Santo Island in the New Hebrides to build an airstrip large enough to accommodate bombers for future support of a planned offensive against the Solomons. Swampy ground and an outbreak of malaria delay construction. Admiral Nimitz, CinCPOA, rejects MacArthur's proposal to use his carriers to support an offensive against Rabaul. Instead, Nimitz offers to capture Tulagi with a marine Raider battalion.

May 29
ATLANTIC: Vyacheslav Molotov, Soviet commissar for foreign affairs, arrives in Washington, D.C., to meet with President Roosevelt. Molotov had been in London earlier arranging details of an Anglo-Soviet mutual support treaty. He is now in

Washington to push Roosevelt for a second front against the Germans in Europe in 1942.

SOUTHWEST PACIFIC AREA: U.S. submarine *Swordfish* sinks a Japanese cargo ship near Balbac Strait.

May 30

CBI: Tenth Air Force B-17s attack Myitkyina airfields, but find no activity there.

ATLANTIC: U.S. freighter is sunk by German submarine *U-404* off the East Coast. General Arnold, in a conference with British planners in London, announces that the USAAF will have 66 combat groups in the United Kingdom by March of 1943.

PACIFIC: Rear Admiral Frank Jack Fletcher's Task Force 17, with the carrier USS *Yorktown*, leaves Pearl Harbor for Midway. U.S. submarine *Pompano* sinks a Japanese transport off Okinawa.

May 31

SOUTHWEST PACIFIC AREA: Three Japanese midget submarines from submarines *I-22*, *I-24*, and *I-27* enter the harbor at Sidney, Australia, sinking one Australian naval vessel and severely damaging a Dutch submarine. The three midget submarines are destroyed.

Fifth Air Force B-17s attack Lae and Salamaua in New Guinea.

PACIFIC: U.S. submarine *Pollack* sinks a Japanese submarine chaser off the southern coast of Japan.

June 1

CARIBBEAN: German submarines *U-106* and *U-158* each torpedo and sink a U.S. freighter off the coast of Mexico.

ATLANTIC: A U.S. freighter is torpedoed and sunk by German submarine *U-404* off the coast of North Carolina; a U.S. freighter is torpedoed and sunk by German submarine *U-172* off the East Coast.

June 2

CARIBBEAN: A U.S. freighter is torpedoed and sunk by German submarine *U-159* off Puerto Rico.

PACIFIC: Admiral Frank Jack Fletcher's Task Force 17 and Admiral Raymond Spruance's Task Force 16 rendezvous northeast of Midway. Fletcher is the senior officer. U.S. naval forces consist of three carriers, seven heavy cruisers, 16 destroyers, oilers, and a light cruiser. The U.S. task force is screened by 25 submarines surrounding Midway. Fifth Air Force bombers attack Rabaul.

June 3

ALEUTIANS: Japanese carriers from the second strike force make a surprise raid on Dutch Harbor in the Aleutians, killing 52 Americans. The base is moderately damaged in the attacks. A counterstrike by nine P-40s and six B-26 Marauders fails to locate the Japanese fleet. According to the Japanese plan, this attack is intended as a diversion to confuse the Americans about Japanese intentions and divert forces away from Midway.

ATLANTIC: A U.S. tanker is torpedoed and sunk by German submarine *U-502* off the Florida coast.

PACIFIC: The Battle of Midway. Unknown to the Japanese, American code breakers have provided Nimitz with the true Japanese operational objective—Midway. A Japanese occupation force of four heavy cruisers, two destroyers, and transport ships carrying 5,000 men is located 600 miles from Midway. B-17 bombers sent to attack the fleet cause no damage. The American task forces change course to approach the Japanese.

June 4

ALEUTIANS: A second Japanese raid on Dutch Harbor in the Aleutians is met by P-40 fighters. Two B-17s and eight B-26 Marauders attack the Japanese fleet, but miss their targets.

CARIBBEAN: A U.S. freighter is torpedoed and sunk by German submarine *U-158* off Mexico.

PACIFIC: The Battle of Midway. U.S. aircraft sink a Japanese tanker. The Japanese send 108 planes from their carrier strike group to attack Midway, causing extensive damage. Seventeen of 26 Marine F2A Brewster Buffalo and F4F Wildcat fighters are lost. A U.S. counterstrike of six Avengers and four B-26 Marauder bombers against the Japanese carriers fails; only one Avenger and two B-26s return to Midway. B-17 bombers are also employed, but cause no damage to the fleet. Carrier aircraft from USS *Enterprise* and USS *Hornet* take off to locate the Japanese carriers, followed shortly after by USS *Yorktown*'s aircraft. *Hornet*'s 15 TBD torpedo planes are all destroyed in making their attack; the *Enterprise*'s 14 TBD torpedo planes have no effect, and 10 are lost. At this time the *Yorktown* and *Enterprise*'s SBD Dauntless dive-bombers locate the Japanese carriers and conduct an attack, catching the Japanese by surprise. Two carriers, the *Kaga* and the *Akagi,* are hit. The *Kaga* later sinks. The third Japanese carrier, *Soryu,* is attacked by the *Yorktown*'s SBDs and TBD torpedo planes and is sunk. Meanwhile, Japanese planes from *Hiryu* locate the *Yorktown*. Hit with bombs and torpedoes, the ship is abandoned with the intention to tow it back to Pearl Harbor. Aircraft from the *Hornet* and *Enterprise* locate the *Hiryu*, and heavily damage it.

The Japanese carrier *Hiryu* attempts to avoid American air attack during the Battle of Midway, June 4, 1942. Antiaircraft bursts are visible at top left. The air attack fatally damages the carrier and on the following day she is abandoned and sunk.

June 5

ALEUTIANS: Japanese forces occupy Attu Island in the Aleutians. Dutch Harbor is attacked by Japanese carrier aircraft.

CARIBBEAN: A U.S. tanker is torpedoed and sunk by German submarine *U-68.*

TBD-1 Devastator torpedo bombers on the deck of USS *Enterprise* at the opening stages of the Battle of Midway. These planes will contribute to the destruction of four Japanese aircraft carriers and a cruiser. Most of the planes and their pilots will not return.

ATLANTIC: The U.S. Congress declares war on Bulgaria, Hungary, and Romania.
PACIFIC: The Battle of Midway. The carriers *Akagi* and *Hiryu,* now useless hulks, are sunk by Japanese destroyers. Two Japanese cruisers collide while trying to avoid the U.S. submarine *Tambor.*

June 6
PACIFIC: The Battle of Midway. The cruiser *Mikuma* is sunk by SBD Dauntless dive-bombers from USS *Enterprise* and USS *Hornet.* The carrier USS *Yorktown* and the destroyer USS *Hammann* are simultaneously torpedoed by Japanese submarine *I-168. Hammann* sinks, but the *Yorktown* stays afloat.

Midway will be the strategic turning point in the war in the Pacific. With the loss of four carriers and their 322 planes and pilots, the Japanese can no longer mount large-scale offensive operations. U.S. losses are 147 aircraft. The Japanese high command will continue its strategy of establishing a defensive perimeter by establishing control of New Guinea, using the southern Solomons as a base of support.

June 7
ALEUTIANS: Japanese forces land on Kiska Island.
CARIBBEAN: German submarines *U-159* and *U-107* each torpedo and sink a U.S. freighter.
PACIFIC: The carrier USS *Yorktown* sinks after efforts to save it fail.

June 8
CARIBBEAN: A U.S. tanker is torpedoed and sunk by German submarine *U-50.*

The crew of the carrier USS *Yorktown* fights to save their ship. She was hit by three bombs from Japanese aircraft of the carrier *Hiryu*. On June 4, 1942, the *Yorktown* was abandoned and later sank.

ATLANTIC: The European Theater of Operations, United States Army (ETOUSA), is established.

SOUTHWEST PACIFIC AREA: General MacArthur again argues with Army Chief of Staff George C. Marshall for an offensive, directed at New Britain and New Ireland. To support this offensive, he requires amphibious-capable forces and aircraft carriers to provide air support. The three divisions he has available, the Australian 7th Division and the 41st and 32nd U.S. Infantry Divisions are not trained to conduct the kind of amphibious assaults MacArthur has in mind.

June 9
CARIBBEAN: A U.S. freighter is torpedoed and sunk by German submarine *U-107* off the coast of Honduras.

June 10
CARIBBEAN: A U.S. tanker is torpedoed and sunk by German submarine *U-157* off the coast of Cuba.

June 11

ATLANTIC: German submarine *U-87* lays mines off Boston harbor; *U-373* lays mines at the mouth of Delaware Bay.

June 12

ALEUTIANS: Eleventh Air Force B-24 Liberators attack Kiska, damaging a Japanese destroyer.

CARIBBEAN: A U.S. tanker is sunk by German submarine *U-158* in the Gulf of Mexico; *U-159* sinks a U.S. steamship off the coast of Panama.

ATLANTIC: General Marshall meets with Admiral King to discuss options for a Pacific offensive. Marshall is inclined to support MacArthur's plan, presented on June 8, noting that the 1st Marine Division could be available in Australia in early July. The Australian and U.S. divisions available could be used as follow-on forces to clear the objectives once a beachhead is established. Nearly 150 heavy and light bombers will be available, as well as 371 fighter aircraft to provide air support. Lae and Salamaua in New Guinea are within range of these land-based aircraft, but attacking Rabaul with the land-based bombers would require aircraft carriers to provide the long-range air support.

German submarine *U-701* lays mines off Cape Henry, Virginia.

MIDDLE EAST: A detachment of 13 B-24 Liberators under command of Colonel Harry Halverson and en route to China, takes off from Fayid, Egypt, and attacks the oil fields at Ploeşti, Romania. The attack causes little damage, but it is the first American airstrike from the European-African-Middle East (EAME) Theater.

SOUTHWEST PACIFIC AREA: U.S. submarine *Swordfish* sinks Japanese freighter in the Gulf of Siam. Fifth Air Force B-17s attack Rabaul.

June 13

CARIBBEAN: A U.S. Coast Guard cutter sinks *U-157* off the coast of Cuba. *U-159* sinks U.S. freighter near the Panama Canal.

ATLANTIC: German submarine *U-584* puts four agents ashore at Amagansett, Long Island. A Coast Guard patrol spots the activity.

President Roosevelt signs an executive order creating the Office of War Information under Elmer Davis to deal with dissemination of information both within the United States and in all foreign countries. The Office of Coordinator of Information is redesignated as the Office of Strategic Services under the Joint Chiefs of Staff. The Office of Strategic Services has the following functions: collect and analyze strategic information and plan and operate special services. William J. Donovan is appointed director.

June 14

ALEUTIANS: Eleventh Air Force B-17s and B-24 Liberators hit two Japanese cruisers at Kiska.

CARIBBEAN: German submarines *U-172* and *U-161* each sink a U.S. merchant ship near the Canal Zone.

PACIFIC: The first elements of the 1st Marine Division arrive at Wellington, New Zealand.

June 15

CARIBBEAN: A U.S. freighter is torpedoed and sunk by German submarine *U-502* off Trinidad; *U-502* and *U-126* each sink a U.S. freighter.

ATLANTIC: Two U.S. tankers in convoy KN 109 (Key West to Norfolk) leaving the Chesapeake Bay strike mines laid by German submarine *U-701*. A U.S. tanker in convoy XB 25 (Halifax to Boston) hits a mine outside of Boston harbor laid by German submarine *U-87*.

PHILIPPINES: U.S. submarine *Seawolf* sinks Japanese gunboat off Corregidor.

June 16

CARIBBEAN: A U.S. freighter is torpedoed and sunk by German submarine *U-126* after it has completed rescuing survivors from a freighter sunk by *U-161* on June 14.

June 17

CARIBBEAN: A U.S. freighter is torpedoed and sunk by German submarine *U-129* near Cuba.

ATLANTIC: German submarine *U-202* puts four agents ashore at Ponte Vedra Beach, Florida, but the landing is compromised when American fisherman come upon them. A U.S. collier in convoy KS 511 (Norfolk to Key West) near the Chesapeake Bay hits a mine laid by *U-701*.

June 18

ALEUTIANS: Eleventh Air Force bombers attack Kiska, sinking a Japanese tanker.

ATLANTIC: British prime minister Winston Churchill arrives in Washington to meet with President Roosevelt to discuss assistance to China, war production, and a second front in Europe. In London, Lieutenant General Carl Spaatz takes command of the U.S. Eighth Air Force. A U.S. freighter is torpedoed and sunk by German submarine *U-124*.

June 19

ATLANTIC: A U.S. patrol vessel is torpedoed and sunk by German submarine *U-701* off Cape Hatteras, North Carolina.

MIDDLE EAST: Headquarters, U.S. Army Forces in the Middle East (USAFIME), is established in Cairo, Egypt. General Russel L. Maxwell assumes command.

PACIFIC: Vice Admiral Robert L. Ghormley takes command of the South Pacific Area and the South Pacific Force, with headquarters in Auckland, New Zealand.

Fifth Air Force B-17s attack Rabaul.

June 20

CARIBBEAN: A U.S. freighter is torpedoed and sunk by German submarine *U-128* off Barbados.

ATLANTIC: Roosevelt and Churchill in private session agree upon a combined invasion of North Africa.

General Marshall provides incoming commander of the European Theater of Operations (ETOUSA), Major General Dwight D. Eisenhower, with strategic guidance for the employment of Army Air Forces in the ETO. The objective is air superiority over the European continent in support of an eventual invasion.

SOUTHWEST PACIFIC AREA: Fifth Air Force B-17s bomb airstrip at Lae in New Guinea.

PACIFIC: Major General William H. Hale takes command of the U.S. Seventh Air Force in Hawaii. The navy still maintains operational control of army assets.

June 21

PACIFIC: Japanese submarine *I-25* shells Fort Stevens, Oregon. U.S. submarine *S-44* sinks Japanese gunboat off the island of Gavutu in the Solomons.

June 22

CBI: Lieutenant General Joseph W. Stilwell's command is retitled American Forces in India, China, and Burma by order of the War Department. Stilwell is charged with accomplishing U.S. political and military goals in the theater. First he must maintain the cohesion of the Chinese army of about 3.8 million men, which is divided between support for Chiang Kai-shek and the Kuomintang, local warlords, and the Communists. The Communists are fighting a guerrilla war against not only the Japanese, but the Nationalist Kuomintang as well. Stilwell is troubled that Chiang keeps his most capable units focused on the Communists, not the Japanese.

Second, Stilwell must find a way to maintain logistical support to China so that the Nationalists can continue to fight the Japanese. If China's armies collapse, the Japanese could release tens of thousands of troops to other areas on their defensive perimeter. But the Germany-first strategy in Washington puts China near the bottom of the priority list. To build the 30-division army and 500 aircraft air force that has been promised to the Chinese, Stilwell will have to provide 7,500 tons of supplies a month. At best, only 3,500 tons a month can be delivered, based on priorities and airlift available. Stilwell has only 57 transport aircraft in theater.

CARIBBEAN: A U.S. tanker is torpedoed and sunk by German submarine *U-67* off Louisiana.

SOUTHWEST PACIFIC AREA: Major General Robert L. Eichelberger takes command of the U.S. I Corps.

June 23

ATLANTIC: Lieutenant General Carl Spaatz is informed that Roundup, the plan for a cross-Channel invasion of Europe, has been postponed in favor of Torch, the combined invasion of North Africa. He is ordered to prepare to divert Eighth Air Force assets to support the new plan.

MIDDLE EAST: General Brereton deploys U.S. bombers from the CBI theater to the Middle East after the German army captures Tobruk and threatens the British defense of Egypt. B-17 bombers destined for Stilwell are diverted to Khartoum, Egypt. An Iran-Iraq Service Command is established in Basra, Iraq, under USAFIME command.

June 24

ATLANTIC: A U.S. freighter is torpedoed and sunk by German submarine *U-404.*

ETO: Major General Dwight D. Eisenhower arrives in London to assume command of the European Theater of Operation, USA (ETOUSA).

MIDDLE EAST: U.S. B-24 Liberators support British air attacks on German positions in Benghazi, Libya.

June 25

ATLANTIC: President Roosevelt and Prime Minister Churchill conclude their meeting in Washington. They agree to a joint effort to develop an atomic weapon.

Admiral King offers an alternate plan (discussed on June 12) to General Marshall's for the Pacific offensive. King argues that Admiral Nimitz should lead an operation beginning August 1, directed against New Guinea and New Britain, with intermediate objectives in the Solomon and Santa Cruz islands. King agrees that the 1st Marine Division and at least two carriers be included in the force list. The Southwest Pacific Theater would support with both ships and land-based aircraft to augment the navy and marine units. The islands captured would be occupied by MacArthur's infantry divisions. MacArthur would support the offensive with diversionary attacks against the island of Timor in the Netherlands East Indies. General Marshall argues that King's plans for an offensive in the Solomons, which lie in the Southwest Pacific, should be under General MacArthur's command as CinCSWPA. King, desiring an offensive to begin as quickly as possible, does not want to be troubled by arbitrary lines that divide up the geography. He asserts that Nimitz as CinCPac be designated commander for the operation.

A Norwegian freighter is damaged by a torpedo from German submarine *U-701* off Cape Hatteras, North Carolina.

PACIFIC: Admiral King, CominCh, orders CinCPac (Admiral Nimitz) and ComSOPAC (Admiral Ghormley) to prepare for offensive operations in the southern Solomons. The initial objectives were to be Santa Cruz and Tulagi Islands. Marines are to be the ground forces involved, with army forces in Australia acting as follow-on forces. D-day for the operation is set for August 1. Nimitz notifies Admiral Ghormley, commander of the South Pacific Area to begin preparations.

U.S. submarine *Nautilus* sinks a Japanese destroyer off the coast of Japan near Yakosuka. U.S. submarine *Grouper* sinks Japanese oiler near the Ryukyus.

June 26

ATLANTIC: Germany announces unrestricted submarine warfare will be conducted along the Atlantic coast of the United States.

CBI: Brigadier General Earl L. Naiden takes command of the Tenth Air Force, replacing General Brereton who departs for the Middle East.

PACIFIC: Major General Alexander A. Vandegrift, commander of the 1st Marine Division, receives the warning order for the Solomons offensive from CinCPac.

June 27

ATLANTIC: German agents who landed at Long Island and in Florida are captured by the FBI before undertaking any operational activities. A total of eight are arrested; six are later tried and executed.

Two U.S. freighters are sunk by German submarines *U-128* and *U-153* off the Atlantic coast. Convoy PQ 17 leaves Iceland for Archangel, USSR with 33 ships, four cruisers, and six destroyers.

MIDDLE EAST: U.S. B-24 Liberators attack the harbor at Tobruk, Libya, to disrupt German resupply efforts.

PACIFIC: Plans for Operation TULSA I, the campaign against the Japanese-held areas on New Britain, New Ireland, and in the Admiralty Islands, are completed.

U.S. submarine *Nautilus* sinks Japanese minesweeper off the coast of Japan.

June 28

ATLANTIC: German submarines *U-332*, *U-203*, *U-505*, *U-701*, and *U-153* sink a total of four U.S. freighters and a tanker off the Atlantic coast.

MIDDLE EAST: Lieutenant General Brereton assumes command of U.S. Army Middle East Air Forces (USAMEAF) with headquarters in Cairo, Egypt. All U.S. military air assets in the theater are consolidated under his command.

PACIFIC: Navy PBY Catalinas bomb Tulagi. U.S. submarine *Stingray* sinks Japanese gunboat off Yap.

June 29

CBI: Generalissimo Chiang Kai-shek demands support from the United States in a meeting with General Stilwell. Chiang requires 500 combat aircraft, three U.S. divisions, and 5,000 tons of supplies per month delivered by air from India.

ATLANTIC: German submarine *U-505* torpedoes and sinks a U.S. freighter.

SOUTHWEST PACIFIC AREA: U.S. Army engineers arrive at Milne Bay to begin work to improve a base for Australian units defending Port Moresby, New Guinea.

PACIFIC: Questions arise over which service will have overall control of the planned Pacific offensive. Admiral King proposes to the Joint Chiefs that Admiral Ghormley command the lower Solomon Islands offensive, while General MacArthur deals with the New Guinea and New Britain offensive.

June 30

CBI: The inability of Allied forces to move supplies from India over the Himalaya Mountains (known as the Hump) air route to China begins to show. The Chinese are expecting 5,000 tons a month. Only 57 aircraft are available for the airlift and only 186 tons have been delivered over the past 60 days.

ATLANTIC: German submarine *U-158* is sunk by a Navy PBM Mariner patrol bomber off Cape Hatteras, North Carolina. *U-202* torpedoes and sinks a U.S. steamship off the North Carolina coast.

MIDDLE EAST: General Brereton moves his headquarters from Cairo to Palestine as a precaution against German advances in eastern Egypt. U.S. B-24 Liberators bomb the harbor at Tobruk.

SOUTHWEST PACIFIC AREA: Fifth Air Force B-24 Liberators and B-25 Mitchells attack Japanese positions near Lae in New Guinea.

PACIFIC: U.S. submarine *Plunger* sinks Japanese freighter off the coast of China near Shanghai.

A U.S. freighter is torpedoed and sunk by Japanese submarine *I-10* off the east coast of Africa.

July 1

CBI: Chinese Air Task Force (CATF) aircraft from Tenth Air Force based in Hengyang, attack Japanese positions near Hangkow.

CARIBBEAN: A U.S. freighter is torpedoed and sunk by German submarine *U-126* off Trinidad.

MIDDLE EAST: U.S. B-24 Liberators bomb the harbor at Tobruk.

SOUTHWEST PACIFIC AREA: U.S. submarine *Sturgeon* sinks a Japanese transport ship off Luzon. The ship was carrying U.S. prisoners of war to Hainan Island. More than 1,000 Americans are killed.

PACIFIC: Major General Millard F. Harmon takes control of all army forces in South Pacific, as a subordinate command to Admiral Ghormley, ComSOPAC.

July 2

CBI: Generalissimo Chiang Kai-shek names General Stilwell the commander of Chinese armies in India. The impressive title, though, carries little authority. Chiang still maintains direct control of the Chinese forces and they will answer only to his orders.

Chinese Air Task Force (CATF) bombers attack Hangkow and cause heavy damage.

U.S. submarine *Plunger* sinks Japanese cargo ship near the mouth of the Yangtze River.

ATLANTIC: The Joint Chiefs of Staff issues a Joint Directive for Offensive Operations in the Southwest Pacific Area (SWPA). This directive represents a compromise between King and Marshall. The directive lays out instructions for an offensive to seize New Britain-New Ireland-New Guinea. The first phase of the offensive, an attack on the Santa Cruz Islands, Tulagi, and nonspecified adjacent islands in the southern Solomons will be given to the navy under Admiral Nimitz. General MacArthur is to support this attack with air and naval forces from the Southwest Pacific Theater. The second phase involves the seizure of Lae, Salamaua, and the northwest coast of New Guinea and will be given to General MacArthur. The third phase is the capture of the Japanese base at Rabaul and the bases in New Britain and New Ireland. This phase will also be led by General MacArthur. The details of the attack on Rabaul and the offensive against New Britain and New Ireland will be determined later by the Joint Chiefs. For the initial phase of the campaign, named Operation Watchtower, all of General MacArthur's air, land, and naval forces will be employed in support, as well as two aircraft carriers, the South Pacific Amphibious Force, and South Pacific Army Forces. The boundary between SWPA and Pacific Ocean Areas (POA) is moved west ever so slightly to place Tulagi, Guadalcanal, and the Florida Islands within Admiral Nimitz's Pacific Ocean Areas theater of operations. Naval task force commanders will command all amphibious operations, and the Joint Chiefs will retain the authority to withdraw the carriers to employ them elsewhere as necessary. The staffs of Nimitz and Ghormley, hard-pressed for time and resources to make the plan work, begin calling Operation Watchtower "Operation Shoestring."

July 3

ALEUTIANS: Eleventh Air Force B-24 Liberators attack and damage Japanese seaplane carriers at Agattu Island.

ATLANTIC: German submarines *U-126*, *U-125*, *U-575*, and *U-215* sink a total of one U.S. tanker and three freighters. Convoy PQ 17 headed for Murmansk is attacked by German submarines and HE-111 torpedo bombers from Norway. Two U.S. freighters are sunk and one is damaged.

SOUTHWEST PACIFIC AREA: Fifth Air Force bombers strike Lae in New Guinea and Tulagi in the Solomons.

July 4

CBI: General Claire Chennault becomes the commander of China Air Task Force (CATF), replacing his previous command, the American Volunteer Group (AVG). Chennault's new command has a B-25 Mitchell bomber and a P-40 fighter squadron. Chennault will require 2,000 tons of supplies per month, further cutting into deliveries provided to China.

ETO: The U.S. Army Air Force conducts its first raid on Europe, participating in a Royal Air Force (RAF) raid on German airfields at Haanstead and Daltonburg in the Netherlands.

MIDDLE EAST: U.S. B-24 Liberators attack an enemy convoy in the Mediterranean, damaging one tanker.

SOUTHWEST PACIFIC AREA: Fifth Air Force bombers attack Lae and Salamaua in New Guinea.

PACIFIC: U.S. submarine *Triton* sinks Japanese destroyer off Agattu Island in the Aleutians.

July 5

ALEUTIANS: U.S. submarine *Growler* sinks a Japanese destroyer and damages two others off Kiska in the Aleutians.

ATLANTIC: German submarine and air attacks on convoy PQ 17 result in the loss of three freighters. Four other freighters are so heavily damaged that they are abandoned by their crews. London orders the convoy to break up and scatter, as reports of a possible attack by German surface ships come in. The reports will turn out to be false. Convoy QP 13 accidentally hits a British minefield in the Denmark Strait. One freighter is damaged, two freighters are sunk, and two others are abandoned.

SOUTHWEST PACIFIC AREA: U.S. submarine *Sturgeon* damages a Japanese oiler off Luzon.

July 6

CBI: General Stilwell establishes the command and control structure for the China-Burma-India theater. The main headquarters is at Chungking, with liaison headquarters at New Delhi, where U.S. and Chinese forces are located, and at Kunming, where the China Air Task Force is located.

ATLANTIC: Admiral William D. Leahy, former chief of naval operations and ambassador to Vichy France, is appointed as chief of staff to the president. General Marshall has argued for several months that the president needs a personal representative to chair JCS meetings, keep track of papers sent to the White House seeking approval from the president on JCS recommendations, and to arbitrate issues that arise between the army and the navy. Leahy, unlike Marshall and King, has no command authority. The command relationship of General Marshall and Admiral King to the president directly is not changed. Leahy's role is to pass on to the Joint Chiefs the general guidance of the president on war planning and strategy, and to represent the consensus of the Joint Chiefs to the president. This command arrangement, never before seen in American history, allows for a rapid exchange of information and decisions. Under Leahy's leadership, the Joint Chiefs of Staff will be responsible for U.S. strategy in the Pacific, China, Europe, and the Mediterranean.

Convoy PQ 17, headed for Murmansk, loses two more freighters to submarine and air attacks.

CARIBBEAN: German submarine *U-153* is damaged in an air attack by U.S. Sixth Air Force bombers from Panama.

July 7

ATLANTIC: A U.S. Army Air Force A-29 Hudson maritime patrol bomber sinks German submarine *U-701* off the coast of North Carolina. Convoy PQ 17 loses two freighters to submarine attacks.

CARIBBEAN: U.S. tanker is sunk by German submarine *U-67* off the coast of Louisiana.

PACIFIC: The Marine 1st Raider Battalion embarks from New Caledonia, headed for the Solomons.

July 8

ATLANTIC: A U.S. tanker is torpedoed and damaged off the coast of Florida by German submarine *U-571*.

MIDDLE EAST: U.S. B-17s attack Tobruk, while B-24 Liberators bomb Benghazi harbor.

PACIFIC: Admiral Nimitz issues orders for Admiral Ghormley to conduct an attack to seize Tulagi Island, Santa Cruz Island, and Guadalcanal. U.S. submarine *S-37* sinks Japanese transport off Rabaul.

July 9

CARIBBEAN: A U.S. tanker is torpedoed and sunk by German submarine *U-67* off the Louisiana coast.

PACIFIC: U.S. submarine *Sailfish* sinks Japanese cargo ship off the coast of Indochina. U.S. submarine *Thresher* sinks Japanese vessel at Kwajalein Atoll.

July 10

ALEUTIANS: A Japanese Mitsubishi A6M Type 0 carrier fighter known as the Zero, which had crash-landed on Akutan Island on June 3, is discovered by a U.S. reconnaissance aircraft. It will later be recovered, restored to flying condition, and studied carefully to design new U.S. aircraft to counter the Zero's capabilities.

ATLANTIC: The Joint Chiefs of Staff refuse requests from both General MacArthur and Admiral Ghormley to postpone the planned offensive in the Solomons until additional reinforcements arrive.

July 11

MIDDLE EAST: U.S. B-24 Liberators attack Benghazi, Libya.

PACIFIC: The loss at Midway leads Japanese Imperial Headquarters strategists to shelve plans for offensive operations against New Caledonia, Fiji, and Samoa. Tulagi in the southern Solomons with its excellent harbor will become a key base for defending Rabaul. The Solomons can serve as a new base for operations against Port Moresby. Japanese planes based at Rabaul and the Solomons can provide air cover for an invasion fleet. The capture of Port Moresby would assure Australia's isolation and allow the Japanese to control the Bismarck Sea and the approaches to Rabaul.

July 12
ATLANTIC: German submarines *U-84* and *U-129* each torpedo and sink a U.S. freighter.
PACIFIC: U.S. submarine *Seadragon* sinks Japanese freighter off the coast of Indochina.

July 13
ATLANTIC: President Roosevelt sends trusted adviser Harry Hopkins to London to obtain a final answer on offensive action in Europe in 1942. The president's instructions to Hopkins are clear: "Under any circumstances I wish Bolero and Roundup to remain an essential objective, even though it must be interrupted."
CARIBBEAN: German submarine *U-153* is sunk by a U.S. destroyer, supported by a subchaser and USAAF aircraft near Panama. *U-166* sinks a U.S. freighter off Cuba; *U-67* sinks a U.S. tanker off the Louisiana coast.
MIDDLE EAST: U.S. B-17s attack Tobruk, while B-24 Liberators attack Benghazi.
SOUTHWEST PACIFIC AREA: TULSA II, the plan by General Headquarters, Southwest Pacific Area, for operations directed at the capture of Rabaul, is completed. Major General George C. Kenney takes command of Fifth Air Force.
PACIFIC: U.S. submarine *Seadragon* sinks a Japanese auxiliary vessel off the coast of Indochina.

July 14
PACIFIC: Major General Millard F. Harmon assumes command of U.S. Army Forces in South Pacific (COMGENSOPAC). Japanese submarine *I-7* sinks a U.S. freighter off the Pacific coast of the United States. The submarine uses machine guns to sink the freighter's lifeboats.

July 15
ATLANTIC: German submarine *U-576* torpedoes three freighters off the coast of North Carolina. The submarine is attacked and sunk by a navy OS2U Kingfisher aircraft. *U-571* damages a U.S. tanker off Key West, Florida.

July 15
PACIFIC: Elements of the 4th Marine Defense Battalion move to Espiritu Santo Island from Efate and establish a heavy antiaircraft and automatic weapons battery.

July 16
CBI: CATF (China Air Task Force) bombers attack Hangkow.

CARIBBEAN: German submarine *U-166* torpedoes and sinks a U.S. fishing boat off Cuba.

ATLANTIC: German submarine *U-161* attacks convoy AS 4 headed for the Persian Gulf, sinking one U.S. steamship.

PACIFIC: Admiral Ghormley issues his operation plan for Watchtower. Task Force 61 commander, Vice Admiral Frank J. Fletcher, has the carriers USS *Saratoga, Wasp,* and USS *Enterprise* and the battleship USS *North Carolina,* along with six cruisers, 16 destroyers, and three oilers. Rear Admiral Richmond K. Turner commands amphibious shipping; Rear Admiral Leigh Noyes commands the air support force, and Task Force 63, under command of Rear Admiral John S. McCain, represents all the land-based air forces in the South Pacific.

U.S. submarine *Seadragon* sinks a Japanese freighter off the coast of Indochina.

July 17

ETO: Admiral King, General Marshall, and President Roosevelt's close adviser Harry Hopkins arrive in London to convince the British to support Sledgehammer, the cross-Channel invasion plan.

MIDDLE EAST: B-17s attack Tobruk and B-24 Liberators attack Benghazi, Libya, to disrupt German lines of supply.

July 18

PACIFIC: Rear Admiral Richmond Kelly Turner reports to Admiral Ghormley as commander of the amphibious force for Operation Watchtower. Ghormley has overall command of the operation, but Major General Alexander A. Vandegrift, Commander of the First Marine Division, is under Turner's command. Admiral Fletcher, although designated the joint expeditionary force commander, is in practice the naval force commander, largely providing air support to the marines.

July 19

CBI: General Stilwell proposes to Generalissimo Chiang Kai-shek that the most rapid way to bring sufficient aid to China is to retake Burma from the Japanese. U.S. B-25 Mitchells support a Chinese army attack on Linchwan, forcing Japanese forces out of the city.

ATLANTIC: As the result of improved U.S. convoy operations, Admiral Karl Dönitz orders German submarines *U-89, U-132, U-402, U-458,* and *U-754* away from the Atlantic coast to pursue more vulnerable targets.

PACIFIC: A Japanese force of 1,800 men leaves Rabaul for Buna, New Guinea.

July 20

CBI: B-25 Mitchells and P-40s attack Japanese supply lines on the Yangtze River.

ATLANTIC: Admiral William D. Leahy assumes his duties as chairman of the Joint Chiefs of Staff.

July 21

ATLANTIC: A U.S. freighter in convoy TAW (Trinidad to Aruba to Key West) is torpedoed by German submarine *U-84* in the Straits of Florida. The ship is recovered and later repaired.

ETO: Major General Eisenhower, CG ETOUSA, issues instructions to Eighth Air Force, requiring that the Allies have air domination over Europe no later than April 1, 1943.
SOUTHWEST PACIFIC AREA: Fifth Air Force B-26 Marauders attack Japanese convoy approaching Buna, New Guinea. Japanese forces land near Gona, New Guinea.
PACIFIC: B-17s attached to ComSOPAC arrive from Hawaii. U.S. freighter is sunk by Japanese submarine *I-11* in the South Pacific.

July 22

ATLANTIC: An unarmed U.S. freighter is torpedoed and sunk by German submarine *U-582* off the west coast of Africa.
ETO: British planners reject U.S. proposal for Sledgehammer.

July 22

NEW GUINEA: Because of the lack of sufficient air cover due to the loss of aircraft carriers after the Battle of Midway, the Japanese land ground forces at Buna in northeast New Guinea with the intention of conducting an overland campaign to capture Port Moresby.
MIDDLE EAST: U.S. Army Middle East Air Force (USAMEAF) B-17s and B-24s attack supply ships and bomb Tobruk.
SOUTHWEST PACIFIC AREA: Japanese forces expand their lodgment in New Guinea, reaching Buna, and advance past Giruwa, headed for Port Moresby. Fifth Air Force B-17s, B-25 Mitchells, and B-26 Marauders attack Japanese shipping off Buna, New Guinea, damaging a destroyer and sinking a cargo ship.

A U.S. freighter is torpedoed by Japanese submarine *I-24* off the coast of Australia.
PACIFIC: Task Force 61, with 1st Marine Division embarked, leaves Wellington, New Zealand.

July 23

CARIBBEAN: A U.S. freighter is torpedoed and sunk by German submarine *U-129* off Cuba.
MIDDLE EAST: U.S. Army Middle East Air Force (USAMEAF) is reinforced by 98th Bomb Group, deployed to Palestine.
SOUTHWEST PACIFIC AREA: Fifth Air Force fighters and bombers attack Japanese troops assembling near Buna and Gona. Salamaua harbor is also attacked.

July 24

ETO: U.S. Joint Chiefs redesignate certain bomber assets for Operation Torch and send orders deploying 15 combat groups from the ETO to the Pacific.
MIDDLE EAST: U.S. Army Middle East Air Force (USAMEAF) B-17s and B-24s attack Tobruk harbor and Benghazi harbor.
PACIFIC: U.S. submarine *Narwhal* sinks a Japanese guardboat and two cargo ships off the coast of Japan.

July 25

ATLANTIC: The Combined Chiefs of Staff establishes the command relationships for the U.S.-British invasion of North Africa. The operation, originally called Gymnast, is renamed Torch.

July 27

CARIBBEAN: German submarine *U-166* mines the waters off the Mississippi River delta.

ATLANTIC: A U.S. freighter is torpedoed and damaged by German submarine *U-582* off the west coast of Africa. The Germans use demolition charges to sink the ship after the crew escapes.

SOUTHWEST PACIFIC AREA: Fifth Air Force B-26 Marauders damage a Japanese transport off Buna, New Guinea.

PACIFIC: U.S. submarine *Spearfish* damages a Japanese submarine depot ship east of Cam Ranh Bay, Indochina.

July 28

ATLANTIC: A U.S. fishing trawler is shelled and sunk by German submarine *U-754* off Nova Scotia. Convoy PQ 17, arrives at the port of Molotovsk, USSR, with only 11 ships, losing 24 ships in transit—the greatest convoy disaster of the war.

Admiral William D. Leahy, as chairman of the U.S. Joint Chiefs of Staff, attends the meeting of the Combined Chiefs of Staff. The Joint Chiefs of Staff and the British Chiefs of Staff functioning as the Combined Chiefs of Staff also must plan Allied strategy in Europe, North Africa, and the Far East.

PACIFIC: Japanese Imperial General Headquarters orders that Port Moresby and Milne Bay be captured as part of the strategy to isolate Australia and threaten U.S. lines of supply in the Pacific. The airfield at Espiritu Santo on the New Hebrides becomes operational.

July 29

SOUTHWEST PACIFIC AREA: Japanese forces consolidate gains in New Guinea after pushing Australian defenders back from Kokoda. Fifth Air Force A-24 Banshees and P-39 Airacobras attack Japanese shipping off Gona.

July 30

CBI: Tenth Air Force P-40s defend CATF (China Air Task Force) airbase at Hengyang from heavy Japanese air attack. The Japanese lose 17 aircraft; three P-40s are lost in the day and night engagements.

ATLANTIC: German submarine *U-166* attacks convoy TAW 7 (Trinidad to Aruba to Key West) near the mouth of the Mississippi River, and sinks a U.S. passenger ship. A U.S. freighter is sunk by German submarine *U-155* near Barbados.

President Roosevelt signs a bill creating "Women Accepted for Volunteer Emergency Service" or WAVES. Lieutenant Commander Mildred H. McAfee is commissioned in the Naval Reserve, the first female line officer in navy history, as director of the WAVES. Within one year 27,000 women would be serving in a variety of maintenance, medical, support, intelligence, and communications positions.

July 31

ALEUTIANS: U.S. submarine *Grunion* torpedoes a Japanese transport off Kiska in the Aleutians, but the transport sinks *Grunion* with gunfire.

ATLANTIC: German submarine *U-751* lays mines off Charleston, South Carolina.

In the first seven months of 1942, 12 U-boats off the Atlantic coast of the United States have sunk 681 ships, nearly 3.5 million tons, representing 73 percent of all Allied and neutral shipping losses since January.

PACIFIC: U.S. submarine *Grenadier* torpedoes a Japanese tanker off Truk. B-17s of the 11th Bomb Group arrive at Espiritu Santo as part of SOPAC's air component.

SOUTH PACIFIC: 11th Bomb Group B-17s from SOPAC attack the airstrip at Guadalcanal and bomb Lunga Point. Rear Admiral John S. McCain's Task Force 63 departs from the Fiji islands, where it has been rehearsing for the Solomons landings.

August 1

CBI: Generalissimo Chiang Kai-shek approves General Stilwell's recommendation for an offensive against Burma, and modifies his previous support requirements from June 29. The offensive will require about 20 Chinese divisions, including two in India and 15 in Yunnan province. The divisions in India will be trained and led by Stilwell at the U.S. base in Ramgarh. Chiang, still unhappy that U.S. advisers and Lend-Lease supplies are slow in arriving, seeks greater concessions from the Americans. He demands a U.S. infantry division, 500 aircraft for the Chinese air force, and an additional 5,000 tons of supplies airlifted over the Hump. Chiang is reluctant to provide Chinese forces in Burma. An Allied victory in Burma would lead to the reestablishment of British colonial authority in the region. He hedges his pledge for an offensive by making impossible demands and siding with General Chennault, whose Tenth Air Force still needs 2,000 tons of supplies a month to keep flying. These demands will force Stilwell to split his resources and therefore delay any offensive in the near future.

For his part, Stilwell puts the majority of his effort toward preparing the Chinese divisions in India and trying to gain operational control of the Chinese divisions in Yunnan (known later as the Y Force).

CARIBBEAN: U.S. Coast Guard J4F bombs and sinks German submarine *U-166* in the Gulf of Mexico.

PACIFIC: U.S. submarine *Narwhal* sinks a Japanese cargo ship and an oiler off the coast of Honshu, Japan.

August 3

PACIFIC: U.S. submarine *Gudgeon* sinks a Japanese transport in the South Pacific.

August 4

CBI: U.S. P-40s attack Japanese headquarters at Linchwan, China.

MIDDLE EAST: USAMEAF B-24 Liberators bomb and damage two merchant ships in the Mediterranean.

PACIFIC: U.S. submarine *Narwhal* sinks a Japanese cargo ship off the coast of Japan.

August 5

MIDDLE EAST: General Brereton describes three major objectives for Allied air forces in the theater. The first objective is air support to ground forces fighting the Afrika

Korps. The second objective is securing the sea and air lines of communication throughout the Mediterranean. The third objective is to conduct an air offensive against Italy and the Ploeşti oil fields in Romania. If captured by German forces, Brereton designates oil fields in the Caucasus as part of the third objective.

PACIFIC: U.S. submarine *Greenling* sinks a Japanese transport and a passenger-cargo ship near Truk.

August 6

ATLANTIC: U.S. schooner is sunk by shellfire from German submarine *U-86* off Newfoundland.

PACIFIC: U.S. submarine *Tautog* sinks a Japanese army transport off Cam Ranh Bay, Indochina.

NEW GUINEA: New Guinea Force is designated, commanding all U.S. and Australian forces in Papua and northeast New Guinea. Major General Sydney F. Rowell, commanding the Australian I Corps, is designated the commander. Fifth Air Force B-24 Liberators and B-17s attack Japanese airfields at Lae and Salamaua.

August 7

ALEUTIANS: Kiska is attacked by a task force of U.S. surface ships.

PACIFIC: Operation Watchtower. Amphibious Force South Pacific (Rear Admiral Richmond K. Turner) lands task groups of the 1st Marine Division at Tulagi and Guadalcanal; the 5th Marine Regiment (without its 2nd Battalion) lands on Red Beach at Guadalcanal. Units push toward the Ilu River. Major General Alexander Vandegrift, commander of the marine landing force, orders that the airfield be captured and that a defensive line be established along the Lunga River. Marine 1st Raider Battalion and 2nd Battalion 5th Marines land on Tulagi. Marines land on Florida Island and Gavutu. Landings are supported by carrier-based aircraft (Rear Admiral Leigh Noyes) and shore-based aircraft (Rear Admiral John S. McCain). Fifth Air Force bombers attack a number of targets in support of the marine landing on Guadalcanal. U.S. submarine *Tambor* sinks a Japanese auxiliary vessel off Wotje, in the Marshall Islands.

August 8

ATLANTIC: German submarine *U-98* mines waters off Jacksonville, Florida. U.S. freighter in convoy SC 94 (Halifax Slow to United Kingdom) is torpedoed and sunk by shellfire of German submarine *U-379* in the Atlantic.

ETO: President Roosevelt and Prime Minister Churchill agree that Major General Dwight D. Eisenhower will command Operation Torch.

PACIFIC: U.S. submarine *Narwhal* sinks a Japanese crab boat off Honshu, Japan. Submarine *S-38* sinks a Japanese transport in the straits between New Britain and New Ireland. U.S. submarine *Silversides* attacks a convoy emerging from Kobe harbor, Japan, and sinks a cargo ship.

GUADALCANAL: General Vandegrift has 10,000 men on Guadalcanal and 6,075 on Tulagi. Japanese aircraft attack and sink a U.S. transport and damage a destroyer, and 21 F4F Wildcats from the carriers are lost in air combat protecting the fleet. Admiral Ghormley authorizes a request from Task Force 61's commander, Vice

Admiral Frank J. Fletcher, to withdraw until sufficient land-based air cover is available. Turner and Fletcher notify Vandegrift that the ships will leave Guadalcanal. The marines are left with 17 days' rations. Troops, supplies (including artillery), and everything else not already landed on the beaches is moved to Espiritu Santo Island. Marines cross Ilu and Lunga Rivers and encounter Japanese forces. The Guadalcanal airfield is captured and units occupy the east bank of the Lunga River.

The Battle of Savo Island. After midnight, a Japanese naval force of seven cruisers and one destroyer under Vice Admiral Mikawa Gunichi, slips past U.S. destroyers guarding the approach to the Amphibious Task Force and attacks Allied ships off Savo Island, sinking one Australian cruiser and three U.S. cruisers before returning to Rabaul. It is one of the greatest defeats in U.S. naval history.

August 9
CBI: CATF (China Air Task Force) bombers attack Haiphong harbor in French Indochina.
GUADALCANAL: Task Force 61 departs for Noumea. General Vandegrift's force is stranded without air or naval support. Tulagi Island and Tanambogo, near Tulagi, are secured by the marines. Gavutu Island is secured, along with several smaller surrounding islands. A U.S. destroyer, damaged the day before, is sunk by Japanese torpedo planes.

August 10
ALEUTIANS: Eleventh Air Force B-17s and B-24 Liberators attack Kiska; one B-24 is lost.
PACIFIC: U.S. submarine *S-44* sinks a Japanese heavy cruiser near Kavieng, New Ireland. This is the first major warship sunk by a U.S. submarine.

August 11
MIDDLE EAST: Persian Gulf Service Command (PGSC) is established, replacing the Iran-Iraq Service Command. PGSC is under command of U.S. Army Forces in the Middle East (USAFIME).
GUADALCANAL: Admiral Ghormley orders Task Force 63 to provide logistics support to the marines on Guadalcanal. U.S. logistics base is established at Port Moresby by U.S. Army Service of Supply (USASOS).

August 12
ETO: U.S. 31st Fighter Group is declared fully operational. The Royal Air Force (RAF) retains operational control of the unit.

August 13
ATLANTIC: U.S. tanker is torpedoed, shelled, and sunk by German submarine *U-171* off the Texas coast; *U-171* sinks a U.S. freighter later the same day. U.S. freighter in convoy TAW 12 (Trinidad to Aruba to Key West) is torpedoed and sunk by German submarine *U-600*.
PACIFIC: Japanese Imperial General Headquarters orders the Seventeenth Army to conduct offensive operations to defeat American forces on Guadalcanal.

New Guinea: Japanese convoy with 3,000 reinforcements arrives near Gona.

August 14

Atlantic: A U.S. freighter is torpedoed, shelled, and sunk by Italian submarine *Reginaldo Giuliani.*

ETO: Lieutenant General Dwight D. Eisenhower, Commanding General, European Theater of Operations, is appointed Commander in Chief of Allied Expeditionary Forces for Operation Torch; the deputy commander is Major General Mark W. Clark. Admiral Sir Andrew B. Cunningham (RN) is appointed Allied naval commander. Brigadier General James Doolittle commands the American air forces, and Air Marshal Sir William Welsh will command the British air forces. The Combined Chiefs of Staff issues a directive to Eisenhower for Allied forces to establish lodgments in Oran-Algiers-Tunis with the intent of gaining control of French Morocco, Algeria, and Tunisia. Allied forces are to ensure the annihilation of Axis forces in order to conduct air and sea operations against Axis installations in the Mediterranean, open lines of communication, and facilitate further operations against the Axis on the continent of Europe.

Two U.S. fighters shoot down a German fighter off the coast of Iceland. This is the first aerial victory by U.S. pilots in the ETO.

August 15

Atlantic: U.S. freighter in convoy SC 95 (Halifax Slow to United Kingdom) is torpedoed and sunk by German submarine *U-705* southeast of Iceland.

August 17

CBI: Major General Clayton Bissell is designated as commander of Tenth Air Force.

Caribbean: U.S. tanker is torpedoed and sunk by German submarine *U-108* off Dutch Guiana. Convoy TAW 13 (Trinidad to Aruba to Key West) comes under attack from German submarine *U-553.* A Swedish merchantman, a British freighter, and a U.S. freighter are torpedoed and sunk south of Cuba.

ETO: Eighth Air Force B-17s, escorted by British fighters, attack the marshaling yard at Rouen-Sotteville. A German fighter is downed by a B-17 gunner—the first aerial kill on a bombing run over Europe.

Pacific: Two companies of the Marine 2nd Raider Battalion, transported in submarines *Nautilus* and *Argonaut,* conduct a raid on Makin Atoll in the Gilbert Islands. The *Nautilus* provides gunfire support for the raid, intended to divert the Japanese from Guadalcanal and gather intelligence. The Japanese garrison of 83 men is eliminated in the attack. The Raiders suffer 30 casualties.

U.S. submarine *Gudgeon* damages two Japanese oilers near Truk.

August 18

Caribbean: Convoy TAW (Trinidad to Aruba to Key West), with 15 ships escorted by a U.S. gunboat, a British corvette, two Coast Guard cutters, and four submarine chasers, is attacked by German submarine *U-162,* which torpedoes U.S. freighter off Grenada.

GUADALCANAL: Japanese destroyers land 900 reinforcements at Taivu Point on Guadalcanal. Colonel Ichiki Kiyanao commands this group, the advance element of 1,500 more soldiers from the 28th Regiment. The captured airfield at Guadalcanal is ready to receive aircraft. It is called Henderson Field in honor of Major Lofton Henderson, a marine pilot shot down while leading an attack on the Japanese carrier *Hiryu* during the Battle of Midway.

NEW GUINEA: Reinforcements bring Japanese forces to over 11,400 army and naval troops in New Guinea. The Japanese begin an advance along the Kokoda-Buna trail.

August 19

CARIBBEAN: German submarine *U-162* attacks the TAW convoy again, torpedoing a U.S. freighter and causing it to be abandoned. German submarine *U-564* later attacks the convoy, torpedoing and sinking a British tanker and a freighter.

ETO: A Canadian and British landing force conducts a raid on Dieppe. Eighth Air Force B-17s bomb Abbeville/Drucat airfield to create a diversion for the Allied raid on Dieppe. The raid itself is a disastrous failure. The first American soldier to die in occupied Europe is a member of the 50-man Ranger unit that accompanies the Allied force.

GUADALCANAL: Marines conduct company-sized patrols to clear coastal villages; one company of marines ambushes a 34-man detachment of recently landed Japanese soldiers near Taivu Point. A Japanese convoy with 1,500 reinforcements leaves Rabaul for Guadalcanal. Fifth Air Force B-17s, flying from Espiritu Santo, bomb Japanese destroyers off Guadalcanal, damaging one off Tulagi.

August 20

ATLANTIC: U.S. Navy PBY-5A sinks German submarine *U-464* in the North Atlantic. Twelfth Air Force is activated at Bolling Field.

ETO: Eighth Air Force bombers attack marshaling yard at Amiens.

GUADALCANAL: Henderson Field is home to 19 F4F-4 Wildcat fighters and 12 SBD-3 Dauntless dive-bombers of Marine Aircraft Group 23. Japanese forces prepare for an attack on Milne Bay in New Guinea.

August 21

ETO: Lieutenant General Carl Spaatz is designated as air officer for ETOUSA, ensuring that Eighth Air Force will be integrated into theater planning.

PACIFIC: U.S. submarine *Cuttlefish* damages a Japanese ammunition ship off the coast of Japan.

U.S. submarine *Tambor* sinks a Japanese collier off Ponape Island in the Carolines.

GUADALCANAL: The Battle of Tenaru. A Japanese attack across the Ilu River to capture Henderson Field is halted. Marine counteroffensive with troops and tanks surrounds the enemy force, leaving 800 killed and 15 men captured. Marine losses are 35 killed and 75 wounded. Colonel Ichiki and the survivors retreat. Taking the regimental flag, Ichiki burns it, then shoots himself.

NEW GUINEA: A Japanese convoy reaches New Guinea, unloading troops and supplies for an overland march to Port Moresby.

August 22
ATLANTIC: Brazil declares war on Germany and Italy.

August 22
CARIBBEAN: Sixth Air Force plane from the 45th Bombardment Squadron sinks German submarine *U-654* north of Panama.

PACIFIC: U.S. destroyer is torpedoed by Japanese destroyer off Guadalcanal and is scuttled; U.S. submarine *Haddock* torpedoes and sinks Japanese transport off the China coast, near Foochow.

GUADALCANAL: Five P-400 fighter aircraft from SOPAC arrive at Henderson Field on Guadalcanal. Fifth Air Force B-17s bomb Rabaul and Lae.

NEW GUINEA: P-400s arrive from the New Hebrides. Major General Cyril A. Clowes, Australian army, takes command of the combined U.S.-Australian force protecting Port Moresby. Of the nearly 9,500 men who make up the Milne force, there are nearly 1,400 Americans, most of them engineers and antiaircraft personnel.

August 23
ETO: U.S. heavy cruiser, escorted by two U.S. destroyers and a British destroyer, arrives at Murmansk, USSR, delivering men and equipment from two RAF Bomber Command squadrons transferred to the USSR.

SOUTHWEST PACIFIC AREA: U.S. submarine *Skipjack* damages a Japanese oiler southwest of Ambon, Netherlands East Indies.

August 24
ETO: Eighth Air Force bombers attack shipyards at Le Trait, France.

GUADALCANAL: The Battle of Eastern Solomons. U.S. Navy Task Force 61, under command of Vice Admiral Frank Jack Fletcher, with carriers *Enterprise* and *Saratoga*, engages a Japanese fleet east of Guadalcanal and bringing reinforcements to the island. Both carrier-based and land-based U.S. aircraft are employed. The *Enterprise* and a destroyer are damaged. The Japanese lose a carrier, a light cruiser, and a seaplane carrier before retiring to the north. Henderson Field is attacked by sea and air. Japanese aircraft attacking Henderson suffer heavy losses. The Japanese offensive in New Guinea begins. Troop transports from Rabaul move toward Milne Bay, while barges move Japanese troops from Buna along the coast.

SOUTHWEST PACIFIC AREA: U.S. submarine *Saury* torpedoes a Japanese army transport off Luzon in the Philippines.

PACIFIC: U.S. submarine *Guardfish* torpedoes and sinks a Japanese passenger-cargo ship off the coast of Honshu, Japan.

NEW GUINEA: The Japanese offensive in New Guinea begins. Troop transports from Rabaul move toward Milne Bay, while barges move Japanese troops from Buna along the coast.

August 25
SOUTHWEST PACIFIC AREA: The Japanese land 1,500 men near Milne Bay. U.S. P-40s from Milne Bay attack the Japanese barges coming from Buna, stranding the

Japanese force on two small islands. Japanese force from Rabaul lands near Rabi, New Guinea, and moves westward.

U.S. submarine *Seawolf* sinks a Japanese cargo ship off the northeast coast of Borneo.

PACIFIC: U.S. submarine *Growler* sinks a Japanese gunboat off Formosa.

GUADALCANAL: The Battle of Eastern Solomons. SOPAC B-17s from Espiritu Santo sink a Japanese destroyer off Santa Isabel, Solomons; aircraft from *Enterprise* sink a transport north of Guadalcanal. Marine SBD Dauntless dive-bombers from Henderson Field damage a light cruiser and destroyer off Guadalcanal.

August 26

CBI: Tenth Air Force B-25 Mitchells attack the rail center at Laisho, China.

PACIFIC: U.S. submarine *Haddock* sinks a Japanese merchant ship off Formosa.

SBD Dauntless dive-bombers from carrier USS *Wasp* damage Japanese submarine *I-17* in the Solomons.

NEW GUINEA: From Milne Bay and Port Moresby, Fifth Air Force B-17s, B-25 Mitchells, B-26 Marauders, and P-40s, along with Royal Australian Air Force (RAAF) Hudsons, attack beaches and transports and the Japanese landing force, damaging a transport and destroying supplies stockpiled on shore. Additional reinforcements arrive from New Ireland, and the Japanese advance against the Australian defenders. The U.S.-Australian Milne Force, consisting of three Australian infantry brigades, a U.S. engineer company, and a battery of U.S. antiaircraft artillery, defends two key airfields at Milne Bay against Japanese infantry assaults.

August 27

ALEUTIANS: Japanese begin withdrawal of units occupying Attu and redeploying them to Kiska Island.

ATLANTIC: German submarine *U-165* attacks convoy SG 6 (Sydney or St. Johns, Newfoundland to Greenland), torpedoing a U.S. oiler and a freighter. German submarine *U-517* attacks convoy SG 6F, torpedoing an army transport; 514 passengers and crew survive.

ETO: Eighth Air Force bombers attack the shipyards in Rotterdam, the Netherlands.

GUADALCANAL: Marines pursue Japanese toward Kokumbona; Henderson Field receives nine more P-400 fighters. Japanese continue advance toward Port Moresby.

August 28

CARIBBEAN: A U.S. Navy PBY Catalina and a Canadian corvette sink German submarine *U-94* in the Caribbean. German submarine *U-511* torpedoes and damages a U.S. tanker, and sinks a British and a Dutch tanker in convoy TAW 15 (Trinidad to Aruba to Key West) near Cuba.

ATLANTIC: U.S. freighter is torpedoed and sunk by German submarine *U-66*.

Eighth Air Force B-17s bomb an aircraft factory at Meaulte that repairs German fighters.

GUADALCANAL: Japanese submarine *I-123* is sunk near Guadalcanal. USMC and Navy SBD Dauntless dive-bombers bomb and sink a Japanese destroyer and damage three other destroyers bringing reinforcements to Guadalcanal, off Santa Isabel, Solomons. This nearly continuous effort to deliver men and supplies to Guadalcanal is termed "The Tokyo Express."

August 29

ETO: Eighth Air Force B-17s attack a German air base at Courtrai/Wevelghem.
NEW GUINEA: Japanese attempts to capture Airstrip No. 3 are halted by Milne Force. Fifth Air Force B-26 Marauders and P-400 Airacobras attack Buna; B-17s hit Rabaul; P-40s support ground forces at Milne Bay.

August 30

ALEUTIANS: Adak, chosen as the area for an advanced base to attack the Japanese-held island of Kiska, is occupied without opposition.
CARIBBEAN: U.S. freighter bound for Trinidad is torpedoed by German submarine *U-162* and abandoned. U.S. freighter is torpedoed and sunk by German submarine *U-66* off Trinidad.
ATLANTIC: U.S. tanker bound for Aruba fires on German submarine *U-705*; the tanker is torpedoed and sinks.
GUADALCANAL: A U.S. transport is sunk by Japanese aircraft near Guadalcanal. More than 6,000 Japanese troops land west of Lunga Point near Tasimboko.
NEW GUINEA: Japanese forces withdraw after another unsuccessful attack on Airstrip No. 3 in New Guinea.

August 31

ALEUTIANS: A U.S. destroyer and navy PBY Catalinas sink Japanese submarine *RO-61* off Atka Island.
MIDDLE EAST: USAMEAF B-24s attack Tobruk harbor; U.S. and RAF fighters provide ground support to British forces near El Alamein.
PACIFIC: U.S. submarine *Growler* sinks a Japanese merchant ship in Formosa Strait.
GUADALCANAL: U.S. carrier USS *Saratoga* is damaged by torpedo from Japanese submarine *I-26* west off Santa Cruz Islands. Marine Raider Battalion and the Marine 1st Parachute Battalion arrive from Tulagi to reinforce the Guadalcanal perimeter. Japanese destroyers put 1,000 troops ashore on Guadalcanal.
NEW GUINEA: The Australians take the offensive against Japanese in Milne Bay. U.S. P-40s support the Australians. Fifth Air Force B-26 Marauders and A-20 Havocs attack Lae airfield. B-17s bomb ammunition supplies at Buna.

September 1

ALEUTIANS: U.S. forces complete occupation of the airbase at Adak.
ATLANTIC: U.S. Navy PBY *Catalina* bombs and sinks German submarine *U-756*.
PACIFIC: Air Force, Pacific Fleet is established under command of Vice Admiral Aubrey W. Fitch.
GUADALCANAL: Guadalcanal receives 200 men from the 6th Naval Construction Battalion to improve Henderson Field. SOPAC B-17s bomb and damage a Japanese

destroyer off Buka Island, Solomons. Adequately supplying the marines at Guadalcanal continues to be a problem.

September 2
PACIFIC: U.S. submarine *Guardfish* sinks Japanese cargo ship off Hokkaido, Japan.
MIDDLE EAST: USAMEAF B-24s attack Tobruk harbor; U.S. and RAF fighters provide ground support to British forces near Alam-el-Halfa.
NEW GUINEA: Japanese reinforcements from Rabaul land at Basabua.

September 3
ALEUTIANS: Two Eleventh Air Force P-38 Lightnings make a 1,260-mile round trip to attack Kiska harbor. It is the longest overwater attack flight in the war up to this time.
SOUTHWEST PACIFIC AREA: The Fifth Air Force is established in Brisbane, Australia, under the command of Lieutenant General George C. Kenney.

September 3
SOUTHWEST PACIFIC AREA: General Kenney, commander Fifth Air Force, releases the Royal Australian Air Force to defend Australian airspace.

U.S. submarine *Seal* damages Japanese merchant ship off the coast of French Indochina.

September 4
PACIFIC: U.S. submarine *Growler* sinks Japanese ammunition ship in Formosa Straits; U.S. submarine *Guardfish* sinks two merchant ships and a passenger cargo ship off Honshu; U.S. submarine *Pompano* sinks a guardboat off Honshu.
NEW GUINEA: Australian forces reach Goroni, forcing the Japanese to withdraw by transport. Japanese forces evacuate Milne Bay after taking over 600 casualties. Fifth Air Force P-40s support the Australian advance along Milne Bay toward Goroni.

September 5
ETO: After significant debate between U.S. and British planners, the Allies agree that the primary landing areas will be at Algiers and Oran in Algeria and at Casablanca in Morocco. Eighth Air Force B-17s attack the marshaling yard at Rouen-Sotteville in France.
PACIFIC: U.S. submarine *Seal* sinks a Japanese merchant ship off the coast of French Indochina.
GUADALCANAL: Two U.S. transports are sunk by Japanese destroyers off Lunga Point, Guadalcanal.
NEW GUINEA: General Eichelberger takes command of the 32nd and 41st Infantry Divisions as part of I Corps. Fifth Air Force P-400 Airacobras and A-20 Havocs attack Buna airfield. About 1,300 Japanese are evacuated from Milne Bay.

September 6
ETO: Eighth Air Force loses two B-17s in bombing raid on Meaulte aircraft plant.

September 7
PACIFIC: U.S. submarine *Growler* sinks a Japanese merchant ship near Formosa.

New Guinea: Fifth Air Force A-20 Havocs and P-400 Airacobras support Australian forces defending along the Owen Stanley Range.

September 8

ETO: Lieutenant General Carl Spaatz and the RAF reach an agreement on fighter support for Eighth Air Force bombing operations. The RAF will support the U.S. daylight bombing raids, while the British will concentrate on night bombing. Spaatz orders priority of effort to be given to Torch, including the buildup of the Twelfth Air Force, which is to support Operation Torch in North Africa.

September 9

Atlantic: German submarine *U-755* torpedoes and sinks a U.S. Coast Guard weather ship in the Atlantic.

Pacific: A reconnaissance seaplane from Japanese submarine *I-25* drops incendiary bombs on a forest near Mount Emily, Oregon, in an attempt to start a forest fire. It is the first Japanese air attack on North America.

September 10

Atlantic: German submarine *U-69* lays mines at the mouth of Chesapeake Bay.

September 11

Pacific: U.S. submarine *Saury* sinks a Japanese aircraft transport in the Makassar Strait. Fifth Air Force B-17s and Royal Australian Air Force (RAAF) Hudsons sink a Japanese destroyer off Normanby Island in the D'Entrecasteaux Islands.

New Guinea: Fifth Air Force A-20s and B-26 Marauders attack Japanese positions on the Owen Stanley Range.

September 12

Atlantic: U.S. Navy takes operational control of the Brazilian navy. A U.S. tanker fires on German submarine *U-512* but the submarine's accurate gunfire forces the crew to abandon the tanker.

ETO: Advance elements of the Twelfth Air Force arrive in Britain.

Guadalcanal: Japanese light cruiser and three destroyers bombard Henderson Field; Japanese ground forces make a limited attack against Lieutenant Colonel Merritt A. Edson's 1st Marine Raider Battalion, defending the ridge that marks the main approach to Henderson Field from the south. It becomes known as Edson's, or more famously, Bloody Ridge.

September 13

Aleutians: Eleventh Air Force B-24 Liberator bombers land at Adak.

ETO: German aerial and submarine attacks begin against convoy PQ 18, bound for Archangel, USSR; one U.S. freighter is torpedoed by German submarine *U-589* off the coast of Norway and abandoned, and two other freighters are abandoned after German torpedo planes attack.

Guadalcanal: Colonel Merritt A. Edson's battalion, supported by the 2nd Battalion 5th Marines, defends the ridge that blocks the Japanese advance to Henderson Field. The Japanese turn back a marine counterattack on Bloody Ridge, and attack the center and right of the marine defensive line. Major Kenneth D. Bailey, the commander of Company C, 1st Marine Raider Battalion, defends the right flank while covering the forced withdrawal of the main defensive line with protective fire. As the defensive line is reorganized, Major Bailey repeatedly leads his troops in brutal hand-to-hand combat with the enemy for nearly 10 hours. He continues fighting even though severely wounded. Although he will die of his wounds, his heroic actions allow the battalion to hold the ridge and will win him the Medal of Honor.

September 14
ALEUTIANS: Eleventh Air Force makes its first combined mission over Kiska. One B-17, 13 B-24 Liberators, 14 P-38 Lightnings, and 14 P-39 Airacobras bomb and strafe a number of targets. The Japanese lose five float planes, a flying boat, two minesweepers, and an ammunition ship. Several other vessels are damaged as well, including submarines *RO 63* and *RO 64*.
ETO: Eighth Air Force takes over the training and support for Twelfth Air Force units arriving in Britain. A U.S. freighter in a convoy bound for Archangel, USSR, is lost off the coast of Norway, and attacked by German torpedo bombers.
PACIFIC: SOPAC B-17s damage a Japanese heavy cruiser sailing from Truk to Guadalcanal.
GUADALCANAL: Marines hold Bloody Ridge against fierce Japanese assaults. The Japanese suffer over 1,200 casualties in the two-day fight. The 1st Marine Raider Battalion is no longer an effective fighting force. With over 200 casualties, only 89 men of the gallant unit are able to leave Bloody Ridge on their own two feet.

September 15
GUADALCANAL: Task Force 18, escorting 4,000 marines of the 7th Marine Regiment from Espiritu Santo to Guadalcanal, is attacked by Japanese submarine I-19. The carrier *Wasp*, the battleship *North Carolina*, and a destroyer are all damaged. The *Wasp* is later scuttled. Japanese battleships bombard U.S. positions at Guadalcanal.
NEW GUINEA: Fifth Air Force B-17s attack Rabaul. Elements of U.S. 32nd Infantry Division arrive at Port Moresby.

September 16
ALEUTIANS: Japanese complete withdrawal of forces from Attu to Kiska.
CARIBBEAN: A U.S. freighter is torpedoed and sunk by German submarine *U-558* off Trinidad.
ATLANTIC: U.S. B-24 Liberator from Ascension Island attacks three German submarines and one Italian submarine conducting rescue operations to save over a thousand Italian POWs aboard the British transport *Laconia*, torpedoed on September 12. The 3rd Marine Division is activated at Camp Elliott, California.

September 17
ATLANTIC: Chief of the Kriegsmarine Admiral Karl Dönitz issues the *Laconia* order, which no longer allows U-boats to rescue survivors of ships sunk in combat operations. A U.S. freighter is torpedoed and sunk by German submarine *U-515* north of British Guiana.

MIDDLE EAST: USAMEAF B-24s attack ports in Greece.

NEW GUINEA: Fifth Air Force P-400s, P-40s, and P-39s attack Japanese barges at Buna and Sanananda Point.

September 18

ATLANTIC: German submarine *U-455* lays mines off Charleston, South Carolina.

ETO: U.S. freighter in a convoy bound for Archangel, USSR, is lost off the coast of Norway when attacked by German torpedo bombers.

GUADALCANAL: The 7th Marine Regiment lands on Guadalcanal along with critically needed supplies.

September 19

CARIBBEAN: A U.S. freighter is torpedoed and sunk by German submarine *U-516* northeast of Barbados.

ETO: A U.S. freighter in convoy QP 14 is torpedoed and sunk by German submarine *U-225* north of Norway.

SOUTH PACIFIC: U.S. submarine *Amberjack* sinks a Japanese transport at northern entrance of Bougainville Strait.

September 20

ETO: The operational plan for Torch is finalized. It has simultaneous landings at Casablanca, Oran, and Algiers. The plan involves 370 merchant ships, 300 warships, over 400 fighters, and 107,000 troops. Three task forces are formed: a Western Task Force (35,000 men) will originate in the United States and land at Casablanca, Morocco, commanded by Major General George S. Patton, Jr. The naval commander will be Rear Admiral Henry K. Hewitt. The Central Task Force (39,000 men) from Great Britain will land at Oran, commanded by Major General Lloyd Fredendall. Admiral Sir Andrew Cunningham will be the naval force commander. The Eastern Task Force (33,000 men), with both British and American forces from Great Britain, will land at Algiers under the command of Lieutenant General Kenneth A. N. Anderson, with U.S. forces under command of Major General Charles W. Ryder. Vice Admiral Sir Harold Burrough will be the naval commander. Brigadier General James Doolittle will command the American air forces, and Air Marshal Sir William Welsh will command British air forces.

NEW GUINEA: Fifth Air Force A-20s provide air support to Australian forces defending on the Owen Stanley Range. P-40s attack Japanese positions on the Kokoda Trail.

September 21

PACIFIC: U.S. submarine *Grouper* sinks a Japanese cargo ship off Shanghai; U.S. submarine *Trout* sinks Japanese auxiliary vessel south of Truk.

GUADALCANAL: Marines from the 7th Marine Regiment, attempting to cross the Matanikau River, are stopped by strong Japanese defenses.

September 22

ATLANTIC: A U.S. tanker is torpedoed and sunk by German submarine *U-211* south of Cape Farewell, Greenland. U.S. freighter in convoy QP 14 is torpedoed and sunk by German submarine *U-435*.

MIDDLE EAST: USAMEAF B-24s attack Benghazi harbor.

INDIAN OCEAN: U.S. freighter is torpedoed and sunk by Japanese submarine *I-29* off the coast of India.

NEW GUINEA: P-40s attack Japanese positions at Buna and on the Kokoda Trail; B-26 Marauders attack Buna airfield; A-20 Havocs attack a number of areas occupied by Japanese forces. Fifth Air Force B-17s attack Rabaul.

September 23

ATLANTIC: A U.S. freighter is torpedoed and damaged by German submarine *U-515* off Georgetown, British Guiana. The submarine is chased off by gunfire from the freighter. The crew abandons, then reboards the ship, only to be torpedoed and sunk by *U-512* the following day.

U.S. freighter in convoy SC 100 (Halifax Slow to United Kingdom) is torpedoed and sunk by German submarine *U-432* near Iceland.

ETO: General Jimmy Doolittle takes command of Twelfth Air Force in Britain.

PACIFIC: SOPAC receives additional B-17s at Espiritu Santo from Seventh Air Force in Hawaii.

GUADALCANAL: Marines fail to cross the Matanikau River after encountering strong Japanese defenses. An attempt to make an amphibious assault west of Point Cruz fails.

NEW GUINEA: Fifth Air Force bombers and fighter aircraft attack the Buna airfield and Japanese positions along the Buna-Kokoda Trail.

September 24

ATLANTIC: U.S. freighter from convoy ON 131 (Liverpool to New York, fast) is torpedoed and sunk by German submarine *U-619* south of Iceland.

CARIBBEAN: U.S. freighter is torpedoed and sunk by German submarine *U-175* north of British Guiana.

INDIAN OCEAN: U.S. freighter is torpedoed and sunk by Japanese submarine *I-165* off the coast of India.

September 25

ALEUTIANS: The first U.S.-Canadian mission is flown over Kiska. Eleventh Air Force B-24 Liberators and B-17s, escorted by 15 P-39s, attack Kiska, damaging a radar station, a transport ship, Japanese submarine *RO-67*, and two float planes, as well as destroying several biplanes.

CBI: Tenth Air Force B-25 Mitchells escorted by P-40s attack Hanoi. The P-40s shoot down nine Japanese fighters.

PACIFIC: U.S. submarine *Sargo* sinks a Japanese merchant ship off the coast of French Indochina.

September 26

NEW GUINEA: Fifth Air Force B-17s attack Rabaul; A-20s provide air support to Australian forces counterattacking in Papua.

September 27

ATLANTIC: U.S. freighter with an armed guard fights a German auxiliary cruiser and supply ship in the central South Atlantic. The freighter is sunk, but only after damaging the German cruiser so badly that it also sinks.

GUADALCANAL: The attempt by Vandegrift's marines to drive the Japanese from the Matanikau River fails. A landing attempt west of Point Cruz runs into an ambush and is evacuated; two other separate attacks fail to cross the river. A total of 60 marines are killed and 100 are wounded. In the evacuation attempt, U.S. Coast Guard coxswain Douglas A. Munro brings his landing boat into shore, steering with one hand and firing at the Japanese with the other to draw fire so that marines can get on other boats. Munro is killed in the fight. For his extraordinary heroism, Munro will be awarded the Medal of Honor.

September 28

ALEUTIANS: Eleventh Air Force B-24 Liberators and B-17s attack Kiska. Five Japanese floatplanes are destroyed and one submarine is sunk.

CARIBBEAN: A U.S. freighter is torpedoed and sunk by German submarine *U-175* near the mouth of the Orinoco River.

PACIFIC: U.S. submarine *Nautilus* torpedoes and sinks a Japanese merchant ship east of Japan; U.S. submarine *Sculpin* torpedoes a Japanese seaplane carrier off Kokoda Island; U.S. submarine *Trout* torpedoes a Japanese escort carrier east of Truk.

NEW GUINEA: Fifth Air Force P-400 Airacobras and P-40s attack Wairopi bridge and targets along the Buna-Kokoda Trail. The U.S. 126th Infantry Regiment of the 32nd Infantry Division arrives at Port Moresby and is assigned to New Guinea Force to support the Australian advance on Wairopi.

September 29

PACIFIC: A reconnaissance seaplane from Japanese submarine *I-25* drops incendiary bombs on an Oregon forest in an attempt to ignite forest fires. This is the last Japanese attack on the U.S. mainland.

October 1

ATLANTIC: The Marine First Amphibious Corps is established at San Diego, California, under the command of Major General Clayton B. Vogel.

PACIFIC: U.S. submarine *Grouper* torpedoes and sinks a Japanese army transport in the East China Sea. U.S. submarine *Kingfish* torpedoes and sinks a Japanese merchant cargo ship off Japan. U.S. submarine *Nautilus* torpedoes and sinks a merchant cargo ship off Japan. U.S. submarine *Sturgeon* damages a Japanese aircraft transport off New Ireland.

NEW GUINEA: Fifth Air Force B-17s and P-400s bomb Menari, Kagi, Kokoda, and Wairopi bridge and the Buna-Wairopi Trail.

MacArthur's staff develops a plan for countering the Japanese advance in New Guinea. The Australian 7th Infantry Division, commanded by Major General George A. Vasey, is ordered to move from Port Moresby to Wairopi. The U.S. 2nd Battalion 126th Infantry Regiment is to move overland from Port Moresby to Jaure in support of the Australians. The 18th Australian Brigade is ordered to move along the northern coast to Wanigela and link up with the U.S. 128th Infantry Regiment, which will be moved by air from Port Moresby. After linkup the combined force will move to Embogo. The Japanese hold the Gona valley, Sanananda point, and Buna village. The intent is to force the Japanese to deal with multiple threats to their flanks and rear.

October 2

CARIBBEAN: German submarine *U-512* is sunk by U.S. aircraft off French Guiana. U.S. freighter is torpedoed and sunk by German submarine *U-201* near Trinidad.

ETO: Eighth Air Force B-17s, escorted by 400 Allied fighters, attack the Meaulte aircraft factory.

SOUTHWEST PACIFIC AREA: Fifth Air Force B-17s bomb Rabaul harbor, damaging a Japanese light cruiser.

October 3

ALEUTIANS: Japanese bombers attack Adak airfield but cause no damage.

CBI: The India Air Task Force is established and includes all AAF combat units in India. Its mission is to defend Assam province, attack Japanese lines of supply in southern Burma and shipping in the Andaman Sea, and raid Bangkok and Rangoon. The task force is composed of the 7th Bombardment Squadron (Heavy) with B-24 Liberators, the 51st Fighter Group with P-40s, and the 341st Bombardment Group (Medium) with B-25 Mitchells.

PACIFIC: U.S. submarine *Greenling* sinks a Japanese merchant cargo ship off the east coast of Japan.

GUADALCANAL: U.S. aircraft from Henderson Field attack a Japanese supply convoy headed for Guadalcanal.

October 4

ATLANTIC: A U.S. freighter is torpedoed and sunk by German submarine *U-175* off the mouth of the Orinoco River. A U.S. tanker in convoy HX 209 (New York to Liverpool) is torpedoed and sunk by German submarine *U-254* off Iceland.

PACIFIC: U.S. submarine *Greenling* sinks a Japanese merchant cargo ship off the coast of Japan. U.S. tanker is torpedoed by Japanese submarine *I-25* off the coast of Oregon and then abandoned.

NEW GUINEA: Fifth Air Force P-40s attack Japanese positions at Myola Lake, Kokoda, Wairopi, and Buna. A reconnaissance element from 126th Infantry Regiment 32nd Division locates and assesses the Kapa-Jauri trail as a possible approach for an attack on the Buna-Gona defenses.

October 5

CARIBBEAN: A U.S. freighter is torpedoed and sunk by German submarine *U-175* off the coast of Venezuela.

ATLANTIC: U.S. Navy PBY Catalina sinks German submarine *U-582* in the waters south of Iceland.

GUADALCANAL: Carrier aircraft from USS *Hornet* operate against Japanese targets in the Solomons. U.S. aircraft from Henderson Field attack a Japanese convoy and damage two destroyers. A navy PBY Catalina from COMAIRSOPAC sinks Japanese submarine *I-22* near Indispensable Strait in the Solomons.

NEW GUINEA: Fifth Air Force B-25 Mitchells attack a Japanese convoy off Buna; B-17s attack Buna airfield and Rabaul airfields; A-20 Havocs attack Sanananda Point.

October 6

ALEUTIANS: Eleventh Air Force B-24 Liberators, a B-17, and 10 P-38s attack Kiska. A transport ship and two other ships are badly damaged; several aircraft are damaged as well.

PACIFIC: A U.S. tanker is torpedoed by Japanese submarine *I-25* off the coast of Oregon and abandoned.

NEW GUINEA: Fifth Air Force supports airlift of Australian 18th Brigade to forward positions in preparation for the attack on Buna and Gona.

October 7

ATLANTIC: A U.S. freighter is torpedoed and sunk by German submarine *U-172* south of Cape Town, South Africa.

MIDDLE EAST: USAMEAF B-24s attack a tanker and fuel depot at Suda Bay, Crete. U.S. P-40s escort bombers providing ground support to British forces west of El Alamein.

PACIFIC: U.S. submarine *Amberjack* sinks a Japanese supply ship in the southern Carolines; U.S. submarine *Sculpin* sinks a Japanese army transport off Rabaul.

GUADALCANAL: Elements of the 5th Marines attempting to extend the defensive perimeter past the Matanikau River encounter a Japanese force attempting to move artillery closer to the marines' defensive lines. Heavy fighting ensues and continues through the next day, slowed only by a tropical downpour.

U.S. Navy Task Group 64.2, composed of two heavy cruisers, two light cruisers, and five destroyers under command of Rear Admiral Norman Scott, arrives near the Russell Islands in the Solomons with orders to intercept Japanese convoys headed to Guadalcanal.

October 8

ATLANTIC: A U.S. freighter is torpedoed, then shelled by German submarine *U-202* off the coast of Africa.

PACIFIC: U.S. submarine *Drum* sinks a Japanese merchant cargo ship off the east coast of Japan.

NEW GUINEA: Fifth Air Force A-20 Havocs attack Japanese positions on the Buna-Kokoda Trail.

October 9

ALEUTIANS: Eleventh Air Force B-17s and B-24 Liberators, escorted by P-38s and P-39s, attack Japanese ships in Kiska harbor.

CARIBBEAN: German submarine *U-505* is damaged by U.S. aircraft patrolling off Trinidad.

ATLANTIC: A U.S. freighter is torpedoed and sunk by German submarine *U-159* southwest of Cape Town, South Africa. Another U.S. freighter is sunk by German submarine *U-68* south of the Cape of Good Hope.

ETO: Eighth Air Force conducts bombing raid on the steel and locomotive works at Lille, France. A total of 69 B-24 Liberators and B-17s, escorted by U.S. and British fighters, attack these targets, part of a force of 100 bombers attacking a number of other targets in the area. Over 100 German planes are damaged or destroyed in the attack.

PACIFIC: Fifth Air Force B-17s attack Rabaul and Lae. The U.S. Army's 164th Infantry Regiment of the American Division departs from Nouméa, New Caledonia, for Guadalcanal. U.S. submarine *Drum* torpedoes and sinks a Japanese merchant cargo ship off the east coast of Japan.

GUADALCANAL: Elements of the 5th Marines, supported by a flanking attack by the 7th Marines, cross the Matanikau River and eliminate the Japanese defensive perimeter. Over 700 Japanese are killed. American casualties number nearly 200.

October 10

SOUTHWEST PACIFIC AREA: U.S. submarine *Amberjack* damages two Japanese vessels off Kavieng, New Ireland. U.S. submarine *Seadragon* torpedoes and sinks a Japanese transport off Borneo. U.S. submarine *Wahoo* sinks a Japanese collier off Bougainville, Solomons.

GUADALCANAL: A total of 12 P-39 Airacobras of the 67th Fighter Squadron arrive at Henderson Field.

October 11

GUADALCANAL: SOPAC B-17s spot Japanese cruisers and destroyers headed for Guadalcanal. Rear Admiral Scott is ordered to intercept a Japanese convoy arriving at midnight near Cape Esperance. In a confused battle, U.S. and Japanese ships fire at each other in the darkness. A U.S. heavy cruiser, a light cruiser, and a destroyer are damaged; one U.S. destroyer is sunk. A Japanese heavy cruiser and destroyer are sunk, and a heavy cruiser and destroyer are damaged.

October 12

CBI: General Stilwell requests assistance from the War Department to equip 30 more Chinese divisions.

PACIFIC: Navy SBD Dauntless dive-bombers sink a Japanese destroyer off Savo Island. A Japanese destroyer is scuttled off New Georgia Island after an air attack by navy and marine aircraft.

October 13

ATLANTIC: A U.S. freighter in convoy SC 104 (Halifax Slow to United Kingdom) is torpedoed and sunk by German submarine *U-221* in the waters west of Great Britain.

GUADALCANAL: The 164th Infantry Regiment of the American Division arrives at Guadalcanal. Japanese air strikes destroy fuel supplies at Henderson Field.

October 14

SOUTHWEST PACIFIC AREA: U.S. submarine *Sculpin* sinks Japanese cargo ship off Kavieng, New Ireland.

PACIFIC: U.S. submarine *Finback* sinks a Japanese army transport off Formosa. U.S. submarine *Greenling* torpedoes and sinks a Japanese cargo ship off the coast of Honshu, Japan. U.S. submarine *Skipjack* sinks a Japanese cargo ship near Truk.

GUADALCANAL: A Japanese surface force of two battleships, a light cruiser, and seven destroyers bombards Henderson Field, destroying 48 of 90 U.S. aircraft there, killing 40 Americans, and temporarily putting the airstrip out of action. Japanese destroyers prepare to land reinforcements at Tassafaronga.

New Guinea: Fifth Air Force airlifts the U.S. 128th Infantry Regiment and Australian units to Wanigela.

October 15
Guadalcanal: Japanese complete landing of nearly 4,000 reinforcements and supplies on Guadalcanal; marine and navy SBD Dauntless dive-bombers and F4F Wildcats from Henderson Field, along with SOPAC B-17s, P-39, and P-400 Airacobras, attack the transports and their escort ships. Two transports and a merchant cargo ship are sunk, and a destroyer is damaged. Japanese combat strength on Guadalcanal is about 20,000 men, roughly equal to U.S. force strength.

October 16
Aleutians: Eleventh Air Force B-26 Marauders and a B-17 attack Kiska and sink two Japanese destroyers. One B-26 is lost.
Pacific: USS *Thresher* conducts the first U.S. submarine mining operation of the war, laying mines off Bangkok, Thailand.
Guadalcanal: Twenty F4F Wildcats and 12 SBD Dauntless dive-bombers are added to Henderson Field, bringing the total number of aircraft to 66. SOPAC P-400s and P-39 Airacobras attack a Japanese landing force at Kokumbona, just a few miles from Henderson Field. Task Force 17, formed around carrier USS *Hornet,* conducts air strikes on Japanese troops. Japanese heavy cruisers, a light cruiser, and seven destroyers shell Henderson Field.

October 17
Atlantic: A U.S. freighter from convoy ON 137 (Liverpool to New York, fast) is torpedoed by German submarine *U-618* and later abandoned.
    Torch convoys begin assembling in Great Britain.
Pacific: A U.S. submarine, *Trigger,* torpedoes and sinks a Japanese merchant ship off Kyushu.

October 18
Pacific: Admiral William F. Halsey replaces Admiral Ghormley as COMSOPAC at Nouméa, New Caledonia. U.S. submarine *Grampus* torpedoes a Japanese light cruiser near Truk, but the torpedo fails to explode. U.S. submarine *Greenling* sinks Japanese transport off the coast of Honshu, Japan.
New Guinea: The air movement of the 128th Infantry, 32nd Division to Wanigela, New Guinea, is completed.

October 19
CBI: U.S. War Department approves General Stilwell's request of equipment for 30 Chinese divisions.
Guadalcanal: Navy SBD Dauntless dive-bombers from Henderson Field attack three Japanese destroyers north of Guadalcanal, damaging one.

October 20
Middle East: Brigadier General Donald H. Connolly takes command of Persian Gulf Service Command (PGSC) in Basra, Iraq. The command includes 1,400 army and civilian workers

PACIFIC: A U.S. heavy cruiser is torpedoed by Japanese submarine *I-176* near San Cristobal, Solomons. U.S. submarine *Drum* torpedoes and sinks a Japanese merchant cargo ship off Honshu, Japan. U.S. submarine *Finback* attacks a Japanese convoy off Formosa and damages two cargo ships. U.S. submarine *Tautog* sinks a Japanese merchant trawler in the South China Sea.

GUADALCANAL: A Japanese attack across the Matanikau River, supported by tanks, is stopped by marine antitank and artillery fire. Admiral Halsey orders the 147th Infantry Regiment to reinforce Guadalcanal.

October 21

CBI: Air Transport Command is established to deliver supplies to China.

ATLANTIC: Admiral King informs Admiral Nimitz that the JCS has approved a request for additional air forces to be moved to the South Pacific before the beginning of 1943.

ETO: Eighth Air Force B-17s attack German submarine bases in an effort to prevent their interference with convoys headed for North Africa from Britain as part of Operation Torch. Three B-17s are lost.

NORTH AFRICA: Major General Mark W. Clark, the deputy commander of Allied forces for Operation Torch, Brigadier General Lyman M. Lemnitzer, two other army officers, and Captain Jerauld Wright (USN) are landed at Cherchel, French North Africa, from British submarine HMS *Seraph* to meet with a French military delegation and ascertain French attitudes toward impending Allied operations. Major General Charles Mast, a pro-Allied commander of the Algiers Division of Vichy French forces in North Africa, and U.S. Consul General Robert Murphy meet the officers. Mast states that with four days notice he can neutralize French resistance to the Allied landings. The meeting is twice interrupted by suspicious police, forcing Clark and others to hide in the wine cellar. The group returns to the submarine shortly before dawn.

PACIFIC: U.S. submarine *Guardfish* torpedoes and sinks a Japanese merchant ship off Formosa; U.S. submarine *Gudgeon* attacks a convoy in the Bismarck Sea and sinks a transport ship near Rabaul.

October 22

ETO: Twelfth Air Force headquarters begins deployment from Britain to North Africa.

MEDITERRANEAN: Major General Mark W. Clark and U.S. Consul Robert Murphy meet with French general Charles Mast, who supports U.S. plan to bring French forces in North Africa under Allied control, with the French accepting the command of General Henri Giraud.

Operation Torch convoy from Britain leaves for North Africa.

PACIFIC: At a conference at Nouméa, General Vandegrift informs Admiral Halsey, the new ComSOPAC, that to hold Guadalcanal he needs additional army and marine combat troops. Halsey tells Vandegrift: "You go back there. . . . I promise to get you everything I have."

October 23

MIDDLE EAST: British Eighth Army begins its El Alamein counteroffensive. USAMEAF fighters and bombers unable to hit targets because of bad weather.

SOUTHWEST PACIFIC AREA: Fifth Air Force B-17s damage two Japanese submarine chasers in a raid on Rabaul.

PACIFIC: U.S. submarine *Kingfish* sinks a Japanese gunboat off Honshu, Japan.

GUADALCANAL: An uncoordinated Japanese attack across the Matanikau River, supported by tanks, is stopped by marines supported by artillery. Over 650 Japanese are killed.

October 24

ATLANTIC: The Western Task Force for Operation Torch sets sail from Hampton Roads, Virginia, headed for Casablanca, Morocco.

President Roosevelt informs the JCS that Guadalcanal must be reinforced.

PACIFIC: U.S. submarine *Nautilus* torpedoes and sinks a Japanese merchant ship off northern Honshu, Japan. U.S. submarine *Trigger* damages a Japanese oiler off Kyushu, the southernmost of the Japanese home islands.

GUADALCANAL: Japanese forces launch a regimental-level attack in a driving rainstorm against the south flank of the Guadalcanal defensive perimeter, the full brunt falling on 1st Battalion, 7th Marines. Sergeant John Basilone's heavy machine-gun sections are the main target of Japanese grenade attacks and mortar fire. When his gun crews suffer heavy casualties, Sergeant Basilone rallies the survivors and personally repairs and fires one machine gun, holding the line under continuous enemy fire until reinforced. Throughout the night, in a pouring rain, Sergeant Basilone takes great personal risks to locate ammunition and bring it forward to keep his guns in action. For his extraordinary gallantry in the face of nearly impossible odds, Sergeant Basilone will receive the Medal of Honor. As Japanese attacks continue throughout the night, the army's 3rd Battalion, 164th Infantry Regiment, led by Lieutenant Colonel Robert K. Hall, joins the marines, led by Lieutenant Colonel Lewis B. "Chesty" Puller, and together they hold Bloody Ridge once more. At least 900 Japanese are killed in the failed attack.

October 25

CBI: CATF (China Air Task Force) B-25 Mitchells, with seven P-40s escorting, attack the docks at Hong Kong. One B-25 and one P-40 are lost. The Japanese lose nearly 21 fighters.

PACIFIC: U.S. submarine *Whale* lays mines off Honshu, Japan, at the entrance to Japan's Inland Sea.

GUADALCANAL: Japanese air and naval forces conduct heavy attacks on Henderson Field. A second Japanese assault is repulsed by 1st Battalion 7th Marines and the army's 3rd Battalion 164th Infantry Regiment. The Japanese assault on the Matanikau River is also stopped.

NEW GUINEA: The army's 2nd Battalion 126th Infantry Regiment reaches Jaure, but has suffered high casualties from disease, especially malaria, in its overland march. The 32nd Infantry Division commander, Major General Edwin F. Harding, requests that the remainder of his division be airlifted to required locations to maintain the combat effectiveness of his units.

October 26

CBI: Japanese aircraft attack airfields in India that are supporting the China air bridge over the Himalayas (the Hump). Numerous logistics storage areas are destroyed.

MIDDLE EAST: USAMEAF fighters and bombers provide air support to the Eighth Army's attack at El Alamein, destroying transportation and attacking Axis troop concentrations. B-17s and B-24 Liberators attack shipping off the coast of Libya.

SOLOMONS: The Battle of the Santa Cruz Islands. Task Force 16, centered around the carrier USS *Enterprise* under command of Rear Admiral Thomas C. Kinkaid, and Task Force 17, centered around the carrier USS *Hornet* under command of Rear Admiral George D. Murray, engage a numerically superior Japanese force with four carriers, four battleships, eight cruisers, and 30 destroyers. *Hornet* is severely damaged and is later sunk. The *Enterprise,* a light cruiser, and a battleship are both heavily damaged and a destroyer is scuttled. The Americans lose 74 aircraft. Two Japanese carriers are damaged, along with the loss of 100 aircraft; a heavy cruiser and a destroyer are also damaged.

GUADALCANAL: The naval victory at Santa Cruz Islands counts for little. The Japanese attack against the perimeter defended by the 1st Battalion of the 164th Infantry is stopped; Japanese forces make a short penetration in the lines defended by 2nd Battalion 7th Marines, but the enemy is repulsed in a counterattack led by Major Odell M. Conoley, the 2nd Battalion's executive officer. The 173rd Infantry Regiment of the 43rd Infantry Division arrives at Espiritu Santo Island.

The USS *Enterprise* receives slight damage from a bomb during an attack by 20 Japanese dive-bombers and torpedo planes during the Battle of the Santa Cruz Islands, October 26, 1942.

October 27

CBI: Generals Wavell and Stilwell map out a plan for an offensive in Burma. U.S. forces will advance into Hukwang Valley, seize Myitkyina, and link with Chinese forces in Yunnan. U.S. engineers will construct a road from Ledo to link with the Burma Road.

ATLANTIC: German submarines attack convoy HX 212 (New York to Liverpool); U.S. tanker is torpedoed by *U-436* and abandoned.

October 29

ALEUTIANS: Japanese forces reoccupy Attu Island.

ATLANTIC: President Roosevelt establishes a production objective of 107,000 aircraft for 1943.

German submarines attack convoy HX 212. A U.S. tanker is torpedoed and sunk by *U-624; U-224* torpedoes and sinks a Canadian tanker.

PACIFIC: U.S. submarine *Grenadier* lays mines off Haiphong, French Indochina. A U.S. Navy PBY Catalina sinks Japanese submarine *I-172* off San Cristobal Island, Solomons.

GUADALCANAL: Japanese forces on Guadalcanal begin a withdrawal to Koli Point and Kokumbona. Marines prepare to continue advance westward toward Point Cruz to pressure the Japanese.

October 30

GUADALCANAL: U.S. Task Group 64.2, commanded by Rear Admiral Norman Scott, with a light cruiser and four destroyers, bombards Japanese positions at Point Cruz, Guadalcanal, in support of an American ground advance west.

October 31

SOUTHWEST PACIFIC AREA: U.S. submarine *Grayback* damages a Japanese cargo ship off Rabaul.

November 1

GUADALCANAL: Marine and army units begin to expand the Guadalcanal perimeter out to the east and west to help protect Henderson Field from Japanese artillery fire. Marines begin an advance across the Matanikau River to isolate Point Cruz; Japanese land reinforcements to the east of the American defenses, near the Metapona River.

November 2

MIDDLE EAST: USAMEAF and RAF provide air support to Eighth Army's attack named Supercharge. U.S. B-25 Mitchells bomb targets in support of British 9th Armored Division; B-17s bomb Tobruk harbor; B-25s and P-40s attack Axis tanks and troops.

SOUTHWEST PACIFIC AREA: U.S. submarine *Seawolf* torpedoes and sinks a Japanese vessel off the island of Mindoro. U.S. submarines *Tambor* and *Tautog* lay mines in various sea lanes approaching French Indochina.

GUADALCANAL: Japanese land an additional 1,500 reinforcements and supplies near Koli Point on Guadalcanal.

NEW GUINEA: Fifth Air Force attacks Japanese shipping near Buna, sinking a cargo ship, and supports the Australian assault to seize Kokoda airfield on the Owen Stanley Range. The 7th Australian Infantry Division captures Kokoda airfield.

November 3

CBI: Generalissimo Chiang Kai-shek agrees to support U.S.-British offensive in Burma, and allows Stilwell to command Chinese forces in India. If backed by Allied air support, Chiang promises to supply the Y Force, the Yunnan divisions.

ATLANTIC: A U.S. tanker in convoy SC 107 (Halifax Slow to United Kingdom) is torpedoed and sunk by German submarine *U-521*; a U.S. freighter is sunk by German submarine *U-181* off the Cape of Good Hope.

SOUTHWEST PACIFIC AREA: U.S. submarine *Haddock* torpedoes and sinks a merchant ship in the East China Sea. U.S. submarine *Seawolf* sinks a Japanese transport off Davao, Philippines; U.S. submarine *Tambor* sinks a merchant ship in the Tonkin Gulf.

GUADALCANAL: Marine reconnaissance elements meet Japanese near Koli Point. They are reinforced by two tank companies, the army's 2nd Battalion 164th Infantry Regiment, and a marine battalion. These units, along with air strikes and artillery fire, force the Japanese to break contact.

November 4

ATLANTIC: A U.S. freighter headed to Murmansk, USSR, is torpedoed and sunk by German submarine *U-354* north of Iceland.

MIDDLE EAST: Lieutenant General Frank M. Andrews takes command of USAFIME.

MEDITERRANEAN: U.S. submarines *Shad, Gunnel, Herring, Barb,* and *Blackfish* conduct reconnaissance activities off the North African coast in support of Operation Torch, observing Rabat, Fedala, Casablanca, Safi, and Dakar.

GUADALCANAL: The 1st Battalion 164th Infantry supports the marines' western advance, while the 2nd and 3rd Battalions of the 164th support the advance to the east. Marine and army units reach Point Cruz and establish defensive positions.

November 5

CARIBBEAN: U.S. tanker in convoy TAG 18 (Trinidad to Aruba to Guantánamo) is sunk by German submarine *U-129*.

ATLANTIC: A U.S. Navy PBY Catalina sinks German submarine *U-408* off Iceland.

MEDITERRANEAN: Lieutenant General Eisenhower and his staff arrive in Gibraltar to oversee Operation Torch landings.

November 6

PACIFIC: U.S. submarine *Haddock* damages a Japanese cargo ship off the southeast coast of Japan.

NEW GUINEA: General MacArthur arrives at Port Moresby to direct offensive against Gona-Buna.

November 7

ALEUTIANS: The Japanese submarine base at Kiska is attacked by Eleventh Air Force B-24 Liberators and B-26 Marauders.

CARIBBEAN: U.S. freighter convoy TAG 19 (Trinidad to Aruba to Guantánamo) is sunk by German submarine *U-508*.

ATLANTIC: U.S. freighter is torpedoed and sunk by German submarine *U-159* off the Cape of Good Hope, South Africa; U.S. freighter is sunk by German submarine *U-161* off the coast of West Africa.

ETO: Eighth Air Force bombers attack U-boat facilities at Brest. Twelfth Air Force begins deployment from Britain to North Africa.

MEDITERRANEAN: General Henri Giraud arrives in Gibraltar after escaping from Lyons, France. Giraud, a hero of two wars, has been selected as the French commander most likely to command the loyalty of French officers in North Africa and rally them to the Allies. Giraud surprises Lieutenant General Eisenhower by demanding that he take charge of the operation and announces plans to divert some of the Allied landing forces to the southern coast of France.

U.S. transport is torpedoed by German submarine *U-205* in the western Mediterranean; USAMEAF aircraft sink Italian submarine *Antonio Sciesa* off the coast of Libya.

GUADALCANAL: U.S. aircraft from Henderson Field attack a Japanese convoy, damaging two destroyers. The 164th Infantry Regiment and 7th Marines advance east toward Matapona River.

November 8

ETO: Eighth Air Force bombers attack the Lille locomotive works and the Abbeville/Drucat airfield in France.

November 8

MEDITERRANEAN: Operation Torch. Allied forces invade Algeria and Morocco, landing at Casablanca, Oran, and Algiers. The Eastern Assault Force, led by Major General Charles W. Ryder, lands at Algiers. An attempt by two British destroyers to enter the port of Algiers with a battalion from a regimental combat team (RCT) of the U.S. 34th Division is met with heavy fire. Troops are landed but are withdrawn by 0900 hours. The 168th RCT from the 34th Division, the 39th RCT of the U.S. 9th Division, and a brigade from the British 78th Division advance toward Algiers without opposition. Key objectives of Blida and Maison Blanche airfields are captured. Algiers surrenders to Allied forces at 1900 hours.

The Center Assault Force, under command of Major General Lloyd R. Fredendall, lands at Oran. Arzew harbor is captured by U.S. rangers to support the landing of two RCTs of the 1st Infantry Division. One task force from Combat Command B of the 1st Armored Division captures Tafaraoui airfield Fighters from the 31st Fighter Group arrive at Tafaraoui to support operations. U.S. paratroopers of the 509th Parachute Infantry, intended to support the capture of La Senia and Tafaraoui airfields, are dropped far from their drop zones. Two British ships flying large American flags attempt to enter Oran harbor carrying a 400-man assault force of the 6th Armored Infantry Regiment, 1st Armored Division. Harbor defenses and the French sloop *La Surprise* fire on the ships, heavily damaging both as they disembark their landing force. Despite heavy casualties, those members of the assault force that make it ashore capture several objectives, but are later forced to surrender. A second task force from 1st Armored Division captures Lourmel airfield. The 26th RCT, 1st Infantry Division captures Bou Sfer and Aïn et Turk, but is unable to advance farther.

French resistance combined with confusion during the landing delays the Western Task Force, commanded by Major General George S. Patton, Jr. The French battleship *Jean Bart,* cruiser *Primaguet,* eight destroyers, and 13 submarines are at Casablanca harbor. The *Primaguet* and the destroyers leave the harbor and attempt to prevent the landings. The *Jean Bart,* in dry dock, supports with gunfire. U.S. naval gunfire and carrier aircraft knock out the cruiser and two of the destroyers and damage the *Jean Bart.* A beachhead is established at Fedala with the 3rd Infantry Division and a battalion of the 67th Armored regiment of the 2nd Armored Division. The French garrison at Fedala surrenders to American forces. The 60th RCT of 9th Infantry Division and a battalion of the 66th Armored Regiment of the 2nd Armored Division are attacked by French aircraft as they land at Port Lyautey. Port Lyautey and its airfield, key objectives of the task force, are strongly defended and the Americans are unable to advance beyond the beachhead. U.S. naval gunfire suppresses French coastal batteries at Safi harbor, and U.S. destroyers with two companies of infantry aboard enter the harbor and capture key objectives. The 47th RCT of the 9th Infantry Division along with two battalions of the 67th Armored Regiment of the 2nd Armored Division land at Safi and U.S. aircraft stop a French column of tanks and trucks attempting to counter the landings.

German aircraft bomb Allied ships near Algiers. Vichy France, led by Marshal Henri Pétain, breaks diplomatic relations with the United States.

PACIFIC: U.S. submarine *Seawolf* sinks a Japanese gunboat off Mindanao, Philippines. U.S. freighter is torpedoed by Japanese submarine *I-21* off Nouméa, New Caledonia.

GUADALCANAL: Admiral William F. Halsey, commander of SOPAC, visits Guadalcanal and meets with General Alexander A. Vandegrift. The meeting is interrupted by a Japanese air attack that forces both officers to seek shelter in a sandbagged dugout.

NEW GUINEA: The Fifth Air Force airlifts the 126th Infantry Regiment to Fasari and Pongani airfields in northern New Guinea and moves the remainder of the 128th Infantry Regiment, 32nd Infantry Division into Wanigela, as General MacArthur prepares for assault on the Buna-Gona defenses.

November 9

ALEUTIANS: One Eleventh Air Force B-17 and four P-38s attack Holtz Bay and Attu airfield, destroying eight Japanese floatplanes.

ETO: Eighth Air Force B-17s attempt to conduct low-level bombing runs (below 10,000 feet) on the U-boat base at St. Nazaire in France. Of the 31 aircraft participating in the attack, three are lost and 22 are damaged by antiaircraft fire. B-24 Liberator bombers attacking at 17–18,000 feet suffer minor damage from antiaircraft fire.

ALGERIA, OPERATION TORCH: General Henri Giraud's broadcasted appeals to French forces to join the Allies are ignored. La Senia airfield outside of Oran is captured. U.S. forces land supplies at Safi and on beaches near Casablanca. French troops continue to resist at Port Lyautey and the airfield. The British First Army is landed under command of General Kenneth A.N. Anderson at Algiers and prepares to advance along the coast road to Tunisia. German aircraft begin landing in Tunis.

A U.S. transport is sunk by German submarine *U-173* near Algiers.

British Spitfires of the Twelfth Air Force attack a French armored unit moving toward Tafaraoui, south of Oran.

NEW GUINEA: Fifth Air Force B-26 Marauders bomb Buna; airlift of the U.S. 126th Infantry Regiment to Pongani begins.

November 10

ATLANTIC: German submarine *U-608* lays mines off New York City.

MEDITERRANEAN, OPERATION TORCH: Major General Mark W. Clark meets with Admiral François Darlan, commander of all Vichy French military forces, seeking to end hostilities as quickly as possible. Darlan by pure chance has been in Algiers visiting his sick son when the Allies land. Deciding to act on Pétain's behalf, Darlan assumes full civil and military authority over French North Africa and orders a cease-fire. U.S. forces capture Oran after a coordinated armor assault against the defenses. Destroyer USS *Dallas* lands troops close to the Port Lyautey airfield, supported by two U.S. infantry battalions attacking from the beachhead. U.S. carrier *Chenango* launches 72 P-40s, which land at Port Lyautey airfield. Casablanca is still defended by French forces, which refuse to surrender. Patton prepares for an all-out assault on the city the next day.

A French submarine attacks U.S. carrier *Ranger* off the coast of French North Africa without effect; two French submarines attack the battleship *Massachusetts* and a U.S. heavy cruiser, but have no effect. Oran surrenders to U.S. forces. Allied forces sail from Algiers to occupy Bougie and Bône in preparation for an overland movement to Tunisia.

SOUTH PACIFIC: A U.S. minesweeper sinks Japanese submarine *I-15* off San Cristobal Island, Solomons.

November 11

CBI: P-40s from the Tenth Air Force attack Shinghbwiyang in Burma.

ALGIERS, OPERATION TORCH: Admiral François Darlan and General Alphonse Juin agree to an armistice, and all resistance ends. Casablanca surrenders to U.S. forces. British troops begin overland movement eastward toward Tunisia. Marshal Pétain rejects the cease-fire order. Darlan is put under house arrest by the Allies to prevent him from following Pétain's orders. Darlan also refuses to order the French fleet at Toulon to sail to Algiers to avoid capture by the Germans. German troops invade unoccupied France. Italian troops land on Corsica and move into France. The collapse of the Vichy government leaves Darlan as the default political head of North Africa. By agreement, Giraud is given command of all French forces, General Juin (previous commander in chief of all French forces in North Africa) is named commander of French land forces.

German submarine *U-173* torpedoes and sinks a U.S. transport and damages a destroyer and an oiler off the North African coast.

Twelfth Air Force fighters land at the Port Lyautey airfield after French end resistance. British 78th Infantry Division and a battalion of the 17th Lancers accompanied by light tanks from the U.S. 1st Armored Division land at Bougie, the first objective on the way to Tunis.

MEDITERRANEAN: USAMEAF B-24 Liberators attack Axis shipping near Benghazi.

PACIFIC: U.S. submarine *Haddock* torpedoes and sinks a Japanese cargo ship in the Yellow Sea.

GUADALCANAL: The 182nd Infantry Regiment of the army's Americal Division lands at Guadalcanal.

November 12

ALGERIA, OPERATION TORCH: The U.S. 509th Parachute Infantry is placed under operational control of the British to support the advance into Tunisia. Elements of the 509th are dropped at Duzerville airport near Bône.

Axis troops in Tunisia grow to 15,000; 581 tons of supplies are landed by air and sea at Tunis.

Three U.S. transports are sunk by German submarine *U-130* off French Morocco.

MIDDLE EAST: The U.S. Ninth Air Force, replacing USAMEAF, is established under General Brereton.

GUADALCANAL: Japanese torpedo planes escorted by Zero fighters attack Task Force 67, commanded by Rear Admiral Richmond K. Turner, while the 182nd Infantry Regiment is unloading at Guadalcanal. A heavy cruiser and a destroyer are damaged. A SOPAC B-17 on a reconnaissance mission spots a Japanese carrier and reports its position for two hours while driving off Japanese Zero fighters and downing six of them.

The Japanese have moved into the area three fleets with more than 60 ships, including two battleships, 11 cruisers, 39 destroyers, two aircraft carriers, and 11 transports, with 11,000 infantrymen and 3,000 naval infantry. While an escort of six cruisers and six destroyers supports the landing of troops at Tassafaronga, the battleships, cruisers, and destroyers will bombard Henderson Field; simultaneously, another fleet centered on the aircraft carriers will attack Henderson Field as well. The Japanese intend to win the Battle of Guadalcanal once and for all. Turner receives reports of a Japanese force headed toward Guadalcanal and sends Task Group 67.4, with two heavy cruisers, three light cruisers, and eight destroyers commanded by Rear Admiral Daniel J. Callaghan, to block the Japanese and protect Henderson Field.

NEW GUINEA: Units of the 126th Infantry Regiment, 32nd Infantry Division begin advance in New Guinea. The 3rd Battalion of the 126th is airlanded at Pongani.

November 13

ALGERIA, OPERATION TORCH: Lieutenant General Eisenhower arrives at Algiers to finalize the agreement with Admiral Darlan concerning the administration of North Africa.

November 13

SOUTH PACIFIC: The Naval Battle of Guadalcanal. Just after one o'clock in the morning, Naval Task Group 67.4 encounters 14 Japanese ships, including two battleships, preparing to bombard Henderson Field. Firing in the darkness at 3,000 yards, the Americans and Japanese fight a confused and brutal battle. Rear Admiral Callaghan and most of his officers are killed by a direct hit on his flagship. A cruiser is so badly damaged that it is later scuttled; another badly damaged cruiser, USS *Juneau,* is torpedoed and sunk by Japanese submarine *I-26* with a loss of 700 men; among the lost are the five Sullivan brothers. Four destroyers are sunk and three are damaged along with two cruisers sunk and the rest damaged. The Japanese lose two destroyers in the encounter. A Japanese battleship, badly damaged in the fight, will later be sunk by aircraft from both USS *Enterprise* and Henderson Field. Five Japanese destroyers are also damaged.

Boatswain's Mate First Class Reinhardt J. Keppler is aboard the heavy cruiser USS *San Francisco* when a Japanese torpedo plane crashes on the aft machine gun platform during an air attack. Keppler treats the injured sailors in the area. That night, as the *San Francisco* fights off Savo Island, Keppler mans a hose to fight a major onboard fire as Japanese gunfire rakes the ship. Mortally wounded, Keppler directs the fire fighting efforts and assists in treating wounded sailors until he collapses from loss of blood. For his great personal valor and dedication to his shipmates he will receive the Medal of Honor.

NEW GUINEA: The 7th Australian Infantry Division takes Wairopi.

November 14

ETO: Eighth Air Force B-17s attack U-boat pens at St. Nazaire.

GUADALCANAL: Henderson Field comes under heavy shellfire for 45 minutes from three Japanese cruisers and four destroyers, but they cause little lasting damage. Aircraft from the *Enterprise* and from Henderson Field attack the group, and Marine SBD Dauntless dive-bombers sink a heavy cruiser. Five other ships are damaged. This leaves the 11 transports headed to Guadalcanal virtually defenseless. Although the Japanese attempt to protect the convoy with air cover, it is insufficient. Carrier aircraft, marine and navy aircraft from Henderson Field, and SOPAC B-17s all participate in sinking six transports and damaging another. A cargo ship is sunk and another damaged. Just before midnight, Task Force 64, with two battleships and four destroyers commanded by Rear Admiral Willis A. Lee, Jr., intercepts another Japanese naval force with a battleship, a light cruiser, and six destroyers. In the narrow waters between Savo Island and Guadalcanal, where the major naval engagements have taken place—an area now known as Iron Bottom Sound—another Battle of Guadalcanal is fought. In this fight the Americans are able to get off the first shots, but the Japanese rapidly engage the Americans, sinking two destroyers and damaging another. One U.S. battleship is badly damaged, leaving the one remaining battleship, Lee's flagship USS *Washington,* to fight on alone. *Washington* cripples and sinks the Japanese battleship and a destroyer, and damages several cruisers so badly that the Japanese retreat.

November 15

ALGERIA, OPERATION TORCH: U.S. paratroopers of the 509th Parachute Infantry conduct assault on Youk-les-Bains near Tébessa in support of the British advance into Tunisia. Axis strength in Tunisia grows to 24,000; 213 tanks are now available.

GUADALCANAL: The four remaining Japanese transport ships are intentionally beached to allow troops to offload as quickly as possible. The ships are struck by

Destroyer Squadron 12 maneuvers off Savo Island during the Guadalcanal campaign. (*U.S. Navy*)

artillery fire, air attack, and naval gunfire. About 2,000 men escape the attack to join their comrades in the jungle. The Japanese have attempted an all or nothing offensive intending to drive the Americans off Guadalcanal and regain the strategic initiative in the South Pacific. The U.S. Navy, in perhaps its finest hour, supported by the Marine Corps and the U.S. Army, succeeds in breaking the back of Japanese land and naval power. The turning point in the Pacific war has been reached and everyone seems to know it. In Washington, Secretary of the Navy Frank Knox tells reporters: "We can lick them. I don't qualify that. We'll defeat them." Admiral Halsey put it more directly: "We've got the bastards licked."

November 16

MEDITERRANEAN, OPERATION TORCH: U.S. paratroopers of the 509th Parachute Infantry conduct assault on Souk el Arba near Tabarka in support of the British advance into Tunisia. Allied troops make first contact with Axis forces in Tunisia.

U.S. destroyers sink German submarine *U-173* off Casablanca.

NEW GUINEA: The U.S. 32nd Infantry and the Australian 7th Division begin an attack on Japanese strongholds at Gona and on the Buna defenses. The Australians make some small gains against Gona, but are forced to retreat. Fifth Air Force A-20s attack targets around Gona, while B-25 Mitchells and B-26 Marauders attack Buna.

U.S. submarine *Haddock* torpedoes and sinks a Japanese cargo ship off the southern coast of Japan.

U.S. submarine *Seal* sinks a Japanese cargo ship in the Palau Islands.

November 17

ATLANTIC: President Roosevelt issues a statement that maintaining Admiral Darlan in his position as high commissioner is only a temporary expedient applying to local conditions. Roosevelt makes the statement in an attempt to diffuse criticism from American lawmakers in Congress over the appointment of a known anti-Semite and pro-fascist as leader of newly-liberated French North Africa.

ETO: B-17s from Eighth Air Force drop 102 tons of bombs on U-boat facilities at St. Nazaire, France.

NORTH AFRICA, OPERATION TORCH: The U.S. 509th Parachute Infantry occupies Gafsa airfield in Tunisia.

SOUTHWEST PACIFIC AREA: U.S. submarine *Salmon* attacks a convoy off the west coast of Luzon, sinking a Japanese ship.

PACIFIC: U.S. submarine *Searaven* torpedoes and sinks a Japanese transport off Christmas Island.

November 18

ATLANTIC: German submarines attack convoy ONS 144 (Liverpool to Halifax, slow). Two U.S. freighters are torpedoed by *U-624* in the North Atlantic past Iceland. One sinks, the other is abandoned by its crew. A U.S. tanker in convoy SC 109 (Halifax Slow to United Kingdom) is torpedoed and set afire by German submarine *U-43* in the mid-North Atlantic.

MEDITERRANEAN: Bombers from Ninth Air Force attack the railyard and port at Benghazi.

SOUTH PACIFIC: U.S. Fifth Air Force B-17s sink a Japanese cargo ship off Kahili airfield, Bougainville.

GUADALCANAL: U.S. Army 182nd and 164th Infantry Regiments, and the 8th Marine Regiment under command of Brigadier General Edmund B. Sebree, assistant commanding general of the Americal Division, advance to Point Cruz to find the Japanese. In a daylong battle, strong and determined Japanese attacks stop the Americans.

NEW GUINEA: Japanese aircraft attack the 32nd Infantry Division's supply boats carrying the division's food, ammunition, communications and medical equipment, and heavy weapons, sinking most of the boats. Major General Harding, who was traveling on one of the boats, narrowly escapes being killed.

November 19

ETO: Eighth Air Force adds the German U-boat yards at Kiel, Bremen, and Vegesack to its priority target list.

NEW GUINEA: The U.S. 128th Infantry Regiment attacks Buna. The 1st and 3rd Battalions, 128th Infantry, make contact with dug-in Japanese forces near the Duropa Plantation in heavy jungle. The inexperienced Americans are unable to locate the Japanese positions and their attack is stopped. General Harding requests tanks to support his attack against the extremely well camouflaged Japanese bunkers. Fifth Air Force B-26 Marauders conduct bombing and strafing runs on Japanese positions.

November 20

CBI: Tenth Air Force bombers attack Mandalay, Burma.

MEDITERRANEAN: Ninth Air Force P-40s support British forces capturing Benghazi.

NEW GUINEA: At Buna, without heavy weapons and with limited ammunition and little food, the 1st Battalion, 128th Infantry gains 200 yards; the 3rd Battalion makes no progress. The 1st Battalion, 126th Infantry arrives after completing an overland movement from Pongani.

November 21

ATLANTIC: A U.S. destroyer attacks the German blockade runner *Anneliese Essberger* in the South Atlantic, forcing the crew to scuttle the ship.

GUADALCANAL: The U.S. 182nd Infantry clears Japanese defenders from Point Cruz at Guadalcanal; well dug-in Japanese defenders halt advance of U.S. 164th Infantry. The Japanese begin surveying a runway at Munda, New Georgia Island. The new airfield, 150 miles northwest of Henderson Field at Guadalcanal, is intended to contest control of the air over the Solomons and establish a strongpoint against further American advances.

NEW GUINEA: The U.S. 126th Infantry Regiment is transferred to augment the 7th Australian Infantry Division's attack toward Sanananda. For the attack on Buna, General Harding designates the 1st and 3rd Battalions of the 128th Infantry Regiment, a detachment of 1st Battalion of the 126th Infantry Regiment, and an Australian infantry company as Warren Force. The 2nd Battalion 128th Infantry and the 2nd Battalion of the 126th Infantry Regiment are designated Urbana Force. Warren Force makes no progress, even with air and artillery support.

November 22

NORTH AFRICA, OPERATION TORCH: The final agreement is signed that commits the French to support the Allies against Axis forces in Tunisia and, later, France. French units are added to the Allied forces. Twelfth Air Force B-17s attack El Aouina airfield in Tunis. Algiers airfield is attacked by Axis aircraft, one B-17 is destroyed.

November 23

CBI: B-25 Mitchells with P-40 escorts of the China Air Task Force (CATF) bomb Haiphong harbor, sinking one freighter and damaging two others. Another B-25 mission attacks Tien Ho airfield, destroying as many as 40 Japanese aircraft.

ATLANTIC: A U.S. tanker is torpedoed and sunk by German submarine *U-518* in the mid-Atlantic on its way to Iceland.

The U.S. Coast Guard accepts women into service under the title SPARS (*Semper Paratus* Always Ready). Captain Dorothy Stratton is the commander.

November 24

TUNISIA, OPERATION TORCH: Allied attacks begin and are intended to capture Tunis-Bizerte. The British 78th Infantry Division attacks on three axes, each with one brigade, supported by tanks from the U.S. 13th and 1st Armored regiments, plus an artillery battalion and the 701st Tank Destroyer Battalion. Combat Command B of

U.S. 1st Armored Division begins movement into Tunisia. Twelfth Air Force fighters attack ground targets near Gabès.

PACIFIC: Japanese forces land at Munda Point on New Georgia Island in the Solomons.

Fifth Air Force B-17 bombers and Australian fighters sink a Japanese destroyer and damage torpedo boats off the northern New Guinea coast.

November 25

TUNISIA, OPERATION TORCH: Allied advance is stopped west of Mateur and at Djedeida and Medjez el Bab. The British 6th Armored Division and Combat Command B of the U.S. 1st Armored Division are stopped at Souk el Arba by Axis airpower and tanks.

GUADALCANAL: Japanese submarine *I-17* lands 11 tons of supplies for soldiers on Guadalcanal.

November 26

ALEUTIANS: Eleventh Air Force B-26 Marauders escorted by four P-38s damage Japanese cargo ship off Attu.

TUNISIA: The first U.S.-German tank battle of the war is fought at Chouigui Pass, near Teboura.

NEW GUINEA: Warren Force's attack is supported by air, artillery, and heavy machine gun fire. The 3rd Battalion, 128th Infantry Regiment, moving through swamps, encounters Japanese defenders in well concealed, heavily fortified positions and is unable to make any progress. Urbana Force halts several Japanese counterattacks. Fifth Air Force P-40s, A-20 Havocs, and B-25 Mitchells attack targets to suppress Japanese air defenses and win air superiority over Buna-Gona.

November 27

CBI: Hong Kong harbor is hit by 10 B-25 Mitchells and 20 P-40s of the Chinese Air Task Force of the Tenth Air Force in the largest raid to date.

November 28

TUNISIA: Effective Axis defenses and superior air power halt the Allied offensive. U.S. 2nd Battalion, 13th Armored Regiment of 1st Armored Division reaches Djedeida, about 15 miles west of Tunis. Twelfth Air Force B-26 Marauders attack facilities at Sfax.

November 29

SOUTH PACIFIC: Navy and marine aircraft from Henderson Field sink two Japanese cargo ships at New Georgia Island.

GUADALCANAL: The 1st Marine Division is relieved in place on Guadalcanal. Marine and army units land near Koli Point to construct an airfield.

NEW GUINEA: Fifth Air Force B-17s, P-40s, and A-20 Havocs attack Japanese positions at Gona.

Fifth Air Force B-17s damage two Japanese destroyers carrying reinforcements to Gona, New Guinea, near Vitiaz Strait; the other two destroyers depart without unloading troops.

November 30

GUADALCANAL: The Battle of Tassafaronga. Rear Admiral Carlton H. Wright, commander of Task Force 67, with four heavy cruisers, one light cruiser, and six destroyers, arrives at Iron Bottom Sound to intercept Japanese ships. Wright finds eight Japanese destroyers off Tassafaronga Point landing supplies to troops on Guadalcanal. The Japanese take aggressive action and torpedo four U.S. cruisers, damaging them all. One cruiser later sinks. One Japanese destroyer is hit by gunfire and later sinks. Although the resupply effort fails, the Japanese have a convincing victory.

NEW GUINEA: Elements of U.S. 126th Infantry Regiment near Sanananda are stopped by counterattacks. Urbana Force is unable to clear Japanese defenses to advance on Buna village; Warren Force encounters Japanese defenses at Duropa Plantation and is stopped.

December 1

ATLANTIC: Gas rationing begins in the United States to save wear on tires and conserve rubber.

TUNISIA: Axis counterattacks at Djedeida and Tebourba force the Allies to retreat. Twelfth Air Force B-17s bomb El Aouina airfield. P-38s attacks German forces at Djedeida. Lieutenant General Carl Spaatz arrives in Algeria to serve as Lieutenant General Eisenhower's air adviser. General Ira C. Eaker from VIII Bomber Command takes Spaatz's place as Eighth Air Force commander.

December 2

ATLANTIC: U.S. steamship is torpedoed and sunk by German submarine *U-604* off Bermuda.

At the University of Chicago scientists led by Enrico Fermi are able to initiate a self-sustaining nuclear chain reaction for the first time. The reaction is a critical step in the Manhattan Project, the secret plan to develop an atomic bomb.

NEW GUINEA: Both American and Australian forces are unable to break the Japanese defensive lines. The U.S. 126th Infantry continues to hold a roadblock before Sanananda against numerous Japanese attacks intended to eliminate it. Malaria, dengue fever, dysentery, and typhus have taken a serious toll on the Allied troops. Told by General MacArthur to take Buna or die in the attempt, Major General Robert L. Eichelberger, commander of I Corps, inspects the 32nd Division and finds that 66 percent of the men are too sick to fight at any given time. Major General Harding and several subordinates are relieved of command. Brigadier General Albert W. Waldron takes command in Harding's place.

December 3

GUADALCANAL: U.S. aircraft from Henderson Field attack a convoy attempting to resupply Japanese forces on Guadalcanal. A destroyer is damaged, and the resupply attempt is only marginally successful.

December 4

MEDITERRANEAN: Ninth Air Force B-24 Liberators conduct first American bombing raid on Italy. Attacking the port of Naples, the 20 bombers sink an Italian light cruiser and damage two other light cruisers as well as four destroyers.

Tunisia: Twelfth Air Force B-17s attack Bizerte harbor; A-20 Havocs with P-38 escorts attack El Aouina airfield. Fighters attack Gabès.

December 5

Atlantic: President Roosevelt establishes the Office of Economic Stabilization to control wartime inflation and limit economic dislocation.

North Africa: Lieutenant General Carl Spaatz is named deputy commander in chief for air operations.

Tunisia: Twelfth Air Force B-17s attack Tunis; B-25 Mitchells and A-20 Havocs escorted by P-38 Lightnings attack Sidi Ahmed airfield.

Pacific: Army Air Force Units in SOPAC are notified that they will be designated as Thirteenth Air Force.

New Guinea: Fifth Air Force B-25 Mitchells and A-20 Havocs support the ground attack on Buna. During Urbana Force's attack on Buna village, Lieutenant Robert H. Odell, the commander of F Company, 2nd Battalion 126th Infantry Regiment, finds himself taking orders directly from Major General Eichelberger, who is initially supervising the attack to assess the capabilities of the 32nd Division. The fighting becomes so heavy and confused that Eichelberger finds himself taking an active role. The general discovers firsthand the difficulty of the task for the infantrymen without additional artillery and tank support. Buna village is isolated. Warren Force attacks with Australian-supplied Bren gun carriers (small armored transports), but is unsuccessful. Brigadier General Waldron is wounded in the attack and Brigadier General Clovis E. Beyers takes command of the 32nd Infantry Division.

December 6

ETO: Eighth Air Force bombers attack Lille locomotive works and Abeville-Drucat airfield in France.

New Georgia: SOPAC aircraft locate construction equipment at Munda on New Georgia Island, indications that the Japanese are building at least one airfield there. This discovery initiates almost daily bombing of Munda by U.S. aircraft.

December 7

Atlantic: A U.S. freighter attempting to join convoy HX 217 (New York to Liverpool) is torpedoed and sunk by German submarine *U-600* east of Newfoundland.

Tunisia: Twelfth Air Force B-17s attack Bizerte; A-20 Havocs attack German troops and tanks near Tebourba in support of the Allied defense.

Pacific: U.S. submarine *Kingfish* torpedoes and sinks a Japanese transport west of the Bonin Islands.

Guadalcanal: U.S. aircraft from Henderson Field attack a 12-ship convoy with reinforcements and supplies bound for Guadalcanal. Two destroyers are damaged. A U.S. cargo ship is damaged by an attack from a Japanese midget submarine launched by submarine *I-24* off Lunga Point, Guadalcanal.

December 8

Atlantic: President Roosevelt receives the JCS plan for the offensive to recapture Burma. The assessment is that Stilwell requires additional resources to support the British, who have the primary responsibility for the campaign.

ETO: Eighth Air Force discovers that bombing of U-boat facilities in France is having no effect.

GUADALCANAL: The army's 132nd Infantry Regiment lands at Guadalcanal. Units on Guadalcanal include the American Division, the 147th and 132nd Infantry Regiments, two marine regiments, and four field artillery battalions.

Eight U.S. motor torpedo (*PT*) boats prevent eight Japanese destroyers from landing reinforcements at Guadalcanal. U.S. submarine *Gar* sinks a Japanese cargo ship off Borneo.

NEW GUINEA: Fifth Air Force B-17s and one B-24 Liberator damage two Japanese destroyers off Buna, New Guinea, attempting to land reinforcements.

December 9

SOUTH PACIFIC: Aircraft from Henderson Field attack the Japanese base at Munda, New Georgia.

GUADALCANAL: Major General Alexander A. Vandegrift and the 1st Marine Division depart Guadalcanal. Major General Alexander M. Patch, former commander of the army's American Division, takes over as commander of U.S. forces on Guadalcanal. It is estimated that one-third of all the marines who left with Vandegrift are unfit for duty due to illness. Vandegrift tells his soldiers, sailors, and marines that their "unbelievable achievements have made the name 'Guadalcanal' a synonym for death and disaster in the language of our enemy. . . ."

Motor torpedo boat *PT-59* sinks Japanese submarine *I-3* as it attempts to drop off supplies to Japanese troops on Guadalcanal.

NEW GUINEA: The Australian 7th Infantry Division captures Gona village. The 3rd Battalion of the 127th Infantry Regiment is airlifted to the vicinity of Buna. Fifth Air Force B-26 Marauders attack Buna; P-40s fly support missions for the 126th Infantry Regiment holding a blocking position near Sanananda.

December 10

ATLANTIC: A U.S. Navy PBY Catalina sinks German submarine *U-611* in the North Atlantic.

TUNISIA: Heavy rains prevent any air support missions for Allied forces.

PACIFIC: U.S. submarine *Halibut* torpedoes and sinks a Japanese merchant ship and damages a Japanese transport off Hokkaido.

SOUTH PACIFIC: U.S. submarine *Wahoo* sinks a Japanese collier and B-17s damage two Japanese oilers off Bougainville.

NEW GUINEA: At Buna, the 3rd Battalion, 127th Infantry relieves the 2nd Battalion, 126th Infantry Regiment, now reduced to about 150 men.

December 11

NORTH AFRICA: Twelfth Air Force establishes five area commands to support Allied operations throughout North Africa.

MEDITERRANEAN: Ninth Air Force B-24 Liberators bomb Naples harbor

SOUTH PACIFIC: U.S. submarine *Seadragon* torpedoes and damages a Japanese cargo ship in the eastern Solomons.

December 12

TUNISIA: Twelfth Air Force B-17s with P-38 escorts attack facilities at Tunis.

PACIFIC: U.S. submarine *Drum* torpedoes and damages Japanese aircraft carrier *Ryuho* in the northern Bonin Islands. U.S. submarine *Halibut* torpedoes and sinks a Japanese merchant cargo ship off the northeast coast of Honshu, Japan.

GUADALCANAL: Five U.S. motor torpedo boats attack 11 Japanese destroyers attempting a resupply mission off Cape Esperance, Guadalcanal. One motor torpedo boat and one destroyer are sunk in the engagement.

December 13

NEW GUINEA: Fifth Air Force B-17s and B-24 Liberators attack a convoy of five Japanese destroyers carrying more than 800 men off Madang, but do no damage. Buna village is heavily bombarded in preparation for an attack. The remaining Japanese defenders evacuate the village during the night.

December 14

PACIFIC: Fleet Air Command is established at Nouméa, New Caledonia, commanded by Rear Admiral Marc A. Mitscher. U.S. submarine *Sunfish* mines the entrance to Iseno Umi Bay, Japan.

NEW GUINEA: Buna village falls to Urbana Force. Fifth Air Force aircraft attack Japanese troops and supplies landed at Mambare River by the five destroyers previously attacked.

December 15

CBI: The all-black 45th Engineer General Service Regiment and the 823rd Engineer Aviation Battalion begin construction of the Ledo Road. Beginning at Ledo in India, the goal is to connect with the old Burma Road at Kunming, 271 miles away.

ATLANTIC: U.S. freighter is torpedoed and sunk by German submarine *U-174* en route from Trinidad to Brazil. U.S. Coast Guard cutter sinks German submarine *U-626* in the North Atlantic.

TUNISIA: Twelfth Air Force B-26s attack El Aouina airfield in Tunis, while B-17s attack the port. Other B-17s attack Bizerte. Ninth Air Force B-24 Liberators attack facilities at Sfax.

NEW GUINEA: As the 2nd Battalion, 128th Infantry Regiment attempts to clear Japanese defenders southeast of Buna village, three general officers are wounded in the day's fighting. General Eichelberger, the only U.S. general officer available, takes command of the battle.

December 16

PACIFIC: U.S. submarine *Halibut* torpedoes and sinks a Japanese merchant ship off Honshu, Japan.

December 17

CBI: CATF (China Air Task Force) bombers attack Laisho.

TUNISIA: Twelfth Air Force B-17s attack Bizerte and Tunis; A-20 Havocs attack Gabès.

PACIFIC: U.S. submarine *Drum* mines the Bungo Strait in the Japanese home islands.

SOUTH PACIFIC: U.S. submarine *Grouper* torpedoes and sinks a Japanese cargo ship in the Solomons.

GUADALCANAL: The U.S. 132nd Infantry of the Americal Division begins an attack on Mount Austen to protect Henderson Field and support offensive operations to the west. The attack is supported by the 1st Battalion, 2nd Marines, as well as by P-38s and marine SBD Dauntless dive-bombers providing air support. The Japanese are well entrenched and the attack fails.

The U.S. 35th Infantry Regiment, 25th Infantry Division arrives at Guadalcanal.

NEW GEORGIA: At Munda Point, New Georgia, the Japanese complete construction of a 4,700-foot-long airfield.

December 18

TUNISIA: Axis forces in Tunisia number 47,000, with 25,000 of them German combat veterans. Twelfth Air Force B-17s with P-38 Lightning escorts attack Bizerte; one bomber and three fighters are lost to enemy fighters. B-26 Marauders and P-38s attack Sousse; two bombers are lost. A-20 Havocs attack railyards in Mateur. Ninth Air Force B-17s attack Sousse.

PACIFIC: U.S. submarine *Sunfish* torpedoes and damages a Japanese transport west of the Bonin Islands.

NEW GUINEA: The Warren Force, directed by Australian brigadier general George F. Wootten and reinforced by two Australian infantry battalions and tanks, supports the 128th Infantry's attack on Buna.

Fifth Air Force B-17s attack Japanese convoy off Madang; B-24 Liberators bomb Lae airfield; other bombers and fighters provide air support to Allied ground attacks.

U.S. submarine *Albacore* torpedoes and sinks a Japanese light cruiser off Madang harbor in eastern New Guinea and torpedoes an armed merchant cruiser.

December 20

ALEUTIANS: Eleventh Air Force B-26 Marauders, B-24 Liberators, B-25 Mitchells, and nine P-38 Lightnings attack Kiska harbor, focusing on the submarine base and facilities. An ammunition dump is hit and a cargo ship is damaged by strafing P-38s.

ETO: The air depot at Romilly-sur-Seine is attacked by 72 Eighth Air Force B-17s. Six bombers are lost to enemy fighters.

PACIFIC: A Japanese merchant ship sinks off Honshu, Japan, after striking a mine laid moments earlier by U.S. submarine *Trigger*.

SOUTH PACIFIC: U.S. submarine *Seadragon* torpedoes and sinks Japanese submarine *I-4* in the waters between New Britain and New Ireland, as *I-4* attempts to resupply Japanese troops on Guadalcanal.

December 21

NEW GUINEA: Fifth Air Force B-17s attack Finschhafen harbor; B-24 Liberators attack Japanese supplies at the mouth of the Mambare River.

December 22

PACIFIC: U.S. submarine *Trigger* torpedoes and damages a Japanese merchant ship near the entrance of Tokyo Bay.

SOUTH PACIFIC: U.S. submarine *Greenling*, attacking a Japanese convoy, torpedoes and sinks a Japanese patrol boat near Bougainville.

December 23

TUNISIA: After relieving the British Coldstream Guards, the U.S. 18th RCT of the 1st Infantry Division is driven off Djebel el Ahmera, later known as Longstop Hill, by a German counterattack. Twelfth Air Force aircraft are completely grounded due to bad weather.

December 24

TUNISIA: The End of Operation Torch. Lieutenant General Eisenhower calls off further offensive action in order to regroup the Allied effort and resupply his exhausted units.

Admiral Darlan is assassinated by a young monarchist, leaving General Henri Giraud as the leader of French North Africa.

GUADALCANAL: The 132nd Infantry reaches the Japanese Gifu defensive lines on the west side of Mount Austen. Over 500 Japanese soldiers are in prepared positions.

NEW GEORGIA: U.S. SBD Dauntless dive-bombers, P-40s, and F4F Wildcats from Henderson Field attack and sink nine of 13 Japanese barges carrying reinforcements headed for Munda, New Georgia. SOPAC P-39 Airacobras assist in destroying 24 Japanese fighters at Munda.

NEW GUINEA: During an attack near Buna, First Sergeant Elmer J. Burr, of Company I, 127th Infantry Regiment, 32nd Infantry Division, sees a Japanese grenade land near his company commander. Without hesitation, he covers the grenade with his body and is killed instantly by the explosion. For his heroic act of self-sacrifice, First Sergeant Burr will receive the Medal of Honor.

December 25

SOUTH PACIFIC: U.S. submarine *Seadragon* torpedoes and damages a Japanese transport off New Britain.

NEW GUINEA: The Australians and Americans of Warren Force conduct an attack through heavily forested swamp against strong Japanese resistance. Colonel Clarence A. Martin climbs a tree to locate Japanese positions. Using his rifle, he kills several enemy soldiers. Working in coordination with tanks and artillery, the Allies begin to make progress.

U.S. submarine *Tautog* torpedoes and sinks a Japanese cargo ship off Timor; U.S. submarine *Thresher* torpedoes and sinks a Japanese army transport south of Borneo.

December 26

ALEUTIANS: Eleventh Air Force B-24 Liberators and P-38 Lightnings attack Sarana Bay and Attu. Japanese antiaircraft fire downs one P-38.

TUNISIA: Twelfth Air Force B-17s attack Bizerte and Sfax. Two bombers and two P-38s are lost; P-40s strafe barges off Sousse. C-47 transports drop a detachment of U.S. paratroopers near El Djem. Ninth Air Force B-24 Liberators attack Tunis, Sfax, and Sousse.

GUADALCANAL: Brigadier General Francis P. Mulcahy, commander of the 2nd Marine Aircraft Wing on Guadalcanal, relieves Brigadier General L. E. Woods as commander of air forces on Guadalcanal.

NEW GEORGIA: U.S. SBD Dauntless dive-bombers, F4F Wildcats, and P-38 Lightnings from Henderson Field sink three Japanese merchant cargo ships at Wickham Anchorage in New Georgia.

December 27

NEW GUINEA: Fifth Air Force B-17s attack Rabaul and B-26 Marauders support the attack on Gona.

December 28

TUNISIA: Twelfth Air Force B-17s bomb Sousse. P-38 and P-40 escort fighters down four enemy fighters. Ninth Air Force bombers attack Sousse.

PACIFIC: U.S. submarine *Kingfish* torpedoes and sinks a Japanese merchant ship off Formosa; U.S. submarine *Triton* torpedoes and sinks a Japanese merchant ship in the Central Pacific.

NEW GUINEA: The Warren Force meets the Urbana Force and begins to eliminate the final Japanese resistance in the Gona and Buna area.

December 29

CBI: Rangoon is attacked by 12 B-24 Liberators from Tenth Air Force.

December 30

ALEUTIANS: An initial attack by B-25 Mitchells with P-38 Lightning escorts at Kiska harbor is met by Japanese fighters, which shoot down two P-38s; a B-25 is also lost. A follow-on attack by B-24 Liberators, B-25 Mitchells, and B-26 Marauders targets two Japanese ships and three submarines in the harbor.

TUNISIA: An attack by Twelfth Air Force B-17s on Sfax continues with a second strike by B-25 Mitchells escorted by P-38s. German troop concentrations at Gabès are hit by B-17s. Gabès airfield is hit by P-40s and P-38 Lightnings. P-40s fly close air support missions near El Guettar.

PACIFIC: U.S. submarine *Greenling*, attacking a Japanese convoy in the central Pacific, torpedoes and sinks one cargo ship and damages another.

NEW GUINEA: U.S. submarine *Searaven* lands agents on the south coast of Ceram Island, Netherlands East Indies. U.S. submarine *Thresher* torpedoes and sinks a Japanese merchant ship off Borneo. Fifth Air Force B-17s attack Rabaul and sink a Japanese merchant ship in port.

December 31

ALEUTIANS: B-24 Liberators from Eleventh Air Force with nine P-38s as escort damage two Japanese merchant cargo ships off Kiska.

ATLANTIC: U-boats operating in the Atlantic have sunk a total of 1,160 ships (about 6.3 million tons) in 1942. U-boats have claimed nearly 70 percent of all Allied and neutral shipping losses (about 7.8 million tons). The German navy is winning the race, sinking one million more tons of shipping than has been built in 1942.

PACIFIC: Japanese Imperial Headquarters orders the evacuation of Guadalcanal. This is intended as a local withdrawal to consolidate severely stretched air, sea, and land forces. The Japanese cannot match the ability of the United States to supply and reinforce. Although giving up Guadalcanal, Japanese strategists intend to continue the campaign for New Guinea.

GUADALCANAL: The 2nd Battalion of the 132nd Infantry Regiment supports the attack on Mount Austen, but the Japanese defend tenaciously, forcing the American commander to call off the attack. B-26 Marauder bombers land at Guadalcanal.

1943

January 1

MEDITERRANEAN: German submarine *U-73* torpedoes and sinks U.S. freighter off Oran, Algeria.

In Tunisia, 15 Ninth Air Force B-24 Liberators attack Tunis harbor, along with Twelfth Air Force B-17s. B-26 Marauders from Twelfth Air Force hit the railyard at Tunis.

TUNISIA: Lieutenant General Eisenhower orders U.S. II Corps under command of Major General Lloyd R. Fredendall to concentrate in the Tebessa-Kasserine area in preparation for an attack on the Axis flank near the Tunisian-Libyan border.

SOUTHWEST PACIFIC AREA: Fifth Air Force B-24 Liberators and B-17s bomb Japanese ships and airfields at Rabaul.

PACIFIC: U.S. submarine *Porpoise* torpedoes and sinks a Japanese merchant cargo ship, and U.S. submarine *Trigger* damages a Japanese transport off the coast of Honshu, Japan.

NEW GUINEA: Urbana Force makes little progress in its attack toward Buna Mission; Warren Force surrounds Japanese defenders.

January 2

CBI: CATF (China Air Task Force) fighters attack a truck convoy on the Burma Road, destroying five trucks.

MEDITERRANEAN: B-25 Mitchells and B-24 Liberators of the Ninth Air Force attack airfields on Crete, destroying over 20 Axis aircraft. Twelfth Air Force B-17s bomb La Goulette harbor in Tunisia. Two escorting P-38 Lightnings are lost to German fighters. A-20 Havocs and Boston Mk IIIs, with fighter escorts, bomb Sousse harbor. B-26 Marauders with fighter escort bomb a bridge near El Djem.

PACIFIC: U.S. submarine *Argonaut* torpedoes and sinks a Japanese guardboat in the Bismarck Sea. U.S. submarine *Spearfish* damages a Japanese cargo ship off New Ireland.

GUADALCANAL: The army's American and 25th Infantry Divisions and units of the 2nd Marine Division are designated on Guadalcanal as XIV Corps with Major General Alexander M. Patch commanding. The 132nd Infantry Regiment overruns the Gifu defenses. The 25th Infantry Division and a portion of the 2nd Marine Division arrive on Guadalcanal. SBD Dauntless dive-bombers, F4F Wildcats, B-17s, B-26

Marauders, and P-38 Lightnings attack 10 Japanese destroyers carrying supplies to Guadalcanal. The SBDs damage a destroyer.

NEW GUINEA: Urbana Force captures Buna Mission; Warren Force completes clearing operations.

January 3

ETO: Eighth Air Force launches its heaviest attack on the St-Nazaire U-boat base. Although 85 B-17s and 13 B-24 Liberators begin the mission, only 60 B-17s and eight B-24s hit the target. Using formation precision bombing tactics for the first time, the bombers drop 171 tons of bombs, damaging the docks. The Germans lose approximately 14 aircraft; seven B-17s are lost, 51 B-17s and six B-24s are damaged. American casualties are 34 crewmen dead and wounded and 70 missing.

TUNISIA: An Axis tank and infantry attack breaks through French defenses at Fondouk. A-20 Havocs and Boston Mk IIIs of the Twelfth Air Force attack German tanks moving west from Fondouk, destroying several enemy vehicles.

American M3 Stuart tanks are employed against the Japanese Gifu stronghold on Guadalcanal.

January 4

CBI: Tenth Air Force bombers attack the railyard at Mandalay, causing heavy damage; a Japanese transport ship at the mouth of the Rangoon River is also damaged.

ATLANTIC: U.S. submarine *Shad* torpedoes and sinks a German minesweeper in Bay of Biscay.

GUADALCANAL: Japanese forces on Guadalcanal are ordered to move to New Georgia. The U.S. 132nd Infantry clears the Gifu area of resistance, suffering nearly 400 casualties in the dense jungle and hills. The Japanese reportedly have lost 500 men. The 161st RCT of the 25th Infantry Division arrives, as does the 6th Marine Regiment of the 2nd Marine Division.

January 5

MEDITERRANEAN: The U.S. Fifth Army is activated at Oujda, Morocco, under command of Lieutenant General Mark W. Clark. Lieutenant General Eisenhower creates Allied Air Force, under Lieutenant General Carl Spaatz. The command includes Twelfth Air Force, Eighth Air Force, and Eastern Air Command in the China-Burma-India Theater.

GUADALCANAL: Major General Patch orders the 25th Infantry Division, commanded by Major General J. Lawton Collins, to relieve the 132nd Infantry and attack west, supported on its right flank by the 2nd Marine Division.

NEW GEORGIA: Naval Task Group 67.2 under Rear Admiral Walden L. Ainsworth bombards Munda airfield on New Georgia Island.

January 6

ALEUTIANS: U.S. PBY Catalina sinks a Japanese cargo ship near Kiska; Eleventh Air Force B-24 Liberators sink a Japanese cargo ship off Holtz Bay.

ATLANTIC: A U.S. PBY-5A Catalina sinks German submarine *U-164* off Brazil.

January 7

NEW GUINEA: Fifth Air Force B-17s, B-24 Liberators, B-25 Mitchells, and B-26 Marauders, along with Australian and New Zealand air force aircraft, supported by U.S. P-38 Lightnings and P-40s, attack a Japanese convoy headed for Lae, New Guinea. One enemy cargo ship is sunk, but the convoy arrives at Lae.

January 8

CBI: Chiang Kai-shek notifies President Roosevelt that the Chinese army will not undertake offensive operations in spring of 1943.

ATLANTIC: German submarine *U-124* attacks the 12-ship convoy TB 1 (Trinidad to Bahia), torpedoing a U.S. tanker and freighter.

TUNISIA: Twelfth Air Force B-17s bomb the naval base at Bizerte. B-26 Marauders bomb Kairouan airfield. A-20 Havocs with P-40 escorts attack Axis tanks near Gabès.

NEW GUINEA: Troops of the 127th Infantry Regiment, 32nd Infantry Division capture Tarakena; the 163rd Infantry Regiment, 41st Infantry Division begins the advance on Sanananda. Fifth Air Force B-17s, B-24 Liberators, B-25 Mitchells, and A-20 Havocs, supported by P-38 Lightnings, attack the Japanese ships unloading at Lae.

January 9

ATLANTIC: German submarine *U-384* attacks and sinks U.S. freighter in the North Atlantic after a prolonged fight by the freighter's crew. German submarine *U-124* attacks convoy TB 1 (Trinidad to Bahia) again, torpedoing and sinking two U.S. freighters off Dutch Guiana.

PACIFIC: U.S. submarine *Gar* torpedoes and damages a Japanese oiler in the Makassar Strait, Netherlands East Indies; U.S. submarine *Nautilus* torpedoes and sinks a Japanese transport ship near Bougainville; U.S. submarine *Searaven* torpedoes and damages a Japanese cargo ship off the far northwest corner of New Guinea; U.S. submarine *Tautog* torpedoes and damages a Japanese light cruiser northeast of Timor.

January 10

TUNISIA: Twelfth Air Force B-26 Marauders, with P-38 Lightnings escorting, attack the railyard and oil storage tanks at Gabès.

GUADALCANAL: The U.S. 25th Infantry Division, after gaining control of the Gifu-Mt. Austen area, crosses the Matanikau River and ties in with the U.S. 2nd Marine Division. The U.S. 182nd and 132nd Infantry Regiments of the Americal Division support the XIV Corps advance. Japanese forces defend a collection of hills called Galloping Horse, Sea Horse, and the Gifu Strongpoint, employing a system of interlocked, heavily fortified bunkers supported by heavy artillery. Two battalions of the 27th Infantry Regiment of the 25th Infantry Division attack the hill complex, taking half of Galloping Horse, but are slowed by the steep terrain and Japanese defenses on Hill 53. Two battalions of the 35th Infantry Regiment of the 25th Infantry Division attack another hill mass called Sea Horse. Another battalion of the 35th continues to clear the Gifu area of enemy stragglers. The attacks are hampered by a lack of water resupply and formidable terrain. The 3rd Battalion, 35th Infantry attacks Sea Horse after calling for artillery fire. As K and L Companies moved forward to attack, K Company begins crossing a stream that is a branch of the Matanikau River. To protect the company's flank as it crosses the open area, two light machine guns from M Company are posted in an overwatch position along with a few riflemen. A sudden Japanese counterat-

A wounded soldier of the 25th Infantry Division receives first aid in the Guadalcanal jungle while litter bearers stand by, January 10, 1943.

tack hits the overwatch position, destroying one machine gun and killing and wounding the crew of the second machine gun. The riflemen are driven off, leaving the company exposed to a devastating attack when they are most vulnerable as they cross the river. Although ordered to withdraw, Sergeant William G. Fournier, the machine gun section leader, and Technical Sergeant/5 Lewis Hall of M Company charge up to the unmanned machine gun and begin firing on the Japanese, who are moving along the stream bed. Because the machine gun cannot be depressed low enough to fire on the enemy, Sergeant Fournier lifts it by its tripod while Hall fires the gun. Standing completely exposed to the enemy, Fournier and Hall continue to fire on the Japanese until both men are mortally wounded. The enemy withdraws and the company is saved. For their singular act of heroism Sergeant Fournier and Technical Sergeant/5 Hall will receive the Medal of Honor.

January 11

MEDITERRANEAN: Ninth Air Force B-24 Liberators bomb Naples harbor.

PACIFIC: U.S. submarine *Trigger* torpedoes and sinks a Japanese destroyer off Honshu. U.S. submarine *Trout* torpedoes and damages a Japanese oiler off Borneo.

GUADALCANAL: The Sea Horse area is under American control. Eight Japanese destroyers off Cape Esperance, Guadalcanal, are attacked by nine U.S. motor torpedo boats from Tulagi. A Japanese destroyer and a U.S. PT boat are damaged; one PT boat is sunk.

January 12

GUADALCANAL: Captain Charles W. Davis is the battalion executive officer of 2nd Battalion, 27th Infantry Regiment, 25th Infantry Division, facing Japanese defenders defending the ridge between Hills 52 and 53 on Guadalcanal. He volunteers to carry instructions to the battalion's forward companies now trapped in a crossfire from Japanese machine guns. He remains with the companies all day and throughout the night. The following day he leads an assault on the Japanese position. As he moves forward, his rifle jams, but he draws his .45 caliber automatic pistol and leads the men forward. Inspired by his heroic example, the soldiers seize the hill. For his decisive leadership and heroic example in the face of a determined enemy, Captain Davis will receive the Medal of Honor.

New Georgia: SOPAC B-26 Marauders, P-38 Lightnings, P-39 Airacobras, and P-40s attack Munda. Two B-26s are lost.

January 13

Atlantic: U.S. PBY-5A Catalinas sink German submarine *U-507* off Brazil.

ETO: Eighth Air Force sends 72 B-17s against industrial targets at Lille, France, dropping 125 tons of bombs and damaging the locomotive construction and repair works at the cost of three B-17s. At least three German aircraft are destroyed and five damaged in the raid.

South Pacific: Major General Millard F. Harmon, commander of U.S. Army forces in the South Pacific Area (COMGENSOPAC), establishes the Thirteenth Air Force, under the command of Brigadier General Nathan F. Twining, with headquarters at Espiritu Santo Island, New Hebrides. The Thirteenth Air Force takes operational control of all U.S. Army Air Forces in the Southern Pacific, except for Army Air Force units on Guadalcanal, which are under the operational control of the Marine Corps.

U.S. submarine *Whale* torpedoes and sinks a Japanese collier north of Kwajalein; U.S. submarine *Triton* damages a Japanese oiler north of New Ireland.

Guadalcanal: Galloping Horse falls to the 25th Infantry Division, supported by massed artillery fire. The 2nd Marine Division begins its advance along the coast past Point Cruz, eliminating enemy positions with flamethrowers, and supported by naval gunfire, artillery, and tanks. The Gifu strongpoint still holds out. American infantrymen suffer from a lack of water in the thick jungle terrain.

New Guinea: Fifth Air Force A-20 Havocs provide ground support to Allied forces near Sanananda. Bombers attack docks and airfields at both Lae and Salamaua.

January 14

Mediterranean: The Casablanca Conference. The Casablanca conference to outline Allied strategy for 1943 begins. This is the first great Allied wartime conference. President Franklin D. Roosevelt, Prime Minister Winston S. Churchill, the military chiefs of staff of both Britain and the United States, and the French leaders General Henri Giraud and Charles de Gaulle, leader of the French government-in-exile in Britain. Roosevelt arrives in secret and is the first American president to visit Africa while in office.

Tunisia: Twelfth Air Force B-17s, with 17 P-38 Lightnings providing escort, bomb enemy shipping and the harbor facilities at Sfax.

Pacific: U.S. submarine *Searaven* attacks a Japanese convoy northwest of the Palaus, sinking the escort vessel and a cargo ship.

Guadalcanal: Thirteenth Air Force P-39 Airacobras drop improvised gasoline bombs on the Japanese defenders near Mount Austen and defending at Kokumbona.

January 15

CBI: Tenth Air Force B-24 Liberators attack a Japanese convoy off the coast of Burma, sinking one cargo ship and damaging another. The cargo ship was moving Allied prisoners, and 500 men perish.

SOUTH PACIFIC: Navy SBD Dauntless dive-bombers, escorted by F4F Wildcats and P-39 Airocobras, attack a Japanese cargo ship off Munda, New Georgia. Seven enemy aircraft are shot down; one American fighter is lost. B-17s and PBY Catalinas bomb Kahili, Bougainville Island. B-24 Liberators bomb the airfield on Gasmata Island in the Bismarck Archipelago.

GUADALCANAL: The 2nd Marine Division makes little progress against Japanese defenses along the coast of Guadalcanal. SBD Dauntless dive-bombers from Henderson Field, with F4F Wildcats and P-39 Airacobras escorting, attack nine Japanese destroyers and pilots report four ships damaged. Eight enemy aircraft are shot down, but one SBD and five fighters are lost.

NEW GUINEA: Fifth Air Force A-20s provide support to the U.S. 163rd Infantry Regiment at Sanananda. B-25 Mitchells attack Japanese supply points at Lae.

January 16

CBI: Tenth Air Force China Air Task Force (CATF) P-40s intercept a Japanese attack on Yunnani. Pilots report that seven enemy aircraft are shot down.

SOUTH PACIFIC: Thirteenth Air Force B-17s bomb the Kahili airfield on Bougainville Island. U.S. submarine *Greenling* torpedoes and sinks a Japanese transport west of Kavieng, New Ireland; U.S. submarine *Growler* attacks a Japanese convoy, torpedoing a cargo ship north of Kavieng.

GUADALCANAL: Major General Alexander M. Patch, commander of XIV Corps, creates a composite unit, combining the 6th Marines, the 2nd Marine Division, and the 182nd and 147th Infantry Regiments, along with the Americal Division artillery, into an army-marine division known as CAM. This unit is to advance along the coast, while the 25th Infantry Division on CAM's flank attempts to clear Japanese defensive positions to the south and west, then drive north to encircle the enemy.

NEW GUINEA: The attack on Sanananda begins. The U.S. 163rd Infantry Regiment clears Japanese strongpoints in coordination with the Australian 18th Brigade. Fifth Air Force A-20 Havocs provide air support for the attack.

January 17

CBI: Tenth Air Force B-25 Mitchells bomb railroad targets in Burma.

MEDITERRANEAN: Ninth Air Force B-24 Liberators bomb Tripoli harbor in Libya. P-40s support the British Eighth Army's advance toward Tripoli.

PACIFIC: U.S. submarine *Finback* attacks and damages a Japanese cargo ship off southern Kyushu, Japan; U.S. submarine *Whale* damages a Japanese troopship near Truk. Fifth Air Force B-17s bomb Japanese airfields and shipping at Rabaul.

GUADALCANAL: Thirteenth Air Force P-39 Airacobras attack Japanese defenses near Mount Austen. B-17s from Henderson Field drop supplies, including much needed water, by parachute or by simply wrapping ammunition and food in burlap or canvas and dropping them out of the aircraft.

January 18

ALEUTIANS: Eleventh Air Force B-24 Liberators and B-26 Marauders, one B-25 Mitchell, and six P-38 Lightnings attempt a bombing run on Japanese ships reported at Kiska harbor. The attack scores no hits, but bad weather leads to six aircraft lost, including three B-24s. One B-24 crew will later be rescued.

SOUTHWEST PACIFIC AREA: A U.S. tanker is torpedoed and damaged by Japanese submarine *I-21* off the coast of southern Australia.

PACIFIC: U.S. submarine *Greenling* damages a Japanese ammunition ship north of Kavieng. U.S. submarine *Silversides* torpedoes and sinks a Japanese fleet tanker near Truk.

GUADALCANAL: The CAM Division advances 1,500 yards beyond Point Cruz.

January 19

CBI: Tenth Air Force P-40s and one B-25 Mitchell attack Japanese positions at Kamaing.

TUNISIA: Ninth Air Force B-24 Liberators bomb the harbor at Sousse; Twelfth Air Force B-17s, with P-38 Lightnings providing cover, bomb industrial targets south of Tunis. B-25 Mitchells attack Medenine. U.S. and British forces, including Combat Command B of the 1st Armored Division, move to reinforce French forces hard-pressed by an Axis attack in the Rebaa Valley.

SOUTHWEST PACIFIC AREA: U.S. submarine *Greenling* damages a Japanese cargo ship north of Rabaul.

PACIFIC: U.S. submarine *Swordfish* near Truk attacks a Japanese convoy headed for the Solomons and sinks a cargo ship. U.S. submarine *Haddock* attacks a Japanese convoy off southern Honshu, Japan, and damages a transport. U.S. submarine *Nautilus* damages a Japanese destroyer in the vicinity of Tulagi. U.S. submarine *Spearfish* is attacked and damaged by Japanese aircraft near the Gilberts while headed for Pearl Harbor.

NEW GEORGIA: Thirteenth Air Force B-17s with P-38 Lightnings and P-40s flying escort bomb the airfield at Munda, New Georgia.

NEW GUINEA: Japanese forces begin to withdraw from Sanananda. Pockets of resistance on the Soputa-Sanananda trail hold up the 163rd Infantry Regiment.

January 20

MEDITERRANEAN: Twelfth Air Force B-25 Mitchells, escorted by P-38 Lightnings, attack Axis ships in the Straits of Sicily and sink a tanker.

PACIFIC: U.S. submarine *Silversides* south of Truk attacks a Japanese convoy headed for the Solomons, torpedoing and sinking one transport ship and damaging another.

January 21

TUNISIA: Twelfth Air Force B-26 Marauders attack Axis shipping off Cape Bon, sinking a freighter and damaging another. Escorting P-38 Lightnings lose two aircraft while destroying five enemy aircraft. A-20s supporting Combat Command B of the U.S. 1st Armored Division attack enemy tanks and trucks near Ousseltia; P-38s attack Axis ground forces moving on the Gabès-Medenine-Ben Gardane road, destroying 65 vehicles and two enemy fighters.

SOUTHWEST PACIFIC AREA: Fifth Air Force B-17s bomb the airfield and shipping at Rabaul.

SOUTH PACIFIC: U.S. submarine *Gato* off Bougainville Island attacks a portion of the Japanese convoy headed for the Solomons, damaging a transport ship. Thirteenth Air Force transfers its headquarters from Nouméa, New Caledonia, to Espiritu Santo in the New Hebrides.

GUADALCANAL: Marine tanks support the army's 2nd Battalion, 35th Infantry Regiment in clearing Japanese positions at Gifu.

January 22

TUNISIA: Twelfth Air Force B-17s bomb El Aouina airfield, followed later by B-26 Marauders and B-25 Mitchells. P-39 Airacrobras and P-40s support the Allied attack in the Ousseltia Valley, which is stopped by strong enemy defenses. B-26s damage an Axis cargo ship in the Straits of Sicily.

GUADALCANAL: The CAM Division advances toward Kokumbona, making contact with U.S. 27th Infantry Regiment of the 25th Infantry Division coming from the south. U.S. freighter is torpedoed and damaged by Japanese submarine *I-21* off the southern coast of Australia, near Sidney.

NEW GUINEA: Sanananda, the final remaining position of the Japanese in Papua, is captured. The U.S. 163rd Infantry Regiment, 41st Infantry Division participates, with elements of the 32nd Infantry Division. The Japanese have been without food or ammunition for several weeks and can no longer mount serious resistance. The campaign has cost the Australians nearly 5,700 killed and wounded; the Americans suffered nearly 2,900 casualties. Over 27,000 cases of malaria have been reported. The 126th Infantry Regiment began the campaign with 131 officers and 3,040 enlisted men. When it is over, only 32 officers and 579 men can report for duty. Lacking training and experience, the U.S. Army has paid heavily in combat but gained important lessons that will bring success in the future.

January 23

ATLANTIC: German submarine *U-175* torpedoes and sinks a U.S. freighter off Liberia.

ETO: Eighth Air Force B-17s bomb the port of Lorient and the U-boat base at Brest, France. The attack on Lorient has 35 B-17s, which drop 86 tons of bombs on the target. Five of the bombers are lost. The U-boat base is raided by 19 B-17s; 45 tons of bombs are dropped on the target.

MEDITERRANEAN: The Casablanca conference is concluded. The U.S. Joint Staff planners find themselves outmaneuvered and outclassed in every way by their British staff counterparts, who have a clear political-military strategy. The Americans, plagued by a lack of consensus both within the military services and among the political leadership, find themselves following the British proposals for an overall strategic concept of the Allies in the prosecution of the war and specific tasks for the Allied forces against Axis forces in Europe and Asia. Major General Albert C. Wedemeyer, the chief army planner at the Casablanca meetings, will later say "We lost our shirts." He also wryly observed, "One might say we came, we listened and we were conquered." The Americans, angered and embarrassed by the lack of basic political-military coordination that is essential to any successful wartime activity, vow not to be caught short again. Overall, the British are able to implement their peripheral strategy focused on the Mediterranean and avoiding a commitment to a cross-Channel invasion. Giraud and de Gaulle refuse to cooperate with each other, but issue an empty statement, largely to placate the British and the Americans: "We have met. We have talked. We have registered our entire agreement on the end to be achieved, which is the liberation of France. . . . This end will be attained by a union in war of all Frenchmen."

The conference produces the following guidance:

The overall goal of the Allies is to force an unconditional surrender of the Axis powers in Europe while simultaneously maintaining pressure against Japan to reduce its military power and attain positions to force Japan's unconditional surrender at some time in the future.

In the Atlantic, the Allies are to secure the lines of communication by defeating the U-boat threat and other threats to sea communications. The Allies will conduct a full-scale assault from the United Kingdom against the European continent in the spring of 1944. Concurrently, the Allies will conduct a vigorous air offensive to reduce Germany's war potential and to make the cross-Channel attack feasible. The U.S. VIII Bomber Command and RAF Bomber Command are tasked to destroy submarine construction yards, aircraft production facilities, transportation centers, and oil production facilities. The appropriate forces to conduct the invasion will be built up in the United Kingdom.

In the Mediterranean, the Allies will accomplish Husky, the invasion of Sicily in June or July of 1943. After Husky, the Allies will conduct limited offensive operations intended to destroy Italian war potential by continuing air attacks from Mediterranean bases. The intent is to support the diversion of Axis forces and materials away from the USSR, while dispersing other Axis forces in France to facilitate a cross-Channel operation and maintain secure lines of communication in the Mediterranean. The strength of the forces to be employed in the Mediterranean will be limited so that priority of effort is directed to preparations for the cross-Channel invasion in 1944.

In the Pacific and Far East, the Allies will protect the lines of communication to Australia, maintain pressure on Japan, retain the initiative in preparation for a future full-scale offensive against Japan, and keep China in the war. Offensive operations in the Pacific and Far East in 1943–44 will have the following objectives: conduct air operations in and from China; gain control of Burma; drive the Japanese from the Aleutian Islands; seize the Marshall and Caroline Islands; seize the Solomons, the Bismarck Archipelago, and the Japanese-held areas of New Guinea. The Allies will also to the greatest extent possible, continue to sustain Soviet and Chinese forces, while also supporting the French forces in Northwest Africa.

General Joseph Stilwell's proposal for an offensive from India into Burma with three Chinese divisions, while 30 Chinese divisions attack from China westward, is favored by the U.S. Joint Chiefs of Staff; the British are not impressed. Political unrest in India and a lack of capability to conduct a sustained offensive in Burma lead to the plan collapsing later in the year. Instead, Major General Claire Chennault proposes airpower as the solution, offering a cheap and decisive effect on the Japanese in Burma and China. Both President Roosevelt and Generalissimo Chiang like the idea; although Stilwell thought it nonsense, the Tenth Air Force will be given the opportunity to prove itself.

Ninth Air Force B-24 Liberators bomb Palermo harbor in Sicily; P-40s fly support missions for British ground forces as the Eighth Army captures Tripoli.

TUNISIA: Twelfth Air Force B-17s bomb Bizerte naval base and are opposed by as many as 100 enemy fighters. The escorting P-38 Lightnings claim 20 enemy aircraft destroyed. The P-38s suffer six casualties. A-20 Havocs and P-40s support U.S. forces near Ousseltia.

SOUTHWEST PACIFIC AREA: U.S. submarine *Guardfish* torpedoes and sinks a Japanese destroyer near Kavieng, New Ireland.

GUADALCANAL: U.S. XIV Corps at Guadalcanal captures Kokumbona; after a Japanese night attack fails, U.S. forces eliminate the last defenders at Gifu.

January 24

CBI: Tenth Air Force B-24 Liberators attack the port facilities at Rangoon, Burma. P-40s attack Japanese ammunition storage base at Shaduzup, Burma.

TUNISIA: Ninth Air Force B-24 Liberators attack Medenine airfield. Twelfth Air Force B-25 Mitchells and B-26 Marauders also make sequential attacks on Medenine airfield. B-17s bomb ships in Sousse harbor. Combat Command B of U.S. 1st Armored Division, supported by infantry from the U.S. 1st Infantry Division, advances to clear enemy defenders from Ousseltia Valley.

SOUTHWEST PACIFIC AREA: Fifth Air Force B-17s bomb the airfield and harbor at Rabaul.

SOUTH PACIFIC: B-24 Liberators attack the airfield at Cape Gloucester, New Britain.

GUADALCANAL: The CAM Division reaches Kokumbona and begins movement to Cape Esperance.

NEW GUINEA: B-25 Mitchells hit supply areas at Lae. U.S. submarine *Wahoo* damages a Japanese destroyer in the waters off Wewak.

January 25

ATLANTIC: German submarine *U-575* torpedoes and sinks a U.S. freighter from convoy UGS 4 (United States to Mediterranean, Slow) south of the Azores.

GUADALCANAL: The U.S. XIV Corps begins to pursue retreating Japanese over the Poha River.

January 26

CBI: The first elements of Detachment 101 parachute behind Japanese lines in northern Burma to establish a guerrilla force of Kachins, the ethnic group that lives in the region and is hostile to Japanese occupation. Detachment 101 is commanded by Captain (later Colonel) William R. Peers.

SOUTHWEST PACIFIC AREA: U.S. submarine *Grayling* torpedoes and sinks a Japanese cargo ship near Mindoro, Philippines. U.S. submarine *Wahoo* attacks Japanese convoy off the northwestern coast of New Guinea, torpedoing and sinking two cargo ships. The submarine then surfaces and attacks other ships in the convoy.

PACIFIC: U.S. submarine *Flying Fish* damages a Japanese transport at Port Apra, Guam.

January 27
ATLANTIC: A U.S. freighter from Charleston, South Carolina, sailing to Sierra Leone, is torpedoed and sunk by German submarine *U-105* in the waters north of Puerto Rico. An armed U.S. freighter from convoy UGS 4 (United States to Mediterranean, Slow) is torpedoed by German submarine *U-514* southwest of the Azores, but fires on her attacker when the submarine surfaces nearby. The U-boat makes a hasty retreat from the accurate fire.

ETO: Eighth Air Force makes its first bombing raid on Germany. The Wilhelmshaven naval base is attacked by 53 B-17s dropping 137 tons of bombs on the target. Over 20 enemy aircraft are destroyed or damaged.

MEDITERRANEAN: Ninth Air Force B-24 Liberators bomb Naples and Messina. Twelfth Air Force B-25 Mitchells bomb two Axis warships off the coast of Algeria, damaging one destroyer.

NEW GUINEA: Fifth Air Force B-24 Liberators bomb Finschhafen.

January 28
CBI: General Stilwell reaches an agreement with the Chinese political and military leadership on the outlines of the program to train and equip 30 Chinese divisions.

ATLANTIC: German submarine *U-514* succeeds in sinking the freighter it has pursued. The survivors are questioned and released. German submarine *U-442* torpedoes and sinks another U.S. freighter from convoy UGS 4 south of the Azores.

TUNISIA: Twelfth Air Force B-17s, B-25 Mitchells, and B-26 Marauders, escorted by P-38 Lightnings, attack the harbor, shipping, and railyards at Sfax. P-40s fly missions against Axis defenders in the Ousseltia Valley.

NEW GUINEA: Fifth Air Force A-20 Havocs bomb Garrison Hill and B-17s bomb Wewak area. B-24 Liberators bomb Salamaua.

January 29
ATLANTIC: Mrs. Ruth Cheney Streeter is commissioned a major and designated as director of the Marine Corps Women's Reserve (MCWR).

TUNISIA: Twelfth Air Force B-17s attack the port facilities at Bizerte; B-26 Marauders bomb El Aouina airfield.

SOUTH PACIFIC: U.S. submarine *Gato* torpedoes and sinks a Japanese cargo ship off Bougainville, Solomons. Japanese aircraft attack U.S. cruisers and destroyers near Rennell Island, protecting a convoy headed for Guadalcanal. One heavy cruiser is damaged.

GUADALCANAL: U.S. XIV Corps at Guadalcanal continues drive toward Cape Esperance.

January 30
ATLANTIC: Grossadmiral Karl Dönitz is named Commander in Chief of the Kriegsmarine.

TUNISIA: German forces attack and seize Faid Pass. Units of the 1st Armored Division along with the 168th RCT of the 34th Infantry Division begin movement toward Maknasy.

Twelfth Air Force B-17s bomb the port facilities at Ferryville; B-25 Mitchells attack rail lines and storage facilities El Aouinet; A-20 Havocs support Allied ground forces near El Guettar.

SOUTH PACIFIC: Japanese continue the attack on the U.S. task group near Rennell Island, sinking the heavy cruiser damaged in the attack of the previous day, and damaging a destroyer. Japanese submarine *I-10* torpedoes and sinks U.S. freighter off New Caledonia.

GUADALCANAL: The U.S. 147th Infantry Regiment advances against Japanese troops attempting to cover the retreat to Cape Esperance.

NEW GEORGIA: Thirteenth Air Force B-17s and B-26 Marauders, escorted by P-39 Airacobras and P-40s, bomb Japanese antiaircraft defenses and the airfield at Munda, New Georgia.

January 31

CBI: C-46 Commando cargo aircraft prove unreliable for flying over the Hump, forcing many crewmen to abandon their aircraft and parachute into the jungle. Detachment 101 rescues more than 100 of them.

ATLANTIC: U-boats have sunk 37 ships (a total of 203,128 tons of shipping) in January. At present, 37 U-boats are near Greenland, 11 are northwest of the Azores, and 25 are south of the Azores and patrolling the west coast of Africa. Another 27 U-boats are in transit either to or from Atlantic patrol.

MEDITERRANEAN: Lieutenant General Lewis H. Brereton, commander of the Ninth Air Force, takes command of U.S. Army Forces in the Middle East (USAFIME) from Lieutenant General Frank M. Andrews. Lieutenant General Andrews will take command of U.S. forces in the ETO.

TUNISIA: Combat Command B of the U.S. 1st Armored Division attacks Faid Pass without success. Twelfth Air Force B-26 Marauders attack the Gabès airfield; B-17s bomb the port facilities at Bizerte.

NEW GEORGIA: Marine SBD Dauntless dive-bombers, F4F Wildcats, and Thirteenth Air Force P-39 Airacobras from Henderson Field sink a Japanese transport between the islands of Vella Lavella and Kolombangara in New Georgia. Off Kolombangara Island, First Lieutenant Jefferson DeBlanc is the leader of a section of six fighters escorting the dive-bombers and TBF Avenger torpedo bombers attacking the Japanese ships. When a large number of enemy fighters arrive to protect the ships, First Lieutenant DeBlanc engages the enemy aircraft and then quickly moves down to 1,000 feet to protect the dive-bombers and torpedo bombers under attack by enemy floatplanes. He provides cover so that the bombers can complete their runs on the targets. DeBlanc remains behind to continue fighting the enemy, scoring five kills, until, low on fuel and ammunition and his plane no longer airworthy, he bails out at tree-top level over Kolombangara. First Lieutenant DeBlanc's extraordinary skills and his courage and ferocity in combat will win him the Medal of Honor.

February 1

CBI: The Allies open a conference at New Delhi to develop a campaign plan for the reconquest of Burma and to open a land supply route to China. The operation, scheduled to begin in November of 1943, is code named Anakim.

TUNISIA: U.S. Combat Command A of 1st Armored Division attacks Faid, but fails to drive defenders from the town. Combat Command D of 1st Armored Division, supported by 1st Battalion 168th Infantry of the 34th Infantry Division, captures Sened Station. Twelfth Air Force B-17s bomb Tunis harbor. A-20 Havocs and P-40s bomb enemy troop concentrations.

SOUTHWEST PACIFIC AREA: Fifth Air Force B-17s bomb the airfield at Rabaul.

PACIFIC: U.S. submarine *Tarpon* torpedoes and sinks a Japanese cargo ship off the southern coast of Japan.

GUADALCANAL: Japanese destroyers take aboard 2,300 Japanese soldiers at Cape Esperance, evacuating the island secretly by night. The 2nd Battalion of the 132nd Infantry Regiment lands at Verahue in an attempt to cut off Japanese forces. One U.S. destroyer is sunk by Japanese air attack south of Savo Island.

February 2

ATLANTIC: German submarine *U-456* attacks convoy HX 224 (New York to Liverpool) in the North Atlantic and torpedoes a U.S. freighter, which is later abandoned and scuttled.

TUNISIA: Combat Command D of the U.S. 1st Armored Division stops an Axis counterattack east of Sened. Twelfth Air Force P-40s and P-39s fly missions to provide support to the ground forces. B-25 Mitchells and B-26 Marauders bomb an airfield at Sfax.

February 3

ATLANTIC: German submarine *U-223* attacks convoy SG 19 (Sydney or St. Johns, Newfoundland to Greenland) off Greenland, torpedoing and sinking one transport and damaging a Norwegian freighter. The transport sinks with 675 men on board. Among them are four army chaplains, representing four different faiths, who offer their life preservers to other soldiers, sacrificing their lives to save others.

German submarine *U-255* attacks a convoy northeast of Iceland, torpedoing and sinking a U.S. freighter.

PACIFIC: U.S. submarine *Tunny* torpedoes and damages a Japanese army transport ship in the South China Sea.

February 4

ALEUTIANS: Eleventh Air Force B-17s, B-24 Liberators, and B-25 Mitchells escorted by P-38 Lightnings and P-40s attack Japanese installations. Five Japanese bombers conduct a strike on Amchitka.

CBI: Tenth Air Force B-25 Mitchells and B-24 Liberators bomb the Myitnge bridge and railway facilities, located south of Mandalay. The bridge is not damaged.

ATLANTIC: German submarines attack convoy SC 118 (Halifax Slow to United Kingdom) in the North Atlantic, but are driven off. British destroyers sink German submarine *U-187*.

ETO: Eighth Air Force B-17s, diverted from the Hamm marshaling yard because of weather conditions, bomb the port and industrial sites at Emden, Germany. The bombers encounter German Ju-88 Junkers and Me-110 Messerschmitt twin-engine fighters for the first time. The fighters shoot down five of the 39 B-17s involved in the raid. Enemy losses are estimated at eight fighters destroyed.

MEDITERRANEAN: At Algiers, Lieutenant General Eisenhower takes command of the newly designated headquarters, North African Theater of Operations (NATOUSA). The boundary of NATOUSA includes Spain and Italy. Eisenhower is commander in chief, North Africa. The command of the European Theater of Operations (ETO) passes from Eisenhower to Lieutenant General Frank M. Andrews.

PACIFIC: U.S. submarine *Tunny* torpedoes and damages a Japanese transport in the South China Sea.

SOUTH PACIFIC: Thirteenth Air Force SBD Dauntless dive-bombers and TBF Avenger torpedo bombers damage four Japanese destroyers attempting to evacuate Japanese ground forces from Guadalcanal. U.S. losses are three F4F Wildcats, three SBDs, four TBFs, and one P-40.

February 5

CBI: Tenth Air Force B-25 Mitchells attack the Myitnge bridge, but fail to destroy it.

ATLANTIC: German submarine *U-413* torpedoes and sinks a U.S. freighter in the North Atlantic that is unable to keep up with convoy SC 118.

SOUTHWEST PACIFIC AREA: Fifth Air Force B-17s bomb Rabaul airfield; A-20 Havocs provide ground support to Allied forces in New Guinea.

February 6

ATLANTIC: A U.S. destroyer drives off three U-boats attempting to attack convoy SC 118.

February 7

ATLANTIC: A U.S. Coast Guard cutter escorting convoy SC 118 initially drives off German submarine *U-402*, but the U-boat later torpedoes and sinks a U.S. tanker and a U.S. passenger ship.

In the South Atlantic, German submarine *U-160* torpedoes and sinks a U.S. freighter headed to Brazil.

MEDITERRANEAN: Ninth Air Force B-24 Liberators bomb Naples harbor; Twelfth Air Force B-17s and B-26 Marauders bomb an airfield and a seaplane base in Sardinia.

SOUTHWEST PACIFIC AREA: U.S. submarine *Growler* rams a Japanese storeship northwest of Rabaul while making a night surface attack. *Growler,* with 18 feet of its bow bent sideways, comes under heavy Japanese fire. On the bridge, the submarine's commanding officer, Commander Howard W. Gilmore, makes an immediate decision. Although wounded, he orders the bridge cleared, and then gives the command, "Take her down!" He sacrifices himself to save his ship, and for this act of extraordinary gallantry, Commander Gilmore will receive the Medal of Honor.

GUADALCANAL: The last elements of the Japanese rear guard are evacuated from Guadalcanal. About 13,000 Japanese soldiers escape to fight another day.

February 8
ALEUTIANS: Eleventh Air Force B-24 Liberators and B-25 Mitchells bomb the Japanese base at Kiska.
CBI: Tenth Air Force B-24 Liberators of the India Air Task Force bomb the marshaling yard at Rangoon.
ATLANTIC: German submarine *U-608* makes an unsuccessful torpedo attack on a U.S. destroyer escorting convoy SC 118 (Halifax Slow to United Kingdom).
TUNISIA: Twelfth Air Force B-17s bomb the docks and shipping at the port of Sousse; B-26 Marauders and B-25 Mitchells bomb the airfield marshaling yard at Gabès. A-20 Havocs bomb enemy troops near Faid.
PACIFIC: U.S. submarine *Tunny* torpedoes and sinks a Japanese merchant ship southwest of Formosa.

February 9
ATLANTIC: After five days of running battle, convoy SC 118 (Halifax Slow to United Kingdom), with 63 ships, 10 escort ships, and land-based air cover, overcomes the constant attack of 20 U-boats. The losses are severe on both sides: three U-boats are sunk and two are damaged. The convoy suffers the loss of 13 ships.
PACIFIC: U.S. submarine *Tarpon* torpedoes and sinks a Japanese transport off the southeast coast of Japan.
GUADALCANAL: Guadalcanal is secured. The campaign has cost the United States nearly 1,600 killed and over 4,000 wounded. The Japanese have suffered approximately 25,000 men lost, including 600 aircraft. The epic land, air, and sea battle forces the Japanese to consolidate their gains while conceding the strategic initiative to the Americans. American losses in ships and planes can be rapidly replaced, but the Japanese cannot replace these critical combat assets.

February 10
ALEUTIANS: Eleventh Air Force B-17s, B-24 Liberators, and B-25 Mitchells, escorted by eight P-38 Lightnings, attack the airfield on Kiska Island.
ATLANTIC: B-24 Liberators of the 2nd Antisubmarine Squadron, attached to the 1st Antisubmarine Group (Provisional), sink German submarine *U-519* northwest of Spain.
SOUTHWEST PACIFIC AREA: Japanese submarine *I-21* torpedoes and damages U.S. freighter near Sidney, Australia. The freighter will sink while being towed to port.
PACIFIC: U.S. submarine *Pickerel* torpedoes and sinks a Japanese cargo ship off the western shore of Hokkaido, Japan.

February 11
SOUTHWEST PACIFIC AREA: U.S. submarine *Grayling* torpedoes and damages a Japanese army cargo ship off Corregidor.
SOUTH PACIFIC: U.S. destroyer sinks Japanese submarine *I-18* in the Coral Sea.
NEW GEORGIA: Thirteenth Air Force B-26 Marauders, P-38 Lightnings, and P-39 Airacobras bomb the Munda airfields on New Georgia Island and Vila airfield on Kolombangara Island, Solomons.

February 12

CBI: Tenth Air Force B-24 Liberators of the India Air Task Force use 2,000-pound blockbusters bombs in an attempt to destroy the Myitnge bridge. Twelve other B-24s bomb the marshaling yard at Rangoon.

ATLANTIC: The official statement of the Casablanca Conference (January 14–23) is issued. It says in part:

> In an attempt to ward off the inevitable disaster, the Axis propagandists are trying all of their old tricks in order to divide the United Nations. They seek to create the idea that if we win this war, Russia, England, China, and the United States are going to get into a cat-and-dog fight. This is their final effort to turn one nation against another, in the vain hope that they may settle with one or two at a time—that any of us may be so gullible and so forgetful as to be duped into making "deals" at the expense of our Allies.
>
> To these panicky attempts to escape the consequences of their crimes we say—all the United Nations say—that the only terms on which we shall deal with an Axis government or any Axis factions are the terms proclaimed at Casablanca: "Unconditional Surrender." In our uncompromising policy we mean no harm to the common people of the Axis nations. But we do mean to impose punishment and retribution in full upon their guilty, barbaric leaders . . .

SOUTHWEST PACIFIC AREA: SWPA headquarters drafts plans for an attack on New Britain and New Guinea, codenamed Elkton.

February 13

ALEUTIANS: Eleventh Air Force bombers, escorted by 10 P-38 Lightnings, attack facilities at Kiska.

TUNISIA: Twelfth Air Force B-26 Marauder bombers attack the airfield at El Aouina. Fighters escorting the B-26s strafe targets of opportunity around Sened Station and Faid.

February 14

TUNISIA: Axis offensive in the Faid-Sidi Bou Zid sector isolates the 168th RCT of the U.S. 34th Division. Combat Command A of the U.S. 1st Armored Division counterattacks to attempt to restore the line. The 168th is almost eliminated as an effective unit.

SOUTHWEST PACIFIC AREA: U.S. submarine *Thresher* torpedoes and damages Japanese submarine *I-62* off the Lesser Sunda Islands. U.S. submarine *Trout* sinks a Japanese gunboat at south entrance to Makassar Strait after a surface gun battle, which wounds several U.S. sailors.

SOUTH PACIFIC: After the loss of eight P-38 Lightnings, three B-24 Liberators, two PB4Y Privateers (a B-24 variant), two P-40s, and two F4U Corsairs to Japanese defenses in the Bougainville area in the space of two days, Thirteenth Air Force calls off all daylight bombing missions in the northern Solomons until adequate fighter cover is available.

NEW BRITAIN: Fifth Air Force B-17s and B-24 Liberators bomb Japanese facilities at Rabaul.

U.S. submarine *Amberjack* is probably sunk by Japanese naval aircraft and surface vessels off New Britain.

February 15

ALEUTIANS: Six Japanese aircraft attack the runway on Amchitka Island.

ATLANTIC: German submarine *U-607* torpedoes and sinks a U.S. tanker separated from convoy ON 165 (Liverpool to New York, fast) in the North Atlantic.

ETO: Eighth Air Force B-24 Liberators bomb the port and shipping at Dunkirk, France. Two of 23 B-24s are lost.

MEDITERRANEAN: A portion of Ninth Air Force is designated the Desert Air Task Force (DATF). Commanded by Brigadier General Auby C. Strickland, the DATF's headquarters is established in Tripoli, Libya. Twelfth Air Force B-17s bomb the harbor and ships at Palermo, Sicily.

TUNISIA: Combat Command C of the U.S. 1st Armored Division with British armored infantry in support counterattacks at Sidi Bou Zid, suffering heavy tank losses. Axis forces capture the remnants of the 168th RCT. Twelfth Air Force B-25 Mitchells and B-26 Marauders bomb the airfield at Kairouan. Fighters provide ground support to Allied forces, and the air base at Sbeitla is evacuated as German forces advance.

PACIFIC: U.S. submarine *Pickerel* attacks a Japanese convoy off the east coast of Honshu, Japan, and sinks a cargo ship.

SOUTH PACIFIC: Thirteenth Air Force B-26 Marauders, P-39 Airacobras, and P-40s attack the airfield on Kolombangara Island. B-24 Liberators attack the airfields at Bougainville and Ballale Islands. Two B-24s are lost.

U.S. submarine *Gato* torpedoes and sinks a Japanese ship in Bougainville Strait.

February 16

ATLANTIC: A U.S. freighter is torpedoed by German submarine *U-607* off Port Elizabeth, South Africa, and later sinks.

ETO: Eighth Air Force B-17s and B-24 Liberators bomb the U-boat base at St-Nazaire, France. Six of 71 B-17s and two of 18 B-24 Liberators participating in the raid are lost; 28 B-17s and two B-24s are damaged. It is estimated that over 30 German aircraft are shot down.

TUNISIA: U.S. II Corps commander Major General Fredendall orders the 1st Armored Division to hold at Sbeitla for as long as possible to buy time for U.S. troops defending Kasserine Pass. U.S. tank losses mount under heavy enemy pressure. Germans advance past Gafsa and occupy Tozeur. A-20 Havocs bomb enemy positions west of Sidi bou Zid.

SOUTHWEST PACIFIC AREA: The U.S. Sixth Army is established in SWPA under command of Lieutenant General Walter Krueger. The U.S. I Corps, under General Eichelberger, the 2nd Engineer Special Brigade, the 503rd Parachute Infantry, and the attached 1st Marine Division make up Krueger's new organization.

PACIFIC: U.S. submarine *Flying Fish* torpedoes and sinks a Japanese ship off Pagan Island, in the Marianas.

SOUTH PACIFIC: Rear Admiral Charles P. Mason assumes command of Air Command Solomons (COMAIRSOLS), a composite force of U.S. Army, Navy, and

Marine Corps, and New Zealand aircraft. Mason has operational control of all U.S. Army, Navy, and Marine Corps, and Royal New Zealand Air Force (RNZAF) aircraft in the Solomon Islands.

February 17
MEDITERRANEAN: Air Chief Marshal Sir Arthur W. Tedder takes command of the newly designated Mediterranean Air Command (which absorbs Ninth Air Force, Twelfth Air Force, and British RAF). General Sir Harold Alexander is named deputy commander in chief of Allied forces and commands Allied ground forces under the Eighteenth Army Group, which includes the British First and Eighth armies, the U.S. II Corps, and the French XIX Corps. Admiral Sir Andrew Cunningham is commander in chief of all Allied naval forces in the Mediterranean.
TUNISIA: Elements of 1st Armored Division defend at Sbeitla, then move to defensive positions near Tebessa, while the U.S. 34th Infantry Division (minus the 168th RCT) takes up defensive positions at Sbiba to protect Kasserine Pass.

February 18
ALEUTIANS: A naval task group under command of Rear Admiral Charles H. McMorris, with one light and one heavy cruiser and four destroyers, fires on Japanese installations at Attu.
MEDITERRANEAN: The subordinate commands of Twelfth Air Force become the core of the North African Air Force (NAAF), subordinate to Mediterranean Air Command (MAC). Lieutenant General Carl Spaatz commands NAAF. Twelfth Air Force ceases to exist as an operational command.
TUNISIA: A battalion of the 39th Infantry Regiment, 9th Infantry Division reinforces engineers and elements of the 26th Infantry Regiment, 1st Infantry Division holding Kasserine Pass.
SOUTHWEST PACIFIC AREA: U.S. submarine *Grampus* torpedoes and damages a Japanese transport north of the Admiralty Islands.
NEW GEORGIA: Thirteenth Air Force B-24 Liberators attack the Munda airfield.
NEW GUINEA: B-17s attack Japanese shipping near Bougainville. Fifth Air Force B-24s bomb Finschhafen and Madang in New Guinea.

February 19
ALEUTIANS: A portion of Admiral McMorris's naval task group attacks a Japanese army cargo ship bound for Attu. The ship sinks the following day.
ATLANTIC: U.S. submarine *Blackfish* is damaged by depth charges after she torpedoes and sinks a German patrol boat in the Bay of Biscay.
TUNISIA: A mixed force of British, French, and American units holds at Sbiba Pass. German forces begin assault on Kasserine Pass.
SOUTHWEST PACIFIC AREA: Naval forces attached to SWPA are designated as Seventh Fleet.

U.S. submarine *Grampus* torpedoes and sinks a Japanese transport off New Ireland.
SOLOMONS: Fifth Air Force B-17s bomb Japanese shipping and facilities around Bougainville Island.

U.S. submarine *Gato* torpedoes a Japanese ammunition ship off Bougainville, causing it to run aground.

NEW GUINEA: U.S. Navy cryptanalysts provide information that the Japanese intend to reinforce Lae in early March.

February 20

ALEUTIANS: Eleventh Air Force B-24 Liberators, B-25 Mitchells, and P-38 Lightnings attack Japanese facilities on Kiska Island.

TUNISIA: German forces break through Kasserine Pass and attack Thala, defended by an ad hoc collection of British infantry, artillery, and armor. Bad weather limits Allied air power; a few P-39 Airacobras attack German forces as they move through Kasserine Pass.

SOUTHWEST PACIFIC AREA: U.S. submarine *Albacore* torpedoes and sinks a Japanese destroyer near the Admiralty Islands.

PACIFIC: U.S. submarine *Halibut* torpedoes and sinks a Japanese transport north of Ponape Island in the Carolines.

SOLOMONS: Thirteenth Air Force B-17s and navy PBY Catalinas bomb Bougainville Island. B-24 Liberators bomb Kolombangara Island. Fifth Air Force B-17s bomb targets near Kahili on Bougainville Island.

February 21

ATLANTIC: German submarines converge on Convoy ON 166 (Liverpool to New York, fast) in the mid-North Atlantic. *U-332* and *U-603* torpedo and sink a Norwegian ship. *U-92* torpedoes a British steamer, which is later scuttled. Two other German submarines, *U-454* and *U-753*, as well as *U-332*, are driven off by escorts. A U.S. Coast Guard cutter sinks German submarine *U-225*. A U.S. freighter in convoy ON 167 is torpedoed and sunk by German submarine *U-664*.

MEDITERRANEAN: Lieutenant General Carl Spaatz's North African Tactical Air Force (NATAF) gains operational control of the Western Desert Air Force, but Ninth Air Force maintains administrative control.

TUNISIA: Combat Command B of the 1st Armored Division, along with an infantry battalion from 1st Infantry Division, moves toward Kasserine to protect retreating U.S. troops moving to Tebessa and to halt the German advance. Weather continues to limit Allied air support to the ground forces.

SOUTHWEST PACIFIC AREA: U.S. submarine *Thresher* attacks a Japanese convoy in the Lesser Sunda Islands of the Netherlands East Indies, damaging a cargo ship.

PACIFIC: U.S. submarine *Sawfish* torpedoes and damages a Japanese oiler off Oagari Jima.

SOLOMONS: Operation Cleanslate begins. The Russell Islands are occupied to establish a forward airbase and logistics base for future operations in the Solomons. The Marine 3rd Raider Battalion lands on Pavuvu Island and two regiments of the 43rd Infantry Division land on Barrika Island. Both islands are unoccupied.

About 9,000 troops are involved, and no enemy forces are encountered. Four light cruisers and four destroyers of Task Force 68, under command of Rear Admiral Aaron S. Merrill, and Thirteenth Air Force fighters from Guadalcanal provide air support.

February 22

CBI: Tenth Air Force B-24 Liberators mine the Gulf of Martaban near Rangoon.

ATLANTIC: Continuing their attack on convoy ON 166, German submarines *U-92* and *U-753* torpedo and damage a Norwegian ship, which is later scuttled. German submarine *U-606* torpedoes and sinks a U.S. freighter and a British steamship, and damages another U.S. freighter (later torpedoed by *U-303*). A Canadian corvette and a Polish destroyer conduct a depth charge attack on *U-606*. When it is forced to surface, the U.S. Coast Guard cutter *Campbell* rams and sinks the U-boat.

TUNISIA: North African Air Force A-20 Havocs fly close air support missions for Allied ground forces. One A-20 is lost when it is attacked by three Bf-109 Messerschmitts. B-17s bomb the Kasserine Pass while P-38 Lightnings attack German forces retiring from Kasserine. B-25 Mitchells bomb the railyards at Gafsa.

February 23

CBI: Tenth Air Force P-40s destroy a railroad bridge west of Myitkyina. B-24 Liberators attack the bridge at Myitnge but fail to damage the bridge.

ATLANTIC: The attack on convoy ON 166 continues. German submarine *U-186* torpedoes and sinks a U.S. freighter and a British ship; *U-707* torpedoes and sinks a U.S. freighter lagging behind the convoy.

Convoy UC 1 (United Kingdom to New York) is attacked by German submarine *U-382*, which torpedoes a Dutch ship; *U-202* torpedoes two British tankers and a U.S. tanker.

TUNISIA: North African Air Force B-17s bomb the airfield at Kairouan. B-25 Mitchells, A-20 Havocs, and B-26 Marauders bomb retreating German forces near Kasserine.

February 24

ATLANTIC: German submarine *U-604* is damaged by depth charges from escort ships guarding convoy ON 166. *U-621* conducts an unsuccessful attack on a U.S. Coast Guard cutter.

February 25

ALEUTIANS: Eleventh Air Force P-40s, B-24 Liberators, and B-25 Mitchells attack Japanese facilities on Kiska Island.

CBI: Tenth Air Force fighters seriously damage a bridge west of Myitkyina. Over 40 Japanese aircraft attack Dinjan airfield in India. Defending P-40s shoot down at least 14 enemy fighters.

ATLANTIC: Before losing contact with convoy ON 166, German submarine *U-92* and *U-600* continue to attack the U.S. Coast Guard cutter, but are unsuccessful. German submarine *U-628*, however, is able to torpedo and sink a British steamship.

MEDITERRANEAN: Ninth Air Force B-24 Liberators bomb Naples harbor.

TUNISIA: Allies regain control of Kasserine Pass. North African Air Force B-17s bomb the airfield at El Aouina, while A-20 Havocs attack German forces around Kasserine and Sbeitla, and along the main road between Gafsa and Feriana.

February 26
ETO: Because of bad weather conditions over their primary target at Bremen, Germany, Eighth Air Force B-17s and B-24s bomb the docks at Wilhelmshaven, Germany. Over 30 enemy aircraft are assessed as destroyed or damaged, while five B-17s out of 59 and two B-24 Liberators out of six are lost.

February 27
CBI: Tenth Air Force B-24 Liberators sink a Japanese cargo ship off Rangoon, Burma.

ETO: Eighth Air Force B-17s and B-24 Liberators bomb the U-boat pens and port facilities at Brest, France. Of the 60 bombers that participate in the raid, only two B-24s are damaged.

PACIFIC: U.S. submarine *Plunger* torpedoes and damages a Japanese oiler west of Jaluit Atoll in the Marshall Islands.

NEW GUINEA: U.S. 162nd Infantry Regiment, 41st Infantry Division occupies Milne Bay.

February 28
CBI: U.S. engineers building the Ledo Road cross into Burma. Major General Lewis A. Pick, the chief engineer for the project, overcomes exceptionally difficult problems with terrain. The Ledo Road project is assisted by the efforts of a civilian-military team from the Office of Strategic Services (OSS) known as Detachment 101. Under the command of Major Carl Rifler, Detachment 101 conducts reconnaissance, trains native guerrillas, and rescues downed pilots. Stilwell orders an increase in the number of guerrillas trained and ready for operations by the end of the year.

ATLANTIC: In the month of February, German U-boats have sunk 63 ships, totaling over 359,000 tons.

March 1
ATLANTIC: A U.S. freighter straggling from convoy HX 227 is torpedoed and sunk by German submarine *U-405* in the White Sea. A U.S. freighter in convoy BT 6 (Bahia, Brazil to Trinidad) is torpedoed by German submarine *U-518* off the coast of Brazil and abandoned. The crew is rescued and the freighter later sinks.

MEDITERRANEAN: Lieutenant General Carl Spaatz takes command of Twelfth Air Force, now an administrative headquarters for the Northwest African Air Force.

March 2
ATLANTIC: German submarines *U-759* and *U-634* combine to attack and sink a U.S. freighter straggling from convoy HX 227 (New York to Liverpool) southwest of Iceland.

MEDITERRANEAN: Northwest African Air Force B-17s bomb Palermo harbor. In Tunisia, B-26 Marauders attack bridges and enemy air defenses at La Hencha.

PACIFIC: U.S. submarine *Permit* torpedoes and damages a Japanese army cargo ship off the northeast coast of Honshu. U.S. submarine *Thresher* torpedoes and sinks a Japanese tanker in the southern Makassar Strait.

NEW GUINEA: Battle of the Bismarck Sea. Fifth Air Force bombers attack a Japanese convoy escorted by eight destroyers and headed for Lae. One cargo ship is sunk by B-17s.

March 3
ATLANTIC: A U.S. freighter, headed to Rio de Janeiro from New York, is torpedoed and sunk by Italian submarine *Barbarigo* off the coast of Brazil.
TUNISIA: Northwest African Air Force B-17s bomb the docks and shipping at Tunis harbor.
NEW GUINEA: Battle of the Bismarck Sea. In Huon Gulf, off Finschhafen, New Guinea, a Japanese destroyer is sunk by Fifth Air Force B-25 Mitchells, one destroyer is sunk by B-17s, and two destroyers and a supply ship are sunk by other aircraft. Another cargo ship damaged by U.S. and Australian aircraft is sunk by U.S. motor torpedo boats *PT-143* and *PT-150*. U.S. and Australian aircraft sink four army cargo ships and a transport. In all, the Japanese lose eight transports and four destroyers. Only 1,000 of the approximately 7,000 soldiers of the Japanese 51st Division reach Lae.

March 4
ETO: Eighth Air Force launches its first attack against strategic industrial targets in the vital Ruhr area of Germany. With 14 B-24 Liberators flying a diversionary mission, 16 B-17s bomb the marshaling yard at Hamm. Enemy losses are estimated to be about 16 aircraft; four B-17s are lost and nine are damaged. In the same strike, 28 B-17s bomb the Rotterdam shipyards. One B-17 is lost and 15 are damaged.

March 5
ATLANTIC: Escort carrier USS *Bogue* begins escorting convoys to provide extended air cover during their transit of the North Atlantic.
NEW GEORGIA: A U.S. naval task force of destroyers and cruisers bombarding Japanese positions on Vila and Munda, New Georgia Island, uses radar and torpedoes to sink two Japanese destroyers in Kula Gulf.
NEW GUINEA: Fifth Air Force A-20 Havocs bomb the airfield at Lae.

March 6
ETO: Eighth Air Force B-17s attack industrial targets at Lorient, France. Of the 65 B-17s involved, three are lost and eight others are damaged; enemy losses are estimated at around seven aircraft destroyed. A diversionary mission of 15 B-24 Liberators attacks the U-boat facilities at Brest, France. No bombers are lost and at least two enemy aircraft are downed.
TUNISIA: Major General George S. Patton, Jr., takes command of U.S. II Corps, relieving Major General Fredendall. Major General Omar Bradley becomes Patton's deputy commander.
SOUTHWEST PACIFIC AREA: U.S. submarine *Triton* sinks a Japanese cargo ship north of the Admiralties; after making its report, it will never be heard from again.
PACIFIC: U.S. submarine *Sawfish* torpedoes and damages a Japanese cargo ship off Toizaki, Japan.

March 7

ALEUTIANS: B-25 Mitchell bombers arrive at Amchitka Island, allowing Eleventh Air Force to increase attacks on Kiska. B-24 Liberators and P-38 Lightnings, along with B-25s, hit a number of Japanese installations on Kiska.

TUNISIA: Northwest African Air Force B-25 Mitchells bomb Axis supply ships traveling between Tunisia and Sicily. B-17s bomb an enemy convoy in the Gulf of Tunis and the marshaling yard at Sousse.

SOUTHWEST PACIFIC AREA: U.S. submarine *Tautog* lays mines off the southeast coast of Borneo.

SOUTH PACIFIC: Thirteenth Air Force B-24 Liberators bomb airfields on Kolombangara and Bougainville. Other B-24s attack Munda airfield on New Georgia.

March 8

CBI: Tenth Air Force B-25 Mitchells attempt to destroy the Myitnge bridge and eliminate enemy air defenses, but the 12 bombers sent against the target do little damage.

ATLANTIC: A navy PBY-5 Catalina sinks German submarine *U-156* in the West Indies. A U.S. freighter is torpedoed by German submarine *U-160* off the coast of South Africa and is later scuttled near Durban.

ETO: Eighth Air Force B-24 Liberators and B-17s attack industrial targets at Rouen, France. Two of the 13 B-24 Liberators are lost and four are damaged. Enemy losses are estimated at about 14 aircraft destroyed. Of the 54 B-17s that hit the target 30 minutes later, two are lost and 10 are damaged. The bombing attack is disrupted by waves of German fighters, the first of which draw off the fighter cover, allowing the second wave to attack the bombers directly.

PACIFIC: U.S. submarine *Permit* attacks a Japanese convoy off the northern tip of Honshu, Japan, and sinks a cargo ship.

March 9

ATLANTIC: German submarine *U-409* torpedoes U.S. freighter in convoy SC 121 (Halifax Slow to United Kingdom). The freighter is abandoned and later sinks. German submarine *U-510* attacks convoy BT 6 (Bahia to Trinidad) off the coast of French Guiana, torpedoing several U.S. freighters. A U.S. freighter from convoy RA 53 is torpedoed and sunk by German submarine *U-586* northeast of Iceland.

SOLOMONS: Thirteenth Air Force B-24 Liberators bomb airfields at Munda, New Georgia, and at Bougainville.

March 10

ALEUTIANS: Eleventh Air Force B-25 Mitchells and B-24 Liberators, escorted by 12 P-38 Lightnings and one F-5A (an unarmed P-38 variant: it carried cameras in the nose), attack facilities on Kiska.

CBI: The Fourteenth Air Force is created by special order of President Roosevelt under the command of Claire L. Chennault, who is promoted from brigadier to major general.

ATLANTIC: German submarine *U-185* attacks convoy KG 123 (Key West to Guantánamo), torpedoing a U.S. tanker and freighter.

German submarines *U-221* and *U-444* attack convoy HX 228 (New York to Liverpool), each torpedoing a U.S. freighter; *U-432* sinks a British destroyer escorting the convoy.

German submarine *U-255* torpedoes and damages a U.S. freighter straggling from convoy RA 53.

March 11

CBI: U.S. Fourteenth Air Force is organized under command of General Claire Chennault at Kunming and assigned to U.S. Army Forces in the China-Burma-India theater.

March 12

ATLANTIC: U.S. destroyers escorting convoy UGS 6 (United States to Mediterranean, Slow) sink German submarine *U-130*.

German submarine *U-68* attacks convoy GAT 49 (Guantánamo to Aruba to Trinidad) and torpedoes a U.S. tanker in the Caribbean. German submarine *U-172* torpedoes U.S. freighter straggling from convoy UGS 6 (United States to Mediterranean, Slow).

The Pacific Military Conference is held in Washington, D.C. Major General Richard K. Sutherland, MacArthur's chief of staff, represents SWPA interests. Admiral William F. Halsey represents SOPAC interests. The proposal is for a limited offensive against Japanese strongholds on the Huon Peninsula in New Guinea and the capture of Munda airfield on New Georgia Island, and the capture of Japanese airfields on New Britain and Bougainville, with the objective of isolating Rabaul and Kavieng in preparation for seizing both. To do this, MacArthur requests five infantry divisions and 45 air groups. Because all forces are now being directed to the European Theater of Operations, SWPA will have to conduct offensive operations with the ground and air units it currently commands.

TUNISIA: Northwest African Air Force B-17s bomb the docks and marshaling yards at Sousse. B-26 Marauders attack supply dumps and lines of supply. B-25 Mitchells bomb supply ships operating between Tunisia and Sicily.

SOUTHWEST PACIFIC AREA: Fifth Air Force B-17s bomb Rabaul airfield.

PACIFIC: U.S. submarine *Plunger* torpedoes and sinks a Japanese vessel in the Caroline Islands.

March 13

ETO: Eighth Air Force B-17s attack the rail marshaling yard and other targets at Amiens, France, while 16 B-24 Liberators fly a diversionary mission. Of the 71 B-17s involved in the attack, 11 are damaged and two enemy planes are reported destroyed.

SOUTHWEST PACIFIC AREA: U.S. submarine *Grayback* torpedoes and damages a Japanese transport northwest of Bismarck Archipelago.

PACIFIC: U.S. submarine *Sunfish* sinks a Japanese cargo ship in the Ryukyus.

NEW GUINEA: Fifth Air Force B-17s bomb Wewak airfield and Japanese shipping.

March 15

ALEUTIANS: Eighth Air Force B-25 Mitchells with P-38 Lightnings make two separate attacks on Kiska. One P-38 is shot down by enemy antiaircraft fire.

SOUTHWEST PACIFIC AREA: The U.S. Seventh Fleet is created to support SWPA under General Douglas MacArthur's operational control. Vice Admiral Arthur S. Carpenter is the commander. CINCUSFLEET maintains administrative control. The fleet consists of two Australian cruisers and a few U.S. and Australian destroyers. Suspicious of MacArthur, Admiral Ernest J. King, the COMINCH, keeps the majority of U.S. naval power in the area under Third Fleet, commanded by Admiral William F. Halsey, COMSOPAC.

U.S. submarine *Trigger* attacks Japanese convoy northwest of the Admiralty Islands, damaging one transport and sinking a cargo ship.

PACIFIC: Central Pacific Force is redesignated as U.S. Fifth Fleet.

NEW GEORGIA: Thirteenth Air Force B-17s bomb the airfield at Munda, New Georgia, and the airfield on Kolombangara Island.

March 16

CBI: Tenth Air Force B-25 Mitchells damage the Myitnge bridge but do not bring it down.

ATLANTIC: German submarine *U-563* spots convoy HX 229 (New York to Liverpool Fast). Although looking for convoy SC 122 (Halifax Slow to United Kingdom), bad weather has allowed this convoy to pass without being detected. Convoys HX 229 and SC 122 are soon intermingled in the rough seas. A pack of 44 U-boats attacks the convoys: German submarine *U-172* torpedoes and damages a U.S. freighter from convoy UGS 6. *U-758* and *U-435* each torpedo and damage a U.S. freighter.

TUNISIA: U.S. II Corps, made up of the 1st Armored, 1st Infantry, and 9th Infantry divisions, moves to capture Maknassy and divert German armor while General Bernard Montgomery's Eighth Army attacks north to break the Axis defenses at Mareth.

March 17

CBI: Tenth Air Force B-25 Mitchells unsuccessfully bomb the Myitnge bridge; P-40s attack support facilities and bridges at Kadrangyang and around Myitkyina.

ATLANTIC: German submarine *U-167* torpedoes and damages a U.S. freighter in convoy UGS 6. Later in the day *U-521* sinks the ship. German submarine *U-91* sinks three freighters damaged in the previous attack on convoy HX 229. *U-600* torpedoes and damages a U.S. freighter; *U-91* then sinks that ship.

TUNISIA: II Corps occupies Gafsa. Combat Command A of 1st Armored Division occupies Zannouch. Northwest African Air Force flies ground support missions against enemy defensive positions.

PACIFIC: U.S. submarine *Kingfish* torpedoes and damages a Japanese transport in the Formosa Strait.

March 18

CBI: Tenth Air Force B-24 Liberators damage the Pazundaung bridge, while B-25 Mitchells succeed in damaging both the Myitnge bridge and enemy antiaircraft positions defending it.

ATLANTIC: German submarine *U-221* torpedoes and sinks a U.S. freighter from convoy HX 229.

ETO: Nearly a hundred Eighth Air Force B-17 and B-24 Liberator bombers attack the submarine yards at Vegesack, Germany, using automatic flight control linked to bombsights. Two bombers are lost and 24 are damaged. Enemy aircraft losses are estimated at over 50 destroyed. Seven subs are reported damaged in the attack.

First Lieutenant Jack W. Mathis is the leading bombardier for his squadron on this mission. Just as his aircraft is starting its bomb run, Mathis is mortally wounded by enemy flak. Without any hesitation, and with his last breath, Mathis carefully lines up his target in the bombsight and releases his bombs. His squadron is able to follow his strike on the target and gain a maximum effect. First Lieutenant Mathis's act of bravery and dedication to the mission above and beyond the call of duty will win him the Medal of Honor.

TUNISIA: Northwest African Air Force fighters fly reconnaissance missions over Axis defensive lines.

March 19

CBI: Tenth Air Force B-25 Mitchells severely damage the Myitnge bridge with four direct hits.

ATLANTIC: German submarine *U-527* torpedoes and damages a U.S. freighter from convoy HX 229. It is later sunk by *U-523*. German submarine *U-533* torpedoes and sinks a Greek freighter from convoy SC 122. The attack on the convoys ends. In all, 12 ships from HX 229 and nine ships from SC 122 are sunk. No U-boats are lost.

PACIFIC: U.S. submarine *Kingfish* torpedoes and sinks a Japanese army hospital ship in the Formosa Strait. U.S. submarine *Sawfish* torpedoes and damages a Japanese guardboat southeast of Japan. U.S. submarine *Wahoo* torpedoes and sinks a Japanese cargo ship and damages another in the Yellow Sea.

March 20

PACIFIC: U.S. submarine *Scamp* torpedoes and damages a Japanese merchant ship off the east coast of Japan.

SOUTHWEST PACIFIC AREA: U.S. submarine *Trigger* fires a torpedo and hits a Japanese gunboat north of the Admiralty Islands, but the torpedo is a dud and damages only the gunboat.

SOUTH PACIFIC: Navy and marine aircraft of the Thirteenth Air Force lay mines off Bougainville near Buin-Tonolai area, while B-17s and B-24 Liberators conduct a diversionary raid on the airfield.

March 21

ATLANTIC: U.S. submarine *Herring* sinks German submarine *U-163* in the Bay of Biscay.

TUNISIA: U.S. 1st Armored Division captures Sened and advances to Maknassy, but further advances are halted by strong Axis defenses. U.S. 1st Ranger Battalion and the 26th Infantry Regiment of 1st Infantry Division capture 700 prisoners in the vicinity of El Guettar.

PACIFIC: U.S. submarine *Finback* torpedoes and damages a Japanese transport ship south of the Caroline Islands. U.S. submarine *Scamp* torpedoes and damages a Japanese transport ship off the east coast of Honshu, Japan. U.S. submarine *Wahoo* torpedoes and sinks two Japanese cargo ships in the Yellow Sea.

March 22

ATLANTIC: Northwest African Air Force heavy bombers of the 1st Antisubmarine Squadron sink German submarine *U-524* north of the Canary Islands.

ETO: Eighth Air Force B-17s and B-24 Liberators bomb the U-boat yards at Wilhelmshaven, Germany. Three bombers are lost, 22 are damaged. Enemy losses are reported to be nearly 40 aircraft lost or damaged. A German tanker is also sunk.

TUNISIA: Maknassy is occupied, but farther advance of the U.S. II Corps is stopped near Djebel Naemia. The 1st and 9th Infantry Divisions make unsuccessful attacks against enemy defenses past El Guettar. Northwest African Air Force fighters fly reconnaissance and ground support missions.

SOUTHWEST PACIFIC AREA: U.S. submarine *Gudgeon* attacks a Japanese convoy, torpedoing and sinking a cargo ship near Surabaya, Java. U.S. submarine *Tambor* torpedoes and damages a Japanese transport ship in the Sulu Sea.

March 23

PACIFIC: U.S. submarine *Whale* torpedoes and sinks a Japanese transport northwest of Saipan.

SOUTH PACIFIC: In response to the disaster in the Bismarck Sea, the Japanese plan to regain air superiority over Guadalcanal and Tulagi and over Papua. A total of 300 aircraft are to be employed in this effort. The Solomons are the target for the first half of April, to be followed by Papua in the second half of April. The Japanese stake inexperienced pilots against an increasingly confident and powerful U.S. air fleet.

March 24

ALEUTIANS: The plan for occupying Attu Island is approved by the JCS. Eleventh Air Force B-24 Liberators, B-25 Mitchells, and P-38 Lightnings conduct five attack missions over Kiska.

CBI: Tenth Air Force B-24 Liberators, along with two B-17s attacking from a height of 50 feet, are unable to damage the Myitnge Bridge.

MEDITERRANEAN: Ninth Air Force B-24 Liberators cause heavy damage to facilities at Messina.

TUNISIA: Major General Orlando Ward, commander of the U.S. 1st Armored Division, personally leads a night assault up Djebel Naemia after Patton orders that the objective be taken. Northwest African Air Force A-20 Havocs and B-25 Mitchells attack enemy troop concentrations.

PACIFIC: U.S. submarine *Wahoo* torpedoes and sinks three Japanese cargo ships in the Yellow Sea.

March 25

TUNISIA: Ward's attack on Djebel Naemia makes no progress; the 18th Infantry Regiment of the 1st Infantry Division is forced off Djebel Berda by an enemy attack. Northwest African Air Force B-17s bomb the docks and ships at Sousse.

The escort carrier USS *Bogue* on convoy duty in the Atlantic, camouflaged to break up her outline against the sea.

March 26

ALEUTIANS: Near the island of Komandorskiye Ostrova, Rear Admiral Charles H. McMorris's naval task group engages a Japanese force of two heavy cruisers, two light cruisers, and four destroyers escorting two transports with reinforcements for Kiska Island. The U.S. force, with one heavy cruiser, one light cruiser, and four destroyers drives the Japanese off. The U.S. heavy cruiser and two U.S. destroyers are damaged. One Japanese heavy cruiser is damaged. This engagement prevents the Japanese from reinforcing or supplying the Aleutians, except by submarine.

CBI: Tenth Air Force B-24 Liberators mine the Rangoon River while other B-24s conduct a diversionary raid on the city of Rangoon.

ATLANTIC: Escort carrier USS *Bogue* proves her worth to convoy SC 123 (Halifax Slow to United Kingdom) by launching aircraft and preventing German submarines *U-443* and *U-415* from approaching the convoy.

March 27

TUNISIA: The 135th and 168th Infantry Regiments of the U.S. 34th Infantry Division attempt to break through Fondouk Gap. The infantry moving on foot across open ground and through barbed wire and minefields make three separate attacks, but make no progress against heavy enemy fire.

NEW GUINEA: Fifth Air Force B-25 Mitchells bomb targets at Lae and Salamaua.

March 28

ETO: Eighth Air Force B-17s bomb the marshaling yard at Rouen-Sotteville, France. Of the 70 B-17s involved, one bomber is lost and nine are damaged. Enemy losses are estimated at 10 aircraft.

SOUTHWEST PACIFIC AREA: With approval of JCS, General MacArthur, COM-SWPA, issues orders that outline the objectives for an offensive plan code-named Cartwheel. The Elkton plan would implement Cartwheel. It is a campaign intended to envelop and isolate Rabaul in a series of coordinated alternating operations between SWPA and SOPAC. The objectives for SWPA are in northeast New Guinea and the Bismarck Archipelago. SOPAC's objectives are to advance from Guadalcanal to clear the Solomon Islands to Bougainville Island. MacArthur's forces will capture Woodlark and Kiriwina Islands to establish airbases in order to support future amphibious operations. Admiral William F. Halsey, COMSOPAC, then will take the offensive to capture New Georgia Island. SWPA will then move against northeast New Guinea at Lae, Salamaua, and Finschhafen. SOPAC will then move on the Shortland Islands and southern Bougainville Island, and SWPA on Madang and Cape Gloucester, clearing the Japanese from western New Britain. As outlined by the JCS, MacArthur will not have direct command of Admiral Halsey's forces, but will be able to provide general direction to COMSOPAC. This does not become a problem, as Halsey and MacArthur discover they work well together as a team.

PACIFIC: U.S. submarine *Tunny* torpedoes and damages a Japanese troopship off Wake Island, which subsequently runs aground on the island.

March 29

ATLANTIC: German submarine *U-160* torpedoes and sinks a U.S. freighter separated from convoy HX 230 (New York to Liverpool).

The War Production Board begins rationing fat (which is used for munitions) as well as meat and cheese.

SOUTHWEST PACIFIC AREA: A JCS directive designates the South Pacific Area as the water and land lying west of the 159th parallel to differentiate it from MacArthur's Southwest Pacific Area (SWPA).

U.S. submarine *Gudgeon* torpedoes and sinks a Japanese fleet tanker and damages another tanker in Makassar Strait.

PACIFIC: U.S. submarine *Wahoo* sinks a Japanese ship south of Kyushu.

March 30

ALEUTIANS: Eleventh Air Force B-24 Liberators, B-25 Mitchells, and P-38 Lightnings attack Kiska and Attu. One B-24 is lost to enemy antiaircraft fire.

TUNISIA: Northwest African Air Force A-20 Havocs bomb enemy forces and tanks in support of the 9th Infantry Division's attack on Djebel Berda.

SOUTHWEST PACIFIC AREA: U.S. submarine *Tuna* attacks a Japanese convoy north of Manus Island in the Admiralties and sinks a cargo ship.

NEW GUINEA: Fifth Air Force B-17s, B-25 Mitchells, B-24 Liberators, and A-20 Havocs attack Japanese ships and facilities at Finschhafen.

March 31

CBI: General Stilwell's 124 transport aircraft in theater can deliver only about 4,000 tons of supplies a month to China. General Chennault's Tenth Air Force uses 1,500 tons of these supplies. Chinese units are being trained at Kunming, but at a far lower rate than Stilwell expects. Chennault claims that with more support, he will be able to attack the Japanese home islands by 1943. This outrageously optimistic proposal appeals to President Roosevelt, who raises the authorized supply tonnage to Chennault.

ETO: Eighth Air Force bombers attack the port facilities at Rotterdam, the Netherlands. Three B-17s and one B-24 are lost; eight bombers are damaged. Enemy losses are negligible.

TUNISIA: Ninth Air Force B-25 Mitchells bomb the airfield at Sfax, damaging several enemy aircraft; P-40s attack enemy transportation north of Gabès. Northwest African Air Force fighters and bombers attack enemy positions between the El Guettar-Gabès road in support of U.S. II Corps.

April 1

ALEUTIANS: Eleventh Air Force B-24 Liberators, B-25 Mitchells, and P-38 Lightnings attack Kiska. The Joint Chiefs of Staff approves the plan to retake Attu. Major General Albert E. Brown's 7th Infantry Division is identified as the land force to conduct Operation Sandcrab, scheduled to begin 7 May. Vice Admiral Thomas C. Kinkaid, Commander, North Pacific Force, will lead the operation.

ATLANTIC: U.S. submarine *Shad* torpedoes an Italian blockade runner in the Bay of Biscay.

TUNISIA: Northwest African Air Force A-20 Havocs bomb airfields while fighters continue to attack enemy motor transports and tanks.

SOLOMONS: Six U.S. fighters of 42 engaged are lost in a three-hour battle over the Russell Islands in the Solomons during a Japanese air attack on Guadalcanal, Tulagi, and the airfield under construction in the Russells. U.S. pilots claim 20 Japanese aircraft shot down.

April 2

PACIFIC: U.S. submarine *Tunny* torpedoes and sinks a Japanese transport west of Truk.

U.S. submarine *Haddock* torpedoes and sinks a Japanese tanker north of Palau; U.S. submarine *Pickerel* is sunk off northern Honshu, Japan.

April 3

ATLANTIC: German submarine *U-155* torpedoes and sinks a U.S. tanker off Key West, Florida.

TUNISIA: General Alexander alerts Patton's II Corps to be prepared to move north of the British First Army for the final offensive directed against Tunis.

April 4

ETO: Eighth Air Force B-17s attack the Renault armament and motor works in Paris against heavy German fighter attack. Of the 85 bombers involved, four B-17s are lost and 16 are damaged. German aircraft losses are estimated at over 50.

MEDITERRANEAN: Ninth Air Force B-24 Liberators bomb the docks at Naples; Northwest African Air Force B-17s bomb the airfield and the marshaling yards.

SOUTHWEST PACIFIC AREA: B-17s bomb the town and airfield at Kavieng, New Ireland.

SOUTH PACIFIC: Vice Admiral Marc A. Mitscher becomes Commander Air Solomons (COMAIRSOL), with operational control of all Royal New Zealand Air Force (RNZAF), U.S. Army, Navy, and Marine Corps aircraft in the South Pacific.

NEW GUINEA: Fifth Air Force B-25 Mitchells and A-20 Havocs attack Japanese positions near the Huon Gulf; B-17s bomb Salamaua.

April 5

ALEUTIANS: Eleventh Air Force B-24 Liberators and B-25 Mitchells bomb the airfields on Attu and Kiska, escorted by P-38 Lightnings and P-4Os.

CBI: Tenth Air Force B-25 Mitchells bomb rail targets at Mandalay.

ATLANTIC: German submarine *U-563* torpedoes and sinks a U.S. tanker separated from convoy HX 231 (New York to Liverpool).

ETO: Eighth Air Force B-17s bomb an aircraft factory and related industrial targets at Antwerp, Belgium. German fighters knock down four B-17s and damage 13 others out of the 82 bombers involved in the attack. At least 23 enemy aircraft are lost.

TUNISIA: Northwest African Air Force and Western Desert Air Force fighters and bombers concentrate on denying the enemy the ability to transport supplies and reinforcements to Tunisia. Pilots report over 60 enemy aircraft downed in air combat. Frustrated with what he believes to be Major General Orlando Ward's lack of action, Patton replaces Ward with Major General Ernest Harmon as commander of 1st Armored Division.

SOUTH PACIFIC: U.S. destroyer sinks Japanese submarine *RO-34* near Russell Island, Solomons.

April 6

CARIBBEAN: German submarine *U-185* torpedoes and sinks a U.S. freighter off Cuba.

MEDITERRANEAN: Ninth Air Force B-24 Liberators bomb Messina harbor in Sicily, while Northwest African Air Force B-17s bomb docks and shipping at Trapani, Sicily, and B-25 Mitchells and P-38 Lightinings attack enemy shipping in the Straits of Sicily.

TUNISIA: Axis forces abandon the key defensive positions in front of U.S. II Corps that had kept 1st Infantry Division and 9th Infantry Division units virtually frozen in place.

April 7

TUNISIA: U.S. II Corps patrols make contact with British Eighth Army patrols east of El Guettar. The 133rd and 135th Infantry Regiments of the U.S. 34th Infantry Division, along with tanks and infantry of the British IX Corps, attacks Fondouk Pass. Artillery and anti-tank fire cause the British-American advance to collapse.

Western Desert Air Force aircraft provide support to ground forces and attack enemy convoys between Sfax and Sousse.

MEDITERRANEAN: Ninth Air Force B-24 Liberators attack Palermo harbor in Sicily.

SOUTHWEST PACIFIC AREA: U.S. submarine *Trout* lays mines near Sarawak, Borneo.

PACIFIC: U.S. submarine *Tunny* torpedoes a Japanese ship northwest of Truk. The ship later sinks. U.S. submarine *Pickerel* torpedoes and sinks a Japanese cargo ship off Honshu, Japan.

GUADALCANAL: Nearly 400 Japanese bombers and fighters launched from carriers attack and sink a U.S. destroyer and a New Zealand corvette south of Guadalcanal. Two U.S. oilers are damaged. Thirteenth Air Force P-38 Lightnings and P-39 Airacobras, along with marine and navy F4F Wildcats and F4U Corsairs engage Japanese dive-bombers and fighters attempting to attack U.S. supply ships off Guadalcanal. Enemy losses are estimated at 39 aircraft; U.S. losses are seven fighters. Marine pilot Lieutenant James Swett, flying with four other Wildcats over Tulagi Harbor, spots about 20 enemy dive-bombers headed for the American ships. Swett is new to the theater and has never been in combat, yet he attacks the enemy formation with great skill, shooting down seven dive-bombers before receiving serious damage to his aircraft. Out of ammunition and with the engine dead, Lt. Swett ditches off Florida Island and is later rescued. For his exceptional skill and daring in taking on an entire enemy formation, Lieutenant Swett will receive the Medal of Honor.

April 8
CBI: Tenth Air Force B-25 Mitchells bomb the airfield at Meiktila. A Japanese storage depot at Ningam is attacked by P-40s and one B-25.

April 9
TUNISIA: The 133rd and 135th Infantry Regiments of the 34th Infantry Division attack to clear enemy positions above Fondouk Pass, while the British 6th Armored Division charges through the pass but fails to trap the retreating enemy. The performance of the demoralized 34th Division is so poor that the British 6th Armored Division commander recommends to General Eisenhower that the 34th be moved to the rear for retraining by British officers. This angers the Americans a great deal, especially since the British plan to attack the pass was seriously flawed.

During the battle at Fondouk, Private Robert D. Booker of the 34th Infantry Division advances alone over 200 yards of open ground with a light machine gun and a box of ammunition to a position where he can directly engage the enemy. Although under constant machine gun and mortar fire, Private Booker ignores a wound and puts his own machine gun into action, knocking out an enemy position. Shortly thereafter, Booker is mortally wounded but continues to fight, encouraging his squad and pointing out targets. For his courage and fortitude against great odds, Private Booker will receive the Medal of Honor.

The U.S. 1st Armored Division begins to move north to positions in anticipation of II Corps movement of 100,000 men 200 miles across Tunisia to take up attack positions on the northern coast. The mission is to attack toward Mateur in order to outflank Axis defenses in support of the British offensive to capture Bizerte.

SOUTHWEST PACIFIC AREA: U.S. submarine *Drum* attacks Japanese convoy, sinking a cargo ship north of Kavieng, New Ireland. U.S. submarine *Grayling* attacks a Japanese convoy, sinking a cargo ship off Mindoro in the Philippines. U.S. submarine

Tautog attacks a Japanese convoy south of Celebes Island, sinking a cargo ship and a destroyer.

April 10
TUNISIA: Tunisian offensive plan from General Alexander's headquarters, Operation Vulcan, is approved. While the British First Army makes the main attack to capture Tunis, the British Eighth Army is to maintain pressure on the Axis south flank. The corps mission is to attack toward Mateur in order to outflank Axis defenses in support of the British offensive.
NEW GUINEA: Fifth Air Force B-17s and B-24 Liberators bomb Wewak.

April 11
ALEUTIANS: Eleventh Air Force B-25 Mitchells, escorted by P-40s and P-38s, attack Kiska.
ATLANTIC: German submarine *U-615* torpedoes and sinks a U.S. freighter in convoy HX 232 (New York to Liverpool). German submarine *U-195* torpedoes and sinks a U.S. freighter in convoy UGS 7 (United States to Mediterranean).
MEDITERRANEAN: Ninth Air Force B-24 Liberators attack Naples harbor, losing one bomber to enemy fighters and antiaircraft fire.
TUNISIA: B-25 Mitchells bomb enemy locations near Sfax. Northwest African Air Force B-17s bomb Tunis harbor; P-38 Lightnings attack enemy fighter and transport aircraft; B-26 Marauders and B-25s bomb enemy-held airfields in northeast Tunisia.

April 12
CBI: Tenth Air Force B-25 Mitchells attack Magwe airfield. P-40s attack Japanese ammunition and supplies at Walawbum.
TUNISIA: Northwest African Air Force B-17s bomb Bizerte harbor. B-25 Mitchells and A-20 Havocs bomb enemy airfields in northeast Tunisia.
PACIFIC: U.S. submarine *Flying Fish* torpedoes and sinks a Japanese cargo ship off Honshu, Japan.

April 13
ALEUTIANS: Eleventh Air Force B-25 Mitchells and B-24 Liberators, escorted by 28 P-38 Lightnings and 20 P-40s, attack Kiska, dropping 43 tons of bombs on the runway and other targets. Enemy antiaircraft fire downs one P-38. A B-25 and another P-38 are damaged.

April 14
ALEUTIANS: Eleventh Air Force bombers and fighters attack Kiska, dropping 85 tons of bombs. One B-24 is shot down.
CBI: Tenth Air Force P-40s, carrying 1,000-pound bombs as an experiment, hit airfields at Myitkyina and Manywet and cause heavy damage.
PACIFIC: U.S. submarine *Pike* torpedoes and damages a Japanese cargo ship north of the Admiralty Islands.
NEW GUINEA: Fifth Air Force P-40s and P-38 Lightnings drive off an attack by the Japanese on Milne Bay, destroying 14 enemy aircraft. Fifth Air Force B-17s sink a Japanese cargo ship in Hansa Bay, New Guinea.

April 15

TUNISIA: Major General Omar N. Bradley takes command of U.S. II Corps, replacing Major General George S. Patton, Jr., who is now assigned to prepare the plan for the Allied attack on Sicily.

Northwest African Air Force A-20 Havoc and P-38 Lightning fighters fly ground support missions for Allied troops.

SOUTHWEST PACIFIC AREA: Fifth Air Force B-17s bomb Rabaul airfields and the airfield at Lae in New Guinea.

PACIFIC: U.S. submarine *Seawolf* torpedoes and sinks a Japanese transport south of Marcus Island.

SOUTH PACIFIC: Two new airfields to support future offensive operations in the Solomons are completed on Barrika Island in the Russell Islands.

April 16

CBI: Tenth Air Force P-40s bomb railroad bridges near Mogaung and Pinbaw. B-24 Liberators bomb the marshaling yard in Rangoon, and B-25 Mitchells bomb rail targets in Mandalay.

ETO: Eighth Air Force B-24 Liberators and B-17s raid U-boat bases at Brest and at Lorient in France. Enemy fighters and ground smoke limit the accuracy of the bombers. Enemy aircraft losses are estimated at over 14. U.S. losses are three B-24s out of 19 and one B-17 out of 59. A total of 18 other bombers are damaged.

MEDITERRANEAN: Ninth Air Force B-24 Liberators bomb Catania harbor in Sicily. Northwest African Air Force B-17s bomb docks at Palermo, Sicily.

NEW GUINEA: Fifth Air Force B-24 Liberators and B-17s bomb Wewak.

April 17

ALEUTIANS: Eleventh Air Force B-24 Liberators bomb and damage the runway at Attu. B-25 Mitchells, P-38 Lightnings, and P-40s attack Kiska.

CBI: Tenth Air Force bombers and P-40s attack bridges at Myitnge, Kamaing, Namti, and Pazundaung.

ATLANTIC: A U.S. Coast Guard cutter, escorting convoy HX 233 (New York to Liverpool), sinks German submarine *U-175* as it shadows the convoy.

ETO: Eighth Air Force B-17s attack an aircraft production facility at Bremen, Germany. Enemy fighters and antiaircraft defenses hit the 115-plane formation hard, destroying 16 and damaging 39 others. Over 60 enemy fighters are reported destroyed and 159 American crewmen are reported as missing.

MEDITERRANEAN: Ninth Air Force P-40Fs and 11 RAF Spitfires attack a massive German air formation of 65 transports with fighter escort, en route to Sicily. While the Spitfires fly cover, the P-40s attack the transports, destroying nearly all of them and shooting down 16 fighters as well.

PACIFIC: U.S. submarine *Flying Fish* torpedoes and sinks a Japanese cargo ship off Hokkaido, Japan.

April 18

TUNISIA: Allied aircraft are able to heavily damage the Axis aerial supply line, destroying nearly 70 transport aircraft and 16 escorts. U.S. losses are six P-40s.

The U.S. Coast Guard cutter *Spencer,* escorting convoy HX 233, attacks and sinks German submarine *U-175* on April 17, 1943.

SOUTHWEST PACIFIC AREA: U.S. submarine *Drum* torpedoes and sinks a Japanese ammunition ship near the Bismarck Archipelago.

PACIFIC: Using information obtained from intercepted Japanese signals, 16 U.S. P-38 Lightnings locate and shoot down a plane transporting Commander in Chief of the Japanese Combined Fleet, Admiral Yamamoto Isoroku. Admiral Yamamoto was en route from Rabaul to the Solomons for an inspection.

April 19

TUNISIA: The British attack on Axis defenses stretching along the general line of Enfidaville, Bou Arada, Medjez el Bab, and Sedjenane begins. U.S. II Corps is in place on the British First Army's north flank.

PACIFIC: U.S. submarine *Seawolf* torpedoes and sinks a Japanese cargo ship in the area of the Bonin Islands.

April 20

PACIFIC: U.S. submarine *Runner* mines approaches to Hong Kong. U.S. submarine *Scorpion* torpedoes and sinks a Japanese gunboat off Honshu, Japan.

ATLANTIC: German submarine *U-565* torpedoes and sinks a U.S. freighter in convoy UGS 7 (United States to Mediterranean, Slow) off the coast of North Africa.

April 21

ALEUTIANS: Eleventh Air Force commander, Brigadier General William O. Butler, takes operational control of all army and navy air units from Commander North Pacific Forces (NORPACFOR), which are designated as Task Group (TG) 16.1.

ATLANTIC: Italian submarine *Leonardo da Vinci* torpedoes and damages a U.S. freighter off the coast of South Africa. After the freighter is abandoned, the submarine sinks the ship with gunfire.

April 23

ATLANTIC: In the North Atlantic, German submarine *U-306* and *U-129* each torpedo and sink a U.S. freighter. *U-306*'s victim is in convoy HX 234 (New York to Liverpool); *U-129*'s victim was bound for Iraq.

ETO: Combined Chiefs of Staff designates Lieutenant General Sir Frederick E. Morgan as chief of staff to the Supreme Allied Commander responsible for an Allied planning organization tasked to prepare initial plans for a cross-Channel invasion. The new organization is referred to as COSSAC, after Morgan's title.

TUNISIA: U.S. II Corps makes its attack in zone to support the British advance. The 9th Infantry Division and 1st Infantry Division attack enemy defenses on key hills along the Tine River valley toward Mateur. Ninth Air Force B-25 Mitchells and P-40s provide support to the ground forces. The Northwest African Air Force B-25s, B-26 Marauders, and A-20 Havocs bomb enemy positions and vehicles.

CENTRAL PACIFIC: Seventh Air Force B-24 Liberators from Funafuti attack Japanese facilities on Tarawa Atoll.

April 24

ALEUTIANS: The U.S. 7th Infantry Division sails from San Francisco bound for Cold Harbor, Alaska.

TUNISIA: At Djebel Dardys near Sedjenane, Sergeant William L. Nelson, a heavy mortar section leader in the 60th Infantry Regiment, 9th Infantry Division, leads his men forward under heavy enemy fire. Placing himself in an exposed position forward of his gunners, he directs mortar fire on enemy soldiers attempting to form a counterattack. Although wounded, Sergeant Nelson crawls to a position only 50 yards from the enemy and continues to direct accurate fire on them. His skill and courage in employing his section against heavy odds and his devotion to duty at the cost of his life will win him the Medal of Honor.

PACIFIC: U.S. submarine *Flying Fish* torpedoes and sinks a Japanese cargo ship in Tsugaru Strait, Japan. U.S. submarine *Runner* torpedoes and damages a Japanese army hospital ship off Hong Kong.

April 25

ALEUTIANS: Eleventh Air Force bombers and fighters attack Kiska and Attu.

April 26

ALEUTIANS: Three light cruisers and six destroyers of Rear Admiral Charles H. McMorris's naval task group bombard Japanese installations at Attu.

April 26

TUNISIA: U.S. II Corps, with four divisions on the attack, attempts to break enemy first line defenses and prepares to send 1st Armored Division toward Mateur. The 34th Infantry Division attacks to seize a cluster of hills identified as Hill 609.

SOUTHWEST PACIFIC AREA: SWPA headquarters issues the Elkton III plan, which lays out the coordinated attack by SWPA and SOPAC forces on Rabaul. The entire operation against Rabaul is codenamed Cartwheel.

April 27

ATLANTIC: U.S. Navy PV-1 patrol bombers, providing coverage for convoy SC 128 (Halifax Slow to United Kingdom), sink German submarine *U-174*.

PACIFIC: Japanese submarine *I-178* torpedoes and sinks a U.S. freighter off Sydney, Australia. U.S. submarine *Scorpion* attacks a Japanese convoy and torpedoes and sinks a cargo ship off Honshu, Japan.

April 28

CBI: Japanese medium bombers and fighters attack Fourteenth Air Force airfields at Kunming, China, but the raid does little damage. P-40 pilots report shooting down 10 enemy aircraft.

ATLANTIC: Escort carrier USS *Bogue* and four destroyers protecting convoy HX 235 (New York to Liverpool) succeed in preventing attacks from five German submarines following the convoy.

MEDITERRANEAN: Ninth Air Force B-24s attack Naples harbor and Messina.

TUNISIA: Company A, 6th Armored Infantry Regiment, 1st Armored Division, encounters heavy enemy resistance as it begins an attack on German entrenchments near Medjez el Bab. A German machine gun position on the company's flank is especially dangerous, holding up the company's advance. Private Nicholas Minue, on his own and completely alone, charges the entrenched enemy position in the face of heavy fire. With only the bayonet on his M-1 rifle, Private Minue kills about 10 enemy soldiers in a trench. As soon as he has cleared this position, he moves forward, driving the enemy until he is mortally wounded. For his extraordinary act of courage and indomitable spirit, Private Minue will receive the Medal of Honor.

SOUTHWEST PACIFIC AREA: U.S. submarine *Gudgeon* torpedoes and sinks a Japanese ship off Panay Island, Philippines.

April 29

ATLANTIC: German submarine *U-258* torpedoes and damages a U.S. freighter in convoy ONS 5 (Liverpool to Halifax, slow). The crew abandons the freighter. Navy PBY Catalinas damage German submarine *U-528* as it attempts to attack the same convoy.

MEDITERRANEAN: At a planning conference in Algiers for Husky, the invasion of Sicily, Supreme Allied Commander General Dwight D. Eisenhower hears from General Bernard Montgomery's representative, who proposes a combined U.S.-British assault on the southeast corner of the island.

TUNISIA: A battalion of the 16th Infantry Regiment of the 1st Infantry Division captures Hill 523 and holds off determined enemy counterattacks during the day until overwhelmed and captured.

April 30
ATLANTIC: British and Canadian naval forces take responsibility for escorting the ONS (Halifax to Liverpool) convoys.
MEDITERRANEAN: Ninth Air Force P-40s attack Axis shipping, sinking one destroyer and damaging two others. Five enemy fighters and three P-40s are lost.
TUNISIA: The 135th Infantry Regiment of the 34th Infantry Division captures Hill 609, a key defensive position, and defends it against enemy counterattack. The U.S. 9th Infantry Division, with French units, advances on the Sedjenane Valley.
SOUTHWEST PACIFIC AREA: U.S. submarine *Gudgeon* lands men and equipment on Panay Island, Philippines.
PACIFIC: Japanese submarine *I-19* torpedoes and sinks a U.S. freighter south of the Fiji Islands. U.S. submarine *Snook* lays mines off Saddle Island, China.

May 1
ALEUTIANS: Eleventh Air Force B-24 Liberators and B-25 Mitchells with P-38 Lightnings and P-40s flying escort attack installations on Kiska. Installations at Holtz Bay and Chichagof Harbor on Attu are also attacked.
CBI: Fourteenth Air Force elements move into eastern China to allow U.S. aircraft to strike deeper into Japanese-occupied areas in China, Indochina, and Thailand.
ETO: Eighth Air Force B-17s attack the St-Nazaire, France, U-boat base and ship-yard while a diversionary group of 24 B-24 Liberators flies along the coast of Brittany. Of the 29 B-17s that bomb the target, seven are lost and 22 are damaged. Enemy losses are estimated at about 20 fighters.
MEDITERRANEAN: Ninth Air Force B-24 Liberators bomb the harbor at Reggio di Calabria in Italy.
TUNISIA: The Tine Valley is open as the German defenders withdraw.

May 2
ALEUTIANS: Eleventh Air Force B-25 Mitchells, P-40s, and eight P-38 Lightnings attack antiaircraft positions and buildings on Kiska.
CBI: Fourteenth Air Force P-40s engage in air combat with about 30 Japanese fighters near Lingling and Changsha. Pilots claim seven enemy Zeroes downed with the loss of one P-40 out of the 17 involved.
MEDITERRANEAN: British Eighth Army commander, General Sir Bernard L. Montgomery, himself arrives in Algiers to press home his plan for Husky, even to the point of pursuing Eisenhower's Chief of Staff, General Walter Bedell Smith, into the men's latrine to win his point.
TUNISIA: Northwest African Air Force fighters fly reconnaissance missions and attack enemy tanks and troops near Massicault and Tebourba.
PACIFIC: Japanese submarine *I-19* torpedoes and sinks a U.S. freighter near the Fiji Islands.

New Georgia: Thirteenth Air Force B-17s along with P-38 Lightnings and P-39 Airacobras bomb Munda airfield in New Georgia.

May 3

Aleutians: Eleventh Air Force B-24 Liberators and B-25 Mitchells, with P-38 Lightnings and P-40s escorting, attack installations and the airfield on Kiska.

Mediterranean: General Dwight D. Eisenhower is the supreme allied commander for Husky, the invasion of Sicily; however, his deputy commander as well as all of his component commanders are British. General Sir Harold Alexander is both the deputy commander and the commander of the Fifteenth Army Group. The air commander is Air Chief Marshal Tedder, and the sea commander is Admiral Sir Andrew B. Cunningham. The Fifteenth Army Group consists of the British Eighth Army, commanded by General Sir Bernard L. Montgomery, and the Seventh Army, commanded by Lieutenant General George S. Patton, Jr.

The plan for Husky is very basic. The British will make the main attack and the Americans will support the British left flank as Montgomery's army marches on Messina. The U.S. forces are to land in the Gulf of Gela, stretching from Licatta eastward to the Pachino peninsula, which marks the boundary between the two armies. From the Pachino peninsula eastward, the British Eighth Army will land, capture Syracuse, advance on Catania and then to Messina. The Americans are given two limits of advance from the beachhead, the Yellow and Blue Lines. Control of this area will bring the U.S. forces to the high ground overlooking the beaches and provide a good defensive position to protect Montgomery's advance. After that, Alexander has no plan. He intends to sort things out once the armies have established themselves on the beach. The British also have the advantage of major ports, which, once captured, will supply their forces. The Allied amphibious landings will be preceded by a major airborne landing of U.S. paratroopers and British glider-borne infantry. The British 1st Airborne Division troops will land at Catania to seize key bridges along the British intended line of advance. The American 82nd Airborne Division will drop near Gela. The Americans will have no major port facility and will have to depend on ship-to-shore transport to maintain their supply lines. This transportation is in the form of the 2 ½-ton amphibious truck called the DUKW. The air attack on Sicily and Sardinia is intended to defeat Axis airpower. After the landings, there will be little coordination between air and ground forces. The intention is to allow the air forces the flexibility to attack targets they determine to be the priority. This plan, run by the British, for the British, leaves the Americans cold and puts further strain on a relationship which has not been all that amicable since the beginning of the Tunisian campaign.

Tunisia: 1st Armored Division captures Mateur. Northwest African Air Force B-17s bomb Bizerte and fighters conduct reconnaissance missions.

May 4

Aleutians: A planned strike on Kiska is cancelled due to bad weather. Eleventh Air Force B-24 Liberators and B-25 Mitchells, along with P-38 Lightnings and P-40s, attack Attu Island targets at Chichagof Harbor and antiaircraft positions at Holtz Bay.

CBI: From French Indochina Fourteenth Air Force B-24 Liberators bomb installations on Hainan Island; B-25 Mitchells and B-17s with P-40 escort bomb the docks at Haiphong and Hanoi.

ATLANTIC: German submarine *U-264* torpedoes and sinks a U.S. freighter in convoy ONS 5 (Halifax to Liverpool).

ETO: Eighth Air Force B-17s are dispatched against factories at Antwerp, Belgium, while a diversion flight of 20 B-17s and 13 B-24 Liberators heads toward France. The 65 bombers that hit the target are covered by 117 P-47C Thunderbolts for nearly 175 miles. Pilots report 10 enemy aircraft lost and 16 B-17s damaged.

TUNISIA: Northwest African Air Force A-20 Havocs attack enemy positions near Zaghouan.

SOUTHWEST PACIFIC AREA: U.S. submarine *Gudgeon* sinks a Japanese trawler west of Panay, Philippines.

PACIFIC: U.S. submarine *Seal,* attacking a Japanese convoy, torpedoes and sinks a fleet tanker southeast of the Palau Islands.

NEW GUINEA: Fifth Air Force B-24 Liberators bomb the harbor and shipping at Wewak.

May 5

ALEUTIANS: Eleventh Air Force B-24 Liberators and B-25 Mitchells, with P-38 Lightnings and P-40s escorting, attack installations on Attu and Kiska. Royal Canadian Air Force (RCAF) pilots support the attack on Kiska.

ATLANTIC: German submarine *U-707* torpedoes and sinks a U.S. freighter in convoy ONS 5.

TUNISIA: Northwest African Air Force B-17s and fighters attack docks and shipping in Tunis harbor.

PACIFIC: U.S. submarine *Permit* attacks and damages a Japanese transport ship in Apra Harbor, Guam. U.S. submarine *Sawfish* torpedoes and sinks a Japanese gunboat off Honshu, Japan. U.S. submarine *Snook* torpedoes and sinks a Japanese cargo ship in the Yellow Sea.

May 6

ALEUTIANS: Eleventh Air Force B-24 Liberators and B-25 Mitchells, with P-38 Lightnings and P-40s escorting, attack installations on Attu and Kiska, dropping over 52 tons of bombs.

ATLANTIC: German submarine *U-195* torpedoes and sinks a U.S. freighter in the South Atlantic.

MEDITERRANEAN: Northwest African Air Force B-17s bomb Marsala and Trapani in Sicily. B-25 Mitchells and B-26 Marauders bomb ships off Marettimo Island and the port of Favignana.

TUNISIA: Ninth Air Force B-25 Mitchells attack Massicault and surrounding areas, while P-40s attack shipping in the Gulf of Tunis. Fighters, A-20 Havocs, and bombers fly over 1,400 sorties, attacking airfields, enemy vehicles, and troops. B-25s and B-26 Marauders bomb ships and aircraft.

SOUTHWEST PACIFIC AREA: SWPA headquarters issues orders for the occupation of Kiriwina and Woodlark Islands by U.S. forces and the capture of the northern coast of New Guinea, including the Huon Peninsula, by Australian forces. Southern Bougainville and western New Britain are also to be occupied. Kiriwina and Woodlark Islands can support advance airfields to support future operations against Rabaul. The Allies will also be able to control the Vitaz Strait and have free access to the Bismarck Sea. The capture of Bougainville will give SOPAC forces a base of operations for strikes on Buka and Kavieng. Occupation of western New Britain will provide a base of operations to support SOPAC and threaten Rabaul.

U.S. submarine *Gar* torpedoes and sinks a Japanese cargo ship in Tarakan harbor, Borneo.

PACIFIC: U.S. submarine *Snook* torpedoes and sinks two Japanese cargo ships in the Yellow Sea. U.S. submarine *Wahoo* sinks Japanese cargo ship off Honshu, Japan.

NEW GEORGIA: U.S. ships lay mines in the western approaches to Kula Gulf, New Georgia Island.

May 7

TUNISIA: U.S. 9th Infantry Division enters Bizerte; Combat Command A of the 1st Armored Division reaches Ferryville.

May 8

CBI: Fourteenth Air Force B-24 Liberators and B-25 Mitchells bomb airfields and support facilities at Canton. The P-40s escorting the bombers destroy nearly 20 enemy aircraft.

ATLANTIC: JCS approves a planning estimate that projects 36 Allied divisions ready for a cross-Channel invasion by April 1944. German forces available in France to oppose the invasion are estimated at 32 divisions and 1,200 aircraft. Planners estimate that the Germans can reinforce these divisions in three weeks, increasing the total to 60 divisions and 1,700 aircraft. To succeed, the planners stress the need for a firm lodgment so that the Allied divisions can maintain a beachhead to support the flow of forces into France. To do this, ports are essential to build up sufficient supplies before an offensive can begin.

TUNISIA: Ninth Air Force P-40s attack shipping near Cap Bon and the Gulf of Tunis. P-40 fighter pilots claim five enemy fighters destroyed. Northwest African Air Force B-25 Mitchells bomb rail junctions and highways. P-40s and A-20 Havocs bomb shipping between Tunisia and Sicily as well as troop convoys and road networks around Tunis and Cap Bon.

SOUTHWEST PACIFIC AREA: Fifth Air Force B-17s bomb Rabaul airfield.

NEW GEORGIA: Thirteenth Air Force P-40 and P-38 Lightnings hit antiaircraft positions at Vila in New Georgia. Two Japanese destroyers hit the U.S. mines at Kula Gulf. One sinks, the other is damaged and later sunk in a U.S. air attack. U.S. aircraft attack two other destroyers, sinking one and damaging another off Rendova, New Georgia Islands.

May 9

MEDITERRANEAN: Ninth Air Force B-24 Liberators bomb the harbor facilities at Messina.

TUNISIA: Combat Command B of the U.S. 1st Armored Division cuts the Bizerte-Tunis Road and makes contact with elements of the British 7th Armored Division north of Tunis. P-40s fly reconnaissance, escort, and ground attack missions against enemy ships, troop concentrations, choke points, and gun positions in the vicinity of Cap Bon. The German commander meets with General Omar Bradley, commander of U.S. II Corps, and surrenders nearly 50,000 soldiers. General Bradley later passes the following message to his subordinates: "With their practical sense, their understanding of the enemy, their firsthand knowledge of the hardships and dangers of war, and above all else, their courage and loyalty, soldiers of the II Corps have played a major role in the winning of a great Allied victory."

SOUTHWEST PACIFIC AREA: U.S. submarine *Gar* torpedoes and sinks a Japanese gunboat off Mindanao, Philippines.

PACIFIC: U.S. submarines *Pogy* and *Wahoo*, both operating off Honshu, Japan, score hits in separate attacks. *Pogy* torpedoes and damages a Japanese transport. *Wahoo* torpedoes and sinks two cargo ships.

May 10

CBI: Fourteenth Air Force P-40s attack an enemy troop train and riverboats in the vicinity of Hanoi.

MEDITERRANEAN: Ninth Air Force B-25 Mitchells and P-40s bomb Pantelleria Island.

SOUTHWEST PACIFIC AREA: Fifth Air Force B-25 Mitchells bomb the Cape Gloucester airfield on New Britain Island in the Bismarck Archipelago.

PACIFIC: U.S. submarine *Plunger* attacks a Japanese convoy in the open ocean east of Saipan, sinking a cargo ship and damaging a transport.

NEW GEORGIA: Thirteenth Air Force P-38 Lightnings, along with navy and marine aircraft, attack Munda airfield in New Georgia.

May 11

ALEUTIANS: Operation Landgrab. The U.S. 7th Infantry Division begins landing on Attu Island. U.S. submarines *Nautilus* and *Narwhal* land scouts on the island. A provisional battalion lands and moves inland, while the 1st Battalion of the 17th Infantry Regiment lands at Holtz Bay, headed for Hill X, its initial objective and the linkup point with the advancing provisional battalion. Meanwhile, at Massacre Bay, delayed by heavy fog and threatening seas, the 2nd and 3rd Battalions of the 17th land and advance toward Jarmin Pass. Both the 1st and 3rd Battalions are stopped by enemy fire short of their objectives. Eleventh Air Force B-24 Liberators conduct several missions supporting the 7th Infantry Division on Attu. The bombers drop supplies, make bombing runs, and drop leaflets to convince the Japanese at Chichagof Harbor to surrender.

MEDITERRANEAN: Northwest African Air Force B-17s, B-26 Marauders, and B-25 Mitchells bomb Marsala in Sicily, targeting transportation and support sites.

SOUTHWEST PACIFIC AREA: Fifth Air Force B-17s and B-24 Liberators bomb Rabaul airfield. B-25 Mitchells bomb Penfoei and Dili in Timor.

U.S. submarine *Grayback* attacks a Japanese convoy northwest of Kavieng, New Ireland, and sinks a collier.

Pacific: Off Saipan, U.S. submarine *Plunger* sinks the damaged Japanese transport it had attacked previously.

May 12

Aleutians: The 2nd Battalion, 32nd Infantry Regiment, attached to the 7th Infantry Division, lands at Massacre Bay. The 1st Battalion of the 17th Infantry Regiment takes the crest of Hill X, but fails to drive the Japanese off the hill. U.S. battleship *Pennsylvania* provides naval gunfire support to the Hill X attack. The battleship *Nevada* supports the landing at Massacre Bay with naval gunfire. Two Japanese submarines conduct torpedo attacks, but miss their intended targets. Shortly thereafter Japanese submarine *I-31* is detected and two U.S. destroyers sink the sub northeast of Chichagof Harbor. Eleventh Air Force B-24 Liberators, B-25 Mitchells, and P-38 Lightnings conduct ground support missions.

Atlantic: The Trident Conference begins. U.S. planners seek to obtain an agreement with the British that conforms to U.S. strategic interests. While supporting the British peripheral approach to defeating the Axis powers through offensive operations in the Mediterranean, these operations will be limited and subordinate to a cross-Channel invasion with a specific date in 1944. In addition, the United States will continue to pursue the strategic initiative gained in the Pacific during the summer of 1942. This includes keeping China in the war through offensive action in Burma, MacArthur's advance in the Southwest Pacific, as well as Nimitz's planned advance in the Central Pacific. Well coordinated among the army and navy, and the state Department, the American position is intended to overcome the lack of preparation that allowed British strategic priorities to dominate the Casablanca conference in January.

Tunisia: The End of the Tunisian Campaign. Colonel General Jurgen von Armin formally surrenders to the British. About 275,000 Axis troops become prisoners of war. The Italian commander will surrender a day later, ending the campaign. The North African campaign has cost the United States 18,558 casualties. The inexperienced Americans have learned some brutal lessons about combat, yet have performed doggedly and, at times, exceptionally, and made significant contributions to the final phases of the campaign.

Southwest Pacific Area: U.S. submarine *Gudgeon* torpedoes and sinks a Japanese cargo ship off southern Luzon, Philippines.

Pacific: U.S. submarine *Steelhead* conducts mine-laying activities off Japan.

May 13

Aleutians: The Japanese continue to hold Jarmin Pass, despite the efforts of the 2nd Battalion 32nd Infantry and the 3rd Battalion of the 17th Infantry to capture the position. The 3rd Battalion of the 32nd Infantry Regiment lands at Holtz Bay to reinforce the attack on Hill X. The battleship USS *Idaho* and a destroyer support the landing with naval gunfire. The American troops, anticipating a quick victory against minimal enemy resistance, have no winter clothing. The extreme weather conditions on the island and lack of supplies will limit the effectiveness of the combat troops.

Caribbean: German submarine *U-176* torpedoes and sinks two tankers off Hispaniola.

U.S. B-17s releasing bombs over a target in Germany *(National Archives and Records Administration)*

ETO: Eighth Air Force B-17s bomb the aircraft factory at Meaulte and the airfields at St. Omer, France. Of the 88 bombers that attack Meaulte, three B-17s are lost and 11 are damaged. Enemy losses are estimated at 11 aircraft destroyed. Of the 31 B-17s flown against the airfields, one bomber is lost and one damaged.

SOUTH PACIFIC: Thirteenth Air Force B-17s bomb Kahili airfields on Bougainville Island and on Ballale Island. Royal New Zealand Air Force (RNZAF) P-40s, U.S. P-38 Lightnings, P-39 Airacobras, and P-40s, along with navy and marine fighters, intercept and destroy 16 enemy aircraft over Russell Island and Tulagi.

NEW GEORGIA: Rear Admiral Walden L. Ainsworth's Naval Task Force 18 bombards Munda and Vila airfields in New Georgia. During the bombardment, minelayers cover the northwestern approaches to Kula Gulf.

NEW GUINEA: Fifth Air Force B-17s bomb the Rabaul airfields and targets at Wewak and Boram in New Guinea. A-20 Havocs attack the airfield at Cape Gloucester on New Britain Island.

May 14

ALEUTIANS: Eleventh Air Force B-24 Liberators and B-25 Mitchells conduct ground support bombing missions over Attu. One B-24 is lost dropping supplies for the infantry.

ATLANTIC: Navy PBY Catalinas sink German submarine *U-657* tracking convoy ONS 7 (Halifax to Liverpool, slow) in the North Atlantic.

ETO: Over 200 Eighth Air Force bombers fly missions against four targets in Europe. The submarine yards and naval base at Kiel, Germany, are attacked by 126 B-17s and 17 B-24 Liberators. Over 60 enemy aircraft are reportedly destroyed; eight U.S. bombers are lost and 37 are damaged. Over Antwerp, Belgium, 38 B-17s bomb industrial targets. One B-17 is lost in the attack and 15 others damaged; enemy aircraft losses are estimated at five destroyed. The B-17s are escorted by 118 P-47 Thunderbolts. At least four German fighters are downed, but three P-47s are lost and one is damaged. All three pilots are listed as missing. At Courtrai, France, 34 B-17s bomb the airfield. Two bombers are shot down and 10 others are damaged. Of the 11 B-26 Marauders that attack the Velsen power station at Ijmuiden, Netherlands, 10 are damaged. This is the first time that the B-26 is used in the strategic air offensive in Europe.

NEW BRITAIN: Fifth Air Force B-25 Mitchells bomb the airfield at Gasmata, New Britain; B-24 Liberators and B-17s bomb the airfield at Rabaul. B-25s bomb the Penfoei airfield and Dili in Timor.

NEW GUINEA: Two U.S. motor torpedo (PT) boats sink Japanese submarine *RO-102* in Vitiaz Strait, off Saidor.

May 15

ALEUTIANS: Eleventh Air Force P-38 Lightnings attack antiaircraft positions while B-24 Liberators bomb Holtz Bay and Chichagof Harbor. The Japanese fall back to Moore Ridge behind Hill X, continuing to delay the advance of the Americans, who are also hampered by a mistaken U.S. airstrike on their position. The provisional battalion finally links up with the 1st Battalion of the 17th Infantry.

CBI: Fourteenth Air Force P-40s intercept a Japanese raid on Kunming airfield. The bombers cause little damage and the P-40s claim 13 fighter and two bomber kills.

CARIBBEAN: U.S. OS2U Kingfisher observation scout aircraft and a Cuban submarine chaser sink German submarine *U-176* off Cuba.

ATLANTIC: The Trident Conference begins. President Franklin Roosevelt, Prime Minister Churchill, the Combined Chiefs of Staff, and Generals Wavell, Chennault, and Stilwell from the China-Burma-India (CBI) theater. U.S. strategists, taking a hard look at U.S. wartime objectives, assess that China's manpower and geographical position are the keys to victory in the war against Japan, just as the USSR's manpower and geography are the keys to victory over Germany in Europe. Unlike the British, the Americans want to press for a swift and decisive victory against Germany in order to put their full resources against what many U.S. military officers (especially in the navy) consider to be the main threat, Japan. Therefore, the centerpiece of this conference for the Americans is to get a commitment from the British on a firm date for the cross-Channel invasion.

    Well coordinated among the Army, Navy, and State Departments, the American position is intended to overcome the lack of preparation that allowed British strategic priorities to dominate the Casablanca conference in January. The Americans obtain an agreement from the British for a cross-Channel invasion with a target date of May 1, 1944. While supporting the British peripheral approach to defeating the Axis powers through offensive operations in the Mediterranean, these operations will be limited and will be subordinate to a cross-Channel invasion. They agree to continue the Mediterranean offensive with the aim of knocking Italy out of the war.

The Allies reaffirm their commitment to a strategic air offensive as preparation for the invasion. But the Americans win support for an increased operational tempo in the Pacific. The United States will continue to pursue the strategic initiative gained in the Pacific during the summer of 1942. This includes keeping China in the war through offensive action in Burma, MacArthur's advance in the Southwest Pacific, as well as Nimitz's planned advance in the Central Pacific.

ETO: Eighth Air Force B-17s attack naval facilities and submarine construction at Helgoland Island and Wilhelmshaven, Germany. Over 30 enemy aircraft are declared destroyed; of the 76 B-17s, five are lost and 27 are damaged. Over Emden, Germany 59 B-17s attack the U-boat yard, marshaling yard, and airfield. One B-17 is lost and nine others are damaged. Enemy losses are estimated at 14 aircraft. The attack is preceded by a fighter sweep of 116 P-47 Thunderbolts over Amsterdam and Rotterdam. Two enemy aircraft are reported shot down, but one P-47 is lost and the pilot is reported as missing.

SOUTHWEST PACIFIC AREA: U.S. submarine *Gar* attacks a Japanese convoy, torpedoing and sinking two cargo ships between Mindoro and Marinduque Islands, in the Philippines.

CENTRAL PACIFIC: Seventh Air Force B-24 Liberators from Midway bomb Wake Island. They are attacked by 22 enemy fighters, which shoot down one B-24. Four enemy aircraft are claimed lost.

NEW GUINEA: Fifth Air Force B-25 Mitchells and A-20 Havocs bomb the Lae airfield on New Guinea.

May 16

ALEUTIANS: Admiral Kinkaid, dissatisfied with Major General Brown's performance, relieves him and puts Major General Eugene M. Landrum in command of the operation. Moore Ridge is captured. The Japanese withdraw to prepared defensive positions around Chichagof Harbor. Eleventh Air Force B-24 Liberators bomb Chichagof Harbor, while other B-24s drop supplies to ground forces. B-25 Mitchells and P-38 Lightnings fly ground support missions.

ATLANTIC: A U.S. destroyer sinks German submarine *U-182* west of Madeira Islands in the North Atlantic near the convoy routes to the Mediterranean.

SOUTHWEST PACIFIC AREA: U.S. submarine *Grayback* torpedoes and damages a Japanese destroyer northwest of Kavieng, New Ireland.

PACIFIC: Japanese submarine *I-19* torpedoes and sinks a U.S. freighter off the Fiji Islands. The submarine surfaces, fires on the survivors, then questions and releases the men.

May 17

ALEUTIANS: Jarmin Pass is captured after Japanese defenders abandon their positions.

ATLANTIC: A U.S. PBM Mariner patrol bomber damages German submarine *U-128* in the South Atlantic, and two U.S. destroyers then sink the U-boat.

SOUTHWEST PACIFIC AREA: U.S. submarine *Grayback* torpedoes and sinks a cargo ship northwest of the Saint Matthias Group Islands.

May 18

ALEUTIANS: The 1st Battalion of the 4th Infantry Division arrives to reinforce the 7th Infantry Division.

Eleventh Air Force B-24 Liberators bomb Kiska Island, while P-40s and a B-25 Mitchell conduct reconnaissance.

ATLANTIC: The Trident Conference. The CCS agrees to a two-phase approach to the cross-Channel invasion, specifically lodgment and buildup. Air superiority is identified as an essential factor in the success of the plan.

MEDITERRANEAN: Northwest African Air Force begins sustained air attacks on Pantelleria Island. The first attack against docks and airfields involves over 80 B-25 Mitchell and B-26 Marauder bombers escorted by P-38 Lightnings.

PACIFIC: U.S. submarine *Pollack* torpedoes and sinks a Japanese gunboat off Maloelap Atoll in the Marshall Islands. Japanese submarine *I-25* torpedoes then surfaces to finish off a U.S. tanker with gunfire off Villa Efate in the New Hebrides Islands.

May 19

ATLANTIC: The Trident Conference. The CCS accepts the JCS draft strategic plan for the defeat of Japan. The plan calls for a two-pronged offensive from the Southwest Pacific and from the Central Pacific, with the Central Pacific as the main effort. The objectives are to capture the Philippines, secure the coastal area of China, and retake Hong Kong. From air bases in China, U.S. bombers will initiate an attack on the Japanese home islands. If necessary, an amphibious invasion will be launched to conquer Japan. This planning outline has no specific timetable, and no additional resources are to be provided to accomplish these objectives.

The CCS also approves the general concept for the cross-Channel invasion. The initial assault will be made with nine divisions to establish the lodgment and be reinforced with three to five divisions per month to prepare for the breakout.

ETO: Eighth Air Force VIII Bomber Command conducts attacks on the U-boat yards at Kiel and the naval facilities at Flensburg, Germany. Of the 103 B-17s that attack Kiel, six are shot down and 28 others are damaged. Enemy aircraft losses are estimated to be over 50. Over Flensburg, 55 B-17s bomb the target and claim 12 enemy aircraft destroyed and have nine B-17s damaged.

MEDITERRANEAN: Northwest African Air Force B-25 Mitchells and B-26 Marauders bomb airfields in Sardinia. B-17s bomb Milo Airfield at Trapani in Sicily.

SOUTHWEST PACIFIC AREA: U.S. submarine *Gar* torpedoes and sinks a Japanese guardboat in the Makassar Strait.

NEW BRITAIN: Fifth Air Force B-24 Liberators bomb the airfield at Gasmata Island in the Bismarck Archipelago.

NEW GUINEA: Fifth Air Force B-25 Mitchells bomb Japanese positions around Salamaua.

May 20

ATLANTIC: Admiral Ernest J. King, COMINCH, establishes under his command the Tenth Fleet with headquarters in Washington, D.C. Tenth Fleet's responsibility is to oversee Atlantic antisubmarine operations.

MEDITERRANEAN: In Sardinia, Northwest African Air Force P-38 Lightnings bomb the docks at Gulfo Aranci and rail lines near Macomer. B-17s bomb the airfield at Grosseto in Italy.

PACIFIC: U.S. submarine *Pollack* torpedoes and sinks a Japanese armed merchant cruiser near Jaluit Atoll, Marshall Islands.

May 21

ALEUTIANS: Elements of the 32nd Infantry and 1st Battalion, 4th Infantry, clear the main passes that cover the approaches to Chichagof Harbor.

ATLANTIC: TBF Avenger torpedo bombers from the U.S. escort carrier USS *Bogue* damage German submarine *U-231* as it tracks convoy ON 184 (Liverpool to New York, fast). A U.S. and Canadian destroyer each drive off other U-boats threatening the convoy.

ETO: Eighth Air Force VIII Bomber Command attacks two targets over Germany, the U-boat yards at Wilhelmshaven and Emden. The 77 B-17s that attack Wilhelmshaven report over 50 enemy aircraft destroyed; seven B-17s are lost and 24 are damaged. The 46 B-17s attacking Emden lose five over the target and 11 other bombers are damaged. Over 30 enemy aircraft are claimed shot down. Over 100 P-47 Thunderbolts conduct a fighter sweep over Ostend and Ghent in Belgium. Three aircraft and pilots are lost.

MEDITERRANEAN: U.S. destroyer sinks Italian submarine *Gorgo* off Algeria as it attempts to make an attack on a U.S. convoy. Ninth Air Force B-24 Liberators attack San Giovanni and Reggio di Calabria in Italy. Crews report four enemy fighters shot down. Northwest African Air Force B-25 Mitchells and B-26 Marauders bomb Villacidro and Decimomannu airfields in Sardinia. B-17s bomb support facilities at Castelvetrano on Sicily.

SOUTHWEST PACIFIC AREA: Fifth Air Force B-17s bomb airfields around Rabaul and B-24 Liberators attack the airfield on Gasmata Island.

May 22

ATLANTIC: TBF Avengers from U.S. escort carrier USS *Bogue* protecting convoy ON 184 (Liverpool to New York, fast) sink German submarine *U-569* and damage *U-305*.

May 23

ALEUTIANS: Eleventh Air Force B-24 Liberators and 18 P-38 Lightnings flying air cover missions to Attu hear a report that 16 Japanese bombers are in the air. Five P-38s attack the bombers, shooting down five enemy planes and reporting seven others destroyed. Two P-38s are shot down in the battle over Attu.

MEDITERRANEAN: Northwest African Air Force P-40s attack gun positions as B-25 Mitchells and B-26 Marauders bomb the docks and airfield on Pantelleria Island.

SOUTH PACIFIC: Japanese submarine *I-17* torpedoes and sinks a U.S. tanker off Nouméa, New Caledonia.

NEW BRITAIN: Fifth Air Force B-24 Liberators and B-17s bomb Kavieng Harbor and the airfield. The bombers also attack Gasmata Island airfield off New Britain.

May 24

MEDITERRANEAN: Ninth Air Force B-24 Liberators bomb facilities supporting the ferry terminal at Villa San Giovanni. Northwest African Air Force P-40s, P-38 Lightnings,

B-25 Mitchells, B-26 Marauders, and B-17s bomb airfields, facilities, and transportation targets across Sardinia.

May 25
ALEUTIANS: Eleventh Air Force B-25 Mitchells and B-24 Liberators conduct ground support missions on Attu while P-38 Lightnings fly air cover. At Kiska and Little Kiska, 18 P-40s fly reconnaissance and attack missions.

ATLANTIC: The Trident Conference ends. The meetings between the British and the Americans are often stormy, as the Combined Chiefs of Staff hammer out a compromise that is decidedly slanted in favor of the American approach. The outcome is an agreed target date of May 1, 1944, for the cross-Channel invasion of Europe. Operation Husky, the invasion of Sicily, will be launched with the objective of knocking Italy out of the war. China will be supported through additional matériel and reinforcements to the U.S. Fourteenth Air Force. Japan's occupation force in the Aleutians will be eliminated; and as part of the U.S. strategic plan to defeat Japan, an attack through the Central Pacific will continue to pressure the Japanese. Offensive air operations will proceed in the ETO as a prelude to the invasion. In the Mediterranean, offensive air operations will be directed against the Ploeşti oil fields in Romania. General Stilwell's request for additional American ground forces for CBI is disapproved, although limited amphibious operations along the coast of Burma are considered possible.

U.S. PBY Catalina sinks German submarine *U-467* south of Iceland.

May 26
ALEUTIANS: U.S. forces are able to consolidate and conduct a coordinated effort to capture Fish Hook Ridge, on which Japanese defenders in deep entrenchments and hidden positions have halted the American advance for nearly a week. A reinforced battalion attempts to conduct a coordinated attack on this position. Private Joe P. Martinez, an automatic rifleman in K Company, 32nd Infantry Regiment, 7th Infantry Division, sets the example to press forward even in the face of heavy machine-gun, rifle, and mortar fire. Those who have dropped to the ground when the enemy began to fire are amazed that Private Martinez is still on his feet and gesturing to his comrades to follow. Martinez uses his Browning Automatic Rifle (BAR) and hand grenades to capture the first position. But the Japanese guarding the Chichagof Pass have a number of defensive positions along the ridges. Undaunted, Private Martinez pushes forward, leading by example and continuing to clear successive enemy trenches with his BAR until he is mortally wounded. The Japanese can no longer hold the key pass, and Martinez's exploits allow American forces to gain an important objective. For his courageous example and extraordinary dedication to duty, he will receive the Medal of Honor.

MEDITERRANEAN: Northwest African Air Force P-40s bomb Pantelleria Island.

SOUTHWEST PACIFIC AREA: U.S. submarine *Trout* lands advisers and supplies to support guerrilla operations on Basilan Island, Philippines.

PACIFIC: U.S. submarine *Whale* torpedoes and sinks a Japanese gunboat off Rota Island in the Marianas. U.S. submarine *Pogy* attacks a convoy off Honshu, Japan, and sinks a cargo ship. U.S. submarine *Saury* attacks a convoy south of Kyushu, Japan, and sinks a transport ship.

May 27
ATLANTIC: German submarine *U-154* attacks convoy BT 14 (Bahia, Brazil to Trinidad) off the coast of Brazil. The U-boat torpedoes and sinks two U.S. freighters and damages a tanker.

In Washington, D.C., Joint Staff planners begin examining forces and support necessary for offensive action against the Marshall Islands in the Pacific Operations Area.
MEDITERRANEAN: Northwest African Air Force P-40s attack targets on Pantelleria Island.
PACIFIC: U.S. submarine *Finback* torpedoes and sinks a Japanese cargo ship northwest of the Palau Islands. U.S. submarine *Runner* begins a patrol from Midway, but is never heard from again.

May 28
CBI: Fourteenth Air Force P-40s attack railroad facilities at Yoyang, China.
ATLANTIC: German submarine *U-177* torpedoes and sinks a U.S. freighter in the North Atlantic.
MEDITERRANEAN: Northwest African Air Force B-17s bomb the oil refinery, marshaling yard, harbor, and shipbuilding yards at Leghorn in Italy. P-40s and A-20 Havocs bomb Pantelleria Island.
SOUTHWEST PACIFIC AREA: Headquarters SWPA approves Alamo Force's plan for Kiriwina and Woodlark Islands assault. The plan is called Chronicle. The day for the assault is June 30.
PACIFIC: U.S. submarine *Saury* torpedoes and sinks a Japanese fleet tanker northwest of Okinawa.

May 29
ALEUTIANS: Nearly 1,000 Japanese soldiers make a night attack on U.S. positions in a desperate attempt to break out. Most of them are killed.
ETO: Eighth Air Force VIII Bomber Command attacks three targets in France. The submarine pens and locks at St-Nazaire are attacked by 147 B-17s. Eight bombers are lost and 59 are damaged. Enemy losses are six aircraft. Several armored versions of the B-17, the YB-40, accompany the bombers, but are unable to keep up with the formation and are largely ineffective. At the Rennes naval depot, 57 B-17s bomb the target, but six planes are lost and 31 are damaged. Enemy losses are estimated at over 20 aircraft. B-24 Liberators bomb the U-boat yards at La Pallice with no losses.
MEDITERRANEAN: Northwest African Air Force P-40s, P-38 Lightnings, and B-26 Marauders attack gun positions and a radar site on Pantelleria Island.
PACIFIC: U.S. submarine *Scamp* torpedoes and sinks a seaplane carrier north of Kavieng, New Ireland. U.S. submarine chaser sinks Japanese submarine *I-178* off Espiritu Santo Island in the New Hebrides. U.S. submarine *Tambor* torpedoes and sinks a cargo ship in the South China Sea. U.S. submarine *Gar* torpedoes and sinks a Japanese gunboat in the Sulu Sea.

May 30
ALEUTIANS: Eleventh Air Force P-40s conduct ground attack missions while B-24 Liberators and B-25 Mitchells conduct bombing missions over Kiska. B-24 Liberators and P-38 Lightnings fly air cover and patrol missions over Attu.

ATLANTIC: German submarine *U-126* torpedoes and sets afire a U.S. freighter off the coast of West Africa.

MEDITERRANEAN: Ninth Air Force B-24 Liberators bomb the airfield at Foggia, Italy, damaging facilities and aircraft, while B-25 Mitchells bomb Pantelleria Island. Northwest African Air Force P-38 Lightnings and B-17s bomb industrial and transportation targets in Sardinia.

PACIFIC: U.S. submarine *Saury* torpedoes and sinks two Japanese cargo ships off Shanghai, China. U.S. submarine *Steelhead* conducts mining operations off the coast of Japan.

May 31

ALEUTIANS: Operation Landgrab Ends. The U.S. 7th Infantry Division eliminates the last resistance on Attu. Of the estimated 2,500 defenders on the island, only 28 are alive as prisoners. The U.S. casualties are stunning: 549 killed, 1,148 wounded, and over 2,000 evacuated as nonbattle casualties, most due to exposure and trench foot. The capture of Attu will be one of the costliest campaigns in World War II for the United States.

CBI: Fourteenth Air Force B-24 Liberators, with U.S. and Chinese P-40s flying escort, bomb the airfield at Ichang, China. Enemy aircraft losses are reported at five shot down; one Chinese P-40 is lost.

MEDITERRANEAN: Northwest African Air Force B-17s bomb the airfield and marshaling yard at Foggia, Italy.

NEW GUINEA: Fifth Air Force B-24 Liberators bomb the airfield and other targets at Lae.

June 1

ALEUTIANS: Eleventh Air Force B-25 Mitchells, P-38 Lightnings, and P-40s attack facilities, radar sites, and gun positions on Kiska Island.

CBI: Fourteenth Air Force P-40s bomb warehouses and rail facilities at Changanyi, China.

ALEUTIANS: Planning begins for the invasion of Kiska. The Eleventh Air Force is directed to intensify air attacks on the island, and ground forces begin intensive training at Fort Ord, California.

MEDITERRANEAN: Northwest African Air Force P-38 Lightnings and B-17s bomb Pantelleria while P-40s attack gun positions. P-40s attack the seaplane base on Stagnone Island and P-38 Lightnings bomb the railroad near Balesrate in Sicily. In Sardinia, P-38 Lightnings, B-26 Marauders, and B-25 Mitchells bomb harbors.

PACIFIC: U.S. submarine *Trigger* torpedoes and sinks a Japanese collier off Honshu, Japan.

June 2

ATLANTIC: U.S. submarine chaser sinks German submarine *U-521* off the coast of Virginia.

SOUTHWEST PACIFIC AREA: Alamo Force plans the assaults on Kiriwina and Woodlark islands (Operation Chronicle). Two battalions of the 158th RCT, reinforced by the 46th Engineer Regiment, antiaircraft and support units, will capture Kiriwina. Colonel Prugh J. Herndon is to command the assault. Woodlark Island is the assignment of the 112th Cavalry Regiment, supported by the 12th Marine Defense Battalion, Seabees, and support units. Brigadier General Julian W. Cunningham, the commander of the 112th, will command the assault. One battalion of the 158th RCT will be the Alamo Force reserve.

PACIFIC: U.S. submarine *Tambor* torpedoes and sinks a Japanese cargo ship in the South China Sea.

June 3

INDIAN OCEAN: Japanese submarine *I-27* torpedoes and sinks a U.S. freighter off Oman.

SOUTH PACIFIC: Admiral Halsey (COMSOPAC) develops plans for Toenails, the attack on New Georgia Island, with the intent to seize Munda airfield. Halsey designates Major General John H. Hester, commander of the 43rd Infantry Division, as commander of ground forces for Toenails. Lieutenant General Millard F. Harmon, the commander of U.S. Army forces in the Southern Pacific (SOPAC), is concerned about the command arrangement for Hester and orders XIV Corps on Guadalcanal, under the command of Major General Oscar W. Griswold, to be prepared to take command of the New Georgia occupation force, so that neither Hester nor the 43rd Infantry Division staff is overburdened with commanding at two separate echelons. Marine forces designated for Toenails are the 1st and 4th Marine Raider Battalions.

BOUGAINVILLE: Thirteenth Air Force B-17s bomb the airfield at Kahili and other targets on Bougainville Island.

June 4

ATLANTIC: TBF Avenger torpedo bombers from the U.S. escort carrier USS *Bogue* damage German submarines *U-228, U-603,* and *U-641.*

NEW GUINEA: Fifth Air Force B-17s and B-24 Liberators bomb airfields in New Guinea, while B-25 Mitchells bomb targets on Timor.

June 5

ATLANTIC: TBF Avengers from USS *Bogue* sink German submarine *U-217.*

MEDITERRANEAN: Northwest African Air Force B-25 Mitchells and P-38 Lightnings attack gun positions on Pantelleria Island. B-17s bomb the harbor and shipping at La Spezia, Italy. B-26 Marauders bomb a port facility, while P-38s attack airfields in Sardinia.

June 6

MEDITERRANEAN: Ninth Air Force B-24 Liberators bomb the harbors at Villa San Giovanni and Reggio di Calabria in Italy; the ferry and railroad yards at Messina in Sicily are also attacked. Eight enemy fighters are reportedly destroyed. B-25 Mitchells bomb Pantelleria Island. Northwest African Air Force P-40s, P-38 Lightnings, B-26 Marauders, A-20 Havocs, A-36 Invaders (Apaches), and B-25 Mitchells bomb gun positions on Pantelleria, initiating the second phase of the air offensive against the tiny island.

June 6

SOUTHWEST PACIFIC AREA: U.S. submarine *Tautog* torpedoes and sinks a Japanese cargo ship in the Sulu Sea.

PACIFIC: U.S. submarine *S-30* torpedoes and sinks a Japanese cargo ship south of Kamchatka.

BOUGAINVILLE: Thirteenth Air Force P-38 Lightnings, P-40s, navy and marine F6F Hellcats, F4U Corsairs, TBF Avenger torpedo bombers, and SBD Dauntless dive-bombers attack Japanese shipping off Buin, on Bougainville Island, damaging a destroyer and two other vessels. A total of 15 enemy aircraft are reported shot down. P-38s and P-40s attack targets on Choiseul Island.

June 7

MEDITERRANEAN: Ninth Air Force B-25 Mitchells bomb gun positions and the airfield on Pantelleria Island.

GUADALCANAL: Thirteenth Air Force P-38 Lightnings and P-40s, navy and marine F6F Hellcats and F4U Corsairs, along with Royal New Zealand Air Force P-40s, intercept Japanese dive-bombers and fighters headed to attack shipping at Guadalcanal. Over 20 enemy aircraft are shot down. Although nine Allied fighters are lost, there are no pilot casualties.

June 8

ALEUTIANS: U.S. engineers complete the fighter airfield on Attu. An Eleventh Air Force C-47 is the first aircraft to land on the airfield.

June 8

CBI: Fourteenth Air Force B-24 Liberators and B-25 Mitchells, escorted by P-40s, bomb shipping, rail, and power facilities near Hanoi, French Indochina.

ATLANTIC: TBF Avenger torpedo bombers from the U.S. escort carrier USS *Bogue* damage German submarine *U-758.*

MEDITERRANEAN: Ninth Air Force B-25 Mitchells bomb Pantelleria Island. Northwest African Air Force aircraft, in addition to conducting bombing runs on the island, scatter surrender leaflets to further demoralize the defenders. P-38 Lightnings attack targets in Sardinia.

BOUGAINVILLE: Thirteenth Air Force B-24 Liberators bomb Kahili airfield on Bougainville Island. Fifth Air Force B-25 Mitchells bomb Koepang and areas near Dili in Timor. U.S. submarine *Finback* attacks a Japanese convoy about 100 miles north of Palau, sinking an auxiliary minelayer.

June 9

MEDITERRANEAN: Ninth Air Force B-24 Liberators bomb near Gerbini and Catania airfield in Sicily. B-25 Mitchells bomb Pantelleria Island. Northwest African Air Force P-40s, P-38 Lightnings, B-26 Marauders, A-20 Havocs, and B-25 Mitchells attack targets on Pantelleria as well.

PACIFIC: Thirteenth Air Force B-17s, P-40s, and P-38 Lightnings attack the airfields at Munda and Vila in New Georgia. U.S. submarine *Greenling* damages a Japanese oiler en route to Truk in the Marianas.

June 10

ALEUTIANS: Eleventh Air Force B-24 Liberators, B-25 Mitchells, and P-40 fighters conduct attacks on facilities at Kiska Island, while F-5As (unarmed P-38 variant) fly photo missions. A U.S. submarine chaser intentionally rams and sinks Japanese submarine *I-24* off Shemya Island.

CBI: Fourteenth Air Force P-40 fighters intercept about 25 Japanese bombers and fighters over Hengyang, China, destroying one bomber.

ATLANTIC: German submarine *U-66* torpedoes and sinks a U.S. tanker off the coast of Florida. Despite a raging fire that kills most of the crew and the armed guard aboard, the crewmen still serve the forward deck gun in an attempt to sink the U-boat.

President Roosevelt signs the tax withholding bill into law. It increases the number of U.S. taxpayers by 60 million and will bring a revenue increase of $43 billion by the end of the war.

ETO: The Combined Chiefs of Staff issues a directive to initiate the Combined Bomber Offensive against strategic targets in Germany. The Combined Operational Planning Committee is established to coordinate the offensive. The U.S. Army Air Force will use precision bombing to attack strategic targets during the day. The Royal Air Force will conduct bombing attacks against strategic city areas at night.

MEDITERRANEAN: Ninth Air Force B-25 Mitchells with P-40 escorts bomb Pantelleria Island. Northwest African Air Force P-40s, P-38 Lightnings, B-26 Marauders, A-20 Havocs, and B-25s conduct over 1,000 sorties against Pantelleria.

PACIFIC: U.S. submarine *Flying Fish* torpedoes but does not damage a Japanese cargo ship in the North Pacific. U.S. submarine *S-30* torpedoes and sinks a Japanese cargo ship in the northern Kurile Islands. U.S. submarine *Tinosa* damages an oiler off Kyushu, Japan. U.S. submarine *Trigger* damages the carrier *Hiyo* off eastern Honshu, Japan.

BOUGAINVILLE: Thirteenth Air Force B-17s and B-24 Liberators bomb the Kahili airfield on Bougainville Island.

NEW BRITAIN: Fifth Air Force B-17s and B-24 Liberators bomb the main airfields around Rabaul, New Britain.

June 11

ALEUTIANS: Eleventh Air Force B-24 Liberators, B-25 Mitchells, P-40s, and P-38 Lightnings conduct attacks on facilities at Kiska Island. Two F-5As (unarmed P-38 variant) conduct photo and reconnaissance missions.

ETO: Eighth Air Force VIII Bomber Command conducts an attack against two targets in Germany. A total of 218 B-17s, far beyond the range of fighter escort, attempt to bomb the U-boat yard at Wilhelmshaven and the port at Cuxhaven, Germany. Enemy fighters prevent an accurate bombing run and shoot down eight bombers and damage 62 others. At least 85 enemy aircraft are reported destroyed.

MEDITERRANEAN: Ninth Air Force B-25 Mitchells along with Northwest African Air Force B-26 Marauders and B-25s support the landing of the British 1st Division on Pantelleria Island. The landing is unopposed and the defenders surrender unconditionally.

PACIFIC: U.S. submarine *Finback* attacks a Japanese convoy in the Palau Islands, sinking a Japanese cargo ship just west of Babelthuap. U.S. submarine *Runner* torpedoes and sinks a Japanese cargo ship off northwest Honshu, Japan. U.S. submarine *S-30* torpedoes and sinks a cargo ship in the Kuriles; U.S. submarine *Silversides* attacks a Japanese convoy, sinking a transport north of New Ireland.

NEW GUINEA: Fifth Air Force B-25 Mitchells attack targets along the Huon Gulf coast of New Guinea. B-24 Liberators bomb the Rabaul airfields on New Britain. B-24s and B-25s bomb targets in Timor.

June 12

ATLANTIC: TBF Avenger torpedo bombers from the escort carrier USS *Bogue* sink German submarine *U-118*. U.S. submarine *R-12* sinks off Key West, Florida; cause is unknown.

MEDITERRANEAN: Ninth Air Force B-25 Mitchells and P-40s attack Lampedusa Island in preparation for a landing by British forces. The island garrison surrenders without a fight. Northwest African Air Force B-17s and B-26 Marauders bomb airfields at Castelvetrano, Boccadifalco, and Milo in Sicily.

PACIFIC: U.S. submarine *Trout* lands men and supplies on Mindanao in the Philippines.

GUADALCANAL: Thirteenth Air Force P-38 Lightnings and P-40s, navy and marine F6F Hellcats and F4U Corsairs, along with Royal New Zealand Air Force P-40s, intercept Japanese bombers and fighters headed to attack Guadalcanal. Over 30 aircraft are shot down and eight Allied aircraft are lost.

June 13

ALEUTIANS: U.S. destroyer sinks Japanese submarine *I-9* off Kiska Island.

CBI: In Burma, nine B-25 Mitchells from Tenth Air Force attack a railroad bridge on the Mandalay to Myitkyina railroad. Damage to the bridge is minor. Fourteenth Air Force B-25 Mitchells with 14 P-40 fighters as escorts attack Nanchang airfield in China.

ETO: Eighth Air Force VIII Bomber Command conducts two attacks on targets in Germany. The Bremen U-boat yards are hit by 122 B-17s; four bombers are lost and 31 are damaged. Only two enemy aircraft are reported destroyed. The U-boat yards at Kiel are attacked by 60 B-17s against the heaviest German fighter attack yet seen. The losses are serious—22 bombers are shot down and 24 are damaged, with nearly 240 crewmen killed, wounded, or missing. Enemy aircraft losses are reported to be over 40.

MEDITERRANEAN: Ninth Air Force B-24 Liberators and Royal Air Force heavy bombers conduct a combined attack on the airfields at Catania and Gerbini in Sicily. Five enemy fighters are reported destroyed and two B-24s are shot down.

PACIFIC: U.S. submarine *Guardfish* torpedoes and sinks a Japanese cargo ship off the southwest coast of New Ireland; U.S. submarine *Sargo* attacks a Japanese convoy in the Carolines and sinks an army transport ship.

BOUGAINVILLE: Thirteenth Air Force B-17s and B-24 Liberators bomb the airfield at Kahili on Bougainville Island.

New Britain: Fifth Air Force B-17s and B-24s bomb the airfields at Rabaul and on Gasmata Island. B-25 Mitchells bomb Dili and Koepang on Timor.

June 14
CBI: Fourteenth Air Force P-40s intercept eight Japanese bombers and 20 fighters near Nanchang, China. The eight P-40s report seven enemy fighters shot down.
New Georgia: Thirteenth Air Force B-25 Mitchells, escorted by F4U Corsairs, bomb the airfield at Vila in New Georgia. B-17s and B-24 Liberators bomb the airfield at Kahili on Bougainville Island.

June 15
CBI: Tenth Air Force B-25 Mitchells bomb the bridge at Myitnge in Burma and cause major damage. Fourteenth Air Force B-25s, escorted by P-40s, conduct ground support operations for Chinese ground forces at Owchihkow, China.
Mediterranean: Northwest African Air Force B-17s, B-25 Mitchells, B-26 Marauders, and P-38 Lightnings bomb airfields at Bo Rizzo, Milo, Sciacca, Castelvetrano, and Boccadifalco in Sicily. Radio stations near Marsala are also attacked.
Southwest Pacific Area: U.S. submarine *Trout* damages a Japanese oiler in the Celebes Sea.
Pacific: U.S. submarine *Gunnel* torpedoes and sinks a Japanese cargo ship in Tsushima Straits; U.S. submarine *Sailfish* torpedoes and sinks a cargo ship off Honshu, Japan.
New Britain: Fifth Air Force B-24 Liberators bomb the airfields at Rabaul, then rearm and refuel and bomb the airfield at Kendari in the Celebes later in the day.

June 16
Guadalcanal: Thirteenth Air Force P-38 Lightnings and P-40s, navy and marine F6F Hellcats and F4U Corsairs, along with Royal New Zealand Air Force P-40s, intercept about 120 Japanese aircraft attempting to attack Allied shipping off Tulagi and Guadalcanal. Over 100 Allied fighters are involved, as well as shipboard and ground-based antiaircraft fire. Although the Japanese hit an LST (Landing Ship Tank) and a cargo ship, they lose 79 aircraft to fighters and 17 other planes to antiaircraft fire. Only six Allied aircraft are lost in this lopsided victory.

Second Lieutenant Joseph R. Sarnoski volunteers to serve as the bombardier of a crew on an important photographic mapping mission covering Buka Island, near Bougainville. As the photoreconnaissance mission is ending, about 20 Japanese fighters swarm the aircraft. Second Lieutenant Sarnoski mans the nose guns and fights off the first attack, allowing the pilot to complete his track over the target area. The second attack wounds five of the crew and seriously damages the bomber. Sarnowski, also wounded, continues to fight, shooting down two enemy fighters. When a 20 millimeter explosive shell wounds him again and knocks him from the guns, he crawls back and continues to engage the enemy until he collapses and dies. Second Lieutenant Sarnoski's example of resolute courage under fire and dedication to the mission not only allows the bomber to return safely, but also will win him the Medal of Honor.

New Guinea: Fifth Air Force B-25 Mitchells bomb Koepang and Oeikoesi on Timor. B-25s and A-20 Havocs attack barges and shore targets around New Guinea and New Britain.

June 17

Atlantic: JCS planners submit a concept of operations to support the strategic plan approved by the CCS on May 19. The planners propose an offensive against the Japanese in the Marshall Islands in December. Kusaire and Eniwetok are proposed as the targets of a combined amphibious invasion. These islands will then be used as airbases for an attack on Truk, the main base of the Japanese Combined Fleet. This approach is intended to attack directly into the center of the Japanese outer defensive perimeter without land-based air cover and will require resources from MacArthur's theater. MacArthur is already concerned that the limited resources he has available may not be sufficient to support the execution of Cartwheel, the campaign to capture Rabaul. Nimitz also has doubts about the concept. He is hesitant to move into the Marshalls without having some support from airbases in the Gilbert Islands first.

Mediterranean: Ninth Air Force B-24 Liberators attack airfields at Biscariy and Comiso in Sicily.

Southwest Pacific Area: U.S. submarine *Drum* attacks a Japanese convoy north of Kavieng, New Ireland, and sinks a transport ship.

Central Pacific: Seventh Air Force B-24 Liberators take off from Funafuti Atoll in the Ellice Islands to conduct a diversionary raid on Tarawa Atoll in the Gilbert Islands. Of the four bombers dispatched, only two find their target. These two bombers are able to damage the runways, knock out an antiaircraft battery, and blow up an ammunition storage area. The diversion succeeds in allowing three B-24s to conduct a night photoreconnaissance mission over Mille Atoll in the Caroline Islands and areas near the Marshall Islands.

New Guinea: Fifth Air Force B-25 Mitchells bomb targets around Madang and Salamaua. B-24 Liberators bomb Sorong, New Guinea, and Boela in the Molucca Islands.

June 18

Mediterranean: Northwest African Air Force B-17s bomb the ferry and railyards in Messina, Italy. P-38 Lightnings bomb the airfield at Milo in Sicily. B-26 Marauders and B-25 Mitchells escorted by P-38s bomb docks and shipping in Sardinia.

Bougainville: Thirteenth Air Force B-24 Liberators bomb the airfield at Kahili on Bougainville Island.

New Guinea: Fifth Air Force B-25 Mitchells bomb and strafe Japanese vessels off Cape Gloucester, New Britain, and at Finschhafen in New Guinea.

June 19

Mediterranean: Ninth Air Force B-24 Liberators bomb the ferry and railyards at Villa San Giovanni, ferries in the Straits of Messina, and the harbor of Reggio di Calabria in Italy.

June 19

SOUTHWEST PACIFIC AREA: U.S. submarine *Growler* attacks a Japanese convoy and sinks a cargo ship north of Mussau Island in the Saint Matthias Group north of New Ireland.

PACIFIC: U.S. submarine *Gunnel* torpedoes and damages a Japanese gunboat and sinks a cargo ship and a coastal minesweeper off southern Kyushu, Japan. U.S. submarine *Sculpin* torpedoes and sinks a Japanese guardboat and a cargo ship off eastern Honshu, Japan.

CENTRAL PACIFIC: Seventh Air Force B-24 Liberators take off from Funafuti Atoll in the Ellice Islands to conduct a night photoreconnaissance mission over Jaluit Atoll in the Marshall Islands.

NEW GUINEA: Fifth Air Force B-17s and B-24 Liberators attack the airfield at Vunakanau on New Britain. A-20 Havocs hit targets in New Guinea.

June 20

ATLANTIC: U.S. Navy PBY Catalinas sink German submarine *U-388* and damage submarine *U-420* in the North Atlantic. A U.S. freighter is damaged by a mine laid by German submarine *U-214* and is towed into port at Dakar, French West Africa.

MEDITERRANEAN: Northwest African Air Force B-26 Marauders bomb the airfields at Milo, Castelvetrano, and Bo Rizzo in Sicily.

PACIFIC: U.S. submarine *Seawolf* torpedoes and sinks a Japanese cargo ship in the South China Sea; U.S. submarine *Tautog* torpedoes and sinks a Japanese transport ship west of the Marianas.

CENTRAL PACIFIC: Seventh Air Force B-24 Liberators take off from Funafuti Atoll in the Ellice Islands to conduct a night photoreconnaissance mission over Jaluit Atoll in the Marshall Islands.

BOUGAINVILLE: B-24 Liberators bomb the airfield at Kahili and other targets on Bougainville Island.

NEW GEORGIA: Thirteenth Air Force P-40s, along with marine and navy F6F Hellcats and F4U Corsairs, attack the airfield at Vila in New Georgia, damaging the runway.

NEW GUINEA: General MacArthur redesignates U.S. Sixth Army as Alamo Force in order to have direct control of U.S. ground forces for upcoming operations. Alamo Force, under command of Lieutenant General Walter Krueger, establishes headquarters at Milne Bay. This subterfuge is intended to bypass Australian general Sir Thomas Blamey's authority as commander of all land forces in the Southwest Pacific Theater. Fifth Air Force B-24s bomb the airfields at Rapopo, Keravat, and Rabaul. In New Guinea, A-20 Havocs attack the airfield at Lae, and B-25 Mitchells and one A-20 attack Finschhafen and targets along the coast of New Britain.

June 21

CBI: Fourteenth Air Force B-25 Mitchells with an escort of eight P-40s, bomb Shihshow, China. Eight other B-25s, with P-40 escort, misidentify the village of Nanhsien as a different enemy-held village and bomb it, killing a number of Chinese civilians.

MEDITERRANEAN: Ninth Air Force B-24 Liberators bomb the ferry at Villa San Giovanni and the harbor facilities and railyards at Reggio di Calabria in Italy. Northwest African Air Force B-17s bomb the Naples railyards, the marshaling yard and trestle in Salerno, the marshaling yard in Battipaglia, and the airfield at Cancello Arnone.

PACIFIC: U.S. submarine *Harder* torpedoes and damages a Japanese oiler off eastern Honshu, Japan.

CENTRAL PACIFIC: A Seventh Air Force B-24 conducts armed photoreconnaissance over Nonouti Island, Beru Island, and Nukunau Island in the Gilberts.

NEW GEORGIA: Rear Admiral Richmond Kelly Turner, the commander of amphibious forces for Toenails, sends a detachment of the Marine 4th Raider Battalion to Segi Point on Vangunu Island, which is intended as a site for a future airfield.

NEW GUINEA: Fifth Air Force A-20 Havocs attack the airfields at Lae and Malahang, while B-25s bomb the airfield at Salamaua. B-25 Mitchells attack Koepang on Timor.

June 22

ALEUTIANS: U.S. destroyer damages Japanese submarine *I-7,* which runs aground 12 miles southwest of Kiska Island.

CBI: Tenth Air Force B-25 Mitchells bomb transportation targets in Ywataung and Monywa in Burma.

ETO: Eighth Air Force VIII Bomber Command conducts its first large-scale daylight raid on the heart of German industrial strength in the Ruhr. The targets are the chemical works and synthetic rubber plant at Huls. Of the 183 B-17s that hit the targets, 16 bombers are shot down and 75 others are damaged. Enemy aircraft losses are estimated at over 40 destroyed. The plants are heavily damaged. The mission had 11 YB-40s (an armored version of the B-17) dispatched to accompany the bombers, and one is lost. A second bombing raid involves the industrial plants at Antwerp, Belgium. Of the 39 B-17s that hit the target, four are lost and 18 are damaged. Only one enemy aircraft is reported destroyed. A diversion effort by 21 B-17s is apparently unsuccessful.

SOUTHWEST PACIFIC AREA: U.S. submarine *Grayling* torpedoes and damages a Japanese oiler in the Strait of Malacca.

CENTRAL PACIFIC: Three Seventh Air Force B-24 Liberators from Canton Island in the Phoenix Islands fly a photoreconnaissance mission over Beru Island, Nukunau Island, Tabiteuea Island, Onotoa Island, Tarawa Atoll, and Arorae Island in the Gilberts. While the bombers are conducting the mission, one bomber uses its guns on Arorae Island.

NEW GEORGIA: Two companies of the 103rd Infantry Regiment, 43rd Infantry Division, are landed to reinforce the marines. The combined force is to occupy Viru Harbor on D-day (June 30).

NEW GUINEA: An advance party of the U.S. 112th Cavalry makes an unopposed landing on Woodlark Island.

June 23

PACIFIC: U.S. submarine *Harder* torpedoes and damages a Japanese seaplane carrier off southern Honshu, Japan.

GUADALCANAL: Japanese submarine *RO-103* attacks a convoy off Guadalcanal and torpedoes and sinks one U.S. cargo ship and damages another. The second cargo ship is later scuttled.

NEW GUINEA: The 158th RCT lands on Kiriwini Island without opposition.

June 24

ATLANTIC: A U.S. Navy PBY Catalina sinks German submarine *U-200* in the North Atlantic southwest of Iceland.

SOUTHWEST PACIFIC AREA: Fifth Air Force B-24 Liberators bomb shipping, docks, and industrial targets at Makassar, Celebes Island. The 17 bombers cause extensive damage, including two light cruisers, which are also hit.

PACIFIC: U.S. submarine *Snook* torpedoes and damages a Japanese oiler in the East China Sea.

June 25

ALEUTIANS: Eleventh Air Force B-25 Mitchells, B-24 Liberators, and P-38 Lightnings attack facilities on Kiska Island. Two B-24s conduct photo and weather reconnaissance missions.

ATLANTIC: The Army Air Force Antisubmarine Command transfers the B-24 Liberators of the 19th Antisubmarine Squadron (Heavy), originally stationed in Newfoundland, to Britain. U.S. tanker en route to Bahia is torpedoed and damaged by German submarine *U-513* off Brazil. The armed guard defends the ship with gunfire to keep the U-boat submerged, allowing the ship to reach Rio de Janeiro for repairs.

ETO: Eighth Air Force bombers attempt to hit targets at Bremen and Hamburg, Germany, but cloud-cover cancels the mission. About 160 B-17s then make a number of attacks on various targets, with the loss of 18 bombers and over 60 others damaged. Seven YB-40 escort bombers (an armored version of the B-17) are included in the mission, but only four actually keep up with the bombers. Enemy losses are estimated at over 60 aircraft.

MEDITERRANEAN: Northwest African Air Force B-17s drop over 300 tons of bombs on storage areas, port facilities, and the marshaling yard in Messina, Sicily.

PACIFIC: U.S. submarine *Sailfish* attacks a Japanese convoy, sinking a collier off the northeast coast of Honshu, Japan.

BOUGAINVILLE: Thirteenth Air Force B-24 Liberators attack targets near Kahili on Bougainville Island and hit the airfield on Buka Island. B-25 Mitchells, escorted by P-40s, bomb the airfield at Vila in New Georgia.

June 26

ALEUTIANS: Eleventh Air Force bombers and P-38 Lightnings conduct weather and photo reconnaissance and attack missions to Kiska and Little Kiska Islands. Four P-38s are damaged by machine-gun fire.

ETO: Eighth Air Force B-17s attack several targets in France; five YB-40 escort bombers are unable to complete the mission. The Vilacoublay air depot is bombed by 12 B-17s; six bombers attack the airfield at Poissy, and another 39 bombers hit the airfield at Tricqueville. Five bombers are lost and 17 are damaged. Over 20 enemy aircraft are reported destroyed.

Air Marshal Trafford L. Leigh-Mallory is selected to oversee air support planning for the cross-Channel invasion.

PACIFIC: U.S. submarine *Jack* attacks a Japanese convoy, sinking two transports off southern Honshu, Japan. U.S. submarine *Runner* claims one Japanese cargo ship sunk off Matsuwa Island in the Kuriles.

NEW GUINEA: Fifth Air Force B-17s and B-24 Liberators bomb Rabaul and then attack Lae in New Guinea. B-25 Mitchells also bomb Lae and Salamaua and conduct an attack on Penfoei on Timor Island.

June 27

ATLANTIC: U.S. freighter en route from Mombasa, Kenya, to Bahia, Brazil, is torpedoed and sunk by German submarine *U-511* off the southern coast of Brazil.

MEDITERRANEAN: Ninth Air Force B-24 Liberators bomb airfields at Kalamaki and Eleusis in Greece. Aircrews report seven enemy fighters shot down.

June 27

BOUGAINVILLE: Thirteenth Air Force B-24 Liberators bomb the airfield at Kahili on Bougainville Island.

NEW GEORGIA: Marine Raiders reach positions to begin attack on Viru Harbor, the site of an intended PT boat base.

NEW GUINEA: Fifth Air Force B-25 Mitchells and A-20 Havocs attack a number of targets in New Guinea. B-24 Liberators bomb Taka, Saumlakki, and Malo Islands in the Moluccas and Boeroe Island in the Sunda Islands.

June 28

ALEUTIANS: Eleventh Air Force B-25 Mitchells bomb Gertrude Cove on Little Kiska Island.

ETO: Eighth Air Force B-17s attack two targets in France. The first target is the submarine pens at St-Nazaire and the second is the airfield at Beaumont-le-Roger. Of the 158 bombers that hit the target at St-Nazaire, eight bombers are lost to enemy fire and 57 are damaged. Nearly 30 enemy aircraft are reported destroyed. Against the Beaumont-le-Roger airfield, the 43 bombers that hit the target suffer only six aircraft damaged.

MEDITERRANEAN: Northwest African Air Force B-17s bomb support facilities in Leghorn, Italy. B-25 Mitchells bomb airfields in Sardinia and Sicily. B-26 Marauders attack airfield targets in Sardinia.

PACIFIC: U.S. submarine *Tunny* torpedoes and sinks a Japanese gunboat off Rota Island in the Marianas.

CENTRAL PACIFIC: Seventh Air Force B-24 Liberators on Funafuti Atoll in the Ellice Islands attempt a bombing mission against Nauru Island in the Gilberts; of the six bombers dispatched, only two attack the target. The others either abort the mission or are unable to locate the target.

June 29

ETO: Eighth Air Force B-17s attack three targets in France. The first is the air depot at Villacoublay, the second is the Tricqueville airfield, and the third is the aero engine works at Le Mans. Heavy cloud cover prevents the first two targets from being hit. Nevertheless, 14 B-17s are damaged and aircrews report three possible enemy aircraft shot down. Over Le Mans, 76 B-17s hit the target. Two YB-40 escort bombers fail to support the mission. The Eighth Air Force commander, Lieutenant General Ira C. Eaker, decides that if the escort bombers are to be useful at all, they must carry bomb loads and must be able to fly complete missions as expected of the other B-17s.

SOUTHWEST PACIFIC AREA: U.S. submarine *Gurnard* attacks a Japanese convoy in the south Philippine Sea but no ships are damaged.

BOUGAINVILLE: Four cruisers and four destroyers of Rear Admiral Aaron S. Merrill's Task Unit 36.2.1 bombard Vila on Kolombangara Island in New Georgia and Buin on Bougainville Island. A task unit, 36.2.2, of minelayers drop off mines near Shortland Harbor, Bougainville, between Alu and Munda Islands, and off New Georgia.

NEW GUINEA: Fifth Air Force B-25 Mitchells and A-20 Havocs attack Japanese positions on the Bitoi River and Nassau Bay in preparation for amphibious landings.

June 30

ETO: The Royal Air Force releases operational control of Eighth Air Force's VIII Fighter Command. U.S. fighter groups are now under control of the 4th Air Defense Wing.

MEDITERRANEAN: Over Sicily, Northwest African Air Force B-17s bomb the airfields at Palermo and Boccadifalco, while B-25 Mitchells hit the airfield at Sciacca and B-26 Marauders bomb the Bo Rizzo airfield.

The Germans have moved five divisions into Italy, and put two in Sicily.

PACIFIC: B-25s bomb Timor Island, while B-24 Liberators and B-17s bomb Rabaul. A Japanese cargo ship is hit off Cape Gloucester, New Britain.

NEW GEORGIA: A battalion of the 172nd Infantry Regiment of the 43rd Infantry Division lands on Rendova Island, encountering light resistance. Units also land on Kokorana Island to establish artillery and antiaircraft positions. The Japanese attempt to disrupt the landings with a heavy air attack of 49 bombers with fighter escort. Although 17 bombers are shot down by F4U Corsairs, F4F Wildcats, and antiaircraft fire, Admiral Turner's flagship, the attack transport *McCawley*, is hit and damaged by a torpedo. A U.S. PT boat accidentally torpedoes and sinks the ship later that night. Torrential rains begin, causing equipment and supplies to pile up on the beaches. Another attack early in the evening by about 30 aircraft is blunted by U.S. fighters. Later the pilots report 18 Japanese aircraft shot down. A B-24 Liberator attack on Kahili at Bougainville Island is aborted because of bad weather. At Munda airfield, 25 B-25 Mitchells with 18 SBD Dauntless and 18 TBF Avengers conduct bombing attacks. Another 16 Avenger torpedo bombers and 12 SBD Dauntless dive-bombers attack Vila airfield. A Japanese shore battery at Munda damages a U.S. destroyer.

Commander Aircraft Solomons (COMAIRSOLS), Rear Admiral Mark A. Mitscher, establishes ComAir New Georgia under Brigadier General Francis P. Mulcahy to provide coordination and control of all air missions flown over New Georgia.

Marine Raiders and a battalion of the 103rd Infantry Regiment, 43rd Infantry Division, land at Oliana Bay on Vangunu Island and move inland to assault Kaeruka.

NEW GUINEA: The remainder of the U.S. 112th Cavalry Regiment lands at Woodlark Island; the U.S. 158th Infantry Regiment lands at Kiriwina Island.

Air bases and supply bases are established for future amphibious operations. The 1st Battalion of the 162nd Infantry Regiment of the 41st Infantry Division lands at Nassau Bay. The assault unit is patched together, consisting of three PT boats, 29 LCVP landing craft, one LCV landing craft, mechanized, and two captured Japanese supply barges. Although heavy surf destroys 18 landing craft, the troops move off toward Salamaua. Fifth Air Force B-25 Mitchells conduct ground support missions for both the American troops landing and Australian troops attacking Japanese positions in support of the landing.

July 1

ATLANTIC: The Women's Army Auxiliary Corps (WAAC) is redesignated as the Women's Army Corps (WAC) under the direction of Colonel Oveta Culp Hobby. WACs receive basic military training and are sent to fill support jobs to free men to fight. WACs will serve in the Mediterranean theater, the ETO, the Southwest Pacific Area, and Southeast Asia Command.

CBI: Fourteenth Air Force commander General Claire Chennault designates port facilities and shipping as the primary targets for future air missions.

ETO: Brigadier General Frederick L Anderson, Jr., takes over VIII Bomber Command from Brigadier General Newton Longfellow.

SOUTHWEST PACIFIC AREA: U.S. submarine *Gar* lands commandos on south coast of Timor Island. U.S. submarine *Gurnard* unsuccessfully attacks a Japanese transport ship in the southern Philippine Sea; U.S. submarine *Thresher* attacks a Japanese convoy in the Straits of Makassar, damaging a destroyer and sinking a cargo ship. The destroyer is later salvaged in Sibaya harbor, Celebes.

NEW GEORGIA: Navy and marine Dauntless dive-bombers hit Japanese positions defending Viru Harbor. Marine Raiders capture Tombe and Tetemara villages, opening the port to U.S. supply ships. Japanese attempt to land supplies and reinforcements at Kaeruka, not knowing that U.S. forces already occupy the area. The enemy group is destroyed.

NEW GUINEA: The 1st Battalion of the 162nd Infantry Regiment is attacked by the Japanese at Nassau Bay. In a pouring rainstorm, in a fight that lasts most of the day, the Japanese finally retreat, leaving 50 dead. American losses are 18 killed and 27 wounded. The battalion pushes forward to threaten the Japanese holding Salamaua. Australian forces are simultaneously moving toward Lae from Wau.

Fifth Air Force A-20 Havocs support the advance of U.S. infantry and attack targets around Lae. B-25 Mitchells attack Kela Point and Logui. B-17s and B-24 Liberators bomb the Rabaul airfields.

July 2

ALEUTIANS: After several reconnaissance flights, Eleventh Air Force B-24 Liberators and B-25 Mitchells attack Kiska Island. Two of the five bombing missions against the facilities are radar-guided. Three bombers are damaged by antiaircraft fire.

ATLANTIC: Off the Carolina coast, German submarine *U-66* torpedoes and sinks a U.S. tanker en route from Houston, Texas, to New York City.

MEDITERRANEAN: In Italy, Ninth Air Force B-24 Liberators attack the airfields at Lecce, Grottaglie, and San Pancrazio Salentino. In Sicily, B-25 Mitchells, escorted by P-40 fighters, bomb the Sciacca airfield. One enemy fighter is shot down and one damaged, but two P-40s are shot down in the air battle. Northwest African Air Force B-25 Mitchells bomb Castelvetrano. The Tuskegee Airmen of the 99th Fighter Squadron escort the B-25s over Sicily.

SOUTHWEST PACIFIC AREA: U.S. submarine *Trout* torpedoes and sinks a Japanese cargo ship off the north coast of Marinduque Island, Philippines.

PACIFIC: U.S. submarine *Flying Fish* torpedoes and sinks a Japanese troopship in the Formosa Strait. U.S. submarine *S-35* torpedoes and sinks a Japanese cargo ship off the west coast of the Kamchatka Peninsula.

NEW GEORGIA: A five-ton dynamite storage area established by the 24th Naval Construction Battalion (Seabees) is blown up. Eighteen Japanese bombers with fighter escort attack Rendova Island, hitting fuel and explosives dumps and causing over 200 casualties. After the attack the area is called "Suicide Point." Later that night, a Japanese cruiser and nine destroyers bombard Rendova, but cause no damage. Thirteenth Air Force B-25 Mitchells and navy F4U Corsairs attack a Japanese auxiliary minelayer in the anchorage at Bairoko.

NEW GUINEA: Fifth Air Force B-25 Mitchells attack Japanese defenses around Kela Point. U.S. forces link up with Australian troops. B-24 Liberators and B-17s bomb the Rabaul airfields.

July 3

CBI: Tenth Air Force B-25 Mitchells bomb the bridge at Myitnge, Burma, and succeed in knocking one of the bridge spans out.

ATLANTIC: The B-24 Liberators of the 15th Antisubmarine Squadron (Heavy) under the Army Air Force Antisubmarine Command return to Jacksonville Municipal Airport, Florida, from their operating base at Langley Field, Virginia. German submarine *U-513* torpedoes and sinks a U.S. freighter off the coast of Brazil.

ETO: Lieutenant General Jacob L. Devers, Commanding General European Theater of Operations, U.S. Army (ETOUSA), notes in a report to General Henry H "Hap" Arnold, Commanding General USAAF, that while VIII Bomber Command bombardiers are well trained, high-altitude gunnery skills are less than satisfactory. Not only are bombers taking losses because of a lack of adequate fighter escort on strategic bombing missions, they are also less effective in defending themselves from fighter attack.

MEDITERRANEAN: Ninth Air Force B-25 Mitchells, with P-40s flying escort, bomb the Comiso airfield in Sicily. Northwest African Air Force B-17s, B-26 Marauders, and B-25 Mitchells bomb airfields in Sardinia, while fighters attack radar stations at Pula and Alghero. A-20 Havocs attack airfields at Sciaccay and Trapani in Sicily.

PACIFIC: U.S. submarine *Scorpion* attacks a Japanese convoy in the Yellow Sea and sinks two cargo ships.

NEW GEORGIA: Army and marine 155 mm artillery batteries begin firing on Munda airfield. The Southern Landing Group—composed of the 172nd and 169th Infantry Regiments of the 43rd Infantry Division, the 136th Field Artillery Battalion, and the 9th Marine Defense Battalion—lands at Zanana Beach. The landing group, commanded by Major General Leonard F. Wing, is to capture Munda. Meanwhile, Thirteenth Air Force B-25 Mitchells bomb the antiaircraft guns and the airfield at Munda.

NEW GUINEA: Fifth Air Force B-24 Liberators bomb the Rabaul airfields and the airfield at Kendari on Celebes Island. Two B-25 Mitchells bomb Koepang on Timor Island.

July 4

CBI: Tenth Air Force B-24 Liberators attack the Shweli bridge on the Burma Road.

ETO: Eighth Air Force B-17s strike the aircraft factories at Le Mans and Nanes and the submarine yards at La Pallice, France. The attack by 166 bombers over the aircraft factories is reported as very effective; over 50 enemy aircraft are reported destroyed. Seven bombers are lost and 54 others are damaged. The 71 B-17s that attack the submarine yards are also successful. One bomber is lost and another damaged. One enemy fighter is believed to have been killed.

MEDITERRANEAN: Ninth Air Force B-25 Mitchells, with P-40s flying escort, attack the Comiso airfield at Sicily. Fighters report three enemy aircraft shot down. American losses are four P-40s. Northwest African Air Force B-17s, B-25 Mitchells, and B-26 Marauders bomb the Catania and Gerbini airfields in Sicily. A-20 Havocs attack airfields in western Sicily. Bombers drop leaflets on Rome.

The 45th Infantry Division, fully loaded for combat, arrives in Oran from the United States and sails for Sicily.

PACIFIC: U.S. submarine *Jack* attacks a Japanese convoy off the southeast coast of Honshu, sinking a cargo ship. Off eastern Honshu, U.S. submarine *Pompano* torpedoes and sinks the seaplane carrier attacked by the U.S. submarine *Harder* on June 23. U.S. submarine *Snook* attacks a Formosa-bound Japanese convoy in the East China Sea, damaging a transport and sinking two cargo ships.

NEW GEORGIA: Sixteen Japanese bombers with fighter escort are hit by heavy marine antiaircraft fire. Marine gunners shoot down 12 bombers and one fighter using only 88 rounds of ammunition. Thirteenth Air Force B-17s bomb Bairoko.

July 5

CARIBBEAN: German submarine *U-759* torpedoes and sinks a U.S. freighter in convoy GTMO 134 (Guantánamo Bay, Cuba, to Ponce, Puerto Rico) south of Hispaniola.

ATLANTIC: The JCS receives the COSSAC Overlord concept of operations based on the planning guidelines provided by the CCS after the Trident Conference. In COSSAC's assessment, the Pas-de-Calais area of France, even though the shortest and most sustainable site for an invasion, is also the most heavily defended. The

Cotentin Peninsula has poor terrain for establishing and sustaining a lodgment, but the port of Cherbourg could provide the Allies with facilities to bring in supplies. Caen has a good port, is weakly defended, and has good surrounding terrain that can support airfields. It also has good defensive terrain to protect a beachhead. Based on this analysis, COSSAC recommends Caen as the site for the cross-Channel invasion. The staff notes that no matter what site is chosen, the destruction of the German air force is essential—not only the enemy's current fighter strength, but also fighter production facilities. The COSSAC planners have examined using airborne and amphibious forces to establish a beachhead at Caen (designated as D-day), followed by the seizure of Cherbourg 14 days after the initial landings (D+14). The Allies will have 18 divisions landed in France and 18 airfields operational by this time. By D+50, planners estimate 30 divisions in France. After this buildup, the Allies will attack to capture Paris and the Seine River ports, followed by an advance into Belgium and northern France.

MEDITERRANEAN: Over Sicily, Ninth Air Force B-24 Liberators attack harbor facilities, railyards, and oil storage areas at Messina. B-25 Mitchells bomb the Sciacca and Biscari airfields. Northwest African Air Force B-17s, B-25 Mitchells, and B-26 Marauders bomb the Gerbini airfields and the radar stations at Marsala and Licata. A-20 Havocs attack Sciacca and the Trapani, Comiso, and Biscari airfields. The 1st Infantry Division sails from Algiers for Sicily.

INDIAN OCEAN: Japanese submarine *I-27* torpedoes and damages a U.S. freighter off Oman. The freighter is in convoy PA 44, en route from Abadan, Iran, to Montevideo, Uruguay.

NEW GEORGIA: The Northern Landing Group, composed of the 1st Marine Raider Battalion and a battalion each of the 145th and 148th Infantry Regiments, 37th Infantry Division, under command of Marine Colonel Harry B. Liversedge, lands in a heavy rain at Rice Anchorage. The group's mission is to conduct a landing in northern New Georgia, attack Japanese positions at Enogai Inlet, and capture Bairoko Harbor to prevent Japanese reinforcements and supplies from reaching the defenders at Munda. Lightly armed and with three days' rations, the men struggle inland through dense jungle.

During a commander's meeting, Major General Millard Harmon requests Major General Oscar Griswold's XIV Corps headquarters be deployed to assist the over-stretched 43rd Infantry Division staff, which is attempting to serve as both ground command for Admiral Kelly Turner and the command element for the New Georgia Occupation Force. Admiral Halsey gives his approval.

Thirteenth Air Force B-24 Liberators, unable to find their primary target at Buin, Bougainville Island, bomb Munda airfield.

During the night, while Rear Admiral Walden L. Ainsworth's Task Group 36.1 bombards Vila, Kolombangara, and Bairoko Harbor, a group of Japanese destroyers makes a torpedo attack on the U.S. ships in Kula Gulf, sinking one destroyer.

NEW GUINEA: Fifth Air Force B-25 Mitchells bomb and strafe the airfield and headquarters at Salamaua.

July 6

ALEUTIANS: Eleventh Air Force B-24 Liberators and P-40s conduct weather reconnaissance missions over Kiska and Segula Islands. Six B-24s bomb the main camp on Kiska. Three heavy cruisers, one light cruiser, and four destroyers of Task Group 16.7 under command of Rear Admiral Robert C. Giffen also bombard the island.

MEDITERRANEAN: Ninth Air Force B-24 Liberators and B-25 Mitchells, with P-40 escort, attack airfields at Gerbini and Biscari. Northwest African Air Force A-20 Havocs, B-25 Mitchells, and B-26 Marauders also bomb Biscari airfield and the airfields at Sciacca, Trapani, and Comiso. B-17s bomb Gerbini airfield.

PACIFIC: U.S. submarine *Permit* torpedoes and sinks a Japanese cargo ship in the Sea of Japan off Hokkaido, Japan.

SOLOMONS: Lieutenant Commander Bruce Van Voorhis, commander of Bombing Squadron 102, voluntarily takes a PB4Y-I Privateer (a B-24 variant) patrol bomber on a 700-mile flight without escort or support to attack a critical target on Greenwich Island. Arriving at the target after battling difficult winds and poor visibility, Lieutenant Commander Van Voorhis conducts six passes over the target even as antiaircraft fire bursts around his aircraft. Enemy aircraft also pursue him, but he manages to destroy one fighter plane in the air and three others on the water. Forced close to the ground by enemy fighters, Van Voorhis's plane is caught in an explosion created by the bomb he dropped over the target. Lieutenant Commander Van Voorhis's daring and selfless dedication to victory will win him the Medal of Honor.

BOUGAINVILLE: Thirteenth Air Force B-17s and B-24 Liberators attack the airfields at Kahili on Bougainville Island, on Ballale Island, and on Buka Island. B-25 Mitchells bomb a beached destroyer at Bamberi on New Georgia. Fifth Air Force B-25s attack the Penfoei airfield on Timor Island.

NEW GEORGIA: The task group of Rear Admiral Walden L. Ainsworth engages in a second encounter with the Japanese in Kula Gulf. Just before dawn, three light cruisers and four destroyers engage a Japanese reinforcement force of seven destroyers. Four of the enemy ships are carrying troops and supplies to Kolombangara. Japanese destroyers sink a light cruiser, and one Japanese destroyer is sunk and three destroyers are damaged by gunfire. One of the damaged troop-carrying destroyers is grounded and abandoned on the southeastern coast of Kolombangara. SBD Dauntless dive-bombers, TBF Avenger torpedo bombers, and F4F Wildcats will later bomb the grounded destroyer. This battle of Kula Gulf cuts off the Northern Landing Group from supply and naval gunfire support.

The 3rd Battalion of the 148th Infantry moves to block the Bairoko Trail while the rest of the group moves toward Enogai Inlet. The Southern Landing Group begins a cautious advance into the jungle from Zanana Beach.

July 7

CBI: Fourteenth Air Force B-25 Mitchells, with P-40 escort, attack shipping at Canton, China. The fighters claim two enemy aircraft shot down.

ATLANTIC: German submarine *U-185* attacks convoy BT 18 (Bahia to Trinidad) off the coast of Brazil, and torpedoes a U.S. freighter and a tanker. The freighter is abandoned and the tanker is scuttled. Later, *U-185* torpedoes and damages another tanker and freighter. The tanker is able to continue to Trinidad, but the freighter is later scuttled.

A B-24 Liberator of the 1st Antisubmarine Squadron (Heavy) sinks German submarine *U-951* off the coast of Portugal.

MEDITERRANEAN: Over Sicily, Ninth Air Force B-24 Liberators bomb rail lines and the airfields. B-25 Mitchells bomb airfields. In Italy, P-40s bomb and strafe Lucca airfield. As P-40s fly a diversionary sweep over the western portion of Sicily, Northwest African Air Force B-17s, B-25 Mitchells, and B-26 Marauders bomb airfields in Sicily. A-20 Havocs bomb Sciacca and airfields. The A-20s also attack the radar station at Marsala and other targets.

PACIFIC: U.S. submarine *Permit* torpedoes and sinks a Japanese cargo ship off Hokkaido, Japan. U.S. submarine *Peto* torpedoes and damages a Japanese oiler off eastern Honshu, Japan. U.S. submarine *Plunger* torpedoes and damages a Japanese cargo ship in the Sea of Japan.

SOLOMONS: Thirteenth Air Force B-25 Mitchells and P-38 Lightnings attack Vila airfield. B-24 Liberators bomb Kahili airfield on Bougainville Island.

NEW GUINEA: Fifth Air Force B-24 Liberators, B-25 Mitchells, and Royal Australian Air Force (RAAF) aircraft conduct ground support missions for Australian forces.

July 8

CBI: Fourteenth Air Force B-24 Liberators, escorted by P-40s, attack Haiphong harbor, bombing shipping, docks, and the cement works.

ATLANTIC: A B-24 Liberator sinks German submarine *U-232* off Portugal. German submarine *U-510* attacks convoy TJ 1 (Trinidad to Rio de Janeiro) northeast of Cayenne, French Guiana, and sinks a U.S. freighter.

German submarine *U-232* is sunk off the coast of Portugal by a B-24 Liberator of the 2nd Antisubmarine Squadron (Heavy).

ETO: Army Air Force Antisubmarine Command establishes the headquarters of the 479th Antisubmarine Group at St. Eval, England. The group is responsible for all antisubmarine squadron operations in England.

MEDITERRANEAN: Ninth Air Force B-24 Liberators attack transportation, industrial, and communication targets in Sicily. B-25 Mitchells and P-40s attack the airfields at Biscari and Comiso. Northwest African Air Force B-17s, B-25 Mitchells, and B-26 Marauders attack Gerbini airfield; P-38 Lightnings strafe radar installations in eastern Sicily, and A-20 Havocs bomb Sciacca airfield. B-26 Marauders bomb the airfields at Biscari and Comiso. A-36 Invaders (Apaches) attack targets throughout Sicily.

General d'Armata Alfredo Guzzoni, the commander of Axis forces in Sicily, orders the ports of Licata, Porto Empedocle, and Sciacca readied for demolition.

PACIFIC: Major General William H. Rupertus replaces Major General Alexander A. Vandegrift as commander of the 1st Marine Division.

NEW GUINEA: Fifth Air Force B-25 Mitchells fly ground support missions for Australian troops.

July 9

ALEUTIANS: U.S. destroyer bombards Japanese positions on Kiska Island.

CBI: Tenth Air Force B-25 Mitchells bomb the railroad bridge on the Mu River in Burma, causing moderate damage.

ATLANTIC: B-25 Mitchells of the 23rd Antisubmarine Squadron (Heavy), based at Drew Field, Tampa, Florida, begin operating from Langley Field, Virginia. PBY Catalina sinks German submarine *U-590* at the mouth of Amazon River, Brazil.

MEDITERRANEAN: In Sicily, General Guzzoni puts his forces on full alert. He has available on paper a sizable force of 200,000 Italian and 30,000 German troops, but only one Italian unit, the 4th Livorno Division located at Licata, is considered reliable. He commands two German divisions, the Hermann Göring Panzer Division (located near Gela) and the 15th Panzer Grenadier Division (located in western Sicily). His intent is to contain the Allied beachhead as quickly as possible, then counterattack to drive the invaders into the sea. The ports of Trapani and Marsala are rendered useless.

The Allies arrive off Sicily with 3,000 ships in two task forces, one under command of Admiral Henry K. Hewitt and the other commanded by Vice Admiral Sir Bertram H. Ramsey.

Over Sicily, Ninth Air Force B-24 Liberators bomb airfields at Comiso and Taormina, while B-25 Mitchells bomb Sciacca and Biscari airfield and P-40s escort bombers over Castelvetrano and Milo airfields. B-25s also bomb Maleme, Crete. Northwest African Air Force B-17s, B-25s, B-26 Marauders, and fighters attack Sciacca, Gerbini, Milo, and Biscari airfields, the Cape Passero Island radar stations, Sciacca, Porto Empedocle, key terrain northeast of Gela, and targets of opportunity. Northwest African Air Force Troop Carrier Command drops British and U.S. airborne units on Sicily in the first major airborne operation to be undertaken by the Allies in World War II.

That night, 266 C-47 transports pass over Sicily to drop 3,400 paratroopers of the 505th and 504th Parachute Infantry Regiments of the 82nd Airborne Division under command of Colonel James M. Gavin. They land in 35 MPH winds and are scattered from Nisconi to San Croce Camerina. Some are dropped over water and drown, some land in the British area. About 100 men land on Objective Y, the main target of the paratroopers. This road intersection north of Gela provides direct access to the beaches. They stop a column of Italian tanks, supported by naval gunfire and infantry from the 16th RCT. Paratroopers, working in small groups, take the initiative in ambushing enemy units, cutting communication lines, and generally slowing the Axis response to the landings.

PACIFIC: U.S. submarine *Thresher* lands men and supplies on Negros Island, Philippines. German submarine *U-511* torpedoes and sinks a U.S. freighter off Ceylon.

BOUGAINVILLE: Thirteenth Air Force B-24 Liberators bomb Kahili airfield and Buin on Bougainville Island, and Poporang Island. B-25s and several fighters strafe Buki and Ganongga Islands, and a destroyer beached on Kolombangara Island in New Georgia.

NEW GEORGIA: There is only one marine raider battalion on New Georgia. A marine Raider battalion attacks Japanese defenses at Enogai after an airstrike. The battle is halted by the onset of darkness.

After a heavy and continuous bombardment by naval gunfire, artillery, and aircraft, an intended major assault by the 172nd and 169th Infantry Regiments, 43rd Infantry Division, is delayed; when conducted, it advances only a few hundred yards along the Munda Trail before halting in a confused and frightened mass without having encountered the enemy in force.

NEW GUINEA: Fifth Air Force B-25 Mitchells bomb airfields at Dili and Cape Chater on Timor Island.

July 10

ALEUTIANS: Eleventh Air Force attacks the Japanese homeland. Using dead reckoning runs, eight B-25 Mitchells attack Paramushiru Island in the Kuriles; the B-25s stage through Attu Island and recover to Adak Island. A Japanese convoy off Attu Island is attacked by six B-24 Liberators and five B-25s. The bombers, conducting runs on the ships at deck level, reportedly sink two freighters.

CBI: Fourteenth Air Force B-24 Liberators bomb the dock area at Haiphong, French Indochina.

ATLANTIC: JCS planners revise their concept for the Central Pacific offensive, proposing that the Gilbert Islands be neutralized before the Marshalls. They propose a December 1 attack focusing on Tarawa, Makin, and Nauru. MacArthur will neutralize Rabaul and the Bismarcks to free marine forces under his command to support the offensive in the Gilberts.

German submarine *U-177* torpedoes and sinks a U.S. freighter off Durban, South Africa.

ETO: Eighth Air Force conducts three attacks on targets in France. The first target is the Caen/Carpiquet airfield. The second is the Abbevile/Drucat airfield. The third is Le Bourget airfield near Paris. Over Caen, 34 bombers hit the target; over Abbeville, 36 bombers hit the target. One B-17 is lost and 33 others are damaged. Enemy losses are estimated at over 17 aircraft. Over Le Bourget, cloud cover prevents the 101 bombers from hitting the target.

MEDITERRANEAN: Operation Husky. Operation Husky is the largest amphibious operation of World War II, in terms of both divisions landed and the size of the landing area. The Fifteenth Army Group consists of the British Eighth Army, commanded by General Sir Bernard Montgomery, and the Seventh Army, commanded by Lieutenant General George S. Patton, Jr. Montgomery commands six infantry divisions (one of these Canadian), one armored division, one airborne division, a tank brigade (Canadian), and an infantry brigade. Patton has under his command the 1st Infantry Division, the 3rd Infantry Division, the 45th Infantry Division, and the 9th Infantry Division; the 82nd Airborne Division, the 2nd Armored Division, and a Ranger battalion. The major maneuver element for the army is II Corps, under command of Major General Omar N. Bradley, which has the 45th Infantry Division, two regiments of the 1st Infantry Division, two Ranger battalions, a tank regiment from the 2nd Armored Division, and the 505th Parachute Regiment and the 504th Parachute Infantry Brigade, to link up with the main force from the beachhead. Afloat in reserve are the remaining Regimental Combat Team of the 1st Infantry Division and the remainder of the 2nd Armored Division. Awaiting movement from Africa if needed is the remainder of the 82nd Airborne and the 9th Infantry Division. The II Corps has 57 miles of beach to control. Naval gunfire hits Syracuse, Catania, Taorima, Augusta, and Trapani. Axis planes bomb the invasion fleet, sinking a destroyer, an LST (Landing Ship Tank), and a minesweeper.

The 45th Infantry Division will land on the eastern edge of the American landing area to link up with British forces near Comiso and Ragusa. The center sector at Gela is the responsibility of the 1st Infantry Division, commanded by Major General Terry de la Mesa Allen, and a battalion of Rangers. Elements of the 82nd Airborne Division will capture and hold the high ground above Gela to assist the 1st Infantry Division. The 3rd Infantry Division under command of Major General Lucian K. Truscott will land at Licata. The 1st and 45th Infantry Divisions will then advance to Route 124, the main east-west road and the approximate boundary of the Yellow Line. The landings go according to plan and there is little opposition. The beach landing sites are poor and rough seas have scattered the 180th Regiment of the 45th Infantry Division. At Gela, Rangers, engineers, and a mortar battalion supported by naval gunfire stop a poorly coordinated attack by two Italian infantry battalions supported by 13 tanks.

Ninth Air Force B-24 Liberators attack the marshaling yard at Catania and the Vibo Valentia airfield. B-25 Mitchells bomb Palazzolo, Sciacca, Catania, Agrigento, Floridia, Giarratana, Biscari, Syracuse, and Piazza Armerina while P-40 fighters cover the assault beaches. A-36 Invaders (Apaches) hit railroads, road junctions, trains, and vehicles while P-40s fly cover for amphibious landings. A-20 Havocs and B-26 Marauders bomb airfields at Sciacca, Canicatti, Ponte Olivo, and Trapani, as well as targets in Caltagirone and Palazzolo. B-17s and B-25s bomb Gerbini, Milo and Sciacca airfields, and targets in Palazzolo and Caltanissetta. P-38 Lightnings strafe radar installations. German submarine *U-371* attacks a convoy off the coast of Algiers, damaging a U.S. freighter and tanker. Both ships eventually are brought to port and salvaged.

PACIFIC: U.S. submarine *Pompano* damages a Japanese oiler off Honshu, Japan. U.S. submarine *Steelhead* damages a Japanese escort carrier north off the Carolines. U.S. submarine *Halibut* damages a Japanese transport near Guam.

BOUGAINVILLE: Thirteenth Air Force B-24s bomb Kahili airfield on Bougainville Island.

NEW GEORGIA: Enogai village is captured by marine Raiders but is exhausted by the effort and receives resupply by air. The Japanese coastal artillery battery at Enogai is also captured, allowing U.S. warships free access to Kula Gulf. The 3,300-foot-long Segi Point fighter airstrip is completed.

NEW GUINEA: Fifth Air Force B-25 Mitchells conduct ground support missions around Salamaua as Allied ground forces link up at Buigap Creek, cutting communications between Salamaua and Mubo.

July 11

ALEUTIANS: Eleventh Air Force B-24 Liberators attempt to conduct a second attack on Paramushiru Island, but are prevented by bad weather. B-25 Mitchells and B-24s attack facilities on Kiska Island. U.S. destroyer bombards Japanese positions at Gertrude Cove.

CBI: Tenth Air Force B-24 Liberators bomb the port of Haiphong, French Indochina.

Fourteenth Air Force B-24s also bomb Haiphong harbor, while other B-24s bomb shipping, enemy positions, and barracks in China. P-40s strafe enemy vehicles and an oil storage area near Lao Kay.

SICILY: The Axis forces begin their counterattack on U.S. forces. The Hermann Goering Division is to attack the 45th Infantry Division, commanded by Major General Troy Middleton, on the east flank, while the Livorno and 15th Panzer Grenadier Division attack the 3rd Infantry Division. The German advance is fiercely contested as enemy armor move within two kilometers of the beachhead before being stopped by U.S. naval gunfire in direct support of the infantry defending Gela. The Germans lose one-third of their tanks in the attack. At Biazzo Ridge, paratroopers and 45th Infantry Division troops stop a major German attack. The 45th Infantry Division captures Comiso and its airfield with 125 aircraft. The 3rd Infantry Division advances, moving beyond Licata, Naro, and Campobello. Off Gela, a U.S. freighter carrying ammunition is set afire by a bomb during a German air attack, is abandoned, and later explodes. Even after detailed coordination between Patton and Cunningham to prevent any mistakes, the 144 C-47 aircraft carrying over 2,000 reinforcements from the 1st and 2nd Battalions, 504th Parachute Infantry Regiment, the 307th Airborne Engineer Battalion, and the 376th Field Artillery Battalion, 82nd Airborne Division, to the landing zone in Gela are fired on by the naval task force. Twenty-three Northwest African Air Force Troop Carrier Command C-47s are shot out of the sky by friendly antiaircraft fire; 37 are damaged and 229 paratroopers are casualties of friendly fire. The survivors are added to the defenses at Gela. The airborne landing is intended to support the 1st Infantry Division in its advance to capture Ponte Olivo and Niscemi.

During the advance of the 15th Infantry Regiment, 3rd Infantry Division, Second Lieutenant Robert Craig volunteers to locate and destroy a machine-gun position at Favoratta that is preventing his company from moving forward. Craig locates the position, jumps up and runs 35 yards in the face of enemy fire and kills three soldiers in the position. Later in the day, as Craig's platoon advances down the exposed face of a ridge, it encounters 100 enemy soldiers. Craig orders his platoon to return to cover on the opposite side of the ridge while he stands alone to face the enemy. Charging forward until he is only 25 yards away, Second Lieutenant Craig kneels down and fires, killing five and wounding three others before he himself is killed. The platoon counterattacks and drive the enemy back, inflicting heavy casualties. Second Lieutenant Craig's singular act of courage will win him the Medal of Honor. Over Italy, Ninth Air Force B-24 Liberators bomb airfields at Vibo Valentia, Sicily, and Reggio di Calabria. Over Sicily, B-25 Mitchells, escorted by P-40s, bomb the airfields at Trapani, Milo, and Bo Rizzo, as well as areas between Sciacca and Enna. P-40s conduct ground support missions for invasion forces. Northwest African Air Force B-26 Marauders hit Milo, Sciacca, and Gerbini airfields as well as assembly areas, vehicle convoys, bridges, trains, and roads. B-17s bomb the Catania marshaling yard and B-25s and P-38 Lightnings hit Sciacca airfield and the town of Caltanissetta as well as truck convoys and gun positions.

PACIFIC: U.S. submarine *Flying Fish* torpedoes and sinks a Japanese guardboat near the Daito Islands. U.S. submarine *Gurnard* attacks a Japanese convoy, sinking a cargo ship northeast of Palau. PBY Catalinas sink one Japanese guardboat and damage another off Kamchatka.

CENTRAL PACIFIC: Seventh Air Force B-24s from Funafuti Island in the Ellice Islands fly a photoreconnaissance mission to Little Makin Island in the Gilbert Islands. Two of the three B-24s also bomb the island.

BOUGAINVILLE: Thirteenth Air Force B-24s and B-17s bomb Kahili airfield on Bougainville Island. Admiral Halsey, COMSOPAC, issues a directive for an attack on Bougainville. Lieutenant General Alexander A. Vandegrift, commander of the I Marine Amphibious Corps, is tasked to lead the invasion. Bougainville, with its six airbases and 45–65,000 Japanese troops, represents the outer Japanese defense barrier protecting Rabaul, only 250 miles distant. Capturing the island and its airbases opens Rabaul to sustained attack.

NEW GEORGIA: Major General Griswold, commander of XIV Corps, and his staff arrive on Rendova Island to size up the situation. The Americans have encountered the Japanese main line of resistance along hills and ridges; the center of the Japanese line is named Horseshoe Hill. A series of interconnected bunkers and pillboxes, 12 feet square and 10 feet deep, expertly camouflaged with rifle and machine-gun ports that provide interlocking lanes of fire, is supported by numerous spider holes and individual fighting positions for riflemen. Behind these positions are mortars that are targeted on selected areas intended to break up any organized attack. American supply lines are overstretched in the difficult jungle terrain. A battalion of the 169th Infantry becomes combat ineffective due to a large number of psychoneurosis casualties.

NEW GUINEA: Fifth Air Force A-20 Havocs and B-25 Mitchells conduct ground support missions around Salamaua. B-25s also bomb Penfoei on Timor Island, while B-17s and B-24 Liberators bomb the airfields at Rabaul.

July 12

CBI: Fourteenth Air Force B-24 Liberators attack docks, shipping, railroad yards, a power plant, and warehouses at various sites in French Indochina. Two cargo ships are sunk. P-40s attack trucks near Ha Giang.

ATLANTIC: A B-24 of the 1st Antisubmarine Squadron (Heavy) sinks German submarine *U-506* off Portugal. German submarine *U-172* torpedoes and sinks a U.S. freighter off the coast of Brazil. The entire crew of 56 safely abandons ship. Some of the men are questioned by the U-boat commander, who also gives the men directions to the nearest shoreline.

SICILY: Adolf Hitler decides to take personal command of the battle in Sicily and orders reinforcements shifted west. He intends to hold the island for as long as possible. In doing so, he cancels a scheduled major offensive on the eastern front. German paratroopers of the 1st Parachute Division land near Catania, while German tanks and infantry attack the 1st Infantry Division south of Nicosia. The division, supported by tanks from the 2nd Armored Division, stops the enemy, destroying 43 tanks and capturing 4,200 prisoners. The 1st Infantry Division captures

Ponte Olivo; the 45th Infantry Division captures Biscari; the 3rd Infantry Division advances to Canicatti.

Ninth Air Force B-24 Liberators attack the harbor, ferry slip, and marshaling yard at Reggio di Calabria, and the ferry slip and railroad yards at Villa San Giovanni in Italy. Over Sicily, B-25 Mitchells hit Bo Rizzo airfield while P-40s patrol over the Licata area. Northwest African Air Force B-17s bomb Messina railroad bridges, while B-26 Marauders and A-20 Havocs bomb Gerbini, Agrigento, Canicatti, and Milo airfields. P-40s attack Termini harbor, rail junctions, rail cars, vehicles, and communication targets throughout Sicily.

SOUTHWEST PACIFIC AREA: Fifth Air Force B-24 Liberators bomb the airfields at Rabaul. B-25 Mitchells bomb Lingat airfield and villages on Selaroe Island in the Moluccas.

PACIFIC: U.S. submarine *Mingo* attacks a Japanese convoy to the east of Sakhalin Island, but fails to cause any damage. U.S. submarine *Plunger* torpedoes and sinks a Japanese cargo ship in the Sea of Japan. U.S. submarine *Spearfish* torpedoes and damages a Japanese destroyer near Eniwetok Atoll.

NEW GEORGIA: Thirteenth Air Force B-25 Mitchells and B-24 Liberators attack Vila airfield; fighters join U.S. Navy SBD Dauntless dive-bombers to attack the Munda area. Four light cruisers and two destroyers of TG 36.9, under command of Rear Admiral Aaron S. Merrill, bombard Munda. U.S. destroyer sinks Japanese submarine *RO-107* east of Kolombangara Island.

July 13

CBI: In Burma, Tenth Air Force B-25 Mitchells lay mines in the Irrawaddy River.

ATLANTIC: TBF Avenger torpedo bombers from escort carrier *Core* sink German submarine *U-487* south of the Azores.

ETO: Eighth Air Force sends B-17s and five YB-40s (an armored version of the B-17) against three targets in France. Against the aircraft works at Villacoublay, 101 B-17s hit the target. Three bombers are lost and 67 are damaged. Enemy losses are reported at more than 15 aircraft destroyed. Another 53 B-17s bomb the Amiens/Glisy airfield. One bomber is lost, 37 are damaged. Enemy losses are nine aircraft. Of the 52 B-17s that bomb Le Bourget airfield in Paris, four are lost and 51 are damaged, and over 40 enemy aircraft are reported destroyed.

SICILY: Axis forces begin a withdrawal to the San Stefano defensive line and await the arrival of the Hermann Göring Panzer Division. General Montgomery, making no progress after capturing Syracuse and Augusta almost without a fight, convinces Alexander to shift the Eighth Army's boundary past Route 124 to allow him to maneuver westward using the main road to outflank the Axis defenses. With this shift in boundary come new orders from Alexander: the Americans will have a purely supporting role and have no other responsibility except to cover Montgomery's advance. However, General Alexander approves Patton's request for the 3rd Infantry Division to conduct a reconnaissance-in-force westward toward Agrigento and Porto Empedocle. The shift in boundary actually provides the Axis forces with an opportunity to consolidate their defenses as II Corps complies with Alexander's new order. Patton orders II Corps to advance northwest toward Caltanissetta in order to divide the island in two.

Ninth Air Force B-24 Liberators bomb the airfields at Crotone in Italy and at Vibo Valentia in Sicily. B-25 Mitchells bomb the Leonforte road and harbor at Termini in support of British forces. Northwest African Air Force B-17s, B-25s, B-26 Marauders, and fighters attack Enna and Milo airfields, Carcitella landing ground, and other targets. Fighters attack truck convoys, trains, railway stations, and troops throughout Sicily.

German air attacks cripple a U.S. freighter with British troops embarked. All but one of the soldiers are killed, as are most of the crew and the armed guard on board.

NEW GEORGIA: Elements of the 169th Infantry advance 500 yards, and take over 100 casualties to capture a Japanese strongpoint on a key ridge south of Munda Trail—now named Reincke Ridge after the regiment's 3rd Battalion commander.

General Griswold assesses that the mission against Munda is too big for the two understrength regiments of the 43rd Infantry Division alone. He recommends committing the 37th Infantry Division and bringing the 25th Infantry Division from Guadalcanal immediately.

During the night off Kolombangara Island, Rear Admiral Walden L. Ainsworth's three light cruisers and 10 destroyers of TG 36.1 engage a Japanese light cruiser and five destroyers escorting troop-carrying destroyers. Torpedoes damage two U.S. light cruisers. A New Zealand light cruiser and a U.S. destroyer are also damaged by a torpedo attack. The destroyer is later scuttled by gunfire. A Japanese light cruiser is sunk and a destroyer is damaged.

NEW GUINEA: Fifth Air Force B-17s and B-24 Liberators bomb the airfield and harbor at Lae. B-25 Mitchells bomb Salamaua area, hitting antiaircraft guns and enemy positions.

July 14

ALEUTIANS: U.S. destroyer bombards Japanese positions at Gertrude Cove, Kiska, but receives no return fire.

ATLANTIC: German submarine *U-178* torpedoes and sinks a U.S. freighter off Mozambique. The U-boat captain questions crew members before giving them directions to the nearest land.

TBF Avengers and F4F Wildcats from escort carrier *Santee* sink German submarine *U-160* south of the Azores.

MEDITERRANEAN: Benito Mussolini receives a report from General Vittorio Ambrosio of the *Commando Supremo* that Sicily's defenders cannot hold out for long. Mussolini is told Italy has no more resources to continue the war. He is urged to end the alliance with Hitler and end the war as soon as possible.

SICILY: The Axis leadership agrees to concentrate German-Italian defenses in the northeast part of Sicily. The 1st Infantry Division captures Niscemi and Mazzarivo. Ninth Air Force B-24 Liberators and Royal Air Force heavy bombers hit railroad, marshaling yard, harbor, and oil storage facilities at Messina. B-25 Mitchells bomb Enna and Palermo, while P-40s attack the Lentini area. Northwest African Air Force fighters attack supplies, trains, rail junctions, bridges, and convoys in Sicily. B-17s, B-26 Marauders, and B-25 Mitchells bomb Messina, Enna, Marsala, and Randazzo. U.S. light cruiser is damaged by mine off Licata.

NEW GEORGIA: In an attempt to break the stalemate along the main line of defense, a battalion of the 103rd Infantry Regiment lands at Laiana Beach, arriving from previous operations on Vangunu Island. Tanks from the 9th Marine Defense Battalion also land to support the infantry. Thirteenth Air Force B-25 Mitchells and P-40s strike barges and a small vessel off New Georgia Island. B-24 Liberators and B-17s bomb the Kahili airfield on Bougainville Island and the airfields on Ballale Island and Buka Island.

NEW GUINEA: Fifth Air Force B-24 Liberators bomb Koepang on Timor Island.

July 15

ALEUTIANS: Eleventh Air Force B-24 Liberators and B-25 Mitchells bomb the antiaircraft positions on Kiska Island. One B-25 is damaged by enemy fire.

ATLANTIC: A U.S. PBY Catalina, a British destroyer, and two frigates sink German submarine *U-135* off the coast of Morocco. U.S. PBM Mariner patrol bomber sinks German submarine *U-159* in the central Caribbean. TBF Avengers and F4F Wildcats from escort carrier USS *Santee* sink German submarine *U-509* south of the Azores.

SICILY: Patton, gaining approval from Alexander to conduct reconnaissance forward allows the 3rd Infantry Division to capture Agrigento. Northwest African Air Force fighters attack trains, road junctions, radar installations, convoys, and railway stations.

SOUTHWEST PACIFIC AREA: SWPA GHQ circulates a plan for an attack on New Britain to control the western part of the island from Gasmata to Talasea. The plan outlines an attack by three separate elements to seize Cape Gloucester, neutralize Gasmata, and capture Talasea by a series of amphibious hops along the northern coastline. The Gasmata operation will take place seven days before the main attack on Cape Gloucester.

PACIFIC: U.S. submarine *Narwhal* shells the airfield on Matsuwa Island in the Kuriles. U.S. submarine *Tinosa* torpedoes and sinks a Japanese armed merchant cruiser north of Truk. A mine laid off Kavieng, New Ireland, by U.S. submarine *Silversides* on June 4 damages a Japanese light cruiser.

NEW GEORGIA: General Griswold takes command of the ground forces on New Georgia. Deputy SOPAC Commander Rear Admiral Theodore S. Wilkinson (who shows a great deal more willingness to cooperate with the army) replaces Rear Admiral Kelly Turner, who leaves to take command of Fifth Amphibious Corps. Griswold orders offensive operations suspended to rest, refit, and resupply the ground units. Admiral Halsey decides not to take on the strong Japanese defenses at Kolombangara Island, and shifts objectives to Vella Lavella. A force of about 27 Japanese bombers, with 40 to 50 fighters flying escort, is intercepted over Vella Lavella Island by Thirteenth Air Force and Allied fighters. Fifteen bombers and 30 fighters are shot down. Three Allied planes are lost.

July 16

ATLANTIC: TBF Avenger torpedo bombers from escort carrier USS *Core* sink German submarine *U-67* in the mid-Atlantic. German submarine *U-513* torpedoes and sinks a U.S. freighter off the coast of Brazil.

General George C. Marshall proposes an operation directed against Rome by seizing Naples and the airfields at Foggia. His proposal is code named Avalanche.

ETO: Eighth Air Force B-26B Marauders bomb the marshaling yard at Abbeville, France. Ten of the 14 are damaged. This is the first use of the B-26 in Europe. It will become one of the most reliable medium bombers in theater.

MEDITERRANEAN: In Italy, Ninth Air Force B-24 Liberators attack Bari airfield and lose three bombers to enemy fighters, but claim 11 fighters destroyed. Royal Air Force (RAF) heavy bombers bomb Reggio di Calabria airfield.

SICILY: The 3rd Infantry Division captures Agrigento and the Rangers capture Porto Empedocle. The British flanking maneuver is quickly halted as the Axis forces, reinforced by Hitler's order, hold along the defensive line from San Stefano through Adriana and on to Catania. Hitler orders German forces to take over the battle and delay the Allies as long as possible.

Over Sicily, B-25 Mitchells bomb Randazzo and Valguarnera. Northwest African Air Force fighters and light and medium bombers support ground operations.

BOUGAINVILLE: Thirteenth Air Force B-17s and B-24 Liberators attack Kahili airfield on Bougainville Island. Off Buin, seven B-24s along with over 70 navy SBD Dauntless dive-bombers and over 100 Allied fighters attack a Japanese convoy. Over 40 enemy aircraft are reported destroyed and seven vessels, including a destroyer, are reported sunk.

NEW GEORGIA: An airstrike of 84 navy-marine SBD Dauntless dive-bombers and TBF Avenger torpedo bombers attacks Lambetti plantation and Munda airfield. The 172nd Infantry attacks Japanese defenses north of Laiana, but is unable to advance because of poor coordination between the infantry and the marine tanks supporting them. The 3rd Battalion of the 169th Infantry captures Kelley Hill, named after Second Lieutenant John Kelley, killed after the hill was taken.

July 17

ATLANTIC: The B-18 Bolos of the 7th Antisubmarine Squadron (Heavy) cease conducting antisubmarine operations from their temporary base in Trinidad. The unit's home base is Jacksonville Municipal Airport, Florida.

ETO: While B-26s fly a diversion to Cayeux, France, Eighth Air Force B-17s attack two industrial targets in Germany, one at Hanover, the other at Hamburg. Bad weather prevents the main targets from being hit, and only 33 of the 205 B-17s and two YB-40s attack a target over Hannover. One B-17 is lost and 52 are damaged; enemy losses are reported at over 30 aircraft destroyed. The 125 B-17s sent against Hamburg find no targets, but 21 bombers attempt a bombing run on the cloud-shrouded Fokker plant at Amsterdam, Holland. The bombs miss their intended target and kill 150 civilians. This attack costs one B-17 lost and 42 others damaged. Aircrews report about 30 enemy aircraft destroyed.

MEDITERRANEAN: Patton meets Alexander in La Marsa, Tunisia, and requests permission to move on Palermo, the capital of Sicily. Alexander, however, decides to place significant restrictions on the advance to Palermo to ensure that Montgomery's flank and rear are protected. Patton's chief of staff, Brigadier General Hobart L. Gay, receives Alexander's revised order, but uses selective decoding, plus a request for retransmission to clarify the order. It is enough of a delay to allow Patton to continue with his original intent to capture Palermo without any limits on the use of his forces.

Based on events in Sicily, and the endorsement from General Marshall, Eisenhower begins examining opportunities for the invasion of the Italian mainland. Ironically and on the same day, Hitler comes to the conclusion that Sicily cannot be held.

Ninth Air Force B-24 Liberators bomb the marshaling yard in Naples, and Royal Air Force (RAF) heavy bombers hit Reggio di Calabria in Italy. One B-24 is shot down and enemy fighters damage several others. Aircrews report 23 enemy fighters destroyed. Over Sicily, B-25 Mitchells bomb Catania and the rail yards and roads at Paterno. P-40s fly escort to Gela and Comiso. Over 200 B-25 Mitchells, B-26 Marauders, and B-17s of the Northwest African Air Force bomb the marshaling yard at Naples, Italy.

SICILY: First Lieutenant David C. Waybur of the 3rd Reconnaissance Troop, 3rd Infantry Division, volunteers to lead a three-vehicle patrol to locate a Ranger unit. The patrol moves at night until it reaches a destroyed bridge near Agrigento. Lieutenant Waybur is in the lead vehicle, when suddenly four enemy tanks appear. Surprised and outmatched, the patrol opens fire with machine guns in a desperate attempt to break contact. The men in Waybur's vehicle are quickly out of action. Although he is seriously wounded, Waybur climbs out of his vehicle and stands directly in front of the first enemy tank with only a Thompson submachine gun. At 30 yards, his fire kills the tank crew and the tank itself tumbles off the damaged bridge. He organizes a hasty defense and sends for help, holding his position until help arrives the next morning. For his extraordinary courage and willingness to sacrifice himself for his comrades, First Lieutenant Wayburn will receive the Medal of Honor.

BOUGAINVILLE: Thirteenth Air Force B-24s and navy and Marine Corps SBD Dauntless dive-bombers and navy TBF Avenger torpedo bombers, escorted by over 100 Allied fighters (marine F4U Corsairs, P-39 Airacobras, U.S. and Royal New Zealand AF P-40s), attack Japanese shipping off Bougainville Island. The B-24s claim hits on two merchant cargo ships and the dive-bombers claim serious damage to two destroyers, an auxiliary minesweeper, a patrol ship, an oiler, and a merchant cargo ship. One Japanese destroyer is sunk. The Allied fighters claim over 40 enemy aircraft and four floatplanes shot down.

NEW GEORGIA: About 150 Japanese infantrymen attack Zanana Beach in an attempt to disrupt the flow of supplies to the front lines. The Japanese overrun a casualty clearing station, massacring the wounded. Marine antiaircraft gunners and army rear area personnel form a hasty defense under the command of an army lawyer and stop them. The 169th Infantry Regiment defends against Japanese attacks near Munda, but the 43rd Infantry Division has suffered over 700 combat casualties and has more than 1,000 men sick from malaria and dysentery. Psychoneurosis casualties average 150 men per day.

NEW GUINEA: Fifth Air Force B-25 Mitchells bomb Timor Island. B-24 Liberators bomb Adaoet Island in the Moluccas. B-25s attack the airfield, a headquarters compound, and various defensive positions around Salamaua.

July 18

ALEUTIANS: Eleventh Air Force B-24 Liberators and B-25 Mitchells bomb Kiska Island. Over the Kurile Islands, six B-24s attack cargo ships and the runway at Murakami Bay on Paramushiru Island.

CBI: Fourteenth Air Force B-24 Liberators bomb shipping at the harbors at Haiphong and Hongay in French Indochina.

ATLANTIC: U.S. Navy airship K-74 is shot down by German submarine *U-134* in the Florida Straits. This is the only airship lost to hostile fire in the war.

SICILY: The 1st Infantry Division captures Enna, a key position that allows the British to move freely eastward. The 45th Infantry Division moves toward the northern coast of the island. Ninth Air Force B-25 Mitchells attack targets near Randazzo and Catania. The Northwest African Air Force A-36 Invaders (Apaches) bomb targets at Santa Caterina, Adrano, Lercara, and Termini Imerese.

CENTRAL PACIFIC: Seventh Air Force B-24 Liberators from Funafuti in the Ellice Islands, bomb Japanese defensive works on Betio Island, Tarawa Atoll, Gilbert Islands.

GUADALCANAL: Japanese submarine *RO-106* torpedoes and sinks a U.S. LST (Landing Ship Tank) off Guadalcanal.

BOUGAINVILLE: Thirteenth Air Force B-24 Liberators, P-40s, and P-38 Lightnings, and over 140 navy and Marine Corps SBD Dauntless dive-bombers, TBF Avenger torpedo bombers and fighters attack Kahili airfield and shipping off Bougainville Island. The airfield is bombed by five B-24 Liberators, which suppress antiaircraft positions and crater the runways. Other U.S. aircraft attack shipping, claiming damage to two destroyers and one light vessel sunk. Enemy losses are estimated at 21 fighters. U.S. losses are nine navy aircraft.

NEW GEORGIA: The 4th Raider Battalion arrives to reinforce the Raiders at Enogai. The battalion of the 148th Infantry, having no effect on the Bairoko Trail, joins the marines.

NEW GUINEA: Fifth Air Force B-24 Liberators bomb the Makassar harbor area of Celebes Island. B-25 Mitchells, one B-24, and an A-20 Havoc bomb and strafe targets around Salamaua. Other B-25s attack shipping off New Britain Island.

July 19

ALEUTIANS: Eleventh Air Force receives three A-24-equipped dive-bomber squadrons from Tampa, Florida, which will fly from Amchitka Island. The A-24 Banshee is the SBD Dauntless dive-bomber without carrier landing equipment.

ATLANTIC: The B-24 Liberators of the 14th Antisubmarine Squadron (Heavy), 25th Antisubmarine Wing, relocate from Massachusetts and begin operations from Langley Field in Hampton, Virginia. US PBM Mariner patrol bomber sinks German submarine *U-513* off Santos, Brazil.

MEDITERRANEAN: Hitler meets with Mussolini at Feltre, Italy, and spends the entire meeting haranguing his gloomy and wavering partner on the need to stand firm. In Italy, over 100 Ninth Air Force B-24 Liberators attack the marshaling yards and airfield at Littoria and the rail lines at Anzio. The previous night, Northwest African Air Force bombers dropped over 800,000 leaflets on Rome.

Over Rome, 150 B-17s of the Northwest African Air Force bomb the railroad yards. B-25 Mitchells and B-26 Marauders attack Ciampino airfield outside of Rome. In Sicily, P-40s bomb rail facilities and A-36 Invaders (Apaches) attack trains and transports.

PACIFIC: U.S. submarine *Porpoise* torpedoes and sinks a Japanese transport south of Wake Island.

BOUGAINVILLE: Thirteenth Air Force B-17s bomb Kahili airfield at Bougainville Island. B-17s and B-25 Mitchells also bomb the airfield on Ballale Island. B-25s conduct ground support missions near Bairoko on New Georgia.

July 20

ALEUTIANS: Over Kiska Island, nine B-24 Liberators of the Eleventh Air Force bomb the airfield and facilities.

ATLANTIC: A B-24 Liberator of the 19th Antisubmarine Squadron (Heavy) sinks German submarine *U-588* in the Bay of Biscay.

PACIFIC: The Joint Chiefs of Staff issues orders to Admiral Chester W. Nimitz, Commander in Chief, Pacific Ocean Areas (CincPOA), to prepare to mount an offensive in the Gilberts in order to put pressure on the Japanese from another direction and to protect strategic lines of communications to the Solomons. The Gilberts will be the first islands to be captured, followed by Kwajalein, Eniwetok, Saipan, Guam, Iwo Jima, and Okinawa.

U.S. submarine *Pompano* torpedoes and damages a Japanese transport east of Kyushu, Japan.

BOUGAINVILLE: Over Bougainville, 18 B-24 Liberators from Thirteenth Air Force bomb airfields at Kahili and on Ballale Island. A Japanese surface force is spotted sailing between Vella Lavella and Choiseul Islands. TBF Avenger torpedo bombers from Henderson Field sink one destroyer and damage another. A heavy cruiser is also damaged. A later attack by B-25 Mitchells sinks a destroyer.

NEW GEORGIA: Marines attack Japanese defenses at Bairoko Harbor and are thrown back with 30 percent casualties. Marine colonel Harry B. Liversedge, commanding the Northern Landing Group, composed of the 1st Marine Raider Battalion and a battalion each of the 145th and 148th Infantry Regiments, 37th Infantry Division, decides to hold at Enogai. Japanese conduct an air attack on Rendova Island. Fighters strafe barges in Pakoi Bay.

NEW GUINEA: Fifth Air Force A-20 Havocs and B-25 Mitchells bomb Madang airfield and other Japanese defensive positions. On Timor Island, B-25s bomb airfields at Lautem, Dili, and Cape Chater.

July 21

ALEUTIANS: Two U.S. destroyers bombard suspected Japanese positions at Gertrude Cove, Kiska Island.

ATLANTIC: A navy PBY Catalina sinks German submarine *U-662* at the mouth of Amazon River, Brazil.

SICILY: Patton forms a Provisional Corps of the 3rd Infantry Division, the 82nd Airborne Division, an RCT of the 9th Infantry Division, along with elements of the 2nd Armored Division, and the 1st and 4th Ranger Battalions under command of

Major General Geoffrey Keyes, to move westward toward Palermo, the capital of Sicily. Allied forces have captured six airfields.

SOUTHWEST PACIFIC AREA: U.S. submarine *Haddock* torpedoes and sinks a Japanese army transport with 180 geishas on board in the Philippine Sea.

NEW GEORGIA: Major General J. Lawton Collins, commander of the 25th Infantry Division, arrives from Guadalcanal accompanied by the remainder of the 37th Infantry Division. Thirteenth Air Force B-25 Mitchells and over 170 navy dive-bombers supported by over 50 fighters attack Japanese defenses around Bairoko.

NEW GUINEA: Fifth Air Force B-25 Mitchells bomb Madang and other ground support targets, while B-26 Marauders bomb barges. The C-47-equipped 66th Troop Carrier Squadron arrives at Port Moresby from the United States.

July 22

ALEUTIANS: Eleventh Air Force B-25 Mitchells and B-24 Liberators, escorted by 13 P-40s and 20 P-38 fighters, attack a number of targets on Kiska Island. A B-25 is shot down by antiaircraft fire, and another 18 aircraft are damaged. One B-25 conducts a photoreconnaissance mission and a B-24 flies a radar reconnaissance mission over Kiska. Rear Admiral Robert C. Giffen's Task Group 16.21 and Rear Admiral Robert M. Griffin's TG 16.22, with two battleships, three heavy cruisers, one light cruiser, and nine destroyers, bombard the island.

ATLANTIC: German submarine *U-66* torpedoes and damages a U.S. tanker en route from New York to Aruba. When the U-boat surfaces to finish off the tanker with gunfire, the tanker's armed guard defends the ship with accurate fire from its deck gun and drives off the enemy. The tanker is able to reach port at San Juan, Puerto Rico, with no casualties.

ETO: A report issued by the British Joint Intelligence Committee claims the Combined Bomber Offensive is having an effect on Germany, noting German fighter strength is now directed mainly against Allied bombing missions in Europe, drawing assets away from other areas. The report claims strategic bombing is having an effect on strategic raw materials production, especially synthetic rubber, fuel, iron, and coal in the Ruhr industrial area of Germany.

MEDITERRANEAN: Over Italy, more than 100 B-17s of the Northwest African Air Force bomb the marshaling yard at Battipaglia and Foggia. B-26 Marauders attack a bridge and the marshaling yard at Salerno.

SICILY: The 45th Infantry Division reaches Termini Imerese on the northern coast. Patton's Provisional Corps is ready to assault the city of Palermo, but the attack is not necessary as city officials surrender to General Keyes.

PACIFIC: U.S. submarine *Sawfish* torpedoes and damages a Japanese ammunition ship in the East China Sea.

BOUGAINVILLE: Thirteenth Air Force B-17s and B-24 Liberators, along with more than 40 navy SBD Dauntless dive-bombers and over 100 Allied fighters attack Japanese shipping off Buin at Bougainville Island. A seaplane carrier is sunk and several other vessels are damaged.

NEW GEORGIA: Major General Griswold orders Major General Robert Beightler to take command of his 37th Infantry Division. The 161st Infantry Regiment from the

25th Infantry Division arrives and is placed under Beighter's command. Griswold issues orders for a coordinated attack on Munda to begin on July 25. The 37th Division takes the northern sector of the enemy line and the 43rd Division takes the southern sector. The 2nd Battalion of the 103rd Infantry Regiment from Vangunu Island reinforces the 43rd Division. The 169th Infantry is moved to the rear for rest and refitting.

A convoy with a Japanese seaplane tender and five destroyers with troops and supplies bound for New Georgia is attacked by 16 SBD Dauntless dive-bombers, 18 TBF Avenger torpedo bombers, and 16 heavy bombers.

NEW GUINEA: Fifth Air Force B-24 Liberators, B-25 Mitchells, and B-26 Marauders attack Japanese defensive positions and antiaircraft placements around Salamaua. B-24s bomb an oil refinery and transportation targets at Surabaya, Java. B-25s bomb targets on Selaroe Island in the Moluccas.

July 23

CBI: Japanese bombers and fighters begin a three-day attack on Kweilin, Hengyang, Lingling, Kanchow, and Suichan.

ATLANTIC: A U.S. destroyer sinks German submarine *U-613* south of Azores. TBF Avenger torpedo bombers from escort carrier USS *Bogue* attack German submarines *U-527* and *U-648* south of the Azores. The Avengers sink *U-527* and *U-648* escapes. Navy PB4Y Privateers sink German submarine *U-598* off Brazil.

The 23rd Antisubmarine Squadron (Heavy), which has operated B-25 Mitchells from Langley Field, Hampton, Virginia, returns to its base at Jacksonville, Florida.

MEDITERRANEAN: The CCS directs General Eisenhower to develop plans for an invasion of Italy, directed in the vicinity of Naples. In Italy, Northwest African Air Force B-17s, B-25 Mitchells, and B-26 Marauders bomb Leverano and Crotone.

SICILY: With Montgomery unable to make any progress, Alexander orders Patton to advance east with his army on the northern Route 113 and Route 120. The 82nd Airborne Division is in Trapani and moving toward Marsala. The 1st Infantry Division captures Enna with elements of the 1st Canadian Division, and prepares to advance on Petrali. The 45th Infantry Division attacks along the coastal road at Termini Imerese, but is halted by elements of the 29th Panzer Grenadier Division, one of the units ordered to Sicily by Hitler. Patton orders his reserve, the 9th Infantry Division, to be moved to Sicily. The II Corps is ordered to move along the coastal road and along Route 120, the main road in the center of the island, to capture Nicosia, Troina, and Randazzo. The 45th Infantry Division is ordered to advance along the coast, while the 1st Infantry Division advances west on Route 120. Northwest African Air Force light bombers support ground operations at Adrano, Paterno, and Troina.

NEW GUINEA: Fifth Air Force B-17s, B-26 Marauders, B-25 Mitchells, and B-24 Liberators bomb a number of targets along the northeast coast.

The airfield constructed on Woodlark Island is operational. The 67th Fighter Squadron, flying P-39 Airacobras, deploys to the island.

July 24

ALEUTIANS: Over Kiska and Little Kiska Islands, 62 U.S. P-40s, with two of the fighters piloted by men of the Royal Canadian Air Force, attack the airfield runway and antiaircraft positions. Although one battery is severely damaged, an Eleventh Air Force P-40 is lost to Japanese antiaircraft fire.

CBI: P-40 pilots report 25 enemy aircraft shot down defending the airspace over Fourteenth Air Force airfields.

ATLANTIC: TBF Avengers and F4F Wildcats from escort carrier *Santee* damage German submarine *U-373* west of the Madeira Islands. B-24 Liberators damage German submarine *U-466* off Cayenne, French Guiana.

ETO: Eighth Air Force conducts its first long-range attack on Norway. The three missions will involve a total distance of 1,900 miles to and from the targets. Against the nitrate works at Heroya, 167 B-17s and a YB-40 bomb the target and disrupt it sufficiently to halt production for at least three months. Enemy losses are reported at nine aircraft destroyed. U.S. losses are one B-17 destroyed and 53 damaged. The Trondheim port area is attacked by 41 B-17s. One B-17 is lost and nine others are damaged; enemy losses are estimated at nine aircraft. The Bergen port area is under cloud cover, and the 84 B-17s cancel the mission.

MEDITERRANEAN: The Fascist Grand Council meets at Mussolini's direction. After a debate over the direction of the war, 19 of 28 members vote against Mussolini remaining in power. The king of Italy, Victor Emmanuel III, orders Mussolini to resign in favor of Field Marshal Pietro Badoglio. Mussolini is put in an ambulance and moved to a secret location, where he is informed he is under arrest.

Northwest African Air Force B-17s and B-25 Mitchells bomb the Bologna railroad yards. B-26 Marauders bomb the Paola railroad yards.

SICILY: The 39th RCT occupies Marsala. Patton's Provisional Corps controls western Sicily. The engineers open Palermo for port operations. The Provisional Corps has captured 53,000 Italians and 400 vehicles.

PACIFIC: U.S. submarine *Tinosa* fires a total of 15 torpedoes at a Japanese oiler in the Carolines—13 are hits but only two explode. The oiler is damaged, but it is towed to Truk and salvaged. U.S. torpedo problems are common, forcing submariners to expend numerous torpedoes in order to get an explosion.

CENTRAL PACIFIC: Seventh Air Force B-24 Liberators from Midway Island attack Wake Island, bombing the oil storage area, barracks, and a gun emplacement. About 30 Japanese fighters attack the eight bombers over the target. One B-24 is lost in a collision with a falling Japanese fighter and nine enemy aircraft are reported destroyed.

NEW GEORGIA: U.S. Navy and marine SBD Dauntless dive-bombers along with 48 Thirteenth Air Force fighters support ground forces around Bairoko and at Bibilo Hill.

NEW GUINEA: Fifth Air Force B-25 Mitchells bomb the airfield and other targets at Lae. B-25s also bomb targets on Timor Island.

July 25

ALEUTIANS: Over Kiska and Little Kiska Islands, 40 U.S. P-40s, with two of the fighters piloted by men of the Royal Canadian Air Force, attack the airfield runway and antiaircraft positions.

CBI: Fourteenth Air Force B-25 Mitchells, escorted by P-40s and P-38 Lightnings, bomb the airfield at Hankow, China, in retaliation for Japanese air attacks on U.S. airfields.

ATLANTIC: The B-24 Liberators of the 15th Antisubmarine Squadron (Heavy) at Jacksonville, Florida, move operations to Battista Field in Cuba.

ETO: Eighth Air Force VIII Bomber Command attacks three targets in Germany. The first target is the diesel engine works at Hamburg, where during the previous night nearly 750 Royal Air Force heavy bombers damaged the city. Because of cloud cover during the day, 100 B-17s hit the shipyard as an alternate target. German fighters shoot down 15 bombers and damage 67 others. Enemy losses are estimated at over 40 aircraft destroyed. Against the shipyard at Kiel, 59 B-17s are unable to attack the target due to heavy cloud cover. Although 141 B-17s are sent against an aviation industrial target at Warnemunde, 118 bombers attack the shipyard at Kiel instead, losing four B-17s to enemy fighters. They return with 51 other bombers damaged and claim six German aircraft destroyed. Over Ghent, Belgium, 13 B-26B Marauders of the VIII Air Support Command bomb the coke ovens used for making steel. Six aircraft are damaged in the attack.

MEDITERRANEAN: Celebrations begin in Rome at the news of Mussolini's resignation. The king selects Pietro Badoglio, a former *Commando Supremo,* to lead the new government. The Italian Fascist Party is dissolved. Badoglio publicly announces that the war will continue, even though the king has instructed Badoglio to break the alliance with Germany and come to terms with the Allies. Badoglio's announcement is intended to keep the Germans from taking any precipitous action before he can carry out his instructions. Hitler, suspicious of Badoglio's motives, orders two divisions from southern France to move to the Italian border.

SICILY: Ninth Air Force B-25 Mitchells bomb docks and shipping at Milazzo. Nearly 100 P-40s strafe and bomb Catania harbor and targets at Milazzo and Taormina.

SOUTHWEST PACIFIC AREA: U.S. submarine *Pompon* torpedoes and sinks a Japanese cargo ship and damages a transport north of the Saint Matthias Group near the Bismarck Archipelago.

SOLOMONS: Lieutenant General Nathan F. Twining, USAAF, becomes Commander Air Solomons (COMAIRSOLS). Brigadier General Dean C. Strother becomes commander of Fighter Command Solomons (he remains the commander of XIII Fighter Command). Colonel William A. Matheny takes command of Bomber Command Solomons.

NEW GEORGIA: The general attack on Munda begins. Preceding the attack, 66 B-17s and B-24 Liberators bomb Lambetti plantation. Another strike of 84 aircraft hits Bibilo hill. The attack begins against Japanese positions on Shimuzu hill, supported by tanks and flamethrowers. The 43rd Infantry Division's two regiments, the 103rd and the 172nd, move along the coast, while three regiments of the 37th Infantry Division (the 148th, 161st, and the 145th) attack the Japanese strongpoint from the front and flank. Supported by marine tanks, the infantrymen fight yard by yard into the midst of the well camouflaged, heavily fortified positions.

The infantry attacks are supported by naval gunfire from seven destroyers. But within 30 minutes, over 170 B-17s, B-24 Liberators, B-25 Mitchells, SBD Dauntless dive-bombers, and TBF Avenger torpedo bombers, escorted by more than 70 fighters, drop 145 tons of bombs on enemy positions. Another 10 B-24s bomb Bibilo hill, while SBDs and TBFs hit Japanese gun positions. A Japanese air attack on U.S. forces on Rendova Island fails as Allied fighters shoot down at least eight fighters and disrupt the bombers so that they are unable to cause any damage.

July 26

ALEUTIANS: Eleventh Air Force B-24s, 38 P-40s, and 24 P-38s attack targets on Kiska Island and Little Kiska Island, dropping over 140 tons of bombs. One P-40 is shot down and three others are damaged by antiaircraft fire.

CBI: Fourteenth Air Force B-25 Mitchells escorted by 12 P-40s bomb the airfield at Hankow, China. An estimated 30 to 50 fighters intercept the attackers. The U.S. crews claim 14 enemy aircraft shot down and 17 probables. One P-40 is lost.

ATLANTIC: The CCS, responding to the news from Italy, decides to speed up the invasion of the mainland in order to bolster the new Italian government and forestall a German reaction.

PBM Mariner patrol bomber sinks German submarine *U-759* in the Caribbean.

ETO: Eighth Air Force VIII Bomber Command attacks two targets in Germany. Over Hannover, 96 B-17s and two YB-40s (an armored version of the B-17) hit rubber production factories. U.S. losses are 16 B-17s, while enemy aircraft losses are estimated to be nearly 50 destroyed. Another raid on Hannover by 61 B-17s turns into 49 bombers attacking targets of opportunity. Crews claim at least 15 enemy aircraft destroyed and six B-17s are lost to enemy fire. Another 54 of 121 B-17s sent against targets in Hannover, bomb the U-boat yards, losing two B-17s and destroying five enemy aircraft. A total of 89 B-17s are damaged on this mission. Over France, 15 B-26B Marauders of the VIII Air Support Command hit the Saint-Omer/Longuenesse airfield. Four bombers are damaged in the attack.

MEDITERRANEAN: In Italy, Northwest African Air Force B-26 Marauders bomb the marshaling yard at Marina di Paola. A German bomber damages a U.S. destroyer off Palermo, Sicily.

CENTRAL PACIFIC: Seventh Air Force B-24 Liberators flying from Midway Island attack Wake Island, hitting the oil storage area. The eight bombers are attacked by at least 20 fighters. The B-24 crews report 11 enemy fighters destroyed.

BOUGAINVILLE: Thirteenth Air Force B-24 Liberators, P-38 Lightnings, P-40s, and navy aircraft attack the airfield at Kahili on Bougainville Island. B-25 Mitchells, P-40s, and U.S. Navy fighters attack targets over Kolombangara Island in New Georgia.

NEW GEORGIA: Army infantry, with marine tanks, assault Lambetti plantation. Ilangana village falls to the 3rd Battalion of the 103rd Infantry, which advances 800 yards along a 600-yard frontage. Within this area the Americans have had to destroy 74 fortified defensive positions. The 161st Infantry Regiment meets heavy opposition on Bartley Ridge, named after Second Lieutenant Martin Bartley, killed during the attack.

NEW GUINEA: Fifth Air Force B-17s and B-24 Liberators bomb targets around Salamaua and Lae airfield. The 65th Troop Carrier Squadron, equipped with C-47s, arrives at Port Moresby from the United States.

July 27

CBI: Fourteenth Air Force B-24 Liberators attack shipping at Hainan Island, claiming two vessels severely damaged. The 10 bombers are attacked by between 25 and 30 fighters. Crews claim 13 enemy fighters shot down with no U.S. losses. Another six B-24s, supported by 14 fighters, attack targets of opportunity on Stonecutters Island near Hong Kong.

CBI: The Chinese-American Composite Wing (CACW) is activated. The wing has Chinese pilots and aircraft, led by Chinese and American officers. The wing consists of the 1st Bomber Group with B-25 Mitchells and the 3rd and 5th Fighter Groups with P-40s.

ETO: Eighth Air Force VIII Air Support Command B-26B Marauders bomb the Tricqueville airfield in France.

MEDITERRANEAN: In Italy, Northwest African Air Force B-17s bomb the Capua airfield and the rail lines at Lioni.

SICILY: The 1st Infantry Division captures Nicosia. The German forces begin a withdrawal in preparation for evacuation through Messina to the Italian mainland. Ninth Air Force P-40s attack both tactical targets on the island and shipping targets at Catania. Northwest African Air Force B-25 Mitchells and B-26 Marauders bomb the landing ground at Scalea.

PACIFIC: U.S. submarine *Sawfish* torpedoes and damages a Japanese minelayer off Kyushu, Japan. U.S. submarine *Scamp* torpedoes and sinks Japanese submarine *I-168* and damages an oiler near the Saint Matthias Group. U.S. submarine *Seadragon* off Wake Island adds damage to a crippled Japanese transport. Japanese cargo ship sinks off Hainan Island when it strikes a mine laid by U.S. submarine *Tambor* on November 2, 1942.

BOUGAINVILLE: Thirteenth Air Force B-17s bomb the Kahili airfields at Bougainville and Ballale islands. Brigadier General Ray L. Owens becomes the commanding general of Thirteenth Air Force.

NEW GEORGIA: P-38 Lightnings, along with navy and Marine Corps aircraft, attack Japanese positions on Bibilo hill, Gurasai, and Munda. Private First Class Frank J. Petrarca, a medic with the 145th Infantry Regiment, 37th Infantry Division, accompanies the infantry's attack on Japanese defenses near Horseshoe Hill. At 100 yards, the enemy opens fire on the Americans, causing several casualties. Petrarca locates the most seriously wounded soldiers, including one who is only 75 yards from the Japanese bunkers. Unable to move him from the direct line of fire, Petrarca provides first aid where the soldier fell, shielding the wounded man with his own body. He then moves to two other wounded soldiers. Petrarca will continue to perform extraordinary feats of heroism to save his comrades until he is killed on July 31 going to the aid of a wounded soldier only 20 yards from the enemy. His last conscious act will be to rise to his knees and shout his defiance to the Japanese. Private First Class Petrarca's numerous acts of selflessness and his indomitable will win him the Medal of Honor.

NEW GUINEA: The Salamaua area is hit by 35 B-25 Mitchells and 18 B-24 Liberators of the Fifth Air Force, representing one of the largest single-strike attacks to take place within the Southwest Pacific Area.

July 28

ALEUTIANS: In a masterstroke of deception and stealth, the Japanese bring in cruisers and destroyers to evacuate over 5,000 men from Kiska Island.

CBI: Fourteenth Air Force B-25 Mitchells, with an escort of nine P-40s, bomb the docks at Taikoo in Hong Kong.

ATLANTIC: A B-24 Liberator of the 4th Antisubmarine Squadron (Heavy) and a Royal Air Force B-24 sink German submarine *U-404* in the Bay of Biscay. A U.S. PBY Catalina sinks German submarine *U-359* in the West Indies. In a heavy fog, a U.S. freighter straggling from convoy BX 65 (Boston to Halifax) encounters a mine laid by German submarine *U-119,* but reaches port under tow.

ETO: Eighth Air Force VIII Bomber Command conducts the deepest U.S. bomber raid into Germany up to this time. For the first time, the bombers are escorted by 105 P-47 Thunderbolts, equipped with jettisonable belly tanks. Two aviation industry targets are selected; one is the Fieseler Works at Kassel and the other is the Focke-Wulf plant at Oschersleben. Weather over the targets limits the effectiveness of the strikes. Although 182 B-17s are launched against Kassel, only 58 hit the target; seven B-17s are shot down and 58 are damaged. Enemy aircraft losses are estimated at nearly 40 destroyed. Of the 120 B-17s intended for Oschersleben, only 37 hit the target; U.S. losses are 15 shot down and 65 damaged. Almost 80 enemy fighter kills are reported. P-47s meet the returning bombers and jump about 60 German fighters, destroying nine. The VIII Air Support Command conducts two strikes on targets in Belgium and France. The coke ovens at Zeebrugge, Belgium, are the target of 17 B-26B Marauders. Three B-26s are damaged in the attack. Another 18 B-26Bs head for Tricqueville airfield in France, but turn back when the fighter escort fails to meet them.

SICILY: Palermo receives supply ships for Patton's army. Lines of supply shift from the beaches to the road and rail lines in western Sicily. The 1st Infantry Division captures Nicosia and advances toward Cerami. Because of the mountainous terrain, the divisions of the II Corps will have to advance separately, unable to support each other. The German defenses have forced the Allies to fight on difficult terrain along narrow twisting roads, which limits maneuver and forces them to make frontal assaults on heavily fortified strongpoints. Destroyed bridges and minefields slow the advance even further. Ninth Air Force P-40s attack targets in Sicily. Over 100 aircraft are involved in the strikes. Northwest African Air Force A-36 Intruders (Apaches) and P-40s bomb enemy movements on the Troina-Randazzo road, attack the bridges and roads near Cesaro, and hit targets near Falcone and Randazzo.

SWPA: Fifth Air Force B-25 Mitchells attack the airfield at Cape Gloucester, New Britain Island, and sink two destroyers offshore. B-24 Liberators bomb targets in the Molucca Islands.

NEW GEORGIA: Two battalions of the 145th Infantry Regiment, 37th Infantry Division, attack to capture Horseshoe Hill.

NEW GUINEA: Fifth Air Force B-25s bomb the town of Lautem and the airfield at Cape Chater.

July 29

CBI: Fourteenth Air Force B-24 Liberators, with fighter escort, bomb shipping and dockyard installations at Hong Kong, Kowloon, and the docks at Taikoo. A force of 23 bombers and 30 fighters attacking Hengyang, China, is attacked by four P-40s. One Japanese fighter is shot down.

ETO: Eighth Air Force VIII Bomber Command attacks two targets in Germany: the Kiel shipyards and the Heinkel Aircraft Works at Warnemunde. Over Kiel, 91 B-17s hit the shipyard and 48 hit targets of opportunity, U.S. losses are six B-17s and 64 damaged. Enemy losses are estimated at over 50 aircraft destroyed. Over Warnemunde 54 B-17s hit the target, losing four B-17s and seven damaged. Enemy losses are light; only two are reported as probable kills. The VIII Air Support Command sends 18 B-26B Marauders against the Schipol airfield at Amsterdam, but a navigational error scrubs the mission. Over the Ft. Rouge airfield in France, 19 B-26Bs hit the target and eight bombers are damaged.

SICILY: Ninth Air Force sends over 200 P-40s against Axis targets on the northeast section of the island. Northwest African Air Force B-26 Marauders bomb the Aquino airfield.

NEW GEORGIA: Major General John Hester, commander of the 43rd Infantry Division, asks to be relieved due to illness. He is replaced by Major General John Hodge from the Americal Division. The 161st Infantry captures Bartley Ridge. The ridge contains 78 separate defensive positions, all of which have to be cleared individually. The Japanese begin a withdrawal to defensive positions around Munda airfield. The 148th Infantry Regiment stops a Japanese counterattack.

Lieutenant Robert S. Scott of the 172nd Infantry Regiment, 43d Infantry Division, advances with the leading platoon of his company to attack a Japanese position on a hilltop near Munda airfield. Although his battle-shaken and exhausted men retreat in the face of a sudden Japanese counterattack, Lieutenant Scott refuses to give up. Using grenades and his carbine, he single-handedly stops the attack. Scott's valiant act allows his men to move forward and capture the position. For his extraordinary courage, he will receive the Medal of Honor.

NEW GUINEA: Fifth Air Force B-17s, B-25 Mitchells, and B-24 Liberators bomb Salamaua. On New Britain Island, B-25s, B-26s, and a B-24 attack army HQ, barges, and villages. The bombers also attack shipping off Cape Gloucester.

July 30

ALEUTIANS: U.S. destroyers bombard the Gertrude Cove and main camp areas on Kiska Island. The Americans do not know that the Japanese have evacuated.

CBI: Fourteenth Air Force P-40s intercept 39 Japanese fighters and 24 bombers over Hengyang, China. The 15 P-40s destroy three bombers and two fighters and lose two of their own fighters.

ATLANTIC: Army Air Force Antisubmarine Command, which has been conducting antisubmarine patrols since January of 1942, ceases operations on the east and west coasts of the United States. These include the B-24 Liberators of the 3rd Antisubmarine Squadron (Heavy) at Fort Dix Army Air Base, New Jersey, the B-25 Mitchells of the 16th Antisubmarine Squadron (Heavy) at Charleston Army Air Field, South

Carolina, and the B-24s of the 27th, 30th, and 392nd Bombardment Squadrons (Heavy) at March Field, California. Only B-24s with the 8th Antisubmarine Squadron (Heavy) at Miami Army Air Field, Florida, will continue operation, but this unit will move to bases in the Caribbean. This marks the dominance of the Allies in the desperately fought Battle of the Atlantic.

German submarine *U-230* lays mines near the entrance to Chesapeake Bay. A PV-1 patrol bomber providing coverage for convoy TJ-2 (Trinidad to Rio de Janeiro) sinks German submarine *U-591* off the coast of Brazil. A PV-1 attacks German submarine *U-604* in the South Atlantic. Aircraft from escort carrier *Santee* sink German submarine *U-43* in the mid-Atlantic. *U-43*'s mission was to lay mines off Lagos, Nigeria. A U.S. submarine chaser sinks German submarine *U-375* off Tunisia.

ETO: Eighth Air Force VIII Bomber Command attacks two aviation-related industrial targets in the Kassel area, escorted by 107 P-47 Thunderbolts with auxiliary tanks. The Fieseler Works are bombed by 94 B-17s. Aircrews claim nearly 50 enemy aircraft destroyed; six B-17s are lost and 69 are damaged. Another 40 B-17s hit the Waldau Fieseler Works, losing six bombers and damaging 18. German aircraft losses are estimated at around 14. The P-47s are effective in countering the German fighters, who by now used to attacking bombers without fighter escort. Over Bocholt, Germany, the P-47s claim nearly 30 enemy aircraft destroyed. During the battle, seven P-47s are lost and one damaged. Six of the pilots are reported missing.

The VIII Air Support Command attacks airfields in the Netherlands and France. Over the Woensdrecht airfield, 11 B-26B Marauders hit the target. One B-26 is lost and six are damaged. The 24 B-26Bs sent against the Courtrai/Wevelghem airfield are recalled when fog prevents the fighter escort from joining the bombers. During the mission, however, the B-26 crews claim around 11 aircraft shot down.

SICILY: The 3rd Infantry Division replaces the 45th Infantry Division for the advance to Messina. The 39th RCT of the 9th Infantry Division is attached to the 1st Infantry Division. Ninth Air Force P-40s attack shipping at Milazzo, Messina, and Riposto. Over 100 P-40s are involved in ground support missions. Northwest African Air Force B-17s bomb Grottaglie airfield. B-25 Mitchells bomb the Pratica di Mare airfield. A-20 Havocs bomb Milazzo and attack Axis gun positions, while fighters hit shipping off Milazzo.

INDIAN OCEAN: U.S. freighter en route to Durban, South Africa, from Basra, Iraq, is torpedoed by German submarine *U-197,* but is able to reach its destination.

SOLOMONS: Thirteenth Air Force B-24 Liberators, with an escort of 16 P-38s and P-40s, along with more than 40 navy F4U Corsairs, attack the Ballale Island airfield.

NEW GUINEA: Fifth Air Force B-25 Mitchells hit barges off the Huon Peninsula and villages near Finschhafen. B-24s bomb Salamaua and Kela. A-20 Havocs destroy barges at Hanisch Harbor and Langemak Bay.

July 31

CBI: During the night, nine B-24 Liberators of the Tenth Air Force mine the Rangoon River in Burma.

ATLANTIC: A U.S. PBM Mariner patrol bomber and a Brazilian aircraft sink German submarine *U-199* off Rio de Janeiro, Brazil.

ETO: Eighth Air Force VIII Air Support Command launches raids on four targets in France. Against the airfield at Merville, 20 B-26B Marauders hit the target and two bombers are damaged. Against the airfield at Poix/Nord, 19 B-26Bs hit the target. One bomber is lost and five are damaged. Against the airfield at Abbeville/ Drucat, 21 B-26Bs hit the target. Against the airfield at Tricqueville, 18 B-26Bs hit the target. One enemy fighter is believed destroyed and five bombers are damaged. Royal Air Force bombers strike Lille and Amiens in conjunction with the American attacks.

SICILY: The 1st Infantry Division, supported by the 39th Infantry Regiment of the 9th Infantry Division, begins the battle for Troina. Troina is a natural strongpoint and the key to the German defensive line. A 10-man detachment, with Sergeant Gerry H. Kisters and an officer, is sent forward to fill a large crater in the road so that the 1st Infantry Division can move its vehicles through Gagliano. Two hidden enemy machine guns fire on the group as they advance. Sergeant Kisters and the officer move forward and assault the first position, capturing the machine gun and four soldiers. Sergeant Kisters then begins crawling toward the other machine gun position. Although wounded five separate times, he kills three enemy soldiers, runs off the fourth, and captures the position. For his courage in the face of the enemy and willingness to sacrifice his life for his comrades, Sergeant Kisters will receive the Medal of Honor.

SOUTHWEST PACIFIC AREA: U.S. submarine *Finback* torpedoes and sinks a Japanese cargo ship south of Borneo. U.S. submarine *Grayling* lands supplies and equipment at Panay, Philippines. U.S. submarine *Saury* in the Philippine Sea is rammed by Japanese destroyer and damaged; *Saury* returns to base.

PACIFIC: U.S. submarine *Pogy* torpedoes and sinks a Japanese aircraft transport northwest of Truk.

BOUGAINVILLE: U.S. submarine *Guardfish* lands a survey party on the west coast of Bougainville Island.

NEW GEORGIA: Thirteenth Air Force P-40s and P-39 Airacobras, along with over 90 navy and Marine Corps aircraft, attack Japanese defensive positions on Bibilo hill. B-17s, B-25 Mitchells, P-40s, and navy aircraft attack the Vila airfield on Kolombangara Island. Private Rodger W. Young of the 148th Infantry Regiment, 37th Infantry Division, is a member of a platoon ordered to make a limited withdrawal in order to align the battalion's night defensive position. The platoon suddenly is pinned down by intense fire from a Japanese machine gun concealed on higher ground only 75 yards away. Private Young is wounded but can see the enemy position. As the platoon attempts to break contact, Young begins crawling toward the position. Another burst of fire wounds him again, but he continues to move forward, firing his rifle as he goes. He gets close enough to throw hand grenades, but is killed in the attempt. Private Young's great courage and heroic sacrifice will win him the Medal of Honor.

NEW GUINEA: Fifth Air Force B-25 Mitchells bomb the Finschhafen area and barges at Hanisch Harbor and Mange. At New Britain Island, B-25s and A-20 Havocs bomb barges near Cape Gloucester area and B-24 Liberators bomb Waingapoe on Sumba Island in the Sundas.

August 1

ALEUTIANS: Despite overcast skies, seven B-24 Liberators of the Eleventh Air Force bomb the Main Camp area on Kiska Island.

CBI: Tenth Air Force: B-25 Mitchells bomb the road bridge at Shweli, Burma, causing minor damage.

ATLANTIC: U.S. gunboat attacks German submarine *U-732*, diverting it away from convoy NG 376 (New York to Guantánamo).

ETO: The 392nd Bombardment Group (Heavy) arrives at Wendling, England, from the United States with B-24 Liberators.

MEDITERRANEAN: The Raid on Ploeşti. Brigadier General Uzal G. Ent, one of the primary planners for the attack on the oil refineries in Ploeşti, Romania, leads 179 B-24 Liberators carrying over 1,700 Americans and over 300 tons of bombs, on an 18-hour, 2,400-mile round-trip mission to destroy Nazi Germany's critical source of fuel. The plan, called TidalWave, has a large-scale attack with the bombers sweeping over Ploeşti low and fast—225 miles an hour at 30 to 100 feet above the ground— using delayed fuse bombs as well as other munitions intended to cause large fires and prevent the refinery from being used for months, even years. To get a sufficient number of aircraft for the mission, the 376th and 98th Bomb Groups of the Ninth Air Force are reinforced by the 93rd, 44th, and 389th Bomb Groups from Eighth Air Force. Launching from Benghazi, the groups maintain contact until three hours into the mission, when the lead aircraft carrying the primary navigator goes out of control and crashes. The plane carrying the second navigator goes down low to search for survivors and cannot return to the formation. Thus, the rest of the flight to the target will be done by dead reckoning. Over time, another 12 bombers abort due to mechanical trouble.

High cloud cover forces the formation to separate into two groups. The 58 B-24s of the 376th Bomber Group and the 93rd Bomber Group fly over the clouds, while Colonel John R. Kane's 98th Bomber Group, Colonel Leon W. Johnson's 44th Bomber Group, and the 389th Bomber Group fly through the clouds and are trailing the leaders by 15 minutes. The lead group becomes disoriented for a short period and arrives over the target from the south, where it is met by heavy antiaircraft fire. General Ent orders the bombers to move east, then approach from the north and attack whatever targets are available. As a result, the bombers of the first group begin to hit targets originally designated for the 44th and the 98th Bomber Groups. Within a short time, Colonel Kane's 98th, followed by Colonel Johnson's 44th and the 389th, fly in over Ploeşti at near-rooftop level as planned. The enemy is waiting and the antiaircraft fire begins to take a heavy toll on the formation. Even though it is clear that many of their assigned targets have already been bombed, Colonel Kane and Colonel Johnson decide to complete the mission, plunging through towering smoke and flames, not knowing what dangers lay on the other side.

Of the 179 B-24s planned for the mission, 165 actually attack Ploeşti. Antiaircraft fire destroys 33 bombers over the target and enemy fighters shoot down another 10. Casualties are heavy—532 airmen are lost. The rest of the bombers either return to Benghazi or are forced to land at other airfields. Nearly all of the aircraft that return from the mission are heavily damaged. Two targets attacked as planned are put out of commission for the rest of the war. The damage to the Ploeşti refineries ranges from total destruction of two targets to minor damage on other targets. Unfortunately for the Allies, the bomb damage does not seriously affect fuel production. The refinery was not operating at peak capacity before the raid, so idle capacity makes up quickly for the damaged areas.

The bombing raid on Ploeşti has required coolness, decisiveness, and, above all, courage. Five officers stand out in this action, the most highly decorated mission in American military history:

Major John L. Jerstad is the pilot of the lead aircraft in his group. Three miles from the target his airplane is badly damaged and begins to burn. Ignoring the damage, he continues toward the target as the flames spread through the aircraft. After dropping his bomb load over the target, Jerstad's B-24 crashes. Jerstad's heroic action to continue the mission regardless of cost and carry on beyond the call of duty will win him the Medal of Honor.

Second Lieutenant Lloyd H. Hughes is flying in the last bomber formation to attack the target. Approaching at the required low altitude, his bomber is seriously damaged by antiaircraft fire and leaking gasoline. The target area is already engulfed in flames, which means that Hughes would have to take his B-24 through the flames. Without hesitation, he flies into the inferno, holds his plane in formation at 30 feet, and drops his bomb load on target. The leaking gasoline from the wing catches fire and Hughes attempts to make an emergency landing, but the bomber is quickly engulfed and crashes. Second Lieutenant Hughes decided to complete the mission, even at the risk of his own life. His heroic sacrifice and dedication to duty will win him the Medal of Honor.

Lieutenant Colonel Addison E. Baker is approaching his target at Ploeşti when his B-24 is hit by antiaircraft fire. Although the aircraft has obviously suffered serious damage, Baker decides to continue to lead his formation. After dropping his bomb load early, Baker guides the bombers to their targets, even maneuvering between 50-foot smokestacks. Baker then leaves the formation and attempts to gain altitude, but the plane crashes soon afterward. Baker's sense of duty and dedication to the mission by exhibiting selfless leadership will win him the Medal of Honor.

Colonel John R. Kane leads the third element of B-24 Liberators over the target. Although separated from the formation to avoid cloud conditions over mountainous terrain, Kane continues the mission and arrives at Ploeşti to discover that another element has already bombed his assigned target. Kane's bombers fly through the heavy smoke of roiling oil fires and intense antiaircraft fire to hit the prescribed target. Kane's cool leadership, exceptional courage, and flying skill overcome an impossibly dangerous situation. Colonel Kane's exceptional devotion to duty wins him the Medal of Honor.

Colonel Leon W. Johnson leads the fourth element of the formation. Though the elements have become separated in the approach to the target and Johnson is lost, he joins the third element and continues to the target. Despite having discovered that his targets had already been hit by another element, Johnson decides to continue his attack in the face of heavy antiaircraft fire, enemy fighters, and the flames of the bombed refinery. Johnson's conspicuous gallantry in action, and intrepidity at the risk of his life above and beyond the call of duty wins him the Medal of Honor.

ITALY: Northwest African Air Force B-17s bomb Capodichino airfield.

SICILY: The remainder of the 9th Infantry Division arrives in Palermo. Northwest African Air Force B-25 Mitchells attack Milazzo.

SOUTHWEST PACIFIC AREA: U.S. submarine *Finback* torpedoes and damages a Japanese transport south of Borneo.

PACIFIC: U.S. submarine *Mingo* bombards Sorol Island in the Carolines. U.S. submarine *Steelhead* attacks the same Japanese convoy attacked by *Pogy* the previous day near Truk and damages an auxiliary vessel.

NEW GEORGIA: The 145th and 161st Infantry under command of the 37th Infantry Division capture Horseshoe Hill; the 169th and 103rd Infantry of the 43rd Infantry Division advance 800 yards without meeting opposition. The American ground attack is supported by 36 SBD Dauntless dive-bombers and TBF Avenger torpedo bombers. Thirteenth Air Force P-40s and U.S. Navy F4U Corsairs attack Munda, bombing anti-aircraft positions, ammunition storage dumps, and targets of opportunity. Kahili airfield on Bougainville Island is struck by 21 B-24 Liberators, 16 P-38 Lightnings, P-40s, and over 30 U.S. Navy aircraft. Japanese shipping off the island is attacked by P-40s and more than 80 navy aircraft. The 27th Infantry Regiment of the 25th Infantry Division arrives at Laiana.

August 2

ALEUTIANS: Eight Eleventh Air Force B-24 Liberators, nine B-25 Mitchells, and eight P-38 Lightnings hit Kiska and Little Kiska Islands in two separate attacks. Two naval task groups consisting of two battleships, two heavy cruisers, three light cruisers, and nine destroyers, bombard Kiska.

ATLANTIC: One B-24 of the 4th Antisubmarine Squadron (Heavy), 479th Antisubmarine Group, sinks German submarine *U-706* in the eastern Atlantic.

ETO: Eighth Air Force B-26 Marauders are sent against two airfields in France. Over Merville airfield, 31 B-26 Marauders hit the target; 16 bombers are damaged. Another 18 B-26s bomb the St. Omer/Ft. Rouge airfield; 13 aircraft are damaged.

MEDITERRANEAN: The 26th Infantry Regiment of the 1st Infantry Division assaults the key defensive position at Monte Basilio, holding it against powerful counterattacks for three days. Field Marshal Badoglio, through intermediaries in the Vatican, asks the Allies under what conditions can Rome be declared an open city.

General Eisenhower proposes a two-pronged invasion of Italy, using Montgomery's Eighth Army to cross the Straits of Messina, while U.S. forces land at Salerno.

Ninth Air Force P-40s attack shipping in the Straits of Messina. Northwest African Air Force P-40 fighters, B-25 Mitchells, and A-20 Havocs attack motor transport, storage areas, and roadways in northeast Sicily. Docks and shipping at Milazzo and Messina in Sicily are hit, as well as the area around Reggio di Calabria in Italy.

NEW GEORGIA: Thirteenth Air Force B-25 Mitchells, B-17s, P-40s, and U.S. Navy F4U Corsairs attack Bairoko harbor. Japanese supply points at Webster Cove are bombed by B-24 Liberators, B-25s, P-40s and U.S. Navy Corsairs. Motor torpedo boat *PT-109* is rammed and sunk by Japanese destroyer *Amagiri* in Blackett Strait; the commander, Lieutenant (j.g.) John F. Kennedy, and surviving crewmembers will be rescued.

NEW GUINEA: Fifth Air Force B-17s bomb supply dumps on the shore of Hansa Bay; A-20 Havocs attack Buiambun, and B-25 Mitchells bomb barges along the coast in the vicinity of Lae; B-24 Liberators bomb Lae harbor, Salamaua, and Voco Point. Fifteenth Air Force B-25s and P-38 Lightnings sink two Japanese motor torpedo boats off Lae.

August 3

ALEUTIANS: Eleventh Air Force B-24 Liberators, B-25 Mitchells, P-38 Lightnings, and P-40s attack a number of targets on Kiska Island.

ATLANTIC: PBM Mariner patrol bomber sinks German submarine *U-572* north of Dutch Guiana. TBF Avengers from escort carrier USS *Card* damage German submarine *U-66* near the Azores. PB4Ys (a B-24 variant) damage German submarine *U-60* in the South Atlantic.

ETO: Major General William E. Kepner becomes commanding general, VIII Fighter Command.

MEDITERRANEAN: Ninth Air Force B-25 Mitchells bomb the highway and town of Adrano; over 300 P-40s attack harbors and shipping at Milazzo and Messina. Northwest African Air Force A-20 Havocs conduct ground support missions; P-40s, A-20s, and B-25 Mitchells attack shipping in the Straits of Messina and Milazzo and attack enemy gun emplacements at Adrano and Biancavilla. U.S. destroyer sinks an Italian submarine off Tunisia. U.S. tanker in convoy KMS 20 (United Kingdom to Mediterranean) strikes a mine near Bizerte, Tunisia, and is heavily damaged.

SICILY: The 3rd Infantry Division attacks German defenses at San Fratello that control access to the coastal highway, but fail in an attempt to cross the Furiano River.

SOUTHWEST PACIFIC AREA: General MacArthur proposes his own outline of operations for an offensive in the Pacific. MacArthur proposes that the Philippines are the main objective of offensive operations. The capture of southern islands in the Philippines cuts the critical sea lines of supply to French Indochina and the Netherlands East Indies that the Japanese rely upon for raw materials. Capturing Mindanao and establishing airbases there will also allow a later attack on Luzon. Rabaul must be captured, not neutralized. The Admiralties also must be captured. MacArthur argues that no offensive will succeed without land-based airpower supporting ground and naval operations. The Vogelkop Peninsula and the Palau Islands need to be captured in order to protect the flanks of the main offensive thrust northward. MacArthur believes his forces can be invading Mindanao by early 1945.

NEW GEORGIA: Air and artillery attacks on Kokengolo Hill. A battalion from the 103rd and a battalion from the 169th Infantry sweep forward to Munda airfield. Japanese defenders on Bibilo hill stop the advance. Companies of the 145th Infantry gain the northern part of the hill, while the 2nd Battalion of the 148th Infantry cuts the Munda-Bairoko Trail.

August 4

ALEUTIANS: Over Kiska Island, three B-24 Liberators bomb through clouds, escorted by two P-40s. Two F-5As (photo reconnaissance P-38 Lightnings) take photos of

Main Camp and Little Kiska Island. This attack is followed by 48 B-25 Mitchells, 22 B-24s, 16 A-24 Dauntless dive-bombers, eight P-40s, and 40 P-38 Lightnings, which attack buildings and a gun battery. A radar-equipped PBY Catalina bombs the submarine base and main camp area on Kiska. A total of 153 tons of bombs are dropped on this day.

ETO: Eighth Air Force B-26 Marauders attack the shipyards at Le Trait, France; the 33 bombers hit the target without loss or casualties.

MEDITERRANEAN: Ninth Air Force P-40s attack shipping at Messina and conduct ground support missions. B-17s bomb the submarine base at Naples; B-26 Marauders and B-25 Mitchells bomb the railroad bridge at Catanzaro and railroad at Paola. In Sicily, P-40s, A-20s, and B-25s attack communication targets, gun positions, and logistics bases near Milazzo, Adrano, and Biancavilla and in the area near Bronte, Riposto, and Fiumefreddo. Other Northwest African Air Force aircraft hit rail sidings on the toe of Italy and attack shipping off the Straits of Messina. A U.S. destroyer is damaged by an Axis dive-bomber off Palermo, Sicily.

SICILY: The 9th Infantry Division, under command of Major General Manton S. Eddy, moves to Nicosia behind the 1st Infantry Division. The 3rd Infantry Division makes no progress against enemy defenses at San Fratello, suffering 103 casualties.

SOUTHWEST PACIFIC AREA: U.S. submarine *Finback* torpedoes and sinks a Japanese army cargo ship south of Borneo.

Fifth Air Force B-25 Mitchells bomb and strafe the Itni River area on New Britain Island and hit several villages on Selaroe in the Tanimbar Islands.

PACIFIC: U.S. submarine *Seadragon* torpedoes and damages a Japanese transport near Ponape in the Carolines.

NEW GEORGIA: Thirteenth Air Force B-25 Mitchells and U.S. Navy Dauntless dive-bombers attack Gurasai-Kindu village area; P-38 Lightnings and P-40s claim 11 Japanese fighters downed in a series of dogfights over the central Solomons. U.S. motor torpedo boats engage Japanese guardboats off Kolombangara, sinking one and damaging another.

August 5

ATLANTIC: AAF Antisubmarine Command: The B-25 Mitchells of the 23rd Antisubmarine Squadron (Heavy), 26th Antisubmarine Wing, transfer from Drew Field, Tampa, Florida, to Edinburgh Field, Trinidad. German submarine *U-566* torpedoes and sinks a U.S. gunboat off Cape Henry, Virginia.

The Women Airforce Service Pilot (WASP) organization is formed under Jacqueline Cochran, director of women pilots. More than 1,000 women civil service volunteers are recruited and pass flight training to fly Army Air Force aircraft from factories to training bases.

ETO: The Eighth Air Force's 351st Fighter Squadron, 353rd Fighter Group, transfers from Goxhill to Metfield, England, with P-47 Thunderbolts.

MEDITERRANEAN: Ninth Air Force B-25 Mitchells bomb Francavilla and shipping in the Straits of Messina. Northwest African Air Force P-40s, A-20s, and B-25s attack troops, roads, motor transport, and gun positions at Adrano and Troina. They also sink or damage over 20 small vessels at Milazzo and in the Straits of Messina. B-17s bomb the docks and railroad yards at Messina. B-25s bomb a switching station in Sardinia, and P-40s, escorting the B-25s, attack and claim to have sunk a U-boat off Sardinia.

SICILY: The 3rd Infantry Division is stalemated at San Fratello, despite naval gunfire and artillery support. After conducting nearly 24 separate counterattacks against the 1st Infantry Division, German forces pull out of Troina at night. During one of these counterattacks, Private James W. Reese of the 26th Infantry Regiment is the acting squad leader of a 60 millimeter mortar squad. Reese maneuvers his squad forward to a position where he is able to direct fire on the enemy and break up the attack. Ordering the squad to take up a safer position, Private Reese moves forward with his mortar and uses his remaining three rounds to destroy an enemy machine gun position. Picking up his M-1 rifle, he then moves forward so that he can engage the enemy directly. He remains there, firing upon the enemy, until he is killed. His bravery, leadership, and complete determination to inflict the greatest damage upon his enemies win him the Medal of Honor.

PACIFIC: U.S. submarine *Pike* torpedoes and sinks a Japanese transport west of Marcus Island. U.S. submarine *Silversides* damages a Japanese minelayer off Rabaul.

NEW GEORGIA: Bibilo hill falls to American soldiers of the 145th Infantry Regiment. Munda is captured as the 3rd Battalion of the 172nd Infantry eliminates the last major Japanese defensive position.

NEW GUINEA: Fifth Air Force B-25 Mitchells attack barges near Madang and at Alexishafen, the Nuru River bridge, and towns of Bogadjim and Saidor.

August 6

CARIBBEAN: A PV-1 patrol bomber, PBM Mariner patrol bombers, and a B-18 Bolo medium bomber sink German submarine *U-615*.

ATLANTIC: JCS planners present an outline of operations in the Pacific from the present to the end of 1944. MacArthur's mission in the Southwest Pacific Area is to neutralize Rabaul and advance west along the north coast of New Guinea to the Vogelkop Peninsula. British forces will conduct an offensive in Burma to open the overland route to China. Forces in Nimitz's Central Pacific Area will attack to seize the Gilbert and Marshall Islands, and then advance to capture the Japanese naval base at Truk. An assault on the Palau Islands will follow. Airbases will be established in China to mount an air offensive against the Japanese home islands. The outline provides no direction for either SWPA or Central Pacific Area forces after accomplishing these objectives, nor are any details provided concerning how U.S. bombers will be supplied in China.

Operating as part of one B-25 Mitchell bomber of the 10th Bombardment Squadron (Medium), 25th Bombardment Group (Medium), and land-based navy aircraft sink German submarine *U-615* off Venezuela.

AAF Antisubmarine Command Headquarters of the 479th Antisubmarine Group and the B-24 Liberators of the 4th and 19th Antisubmarine Squadrons (Heavy) transfer from St. Eval to Dunkeswell, England.

ETO: Eighth Air Force's 352nd Fighter Squadron, 353rd Fighter Group, transfers from Goxhill to Raydon, England, with P-47 Thunderbolts.

MEDITERRANEAN: Hitler meets with Badoglio at Treviso, Italy. The meeting focuses on future plans and combined strategy. Secretly, neither trusts the other. In fact, Badoglio is awaiting word from the Allies in response to envoys he has sent to Lisbon and Tangiers to discuss surrender terms. Hitler has sent instructions to the German High Command to prepare plans for the capture of Rome, the seizure of the Italian fleet, and the occupation of northern Italy by German forces if the Italians surrender to the Allies or attempt to back out of the war.

SICILY: In Sicily, over 60 Ninth Air Force B-26 Marauders bomb Bronte, Catania, and Randazzo and the area near the Adrano-Biancavilla road; another 20 Marauders bomb road intersections in Adrano and Bronte. Over 100 P-40s attack shipping targets near Messina. Northwest African Air Force B-17s bomb coastal roads near Messina; B-26 Marauders and B-25 Mitchells attack road and rail transportation. A-20 Havocs and B-25 bombers hit transportation targets at Troina, Adrano, Biancavilla, Tortorici, Bronte, Piranino, and Randazzo. Other aircraft attack shipping in the Straits of Messina.

SOLOMONS: Over Santa Isabel Island, Thirteenth Air Force P-39 Airacobras and P-40s attack Tanagaba Harbor; 24 B-17s and B-24 Liberators, 24 B-25 Mitchells, and more than 50 U.S. Navy and Marine Corps F4U Corsairs, F4F Wildcats, and SBD Dauntless dive-bombers attack Japanese bivouac sites and supply points near Rekata Bay.

NEW GEORGIA: The Battle of Vella Gulf. Six U.S. destroyers of Task Group 36.2, commanded by Commander Frederick Moosbrugger, conduct a night attack on four Japanese destroyers attempting to bring troops and supplies to Kolombangara. Three enemy destroyers are sunk with no U.S. casualties.

U.S. submarine *Pike* torpedoes but fails to damage a Japanese aircraft carrier near Marcus Island.

NEW GUINEA: Fifth Air Force B-24 Liberators bomb Laha airfield on Amboina Island in the Celebes.

August 7

ATLANTIC: TBF Avengers from escort carrier USS *Card* sink German submarine *U-117* in the North Atlantic.

SICILY: Major General Lucian K. Truscott, commander of the 3rd Infantry Division, attempts to outflank the German defenses at San Fratello with an amphibious landing by the 2nd Battalion 30th Infantry, supported by tanks, artillery, and engineers, while the 3rd Battalion of the 15th Infantry and the 3rd Battalion of the 30th Infantry conduct a holding attack on the enemy's main defensive line. The Germans, withdrawing during the night, escape the threat to their rear. Ninth Air Force B-25 Mitchells attack Randazzo, while P-40s attack shipping at the Straits of Messina. Northwest African Air Force A-20 Havocs also attack Randazzo. P-40s and A-36 Intruders (Apaches) strafe and bomb small craft in the Straits of Messina, supply dumps on the toe of Italy, and vehicles and communication targets. In Italy, B-25 Mitchells and B-26 Marauders bomb railroad and highway bridges.

NEW GEORGIA: Thirteenth Air Force B-24 Liberators and B-25 Mitchells, plus nearly 30 navy aircraft, bomb the harbor and shore on Bairoko Island.

NEW GUINEA: Fifth Air Force B-24 Liberators bomb Salamaua and Kela Village. B-25 Mitchells bomb Cape Chater airfield and Lautem on Timor Island.

August 8

ATLANTIC: TBF Avengers from escort carrier USS *Card* damage German submarine *U-262* in the North Atlantic, but *U-262* continues to attack, missing a U.S. destroyer, while *U-664* conducts an unsuccessful attack on the escort carrier.

SICILY: Ninth Air Force B-25 Mitchells bomb Randazzo area and P-40s attack shipping at Messina and provide ground support to Allied forces. Northwest African Air Force B-26 Marauders attack highway and rail bridges at Angitola, Italy, while P-38 Lightnings strafe trains.

PACIFIC: U.S. submarine *Salmon* torpedoes but fails to damage a Japanese vessel off the Kurile Islands. U.S. submarine *Whale* torpedoes and sinks a Japanese ammunition ship northwest of the Marianas.

NEW GEORGIA: Thirteenth Air Force B-25 Mitchells, with P-38 Lightnings, P-39 Airacobras, and U.S. Navy F4U Corsairs flying cover, bomb Vila and Buki harbors on Kolombangara Island.

August 9

ATLANTIC: TBF Avengers from escort carrier USS *Card* sink German submarine *U-664* west of the Azores.

ETO: Eighth Air Force VIII Air Support Command sends 72 B-26 Marauders to bomb the St. Omer/Ft. Rouge airfield in France. Because of heavy cloud cover, only one bomber hits the target. Nevertheless, 11 aircraft are damaged on the mission.

SICILY: Ninth Air Force P-40s attack shipping at Messina, Milazzo, and Palmi. Northwest African Air Force B-17s bomb a road intersection near Messina; P-40 fighters attack highways, rail transport, and gun positions. Over Italy, B-25 Mitchells attack the Catanzaro and Soverato River bridges, while B-26 Marauders bomb the bridges over the Angitola River. P-38 Lightnings attack targets of opportunity.

PACIFIC: U.S. submarine *Sculpin* torpedoes and sinks a Japanese merchant ship off Formosa.

NEW GEORGIA: An element of the 25th Infantry Division links up with Colonel Harry B. Liversedge's (USMC) Northern Landing Group (composed of the 1st Marine Raider Battalion and a battalion each of the 145th and 148th Infantry Regiments, 37th Infantry Division) at Enogai and assumes operational control of the marine-army force. Thirteenth Air Force B-25 Mitchells, followed by B-24 Liberators, bomb Vila on Kolombangara Island.

August 10

ALEUTIANS: Eleventh Air Force P-38 Lightnings, P-40s, A-24 Dauntless dive-bombers, B-24 Liberators, and B-25 Mitchells bomb and strafe targets on Kiska Island.

ATLANTIC: Headquarters AAF redesignates Bombardment Groups and Squadrons (Dive) equipped with A-24s and A-36 Intruders (Apache) as Fighter-Bomber Groups and Squadrons, primarily because these type aircraft are not employed as dive-bombers.

The 14th Antisubmarine Squadron (Heavy), 25th Antisubmarine Wing, with B-24 Liberators, ceases operating from Langley Field, Virginia, and returns to Camp Edwards Army Airfield, Falmouth, Massachusetts.

MEDITERRANEAN: Ninth Air Force B-25 Mitchells bomb Randazzo, while P-40s attack shipping in the Straits of Messina. Northwest African Air Force P-38 Lightnings attack communication targets on the toe of Italy; other aircraft attack the straits, bomb Randazzo, and conduct ground support missions in Sicily.

PACIFIC: U.S. submarine *Salmon* torpedoes and sinks a Japanese merchant fishing boat near Sakhalin Island.

NEW GEORGIA: Thirteenth Air Force P-40s and P-39 Airacobras turn back about 40 Japanese fighters attacking engineers working on Munda airfield.

NEW GUINEA: Fifth Air Force B-24 Liberators bomb airfields in the Salamaua area. B-25 Mitchells hit Japanese barges near Lae. At New Britain, B-25s attack antiaircraft positions near Borgen Bay and A-20 Havocs attack barges and positions on Gasmata Island.

August 11

ALEUTIANS: Eleventh Air Force B-24 Liberators, B-25 Mitchells, A-24 Dauntless dive-bombers, and P-38 Lightnings attack Kiska Island. B-24s from Attu Island bomb an airfield on Paramushiru Island and a naval base on Shimushu Island in the Kuriles. The nine bombers report 40 enemy aircraft attacked them. They claim four confirmed kills, one probable, and four possibles.

ATLANTIC: TBF Avengers from escort carrier *Card* sink German submarine *U-525* near the Azores. German submarine *U-604*, previously damaged, is scuttled near Ascension Island.

MEDITERRANEAN: Northwest African Air Force B-17s bomb the marshaling yard at Terni; B-25 Mitchells bomb the Angitola River bridges, and B-26 Marauders and P-38 Lightnings attack a bridge at Catanzaro.

SICILY: German forces begin the evacuation of Sicily. On Patton's order, the 2nd Battalion, 30th Infantry, 3rd Infantry Division conducts another amphibious landing to cut off retreating German forces at Brolo. The landing force musters one LST (Landing Ship Tank), two LCI (Landing Craft Infantry), and six LCTs, supported by a battleship and six destroyers. There is no opposition, and the Americans advance to the dominant high ground of Monte Cipola and dig in. Although initially providing naval gunfire support, the ships move off once communications are lost. The battalion is quickly surrounded by German forces attempting to break through the defensive position that lies astride their line of retreat. Even though the Americans are supported with air and naval bombardment, the Germans are able to escape before the main body of the 3rd Infantry Division can link up. The battalion suffers 177 casualties. Ninth Air Force B-25 Mitchells bomb transportation targets near Randazzo. P-40s attack Messina, concentrating on shipping, transport, and troops. A-20 Havocs conduct ground attack missions in support of 3rd Infantry Division.

In the final stages of the Sicily campaign, Lieutenant General George S. Patton, Jr., commander of the U.S. Seventh Army, talks with a weary soldier of the 30th Infantry Regiment, 3rd Infantry Division, August 1943.

PACIFIC: U.S. submarine *Finback* torpedoes and sinks a Japanese auxiliary vessel bound for Singapore in the Flores Sea. Japanese submarine *I-11* torpedoes and damages a U.S. freighter near Espiritu Santo.

August 12
ALEUTIANS: Eleventh Air Force B-24 Liberators and B-25 Mitchells from Adak Island fly a number of sorties over Kiska Island. P-40s, P-38 Lightnings, B-24s, B-25s, and A-24 Dauntless dive-bombers fly from Amchitka Island to conduct bombing runs, while other B-24s, P-40s, and F-5As (photo reconnaissance variant of the P-38 Lightning) fly reconnaissance and photo missions over the island. A navy task unit consisting of two heavy cruisers, two light cruisers, and five destroyers bombards Kiska.

ETO: Eighth Air Force VIII Bomber Command targets manufacturing and synthetic oil production in the Ruhr. B-17s bomb synthetic oil production facilities at Bochum, Gelsenkirchen, and Recklinghausen. Of the 133 bombers that hit the targets, 23 B-17s are shot down and 105 suffer damage. German losses are reported to be about 30 aircraft destroyed. B-17s also bomb manufacturing plants at Bonn. Of the 110 bombers that hit the target, two are shot down and 70 are damaged. Enemy fighter losses are estimated at four confirmed kills. The raids are costly: Six crewmen are killed, 56 are wounded, and 253 are missing. Actor Clark Gable flies with the 351st Bomber Squadron on this mission. B-26 Marauders of the VIII Air Support Command bomb the Poix/Nord airfield in France. Nearly half of the 34 bombers that hit the target are damaged.

BOUGAINVILLE: Thirteenth Air Force B-24 Liberators, with P-40s and F4U Wildcats flying cover, attack Kahili airfield; they claim 11 enemy fighters shot down. U.S. losses are one P-40 and one Wildcat.

NEW BRITAIN: Fifth Air Force A-20 Havocs attack Gasmata Island and Japanese barges. A lone B-24 Liberator attacks Cape Gloucester airfield.

August 13

ALEUTIANS: B-25 Mitchells of the 406th Bombardment Squadron (Medium), 41st Bombardment Group (Medium), redeploy from Adak Island to Elmendorf Field, Anchorage, Alaska. The A-24 Douglas dive-bombers of the 515th and 516th Fighter-Bomber Squadrons, 407th Fighter-Bomber Group, will also redeploy from Amchitka Island to Drew Field, Tampa, Florida.

CBI: Fourteenth Air Force P-40s attack Japanese installations at Lungling, China.

MEDITERRANEAN: Ninth Air Force sends 61 B-24 Liberators on a 1,200-mile round trip to Austria to bomb the aircraft production facility at Wiener-Neustadt. This facility and the facility at Regensburg, Germany, account for nearly all the fighter aircraft produced for the German Luftwaffe. The same bombers had participated in the Ploeşti raid and are in poor condition; the bombing is largely ineffective. One bomber is shot down and one crash-lands in Switzerland on the return flight. German planes attack convoy off the coast of Algeria, damaging three U.S. freighters. The B-24 Liberators of the 67th Bombardment Squadron (Heavy), 44th Bombardment Group (Heavy), redeploy from Libya to England.

SICILY: Ninth Air Force B-25 Mitchells attack targets in Sicily and P-40s attack shipping at Messina. Northwest African Air Force P-40s, A-20 Havocs, and A-36 Intruders (Apache) attack shipping in the Straits of Messina. Despite the effort of the Allied air forces, the Germans move 15,000 troops, 1,300 vehicles, 21 tanks, and 22 assault guns to the mainland via ferries from Messina.

PACIFIC: Japanese Imperial Headquarters orders Japanese forces to withdraw from the central Solomons and consolidate forces for an anticipated attack from the Central Pacific area.

U.S. submarine *Paddle* torpedoes and damages a Japanese transport in the Sea of Japan. U.S. submarine *Sunfish* torpedoes and sinks a Japanese gunboat off Chichi Jima.

SOLOMONS: Japanese bomber and torpedo planes attack and sink a U.S. transport at Guadalcanal. Japanese submarine *I-19* torpedoes and damages a U.S. freighter near Espiritu Santo.

BOUGAINVILLE: Thirteenth Air Force B-24 Liberators bomb Kahili airfield on Bougainville Island.

NEW GEORGIA: Thirteenth Air Force P-40 fighters are the first to land on the reconstructed, U.S.-controlled airbase at Munda. After refueling, they conduct a sweep over Kolombangara Island.

NEW GUINEA: Fifth Air Force B-24 Liberators, B-17s, and B-26 Marauders bomb the Salamaua area, dropping 175 tons of bombs. On a night raid that covers 1,200 miles round-trip, nine B-24s bomb the oil production area at Balikpapan, Borneo.

August 14

ATLANTIC: Quadrant Conference. In Quebec, Canada, President Franklin D. Roosevelt, Prime Minister Winston S. Churchill, and their military chiefs of staff meet to discuss the primary operational objective of American strategy for 1944, the cross-Channel invasion of Europe, codenamed Overlord. The leaders approve the outline plan developed by the Combined Chiefs of Staff for use by the Supreme Allied Commander (COSSAC) staff and authorize preparations. Because the COSSAC planners are concerned about German fighter strength in western Europe interfering with the invasion, the combined bomber offensive against airfields and aircraft in France, Belgium, and the Netherlands is to continue with the "highest strategic priority." Although the Allies will continue offensive operations in Italy, they are clearly to be a low priority. An invasion of southern France as a companion to Overlord is to be planned, with the bulk of the forces for that operation coming out of Italy. The British agree to the U.S. timetable for offensive operations in the Central and South Pacific and recognize China's important role in American strategy; the Southeast Asia Command in the CBI theater will be formed. The idea of an Allied offensive into Burma is revisited. They agree that in early 1944, Chinese forces will advance from Yunnan into Burma, the British from India; the Americans with a Chinese-American force will attack from Shingbwiyang toward Myitkyina. The capture of Myitkyina will allow transport aircraft to fly the "Hump" route over the Himalayas easier and allow the Ledo Road to progress faster. With the overland route opened, 65,000 tons of supplies can be delivered to the Chinese. The plan to equip 30 Chinese divisions is quietly set aside. The program to establish airbases to put B-29s in China to attack the Japanese home islands will soon come to dominate all other support priorities in the CBI Theater.

In the Pacific, the Allies decide that Rabaul will be neutralized, not captured. The Japanese air and naval base at Rabaul is the centerpiece to MacArthur's Cartwheel campaign. This decision leaves the SWPA with what amounts to a holding mission while Nimitz's Central Pacific offensive takes priority.

The Allies agree that once Germany has surrendered, forces in Europe will be moved to the Pacific with the intent to defeat Japan within a year. With this conference, American strategic priorities and proposals now dominate Allied strategy.

MEDITERRANEAN: Ninth Air Force, using 61 B-24 Liberators from Eighth Air Force, bombs the aircraft production facility at Wiener-Neustadt, Austria.

The Italian government declares Rome an open city.

New Guinea: Fifth Air Force B-24 Liberators, B-17s, and B-25 Mitchells bomb the Salamaua area for a second day. A-20 Havocs strafe barges near Finschhafen. B-25 Mitchells bomb targets on New Britain Island.

August 15

Aleutians: Rear Admiral Thomas C. Kinkaid, Commander, North Pacific Force, launches Operation Cottage, the assault on Kiska Island. Major General Charles H. Corlett commands nearly 40,000 U.S. and Canadian troops, with full Arctic equipment, in the effort to capture the island from an estimated 10,000 Japanese defenders.

The 635th Bombardment Squadron (Dive), 407th Fighter-Bomber Group, operating from Amchitka Island, is disbanded and its A-24 Dauntless dive-bombers are transferred to other units.

Atlantic: The B-25 Mitchells of 17th Antisubmarine Squadron (Heavy), 26th Antisubmarine Wing, based at Miami, Florida, are reassigned from antisubmarine duty. The squadron will transfer to New Mexico and transition to B-24 Liberators. The squadron will be redesignated as the 855th Bombardment Squadron (Heavy) and assigned to the Eighth Air Force.

ETO: Eighth Air Force VIII Bomber Command attacks Vlissingen airfield in the Netherlands and the airfields at Amiens and Poix in France. The B-17s hit the targets, but 48 of the 147 bombers are damaged. Another 143 B-17s attack the airfields at Merville, Lille/Vendeville, and Vitry en Artois. Enemy losses are nine aircraft; U.S. losses are two bombers shot down and 11 damaged. The B-26 Marauders of the VIII Air Support Command also attack German airfields in France. Over St. Omer/Ft Rouge, 31 bombers hit the target and 18 are damaged. The marshaling yard at Abbeville is bombed by 19 B-26 Marauders and nine are damaged.

Italy: Northwest African Air Force B-25 Mitchells and B-26 Marauders bomb a railroad junction and marshaling yard. P-38 Lightnings attack rail lines, trains, and troops.

Pacific: U.S. submarine *Wahoo* torpedoes and damages a Japanese fleet tanker in the Sea of Japan.

New Georgia: The 35th Regimental Combat Team of the 25th Infantry Division lands on Vella Lavella Island under Brigadier General Robert B. McLure to establish a beachhead. The marine 4th Defense Battalion supporting the assault shoots down 42 Japanese planes. Fighters from Munda airfield are sent to cover the landings at Vella Lavella. The pilots claim that about 25 Japanese aircraft attempting to interfere with the landings are shot down. F4U Corsair pilots also claim 10 Japanese shot down over Kahili, Bougainville Island.

New Guinea: Japanese bombers with fighter escort attempting an attack are met by Fifth Air Force P-39 Airacobras, which claim 14 enemy aircraft destroyed. Three of the Airacobras are lost in the battle.

August 16

Atlantic: The 4th Marine Division, commanded by Major General Harry Schmidt, is activated at Camp Pendleton, California.

ETO: Eighth Air Force VIII Bomber Command attacks the Le Bourget air depot with 171 B-17s and one YB-40, escorted all the way to the target by P-47 Thunderbolts using drop tanks. U.S. losses are four bombers shot down and 46 damaged. Enemy losses are estimated at over 30 aircraft destroyed. The airfields at Poix and Abbeville are bombed by 66 B-17s. More than half of the aircraft are damaged. The VIII Air Support Command sends B-26 Marauders against the Bernay St. Martin airfield. Of the 31 bombers that hit the target, two are damaged. Another 29 B-26s attack Beaumont Le Roger airfield. Three bombers are damaged.

MEDITERRANEAN: Northwest African Air Force A-36 Intruders (Apache) and P-40s attack targets on the toe of Italy, concentrating on trains, trucks, railroad yards, and sidings. German torpedo bomber hits a U.S. freighter near Bône, Algeria, killing or wounding over 400 of the 1,800 Italian prisoners of war on board.

General Eisenhower issues a final plan for Operation Avalanche. He will use the Fifth Army, commanded by Lieutenant General Mark W. Clark, and the British Eighth Army, under Field Marshal Bernard L. Montgomery, to invade Italy. Montgomery will cross the Straits of Messina between September 1 and 4, advance up the toe of the Italian boot, capture Calabria and Taranto, and draw German forces south. As the Germans move to attack Montgomery, the Fifth Army will land at Salerno about September 9 to outflank the enemy. Salerno is chosen because it is closer to Montgomery's Eighth Army and it is within the limits of Allied air cover. From Salerno, the Fifth Army, composed of the British X Corps and the U.S. VI Corps, will capture Naples, the largest port in southern Italy and the large airfield at Capodichino in order to establish a base for further operations. Salerno's easy surf, 20-mile beach, and road network into the interior attract the planners' attention. The Salerno plain is dominated by mountains that resolute defenders can use to trap the invaders on the beach. The Calore and Sele rivers parallel each other, then join about four miles from the coast. This obstacle divides the plain into two sectors, limiting the support the X and VI Corps can provide each other. Capturing the Montecorvino airfield near the town of Salerno would support four Allied fighter squadrons.

SICILY: A regimental-size amphibious landing at Bivo Salica by the 3rd Infantry Division is useless, as the Germans have withdrawn and the remainder of the division is moving rapidly against light resistance. The 7th Infantry Regiment, 3rd Infantry Division, enters Messina. General Truscott meets the civilian leaders of the city, and General Patton formally accepts the surrender of the city. The Germans have evacuated 40,000 men, 9,600 vehicles, 94 guns, 47 tanks, nearly 2,000 tons of ammunition and fuel, and over 15,000 tons of other equipment. The Italians have evacuated about 75,000 men, 500 vehicles, and almost 100 artillery pieces with little or no interference from the Allies. U.S. casualties are 2,200 killed and 6,500 wounded. British casualties total 12,800. The Axis casualties are estimated at 29,000 and 147,000 prisoners. The Allies capture 70 tanks and over 280 artillery pieces. More importantly, over 100 aircraft are captured and 500 others are estimated destroyed on the ground. This is the first time the American forces fight as a separate army and they have proven themselves as a capable fighting force even in the face of British doubts about their abilities.

New Georgia: Thirteenth Air Force B-25 Mitchells, B-17s, and over 30 navy aircraft attack Vila airfield on Kolombangara Island.

New Guinea: Fifth Air Force B-24 Liberators bomb oil tanks at Balikpapan, Borneo. P-38 Lightnings and 32 P-47 Thunderbolts, operating for the first time in combat in the Pacific, intercept 25 Japanese fighters. Nearly half of the enemy aircraft are shot down.

August 17

CBI: Fourteenth Air Force B-24 Liberators bomb the barracks at Cau Lo, in French Indochina.

ETO: The Attack on Schweinfurt. Eighth Air Force launches a two-pronged attack into Germany. The 4th Bomb Wing with B-17Fs (a modified B-17 that can carry extra fuel for long-range missions) is to bomb the facilities at Regensburg where half of Germany's fighters are produced, then continue to North Africa. The standard approach for German fighters would be to attack the incoming bombers, then land to refuel and rearm in time to launch and attack the bombers on their expected return flight. The 1st Bomb Wing, following the 4th by 15 minutes, will pass over Schweinfurt to hit the four factories that produce more than half of the ball bearings for the German military. The plan is to catch the German fighters while they are on the ground preparing for the 4th Bomb Wing to make its return flight, leaving the 1st untouched over Schweinfurt.

At 1148, 127 B-17s begin bombing Regensburg at less than 20,000 feet. The 4th Bomb Wing loses eight bombers on the way in and another 14 on the raid itself. Over 50 bombers are damaged. Regensburg loses the equivalent of three weeks' production of fighter aircraft as a result of the accurate bombing. The bombers continue on to bases in North Africa. The 1st Bomb Wing arrives over Schweinfurt with 188 B-17s at 1459, more than five hours behind schedule. They find over 300 German fighters waiting for them after their fighter escorts drop off. German fighters shoot down 24 B-17s on the way to Schweinfurt. They approach from west to east over the target, the exact opposite track intended, which causes problems for the lead bombardier in locating the factories. In addition, the factories are protected by an artificial generator-produced fog. On the return trip, German fighters again assemble to harry the 1st Bomb Wing. The U.S. 56th Fighter Group with P-47 Thunderbolts comes to the heavy bombers' rescue over Belgium, shooting down 11 German aircraft in almost as many minutes. The wing loses 36 B-17s and over 120 are damaged. The damage to the ball bearing plants has no effect on production.

A total of 60 B-17s are lost in the fierce air battle; along with damaged aircraft, this represents 40 percent of the force dispatched. Crew losses are also heavy: Seven are killed, 21 are wounded, and 552 are missing. The bomber crews for the two missions together claim a total of 288 enemy aircraft shot down, 27 probable kills, and 99 possible kills. In reality, the Germans actually lose only 48 aircraft all together—36 shot down (mostly by fighters) and 12 damaged beyond repair. This is typical of the inflated reporting from gun crews on the bombers.

As a diversion for the Schweinfurt attack, VIII Air Support Command launches B-26 Marauders against two airfields in France. Over Bryas Sud airfield, 29 Marauders hit the target; two bombers are damaged. Over Poix/Nord airfield, 35 B-26s hit the target with 20 aircraft receiving damage.

During the night, the Royal Air Force begins Operation Crossbow, massive attacks on German V-weapon sites (from the German word *Vergeltungswaffen*—revenge weapons). The V-1 is a pilotless flying bomb launched from a ramp or by aircraft. It carries a 1,875-pound warhead, and uses a pulse jet engine guided by a gyroscope on automatic pilot. The entire missile weighs 4,800 pounds and travels at speeds near 400 miles per hour. At a predetermined time of flight, the fuel will be expended (usually between 10 and 125

V-1s captured by the Allies *(Library of Congress)*

miles) and the bomb will drop. Targeted at London, they are intended to cause terror and weaken civilian morale. Once intelligence reveals that Peenemünde, Germany, is a main research and launching site, the British immediately launch 570 Lancaster bombers to drop 2,000 tons of bombs on the target, crippling activities there for more than a month, but 40 bombers are lost.

MEDITERRANEAN: Northwest African Air Force B-17s bomb Istres-Le-Tube airfield and Salon-de-Provence airfield in southern France. B-26 Marauders and B-25 Mitchells attack communication targets on the toe of Italy, while P-38 Lightnings escorting the bombers attack military vehicles.

NEW GUINEA: Fifth Air Force B-24 Liberators and B-17s make a predawn attack on Wewak and other smaller airfields and are followed by more than 30 B-25 Mitchells, with over 80 P-38 Lightnings providing cover. At Wewak, 100 Japanese aircraft are destroyed on the ground. The intent is to neutralize Japanese airfields in preparation for offensive operations against Lae. A-20 Havocs attack Japanese forces around the Salamaua area.

B-24 Liberators bomb the oil storage facilities at Balikpapan, Borneo.

August 18

ALEUTIANS: After three days of friendly fire casualties and evacuations for illness, the Allies find that there are no Japanese on the island. A U.S. destroyer strikes a mine offshore, causing over 100 casualties, including 70 dead.

The Eleventh Air Force since June 3, 1942, has destroyed 69 Japanese aircraft, sunk 21 ships, and damaged 29 others, with the loss of 29 aircraft.

ETO: B-26 Marauders bomb the Ypres/Vlamertinge airfield in Belgium. Every aircraft bombing the target is damaged, but there are no casualties. Over Woensdrecht airfield in the Netherlands, 32 B-26s hit the target; eight bombers are damaged and there are no casualties.

ITALY: Two U.S. light cruisers and four destroyers fire on the towns of Gioia Tauro and Palmi.

PACIFIC: U.S. submarine *Plunger* torpedoes and damages a Japanese merchant ship in the Sea of Japan.

NEW GUINEA: Fifth Air Force sends over 70 B-24 Liberators, B-25 Mitchells, and B-17s, with about 100 fighters flying cover, to attack Wewak and other smaller airfields. At least 28 more Japanese aircraft are destroyed. The Japanese have lost 75 percent of their air combat power in New Guinea in just 48 hours.

Near Wewak, New Guinea, Major Ralph Celi is leading his squadron in an attack on the Dagua airfield. Japanese fighters intercept the formation and concentrate on Celi's aircraft, which quickly bursts into flame. Disregarding the danger, Major Celi continues the attack, bringing his squadron down to make effective hits on the target. With the mission complete, Major Celi turns over command to his wingman before he is forced to crash into the sea. For his supreme act of courage and dedication to duty, major Celi is later awarded the Medal of Honor.

August 19

CBI: Brigadier General Howard C. Davidson takes command of Tenth Air Force.
ATLANTIC: Aircraft from escort carrier USS *Croatan* unsuccessfully attack German submarine *U-134* northwest of the Azores.
ETO: Eighth Air Force VIII Bomber Command attacks airfields in the Netherlands. With 175 P-47 Thunderbolts flying escort, 38 B-17s hit the Gilze-Rijen airfield; another 55 hit Flushing airfield. U.S. losses are four B-17s downed and 42 bombers damaged. The bomber crews claim about 30 German aircraft destroyed. The fighters report another nine German aircraft shot down. One P-47 is lost and the pilot is listed as missing. The VIII Air Support Command attacks two airfields in France: the Amiens/Glisy airfield and the Poix/Nord airfield. Against the former, 36 B-26 Marauders hit the target and have 10 bombers damaged and claim one enemy aircraft destroyed. Against the latter airfield, 35 Marauders hit the target with one bomber damaged and no casualties.
ITALY: Ninth Air Force B-24 Liberators bomb the marshaling yard at Foggia, while P-40s fly coastal reconnaissance over the toe of Italy, bombing targets of opportunity. With P-38 Lightnings escorting the bombers, over 150 B-17s of the Northwest African Air Force also bomb the Foggia marshaling yard, while B-26 Marauders and B-25 Mitchells attack marshaling yards at Sapri and Salerno. Enemy losses are reported at 34 aircraft shot down. A-36 Intruders (Apache) attack the Catanzaro marshaling yard, while P-40s conduct sweeps over the toe of Italy to attack transportation targets.
SOUTHWEST PACIFIC AREA: A U.S. Navy OS2N Kingfisher scout plane sinks Japanese submarine *I-17* off eastern Australia. U.S. submarine *Finback* torpedoes and sinks a Japanese auxiliary submarine chaser off the east coast of Celebes.
NEW GEORGIA: Thirteenth Air Force B-25 Mitchells, with fighter escort, attack barges off Vella Lavella Island. The Japanese continue to lose fighters to ground fire and air attack over New Georgia.

August 20

CBI: Army Air Forces, India-Burma Sector, China-Burma-India theater, is activated at New Delhi, India, under the command of Lieutenant General George E. Stratemeyer. The main component of this new command is Tenth Air Force. Fourteenth Air Force B-25 Mitchells bomb Tien Ho airfield at Canton. Fighters flying escort report five enemy aircraft shot down over the target. Over Kweilin, 15 P-40s intercept 21 Japanese fighters. During the air battle, two P-40s and two Japanese fighters are shot down.

ETO: AAF Antisubmarine Command dispatches the B-24 Liberators of the 22nd Antisubmarine Squadron (Heavy), 479th Antisubmarine Group, to Dunkeswell, England.

ITALY: Northwest African Strategic Air Force B-26 Marauders bomb the marshaling yards at Capua and Aversa, while B-25 Mitchells bomb the Benevento marshaling yard.

SOUTHWEST PACIFIC AREA: U.S. submarine *Gar* torpedoes and sinks a Japanese transport in the Celebes Sea.

PACIFIC: Admiral Chester W. Nimitz, CINCPOA, submits an outline plan for an offensive against the Marshalls.

U.S. submarine *Pompano* departs Midway on her seventh war patrol and disappears. U.S. submarine *Plunger* torpedoes and sinks a Japanese cargo ship off the southwest coast of Hokkaido, Japan. U.S. submarine *Wahoo* torpedoes and sinks a Japanese merchant vessel near the Kurile Islands.

NEW BRITAIN: Fifth Air Force B-25 Mitchells strafe Japanese supply barges near Cape Gloucester on New Britain Island. Kiriwina Island airfield is operational. The Royal Australian Air Force takes control of the field.

NEW GUINEA: Fifth Air Force B-24 Liberators attack Boram airfield; the 46 P-38 Lightnings report 19 enemy fighters shot down. A-20 Havocs bomb Lae and the Salamaua area.

August 21

CBI: Fourteenth Air Force B-24 Liberators and B-25 Mitchells, escorted by 12 P-40s, bomb the docks and the airfield at Hankow. Over 50 Japanese fighters attack the formation. Two Liberators are shot down and 10 are damaged. Bomber aircrews and fighter pilots report 57 confirmed kills and 13 probables. In the Hengyang area, 19 P-40s encounter 33 enemy aircraft and shoot down five fighters. Near Changsha, nine P-38 Lightnings take on 12 enemy fighters and shoot down three of them.

ATLANTIC: Quadrant Conference Report to Stalin. President Roosevelt and Prime Minister Churchill send a summary message to Stalin advising him of the outcome of the Quadrant Conference.

> In our conference at Quebec, just concluded, we have arrived at the following decision as to military operations to be carried out during 1943 and 1944.
>
> The bomber offensive against Germany will be continued on a rapidly increased scale from bases in the United Kingdom and Italy. The objectives of this air attack will be to destroy the German air combat strength, to dislocate the German military, industrial, and economic system, and to prepare the way for a cross-Channel invasion.
>
> A large-scale buildup of American forces in the United Kingdom is now underway. It will provide an initial assault force of British and American divisions for cross-Channel operations. A bridgehead in the continent once secured will be reinforced steadily by additional American troops at the rate of from three to five

divisions per month. This operation will be the primary British and American ground and air effort against the Axis.

The war in the Mediterranean is to be pressed vigorously. Our objectives in that area will be the elimination of Italy from the Axis alliance, and the occupation of that country as well as Sardinia and Corsica as bases for operations against Germany.

Our operations in the Balkans will be limited to the supply of Balkan Guerrillas by air and sea transport, to minor raids by Commandos, and to the bombing of strategic objectives.

We shall accelerate our operations against Japan in the Pacific and in Southeast Asia. Our purposes are to exhaust Japanese air, naval, and shipping resources, to cut the Japanese communications and to secure bases from which to bomb Japan proper.

Roosevelt and Churchill reaffirm the unconditional surrender policy for the Axis powers. The Allies agree to reallocate seven divisions from Italy to Britain to prepare for the cross-Channel invasion.

ETO: AAF Antisubmarine Command dispatches the B-24 Liberators of the 6th Antisubmarine Squadron (Heavy), 479th Antisubmarine Group, from Gander Lake, Newfoundland, to Dunkeswell, England.

ITALY: Ninth Air Force B-24 Liberators attack a railroad station, marshaling yard, and air depot at Cancello Arnone. Northwest African Strategic Air Force B-26 Marauders and B-17s, escorted by P-38 Lightnings, bomb marshaling yards at Villa Literno and Aversa and report over 20 enemy fighters shot down.

SOUTHWEST PACIFIC AREA: SWPA planners identify a list of possible ground forces for an attack on New Britain. These include 1st Marine Division, the 32nd Infantry Division, and the 503rd Parachute Infantry Regiment.

August 22

CBI: Fourteenth Air Force P-40s bomb a supply depot, a unit headquarters, troops, and vehicles at Tengchung.

ETO: Eighth Air Force VIII Air Support Command B-26 Marauders bomb the Beaumont-le-Roger airfield in France. Of the 35 bombers that hit the target, one B-26 is lost and eight are damaged. Aircrews claim three enemy aircraft destroyed.

MEDITERRANEAN: All fighter and medium bomber groups of the Ninth Air Force are transferred to the Twelfth Air Force. This includes B-25 Mitchells of the 12th and 340th Bombardment Groups (Medium) in Sicily, the P-40s of the 57th Fighter and 79th Fighter Groups in Sicily, and the P-40s of the 324th Fighter Group in El Haouaria, Tunisia.

Northwest African Air Force B-26 Marauders, with A-36 Intruders (Apache) providing escort, bomb the Salerno marshaling yard. Aircrews claim 26 enemy fighters destroyed.

PACIFIC: U.S. submarine *Pike* torpedoes and damages a Japanese cargo ship near Yap. U.S. submarine *Plunger* torpedoes and sinks a Japanese merchant fishing ship in the Sea of Japan. U.S. submarine *Swordfish* torpedoes and sinks a Japanese cargo ship off Palau. U.S. submarine *Tullibee* torpedoes and sinks a Japanese transport west of Truk.

New Georgia: Thirteenth Air Force B-25 Mitchells and U.S. Navy SBD Dauntless dive-bombers attack supply barges on the coast of Vella Lavella Island.

August 23
CBI: Tenth Air Force B-25 Mitchells take out the center span of the Myitnge bridge in Burma using a low-level approach to the target.

Mediterranean: Ninth Air Force B-24 Liberators hit a marshaling yard at Bari, Italy.

Northwest African Air Force B-26 Marauders bomb the marshaling yard at Battipaglia, Italy. German submarine *U-380* torpedoes and damages a U.S. freighter en route from Sicily to Bizerte, Tunisia.

Southwest Pacific Area: U.S. submarine *Grayling* delivers supplies to Filipino guerrilla forces on Panay.

Pacific: U.S. submarine *Paddle* torpedoes and sinks an Italian cargo ship off Hamamatsu, Japan.

New Guinea: Fifth Air Force B-26 Marauders bomb Kela; B-25 Mitchells bomb Marawasa, Finschhafen, and Lillum Saun.

August 24
Aleutians: Kiska Island is declared secured. About 140,000 troops will remain on the island for the next year, having absolutely no operational use.

CBI: Fourteenth Air Force B-24 Liberators and B-25 Mitchells, escorted by P-40s and P-38 Lightnings, bomb the airfields at Hankow and Wuchang. U.S. losses are four B-24s shot down and three damaged. Aircrews report 24 enemy fighters shot down.

Atlantic: Quadrant Conference ends. The Combined Chiefs of Staff accepts COSSAC's concept plan for Overlord and authorizes detailed planning. The British advocate a major campaign in Italy to keep German forces occupied in order to support a cross-Channel invasion, arguing that an advance into northwest Italy would allow the Allies to establish airbases to support the strategic bomber offensive. Unwilling to commit any additional resources to Italy and to ensure that Overlord is the priority of effort, Quadrant reaffirms a cross-Channel invasion for May of 1944, along with a simultaneous 10-division invasion of southern France. Objectives in Italy are designated as Rome and its surrounding air bases. After the fall of Rome, the Allies will advance as far as practicable.

President Roosevelt and Prime Minister Churchill issue a statement at the completion of the Quadrant Conference in Quebec. *"The whole field of world operations has been surveyed in the light of the many gratifying events which have taken place since the meeting of the President and the Prime Minister in Washington at the end of May, and the necessary decisions have been taken to provide for the forward action of the fleets, armies, and air forces of the two nations."* While the statement emphasizes Allied successes in recent months, it masks the British unease over the cross-Channel invasion and the American suspicion of British goals in the Mediterranean.

The CCS also approves a concept for offensive operations in the Pacific for 1944–45. In the Central Pacific, the intent is to seize the Gilbert Islands and then prepare to attack the Marshalls and the Carolines. Truk would be captured and used as an airbase. The Palaus would follow, with a move to capture bases in the Mariana Islands. These islands would be used to support the strategic bomber offensive against the Japanese home islands. The Central Pacific theater has the priority of effort primarily because capture of bases in the islands would support extended air operations, and most likely force the Japanese navy into a major battle to protect the home islands. Southwest Pacific Area objectives are New Guinea and the Admiralty Islands, to isolate Rabaul. Central Pacific theater has the priority of effort.

The Army Air Forces Antisubmarine Command is redesignated I Bomber Command and reassigned to the First Air Force as the Army Air Forces turn over responsibility for antisubmarine operations to the U.S. Navy. As a result, four antisubmarine squadrons (heavy) along the east coast are given new missions.

Aircraft from escort carrier *Core* sink German submarines *U-84* and *U-185* southwest of the Azores.

ETO: Eighth Air Force VIII Bomber Command attacks the Villacoublay air depot and airfields in France. The air depot is hit by 86 B-17s and 64 of them are damaged. One enemy fighter is claimed destroyed. Against the Conches and Evreux/Fauville airfields, 22 B-17s bomb the targets with the loss of one B-17 and 15 damaged. Two enemy fighters are reported as possible kills. The 85 B-17s of the 4th Bomb Wing, which had flown to North Africa after attacking Regensburg, Germany, on August 17, return to England by way of the Bordeaux/Merignac airfield. Three B-17s are lost over the target and two are damaged. Another nine bombers are forced to return to North Africa. The aircrews claim three enemy aircraft shot down. The VIII Air Support Command sends B-26 Marauders to fly two diversion missions for the VIII Bomber Command missions.

PACIFIC: U.S. submarine *Whale* torpedoes and damages a Japanese fleet tanker in the East China Sea.

NEW GEORGIA: The 3rd Battalion, 145th Infantry Regiment, 37th Infantry Division, captures Bairoko without a fight. The Japanese defenders evacuated the previous night to Arundel, Kolombangara, and Baanga. Thirteenth Air Force B-24 Liberators, with fighter escort, bomb Papatura Fa Island and attack the Ringa cove. P-39 Airacobras strafe barges off Choiseul Island.

NEW GUINEA: Fifth Air Force B-24 Liberators bomb Wewak and Salamaua, while B-25 Mitchells bomb Larat and barges near Wotap.

August 25

CBI: Fourteenth Air Force B-25 Mitchells, with fighter escort, bomb the Kowloon Docks at Hong Kong.

Admiral Louis F. Mountbatten is appointed Supreme Allied Commander, Southeast Asia Command (SEAC).

ETO: VIII Air Support Command attacks two targets in France. Against the power station at Rouen, 21 B-26 Marauders hit the target and have two bombers damaged. The Tricqueville airfield is hit by 31 B-26 Marauders. Two bombers are damaged and aircrews report one enemy aircraft destroyed.

ITALY: Ninth Air Force B-24 Liberators bomb the marshaling yard at Foggia, while 135 B-17s and 140 P-38 Lightnings of the Northwest African Air Force attack airfields around Foggia.

BOUGAINVILLE: Thirteenth Air Force B-24 Liberators with 24 fighters flying escort attack Kahili airfield.

NEW GEORGIA: Thirteenth Air Force B-25 Mitchells, along with more than 40 U.S. Navy SBD dive-bombers attack barge areas at Webster and Ringa Coves. Navy Task Group 34.4, covered by four destroyers, lays mines off Wilson Cove on western Kolombongara Island.

NEW GUINEA: Fifth Air Force sends nearly 100 B-24 Liberators, B-25 Mitchells, and B-17s to bomb the area around Hansa Bay. B-24s also attack Finschhafen. A-20 Havocs attack Gasmata Island off New Britain.

August 26

ALEUTIANS: Eleventh Air Force begins redeploying two heavy bomber squadrons (B-24 Liberators) and two medium bomber squadrons (B-25 Mitchells) to other duties in the continental United States.

CBI: Fourteenth Air Force B-24 Liberators, escorted by 17 fighters, bomb the Kowloon Docks at Hong Kong. A total of five enemy aircraft are reported downed. Over Tien Ho airfield in Canton, B-25 Mitchells, escorted by P-40s, take on enemy fighters. One P-40 is lost and five enemy aircraft are reported destroyed. The 449th Fighter Squadron, activated at Kunming, is established at Lingling and begins transition training with P-38 Lightnings. The squadron is under the 23rd Fighter Group.

ETO: VIII Air Support Command sends 36 B-26 Marauders against the Caen/Carpiquet airfield in France. One bomber crashes on the return landing.

MEDITERRANEAN: The C-47s of the 316th Troop Carrier Group, Ninth Air Force, are transferred to Twelfth Air Force. The USAAF and Royal Air Force units assigned to the Desert Air Force (DAF) are assigned to the Northwest African Air Force. B-17s and P-38 Lightnings of the Northwest African Air Force bomb Capua airfield. German submarine *U-410* attacks convoy UGS 14 (United States to Mediterranean, Slow) off the coast of Algeria, torpedoing two U.S. freighters, which later sink.

SOUTHWEST PACIFIC AREA: New Britain is the next target for offensive operations in SWPA. The objective is to seize the Cape Gloucester area and neutralize Gasmata, then establish control over the western half of New Britain to a point along a line from Gasmata to Talasea and from the Vitu Islands to Long Island.

PACIFIC: U.S. submarine *Tunny* unsuccessfully attacks a Japanese convoy off the Palau Islands.

BOUGAINVILLE: Fifteenth Air Force B-24 Liberators bomb Japanese destroyers near Buka Island, damaging one destroyer.

NEW GEORGIA: Thirteenth Air Force B-25 Mitchells and navy SBD Dauntless dive-bombers, escorted by fighters, attack enemy antiaircraft positions and barges at Ringa and Webster Coves. B-24 Liberators, escorted by fighters, bomb Kahili airfield on Bougainville Island.

August 27

CBI: Fourteenth Air Force P-40s attack a truck convoy between Sintsiang and Yoyang, destroying at least five vehicles. One P-40 is lost to ground fire. Another six P-40s attack targets of opportunity along the Japanese line of communication between Yoyang and Hankow.

ATLANTIC: TBF Avengers from escort carrier USS *Card* conduct an unsuccessful attack on German submarine *U-508*. Other aircraft sink *U-847* in the mid-Atlantic.

ETO: Eighth Air Force VIII Bomber Command Mission conducts its first raid on German V-weapons, in this case a launching site under construction at Watten, France. Escorted by 173 P-47 Thunderbolts, 187 bombers hit the target; four B-17s are lost and 99 are damaged. Aircrews claim seven enemy fighters destroyed. U.S. fighter pilots report eight probable kills with the loss of one P-47. The pilot is listed as missing. B-26 Marauders of the VIII Air Support Command bomb the Poix Nord airfield with no aircraft or personnel losses.

ITALY: Northwest African Air Force B-17s bomb marshaling yards at Sulmona and B-26 Marauders bomb the marshaling yards at Benevento and Caserta, escorted by about 150 P-38 Lightnings.

SOUTHWEST PACIFIC AREA: U.S. submarine *Drum* torpedoes and damages a Japanese transport north of the Admiralty Islands. U.S. submarine *Grayling* sinks a Japanese cargo ship off western Luzon Island in the Philippines.

PACIFIC: U.S. submarine *Pollock* torpedoes and sinks a Japanese cargo ship south of Kyushu, Japan.

NEW GEORGIA: The 172nd Infantry Regiment of the 43rd Infantry Division lands on Arundel Island, followed by the 169th Infantry Regiment from the 43rd and two battalions of the 27th Infantry Regiment of the 25th Infantry Division. Thirteenth Air Force P-39 Airacobras strafe barges and shore targets at Ringa Cove. Over Choiseul Island, 12 B-25 Mitchells, eight P-40s, and eight U.S. Navy F4U Corsairs strafe barges and shoreline targets at Kakasa.

NEW GUINEA: Fifth Air Force B-26 Marauders attack bridges in the Bogadjim area. A-20 Havocs attack barges and troops near Lae. B-25 Mitchells bomb the Dili and Cape Chater airfields on Timor Island.

August 28

ITALY: Northwest African Air Force B-17s bomb the marshaling yard at Terni. B-26 Marauders bomb the Aversa and Sparanise marshaling yards. B-25 Mitchells bomb the Cancello Arnone marshaling yard.

PACIFIC: U.S. submarine *Tarpon* torpedoes and damages a Japanese ship east of Shikoku, Japan.

SOLOMONS: Thirteenth Air Force B-25 Mitchells, P-40s, and U.S. Navy F4U Corsairs attack barges, personnel, and buildings on Sigolehe Island and Barora Ite Island.

NEW GUINEA: Fifth Air Force B-25 Mitchells bomb supplies and shipping in the Hansa Bay area. Several vessels are sunk in the attack. B-17s and A-20 Havocs bomb jetties at Lae and Voco Point and attack barges in Samoa harbor.

August 29

CBI: Fourteenth Air Force B-25 Mitchells, with fighter escort, bomb the airfield at Chingmen.

ETO: Major General William E. Kepner takes command of VIII Fighter Command.

ITALY: Northwest African Air Force B-17s bomb the marshaling yard at Orte.

New Guinea: Fifth Air Force sends 35 B-24 Liberators, escorted by 44 P-38 Lightnings, to attack the airfields at Wewak and Boram. The Alexishafen and Bogadjim areas are attacked by 48 B-25 Mitchells and two B-17s. A-20 Havocs attack supply points on Gasmata Island off the coast of New Britain.

August 30

CBI: Fourteenth Air Force B-25 Mitchells bomb fuel storage sites at Owchihkow and Shihshow, while P-40s attack enemy gun positions. Four P-40s attack a ship convoy east of Hong Kong, damaging a freighter and two other vessels.

ETO: B-26 Marauders of the VIII Air Support Command bomb an ammunition dump near Saint-Omer, France. Of the 33 bombers that hit the target, 14 are damaged and three crewmen are wounded.

Italy: Northwest African Air Force B-17s bomb Viterbo airfield. B-25 Mitchells bomb the marshaling yard at Civitavecchia, while B-26 Marauders bomb the Aversa marshaling yard. A-36 Intruders (Apache) bomb the marshaling yards at Sapri and Lamezia.

Pacific: U.S. submarine *Halibut* torpedoes and sinks a Japanese cargo ship in the Sea of Japan.

Bougainville: Kahili airfield is attacked by 24 B-24 Liberators, along with 20 P-40s, P-39 Airacobras, and U.S. Navy F4U Corsairs. The Japanese reportedly lose 30 aircraft; six American planes are lost.

New Britain: Thirteenth Air Force B-26 Marauders bomb Cape Gloucester airfield. B-25 Mitchells attack villages along the northwest coast of the island, bombing supply points and barges.

August 31

CBI: Fourteenth Air Force B-24 Liberators, with P-40s and P-38 Lightnings, attack Gia Lam airfield and a dike near Co Bi barracks in French Indochina. In China, B-25 Mitchells bomb Ichang airfield and P-38 Lightnings bomb the Yoyang railroad yards. Enemy ground fire shoots down one P-38.

ETO: Eighth Air Force VIII Bomber Command B-17s attack two air-related targets in France. The Amiens/Glisy airfield is hit by 105 bombers; three B-17s are lost and 36 are damaged. Enemy losses are reported to be five confirmed kills. Escorted by 160 P-47 Thunderbolts, 149 B-17s are sent against the aircraft plant at Meulan. Unable to see the target because of cloud cover, one bomber drops its bombs on a rail target near Rouen. The attack leaves 19 B-17s damaged with one crewman wounded. The U.S. fighters claim two confirmed kills on the enemy, but two P-47s are lost with both pilots reported as missing. VIII Air Support Command attacks three targets in France: the Rouen and Mazingarbe power stations; Poix/Nord and Lille/Nord airfields; and the fuel depot at Hesdin. Of the 104 B-26 Marauders that hit the target, one B-26 is lost and 13 are damaged.

Italy: Ninth Air Force B-24 Liberators bomb the marshaling yard at Pescara and report nine enemy fighters destroyed. Northwest African Air Force sends 150 B-17s against the marshaling yard at Pisa, causing widespread damage to the target.

Southwest Pacific Area: The 1st Marine Division in Australia is alerted to prepare to conduct operations on New Britain.

PACIFIC: U.S. submarine *Seawolf* torpedoes and damages a Japanese torpedo boat and sinks two cargo ships in the East China Sea.

Japanese submarine *I-20* torpedoes and damages a U.S. tanker near Espiritu Santo, New Hebrides.

CENTRAL PACIFIC: Task Force 15, commanded by Rear Admiral Charles A. Pownall, consisting of two carriers, one small carrier, one battleship, two light cruisers, 11 destroyers, and with the submarine *Snook* in support, bombs Marcus Island with TBF Avenger torpedo bombers, SBD Dauntless dive-bombers, and F6F Hellcats. TBF Avenger aircrews from the small carrier USS *Independence* report sinking three Japanese small craft.

NEW GEORGIA: Thirteenth Air Force P-40s intercept Japanese fighters over Vella Lavella Island, and claim five aircraft destroyed. P-40s also attack barges in Timbala Bay on Vella Lavella. Enemy gun positions and the radio station at Vila on Kolombangara Island are attacked by 22 B-25 Mitchells and 50 U.S. Navy aircraft.

September 1

CBI: Fourteenth Air Force B-25 Mitchells, supported by P-40s, attack a Japanese destroyer at Shihhweiyao, but cause no damage. Other P-40s attack vessels between Ocheng and Shihhweiyao, and troops at Ocheng on the Yangtze River. They also damage a small ship at Swatow harbor and strafe the nearby airfield. P-38 Lightnings and a P-40 attack a barracks and destroy locomotives at Yangsin, destroy a small steamer at Wuchang, a tug at Kutang, and attack a train and an antiaircraft position near Puchi.

ATLANTIC: The JCS allocates the 4th Marine Division and the 7th Infantry Division as ground forces for Nimitz's planned offensive in the Marshall Islands. The objectives of the offensive are initially designated as Wake, Eniwetok, and Kusaie.

The War Department begins recruiting for a specialized force of 3,000 American combat troops for operations in Burma.

MEDITERRANEAN: Twelfth Air Force takes administrative control of the Army Air Force elements of the Northwest African Air Force, which are transferred to the appropriate Twelfth Air Force organizations, although operational control remains with the Northwest African Air Force.

PACIFIC: U.S. destroyer sinks Japanese submarine *I-182* off Espiritu Santo, New Hebrides. U.S. submarine *Pompano* torpedoes and sinks a Japanese merchant vessel off Miyako.

NEW GUINEA: Fifth Air Force B-24 Liberators and B-25 Mitchells hit the Alexishafen-Madang area with its heaviest bombing attack to date—201 tons of bombs are dropped on the target. The C-47s of the 68th and 69th Troop Carrier Squadrons, 433rd Troop Carrier Group, arrive at Port Moresby, New Guinea.

September 2

CBI: Fourteenth Air Force sends 10 B-25 Mitchells, with five P-40s as escorts, to bomb shipping at Hong Kong.

ETO: Eighth Air Force VIII Bomber Command B-17s, escorted by 182 P-47 Thunderbolts, attack Mardyck and Denain/Prouvy airfields in France. Of the 34 bombers that hit the target, nine B-17s are damaged. Three P-47s are lost and five are damaged in a series of fighter sweeps. VIII Air Support Command launches 216 B-26 Marauders against five targets in France. Two are aborted due to weather, but 35 B-26s bomb the power station at Mazingarbe and 69 other bombers attack a fuel depot at Hesden. One B-26 is lost and 13 are damaged.

MEDITERRANEAN: First Air Force B-24 Liberators of the 1st Antisubmarine Squadron (Heavy), 480th Antisubmarine Group, based at Port Lyautey, French Morocco, begin operating from Protville, Tunisia.

ITALY: Twelfth Air Force XII Bomber Command sends almost 200 B-17s and B-25 Mitchells to bomb the marshaling yards at Bologna, Trento, Bolzano, and Cancello Arnone. Aircrews and escort fighters report 28 enemy aircraft destroyed.

SOUTHWEST PACIFIC AREA: U.S. submarine *Bowfin* delivers supplies and evacuates guerrillas from Binuni Point, Mindanao.

PACIFIC: U.S. submarine *Seawolf* torpedoes and sinks a Japanese cargo ship in the East China Sea. U.S. submarine *Snapper* torpedoes and sinks a Japanese escort vessel northwest of Truk.

NEW GEORGIA: Thirteenth Air Force B-25 Mitchells and U.S. Navy aircraft attack antiaircraft and artillery positions at Vila on Kolombangara Island. B-24 Liberators, P-40s, P-39 Airacobras, and navy aircraft attack the airfield and other targets surrounding the airfield at Kahili on Bougainville Island.

NEW GUINEA: Fifth Air Force B-25 Mitchells escorted by P-38 Lightnings attack shipping at Wewak harbor. Several ships are damaged and 10 enemy aircraft are reported destroyed. The ships are protected by barrage balloons, an unusual tactic by the Japanese.

September 3

CBI: Fourteenth Air Force P-40s and P-38 Lightnings attack the troop barracks at Pho Lu, in French Indochina.

ETO: Eighth Air Force VIII Bomber Command B-17s, with P-47 Thunderbolts escorting, attack German airfields, support installations, and industrial targets in France. The Romilly sur Seine air depot is hit by 100 B-17s; 28 hit the St. Andre de L'Eure airfield, and 12 bomb the Evreux/Fauvill airfield, a target of opportunity. German fighter losses are reported to be 11 confirmed kills; four B-17s are lost and 55 are damaged. Over Mureaux airfield, 38 B-17s hit the target and another 18 bombers hit a deception target made to look like an airfield near Dieppe. Two B-17s are damaged in the attack. The Caudron-Renault industrial area near Paris is bombed by 37 B-17s. Aircrews claim 15 confirmed kills on German fighters. Five B-17s are lost and 18 are damaged. P-47 pilots report four confirmed kills on enemy aircraft. Although one P-47 is lost and two are damaged, there are no casualties. VIII Air Support Command sends B-26 Marauders against the Beaumont le Roger, the Lille/Nord, and the Beauvais/Tille airfields.

MEDITERRANEAN: Italy signs an instrument of surrender, but the news is kept quiet; the Allies hope that it will give the Italians time to surrender and also forestall any German action to occupy Italy. Italy agrees to transfer its air and naval units to the Allies, withdraw ground forces from all battlefronts, and withdraw from any territory occupied by Axis forces. Eventually, nine Italian divisions will join the Allies.

The Germans will disarm another 43 divisions in France, the Balkans, and in Italy. The Italian navy, with six battleships 27 destroyers, 19 submarines, and eight cruisers, will join the Allies as well. The Germans sink one Italian battleship as it attempts leaves port. Another 10 destroyers and 10 cruisers, along with one partially completed battleship, fall into German hands.

ITALY: Ninth Air Force B-24 Liberators bomb the marshaling yard at Sulmona. Six bombers are shot down and aircrews report 11 German fighters destroyed. Twelfth Air Force A-20 Havocs, A-36 Intruder (Apache) fighters, and RAF light bombers bomb troops, airfields, gun positions, roads, and bridges throughout the toe of Italy in support of the British Eighth Army, which begins Operation Baytown with the crossing of the Straits of Messina. The British advance rapidly, facing little or no resistance.

PACIFIC: U.S. destroyer *Ellet* torpedoes and sinks Japanese submarine *I-25* northeast of Espiritu Santo. U.S. submarine *Pollack* torpedoes and sinks a Japanese transport off Mikura Jima. U.S. submarine *Pompano* torpedoes and sinks a Japanese cargo ship east of Hokkaido, Japan.

NEW GEORGIA: Thirteenth Air Force B-24 Liberators and U.S. Navy aircraft bomb Vila airfield on Kolombangara Island. P-40s strafe a wharf at Webster Cove. B-24 Liberators, P-40s, and navy aircraft attack Kahili airfield on Bougainville Island.

September 4

CBI: Fourteenth Air Force B-25 Mitchells and P-40s bomb the Tien Ho airfield at Canton. Aircrews report three enemy fighters shot down.

ETO: Eighth Air Force VIII Air Support Command attacks the marshaling yards at Courtrai Lille/Deliverance, St. Pol, and Hazebrouck in France with 144 B-26 Marauders.

PACIFIC: U.S. submarine *Albacore* torpedoes and sinks a Japanese gunboat southwest of Ponape in the Carolines. U.S. submarine *Pargo* torpedoes and damages a Japanese fleet tanker in the East China Sea. U.S. submarine *Sunfish* torpedoes and sinks a Japanese cargo ship southwest of Formosa. U.S. submarine *Tarpon* torpedoes and sinks a Japanese guardboat in the North Pacific.

NEW GEORGIA: Thirteenth Air Force B-25 Mitchells attack the area near Dulo Cove.

NEW BRITAIN: Fifth Air Force A-20 Havocs and Royal Australian Air Force aircraft bomb the airfield on Gasmata Island. P-38 Lightnings intercept enemy fighters and bombers and report 20 confirmed kills.

NEW GUINEA: Naval Task Force 76, commanded by Rear Admiral Daniel E. Barbey, lands 7,800 men of the Australian 9th Division in Operation Postern, about 18 miles east of the key Japanese base at Lae. Japanese aircraft sink one of the landing craft and damage a destroyer and two LSTs (Landing Ship Tank). Seaman First Class Johnnie D. Hutchins is serving on board an LST during the assault on Lae. The LST is hit by Japanese shore batteries and aerial attack as it approaches the beach. The LST's pilothouse is hit by a bomb, leaving the ship helpless. Hutchins, although mortally wounded in the attack, takes control of the wheel and uses the last of his strength to steer clear of an air-launched torpedo. He dies at the wheel, thinking only of saving his ship and shipmates. His courage and fortitude wins him the Medal of Honor.

Fifth Air Force B-24 Liberators and B-25 Mitchells support the Allied landings at Hopoi and at the mouth of the Buso River.

September 5

ETO: Eighth Air Force VIII Air Support Command attacks the marshaling yards at Ghent, Belgium, with 63 B-26 Marauders.

MEDITERRANEAN: The main body of the U.S. convoy for Operation Avalanche leaves Oran for Salerno.

ITALY: Twelfth Air Force XII Bomber Command sends over 130 B-17s to bomb the Viterbo airfield and Civitavecchia. B-25 Mitchells and B-26 Marauders bomb the landing grounds at Grazzanise.

PACIFIC: U.S. submarine *Albacore* attacks a Japanese transport south of the Carolines, launching two torpedoes that fail to explode. U.S. submarine *Swordfish* torpedoes and sinks a Japanese army transport north of New Guinea.

NEW GUINEA: Fifth Air Force B-24 Liberators and B-25 Mitchells bomb Nadzab and Lae airfields and A-20 Havocs spread a smokescreen over the target as C-47s of the 433rd Troop Carrier Group drop the U.S. 503rd Parachute Infantry Regiment at Nadzab near Lae to seize an airhead for the arrival of the 7th Australian Infantry Division. Japanese forces begin a retreat from Lae to Finschhafen, about 50 miles to the east. In the retreat, the jungle kills more Japanese troops than Allied firepower. Of the 8,000 that begin the overland trek to Finschhafen, 2,000 will die along the way.

September 6

ETO: Eighth Air Force VIII Bomber Command aims for industrial targets at Stuttgart, Germany. Cloud cover disperses the bomber formations, which then begin to attack targets of opportunity. The mission costs 45 B-17s lost and 116 others damaged. Aircrews report over 110 confirmed or probable kills on enemy aircraft. Casualties are two killed, 27 wounded, and 333 missing. Although 176 P-47 Thunderbolts fly escort for the B-17s, they are unable to stave off the German fighter attacks on the dispersed bombers. One P-47 is lost and pilots claim only one enemy fighter shot down. VIII Air Support Command attacks the marshaling yards at Amiens, Rouen, and Serqueux, France, with 192 B-26 Marauders. Six bombers are damaged over the targets.

ITALY: Twelfth Air Force XII Bomber Command sends B-17s against the airfield at Capodichino, the Villa Literno marshaling yard, the railroad facilities at Minturno, and the Gaeta harbor facilities. B-25 Mitchells and B-26 Marauders bomb Capua airfield and landing grounds at Grazzanise.

PACIFIC: U.S. submarine *Halibut* torpedoes and sinks a Japanese cargo ship east of Hokkaido, Japan, and torpedoes a heavy cruiser, but the warhead fails to explode.

U.S. submarine *Seahorse* is damaged by depth charges off the Palau Islands.

SOLOMONS: Thirteenth Air Force B-24 Liberators blast gun positions at Vila on Kolombangara Island. B-25 Mitchells and P-39 Airacobras attack enemy positions

at Kakasa on Choiseul Island. P-39 Airacobras and U.S. Navy aircraft attack a radar site on Morgusaia Island and shoot down five enemy fighters; two P-39s are lost.
NEW GUINEA: Fifth Air Force B-24 Liberators and B-25 Mitchells attack Lae airfield and defenses in Malahang as Allied ground forces push toward Lae. Eight enemy aircraft are shot down over Lae. B-25 Mitchells fly a sweep against supply barges along the coast of New Britain.

September 7

ETO: Eighth Air Force VIII Bomber Command B-17s, escorted by 178 P-47 Thunderbolts, attack the Brussels/Evere airfield in Belgium and the V-weapon site at Watten, France. Of the 105 B-17s that hit the airfield, 11 bombers are damaged. Weather over the rocket site results in only 58 of the 147 B-17s dispatched hitting the target, and 39 B-17s are damaged. The fighter pilots report three enemy fighters as confirmed kills. One P-47 is lost and another is damaged. B-24 Liberators bomb the Bergen/Alkmaar airfield in the Netherlands. Only three bombers hit the assigned target; another 19 bombers attack a convoy off Texel Island. The VIII Air Support Command targets the Lille and St. Pol marshaling yards in France, but only St. Pol is hit due to confusion at the rendezvous point. The 81 B-26 Marauders that do bomb the target have two bombers damaged but suffer no casualties. Aircrews claim only one enemy fighter as a possible kill.
MEDITERRANEAN: Lieutenant General Lewis H. Brereton, commander of the Ninth Air Force, is directed to transfer his headquarters from Africa to Britain and reform his command in the European Theater of Operations by absorbing the VIII Air Support Command.
ITALY: Twelfth Air Force XII Bomber Command B-17s bomb outlying airfields at Foggia. B-25 Mitchells and B-26 Marauders attack road and rail bridges at Saptri and Trebisacce and roads at Lauria.
INDIAN OCEAN: Japanese submarine *I-27* torpedoes a U.S. freighter en route to Durban, South Africa, from Colombo, Ceylon, but its warhead fails to explode. The submarine surfaces and makes an ineffective attack with gunfire.
NEW GEORGIA: Thirteenth Air Force B-25 Mitchells bomb supplies and barges near Ringa Cove.
NEW GUINEA: Fifth Air Force B-24 Liberators and B-26 Marauders bomb the Lae area. B-25 Mitchells bomb and strafe targets on road to Markham. P-38 Lightnings flying air cover drive off Japanese bombers attacking Morobe. C-47s begin airlifting the Australian 7th Division to Nadzab. A-20 Havocs attack supply sites on Gasmata Island at New Britain.

September 8

CBI: Tenth Air Force B-24 Liberators mine the Rangoon River during the night.
ETO: The veterans of Ploeşti, the 44th and 93rd Bombardment Groups (Heavy), resume operations in-theater with the Eighth Air Force. VIII Air Support Command B-26 Marauders attack three targets in France. Over Lille/Nord airfield, 68 bombers hit the target and suffer no casualties, even though three B-26s are damaged. Another 68 bombers hit the Lille/Vendeville airfield and lose one B-26; 22 others

are damaged. A coastal defense target at Boulogne is hit by 68 B-26 Marauders, with 26 of them returning with damage.

ITALY: General Eisenhower announces Italy's surrender just before Allied forces are to land on Salerno beach. "Hostilities between the United Nations and Italy have terminated effective at once." Due to a limit on landing craft, two divisions from the British X Corps, commanded by Lieutenant General Sir Richard L. McCreery, and one division from the U.S. VI Corps, commanded by Major General Ernest J. Dawley, will make the initial landing. Major General Fred L. Walker's 36th Infantry Division is chosen for the task. Three Ranger battalions, commanded by Lieutenant Colonel William O. Darby, and two British commando battalions are to guard the left flank of X Corps and seize the Nocera-Pagani pass. Two regimental combat teams from the 45th Infantry Division, commanded by Major General Troy Middleton, remain shipboard as reserve. The Allied force is 169,000 men and 20,000 vehicles.

Ninth Air Force B-24 Liberators bomb Foggia. About 130 B-17s of the Twelfth Air Force's XII Bomber Command hit Frascati. B-25 Mitchells and B-26 Marauders attack a highway at Lauria, and bridges at Trebisacce and Saptri. A convoy bound for Salerno to participate in Operation Avalanche is attacked by German dive-bombers.

NEW GEORGIA: Thirteenth Air Force B-25 Mitchells bomb the Vila airfield area on Kolombangara Island.

NEW GUINEA: In support of Australian ground forces, Fifth Air Force B-17s, B-24 Liberators, B-25 Mitchells, and B-26 Marauders bomb the area around Lae, while A-20 Havocs bomb Salamaua. U.S. destroyers bombard Lae. U.S. submarine *Drum* torpedoes and sinks a Japanese cargo ship off Hollandia.

September 9

CBI: During the night, Tenth Air Force B-24 Liberators mine the Rangoon River in Burma.

In China, Fourteenth Air Force B-25 Mitchells and P-40s bomb the airfield at Canton. P-38 Lightnings bomb the docks at Whampoa, and P-40s and P-38 Lightnings hit shipping on the Yangtze River and strafe targets of opportunity.

CARIBBEAN: German submarine *U-214* lays mines off Colon, near the Panama Canal Zone.

ETO: Eighth Air Force sends 330 B-17s and B-24 Liberators over France with an escort of 215 P-47 Thunderbolts in an attempt to bring German fighters into the skies so that they can be destroyed. The targets are German airfields. The Beaumont Suroise airfield is hit as a secondary target by 48 B-17s; two bombers are lost and 21 are damaged. Aircrews report 16 confirmed kills on enemy fighters. A total of 59 B-17s hit the Beauvais/Tille airfield; six B-17s suffer damage. The Lille/Nord airfield is hit by 37 B-17s; 10 are damaged and two crewmen are wounded. The Lille/Vendeville airfield is hit by 52 B-17s; seven bombers are damaged. The Vitry-en-Artois airfield is hit by 51 B-17s with no losses. The St. Omer/Ft. Rouge and St. Omer/Longuenesse airfields are hit by 28 B-24 Liberators; three bombers are damaged and one crewman is wounded. The Abbeville/Drucat airfield is hit by 35 B-24s with no losses; P-47 pilots report only one confirmed fighter kill. Two P-47s are shot down, with one pilot missing. VIII Air Support Command sends 217 B-26 Marauders to bomb coastal defense targets near Boulogne, France. Of the 202 bombers that hit the targets, three B-26s are lost and 26 are damaged. Aircrew casualties are 11 killed, eight wounded, and 19 missing.

ITALY: Operation Avalanche. The 141st and 142nd Regimental Combat Teams of the 36th Infantry Division land on the beach before Paestum and immediately take fire from German defenders. Reinforced by the 143rd Regimental Combat Team, the Americans fight through obstacles, mines, and sniper and machine-gun fire to advance to the foothills about five miles inland, forcing the defenders to withdraw. From these hills, the division controls the entire southern half of the Salerno plain.

A number of tanks from the 16th Panzer Division conduct counterattacks against the American beachhead but are driven off by close air support, artillery, naval gunfire, engineers, and antiaircraft guns, which are fired directly at the enemy. Infantrymen using grenades, rifles, and pistols stop several tanks. Elements of the U.S. 45th Division are sent ashore during the night to reinforce the 36th Division. The British X Corps, supported by naval gunfire, advances three miles against strong German resistance to the Montecorvino airfield just west of Highway 18 and has patrols in Battipaglia. The Rangers land unopposed at Maiori and the British commandos meet some opposition but overcome it and are moving into Salerno. The British and American landings, like the previous landing at Sicily, are essentially two independent operations. There is little coordination and a 10-mile gap lies between the two corps, marked by the Sele River. Nearly 130 miles away, General Montgomery orders a two-day halt for the Eighth Army, allowing German forces of the LXXVI Panzer Corps to move north to support the defense of the Salerno beaches. Ninth Air Force B-24 Liberators hit the airfield at Foggia; Twelfth Air Force XII Bomber Command sends over 100 B-17s to bomb bridges at Capua and Cancello Arnone. B-25 Mitchells and B-26 Marauders hit railroad bridges at Potenza and the landing ground at Scanzano. XII Air Support Command fighters maintain patrols over Salerno.

Sergeant James M. Logan of Company I, 3rd Battalion of the 141st Infantry Regiment, 36th Infantry Division, lands with the first wave at Salerno and advances about 800 yards inland when the Germans counterattack. The Germans have taken positions behind a rock wall and are firing on Logan's company. Sergeant Logan exposes himself to enemy fire to stop the initial advance, then runs 200 yards to reach the machine-gun position at the wall. He jumps the wall, kills the soldiers on the machine gun, then turns the weapon on the enemy until the ammunition is expended. He also succeeds in capturing an officer and private. Later in the morning, Sergeant Logan will singlehandedly clear a sniper from a house. Sergeant Logan's fearlessness and his inspiring actions will win him the Medal of Honor.

SOUTHWEST PACIFIC AREA: U.S. submarine *Grayling* is sunk in the South China Sea west of Luzon.

PACIFIC: U.S. submarine *Harder* torpedoes and sinks a Japanese cargo ship east of Honshu, Japan. U.S. submarine *Permit* torpedoes and damages a Japanese cargo vessel near Kwajalein Atoll. U.S. submarine *Pompano* torpedoes and damages a Japanese cargo ship east of Hokkaido, Japan.

NEW GEORGIA: Thirteenth Air Force B-25 Mitchells and U.S. Navy SBD Dauntless dive-bombers attack Vila airfield on Kolombangara Island. B-24 Liberators, with fighter escort, bomb Kahili airfield on Bougainville Island.

NEW GUINEA: Fifth Air Force B-25 Mitchells bomb and strafe coastal area from Alexishafen to Finschhafen and attack suspected supply points on New Britain Island.

September 10

CBI: Tenth Air Force B-25 Mitchells bomb the Gokteik viaduct in Burma. In China, Fourteenth Air Force sends 10 B-25 Mitchells and seven P-40s to attack warehouses near Wuchang and the docks at Hankow. P-40 pilots report nine Japanese aircraft destroyed. Nine P-38 Lightnings bomb the Whampoa docks.

ITALY: Salerno Beachhead. The Germans, with one division immediately available and two others arriving, are confident that the Allies can be driven into the sea. The expected arrival of the LXXVI Panzer Corps only reinforces that belief. The 179th RCT of the 45th Infantry Division lands and prepares for an advance toward Ponte Sele, near the area bound by the Sele and Calore Rivers. German aircraft conduct attacks on Allied ships in the Gulf of Salerno.

Ninth Air Force B-24 Liberators bomb an airfield at Foggia. Twelfth Air Force XII Bomber Command sends B-25 Mitchells, B-24 Liberators, and B-17s to bomb rail and road junctions and bridges to prevent the arrival of German reinforcements to Salerno. XII Air Support Command aircraft and RAF fighters of the Northwest African Air Force attack enemy road movement and cover the Salerno beachheads. B-25 Mitchells conduct a night bombing attack on communications centers at Corleto, Perticara, Auletta, and Saptri.

NEW BRITAIN: Fifth Air Force B-25 Mitchells bomb supply barges along the coast of the island.

September 11

ALEUTIANS: Eleventh Air Force sends 12 B-25 Mitchells and eight B-24 Liberators to attack Paramushiru Island in the Kuriles. Aircrews report one cargo ship and a transport are sunk, and a transport and two cargo ships are damaged. The bombers also attack structures and an antiaircraft position on Shimushu Island. Japanese defend the islands with 40 fighters. Aircrews report 13 enemy fighters are shot down and three more are probables. Two B-24 Liberators are forced to land in the Soviet Union, but seven B-25s and two B-24s are lost.

CBI: In China, Fourteenth Air Force sends 10 B-25 Mitchells and 11 P-40s to attack the docks at Hankow and the Wuchang cotton mills. A group of three P-38 Lightnings bomb supply depots at Tayeh and strafe warehouses and barracks at Yangsin.

ATLANTIC: German submarine *U-107* lays mines off Charleston, South Carolina.

ETO: Eighth Air Force VIII Air Support Command sends B-26 Marauders to attack the Rouen power station and the Beaumont le Roger airfield. Unable to attack the primary target at Rouen due to heavy clouds, 19 B-26s hit a secondary target, the shipyard at Le Trait. Fourteen bombers are damaged and one airman is wounded.

Over the Beaumont le Roger airfield, 32 B-26 Marauders hit the target. One bomber is damaged and four crewmen are reported killed.

ITALY: Salerno Beachhead. The 142nd RCT of the 36th Infantry Division advances toward the Altavilla hills, which dominate the Salerno plain. The 179th RCT of the 45th Infantry Division, with tanks and artillery, advances up Highway 18 to secure Ponte Sele and control the main corridor of advance into the U.S. beachhead. A German counterattack with tanks and infantry and supported by heavy artillery fire nearly surrounds the regiment and forces it into a defensive position. The 157th RCT is committed from the U.S. VI Corps reserve to attack and protect the 179th's vulnerable flank, but is stopped short by German troops near a cluster of five stone buildings known as the Tobacco Factory. A battalion from the 143rd RCT is shipped on landing craft to the British X Corps area near Maiori to stop a German attack.

Twelfth Air Force XII Bomber Command B-17s bomb the Benevento marshaling yard and bridge. B-25 Mitchells and B-26 Marauders attack lines of communication at Castelnuovo, Ariano, Mignano, and Isernia. U.S. and RAF aircraft of the Northwest African Air Force conduct ground support missions around Salerno. A U.S. destroyer is sunk by German motor torpedo boats and two light cruisers are damaged by radio-controlled bombs from German aircraft.

PACIFIC: U.S. submarine *Harder* torpedoes and sinks a Japanese transport south of Kyushu, Japan. U.S. submarine *Narwhal* torpedoes and sinks a Japanese transport northwest of Nauru Island. U.S. submarine *Spearfish* torpedoes and damages a Japanese army transport off Kyushu, Japan.

NEW GEORGIA: Thirteenth Air Force B-25 Mitchells bomb Japanese positions near Vila airfield on Kolombangara Island. B-24 Liberators also bomb the airfield. P-40s and P-39 Airacobras support SBD Dauntless dive-bombers in striking gun positions at Hamberi on New Georgia Island. Over Bougainville Island, 25 B-24 Liberators, with fighter escort, bomb Kahili airfield. Aircrews report seven Japanese fighters shot down.

NEW GUINEA: Fifth Air Force B-24 Liberators bomb Makassar.

September 12

CBI: In China, Fourteenth Air Force P-38 Lightnings bomb shipping near Hong Kong. Others attack Yangtze River traffic, and P-40s strafe a barracks and destroy a locomotive near Shihhweiyao.

MEDITERRANEAN: Ninth Air Force B-24 Liberators bomb Kalathos and Maritsa airfields on Rhodes.

ITALY: At Salerno, elements of two German divisions arrive to face the U.S. VI Corps. The 1st Battalion of the 142nd Infantry Regiment, occupying the key hills near Altavilla, takes heavy casualties and is driven off Hill 424. The 157th Infantry Regiment forces German defenders out of the Tobacco Factory. During the night the VI Corps commander, Major General Ernest J. Dawley, changes troop dispositions on his left flank to defend against a possible German counterattack from the British X Corps sector.

Twelfth Air Force XII Bomber Command B-17s bomb lines of communication at Mignano, Benevento, and Frosinone airfield. B-25 Mitchells attack roads and truck traffic at Ariano, Isernia, Castelnuovo, and Formia road junctions. U.S. and RAF aircraft of the Northwest African Air Force attack lines of communication around Potenza and Auletta, and fly ground support missions for the hard-pressed Fifth Army at Salerno.

German commandos led by Colonel Otto Skorzeny conduct a surprise glider assault on a mountaintop where Mussolini is being held at a ski lodge. The deposed Italian leader is whisked away to German-controlled territory and is eventually taken to Hitler's headquarters in East Prussia.

PACIFIC: U.S. submarine *Permit* torpedoes and damages a Japanese aircraft transport south of Kwajalein.

NEW GUINEA: Fifth Air Force B-17s and B-24 Liberators bomb Lae as the Australians advance. The Australian 5th Division captures Salamaua, while B-25 Mitchells strafe the area between Saidor and Langemak Bay.

American losses after landing at Nassau Bay in June in support of the Australian advance are 81 killed and 396 wounded, in a series of small-unit battles fought in the jungles where the enemy is usually within an arm's length. Disease and weather further weaken the troops.

B-25 Mitchells attack supply barges near Cape Gloucester on New Britain Island. A-20 Havocs bomb a radio station on Gasmata Island.

The neuropsychotic casualty rate for U.S. forces in the SWPA is 43.9 percent per 1,000 men.

September 13

ALEUTIANS: Major General William O. Butler gives up command of the Eleventh Air Force to Major General Davenport Johnson.

ETO: Eighth Air Force activates the 1st, 2nd, and 3rd Bombardment Divisions in England. They are commanded by Major General Robert B. Williams, Brigadier General James P. Hodges, and Major General Curtis E. LeMay, respectively. VIII Bomber Command's four bombardment wings are now redesignated as Combat Bombardment Wings (Heavy).

ITALY: At Salerno, General Dawley continues to reinforce his left flank with elements of the 36th Infantry Division, sending two battalions of the 141st Infantry Regiment and a battalion of the 143rd Infantry Regiment to defensive positions in support of the 157th and 179th Infantry Regiments of the 45th Infantry Division. The Americans are attacked by strong German combat formations with tanks and infantry. Two battalions of the 179th Infantry are driven back, opening a large gap in the lines. The 2nd Battalion 143rd Infantry Regiment is partially surrounded and suffers over 500 casualties. As the enemy advances south toward the beachhead, two artillery battalions, including the division artillery band, headquarters staff, and mechanics are turned into infantry to stop the advance. The two artillery battalions fire 3,600 rounds on the enemy and the attack is halted. The situation is so precarious toward the end of the day that Lieutenant General Clark orders the Fifth Army staff to begin planning to evacuate one of the two beachheads and consolidate British and American forces.

Two battalions of the 142nd Infantry attempt to retake Hill 424 supported by a battalion of the 143rd Infantry Regiment. The Germans are dug in and supported by artillery fire. Despite repeated attempts, Hill 424 remains in enemy hands.

Twelfth Air Force XII Bomber Command B-17s attack lines of communication at Torre del Greco, Sala, Consilina, and Atena Lucana. B-25 Mitchells bomb lines of communication around Pompeii, Castellammare di Stabia, and Torre Annunziata. XII Air Support Command A-36 Intruder (Apache) fighter-bombers destroy 25 to 30 vehicles near Potenza. U.S. and RAF A-20 Havocs and B-25 Mitchells of the Northwest African Air Force attack roads and vehicles around Auletta, Pompeii, Sala, Consilina, and San Severino Rota. More than 80 C-47s drop paratroopers of the U.S. 82nd Airborne Division south of the Sele River to protect the Salerno beachhead and reinforce the perimeter. A U.S. freighter is damaged by German air attack off Salerno.

At Altavilla, a company of the 36th Infantry Division attacks Hill 424. First Lieutenant Arnold L. Bjorklund, leading the first platoon around the right flank, encounters heavy machine-gun and rifle fire. As the platoon returns fire, Bjorklund crawls forward to within a few yards of a German machine-gun position. Using a hand grenade, he destroys the position. Taking fire from another machine-gun position, he moves forward and again, within a few yards of the enemy, throws a hand grenade and destroys the position. His platoon advances about 150 yards up the slope, but takes fire from a heavy mortar. Once more, First Lieutenant Bjorklund makes his way within 10 yards of the enemy and uses a hand grenade to knock out the mortar. Bjorklund's courage and dedication to his men will win him the Congressional Medal of Honor. During the same attack on Hill 424, the third platoon also encounters strong enemy resistance. Private William J. Crawford, without orders and on his own initiative, attacks an enemy machine-gun position, destroying it with a hand grenade. When the platoon's advance is stopped by two machine-gun positions, Private Crawford, faces intense fire to destroy both positions singlehandedly with grenades and rifle fire. His extraordinary courage and coolness under fire will win him the Medal of Honor.

PACIFIC: U.S. submarine *Permit* torpedoes and damages a Japanese fleet tanker south of Kwajalein. U.S. submarine *Snook* torpedoes and sinks Japanese army transport in the South China Sea, and narrowly avoids being sunk by an escorting destroyer.

NEW GUINEA: Fifth Air Force B-24 Liberators, with P-38 Lightnings flying escort, bomb airfields and ammunition dumps near Wewak. B-25 Mitchells bomb Lae.

September 14

CBI: Tenth Air Force receives A-36 Intruder (Apache) fighter-bombers from the United States to establish the 382nd Bombardment Squadron (Dive) at Nawadih, India.

Fourteenth Air Force B-24 Liberators bomb docks and shipping at Haiphong harbor in French Indochina. Three B-24s are lost and two are damaged. P-38 Lightnings severely damage two vessels on the Yangtze River at Chiuchiang, China.

ETO: Eighth Air Force VIII Air Support Command B-26 Marauders attempt to attack airfield targets in France and the Netherlands, but cloud cover over the targets aborts the mission. Of the 108 bombers involved, 18 B-26s are damaged. Three crewmen are wounded.

ITALY: At Salerno, the shattered 36th Infantry Division is retired from the front lines to reorganize, except for one company of the 143rd Infantry Regiment trapped on Hill 424, and two battalions of the 141st Infantry. A new defensive line is cobbled together from engineer units, tank destroyer units, and infantry units. The 45th Infantry Division holds the far left flank. German attacks on the 45th are stopped, and an enemy tank and infantry attack is stopped at the Calore River crossing by tank destroyers, naval gunfire, artillery, and infantry. The total artillery rounds expended during the day by the 45th and 36th divisions tops 10,000. The 180th Infantry Regiment of the 45th Infantry Division lands and becomes the VI Corps reserve. The British X Corps links with the 45th Infantry Division to close the gap between the two corps that has existed since the initial landings. About 2,000 men of the 505th RCT of the 82nd Airborne Division are dropped to strengthen the defenses. Another battalion of the 509th is dropped behind enemy lines in front of the British X Corps, but the troops are scattered away from their drop zones and have little effect. Of the 600 men who jump, 400 will return to friendly lines.

Ninth Air Force B-24 Liberators bomb the Pescara marshaling yard. Twelfth Air Force XII Bomber Command B-17s, B-25 Mitchells, and B-26 Marauders attack highways, road junctions, bridges, railroads, marshaling yards, and gun positions. Allied aircraft of the Northwest African Tactical Air Force conduct ground support missions.

A U.S. freighter is damaged by German air attack off Salerno.

SOLOMONS: Japanese aircraft attack U.S. airfields at Guadalcanal and at Barakoma and Munda on New Georgia Island. Thirteenth Air Force B-24 Liberators, escorted by army and navy fighters, bomb Kahili airfield on Bougainville Island. Aircrews report eight Japanese fighters downed. B-25 Mitchells and B-24 Liberators bomb Vila airfield and other targets on Kolombangara Island. P-39 Airacobras and U.S. Navy fighters and dive-bombers attack Ballale Island airfield.

NEW GUINEA: Fifth Air Force B-25 Mitchells attack Lae and barges in Hansa Bay.

September 15

CBI: In China, Fourteenth Air Force sends five B-24 Liberators to bomb a cement plant at Haiphong, French Indochina. The bombers are attacked by over 50 Japanese fighters, which shoot down four of the bombers. The aircrew of the surviving B-24 reports 10 enemy fighters destroyed. B-25 Mitchells, escorted by P-40s, attack a cotton mill near Wuchang, China.

ETO: Eighth Air Force VIII Bomber Command B-17s attack facilities in France. Over the Romilly-sur-Seine air depot, 87 B-17s hit the target and nine bombers are damaged. Over the Caudron-Renault industrial area in Paris, 40 B-17s hit the target; another 21 hit the Billancourt-Renault works, and 78 hit the Hispano-Suiza aircraft engine works in Paris. Aircrews report at least 12 enemy aircraft destroyed. U.S. losses are five B-17s lost and 33 damaged. B-24 Liberators bomb the airfield at Chartres. One B-24 is lost and three enemy aircraft are reported shot down. Five B-17s join the RAF on a night attack on the Dunlop factory at Montlucon, France. The VIII Air Support Command attacks the Merville airfield in France with 68 B-26 Marauders. All of the bombers return, but 27 are damaged and only two crewmen are wounded.

ITALY: General Bernard L. Montgomery's Eighth Army advance forces the Germans to begin a withdrawal that eases the pressure on U.S. forces at Salerno.

Ninth Air Force B-24 Liberators bomb the marshaling yard at Potenza. Twelfth Air Force XII Bomber Command B-17s bomb highways and rail lines. B-25 Mitchells and B-26 Marauders bomb highways and road junctions. XII Air Support Command and Northwest African Air Force fighters attack buildings, railroads, and highways in support of U.S. Fifth Army at Salerno.

PACIFIC: U.S. submarine *Haddock* torpedoes and sinks a Japanese collier north of Truk.

SOLOMONS: Thirteenth Air Force B-25 Mitchells bomb Vila airfield on Kolombangara Island and Kahili airfield on Bougainville Island. B-24 Liberators, with fighter escort, also bomb Kahili and Parapatu Point on New Georgia Island. The airfield facilities at Ballale Island are attacked by navy SBD Dauntless dive-bombers, supported by army, navy, and marine fighters. A U.S. destroyer and a PBY Catalina sink Japanese submarine *RO-101* near San Cristobal.

NEW GEORGIA: The 12,400 Japanese troops occupying Kolombangara Island are ordered to evacuate. A New Zealand brigade relieves U.S. Army forces on Vella Lavella, the initial transition to Allied forces occupying New Georgia.

NEW GUINEA: Fifth Air Force B-24 Liberators, with P-38 Lightnings escorting, bomb airfields near Wewak. Aircrews report 10 enemy aircraft destroyed on the ground and 14 others shot down. B-17s bomb the Lae area and B-25 Mitchells sink about 15 supply barges between Alexishafen and Finschhafen.

September 16

CBI: Fourteenth Air Force sends eight B-25 Mitchells with 12 P-40s flying escort against logistics targets at Liujenpa, China.

ETO: Eighth Air Force VIII Bomber Command attacks airfields and harbors in France. Escorted by 79 P-47 Thunderbolts, 79 B-17s hit the Nantes harbor and 52 B-17s hit the Nantes/Chateau-Bougon airfield. The bomber crews report over 22 enemy aircraft shot down, the fighter pilots report two confirmed kills and one possible kill. U.S. losses are severe: 7 B-17s lost and 48 damaged. La Pallice harbor, the La Rochelle/Laleau airfield, and the Cognac/Chateaubernard airfield are bombed by another 93 B-17s. Four bombers are lost and 22 are damaged. Aircrews report over 22 enemy fighters shot down. Five B-17s participate in a night attack with the RAF against the marshaling yard at Modane, France. VIII Air Support Command raids the Beaumont le Roger and the Tricoueville airfields with 67 B-26 Marauders. Two bombers are damaged.

ITALY: Lieutenant General Mark Clark and his staff establish Fifth Army headquarters ashore at Salerno, mostly in an effort to raise the morale of American troops. Two battalions of the 504th Parachute Infantry Regiment move to capture Altavilla and are held up by German infantry and artillery. Ninth Air Force B-24 Liberators bomb road junctions and a supply base at Potenza. Twelfth Air Force XII Bomber Command B-17s bomb bridges, rail lines, a marshaling yard, and trains around Benevento and Caserta. XII Air Support Command and Northwest African Tactical Air Force aircraft conduct ground support operations over Salerno.

SOLOMONS: Thirteenth Air Force P-40s and navy fighters support navy SBD Dauntless dive-bombers attacking the airfield on Ballale Island.

NEW GUINEA: Fifth Air Force B-17s, B-26 Marauders, B-25 Mitchells, and A-20 Havocs attack Japanese positions at Lae in support of the Australian attack. The Japanese later evacuate the area.

September 17

ITALY: Ninth Air Force B-24 Liberators bomb the marshaling yard and a road and rail junction at Pescara. Twelfth Air Force XII Bomber Command B-17s and B-26 Marauders bomb the Ciampino and Pratica di Mare airfields. B-25 Mitchells attack vessels at the mouth of the Tiber River. P-38 Lightnings conduct widespread dive-bombing missions against roads, rail lines, bridges, and targets of opportunity. XII Air Support Command and Northwest African Tactical Air Force aircraft bomb rail and road junctions, motor transport, and targets of opportunity.

September 18

CBI: Fourteenth Air Force sends four B-25 Mitchells and seven P-40s to attack rail and industrial targets at Shihhweiyao, China.

ATLANTIC: German submarine *U-260* torpedoes and damages a U.S. freighter in the mid-North Atlantic. The B-24 Liberators of the 12th Antisubmarine Squadron (Heavy), 25th Antisubmarine Wing, at Langley Field, Virginia, cease antisubmarine operations.

ETO: Eighth Air Force VIII Air Support Command B-26 Marauders bomb Beauvais/Tille airfield. Of the 25 B-26s that hit the target, 12 are damaged.

ITALY: At Salerno, the 45th Infantry Division encounters no enemy forces and advances to Persano. The 3rd Infantry Division commanded by Major General Lucian K. Truscott, begins landing at Salerno. Ninth Air Force B-24 Liberators bomb the marshaling yard at Pescara. Twelfth Air Force XII Bomber Command B-17s bomb the airfield at Viterbo. B-25 Mitchells and B-26 Marauders bomb the Ciampino and Pratica di Mare airfields. P-38 Lightnings strafe the airfields at Foggia and bomb roads, rail lines, and bridges.

PACIFIC: U.S. submarine *Spearfish* torpedoes but only damages a Japanese torpedo boat south of Kyushu, Japan, due to the premature explosion of two torpedoes. U.S. submarine *Trigger* torpedoes and sinks a Japanese cargo ship in the South China Sea.

CENTRAL PACIFIC: During the night, Seventh Air Force sends 24 B-24 Liberators from Funafuti Island and Canton Island to bomb Betio Island, Tarawa Atoll, and Maiana and Abemama Islands in the Gilberts. Navy Task Force 15, under command of Rear Admiral Charles A. Pownall, attacks the same targets with TBF Avengers, SBD Dauntless dive-bombers, and F6F Hellcats from fast carrier USS *Lexington* and small carriers *Princeton* and *Belleau Wood*. Thirteenth Air Force B-24 Liberators bomb the airfield and facilities on Nauru Island and Makin Atoll in the Gilberts.

NEW GUINEA: Fifth Air Force A-20 Havocs attack targets around Lae. B-26 Marauders strafe targets near Finschhafen. U.S. submarine *Scamp* attacks a Japanese convoy north of New Guinea, sinking a cargo ship. The C-47s of the 65th Troop Carrier Squadron, 54th Troop Carrier Wing move from Port Moresby to Tsili Tsili.

September 19

ETO: Eighth Air Force VIII Air Support Command targets the Lille/Nord airfield with 72 B-26 Marauders. Only 18 bombers hit the target and 10 B-26s are damaged. Four crewmen are wounded.

ITALY: Elements of the 504th Parachute Infantry Regiment, supported by tanks, capture Altavilla after the Germans withdraw.

PACIFIC: U.S. submarine *Harder* torpedoes and sinks a Japanese cargo ship off east Shikoku, Japan. U.S. submarine *Scamp* torpedoes and sinks a Japanese cargo ship north of the Admiralty Islands.

CENTRAL PACIFIC: From Funafuti Island and Canton Island, 20 Seventh Air Force B-24 Liberators bomb Tarawa Atoll and Abemama Island in the Gilberts and conduct photo reconnaissance of Betio Island and Tarawa Atoll. Japanese fighters shoot down one B-24.

NEW BRITAIN: Thirteenth Air Force B-25 Mitchells and navy SBD Dauntless dive-bombers, with fighter cover, bomb Vila airfield on Kolombangara Island and enemy positions on New Georgia Island.

NEW GUINEA: Fifth Air Force B-25 Mitchells and B-26 Marauders bomb Finschhafen as a preparation for Allied landings. B-17s and B-24 Liberators bomb the airfield and surrounding area at Cape Gloucester on New Britain Island.

September 20

CBI: The Fourteenth Air Force airfield at Kunming, China, is attacked by 27 Japanese bombers and 20 fighters. The attack causes little damage as 24 P-40s and three P-38 Lightnings intercept and attack the enemy formation, reporting 17 aircraft destroyed. One U.S. fighter is lost.

ATLANTIC: German submarine *U-238* attacks New York-bound convoy ON 202 (Liverpool to New York, Fast), torpedoing and sinking one U.S. freighter and forcing another to be abandoned in the mid-North Atlantic. *U-645* later finishes off the abandoned freighter.

ITALY: At Salerno, Lieutenant General Mark Clark, disappointed with Major General Dawley's performance during the crisis on the Salerno beaches, relieves him as VI Corps commander in favor of Major General John P. Lucas. The 36th Infantry Division is allowed to rest and refit as the corps reserve. The 3rd Infantry Division and the 45th Infantry Division enter the mountains in pursuit of the retreating Germans. The 3rd Division takes Highway 7, the 45th Division takes Highway 91. Ninth Air Force B-24 Liberators of the 98th and 376th Bombardment Groups (Heavy) are transferred to the Twelfth Air Force after raiding marshaling yards at Castelfranco Veneto and Pescara. Twelfth Air Force XII Bomber Command B-17s and B-26 Marauders bomb the Castelnuovo road junction, and roads and railroad near Sarno. XII Air Support Command A-36 Intruder (Apache) fighter-bombers attack enemy tank and troop concentrations forming near Nocera. Allied aircraft of the Northwest African Tactical Air Force attack enemy troop movements in the area around Naples and Benevento.

PACIFIC: U.S. submarine *Haddock* torpedoes and damages a Japanese fleet tanker east of the Palaus. U.S. submarine *S-28* torpedoes and sinks a Japanese gunboat off the Kuriles.

NEW GUINEA: Fifth Air Force B-24 Liberators bomb Wewak and Boram airfields. B-25 Mitchells bomb Penfoei on Timor Island.

September 21

CBI: Fourteenth Air Force sends eight B-25 Mitchells and eight P-40s to attack railroad yards and warehouses at Chiuchiang, China.

ETO: Eighth Air Force VIII Air Support Command attacks the Beauvais/Tille airfield in France, but bad weather limits the effectiveness of the 44 B-26 Marauders that make it over the target. One enemy aircraft is reported destroyed and one B-26 is lost and 13 are damaged.

MEDITERRANEAN: Ninth Air Force IX Fighter Command headquarters at Tripoli, Libya, is inactivated. It will move to Middle Wallop, in England. German submarine *U-238* torpedoes and damages a U.S. freighter in a convoy bound for Salerno. The ship later sinks despite efforts to save her.

ITALY: The 133rd Infantry Regiment of the 34th Infantry Division arrives at Salerno to reinforce VI Corps.

Twelfth Air Force XII Bomber Command B-17s bomb a bridge and the approaches to Benevento. B-25 Mitchells and B-26 Marauders bomb bridges at Cancello Arnone and Capua. B-24 Liberators on detached service from the Eighth Air Force bomb Leghorn and Bastia. B-25 Mitchells and A-36 Intruder (Apache) fighter-bombers of the Northwest African Air Force and XII Air Support Command attack enemy troop concentrations, trucks, tanks, and targets of opportunity near Solofra, Avellino, and Benevento.

INDIAN OCEAN: German submarine *U-188* torpedoes a U.S. freighter off the Horn of Africa. The U-boat confidently surfaces to finish off the ship with gunfire, but encounters a crew fully armed and ready to fight. The accurate fire forces the U-boat to submerge and attack with torpedoes. The crew finally abandons ship.

PACIFIC: U.S. submarine *Haddock* torpedoes and sinks a Japanese collier northwest of Truk. U.S. submarine *Trigger* torpedoes and sinks two Japanese fleet oilers and damages another and sinks a cargo ship north of Formosa. U.S. submarine *Wahoo* torpedoes and sinks a Japanese merchant fishing vessel northeast of Hokkaido, Japan.

NEW GEORGIA: Thirteenth Air Force B-24 Liberators bomb the airfield on Buka Island. Two Japanese fighters are reported shot down in the attack.

NEW GUINEA: Fifth Air Force A-20 Havocs, B-26 Marauders, and Australian aircraft attack Tami Island and bomb Finschhafen. B-25 Mitchells bomb and strafe the Bogadjim area and Langgoer. B-24 Liberators attack Cape Gloucester and a freighter near Talasea on New Britain and sink a transport southeast of the Admiralties. A-20 Havocs and Australian aircraft bomb Gasmata Island.

September 22

ETO: Eighth Air Force VIII Air Support Command attacks the Evreux/Fauville airfield with 70 B-26 Marauders. There are no losses or casualties. A fighter sweep over northeast France and Belgium by 240 P-47 Thunderbolts results in one fighter lost and another damaged; two enemy fighters are reported destroyed. Another 155 P-47 Thunderbolts sweep over northern Belgium and the coastal islands of the

Netherlands. VIII Bomber Command sends five B-17s with the RAF in a night raid on the city of Hannover, Germany.

MEDITERRANEAN: The Ninth Air Force IX Bomber Command B-24 Liberators are transferred to the Twelfth Air Force.

ITALY: The 30th Infantry Regiment of the 3rd Infantry Division captures Acerno after a strong defense by German infantry supported by self-propelled guns. The 180th Infantry Regiment of the 45th Infantry Division, with tank support, captures Oliveto. The 36th Engineer Regiment (Combat) follows the divisions, performing near-miracles in repairing bridges and roads destroyed by the retreating Germans.

Twelfth Air Force XII Bomber Command B-25 Mitchells and B-26 Marauders bomb roads, railroads, and bridges near Grottaminarda; XII Air Support Command aircraft attack troop concentrations, tanks, and trucks in the Foggia area, and the landing ground at Capua.

PACIFIC: U.S. submarine *Harder* torpedoes and sinks a Japanese merchant tanker and cargo ship east of Honshu, Japan. U.S. submarine *Hoe* torpedoes and sinks a Japanese fleet tanker east of Guam. U.S. submarine *Snook* torpedoes and sinks one Japanese cargo ship in the Yellow Sea and damages another. U.S. submarine *Trigger* torpedoes and damages a Japanese cargo ship in the East China Sea.

SOUTH PACIFIC: The planned landings on New Britain are postponed until December 26. Admiral William F. Halsey, COMSOPAC, requests a study on the possibility of landing at Empress Augusta Bay on Bougainville Island. Rear Admiral Theodore S. Wilkinson is named the commander of the planned offensive.

NEW GUINEA: Elements of the Australian 9th Division land at the mouth of the Song River north of Finschhafen. The Japanese occupy the Satelberg Ridge, which covers the approaches to Finschhafen. Fifth Air Force B-25 Mitchells bomb enemy defenses near Finschhafen. A-20 Havocs and B-25 Mitchells bomb the Lae area. The Japanese reportedly lose 38 aircraft to Allied fighters. B-24 Liberators and B-25 Mitchells bomb the airfield on Gasmata Island off New Britain. B-24 Liberators bomb Amboina Island in the Moluccas.

September 23

ALEUTIANS: Eleventh Air Force comes under the operational control of Commander Northern Pacific (COMNORPAC) Forces.

ATLANTIC: German submarine *U-952* torpedoes and sinks a U.S. freighter in convoy ONS 202 (Liverpool to Halifax, slow) off Newfoundland.

ETO: Eighth Air Force VIII Bomber Command B-17s attack the Nantes port area, the Vannes/Meucon airfield, and the Kerlin/Bastard airfield in France during the morning. Over Nantes, 43 of the 46 bombers that hit the target are damaged. Aircrews report at least 22 enemy aircraft destroyed. At Vannes/Meucon airfield, 55 bombers hit the target and seven B-17s are damaged. The 53 B-17s that hit the Kerlin/Bastard airfield lose one bomber and 10 others are damaged. Two enemy aircraft are reported destroyed. Later in the evening the Nantes port area is hit again by 61 B-17s and the Rennes/St. Jacques airfield is hit by 19 B-17s. Two B-17s are lost and 18 are damaged. Four of five B-17s accompany the RAF on a night raid on Mannheim, Germany. One B-17 is damaged in the attack.

ITALY: Twelfth Air Force XII Bomber Command B-26 Marauders bomb bridges near Capua. XII Air Support Command aircraft attack motor transport, roads, railroads, gun positions, and targets of opportunity in the mountains north and west of Salerno.

Corporal James D. Slaton, 157th Infantry Regiment, 45th Infantry Division, is the lead scout of an infantry squad with the mission of outflanking a German position, that has been holding the advance of two platoons near Oliveto. Moving ahead of his squad, Corporal Slaton approaches an enemy machine-gun position and uses his bayonet to kill the gunner. Unable to remove the bayonet from the body, he detaches it, then kills the other gunner with rifle fire. When he begins taking fire from another machine-gun position, Corporal Slaton attacks over open ground and destroys it with a hand grenade. When a third machine-gun position engages him, Corporal Slaton fires his rifle to kill the two gunners. Corporal Slaton stands alone until he is able to withdraw under the cover of friendly mortar fire. Slaton's tremendous courage and skills as a soldier win him the Medal of Honor.

SOUTHWEST PACIFIC AREA: Fifth Air Force P-40s bomb Gasmata Island off New Britain.

PACIFIC: U.S. submarine *Trout* torpedoes and sinks a Japanese transport and a cargo ship northwest of the Marianas. U.S. submarine *Tuna* torpedoes and attacks a Japanese cargo vessel east of Malaya.

SOLOMONS: The new commander of COMAIRSOLS is Brigadier General James T. Moore, relieving Brigadier General Francis Mulcahy. Moore takes command of 314 fighters and 317 bombers from the Royal New Zealand Air Force, Thirteenth Air Force bombers, and the 1st and 2nd Marine Air Wings. Most are located at Guadalcanal, but will redeploy to Munda and Vella Lavella airfields after New Georgia is secure.

BOUGAINVILLE: Thirteenth Air Force sends 23 B-24 Liberators, with 16 P-38 Lightnings and over 60 SBD Dauntless dive-bombers, to attack Kahili on Bougainville Island. It is reported that nine enemy fighters are shot down. Another 21 B-24 Liberators conduct a bombing raid on Kolombangara Island. U.S. submarine *Gato* lands a reconnaissance team off the northwest coast of the island to look for possible landing sites, while the *Guardfish* does the same for a team examining Empress Augusta Bay.

NEW GEORGIA: Barakoma airfield on Vella Lavella is operational.

September 24
ETO: Eighth Air Force VIII Air Support Command B-26 Marauders bomb the Evreux/Fauville airfield and the Beauvais/Tille airfield in France. Of the 71 B-26s that hit Evreux/Fauville airfield four bombers are damaged; aircrews claim one probable enemy fighter kill. Of the 66 B-26s that hit Beauvais/Tille airfield, 17 are damaged.

ITALY: Twelfth Air Force XII Bomber Command B-25 Mitchells and B-26 Marauders bomb roads, railways, and bridges, at Grottaminarda, Benevento, Avellino, and Capua.

INDIAN OCEAN: Japanese submarine *I-10* torpedoes and sinks a U.S. freighter southeast of Aden.

PACIFIC: U.S. submarine *Cabrilla* torpedoes and damages the Japanese carrier *Taiyo* northwest of Chichi Jima. The submarine fires six torpedoes at the carrier; three hit, but only one explodes. The *Taiyo* is towed by an escort carrier to Yokosuka.

September 25

ETO: Eighth Air Force VIII Air Support Command B-26 Marauders bomb the St. Omer/Longuenesse airfield. Four of the 68 bombers that hit the target are damaged.

ITALY: Twelfth Air Force XII Bomber Command B-17s bomb the Bologna marshaling yard and the railroad bridge at Bolzano. B-25 Mitchells and B-26 Marauders bomb airfields at Pisa, Lucca, and Bastia/Borgo, and road junctions, bridges, and rail lines. XII Air Support Command and RAF Desert Air Force aircraft attack roads near Serino, troops at Sarno, and supplies stored near Foggia. A U.S. minesweeper is sunk by German submarine *U-593* in the Gulf of Salerno.

PACIFIC: U.S. submarine *Bluefish* torpedoes and damages a Japanese cargo ship in the Flores Sea. U.S. submarines *Bowfin, Billfish,* and *Bonefish* attack a Japanese convoy. *Bowfin* sinks a tanker north of Nha Trang, French Indochina, in the South China Sea.

NEW GEORGIA: Thirteenth Air Force B-25 Mitchells with navy TBF Avengers and SBD Dauntless dive-bombers attack Japanese gun positions around Vila airfield on Kolombangara Island and at Disappointment Cove on New Georgia. Tank landing ship *LST-167* is damaged by a Japanese dive-bomber off Vella Lavella.

NEW GUINEA: Fifth Air Force B-17s, B-24 Liberators, and B-25 Mitchells bomb enemy installations and supply lines, while A-20 Havocs and Australian aircraft conduct ground support missions for the Australian 9th Division near Finschhafen. B-25s bomb and strafe antiaircraft positions on New Britain Island.

September 26

ETO: Eighth Air Force VIII Bomber Command B-17s attack the Reims/Champagne airfield and targets near Paris. One B-17 is lost and 31 are damaged in the two raids.

ITALY: The 45th Infantry Division captures Teora, controlling the key road junction of Highways 7 and 91. Twelfth Air Force XII Bomber Command cannot fly any missions due to weather. XII Air Support Command fighters conduct ground support missions in the Benevento area and at Foggia, and attack troops near Sarno.

BOUGAINVILLE: Thirteenth Air Force B-24 Liberators, escorted by 14 P-38 Lightnings, bomb troops near Kahili. P-40s, P-39 Airacobras, and 15 U.S. Navy F4U Corsairs supporting more than 50 navy SBD Dauntless dive-bombers attack the Kahili airfield as well as other targets on the island.

September 27

ATLANTIC: PBM Mariner patrol bombers sink German submarine *U-161* off Brazil.

ETO: An Eighth Air Force VIII Bomber Command attack on the port of Emden, Germany, is led by two H2S radar-equipped B-17s of the 482nd Bombardment

Group (Pathfinder). This squadron has been created to allow bombers to conduct missions over cloud-covered targets. Pathfinders lead the bombers over the target and when the Pathfinder releases its bombs, it is the signal for all the other bombers in the formation to release their bomb load.

The 246 B-17s that hit the Emden area are escorted by 262 P-47 Thunderbolts. A total of seven bombers are lost and 79 are damaged. Aircrews report at least 32 confirmed enemy kills. The fighter pilots report 21 confirmed kills and two probables. One P-47 is lost and two damaged. Four of five B-17s accompany the RAF on a night raid on Hannover, Germany. One B-17 is shot down and the 10 crewmen are reported missing. VIII Air Support Command B-26 Marauders bomb airfields in France. Over the Beauvais/Tille airfield, 65 B-26s hit the target and 24 bombers are damaged. Aircrews report at least four enemy aircraft destroyed. Over the Conches airfield, 68 B-26s hit the target. One bomber is lost and four are damaged. Six crewmen are listed as missing.

ITALY: Twelfth Air Force is nearly grounded by weather conditions. XII Air Support Command fighters attack Viterbo airfield and bomb a road junction at San Severo.

PACIFIC: U.S. submarine *Bluefish* torpedoes and sinks a Japanese torpedo boat south of the Flores Sea, Netherlands East Indies. In the South China Sea, U.S. submarine *Bonefish* torpedoes and sinks a Japanese army transport and damages a cargo ship south of Nha Trang, French Indochina.

Major General Charles D. Barrett takes command of I Marine Amphibious Corps from Lieutenant General Alexander A. Vandegrift. I Marine Amphibious Corps issues orders for 3rd Marine Division to land near Cape Torokina on Bougainville Island to "seize, occupy and defend" a beachhead, then be prepared to expand the beachhead with the arrival of the 37th Infantry Division.

BOUGAINVILLE: Thirteenth Air Force B-24 Liberators, P-40s, P-39 Airacobras, and navy fighters bomb the Kahili area. P-39 Airacobras over Choiseul Island strafe supply barges.

NEW GUINEA: Fifth Air Force sends 117 B-24 Liberators and B-25 Mitchells, escorted by 129 P-38 Lightnings and P-40s, to attack airfields and shipping near Wewak. Some 40 Japanese aircraft are destroyed on the ground and eight others are reported shot down. Bomber aircrews report extensive damage to 10 Japanese cargo ships.

September 28

ITALY: Bad weather allows only a few Twelfth Air Force fighter-bombers to attack motor transport in the area around Benevento and Caserta.

SOUTHWEST PACIFIC AREA: U.S. submarine *Cisco* is sunk off Panay Island. U.S. submarine *Grouper* lands men and supplies on south coast of New Britain.

PACIFIC: U.S. submarine *Gudgeon* torpedoes and sinks a Japanese merchant cargo ship near Guam.

CENTRAL PACIFIC: The 27th Infantry Division staff, which has been planning for an assault on Nauru in the Gilberts, is notified that its new objective will be Makin Atoll. Japanese troops on the atoll were estimated to be about 800, with antiaircraft guns and as many as 40 machine guns. Two battalions of the 165th RCT will make the initial landing as part of Task Force 54, under command of Rear Admiral Richmond Kelly Turner. The second battalion will initially be held in reserve, then conduct a second landing.

NEW GEORGIA: Japanese forces begin evacuating Kolombangara Island. The New Georgia campaign has been characterized by continuous, close combat in dreadful conditions and under extreme hardship. Lacking firepower and experience, and slowed by a lack of adequate supplies and disease, U.S. soldiers and marines have fought in the jungle against an invisible, disciplined enemy occupying defensive positions that could be taken only by direct assault. As the battles at Buna and Gona in New Guinea have proven earlier, infantry working with tanks and flamethrowers make the difference in overwhelming Japanese defenses. But the victory has taken a heavy toll. U.S. forces have suffered 5,100 casualties.

NEW GUINEA: Fifth Air Force sends 40 B-24 Liberators, escorted by 29 P-38 Lightnings, against Japanese defenses around Wewak. Enemy losses are estimated at eight fighters shot down. A-20 Havocs and Australian aircraft attack the Finschhafen and Lae area.

September 29

CBI: Fourteenth Air Force B-24 Liberators bomb Myitkyina and Sadon in Burma.

ITALY: The 3rd Infantry Division captures Avellino in a surprise night attack before German engineers can complete laying demolition charges.

Twelfth Air Force XII Bomber Command B-25 Mitchells, B-26 Marauders, and P-38 Lightnings bomb bridges at Piana, Castelvenere, Amorosi, and Cancello Amone, while U.S. and RAF aircraft attack San Giorgio del Sannio and roads near Benevento.

The 100th Infantry Battalion, a unit comprised of Japanese-American volunteers, is attached to Fifth Army and joins the 133rd Infantry Regiment, 34th Infantry Division.

PACIFIC: U.S. submarine *Bluefish* torpedoes and sinks a Japanese cargo ship in the Banda Sea. U.S. submarine *Gudgeon* torpedoes and damages a Japanese gunboat off Saipan.

SOLOMONS: Thirteenth Air Force P-40s, P-38 Lightnings, and P-39 Airacobras support navy fighters and SBD Dauntless dive-bombers in an attack on a barge depot at Kakasa on Choiseul Island.

September 30

ATLANTIC: The B-25 Mitchells of the 10th Antisubmarine Squadron (Heavy), 26th Antisubmarine Wing, cease antisubmarine operations from Galveston, Texas.

ITALY: Twelfth Air Force XII Bomber Command P-38 Lightnings, B-25 Mitchells, and B-26 Marauders bomb roads and bridges at Ausonia, Piana, Castelvenere, Amorosi, and Capua. B-25s bomb Benevento and road and rail networks. XII Air Support Command fighter-bombers conduct ground support missions outside of Naples.

SOUTHWEST PACIFIC AREA: U.S. submarine *Bowfin* delivers supplies and evacuates guerrillas from Siquijor Island in the Philippines. The submarine also torpedoes and sinks a cargo ship in the Celebes Sea.

PACIFIC: Japanese Imperial Headquarters issues an order to subordinate units to make every effort to hold the important southeastern area extending eastward from the eastern part of New Guinea to the Solomon Islands by repulsing all enemy attacks in the area. To accomplish this, Rabaul is considered as the center and every effort will be made for a protracted defense of important positions in the Bismarck Archipelago and on Bougainville. The Japanese realize that important positions in northern New Guinea area must be reinforced. Air and naval forces will be used to destroy the attacking enemy before landings are made. If landings are successful, the enemy must be destroyed as quickly as possible before any consolidation of the beachhead. Supply lines that can transport supplies to outposts rapidly, especially in New Guinea, must be maintained.

U.S. submarine *Harder* torpedoes and sinks a Japanese auxiliary submarine chaser in the North Pacific. U.S. submarine *Pogy* torpedoes and sinks a Japanese army transport near Palau.

BOUGAINVILLE: Thirteenth Air Force B-24 Liberators, escorted by P-38 Lightnings, P-40s, and navy F4U Corsairs, attack Kahili airfield and supply sites. Another six B-25s bomb Kakasa on Choiseul Island.

October 1

CBI: Fourteenth Air Force sends 21 B-24 Liberators and 24 fighters of the Chinese-American Composite Wing (CACW) against a power plant and port facilities at Haiphong, French Indochina. More than 65 Japanese fighters attack the formation, shooting down two aircraft. Aircrews report 30 enemy fighters destroyed. Three P-40s are lost and fighter pilots report two confirmed kills.

ATLANTIC: Navy PV-1 Ventura patrol planes attack German submarines *U-402* and *U-448* tracking convoy HX 258 (New York to Liverpool) in the North Atlantic.

ETO: Despite the Eighth Air Force's attempt to destroy the German Air Force in France as a precondition for the cross-Channel invasion, intelligence reports show that German fighter production has actually increased, as has the number of fighters available for combat in western Europe.

MEDITERRANEAN: Ninth Air Force and IX Bomber Command begin to redeploy from Egypt and Libya to England.

ITALY: Lieutenant General Sir Richard L. McCreery's X Corps captures Naples. Marshal Montgomery's Eighth Army captures the airfield at Foggia. Twelfth Air Force XII Bomber Command B-26 Marauders attack communication targets in the Capua, Grazzanise, Arce, and Mignano areas. B-24 Liberators bomb the aircraft factory at Wiener-Neustadt in Austria. XII Air Support Command aircraft attack Benevento, the bridge at Capua, and transportation targets near Isernia and Avezzano.

PACIFIC: U.S. submarine *Peto* torpedoes and sinks a Japanese transport and a cargo ship in the Carolines. U.S. submarine *Wahoo* torpedoes and sinks a Japanese cargo ship in the Sea of Japan.

SOLOMONS: Admiral William F. Halsey, COMSOPAC, informs General MacArthur of his intention to invade Bougainville on November 1.

NEW GEORGIA: Thirteenth Air Force B-24 Liberators bomb Japanese supply point and troops near Vila airfield on Kolombangara Island. B-25 Mitchells and P-38

Lightnings, along with navy SBD Dauntless dive-bombers, attack the barge depot at Kakasa on Choiseul Island.

NEW GUINEA: Fifth Air Force A-20 Havocs and Australian aircraft bomb and strafe the Finschhafen area in support of Australian ground forces.

October 2

CBI: Fourteenth Air Force P-40s attack Yangtze River shipping in the area near Chiuchiang, China.

The 51st Fighter Group receives the 25th and 26th Fighter Squadrons (with P-40s).

ETO: Eighth Air Force VIII Bomber Command attacks Emden, Germany, with 349 B-17s led by two B-17 Pathfinders with H2S radar and escorted by 227 P-47 Thunderbolts. Of the 339 bombers that hit the target, two B-17s are lost and 34 are damaged; aircrews claim at least 15 enemy fighters as confirmed kills. The P-47 pilots report one P-47 damaged and claim five enemy confirmed kills, two probable kills, and one possible. The VIII Air Support Command sends 72 B-26 Marauders against the St. Omer/Longuenesse airfield in France. Only six bombers hit the target due to cloud cover, but 12 B-26s are nevertheless damaged with one crewman killed and four wounded. Two B-17s join the Royal Air Force on a night raid against Munich, Germany.

ITALY: The 82nd Airborne Division enters Naples acting as the Allied security and occupation force. Despite bad weather, fighter-bombers of the XII Air Support Command attack targets and conduct reconnaissance missions in the Volturno Valley.

SOUTHWEST PACIFIC AREA: Fifth Air Force B-25 Mitchells strafe villages in the Talasea area and barges off Gasmata Island, while B-26 Marauders bomb Hoskins airfield. One B-24 bombs Cape Gloucester airfield.

U.S. submarine *Kingfish* lays mines off southern Celebes.

NEW GEORGIA: Thirteenth Air Force B-25 Mitchells and navy SBD Dauntless dive-bombers attack barges near Vila on Kolombangara Island.

October 3

CBI: In China, Fourteenth Air Force P-40s damage a vessel on the Yangtze River near Chiuchiang as four P-38 Lightnings bomb the docks at Chiuchiang. Off Hainan Island, six B-24 Liberators damage a freighter.

ETO: Eighth Air Force VIII Air Support Command B-26 Marauders attack the Amsterdam/Schiphol, Woensdrecht, and Haamstede airfields in the Netherlands. Of the 131 bombers that hit the targets, 47 B-26s are damaged. Another 63 B-26s bomb the Beauvais/Tille airfield in France. One bomber is lost and 27 are damaged. Only five crewmen are wounded in the raids.

ITALY: Twelfth Air Force XII Bomber Command B-26 Marauders, B-25 Mitchells, and P-38 Lightnings bomb rail and road bridges and a road junction at Capua, Castel Volturno, Piana, Arce, Mignano, and Isernia.

SOLOMONS: Thirteenth Air Force P-39 Airacobras strafe several barges west of Choiseul.

NEW BRITAIN: Fifth Air Force B-25 Mitchells attack supply barges along the west coast of the island.

NEW GUINEA: Japanese submarine *RO-108* torpedoes and sinks U.S. destroyer off eastern New Guinea.

October 4
CBI: The Fourteenth Air Force airfield at Kweilin is attacked by 17 Japanese bombers with 25 fighters providing escort. The bombers, avoiding U.S. fighters by flying above 20,000 feet, miss their target.

ATLANTIC: Aircraft from the carrier USS *Ranger* operating off the Norwegian coast attack a German-Norwegian convoy. TBF Avengers, SBD Dauntless dive-bombers, and F4F Wildcats sink four cargo ships and a German transport and damage a German tanker and three cargo ships. The Wildcats shoot down two German aircraft.

TBF Avengers from escort carrier USS *Card* with convoy UGS 19 (United States to Mediterranean, Slow) attack three German submarines north of the Azores, sinking *U-460* and *U-422*. *U-460* was in process of resupplying two other U-boats. In the North Atlantic, PV-1 patrol bombers overwatching convoy ONS 204 (Liverpool to Halifax, Slow) sink German submarine *U-336*.

ETO: Eighth Air Force VIII Bomber Command attacks industrial targets in Germany, escorted by 223 P-47 Thunderbolts. B-17s bomb Wiesbaden and Frankfurt. Five bombers are lost and 45 are damaged. Aircrews report 19 enemy aircraft destroyed. Another 37 B-17s bomb Frankfurt later in the morning, losing three bombers, and 35 others are damaged. Aircrews report 18 enemy fighters shot down. Over the Saarlautern industrial area and the St. Dizier/Robinson airfield, 105 bombers attack the targets, losing four B-17s while 23 others suffer damage. Aircrews report 37 enemy fighters destroyed. Over the Sarreguemnines and Saarbrucken marshaling yards, 47 B-17s hit their targets, with only two bombers damaged. A diversion flown by 38 B-24 Liberators results in four bombers lost and 19 damaged. Aircrews report that 13 enemy aircraft have been destroyed. The fighter pilots report 19 confirmed kills, one probable kill, and two possibles. U.S. losses are 16 P-47s damaged. Total casualties for these missions are four crewmen killed, 27 wounded, and 142 missing.

During the night four B-17s drop over 240,000 leaflets over Paris.

ITALY: Twelfth Air Force XII Bomber Command sends over 100 B-17s against the Pisa marshaling yard and Bolzano bridges. XII Air Support Command fighter-bombers attack trains, roads, rail lines, and vehicles near Isernia, Avezzano, Pescara, and Isolella.

MEDITERRANEAN: German bombers attack convoy UGS 18 (United States to Mediterranean, Slow) and damage a U.S. freighter off the coast of Algeria.

BOUGAINVILLE: Thirteenth Air Force B-24 Liberators, escorted by P-38 Lightnings and U.S. Navy F4U Corsairs, bomb Kahili airfield. About 30 Japanese fighters attempt to break up the attack and nine enemy aircraft are reported shot down. P-39 Airacobras and four Corsairs sink 18 supply barges located on the west coast of Choiseul Island.

October 5
MEDITERRANEAN: German bombers make another attack on convoy UGS 18 (United States to Mediterranean, Slow) and damage a second U.S. freighter off the coast of Algeria.

ITALY: Twelfth Air Force XII Bomber Command B-17s bomb the marshaling yard at Bologna. B-25 Mitchells and B-26 Marauders bomb the Formia road and Isernia. XII Air Support Command and RAF Desert Air Force aircraft bomb numerous targets around Isernia and Venafro.

PACIFIC: Navy Task Force 14, under command of Rear Admiral Alfred E. Montgomery and composed of six carriers, three heavy cruisers, four light cruisers, and 24 destroyers, bombards Wake Island. U.S. submarine *Wahoo* torpedoes and sinks a Japanese army transport in the Tsushima Straits.

CENTRAL PACIFIC: CINCPOA issues plans for a Central Pacific offensive. In the Gilbert Islands, Admiral Spruance is tasked to capture Makin, Tarawa, and Abemama. He is also to deny the Japanese the use of bases in the Marshall Islands and at Nauru. The offensive is to begin on November 19.

October 6

CBI: Fourteenth Air Force P-40s from Suichwan intercept 27 Japanese bombers and 21 fighters. The enemy loses one bomber and one fighter before turning back.

ITALY: The U.S. VI Corps establishes itself on the south bank of the Volturno River. Across the river valley are high hills where German forces are waiting. Since September 9, U.S. casualties have totaled nearly 4,900 men, with the 36th Infantry Division taking nearly 40 percent of these casualties. Some battalions of the 36th Infantry are down to less than 100 men.

Twelfth Air Force XII Bomber Command B-17s bomb the marshaling yard at Mestre. B-26 Marauders attack Isernia and the road junction at Formia. Northwest African Air Force aircraft hit targets at Teano, Alfedena, and Capua. XII Air Support Command P-40s and A-36 Intruder (Apache) fighter-bombers attack roads and vehicles in support of Fifth Army.

SOUTHWEST PACIFIC AREA: U.S. submarine *Kingfish* lands men and supplies on northeast coast of Borneo.

Fifth Air Force B-25 Mitchells bomb and strafe targets of opportunity on New Britain.

PACIFIC: U.S. submarine *Skate* is attacked and damaged by Japanese aircraft off Wake Island, but remains on patrol. U.S. submarine *Steelhead* torpedoes and damages a Japanese fast fleet tanker southwest of Guam. U.S. submarine *Tinosa* later finishes off the tanker northwest of Truk. U.S. submarine *Wahoo* torpedoes and sinks a Japanese army cargo ship in the Sea of Japan.

Navy Task Force 14 continues to bombard Wake Island. Fearing that the bombardment is a prelude to an amphibious landing, Rear Admiral Sakaibara Shigematsu orders the execution of 98 American civilian contractors, who have been kept on the island since its capture by the Japanese on December 23, 1941.

BOUGAINVILLE: Kahili airfield is attacked by 24 B-25 Mitchells and 14 P-38 Lightnings. Thirteenth Air Force P-39 Airacobras and U.S. Navy F4U Corsairs strafe barges off the west coast of Choiseul Island.

NEW GEORGIA: BATTLE OF VELLA LAVELLA As nine Japanese destroyers begin a nighttime evacuation of troops from Vella Lavella Island, three U.S. destroyers attack. All three U.S. destroyers are damaged by torpedoes and one destroyer is scuttled. U.S. torpedoes sink one Japanese destroyer.

October 7

CBI: Fourteenth Air Force B-25 Mitchells attack a freighter south of Amoy, China, causing heavy damage. B-24 Liberators bomb the cement plant at Haiphong, French Indochina.

ATLANTIC: German submarine *U-645* torpedoes and sinks a U.S. freighter in convoy SC 143 (Halifax Slow to United Kingdom) in the North Atlantic.

ETO: Four B-17s from Eighth Air Force drop 240,000 leaflets over Paris during the night. Ninth Air Force's 434th Troop Carrier Group with C-47s arrives at Fulbeck, England, from the United States.

PACIFIC: U.S. submarine *S-44* is sunk by Japanese escort destroyer east of the Kamchatka Peninsula.

October 8

CBI: Fourteenth Air Force B-24 Liberators, supported by P-40s, bomb Gia Lam airfield in French Indochina. B-24 Liberators bomb facilities and a headquarters at Tengchung, China.

ETO: Eighth Air Force VIII Bomber Command B-17s attack the Bremen shipyard and industrial facilities using airborne transmitters for the first time to jam German radar. The shipyard is hit by 105 B-17s. U.S. losses are nine bombers shot down and 61 damaged; aircrews report over 40 enemy aircraft destroyed. Another 53 B-17s hit the industrial area, losing four bombers and suffering damage to 44 others; aircrews report 24 enemy fighters destroyed. The U-boat yards at Vegesack are bombed by 43 B-24 Liberators. Three B-24s are lost and 21 are damaged; aircrews report 17 fighters destroyed. Later in the afternoon Bremen is again bombed by 156 B-17s. This time 14 bombers are shot down and 112 are damaged; aircrews report over 90 enemy fighters shot down. The raid over Bremen is escorted by 274 P-47 Thunderbolts. The pilots report 12 confirmed kills, two probables, and four possibles. Three P-47s are lost and five are damaged. Total casualties for this raid are four crewmen killed, 58 wounded, and 304 missing. VIII Air Support Command B-26 Marauders attack the Lille/Vendeville and Chievres airfields in France. Although the mission is aborted due to bad weather over the target, four B-26s are damaged. Two VIII Bomber Command B-17s drop 266,000 leaflets over Rennes during the night.

ITALY: The 30th Infantry Regiment of the 3rd Infantry Division drives the last German defenders over the Volturno River. General Lucian K. Truscott outlines a plan for the division to assault German positions on the hills across the Volturno River. The 7th and 15th Infantry Regiments will make the main attack while a battalion of the 15th Infantry conducts a diversion on the left flank.

MEDITERRANEAN: Twelfth Air Force XII Bomber Command B-24 Liberators bomb airfields in Athens and on Crete and Rhodes, in Greece. B-25 Mitchells also bomb an airfield in Athens.

SOUTHWEST PACIFIC AREA: U.S. submarine *Guardfish* torpedoes and sinks a Japanese cargo ship near the Admiralty Islands. U.S. submarine *Gurnard* torpedoes and sinks a Japanese cargo ship and a transport off northern Luzon, Philippines.

PACIFIC: Major General Charles D. Barrett, commander of I Marine Amphibious Corps, dies suddenly and Lieutenant General Alexander A. Vandegrift returns to temporary command.

U.S. submarine *Gato* torpedoes a Japanese cargo ship south of Truk, but the torpedo fails to explode. *Gato* escapes the attack of an escorting torpedo boat.

October 9

ALEUTIANS: Attu Island is bombed by 12 Japanese bombers based in the Kuriles.

CBI: Fourteenth Air Force B-25 Mitchells attack a tanker, other vessels, near Amoy and Quemoy islands off the coast of China. One B-25 is lost. P-40s bomb a fuel storage area and a barracks at Mangshih, China; one P-40 is shot down by ground fire.

ETO: Eighth Air Force VIII Bomber Command attacks targets in Germany and Poland to assist the advance of the Soviet army. Over Anklam, Germany, 106 B-17s hit the industrial area and lose 18 bombers and another 52 damaged; aircrews report at least 65 enemy fighters shot down. Over the Marienburg, Germany, industrial area, 96 B-17s hit the target with a loss of two bombers and damage to 13 others; aircrews report nine enemy fighters destroyed. The U-boat yards and the port area of Danzig (Gdańsk), Poland, are bombed by 41 B-24 Liberators; two bombers are lost and 20 others are damaged; aircrews report seven enemy fighters destroyed. Over 100 B-17s hit the port area at Gdynia, Poland. Enemy losses are estimated at over 40 aircraft, but six U.S. bombers are lost and 63 are damaged. VIII Air Support Command sends 72 B-26 Marauders to bomb the Woensdrecht airfield in the Neth-

A B-17 bomber of the Eighth Air Force hits an industrial target over Marienburg, Germany, on October 9, 1943.

erlands. Of the 66 bombers that hit the target, 26 are damaged. At the completion of this mission, the B-26s will be transferred from Eighth Air Force to Ninth Air Force. The total casualties for this mission are 35 wounded and 266 missing.

MEDITERRANEAN: Twelfth Air Force XII Bomber Command B-17s bomb airfields at Larissa, Athens, and Salonika in Greece. B-24 Liberators hit Kastelli/Pediada airfield on Crete.

ITALY: A U.S. destroyer is torpedoed and sunk by German submarine *U-616* in the Gulf of Salerno.

SOUTHWEST PACIFIC AREA: U.S. submarine *Kingfish* torpedoes and sinks a Japanese oiler in the Sulu Sea. U.S. submarine *Puffer* torpedoes and sinks a Japanese tanker in Makassar Strait but suffers damage from a depth charge attack and must terminate its patrol. U.S. submarine *Rasher* torpedoes and sinks a Japanese cargo ship in the Banda Sea.

PACIFIC: U.S. submarine *Wahoo* torpedoes and sinks a Japanese cargo ship in the Sea of Japan.

SOLOMONS: Thirteenth Air Force B-25 Mitchells and P-40s attack barges and troop concentrations on Choiseul Island. P-39 Airacobras and navy F4U Corsairs strafe buildings, a radar station, and gun positions at Poporang Island.

NEW GUINEA: Fifth Air Force A-20 Havocs and Australian aircraft bomb and strafe Japanese defensive positions near Finschhafen. B-24 Liberators bomb Makassar on Celebes Island.

October 10

CBI: Tenth Air Force sends seven B-24 Liberators against the Meza railroad bridge in Burma, causing serious damage. Fourteenth Air Force B-24 Liberators, with an escort of 18 P-40s, attack port facilities at Haiphong, French Indochina. In China, P-40s bomb ammunition supplies at Tengchung and a supply dump and targets of opportunity in the Lungling area.

ETO: Eighth Air Force VIII Bomber Command B-17s escorted by 216 P-47 Thunderbolts attack transportation targets near Munster, Germany. A total of 236 bombers hit the target as well as targets of opportunity at Coesfeld, Germany, and at the Enschede airfield in the Netherlands. Aircrews report over 180 enemy aircraft destroyed, but 30 B-17s are lost and 105 are damaged. Fighter pilots report 19 confirmed enemy kills; one P-47 is lost and three are damaged. Total U.S. losses for this mission are two crewmen killed, 18 wounded, and 307 missing.

ITALY: The 34th Infantry Division completes preparations for its attack across the Volturno River on the 3rd Infantry Division's right flank. The three regiments are to seize the hills behind the town of Squille. The 45th Infantry Division, approaching the Volturno River on VI Corps's right flank, continues to clear enemy delaying its advance.

MEDITERRANEAN: Twelfth Air Force B-17s bomb airfields at Athens, Greece. B-24 Liberators bomb the Maritsa airfield on Rhodes and the Calato and Heraklion airfields on Crete.

PACIFIC: U.S. submarine *Bonefish* torpedoes and sinks a Japanese cargo ship and a merchant transport off Cam Ranh Bay, French Indochina. U.S. submarine *Grayback* makes an unsuccessful attack on a Japanese troopship east of the Ryukyu Islands. U.S. submarine *Kingfish* lays mines in Makassar Strait.

BOUGAINVILLE: Thirteenth Air Force sends 24 B-24 Liberators, escorted by P-38 Lightnings, P-40s, P-39 Airacobras, and over 50 navy fighters and dive-bombers, to attack Kahili airfield and the supply areas. American pilots report 15 Japanese aircraft are shot down.

October 11

CBI: Fourteenth Air Force sends eight B-24 Liberators to bomb the area near Teng-chung, China, and Sadon and Myitkyina in Burma.

MEDITERRANEAN: Twelfth Air Force XII Bomber Command B-25 Mitchells bomb Garitsa airfield and P-38 Lightnings attack shipping in Corfu harbor.

PACIFIC: U.S. submarine *Skipjack* torpedoes and damages a Japanese transport off Kwajalein. U.S. submarine *Wahoo* is sunk by Japanese naval aircraft, submarine chasers, and a minesweeper in La Perouse Strait off northern Hokkaido, Japan.

GUADALCANAL: Japanese aircraft conduct a torpedo attack on U.S. shipping off Koli Point, damaging two cargo ships.

BOUGAINVILLE: Thirteenth Air Force sends 22 B-24 Liberators and more than 30 U.S. Navy SBD dauntless dive-bombers against Kahili airfield. Supply areas and the airfield are hit. Aircrews report that 12 Japanese airplanes are destroyed.

NEW BRITAIN: Photoreconnaissance over Rabaul reveals the Japanese building up air power. At least 128 bombers and 145 fighters are located on the three major airfields.

NEW GUINEA: Colonel Neel E. Kearby volunteers to lead a flight of four fighters to conduct an aerial reconnaissance of the Japanese airfield at Wewak. Kearby completes his mission and spots a Japanese fighter below him. Kearby dives down and destroys the fighter; shortly thereafter, Kearby's group spots 12 bombers accompanied by 36 fighters. Kearby gives the signal to attack and he quickly shoots down three fighters. Kearby then shoots down two fighters that are attacking one of his pilots. After breaking off the attack and assembling his flight, Kearby returns to base. For his great skill and daring in facing overwhelming odds, Colonel Kearby will be awarded the Medal of Honor.

October 12

CBI: Fourteenth Air Force sends five B-24 Liberators to bomb the warehouse area and railroad yards at Myitkyina, Burma.

ATLANTIC: TBF Avengers from escort carrier USS *Card* attack a German U-boat refueling operation north of the Azores. *U-731* is damaged in the attack.

PACIFIC: U.S. submarine *Cero* torpedoes and sinks a Japanese stores ship off Chichi Jima.

NEW BRITAIN: Fifth Air Force leads a major air offensive against the main Japanese naval and air base at Rabaul in order to isolate and neutralize it. Almost 350 B-24 Liberators, B-25 Mitchells, P-38 Lightnings, and Australian aircraft bomb Rabaul, the harbor, and the airfields. Aircrews report at least 50 enemy aircraft destroyed. Two transports are sunk, three destroyers and an oiler are damaged, and nine other vessels are hit. Ammunition storage areas are also heavily damaged.

October 13

CBI: Japanese fighters arrive over Sumprabum, Burma, to attack U.S. transports flying supplies to China over the Himalayas (the Hump). Three transports are shot down. To protect the Hump flights, P-40s attack the Japanese fighter base at Myitkyina.

ATLANTIC: TBF Avengers from escort carrier USS *Card* sink German submarine *U-402* in the North Atlantic.

MEDITERRANEAN: Italy declares war on Germany.

German submarine *U-371* torpedoes and sinks a U.S. destroyer off Bône, Algeria.

ITALY: The VI Corps attacks German defenses across the Volturno River. The 7th and 15th Infantry Regiments of the 3rd Infantry Division capture the heights dominating the river valley. The division is able to move all of its battalions across the river by the end of the day. Engineers begin bridging the river to bring tanks, artillery, and supplies to the forward lines. The 34th Infantry Division captures its objectives and moves to the junction of the Calore and Volturno Rivers. The 179th and 180th Infantry Regiments of the 45th Infantry Division clear the enemy from Monte Acero.

Twelfth Air Force XII Bomber Command B-25 Mitchells and B-26 Marauders bomb the town of Alife, a road junction at Sessa Aurunca, and the airfield at Tirana. XII Air Support Command, with RAF Desert Air Force fighters, supports the Fifth Army with attacks on enemy troops, transportation, and lines of communication, especially around Ortona, Giulianova, and Campobasso.

Captain Arlo L. Olson's company leads the advance of the 15th Infantry Regiment, 3rd Infantry Division as it crosses the Volturno River. As he wades into the chest-deep water, a German machine-gun opens fire on him. Upon reaching the opposite side, he knocks out the position with two hand grenades. Another enemy machine-gun position about 150 yards away begins firing at the company. With complete disregard for his own safety, Captain Olson approaches the enemy despite enemy bullets and hand grenades. Olson kills the five German soldiers in the position and continues to advance. The next position, defended by nine soldiers, also falls to Olson's fire. Over the next 13 days, Captain Olson continues to lead his men forward until he is killed on October 27, 1943. On that day, in two extraordinary acts of heroism he destroys an enemy defensive position singlehandedly with only his pistol, then leads a successful attack against German infantry defending the slopes of Monte San Nicola. Severely wounded in the aftermath of the battle, Captain Olson establishes a defensive perimeter and refuses medical aid until all of his men have been taken care of first. He dies as he is being evacuated. Olson's extraordinary dedication to duty and his selfless acts of courage will win him the Medal of Honor.

SOUTHWEST PACIFIC AREA: U.S. submarine *Rasher* attacks a Japanese convoy, sinking a cargo ship in the Banda Sea.

PACIFIC: U.S. submarine *Seadragon* conducts an unsuccessful attack on a Japanese ammunition ship and an auxiliary submarine chaser near Kwajalein. *Seadragon* avoids the response attack.

NEW BRITAIN: Fifth Air Force sends over 100 B-24 Liberators and B-25 Mitchells against Rabaul, but bad weather aborts the mission. B-24 Liberators attack targets at Hoskins, Lindenhafen, Cape Gloucester, and Gasmata Island.

October 14

CBI: Fourteenth Air Force sends four B-25 Mitchells to attack shipping and the airfield near Amoy.

ETO: Eighth Air Force VIII Bomber Command B-17s return to Schweinfurt, Germany, to attack the ball bearing plants. Of the 229 B-17s that hit the target, 60 bombers are lost to especially strong enemy fighter attack and 145 are damaged. Aircrews report over 180 enemy fighters destroyed. The total casualties for this mission are five crewmen killed, 40 wounded, and 594 missing. U.S. bomber crew casualties have been so heavy over the past month that daylight bombing against strategic targets without fighter escort deep into Germany is suspended for a short period.

ITALY: Lieutenant General Mark W. Clark changes the U.S. VI Corps to a two-division front, pulling the 45th Infantry Division back. The 3rd and 34th Infantry Divisions are to advance to take control of the upper Volturno valley. The valley is narrow and broken by deep ravines and steep brush-covered ridges. The weather continues to deteriorate, with rain and fog a constant condition.

Twelfth Air Force XII Bomber Command B-17s bomb the Terni marshaling yard. B-25 Mitchells attack the airfield at Argos, while B-17s and B-24 Liberators attack the Giulianova bridge. XII Air Support Command and RAF Desert Air Force aircraft attack transportation assets near the front lines at the Volturno River.

SOUTHWEST PACIFIC AREA: SWPA headquarters issues an outline plan for the attack on New Britain. The 7th Marine Regiment, 1st Marine Division, will land between Cape Gloucester and Borgen Bay with two battalion landing teams (BLT) organized as Combat Team C. One separate BLT will land near Taual. Combat Team B will act as the reserve.

PACIFIC: Admiral Nimitz, CINCPOA, issues instructions for planners to focus on the capture of Kwajalein, Wotje, and Maloelap. The tentative planning date for the beginning of the Marshalls offensive is January 1, 1944. By use of carrier-based airpower to compensate for land-based aircraft, Nimitz believes the isolated islands can be captured quickly. The Central Pacific offensive has the advantage of being able to cut the Japanese off from oil supplies in the Netherlands East Indies and place American land-based airpower within range of the Japanese home islands. For Nimitz, the offensive also offers the possibility of a major open sea battle against the Japanese fleet, something both American and Japanese naval planners and strategists have been anticipating for years.

U.S. submarine *Grayback* torpedoes and sinks a Japanese fleet tanker in the East China Sea.

NEW BRITAIN: Fifth Air Force sends over 60 B-25 Mitchells against the airfield and supply points at Cape Gloucester.

October 15

ATLANTIC: German submarine *U-371* torpedoes and damages a U.S. freighter in a convoy off the coast of Morocco. The ship is beached and later lost.

ETO: Lieutenant General Ira C. Eaker, Commanding General Eighth Air Force, also commands a new headquarters intended to provide a unified command and control structure for the Eighth and the Ninth Air Forces titled U.S. Army Air Forces in United Kingdom (USAAFUK).

MEDITERRANEAN: Twelfth Air Force XII Bomber Command sends B-25 Mitchells to attack airfields at Salonika and Megalo Mikra in Greece.

ITALY: The 7th Infantry Regiment of the 3rd Infantry Division captures Cisterna.

PACIFIC: U.S. submarine *Tullibee* attacks a Japanese convoy, sinking a transport in the Formosa Straits.

SOLOMONS: The I Marine Amphibious Corps issues an order for an amphibious assault on Bougainville at Empress Augusta Bay to seize Cape Torokina at the south end of the bay and establish a perimeter.

BOUGAINVILLE: Thirteenth Air Force sends 21 B-24 Liberators, with two P-38 Lightnings and 17 navy F4U Corsairs as escort, to bomb Kahili airfield and its supply base. Aircrews report six enemy fighters shot down.

NEW GUINEA: Fifth Air Force P-38 Lightnings and P-40s intercept about 100 Japanese aircraft intending to attack Allied shipping in Oro Bay. The fighter pilots claim 40 confirmed kills. Over Finschhafen, four P-40s report intercepting over 20 Japanese aircraft and shooting down five of them.

October 16

ETO: The Ninth Air Force is established at Sunninghill, England, as a tactical air force. The new commander is Lieutenant General Lewis H. Brereton.

ITALY: Twelfth Air Force XII Bomber Command B-25 Mitchells bomb the marshaling yard, rail lines, and industrial targets around Bologna.

PACIFIC: U.S. submarine *Mingo* makes an unsuccessful attack on the Japanese escort carrier *Chuyo* northwest of Truk and avoids a depth charge attack.

BOUGAINVILLE: Thirteenth Air Force sends eight B-24 Liberators to bomb Kara airfield. Later, six B-25 Mitchells bomb the airfield on Ballale Island.

NEW GUINEA: Fifth Air Force sends over 60 B-25 Mitchells to attack the Alexishafen area and bomb the Wewak airfield. A-20 Havocs bomb and strafe targets on Gasmata Island off New Britain.

October 17

CBI: Colonel Lewis A. Pick arrives in-theater to take charge of the construction of the Ledo Road. Beginning in Ledo, India, it is intended to link with the original Burma Road. Pick will follow as best as possible an old caravan route through northern Burma. The 849th and the 1883rd Aviation Engineer Battalions and the 382nd Construction Battalion will play a large role in the construction. These all-black units, along with the all-white 330th Engineer General Service Regiment and the 209th Engineer Battalion, will do a large share of this enormous undertaking. Black Americans make up about 60 percent of the 15,000 men assigned to this mission.

ITALY: Elements of the 168th Infantry of the 34th Infantry Division capture Alvignano.

Twelfth Air Force Allied aircraft of Northwest African Tactical Air Force attack targets near Teano and Alife and motor transport targets at Benedello, Penna, and

Pedesso. Enemy troops and vehicles are attacked at Vinchiaturo, Benedello, Teramo, and Sparanise.

PACIFIC: U.S. submarine *Tarpon* torpedoes and sinks a German auxiliary cruiser off Chichi Jima.

NEW GUINEA: Fifth Air Force B-25 Mitchells bomb Wewak and Boram airfields and report that 15 enemy aircraft have been destroyed on the ground and four others as confirmed kills in the air. Four P-39 Airacobras intercept 18 Japanese aircraft over Finschhafen and report six enemy aircraft shot down. Over Oro Bay, P-40s and P-38 Lightnings shoot down 24 Japanese aircraft.

Private Nathan Van Noy, Jr., is a member of Headquarters Company, Shore Battalion, Engineer Boat and Shore Regiment at Finschhafen, New Guinea. He is manning a machine-gun position about five yards from the shoreline when he is alerted that three Japanese troop barges are approaching the beach. As Van Noy peers over his sights in the early morning darkness, the barges appear. One barge is immediately hit by direct fire, but the other two land only ten yards from Van Noy's position. Although fully exposed, he engages the enemy troops until his ammunition is expended, killing at least 20 soldiers. During the course of the fight, he is wounded numerous times and, refusing to withdraw, dies at his post. His heroism and fighting spirit not only saved the lives of many of his comrades, but also will win him the Medal of Honor.

ETO: Major General Elwood R. "Pete" Quesada takes command of the IX Fighter Command.

ITALY: XII Air Support Command A-36 Intruder (Apache) fighter-bombers bomb the rail yards at Venafro. Fighters attack airfields around Rome and also hit Viterbo, Grosseto, the seaplane base at Bracciano, and attack trains connecting Rome and Orte and Rome and Naples. A-20 Havocs bomb the road and railway near Cassino and roads, bridges, and vehicles near Minturno and Chieti.

PACIFIC: U.S. submarine *Flying Fish* attacks Yokosuka-bound Japanese escort carrier *Chuyo* north of Guam, but fails to damage the carrier. U.S. submarine *Lapon* torpedoes and sinks a Japanese cargo ship off Shikoku, Japan, and fires two torpedoes at an auxiliary minesweeper, both of which fail to explode. U.S. submarine *Silversides* torpedoes and sinks a Japanese cargo ship north of the Marianas.

SOLOMONS: Thirteenth Air Force B-24 Liberators and SBD Dauntless dive-bombers, with over 50 fighters flying escort, bomb the airfield on Ballale Island. Over Choiseul Island 14 P-39 Airacobras and over 20 navy fighters conduct strafing attacks on Japanese positions.

NEW BRITAIN: Despite bad weather over the target, Fifth Air Force B-25 Mitchells bomb Rabaul from treetop and mast-height level. Aircrews report two vessels sunk and 70 enemy aircraft destroyed on the ground and in the air. B-24 Liberators diverted from Rabaul, bomb Cape Hoskins and Cape Gloucester.

October 19

ATLANTIC: THE MOSCOW CONFERENCE BEGINS U.S. secretary of state Cordell Hull, British foreign minister Anthony Eden, and Vyacheslav Molotov, the Soviet foreign minister, meet to discuss political conditions related to the end of the war in Europe.

ITALY: The 3rd and 34th Infantry Divisions begin to close on Dragoni to capture the important bridges over the Volturno River north of the town. The 168th Infantry Regiment of the 34th Infantry Division captures the town without a fight as the Germans withdraw. The 135th Infantry Regiment prepares to cross the Volturno to cut off the enemy and capture Alife.

XII Air Support Command, Northwest African Tactical Air Force, and RAF Desert Air Force aircraft attack enemy forces, supply bases, and transport near Boiano and Viterbo. Cassino and Anzio are also attacked as well as trains near Barisciano and troops near Mintumo.

BOUGAINVILLE: Thirteenth Air Force B-24 Liberators, PV-1 Ventura medium bombers, P-38 Lightnings, P-40s, and Navy fighters and Dauntless dive-bombers attack Kara and Kahili airfields.

October 20

CBI: Tenth Air Force B-25 Mitchells return to the bridge at Meza, Burma, to prevent further repairs on the bridge.

ATLANTIC: Aircraft from escort carrier *Core* with convoy UGS 20 (United States to Mediterranean, Slow) sink German submarine *U-378* north of the Azores.

At the Moscow Conference, the Soviets are briefed on Overlord (the overall plan for the invasion of Western Europe) but only the broadest details are provided.

ETO: Eighth Air Force VIII Bomber Command sends B-17s against industrial targets at Düren, Germany. Only 97 of the 170 B-17s sent hit the target, largely due to cloud cover and the failure of Oboe radar equipment, intended to allow accurate bombing despite cloud cover over a target. Pathfinder B-17s, guided by Oboe radar receivers on a curved course, will approach the target release point. At that point, the home station sends a second radar signal. The intersection of these two signals is the cue for the lead bombardier to release his bomb load. The other bombers will follow, releasing at the same point.

Another 42 bombers hit the Woensdrecht airfield in the Netherlands, but the target of opportunity costs the U.S. nine B-17s shot down and 11 damaged. Enemy losses are estimated to be at least four aircraft destroyed.

During the night, five B-17s drop over 876,000 leaflets over Rouen and Paris.

ITALY: Twelfth Air Force XII Bomber Command B-17s, B-26 Marauders, B-25 Mitchells, and P-38 Lightnings bomb airfields north and east of Rome. XII Air Support Command, Northwest African Air Force aircraft attack gun positions, trucks, and lines of communication near Cassino, where the Germans are preparing a new defensive line.

SOUTHWEST PACIFIC AREA: General MacArthur responds to the CCS offensive plan in the Pacific with an alternative schedule that proposes Rabaul be neutralized by February 1 by the capture of Hansa Bay, New Guinea, capture of the Admiralties, and the capture of Kavieng, New Ireland. By October, the Vogelkop Peninsula will be captured, along with Halmahera and Manado islands in the northeast Celebes in December. By February 1945 SWPA forces will be ready for an invasion of Mindanao in the Philippines.

PACIFIC: U.S. submarine *Gato* torpedoes and sinks a Japanese transport between Truk and Kavieng, New Ireland. U.S. submarine *Kingfish* torpedoes and sinks a Japanese cargo ship south of Nha Trang, French Indochina.

SOLOMONS: COMAIRSOLS headquarters moves to Munda airfield on New Georgia.
BOUGAINVILLE: Thirteenth Air Force P-40s and nearly fifty navy F4U Corsairs attack Kahili. Corsair pilots report three enemy fighters destroyed. Kakasa on Choiseul Island is attacked by PV-1 Venturas, P-40s, and navy fighters and SBD Dauntless dive-bombers.
NEW BRITAIN: A-20 Havocs attack Gasmata Island.

October 21

CBI: Fourteenth Air Force sends six B-24 Liberators to bomb Nawlang, Burma. Aircrews report destroying an enemy barracks.
ATLANTIC: Aircraft from escort carrier *Core* damage German submarine *U-271* north of the Azores.
ITALY: Twelfth Air Force XII Bomber Command B-17s bomb a railroad viaduct at Terni and rail and road bridges in Albania. B-24 Liberators attack the Orvieto railroad bridge. B-26 Marauders and B-25 Mitchells bomb the bridges and rail lines. P-38 Lightnings bomb a radar station at Pellegrino and the marshaling yard at Skopje, Yugoslavia. Allied aircraft attack troops and the railroad near Cassino.
PACIFIC: U.S. submarine *Steelhead* torpedoes and damages a Japanese aircraft transport east of Yap.
BOUGAINVILLE: Thirteenth Air Force sends 12 B-25 Mitchells with an escort of 36 fighters to attack Kara airfield
NEW GUINEA: Fifth Air Force sends over 50 B-24 Liberators and 19 B-25 Mitchells to bomb Japanese positions near Sattelberg. P-40s bomb Gasmata Island off New Britain and attack two Japanese light cruisers off New Ireland. One cruiser is reported damaged.

October 22

ATLANTIC: The Combined Chiefs of Staff approves the plan proposed by the U.S. Joint Chiefs of Staff to create a new, numbered air force in Italy from part of the Twelfth Air Force to be used to support the strategic bombing campaign in Germany and support Allied ground operations in Italy.
ETO: Ninth Air Force B-26 Marauders bomb Evreux/Fauville airfield in France, but most of the bombers abort due to bad weather.
ITALY: Twelfth Air Force XII Bomber Command B-26 Marauders bomb railroad bridges near Orvieto. B-25 Mitchells bomb a railroad bridge near Grosseto. The XII Air Support Command and Northwest African Air Force aircraft conduct ground support missions north of the Volturno River, attacking gun positions, strongpoints, and targets of opportunity.
PACIFIC: U.S. submarine *Grayback* torpedoes and sinks a Japanese transport in the East China Sea. U.S. submarine *Shad* makes an unsuccessful attack on two Japanese light cruisers in the East China Sea.
SOLOMONS: The I Marine Amphibious Corps develops plans for the 2nd Marine Parachute Battalion to raid Choiseul as a diversion prior to the landing on Bougainville.
BOUGAINVILLE: Thirteenth Air Force sends 22 B-24 Liberators, P-39 Airacobras, and P-40s, along with about 160 navy fighters and dive-bombers against Kahili and Kara airfields. Kahili airfield is rendered unserviceable after this raid. Choiseul Island is

bombed by B-24 Liberators and navy aircraft. One B-24 claims hits on a carrier off Buka Island.

NEW GUINEA: Fifth Air Force B-25 Mitchells bomb Wewak and sink two small cargo ships. The bombers also hit barges and parked aircraft. P-39 Airacobras and Australian air force aircraft strafe targets near Madang. Other P-40s attack Gasmata Island off New Britain.

October 23

CBI: Tenth Air Force B-25 Mitchells conduct a bombing raid on the Meza railroad bridge in Burma in an attempt to halt repairs.

ITALY: Twelfth Air Force XII Bomber Command B-26 Marauders bomb railroad and road bridges at Marsicano and Montalto di Castro. XII Air Support Command, RAF Desert Air Force, and Northwest African Air Force aircraft attack troops, vehicles, lines of communication, and gun positions from Gaeta to Isernia and from Vairano to Ancona. German aircraft attack U.S. shipping off Naples and hit a freighter carrying gasoline. The fire burns for 64 hours.

PACIFIC: U.S. submarine *Silversides* torpedoes and sinks a Japanese fleet tanker and two cargo ships north of the Admiralty Islands.

BOUGAINVILLE: Thirteenth Air Force sends 11 B-24 Liberators and 16 P-38 Lightnings to bomb Kahili airfield. Kara airfield is attacked by 36 P-40s and P-39 Airacobras, along with navy dive-bombers and fighters. Another combined strike by B-24 Liberators, army and navy fighters, and 42 navy SBD Dauntless dive-bombers hits both airfields later in the day. B-24s bomb Kakasa on Choiseul Island.

NEW BRITAIN: Fifth Air Force sends over 40 B-24 Liberators, escorted by P-38 Lightnings, to bomb the Rapopo airstrip. Aircrews report 20 enemy aircraft destroyed on the ground and another 20 fighters destroyed in the air.

October 24

CBI: Fourteenth Air Force B-24 Liberators, with 13 P-40s as escort, attack a barracks compound at Co Bi in French Indochina.

ETO: Ninth Air Force sends 200 B-26 Marauders against the Montdidier, Beauvais/Nivillers, and Saint-Andre-de-L'Eure airfields in France.

MEDITERRANEAN: Twelfth Air Force XII Bomber Command B-24 Liberators bomb the aircraft plant at Wiener-Neustadt in Austria.

ITALY: The 133rd Infantry Regiment of the 34th Infantry Division attacks north past San Angelo d'Alife, battling German tanks, artillery, infantry, and minefields to capture the hills above the town. The battalion suffers over 200 casualties in three days of fighting.

B-25 Mitchells attack the airfield at Tirana, a railroad bridge near Orvieto, and a viaduct at Terni. The XII Air Support Command, the Northwest African Air Force, and the RAF Desert Air Force bomb lines of communication and conduct ground support missions near Formia, Minturno, Sessa Aurunca, and Frosolone.

PACIFIC: Navy PBY Catalinas sink one Japanese destroyer and damage another near Truk.

BOUGAINVILLE: Thirteenth Air Force B-25 Mitchells, Royal New Zealand Air Force P-40s, and U.S. Navy F4U Corsairs attack Kahili airfield, followed shortly by another group of army and navy fighters accompanying over 70 navy SBD Dauntless dive-bombers, which also bomb the target.

New Britain: Fifth Air Force B-25 Mitchells, escorted by over 50 P-38 Lightnings, report destroying 45 Japanese bombers on the ground at Vunakanau, Rapopo, and Tobera airstrips. Aircrews also report 40 enemy fighters destroyed in the air. Marine aircraft sink a Japanese destroyer southwest of Rabaul.

October 25

CBI: Fourteenth Air Force P-40s and B-25 Mitchells attack Haiphong and shipping in the Gulf of Tonkin. Boats, barges, a cargo ship, and a tanker are reported sunk or damaged.

Italy: Twelfth Air Force XII Bomber Command P-39 Airacobras attack the landing ground at Podgorica. XII Air Support Command, Northwest African Air Force, and RAF Desert Air Force attack lines of communication, bridges, radio stations, and trains near Frosinone, Formia, Gaeta, and Cetraro.

Pacific: U.S. submarine *Tullibee* makes an unsuccessful attack on a Japanese transport in the East China Sea.

New Britain: Fifth Air Force sends over 60 B-24 Liberators to bomb Rabaul. Aircrews report over 20 enemy aircraft destroyed on the ground and another 30 in the air. A-20 Havocs conduct ground support missions near Lae in New Guinea.

October 26

CBI: Fourteenth Air Force sends 13 B-24 Liberators and 15 P-40s to attack the railroad yards at Haiphong in French Indochina. B-25 Mitchells attack shipping at Kiungshan, China. Two B-25s are lost; aircrews report a tanker and a transport sunk.

B-24s begin flying the southern Hump route (the aerial resupply route to China flown over the Himalaya Mountains) to prevent Japanese fighters from taking such a heavy toll on unarmed transport aircraft. The heavily armed bombers lure the enemy fighters to make an attack, then blast them at close range with machine-gun fire. Using this tactic, bomber crews report 18 enemy fighters shot down.

Mediterranean: Twelfth Air Force XII Bomber Command B-25 Mitchells and P-38 Lightnings attack Salonika/Sedhes and Megalo Mikra airfields in Greece.

Italy: The XII Air Support Command and RAF Desert Air Force aircraft attack gun emplacements and report destroying vehicles and parked aircraft in the Ancona area.

Southwest Pacific Area: Fifth Air Force B-24 Liberators attack Pombelaa on Celebes Island. Japanese fighters shoot down two B-24 Liberators. Aircrews report 11 enemy fighters shot down.

Pacific: Navy PBY Catalina damages a Japanese destroyer off the eastern coast of New Ireland.

Bougainville: Thirteenth Air Force B-24 Liberators, B-25 Mitchells, P-38 Lightnings, P-40s, P-39 Airacobras, and navy fighters and dive-bombers attack Kahili airfield. Navy fighters and SBD Dauntless dive-bombers, along with army P-39 Airacobras and P-40s, attack Kara airfield. The Buka Island airfield is attacked by B-25 Mitchells and P-38 Lightnings.

October 27

CBI: In China, Fourteenth Air Force sends six B-24 Liberators to bomb Tungting Lake area as 60,000 Japanese troops begin an offensive that will last into December. Aircrews report eight enemy fighters shot down.

ATLANTIC: General Marshall rejects MacArthur's October 20 proposed offensive plan in the Pacific, noting that it requires too many resources to undertake.

MEDITERRANEAN: Twelfth Air Force sends over 150 B-17s and B-24 Liberators to bomb the Wiener-Neustadt aircraft factory and rail lines and bridges at Friedberg and Ebenfurth in Austria.

ITALY: The 2nd Battalion of the 135th Infantry Regiment, reinforced by tanks, attempts to capture Hill 235, the dominant terrain that controls the valley near Raviscanna. The 135th makes no progress and the 2nd Battalion of the 168th moves to the attack. The entire 34th Division's advance is held up for 48 hours until the Germans give up Hill 235 on the 29th of October.

PACIFIC: U.S. submarine *Flying Fish* torpedoes and sinks a Japanese transport east of the Ryukyus. U.S. submarines *Shad* and *Grayback* torpedo and sink a Japanese cargo ship and damage another in the East China Sea. A transport is hit by a torpedo that fails to explode.

BOUGAINVILLE: Thirteenth Air Force B-24 Liberators attack Kahili and Kara airfields. P-40s providing cover over Kahili report three enemy fighters shot down. Navy cruisers and destroyers provide naval gunfire support for the Allied landing on Mono and Stirling Islands in the Treasury Island Group, south of Bougainville. Japanese aircraft damage a destroyer and mortar fire damages two LSTs.

NEW GUINEA: Fifth Air Force P-40s and P-39 Airacobras intercept Japanese bombers attempting to drop supply bundles near Sattelberg. The fighter pilots claim 12 aircraft shot down. A-20 Havocs hit the harbor and supply sites on Gasmata Island off New Britain.

October 28

ATLANTIC: Aircraft from escort carrier USS *Block Island* attack two German submarines east of Newfoundland. *U-220* is sunk and *U-256* escapes.

ITALY: XII Air Support Command A-36 Intruder (Apache) fighter-bombers attack roads, bridges, and gun positions near Vairano, and transportation targets near Rome.

SOUTHWEST PACIFIC AREA: U.S. submarine *Flying Fish* torpedoes and sinks a Japanese fleet oiler in the Philippine Sea.

SOLOMONS: A raiding force of 650 marines of the 2nd Marine Parachute Battalion lands on Choiseul Island as part of a deception plan to draw Japanese attention away from the assault on Bougainville. The battalion lands unopposed and advances inland.

BOUGAINVILLE: Thirteenth Air Force sends 19 B-24 Liberators, P-40s, and P-39 Airacobras, along with navy fighters and dive-bombers, to bomb Kara airfield. The airfield on Ballale Island is also attacked.

NEW BRITAIN: Fifth Air Force P-40s attack Gasmata Island off New Britain. P-47 Thunderbolts attack barges at Talasea.

October 29

CBI: Fourteenth Air Force sends 14 B-24 Liberators and 16 P-40s to attack the smelter area at Quang Yen in French Indochina. Nine P-40s attack transportation targets in the Chiuchiang area of China.

ITALY: Twelfth Air Force XII Bomber Command B-17s, escorted by P-38 Lightnings, bomb the marshaling yard and industrial targets in Genoa.

PACIFIC: U.S. submarine *Seawolf* torpedoes and sinks a Japanese cargo ship off Swatow, China.

SOLOMONS: Patrols from the 2nd Marine Parachute Battalion encounter Japanese on Choiseul as they move toward Sangigai.

BOUGAINVILLE: Thirteenth Air Force B-25 Mitchells, B-24 Liberators, and navy aircraft bomb the airfield on Buka Island and Bonis airfield on Bougainville.

NEW BRITAIN: Fifth Air Force sends 37 B-24 Liberators, escorted by 53 P-38 Lightnings, against Rabaul. Aircrews report 45 enemy aircraft destroyed on the ground and in the air. P-47 Thunderbolts strafe the Cape Gloucester area.

NEW GUINEA: Fifth Air Force B-25 Mitchells bomb Madang and P-47 Thunderbolts attack shipping in Hansa Bay, New Guinea.

October 30

CBI: Fourteenth Air Force sends seven B-25 Mitchells and 12 P-40s to attack support installations at Shayang, China.

ATLANTIC: The Moscow Conference Ends. The conference participants issue a declaration agreeing to continue the war until the Axis powers accept unconditional surrender. The Allies agree to participate in a postwar peace organization. The Allies pledge full cooperation and pledge to consult with each other "with a view to joint action on behalf of the community of nations." A commission will be established to address boundaries, occupation zones, and other questions regarding the status of the defeated nations. An advisory council will be established to deal with the return of Italy to democracy. Austria will be restored to independence, and war crimes will be tried and punished after the war.

The issue of a second front is a main topic at the conference. The USSR offers to join the war with Japan in return for opening a second front as soon as possible.

ETO: Ninth Air Force sends five B-26 Marauders to bomb the Cherbourg/Maupertus airfield in France.

ITALY: Twelfth Air Force XII Bomber Command B-24 Liberators bomb the Genoa marshaling yard and industrial targets. B-17s bomb Savona, Porto Maurizio, and Varazze. Northwest African Air Force B-25 Mitchells bomb Frosinone and XII Air Support Command aircraft attack bridges, roads, vehicles, and gun positions around Giulianova, Ancona, Ortona, Sessa Aurunca, Mignano, and Cassino.

SOLOMONS: Marines on Choiseul call in air strikes on Sangigai. TBF Avengers and 26 fighters bomb the village, but come close to killing a number of marines. The village is occupied after the Japanese withdraw. The enemy loses 72 men in counterattacks on the village. A number of important documents are captured in the village, providing information on Japanese intentions.

BOUGAINVILLE: Thirteenth Air Force sends 16 B-24s and more than 90 U.S. Navy SBD Dauntless dive-bombers against Kara airfield. Six B-25 Mitchells bomb Kieta, along with 12 P-39 Airacobras and navy fighters. P-40s and navy aircraft also attack Tonolai harbor.

NEW BRITAIN: Fifth Air Force B-25 Mitchells strafe supply barges in Rein Bay.

October 31

CBI: The 5307th Composite Unit (Provisional), known as Galahad, arrives in-the-ater. Galahad is the result of a blind call for volunteers for a hazardous mission. The collection of individuals ranges from highly experienced combat soldiers to misfits and dropouts. They are to be trained to become a deep penetration force along the model of the British Chindits. Stilwell is glad to see American combat troops, regardless of their reputation, and is eager to employ them in the upcoming offensive. Galahad becomes known by the last name of its new commander, Brigadier General Frank D. Merrill, a close associate of Stilwell's. Soon afterward the press is calling the unit Merrill's Marauders. The unit will be trained by British instructors of South East Asia Command (SEAC).

In Burma, Tenth Air Force P-40s, carrying 1,000-pound bombs, attack the Japanese airfield at Myitkyina with bomb runs and strafing attacks on antiaircraft positions. B-25 Mitchells attack the Meza railroad bridge. Air transports are delivering an average of over 8,000 tons of supplies in October. Chennault is getting at least half of this. As a result, Stilwell's plan to train and equip Chinese divisions in the Y Force for an offensive in Burma is far behind schedule. Another 30 Chinese divisions, called Zebra Force, is promised by Chiang, and Stilwell provides 2,200 Americans at Kweilin to serve as the cadre. Not enough supplies are provided by the airlift to do more than rudimentary support and training.

The Fourteenth Air Force reports that since February 2, 357 Japanese aircraft have been destroyed to 68 U.S. aircraft lost in combat.

ATLANTIC: TBF Avengers from escort carrier USS *Card* attack two German submarines, sinking *U-584* north of Flores Island, Azores. U.S. destroyer damages German submarine *U-256* north of the Azores.

ETO: Twelfth Air Force XII Bomber Command B-17s bomb the Antheor viaduct in France.

ITALY: Twelfth Air Force B-26 Marauders attack Anzio, while B-25 Mitchells attack docks and shipping at Civitavecchia.

General Mark Clark, commander of Fifth Army, takes operational control of the 1st Italian Motorized Group, a well-trained and eager, but inexperienced, unit that represents Italy's new status in the war.

SOUTHWEST PACIFIC AREA: U.S. submarine *Rasher* (SS-269) torpedoes and sinks a Japanese oiler in the Celebes Sea.

BOUGAINVILLE: Thirteenth Air Force sends over 20 B-25 Mitchells, with fighter support, to bomb Kara airfield.

November 1

CBI: Fourteenth Air Force B-25 Mitchells and P-40s bomb the railyards at Yoyang, China.

ATLANTIC: U.S. destroyer suffers damage in an encounter with German submarine *U-405* north of the Azores. The U-boat is rammed by the destroyer and sunk. The destroyer is scuttled the next day by TBF Avengers from the escort carrier *Card*.

ETO: The Allied Expeditionary Air Force (AEAF) is activated to provide a tactical air force for the Allied cross-Channel invasion of Europe. AEAF takes operational control of the Ninth Air Force to support this mission.

Mediterranean: Lieutenant General James H. Doolittle takes command of the Fifteenth Air Force, activated at Tunis, Tunisia. The B-17s and B-24 Liberators of the XII Bomber Command (Twelfth Air Force) are transferred to the Fifteenth Air Force.

Italy: The 34th Infantry Division advances along the Lete River, advancing on Capriati a Volturno. The 504th Parachute Infantry Regiment advances toward Gallo to protect the 34th Division's right flank. The 3rd Infantry Division, on the west side of the Volturno River, advances toward Mignano.

The XII Air Support Command (Twelfth Air Force) attacks bridges and road junctions near Pontecorvo.

Pacific: U.S. submarine *Haddock* makes an unsuccessful attack on two Japanese vessels north of Truk.

Bougainville: Amphibious Task Force 31, commanded by Rear Admiral Theodore S. Wilkinson, lands two regiments of the 3rd Marine Division and the 2nd Marine Raider Regiment of Lieutenant General Alexander A. Vandegrift's 1st Marine Amphibious Corps on Bougainville. Major General Allen H. Turnage commands the assault, which is preceded by minesweepers and two destroyers that provide close-in fire support and airstrikes by P-40s and P-39 Airacobras, P-38 Lightnings, F4U Corsairs, and SBD Dauntless dive-bombers. In a matter of minutes, nearly 8,000 men are on the beach. Marines on the northern beaches face heavy surf that damages 64 LCVPs and 27 LCMs, but encounter no enemy forces. The Raiders encounter a few bunkers and trenches, but rapidly overcome the enemy resistance. The 1st Battalion 3rd Marines landing along Cape Torokina encounters a major concentration of enemy defenses largely missed by preparatory fire. The beach defenses consist of pillboxes, trenches, and fighting positions dominated by a 75 millimeter gun in a well camouflaged and heavily fortified bunker, protected by two flanking bunkers. The gun hits several LCVPs as they approach the beach. Once on the beach, the marines fight their way through the defenses in what one observer described as the bloodiest fighting in the entire Solomons campaign. Sergeant Robert A. Owens, ordering his men to provide covering fire on the flanking bunkers, charges the 75 mm gun position; although wounded during the assault, he kills the crew and allows his fellow marines a better chance to land on the beach alive. Sergeant Owens's singular act of courage certainly contributes to the success of the landing and will win him the Medal of Honor. Over 150 Japanese troops are killed in this battle. As the marines move off the beach to establish the initial perimeter, they discover that just a few yards beyond the beach lies vast, swampy jungle. LSTs begin landing artillery and supplies as the first day's objectives are reached and a defensive perimeter is established.

TBF Avengers from a carrier task force (TF 38, commanded by Frederick C. Sherman) and naval gunfire support from four light cruisers and eight destroyers in Task Force 39 (Rear Admiral Aaron Merrill) support the landing, attacking airfields and installations in the area near Buka and Bonis and airfields on Shortland Island.

Marines of the 3rd Marine Division land in rough surf on Bougainville, November 1, 1943.

Two U.S. destroyers are damaged. Thirteenth Air Force B-24 Liberators bomb Kahili and Kara airfields. About 26 enemy fighters are reported shot down. B-25 Mitchells strafe barges at Faisi Island. An auxiliary submarine chaser is sunk west of Shortland Island.

NEW GUINEA: Fifth Air Force B-24 Liberators bomb Maniang Island in the Celebes.

November 2

CBI: Fourteenth Air Force B-25 Mitchells and P-40s attack the docks and warehouses at Shasi, China.

MEDITERRANEAN: Fifteenth Air Force B-17s and B-24 Liberators bomb the aircraft factory at Wiener-Neustadt in Austria. Aircrews report more than 50 fighters destroyed. In Italy, B-25 Mitchells bomb the marshaling yard at Ancona. B-26 Marauders bomb Civitavecchia harbor. P-38 Lightnings escort both missions.

BOUGAINVILLE: During the night, Naval Task Force 39, with four light cruisers and eight destroyers commanded by Rear Admiral Aaron S. Merrill, encounters a Japanese force of two heavy cruisers, two light cruisers, and six destroyers in Empress Augusta Bay. The Japanese intend to attack transports off Bougainville. Captain Arleigh Burke takes his destroyer squadron on an aggressive torpedo attack against a superior force. A U.S. light cruiser and two destroyers are lost to enemy gunfire and torpedoes. U.S. destroyers sink a Japanese destroyer and a light cruiser and damage two heavy cruisers. Three Japanese destroyers are damaged in collisions avoiding torpedoes. The Japanese retaliate with an air attack on the task force. The enemy loses 17 planes to shipboard antiaircraft fire, while AIRSOLS fighters claim another

16 aircraft. A U.S. cruiser is slightly damaged by Japanese aircraft. This battle establishes U.S. naval superiority in the Solomons.

TBF Avengers from Task Force 38, commanded by Rear Admiral Frederick C. Sherman, attacks enemy airfields around Buka. The task force has the fast carrier USS *Saratoga* and the light carrier USS *Princeton,* along with two light cruisers and nine destroyers. Thirteenth Air Force B-24 Liberators bomb Kahili airfield.

NEW BRITAIN: Fifth Air Force sends 75 B-25 Mitchells, escorted by 70 P-38 Lightnings, to attack Rabaul to support the marine landing on Bougainville. The bombers sink a stores ship and damage two heavy cruisers, a destroyer, another stores ship, and a minesweeper. Under intense antiaircraft fire, the B-25s and P-38s also report destroying 12 aircraft on the ground and 68 others destroyed in the air. The attack is costly—21 American aircraft are shot down.

Major Raymond H. Wilkins is leading the B-25 Mitchells of the 8th Bombardment Squadron, 3rd Bombardment Group, against Japanese shipping in Simpson Harbor at Rabaul, New Britain. Wilkins has flown 86 combat missions in the previous 22 months, a feat unequaled by any man in the Fifth Air Force. He already holds five Distinguished Flying Crosses for his courage in previous actions in New Guinea. Because previous air strikes have obscured the planned approach, Wilkins's squadron is forced to make a different approach, bringing them directly into heavy Japanese antiaircraft fire. Wilkins's B-25 is hit in the right wing but he continues as the lead aircraft, first strafing a group of small harbor vessels and then making a low-level bombing run on a destroyer, sinking it with a 1,000-pound bomb. Continuing the attack even as he fights for control of the B-25, he bombs a transport ship. Wilkins maneuvers to divert fire from a Japanese heavy cruiser to his own plane to allow the other aircraft of his squadron to escape. His bomber is subsequently downed by enemy fire. For his extreme courage and leadership in one of the most difficult bombing missions of the Pacific war, Major Wilkins will be awarded the Medal of Honor.

November 3

CBI: Fourteenth Air Force sends 21 B-24 Liberators with fighter escort to attack the Kowloon Docks at Hong Kong. Aircrews report four enemy fighters shot down.

ETO: Eighth Air Force VIII Bomber Command B-17s and B-24 Liberators, using both the British H2S and the new U.S. H2X radar, bomb the port at Wilhelmshaven, Germany. Of the 539 bombers that hit the target, seven B-17s are shot down and 49 are damaged. Aircrews report that the radar-assisted bombing improved accuracy and claim over 20 enemy fighters destroyed. The raid is supported by over 300 P-47 Thunderbolts. Another 45 P-38 Lightnings escort the bombers for most of the raid. The pilots report three confirmed kills, five probables, and five possibles. Overnight, two B-17s drop over 1.5 million leaflets on Antwerp and Rotterdam.

Ninth Air Force B-26 Marauders bomb the airfields at Saint-Andre-de-L'Eure and Triqueville in France. Other B-26s bomb the Schiphol airfield in the Netherlands.

ITALY: The 34th Infantry Division with a battalion of Rangers crosses the Volturno River to capture Venafro and cut Highway 6 northwest of Mignano. The 168th Infantry Regiment of the 34th Infantry Division crosses the Volturno River northeast of

Venafro. Twelfth Air Force aircraft conduct a number of ground support and bombing runs on German defenses, railyards, and the road network from Venafro to Cassino.

Southwest Pacific Area: Thirteenth Air Force sends 19 B-24 Liberators to attack a convoy off Mussau Island, reporting three vessels damaged or sunk.

Pacific: The battleship USS *Oklahoma,* sunk on December 7, 1941, is refloated at Pearl Harbor. Navy PB4Ys (a B-24 variant) sink a Japanese stores ship off Ocean Island, near Tarawa in the Gilberts.

The Japanese Second Fleet dispatches seven heavy cruisers, a light cruiser, and four destroyers from Truk to attack the U.S. fleet at Bougainville.

Solomons: The 2nd Marine Parachute Battalion is evacuated from Choiseul. U.S. casualties are six killed, 12 wounded, and one missing.

Bougainville: Major General Turnage adjusts the positions of the 3rd and 9th Marines and moves units forward to occupy the Piva and Mission Trails. No Japanese are encountered.

New Guinea: Fifth Air Force B-25 Mitchells attack supply barges around Alexishafen.

November 4

CBI: Fourteenth Air Force dispatches the Chinese-American Composite Wing against shipping and supply targets at Amoy and Swatow in China. The B-25s report four cargo ships damaged or sunk in the attack. One cargo ship sunk was carrying 100,000,000 yuan in Central Reserve Bank notes. B-24s damage a Japanese cargo vessel and destroyer north of New Ireland. U.S. submarine *Seawolf* torpedoes and sinks a Japanese cargo ship southwest of Hong Kong, China.

Italy: Roca Pipirozzi falls to a battalion of the 180th Infantry Regiment of the 34th Infantry Division. The 2nd Battalion of the 168th Infantry Regiment, 34th Infantry Division, captures the town of Roccaravindola and S. Maria Oliveto. The 34th is able to consolidate its position, but units have suffered heavily from minefields in the hills. The 3rd Battalion of the 179th Infantry Regiment (45th Infantry Division) captures and consolidates its position at Venafro.

Fifteenth Air Force B-17s bomb rail lines between Montalto di Castro and Talamone, and between San Vincenzo and Cecina. P-38 Lightnings carrying bombs hit a tunnel near Terni. XII Air Support Command and RAF aircraft attack trucks and trains near Sora and Avezzano and attack the Furbara and Tarquinia airfields.

Southwest Pacific Area: U.S. submarine *Silversides* lays mines off New Ireland, sinking a surveying ship and a transport and damaging a light cruiser and destroyer.

Pacific: U.S. submarine *Tautog* unsuccessfully attacks Japanese convoy in the Palau Islands.

Solomons: Thirteenth Air Force B-24 Liberators bomb the Buka Island airfield.

The 21st Marine Regiment of the 3rd Marine Division, with 3,500 men and 5,000 tons of supplies, leaves Guadalcanal for Bougainville.

New Britain: Thirteenth Air Force B-24 Liberators damage two tankers and damage a troop transport near Truk. Admiral Halsey orders Rear Admiral Frederick Sherman's Task Force 38 to intercept the Japanese naval force from Truk.

November 5

ATLANTIC: B-25 Mitchell bombers and U.S. Navy PB4Y Privateers on Ascension Island sink German submarine *U-848* off the coast of West Africa.

ETO: Eighth Air Force VIII Bomber Command B-17s, escorted by 47 P-38 Lightnings and 336 P-47 Thunderbolts, attack the marshaling yard and oil plants at Gelsenkirchen, Germany. Of the 323 bombers that hit the target, eight B-17s are shot down and 225 are damaged. Aircrews report at least 18 enemy fighters destroyed. Four P-47s are lost and one is damaged. Over Munster, Germany, 104 B-24 Liberators bomb the city's marshaling yard. Three B-24 Liberators are lost and 44 are damaged. Aircrews report over 20 enemy aircraft shot down. Later in the day five B-17s drop more than a million leaflets over Paris, Amiens, Rouen, and Caen.

ITALY: The 3rd Infantry Division attempts to overcome enemy defenses at the Mignano gap by making flanking attacks. A battalion of the 7th Infantry Regiment is stopped at Monte La Difensa, where impassible cliffs are defended by German positions blasted into the sides of the mountain and backed by artillery and mortar fire. A battalion-level attack of the 15th Infantry Regiment also fails to make any progress against enemy forces dug in at Monte Rotundo.

Fifteenth Air Force B-24 Liberators conduct a low-level bombing run on road and rail bridges between Falconara and Marittima. XII Air Support Command B-25 Mitchells, escorted by Fifteenth Air Force P-38 Lightnings, bomb the Berat-Kucove airfield in Albania. Other XII Air Support Command aircraft attack the road network around Isernia, Cassino, and Atena Lucana.

PACIFIC: U.S. submarine *Halibut* torpedoes and damages Japanese carrier *Junyo* east of Kyushu, Japan.

BOUGAINVILLE: Thirteenth Air Force B-25 Mitchells attack Japanese troops near Kieta and sink barges between Kieta and Banin Harbor. Navy fighter aircraft damage a Japanese cargo ship in Matchin Bay.

NEW BRITAIN: In order to prevent any Japanese counterattack while the landing on Bougainville takes place, Fifth Air Force sends more than 90 B-24 Liberators with fighter escort to attack Rabaul harbor. Naval Task Force 38 sends 16 TBF Avengers, 22 TBD Dauntless dive-bombers from *Saratoga* and seven Avengers from USS *Princeton*, covered by F6F Wildcats, to conduct an additional attack on Rabaul. Flying through intense antiaircraft fire, the navy planes damage five Japanese heavy cruisers, two light cruisers, and two destroyers. The combat air patrol for the task force's ships is provided by 52 F4F Hellcat fighters from Vella Lavella airfield. U.S. losses are five bombers and five fighters. Japanese aircraft losses are estimated at 14 probable kills. The Japanese naval force is ordered back to Truk.

NEW GUINEA: Fifth Air Force P-47 Thunderbolt pilots report shooting down more than 20 enemy aircraft over Wewak.

November 6

CBI: Tenth Air Force B-24 Liberators lay mines in the Rangoon River in Burma during the night.

ETO: Eighth Air Force VIII Bomber Command sends two B-17s to drop over 400,000 leaflets over Paris.

MEDITERRANEAN: German aircraft conduct a torpedo attack on a convoy off Tunisia and bound for Naples, sinking a U.S. destroyer and damaging a troop transport, which is later abandoned.

ITALY: Fifteenth Air Force B-17s bomb bridges over the Fiora River. P-38 Lightnings attack a bridge near Orvieto and Monte Molino. Fighters strafe the airfield at Tarquinia, rail traffic, and enemy vehicles. XII Air Support Command aircraft attack gun positions, bridges and roads, vehicles near Cassino, and rail traffic.

PACIFIC: U.S. submarine *Haddock* attacks a Japanese convoy sailing from Truk to Singapore, torpedoing and sinking a fleet tanker west of Truk. U.S. submarine *Scorpion* torpedoes another fleet tanker in the same vicinity. Although *Haddock* is attacked by an escorting destroyer, it escapes.

CENTRAL PACIFIC: Seventh Air Force's VII Air Force Service Command and VII Bomber Command establish advanced headquarters on Funafuti Atoll in the Ellice Islands. Baker, Nukufetau, and Nanumea Islands in the Ellice Islands will have airfields built on them to support the planned offensives against Tarawa Atoll and Makin in the Gilbert Islands, as well as Japanese strongholds in the Carolines and the Marshalls.

BOUGAINVILLE: The 21st Marine Regiment lands at Empress Augusta Bay. A hastily organized Japanese landing force of 800 men attacks the left flank of the perimeter defended by 3rd Battalion 9th marines near the Laruna River. In a daylong, confused fight both the marines and Japanese are surprised by what they encounter after U.S. Marine combat patrols beyond the perimeter stumble upon Japanese infantry in the swampy jungle. The Japanese establish a small defensive perimeter and hold off an attack by elements of 1st Battalion 3rd Marines.

Thirteenth Air Force sends 24 B-25 Mitchells with fighter escort to support an initial attack by navy SBD Dauntless dive-bombers and fighters on Kara airfield. In a follow-on attack, 17 B-24 Liberators bomb Bonis airfield. B-25 Mitchells attack Japanese shipping west of Buka, sinking a submarine chaser, an auxiliary submarine chaser, and a cargo vessel. Four other vessels are sunk in the same vicinity.

NEW BRITAIN: Fifth Air Force P-40s attack Gasmata Island.

NEW GUINEA: Japanese aircraft succeed in attacking Nadzab, Dumpu, and Finschhafen but cause little damage.

November 7

CBI: Fourteenth Air Force B-25 Mitchells bomb Amoy harbor in China, sinking two cargo ships and another vessel.

ETO: Eighth Air Force VIII Bomber Command attacks industrial targets in Wesel and Düren, Germany. Poor weather conditions limit the effectiveness of the attacks. Of the 53 B-17s that hit Wesel, four B-17s are damaged; one crewman is killed and two are wounded. Over Düren, only 37 B-17s hit the primary target because the two B-17 Pathfinders are unable to use the Oboe radar guidance system. Another 20 B-17s hit the secondary target at Randerath; two B-17s are damaged. The bombers are escorted by 283 P-47 Thunderbolts. Pilots report one confirmed enemy kill at a cost of six P-47s lost; the six pilots are reported as missing.

Ninth Air Force sends over 200 B-26 Marauders against the Montdidier and Meulan-Les Mureaux airfields in France, but the mission is aborted due to weather conditions over the target area. Nevertheless, two escorting P-38 Lightnings are lost.

MEDITERRANEAN: XII Air Support Command and Northwest African Air Force aircraft bomb the harbor and shipping at Split, Yugoslavia.

ITALY: XII Air Support Command and Northwest African Air Force aircraft attack bridges, road junctions, and transportation around Mignano-Cassino and Pontecorvo.

SOLOMONS: Task Force 53, the navy and marine element for the attack on Tarawa, departs in secrecy from the New Hebrides.

BOUGAINVILLE: The Japanese make attacks on the trail blocks established by the marines at the Piva and Numa Numa Trails. At the Koromokina River, Sergeant Herbert Joseph Thomas of the 3rd Marines, 3rd Marine Division, leads his squad against Japanese positions in the dense jungle. After successfully destroying two machine-gun positions, Sergeant Thomas prepares his men to assault a third position. Taking a hand grenade, Thomas throws it toward the enemy, but it strikes some vines and lands in the midst of the squad. Without hesitation, Sergeant Thomas covers the grenade with his body, saving the lives of his men. His selfless act of courage allows his men to capture the enemy position and wins him the Medal of Honor.

Thirteenth Air Force sends 21 B-24 Liberators to attack the Buka Island airfield.

NEW BRITAIN: Fifth Air Force sends 25 B-24 Liberators, escorted by over 60 P-38 Lightnings, to bomb Rapopo airfield. Japanese fighters intercept the formation and shoot down five P-38 Lightnings. Aircrews report more than 20 fighters destroyed in the air and several more destroyed on the ground.

NEW GUINEA: Fifth Air Force B-25 Mitchells bomb Wewak and Japanese aircraft attack Nadzab and Bena Bena, destroying or damaging about 16 U.S. planes. The raid costs the Japanese 14 aircraft shot down by U.S. fighters.

November 8

CBI: Tenth Air Force sends five B-24 Liberators to lay mines in the Rangoon River during the night.

ETO: Eighth Air Force sends two B-17s to drop leaflets over Paris.

MEDITERRANEAN: General Eisenhower, still in command of the Mediterranean theater, decides on a two-pronged attack on Rome. While Montgomery and Clark's armies attack the Winter Line, Clark's VI Corps will conduct an amphibious assault at Anzio, south of Rome and some 45 miles behind the Gustav Line. The Combined Chiefs of Staff approves Eisenhower's request to keep 68 LSTs (landing ship, tank) in the Mediterranean to support this assault but directs him to release them by the end of January 1944 so that they will be available for Overlord.

Fifteenth Army Group commander General Sir Harold Alexander orders Lieutenant General Mark Clark's Fifth Army to prepare plans for an amphibious attack using one division on the west coast of Italy to outflank the Gustav Line. Simultaneous attacks by the Eighth and Fifth Armies will leave the Germans unable to respond to an amphibious landing south of Rome. The initial target date of December 20 for the landing of one division has to be postponed due to a lack of progress against the Germans and a lack of landing craft.

Fifteenth Air Force attacks the Turin ball bearing factory and other nearby industrial targets with 81 B-17s. Northwest African Air Force bombers and RAF Desert Air Force fighters attack targets west of the Sangro River and trains at Civitanova and Pescara.

ITALY: A battalion of the 30th Infantry Regiment of the 3rd Infantry Division captures Monte Rotundo, while a battalion of the 15th Infantry Regiment captures Hill 253. Both hold against a number of strong German counterattacks. The 135th Infantry Regiment of the 34th Infantry Division along with an ad hoc task force of infantry, tanks, tank destroyers, and engineers captures Montaquila. The 45th Infantry Division advances past Pozzilli against strong resistance. The entire VI Corps suffers increasingly from the accumulated effects of rain, mud, and exposure as the infantrymen battle up hills so steep they often have to advance on their hands and knees. German troops are solidly protected in heavily fortified positions and are difficult to dislodge.

PACIFIC: U.S. submarine *Bluefish* torpedoes and sinks a Japanese army tanker in the South China Sea. U.S. submarine *Rasher* torpedoes and sinks a Japanese merchant tanker in the Makassar Straits, escaping from an auxiliary submarine chaser.

BOUGAINVILLE: A counterattack by 1st Battalion 21st Marines, preceded by a barrage from five artillery battalions, breaks the Japanese defensive positions. The transports carrying the 148th Regimental Combat Team of the 37th Infantry Division are attacked by Japanese aircraft as they enter Empress Augusta Bay. The attackers kill five soldiers and wound 20 more. The Japanese begin heavy attacks along the Piva Trail, but are repulsed by artillery, tanks, and mortar fire.

Thirteenth Air Force sends 22 B-24 Liberators to bomb Bonis airfield. B-25 Mitchells bomb targets at the month of the Laruma River and Kieta. Japanese divebombers attack U.S. ships off Cape Torokina, damaging a light cruiser.

The I Amphibious Corps takes control of the battle from 3rd Marine Division.

November 9

ITALY: Fifteenth Air Force B-24 Liberators attack the Turin ball bearing works, and B-17s bomb the Genoa-Ansaldo steel works. P-38 Lightnings provide escort for both raids. Northwest African Air Force aircraft attack Formia and Itri, while XII Air Support Command aircraft attack roads and bridges in the Mignano-Ceprano area and rail targets in the Rome-La Spezia area.

SOUTHWEST PACIFIC AREA: U.S. submarine *Rasher* makes an unsuccessful attack on a Japanese fleet oiler in the Celebes Sea. U.S. submarine *Sargo* torpedoes and sinks a Japanese cargo ship in the Philippine Sea.

PACIFIC: U.S. submarine *Seawolf* makes an unsuccessful attack on a Japanese cargo vessel in the South China Sea.

Major General Ray S. Geiger takes command of the I Marine Amphibious Corps from Lieutenant General Alexander A. Vandegrift, who leaves for Washington, D.C., to become commandant of the Marine Corps.

BOUGAINVILLE: Upon moving inland from the beach the marines discover that western Bougainville Island is covered by swamps. Any high ground is of important military value, as are trails that allow easy movement. Control of the trails becomes a key task for both the marines and the Japanese.

The Marine Raiders attack to clear Japanese away from Piva trail and run immediately into an advancing Japanese force preparing to attack. The Japanese attack is thrown back and the Raiders advance to the important junction of Numa Numa and Piva trails. In the first few minutes of the attack, Private First Class Henry Gurke and another Raider find themselves in the midst of a major fight. As Gurke's buddy is laying down suppressive fire with a Browning Automatic Rifle, a Japanese grenade drops into their foxhole. Gurke pushes his buddy aside and covers the grenade with his body. His act of devotion to a comrade by sacrificing his life will win him the Medal of Honor.

The 148th Infantry Regiment, 37th Infantry Division takes control of the left half of the perimeter.

Thirteenth Air Force B-25 Mitchells bomb Buka Island airfield. B-25s bomb Kieta and B-24 Liberators attack Kara and Kahili airfields. P-39 Airacobras along with navy aircraft also attack Kara airfield and the Ballale Island airfield.

NEW BRITAIN: B-25 Mitchells bomb fuel supplies and shipping in the Rein Bay area, while P-40s bomb supply dumps on Gasmata Island. B-24 Liberator aircrews report sinking a destroyer near Kavieng, New Ireland.

NEW GUINEA: Fifth Air Force B-25 Mitchells and A-20 Havocs, escorted by P-38 Lightnings and P-47 Thunderbolts, attack the airfield at Alexishafen, reporting at least 12 enemy airplanes destroyed on the ground. Another 10 to 15 Japanese fighters are reported destroyed in the air.

November 10

ATLANTIC: Navy PB4Y-1 Privateers and an RAF Wellington bomber sink German submarine *U-966* in the Bay of Biscay.

ETO: Eighth Air Force sends five B-17s to drop leaflets over Paris, Rennes, Le Mans, and Rouen, France.

Ninth Air Force B-26 Marauders bomb an airfield in Chievres, Belgium.

MEDITERRANEAN: Fifteenth Air Force B-24 Liberators bomb the Turin ball bearing works and B-17s bomb a bridge and the marshaling yards at Bolzano. P-38 Lightnings escort the B-24s completely through the mission and provide partial coverage to the B-17s.

Northwest African Air Force bombers attack shipping at Split, Yugoslavia, and Durazzo, Albania.

ITALY: The 3rd Infantry Division faces heavy counterattacks from the Germans. In one representative action north of Mignano, Lieutenant Maurice L. Britt and a small group of infantrymen stop an attack by over 100 enemy soldiers. Although repeatedly wounded by bullets and grenade fragments, Lieutenant Britt refuses treatment. Fighting valiantly against nearly impossible odds, he kills five enemy soldiers and knocks out a machine-gun crew, using every weapon he can lay his hands on. In the end, he holds his position and captures four prisoners. Lieutenant Britt's exemplary courage and determination stop the German counterattack and save his company. He will receive the Medal of Honor.

XII Air Support Command and RAF aircraft attack German positions at Rocca and Rome and attack truck and rail traffic in the Rome-La Spezia and Piombino-Leghorn areas.

Southwest Pacific Area: U.S. submarine *Albacore* is damaged by a U.S. bomber off New Ireland, but continues on patrol.

Pacific: U.S. submarine *Barb* makes an attack on a Japanese convoy, damaging a cargo ship. *Barb* is forced to evade an auxiliary minesweeper escorting the convoy. U.S. submarine *Scamp* torpedoes and sinks a Japanese transport between Truk and New Ireland.

Task Force 52, the navy and army element for the attack on Makin atoll in the Gilberts, leaves Pearl Harbor. The task force consists of three escort carriers, four battleships, four heavy cruisers, and four destroyers. The 27th Infantry Division Task Force is composed of the 165th Regimental Combat Team, two companies of the 193rd Tank Battalion, the 152nd Engineer Battalion, and an antiaircraft battalion.

Central Pacific: B-24 Liberators of the 30th Bombardment Group (Heavy), Seventh Air Force, arrive from Hawaii to be stationed at Nanumea in the Ellice Islands and at Canton Island in the Phoenix Islands.

Bougainville: Thirteenth Air Force B-25 Mitchells bomb the Kara airfield.

New Britain: Fifth Air Force B-24 Liberators bomb Lakunai airfield and attack a new landing ground on Duke of York Island east of Rabaul.

New Guinea: Fifth Air Force B-25 Mitchells attack the Alexishafen airfield.

November 11

CBI: Fourteenth Air Force sends six B-24 Liberators to bomb the Burma Road, causing heavy damage.

ETO: Eighth Air Force VIII Bomber Command attempts to attack two targets in Germany, the marshaling yard at Munster and industrial targets in Wesel. Weather limits the effectiveness of the raids. Only 57 of the 167 B-17s hit the target at Munster. Aircrews report 10 enemy fighters shot down while four B-17s are lost and 27 others damaged. The 180 B-17s sent to bomb Wesel, abort the mission over the English Channel. One B-17 is damaged and no casualties are reported. The two missions are escorted by 59 P-38 Lightnings and 342 P-47 Thunderbolts. The P-47 pilots report eight confirmed kills, one probable, and two possibles. Two P-47 Thunderbolts are lost and one is damaged. The two pilots are reported as missing. Ninth Air Force sends 157 B-26 Marauders to bomb targets near Cherbourg, France. Fifteenth Air Force sends 28 B-24 Liberators to bomb the ball bearing plant at Annecy, France. One Pathfinder B-17 flies an Oboe radar test over Emmerich, Germany.

Italy: The 2nd Battalion 509th Parachute Infantry and the 1st Ranger Battalion capture Mount Santa Croce, after relieving a battalion of the 180th Infantry Regiment, 45th Infantry Division. The rest of the division makes only limited progress in trying to push the Germans from the hills guarding Acquafondata.

Twelfth Air Force A-20 Havocs and RAF aircraft attack troop concentrations and communication sites near Rocca and Palena. Northwest African Air Force aircraft bomb an explosive works near Popoli and the docks at Civitavecchia. Enemy strongpoints at Roccaraso and Atessa are attacked. Transportation targets between the Sangro and Pescara rivers are attacked.

In one of the attacks by the 3rd Infantry Division near Mignano, an infantry company is counterattacked by German infantry. Heavily outnumbered, Private First Class Floyd K. Lindstrom turns his machine gun on the attackers. Unable to get a clear shot at the enemy occupying the high ground, Lindstrom picks up his machine gun and carries it uphill until he is only 10 yards away from the enemy position. He begins firing again, even as bullets slam into the rocky ground all around him. Still unable to suppress the enemy, he abandons the machine gun and charges forward, drawing his pistol. He kills the two soldiers and takes their machine gun, employing it now against the enemy. As his men respond to his orders, Lindstrom retrieves two ammunition boxes from the enemy position, all the while ignoring the intense rifle fire directed his way. The heavy volume of fire from Lindstrom's guns stops the German counterattack. Lindstrom's initiative and aggressive action with total disregard for his own life in order to protect his comrades will win him the Medal of Honor.

SOUTHWEST PACIFIC AREA: U.S. submarine *Capelin* torpedoes and sinks a Japanese cargo ship northwest of Ambon, in the Banda Sea.

Japanese submarine *I-21* torpedoes a U.S. freighter with over 1,300 troops on board bound for Townsville, Australia. Over 200 men are killed or drowned.

PACIFIC: U.S. submarine *Drum* makes an unsuccessful attack on a Japanese convoy sailing from Truk to Rabaul. U.S. submarine *Sargo* torpedoes and sinks a Japanese transport in the Ryukyus.

CENTRAL PACIFIC: Japanese aircraft attack the airfield on Nanumea Island in the Ellice Islands, destroying a B-24 Liberator, even as more B-24s of the 11th Bombardment Group (Heavy) arrive from Hawaii to be stationed at Nukufetau Island and Funafuti Atoll in the Ellice Islands.

BOUGAINVILLE: Thirteenth Air Force B-25 Mitchells and Navy F4U Corsair fighters strafe barges and shore installations in Matchin Bay. Additional elements of the 21st Marines land at Empress Augusta Bay.

NEW BRITAIN: Fifth Air Force B-24 Liberators bomb Lakunai airfield near Rabaul. Thirteenth Air Force B-24s join Fifth Air Force aircraft and Royal Australian Air Force aircraft in a concentrated attack on Rabaul harbor. TBF Avengers and TBD Dauntless dive-bombers from Rear Admiral Frederick C. Sherman's Task Force 38 and Task Group 50.3 also participate. TG 50.3 has two new carriers, the USS *Essex* and USS *Bunker Hill*, and a light carrier USS *Independence*. This task group, under command of Rear Admiral Alfred Montgomery, was originally assigned to Admiral Spruance's Makin and Tarawa operation, but Admiral Halsey has requested additional carrier support, and Admiral Nimitz passes operational control to Halsey.) Fighter pilots report 17 Japanese fighters shot down; bomber aircrews report five enemy fighters destroyed. A destroyer is sunk and two light cruisers and three destroyers are damaged.

The new carriers from TG 50.3 employ 33 SB2C Helldiver dive-bombers for the first time in the Pacific. The task group is attacked by 199 Japanese aircraft, including 27 dive-bombers and 14 torpedo bombers. Air cover is provided by navy F4U

Corsairs and F4F Hellcats from Vella Lavella airfield on New Georgia. The fighters land on the carriers to refuel and rearm. Only three enemy bombers are able to release their ordnance near the carriers, causing only minor damage.

Although the Japanese attack reminds many Japanese of Midway in terms of the number of aircraft involved, this battle bears little resemblance to the original. These are not the superb airmen of the Imperial Japanese Navy of 1942. Instead, these are marginally trained pilots facing combat-experienced and highly trained American flyers. The Japanese pilots, for all their courage, have little chance of success. This devastating loss of pilots and aircraft marks the effective end of the ability of the Japanese to challenge American control of the air or sea. As a result of this attack, Rabaul is effectively neutralized, accomplishing the operational objective of the Cartwheel campaign. The Americans, however, will not realize this fact for several more weeks.

Small and elite, the U.S. Marines maintained their own aviation units, flying aircraft such as this F4U Corsair equipped with five-inch rockets, which prepares to take off from a carrier before dawn. *(National Archives and Records Administration)*

November 12

CBI: In Burma, Tenth Air Force sends two B-24 Liberators to mine the Rangoon River during the night.

In China, Fourteenth Air Force B-25 Mitchells and P-40s attack the railyard and warehouses at Yoyang. B-25s also bomb targets along the waterfront at Yangchi Kang and Puchi.

ATLANTIC: A U.S. Navy PB4Y-1 Privateer (a B-24 variant) patrol bomber sinks German submarine *U-508* in the Bay of Biscay.

ITALY: Fifteenth Air Force B-26 Marauders attack railroad bridges and rail lines near Montalto di Castro and Orbetello. Northwest African Air Force A-20 Havocs provide ground support near Palena and Atina, and attack targets along the road at Acquafondata. A-20s also bomb the Arezzo marshaling yard and Perugia airfield.

PACIFIC: U.S. submarine *Harder* torpedoes and sinks an auxiliary minesweeper and another vessel in a Japanese convoy in the northern Marianas. U.S. submarine *Scamp* torpedoes and sinks a Japanese light cruiser north of the Marianas, which had been damaged in the raid on Rabaul on November 11. U.S. submarine *Thresher* torpedoes and sinks a Japanese transport north of Truk, but is forced to terminate its patrol after sustaining damage from a depth charge attack.

CENTRAL PACIFIC: Seventh Air Force continues receiving B-24 Liberators from Hawaii from the 30th Bombardment Group (Heavy), stationing them on Nanumea Island in the Ellice Islands.

BOUGAINVILLE: The 129th and 145th Regimental Combat Teams of the 37th Infantry Division complete their landing, adding 10,277 men to the expanding perimeter.

Thirteenth Air Force attacks Tarlena with 18 B-25 Mitchells. B-25s also bomb the area near Matchin Bay. Eight P-38 Lightnings strafe Bonis airfield.

NEW GUINEA: Fifth Air Force B-25 Mitchells and B-26 Marauders bomb Japanese positions between Finschhafen and Saidor. B-24 Liberators bomb targets on Java and on Amboina Island in the Moluccas.

November 13

ETO: Eighth Air Force VIII Bomber Command B-17s, B-24 Liberators, and three B-17 Pathfinder aircraft, escorted by 45 P-38 Lightnings and 345 P-47 Thunderbolts, attack the port of Bremen and targets in Kiel-Flensburg in Germany. Weather causes most of the bombers to abort the mission. Over Bremen, 79 B-17s and 61 B-24s hit the target. Three B-17s and 13 B-24s are lost; 15 B-17s and 13 B-24 Liberators are damaged. Aircrews report 20 enemy fighters shot down. Fighters report 10 confirmed enemy kills, three probables, and six possibles. U.S. losses are seven P-38 Lightnings and three P-47 Thunderbolts. A total of nine fighters are damaged. Nine pilots are reported missing.

Ninth Air Force's 354th Fighter Group in England receives P-51 Mustang fighters.

ITALY: Northwest African Air Force A-20 Havocs bomb Palena, Atina, Civitavecchia harbor, and a road near Terracina. XII Air Support Command and RAF aircraft bomb Giulianova harbor and the landing grounds at Aquino, Frosinone, and Marcigliana. Transportation targets in the Pescara-Rieti area are also attacked.

SOUTHWEST PACIFIC AREA: U.S. submarine *Narwhal* lands men and supplies at Paluan Bay, Mindoro, Philippines.

PACIFIC: U.S. submarine *Scorpion* torpedoes and damages a Japanese oiler northwest of the Marianas. U.S. submarine *Trigger* torpedoes and sinks a Japanese transport in the East China Sea, and receives slight damage from a depth charge attack.

CENTRAL PACIFIC: Seventh Air Force begins air operations in support of Operation Galvanic, with 18 B-24 Liberators flying from Funafuti Atoll in the Ellice Islands to bomb Tarawa atoll. One B-24 is lost in the raid.

BOUGAINVILLE: The 2nd Battalion 21st Marines fights Japanese troops in what is called the Battle of Coconut Grove. The marines expand the northern and eastern perimeter, encountering Japanese defending a coconut grove, one of the few identifiable terrain features in the swampy jungle. The 37th Infantry Division takes control of its assigned sector. The division's commander, Major General Robert S. Beightler, arrives on the island.

Thirteenth Air Force attacks antiaircraft positions, dispersal areas, and the runway at Bonis airfield with 17 B-24 Liberators. Six B-25 Mitchells conduct low-level bombing runs on the Buka Island airfield. Japanese aircraft attack Naval Task Force 39 off Empress Augusta Bay and damage a U.S. light cruiser.

NEW GUINEA: Fifth Air Force sends nearly 120 B-24 Liberators and B-25 Mitchells to bomb Alexishafen. P-40s conduct strafing attacks as well.

November 14

MEDITERRANEAN: Northwest African Air Force B-25 Mitchells, escorted by Fifteenth Air Force P-38 Lightnings, bomb the Sofia marshaling yard. Fighter pilots report shooting down five enemy aircraft.

PACIFIC: Just north of Truk U.S. submarine *Apogon* makes an unsuccessful attack on a Japanese convoy headed for the island.

CENTRAL PACIFIC: Seventh Air Force sends nine B-24 Liberators from Nukufetau Island in the Ellice Islands to bomb Tarawa Atoll. Another nine B-24s from Nanumea Island attack Mille Atoll in the Carolines.

BOUGAINVILLE: The 2nd Battalion 21st Marines, now reinforced, drives the Japanese defenders from the coconut grove and advances 1,500 yards. The attack is supported by 20 TBF Avengers flying ground support missions and a heavy pre-assault bombardment by artillery. The marines capture the key intersection of Numa Numa Trail and East-West Trail.

NEW GUINEA: Fifth Air Force B-25 Mitchells bomb Japanese supply and troop concentration near Sio.

November 15

CBI: Fourteenth Air Force B-24 Liberators bomb the docks in the Kowloon area of Hong Kong.

ATLANTIC: The JCS planners anticipate strikes on the Japanese homeland from the Marshall Islands by December 1944 with the B-29 Stratofortress, a strategic bomber capable of flying long distances.

MEDITERRANEAN: Fifteenth Air Force B-24 Liberators, with P-38 Lightnings flying escort, bomb Eleusis airfield. Twelfth Air Force XII Air Support Command B-25 Mitchells bomb Kalamaki airfield.

ITALY: Fifth Army commander Mark Clark orders an end to the offensives by X Corps and VI Corps. Weather, terrain, and exhaustion have forced the Allies to culminate as the divisions are unable to make any further progress. The Germans are able to reinforce with two divisions and assess that the Allies can be held south of Rome during the winter months. The Fifth Army begins a period of reorganizing and consolidating in preparation for a second offensive. Between October 7 and this day, VI Corps has taken nearly 9,700 casualties. The British X Corps suffers 2,800 casualties. Northwest African Air Force fighters attack road transports near Ancona.

SOUTHWEST PACIFIC AREA: U.S. submarine *Crevalle* torpedoes and sinks a Japanese cargo ship west of Luzon in the Philippines. U.S. submarine *Narwhal* lands supplies and evacuates fighters at Mindanao, Philippines.

PACIFIC: The V Amphibious Corps develops the operational plan for the invasion of the Marshalls. Major General Holland M. Smith commands the V Amphibious Corps. The 4th Maine Division, commanded by Major General Harry Schmidt, will seize Roi-Namur Islands. The army's 7th Infantry Division commanded by Major General Charles H. Corlett will seize Kwajalein. Eniwetok Atoll will be captured by an army-marine force led by marine brigadier general Thomas E. Watson. The small island of Majuro will be assigned to the V Amphibious Corps Reconnaissance Company and a battalion of the 106th Infantry Regiment of the 7th Infantry Division.

CENTRAL PACIFIC: Seventh Air Force B-24 Liberators from Canton Island and Nanumea Island bomb Jaluit Atoll in the Marshalls, Mille Atoll in the Carolines, and Makin Island in the Gilberts.

BOUGAINVILLE: Thirteenth Air Force B-24 Liberators bomb Kahili airfield. Fighters attack and destroy several barges along the coast and destroy two fuel supply points at Tonolai. The 419th Night Fighter Squadron, XIII Fighter Command, arrives on Guadalcanal Island from the United States with P-38 Lightnings and P-70 Havoc night fighters.

NEW GUINEA: Fifth Air Force sends over 30 B-24 Liberators against targets near Alexishafen. A group of 88 B-25 Mitchells with an escort of 16 P-40s heading for Wewak and Boram is intercepted by fighters escorting Japanese bombers headed for Gusap. The B-25s abort the mission and the P-40 pilots report 20 enemy aircraft destroyed with the loss of two fighters. P-47 Thunderbolt pilots report five enemy kills over Wewak.

November 16

CBI: Fourteenth Air Force sends 11 B-24 Liberators, two B-25 Mitchells, and four P-40s to attack the Kowloon docks at Hong Kong.

ETO: Eighth Air Force VIII Bomber Command attacks two targets in Norway, the industrial areas at Knaben and Rjukan, with B-17s. Over Knaben, 130 bombers hit the target. One B-17 is lost and seven others are damaged; aircrews report two enemy fighters shot down. Over Rjukan, 147 bombers hit the target; one B-17 is lost and one damaged. A later strike on Rjukan by 29 B-24 Liberators results in no losses or casualties.

Air Marshal Sir Trafford L. Leigh-Mallory, RAF, is named Air Commander in Chief, Allied Expeditionary Air Force (AEAF). Brigadier General William O. Butler, USAAF, is named deputy commanding general.

MEDITERRANEAN: Fifteenth Air Force B-17s bomb the airfield at Istres-Le-Tube, while B-26 Marauders, escorted by P-38 Lightnings, bomb the Salon-de-Provence airfield.

Northwest African Air Force and Twelfth Air Force B-25 Mitchells attack the Eleusis airfield in Greece. Fifteenth Air Force P-38 Lightnings provide cover for the raid.

ITALY: The U.S. 36th Infantry Division relieves the 3rd Infantry Division in the Mignano area.

PACIFIC: U.S. submarine *Corvina* is sunk by Japanese submarine *I-176*, south of Truk.

CENTRAL PACIFIC: Seventh Air Force B-24 Liberators from Nanumea and Nukufetau Islands bomb Jaluit and Maloelap Atolls in the Marshalls. Kwajalein Atoll in the Marshalls and Little Makin Island and Tarawa Atoll in the Gilberts are attacked by individual bombers.

BOUGAINVILLE: Thirteenth Air Force B-25 Mitchells and B-24 Liberators bomb the Buka Island airfield, while other B-25 Mitchells attack logistics targets along the coastline of Bougainville. P-40s and P-39 Airacobras also carry out attacks on gun positions along the coast and near Kieta and Tonolai Harbors.

NEW GUINEA: Fifth Air Force B-25 Mitchells bomb targets near Finschhafen. P-39 Airacobras, with P-40s providing cover, strafe barges from Saidor to Madang. P-38 Lightnings encounter a large force of Japanese fighters over Wewak. Pilots report six enemy aircraft shot down and two P-38s lost. PBY Catalinas attack Japanese shipping off New Guinea, sinking a Japanese cargo vessel.

November 17

CBI: Fourteenth Air Force sends eight P-40s to strafe the airfield and barracks at Kengtung, China. In French Indochina, four P-40s attack construction equipment at Dong Cuong airfield.

MEDITERRANEAN: Fifteenth Air Force B-17s, escorted by P-38 Lightnings, attack the Eleusis airfield, destroying several aircraft on the ground and damaging the runways and support buildings. Northwest African Air Force B-25 Mitchells attack the airfield at Kalamaki.

PACIFIC: U.S. submarine *Capelin* departs Darwin, Australia, and disappears without a trace. U.S. submarine *Drum* torpedoes and sinks a Japanese submarine depot ship northwest of New Ireland.

CENTRAL PACIFIC: Seventh Air Force sends more than 20 B-24 Liberators to bomb Mille atoll in the Carolines, Maloelap Atoll in the Marshalls, and Tarawa Atoll in the Gilberts.

BOUGAINVILLE: Thirteenth Air Force B-24 Liberators bomb Buka and Bonis. B-25 Mitchells also bomb Kieta. Destroyers conduct naval gunfire missions against Buka airfield. Japanese aircraft attack convoy bringing reinforcements from the 21st Marine Regiment to the island. A high-speed transport is sunk.

November 18

CBI: Fourteenth Air Force P-40s strafe troops and sink a troop barge at Shihmen, China.

ETO: Eighth Air Force VIII Bomber Command sends B-24 Liberators against the Oslo/Kjeller airfield in Norway. Of the 82 bombers that hit the target, nine are lost and 13 are damaged; aircrews report 10 enemy aircraft destroyed. Over France, five B-17s drop 980,000 leaflets over Paris, Orleans, Chartres, Rennes, and Le Mans.

Ninth Air Force C-47s of the IX Troop Carrier Command conduct a rehearsal of the cross-Channel airborne operation with paratroopers of the U.S. 101st Airborne Division.

MEDITERRANEAN: Fifteenth Air Force B-17s, with P-38 escort, bomb Eleusis airfield.

ITALY: Major General Geoffrey Keyes arrives from Sicily and takes command of the newly reorganized II Corps, made up of the 3rd and 36th Infantry Divisions. The Fifth Army is now made up of three corps: the British X Corps with two infantry divisions east of the Garigliano River Valley; the II Corps covering a five-mile front south of the town of Mignano and north of Route 6; and the VI Corps, commanded by Major General John P. Lucas, composed of the 45th and 34th Infantry Divisions, holding the area from Monte Sammucro north of Route 6 to the town of Pozzilli, then to the area north of the town of Coli, covering a front of about 15 miles.

SOUTHWEST PACIFIC AREA: U.S. submarine *Bluefish* sinks a Japanese destroyer and damages an oiler *Ondo* in the Celebes Sea. U.S. submarine *Crevalle* unsuccessfully attacks a Japanese landing ship/aircraft transport in the Sulu Sea.

CENTRAL PACIFIC: Seventh Air Force sends 19 B-24 Liberators to bomb Mille Atoll, while two B-24s bomb Tarawa Atoll. Carrier Task Group 50.4, commanded by Rear Admiral Frederick C. Sherman, sends aircraft to attack Nauru.

BOUGAINVILLE: THE BATTLE OF PIVA FORKS Continuing to expand the perimeter to clear an area believed to be suitable for an airfield, the 2nd and 3rd Battalions, 3rd Marines, attack along the east fork of the Piva River, a meandering stream that cuts through the swamp.

Thirteenth Air Force B-24 Liberators bomb the airfields at Kara and on Buka Island.

NEW GUINEA: Fifth Air Force B-25 Mitchells and B-26 Marauders attack enemy positions near Sattelberg.

November 19

CBI: Fourteenth Air Force B-25 Mitchells attack Japanese shipping in the South China Sea, damaging a number of vessels and attacking warehouses and wharves at Swatow, China.

ETO: Eighth Air Force VIII Bomber Command sends 161 B-17s and three Pathfinder B-17s against targets near Gelsenkirchen, Germany. The bombers are unable to acquire the target due to a combination of weather and malfunctioning radar equipment and head to alternate targets. Over France, six B-17s drop over leaflets on Amiens and Reims, then head for the Netherlands and Belgium to drop leaflets over Amsterdam, The Hague, Brussels, and Ghent. Over two million leaflets are dropped on this mission.

MEDITERRANEAN: As the Fifth Army reorganizes, the British Eighth Army begins attacks against German defenses on the Adriatic coast of Italy. The Germans have established a forward line of defense called the Winter Line, anchored on the Garigliano River and stretching across the high hills guarding the Rapido River Valley and ending in the Apennines. The second line of defense is far more elaborate and is called the Gustav Line. It controls the dominating heights of the Rapido River Valley at the heights of Cassino, blocking Route 6, the main road to Rome. The plan is to draw German reinforcements away from the center, leaving weak defenses vulnerable to attack by the Fifth Army, which will push the enemy to the entrance of the Liri River Valley. The approach is marked by mountain peaks that stand like sentinels, providing clear observation and preventing any advance. The Germans have built log and earth fortifications on these peaks, and have carefully covered the approaches with mines and obstacles, all covered by machine guns, mortars, or artillery. There are three roads leading into Cassino, all of them covered by fire from the dominating hills above. No advance can be made until the mountain peaks are controlled by infantry.

ITALY: Twelfth Air Force XII Air Support Command A-36 Intruder (Apache) fighter-bombers and P-40s bomb a bridge near Cassino and the bridge at Pontecorvo.

BOUGAINVILLE: Thirteenth Air Force B-25 Mitchells bomb the Matchin Bay area and bomb the airfield on Ballale Island.

PACIFIC: U.S. submarine *Harder* attacks Japanese convoy and sinks two transports.

Captain John P. Cromwell, commanding a Submarine Coordinated Attack Group from USS *Sculpin*, possesses secret intelligence information concerning U.S. submarine and surface fleet operations, as well as future military plans. While establishing a line of submarines near Truk, the *Sculpin* is severely damaged by a

Japanese depth-charge attack. He orders the sub to surface and engage the enemy directly, buying time so the crew can abandon ship. Knowing his capture will provide the enemy with valuable intelligence information, Captain Cromwell decides to remain on board as the *Sculpin* sinks. By saving the crew and sacrificing himself in an unselfish act of gallantry Captain Cromwell will receive the Medal of Honor.

CENTRAL PACIFIC: Seventh Air Force sends 31 B-24 Liberators from Ellice Island bases to bomb Makin Island and Tarawa atoll.

BOUGAINVILLE: The Japanese roadblock on the Numa Numa Trail is captured by 3rd Battalion 3rd Marines, using light tanks. The 145th Infantry Regiment of the 37th Infantry Division arrives, along with the 135th, 136th, and 140th Artillery Battalions.

NEW GUINEA: Fifth Air Force B-25 Mitchells and B-26 Marauders bomb Japanese positions near Sattelberg and A-20 Havocs bomb enemy positions near Finschhafen.

November 20

ITALY: Northwest African Air Force B-25 Mitchells bomb the railway junction at Porto Civitanova, and attack targets around Pedaso, Giulianova, and Loreto.

SOUTHWEST PACIFIC AREA: Navy PBY Catalinas sink a Japanese cargo vessel north of New Ireland.

PACIFIC: U.S. submarine *Harder* torpedoes and sinks a Japanese transport northeast of the Marianas.

CENTRAL PACIFIC: Tarawa Operation Galvanic. The plan is for the V Amphibious Corps to capture three important objectives in the Carolines: Betio Island in Tarawa Atoll, which has an airstrip on it, Apamama atoll, which is suitable for an airfield, and Makin Atoll, which can be used as a base for future operations against the Marshalls. Marines of the 2nd Marine Division are assigned Betio Island, Tarawa Atoll, and Apamama. The 165th RCT of the 27th Infantry Division is to land on Makin Atoll. Vice Admiral Raymond A. Spruance, Commander of Central Pacific Forces, is the overall commander. The V Amphibious Corps is commanded by marine major general Holland "Howlin Mad" Smith. Rear Admiral Harry W. Hill commands Task Force 53, which has overall command and control of the amphibious landing on Tarawa. Major General Julian C. Smith is the 2nd Marine Division commander. Rear Admiral Richmond Kelly Turner commands Task Force 52, and has command and control of the amphibious assault on Makin. The army component is the 27th Infantry Division, commanded by Major General Ralph C. Smith. Admiral Chester W. Nimitz, concerned that the Japanese will attack the task forces with air and naval forces, has ordered the quick capture of the objectives. This has affected the support plan for the assaults.

Betio is about three miles long and 800 yards at its widest point and is surrounded completely by a coral reef that prevents landing craft from crossing and reaching shore. Sitting about 10 feet above sea level, it is one of the most heavily fortified positions in the world. There are nearly 500 pillboxes and reinforced bunkers, covered with obstacles, mines, and barbed wire, all covered by heavy caliber

Infantrymen from 2nd Battalion, 165th Infantry Regiment, approach Yellow beach on Makin Atoll, November 20, 1943.

guns and machine guns. Nearly 3,000 Japanese troops of the Special Naval Landing Force have been training and preparing for this attack for months.

The marine planners account for the limitations imposed by the coral reef by using LVT (Land Vehicle Tracked) amphibious tractors for the first wave. These tractors can swim from the ships and drive across the reef. The LVTs have no armor protection and no ramp, forcing troops to clamber over the sides. After a poorly coordinated air and naval bombardment, the initial assault makes the 10-mile approach to the island and lands three reinforced battalion landing teams on the northwest side of the island, centered on a lagoon, which has a long pier jutting into the ocean. Farthest west is Red Beach One, the target of 3rd Battalion 2nd Marines (3/2); in the center is Red Beach Two, the target of 2nd Battalion 2nd Marines (2/2); Red Beach Three is the responsibility of 2nd Battalion 8th Marines (2/8). Two destroyers enter the lagoon, preceded by minesweepers, but do not provide gunfire support until later. The LVTs are stopped at the seawall, and the marines jump over the sides of the Alligators into an intense volume of gunfire. About 1,500 Marines land in about 10 minutes, but are almost immediately pinned down on the narrow strip of sand against the seawall. Landing teams 3/2 and 2/2 take heavy casualties, but landing team 2/8 is able to land without serious casualties. Major Henry P. "Jim" Crowe commands on Red Beach Three; he wades in carrying a shotgun with a cigar clenched in his teeth. "Look," he calls to his men, "The sons of bitches can't hit me. Do you think they can hit you?" Get moving!" "Go!" Crowe's men are unable to join with 2/2. The initial assault bogs down as shocked and disorganized marines cluster in small groups. One group clusters on the western side of the island called Green Beach. Major Michael P. Ryan takes charge and organizes them to fight and moves about 500 yards eastward behind Red Beach One.

Colonel David M. Shoup, who had planned the entire operation, also commands the landing force and comes in with the first wave. Attempting to bring order out of chaos with only minimal communications to subordinates or to the division, Shoup orders reinforcements. The regimental reserve, landing team 1st Battalion 2nd Marines and the division reserve, 3rd Battalion 8th Marines in LCVP (Landing Craft Vehicle Personnel), cannot cross the reef, forcing the marines to wade in from 500 to 1,000 yards onto the beachhead. Japanese fire tears into the struggling ranks. Sherman tanks are landed, but only two of the 14, which make it to the shore, are operational at the end of the day. By the end of the day, five battalions are ashore, maybe 5,000 men—but at least 1,500 are casualties. General Julian Smith and Admiral Hill report to Spruance, "Issue in doubt." Yard by yard, individuals and small groups of marines advance into the teeth of enemy fire to take out Japanese positions close to the seawall.

Staff Sergeant William J. Bordelon is a member of the assault engineer platoon of the 1st Battalion, 18th Marines, attached to the 2nd Marine Division. Bordelon is one of only four survivors of his assault team who made it to the seawall. Staff Sergeant Bordelon begins improvising explosive charges and then scrambles from cover to attack and destroy two of the closest Japanese pillboxes. Painfully wounded when one of the demolition charges explodes in his hand, he continues to work, even after being wounded by enemy machine-gun fire as he tries to assault a third pillbox. Without explosives, he provides covering fire with his rifle to assist other marines as they scale the seawall. Disregarding his own wounds, Staff Sergeant Bordelon goes to the aid of one wounded marine demolition man and another marine wounded while trying to assist. He obtains additional explosives and sets out to attack a fourth Japanese machine-gun position when he is killed by enemy fire. Staff Sergeant Bordelon's exceptional heroism, his unselfish devotion to his fellow marines, and the skill he displayed in action against a determined and prepared enemy will win him the Medal of Honor.

First Lieutenant William Deane Hawkins, commanding a Scout Sniper Platoon, is among the first to land at Tarawa, taking on enemy defenders at the end of the Betio pier. As the situation becomes more desperate, First Lieutenant Hawkins leads his men in attacks on pillboxes and defensive positions using grenades and explosives. At dawn on 21 November, First Lieutenant Hawkins again leads an assault on a formidable position protected by five machine-guns. Ignoring the heavy fire directed against him, Hawkins returns fire, suppressing the enemy until he can destroy the position with hand grenades. Although wounded in the chest, he refuses to fall back, destroying three more pillboxes before he is fatally wounded. His extraordinary courage and relentless fighting spirit in the face of formidable opposition will win him the Congressional Medal of Honor.

Although suffering a serious and painful leg wound, Colonel Shoup rallies the broken elements that huddle along the sea wall and organizes the effort to advance against reinforced Japanese positions that have unrestricted fields of fire. Over the two days of major combat, Colonel Shoup has organized attacks against these exceptionally strong and fanatically defended positions. His personal leadership, indomitable will, and fearlessness in the face of enormous odds directly lead to the capture of the island, make him a legend in the Marine Corps, and he will win the Medal of Honor.

A turret fire on the battleship USS *Mississippi* kills 40 sailors and injures nine others.

CENTRAL PACIFIC: Makin Operation Galvanic. Preceded by closely coordinated naval gunfire and carrier air strikes, three battalion landing teams (designated as 1, 2, and 3 BLT) of the 165th Regimental Combat Team land on three beaches on Butaritari Island. The preparation includes 2,000-pound "daisy cutter" bombs on suspected Japanese positions in the center of the island. 1 BLT and 3 BLT land first on the far western side of the island and advance eastward encountering only light harassing fire from a few snipers. After another interval of naval and aerial bombardment, 2 BLT lands in the face of machine-gun fire on the northwestern side of the island in the lagoon and moves into the center of the Japanese defenses. The troops land with light and medium tanks and bring on communications equipment and immediately are able to emplace artillery. On order from Major General Holland Smith, V Amphibious Corps commander, 3 BLT goes into reserve in case it is needed on Tarawa. Some natives emerge from cover, shell-shocked but happy to see the Americans. They report that between 400 and 500 Japanese troops are on the island.

Encountering a formidable tank barrier, along with trenches, pillboxes, and gun emplacements, the infantrymen make a coordinated assault using tanks, engineers, and artillery to clear the eastern half of the island and consolidate their positions for the night. Major General Ralph C. Smith, the 27th Infantry Division commander, lands during the evening to take charge of the battle. Losses have been light, 25 killed and 62 wounded. One of the dead is Colonel J. G. Conroy, commander of the 165th RCT, killed while he was directing tanks against snipers.

BOUGAINVILLE: The Japanese counterattack the 3/3 Marines holding the Numa Numa roadblock. The enemy is thrown back after taking heavy losses.

Thirteenth Air Force attacks Bonis airfield with 45 B-25 Mitchells, Royal New Zealand Air Force Venturas, and P-38 Lightnings. B-25s also strafe coastal villages around Empress Augusta Bay.

NEW GUINEA: Fifth Air Force B-25 Mitchells and B-26 Marauders attack Japanese positions near the Sattelberg area and sink or damage transports in Hansa Bay. A-20 Havocs attack targets in the Lae area. B-24 Liberators bomb Gasmata Island off New Britain.

November 21

CBI: Fourteenth Air Force P-40s and four B-25 Mitchells attack the town of Tzeli, China. Four B-25s attack Japanese shipping on the South China Sea, damaging a cargo ship and buildings at Taiping-hsu airfield.

MEDITERRANEAN: Field Marshal Albert Kesselring takes command of Army Group C, the German command responsible for Italy. Army Group C consists of two armies, the Tenth Army, defending Rome and the southern area of Italy, and the Fourteenth Army, defending central and northern Italy. Kesselring intends to make the Allies fight for every mile gained, use the mountainous terrain to the best advantage, and wear them down with casualties.

ITALY: Fifteenth Air Force B-26 Marauders bomb the Civitavecchia harbor, a bridge at Fano, and the marshaling yard at Chiusi. Northwest African Air Force B-25 Mitchells bomb gun emplacements at Gaeta. Allied aircraft attack strongpoints in the Santa Maria Imbaro and Poggiofiorito areas.

PACIFIC: U.S. submarine *Trigger* sinks Japanese cargo ship in the Yellow Sea.

CENTRAL PACIFIC: Seventh Air Force B-24 Liberators from Funafuti Atoll and Nanumea Island in the Ellice Islands bomb Nauru Island in the Gilberts. U.S. submarine *Nautilus* lands a marine reconnaissance company on Abemama Island in the Gilberts.

TARAWA: Having gained some level of organization, Colonel Shoup orders each landing team to attack. Major Ryan is ordered to take all of Green Beach. 1st Battalion 8th Marines is to land on Red Beach Two near the pier. Unfortunately the marines of 1/8 begin to wade into the lagoon in the wrong direction and immediately are taken under fire from the Japanese positions. They suffer 300 casualties getting to the beachhead. Destroyers USS *Ringold* and USS *Dashiell* support with naval gunfire and are quite effective. Air support, however, is not. Ryan, making progress with his makeshift team, now supported by tanks, is reinforced with the 1st Battalion, 6th Marines. The 2nd Battalion 6th Marines lands on nearby Bairiki Island to secure the island for the landing of the artillery to land, which will fire support. Shoup sends a message to General Julian Smith: "Casualties many. Percentage dead: unknown. Combat efficiency: we are winning." On the night of November 21, Colonel Merritt A. "Red Mike" Edson, who won the Medal of Honor at Guadalcanal, takes command of the battle from Colonel Shoup.

The V Amphibious Corps Reconnaissance Unit, with a squad of army engineers supported by the submarine USS *Nautilus,* attacks Japanese defenders on Apamama Atoll. The *Nautilus* provides gunfire for the assault, but the Japanese are well prepared and the assault fails.

MAKIN: Supported by carrier air strikes, 1 BLT and 2 BLT clear enemy snipers and eliminate Japanese positions as they advance eastward into the heart of the Japanese defenses. The Japanese offer ineffective resistance, mostly due to the heavy volume of preparatory fire the day before. Again there is effective use of engineers, artillery, and tanks working with the infantry. Positions are consolidated and Japanese infiltrators are fought off during a long night. U.S. casualties are 18 killed, 26 wounded. Another two soldiers are killed and 13 wounded by a daisy cutter bomb from a navy aircraft that is mistakenly dropped on friendly lines.

SOLOMONS: Major General Ralph J. Mitchell (USMC) replaces Brigadier General Nathan F. Twining (USAAF) as Commander Air Solomons (COMAIRSOLS).

NEW GUINEA: Fifth Air Force A-20 Havocs attack the Finschhafen area. B-24 Liberators bomb Gasmata Island off New Britain.

November 22

CARIBBEAN: German submarine *U-516* torpedoes and sinks U.S. tanker off Panama.

MEDITERRANEAN: Sextant Conference. President Franklin D. Roosevelt, Prime Minister Winston S. Churchill, and Generalissimo Chiang Kai-shek confer in Cairo, Egypt. Talks are held concerning Operation Overlord (the overall plan for the invasion of western Europe) and the possibility of expanding operations in the Mediterranean Theater of Operations. Churchill desires an Allied operation to capture the Greek island of Rhodes (Operation Accolade), which could delay Overlord. The leaders also discuss future operations against Japan and plans for the China-Burma-India Theater (CBI). These included a plan for an amphibious landing and offensive in Burma (Operation Buccaneer and Champion) and basing the new long-range B-29 bombers in the CBI (Operation Twilight).

ITALY: Fifteenth Air Force B-26 Marauders, escorted by P-38 Lightnings, bomb the rail lines at Foligno and a bridge at Ciciana. Twelfth Air Force XII Air Support Command sends over 100 P-40s, B-25 Mitchells, and RAF aircraft against German positions in the Lanciano-Fossacesia area. P-40s also attack transportation targets at Fabriano, Viticuso, Vallerotonda, and Urbino. A-36 Intruder (Apache) fighter-bombers attack the chemical works, harbor, and railyards at Civitavecchia and bomb San Vittore del Lazio.

SOUTHWEST PACIFIC AREA: U.S. submarine *Drum* is damaged by depth charges north of New Guinea and ends its patrol.

PACIFIC: U.S. submarine *Seahorse* sinks a Japanese cargo ship in the East China Sea. U.S. submarine *Tinosa* sinks two Japanese cargo ships off Palau and receives minor damage in a depth charge attack.

CENTRAL PACIFIC: Seventh Air Force sends 11 B-24 Liberators to bomb Mille Atoll in the Carolines. Aircrews report two Japanese fighters shot down.

TARAWA: Colonel Edson orders 1/6, assembled on Green Beach and in good order, to attack eastward and make contact with marines on Red One. The 1/8 is to attack west to eliminate Japanese resistance facing the lagoon in front of Red One. The rest of the 8th Marines (2/8 and 3/8) are to attack east. The marines, better organized and receiving resupply, now launch coordinated attacks with engineers, tanks, and artillery. The 3rd Battalion 6th Marines lands on Green Beach.

On Red Beach Three, the 8th Marines are unable to advance against three heavily fortified strongpoints. A shore party led by First Lieutenant Alexander "Sandy" Bonnyman appears on the beach, and on his own initiative he organizes a team of 21 engineers with flamethrowers and demolition charges to make a coordinated assault on the positions. As the marine riflemen provide covering fire, Bonnyman leads his group into a maelstrom of fire, methodically taking down each position. As the Japanese begin to break, Bonnyman is killed in the firefight. Only 13 of his men survive the attack. Bonnyman's cool courage and leadership in turning the tide of battle for the 8th Marines will win him the Medal of Honor.

General Julian Smith links up with Colonel Edson after nearly being killed when he attempts to enter the lagoon. The exhausted marines are unable to sustain the

Marines of the 2nd Marine Division, working in teams, assault a Japanese defensive position on Tarawa about November 22, 1943.

momentum of their attacks. The 2/8 and 3/8 are rotated out of the battle line to Bairiki, while artillery is landed on Green Beach.

During the night, the Japanese attempt a furious coordinated counterattack on the marine positions. They are stopped by artillery, naval gunfire from destroyers (who use up every one of their five-inch gun shells during the night), and by determined marines, who often fight the enemy hand-to-hand.

U.S. destroyer rams Japanese submarine *I-35*.

MAKIN: General Holland Smith authorizes the release of 3 BLT to conduct the final attack on Butaritari Island. The fresh battalion makes a rapid advance, supported by tanks, artillery, and carrier air strikes. A water-borne flanking movement lands troops on the backside of the island to cut off the Japanese retreat and to clear Kuma Island of any enemy troops. The infantry stops about 5,000 yards short of the end of the island as night begins to fall. The advance results in six killed and 17 wounded. During the night, Japanese troops make several attacks on the American positions. It becomes quickly apparent to the men that many of the Japanese are drunk.

BOUGAINVILLE: Thirteenth Air Force P-40s encounter Japanese fighters over Empress Augusta Bay and report five enemy kills. P-38 Lightnings strafe barges and shore targets at Chabai.

NEW BRITAIN: Fifth Air Force sends over 100 B-25 Mitchells and B-24 Liberators to bomb Cape Gloucester and Gasmata Island.

November 23

CBI: Fourteenth Air Force sends 13 B-25 Mitchells, 24 P-40s, and seven P-51 Mustangs against the railroad yards and warehouse area of Yoyang, China.

ETO: Ninth Air Force B-26 Marauders bomb the Berck-sur-Mer and Saint-Omer/ Longuenesse airfields in France.

ITALY: The 1st Special Service Force, a group of Canadian and American commandos led by Colonel Robert T. Frederick, is attached to the U.S. 36th Infantry Division.

SOUTHWEST PACIFIC AREA: U.S. submarine *Blackfish* sinks a Japanese transport off northern New Guinea. U.S. submarine *Capelin* sinks a Japanese cargo ship in the Molucca Sea.

PACIFIC: U.S. submarine *Gudgeon* attacks a Japanese convoy, sinking an escort vessel and transport and damaging two fleet tankers in the East China Sea.

CENTRAL PACIFIC: Seventh Air Force sends six B-24 Liberators to bomb Emidj and Jabor islands in the Jaluit Atoll in the Marshalls.

TARAWA: Japanese resistance is shattered and 3/6 advances in a coordinated assault with tanks and engineers to the eastern tip of the island, killing 450 of the enemy and

Marines clear the final Japanese defensive positions on Tarawa with flamethrowers, November 23, 1943.

suffering 34 casualties. The last area to fall is the defenses in front of Red One, as both 1/8 and 3/2 attack to clear out the last few Japanese left alive. Many of the enemy kill themselves rather than be captured. By 1305, General Julian Smith notifies General Holland Smith that the island is secure. U.S. aircraft begin landing on the airstrip almost immediately. It is named Hawkins Field after Lieutenant Deane Hawkins, whose bravery on the first day of the battle as the scout-sniper platoon leader stood out among innumerable acts of bravery. The Americans capture 146 prisoners, but these are almost all Korean laborers. Only eight members of the Special Naval Landing Force are captured—the rest of the nearly 3,000 who defended the island are dead.

In the three-day assault on Tarawa, 18,088 marines and sailors landed and suffered 3,407 casualties. The marines lost 997 killed, 2,233 wounded, and 88 missing. Navy casualties are 30 killed and 59 wounded. The American public is shocked by the casualties and by the headlines of American newspapers, reporting that marines were slaughtered wholesale. Congress even talks of an investigation. But General Alexander Vandegrift, the new commandant of the Marine Corps, and Colonel Edson both provide full facts to the press and the shock is replaced by a resolve to face such terrible losses in the future.

The experience on Tarawa shapes the American approach to amphibious operations in the Central Pacific for the remainder of the war. Issues of fire support coordination for air and naval gunfire are resolved; the Japanese defenses are closely studied to make adjustments in the weapons and tactics employed against them. The LVT and the Sherman tank have proved their worth and will be incorporated in future amphibious assaults.

Most of all, Tarawa becomes one of those touchstones in American history, where the word is spoken reverently, like Gettysburg or Valley Forge, unforgettable places where American courage is enshrined forever.

MAKIN: The tip of Butaritari Island is reached by 3 BLT, as tanks and infantrymen kill isolated groups of Japanese. General Ralph Smith reports to General Holland Smith: "Makin Taken." Out of the 284 troops of the Japanese Special Naval Landing Force that occupied the island, three are captured. There are approximately 300 Korean laborers on the island as well, and 101 surrender. U.S. casualties are 66 killed and 150 wounded

GILBERTS: The 2nd Battalion 6th Marines lands on Eita Island in pursuit of the last Japanese defenders on the Gilberts. Japanese sub *I-35* is sunk by two U.S. destroyers.

BOUGAINVILLE: Chabai is attacked by 23 B-25 Mitchells, six Royal New Zealand Air Force Venturas, and 24 Navy F4U Corsairs. Two B-24 Liberators attack the target again, later in the day. Over Buka Island, 19 B-24 Liberators bomb Bonis and Buka airfields. Navy Task Force 39, the cruiser and destroyer force, bombards the area near Buka and Bonis.

NEW GUINEA: Fifth Air Force B-25 Mitchells and A-20 Havocs bomb targets around Finschhafen.

November 24

CBI: Fourteenth Air Force B-25 Mitchells and 16 P-40s bomb Hanshow, China. B-25 Mitchells attack Amoy harbor and make two direct hits on a docked freighter.

CARIBBEAN: German submarine *U-516* torpedoes and sinks a U.S. freighter northwest of Cristobal, near the Panama Canal Zone.

ETO: Eighth Air Force sends seven B-17s to drop 2.4 million leaflets over Lille, France, and Brussels, Antwerp, Charleroi/Gosselies, and Ghent, Belgium.

MEDITERRANEAN: Fifth Army outlines its objectives for the December offensive, Operation Raincoat, the first assault on the German defenses known as the Winter Line. The offensive is aimed at capturing the three peaks that control the entrance to the Liri Valley. In Phase I, the British X Corps will assault the slopes of Monte Camino, while the II Corps attacks the lower hills of Monte la Difensa and Monte Maggiore. X Corps will then relieve II Corps in the area around Monte Maggiore. VI Corps will conduct simultaneous small diversionary attacks. Phase II is the capture of Monte Sammucro and the opening of the Colli-Atina Road. Phase III is an attack up the Liri Valley.

Twelfth Air Force Northwest African Air Force and Allied bombers support the British Eighth Army near Fossacesia. XII Air Support Command A-36 Intruder (Apache) fighter-bombers bomb Civitavecchia harbor.

Fifteenth Air Force B-17s, with P-38 escorts, attack the submarine base at Toulon.

PACIFIC: In successive separate attacks, USAAF B-24s and U.S. Navy PBY Catalinas damage a Japanese light cruiser transporting soldiers and supplies to Garove Island north of New Britain, forcing it to abandon the attempt.

CENTRAL PACIFIC: Seventh Air Force sends 20 B-24 Liberators to bomb Maloelap Atoll in the Marshalls. Aircrews report damage to the landing strip and hits on a cargo vessel. Japanese submarine *I-175* torpedoes and sinks an escort carrier, USS *Linscome Bay*. Over 600 men perish with the ship. *I-175* is damaged by depth charges from escort ships. The first attack in the Gilberts is costly for the navy; along with the loss of the *Linscome Bay*, nine aircraft are also lost in combat and the total casualties for the navy over a four-day period are 752 killed and 291 wounded.

MAKIN: The 165th RCT begins to re-embark, leaving behind an occupation force on Butaritari Island. For weeks afterward, individual Japanese soldiers will rush out from their hiding places to attack American troops.

BOUGAINVILLE: The 2nd and 3rd Battalions, 3rd Marines, advance on the East-West trail behind the heaviest artillery bombardment of the Pacific war. A 20-minute artillery preparation fires over 5,600 rounds on Japanese bunkers, foxholes, and trenches lying in the low swampy ground amidst heavy jungle. The advance is measured in yards. Even in the midst of battle, the frontline troops receive a real turkey dinner for Thanksgiving, an amazing logistical feat in itself. The men sit wherever convenient to eat their meal, completely ignoring the blood and carnage around them. The marines succeed in capturing the high ground beyond the trail but, during the course of the battle, suffer 115 casualties. Japanese losses are estimated at over 1,000.

Thirteenth Air Force sends B-25 Mitchells to hit the airfield at Kahili and a possible radio station at Mutupina Point. Fighters strafe Gazelle and Queen Carola harbors. Buka Island is bombed by 25 B-24 Liberators.

NEW GUINEA: Fifth Air Force B-25 Mitchells, B-26 Marauders, and A-20 Havocs bomb the village of Kalasa. Logistics sites near Finschhafen are bombed by 15 A-20

Havocs and B-25 Mitchells, escorted by P-38 Lightnings. B-24 Liberators, supported by P-38 Lightnings, bomb Gasmata Island.

November 25

CBI: Tenth Air Force B-25 Mitchells, escorted by P-51 Mustangs, bomb the Mingaladon airfield in Rangoon, Burma. Aircrews report two aircraft destroyed on the ground and two destroyed in the air. Two P-51 Mustangs are shot down. Fourteenth Air Force sends 14 B-25 Mitchells, with 16 P-38 Lightnings and P-51 Mustangs as escort, to attack the airfield at Shinchiku, China. Aircrews report damage to the airfield, hangars, and barracks. Enemy losses are estimated at 32 aircraft destroyed.

ATLANTIC: A U.S. Navy PB4Y Privateer (a B-24 variant) sinks German submarine *U-849* in the South Atlantic.

ETO: Eighth Air Force VIII Fighter Command employs P-47 Thunderbolts as bombers to attack the Saint-Omer airfield in France. P-38 Lightnings and P-47 Thunderbolts conduct offensive sweeps near Lille. The 401st Bombardment Group (Heavy) reaches operational status, giving the Eighth Air Force 22 operational heavy bomber groups. The Allied Expeditionary Air Force (AEAF) is activated. The RAF's Second Tactical Air Force and the U.S. Ninth Air Force are to be under the AEAF's operational control.

ITALY: Fifth Army's plan for an amphibious landing at Anzio (Operation Shingle) is approved. Twelfth Air Force XII Air Support Command aircraft bomb German gun positions and strongpoints near Lanciano and Fossacesia.

PACIFIC: U.S. destroyer sinks Japanese submarine *I-19* north of Gilberts. U.S. submarine *Albacore* sinks a Japanese cargo ship off northern New Guinea. U.S. submarine *Searaven* sinks a Japanese fleet tanker north of Ponape Island in the Carolines.

GILBERTS: The V Amphibious Corps Reconnaissance Unit, with a squad of army engineers supported by the submarine *Nautilus,* secures Apamama Atoll after discovering that the Japanese defenders have killed themselves. Work immediately begins on establishing an airfield capable of supporting Seventh Air Force bombers. The airfield will be named after the fighter ace, Lieutenant Commander Edward "Butch" O'Hare, killed in action on November 27. A destroyer sinks Japanese submarine *I-40* in the northern Gilberts.

BOUGAINVILLE: The 1st Battalion 9th Marines passes through the weary 3rd Marines to continue the advance. They encounter strongly entrenched Japanese defenders on a piece of high ground the marines later call Grenade Hill, because of the number of grenades the Japanese throw at the marines.

The Japanese send three destroyer transports with about 900 men and two destroyer escorts to reinforce Buka. Captain Arleigh A. Burke, commanding Destroyer Squadron 23, intercepts the force and in typical style makes an aggressive torpedo attack, sinking the two escort destroyers. The destroyer transports make a run for Rabaul, as Burke pursues.

NEW IRELAND: The Battle of Cape St. George. Destroyer Squadron 23, under command of Captain Arleigh A. Burke, attacks five Japanese destroyers. Three Japanese destroyers are sunk by torpedoes and gunfire and another destroyer is damaged. Burke's ships receive no damage.

November 26

CBI: Fourteenth Air Force B-25 Mitchells bomb Kiangling airfield in China. B-25s damage a freighter in Honghai Bay. Eight P-40s attack the Cam Duong railroad yards in French Indochina. B-25s sink a Japanese auxiliary minesweeper off Canton, China.

ATLANTIC: The Sextant Conference. The first part of the Sextant Conference concludes in Cairo. The CCS in preparation for the Eureka Conference in Teheran, lays out a plan for operations in Europe in 1944. In the Mediterranean, the Allies will advance to the Pisa-Rimini line. The partisans in Yugoslavia would be given aid. Turkey will be induced to enter the war. The Allies will capture the island of Rhodes to secure access to the Dardanelles. An amphibious operation will be conducted in the Bay of Bengal. Overlord, the cross-Channel invasion of Europe, will be delayed.

ETO: Eighth Air Force VIII Bomber Command attacks Bremen, Germany, and attempts to attack Paris, France. Over the port of Bremen, 350 B-17s and 77 B-24 Liberators are guided by 13 radar-equipped Pathfinder B-17s. U.S. losses are 22 B-17s and three B-24 Liberators. Another 142 B-17s, 17 Pathfinder B-17s, and 20 B-24s are damaged. Aircrews report at least 16 German fighters destroyed. Four B-17s are lost and 18 damaged in an attempt to attack Paris aborted due to heavy cloud cover. Aircrews report eight enemy aircraft destroyed. The 28 P-38 Lightnings and 353 P-47 Thunderbolts that escort these two missions report 36 enemy confirmed kills, three probables, and nine possibles. Four P-47s are shot down and the pilots are reported as missing. Another 10 fighters are damaged.

Ninth Air Force sends 140 B-26 Marauders to attack the Cambrai/Epinoy and Roye/Amy airfields in France. Military construction in Audinghen is also bombed.

ITALY: Fifteenth Air Force B-17s bomb the viaduct at Recco and the Rimini marshaling yard and bridge. B-26 Marauders bomb Cassino, and B-24 Liberators bomb bridges in the Fano, Cesano, Senigallia, and Falconara area. Twelfth Air Force B-25 Mitchells and A-20 Havocs attack the Ancona marshaling yard and harbor and German positions near Fossacesia, Lanciano, Castelfrentano, and troop concentrations near Palombaro and Casoli.

SOUTHWEST PACIFIC AREA: Vice Admiral Thomas C. Kinkaid takes command of the Seventh Fleet, replacing Vice Admiral Arthur S. Carpenter.

PACIFIC: U.S. submarine *Bowfin* sinks a Japanese army tanker and merchant cargo ship in the Andaman Sea. U.S. submarine *Raton* damages a Japanese ammunition ship northwest of the Saint Matthias Group. U.S. submarine *Ray* makes an unsuccessful attack on a Japanese cargo vessel between Truk and New Ireland, but sinks a Japanese transport southwest of Truk. U.S. submarine *Tinosa* sinks a Japanese cargo ship and damages another near the Palau Islands.

BOUGAINVILLE: The Japanese evacuate Grenade Hill, allowing the 1/9 Marines an easy victory.

Thirteenth Air Force B-24 Liberators, B-25 Mitchells, and fighter aircraft attack Buka and Bonis airfields.

NEW BRITAIN: Fifth Air Force B-24 Liberators bomb Gasmata Island and report hitting a Japanese cruiser off the coast.

NEW GUINEA: Australian forces clear the last Japanese defenders off Satelberg Ridge, opening the way to Finschhafen. The Japanese begin retreating westward to Saidor.

Fifth Air Force B-25 Mitchells attack barge locations near Sio. P-40s and P-47 Thunderbolts attack Japanese positions around Alexishafen, Madang, and Nubia. Over Finschhafen, P-39 Airacobras attack 40 Japanese fighters and bombers. Pilots report four aircraft shot down.

November 27

CBI: Tenth Air Force B-24 Liberators, escorted by P-38 Lightnings, and B-25 Mitchells, escorted by P-51 Mustangs, bomb Insein, Burma. Japanese fighters intercept the incoming strike and shoot down six fighters and three B-24s. Aircrews report 19 Japanese fighters shot down. B-24s sink Japanese army hospital ship in the Bismarck Sea. Fourteenth Air Force B-25 Mitchells bomb the docks and warehouses at Swatow, China, and attack a convoy of nine vessels heading toward Amoy in the Formosa Strait. Aircrews report one destroyer sunk and a destroyer and cargo ship damaged. In actuality, a transport is sunk and a torpedo boat damaged.

ITALY: Fifteenth Air Force B-17s, escorted by P-38 Lightnings, bomb the marshaling yard and bridges at Rimini and Grizzana and a bridge approach on the Reno River southwest of Bologna. Twelfth Air Force A-20 Havocs and B-25 Mitchells, with fighters and RAF aircraft of Northwest African Air Force, bomb enemy positions, gun emplacements, and transportation targets around Lanciano, Fossacesia, Castelfrentano, and Casoli. B-25s bomb Porto Civitanova.

PACIFIC: U.S. submarine *Bowfin* sinks a Vichy French cargo ship off the coast of French Indochina, near Binh Dinh. U.S. submarine *Seahorse* sinks a Japanese fleet tanker in the East China Sea.

CENTRAL PACIFIC: Seventh Air Force sends eight B-24 Liberators to bomb Mili Atoll in the Marshalls.

GILBERTS: The 2nd Battalion 6th Marines fights the Battle of Buariki on Eita Island in heavy jungle against determined Japanese of the Special Naval Landing Force. The combat is mostly close-in and brutal. Every one of the 175 Japanese is killed; 32 Americans are dead and 59 are wounded. This major combat action is eclipsed by the aftermath of the Battle of Tarawa.

BOUGAINVILLE: Thirteenth Air Force B-25 Mitchells bomb Queen Carola Harbor. B-24 Liberators bomb Bonis airfield. Other B-25 Mitchells and Royal New Zealand Venturas attack targets at the mouth of the Mobiai River and at Mutupina Point. The airfield on Buka Island is bombed by more than 20 B-24 Liberators.

NEW GUINEA: Fifth Air Force B-25 Mitchells and B-26 Marauders bomb the airfields at Boram and Finschhafen, and the town and harbor at Wewak. Aircrews report 15 enemy aircraft destroyed and 12 barges sunk.

November 28

CBI: Tenth Air Force B-24 Liberators bomb the Botataung docks at Rangoon. Aircrews report heavy damage to the docks and four enemy fighters shot down. B-25 Mitchells attack Sagaing. Fourteenth Air Force P-40s bomb and strafe Japanese barracks near Litsaoho, China. P-40s strafe the town area and airfield at Luang Prabang and attack the radio facilities and a barracks at Tran Ninh in French Indochina.

The "Big Three" at Tehran, Iran, during the Eureka conference, held from November 28 to December 1, 1943. Seated from left to right: Premier Joseph Stalin of the Soviet Union, President Franklin D. Roosevelt of the United States, and Prime Minister Winston S. Churchill of Great Britain. This is the first face-to-face meeting of the three war leaders.

MEDITERRANEAN: Twelfth Air Force B-25 Mitchells bomb warehouses, docks, marshaling yards, barracks, shipping, and other targets at Sibenik, Zara, and Dubrovnik.

Eureka Conference begins in Iran. President Franklin D. Roosevelt, Prime Minister Winston S. Churchill, and Marshall Joseph V. Stalin meet in Teheran, Iran, until November 30. Presented with the CCS proposals for operations in Europe in 1944, Stalin agrees with the American strategic approach for 1944 and endorses Overlord (the cross-Channel invasion of western Europe) and Anvil (the complementary plan for the invasion of southern France in support of Overlord), which are to be given priority over all other operations. Stalin promises to initiate an offensive timed with the cross-Channel invasion.

Concerning the Pacific, the United States will continue offensive operations in the Central and South Pacific drives, including seizure of the Marianas as a base for strategic bombing attacks on Japan. Much to the relief of the Americans, Stalin promises to enter the war against Japan once Germany has surrendered. The Allies discuss postwar plans, including a future United Nations organization and the settlement of boundaries for Poland.

SOUTHWEST PACIFIC AREA: U.S. submarine *Raton* sinks two Japanese cargo ships north of New Guinea.

PACIFIC: U.S. submarine *Bowfin* sinks two Japanese cargo ships off Binh Dinh, French Indochina, but is damaged by Japanese gunfire, ending its patrol. U.S. submarines *Pargo* and *Snook* attack a Japanese transport convoy northwest of the Marianas. *Snook* sinks one transport.

CENTRAL PACIFIC: Seventh Air Force sends 11 B-24 Liberators to bomb Nauru Island.

BOUGAINVILLE: Thirteenth Air Force B-25 Mitchells bomb and strafe the area near Mutupina Point. Fighters strafe Tinputs harbor and barges at Tonolai.

NEW GUINEA: Fifth Air Force B-24 Liberators bomb the airfields at Wewak and Boram. More than 40 B-25 Mitchells, B-26 Marauders, and A-20 Havocs attack villages on the Huon Peninsula and targets near Finschhafen.

November 29

CBI: Fourteenth Air Force B-25 Mitchells bomb the airfield and warehouses at Swatow and the power station at Amoy, China.

ATLANTIC: TBF Avengers from escort carrier USS *Bogue* accompanying convoy UGS (United States to Mediterranean, Slow) sink German submarine *U-86* east of the Azores. Two other U-boats are attacked, *U-238* and *U-764*, but escape without damage.

ETO: Eighth Air Force VIII Bomber Command sends 360 B-17s, escorted by 38 P-38 Lightnings and 314 P-47 Thunderbolts, against the port of Bremen, Germany. Only 154 bombers hit the target due to heavy clouds and malfunctioning radar equipment. Aircrews report 15 enemy fighters destroyed, but 13 B-17s are lost and 46 are damaged. The fighter pilots report 15 confirmed kills, four probables, and six possibles. U.S. fighter losses are seven P-38s and nine P-47s shot down; two P-47s are damaged. Over Paris, Reims, Chartres, Amiens, Le Mans, Orleans, and Rouen, France, eight B-17s drop more than a million-and-a-half leaflets.

Ninth Air Force sends 53 B-26 Marauders to bomb Chievres airfield in France.

MEDITERRANEAN: Twelfth Air Force B-25 Mitchells bomb Sarajevo, Yugoslavia.

ITALY: VI Corps makes diversionary attacks before Fifth Army's scheduled December 3 offensive, Operation Raincoat. Division and corps artillery fire on targets around San Pietro and San Vittore. The 3rd Ranger Battalion makes a diversionary reconnaissance in force toward San Pietro, an advance preceded by over 2,200 artillery rounds. Later in the day, after encountering strong German defenses, the battalion retreats, covered by an artillery barrage of 2,600 shells.

Other attacks are intended to capture limited objectives between Monte Corno and Monte Mare in order to draw German reserves north and away from the II Corps, where the main attack is to occur. The 45th Infantry Division is ordered to conduct attacks to seize favorable ground and open the Filignano-Sant' Elia road. The 179th Infantry Regiment attacks La Bandita and Monte La Posta to capture the village of Lagone. The 1st Battalion 179th Infantry attacks are stopped by heavy machine gun, mortar, and rifle fire from the hilltops. The 157th Infantry Regiment attacks to clear the road to Sant' Elia.

The 34th Infantry Division attacks to clear the Coli-Atina road and seize the hills north and south of Cerasuolo. The 1st Battalion 168th Infantry Regiment makes progress on Monte Pantano and stops several strong German counterattacks. The 133rd Infantry Regiment advances against German defenders on hills between Castelnuovo and Cerasuolo.

Seventy Fifteenth Air Force B-26 Marauders bomb the Grosseto airfield and marshaling yards. B-24 Liberators, with P-38 Lightnings flying escort, bomb near Furbara.

Near Cerasuolo, Staff Sergeant Allan M. Ohata, his squad leader, and three men, one of them Private Mikio Hasemoto, are ordered to protect the left flank of a platoon of Company B, 100th Infantry Battalion (Separate). When almost 40 enemy soldiers assault their position under the covering fire of two machine gunners, Private Hasemoto engages them with his Browning Automatic Rifle (BAR). When his weapon is damaged by enemy fire, he runs 10 yards to the rear, grabs another BAR and rejoins the fight. In the meantime, Staff Sergeant Ohata leaves his position and advances 15 yards through heavy fire to give Hasemoto covering fire, killing 10 of the enemy. When the second BAR jams, Hasemoto finds an M-1 rifle. Hasemoto and Ohata continue engaging the enemy until only three soldiers are left standing. The two men then charge forward to finish the fight. The following day Ohata and Hasemoto again defend their position against determined enemy attacks. Although Private Hasemoto is killed by enemy fire, his example of courage under fire and devotion to duty earns him the Medal of Honor. Staff Sergeant Ohata will also be awarded the Medal of Honor for his exemplary courage under fire.

During a flank attack on enemy-held high ground, Private Shizuya Hayashi of Company A charges an enemy machine-gun position singlehandedly, killing or driving off the defenders. Private Hayashi then engages an enemy antiaircraft gun, which opens fire on the company as it advances. Private Hayashi returns fire, killing nine enemy soldiers and capturing four others. Private Hayashi's extraordinary heroism in the face of enemy fire will win him the Medal of Honor.

SOUTHWEST PACIFIC AREA: U.S. submarine *Bonefish* sinks a Japanese cargo ship off Kangean Island, north of Bali. The ship is carrying 546 British prisoners of war.

PACIFIC: U.S. submarine *Paddle* attacks a Japanese fleet tanker near Eniwetok Atoll. U.S. submarines *Pargo* and *Snook* pursue the Japanese transport convoy northwest of the Marianas, each submarine sinking a transport and avoiding the escorts' counterattack. U.S. submarine *Snapper* sinks a Japanese transport off Hachijo Jima.

BOUGAINVILLE: The 1st Marine Parachute Battalion lands before dawn east of Cape Torokina at Koiari beach to attack a Japanese logistics base. Overrunning the site, they encounter heavy Japanese resistance. U.S. destroyer *Fullam* supported by F4U Corsairs provides close supporting fire to allow the marines to be evacuated.

Thirteenth Air Force sends 18 B-25 Mitchells against Tinputs Harbor. B-24 Liberators bomb Kieta, while P-39 Airacobras and navy SBD Dauntless dive-bombers attack warehouses at Mosigetta. Fighters attack Gazelle harbor and gun positions near Torokina Plantation. Navy Task Group 74.2, commanded by Captain Frank R. Walker, with two U.S. destroyers and two Australian destroyers, bombards enemy positions on Gasmata.

NEW BRITAIN: Fifth Air Force B-25 Mitchells and B-26 Marauders bomb Cape Gloucester.

November 30

CBI: Fourteenth Air Force P-40s bomb fuel and ammunition storage areas at Luchiangpa, China.

ATLANTIC: Eureka Conference statement

> We the President of the United States, the Prime Minister of Great Britain, and the Premier of the Soviet Union, have met these four days past, in this, the Capital of our Ally, Iran, and have shaped and confirmed our common policy.
>
> We express our determination that our nations shall work together in war and in the peace that will follow.
>
> As to war—our military staffs have joined in our round table discussions, and we have concerted our plans for the destruction of the German forces. We have reached complete agreement as to the scope and timing of the operations to be undertaken from the east, west and south.
>
> The common understanding which we have here reached guarantees that victory will be ours.
>
> And as to peace—we are sure that our concord will win an enduring Peace. We recognize fully the supreme responsibility resting upon us and all the United Nations to make a peace which will command the goodwill of the overwhelming mass of the peoples of the world and banish the scourge and terror of war for many generations.
>
> With our Diplomatic advisors we have surveyed the problems of the future. We shall seek the cooperation and active participation of all nations, large and small, whose peoples in heart and mind are dedicated, as are our own peoples, to the elimination of tyranny and slavery, oppression and intolerance. We will welcome them, as they may choose to come, into a world family of Democratic Nations.
>
> No power on earth can prevent our destroying the German armies by land, their U Boats by sea, and their war plants from the air.
>
> Our attack will be relentless and increasing.
>
> Emerging from these cordial conferences we look with confidence to the day when all peoples of the world may live free lives, untouched by tyranny, and according to their varying desires and their own consciences.
>
> We came here with hope and determination. We leave here, friends in fact, in spirit and in purpose.

Churchill, Stalin, and Roosevelt agree to support the Yugoslav partisans. They also agree to conduct Overlord in May of 1944, along with Anvil, the supporting attack in southern France. The Soviets will launch an offensive to contain as many German divisions as possible on the eastern front.

At the end of this conference, it is clear to Churchill that Britain has become the junior partner in the Alliance and that Britain's strategic objectives are growing irrelevant to the emerging partnership between Roosevelt and Stalin. Roosevelt leaves Teheran with a strong belief that a strong Soviet-American cooperation will both secure and maintain a peaceful postwar world.

TBF Avengers from escort carrier USS *Bogue* damage German submarine *U-238* east of the Azores.

ETO: Eighth Air Force VIII Bomber Command attacks the industrial area at Solingen, Germany, with B-17s, 29 B-24 Liberators, and three radar-equipped Pathfinder B-17s, escorted by 20 P-38 Lightnings and 327 P-47 Thunderbolts. Cloud cover limits the Liberators' effectiveness, and only 79 B-17s of 349 hit the target, led by one radar B-17. Three B-17s are shot down and 12 bombers are damaged. Aircrews report one enemy fighter destroyed. Fighter pilots report two probable kills and one possible kill. One P-38 is lost and one damaged, and five P-47s are lost and one damaged. The six pilots are listed as missing. Six B-17s drop over 1 million leaflets on Paris, Rouen, and Tours in France, then on Krefeld and Opladen in Germany.

ITALY: In the 45th Infantry Division sector, the 1st Battalion of the 179th continues its attack on La Bandita and attempts to take Langone. Both attacks are halted by enemy fire. In the 34th Division area, the 1st Battalion of the 168th Infantry Regiment holds positions on Monte Pantano against several German counterattacks. The 1st Battalion of the 133rd Infantry Regiment enters Castelnuovo; the 3rd Battalion moves to Monte la Rocca, and the 100th Battalion moves to Croce Hill. The regiment's progress is stopped by mortar and artillery fire.

Fifteenth Air Force B-26 Marauders bomb the Monte Molino railroad bridge, Montalto di Castro, Bastia, and Torgiano. B-24 Liberators, escorted by P-38 Lightnings, bomb Fiume. Twelfth Air Force A-20 Havocs attack German defenses around Lanciano, Fossacesia, Orsogna, Castelfrentano, and Guardiagrele. They also fly ground support missions for the 34th Infantry Division defending Monte Pantano.

SOUTHWEST PACIFIC AREA: Lieutenant General Walter Krueger, commander of Alamo Force, orders the 112th Cavalry Regimental Combat Team (in reality a 1,500-man detachment from the Texas National Guard, without horses) to be prepared to land on Arawe, New Britain, by December 15.

PACIFIC: U.S. submarine *Gato* sinks a Japanese army transport east of the Yap Islands, escaping counterattacks by an escorting submarine chaser. U.S. submarine *Skate* attacks Japanese carrier *Zuiho* with four torpedoes north of Truk. None of the torpedoes score a hit.

CENTRAL PACIFIC: Seventh Air Force B-24 Liberators bomb Maloelap Atoll in the Marshalls. A second strike of 20 additional B-24 Liberators on the atoll is aborted due to bad weather, but two bombers attack a cargo ship near the intended target.

BOUGAINVILLE: Thirteenth Air Force fighter aircraft with navy fighters attack barges and antiaircraft guns at Tonolai. Fighters are also active attacking targets around Numa Numa, Chabai, the Jakohina Mission area, Kangu, Malabita Hill, and Mosigetta.

NEW GUINEA: Fifth Air Force B-24 Liberators bomb Alexishafen and B-25 Mitchells and A-20 Havocs attack Kalasa and Japanese transports near Waroe.

December 1

CBI: Tenth Air Force B-24 Liberators, with P-38 Lightnings flying escort, bomb Insein in Burma. Over the target, they are attacked by Japanese fighters, and six B-24 Liberators are shot down and five others are damaged. B-25 Mitchells attack the newly-repaired Myitnge bridge and cause additional damage. Fourteenth Air Force sends 19 B-25 Mitchells, 24 P-40s, and 10 P-51 Mustangs against the Kowloon shipyards and the Taikoo docks in Hong Kong, China.

ETO: Eighth Air Force VIII Bomber Command attacks the industrial area at Solingen, Germany, with 206 B-17s, 69 B-24 Liberators, and five radar-equipped Pathfinder B-17s, escorted by 42 P-38 Lightnings and 374 P-47 Thunderbolts. U.S. losses are 19 B-17s and five B-24s shot down and 89 bombers damaged. Aircrew losses are 13 killed, 23 wounded, and 227 missing. They report that at least four enemy fighters are shot down. The P-47 pilots report 20 confirmed enemy kills, four probables, and seven possibles. Two P-38s are lost and one damaged; five P-47s are shot down and four are damaged. The seven pilots shot down are reported as missing. Ninth Air Force B-26 Marauders bomb the Chievres, Belgium, airfield and the airfields at Cambrai/Epinoy, Lille/Yendeville, and Cambrai/Niergnies in France.

ITALY: The 2nd Battalion 179th Infantry Regiment of the 45th Infantry Division attempts to take Hill 769, which overlooks Lagone from the south. German fire has been particularly effective in stopping the advance of the 179th. Patrols occupy the heights, but are pushed back by German counterattacks. In the 34th Infantry Division's area, the 168th Infantry Regiment battles to hold a series of small knobs on Monte Pantano. Minefields, steep terrain, and poor communications prevent any advance against the Germans defending in well-prepared positions.

Fifteenth Air Force sends over 100 B-17s against the ball bearing works and marshaling yard at Turin. B-26 Marauders, with fighter escort, attack bridges and railroad facilities at Aulla, Cecina, and Sestri Levante. Twelfth Air Force B-25 Mitchells bomb gun positions near Sant' Ambrogio. Other aircraft attack transportation and ground support targets around Casoli, Lanciano, Guardiagrele, Mignano, Minturno, and Chieti.

PACIFIC: U.S. submarine *Bonefish* sinks a Japanese transport in the Celebes Sea. U.S. submarine *Pargo* sinks a Japanese transport north of Ulithi Atoll near the Yap Islands. U.S. submarine *Peto* sinks a Japanese transport north of the Admiralty Islands, then escapes a counterattack from an escorting torpedo boat.

CENTRAL PACIFIC: Seventh Air Force sends four B-24 Liberators to bomb Mili Atoll in the Marshalls.

BOUGAINVILLE: Thirteenth Air Force B-25 Mitchells and P-38 Lightnings attack Malai. Over Empress Augusta Bay, P-39 Airacobras strafe Tonolai and support U.S. Navy SBD Dauntless dive-bombers attacking Japanese positions near the Jaba River and supply storage areas on Kara and Ballale Islands. Targets at Tenekow, Chabai, and Mutupina Point are also attacked.

NEW GUINEA: Fifth Air Force employs over 40 B-24 Liberators with P-47 escorts to bomb Wewak. About 50 Japanese fighters intercept them over the target. Aircrews report 11 enemy fighters shot down, but three B-24s are lost.

December 2

CBI: Fourteenth Air Force P-40s intercept 18 Japanese bombers and 30 fighters attacking Suichwan airfield in China. One enemy aircraft and two P-40s are shot down. Japanese positions near Changte, China, are attacked by 16 P-40s.

ETO: Four B-17s of Eighth Air Force VIII Bomber Command drop over two million leaflets on Bremen, Oldenburg, and Hamburg, Germany. One Pathfinder B-17 flies an Oboe test over Huls, Germany, dropping two 2,000-pound general purpose bombs and one photoflash bomb. The photoflash bomb is used for night photography and has a peak intensity of approximately 500,000,000 candlepower.

MEDITERRANEAN: Fifteenth Air Force B-17s bomb submarine pens at Marseilles.

ITALY: In the 34th Infantry Division area, the 3rd Battalion 168th Infantry Regiment attacks after a one-hour artillery bombardment and captures a small knob on Monte Pantano, but faces heavy counterattacks throughout the day and night.

Operation Raincoat begins in a steady rain with the heaviest artillery preparation yet seen in the campaign in Italy. A total of 22,500 rounds are fired in the II Corps sector. The 1st Special Service Force clears Monte la Difensa and moves to take Monte la Remetanea.

Fifteenth Air Force B-24 Liberators, with fighter escort, bomb the railroad bridge and marshaling yard at Bolzano. B-26 Marauders bomb the bridge near Orvieto and the marshaling yard at Arezzo. Twelfth Air Force B-25 Mitchells, A-20 Havocs, and RAF aircraft conduct ground support missions near Monte Trocchio and Sant' Ambrogio. B-25s attack the bridge and approaches near Chieti.

German aircraft bomb Allied shipping at Bari, Italy, sinking three cargo ships, two carrying ammunition, and one ship carrying mustard gas. The catastrophic explosions resulting from the German bomb hits on these ships damage five other cargo ships and a tanker. At least 130 merchant seamen and sailors are killed and more than 70 are wounded.

CAIRO: Allied Military Strategy Conference. The CCS outlines a plan for the defeat of Japan. MacArthur's forces in the Southwest Pacific Area will advance along the north coast of New Guinea to capture the Vogelkop Peninsula by August 1944. Nimitz's Central Pacific forces will capture islands in the Marianas for use as bomber bases for the strategic attack on the Japanese home islands. Guam, Saipan, and Tinian are specific targets and will be captured by October 1944, with bombing operations beginning in December of 1944. The British will move into upper Burma to open the overland supply route into China to improve logistics support for U.S. air operations in China.

PACIFIC: U.S. submarine *Narwhal* lands ammunition and stores, and evacuates guerrillas from Mindanao, Philippines.

BOUGAINVILLE: Thirteenth Air Force B-25 Mitchells attack Malai, the Porror River, and Rigu Mission at Kieta. B-24 Liberators bomb Korovo and fighters strafe Chabai.

NEW GUINEA: Fifth Air Force B-25 Mitchells bomb the Borgen Bay area. Japanese positions around Finschhafen are bombed by 20 B-25 Mitchells and B-26 Marauders. B-24 Liberators bomb the area near Sio.

December 3

CBI: Fourteenth Air Force sends eight P-40s to attack barracks at Wanling, China.

ATLANTIC: German submarine *U-193* torpedoes a U.S. tanker in the Gulf of Mexico. While the crew abandons ship, nine sailors and the commander of the armed guard stay on board to fire the aft 5-inch gun at the U-boat. Another torpedo from *U-193* sinks the tanker and only one of the courageous fighters survives.

CAIRO: Allied Strategy Conference. Second Cairo Conference (Sextant) begins, attended by President Roosevelt, Prime Minister Churchill, and Generalissimo Chiang Kai-shek, and lasts until December 7. The proposed amphibious operation in Burma is cancelled to focus priorities on the cross-Channel invasion. The Americans reject Churchill's requests for cancellation of Anvil in favor of offensive operations in Itay and Yugoslavia. Chiang is displeased and refuses to commit Chinese forces for an offensive in Burma. Chiang's stubbornness only reinforces the view that China is seen as less important to the Allied effort than the Soviet Union.

There is a discussion on the best option for securing air bases to force the unconditional surrender of Japan through strategic bombing. Suggested bases for the new B-29 strategic bomber include Tinian, Saipan, and Guam in the Marianas.

ITALY: In the II Corps area, the 142nd Infantry Regiment of the 36th Infantry Division captures Monte Maggiore. The 45th Infantry Division is still stalled before La Bandita and Hill 769. In the 34th Infantry Division area, the 3rd Battalion of the 168th Infantry Regiment relieves the 1st Battalion and continues the attack to capture a small knob on Monte Pantano, but is driven back with heavy casualties. The battalion has suffered over 400 casualties during the six-day fight to capture the position.

Fifteenth Air Force B-24 Liberators, with fighter escort, bomb the Casale airfield near Rome.

MEDITERRANEAN: Twelfth Air Force B-25 Mitchells bomb the harbor and marshaling yard at Sibenik.

PACIFIC: U.S. submarine *Guardfish* sinks a Japanese fleet tanker west of the Palau Islands.

BOUGAINVILLE: Thirteenth Air Force sends 23 B-25 Mitchells to bomb Kieta Harbor and logistics targets. B-24 Liberators bomb Bonis, while fighters, both USAAF and U.S. Navy, attack targets of opportunity.

NEW GUINEA: Fifth Air Force A-20 Havocs attack villages around Finschhafen. P-47 Thunderbolts shoot down several enemy aircraft over Wewak. Over Cape Gloucester on New Britain, more than 60 B-24 Liberators and B-25 Mitchells bomb the airfield.

December 4

CBI: Tenth Air Force B-24 Liberators mine the Rangoon River and the Salween River at Moulmein in Burma. In China, Fourteenth Air Force conducts ground support operations against advancing Japanese forces near Changte with B-25 Mitchells and P-40s.

Changte falls to Japanese forces.

ETO: Eighth Air Force B-17s drop 1.6 million leaflets over Tours, Rouen, Le Mans, Orleans, Laval, Lille, and Paris, France. Ninth Air Force initiates Operation Crossbow and directs IX Bomber Command to begin attacking German missile sites threatening Britain.

MEDITERRANEAN: During the Second Cairo Conference (Sextant), President Franklin D. Roosevelt, Prime Minister Winston S. Churchill, and President Ismet Inonu of

Turkey meet. Churchill discusses the possibility of Turkey entering the war; the plan for the amphibious assault in the Bay of Bengal is cancelled; a tentative timetable is set up for Pacific offensive; and a unified command is established in the Mediterranean effective December 10.

ITALY: On Monte Pantano in the 34th Infantry Division area, the 135th Infantry Regiment replaces the badly battered 168th Infantry Regiment.

In the II Corps area, the 1st Battalion of the 1st Special Service Force is pushed off Monte la Remetanea and returns to defenses established on Monte la Difensa. In the 36th Infantry Division area, the 142nd Infantry Regiment holds positions on Monte Maggiore, but can advance no farther. The divisions are having difficulty resupplying frontline troops on the mountainous terrain.

SOUTHWEST PACIFIC AREA: Brigadier General Julian W. Cunningham, commander of the 112th Cavalry, issues an operations order to his commanders for the assault on Arawe.

PACIFIC: U.S. submarine *Apogon* sinks a Japanese gunboat northeast of Ponape Island. U.S. submarine *Gunnel* sinks a Japanese transport northeast of Haha Jima and escapes an attack by an escorting destroyer. U.S. submarine *Sailfish* torpedoes and sinks Japanese escort carrier *Chuyo* southeast of Honshu. Perishing on the *Chuyo* are survivors from the submarine *Sculpin,* whose commander, Captain John P. Cromwell, had sacrificed himself to save his crew on November 19.

CENTRAL PACIFIC: Seventh Air Force sends 54 B-24 Liberators to bomb Mille atoll in the Carolines, but only 34 hit the target due to bad weather. Eight B-24s bomb Nauru atoll. Navy Task Force 50, commanded by Rear Admiral Charles A. Pownall, attacks Kwajalein and Wotje Atolls. Aircraft from the carrier USS *Lexington* and small carrier USS *Independence* sink a Japanese collier, a cargo ship, an auxiliary submarine chaser, and a guardboat. Two light cruisers are also damaged. Japanese torpedo dive-bombers damage the *Lexington.*

BOUGAINVILLE: Thirteenth Air Force B-24 Liberators and B-25 Mitchells bomb Chabai.

NEW GUINEA: Fifth Air Force A-20 Havocs attack villages and logistics in the Finschaffen area.

December 5

CBI: Tenth Air Force B-24 Liberators mine waters near Moulmein and in the Rangoon River in Burma. Fourteenth Air Force P-40s continue to attack Japanese forces around Changte. Japanese bombers and fighters attack Fourteenth Air Force airfields.

ATLANTIC: The CCS describes the intent for Anvil to support Overlord. The Mediterranean theater is notified to plan to commit two divisions to the landings in southern France.

ETO: Eighth Air Force VIII Bomber Command attacks the Cognac/Chateaubernard airfield in France with 96 B-24 Liberators. One bomber is lost and seven are damaged. Over the Bordeaux/Merignac air depot, only one of 236 B-17s sent hits the target. In this attack, eight bombers are lost and 19 are damaged. Aircrews report 12 German fighters shot down. The two missions are escorted by 34 P-38 Lightnings and 266 P-47 Thunderbolts, along with 36 Ninth Air Force P-51 Mustangs. One P-47 is lost. Total U.S. casualties for these missions are three killed, 14 wounded, and 51 missing. Ninth Air Force B-26 Marauders bomb Ligescourt, Campagne-les-Hesdin, and Saint-Josse, France.

MEDITERRANEAN: President Roosevelt and Prime Minster Churchill agree that General Dwight D. Eisenhower will be the Supreme Allied Commander for Operation Overlord, the cross-Channel invasion of Europe.

The Combined Chiefs of Staff (CCS) issues a directive creating the Mediterranean Allied Air Forces (MAAF), consolidating British and U.S. forces of the Mediterranean Air Command (MAC) and Northwest African Air Force (NAAF).

ITALY: In II Corps area, the 1st Special Service Force stops a German counterattack on Monte La Difensa, supported by concentrated artillery fire. Twelfth Air Force transfers its headquarters from Tunisia to Italy. B-25 Mitchells bomb a bridge at Pescara. Allied aircraft attack transportation targets near Aquino and bomb bridges near Mignano and Ladispoli. The airfields at Piombino and Aviano are also attacked.

SOUTHWEST PACIFIC AREA: U.S. submarine *Narwhal* sinks a Japanese cargo ship in the Sulu Sea.

BOUGAINVILLE: Thirteenth Air Force B-25 Mitchells and navy SBD Dauntless dive-bombers attack Monoitu, the Aitara mission, and Mosigetta.

NEW GUINEA: Fifth Air Force A-20 Havocs attack Japanese positions near Finschhafen. B-25 Mitchells, B-26 Marauders, and P-40s attack along the Bogadjim road. Over New Britain Island, 40 B-24 Liberators bomb Cape Gloucester and A-20s attack and destroy several small vessels.

December 6

CBI: In China, Fourteenth Air Force B-25 Mitchells attack Japanese forces at Changte, Chin and attack the railyard at Hsipaw.

ATLANTIC: The Combined Chiefs of Staff agrees to a general strategy in Europe for 1944. Overlord and Anvil are the supreme operations for the Allies. All resources necessary will be provided to ensure success. The Allies will attack in Italy to reach the Pisa-Rimini line. The amphibious assault in the Bay of Bengal is cancelled and all landing craft in Southeast Asia Command are to be transferred to the ETO for Overlord. In the Mediterranean Theater, 68 LSTs will remain until mid-January, when they will be transferred to support Anvil.

MEDITERRANEAN: Fifteenth Air Force sends 45 B-24 Liberators to bomb the Eleusis airfield and 56 B-17s to attack Kalamaki airfield. One B-24 is lost.

ITALY: In the 45th Division area, the 179th Infantry Regiment succeeds in pushing the Germans off Hill 769, but the enemy still controls the rear slope.

Twelfth Air Force P-40 and A-36 Intruder (Apache) fighter-bombers bomb bridges at Ceprano and Mignano.

BOUGAINVILLE: Thirteenth Air Force B-25 Mitchells bomb the Monoitu Mission area. Another 24 B-25s, with fighter support, bomb Tarlena village. P-40s strafe the Arawa Bay area near Kieta.

NEW GUINEA: Fifth Air Force A-20 Havocs and B-25 Mitchells attack villages and logistics areas around Finschhafen. Over New Britain, nearly 100 B-24 Liberators and B-25 Mitchells bomb Cape Gloucester and Borgen Bay, while P-40s strafe Cape Hoskins.

December 7

CBI: Fourteenth Air Force sends 13 B-25 Mitchells to bomb Japanese positions at Changte, China. In Burma, eight P-40s strafe freight cars on the rail line between Mogaung and Myitkyina.

ATLANTIC: The Allied Leadership Statement. From both the Sextant and Eureka conferences comes a statement that expresses the goals and intent of Britain, the USSR and the United States in dealing with Japan.

> The several military missions have agreed upon future military operations against Japan. The Three Great Allies expressed their resolve to bring unrelenting pressure against their brutal enemies by sea, land, and air. This pressure is already mounting.
>
> The Three Great Allies are fighting this war to restrain and punish the aggression of Japan. They covet no gain for themselves and have no thought of territorial expansion.
>
> It is their purpose that Japan shall be stripped of all the islands in the Pacific which she has seized or occupied since the beginning of the first World War in 1914, and that all the territories Japan has stolen from the Chinese, such as Manchuria, Formosa, and the Pescadores, shall be restored to the Republic of China.
>
> Japan will also be expelled from all other territories which she has taken by violence and greed. The aforesaid three great powers, mindful of the enslavement of the people of Korea, are determined that in due course Korea shall become free and independent.
>
> With these objects in view the three Allies, in harmony with those of the United Nations at war with Japan, will continue to persevere in the serious and prolonged operations necessary to procure the unconditional surrender of Japan.

ETO: The Combined Chiefs of Staff directs that the U.S. Strategic Air Forces in Europe (USSAFE) will coordinate the operations of the Eighth and Fifteenth Air Forces for the air war against Germany.

ITALY: As the last part of Phase I of Operation Raincoat is underway, Fifth Army initiates Phase II of the operation in the II Corps area to prevent the enemy from reorganizing or reinforcing its defenses. San Pietro is the key strongpoint, a village fortified by the Germans and protected by Monte Lungo and Monte Sammucro. German positions are primarily deep bunkers covered by logs and earth and protected by minefields and barbed wire. The approaches to these fortifications are covered by machine guns and by mortar and artillery fire. II Corps intends to capture Monte Lungo while simultaneously sweeping north of San Pietro to outflank it and seize the Monte Sammucro heights.

Two battalions of the 143rd Infantry Regiment of the 36th Infantry Division assemble at Cannavinelle Hill to prepare to attack San Pietro. A Company, 1st Battalion, of the 143rd Infantry Regiment moves toward Monte Sammucro, taking the position in a night attack, but takes heavy casualties when the Germans counterattack. Reinforced, the company holds the position.

The 3rd Ranger Battalion prepares to attack Hill 950 northeast of Monte Sammucro.

The Italian 1st Motorized Group, commanded by Division General Vincenzo Dapino, is attached to II Corps and is ordered to capture Monte Lungo. The Italians relieve the 1st Battalion, 141st Infantry Regiment.

Twelfth Air Force B-25 Mitchells and A-36 Intruder (Apache) fighter-bombers attack the harbor and town of Civitavecchia. B-25 Mitchells also attack rail and road networks near Pescara. A-36s, P-40s, and RAF fighters attack a German gun position near Orsogna and hit other targets near Viticuso, San Vittoria, and a bridge at Civitella Roveto.

PACIFIC: U.S. submarine *Pogy* sinks a Japanese collier north of Truk. U.S. submarine *Sailfish* is attacked by a Japanese aircraft off Kyushu, Japan, and suffers slight damage.

CENTRAL PACIFIC: Seventh Air Force sends 14 B-24 Liberators from Tarawa atoll on a night raid to hit targets on Maloelap and Wotje Atolls in the Marshalls. B-24s from Nukufetau Island also bomb Maloelap Atoll, initiating Operation Flintlock, the offensive against Kwajalein and Majuro Atolls in the Marshalls.

BOUGAINVILLE: Thirteenth Air Force sends 18 B-25 Mitchells to bomb Kahili and Kieta harbor.

NEW GUINEA: Fifth Air Force A-20 Havocs bomb troop encampments and supply areas near Finschhafen. P-40s strafe boats and barges near Madang. Over New Britain, B-24 Liberators and B-25 Mitchells attack Cape Gloucester and Borgen Bay.

December 8

CBI: Fourteenth Air Force B-25 Mitchells, escorted by 16 P-40s, bomb Japanese positions at Changte, China.

ETO: Lieutenant General Carl Spaatz, commanding the Twelfth Air Force, is named as the new commander of U.S. Strategic Air Forces in Europe (USSAFE).

MEDITERRANEAN: Fifteenth Air Force attacks the Tatoi and Eleusis airfields with over 120 B-24 Liberators and B-17s.

ITALY: The attack of the 1st Italian Motorized Group on Monte Lungo is preceded by a heavy artillery barrage. The Italians are stopped by the enemy. The 2nd and 3rd Battalions of the 143rd Infantry Regiment are stopped before San Pietro by strong defenses and mortar and artillery fire from Monte Lungo. The 1st Battalion of the 143rd holds off enemy counterattacks on Monte Sammucro. The 3rd Ranger Battalion attacks Hill 950 and is unable to push the German defenders off the hill despite repeated attempts.

In the VI Corps area, the 1st Special Service Force retakes Monte la Remetanea and is relieved by the 142nd Infantry Regiment, which has extended its position southward. The only way units are resupplied on Monte Maggiore is by men carrying everything on their backs up trails so slippery and steep that even mules cannot be used. Moving the wounded off the mountain takes about 12 hours.

The 34th Infantry Division is relieved by the 2nd Moroccan Infantry Division, commanded by Major General A. M. F. Dody.

Fifteenth Air Force B-26 Marauders bomb Spoleto viaduct, the marshaling yard at Orte, and Civitavecchia harbor. Twelfth Air Force B-25 Mitchells bomb transportation and industrial targets around Pescara, Ancona, and Aquila. A-20 Havocs and A-36 Intruder (Apache) fighter-bombers and Allied aircraft conduct ground support missions near Miplinnico and Orsogna and attack lines of communication at Avezzano, Frosinone, Viticuso, Gaeta, and Sant' Elia Fiumerapido.

PACIFIC: U.S. submarine *Sawfish* sinks a Japanese transport southwest of Chichi Jima.

CENTRAL PACIFIC: Seventh Air Force B-24 Liberators bomb Jaluit Atoll in the Marshalls and Mille Atoll in the Carolines. A naval task group of carriers, battleships, and destroyers under command of Rear Admiral Willis A. Lee bombards Nauru Island. A destroyer is damaged by shore battery fire.

BOUGAINVILLE: Marines advancing to expand the perimeter encounter Japanese defenders on a low ridge. The battle for what the Marines call Hellzapoppin Ridge begins.

Thirteenth Air Force fighters attack targets of opportunity near Kieta, Cape Torokina, and Baniu Plantation.

NEW GUINEA: B-25 Mitchells and B-26 Marauders bomb logistics bases on the Huon Peninsula near Finschhafen.

December 9

CBI: Fourteenth Air Force B-25 Mitchells bomb Japanese positions at Changte, Wuchang, and Hankow, China. These attacks allow Chinese forces to retake Changte.

ITALY: San Pietro holds against attacks by the two battalions of the 143rd Infantry Regiment, 36th Infantry Division. The Americans make progress measured in yards. They fall back to their starting positions in order for the artillery to destroy the enemy positions. The 1st Battalion 143rd Infantry Regiment holds against German counterattacks on Monte Sammucro, supported by accurate and deadly artillery fire from the 133rd Field Artillery Battalion.

In the VI Corps area, the 45th Infantry Division clears Hill 769, but is unable to push the Germans from La Bandita or Legone.

Twelfth Air Force B-25 Mitchells bomb lines of communication targets at Giulianova, Pescara, Teramo, and Terni. A-20 Havocs, A-36 Intruder (Apache) fighter-bombers, and P-40s attack Orsogna, the Avezzano marshaling yard, and German troops and gun positions at San Pietro, Infine, and Viticuso. Trains and trucks around Rome are also attacked.

CENTRAL PACIFIC: Seventh Air Force B-24 Liberators bomb Mille Atoll in the Carolines. Aircrews report five Japanese fighters destroyed.

NEW GUINEA: Fifth Air Force B-25 Mitchells and A-20 Havocs hit barges, coastal installations, and roads near Fortification Point, while over 60 P-39 Airacobras hit Bogadjim Road and barges and enemy positions along the northern coast of Huon

Peninsula and in the Ramu River valley. Over New Britain Island, 50 B-25 Mitchells bomb Japanese supply points along the coast from Borgen Bay to Rein Bay.

December 10

CBI: Fourteenth Air Force sends 12 B-25 Mitchells, escorted by 15 P-40s, to attack the marshaling yard at Hanoi, French Indochina. Aircrews report heavy damage to the warehouse area and railroad station. In China, Japanese aircraft bomb Heng-yang airfield and are intercepted by eight P-40s, shooting down three, but two P-40s are shot down as well. One pilot is killed. Two B-25 Mitchells are damaged on the ground.

ATLANTIC: The Combined Chiefs of Staff orders establishment of the Mediterranean Theater of Operations to become effective.

ETO: Eighth Air Force B-17s drop 1.2 million leaflets over, Paris, Caen, Amiens, and Rouen, France, and Ghent, Belgium, during the night. The Germans strike Ninth Air Force airfields in Britain with 20 aircraft. Casualties are eight killed and over 20 wounded.

MIDDLE EAST: Persian Gulf Service Command is redesignated as Persian Gulf Command (PGC) and is responsible directly to the War Department. The commander, Brigadier General Donald H. Connolly, is responsible for coordinating U.S. activities in the region with Allied nations.

MEDITERRANEAN: Fifteenth Air Force B-24 Liberators, with fighter escort, bomb a marshaling yard at Sofia, Bulgaria.

ITALY: The 3rd Ranger Battalion captures Hill 950 after a pre-assault bombardment of 1,600 rounds of artillery are fired on the hill. The Rangers have suffered heavy loses in the two days of fighting.

Fifteenth Air Force B-26 Marauders attack the bridge approaches at Ventimiglia. Twelfth Air Force P-40s and A-36 Intruder (Apache) fighter-bombers attack oil tanks, warehouses, and railroads at Civitavecchia and Acquafondata.

BOUGAINVILLE: Thirteenth Air Force B-25 Mitchells bomb the logistics sites and the airfield at Kahili. P-39 Airacobras bomb logistics bases and antiaircraft positions at Tonolai and strafe barges in the harbor.

Torokina airfield is opened and a marine fighter squadron lands there to begin flying ground support missions the next day.

NEW GUINEA: Fifth Air Force B-25 Mitchells and B-26 Marauders bomb logistics sites and camps near the Bogadjim Road, while P-39 Airacobras strafe barges near Madang. Over New Britain Island, 27 B-24 Liberators bomb Cape Gloucester.

December 11

CBI: Fourteenth Air Force B-24 Liberators bomb the airfield at Hankow, China. An attack by 30 Japanese aircraft over Suichwan is intercepted by eight P-40s. The pilots report eight enemy kills.

ETO: Eighth Air Force VIII Bomber Command attacks industrial sites at Emden, Germany, with 437 B-17s and 86 B-24 Liberators, escorted by 31 P-38 Lightnings, 313 P-47 Thunderbolts, and 44 P-51 Mustangs from Ninth Air Force. Fifteen B-17s and two B-24s are lost and 121 B-17s and 18 B-24s are damaged. Aircrews report over 80 fighters downed. The fighter pilots report 21 confirmed kills and seven possibles. There are three P-47s and one P-51 lost, with four P-47s and one P-51 damaged. U.S. casualties are three killed, 20 wounded, and 189 missing. During the evening, four B-17s drop 800,000 leaflets over Nantes, Laval, Rennes, and Le Mans in France.

MEDITERRANEAN: German U-boats *U-223*, *U-593*, and *U-73* attack convoy KMS 34 (United Kingdom to Mediterranean, Slow).

ITALY: The Fifth Army shifts corps boundaries, giving the British X Corps the area between Monte la Difensa and Monte Maggiore, and narrowing the II Corps area, centering its line of advance along Route 6. The Fifth Army has met all its objectives for Phase I of Operation Raincoat. The German line has been weakened, but the approach to the Liri Valley is still controlled by the enemy.

The 1st Battalion 143rd Infantry Regiment holds against German counterattacks on Monte Sammucro, but the battalion has lost its commander and is down to 340 men. The 504th Parachute Infantry Regiment reinforces the defenses on Monte Sammucro and relieves the 3rd Ranger Battalion.

Twelfth Air Force P-40s and A-36 Intruder (Apache) fighter-bombers attack Anzio, Nettuno, Viticuso, San Vittore del Lazio, Pontecorvo, Acquafondata, and transportation targets at Arce, Ostia, and Lido di Roma.

SOUTHWEST PACIFIC AREA: U.S. submarine *Bonefish* damages a small Japanese cargo vessel in the Celebes Sea.

BOUGAINVILLE: Thirteenth Air Force B-25 Mitchells bomb Kahili and Arigua Plantation. B-24 Liberators bomb the village and wharf at Tsirogei. P-39 Airacobras bomb Tonolai and Allied night fighters attack Japanese camps along the Jaba River.

NEW GUINEA: Fifth Air Force B-25 Mitchells and B-26 Marauders hit Japanese camps near Fortification Point and Finschhafen. Over New Britain, B-25 Mitchells bomb and strafe the Borgen Bay area. B-24 Liberators bomb Makassar on Celebes Island and Balikpapan on Borneo.

December 12

CBI: Tenth Air Force strikes a major Japanese line of supply crossing the bridge at Myittha in Burma with 28 B-25 Mitchells and 13 B-24 Liberators. Damage is negligible. In China, Fourteenth Air Force P-40s and P-38 Lightnings intercept 11 Japanese bombers and 30 fighters attacking the U.S. airfield at Hengyang. Fighter pilots report five bombers and three fighters shot down. Two P-40s are lost. One pilot is killed, the other is wounded. Hankow airfield is bombed by nine B-24 Liberators.

ATLANTIC: TBF Avengers from escort carrier USS *Bogue* attack two German submarines southwest of the Canary Islands. *U-172* is damaged and *U-219* escapes.

ETO: Eighth Air Force sends four B-17s to drop 800,000 leaflets on Paris, Amiens, and Orleans, France.

ITALY: Twelfth Air Force B-25 Mitchells bomb lines of communication at Terracina. P-40 and A-36 Intruder (Apache) fighter-bombers attack trucks along roads between Chieti and Francavilla and bomb the town of Itri.

SOUTHWEST PACIFIC AREA: U.S. submarine *Tuna* (SS-203) sinks a Japanese naval transport north of Halmahera in the Molucca Sea.

CENTRAL PACIFIC: Seventh Air Force sends 25 B-24 Liberators to bomb Emidj Island in the Marshalls.

BOUGAINVILLE: Thirteenth Air Force B-25 Mitchells strafe Arigua Plantation and logistics at Bonis. B-24 Liberators bomb the Kahili area and Poporang. Fighters strafe Japanese forces between Kieta and the Aropa River and the harbor at Tonolai. Navy SBD Dauntless dive-bombers attack targets near the Ratsua-Porton-Chabai-Soraken areas and the Kieta Harbor-Tobera Bay area. B-24 Liberators bomb the Kahili area and Poporang.

NEW GUINEA: Fifth Air Force P-40s dive-bomb Bogadjim Road. B-24 Liberators bomb Ceram Island in the Moluccas.

December 13

CBI: A Japanese raid of 20 bombers, escorted by 25 fighters, attacks Tenth Air Force's Dinjan airfield in India, but causes little damage. Pilots report 12 bombers and five fighters shot down. Twelve Fourteenth Air Force B-25 Mitchells bomb Li-Chou, Kungan, and Wuchang airfield. P-40s strafe targets of opportunity near Changte, Linli, and Li-Chou.

ATLANTIC: German submarine *U-172* attacks a U.S. destroyer and damages it with gunfire southwest of the Canary Islands. The U-boat in turn is sunk by TBF Avengers from escort carrier USS *Bogue* and three destroyers.

ETO: Eighth Air Force VIII Bomber Command B-17s and B-24 Liberators, escorted by 31 P-38 Lightnings, 322 P-47 Thunderbolts, and 41 Ninth Air Force P-51 Mustangs, attack Bremen and Kiel, Germany. P-51s for the first time fly the limit of their escort range. Of the 171 B-17s that bomb the port of Bremen, 31 B-17s are damaged. Over Kiel, guided by Pathfinder B-17s and B-24 Liberators, 367 B-17s and 93 B-24 Liberators attempt to hit the target. The formation is disrupted and 78 B-17s move off to bomb targets of opportunity in Hamburg. Four B-17s and one B-24 are lost and 137 B-17s and five B-24 Liberators are damaged. Aircrews report seven enemy fighters shot down. Fighter pilots report one confirmed enemy kill and one possible. One P-47 and one P-51 are reported lost. One P-47 and two P-38s are damaged. During the night, five B-17s drop 1 million leaflets on Le Mans, Rennes, Tours, Nantes, and Chartres, France.

Ninth Air Force attacks Schiphol airfield in the Netherlands with nearly 200 B-26 Marauders.

MEDITERRANEAN: A U.S. destroyer and a British frigate sink German submarine *U-593* northeast of Algiers.

Twelfth Air Force B-25 Mitchells bomb an oil depot, harbor, warehouses, and railway yard at Sibenik and Split.

ITALY: In the VI Corps area, night attacks by the 157th Infantry Regiment, 45th Infantry Division, are stopped by strong German resistance on the hills overlooking the Sant' Elia road.

Twelfth Air Force P-40 and A-36 Intruder (Apache) fighter-bombers attack German positions near Miglionico and lines of communication at Terracina, Pontecorvo, Isolella, and near Atina and Acquafondsta.

SOUTHWEST PACIFIC AREA: U.S. submarine *Puffer* makes an unsuccessful attack on a Japanese transport west of Luzon, Philippines. A U.S. Navy PBY Catalina sinks a Japanese cargo vessel north of New Ireland.

PACIFIC: U.S. submarine *Pogy* damages a Japanese cargo ship off the Palau Islands; it is damaged in a depth charge attack and the submarine's patrol must be terminated. U.S. submarine *Pompon* lays mines off the southwest coast of French Indochina. U.S. submarine *Sailfish* sinks a Japanese cargo ship in the Ryukyus.

CENTRAL PACIFIC: Seventh Air Force sends 10 B-24 Liberators to bomb Wotje Atoll in the Marshalls.

BOUGAINVILLE: Thirteenth Air Force B-25 Mitchells bomb Porton and Numa Numa. Fighters strafe Tenekow. B-24 Liberators bomb Bonis.

NEW GUINEA: Fifth Air Force A-20 Havocs attack villages along Bogadjim Road and P-39 Airacobras strafe barges along the Huon Peninsula. Over 100 B-24 Liberators and B-25 Mitchells bomb Gasmata Island.

December 14

CBI: Fourteenth Air Force B-25 Mitchells, with fighter escort, bomb Shasi, China. P-40s strafe supply trucks near Tengchung. Over Gia Lam airfield and railroad yard in French Indochina, six P-40s conduct a low-level attack.

MEDITERRANEAN: Fifteenth Air Force B-17s and B-24 Liberators, with fighter escorts, bomb the Kalamaki, Eleusis, and Tatoi air depots at Athens. B-17s also bomb the docks and shipping at Piraeus. Aircrews report 10 German fighters destroyed.

ITALY: II Corps, in coordination with VI Corps, attacks, ordering the 36th Infantry Division to capture San Pietro and Monte Lungo. On Monte Sammucro, the 1st Battalion 143rd Infantry and the 2nd Battalion of the 504th Parachute Infantry will attack west to outflank San Pietro. The two battalions of the 143rd Infantry Regiment, reinforced by a company of tanks from the 753rd Tank Battalion, will assault San Pietro. Meanwhile, the 1st Italian Motorized Group, reinforced by the 142nd Infantry Regiment, will attack Monte Lungo from two directions.

In the VI Corps area, the 45th Infantry Division advances during the night to attack the village of Lagone, which has resisted numerous American assaults.

Twelfth Air Force B-25 Mitchells bomb the marshaling yard at Orte. A-20 Havocs attack lines of communication near Pontecorvo. P-40s and A-36 Intruder (Apache) fighter-bombers attack bridges near Roccasecca, Atina, Ceprano, and Sora. The docks and town of Civitavecchia are also attacked. The main roads to Sant' Elia and Attina are attacked to slow German reinforcements into the VI Corps area.

PACIFIC: Admiral Nimitz, CINCPOA, reschedules the attack on the Marshalls to January 17, 1944.

U.S. submarine *Herring* sinks a Japanese cargo ship in the East China Sea.

CENTRAL PACIFIC: Seventh Air Force sends 16 B-24 Liberators to bomb Maloelap Atoll in the Marshalls.

BOUGAINVILLE: Thirteenth Air Force fighters support navy SBD Dauntless dive-bombers attacking Japanese antiaircraft positions near Chabai.

NEW GUINEA: Fifth Air Force sends 228 B-24 Liberators, B-25 Mitchells, and A-20 Havocs to bomb Arawe. P-39 Airacobras strafe barges along the Huon Peninsula. B-24s bomb Saidor. B-26 Marauders and B-25s bomb Gasmata Island.

December 15

CBI: The Tenth Air Force and RAF Bengal Air Command are combined to form the Eastern Air Command (EAC), under Lieutenant General George E. Stratemeyer (USAAF). Air Vice Marshall Thomas M. Williams (RAF) is the assistant commander. The headquarters is located in New Delhi, India. This combined U.S.-British command is under the operational control of Southeast Asia Command (SEAC) in New Delhi, India, and is commanded by Admiral Lord Louis Mountbatten.

Fourteenth Air Force attacks the airfield at Pailochi, China, with 25 P-40s. Pilots report three enemy aircraft destroyed on the ground.

ATLANTIC: The Combined Chiefs of Staff estimates availability of forces in ETO by May 1, 1944, the date planned for the cross-Channel invasion (Operation Overlord). The Allies would have 31 2/3 divisions in Britain, 3,783 heavy bombers, 1,000 medium bombers, and 4,200 fighter aircraft. Four divisions per month would enter France. In the Mediterranean, the Allies had 31 divisions and would allocate 10 divisions to participate in Anvil, the landing in southern France supporting Overlord. The U.S. troop strength in the ETO by May 31, 1944, is estimated at 1.4 million.

ETO: In the ETO, the Allies have 3,783 heavy bombers, 1,000 medium bombers, and 4,200 fighter aircraft. The Ninth Air Force officially comes under operational control of the Allied Expeditionary Air Force (AEAF).

MEDITERRANEAN: Twelfth Air Force B-25 Mitchells bomb the airfield at Mostar, Yugoslavia. P-40s and A-36 Intruder (Apache) fighter-bombers attack targets near Mostar and the Zemonico landing ground.

ITALY: In the II Corps area, two battalions of the 142nd Infantry Regiment attack Monte Lungo after a long artillery bombardment. An American first sergeant, leading an infantry platoon, roots several Germans out of a cave and shakes out of one surprised and frightened prisoner information on the location of all the other German positions.

The 143rd Infantry Regiment, with two battalions supported by 16 medium tanks from A Company, 753rd Tank Battalion, renews its attack on San Pietro and meets heavy resistance, advancing about 300 yards. During the attack 12 tanks are lost due to mines and enemy fire.

An attack into the valley toward San Pietro by the 2nd Battalion 141st Infantry is stopped by German artillery fire and suffers heavy casualties. The Americans call the open area "Death Valley." They reorganize and continue the advance.

The 1st Battalion of the 143rd Infantry, reinforced by the 2nd Battalion 504th Parachute Infantry Regiment, moves to attack the hills beyond Monte Sammucro to outflank San Pietro. Both battalions are stopped with heavy losses. The 1st Battalion is down to 155 men and has expended all of its ammunition.

In the VI Corps area, the 1st and 3rd Battalions of the 179th Infantry Regiment of the 45th Infantry Division attack Lagone, while the 1st Battalion attacks to capture a key hill to the south of the village. The 1st and 3rd Battalions of the 157th Infantry Regiment, with a platoon of tanks from the 755th Tank Battalion, reach the top of Hill 470 and advance to La Rava Creek, but cannot advance farther.

Fifteenth Air Force B-17s, with P-38 Lightnings and P-47 Thunderbolts escorting, bomb the Bolzano marshaling yards. B-24 Liberators, with P-38 escort, attack the viaduct at Avisio. Twelfth Air Force B-25 Mitchells and A-20 Havocs bomb lines of communication near Pontecorvo and Frosinone.

SOUTHWEST PACIFIC AREA: Chief of Staff George C. Marshall arrives on Goodenough Island to meet with General MacArthur and Lieutenant General Walter Krueger. Marshall provides MacArthur with the outcomes of the recent Cairo-Teheran meetings and listens to MacArthur's plea for more aircraft and more ground troops. The Cartwheel campaign is moving slowly, and it seems to have no real purpose now, at the end of 1943. At the Sextant Conference at Cairo, Marshall was persuaded by the other members of the JCS that the Central Pacific offensive was the quickest way to win the war. MacArthur's SWPA can continue its offensive in New Guinea, but only as a holding action for the main effort by Nimitz.

MacArthur argues that Nimitz's timetable for an advance through the Marshalls is far too optimistic and will be costly. Cartwheel has been slow, he admits, but it has weakened the Japanese significantly and put the Americans in a position to approach the Philippines. The Philippines are essential to the Pacific campaign, not the Pacific islands and atolls in the Carolines and Marshalls. The Japanese lifeline from the Netherlands East Indies goes through the South China Sea, past the Philippines. The Philippine Islands are an ideal base from which to launch the attack on the Japanese home islands. Australia is a secure base of operations to support and sustain an offensive. The geography of Nimitz's Pacific operation areas lacks such a base, except for Pearl Harbor, which is too far away to be suitable. The Philippines will draw the Japanese navy to the final battle the American navy seeks; above all, a return to the Philippines would fulfill a sacred obligation that MacArthur had voiced in 1942—Americans would return.

MacArthur advocates a year-long campaign plan for Southwest Pacific Area just as Nimitz has for the Central Pacific. MacArthur's plan is to have all of New Guinea under Allied control in order to be ready for an attack on Mindanao in February 1945.

The meeting of these two towering figures of the Second World War is unique. No one called General Marshall by his first name, except the president of the United States, and even he rarely took advantage of the privilege. No one ever called General MacArthur by his first name—ever. Yet at this meeting, both men addressed each other using first names, a symbol of the power and prestige these two men held. It was clear to Marshall that CINCSWPA was determined not to be relegated to a strategic backwater by the navy. He listened sympathetically to MacArthur, but remained noncommittal.

CENTRAL PACIFIC: Seventh Air Force sends 30 B-24 Liberators to bomb Maloelap and Wotje Atolls in the Marshalls. One B-24 is lost over Maloelap. Aircrews report two Japanese fighters shot down.

BOUGAINVILLE: The XIV Corps, under command of Major General Oscar W. Griswold, arrives to take control of Bougainville from I Marine Amphibious Corps.

Thirteenth Air Force sends 23 B-25 Mitchells and 16 fighters to bomb Buka Island.

NEW BRITAIN: Operation Director. Navy Task Force 76, commanded by Rear Admiral Daniel E. Barbey, lands the 112th Cavalry Regiment on Arawe. The regiment is to "seize and defend a suitable location" for light naval facilities. The regiment, reinforced with artillery and engineers, conducts an amphibious assault; one troop attempts a diversionary attack using rubber boats to make a landing. The Japanese make short work of this attempt, but the LVTs that land the remainder of the regiment are unopposed. Fifth Air Force supports the landing on Arawe with B-25 Mitchells attacking villages in the area. Naval gunfire support from destroyers suppresses Japanese defenses to allow the troops to land and move to gain control of the Arawe peninsula and establish defensive positions. The regiment withstands attacks from over 100 Japanese aircraft, which return every day for over a week.

B-24 Liberators bomb Cape Gloucester and P-39 Airacobras strafe barges at Reiss Point. B-25 Mitchell aircrews report two cargo ships hit in an attack on Timor Island in the Sunda Islands.

December 16

CBI: Fourteenth Air Force B-25 Mitchells and 11 P-40s attack near Owchihkow, China. P-40s attack Pailochi airfield. P-38 Lightnings strafe a troop train near Changanyi and sampans on the Yangtze River.

ATLANTIC: German submarine *U-516* torpedoes and sinks a U.S. tanker en route from New York to Aruba (off Venezuela).

ETO: Eighth Air Force VIII Bomber Command attacks Bremen, Germany. Escorted by 31 P-38 Lightnings, 131 P-47 Thunderbolts and 39 P-51 Mustangs from the Ninth Air Force, 402 B-17s, 133 B-24 Liberators, and 10 Pathfinder aircraft hit the target. Ten B-17s are lost and a total of 159 bombers are damaged. Six crewmen are killed, eight wounded, and 104 are reported missing. Aircrews report more than 18 German fighters destroyed. The fighter pilots report two confirmed enemy kills. One P-47 is lost and two P-38s are damaged. One pilot is reported killed and another reported missing. Later that night, four B-17s drop nearly 2 million leaflets over Brussels, Belgium, Hannover, Germany, and Lille, France.

MEDITERRANEAN: German submarine *U-73* attacks a convoy off the Algerian coast, torpedoing and damaging a U.S. freighter. Three U.S. destroyers track and sink the U-boat northwest of Oran, Algeria.

Twelfth Air Force B-25 Mitchells, P-40s, and P-47 Thunderbolts bomb shipping at Zara, Yugoslavia.

ITALY: In II Corps area, the 2nd Battalion 141st Infantry moves toward San Pietro and two companies enter the town, but the battalion suffers nearly 170 casualties, forcing it to retreat.

The 142nd Infantry Regiment clears Monte Lungo and the 1st Italian Motorized Group captures the smaller hills near the mountain.

The Germans counterattack from San Pietro to cover their withdrawal. The attack falls largely on the 3rd Battalion of the 143rd Infantry. One infantry company is so badly pressed by the enemy that a private first class is left to rally the men remaining. Artillery fire on the attacking German infantry ends the threat to the battalion.

The 1st Battalion 143rd Infantry and the 2nd Battalion of the 504th Parachute Infantry hold their positions on the western slope of Monte Sammucro against a heavy counterattack.

In VI Corps area, the 45th Infantry Division's 179th Infantry Regiment advances up La Bandita, occupies Lagone, and moves west toward Monte La Posta after the enemy withdraws. The 2nd Battalion of the 157th Infantry Regiment captures Fialla Hill just below the heights of Monte Cavallo and is forced back after an artillery bombardment and counterattack from German forces.

Fifteenth Air Force B-17s, escorted by P-38 Lightnings and P-47 Thunderbolts, bomb the marshaling yard at Padua. Aircrews report extensive damage to rail lines, rolling stock, and buildings. B-24 Liberators attack the rail lines between Dogna and Chiusaforte. Twelfth Air Force A-20 Havocs attack gun positions near Mignano, while P-40s and A-36 Intruder (Apache) fighter-bombers attack enemy positions near Hill 470, Chieti, Cassino, and Roccasecca. Civitavecchia's docks are also attacked.

BOUGAINVILLE: Thirteenth Air Force B-24 Liberators bomb Monoitu and dispersal areas at Bonis airfield. Fighters support navy SBD Dauntless dive-bomber strikes on gun positions at Bonis.

NEW BRITAIN: Fifth Air Force B-24 Liberators attack Cape Gloucester airfield.

NEW GUINEA: General MacArthur orders Lieutenant General Walter Krueger to organize a task force to capture Saidor, part of Operation Dexterity. Saidor will be used as a naval and air base and will pressure Japanese forces at Finschhafen. Brigadier General Clarence A. Martin, the deputy commander of the 32nd Infantry Division, will command the 126th RCT from his division.

December 17

CBI: Fourteenth Air Force sends six P-40s to bomb and strafe targets of opportunity in Hanoi, French Indochina.

ITALY: The Germans abandon San Pietro. The 1st Battalion 141st Infantry Regiment relieves the battered and depleted 1st Battalion 143rd Infantry on Monte Sammucro. The two battalions of the 143rd Infantry advance beyond San Pietro in pursuit of the Germans.

In VI Corps area, the 180th Infantry Regiment of the 45th Infantry Division captures Monte la Posta after moving forward through the positions occupied by the 179th Infantry Regiment and moves along the Sant' Elia road as far as Monte Molina and Monte Rotundo, the next obstacles to the American advance. The 157th Infantry Regiment discovers that the enemy had abandoned positions on Hill 640 and Fialla Hill. This marks a general withdrawal of German forces to reconsolidate.

Twelfth Air Force A-20 Havocs attack German artillery near Sant' Elia Fiumerapido. P-40s and A-36 Intruder (Apache) fighter-bombers attack enemy positions near Monte Trocchio, Cervaro, and Cardito. The Nettuno and Anzio marshaling yards, barracks, warehouses, and docks are also attacked.

SOUTHWEST PACIFIC AREA: Sixth Army receives orders to capture Saidor on the north coast of New Guinea to cut off retreating Japanese from Finschhafen.

BOUGAINVILLE: Thirteenth Air Force sends 18 B-25 Mitchells against Malai. Another six B-25s support navy SBD Dauntless dive-bombers in an attack on targets near Mutupina Point.

NEW BRITAIN: The 112th Cavalry makes an amphibious movement to the Itini River to contain the Japanese retreat.

Fifth Air Force P-47 Thunderbolts intercept about 40 Japanese aircraft over the Arawe Peninsula and report shooting down at least 10. B-24 Liberators and B-25 Mitchells bomb Cape Gloucester and nearby shipping. The bombers drop 80 2,000-pound bombs on the airfield. The pilots of the Fifth Air Force begin to use the term "Gloucesterizing" to describe the thorough destruction of a target.

NEW GUINEA: Sixth Army is to seize Saidor in support of the 9th Australian Division's advance past Finschhafen in order to cut off the Japanese retreat westward from the Huon Peninsula.

December 18

CBI: Generalissimo Chiang Kai-shek gives General Joseph Stilwell command of Chinese forces in India and those in the Hukawng Valley in Burma. This is a largely symbolic act, for Chinese commanders still secretly take orders from the Generalissimo. Thus, commanders often ignore or respond very slowly to Stilwell's orders.

Fourteenth Air Force B-25 Mitchells conducting a sea sweep report damaging a cargo ship and a tanker in the Hainan Straits. The Namsang airfield in China is attacked by 27 B-24 Liberators, supported by 28 P-40s. Japanese bombers and fighters attack the U.S. airfield at Kunming.

MEDITERRANEAN: Fifteenth Air Force B-26 Marauders bomb two Var River bridges; aircrews report destroying one and heavily damaging another.

ITALY: The 2nd Battalion 504th Parachute Infantry is relieved by the 1st Battalion on Monte Sammucro. Patrols discover enemy forces holding the southern slope of Monte Sammucro, blocking any advance down Route 6.

Twelfth Air Force P-40s attack German positions in Tollo, Canosa Sannita, and Orsogna. A-36 Intruder (Apache) fighter-bombers attack German positions near Monte Trocchio, Cassino, and Viticuso and logistics sites near Tenacina.

PACIFIC: U.S. submarine *Aspro* attacks a Japanese convoy, damaging two fleet tankers east of Formosa and escapes from an escorting destroyer. U.S. submarine *Cabrilla* lays mines off Saracen Bay, Cambodia, French Indochina. U.S. submarine *Grayback* sinks a Japanese cargo ship northeast of Okinawa and escapes from an escorting destroyer.

CENTRAL PACIFIC: Seventh Air Force B-24 Liberators bomb Mille atoll in the Carolines. P-39 Airacobras of the 46th and 72nd Fighter Squadrons, 15th Fighter Group, transfer to Makin Island, joining the A-24s (the AAF version of the navy's SBD Dauntless) of the 531st Fighter-Bomber Squadron on Makin.

BOUGAINVILLE: The 1st Battalion and 3rd Battalions of the 21st Marines conduct a double envelopment of Hellzapoppin Ridge behind the close support of TBF Avengers and TBD Dauntless dive-bombers. The marines lose 12 men killed and 23 wounded in capturing this important piece of key terrain.

Thirteenth Air Force sends 15 B-24 Liberators to bomb logistics bases at Kahili and Bonis. Another 19 bombers attack targets near Chabai-Porton. B-25 Mitchells carry out low-level strikes on troop concentrations at Poroporo and Korovo.

New Britain: Japanese forces land at Omoi to attack the 112th Cavalry's defensive positions at Arawe.

New Guinea: Fifth Air Force sends 33 A-20 Havocs to attack logistics areas near Finschhafen. On New Britain, over 70 B-24 Liberators, B-25 Mitchells, and B-26 Marauders bomb Cape Gloucester. B-25 Mitchells attack Borgen Bay and B-24s bomb Hoskins airfield.

December 19

CBI: Chiang Kai-shek rejects the request of the SEAC commander, Admiral Lord Louis Mountbatten, for Chinese forces to participate in the Burma offensive.

During the night, Tenth Air Force sends 20 B-24 Liberators against the new dock construction at Bangkok, Thailand. Aircrews report major destruction to the target.

In China, Japanese bombers and fighters attack Fourteenth Air Force's airfields at Hengyang and Yunnani. P-40s intercept the enemy and shoot down nine aircraft, but lose two fighters. Nanhsien and Ansiang are attacked by 12 B-25 Mitchells and eight P-40s.

ETO: Eighth Air Force sends five B-17s to drop one million leaflets on Paris, Amiens, and Chartres, France.

Mediterranean: Fifteenth Air Force B-17s attack the Messerschmitt plant at Augsburg and the marshaling yard at Innsbruck. A total of 150 B-24 Liberators and B-17s are involved in the attack, escorted by P-38 Lightnings and P-47 Thunderbolts. U.S. losses are nine bombers, to an estimated 37 German fighters shot down.

Italy: In II Corps area, the 15th Infantry regiment of the 3rd Infantry Division relieves the 142nd Infantry on Monte Lungo. German defenders retreat to a new defensive line at Cedro Hill, Monte Porchia, and the town of San Vittore, and still hold the lower slopes of Monte Sammucro, blocking any advance along Highway 6 or through the Mignano gap. The 143rd and 141st Infantry Regiments attack to clear the way, but are unable to capture the positions. The 143rd Infantry is down to 35 men per company.

In VI Corps area, elements of the 157th Infantry Regiment occupy Monte Cavallo.

Phase II of Operation Raincoat ends with the Fifth Army holding its gains while attempting to deal with increasingly bad winter weather, long supply lines, and units with almost as many non-battle casualties as combat casualties.

Fifteenth Air Force B-26 Marauders bomb the Perugia railroad installations and the marshaling yards at Castiglione della Valle and Foligno. P-47 Thunderbolts strafe Ancona airfield, truck convoys at Porto Civitanova, a train near Senigallia, and a vessel at Roseto degli Abruzzi. Twelfth Air Force B-25 Mitchells bomb the marshaling yards at Terni and Orte. A-20 Havocs attack Cassino, while P-40s bomb Orsogna and supplies near Arce. A-36 Intruder (Apache) fighter-bombers attack Civitavecchia.

Pacific: U.S. submarine *Grayback* sinks the destroyer that pursued it the previous day northeast of Okinawa. Fifteenth Air Force B-24 Liberators and navy PBY Catalinas sink a Japanese cargo ship southwest of Kavieng. A navy PBY damages a Japanese cargo vessel near Kwajalein.

CENTRAL PACIFIC: Seventh Air Force sends 29 B-24 Liberators to bomb barracks, hangars, and wharf areas on Mille and Maloelap Atolls. Aircrews report seven enemy fighters destroyed. P-39 Airacobras strafe Mille Atoll, reporting three enemy aircraft destroyed and an oil storage site set afire. Two P-39s are lost.

BOUGAINVILLE: Thirteenth Air Force sends 24 B-25 Mitchells to bomb logistics sites at Moisuru.

NEW BRITAIN: More than 140 Fifth Air Force B-24 Liberators, B-25 Mitchells, and B-26 Marauders bomb Cape Gloucester. Gasmata Island is bombed by 37 P-40s, and 20 A-20 Havocs attack Japanese positions near Arawe.

NEW GUINEA: Fifth Air Force B-25 Mitchells, A-20 Havocs, and P-39 Airacobras attack supply barges, troop sites, and gun positions near Finschhafen. B-25s and B-26 Marauders also bomb Madang. P-47 Thunderbolts sweep the northeast coastline.

December 20

CBI: Chiang Kai-shek has been pressing President Roosevelt for more money and supplies, but balks at Roosevelt's proposal to join in the Allied offensive against Burma as a means of obtaining additional aid. He tells Roosevelt that unless there is an amphibious operation against Rangoon, Moulmein, or the Andaman Islands, the Chinese divisions in Yunan (the "Y" Force) will not participate.

Fourteenth Air Force sends 11 B-25 Mitchells and six P-40s against the Yoyang railroad yards in China.

ATLANTIC: TBF Avengers from escort carrier USS *Bogue* sink German submarine *U-850* southwest of the Azores.

ETO: Eighth Air Force VIII Bomber Command attacks Bremen, Germany, with 357 B-17s and 103 B-24 Liberators, led by 12 Pathfinder aircraft and escorted by 26 P-38 Lightnings, 418 P-47 Thunderbolts, and 47 Ninth Air Force P-51 Mustangs. For the first time, some bombers deploy Window (today known as chaff), strips of metal foil intended to confuse radar detection equipment and mask the true location of the aircraft. The Germans employ rocket-firing fighters in an attempt to conduct standoff attacks, but these are more frightening than effective. Nevertheless, 27 bombers are lost. Another 216 B-17s and 34 B-24s are damaged. Aircrews report about 21 German fighters destroyed. The fighter pilots report 19 confirmed kills, three probables, and six possibles. Two P-47s and four P-51s are reported shot down and six P-47s are damaged. American casualties for this raid are nine killed, 42 wounded, and 275 missing. Later that night five B-17s drop one million leaflets on Lille and Lens in France and on Ghent and Brussels in Belgium.

Ninth Air Force sends more than 180 B-26 Marauders to attack German rocket bases in northern France. Only 35 actually hit any targets as bad weather forces the majority of the bombers to abort the mission.

Technical Sergeant Forrest T. Vosler is a radio operator-air gunner on the mission over Bremen. After bombing the target, antiaircraft fire severely damages his aircraft, forcing it out of formation. Enemy fighters savagely attack the lone bomber, firing their 20 millimeter cannon. Vosler is wounded and the tail gunner has also been seriously wounded. Without protection from the tail guns, the bomber cannot survive long. Vosler painfully makes his way to the rear and puts the tail guns into action. He is wounded again and loses most of his sight. Nevertheless, Vosler grimly hangs on, and continues to fight. When the pilot decides to make an emergency water landing, Vosler, primarily by touch, gets the radio set working and sends out a distress signal. After hitting the water, Vosler not only manages to find his way out of the aircraft, but also brings out the wounded tail gunner so his fellow crewmembers can load him into the survival raft. Technical Sergeant Vosler's extraordinary courage, dedication, and skill saves his aircraft and his comrades from certain destruction. He will receive the Medal of Honor.

MEDITERRANEAN: More than 100 Fifteenth Air Force B-17s bomb Eleusis airfield in Greece.

The Mediterranean Allied Air Force (MAAF) is established under command of Air Chief Marshall Sir Arthur Tedder of the Royal Air Force. The MAAF is a combined headquarters having operational control over all Allied air forces operating in the Mediterranean Theater of Operations. The reorganization disbands the Mediterranean Air Command and Northwest African Air Force (NAAF) and creates a subordinate component called U.S. Army Air Forces, North African Theater of Operations (USAAFNATO) under command of General Carl Spaatz, who has administrative control of the Twelfth and Fifteenth Air Forces.

ITALY: Twelfth Air Force P-40s attack Chieti, Orsogna, and bomb a fuel storage area near Manoppello. A-36 Intruder (Apache) fighter-bombers attack Terracina and transportation targets near Rome.

PACIFIC: U.S. submarine *Gato* sinks a Japanese transport in the East China Sea and is slightly damaged in a depth charge attack. U.S. submarine *Puffer* sinks a Japanese destroyer west of Manila and makes an unsuccessful attack on a cargo ship. Navy PBY Catalinas sink a Japanese transport off the northwest coast of New Britain.

CENTRAL PACIFIC: Seventh Air Force sends 16 B-24 Liberators to bomb Maloelap Atoll in the Marshalls. Aircrews report eight Japanese fighters shot down, but three B-24s are lost to enemy fire.

BOUGAINVILLE: The Americal Division, commanded by Major General John R. Hodge, relieves the 3rd Marine Division. XIV Corps commander, Major General Oscar W. Griswold, officially relieves Major General Ray S. Geiger and I Marine Amphibious Corps.

NEW BRITAIN: Fifth Air Force A-20 Havocs attack Arawe and P-38 Lightning pilots report downing 10 Japanese aircraft along the south coast of the island. B-24 Liberators bomb a cargo ship off Cape Pomas.

NEW GUINEA: Fifth Air Force B-26 Marauders and B-25 Mitchells attack Japanese camps near Finschhafen area and bomb Alexishafen.

December 21

ALEUTIANS: Navy PBY Catalinas from Attu Island bomb Shimushu and Paramushiru Strait in the Kuriles.

CBI: General Joseph Stilwell arrives in Ledo to take personal command of the upcoming Burma offensive.

Fourteenth Air Force sends 29 B-24 Liberators to bomb the railroad yards at Chiengmai, China. Aircrews report heavy damage to warehouses.

ETO: Ninth Air Force sends 84 B-26 Marauders against German rocket sites in France.

ITALY: Twelfth Air Force B-25 Mitchells and P-40s bomb Terracina. A munitions factory near Sant' Elia Fiumerapido is also attacked. A-36 Intruder (Apache) fighter-bombers attack a fuel storage site and a munitions factory near Cervaro. The A-36s also attack transportation targets around Rome and Civitavecchia.

PACIFIC: U.S. submarine *Grayback* sinks a Japanese auxiliary netlayer and merchant ship southwest of Kagoshima, Japan. U.S. submarine *Sailfish* sinks a Japanese transport south of Kyushu, Japan. U.S. submarine *Skate* sinks a Japanese fleet tanker northwest of Truk.

CENTRAL PACIFIC: Seventh Air Force sends eight B-24 Liberators, accompanied by four navy PB4Y Catalinas, on a photoreconnaissance mission over Kwajalein Atoll in the Marshalls. A-24 Banshees, along with U.S. Navy and Marine Corps aircraft, attack shipping and airfields at Emidj Island, while six P-39 Airacobras strafe fuel storage areas, shipping, and antiaircraft positions on Mille Atoll in the Carolines.

BOUGAINVILLE: Thirteenth Air Force B-25 Mitchells attack Monoitu Mission.

NEW GUINEA: Fifth Air Force A-20 Havocs hit camps near Finschhafen. B-25 Mitchells bomb Madang. P-40s attack Kaukenau. Fifteenth Air Force B-25 Mitchells sink a small Japanese cargo vessel at Wewak. Over New Britain, Cape Gloucester is bombed by over 100 B-24 Liberators, B-25 Mitchells, and A-20 Havocs. P-47 Thunderbolt pilots report 17 enemy fighters shot down over Arawe. P-40s and A-20 Havocs attack Hoskins airfield. P-39 Airacobras strafe targets around Borgen Bay and Rein Bay.

D-day for the Saidor landing is set for January 2, 1944.

December 22

CBI: Fourteenth Air Force's Kunming airfield in China is attacked by 65 Japanese bombers and fighters, destroying two U.S. aircraft on the ground. The attackers are challenged by 10 P-40s and a P-38 Lightning. The fighter pilots report 12 enemy aircraft shot down. Near Chengkung, seven P-40s intercept 58 Japanese aircraft heading toward the airfield and shoot down three. B-25 Mitchells, with fighter escort, bomb Hwajung.

ETO: Eighth Air Force VIII Bomber Command attacks the Osnabruck and Munster marshaling yards in Germany. Both heavy clouds and malfunctioning Pathfinder equipment result in many bombers missing their targets. Over Osnabruck, 147 B-17s and 87 B-24 Liberators led by two Pathfinder aircraft hit the target. Five B-17s and 12 B-24s are lost and 23 B-17s and 12 B-24s are damaged. Aircrews report 18 enemy fighters destroyed. Over Munster, 164 B-17s, 30 B-24 Liberators, and three Pathfinder aircraft hit the target. Three B-17s and two B-24s are lost; 30 B-17s are damaged. The bombers are escorted by 40 P-38 Lightnings, 448 P-47 Thunderbolts, and 28 P-51 Mustangs from Ninth Air Force. Pilots report 15 confirmed kills, one probable kill, and six possibles. Two P-38s and two P-47s are lost and one P-47 is damaged. U.S. total casualties on this raid are six killed, 14 wounded, and 214 missing. Later that night, six B-17s drop over one million leaflets on Paris, Amiens, Chartres, Orleans, and Rennes, France. One B-17 drops two 2,000-pound General Purpose (GP) bombs and one Photoflash (illumination) bomb on Cologne, Germany.

MEDITERRANEAN: General Carl Spaatz is ordered to take command of U.S. Strategic Air Forces in Europe. His replacement as commander of Air Forces Mediterranean Theater of Operation is Lieutenant General Ira C. Eaker.

ITALY: Twelfth Air Force P-40s attack transportation targets near Tortoreto and Benedello.

PACIFIC: U.S. submarine *Gurnard* damages a German cargo ship east of Shikoku, Japan.

CENTRAL PACIFIC: Seventh Air Force A-24 Banshees from Makin Island, escorted by 32 P-39 Airacobras along with navy F6F Hellcats and SBD Dauntless dive-bombers, attack cargo ships in Mille Atoll lagoon in the Marshalls. P-39s attack antiaircraft positions and fuel storage areas. A Japanese transport is sunk.

BOUGAINVILLE: Thirteenth Air Force B-25 Mitchells attack a logistics base at Kahili. B-24 Liberators attack targets near Bonis, Porton, and at Sohano Island.

NEW GUINEA: Fifth Air Force sends about 40 B-25 Mitchells, with P-38 escort, to bomb Wewak and Boram. Aircrews report more than 13 enemy aircraft shot down. B-25s and P-39 Airacobras bomb the airfield and supply barges at Madang and the town of Alexishafen, while A-20 Havocs and B-26 Marauders bomb Japanese positions near Finschhafen. Over New Britain, B-24 Liberators, B-25 Mitchells, and A-20 Havocs bomb Cape Gloucester.

December 23

CBI: The Chinese 38th Division begins operations in the Hukawng Valley in Burma.

Tenth Air Force B-24 Liberators bomb the railroad terminal at Bangkok, Thailand, during the night. Aircrews report heavy explosions and large fires. Fourteenth Air Force B-24 Liberators, escorted by seven P-51 Mustangs and 23 P-40s, bomb White Cloud airfield in China. Fighter pilots report 11 enemy aircraft destroyed. Huang Shan Kou is attacked by 14 P-38 Lightnings, and two B-25 Mitchells report a gunboat sunk in the Formosa Straits.

ATLANTIC: German submarine *U-415* makes an unsuccessful attack on escort carrier *Card* and a destroyer near the Azores, after escorting a convoy to the Mediterranean. German submarine *U-471* makes an unsuccessful attack on the battleship *Arkansas* screening troop convoy TU 5 (United Kingdom to United States) in the North Atlantic.

ETO: Eighth Air Force sends 92 P-47 Thunderbolts to attack the Gilze-Rijen airfield in the Netherlands.

ITALY: Fifteenth Air Force B-26 Marauders bomb the railroad bridge and marshaling yard at Imperia and rail lines at Ventimiglia.

CENTRAL PACIFIC: Seventh Air Force P-39 Airacobras conducting a night combat patrol intercept enemy bombers over Makin Island and shoot down two of them. One P-39 is lost in the battle. B-24 Liberators bomb Kwajalein, Wotje, and Maloelap Atolls. Mili Atoll is attacked by 10 A-24 banshees, escorted by 20 P-39 Airacobras.

NEW BRITAIN: Thirteenth Air Force sends 18 B-24 Liberators to bomb Taharai and Vunakanau airfields in Rabaul. Fighter pilots escorting the bombers report 30 enemy aircraft shot down. B-25 Mitchells bomb targets on Sohano Island and on Choiseul Island. Fifth Air Force sends 61 B-24 Liberators to bomb Cape Gloucester, followed by B-24 Liberators during the night. P-39 Airacobras attack supply barges between Borgen Bay and Rein Bay. P-40s bomb Gasmata Island and strafe Cape Hoskins.

NEW GUINEA: Fifth Air Force sends over 80 B-25 Mitchells, B-26 Marauders, and A-20 Havocs to attack coastal targets from Wewak to Hansa Bay, the Huon Peninsula, and the Alexishafen airfields.

December 24

CBI: Fourteenth Air Force sends 18 B-24 Liberators, escorted by 18 fighters, to bomb a satellite airfield at Tien Ho, China. Aircrews report 20 Japanese aircraft shot down. One B-24 is lost.

ATLANTIC: U.S. destroyer sinks German submarine *U-645* in the North Atlantic. German submarines *U-275* and *U-382* sink a U.S. destroyer northwest of Spain.

ETO: General Dwight D. Eisenhower is officially announced as Supreme Allied Commander, Allied Expeditionary Force. He has responsibility for planning Overlord, the invasion of Europe.

Eighth Air Force VIII Bomber Command attacks 23 German rocket sites around the Pas-de-Calais, France. It is the largest number of aircraft assembled against a target up to this time, a total of 478 B-17s and 192 B-24 Liberators hit the targets, escorted by 40 P-38 Lightnings, 459 P-47 Thunderbolts, and 42 Ninth Air Force P-51 Mustangs. Two P-38s and two P-51s are damaged. Ninth Air Force also sends over 60 B-26 Marauders against the same target set, but only half attack the targets, primarily due to bad weather.

MIDDLE EAST: Brigadier General Donald P. Booth takes command, relieving Brigadier General Donald H. Connolly as commander of Persian Gulf Command.

MEDITERRANEAN: General Sir Henry Maitland Wilson is named Supreme Allied Commander, Mediterranean Theater (SACMED).

ITALY: Fifteenth Air Force B-26 Marauders bomb the Cecina marshaling yard.

PACIFIC: U.S. destroyer escort sinks Japanese submarine *I-39* off Koli Point, Guadalcanal. U.S. submarine *Gurnard* sinks a Japanese transport and auxiliary minesweeper east of Shikoku, Japan. U.S. submarine *Raton* torpedoes a Japanese transport in Kaoe Bay, Halmahera Island. U.S. submarine *Skate* torpedoes Japanese battleship *Yamato* northeast of Truk.

CENTRAL PACIFIC: Seventh Air Force sends 18 B-24 Liberators to bomb Wotje Atoll. B-25 Mitchells of the 396th and 820th Bombardment Squadrons (Medium), of the 41st Bombardment Group (Medium), arrive at Tarawa Atoll.

BOUGAINVILLE: The Japanese abandon a small hill named 600A after a three-day fight. This is the final piece of key terrain that secures the American perimeter.

Navy Task Force 39 with three cruisers and four destroyers bombards the areas near Buka and Bonis.

NEW BRITAIN: Thirteenth Air Force sends B-24 Liberators to bomb Vunakanau airfield and Lakunai at Rabaul. Fighter pilots flying escort report 25 Japanese aircraft shot down. Seven fighters are lost. Fifth Air Force bombs Cape Gloucester with almost 190 B-24 Liberators, B-25 Mitchells, and A-20 Havocs. P-39 Airacobras attack a disabled destroyer offshore. Over Arawe, A-20 Havocs attack Japanese troops.

NEW IRELAND: Navy Task Group 50.2, commanded by Rear Admiral Frederick C. Sherman, attacks Japanese ships at Kavieng with aircraft from carrier USS *Bunker Hill* and small aircraft carrier USS *Monterey*. One transport is sunk and two minesweepers and a transport are damaged.

December 25

MEDITERRANEAN: At a meeting in Tunis, Allied planners draft a new plan for the amphibious assault south of Rome. Instead of one division as originally planned, two divisions, an airborne unit, and armored forces will land. The target date is set between January 20 and January 31, 1944. To support the landing, Fifth Army, reinforced by two divisions from Eighth Army, will cross the Garigliano and Rapido rivers and drive up the Liri Valley toward Rome. Eighth Army will attack to threaten Route 5, the alternate highway to Rome. Pressed on both fronts, the Germans will not be able to react to a landing near Anzio and Nettuno. After landing, the Allies will advance to capture the hills at Colli Laziali, 20 miles from the landing beaches and near Route 7. Once that key terrain is occupied, the German lines of supply will be threatened and both the Gustav Line and Rome will have to be abandoned. The landing force will then link up with the Fifth Army advancing up the Liri Valley. The amphibious assault plan is called Shingle and will be commanded by Major General John P. Lucas. General Sir Harold Alexander, commander of the Fifteenth Army Group (of which the Eighth and Fifth Armies are a part), notes that the Anzio landing will give the Allies an advantage and that to succeed "the two forces operating under the Commander, Fifth Army, join hands at the earliest possible moment."

ITALY: The 1st Regiment 1st Special Service Force captures Hill 730, the key enemy position on Monte Sammucro, but the unit takes heavy casualties. The 504th Parachute Infantry captures another German position and clears Monte Sammucro.

Fifteenth Air Force B-26 Marauders bomb the marshaling yards at Pisa and Porta Nuova. B-17s attack the Bolzano marshaling yard. B-24 Liberators bomb the Pordenone marshaling yard. Twelfth Air Force A-36 Intruder (Apache) fighter-bombers attack transportation targets at Pontecorvo.

CENTRAL PACIFIC: Seventh Air Force attacks the runway, ammunition storage, and an antiaircraft position on Mili Atoll in the Marshalls with 10 A-24 Banshees, supported by P-39 Airacobras.

BOUGAINVILLE: The Americal Division relieves the 3rd Marine Division.

NEW BRITAIN: The Japanese attack 112th Cavalry forward positions on Arawe. A-20 Havocs provide ground support as the cavalrymen fight back concentrated Japanese assaults. The 112th Cavalry suffers 25 killed and 71 wounded. The Japanese losses are estimated at 78 killed.

Fifth Air Force conducts sustained bombing of Cape Gloucester by over 180 B-24 Liberators, B-25 Mitchells, B-26 Marauders, and A-20 Havocs. Thirteenth Air Force B-24 Liberators bomb Lakunai airfield at Rabaul. Fighter pilots report shooting down 13 enemy fighters, but lose two escorting P-38 Lightnings.

NEW IRELAND: Navy Task Force 38 under command of Rear Admiral Frederick C. Sherman launches 86 aircraft against Kavieng harbor, but no shipping targets are located.

December 26

CARIBBEAN: German submarine *U-530* torpedoes and damages a U.S. tanker off the coast of Panama en route from Aruba to the Canal Zone.

ITALY: The 1st Battalion, 143rd Infantry, 36th Infantry Division captures Morello Hill.

Fifteenth Air Force B-26 Marauders bomb the marshaling yards at Prato, Empoli, and Pistoia.

Near Sommocolonia, Italy, Lieutenant John R. Fox from the 598th Field Artillery Battalion is serving as the forward observer with the 366th Infantry Regiment of the 92nd Division. Just before dawn, German infantry attack the town in strength, forcing the Americans to retreat. Lieutenant Fox and other members of the observer team stay in the town to direct artillery fire on the enemy. As the Germans continue the attack Lieutenant Fox continues to call in artillery shells closer and closer to his own position. Acknowledging the danger to himself, he orders a final adjustment to land on his own position just as the enemy is in his midst. Lieutenant Fox sacrifices himself to stop the German attack and allow his comrades to organize an effective counterattack. For this act of valor Lieutenant John Fox will receive the Medal of Honor.

CENTRAL PACIFIC: Seventh Air Force sends 16 B-24 Liberators to bomb Wotje Atoll, while P-39 Airacobras fly reconnaissance and strafing missions over Mili Atoll.

BOUGAINVILLE: Thirteenth Air Force sends seven B-25 Mitchells, with 34 fighters, to attack the Cape Saint George area. Another 25 B-25s attack camp and logistics at Kahili.

NEW BRITAIN: Operation Backhandler. Seventh Amphibious Force, commanded by Rear Admiral Daniel E. Barbey, lands the 1st Marine Division, commanded by Major General William H. Rupertus, at Cape Gloucester. Naval gunfire and LCIs with rocket launchers support the landing. Fifth Air Force supports the landing of the 1st Marine Division at Cape Gloucester with over 270 B-25 Mitchells, B-24 Liberators, and A-20 Havocs. A fuel dump is bombed, resulting in a large explosion and fire.

Three battalion landing teams (BLTs) of the 7th Marine Regiment, commanded by Colonel Julian N. Frisbie, land on a narrow beach to establish a beachhead perimeter. The marines find only a few Japanese and, moving inland toward Target Hill, quickly find themselves in a swamp forest, wading waist-deep in mud and water. The 1st Battalion 7th

The landing vehicle tracked (LVT) carried 6,500 to 8,000 pounds of cargo and was essential to the success of Marine landings from Tarawa to Peleliu. At Cape Gloucester, New Britain, in December 1944, the ground was so saturated and the mud so deep that only an LVT could bring supplies to the Marines pushing forward.

Marines occupies Target Hill protecting the left flank of the beachhead. Two battalions of the 1st Marine Regiment pass through the 3rd Battalion 7th Marines to move toward Gloucester airfield and encounter a Japanese roadblock. About 40 minutes after the initial landing, LSTs begin unloading supplies and tanks. Bulldozers begin cutting paths through the jungle, but as the units advance deeper into the swampy jungle, only LVT amphibious tractors can resupply them. The assistant commander of the 1st Marine Division, Brigadier General Lemuel Shepherd, Jr., takes control of the beachhead.

The Japanese respond to the landing with dive-bomber attacks, sinking one destroyer and damaging three others. One LST is also damaged. Major General William H. Rupertus, upon landing on the beach, requests the 5th Marines from the division reserve.

The 2nd Battalion 1st Marines, supported by 75-millimeter pack howitzers, lands on the western edge of New Britain near Tauali to cut the main coastal road and block any enemy movements to reinforce or retreat from Cape Gloucester. The marines are to locate and destroy any enemy forces in the area.

About 80 Japanese aircraft succeed in sinking a destroyer and damaging two others. P-38 Lightnings, P-40s, and P-47 Thunderbolts report shooting down over 60 enemy aircraft and report five U.S. aircraft as losses. Actual Japanese losses are 13 bombers and four aircraft lost. U.S. B-25 Mitchells, flying over the beach at the time of the enemy attack, are engaged by friendly antiaircraft fire and two are shot down. The bombers then accidentally drop bombs on marines at Silimati Point, killing one and wounding 14.

Engineers land on Long Island to establish a radar site.

The Japanese conduct a night attack on the 2nd Battalion 7th Marine sector in a rainstorm so severe that the marines have to leave their foxholes because they are filled with water. The Japanese attack fails, leaving 200 dead.

December 27

CBI: Brigadier General Lewis A. Pick opens the Ledo Road to Shingbwiyang in the Hakawng Valley.

The Japanese send 36 aircraft to attack Suichwan airfield in China, destroying a Fourteenth Air Force B-25 and fuel storage areas. Fighters intercepting the attackers report four enemy aircraft destroyed. One P-40 is lost.

INDIAN OCEAN: German submarine *U-178* torpedoes and sinks a U.S. freighter bound for Calcutta, India, west of the Maldives.

ETO: Eighth Air Force sends seven B-17s to drop over 1 million leaflets on Paris, Lille, Evreux, Rouen, and Caen in France.

ITALY: Fifteenth Air Force B-26 Marauders bomb the viaducts at Zoagli and Recco. Twelfth Air Force A-36 Intruder (Apache) fighter-bombers attack a factory and rail lines at Anagni and Civitavecchia, and a bridge at Pontecorvo.

SOUTHWEST PACIFIC AREA: U.S. submarine *Flying Fish* sinks a Japanese fleet tanker in the South China Sea north of Luzon, Philippines. U.S. submarine *Ray* sinks a Japanese fleet tanker west of the Celebes.

PACIFIC: U.S. submarine *Gurnard* damages a Japanese transport east of Shikoku, Japan. U.S. submarine *Tautog* damages a Japanese seaplane carrier off Shionomisaki, Japan.

BOUGAINVILLE: Thirteenth Air Force B-25 Mitchells bomb the seaplane anchorage at Buka, while P-38 Lightnings support over 70 navy SBD Dauntless dive-bombers in attacks on antiaircraft positions. B-25s attack logistics bases at Kahili and a camp at Kieta. Two cruisers and four destroyers of Task Force 39 bombard the Kieta area.

NEW BRITAIN: The 1st and 3rd Battalions of the 1st Marines, reinforced with tanks, move toward Cape Gloucester airfield with difficulty. The narrow trail and heavy jungle limits movement. The 1st Battalion 7th Marines consolidates positions on Target Hill, a small hilltop that is valuable as an observation point and controls any movement of troops along the shoreline.

Fifth Air Force A-20 Havocs attack positions on Cape Gloucester. B-25 Mitchells hit villages and roads from Rottock Bay to Riebeck Bay and strafe barges along the southern coast of the island. B-24 Liberators bomb the airfield at Hoskins.

In response to a request from General Cunningham, an infantry company from the 158th Infantry Regiment lands on Arawe to reinforce the 112th Cavalry.

Thirteenth Air Force and Allied fighters conduct a sweep of the Rabaul area and report destroying 17 enemy aircraft.

NEW GUINEA: Fifth Air Force B-24 Liberators bomb Alexishafen. B-25 Mitchells bomb Madang and targets along the Huon Peninsula.

December 28

CBI: The Chinese 38th Division clears Japanese strongpoints along the Tarung River in the Hukawng valley.

Fourteenth Air Force B-25 Mitchells and P-51 Mustangs attack Yangtze River shipping at Chihchow, China.

ATLANTIC: A U.S. PB4Y Privateer discovers five German destroyers and six torpedo boats in the Bay of Biscay. Six PB4Ys are able to conduct an attack, which is later supported by two British light cruisers. One German destroyer and two torpedo boats are sunk.

INDIAN OCEAN: Japanese submarine *I-26* torpedoes and damages a U.S. freighter en route to Mombasa, Kenya, off the Horn of Africa. The crew abandons ship, but the 27-man armed guard maintains a steady and accurate fire on the submarine, which breaks off its attack. The ship is dead in the water and is later towed to Suez, but it is unsalvageable.

ETO: VIII Bomber Command Mission sends one B-17 on an Oboe test, dropping two 2,000-pound bombs and a Photoflash bomb over Dusseldorf, Germany. Six B-17s drop two million leaflets over Osnabruck, Hannover, and Hildesheim, Germany, Amiens, France, and Zwolle in the Netherlands.

ITALY: Fifteenth Air Force sends over 100 B-26 Marauders against airfields and rail lines at Guidonia and Centocelle and railroad bridges near Orvieto. B-17s and B-24 Liberators bomb the marshaling yard at Rimini. Another 17 B-24s sent against the Vicenza marshaling yard without fighter escort are attacked by about 50 fighters.

German fighters claim 10 bombers, while aircrews report 18 fighters are shot down. Twelfth Air Force B-25 Mitchells, A-20 Havocs, and A-36 Intruder (Apache) fighter-bombers bomb the landing grounds at Ciampino, transportation targets at Frosinone, Roccasecca, and Civitavecchia. P-40s attack Anzio harbor and lines of communication in the Pontecorvo and Atina areas.

PACIFIC: U.S. submarine *Muskallunge* unsuccessfully attacks a Japanese convoy west of Truk.

CENTRAL PACIFIC: Seventh Air Force sends 15 B-24 Liberators to bomb Mille Atoll, Maloelap, and Majuro Atolls. Mille Atoll is also attacked by 18 A-24 Banshees escorted by 20 P-39 Airacobras, followed soon thereafter by nine B-25 Mitchells from Tarawa escorted by 12 P-39s.

BOUGAINVILLE: Thirteenth Air Force B-24 Liberators bomb logistics sites at Bonis and 22 B-25 Mitchells bomb the logistics base at Kahili. Over Rabaul, a fighter sweep reportedly nets over 20 enemy aircraft destroyed.

NEW BRITAIN: Advancing behind Fifth Air Force aircraft, two battalions of the 1st Marines battle a Japanese strongpoint in a heavy rainstorm. The marines lose eight killed and 16 wounded in clearing the enemy position. The 2nd Battalion 1st Marines near Tauali encounters Japanese patrols.

General Krueger releases the 5th Marines to reinforce the 1st Marine Division. The 112th Cavalry repels a Japanese counterattack on Arawe.

December 29

CBI: Fourteenth Air Force P-40s strafe the railroad station, railyards, and the town of Hsipaw, China

PACIFIC: Off Palau, U.S. submarine *Silversides* sinks a Japanese transport and two cargo ships and damages another cargo ship north of Yap.

ITALY: Troops from the 143rd Infantry enter San Vittore but are forced back.

The II Corps has reached all of its objectives for Phase II of Operation Raincoat. Fifteenth Air Force B-26 Marauders attack the marshaling yard at Certaldo and Poggibonsi. B-17s bomb the marshaling yards at Ferrara and Rimini. Twelfth Air Force A-36 Intruder (Apache) fighter-bombers attack the railway station at Ferentino, the harbor and railroad yard at Civitavecchia, and trucks near Aquino.

NEW BRITAIN: The Japanese abandon their defensive position, which the marines have named "Hell's Point." The 2nd Battalion of the 5th Marines lands to support the 1st Marines. The plan is to have the 5th Marines sweep around the left flank of the enemy while 1st Marines advances. The 1st Battalion 7th Marines holds Target Hill.

Fifth Air Force sends over 120 B-24 Liberators, B-25 Mitchells, and B-26 Marauders to attack Japanese positions at Cape Gloucester in support of the marine assault to capture the airfield.

The assistant commander of the 1st Marine Division, Brigadier General Lemuel Shepherd, Jr., takes two battalions of the 7th Marines to clear the Japanese from Borgen Bay. The marines are reinforced by artillery and a platoon of tanks from the 1st Tank Battalion.

NEW GUINEA: Fifth Air Force B-24 Liberators bomb camps and communication targets near Sio. B-25 Mitchells bomb Madang.

December 30

CBI: Tenth Air Force sends 20 B-24 Liberators to attack railway facilities at Monywa, Burma. Fourteenth Air Force's Suichuan airfield in China is attacked by eight Japanese fighters with 12 others providing cover. The attack destroys two aircraft on the ground, but eight P-40s intercept the enemy and shoot down three fighters.

Since April, Fourteenth Air Force has transported 2,592 tons of fuel to keep its aircraft flying, all of it brought over the treacherous Himalaya Mountains (the Hump). Since October 1, 39 vessels have been sunk and 19 damaged. At the end of the year the Fourteenth Air Force has 188 fighters, 51 B-24 Liberators, and 35 B-25 Mitchells

ETO: Eighth Air Force VIII Bomber Command targets the port area and oil refinery at Ludwigshafen, Germany. A force of 502 B-17s and 145 B-24 Liberators, led by 11 Pathfinder aircraft and escorted by 79 P-38 Lightnings, 463 P-47 Thunderbolts, and 41 Ninth Air Force P-51 Mustangs, hits the target. Fourteen B-17s and nine B-24s are lost and 110 B-17s and 12 B-24s are damaged. Aircrews report 12 German fighters destroyed. Fighter pilots report eight confirmed kills, three probables, and six possibles. Fighter losses are 11 P-47s and two P-51s. Five P-47s are damaged. Total American losses for this mission are 11 killed, 19 wounded, and 212 missing. Later in the evening, five B-17s drop one million leaflets on Cambrai, France, and on Antwerp, Ghent, and Lens in Belgium.

Ninth Air Force attacks the Saint-Omer airfield and German rocket sites on the northern coast of France with 100 B-26 Marauders.

ITALY: In II Corps area, the 36th Infantry Division is relieved in place by the 34th Infantry Division. The 142nd Infantry Regiment is placed under the 34th Division's operational control to maintain control of Monte Sammucro.

In VI Corps area, the 45th Infantry Division's 180th Infantry Regiment attempts to clear Monte Molino and Monte Rotondo, guarding the Sant' Elia road. Advancing behind a 15-minute artillery barrage, and supported by tanks from the 755th Tank Battalion, the Americans are able to occupy Monte Rotondo with a small force but are driven back everywhere else.

Fifteenth Air Force B-17s, escorted by P-38 Lightnings and P-47 Thunderbolts, bomb the marshaling yards at Rimini and Padua. Two bombers are lost and nine German fighters are reported destroyed. B-26 Marauders bomb the marshaling yard at Borgo San Lorenzo and Viareggio, and a road junction near Roccasecca. Twelfth Air Force A-20 Havocs attack Atina, while P-40s and A-36 Intruder (Apache) fighter-bombers attack enemy positions near Chieti and Miglianico. Gun positions near Arce and Minturno, Sant' Elia Fiumerapido, Ferentino, and Atina are also attacked.

SOUTHWEST PACIFIC AREA: U.S. submarine *Bluefish* sinks a Japanese oiler in the Java Sea.

CENTRAL PACIFIC: Seventh Air Force sends 17 B-24 Liberators to bomb Kwajalein Atoll. B-24s attack a Japanese cargo ship south of Kwajalein. B-25 Mitchells from Tarawa bomb Jabor on Jaluit Atoll in the Marshalls. A-24 Banshees, escorted by 24 P-39 Airacobras, dive-bomb gun positions on Mili Atoll, also in the Marshalls. Seventh Air Force's advanced headquarters moves from Funafuti Atoll to Tarawa.

BOUGAINVILLE: The newly constructed Piva airfield is operational. Thirteenth Air Force sends 16 B-24 Liberators and 35 B-25 Mitchells to bomb the logistics support areas at Kahili. Another six B-25s bomb the Korovo area.

NEW BRITAIN: The 7th Marines move out to expand their perimeter, clearing out Japanese defenses and capturing weapons and ammunition stores.

During the night, the 2nd Battalion 1st Marines fights the Battle of Coffin Corner. A Japanese assault in a heavy rainstorm, supported with mortar and machine-gun fire, temporarily breaks a company's defensive perimeter, but the marines counterattack with a platoon cobbled together by Lieutenant James R. Mallon and throw the enemy back. The Japanese lose 89 men and five prisoners are captured. The marines suffer six killed and 17 wounded.

Elements of the 1st and 5th Marines capture the Cape Gloucester airfield. Fifth Air Force A-20 Havocs hit positions in the Cape Gloucester area in support of the marines. The marines find that the airfield has been heavily damaged ("Gloucesterized" in the air force terminology) by U.S. air attacks.

Thirteenth Air Force B-24 Liberators, with 25 fighters covering, attack shipping at Rabaul and also bomb Tobera airfield. The fighters report aggressive enemy fighter opposition with 12 aircraft shot down. Over the past month, the Thirteenth Air Force has flown 617 sorties and dropped 197 tons of bombs on Rabaul. U.S. losses have been 19 aircraft; Japanese aircraft losses are estimated at over 100.

NEW GUINEA: Fifth Air Force B-24 Liberators and B-25 Mitchells bomb Alexishafen, Sio, and Madang, and targets of opportunity along the coast of the Huon Peninsula. P-39 Airacobras strafe barges along the Huon Peninsula. P-47 Thunderbolts strafe the Madang area.

December 31

ALEUTIANS: Four PBY-5A Catalinas from Attu Island bomb Shimushu and Kashiwabara in the Kuriles.

CBI: Fourteenth Air Force B-24 Liberators bomb the Lampang railroad yards. B-25 Mitchells attack shipping along the Yangtze River and attack a passenger vessel in the Hainan Straits. The Fourteenth Air Force is destroying an average of 50,000 tons of Japanese shipping per month, representing one-third of all enemy shipping losses and crippling the Japanese war effort.

ETO: Eighth Air Force VIII Bomber Command attacks airfields in France escorted by 74 P-38 Lightnings, 441 P-47 Thunderbolts, and 33 Ninth Air Force P-51 Mustangs. Over the Bordeaux-Merignac, Cognac-Chateaubernard, and Landes Bussac airfields 200 B-17s and 57 B-24 Liberators hit their targets. Eighteen B-17s and five B-24s are lost and 118 bombers are damaged. Aircrews report 17 German fighters destroyed. Four of 57 B-17s are damaged on a mission to find a blockade-running ship at Gironde. Over the St. Jean D'Angely airfield, 87 B-24 Liberators hit the target, losing one bomber and having eight damaged. Aircrews report nine enemy aircraft destroyed. Over the industrial areas at Paris-Ivry and Bois-Colombes, 120 B-17s hit the target, losing one B-17 and 50 others damaged. Fighter pilots report nine confirmed enemy kills, one probable kill, and one possible. Four fighters are lost and eight are damaged. Total U.S. casualties for this mission are 11 killed, 46 wounded, and 253 missing. For the month of December 1943, the Eighth Air Force has dropped over 13,000 tons of bombs.

Ninth Air Force sends about 200 B-26 Marauders to bomb German rocket sites on the coast of France.

ITALY: In II Corps area, the 6th Armored Infantry Regiment of the 1st Armored Division relieves the 15th Infantry, 3rd Infantry Division on Monte Lungo.

In VI Corps area, the 45th Infantry Division's 1st Battalion, 180th Infantry Regiment, in rain that later turns to snow, attempts to clear Monte Molino but is unable to advance under enemy fire. U.S. rifle companies in the two battalions are down to 65 men each. The Fifth Army has over 22,000 men being treated for illness and trench foot. Troops in the front lines must often be resupplied by mules. The VI Corps begins to be moved off the front lines, to be replaced by the French Expeditionary Corps, commanded by General Alphonse P. Juin. It is composed of the 2nd Moroccan Division and the 3rd Algerian Division.

Twelfth Air Force A-36 Intruder (Apache) fighter-bombers attack gun positions around Formia.

PACIFIC: U.S. submarine *Greenling* sinks a Japanese transport in the eastern Carolines and escapes the search of a submarine chaser. U.S. submarine *Herring* attacks a Japanese convoy east of Shikoku, Japan.

At the end of the year, U.S. submarines have sunk a total of 335 Japanese ships, totaling about 1.5 million tons. Using intercepted communications from Ultra, the submarine fleet is able to attack critical shipping targets and aims at first starving the outer defenses of the Japanese, while slowly strangling war production on the home islands.

NEW BRITAIN: Major General William H. Rupertus sends the following message to Lieutenant General Krueger: "Situation well in hand due to fighting spirit of troops, the usual Marine luck and the help of God." Fifth Air Force A-20 Havocs attack Japanese troops around Cape Gloucester. The 3/5 Marines complete their landing and relieve the 2/7 Marines, which now becomes the division reserve.

Japanese aircraft attempting to attack marines near Arawe are attacked by nearly 50 P-40s and P-47 Thunderbolts. The Japanese lose 12 aircraft to the American fighters.

Thirteenth Air Force attacks Rabaul with 15 B-24 Liberators, escorted by 48 F6F Hellcats and 25 P-38 Lightnings. They are met by heavy antiaircraft fire and are attacked by nearly 90 Japanese fighters. Three B-24s are lost and aircrews report 20 enemy fighters destroyed.

NEW GUINEA: Fifth Air Force B-24 Liberators and B-25 Mitchells bomb the areas around Madang, Alexishafen, and Bogadjim.

Allied casualties for the year in New Guinea total 24,000 men, 17,000 of those are Australian.

1944

January 1

CBI: The 5307th Composite Unit (Provisional) is activated. It is organized into three battalions, each with two combat teams of 100 men each. Along with infantry, each combat team has a reconnaissance element, a medical detachment, a mortar and machine gun detachment, and engineer, communications, and command sections. All equipment for the unit is packed on mules or carried by individual soldiers. The unit will be resupplied by air. The 1st Provisional Tank Group under command of Colonel Rothwell H. Brown arrives at Ledo. It is composed of 90 M4A4 Sherman medium tanks armed with 76 millimeter main guns and M3A3 Stuart V light tanks armed with 37 millimeter main guns. The unit has a compliment of 29 officers and 222 enlisted men, both Chinese and Americans. Most of the Chinese soldiers, who range between the ages of 15 and 25, had never seen a machine until joining the unit a few weeks prior.

In Burma, Tenth Air Force B-25 Mitchells, along with 16 P-38 Lightnings, attack a bridge on the Mu River. Major Robert A. Erdin's maneuver to avoid a crash leads to the discovery of an effective bombing technique that puts bombs directly on target. The 490th Bombardment Squadron (Medium) of the 341st Bombardment Group (Medium) soon becomes known as the "Burma Bridge Busters."

A-36 Intruder (Apache) fighter-bombers and P-51 Mustangs attack the airfield at Myitkyina.

The 315th Troop Carrier Squadron with C-47s is activated at Dinjan, India, and assigned to Tenth Air Force.

ETO: The Allies have 11 combat divisions in Britain reserved for Overlord.

The 491st, 492nd, and 493rd Bombardment Groups (Heavy) arrive in England from the United States. These units will receive crews and be equipped with B-24 Liberators. The 492nd will fly its first mission on May 11; the 491st will follow on June 2; and the 493rd on June 6.

The U.S. Strategic Air Forces in Europe (USSAFE) is established to take operational control of the Eighth and Fifteenth Air Forces.

ITALY: The Twelfth Air Force's XII Bomber Command, commanded by Brigadier General Robert D. Knapp, is reorganized as a medium bomber command with three B-25 Mitchell groups and three B-26 Marauder groups.

Three B-26 Marauder groups from Fifteenth Air Force are transferred to Twelfth Air Force. The Fifteenth has six heavy bomber groups (four B-17 and two B-24) and four fighter groups (one P-47 and three P-38).

SOUTHWEST PACIFIC AREA: U.S. submarine *Puffer* torpedoes and sinks a cargo ship south of Negros Island in the Philippines.

PACIFIC: U.S. submarine *Herring* torpedoes and sinks an aircraft transport in the North Pacific, 220 miles southeast of the island of Honshu, Japan. The submarine evades an escorting destroyer.

U.S. submarine *Balao* torpedoes and damages a Japanese transport ship south of Truk.

CENTRAL PACIFIC: In the Marshalls, Seventh Air Force sends six P-39 Airacobras to attack Mille Atoll harbor and shipping.

The headquarters of VII Bomber Command is ordered to move from Funafuti Atoll in the Ellice Islands to Tarawa Atoll in the Gilbert Islands.

Four PB4Y-1 Privateers from Apamama Atoll, Gilbert Islands, mine the waters near Maloelap Atoll in the Marshalls. Three, PV-1 Patrol Bombers from Tarawa mine the waters off Jaluit Atoll in the Marshalls, and two PBY-5 Catalinas mine Jabor anchorage at Jaluit.

BOUGAINVILLE: Allied fighters and U.S. Navy SBD Dauntless dive-bombers provide air support to ground forces near Torokina. Thirteenth Air Force B-25 Mitchells and B-24 Liberators bomb Kahili, and four B-24s bomb Manob.

NEW BRITAIN: Thirteenth Air Force B-24 Liberators, escorted by over 70 P-38 Lightnings and navy F6F Hellcats, bomb Lakunai airfield. Antiaircraft fire is heavy over the target and about 90 Japanese fighters intercept the formation. About 20 enemy fighters are reported shot down. One B-24 is lost; two other Liberators are badly damaged and forced down near Torokina on Bougainville Island.

A-20 Havocs attack Japanese troop concentrations around Cape Gloucester; B-25 Mitchells bomb positions at Borgen Bay; and P-39 Airacobras attack barges on the northern coast.

NEW GUINEA: Fifth Air Force sends 60 B-24 Liberators, 48 B-25 Mitchells, and A-20 Havocs to the landing area at Saidor. The bombers drop 218 tons of bombs on the target. B-25 Mitchells bomb Madang and Alexishafen.

Navy Task Group 37.2, commanded by Rear Admiral Frederick C. Sherman, attacks a Japanese convoy escorted by cruisers and destroyers off Kavieng, New Ireland. Carrier pilots report one light cruiser damaged.

U.S. submarine *Ray* torpedoes and sinks a Japanese gunboat at the mouth of Ambon Bay, Netherlands East Indies.

Navy PBY Catalinas sink a Japanese cargo ship near Lorengau in the Admiralty Islands.

January 2

CBI: Major General Daniel L. Sultan arrives to serve as General Stilwell's deputy and handle most of the administrative matters that Stilwell had previously handled alone.

Tenth Air Force B-25 Mitchells escorted by 16 P-39 Airacobras attack industrial targets at Yenangyaung in Burma and damage an oilfield. B-24 Liberators also attack a refinery and a power station. Another 30 A-36 Intruder (Apache) fighter-bombers and P-51 Mustangs bomb the approaches to Loilaw bridge.

In China Fourteenth Air Force P-40s bomb and strafe Japanese barracks at Hopang.

Japanese submarine *I-26* torpedoes and sinks a U.S. freighter off the coast of Arabia.

ATLANTIC: A U.S. Navy PB4Y Privateer tracks a German blockade runner en route from Japan to Germany in the South Atlantic. A U.S. destroyer intercepts the vessel.

ITALY: Fifteenth Army Group directs the Fifth Army to use two infantry divisions to land at Anzio and cut the German lines of communication and supply behind the Gustav Line. The remainder of Fifth Army is to attack at Cassino, break the enemy lines, and link up with the Anzio force.

In the Fifteenth Air Force, B-24 Liberators of the 720th and 722nd Bombardment Squadrons (Heavy) of the 450th Bombardment Group (Heavy) arrive from the United States. The squadrons are scheduled to fly their first mission in early

January. The B-24 Liberators of the 724th, 725th, 726th, and 727th Bombardment Squadrons (Heavy) of the 451st Bombardment Group (Heavy) of the Fifteenth Air Force also arrive from the United States. The group will be ready for combat missions at the end of January.

XII Air Support Command conducts bombing missions on Monte la Chiaia in preparation for the II Corps attack. Twelfth Air Force B-25 Mitchells bomb the Terni marshaling yard, the iron works, and a military barracks.

PACIFIC: U.S. submarine *Finback* torpedoes and sinks a Japanese merchant tanker in the East China Sea.

CENTRAL PACIFIC: Seventh Air Force B-24 Liberators based at Tarawa bomb Maloelap Atoll in the Marshalls. B-25 Mitchells attack targets on Jaluit Atoll and P-39 Airacobras strafe Japanese shipping near Mille Atoll.

Five PV-1 Patrol Bombers from Tarawa and one PBY-5 Catalina conduct aerial mining in the Marshall Islands.

Japanese aircraft attack the airfield on Apamama Atoll, Gilbert Islands, destroying one PB4Y Privateer and damaging two others.

BOUGAINVILLE: Thirteenth Air Force B-25 Mitchells bomb a supply dump on Buka Island.

NEW BRITAIN: Brigadier General Lemuel C. Shepherd, the assistant division commander, leads an advance of the 2/7, 3/7, and 3/5 Marines toward Borgen Bay. As the 3/7 and 3/5 Marines advance to the southeast, the 2/7 Marines are to fall back as the reserve. Jungle movement becomes treacherous and slow. After marines hack their way about 300 yards, Japanese defenders along Suicide Creek stop the advance of the 3rd Battalion 7th Marines and 3rd Battalion 5th Marines. The creek's 12-foot-high banks are covered by interlocking fields of fire from cleverly hidden machine gun positions, making an attack suicidal—thus the name given to the creek by the marines.

Fifth Air Force P-40s strafe the airfield, antiaircraft positions, and supplies at Cape Hoskins.

NEW GUINEA: Task Force 76, commanded by Rear Admiral Daniel E. Barbey, lands the 126th Regimental Combat Team, 32nd Infantry Division (Reinforced), at Saidor. Six destroyers, six LSTs, nine APDs, and 16 LCIs support the landing. The 126th Regimental Combat Team, the 121st Field Artillery Battalion, two engineer battalions, and support troops land with 6,700 men, 300 vehicles, and 1,800 tons of supplies. The landing force is commanded by Major General Clarence A. Martin. B-24 Liberators and B-25 Mitchells, despite bad weather, succeed in dropping 100 tons of bombs on targets behind the beachhead. A-20 Havocs also provide ground support. The landing is intended to cut off the Japanese retreat from the Huon Peninsula before the advancing Australian 9th Division. P-40s attack Japanese bombers and fighters attacking the landing. One P-40 is lost and five Japanese aircraft are shot down. Although the intent is to trap the Japanese between the Americans and the Australians, torrential rains, heavy jungle, and mountainous terrain allow the Japanese to escape the trap. Japanese troops from Madang guard the trails leading west to allow their comrades to escape.

January 3

CBI: Tenth Air Force A-36 Intruder (Apache) fighter-bombers and P-51 Mustangs attack logistics storage sites at Sahmaw in Burma. Another attack by 19 B-25 Mitchells with 16 P-38 Lightnings flying escort bombs the oilfields at Yenangyaung; another 10 B-24 Liberators making a follow-on attack cause heavy damage to the target. Fourteenth Air Force B-24 Liberators bomb the railroad yards at Lampang, China.

ATLANTIC: The CCS temporarily allocates 87 LSTs to the Mediterranean theater to support Operation Shingle, the Anzio landings. General Eisenhower reports to the JCS that he believes the Shingle operation is very risky. The Germans can rapidly concentrate on the beachhead and quickly crush the two-division force. He is also concerned that there is insufficient means to resupply and sustain the landing force by sea. He believes that if the Anzio landing force and the rest of Fifth Army do not make the planned link-up within eight days of the first landing, then the operation must be considered a failure and the landing force must be withdrawn.

A U.S. destroyer sinks a German blockade runner in the South Atlantic, recovering 130 survivors.

ETO: The B-17s of the 728th, 729th, 730th, and 731st Bombardment Squadrons (Heavy) of the 452nd Bombardment Group (Heavy) arrive in England from the United States. The group's first mission is scheduled for early February.

MEDITERRANEAN: Lieutenant General Nathan F. Twining takes command of the Fifteenth Air Force.

B-17s with P-38 Lightnings and P-47 Thunderbolts flying escort bomb the Villarperosa ball bearing works, the marshaling yard at Lingotto, and the Fiat motor works near Turin.

The B-24 Liberators of the 719th Bombardment Squadron (Heavy) of the 449th Bombardment Group (Heavy) arrive from the United States. The B-24 Liberators of the 721st and 723rd Bombardment Squadrons (Heavy) of the 450th Bombardment Group (Heavy) also arrive from the United States. All three squadrons will fly their first mission early this month.

Brigadier General Edward M. Morris takes command of XII Fighter Command. Twelfth Air Force B-25 Mitchells bomb troops at Prijedor and hit other targets at Split and Sibenik in Yugoslavia.

ITALY: Twelfth Air Force P-40s and A-36 Intruder (Apache) fighter-bombers attack gun positions near Cassino, trains between Ceccano and Segni, and the harbor at Civitavecchia. Other P-40s attack vehicles near Avezzano and Sulmona.

SOUTHWEST PACIFIC AREA: U.S. submarine *Bluefish* lays mines off the eastern Malayan coast. U.S. submarine *Raton* torpedoes and sinks a Japanese fleet tanker east of Mindanao in the Philippines.

PACIFIC: U.S. submarine *Tautog* torpedoes and sinks a Japanese transport south of Honshu, Japan.

CENTRAL PACIFIC: Seventh Air Force A-24 Banshees, supported by P-39 Airacobras, attack Japanese antiaircraft positions, radar, radio facilities, oil storage facilities, and runways on Mille Atoll in the Marshalls.

Navy PB4Y-1 Privateers from Apemama Atoll in the Gilbert Islands conduct aerial mining in the Marshalls. Four PV-1 patrol bombers from Tarawa put down mines near Jaluit Atoll.

Japanese aircraft attack the airfield at Apamama, but cause little damage.

BOUGAINVILLE: Thirteenth Air Force B-25 Mitchells bomb a bivouac area near Kahili and 15 other B-25s attack supply storage areas near Buka Passage.

NEW BRITAIN: The 1st Battalion 7th Marines repulses a Japanese attack on Target Hill. Three Sherman medium tanks arrive on the banks of Suicide Creek on a corduroy road built with great difficulty and extraordinary effort by engineers. Engineers begin to rebuild Cape Gloucester airfield.

Thirteenth Air Force fighters attack Rabaul and report six enemy fighters destroyed.

Fifth Air Force B-24 Liberators bomb Kavieng on New Ireland. A-20 Havocs attack Japanese positions at Borgen Bay.

NEW GUINEA: Fifth Air Force B-24 Liberators and B-25 Mitchells bomb the Alexishafen area.

The 388th Bombardment Squadron (Light) of the 312th Bombardment Group (Light) will transition from P-40s to A-20 Havocs in February.

U.S. submarine *Kingfish* attacks a Japanese convoy, sinking two fleet tankers northwest of Borneo.

January 4

ATLANTIC: A U.S. light cruiser and a destroyer intercept and sink a German blockade runner with gunfire off the northeast coast of Brazil.

ETO: Eighth Air Force attacks two targets over Germany. Of the 371 B-17s and 115 B-24 Liberators that hit the port area at Kiel, 11 B-17s and six B-24s are lost; 113 B-17s and 19 B-24s are damaged. Aircrews report four enemy aircraft as confirmed kills, 12 as probable kills, and four as possibles. U.S. casualties are 22 killed, 53 wounded, and 170 missing. The bombers are escorted by 70 P-38 Lightnings and 42 P-51 Mustangs of the Ninth Air Force. The fighter pilots report one enemy fighter as a confirmed kill, one probable kill, and four possibles. One P-38 is shot down and one is damaged; a P-51 is also lost. Both pilots are reported missing.

Of the 68 B-17s that hit Munster, two B-17s are lost and 36 are damaged. One crewman is wounded and 20 others are missing. The 430 P-47 Thunderbolt pilots that escort the bombers report seven enemy fighters destroyed. Only one P-47 is damaged.

Ninth Air Force B-26 Marauders attack V-weapon sites in France.

Over France during the night, four B-17s drop 800,000 leaflets on Orleans, Lorient, Rouen, and Tours.

U.S. aircraft begin Operation Carpetbagger, airdropping supplies to underground resistance groups in western Europe.

The XIX Air Support Command is activated in England, commanded by Major General Elwood R "Pete" Quesada.

ITALY: The last phase of Operation Raincoat begins in the II Corps area. The intent is to drive the Germans back to Cassino at the opening to the Liri Valley and clear Route 6. Monte Majo and a chain of hills to the southwest, Monte la Chiaia, Monte

Porchia, and Cedro Hill guard the approach. Monte Trocchio, standing behind the chain of hills, is the last defensible terrain before Cassino. The 135th and 168th Infantry Regiments will outflank and clear Monte Chiaia. The 1st Special Service Force will capture Monte Majo, and the 6th Armored Infantry, 1st Armored Division, will capture Monte Porchia. The British X Corps is assigned the capture of Cedro Hill.

The 1st Special Service Force begins the offensive with an attack that captures the hills along the front slope of Monte Majo.

Fifteenth Air Force sends over 100 B-17s to bomb the Dupnica area of Bulgaria, but heavy cloud cover prevents all but 29 from bombing the target.

Twelfth Air Force B-25 Mitchells bomb the marshaling yard at Travnik in Yugoslavia.

SOUTHWEST PACIFIC AREA: U.S. submarines *Bluefish* and *Rasher* attack a Japanese convoy off the coast of French Indochina. *Bluefish* torpedoes and sinks a merchant tanker and *Rasher* damages a tanker and conducts mine-laying activities. U.S. submarine *Cabrilla* torpedoes and sinks a Japanese cargo ship off the coast of French Indochina.

PACIFIC: U.S. submarine *Tautog* torpedoes and sinks a Japanese cargo ship off southern Honshu, Japan.

CENTRAL PACIFIC: Two PV-1 patrol bombers and one PBY-5 Catalina from Tarawa, mine near Jaluit Atoll in the Marshalls.

BOUGAINVILLE: Thirteenth Air Force B-25 Mitchells attack gun positions at Tonolai and bomb Chabai.

NEW BRITAIN: After a 15-minute artillery preparation and with the help of engineers using bulldozers to plow over the steep banks of Suicide Creek, the 3rd Battalion 7th Marines and 3rd Battalion 5th Marines overwhelm the Japanese defenses. The 3/7 Marines tie in with the 1/7 Marines on the left flank, and 2/7 Marines moves to lengthen the line to the west, joining with 3/5 Marines.

Fifth Air Force B-25 Mitchells attack artillery positions in the Cape Gloucester area. More than 40 Allied fighters from Thirteenth Air Force attack the Rabaul area and report 10 Japanese aircraft shot down.

NEW GUINEA: Fifth Air Force sends over 100 B-24 Liberators and B-25 Mitchells to attack targets near Alexishafen, Madang, and Bogadjim and bomb Japanese troops and supplies located between Finschhafen and Saidor.

Fifth Air Force attacks Japanese shipping at Timor. Aircrews report one cargo ship sunk.

Navy aircraft from Task Group 37.2, commanded by Rear Admiral Frederick C. Sherman, attack Japanese shipping at Kavieng and damage two destroyers.

January 5

CBI: Tenth Air Force B-25s, supported by eight P-38 Lightnings, attack the Mu River bridge in Burma.

ATLANTIC: A Navy PBM-3S Mariner sights and tracks a German blockade runner while a U.S. light cruiser and destroyer sink the vessel with gunfire off the coast of Brazil.

ETO: Eighth Air Force attacks two targets over Germany and two over France. The first target is the shipyard and industrial area at Kiel. Of the 119 B-17s and 96 B-24 Liberators that hit the target, five B-17s and five B-24s are lost, 64 B-17s and 16 B-24s are damaged. Aircrews report 41 confirmed kills and 19 others unconfirmed. U.S. losses are 36 killed, five wounded and 100 missing. The mission is escorted by Ninth Air Force P-38 Lightnings and P-51 Mustangs. The fighter pilots report 22 enemy aircraft shot down and one probable kill. Seven P-38s are lost. The pilots are reported missing.

The second attack consists of targets of opportunity at Neuss, Geilenkirchen, Dusseldorf, and Wassenburg, Germany. Of the 73 B-17s that hit targets, two B-17s are lost and 23 are damaged. Aircrews report two confirmed enemy aircraft kills and five other probables. U.S. casualties are two wounded and 20 missing.

Over the Bordeaux/Merignac airfield in France 112 B-17s hit their target. Eleven bombers are lost and 51 are damaged. Aircrews report 50 enemy aircraft as confirmed kills and 10 others as probable kills; U.S. losses are 11 killed, 21 wounded, and 110 missing. The mission is escorted by 76 P-47 Thunderbolts. The pilots report two confirmed kills, but five P-47s are lost and two are damaged. The five fighter pilots are reported as missing.

Of the 78 B-17s that hit the Tours airfield in France, one B-17 is lost and 10 are damaged. Aircrews report two confirmed enemy aircraft shot down. The mission is escorted by 149 P-47 Thunderbolts and the pilots report three confirmed kills. Two P-47s are damaged.

ITALY: The 3rd Battalion, 168th Infantry, 34th Infantry Division attacks in very difficult terrain behind an artillery barrage, but makes slow progress. The 3rd Battalion of the 135th Infantry Regiment attacks and seizes half of the village of San Vittore, below Monte Chiaia. The 1st Battalion 135th Infantry calls in an artillery bombardment on German positions. American artillery batteries fire over 1,600 rounds. As the Americans advance, they are stopped by machine-gun fire from the village of Santa Giusta.

The 6th Armored Infantry advances against German positions on Monte Porchia.

Twelfth Air Force A-36 Intruder (Apache) fighter-bombers attack gun positions near Mignano and enemy positions on Monte Porchia.

SOUTHWEST PACIFIC AREA: U.S. submarine *Rasher* torpedoes and sinks a Japanese tanker in the South China Sea off Malaya.

PACIFIC: The V Amphibious Corps staff completes planning and preparation for an attack on the Marshall Islands. The force consists of 380 ships and 85,000 men.

CENTRAL PACIFIC: A U.S. Navy PBY-5 Catalina from Tarawa drops mines near Wotje Atoll.

U.S. submarine *Scorpion,* on her fourth war patrol, makes a scheduled rendezvous with USS *Herring,* but is never heard from again.

BOUGAINVILLE: Thirteenth Air Force B-24 Liberators attack Tonolai and a logistics base at Kahili.

NEW GEORGIA: Thirteenth Air Force B-25 Mitchells bomb troop concentrations near Choiseul Bay.

NEW BRITAIN: The 112th Cavalry at Arawe is reinforced by the 2nd Battalion, 158th Infantry. The Japanese have established themselves about 600 yards from the American perimeter and are able to fire machine guns and mortars into the U.S. lines. The Japanese have dug trenches and foxholes and covered them with vegetation, making them nearly impossible to locate.

NEW GUINEA: Fifth Air Force B-24 Liberators and B-25 Mitchells attack the Alexishafen, Madang, and Bogadjim areas. The bombers also hit supply and transport barges along the coast from Finschhafen to Saidor.

Infantrymen of the 158th Regimental Combat Team take cover from Japanese fire on Arawe, New Britain, January 1944.

January 6

CBI: Tenth Air Force P-51s and A-36 Intruder (Apache) fighter-bombers conduct ground support missions for the Chinese 38th Division at Sumprabum and Taihpa Ga in Burma. They also attack a Japanese cavalry unit and logistics storage areas at Kamaing.

Two Fourteenth Air Force B-25 Mitchells bomb a troop ship on the Yangtze River and report it as sunk.

ETO: Lieutenant General James H. Doolittle takes command of Eighth Air Force, replacing Lieutenant General Ira C. Eaker. Eaker will become commander of the Mediterranean Allied Air Force (MAAF).

General Carl Spaatz assumes command of U.S. Strategic Air Forces in Europe (USSAFE). Fifteenth Air Force's targets as part of the Combined Bomber Offensive will be assigned by Spaatz's headquarters.

The C-47s of 436th Troop Carrier Group and the 79th, 80th, 81st, and 82nd Troop Carrier Squadrons arrive in England from the United States.

During the night, five B-17s drop 984,000 leaflets on Amiens, Lille, Valenciennes, Cambrai, and Reims, France.

ITALY: The 100th and 3rd Battalions of the 34th Infantry Division are attached to 1st Special Service Force, forming Task Force B. Division artillery will be added and Task Force B's mission is to outflank Monte Trocchio. The 1st Battalion of the 168th Infantry, 34th Infantry Division attempts to move beyond German strongpoints, but makes no progress. Another attack by the 2nd Battalion captures the key position on Hill 396 and defends it against furious enemy counterattacks. The 1st Battalion 135th Infantry encounters strong resistance and is replaced by the 2nd Battalion, which makes a rapid advance. The 6th Armored Infantry, supported by tanks and artillery and by the 48th Engineer Combat Battalion, acting as infantry, captures the north end of Monte Porchia and holds off repeated German counterattacks. Combat casualties in one battalion of the 6th Armored Infantry have reduced its strength to 150 men.

The Fifteenth Air Force's 718th Bombardment Squadron (Heavy) of the 449th Bombardment Group (Heavy) arrives from the United States with B-24 Liberators. The squadron will fly its first mission early this month.

Twelfth Air Force B-26 Marauders bomb the marshaling yards at Pontedera and Lucca, the Piaggio aircraft factory, and the railway near Follonica. P-40s and A-36 fighter-bombers attack enemy positions at Monte la Chiaia and Monte Porchia, the Cervaro-Monte Trocchio area, and the town of Fondi.

CENTRAL PACIFIC: A navy PBY-5 Catalina from Tarawa drops mines near Wotje Atoll.

NEW BRITAIN: The 3/7 later moves back to act as the reserve. The 3rd Battalion 5th Marines captures Hill 150, but discovers the Japanese strongly entrenched at Aogiri ridge, located roughly in the center of the marine line of advance. Heavy jungle prevents any flanking maneuver.

Thirteenth Air Force P-38 Lightnings along with 32 F4U Corsairs and 26 F4F Wildcats head for Rabaul, but weather prevents all but 16 P-38 Lightnings and eight Corsairs from making the attack. They are intercepted by at least 40 Japanese aircraft, leading to a giant dogfight in which nine Japanese fighters and two P-38s are shot down.

NEW GUINEA: Fifth Air Force B-24 Liberators and B-25 Mitchells bomb the Alexishafen and Bogadjim areas. A-20 Havocs attack targets along the road from Bogadjim to Yaula. Other B-25s attack targets of opportunity on the Huon Peninsula and in the Borgen Bay area. P-39 Airacobras strafe barges at Borgen Bay and Rein Bay.

The 389th Bombardment Squadron (Light) of the 312th Bombardment Group (Light) will transition from P-40s to A-20 Havocs in February.

January 7

CBI: Tenth Air Force B-25 Mitchells and 15 P-38 Lightnings attack oil storage and production facilities near Lanywa in Burma. A-36 Intruder (Apache) fighter-bombers and P-51 Mustangs bomb supply points and troops at Nanyaseik.

Fourteenth Air Force B-25s and six P-40s report two large boats, a barge, and a small ore craft sunk on the Yangtze River. P-38 Lightnings report nearly 40 sampans destroyed along the river from Hankow to Chiuchiang, and two B-25s report sinking a passenger vessel off Hong Kong.

ETO: General Eisenhower's staff submits initial concept for Anvil to the CCS, proposing an initial assault with two divisions, followed by a buildup to 10 divisions (eight infantry and two armored). Objectives are the ports of Marseilles and Toulon, followed by an advance north to link up with Allied forces moving from northern France.

Eighth Air Force sends 382 B-17s and 120 B-24 Liberators against the I.G. Farben plant at Ludwigshafen, Germany. Of the 351 B-17s and 69 B-24s that hit the target, five B-17s and 17 B-24s are lost. Another 106 B-17s and 20 B-24s are damaged. Aircrews claim 30 enemy aircraft shot down and six others as probable kills. U.S. casualties are 14 killed, 13 wounded, and 121 missing. The mission is escorted by 71 P-38 Lightnings, 463 P-47 Thunderbolts, and 37 Ninth Air Force P-51 Mustangs. The fighter pilots report seven confirmed enemy kills and three possibles. One P-38 and five P-47s are lost and the pilots are reported as missing.

During the night, five B-17s drop over one million leaflets on Paris, Chartres, Caen, and Evreux, France.

ITALY: The 1st Special Service Force attacks to clear enemy positions on Monte Majo, supported by accurate artillery fire that breaks up enemy counterattacks. The 168th Infantry regiment expands its control of the hills and succeeds in breaking the entire German defensive line. The 135th Infantry Regiment captures Monte la Chiaia. The 3rd Battalion of the 135th Infantry moves from the village of San Vittore and clears the hills north of Route 6. The 6th Armored Infantry captures Monte Porchia, and stops another German counterattack.

Fifteenth Air Force B-17s, with P-38 Lightnings providing escort, bomb an aircraft factory at Maribor and a torpedo factory at Fiume. German fighters attack the formation over Maribor and the P-38s find themselves outnumbered. The air battle lasts over 30 minutes and three P-38s are shot down while U.S. fighter pilots claim four fighters as confirmed kills.

Twelfth Air Force B-25 Mitchells bomb Perugia airfield. B-26 Marauders hit the marshaling yards at Foligno and Arezzo. A-36 Intruder (Apache) fighter-bombers hit gun positions, trucks, and trains in the Cervaro-Aquino-Cassino area and bomb the railyards at Velletri. P-40s give close support to American ground troops in the Monte Maio, Monte Chiaia, Monte Porchia, and Cedro Hill areas. A-36 Intruder (Apache) fighter-bombers and P-40s disperse a German troop concentration near Monte Chiaia.

Sergeant Joe C. Specker's company of the 48th Engineer Combat Battalion advances up Monte Porchia. Sergeant Specker, acting as a scout, locates a German machine gun and riflemen barring the advance. Sergeant Specker then begins moving one of his own machine guns into a position to cover the engineers' advance. He is spotted by the enemy and wounded so badly that he is unable to walk. He drags himself into position and sets up the machine gun, then fires on the Germans so effectively that the engineers are able to capture their objective. During the attack Sergeant Specker dies of his wounds. For his act of courage and dedication to duty, Sergeant Specker will receive the Medal of Honor.

SOUTHWEST PACIFIC AREA: U.S. submarine *Kingfish* attacks a Japanese convoy southwest of Palawan Island and sinks a tanker.

PACIFIC: Major General Hubert R. Harmon takes command of Thirteenth Air Force.

NEW BRITAIN: Thirteenth Air Force B-24 Liberators bomb Vunakanau airfield.

Fifth Air Force B-24s bomb the Cape Gloucester area and A-20 Havocs hit Japanese forces near Arawe.

NEW GUINEA: Fifth Air Force B-24 Liberators and B-25 Mitchells, with P-39 Airacobras and P-47 Thunderbolts, bomb the Alexishafen-Madang area. They also attack targets near Erima and Bogadjim and along the Bogadjim Road. Huts and barges near Sidor are also attacked.

January 8

CBI: Tenth Air Force P-51s and A-36 Intruder (Apache) fighter-bombers damage a bridge near Hopin in Burma and damage rail stock at Tigyaingza.

Fourteenth Air Force moves the B-25 Mitchells of the 22nd Bombardment Squadron (Medium), 341st Bombardment Group (Medium), from Chakulia, India, to Yangkai, China.

The 5307th Composite Unit (Provisional) is released from South East Asia Command (SEAC) control and transferred to General Stilwell's Northern Combat Area Command. Stilwell appoints Brigadier General Frank D. Merrill as 5307th commander.

ETO: Eighth Air Force sends five B-17s to drop more than 2 million leaflets over Antwerp and Brussels in Belgium and over Rennes, Brest, and Nantes in France.

MEDITERRANEAN: The B-24 Liberators of the 449th and 450th Bombardment Groups (Heavy) of the Fifteenth Air Force are now operational, giving the Fifteenth a total of eight heavy bomber groups. Fifteenth Air Force B-24s bomb the airfield at Mostar, Yugoslavia, and Twelfth Air Force B-25 Mitchells bomb the harbor, warehouses, and railway at Metkovic.

ITALY: Fifteenth Air Force B-17s, with P-38 Lightnings and P-47 Thunderbolts flying escort, bomb the Reggio Emilia aircraft factory. Twelfth Air Force A-20 Havocs attack the Frosinone and Colleferro-Segni railway stations. B-26 Marauders bomb the Grosseto and Lucca marshaling yards. P-40s support the Fifth Army near Cassino. A-36 Intruder (Apache) fighter-bombers attack railway targets at Aquino, Frosinone, Palestrina, and Castelforte. P-40s attack Avezzano, and A-36s bomb transportation targets near Tarquinia.

SOUTH PACIFIC: Navy Task Force 38, commanded by Rear Admiral Walden L. Ainsworth, with two light cruisers and five destroyers, conducts a bombardment of Japanese shore installations on Faisi, Poporang, and Shortland Islands in the Solomons.

CENTRAL PACIFIC: Seventh Air Force B-24 Liberators and B-25 Mitchells operating from Tarawa bomb shipping, gun positions, and shore installations in the Marshalls.

Eight navy PB4Y-1 Privateers from Apemama Atoll in the Carolines, mine the waters off Wotje Atoll in the Marshalls and strafe facilities and shipping. Seven PBY-5 Catalinas from Tarawa also conduct aerial mining at Wotje.

BOUGAINVILLE: Thirteenth Air Force B-24 Liberators bomb Kahili.

NEW BRITAIN: The assault on Aogiri Ridge fails. Lieutenant Colonel Lewis W. Walt takes command of the 3/5 Marines after the commander and executive officer are wounded.

Fifth Air Force B-25 Mitchells and A-20 Havocs hit Japanese defensive positions near Arawe.

NEW GUINEA: Fifth Air Force B-24 Liberators and B-25 Mitchells bomb the Madang area, Uligan Harbor, Bogadjim, and the Bogadjim Road.

In the Celebes, B-24s bomb Kendari and other targets.

January 9

CBI: Tenth Air Force P-51 Mustangs and A-36 Intruder (Apache) fighter-bombers attack a bridge, barracks, and an ammunition storage area at Loilaw, Burma.

Fourteenth Air Force B-25 Mitchells bomb a cargo vessel near Swatow, China. Aircrews report the vessel sunk. In French Indochina, four B-25s bomb railroad yards and the Lao Kay railroad station.

MEDITERRANEAN: Fifteenth Air Force B-17s bomb the docks and shipping at Pola, Yugoslavia.

ITALY: Twelfth Air Force B-25 Mitchells attack the Ancona marshaling yard and docks. P-40s and A-36 Intruder (Apache) fighter-bombers attack German vehicles and defenses at Palena, Sulmona, and Cervaro.

BOUGAINVILLE: Thirteenth Air Force B-25 Mitchells attack the seaplane base on Buka Island and the supply depots at Kahili.

NEW BRITAIN: The heavy rains and excessive heat are taking a significant toll on the marines at Aogiri Ridge. Visibility in the terrain is less than 10 yards. The Japanese have placed machine guns in the roots of enormous trees that cover the ridge and have built stout log and earth bunkers interconnected with tunnels across the 200-yard front of the ridge. They are nearly invisible. Two companies from 3/7 arrive to support the renewed assault. The marines struggle forward, and occupy the lower slope of the western end of the ridge. In the face of heavy machine-gun fire, Lieutenant Colonel Lewis C. Walt organizes a volunteer crew to push a 37 millimeter gun up the muddy slopes of Aogiri Ridge to knock out enemy positions that have been holding up the assault. Walt and his marines are able to secure only the slightest toehold on the crest of the ridge.

Thirteenth Air Force B-24 Liberators attack Vunakanau airfield.

NEW GUINEA: Fifth Air Force fighters and bombers attack Alexishafen, Madang, Bogadjim, Uligan Harbor, and the area east of Saidor. The airfield outside of Saidor is repaired by engineers.

January 10

CBI: In Burma, Tenth Air Force A-36 Intruder (Apache) fighter-bombers and P-51 Mustangs attack a Japanese troop position at Nanyaseik. P-40s attack a bridge and rail lines at Namti.

B-24 Liberators bomb the marshaling yard and airfield in the Bangkok area and the main jetty at Akyab, Burma. Nine B-25 Mitchells mine the Mokpalin, Burma, ferry crossing over the Sittang River.

During the night, B-24s lay mines in the Menam River near Bangkok, Thailand, and in the Rangoon River.

In China, Fourteenth Air Force P-51 Mustangs bomb the approach to the Kienchang bridge and attack a troop train near Teian. B-25 Mitchells and P-40s sweep from Anking to Chiuchiang and report sinking a large motor launch, two barges, and a tug on the Yangtze River. B-25s and P-40s attack shipping near Wusueh, sinking a launch and damaging three tankers.

The B-25 Mitchells of the 491st Bombardment Squadron (Medium), 341st Bombardment Group (Medium), transfer from Chakulia, India, to Yangkai, China.

ETO: During the evening, Eighth Air Force sends five B-17s over France to drop nearly five million leaflets over Orleans, Chateauroux, Rouen, Le Mans, and Tours.

Ninth Air Force receives the Headquarters 366th Fighter Group and the 390th Fighter Squadron with P-47 Thunderbolts from the United States. The squadron will fly its first mission in early March.

MEDITERRANEAN: Fifteenth Air Force B-24 Liberators bomb the marshaling yard at Skoplje, Yugoslavia. B-17s escorted by P-38 Lightnings and P-47 Thunderbolts bomb the marshaling yards at Sofia, Bulgaria. They are attacked by about 60 enemy fighters, which shoot down two B-17s. Aircrews report 28 enemy aircraft destroyed.

A U.S. freighter is damaged by a German aerial torpedo during an air attack on convoy KMS 37 (United Kingdom to Mediterranean) en route to Augusta and Naples, Italy.

ITALY: The 168th Infantry Regiment of the 34th Infantry Division, advancing toward the village of Cervaro to flank Monte Trocchio, is forced to fight through German defenses reoccupied during the past few days.

PACIFIC: U.S. submarine *Seawolf* begins attacking a Japanese convoy off Okinawa and sinks two cargo ships. During a typhoon, U.S. submarine *Steelhead* attacks a Japanese convoy south of Honshu, Japan, sinking a repair ship.

CENTRAL PACIFIC: Two PBY-5 Catalinas from Tarawa lay mines at Wotje Atoll.

Japanese aircraft raid the airfield at Apamama. Only slight damage is reported.

BOUGAINVILLE: Thirteenth Air Force sends B-24s to bomb the logistics base at Kahili.

NEW BRITAIN: The Japanese counterattack from positions on the rear of the Aogiri ridge. Five times the Japanese attack the marines holding the crest of the ridge. Mortar and artillery fire hitting at times within 50 yards of the marines stops the attackers. The 37 millimeter gun Colonel Lewis C. Walt has brought forward fires canister shells against the enemy infantry. A Japanese officer leading one attack is killed just a few steps from Walt's position.

Thirteenth Air Force sends 10 B-24 Liberators against Vunakanau airfield, then initiates a night heavy bombing effort, sending 20 B-24s to attack Lakunai airfield.

Fifth Air Force P-39s strafe scattered villages and barges along the coast.

NEW GUINEA: Fifth Air Force bombers and fighters attack the Madang, Alexishafen, and Bogadjim areas and the coastline from Madang to Sio.

B-25 Mitchells bomb Koepang on Timor Island

January 11

CBI: The Fourteenth Air Force's airfield at Suichwan, China, is attacked by 14 Japanese bombers, followed by three medium bombers and 15 fighters. The second strike is intercepted by seven P-51 Mustangs and five P-40s. The fighter pilots report all three bombers shot down.

B-24 Liberators bomb the harbor, aluminum plant, and airfield at Takao, Formosa. Other B-24s mine harbors at Takao and at Hong Kong. One B-24 is lost during the mission.

ATLANTIC: President Roosevelt reports on the postwar world in his State of the Union Address:

> . . . when I went to Cairo and Teheran in November, we knew that we were in agreement with our Allies in our common determination to fight and win this war. There were many vital questions concerning the future peace, and they were discussed in an atmosphere of complete candor and harmony. . . . The one supreme objective for the future, which we discussed for each nation individually, and for all the United Nations, can be summed up in one word: Security. . . .
>
> And that means not only physical security which provides safety from attacks by aggressors. It means also economic security, social security, moral security—in a family of nations. In the plain down-to-earth talks that I had with the Generalis-

simo [Chiang Kai-shek] and Marshal Stalin and Prime Minister Churchill, it was abundantly clear that they are all most deeply interested in the resumption of peaceful progress by their own peoples—progress toward a better life. All our Allies have learned by experience—bitter experience that real development will not be possible if they are to be diverted from their purpose by repeated wars—or even threats of war.

The best interests of each nation, large and small, demand that all freedom-loving nations shall join together in a just and durable system of peace. In the present world situation, evidenced by the actions of Germany, and Italy and Japan, unquestioned military control over the disturbers of the peace is as necessary among nations as it is among citizens in any community. And an equally basic essential to peace—permanent peace—is a decent standard of living for all individual men and women and children in all nations. Freedom from fear is eternally linked with freedom from want.

ETO: Eighth Air Force sends a total of 525 B-17s against three aircraft production facility targets in Germany. The Germans protect the target area with over 500 fighters. Against Oschersleben 177 B-17s are dispatched and 139 hit the primary target; 34 bombers are lost and 85 are damaged. Aircrews report destroying nearly 200 enemy aircraft. U.S. casualties are nine killed, 11 wounded, and 349 missing.

Over Halberstadt only 52 of the 114 B-17s dispatched hit the primary target. Eight bombers are lost and 43 damaged. Aircrews report 35 confirmed kills and 11 probable kills. U.S. casualties are one killed, 18 wounded, and 81 missing. The bombers are escorted by 177 P-47 Thunderbolts and 44 Ninth Air Force P-51 Mustangs. The fighter pilots report 29 confirmed kills and 11 probables. Two P-47s are lost, seven are damaged, and one P-51 is damaged. Two pilots are killed and two are missing.

Against Brunswick, 234 B-17s and 138 B-24s are dispatched and only 47 B-17s hit the primary target while the other bombers hit a variety of secondary targets. A total of 16 B-17s and two B-24s are lost. Aircrews report 19 confirmed kills and 16 probables. U.S. casualties are five wounded and 176 missing. The mission is escorted by 49 P-38 Lightnings and 322 P-47 Thunderbolts. The pilots report two confirmed kills and one probable. One P-38 and two P-47s are lost; one P-47 is damaged. One pilot is reported as missing. During this attack four B-24s serve as PFF (Pathfinder) aircraft for the first time.

MEDITERRANEAN: Fifteenth Air Force B-17s, with P-38 Lightnings as escort, bomb the harbor at Piraeus, Greece. Eight enemy fighters are shot down but six B-17s are lost in midair collisions due to heavy overcast conditions.

ITALY: Twelfth Air Force B-26 Marauders attack industrial targets at Piombino; B-25 Mitchells bomb rail targets at Falconara and Fabriano. P-40s and A-36 Intruder (Apache) fighter-bombers attack defenses and gun positions in Cervaro-Monte Trocchio, a gun position near Minturno, road traffic in the Macerata-Aquila-Popoli area, and railroad facilities at San Giorgio del Sannio.

PACIFIC: U.S. submarine *Seawolf* continues attacking the Japanese convoy off Okinawa, sinking a cargo ship. U.S. submarine *Sturgeon* attacks a Japanese convoy off Kyushu, Japan, and sinks a cargo ship. The submarine is undamaged after a depth charge attack by escort ships. U.S. submarine *Tautog* torpedoes and damages a Japanese ammunition ship off Honshu, Japan.

CENTRAL PACIFIC: Seventh Air Force B-25 Mitchells from Tarawa attack vessels and installations at Maloelap Atoll and Wotje, damaging a destroyer.

P-39 Airacobras from Makin Island attack runways on Mille Atoll.

Four navy PBY Catalinas from Tarawa conduct aerial minelaying operations at Wotje and Maloelap Atolls in the Marshalls.

BOUGAINVILLE: Thirteenth Air Force P-39s strafe targets of opportunity from Numa Numa to Koromira.

NEW BRITAIN: The 3rd Battalion 5th Marines captures Aogiri Ridge and discovers a hidden trail, well built and solid, that leads to Brogen Bay. It is the main Japanese supply route. The 1st Battalion 7th Marines, supported by tanks, clears out a Japanese strongpoint between Hill 150 and Aogiri Ridge. The strongpoint was protecting a major logistics base.

NEW GUINEA: The Saidor airfield receives C-47s bringing ammunition and other supplies. The 126th RCT encounters almost no enemy in the area.

Fifth Air Force B-25 Mitchells, P-39 Airacobras, and P-40s attack targets around Uligan Harbor, Bogadjim, Hansa Bay, and Alexishafen.

January 12

CBI: Tenth Air Force B-25 Mitchells and P-38 Lightnings attack the Letpadan marshaling yard in Burma.

The C-47s of the 27th Troop Carrier Squadron, Tenth Air Force (attached to Troop Carrier Command, Eastern Air Command), arrive at Sylhet, India, from the United States.

Fourteenth Air Force B-24 Liberators bomb the Bangsue marshaling yard at Bangkok, Thailand.

ETO: The 389th Fighter Squadron of the 366th Fighter Group, with P-47 Thunderbolts, arrives in England from the United States. The squadron's first mission will be in March.

MEDITERRANEAN: The naval air station at Port Lyautey, French Morocco, is operational.

ITALY: The 34th Infantry Division conducts several attacks. The 2nd Battalion 168th Infantry attacks to capture Cervaro, while the 1st and 3rd Battalions of the 168th attack north of the village to outflank the enemy positions on the hillsides overlooking Route 6. Tanks provide fire support. The 100th Battalion and the 1st Battalion 133rd Infantry Regiment capture Monte Caprono. The 2nd Battalion 135th Infantry pressures the Germans holding Point 189 southwest of Cervaro.

Twelfth Air Force A-20 Havocs attack San Donato; P-40s attack German positions at San Biagio Saracinesa, Sant' Elia Fiumerapido, Monte Trocchio, and Atina. A-36 Intruder (Apache) fighter-bombers attack the Avezzano and Cisterna di Latina railroad facilities and a village near Atina.

The final plan for Shingle (the Anzio landing) is approved. Fifth Army commander Mark Clark selects the VI Corps commander, Major General John P. Lucas, to lead the assault. The assault force will depart Naples and will consist of the U.S.

3rd Infantry Division, the 504th Parachute Infantry Regiment, the 751st Tank Battalion, and U.S. Army Rangers. The British will provide their 1st Division, the 46th Royal Tank Regiment, and Commandos. Each nation will provide support troops as well. This is the main landing force. A second landing force, to arrive within three days after the initial landing, consists of the U.S. 45th Infantry Division and two combat commands of the U.S. 1st Armored Division. The landing date (D-day) is set for January 22. Fifteenth Army Group expects Fifth Army to attack Cassino, crossing the Rapido River on January 20 to draw German reinforcements away from the Anzio area. Once the breakout has occurred, Allied forces will link up and drive German forces north past Rome.

PACIFIC: U.S. submarine *Hake* torpedoes and sinks a Japanese aircraft transport off Okinawa.

CENTRAL PACIFIC: Seventh Air Force A-24 Banshees from Makin Island dive-bomb antiaircraft positions and the storage area on Mille Atoll in the Marshalls. The Banshees are supported by 20 P-39 Airacobras, which strafe runways on the Atoll.

Navy PB4Y patrol bombers attack Japanese shipping in Kwajalein lagoon, sinking a gunboat. Five PBY-5 Catalinas from Tarawa conduct aerial minelaying operations at Maloelap Atoll in the Marshalls. One Catalina is hit by antiaircraft fire near Jaluit.

U.S. submarine *Albacore* torpedoes and sinks a Japanese gunboat off Truk and damages a gunboat being towed.

BOUGAINVILLE: Thirteenth Air Force P-39 Airacobras bomb and strafe Teop, Inus Point, Numa Numa, and Piano Mission.

NEW BRITAIN: Marine Company B, 1st Tank Battalion, arrives with M3A1 Stuart tanks to support the army on Arawe.

Thirteenth Air Force B-25 Mitchells bomb Vunakanau airfield in the morning, and 16 B-24 Liberators follow with a nighttime attack on Lakunai airfield.

NEW GUINEA: Fifth Air Force B-24 Liberators and B-25 Mitchells attack the Alexishafen area; A-20 Havocs attack Warai.

B-24s bomb Balikpapan, Borneo, as well as Makassar on Celebes Island and Dili on Timor Island.

January 13

CBI: In Burma, Tenth Air Force P-51 Mustangs attack Japanese troops at Lalawng Ga and bomb Maran Ga and Shaduzup. P-40s attack a communication center and supply points along the Kamaing-Mogaung Road. Another four P-51 Mustangs and a B-25 Mitchell bomb the airfield and supply area at Myitkyina.

Major General Kenneth B. Wolfe, commander of the Twentieth Air Force, arrives at New Delhi, India, with elements of the XX Bomber Command staff. The unit will direct Operation Matterhorn, the strategic bombing effort against Japan with the new B-29 Superfortress.

ETO: Ninth Air Force sends 193 B-26 Marauders against German V-weapon sites in France. The headquarters of the 368th Fighter Group, and 395th, 396th, and 397th Fighter Squadrons with P-47 Thunderbolts, arrive in England from the United States. The squadrons will fly their first mission in mid-March.

ITALY: Fifteenth Air Force B-17s, with P-38 Lightnings providing escort and P-47 Thunderbolts flying top cover, bomb Centocelle and Guidonia airfields.

Twelfth Air Force B-25 Mitchells and B-26 Marauders bomb Guidonia, Centocelle, and Ciampino airfields. A-20 Havocs bomb the town of Atina. A-36 Intruder (Apache) fighter-bombers attack the town and railway yards at Isola del Liri, a factory at Colleferro, docks at Formia, railroad yards at Valmontone, and a railway station near Frosinone. P-40s attack Sant' Elia Fiumerapido, San Biagio, Saracinesa, and a rail and road junction near Villa Latina.

PACIFIC: Admiral Nimitz outlines the tentative plan for a year-long campaign in the Central Pacific for 1944, called Granite. The focus of offensive operations is the Luzon-China-Formosa area, to be controlled by Allied forces by spring of 1945. Truk will be the target of carrier air raids to isolate the island, followed by an invasion of the Admiralty Islands and Kavieng, New Ireland. Eniwetok Atoll and Vjeland Island in the Marshalls will be captured, followed by the capture of Truk and Mortlock in the Carolines. Saipan, Tinian, and Guam will be captured at the end of the year. If Truk is bypassed as an option, then the Palau Islands can be attacked as early as August. This would allow Central Pacific and SWPA forces to link near the Philippines.

Southern Pacific forces are reorganized to support the emerging strategy in the Pacific. General MacArthur's SWPA will receive the army XIV Corps (25th, 37th, 40th, 43rd, and 93rd Infantry Divisions and the American Division) and will assume operational control of the Thirteenth Air Force. All combat support and service support units not required in the South Pacific Area will also be transferred to SWPA. All naval forces, except those assigned to Seventh Fleet under MacArthur's command, will be transferred to Admiral Nimitz in the Central Pacific Area. Nimitz will receive the 1st and 3rd Marine Divisions of the First Amphibious Corps as well.

The 4th Marine Division leaves San Diego, California, headed for the Marshalls.

U.S. submarine *Swordfish* is damaged by depth charges off Honshu, Japan, but remains on patrol.

CENTRAL PACIFIC: Seventh Air Force B-25 Mitchells from Tarawa attack shipping at Wotje Atoll. A-24 Banshees from Makin Island dive-bomb the dock, a barracks, and storage area on Mille Atoll. P-39 Airacobras escorting the bombers attack ground targets.

Thirteenth Air Force moves its headquarters from Espiritu Santo, New Hebrides Islands, to Guadalcanal, Solomon Islands.

NEW BRITAIN: Thirteenth Air Force B-25 Mitchells bomb a number of targets throughout the area in an early morning raid. Fifth Air Force B-24s bomb Gasmata Island.

The 3rd Battalion 7th Marines, after artillery and air strikes from Fifth Air Force aircraft, moves to take Hill 660, the last key position that can threaten the Marine beachhead. A boulder-strewn ravine cloaked in thick jungle vegetation marks the approach to the area. The Japanese have incorporated natural obstacles into their defenses. The first marine companies to make contact are immediately stopped by machine-gun fire.

The 2nd Battalion 1st Marines is transported from Tauali to Cape Gloucester airfield to rejoin the rest of the regiment.

NEW GUINEA: In Fifth Air Force, Major General Paul B. Wurtsmith becomes commanding general of the V Fighter Command.

Over 130 B-24 Liberators, B-25 Mitchells, and P-40s attack Alexishafen. B-24s and B-25s strike Kaukenau and Timoeka and damage a freighter off Tanimbar Island in the Molucca Islands. Fifth Air Force B-24 Liberators sink a Japanese transport north of the Admiralty Islands.

January 14

CBI: President Roosevelt sends a message to Generalissimo Chiang Kai-shek requesting the commitment of the Chinese Y Force to Burma, and hints broadly that Chiang's decision will affect his Lend-Lease supply shipments.

Fourteenth Air Force B-24 Liberators sink a cargo ship in the South China Sea off Hainan.

ATLANTIC: U.S. destroyers damage German submarine *U-382* off the coast of Spain.

ETO: COSSAC expands into Supreme Headquarters Allied Expeditionary Force (SHAEF) with the arrival of General Eisenhower as supreme Allied commander. He orders detailed planning to begin on Overlord. Air Marshall Sir Arthur Tedder is the deputy commander, Lieutenant General Omar N. Bradley is commander of the U.S. First Army, General Sir Bernard L. Montgomery is commander of the 21st Army Group, and Lieutenant General Carl Spaatz is commander of U.S. Strategic Air Forces Europe. Admiral Sir Bertram Ramsey is the Allied naval commander in chief, Air Marshall Sir Trafford Leigh-Mallory is the air commander in chief, and Lieutenant General Walter Bedell Smith is chief of staff for SHAEF.

Eighth Air Force sends 374 B-17s and 178 B-24 Liberators, escorted by 98 P-38 Lightnings, 504 P-47 Thunderbolts, and 43 Ninth Air Force P-51 Mustangs, against 21 V-weapon sites in France. Two B-17s and one B-24 are lost, 66 B-17s and 10 B-24s are damaged. Aircrews report eight enemy aircraft destroyed. U.S. casualties are one killed, 11 wounded, and 31 missing. The fighter pilots report 14 enemy aircraft as confirmed kills, one as a probable kill. U.S. aircraft losses are one P-38, one P-47, and one P-51 lost; 10 P-47s and one P-51 damaged. Three pilots are missing.

During the night four B-17s drop 840,000 leaflets over Amiens, Lille, Cambrai, and St. Omer in France. Two B-17s conduct an Oboe Mk II radar test over Wesel, Germany. One B-17 aborts while the other drops two tons of high-explosive bombs on the target.

MEDITERRANEAN: Fifteenth Air Force sends nearly 200 B-17s and B-24 Liberators against Mostar, Yugoslavia. P-38 Lightnings and P-47 Thunderbolts provide escort.

ITALY: Twelfth Air Force B-25 Mitchells bomb the bridge at Pontecorvo. A-20 Havocs attack German positions at Monte Trocchio; P-40s and A-36 Intruder (Apache) fighter-bombers attack defensive positions at San Giuseppe, Sant' Elia Fiumerapido, and Monte Trocchio. A-36s also attack enemy positions near Minturno, Isola, del Liri, and the harbor at Anzio.

PACIFIC: U.S. submarine *Seawolf* attacks a Japanese convoy near Okinawa and sinks a fleet tanker.

U.S. submarine *Swordfish* attacks a Japanese convoy and sinks a transport south of Honshu, Japan.

CENTRAL PACIFIC: Seventh Air Force B-24 Liberators staging through Tarawa bomb islands at Kwajalein Atoll. B-25s from Makin Island attack shipping at Wotje Atoll.

U.S. submarines *Scamp* and *Albacore* attack a Japanese convoy near the Palau Islands. *Scamp* sinks a fleet tanker and *Albacore* sinks a destroyer. Another submarine, *Guardfish,* attacks the same convoy later, sinking a fleet tanker.

The crew of the PBY-5 Catalina shot down near Jabor on January 12 is rescued.

BOUGAINVILLE: Thirteenth Air Force P-39 Airacobras together with navy SBD Dauntless dive-bombers attack Wakunai.

NEW BRITAIN: With tanks providing fire support, the 3rd Battalion 7th Marines captures Hill 660 in a heavy downpour.

Thirteenth Air Force B-24 Liberators conduct night bombing attacks on airfields and facilities. Over 50 SBD Dauntless dive-bombers attack Japanese shipping in Simpson harbor at Rabaul. Fifth Air Force B-24 Liberators, B-25 Mitchells, and A-20 Havocs attack targets along the northern and southern coasts.

NEW GUINEA: Fifth Air Force sends over 50 B-24 Liberators, B-25 Mitchells, and P-40s against targets in the Alexishafen and Erima areas.

Navy SBD Dauntless dive-bombers and TBF Avengers, supported by Allied fighters, bomb Japanese shipping in Simpson Harbor at Rabaul. Pilots report one destroyer and a fleet tanker damaged.

January 15

MEDITERRANEAN: Lieutenant General Ira C. Eaker takes command of the Mediterranean Allied Air Force (MAAF) and Army Air Forces Mediterranean Theater of Operations (AAFMTO). Eaker replaces Air Chief Marshall Sir Arthur Tedder, who becomes the deputy commander in chief for Overlord. The MAAF is a new organization that replaces Mediterranean Air Command.

The headquarters for the 455th Bombardment Group (Heavy), and the 740th, 741st, 742nd, and 743rd Bombardment Squadrons (Heavy) equipped with B-24 Liberators, arrive from the United States. The group's first mission is scheduled for mid-February.

ITALY: The Germans abandon their last defensive position on Monte Trocchio without a fight as units of the 34th and 36th Infantry Divisions prepare to attack. The Allies have broken the Winter Line. The Americans are now at the threshold of the Liri Valley, the most rapid avenue of advance to Rome. Between November 15 and this day, Fifth Army has combat losses of nearly 16,000 men. Of that total, 9,000 were Americans. Another 50,000 Americans in Fifth Army are nonbattle casualties.

Fifteenth Air Force B-24 Liberators bomb the marshaling yard and factories at Prato and hit the town of Pistoia. B-17s concentrate on transportation targets near Florence. Twelfth Air Force A-36 Intruder (Apache) fighter-bombers and P-40s attack enemy positions at Picinisco and Atina.

SOUTHWEST PACIFIC AREA: U.S. submarine *Crevalle* lays mines east of Saigon in French Indochina. U.S. submarine *Thresher* attacks a Japanese convoy and sinks a cargo ship and a tanker north of Luzon in the Philippines.

CENTRAL PACIFIC: Seventh Air Force B-25 Mitchells from Tarawa attack Japanese shipping and storage facilities on Maloelap Atoll in the Marshalls. The nine bombers make a low-level attack and one B-25 is downed by antiaircraft fire.

BOUGAINVILLE: Thirteenth Air Force sends 24 B-25 Mitchells, with 60 fighters flying escort, to attack East Cape. P-39 Airacobras attack Chabai.

NEW BRITAIN: Fifth Air Force B-25 Mitchells and P-39 Airacobras attack Japanese positions on the southern coast.

NEW GUINEA: An Australian patrol searching for the enemy near Soi discovers a trunk half submerged in a creek. In the trunk are the complete ciphers of the Japanese army's 20th Division. This allows MacArthur's cryptanalysts to break the Japanese army's cipher system; soon the Allies know the enemy's plans and intentions.

Fifth Air Force B-24 Liberators and B-25 Mitchells attack Uligan Harbor and B-25s with P-40s and P-47 Thunderbolts attack the Madang, Alexishafen, Erima, and Bogadjim areas.

January 16

ATLANTIC: TBF Avengers from escort carrier USS *Guadalcanal* sinks German submarine *U-544* in the mid-Atlantic.

A U.S. freighter straggling from the New York-bound convoy ON 219 (Liverpool to New York, fast) is torpedoed and sunk by German submarine *U-960* in the North Atlantic.

ETO: General Dwight D. Eisenhower assumes duties as Supreme Commander, Allied Expeditionary Force (AEF).

MEDITERRANEAN: Fifteenth Air Force B-17s escorted by P-38 Lightnings bomb the aircraft production facility at Klagenfurt, Austria, and the landing ground at Villaorba, Italy. The fighter pilots report nine enemy fighters shot down; U.S. losses are three P-38s lost.

ITALY: Twelfth Air Force B-25 Mitchells bomb the marshaling yard at Terni and B-26 Marauders attack the marshaling yard and bridge at Orte. A-20 Havocs bomb Atina; P-40s attack bridges near San Giorgio del Sannio and enemy positions near Cassino. A-36 Intruder (Apache) fighter-bombers hit the transportation targets at Cecina and Siena, and the town areas of Avezzano and Formia.

SOUTHWEST PACIFIC AREA: U.S. submarine *Redfin* torpedoes and damages a Japanese destroyer north of the Spratly Islands.

PACIFIC: U.S. submarine *Sturgeon* torpedoes and damages a Japanese destroyer south of Kyushu, Japan. U.S. submarine *Swordfish* torpedoes and sinks a Japanese gunboat off Honshu, Japan. U.S. submarine *Whale* attacks a Japanese convoy and sinks a cargo ship near Okinawa. U.S. submarine *Seawolf* also damages a transport, which USS *Whale* later sinks southeast of Okinawa.

CENTRAL PACIFIC: Seventh Air Force sends 25 A-24 Banshees, 16 P-39 Airacobras, and eight P-40s from Makin Island to attack Japanese barracks, antiaircraft positions,

A group of Marines, most likely from the 2nd Marine Raider Regiment, pause in January 1944 after nearly 60 days of combat on Bougainville Island.

and storage areas at Mille Atoll in the Marshalls. Three Japanese aircraft are reported destroyed and two P-39s are lost.

The B-24 Liberators of the 431st Bombardment Squadron (Heavy), 11th Bombardment Group (Heavy), arrive at Tarawa.

U.S. submarine *Blackfish* attacks a Japanese convoy and sinks a transport near Truk.

U.S. submarine *Seahorse* torpedoes and sinks a cargo ship southeast of the Marianas.

BOUGAINVILLE: The last elements of the 3rd Marine Division are replaced by the Americal Division, giving the army complete control of the defensive perimeter formed on the western side of the island. On the eastern side are still tens of thousands of Japanese soldiers, battered by American airpower, but still capable of offensive action.

NEW BRITAIN: Two companies of Japanese infantry attack to regain Hill 660, but are met with mortar and artillery fire. Over 110 Japanese are killed in the attack, and other infiltration-type attacks are also repulsed. The Japanese retreat toward Talasea and Hoskins Plantation. The marines have accomplished the near-impossible—attacking and defeating an enemy in prepared positions in some of the most challenging terrain in the world and in atrocious weather conditions.

Fifth Air Force B-24s and B-25s attack Japanese positions near Arawe. The 2nd Battalion 158th Infantry, supported by marine tanks, attacks the Japanese positions on Arawe. The tanks bog down in the soft ground as the infantry advances. The Japanese are forced to retreat and the 158th returns to its own lines. Two of the tanks have to be destroyed in place because they are so badly mired in the mud. American casualties in the attack are 20 killed and 40 wounded.

NEW GUINEA: Fifth Air Force B-25 Mitchells, A-20 Havocs, and P-40s attack targets around Madang, Erima, and Bogadjim.

Navy PBY Catalinas attack a Japanese convoy headed for Rabaul near the St. Matthias Group of islands, sinking two cargo ships and a transport. Japanese submarine *I-181* is damaged in the Vitiaz Strait.

January 17

CBI: In Burma, Tenth Air Force A-36 Intruder (Apache) fighter-bombers and P-51 Mustangs support ground forces around Taro and the Shaduzup-Ngamaw Ga area; supply dumps, warehouses, and rolling stock at Sahmaw are also attacked. P-40s attack Myitkyina airfield.

ITALY: The mission of the U.S. II Corps commanded by Major General Geoffrey T. Keyes is to draw German forces away from Anzio by attacking across the Rapido River. The rest of Fifth Army (the British X Corps and the French Expeditionary Corps) will attack along the high ground on both sides of the Liri Valley, opening the way to link up with the VI Corps at Anzio as it breaks out of the beachhead. The 36th Infantry Division commanded by Major General Frederick L. Walker has the mission of crossing the Rapido River. Melting snow makes the river between 25 and 50 feet wide and 10 to 15 feet deep. The French and British attack fails to capture the heights on the flanks of II Corps, leaving the intended river crossing area under direct enemy observation.

The Shingle force begins its final rehearsals for the Anzio landings on beaches near Salerno. The VI Corps is to make three simultaneous assaults. The entire 3rd Infantry Division, commanded by Major General Lucian K. Truscott, will land near Nettuno. Three battalions of Rangers, heavy mortars, and the 509th Parachute Infantry Battalion will land near Anzio harbor to capture the port and destroy any coastal defenses. The British 1st Division will land a brigade and Commandos northwest of Anzio to block routes into the beachhead and link up with American units at Anzio. The 504th Parachute Infantry will serve as Corps reserve and will land behind the 3rd Infantry Division. Airpower will limit any German advance toward the beachhead and destroy German aircraft. XII Air Support Command, led by Major General E. J. House, reinforced with two groups from the Desert Air Force, will provide direct support to the ground forces. Task Force 81 under the command of Rear Admiral F. J. Lowry will land the forces and ensure they are securely established on shore. Lowry has a British and American task force with a total of five cruisers, 16 destroyers, and 17 minesweepers. There will be no preliminary naval bombardment, to maximize surprise. Rocket-launching LCTs will provide the only covering fire approximately 10 minutes before the troops land on the beach. Most of the British 1st Division and the 46th Royal Tank Regiment will remain as a shipboard floating reserve.

Fifteenth Air Force B-17s bomb the marshaling yards at Prato and Pontassieve. B-24 Liberators escorted by P-38 Lightnings and P-47 Thunderbolts bomb the marshaling yard at Arezzo. Twelfth Air Force P-40s attack enemy positions at San Giuseppe and Formia, and the docks at Anzio. A-36 Intruder (Apache) fighter-bombers attack Anzio, Avezzano, and town and factory buildings at Tarquinia.

CENTRAL PACIFIC: Seventh Air Force sends nine B-25s from Abemama Island and four P-40s from Makin Island to attack supply storage area, antiaircraft positions, and the runway at Mille Atoll in the Marshalls.

NEW BRITAIN: Thirteenth Air Force fighters support a navy SBD dauntless dive-bomber attack on Japanese shipping at Rabaul. Pilots report 18 Japanese aircraft shot down. Ten Allied fighters are lost. During the night B-24 Liberators bomb the Rabaul area.

NEW GUINEA: Fifth Air Force sends 47 B-24 Liberators and B-25 Mitchells to bomb the Hansa Bay area. B-24s bomb Bandanaira in the Celebes Islands. Fifth Air Force B-24 Liberators sink two Japanese cargo ships off Manus in the Admiralty Islands.

Navy SBD Dauntless dive bombers and TBF Avengers, supported by fighter aircraft, bomb shipping at Rabaul, sinking a repair ship, a transport, and a cargo ship, and damaging an aircraft transport.

U.S. submarine *Bowfin* attacks a Japanese convoy in the Makassar Strait.

January 18

CBI: In Burma, Tenth Air Force B-24 Liberators and B-25 Mitchells bomb Japanese camps at Kyaukchaw. P-38 Lightnings attack the airfield at Meiktila. A-36 Intruder (Apache) fighter-bombers and P-51 Mustangs attack troops, supply dumps, and repair facilities at Sawnghka. P-40s attack troops and supplies at Shaduzup.

In French Indochina, two Fourteenth Air Force B-25 Mitchells bomb rail lines and the wharf at Campha and oil storage facilities at Mon Cay.

ITALY: The British X Corps attack with two divisions across the Garigliano River near Minturno causes two German Panzer Grenadier divisions to be moved away from Rome to the south, leaving the Anzio area completely unguarded.

Fifteenth Air Force B-17s, with P-38 Lightnings and P-47 Thunderbolts providing escort, attack marshaling yards, a bridge, and an airfield near Florence.

Twelfth Air Force B-25 Mitchells bomb the town and railway viaduct at Terni, and A-20 Havocs attack gun positions near Minturno. P-40s and A-36 Intruder (Apache) fighter-bombers attack troops, trucks, and gun positions in Minturno, Pontecorvo, and Atina.

PACIFIC: U.S. submarine *Flasher* torpedoes and sinks a Japanese oiler far off Marcus Island.

CENTRAL PACIFIC: Seventh Air Force sends 12 B-25 Mitchells from Abemama Island to attack Japanese facilities on Mille Atoll. Another mission sends 25 A-24 Banshees and eight P-40s from Makin to attack the oil storage area on Jabor Island in Jaluit Atoll. Aircrews report a tanker sunk.

NEW BRITAIN: The battered 7th Marines are relieved by the 2nd Battalion 1st Marines and the 2nd Battalion 5th Marines.

Thirteenth Air Force sends 34 B-25 Mitchells supported by more than 70 fighters to attack Tobera.

NEW GUINEA: Fifth Air Force sends 40 B-24 Liberators to attack the Hansa Bay area. More than 70 B-25 Mitchells attack the Madang and Bogadjim areas. Over Wewak, Japanese fighters engage 55 P-40s and P-38 Lightnings. Pilots report 12 Japanese fighters shot down. U.S. losses are three P-38s.

B-24s bomb Laha in the Celebes Islands.

U.S. submarine *Bowfin* torpedoes and sinks a Japanese tanker in the Makassar Strait.

January 19

CBI: Generalissimo Chiang Kai-shek threatens to discontinue providing housing and food to American forces in China unless he receives $1 billion in loans by March 1.

A-36 Intruder (Apache) fighter-bombers and P-51 Mustangs support the Chinese 38th Division in the Hukawng Valley in Burma. Tenth Air Force B-24 Liberators bomb the marshaling yard in Bangkok, Thailand.

In French Indochina, Fourteenth Air Force B-25 Mitchells and P-40s attack the barracks at Mon Cay.

MEDITERRANEAN: Fifteenth Army Group is redesignated as Headquarters, Allied Central Mediterranean Force (ACMF).

ITALY: The Anzio landing force completes its exercises on beaches near Salerno.

Twelfth Air Force A-36 Intruder (Apache) fighter-bombers attack transportation targets north of Rome. The A-36s and P-40s attack enemy positions in support of the British effort to expand the bridgehead on the Garigliano River. The British fail to gain ground, leaving the flank of the U.S. II Corps exposed as it prepares to cross the Rapido River the following day.

CENTRAL PACIFIC: Seventh Air Force sends 17 B-25s from Tarawa to attack Mille Atoll in the Marshalls. The bombers make a low-level run, hitting gun positions, fuel supplies, and the airfield. Japanese antiaircraft fire destroys two of the bombers.

U.S. submarine *Haddock* torpedoes and damage Japanese carrier *Unyo* near Guam.

Fifth Air Force B-24 Liberators sink a Japanese cargo ship at Manus in the Admiralty Islands.

NEW BRITAIN: Marines begin patrolling to locate the vanished enemy, setting ambushes and collecting information from the natives, following trails and looking for signs of the Japanese. There are a series of short, intense, company-sized firefights with Japanese elements delaying the approach of the marines.

Thirteenth Air Force launches 11 B-24 Liberators on a nighttime attack on Rabaul and Vunakanau.

NEW GUINEA: Two battalions of the 128th RCT land at Saidor.

Fifth Air Force B-24 Liberators bomb Amboina Island in the Molucca Islands and Halong in the Celebes Islands.

January 20

CBI: Tenth Air Force A-36 Intruder (Apache) fighter-bombers and P-51 Mustangs attack the railway near Mogaung and supplies at Mohnyin. P-38 Lightnings and B-25 Mitchells bomb rail lines and a bridge near Nattalin.

Fourteenth Air Force B-24 Liberators sink Japanese transports southeast of Swatow, China.

ETO: General Carl Spaatz, Commanding General USSAFE, assumes administrative control for all USAAF units in the United Kingdom.

Ninth Air Force receives headquarters, 437th Troop Carrier Group, and the 83rd, 84th, and 85th Troop Carrier Squadrons from the United States. The group is equipped with C-47s.

During the night, Eighth Air Force dispatches five B-17s to drop 960,000 leaflets on Lille, Brest, Caen, and Chartres in France.

ITALY: In the II Corps area, Major General Frederick L. Walker, commander of the 36th Infantry Division, is ordered to cross the Rapido River with two infantry regiments, one north and one south of Sant' Angelo. They are to capture the town of Sant' Angelo and open the way for Combat Command B of the 1st Armored Division to attack up the Liri Valley and link up with the VI Corps at Anzio.

Completely exposed to enemy fire, two battalions of the 141st Infantry Regiment attempt to cross the river north and about 100 men reach the other shore and dig in. The 143rd Infantry Regiment gets about one battalion across. After a futile effort to advance, the survivors are withdrawn back across the river. The attack fell apart almost immediately from a combination of poor preparation, mines, impassible mud, and poor coordination.

Twelfth Air Force B-26 Marauders bomb the marshaling yard at Viterbo and attack a bridge at Pontecorvo. B-25 Mitchells attack railroads near Carsoli area. A-20 Havocs attack enemy positions near Minturno. A-36 Intruder (Apache) fighter-bombers and P-40s fly nearly 200 sorties supporting the Fifth Army as the 36th Infantry Division attempts to cross the Rapido River. P-40s attack Sant' Angelo and 36 A-20 Havocs and 24 P-40s attack roads and gun positions around Cassino.

PACIFIC: U.S. submarine *Batfish* attacks a Japanese convoy off southern Honshu, sinking a transport.

CENTRAL PACIFIC: Seventh Air Force sends 13 B-24 Liberators, staging through Tarawa Atoll, to make a night raid on Wotje Atoll. P-40s from the Gilberts strafe ships at Jaluit Atoll. B-25 Mitchells sink a transport at Namu Atoll in the Marshalls.

B-24s of the 98th Bombardment Squadron (Heavy) and the Headquarters, 11th Bombardment Group (Heavy) arrive at Tarawa.

U.S. submarine *Gar* attacks a Japanese convoy coming from New Guinea and sinks a cargo ship off Palau. U.S. submarine *Seadragon* torpedoes and damages a stores ship northwest of Truk.

NEW BRITAIN: Thirteenth Air Force dispatches 18 B-25 Mitchells, escorted by about 70 fighters, to attack the airfield, fuel storage area, and gun positions at Vunakanau and Rabaul.

Fifth Air Force A-20s attack Japanese positions between Borgen Bay and Rein Bay and attack supply barges on Gasmata Island.

NEW GUINEA: Fifth Air Force B-25 Mitchells and one B-24 bomb and strafe the Hansa Bay area.

U.S. submarine *Tinosa* lands men and equipment in northeast Borneo.

January 21

ALEUTIANS: Navy PBY-5A Catalinas from Attu and PV-1 Patrol Bombers bomb and photograph Japanese installations on Paramushiru Island in the Kuriles.

ETO: At the supreme commander's conference in England the planning details for Overlord are briefed to the commanders. Overlord is a general plan for a cross-Channel invasion. Now that the exact location and date of the landing are identified in this detailed plan, the operation is called Neptune. General Sir Bernard L. Montgomery will be responsible for all ground forces in the cross-Channel invasion as commander of the 21st Army Group. This army group will be composed of the British Second Army and the U.S. First Army. After examining the plan, Montgomery believes a three-division initial landing is insufficient and the frontage for the attack is too narrow. He asks for five divisions in the first wave, extending from Caen to the Cotentin beaches, supported by an airborne landing in the rear of the enemy. More divisions in the initial assault will mean more landing craft and a certain postponement of the agreed upon landing date of May 1.

Eighth Air Force attacks 36 V-weapon sites in France escorted by 49 P-38 Lightnings, 531 P-47 Thunderbolts, and 48 Ninth Air Force P-51 Mustangs. Of the 302 B-17s and 68 B-24 Liberators that hit the targets, one B-17 and five B-24s are lost and 103 B-17s and 44 B-24s are damaged. Aircrews report five enemy aircraft as confirmed kills. U.S. casualties are two killed, 31 wounded, and 74 missing. The fighter pilots report six confirmed enemy kills in the air and four destroyed or damaged on the ground. One P-47 is lost with the pilot reported missing; two other P-47s are damaged. Ninth Air Force also sends 119 B-26 Marauders to bomb V-weapon sites.

During the night, five B-17s drop 1.2 million leaflets on Reims, Nantes, Le Mans, Tours, and Orleans, France.

MEDITERRANEAN: Fifteenth Air Force B-17s bomb airfields at Istres-Le-Tube and Salon-de-Provence in France.

The 738th and 739th Bombardment Squadrons (Heavy) of the 454th Bombardment Group (Heavy) arrive with B-24 Liberators from the United States. The group's first mission is scheduled for early March.

ITALY: In the II Corps area, the Fifth Army commander, Lieutenant General Mark Clark, orders another attack despite concerns from subordinates; he is convinced that it is essential in drawing German forces away from Anzio. A battalion of the 143rd Infantry attempts another crossing behind heavy smoke and succeeds in reaching the opposite bank. The 141st Infantry crosses the river with two battalions. Accurate and heavy artillery fire limits any advance and prevents the engineers from bridging the river. The units are cut off and exposed to enemy fire all day. The 143rd Infantry withdraws under fire successfully, but the 141st is stranded.

Twelfth Air Force B-26 Marauders attack railroad bridges near Orvieto. B-25 Mitchells bomb the Pontecorvo bridge. P-40s attack German positions supporting the Gargliano and the Rapido River bridgeheads. A-36 Intruder (Apache) fighter-bombers attack targets around Veletri, Minturno, and Viterbo.

CENTRAL PACIFIC: Seventh Air Force sends 16 B-24 Liberators staging through Tarawa on a night raid against Kwajalein Atoll. B-25 Mitchells based at Tarawa attack Arno and Aur Atolls. B-25s from Abemama Island attack facilities and gun positions on Mille Atoll. A-24s and P-40s from Makin Island attack gun positions, storage facilities, and two small vessels at Jaluit Atoll.

NEW BRITAIN: Japanese forces on New Britain are ordered to retreat to Iboki and to prepare for holding the American advance at Talasea.

Fifth Air Force B-25 Mitchells and P-39 Airacobras strafe barges and attack other targets of opportunity along the northern coast of the island.

NEW GUINEA: Fifth Air Force B-25 Mitchells, A-20 Havocs, and P-39 Airacobras bomb the Madang Saidor areas.

U.S. submarine *Seahorse* attacks a Japanese convoy departing Palau for Hollandia and sinks an army transport and a cargo ship near Palau.

January 22

CBI: In Burma, Tenth Air Force A-36 Intruder (Apache) fighter-bombers, P-51 Mustangs, and one B-25 attack enemy supply dumps and communications between Kumnyen and Ngamaw Ga in support of Chinese forces.

In China, Fourteenth Air Force sends 11 P-40s and five P-51 Mustangs to attack the Nanchang airfield. P-38 Lightnings damage bridges at Shektan and Sheklung.

MEDITERRANEAN: Rear Admiral Frank J. Lowry commands the naval force for Operation Shingle. A minesweeper is sunk by mine and *LCI-20* is sunk by German aircraft.

ITALY: In the II Corps area, the Germans conduct a counterattack on the 141st Infantry Regiment holding the bridgehead across the Rapido River, and kill or capture the defenders. The 141st and 143rd Infantry Regiments lose 2,128 troops in their futile attempts to cross the Rapido River. General Mark Clark, Fifth Army commander, believes the sacrifice worthwhile, even if the attack is a failure.

At Anzio, the Allies achieve complete surprise and land with no opposition. The 3rd Infantry Division moves to its initial phase line. General Mark Clark lands a few hours later. The Rangers capture the port of Anzio and the 509th Parachute Infantry Battalion moves east to occupy Nettuno. By 1200, VI Corps has accomplished all of its D-day objectives. Allied aircraft fly over 1,200 sorties in support of the landings, attacking bridges and road junctions at Cisterna and Velletri. One minesweeper is lost to a mine and one LCI is bombed and sunk. By midnight 36,000 men and 3,200 vehicles have been landed. Casualties are 13 killed, 97 wounded, and 44 missing. The Allies have captured 227 German prisoners. The 30th Infantry Regiment has captured all the bridges over the Mussolini Canal, which controls any approaches to the right flank of the beachhead, but loses them during a night counterattack.

Twelfth Air Force supports the Anzio landings with A-20 Havocs and A-36 Intruder (Apache) fighter-bombers isolating the landing area by attacking the main road and rail routes into the bridgehead. Valetri, Valmontone, Colleferro, Ceprano, and Fondi are also targeted to prevent any opportunity for enemy forces to assemble. P-40s cover the airspace over the Anzio landing force, intercepting German fighter-bombers.

Fifteenth Air Force B-17s and B-24 Liberators bomb the marshaling yards at Terni, Arezzo, Pontedera and the bridge and town at Pontecorvo.

As F Company, 143rd Infantry, 36th Infantry Division, begins its night crossing of the Rapido River near San Angelo, the Germans begin dropping mortar and artillery rounds on the bridge while machine-gun fire seeks out the American troops as they reach the opposite bank. Staff Sergeant Thomas E. McCall commands a machine-gun section supporting the infantry. Exposing himself to enemy fire, McCall leads his men forward through a barbed wire obstacle to a firing position where his section can engage the enemy. When his soldiers are wounded by enemy fire, McCall again ignores enemy fire to render aid. When his entire machine-gun section is either killed or wounded, Staff Sergeant McCall charges forward alone, carrying the machine-gun in his arms and destroying two enemy positions; he is last seen attacking another position, firing his weapon from his hip. Staff Sergeant McCall's care for the men under his command, his exemplary leadership and supreme courage will win him the Medal of Honor.

SOUTH PACIFIC: Japanese submarine *RO-37* torpedoes an oiler off San Cristobal in the Solomons, but is sunk by the destroyer USS *Buchanan.*

CENTRAL PACIFIC: Seventh Air Force sends 18 B-24 Liberators from Tarawa against Kwajalein, Jaluit, and Mille Atolls. Nine B-25 Mitchells from Tarawa bomb shipping and targets on Wotje Atoll. Another 10 B-25s from Abemama Island attack Maloelap Atoll. Aircrews report 10 Japanese aircraft shot down and three B-25s lost.

NEW BRITAIN: Thirteenth Air Force attacks Lakunai airfield with 27 B-25 Mitchells, supported by more than 90 fighters. Aircrews report heavy damage to the airfield and 18 Japanese aircraft destroyed. One B-25 and four fighters are lost. Over Rabaul, six B-25s and more than 30 B-24 Liberators bomb facilities in the town.

Fifth Air Force A-20 Havocs and P-40s attack targets of opportunity on the island.

NEW GUINEA: Fifth Air Force B-25 Mitchells and P-38s attack Japanese shipping at Manus in the Admiralties. Pilots report an auxiliary submarine chaser is sunk and a cargo vessel is damaged.

U.S. submarine *Tinosa* attacks a Japanese convoy, sinking two tankers off Borneo.

January 23

ALEUTIANS: Navy PBY-5A Catalinas and PV-1 Patrol Bombers from Attu bomb Japanese installations on Paramushiru Island, Kuriles.

CBI: In Burma, Tenth Air Force B-24 Liberators attack shipping at Mergui harbor on the west coast of Malaysia. B-25 Mitchells and P-38 Lightnings destroy a bridge at Myittha and damage another at Samon. A-36 Intruder (Apache) fighter-bombers, P-51 Mustangs, and one B-25 damage enemy supply points at Kamaing and Mogaung. P-40s attack Myitkyina airfield.

In China, Fourteenth Air Force B-25 Mitchells and P-40s from Kweilin attack Kai Tek airfield in the Hong Kong-Kowloon area.

ETO: Allied planners outline the concept of operations for Neptune. The Americans have the responsibility for the western portion of the landing area closest to Cherbourg while the British have responsibility for the east closest to Caen. A total of 39 divisions are to be involved in the invasion: 20 American, 14 British, three Canadian, one French, and one Polish.

Allied planners evolve an elaborate deception to draw the attention of the Germans toward the Pas-de-Calais, the most obvious landing site, rather than the Cotentin Peninsula, the actual invasion site. A false army group is created near Dover, with giant campsites and inflated rubber tanks, landing craft, and vehicles all open to observation and counting. Naval maneuvers are held off the coast of the empty camps and German listening posts hear a constant stream of radio traffic reports directed to SHAEF headquarters from Lieutenant General George S. Patton, Jr., the well-known American combat leader and ostensible commander of the fictitious army group. The elaborate ruse works. The Germans over time will be convinced that the Pas-de-Calais is the Allied landing area and hold 19 divisions there even after the landings at Normandy.

Ninth Air Force sends almost 200 B-26 Marauders against V-weapon sites in France.

During the night, Eighth Air Force sends five B-17s to drop leaflets on Rennes, Le Mans, Chartres, Lille, and Orleans, France.

ITALY: At Anzio, the 30th Infantry Regiment of the 3rd Infantry Division, along with the 504th Parachute Infantry Regiment, recaptures the bridges over the Mussolini Canal. The 3rd Infantry Division, along with the paratroopers and Rangers, holds the right half of the beachhead, and a brigade of the British 1st Division holds the left half. German divisions are ordered to Anzio.

Fifteenth Air Force B-17s, escorted by P-47 Thunderbolts, bomb bridges at Pontecorvo and Ceprano.

Twelfth Air Force B-26 Marauders and B-25 Mitchells bomb near Avezzano. A-20 Havocs and A-36 Intruder (Apache) fighter-bombers attack Vallecorsa and road junctions at Fondi.

PACIFIC: U.S. submarine *Snook* torpedoes and sinks a Japanese gunboat near Chichi Jima.

Fourteenth Air Force B-25 Mitchells attack a Japanese convoy off Foochow, China, sinking a cargo ship.

CENTRAL PACIFIC: Seventh Air Force sends 21 B-25 Mitchells from Tarawa Atoll and Abemama Island against Taroa Island, Maloelap Atoll. Aircrews report three enemy fighters shot down. Another 23 B-24 Liberators from Makin and Abemama Islands bomb Wotje Atoll.

NEW BRITAIN: Thirteenth Air Force and marine fighters support over 60 navy SBD Dauntless dive-bombers attacking Lakunai airfield and Matupi Harbor. Fighter pilots report 30 Japanese aircraft shot down. Three Allied fighters are lost.

Fifth Air Force A-20 Havocs attack Japanese forces and antiaircraft positions near Cape Raoult and Gasmata Island.

NEW GUINEA: Fifth Air Force sends 35 B-24 Liberators with fighter escort to bomb Wewak. The Japanese intercept the Americans with 50 fighters. American pilots report 12 enemy fighters shot down. U.S. losses are five fighters. P-39 Airacobras attack barges and antiaircraft positions at Uligan Harbor.

U.S. submarine *Gar* attacks a Japanese convoy, sinking a transport near Palau.

January 24

CBI: Fourteenth Air Force B-25 Mitchells sink Japanese ship in Lishen Bay, China.

ATLANTIC: German submarines attack a convoy headed to Murmansk; a U.S. freighter is torpedoed and sunk by *U-278* off North Cape, Norway.

ETO: General Eisenhower informs the Combined Chiefs of Staff that five divisions are required for the initial assault for Neptune. One U.S. and one British division will be added. On D+2, another two divisions will be landed. This leads to a requirement to increase LSTs from 149 to 168. Eisenhower also requests that the Combined Bomber Offensive concentrate on eliminating the German fighter threat, to include fighter production facilities.

Eighth Air Force sends 857 B-17s and B-24 Liberators to attack transportation and industrial targets at Frankfurt-Heddernheim, Frankfurt/Main, and Russelsheim. Due to bad weather, the mission is recalled, but 58 B-17s do attack a power station near Eschweiler. Two bombers are shot down and seven are damaged. Aircrews report one enemy aircraft as a probable kill. Five crewmen are dead and 21 missing. Escorting P-38 Lightnings, P-47 Thunderbolts, and Ninth Air Force P-51 Mustangs report 19 confirmed kills and four probables. American losses are four P-38s, three P-47s, and two P-51 Mustangs; all the pilots are reported as missing. Six P-47s are damaged. The RAF and USAAF in the United Kingdom agree to assign all P-51s to Eighth Air Force to support long-range escort of the heavy bombers. The Ninth Air Force will be assigned all the P-38s and P-47s in theater.

Ninth Air Force sends over 175 B-26 Marauders against V-weapon sites in France.

MEDITERRANEAN: Fifteenth Air Force B-24s escorted by P-38 Lightnings bomb the airfield and town area at Skopje, Yugoslavia. B-17s escorted by P-47 Thunderbolts attack the marshaling yard at Vrattsa and the area near Dolno Tserovene in Bulgaria.

ITALY: General Mark W. Clark decides to attack the flanks of the Liri Valley using the British X Corps and French Expeditionary Corps, with the U.S. II Corps making an advance to the north of Cassino. Major General Charles W. Ryder's 34th Infantry Division will cross the Rapido River and seize three objectives: an Italian barracks area near Monte Villa, the town of Cassino, and Monte Castellone. Once these objectives are taken, the defenses at Monte Cassino can be outflanked and the Liri Valley will be open for the advance of Combat Command B of the 1st Armored Division. The 142nd Infantry of the 36th Infantry Division will conduct a diversionary attack toward Sant'Angelo after crossing the Rapido. The II Corps commander, Major General Geoffrey Keyes, passes Clark's instructions to his subordinates.

At Anzio, units of the 3rd Infantry Division conduct reconnaissance toward Cisterna, a key town on Route 7 that leads to Colli Laziali, the VI Corps objective. Meeting strong German resistance, they fall back to friendly lines. An LST hits a mine off Anzio and begins transferring troops to an LCI, when it, too, hits a mine. Nearly 300 men are killed or wounded.

At Anzio, German aircraft damage a destroyer and a minesweeper. An aerial torpedo damages a destroyer.

Twelfth Air Force A-36 Intruder (Apache) fighter-bombers attack Velletri and the road junction nearby.

PACIFIC: U.S. submarine *Sturgeon* attacks a Japanese convoy off Honshu, Japan, sinking a cargo ship.

CENTRAL PACIFIC: Seventh Air Force sends 24 A-24 Banshees from Makin Island, supported by 12 P-39 Airacobras and seven P-40s, to attack gun positions and storage facilities on Mille Atoll. B-25 Mitchells, staging through Makin Island, bomb the Wotje Atoll airfield. During the night, nine B-25s from Tarawa and 12 B-24s from the Ellice Islands, bomb targets on Maloelap Atoll.

Navy PB4Ys damage a cargo ship and submarine chaser off Kwajalein.

NEW BRITAIN: Thirteenth Air Force fighters, along with navy, marine, and RNZAF fighters, support navy and marine TBF Avengers attacking shipping in Simpson Harbor and Keravia Bay. Fighter pilots report more than 20 enemy aircraft shot down.

ADMIRALTIES: Fifth Air Force sends 38 B-25 Mitchells to attack shipping and harbor installations on Manus Island in the Admiralties.

NEW GUINEA: Fifth Air Force B-24 Liberators bomb airfields at Wewak and Boram, and B-25 Mitchells and P-47 Thunderbolts attack Madang in the Hansa Bay area.

Marine TBF Avengers, supported by navy, marine, New Zealand Air Force and U.S. Army Air Force fighters, attack Japanese shipping at Rabaul. Pilots report a water tanker, aircraft transport, and two cargo ships are sunk.

Japanese aircraft conduct a raid on American shipping in Dreger Bay, New Guinea, damaging a freighter.

Fifth Air Force B-25 Mitchells bomb Japanese shipping and harbor installations at Manus in the Admiralties. Aircrews report a transport and auxiliary minelayer sunk and another auxiliary minelayer damaged.

January 25

ETO: Eighth Air Force sends five B-17s to drop 1.2 million leaflets over Caen, Reims, Chartres, Chateauroux, and Brest in France.

ITALY: In the II Corps area, the 133rd Infantry Regiment of the 34th Infantry Division crosses the Rapido River and establishes a beachhead.

At Anzio, units of about eight German divisions establish a defensive line. An additional five divisions are on the way. German strength is about 40,000 men. The 3rd Infantry Division begins a two-battalion advance on Cisterna, supported by tanks and tank destroyers, but the advance is stopped by German strongpoints supported by tanks and self-propelled guns. A diversionary attack by the 504th Parachute Infantry Battalion across the canal on the right flank of the beachhead captures a few villages, but is driven back by German tanks. Off Anzio, a U.S. minesweeper is sunk by a mine, and a submarine chaser is damaged in a German air attack.

Twelfth Air Force B-25 Mitchells bomb Valmontone. B-26 Marauders bomb the Sezze and Rieti marshaling yard. A-20 Havocs attack Terelle and A-36 Intruder (Apache) fighter-bombers attack Civita Castellana, Itri, and Velletri. P-40s also attack Velletri and strafe trucks near Fondi.

CENTRAL PACIFIC: Seventh Air Force sends 24 A-24 Banshees from Makin Island, supported by 12 P-39 Airacobras, to attack gun positions on Mille Atoll. Eight B-25 Mitchells from Tarawa attack targets at Taroa Island, Maloelap Atoll. B-24s flying from the Gilbert Islands bomb Kwajalein Atoll.

NEW BRITAIN: Thirteenth Air Force conducts a night attack on Lakunai airfield with 19 B-24 Liberators preceded by three flare ships.

Fifth Air Force P-40s and A-20 Havocs attack targets on Gasmata Island.

NEW GUINEA: Fifth Air Force B-24 Liberators bomb the Hansa Bay area and B-25 Mitchells bomb Alexishafen and Madang.

January 26

CBI: President Roosevelt responds to Chiang Kai-shek's threat to reduce support to U.S. forces in China in a letter that states that on March 1 U.S. expenditures in China will be limited to $25 million per month.

In China, Fourteenth Air Force sends 18 P-40s from Kunming to attack the Kengtung airfield. General Claire Chennault proposes that the new B-29 strategic bombers be under his command as part of Fourteenth Air Force.

U.S. submarine *Crevalle* torpedoes and sinks a Japanese gunboat in the South China Sea near French Indochina.

German submarine *U-532* torpedoes and sinks a U.S. freighter south of Diego Garcia.

ATLANTIC: German submarine *U-716* torpedoes and sinks a U.S. freighter in a convoy headed for Murmansk.

ITALY: In the II Corps area, the 133rd Infantry Regiment attacks Hill 213, which must be captured before attacking Monte Castellone, the main objective. Mines and flooded terrain prevent any advance and the ground is too soft for tanks of the 756th Tank Battalion to cross over. Facing heavy enemy fire, the regiment falls back to the banks of the river. The 142nd Infantry Regiment of the 36th Infantry Division is attached to 34th Infantry Division.

At Anzio, the 3rd Infantry Division renews the attack toward Cisterna behind a heavy artillery barrage, but the attack stalls short of Route 7. An LCI (landing craft, infantry) is sunk and an LST is damaged by mines off Anzio. German air attacks damage a U.S. freighter. Another freighter is beached after a German fighter crashes into the ship. The ship is later repaired and returned to sea.

Twelfth Air Force A-20s attack Cisterna and A-36 Intruder (Apache) fighter-bombers and P-40s strafe roads and rail lines, trucks, and supply points.

CENTRAL PACIFIC: Seventh Air Force B-25 Mitchells from Makin Island attack the airfield on Maloelap Atoll and are met by about 20 Japanese fighters. As the bombers reach Aur Atoll, they are rescued by 12 P-40s, which drive off the enemy. Fighter pilots claim at least 10 confirmed kills and the bomber aircrews report five confirmed kills. B-25 Mitchells from Tarawa attack Aineman Island in Jaluit Atoll.

U.S. submarine *Skipjack* torpedoes and sinks a Japanese destroyer and a transport near Ponape in the Carolines.

New Britain: Thirteenth Air Force fighters support U.S. Navy SBD Dauntless dive-bombers on Lakunai. More than 20 Japanese fighters are reported destroyed in the air. Three Allied fighters are lost.

Admiralties: Fifth Air Force sends 42 B-24 Liberators to bomb Momote on Los Negros Island and Lorengau on Manus Island.

New Guinea: Fifth Air Force B-24 Liberators, A-20 Havocs, P-39 Airacobras, and P-40s attack targets in the Alexishafen-Madang area.

Navy Task Group 74.2, commanded by Rear Admiral Russell S. Berkey, with two light cruisers and three destroyers, bombards Japanese installations in Madang-Alexishafen area.

U.S. submarine *Hake* torpedoes and sinks a Japanese auxiliary netlayer off Ambon in the Netherlands East Indies.

January 27

ETO: Eighth Air Force sends five B-17s to drop nearly 1.5 million leaflets on Paris, Rennes, Le Mans, and Orleans in France.

Ninth Air Force receives the 572nd Bombardment Squadron (Medium) of the 391st Bombardment Group (Medium) from the United States. The squadron, equipped with B-26 Marauders, will fly its first mission in mid-February.

Mediterranean: Fifteenth Air Force B-17s bomb the Salon-de-Provence and Montpellier-Frejorgues airfields. B-24 Liberators bomb Istres-Le-Tube airfield. The bombers are escorted by P-38 Lightnings.

Italy: In the II Corps area, the 168th Infantry Regiment of the 34th Infantry Division crosses the Rapido River and, with a few tanks from the 756th Tank Battalion, advances against German defensive positions on Hill 213 and Hill 56. The advance is negated by the panicked retreat of troops back across the river. Two companies reorganize and cross the river again, establishing defensive positions in front of Monte Cairo.

Twelfth Air Force B-25 Mitchells attack supply lines at Velletri, the railway at Colleferro, and the Orte marshaling yard. B-26 Marauders bomb bridges at Ceprano and the marshaling yard at Terni. A-20 Havocs provide close support near Terelle and A-36 Intruder (Apache) fighter-bombers attack rail and road traffic at Poggio Mirteto, Ceccano, and Ciampino. Over 70 P-40s attack German positions at Cisterna and Atina. Allied fighter pilots report 28 enemy aircraft shot down over Anzio. German aircraft damage a submarine chaser.

Pacific: Conference at Pearl Harbor. In a rejection of the Sextant agreement by the CCS that the Central Pacific should be the primary means for the attack on Japan, SWPA, POA, and SOPAC planners believe that New Guinea to the Philippines is the better choice. Two alternatives are discussed. The first is to capture Truk and concentrate on the Mariana and Palau Islands. The other option is to bypass Truk and attack the Palaus directly about one month earlier than planned. Nimitz, shaken by the cost of securing Tarawa, has less faith in his original plans outlined in Granite. The quickest approach to Japan may be through the Philippines and the coast of China. Truk could be bypassed, then an attack through the Marianas to the Palaus could be launched with the objective of supporting MacArthur's New Guinea offensive. The goal is the Philippines, with the main effort in SWPA under MacArthur's command. Admiral King, COMICH, sends Admiral Nimitz a note after the conference stating that "The idea of rolling up the Japanese along the New Guinea coast . . . and up through the Philippines to the exclusion of clearing our Central Pacific line of communications . . . is to me absurd. Further it is not in accordance with the decisions of the Joint Chiefs of Staff."

U.S. submarine *Swordfish* attacks a Japanese convoy sinking a gunboat off Honshu, Japan.

U.S. submarine *Thresher* attacks a Japanese convoy, sinking a transport and a cargo ship southwest of Formosa.

SOUTH PACIFIC: Major General Nathan F. Twining, Commanding General Thirteenth Air Force, and a crew of 14 are down at sea between Guadalcanal Island and Espiritu Santo Island. The entire group is rescued six days later. General Twining's raft has no radio, an item that Lieutenant General Millard F. Harmon, Commanding General U.S. Army Forces in the South Pacific, has been requesting for some time. This incident results in the rapid appearance of dinghy radio sets for aircrews.

CENTRAL PACIFIC: Seventh Air Force sends six B-25 Mitchells from Tarawa to attack Nauru Island. Nine B-25s, staging through Makin, attack Wotje Atoll in the Marshalls. Mille Atoll is attacked by 23 A-24 Banshees, supported by 10 P-39 Airacobras. Seven B-24 Liberators, staging through Makin Island, bomb Taroa Island in the Maloelap Atoll.

BOUGAINVILLE: Thirteenth Air Force P-39 Airacobras attack targets of opportunity.

NEW BRITAIN: Thirteenth Air Force B-25 Mitchells escorted by over 60 army and navy fighters, attack Lakunai airfield. Fighter pilots report more than 20 confirmed kills on Japanese aircraft. Six U.S. fighters are lost. B-24 Liberators bomb the Rabaul area.

ADMIRALTIES: Fifth Air Force sends 41 B-24 Liberators to bomb Lorengau on Manus Island.

NEW GUINEA: Fifth Air Force B-25 Mitchells, A-20 Havocs, and P-39 Airacobras attack targets around Madang and Bogia.

B-24 Liberators damage a cargo ship and bomb the town area at Dili on Timor Island.

January 28

ATLANTIC: A navy PB4Y-1 Privateer sinks German submarine *U-271* off Limerick, Ireland.

ETO: Eighth Air Force sends 54 B-24 Liberators escorted by 122 P-47 Thunderbolts against the Bonnieres V-weapon site in France. The attack is led by two radar-equipped bombers. The equipment malfunctions, targets are misidentified, and only 31 bombers hit the primary target. One bomber is damaged, but there are no casualties.

During the night five B-17s drop more than 1.36 million leaflets over Amiens, Rouen, Cambrai, Reims, and Caen in France.

ITALY: A motor torpedo boat carrying Lieutenant General Mark Clark is damaged by friendly fire from a minesweeper near Anzio. A U.S. submarine chaser is damaged in an air attack.

NEW IRELAND: Thirteenth Air Force B-24 Liberators, and navy PBY Catalinas sink a Japanese transport carrying a midget submarine off Kavieng, New Ireland.

NEW GUINEA: U.S. submarine *Bowfin* torpedoes and damages a Japanese oiler off Makassar on Celebes Island.

January 29

CBI: In Burma, Tenth Air Force B-24 Liberators, with 16 P-38s as escorts, bomb gasoline plants at Yenangyaung.

ETO: Eighth Air Force sends 675 B-17s and 188 B-24 Liberators, led by PFF aircraft and escorted by 89 P-38 Lightnings, 503 P-47 Thunderbolts, and 40 Ninth Air Force P-51 Mustangs against industrial targets at Frankfurt, Germany. Of the 590 B-17s and 170 B-24s that hit the primary target, 24 B-17s and five B-24s are lost and 118 B-17s and 22 B-24s are damaged. Aircrew casualties are 22 killed, 32 wounded, and 299 missing. Aircrews report 75 confirmed kills and 27 probables. The fighter pilots report 47 enemy confirmed kills and six probables. Five P-38s and 10 P-47s are lost; four P-38s are damaged along with one P-47 damaged. A total of 14 pilots are reported missing.

Ninth Air Force sends over 80 B-26 Marauders to bomb V-weapon sites in France.

During the night five B-17s drop 1.2 million leaflets over Lille, Tours, Lorient, Nantes, and Valenciennes in France.

ITALY: At Anzio, the U.S. 3rd Battalion 1st Armored Regiment supports the British advance on the Albano Road at Anzio, while Combat Command A and elements of a tank regiment and the 6th Armored Infantry attempt to support the attack, but the muddy ground with hills and gullies prevents any advance. An attack by over 100 German aircraft on the ships off Anzio sinks one cargo ship and a British cruiser.

Fifteenth Air Force B-17s bomb marshaling yards at Ancona, Fabriano, Rimini, and Bologna while P-47 Thunderbolts conduct sweeps over Rome and Florence.

Twelfth Air Force P-40s and A-36 Intruder (Apache) fighter-bombers attack German defenses at Anzio and attack road and rail communications in the area behind the beachhead.

PACIFIC: U.S. submarine *Tambor* attacks a Japanese convoy and sinks a cargo ship north of Okinawa.

CENTRAL PACIFIC: A pre-landing air and naval bombardment on Kwajalein expends 6,000 tons of ordnance on the island. Seventh Air Force B-24 Liberators operating from the Gilberts conduct nearly continuous attacks on Maloelap, Jaluit, Aur, Wotje, and Mille Atolls in the Marshalls. P-39 Airacobras conduct strafing attacks on Mille all day. B-25 Mitchells from Tarawa attack shipping and shore installations at Wotje. A-24 Banshees, supported by 12 P-40s, bomb Jaluit.

Aircraft from fast carrier force TF 58, commanded by Rear Admiral Marc A. Mitscher, conduct strikes against Japanese aircraft and shipping in the Marshall Islands.

New Britain: Thirteenth Air Force fighters cover a strike by 40 navy SBD Dauntless dive-bombers on Tobera. B-24 Liberators, escorted by P-38 Lightnings and navy fighters, attack Lakunai airfield. Pilots report more than 20 Japanese aircraft shot down. Fifth Air Force sends 45 A-20 Havocs to attack Japanese positions at Cape Gloucester.
New Guinea: Fifth Air Force B-25 Mitchells bomb landing fields at Bogia and Nubia.

U.S. submarine *Bowfin* lays mines off southeastern coast of Borneo.

January 30

ETO: Eighth Air Force attacks aircraft production facilities at Brunswick, Germany, with 623 B-17s and 154 B-24 Liberators, escorted by 635 fighters (P-38 Lightnings, P-47 Thunderbolts, and Ninth Air Force P-51 Mustangs). Cloud cover over the primary target leads 597 B-17s to bomb the city itself as a secondary target. The B-24 Liberators, finding the secondary target obscured, attack Hannover and other targets of opportunity. Aircraft losses are 18 B-17s lost and 107 damaged; two B-24s lost and 11 B-24s damaged. Aircrews report 51 confirmed kills and seven probables. U.S. casualties are four killed, 14 wounded, and 206 missing. The fighter pilots report 45 enemy confirmed kills and 15 probables. Fighter losses are two P-38s and two P-47 Thunderbolts; two P-38s, three P-47 Thunderbolts, and two P-51s are damaged. U.S. casualties are one wounded and four missing.

During the night, five B-17s drop 1.2 million leaflets over Chateauroux, Brest, Chartres, Le Mans, and Caen in France.
Italy: In the II Corps area, the 168th Infantry Regiment captures Hill 213 and Hill 56 and stops several enemy counterattacks. Monte Castellone is now open to attack, which will support the French Expeditionary Corps.

At Anzio, the VI Corps commander, Major General John P. Lucas, orders an attack to break out of the beachhead. On the left, the British 1st Division, supported by the U.S. 1st Armored Division, will attack north, while the 3rd Infantry Division and the 504th Parachute Infantry Battalion and Rangers on the right will attack to cut Route 7 at Cisterna. Two battalions of Colonel William O. Darby's Rangers are to infiltrate enemy lines to assault Cisterna just before dawn. The 3rd Infantry Division would then launch the main attack, while the 504th Parachute Infantry Battalion makes a diversionary attack on the right. The Rangers are surprised and trapped within 800 yards of Cisterna; although a few make it into the outskirts of the town, the two battalions, nearly 700 men, are either killed or taken prisoner. The 15th Infantry Regiment makes little headway against boggy fields and strong German resistance. The 7th Infantry Regiment's attack advances about halfway to Cisterna before being halted by enemy fire.

Fifteenth Air Force adds its ninth heavy bomber Group with the addition of the B-24s of the 451st Bombardment Group. B-17s escorted by P-38 Lightnings bomb airfields at Villaorba, Maniago, and Lavariano. B-24s, also escorted by P-38s, bomb Udine airfield and Fier radar station. Aircrews report more than 60 aircraft destroyed in the air and more destroyed on the ground.

Twelfth Air Force B-25 Mitchells bomb road junctions at Valmontone and Genzano di Roma, and the town of Monte Compatri. A-20 Havocs attack targets near Cori.

Sergeant Truman O. Olson is a light machine gunner with B Company, 7th Infantry Regiment, 3rd Infantry Division. An attack on a German trench line near Cisterna di Littoria is slowed and stopped and most of the company are killed or wounded. Olson is one of the survivors who establish a small defensive perimeter and fight for their lives. Sergeant Olson and his crew operate the only machine gun left. For nearly 24 hours, Olson continues to break up enemy attacks. By daybreak, he is the only man left in his section and, though wounded, continues to engage the enemy. This time more than 200 troops attack his position, supported by mortar and machine-gun fire. Sergeant Olson refuses to be evacuated after being badly wounded again and succeeds in breaking up the attack. For his courage and dedication to duty in the face of overwhelming odds, Sergeant Olson will receive the Medal of Honor.

SOUTHWEST PACIFIC AREA: Navy SBD Dauntless dive-bombers and TBF Avengers, supported by Allied fighters, bomb Japanese shipping at Rabaul. Pilots report sinking a water supply ship and damaging an auxiliary vessel.

PACIFIC: During the night a navy PB2Y Coronado (a long-range maritime patrol bomber) from Midway bombs the airfield on Wake Island. Two motor torpedo boats are sunk.

CENTRAL PACIFIC: Seventh Air Force P-40s and P-39 Airacobras make continuous attacks on the Mille Atoll airfield. B-24 Liberators bomb Kwajalein Atoll throughout the night. During the preinvasion bombardment of Wotje Atoll, a destroyer is damaged by fire from a shore battery.

SBD Dauntless dive-bombers and F4F Hellcats from Naval Task Group 52.8, with the carriers USS *Enterprise, Yorktown,* and *Bunker Hill* and the small carrier USS *Belleau Wood,* sink a number of auxiliary submarine chasers at Kwajalein Atoll and Mille. Carrier aircraft also damage a cargo ship at Eniwetok, which is later sunk by a destroyer. Battleships USS *Washington, Indiana,* and *Massachusetts* and four destroyers bombard Japanese positions on Kwajalein. Battleship USS *North Carolina* sinks a transport off Roi. A destroyer sinks a transport and guardboat off Ujae Atoll.

U.S. submarine *Seahorse* attacks a Japanese convoy moving from Palau and sinks a cargo ship near Palau. U.S. submarine *Spearfish* attacks a Japanese convoy and sinks a transport off Saipan.

BOUGAINVILLE: Thirteenth Air Force sends 20 P-39 Airacobras to attack Kunrai.

Navy Task Group 31.8, with four destroyers, three high speed transports, and two motor torpedo boats, lands New Zealand troops and U.S. Navy personnel on the Green Islands, north of Bougainville, to conduct reconnaissance for suitable airfields and landing beaches.

Staff Sergeant Jesse R. Drowley of the Americal Division is a squad leader at Bougainville and has the mission during a platoon attack to establish a local perimeter defense and act as the platoon reserve. Seeing two men fall, he rushes forward in the face of heavy enemy fire to bring them back to safety. He locates a Japanese pillbox firing into the platoon and moves to an American tank supporting the attack. Climbing on the turret, he obtains a submachine gun and rides on top of the tank firing in the direction of the pillbox to mark the target for the tank crew. Fully exposed to enemy fire, Staff sergeant Drowley is hit in the chest. Ignoring his wound he continues to direct fire on the pillbox until, wounded again in the left eye, he falls off the tank. Pulling himself to his feet, Drowley stays alongside the tank until the pillbox has been eliminated and another behind it destroyed as well. Satisfied that the attack can progress, he walks to the rear for medical treatment. For his conspicuous bravery and extraordinary dedication to duty Staff Sergeant Drowley will receive the Medal of Honor.

NEW BRITAIN: Lieutenant Colonel Lewis B. "Chesty" Puller takes command of southern patrols to locate and clear Japanese forces from Borgen Bay to the Itni River as part of the effort to clear the enemy from western New Britain. Puller's force, consisting of 384 men, departs Agulupella. The force is resupplied periodically by air drops from small planes.

Thirteenth Air Force sends 26 B-25 Mitchells and fighters to bomb Lakunai airfield. B-24 Liberators and fighters bomb Vunakanau airfield. Fighters support a navy SBD Dauntless dive-bomber attack on Japanese shipping in the Rabaul area. Pilots report over 20 Japanese aircraft shot down.

Fifth Air Force A-20 Havocs attack barges along the northern coast and P-39 Airacobras strafe barges and fuel storage areas at Rein Bay.

NEW GUINEA: Fifth Air Force B-25 Mitchells bomb landing areas at Hansa Bay and Nubia.

January 31

ETO: Eighth Air Force attacks V-weapon construction at St-Pol/Siracourt, France. Of the 74 B-24 Liberators that hit the target, two bombers are damaged. P-47 Thunderbolts provide escort for the mission. Gilze-Rijen airfield in the Netherlands is attacked by 70 P-47 fighter-bombers, escorted by 47 P-38s and 87 P-47 Thunderbolts. Fighter pilots report that 13 enemy aircraft shot down and one probable kill. Six P-38s are lost, one P-38 is damaged, and two P-47s are damaged. Aircrew casualties are one wounded and six missing.

MEDITERRANEAN: Fifteenth Air Force B-17s with P-38 Lightnings escorting, bomb Klagenfurt airfield in Austria. Aircrews report 16 enemy aircraft shot down.

Twelfth Air Force A-20 Havocs bomb Artena. P-40s and A-36 Intruder (Apache) fighter-bombers attack German positions at Sezze, Fondi, and Priverno. P-47 Thunderbolts bomb San Benedetto de Marsi.

ITALY: At Anzio, the 7th and 15th Infantry Regiments of the 3rd Infantry Division renew the attack to cut off Route 7 at Cisterna. Supported by a heavy artillery bombardment and air attacks, the infantry advances with tanks in support but makes only a limited advance. On the left, the 6th Armored Infantry supported by tanks from the 1st Armored Regiment makes only a few hundred yards before being stopped by minefields and artillery. The units of the 1st Armored Division are ordered to VI Corps reserve that night.

Twelfth Air Force A-20 Havocs bomb Artena. P-40s and A-36 Intruder (Apache) fighter-bombers attack a road junction at Sezze, the town of Fondi, and Priverno; P-47 Thunderbolts bomb San Benedetto de Marsi.

SOUTHWEST PACIFIC AREA: Within the SWPA, General MacArthur has five army divisions: the 1st Cavalry, the 6th Infantry, the 24th Infantry, the 32nd Infantry, and the 41st Infantry. He also has three regimental combat teams, the 112th Cavalry, the 158th Infantry Regiment, and the 503rd Parachute Infantry Regiment. He can expect the arrival of three more divisions, the 31st Infantry, the 33rd Infantry, and the 43rd Infantry. The Fifth Air Force numbers about 1,000 aircraft, and Vice Admiral Thomas C. Kinkaid, commander of Seventh Fleet, has a greatly expanded amphibious and sea transport capability. In the month of January, 308 B-24, 107 B-25, and nine B-26 sorties have been carried out against Alexishafen and Madang, employing a total of 1,100 tons of bombs against the Japanese holding out against the Australians.

Central Pacific: Operation Flintlock, the campaign to seize the Marshall Islands, is commanded by Vice Admiral Raymond A. Spruance, Commander Central Pacific Force, designated as Task Force 50. It is composed of Southern Attack Force (Task Force 51), commanded by Rear Admiral Richmond K. Turner, the Northern Attack Force (Task Force 53), commanded by Rear Admiral Richard L. Conolly, and Reserve Force and Majuro Attack Group (Task Force 51.2), commanded by Rear Admiral Harry W. Hill. Aircraft from Task Force 58, commanded by Rear Admiral Marc A. Mitscher, and land-based aircraft from Task Force 57 (Rear Admiral John H. Hoover), have responsibility for covering the landings.

Aircraft from fast-carrier group Task Group 58.3 (Rear Admiral Frederick C. Sherman) bomb aircraft and the airfield facilities at Engebi Island, Eniwetok Atoll. TG 58.3 aircraft and a destroyer sink an auxiliary netlayer off Eniwetok.

The Majuro Island force, consisting of a marine reconnaissance company and the 2nd Battalion 106th Infantry Regiment, lands and find only one Japanese soldier serving as a caretaker. Marines land on small islands off Kwajalein to establish artillery firing positions to support the landings. The army's 145th Artillery Battalion occupies positions.

Seventh Air Force A-24 Banshees bomb the airfield on Mille Atoll, while P-39 Airacobras and P-40s provide continuous air cover to prevent any interference with the landings. P-40s attack Jaluit Atoll and during the night eight B-24 Liberators bomb Wotje Atoll.

U.S. submarine *Trigger* (SS-237) sinks a Japanese auxiliary submarine depot ship northwest of Truk and damages a destroyer. U.S. submarine *Tullibee* torpedoes and sinks an auxiliary netlayer off Saipan.

New Britain: Over 1,300 bomber and 1,800 fighter sorties have been flown against Rabaul in January. American losses total 35 bombers and 65 fighters. Thirteenth Air Force fighters support Navy SBD Dauntless dive-bombers on Tobera. This is followed by an attack by 17 B-24 Liberators with fighter support on the same target. Aircrews report eight Japanese aircraft shot down.

New Guinea: Fifth Air Force A-20 Havocs attack Uligan Harbor and P-39 Airacobras strafe a landing strip at Alexishafen. B-24 Liberators sink a Japanese guardboat off Celebes.

A lone Japanese aircraft makes a high-level bombing raid on American shipping in Langemak Bay, New Guinea. A freighter is damaged

February 1

CBI: In Burma, Tenth Air Force B-24 Liberators bomb Mingaladon Nyaungbinwun airfields. P-51 Mustangs and A-36 Intruder (Apache) fighter-bombers and a B-25

Mitchell bomb the Myitkyina airfield. Engineers begin construction of a permanent road in the Hukawng Valley.

ETO: The 21st Army Group issues its initial plan as part of the initial joint plan called Neptune. A landing beach is added part of the Cotentin Peninsula to bring Allied forces closer to the port of Cherbourg, a key objective in the operation. The U.S. First Army is assigned two beachheads between Vierville-sur-Mer and Colleville-sur-Mer. The VII Corps is to land at the beach named Utah to cut of the base of the Cotentin Peninsula and capture Cherbourg. Two airborne divisions are to land before the beach assault. The 101st Airborne Division is to capture the four western causeway exits that lead out from the beach over flooded ground. The 82nd Airborne Division is to land west of the Meredet River to capture Ste. Mère-Eglise and control the roads leading to the beachhead. The V Corps is to land at the beach named Omaha between Carentan and Bayeux and move south to St. Lô to cover the British and Canadian forces of the Second Army as it advances to Caen and Bayeaux. The LST requirement for the initial landings has increased from 149 to 168. Included in the plan is an effort to convince the enemy that Neptune is a diversion and Pas-de-Calais is the actual invasion site.

At the end of the first day (D-day), 8 2/3 divisions are to land. By D+1, 10 1/3 divisions are to be ashore; by D+12, 26–30 divisions are to be ashore. By D+30, these divisions will require 1,800 tons of fuel per day to support the approximately 92,000 vehicles estimated to be in France at that time and 42,000 tons of supplies per day to support nearly 500,000 men.

The Eighth Air Force receives the B-24 Liberators of the 752nd, 753rd, 754th, and 755th Bombardment Squadrons (Heavy) of the 458th Bombardment Group (Heavy), arrived in England from the United States. The group's first mission is scheduled for late February.

In the Ninth Air Force, the headquarters of the 416th Bombardment Group (Light) and 669th, 670th, and 671st Bombardment Squadrons (Light) with A-20 Havocs arrives from the United States. The group's first mission is scheduled for early march. The 30th Photographic Reconnaissance Squadron, III Reconnaissance Command, arrives with F-5 Lightnings.

Major General Elwood R. "Pete" Quesada assumes command of IX Air Support Command, which has operational control over all fighter and reconnaissance units of IX Fighter Command.

MEDITERRANEAN: German aircraft make a torpedo attack on convoy UGS 30 (United States to Mediterranean, Slow) in the western Mediterranean. One U.S. freighter is damaged and another is torpedoed and abandoned.

ITALY: In the II Corps area, the 133rd Infantry attacks the Italian barracks area at Monte Vella; the 135th Infantry attacks toward Monte Castellone. Both regiments belong to the 34th Infantry Division. The 142nd Infantry 36th Infantry Division attacks to support the French attack north of Monte Castellone.

At Anzio, the 3rd Infantry Division attacks toward Cisterna, but German tank and infantry counterattacks force Major General Truscott to order a consolidation of the line and prepare defensive positions.

General Sir Harold Alexander, commander of the Fifteenth Army Group, arrives at Anzio and meets with Major General John P. Lucas. After the meeting Lucas writes, "My head will probably fall in the basket but I have done my best. There were just too many Germans here for me to lick and they could build up faster than I could. As I told Clark yesterday, I was sent on a desperate mission, one where the odds were greatly against success, and I went without saying anything because I was given an order and my opinion was not asked."

The 45th Infantry Division and other units of the 1st Armored Division land at Anzio. German forces defending the area have now reached over 70,000 men. The Allies, even with additional reinforcements, have about 61,000 men ashore.

In the II Corps area the 135th Infantry Regiment of the 34th Infantry Division attacks toward Monte Castellone and captures its objectives, supported by fire from the 168th Infantry Regiment on Hill 213 and Hill 56.

Twelfth Air Force B-25 Mitchells bomb the Albano-Laziale road junction. P-40s bomb Cori, while A-36 Intruder (Apache) fighter-bombers hit Poggio Mieteto and P-47 Thunderbolts attack the station at San Valentino.

Private First Class Alton W. Knappenberger is a Browning Automatic Rifleman in the 3rd Infantry Division facing a German attack against his battalion near Cisterna di Littoria. Knappenberger crawls to an exposed knoll and begins a battle with an enemy machine gun 85 yards away. Rising to a kneeling position, Knappenberger knocks out the gun. When two Germans soldiers approach to throw grenades at him, Private First Class Knappenberger kills them both. As another German machine gun opens fire only 100 yards away, the American eliminates the crew with a burst of fire. Increasingly, Knappenberger finds himself the target of concentrated volumes of fire from a number of weapons. He fires on every target he can engage, then, out of ammunition, he crawls to find more ammunition and returns to the position, stopping the assault of a German platoon armed with automatic weapons. Only when his ammunition is exhausted does Knappenberger fall back to rejoin his unit. Private First Class Knappenberger's extraordinary feat of arms and his exceptional courage in the face of a determined enemy will win him the Medal of Honor.

PACIFIC: Amphibious Forces, Pacific Fleet, is established at Pearl Harbor. Vice Admiral Richmond K. Turner, Commander Fifth Amphibious Force, is selected to serve as the commander.

CENTRAL PACIFIC: Operation Flintlock. The 23rd Marine Regiment lands at Roi Island and the 24th Marine Regiment lands on Namur Island. Navajo code talkers are employed to transmit reports and instructions quickly and efficiently without having to take time to encrypt radio messages to prevent the Japanese from gaining any information.

The 32nd and 184th Infantry Regiments of the 7th Infantry Division land on Kwajalein Island and immediately encounter Japanese defenders in spider holes and camouflaged trenches. Clearing these initial defenses, the Americans face a number of counterattacks.

Seventh Air Force B-24 Liberators from Makin Island bomb beach defenses on Kwajalein. P-40s continue patrols over Mille Atoll.

Marines land on Roi and Namur and army troops land on Kwajalein under cover of heavy naval gunfire from battleships, cruisers, and destroyers. A cruiser is

Men of the 7th Infantry Division use a flamethrower on Japanese positions on Kwajalein Island, February 4, 1944.

damaged by an eight-inch shell ricochet and two destroyers and a minesweeper run aground. Two battleships are damaged in a collision.

U.S. submarine *Guardfish* attacks a Japanese convoy heading for Truk and sinks a destroyer. U.S. submarine *Seahorse* attacks a Japanese convoy moving from Palau to Rabaul and sinks a transport near Woleai Atoll.

First Lieutenant John V. Power, a platoon leader attached to the 4th Marine Division, is severely wounded in the stomach as he tosses a demolition charge against a Japanese bunker position. Without hesitation, he continues the attack, holding his wounded side with one hand while firing his carbine with his right hand. As he reloads he is killed. First Lieutenant Power's exceptional fighting spirit and courage in engaging the enemy will win him the Medal of Honor.

During the assault on Namur Island, Private Richard K. Sorenson and five other marines of the 4th Marine Division occupy a shell hole when a Japanese grenade lands among them. Private Sorenson falls on the grenade to save his comrades. He is severely wounded, but his act of selfless courage will win him the Medal of Honor.

On Roi Island, Private First Class Richard B. Anderson of the 4th Marine Division jumps into a shell crater with three other marines. Attempting to throw a grenade, Private First Class Anderson drops it and watches the live grenade roll toward his comrades. Anderson immediately jumps on the grenade and sacrifices himself to save the lives of his fellow marines. His sacrifice will earn him the Medal of Honor.

BOUGAINVILLE: Two U.S. destroyers sink Japanese submarine *I-171* near Buka Island.

NEW BRITAIN: Operation Appease begins. This is intended to capture Talasea and Hoskins Plantation, the last objectives of the campaign.

NEW GUINEA: The naval base at Finschhafen, New Guinea, is established.

U.S. submarine *Hake* torpedoes and sinks a Japanese cargo ship and transport off Halmahera.

B-24 Liberators damage a Japanese ship en route from Hollandia to Aitape.

February 2

ATLANTIC: Stalin agrees to provide six bases in the western USSR for American aircraft from the ETO.

ETO: Eighth Air Force attacks V-weapon construction at St.-Pol/Siracourt and Watten, France. Of the 95 B-24 Liberators that hit the target, two bombers are lost and three are damaged. The mission is escorted by 183 P-47 Thunderbolts. U.S. casualties are 10 killed and 19 missing.

Ninth Air Force sends 36 B-26 Marauders to attack the airfield at Triqueville, France. Eighth Air Force provides 34 P-38 Lightnings and 44 P-47 Thunderbolts as escort.

The 668th Bombardment Squadron (Light) of the 416th Bombardment Group (Light), with A-20 Havocs, arrives from the United States. The squadron's first mission is scheduled for early March.

MEDITERRANEAN: Fifteenth Air Force B-24 Liberators, with RAF Spitfire escort, bomb the radar station at Durazzo, Albania.

Twelfth Air Force B-25 Mitchells attack the Marino road junction and A-20 Havocs bomb Norma. A-36 Intruder (Apache) fighter-bombers and P-40s bomb transportation and supply targets and the road to Viterbo. P-40s attack Cisterna and Formia.

Major General Gordon P. Saville takes command of XII Air Support Command.

ITALY: In the II Corps area, the 133rd Infantry captures the Italian barracks at Monte Vella; the 135th Infantry seizes Monte Castellone.

At Anzio, the 2nd Battalion 7th Infantry Regiment of the 3rd Infantry Division stops an early morning battalion-size attack on its position, capturing 131 prisoners. Major General John P. Lucas receives orders from General Mark Clark to consolidate the beachhead and prepare for defensive operations. The 1st Special Service Force arrives to reinforce Lucas, guarding the right flank along the Mussolini Canal. German counterattacks west of Cisterna are stopped, largely by concentrated Allied artillery fire.

PACIFIC: U.S. submarine *Plunger* attacks a Japanese convoy south of Honshu, Japan, and sinks two cargo ships. Although depth-charged, the submarine escapes.

CENTRAL PACIFIC: Operation Flintlock. The 24th Marines secure Namur after repulsing a Japanese counterattack at dawn. Roi Island is secured later in the day. After a slow advance, units of the 184th and 32nd Infantry Regiments of the 7th Infantry Division report capturing nearly all of Kwajalein.

Seventh Air Force A-24 Banshees, P-39 Airacobras, and P-40s from Makin bomb Mille Atoll. B-24 Liberators from Tarawa bomb Rongelap Island.

Destroyer USS *Walker* sinks Japanese submarine *RO-39* off Wotje Atoll, Marshall Islands.

NEW GEORGIA: The B-24 Liberators of the 31st Bombardment Squadron (Heavy), 5th Bombardment Group (Heavy), Thirteenth Air Force, begin operating from Munda airfield.

NEW BRITAIN: Fifth Air Force B-25 Mitchells bomb targets along the coast from Cape Gauffre to Rein Bay.

NEW GUINEA: Fifth Air Force B-24 Liberators bomb Sorong and Alexishafen and A-20 Havocs attack installations near Madang.

February 3

CBI: In Burma, Tenth Air Force P-38 Lightnings attack bridges and camps along the Prome-Taungup road, destroying one bridge. P-51 Mustangs hit a Japanese camp at Sawnghka.

ETO: Eighth Air Force sends 671 B-17s and 193 B-24 Liberators against the port at Wilhelmshaven, Germany, escorted by 74 P-38 Lightnings, 508 P-47 Thunderbolts of the Eighth and Ninth Air Force, and 50 Ninth Air Force P-51 Mustangs. The B-24s abort the mission but 553 B-17s hit the main target. The B-17s also drop 1.8 million leaflets. Four bombers are lost and 48 bombers damaged. Aircrews report one probable kill. U.S. casualties are two killed, nine wounded, and 42 missing. The fighter pilots report eight confirmed kills on enemy aircraft. Eight P-47 Thunderbolts and one P-51 are lost; 16 P-47 Thunderbolts are damaged. U.S. casualties are nine pilots missing.

During the night, seven B-17s drop leaflets on Paris, Rouen, Amiens, Reims, Orleans, and Rennes.

ITALY: In the II Corps area, the 133rd Infantry Regiment of the 34th Infantry Division battles German defenders in the streets of Cassino, but cannot dislodge them. The New Zealand 2nd Divisions and the Indian 4th Division under command of Lieutenant General Sir Bernard C. Freyberg are redesignated as the New Zealand Corps and placed under command of Clark's Fifth Army.

A-36 Intruder (Apache) fighter-bombers hit roads and targets south of Rome and attack German positions near Sezze and Fondi.

Private First Class Leo J. Powers of the 133rd Infantry Regiment, 34th Infantry Division, attacks Hill 175 near Cassino. The Germans have machine guns and pillboxes on the hill and are supported by mortars. As his company begins to falter in the face of heavy enemy fire, Powers continues to advance, crawling close enough to attack one of the pillboxes with hand grenades. He stands in full view of the enemy to make an accurate throw and knocks out the position, killing and wounding the defenders. As the infantrymen begin to advance, a second machine gun in a pillbox begins firing on them. Private First Class Powers repeats his first amazing act of courage, approaching the pillbox, then standing in full view of the enemy to throw his grenades. He continues this same tactic against a third pillbox, destroying it, and takes the surrender of four German soldiers. This extraordinary act of courage will win PFC Powers the Medal of Honor.

PACIFIC: U.S. submarine *Tambor* attacks a Japanese convoy in the East China Sea, sinking a fleet tanker and a merchant fleet tanker off Shanghai. The submarine is damaged by depth charges, but remains on patrol.

CENTRAL PACIFIC: Operation Flintlock. The attack on Kwajalein continues as the 184th Infantry encircles one group of enemy defenders while the 32nd Infantry advances to clear the rest of the island.

Cruiser and destroyer gunfire support landings of army troops on Ebeye, Kwajalein Atoll, Marshalls.

NEW BRITAIN: Thirteenth Air Force P-40s and U.S. Navy fighters support a navy SBD Dauntless dive-bomber strike on Tobera. B-24 Liberators, with P-38 Lightning navy fighters escorting, bomb the Lakunai airfield. Aircrews report 13 Japanese aircraft shot down.

NEW IRELAND: Navy PBY Catalinas and Fifth Air Force B-25 Mitchells attack a Japanese convoy west of New Ireland and sink cargo ship.

ADMIRALTIES: Fifth Air Force P-39 Airacobras and B-25 Mitchells attack Momote and Hyane Harbor on Los Negros Island.

NEW GUINEA: Fifth Air Force sends nearly 100 B-24 Liberators and B-25 Mitchells, supported by P-38 Lightnings, P-40s, and P-47 Thunderbolts, to bomb airfields at Wewak. Aircrews report about 80 Japanese aircraft destroyed on the ground and in the air. A-20 Havocs attack targets near Alexishafen and Hansa Bay.

February 4

ETO: Eighth Air Force sends 589 B-17s and 159 B-24 Liberators to attack industrial targets and the railyards at Frankfurt am Main, Germany, escorted by 56 P-38 Lightnings, 537 Eighth and Ninth Air Force P-47 Thunderbolts, and 44 Ninth Air Force P-51 Mustangs. Weather and navigation problems result in only 346 B-17s and 27 B-24 Liberators hitting their target. The other bombers are scattered and hit Giessen, Wiesbaden, Trier, Arloff, Russelheim, Grafenhausen, Darmstadt, Koblenz, and some unidentified targets. Bomber losses are 18 B-17s and two B-24 Liberators; 362 bombers are damaged. Aircrews report four confirmed enemy aircraft kills. U.S. casualties are seven killed, 20 wounded, and 203 missing. Fighter pilots report eight confirmed kills. One P-38 is lost, five P-47 Thunderbolts and five P-38 Lightnings are damaged. One pilot is reported missing. During the night, seven B-17s drop 319 bundles of leaflets over Lorient, Tours, Nantes, Raismes, Lille, and Cambrai in France and over Antwerp, Belgium.

In the Ninth Air Force, Major General Otto P. Weyland takes command of XIX Air Support Command.

MEDITERRANEAN: The combined planning staffs meet to develop a detailed plan for Anvil, the invasion of southern France in support of Overlord. Seventh Army's mission is to make an amphibious and airborne assault on the south coast of France, secure a beachhead east of Toulon, and then capture the city. After Toulon is secured, Seventh Army will advance toward Lyon and join with Allied forces in northern France advancing from Normandy.

ITALY: In the II Corps area, an attack on the slopes of Monte Cassino by a battalion of the 135th Infantry fails. German infantry counterattacking with tanks drive the 133rd

Infantry out of the town of Cassino. The 34th Infantry Division has reached the limit of its capability and is unable to advance before Cassino and cannot reach Route 6.

The German Fourteenth Army, opposing Allied forces at Anzio, is reinforced and now totals five divisions. During the early morning hours, British defenders are driven from outside Campoleone. Both sides suffer heavy losses. One RCT of the 45th Infantry Division defends the left flank of the beachhead along the Moletta River. The 1st Special Service Force holds the right flank of the beachhead along the Mussolini Canal. The British 1st Division and the U.S. 3rd Infantry Division hold the center of the beachhead. The 3rd Infantry Division is responsible for the area from Carano to the Mussolini Canal. The remainder of the 45th Infantry Division and units of the 1st Armored Division are held in reserve to stop any penetrations of the defensive line. American units, depleted by combat losses, find replacements are slow in coming.

PACIFIC: Cruisers and destroyers of Navy Task Group 94.6, commanded by Rear Admiral Wilder D. Baker, bombard Japanese installations at Paramushiru in the Kurile Islands. One cargo ship is damaged.

CENTRAL PACIFIC: Operation Flintlock. Supported by naval gunfire, the 32nd Infantry Regiment of the 7th Infantry Division clears the last defenders of Kwajalein. Wotje, Mille, Maloelap, and Jaluit Islands are now isolated. The Japanese garrisons there will be subject to air attack and play no further role in the war.

Seventh Air Force B-24 Liberators from Tarawa and Makin Island bomb Wotje, Maloelap, and Mille Atolls. P-40s based on Makin bomb and strafe Mille Atoll. B-25 Mitchells from Tarawa and Abemama Island bomb Wotje and Maloelap Atolls.

A destroyer and destroyer escort sink Japanese submarine *I-175* north of Jaluit Atoll.

PV-1 Patrol Bombers sink a Japanese water tanker at Jaluit.

Marine PB4Y Privateers conduct an aerial reconnaissance of Truk.

BOUGAINVILLE: The P-38 Lightnings of the 68th Fighter Squadron, 347th Fighter Group, transfer from Fiji.

U.S. destroyers bombard Japanese positions on the northwest coast of Bougainville. A destroyer is damaged by fire from the shore battery.

NEW GEORGIA: Headquarters of the 5th Bombardment Group (Heavy) redeploys from Guadalcanal to Munda airfield.

NEW BRITAIN: Thirteenth Air Force sends 25 B-25 Mitchells escorted by over 40 fighters to attack the Tobera airfield. B-24 Liberators, escorted by P-38 Lightnings and navy fighters, attack Vunakanau airfield.

NEW GUINEA: Fifth Air Force sends over 170 B-24 Liberators, A-20 Havocs, and B-25 Mitchells to bomb airfields in the Marienberg, Madang, and Alexishafen areas. P-39 Airacobras attack targets of opportunity near Alexishafen.

February 5

ALEUTIANS: Eleventh Air Force B-24 Liberators and P-38 Lightnings provide air cover for light cruisers and destroyers after they bombard installations at the Kurabu Cape-Musashi Bay areas in the Kurile Islands. Eleventh Air Force and U.S. Navy aircraft also attack installations at Paramushiru and Shimushu.

CBI: In Burma, Tenth Air Force B-24 Liberators bomb the Heho and Aungban airfields. B-25 Mitchells also bomb the Heho, Sagaing, and Myittha airfields.

Fourteenth Air Force B-24 Liberators bomb Bangkok, Thailand. Two B-24s and two B-25 Mitchells attack a convoy near Hong Kong. Aircrews report sinking a gunboat and two cargo ships.

ETO: Eighth Air Force attacks the airfields at Chateauroux/Martinerie, Avord, Chateaudun, Orleans/Bricy, Villacoublay, and Romilly-sur-Seine in France with more than 300 B-17s. More than 100 B-24 Liberators are sent to bomb Meslay airfield. Two B-24s are lost and 34 are damaged. The B-24 crews report five confirmed kills. A total of 42 B-17s are damaged; U.S. casualties are one killed, 15 wounded, and 22 missing. The raids have 92 P-38 Lightnings, 496 Eighth and Ninth Air Force P-47 Thunderbolts, and 46 Ninth Air Force P-51 Mustangs escorting. Fighter pilots report six confirmed kills. Two P-47s are lost and two P-38s and two P-47s are damaged. Two pilots are missing.

During the night, five B-17s drop leaflets during a Carpetbagger mission (support to resistance groups in western Europe) on Ghent, Monceau-sur-Sambre, Antwerp, and Brussels, Belgium.

Ninth Air Force B-26 Marauders attack six V-weapon sites in France.

ITALY: The 2nd and 3rd Battalions, 30th Infantry Regiment, 3rd Infantry Division, repulse a German night attack near Ponte Rotto. Although the enemy captures Ponte Rotto, the Americans stabilize the line by a counterattack with tanks and infantry. The Germans begin bombarding the beachhead with 372 artillery pieces, including monster 170 millimeter guns at Colli Laziali and 210 and 240 millimeter railroad guns. A U.S. Navy cruiser and three destroyers return fire in an attempt to knock out some of the artillery.

Twelfth Air Force B-25 Mitchells bomb the Terni marshaling yard. A-20 Havocs attack the Lanuvio and Piedimonte areas. Twelfth Air Force P-40s and A-36 Intruder (Apache) fighter-bombers attack German positions at Cisterna, Vetralla, and Velletri and attack motor transport around Rome.

SOUTHWEST PACIFIC AREA: U.S. submarine *Flasher* torpedoes and sinks a Japanese cargo ship off Mindoro in the Philippines. U.S. submarine *Narwhal* delivers supplies and evacuates personnel from Panay.

CENTRAL PACIFIC: Seventh Air Force P-40s from Makin Island attack the oil storage area and radio facilities on Jaluit Atoll. P-39 Airacobras strafe the airfield on Mille Atoll.

NEW BRITAIN: The Japanese stubbornly resist the Americans on Arawe, but report they are running short on food and ammunition. Thirteenth Air Force P-40s support navy fighters in covering a strike by more than 60 SBD Dauntless dive-bombers on Lakunai. Soon after the first strike, 13 B-24 Liberators with P-38 and navy fighter escort follow up with another attack.

Fifth Air Force sends 48 B-24 Liberators to bomb Hoskins airfield and Gasmata Island.

NEW GUINEA: Fifth Air Force B-25 Mitchells and A-20 Havocs attack the Hansa Bay area.

February 6

CBI: Fourteenth Air Force sends six B-25 Mitchells to bomb bridges and trains at Anxuan, Tien An, Phong Loc, and Dong Hoi, French Indochina.

ATLANTIC: A U.S. Navy PB4Y-1 Privateer sinks German submarine *U-177* west of Ascension Island.

ETO: Eighth Air Force targets the Romilly-sur-Seine depot and the Nancy/Essay and Dijon/Longvic airfields, but most of the over 400 B-17s sent abort or attack other targets. Over 100 B-24 Liberators are dispatched to the St. Pol/Siracourt V-weapon site, but nearly all miss the target. Four B-17s are lost and 44 B-17s and eight B-24 Liberators are damaged. Aircrews report three confirmed kills. U.S. casualties are seven killed, three wounded, and 43 missing. The mission is supported by 85 P-38 Lightnings, 506 Eighth and Ninth Air Force P-47 Thunderbolts, and 47 Ninth Air Force P-51 Mustangs. Fighter pilots report 11 confirmed kills and two probables and report two additional aircraft destroyed on the ground. Three P-38 Lightnings and one P-47 are lost; two P-38s and three P-47s are damaged. Two pilots are wounded and four are missing.

Ninth Air Force sends over 100 B-26 Marauders to bomb V-weapon sites, airfields, and a factory in France.

During the night, in support of a Carpetbagger mission over Belgium, six B-17s drop leaflet bundles over Brussels, Antwerp, Ghent, Liege, and Monceau-sur-Sambre.

ITALY: The U.S. 88th Infantry Division arrives in Italy and begins combat training.

Twelfth Air Force P-40s bomb Cisterna, Santa Lucia (near Campoleone), Cori, and Atina. A-36 Intruder (Apache) fighter-bombers attack San Stefano al Mare, Cisterna, Frascati, and Albano Laziale, as well as vehicles, railroad cars, and targets of opportunity near Rome.

CENTRAL PACIFIC: Operation Flintlock. Marine aircraft begin landing on Roi Island airfield, named Dyess airfield, after a winner of the Medal of Honor. The Roi-Namur battle costs the 4th Marine Division 313 marines killed and 502 wounded. Japanese casualties are 3,563 dead, the majority killed during the opening air and naval bombardment.

Seventh Air Force B-24 Liberators from Tarawa bomb Maloelap and Wotje Atolls. A-24 Banshees and P-40s from Makin Island attack Mille Atoll, and P-39 Airacobras from Tarawa attack Jaluit Atoll.

NEW BRITAIN: Thirteenth Air Force sends 32 B-25 Mitchells escorted by army and navy fighters to bomb Lakunai airfield. Soon afterward another attack by 19 B-24 Liberators is conducted, escorted by nearly 50 Allied fighters. Fighter pilots report 16 Japanese aircraft shot down. Lakunai airfield has been rendered unserviceable.

NEW GUINEA: Fifth Air Force B-25 Mitchells and B-24 Liberators bomb Bunabun Harbor, Madang, and other targets. P-39 Airacobras attack and sink barges near Nubia. Fifth Air Force A-20 Havocs and P-40s sink two Japanese ships and damage another one off Wewak.

February 7

CBI: Fourteenth Air Force B-25 Mitchells damage the powerplant at Thanh Hoa, strafe nearby barracks, and attack the radio station at Vinh in French Indochina.

ITALY: At Anzio, German attacks push the British off Buonripso Ridge and head for Carroceto and the collection of buildings known as the Factory. The 3rd Battalion of the 504th Parachute Infantry moves to Carroceto and counterattacks to support the line. The 3rd Infantry Division conducts company-sized attacks near Ponte Rotto.

German aircraft bomb the Anzio beachhead day and night, targeting supplies, harbor facilities, shipping, and troop concentrations. The area near the evacuation hospital on the beachhead is bombed and shelled so often that the men at Anzio refer to it as "Hell's Half Acre." Allied antiaircraft fire accounts for seven enemy aircraft, while Allied fighters report 16 enemy aircraft destroyed.

Twelfth Air Force B-26 Marauders bomb the bridge approach near Manziana. B-25 Mitchells bomb the Viterbo marshaling yard and the town of Cisterna. A-20 Havocs attack Piedimonte and the road junction and railway station at Campoleone. A-36 Intruder (Apache) fighter-bombers attack Pontecorvo and artillery positions. P-40s attack an observation tower at Littoria, a railroad gun, the Sezze railyards, and German positions at Cisterna.

SOUTHWEST PACIFIC AREA: U.S. submarine *Narwhal* delivers supplies and evacuates personnel from Negros in the Philippines.

CENTRAL PACIFIC: Kwajalein Atoll is declared secured. U.S. casualties are nearly 1,000. About 500 Japanese are killed and 100 are taken prisoner. Operation Catchpole, the attack on Eniwetok, is moved up to mid-February.

Seventh Air Force B-25 Mitchells from Tarawa and Abemama Island bomb Wotje and Maloelap Atolls. P-40s from Makin Island attack storage area on Jaluit Atoll.

NEW BRITAIN: Thirteenth Air Force P-40s and navy fighters support an SBD Dauntless dive-bomber attack on Tobera. The airfield is reported unserviceable and several aircraft and gun positions are destroyed. Aircrews report 11 enemy aircraft shot down. B-24 Liberators, escorted by P-38 Lightnings and navy fighters, bomb Vunakanau airfield.

Fifth Air Force P-39 Airacobras fly strafing sweeps over the island.

February 8

CBI: General Headquarters in India reports that a major Japanese offensive is very probable. General Joseph Stilwell directs planning for a campaign to capture the key transportation hub at Myitkyina, an essential part of the Japanese defense of Burma. Myitkyina's capture is essential as part of the American goal of opening a land supply route to China. He intends to use two Chinese divisions, the 38th and the 22nd, and the U.S. 5307th Composite Unit (Provisional), also known as Merrill's Marauders, to attack through the Hukawng Valley. The Chinese divisions will fix Japanese forces with a frontal attack while the Marauders flank the enemy's defensive positions and force them to retreat to avoid being trapped. British unconventional war specialist general Orde Wingate's deep penetration raiding force, known as the Chindits, will operate south of Myitkyina and act as a diversion.

ETO: Eighth Air Force attacks V-weapon sites at Siracourt and Watten in France. Of the 127 B-24 Liberators that hit the targets, 41 are damaged and 10 crewmen are wounded. The bombers are escorted by 89 Eighth and Ninth Air Force P-47 Thunderbolts. Using blind-bombing techniques, only 88 of 236 B-17s hit their primary target, the marshaling yards at Frankfurt, Germany. Bomber losses are 13 B-17s and 110 damaged. Aircrews report one confirmed kill. U.S. casualties are 11 killed, four wounded, and 130 missing. The Frankfurt mission has 77 P-38 Lightnings, 435 Eighth and Ninth Air Force P-47 Thunderbolts, and 41 Ninth Air Force P-51 Mustangs flying escort. Fighter pilots report 16 confirmed kills and one probable. Aircraft losses are two P-38s, three P-47 Thunderbolts, and four P-51 Mustangs. Five P-47s are damaged. Nine pilots are reported missing.

Ninth Air Force attacks V-weapon sites in France with over 300 B-26 Marauders in a morning and afternoon attack.

The B-26 Marauders of the 494th Bombardment Squadron (Medium) of the 344th Bombardment Group (Medium) arrive from the United States. The squadron's first mission is scheduled for later in February.

Six Eighth Air Force B-17s drop leaflets in a Carpetbagger mission over Caen, Rouen, Paris, Rennes, and Amiens, France.

ITALY: In the II Corps area, the 133rd Infantry supported by a battalion of tanks, attacks the town of Cassino while the 135th and 168th Infantry of the 34th Infantry Division are stopped at the front slopes of Monte Cassino.

Naval gunfire, ground artillery fire, and dive-bombers all work together in an attempt to suppress enemy artillery fire aimed at the Anzio beachhead. A U.S. destroyer is damaged by shore battery fire off Anzio. Twelfth Air B-25 Mitchells bomb Cisterna and B-26 Marauders bomb the Siena marshaling yard. A-20 Havocs bomb Piedimonte and A-36 Intruder (Apache) fighter-bombers attack gun positions near Ausonia and fly strafing and bombing sweeps against motor transport and gun positions near Cisterna di Latina and Pontecorvo. P-40s attack targets near Roccasecca, Castello, Caprile, Piedimonte, and Aquino. P-47 Thunderbolts bomb Atina.

The 301st Fighter Squadron of the 332nd Fighter Group arrives in Italy from the United States. Equipped with P-39 Airacobras, the squadron will fly its first mission in mid-February.

Second Lieutenant Paul F. Riordan of the 34th Infantry Division leads a platoon against German strongpoints in Cassino, located in a jail house. Second Lieutenant Riordan is able to approach the building in spite of heavy enemy fire. Knowing that the rest of the platoon cannot advance any farther, Riordan attacks the building alone. As he enters the building, he kills two of the enemy before himself being killed. Second Lieutenant Riordan's courage and leadership will be worthy of receiving the Medal of Honor.

PACIFIC: U.S. submarine *Snook* attacks a Japanese convoy off the west coast of Kyushu, Japan, and sinks a transport and damages a cargo ship. *Snook* survives an enemy depth-charge attack.

CENTRAL PACIFIC: Seventh Air Force B-24 Liberators from Makin and Abemama Islands hit Maloelap and Mille Atolls.

NEW GUINEA: Fifth Air Force A-20 Havocs and B-25 Mitchells bomb areas near Alexishafen and Madang. P-39 Airacobras strafe targets of opportunity during sweeps over northeast New Guinea.

February 9
CBI: President Roosevelt requests that Generalissimo Chiang Kai-shek allow a U.S. observer mission to visit the Chinese Communist stronghold in Yenan to gather

intelligence on Japanese forces and seek assistance in recovering downed American flyers. Chiang Kai-shek, suspicious of American motives, rejects the request. Chiang has perhaps 500,000 troops in Yenan, all watching the Communists as they conduct a guerrilla campaign against the Japanese. Chiang wants no U.S. contact with Mao Tse-tung (Mao Zedong), the leader of the Chinese Communists.

Tenth Air Force B-25 Mitchells, P-51 Mustangs, P-38 Lightnings, P-40s, and A-36 Intruder (Apache) fighter-bombers carry out 75 attack sorties against Japanese troops, supply points, and roads and bridges.

In China, Fourteenth Air Force P-40s strafe and bomb a barracks and oil storage area at Chefang and areas near Homun and Mangshih. In French Indochina two B-25 Mitchells destroy a radio station near Haiphong.

U.S. submarine *Bonefish* torpedoes and damages a Japanese merchant tanker off French Indochina.

ETO: Ninth Air Force sends 133 B-26 Marauders to bomb V-weapon sites and the marshaling yards at Tergnier in France.

ITALY: At Anzio, the 3rd Battalion, 504th Parachute Infantry counterattacks to support British units holding Carroceto against a strong German assault. The 1st Battalion of the U.S. 1st Armored Division attacks Buonripso Ridge in support of the British 1st Division, while the 3rd Battalion defends the Factory. The 180th Infantry Regiment of the 45th Infantry Division moves into the line to replace a depleted British brigade. After nearly 12 hours of combat, the Germans capture the Factory.

While protecting the right flank of the Anzio beachhead, one company of the 1st Special Service Force conducts an early morning raid on the village of Sessano, nearly wiping out the defenders and holding it for a short time before withdrawing.

Ground artillery, naval gunfire, and air attacks are coordinated against German artillery fire.

Twelfth Air Force B-25 Mitchells, A-20 Havocs, and B-26 Marauders bomb German transportation and troop concentrations near Campoleone. P-40s attack German positions at Cisterna. A-36 Intruder (Apache) fighter-bombers and P-40s attack German forces preparing for a counterattack at the Anzio area, at the villages of Piedimonte and Aquino, and at gun positions near Cassino and Ausonia.

CENTRAL PACIFIC: Seventh Air Force A-24 Banshees from Makin Island and P-40s bomb and strafe oil storage and gun positions on Jaluit Atoll. B-24 Liberators from Tarawa Atoll operate in a continuous cycle, bombing Wotje Atoll and Taroa Island in Maloelap Atoll.

NEW BRITAIN: Moving for 11 days, Lieutenant Colonel Puller's force reaches Gilnit village and occupies the Japanese supply base at Nigol, discovering 34 supply barges, along with weapons, ammunition, and food.

Thirteenth Air Force P-40s and navy fighters support an SBD Dauntless dive-bomber attack on Vunakanau airfield. This attack is followed by 24 B-24 Liberators escorted by navy fighters. B-24 Liberators, with P-38 Lightnings escorting, bomb Tobera airfield.

February 10

CBI: In Thailand, Tenth Air Force sends nine B-24 Liberators to bomb the Ban Mah arsenal at Bangkok and the Don Maung airfield. In Burma, B-24 Liberators bomb

Prome and Akyab. Nine B-25 Mitchells attack Chiradan and Godusara, and 16 P-51 Mustangs strafe a barracks and a road at Chishidu.

In China, Fourteenth Air Force P-40s bomb the supply base and training center at Wanling. Five B-24 Liberators mine the mouth of the Yangtze River. P-40s attack small boats along the river. B-25 Mitchells report two cargo ships sunk near Hainan Island. P-51 Mustangs and P-38 Lightnings strafe boats and aircraft near Chiuchiang.

ETO: Eighth Air Force sends 169 B-17s, escorted by 64 P-38 Lightnings, 357 Eighth and Ninth Air Force P-47 Thunderbolts, and 45 Ninth Air Force P-51 Mustangs, against industrial production at Brunswick, Germany. Of the 141 bombers that hit the target, 29 B-17s are lost and 53 are damaged. Aircrews report 42 confirmed kills and 30 probables. Two crewmen are killed and three are wounded, and 295 are reported as missing. Fighter pilots report 56 confirmed kills and one probable, with two possible aircraft destroyed on the ground. Aircraft losses are five P-38 Lightnings and four P-47 Thunderbolts and one P-38 and one P-51 and six P-47s damaged. One pilot is reported killed, one wounded and nine are missing.

Poor weather conditions limit the 81 B-24 Liberators sent against the Gilze-Rijen airfield in the Netherlands. Only 27 hit the target and four bombers are damaged. Aircrew casualties are 26 killed and 14 wounded. P-47 Thunderbolts escort the bombers and report no losses.

Eighth Air Force B-17s, supporting Carpetbagger missions to resistance groups, drop leaflets over Rennes, Caen, Rouen, and Amiens in France and over Antwerp, Belgium.

The headquarters of the 364th Fighter Group, and 383rd, 384th, and 385th Fighter Squadrons, arrives from the United States. They are equipped with P-38Js, a P-38 Lightning with a modified and improved powerplant. The first mission for the squadrons will be in early March.

Ninth Air Force attacks V-weapon sites, airfields at Poix and Beauvais/Tille, a bridge at Le Crotoy, and a coastal battery in France with 114 B-26 Marauders.

The B-26 Marauders of the 496th Bombardment Squadron (Medium), 344th Bombardment Group (Medium), arrive from the United States. The squadron's first mission is scheduled for late February.

ITALY: At Anzio, tank destroyers of B Company, 894th Tank Destroyer Battalion, and the 3rd Battalion 504th Parachute Infantry cover the withdrawal of British units near Carroceto. Allied artillery and air attacks stop the enemy advance. Most of the British 1st Division is relieved in place by the 180th and 179th Infantry Regiments of the 45th Infantry Division. The 3rd Battalion of the 504th Parachute Infantry along with British infantry units holds a shorter portion of the front line. The 36th Engineer Combat Regiment takes up defenses along the beachhead's left flank.

Fifteenth Air Force B-17s bomb Albano, Laziale, Cisterna, and Cecina while B-24 Liberators bomb Campoleone and Velletri. P-38 Lightnings bomb and strafe the Tivoli, Vicovaro, and Monterotondo areas.

Twelfth Air Force P-40s and A-36 Intruder (Apache) fighter-bombers support the withdrawal in the Carroceto area.

Southwest Pacific Area: U.S. submarine *Pogy* torpedoes and sinks a Japanese destroyer and cargo ship near Formosa. U.S. submarine *Spearfish* torpedoes and damages a Japanese transport, also near Formosa.

Central Pacific: Aircraft from Navy Task Group 58.4, commanded by Rear Admiral Samuel P. Ginder, bomb Japanese installations on Eniwetok Atoll in preparation for Operation Catchpole.

Bougainville: Thirteenth Air Force P-39 Airacobras attack facilities at Bonis and barges in Matchin Bay.

New Britain: Thirteenth Air Force P-40s and navy fighters support an SBD Dauntless dive-bomber attack on Vunakanau airfield. A second attack is carried out by B-25 Mitchells. B-24 Liberators supported by P-38 Lightnings and navy fighters bomb Tobera. Aircrews report more than 30 Japanese aircraft shot down.

Admiralties: Fifth Air Force sends six B-25 Mitchells and a B-24 against Momote airfield on Los Negros Island and jetties at Manus Island.

New Guinea: U.S. forces near Saidor link with the Australians advancing from the Huon Peninsula. This ends the campaign for control of western New Guinea after two years of long and often desperate fighting.

Fifth Air Force sends over 50 B-24 Liberators to bomb the airfield and harbor area at Wewak. A navy PBY Catalina sinks a Japanese fishing boat off Wewak.

U.S. submarine *Hake* attacks a Japanese mine and netlayer escorting a convoy to Manokwari; the Japanese ship is not damaged and drops depth charges.

February 11

CBI: In China, Fourteenth Air Force B-25 Mitchells, escorted by American and Chinese P-40s, bomb the storage area at Kai Tek airfield. The fighter pilots report five Japanese fighters shot down. Japanese aircraft bomb and strafe the Namyung airfield, preventing its use for several days.

U.S. submarine *Gudgeon* torpedoes and sinks a Japanese cargo ship damaged by air attack off Wenchow, China.

ETO: Eighth Air Force B-24 Liberators bomb the Siracourt V-weapon site in France. One bomber is lost and 18 are damaged. One crewman is killed, one wounded, and 10 are missing. The bombers are escorted by 85 Eighth and Ninth Air Force P-47s and 41 P-51 Mustangs. There are no losses to the fighters.

The marshaling yard at Frankfurt, Germany, is hit by 157 B-17s. Bomber losses are five B-17s and 127 damaged; they were escorted by 82 P-38 Lightnings, 486 Eighth and Ninth Air Force P-47 Thunderbolts, and 38 Ninth Air Force P-51 Mustangs. Aircrews report three confirmed kills. One crewman is killed, 26 wounded, and 51 are missing. Fighter pilots report 30 confirmed kills and two probables, with another seven destroyed on the ground. Aircraft losses are eight P-38 Lightnings, four P-47s, and two P-51s. Six P-47 Thunderbolts, two P-38s, and one P-51 are damaged. U.S. casualties are 14 pilots missing.

During the night five B-17s drop leaflets on Ghent, Brussels, and Antwerp in Belgium.

Ninth Air Force receives the B-26 Marauders of the 495th and 497th Bombardment Squadrons (Medium), 344th Bombardment Group (Medium), from the United States. The squadrons' first mission is scheduled for late February.

ITALY: At Anzio, the 1st Battalion, 179th Infantry Regiment of the 45th Infantry Division, supported by tanks from the 191st Tank Battalion, attempts to retake the Factory, the key position on the Albano Road and the main avenue of advance into the Anzio beachhead. Although reaching the outskirts, the infantrymen are unable to hold their gains and are driven back by German counterattacks.

Fifteenth Air Force receives Headquarters, 460th Bombardment Group (Heavy), and 760th, 761st, 762nd, and 763rd Bombardment Squadrons (Heavy) from the United States. Equipped with B-24 Liberators, the squadrons will fly their first mission in mid-March.

NEW BRITAIN: Thirteenth Air Force B-25 Mitchells, escorted by navy fighters, bomb Vunakanau airfield. B-24 Liberators with P-38 Lightnings and navy fighters bomb Tobera airfield.

NEW IRELAND: Fifth Air Force B-24 Liberators escorted by P-38 Lightnings bomb Kavieng airfield, hitting aircraft preparing to launch.

February 12

CBI: Tenth Air Force P-51 Mustangs and A-36 Intruder (Apache) fighter-bombers attack Japanese camps at Walawbum and Padaw and supply points near Chishidu. P-51 Mustangs and B-25 Mitchells attack camps between Tsumhpawng Ga and Walawbum, a supply area near Kamaing, and a convoy on the Myitkyina-Sumprabum road.

The 59th Fighter Squadron, 33rd Fighter Group, arrives at Karachi, India, after being redeployed from Italy. The squadron will receive P-47Ds, a modification of the Thunderbolt with improved cockpit armor, additional fuel capacity, and structural strengthening.

In French Indochina, Fourteenth Air Force P-40s attack a barracks at Vinh and the Dong Cuong airfield, railroad yards at Cam Duong, and sampans at Phu Tho. B-25 Mitchells report sinking two trawlers in the Gulf of Tonkin while attacking targets of opportunity near Haiphong.

In China, 24 American aircraft (P-38 Lightnings, P-51 Mustangs, and P-40s) intercept 25 Japanese fighters near Suichwan. In the resulting dogfight, six Japanese aircraft are reported shot down and six are reported as probable kills. Two P-38 Lightnings are lost. One pilot is killed and the other parachutes safely and is returned to friendly lines.

ATLANTIC: The CCS sends a directive to General Eisenhower, Supreme Commander Allied Expeditionary Force, with the mission statement for Overlord. *"You will enter the continent of Europe, and in conjunction with other United Nations, undertake operations aimed at the heart of Germany and the destruction of her armed forces."*

ETO: Ninth Air Force receives the headquarters of the 370th Fighter Group and the 401st, 402nd, and 485th Fighter Squadrons from the United States. The squadrons will transition to P-38 Lightnings and fly their first missions in May.

ITALY: At Anzio, the 1st Battalion, 179th Infantry Regiment of the 45th Infantry Division, supported by tanks from the 191st Tank Battalion, again attempts to retake the Factory. Storming into the collection of battered buildings, the battalion cannot hold what it has seized. German counterattacks force the Americans out. One company of the battalion has been reduced to three officers and 40 men. With control of Buonriposo Ridge, Carroceto, and the Factory, the Germans can threaten the entire Anzio beachhead. The German Fourteenth Army has nearly 120,000 troops available for an offensive.

Fifteenth Air Force B-17s and B-24 Liberators bomb German troop concentrations and highways near Cecina. Headquarters of the 459th Bombardment Group (Heavy) and 756th Bombardment Squadron (Heavy) arrive from the United States equipped with B-24 Liberators. The squadron's first mission will be in March.

Twelfth Air Force B-25 Mitchells attack gun positions at Campoleone and B-26 Marauders bomb Cecina. A-36 Intruder (Apache) fighter-bombers attack troops and gun positions near Roccasecca, and the towns of Fondi and Lanuvio. P-40s attack Sezze, Cori, and Atina.

PACIFIC: U.S. submarine *Tambor* torpedoes and sinks a Japanese merchant tanker in the East China Sea.

CENTRAL PACIFIC: Seventh Air Force B-25 Mitchells from Tarawa and Abemama Island bomb Wotje and Maloelap Atolls. A-24 Banshees and P-39 Airacobras from Makin Island bomb and strafe Mille Atoll.

Japanese flying boats bomb and destroy logistics storage areas on Roi Island and damage two LCTs (landing craft tank)

NEW BRITAIN: The 1st Marines dispatch a company to land on Rooke Island to locate and destroy Japanese forces. The island, off the western tip of New Britain, is unoccupied.

Thirteenth Air Force B-25 Mitchells, with navy fighters, bomb Tobera airfield. B-24 Liberators, escorted by P-39 Airacobras and navy fighters, attack Vunakanau airfield. P-40s and navy fighters support an SBD Dauntless dive-bomber attack on Lakunai.

NEW GUINEA: Fifth Air Force sends 50 A-20 Havocs to attack Japanese positions near Wewak.

February 13

CBI: Fourteenth Air Force B-25 Mitchells sink a Japanese cargo ship and damage another off Hainan Island.

ATLANTIC: The Combined Chiefs of Staff (CCS) directs changes to targets for the Combined Bomber Offensive (CBO) Plan. The number of targets is reduced and revised to account for relocation of vital industries. Destruction of major lines of communication and reducing the capability of the German Luftwaffe become high priorities in preparation for Overlord.

ETO: Eighth Air Force sends 277 B-17s and 192 B-24 Liberators against V-weapon sites in France. Of the 266 B-17s and 138 B-24s that hit the targets, four B-17s are lost and 75 damaged. The B-24s have 59 damaged. Aircrews report one probable kill. Aircrew losses are seven killed, 23 wounded, and 24 missing. The bombers are escorted by 189 P-47 Thunderbolts and 43 P-51 Mustangs. The pilots report six confirmed kills and one probable as well as four others possibly destroyed on the ground. One P-51 is lost and four P-47s are damaged. There are no casualties among the pilots.

Ninth Air Force sends 182 B-26 Marauders to attack V-weapon sites in France. **ITALY:** Fifteenth Air Force receives the B-24 Liberators of the 757th and 758th Bombardment Squadrons (Heavy), of the 459th Bombardment Group (Heavy), from the United States. The squadrons will fly their first missions in March.

Twelfth Air Force B-25 Mitchells and A-20 Havocs support Allied forces at Anzio. P-40s and A-36 Intruder (Apache) fighter-bombers attack German troop concentrations, a railway tunnel, strongpoints, vehicles, supplies, and gun positions. **SOUTHWEST PACIFIC AREA:** MacArthur's headquarters directs operations to control the Bismarck Archipelago, capturing Kavieng and the Admiralty Islands. Alamo Force is directed to seize the Seeadler harbor area on the Admiralties and establish naval and air facilities. D-day for Operation Brewer is set for April 1.

U.S. submarine *Robalo* attacks but fails to damage two cargo ships off Luzon in the Philippines. **CENTRAL PACIFIC:** U.S. submarine *Permit* is damaged by depth charges far southwest of Truk, but remains on patrol. **NEW BRITAIN:** Thirteenth Air Force B-25 Mitchells bomb Tobera airfield and 23 B-24 Liberators bomb Lakunai airfield. P-40s and U.S. Navy fighters escort navy SBD Dauntless and TBF Avenger torpedo-bombers attacking Vunakanau. **NEW IRELAND:** Fifth Air Force sends 35 B-24 Liberators, with 32 P-38 Lightnings escorting, to bomb the Kavieng airfield. After the attack, the airfield is reported unserviceable. **ADMIRALTIES:** Fifth Air Force B-25 Mitchells bomb Momote airfield on Los Negros Island. **NEW GUINEA:** Fifth Air Force sends 24 A-20 Havocs to attack Japanese positions at Aitape. A-20s sink a Japanese cargo ship off Aitape.

February 14

CBI: Tenth Air Force P-51 Mustangs and A-36 Intruder (Apache) fighter-bombers carry out a number of attacks on Japanese targets in Burma, including logistics bases, transportation routes, convoys, and troop concentrations. **ETO:** General Dwight D. Eisenhower establishes Supreme Headquarters Allied Expeditionary Force (SHAEF). Chief of Staff, Supreme Allied Commander (COSSAC) is now incorporated into SHAEF. **ITALY:** The 133rd Infantry fails to capture the town of Cassino. The 34th Infantry Division is too weakened by casualties to make any further attacks. Lieutenant General Sir Bernard C. Freyberg's New Zealand Corps arrives at Cassino. Towering above the town is Monte Cassino and its Benedictine abbey founded in A.D. 524. General Clark authorizes Freyberg to fire on the ancient monastery if he believes it necessary, although Clark and the II Corps commander, Major General Geoffrey Keyes, both believe that bombing the monastery is unnecessary.

Fifteenth Air Force B-17s escorted by P-47 Thunderbolts attack the Modena, Brescia, and Verona marshaling yards and several targets of opportunity. Aircrews report 20 enemy fighters shot down. B-24 Liberators bomb the Mantua, Verona, Massa Lombarda, Fenara, and Arezzo marshaling yards and targets of opportunity. The B-24-equipped 759th Bombardment Squadron (Heavy), 459th Bombardment

Group (Heavy), arrives from the United States. The squadron will fly its first mission in early March.

Twelfth Air Force A-36 Intruder (Apache) fighter-bombers attack artillery in the Pontecorvo area, the railway yards at Civita Castellana and Frosinone, and motor transport. P-40s bomb and strafe troop concentrations at Anzio and attack tanks, motor transport, and guns near Cisterna, Cori, and Rocca di Papa. P-47 Thunderbolts attack Colleferro and Valmontone.

The Twelfth Air Force transfers the 12th Bombardment Group (Medium) and 33rd and 81st Fighter Groups to the China-Burma-India Theater and transfers the 52nd Troop Carrier Wing to the European Theater of Operations (ETO).

SOUTHWEST PACIFIC AREA: U.S. submarine *Flasher* torpedoes and sinks a Japanese cargo ship and a tanker off Luzon in the Philippines.

PACIFIC: U.S. submarine *Snook* torpedoes and sinks a Japanese cargo ship near Tsushima, Japan.

CENTRAL PACIFIC: Seventh Air Force sends over 40 B-24 Liberators based at Makin Island and Tarawa to attack Ponape Island in the Carolines.

BOUGAINVILLE: Thirteenth Air Force sends 19 B-25 Mitchells to attack Kara and Kahili, while P-39 Airacobras attack the bridges on the Puriata River.

A Japanese dive-bomber damages a U.S. light cruiser supporting the landing on Green Island.

NEW BRITAIN: Thirteenth Air Force B-25 Mitchells bomb Vunakanau airfield while 28 B-24 Liberators bomb Rapopo airfield. P-40s and navy fighters escort a navy SBD Dauntless dive-bomber attack on Tobera; four B-25 Mitchells later bomb the same target.

NEW IRELAND: Fifth Air Force B-24 Liberators bomb the Kavieng and Panapai airfields.

ADMIRALTIES: Fifth Air Force sends over 80 B-25 Mitchells to attack Momote airfield on Los Negros Island.

NEW GUINEA: Fifth Air Force A-20 Havocs, with P-40 support, bomb and strafe Dagua airfield. Pilots report destroying over 20 Japanese aircraft on the ground.

February 15

CBI: In Burma, Tenth Air Force P-40s, P-51 Mustangs, and A-36 Intruder (Apache) fighter-bombers attack targets of opportunity along the Hukawng-Walawbum road and supply points near Kamaing.

Fourteenth Air Force B-25 Mitchells attack targets in French Indochina, damaging a steamer at Haiphong harbor and attacking rail facilities.

Mines laid by Fourteenth Air Force B-24 Liberators on February 10 sink a Japanese cargo ship at the entrance to the Yangtze River.

ETO: Eighth Air Force sends 54 B-24 Liberators to bomb V-weapon sites in France. Although 29 bombers are damaged there are no casualties.

Ninth Air Force sends B-26 Marauders to bomb V-weapon sites in France in a morning and afternoon attack.

ITALY: At Anzio, the 45th Infantry Division takes control of the former British 1st Division area. Reinforcements arrive in the form of a British infantry brigade, artillery, and antiaircraft guns. Allied artillery is now firing an average of 20,000 rounds per day. An LCT (landing craft tank) carrying gasoline is destroyed in a German air attack. One cargo ship is damaged.

Fifteenth Air Force sends 100 B-17s to bomb the Benedictine abbey at Monte Cassino. Twelfth Air Force B-26 Marauders and B-25 Mitchells also bomb the abbey.

At Anzio, Twelfth Air Force A-20 Havocs attack motor transport and road networks near Albano and Valmontone. P-40s bomb enemy troop concentrations near Cisterna and logistics bases near Valmontone and Rocca di Papa. A-36 Intruder (Apache) fighter-bombers attack German troops north of Anzio. Offshore, a destroyer escort is damaged by a radio-controlled German bomb dropped from an aircraft, and an LCI (landing craft infantry) is damaged by mine. A freighter is destroyed by a bomb along with the LCT (landing craft tank) alongside.

SOUTHWEST PACIFIC AREA: U.S. submarine *Tinosa* attacks a Japanese convoy east of Mindanao and sinks a cargo ship.

PACIFIC: U.S. submarine *Snook* torpedoes and sinks a Japanese cargo ship off the south coast of Korea. U.S. submarine *Steelhead* torpedoes and damages a Japanese cargo ship off Chichi Jima.

CENTRAL PACIFIC: U.S. submarine *Aspro* torpedoes and sinks Japanese submarine *I-43* off Guam as it transports sailors to Truk.

BOUGAINVILLE: Navy Task Force 31, commanded by Rear Admiral Theodore S. Wilkinson, lands the New Zealand 3rd Division on Green Island. Task Force 38, commanded by Rear Admiral Walden C. Ainsworth, with two light cruisers and five destroyers, and Task Force 39, commanded by Rear Admiral Aaron S. Merrill, with two light cruisers and five destroyers, cover the landing.

NEW GEORGIA: The B-24 Liberators of the 424th Bombardment Squadron (Heavy), 307th Bombardment Group (Heavy), depart from Munda and return to Guadalcanal Island.

NEW BRITAIN: U.S. submarine *Gato* torpedoes and sinks a Japanese guardboat off Rabaul.

NEW IRELAND: Thirteenth Air Force sends 20 B-24 Liberators to attack Borpop airfield. Aircrews report heavy damage.

Fifth Air Force B-24 Liberators, A-20 Havocs, and B-25 Mitchells bomb Kavieng harbor, the town, shipping, and the Panapai airfield. Eight of the P-38 Lightnings escorting the bombers are shot down by antiaircraft fire. A navy PBY Catalina makes five separate take-offs and landings under heavy enemy fire to rescue downed pilots in the water.

February 16

CBI: Tenth Air Force A-36 Intruder (Apache) fighter-bombers and P-51 Mustangs hit supply dumps, troop concentrations, and camps near Myitkyina, Kamaing, Tonkin, and Walawbum. The 118th Tactical Reconnaissance Squadron arrives in India from the United States. The unit, equipped with P-51 Mustangs, is subordinate to Tenth Air Force.

ATLANTIC: The JCS issues an assessment of operations in the Pacific for 1945. U.S. forces in the Pacific have to be in position by early 1945 to support both an air and amphibious attack on Japan. A U.S. approach through the Philippines, as advocated by MacArthur, will not meet the timeline, nor make the best use of U.S. naval power. It appears that Nimitz's Central Pacific advance offers the fastest approach and best uses the U.S. advantage in naval and air power to allow for both strategic bombing and closing off the Japanese lines of supply in the South China Sea.

ITALY: The main German attack on the Anzio beachhead defensive line falls on the 45th Infantry Division, covering the critical left flank on the Albano Road. The 179th and 157th Infantry Regiments hold the road, repulsing the enemy attacks with heavy losses and supported by the fire of 144 guns massed by the 166th Field Artillery Battalion. German diversionary attacks on both flanks are disrupted by heavy and accurate artillery fire.

German artillery fire is also heavy and accurate. German aircraft bomb the beachhead. Allied aircraft support the 45th Infantry Division and heavy bombers attack the main routes into the battle area from Rome.

Twelfth Air Force P-40s attack Monte Cassino abbey and German positions and troops, and attack Fondi and Roccasecca.

A U.S. destroyer is damaged by a German air attack off Anzio.

SOUTHWEST PACIFIC AREA: U.S. submarine *Tinosa* continues to track a Japanese convoy and sinks a cargo ship off Sarangani Island, south of Mindanao Island in the Philippines.

CENTRAL PACIFIC: Seventh Air Force B-24 Liberators from Tarawa bomb Wotje Atoll and Taroa Island in Maloelap Atoll. P-40s from Makin Island attack Jaluit Atoll and A-24 Banshees bomb Mille Atoll.

Navy aircraft from Task Group 58.4, commanded by Rear Admiral Samuel P. Ginder, bomb Eniwetok.

A U.S. destroyer and a minesweeper sink Japanese submarine *RO-40* off Kwajalein. U.S. submarine *Skate* torpedoes and sinks a Japanese light cruiser north of Truk.

NEW BRITAIN: Lieutenant Colonel Puller's force begins to return to friendly lines after eight days of patrolling. His estimate is that the Japanese have not been in the Gilnit area in any size for at least two months.

Thirteenth Air Force B-24 Liberators, with P-38 Lightnings and navy F4U Corsairs flying escort, bomb Vunakanau airfield.

NEW IRELAND: Fifth Air Force B-25 Mitchells attack a Japanese convoy off New Hanover and Kavieng, New Ireland, sinking two submarine chasers and a transport.

February 17

CBI: In French Indochina, Fourteenth Air Force B-25 Mitchells damage a cargo ship in the Gulf of Tonkin and destroy rail targets.

ITALY: At Anzio, German tanks and infantry, supported by enemy aircraft, attack the 179th Infantry Regiment, 45th Infantry Division, in an attempt to break through the Albano Road and rupture the defensive line at Anzio. Desperate fighting takes place as American infantrymen and tanks fall back over two miles. Tanks from the 1st Armored Division, antiaircraft guns, naval gunfire, artillery, fighters, and bombers combine to halt the attack. Air support from 198 fighter-bombers, 176 medium bombers, and 288 heavy bombers is employed in support of the division.

The commander of the 45th Infantry Division, Major General William W. Eagles, orders two battered battalions of the 179th Infantry to make a night attack to regain lost ground. It is a disaster, as fresh German units already in prepared positions easily stop the attack and leave the men in a dangerously exposed position.

Casualties among British generals leads to General Lucian K. Truscott taking command as deputy commander of VI Corps. Brigadier General John W. O'Daniel takes over Truscott's position as commander of the 3rd Infantry Division.

In an effort to stop the German attack on the Allied beachhead at Anzio, Fifteenth Air Force B-17s and B-24 Liberators attack Campoleone and Grottaferrata and supply bases near Campoleone and Rocca di Papa. They also attack troop concentrations near Frascati and logistics bases near Grottaferrata. Twelfth Air Force B-25 Mitchells bomb the Campoleone and Lanuvio area. A-20 Havocs attack logistics sites and troop concentrations in the Anzio area. P-47 Thunderbolts bomb logistics sites near Valmontone, while A-36 Intruder (Apache) fighter-bombers attack Carroceto, a railroad underpass, and a factory north of Anzio. P-40s attack German transportation assets, guns, bridges, and assembly areas near Cisterna, and stations at Campoleone and Carroceto. A-36 Intruder (Apache) fighter-bombers bomb Monte Cassino Abbey.

Over 500 Allied aircraft drop 1,100 tons of bombs in support of VI Corps.

CENTRAL PACIFIC: Operation Hailstone. Navy Task Force 58, commanded by Vice Admiral Raymond A. Spruance and consisting of nine carriers and six battleships, attacks facilities and shipping at Truk. The carrier USS *Intrepid* is damaged during a Japanese air attack with an aerial torpedo. SB2C Helldivers and TBF Avengers sink a Japanese light cruiser, armed merchant cruiser, three cargo ships, a motor torpedo boat, two support vessels, 17 transports, four fleet tankers, an aircraft transport, and two destroyers. Two destroyers, two submarines, an ammunition ship, a seaplane tender, and several other smaller ships are also damaged. Naval gunfire sinks a destroyer and a submarine chaser.

A destroyer sinks Japanese submarine *I-11* near Wotje Atoll.

U.S. submarine *Cero* torpedoes and sinks a Japanese transport between Truk and New Ireland. U.S. submarine *Sargo* attacks a Japanese convoy about 150 miles northeast of Palau and sinks an ammunition ship and damages an oiler.

U.S. submarine *Tang* attacks a Japanese convoy and sinks a cargo ship and merchant tanker in the vicinity of Truk. *Tang* escapes a depth charge attack.

Operation Catchpole. The naval and air bombardment of Parry and Eniwetok Islands begins. Artillery is landed at Aitsu and Rujoru Islands to support the upcoming assaults.

Seventh Air Force B-24 Liberators from Tarawa and Abemama Island bomb Ponape and Kusaie Islands and attack Jaluit Atoll.

NEW BRITAIN: Thirteenth Air Force P-40s and navy fighters support 70 navy SBD Dauntless dive-bombers attacking shipping in Keravia Bay. Aircrews report eight Japanese aircraft shot down. Two navy fighters are shot down.

NEW GUINEA: Navy SBD Dauntless dive-bombers and TBF Avenger torpedo-bombers attack Japanese shipping in Keravia Bay, near Rabaul, sinking a minesweeper, a guardboat, and a cargo ship.

February 18

CBI: The 58th Fighter Squadron of the 33rd Fighter Group arrives at Karachi, India, from Italy. The squadron will be equipped with P-47D Thunderbolts.

Fourteenth Air Force B-25 Mitchells sink a Japanese transport south of Takhow Island, Wenchow, China.

ITALY: At Anzio, the German attack along the Albano Road all but annihilates two battalions of the 179th Infantry Regiment (45th Infantry Division). One company of the 2nd Battalion, 157th Infantry, defending the road is battered by artillery fire and suffers heavy casualties, but holds its position. The 2nd Battalion 180th Infantry is nearly surrounded. Although the Germans are able to advance about half a mile deeper toward the final line of defense at Anzio, small groups of American infantrymen hold their positions and prevent a breakthrough. The defense is aided by the timely concentration of Allied artillery, with over 200 guns massing fire on German troops. Colonel William O. Darby takes command of the 179th Infantry and organizes a last-ditch defense. Supported by 1st Armored Division tanks, the 180th and 179th hold their positions. After a full day of combat, the Germans finally withdraw at dark. The 2nd Battalion 6th Armored Infantry makes contact with isolated elements of the 157th Infantry. Rear echelon troops are brought up to the front line as infantry, and the 45th Infantry Division consolidates its defenses.

CENTRAL PACIFIC: Operation Catchpole. Rear Admiral Harry W. Hill's Navy Task Group 51.11 lands the 22nd Marine Regiment at Engebi Island near Eniwetok preceded by intense artillery fire, naval gunfire, air strikes, and several rocket-firing LCIs. Tanks land with the marines and the island is captured quickly, with over 1,000 Japanese defenders killed. Documents captured on the island indicate that Parry and Eniwetok islands are more strongly defended than originally estimated. Two battalions of the 106th Infantry Regiment, 7th Infantry Division, land at Eniwetok and are slowed by difficult terrain and formidable enemy defensive positions near the beach. The Japanese launch a counterattack with over 400 men, breaking the American line. The enemy attack is stopped after brutal close combat. The decision is made to support the 106th Infantry Regiment's attack on Eniwetok with tanks and the 3rd Battalion of the 22nd Marines. The army and marines fail to coordinate and the marines are left in an exposed position overnight to fight off numerous Japanese attacks alone.

Seventh Air Force P-40s from Makin Island bomb and strafe Jaluit and Mille Atolls.

Operation Hailstone. Vice Admiral Raymond A. Spruance's TF 58 continues to attack facilities and shipping at Truk. Carrier aircraft sink a Japanese destroyer, a motor torpedo boat, and a submarine chaser.

NEW BRITAIN: Lieutenant Colonel Puller's force returns to friendly lines; the 1/5 Marines is left to garrison Agulupella to protect a radar unit.

Thirteenth Air Force B-25 Mitchells and B-24 Liberators bomb Vunakanau airfield, while two B-25 Mitchells and four P-38 Lightnings attack Tobera airfield.

Destroyer Squadron 12 (Captain Rodger W. Simpson) bombards Rabaul, New Britain.

NEW IRELAND: Destroyer Squadron 23, commanded by Captain Arleigh A. Burke, bombards Japanese positions at Kavieng, New Ireland.

February 19

CBI: Tenth Air Force sends A-36 Intruder (Apache) fighter-bombers and P-51 Mustangs and B-25 Mitchells to attack supply and transportation targets in Burma.

Fourteenth Air Force B-24 Liberators, B-25 Mitchells, and P-40s fly sea sweeps over coastal areas from the Formosa Straits to French Indochina. Aircrews report sinking three ships and damaging rail lines and bridges.

ITALY: At Anzio, a weak German attack on the Albano Road is stopped by heavy concentrations of artillery fire, tanks, and the stubborn refusal of the men of the 45th Infantry Division to give up in the face of determined attacks by the enemy.

VI Corps prepares to counterattack as the enemy offensive wears down. Two battalions of the 6th Armored Infantry and a battalion of tanks, along with the 30th Infantry Regiment from the 3rd Infantry Division, attack west to force the advanced elements of the German forces to retreat. The tanks and infantry advance over a mile, capturing over 200 prisoners.

Twelfth Air Force B-25 Mitchells, A-36 Intruder (Apache) fighter-bombers, and P-40s provide continuous air cover, attacking troops, tanks, and transportation targets to stall the German offensive.

U.S. light cruiser USS *Philadelphia* arrives off Anzio to provide gunfire support.

PACIFIC: U.S. submarine *Grayback* torpedoes and sinks a Japanese cargo ship off Formosa, and sinks another cargo ship as it attempts to rescue survivors. U.S. submarine *Jack* attacks a Japanese convoy of six tankers in the South China Sea, sinking four of them.

CENTRAL PACIFIC: Seventh Air Force B-24 Liberators from Tarawa and Makin Island attack Ponape and Kusaie Islands, while B-25 Mitchells from Tarawa hit Wotje Atoll and P-40s from Makin attack Mille Atoll. The 3rd Battalion of the 22nd Marines lands to reinforce and begins advancing inland.

NEW BRITAIN: U.S. bomber aircraft have flown over 1,100 sorties and fighters have flown over 1,500 sorties since February 1. Shipping in the harbor is almost nonexistent and fighters are attacking more Japanese antiaircraft positions. Most of the Japanese aircraft remaining on Rabaul are relocated to Truk to counter the carrier attacks on the island.

Thirteenth Air Force P-40s and navy fighters escort navy SBD Dauntless dive-bombers attacking Lakunai airfield. Fighter pilots report 22 Japanese aircraft shot down. Soon after the navy strike, six B-24 Liberators bomb the airfield. Meanwhile 14 B-24 Liberators, with P-38 Lightnings and navy fighters escorting, attack Tobera airfield.

NEW IRELAND: Fifth Air Force B-25s, A-20 Havocs, and P-38 Lightnings destroy a Japanese convoy off Kavieng, sinking four ships.

NEW GUINEA: U.S. submarine *Cero* torpedoes a Japanese cargo ship headed for Palau off the northwest coast of New Guinea, but causes no damage.

February 20

CBI: Headquarters, 33rd Fighter Group and 60th Fighter Squadron arrives at Karachi, India, from Italy. The squadron will receive P-47D Thunderbolts.

ATLANTIC: The commander of Southeast Asia Command (SEAC), Admiral Lord Louis Mountbatten, offers an option for future offensive operations. SEAC forces will capture a port in China and move to Sumatra in the Netherlands East Indies once Germany has been defeated and additional forces are made available from the ETO. This offensive will begin no earlier than October of 1944. General Joseph Stilwell, the SEAC deputy commander, offers a different option. Discounting any offensive into the Netherlands East Indies, Stilwell advocates an offensive to capture a Chinese port with the resources at hand rather than waiting for support from another theater.

ETO: Big Week. This is the first day of Big Week, a series of missions directed against aircraft production facilities in German cities. Bombers are escorted to the target and back by fighters equipped with drop tanks, which increases their range and allows them to stay with the bombers for longer distances.

Eighth Air Force sends more than 1,000 bombers to attack the Leipzig/Mockau airfield, the Tutow airfield, and aircraft production facilities. Of the 417 B-17s sent against the airfield, 239 hit the primary target. Aircrews report 14 confirmed kills and five probables. Over Tutow airfield 105 of the 314 sent hit the primary target. Aircrews report 15 confirmed kills and 15 probables. Of the 272 B-24 Liberators sent against aircraft production facilities at Brunswick, Wilhelmtor, and Neupetritor, 76 hit the primary target. Aircrews report 36 confirmed kills and 13 probables. The B-17s and B-24s are escorted by 94 P-38 Lightnings, 668 Eighth and Ninth Air Force P-47 Thunderbolts, and 73 Eighth and Ninth Air Force P-51 Mustangs. Fighter pilots report 61 confirmed kills and seven probables. Fighter losses are one P-38, two P-47 Thunderbolts, and one P-51. Six P-47s are damaged. Four pilots are reported missing.

Bomber losses for the first day of Big Week are 21 bombers lost and 239 damaged. Aircrew losses are 20 killed, 27 wounded, and 209 missing.

Sergeant Archibald Mathies is a ball turret gunner in a B-17 of the 510th Bomber Squadron, 351st Bomber Group. When his bomber is attacked by German fighters, the pilot is wounded and the copilot is killed. Mathies and other members of the crew are able to bring the severely damaged bomber back to the airfield. Mathies and the navigator volunteer to land the bomber to save the life of the wounded pilot. As the other crewmen parachute from the aircraft, Sergeant Mathies and the navigator prepare to make a landing. After several attempts, the bomber crashes, killing the three men. Because Sergeant Mathies would not abandon a comrade and displayed exemplary courage in his willingness to risk his life, he will receive the Medal of Honor.

First Lieutenant William R. Lawley, Jr., 364th Bomber Squadron, 305th Bomber Group, is piloting a B-17 when about 20 German fighters attack his bomber. Severely damaged, with an engine on fire, eight crewmen wounded, and the copilot killed, the aircraft falls out of the protective formation. Lieutenant Lawley has suffered facial wounds but brings the bomber out of a steep dive and is able to fly with only his left hand. Blood has covered the instruments and windshield and, as fire spreads in the aircraft, Lawley gives the order for the crew to bail out before the fire reaches the bomb load the aircraft still carries. Lawley hears that two crewmen are badly wounded and unable to exit the aircraft, so he decides to keep the bomber in the air as long as possible and land safely. Lawley battles to keep the bomber aloft, fighting the damaged controls, evading enemy fighters, and putting out flames in a damaged engine. At one point Lawley passes out, but regains consciousness and guides the bomber back to England where he is able to make a successful crash landing at a fighter airfield. For his dedication to duty, his heroism and exceptional flying skill, First Lieutenant Lawley will be awarded the Medal of Honor.

Second Lieutenant Walter E. Truemper is a navigator on a B-17 of the 510th Bomber Squadron, 351st Bomber Group, on a mission over Europe when German fighters attack the bomber and cause severe damage. The copilot is killed, the pilot and radio operator wounded. Truemper and other members of the crew manage to bring the aircraft back to the airfield. The aircraft is too badly damaged to land and the crew is ordered to bail out. Truemper and an engineer reply that the pilot is too badly injured to bail out and that they will attempt to land the plane. The men make two unsuccessful attempts and crash the bomber into a field on the third attempt, killing all aboard. For his exceptional courage and self-sacrifice, Second Lieutenant Truemper will be awarded the Medal of Honor.

ITALY: The German offensive at Anzio stalls after five days of continuous attack to break the Allied defensive line at the Albano Road. The Germans suffer casualties estimated at over 5,300, with 600 prisoners. VI Corps casualties are nearly 4,500 men with 1,300 captured. Another 1,600 are non-battle casualties. The 45th Infantry Division's boundary is reduced to strengthen the line and account for the heavy losses sustained. The 3rd Battalion 180th Infantry of the 45th Infantry Division, supported by tanks of the 1st Armored Regiment, holds off a strong German attack.

Fifteenth Air Force B-24 Liberators attack German defenses. Twelfth Air Force B-25 Mitchells hit logistics sites and assembly areas and A-20 Havocs bomb troops and vehicles near Carroceto. A-36 Intruder (Apache) fighter-bombers and P-40s attack German troop vehicles, strongpoints, the factory, and tanks near Carroceto and bomb strongpoints at Fondi and targets of opportunity around Piedimonte.

German submarine *U-410* torpedoes and sinks *LST-348* (landing ship tank) south of Naples.

PACIFIC: U.S. submarine *Pogy* torpedoes and sinks a Japanese cable layer and a cargo ship off Formosa.

CENTRAL PACIFIC: Operation Catchpole. The 22nd Marines begin clearing the southwest corner of Eniwetok, while the 106th Infantry clears the east end.

Air and naval bombardment of Parry Island begins. Artillery is landed on Japten Island to support the assault on Parry.

Navy aircraft from Task Group 58.1 (Rear Admiral John W. Reeves, Jr.) bomb facilities on Jaluit Atoll.

BOUGAINVILLE: Thirteenth Air Force P-39 Airacobras attack barges off the Island. Pilots report 20 barges sunk.

NEW BRITAIN: Thirteenth Air Force sends 35 B-25 Mitchells with fighter escort to attack Lakunai airfield

NEW GUINEA: Fifth Air Force sends 38 B-24 Liberators to bomb the Alexishafen-Hansa Bay area. B-24s damage a Japanese cargo vessel northwest of Wewak.

February 21

CBI: Tenth Air Force P-51 Mustangs, A-36 Intruder (Apache) fighter-bombers, and B-25 Mitchells attack bridges, roads, camps, and logistics facilities in Burma.

ETO: Eighth Air Force attacks airfield targets in Germany. A total of 336 B-17s are sent against the Gutersioh, Lippstadt, and Werl airfields, but cloud cover leads 285 of the bombers to hit alternate airfields and marshaling yards. Aircrews report 12 confirmed kills and five probables. Of the 281 B-17s sent against Diepholz and Brunswick airfields, 175 hit the primary targets. Aircrews report two confirmed kills and five probables. Achmer and Handorf airfields are the target of 244 B-24 Liberators, but nearly all hit alternate airfield targets. Aircrews report five confirmed kills and six probables. The mission is escorted by 69 P-38 Lightnings, 542 Eighth and Ninth Air Force P-47 Thunderbolts, and 68 Eighth and Ninth Air Force P-51 Mustangs. The fighter pilots report 33 confirmed kills and five probables. Two P-47s and three P-51s are lost; six fighters are damaged. Five pilots are reported as missing. In the second day of Big Week, 16 bombers are lost and 111 are damaged. Aircrew losses are 24 killed, 20 wounded, and 163 missing.

ATLANTIC: President Roosevelt and the JCS agree that the British proposal to cancel Anvil, the invasion of southern France, and divert the forces to landings in the Adriatic is not within U.S. interests. The British propose that, instead of Anvil, a landing at Trieste will allow Allied forces to advance through the Ljubljana Gap and reach Budapest and Vienna before the Soviets did. The United States argues that such a plan is logistically unsupportable and that the use of French or American forces in the Balkans would have little effect on the outcome of the war. The Americans also fear that the British plan will antagonize the Soviets and put U.S. forces in the Balkans when the war ends.

ITALY: Heavy German artillery fire followed by dive-bombers precedes an attack on the 180th Infantry at Anzio. The Americans are able to stop the enemy with tanks and concentrated artillery fire.

Twelfth Air Force A-20 Havocs attack German troops near Campoleone. P-40s and A-36 Intruder (Apache) fighter-bombers attack troops as well as a fuel storage area, tank and truck assembly areas, and gun positions. The A-36s also bomb and block the road between Itri and Gaeta.

CENTRAL PACIFIC: Operation Catchpole. The combined army-marine force succeeds in clearing Eniwetok Island of Japanese. U.S. losses since the beginning of the attack on the Marshalls are about 1,750 killed and wounded. Japanese casualties are estimated at 8,500 dead. The 3rd Battalion 22nd Marines reembarks in preparation for the attack on Parry.

Seventh Air Force B-24 Liberators from Tarawa and Abemama Island bomb Ponape and Kusaie Islands and Jaluit Atoll. B-25 Mitchells from Abemama bomb

Maloelap Atoll and P-40s from Makin Island attack Mille Atoll. As the campaign for the Marianas progresses, the Seventh Air Force's mission is to neutralize and isolate those islands in the Marianas that will not be occupied by ground forces.

BOUGAINVILLE: Thirteenth Air Force B-24 Liberators bomb Kara airfield while P-39 Airacobras attack buildings, barges, and targets of opportunity.

NEW BRITAIN: Thirteenth Air Force B-24 Liberators bomb Lakunai and Rapopo airfields. P-38 Lightnings and navy fighters support Navy SBD Dauntless dive-bomber strikes on gun positions at Lakunai. Navy SBD Dauntless dive-bombers and TBF Avengers bomb antiaircraft positions and facilities at Rabaul. Pilots report one guardboat sunk.

Fifth Air Force P-39 Airacobras attack Raiven Plantation.

NEW GUINEA: Fifth Air Force A-20 Havocs attack targets in the Madang and the Hansa Bay areas.

Fifth Air Force B-25 Mitchells attack a five-ship convoy headed to Palau off New Hanover in the Bismarck Archipelago, sinking four of the ships.

U.S. submarine *Cero* torpedoes and damages a Japanese cargo ship north of New Guinea.

February 22

CBI: Tenth Air Force sends over 70 aircraft (B-25 Mitchells, P-51 Mustangs, and P-40s) against logistics and transportation targets. A number of bridges are destroyed.

Fourteenth Air Force P-40s strafe the Kengtung airfield and a truck convoy.

U.S. submarine *Ray* lays mines off Saigon, French Indochina.

A Vichy French river gunboat is sunk by mines dropped by Fourteenth Air Force aircraft off the coast of French Indochina near Saigon.

ETO: Eighth Air Force attacks aircraft production facilities and airfields in Germany. A total of 289 B-17s are sent against facilities at Aschersleben, Bernburg, and Halberstadt. Less than 100 hit the primary targets while the others hit secondary targets. Aircrews report 32 confirmed kills and 18 possibles. A mission of 333 B-17s to Schweinfurt is aborted due to weather; 177 B-24 Liberators are recalled and the bombers drop on various towns in the Netherlands, including Arnhem and Nijmegen. Aircrews report two confirmed kills. The missions are escorted by 67 P-38 Lightnings, 535 Eighth and Ninth Air Force P-47 Thunderbolts, and 57 Eighth and Ninth Air Force P-51 Mustangs. The fighter pilots report 59 confirmed kills and seven probables. Eight P-38s and three P-51s are lost and 22 fighters are damaged. Eleven pilots are missing. In the third day of Big Week, 41 bombers are lost and 150 are damaged. Aircrew losses are 35 killed, 30 wounded, and 397 missing.

Ninth Air Force sends nearly 200 B-26 Marauders to bomb Gilze-Rijen airfield in the Netherlands. Only 66 hit the target after bad weather causes most of the bombers to abort the mission.

MEDITERRANEAN: In support of Eighth Air Force's attack, Fifteenth Air Force sends a total of 65 B-17s and 118 B-24 Liberators, escorted by 122 P-38 Lightnings and 63 P-47 Thunderbolts to attack aircraft production facilities at Regensburg, Germany. Over 120 German fighters attack the formations en route to and over the targets.

A total of 19 bombers are lost; one P-47 and one P-38 are lost. B-17s also bomb Zagreb, Yugoslavia, while B-24s bomb Sibenik and the harbor at Zara, also in Yugoslavia. Aircrews report 40 confirmed kills. U.S. losses are 13 bombers and crews.

German submarine *U-969* attacks convoy UGS 31 (United States to Mediterranean, Slow) off the coast of Algeria, damaging two U.S. freighters, which are later beached and salvaged.

ITALY: The New Zealand Corps completes the relief of the 34th Infantry Division at Cassino. General Sir Harold R. L. G. Alexander, Supreme Commander Allied Forces in Italy, decides to use the British Eighth Army to break through the Liri Valley and link with the Allies breaking out of the Anzio beachhead. Clark's Fifth Army will shift to the area bounded by the west coast of the Italian Peninsula and the Liri Valley, about 12 miles wide.

Twelfth Air Force A-20 Havocs attack Campoleone and P-47 Thunderbolts attack German troops, gun positions, and roads in the Carroceto-Roccasecca-Campoleone area. A-36 Intruder (Apache) fighter-bombers attack German guns around Carroceto and Formia. P-40s attack gun positions near Campoleone.

First Lieutenant Jack C. Montgomery commands a rifle company in the 45th Infantry near Padiglione, Italy. As German troops begin establishing a series of positions in front of his unit, First Lieutenant Montgomery attacks the closest position alone with only his M-1 rifle and hand grenades. He quickly overcomes the enemy position, killing eight and capturing four soldiers. After calling for artillery fire, Montgomery then attacks a second position, capturing machine guns and seven German soldiers. Montgomery then clears a house and in the face of enemy fire, moves 32 prisoners to the rear. His inspiring acts of courage and leadership will win him the Medal of Honor.

CENTRAL PACIFIC: Operation Catchpole. The 3rd Battalion 22nd Marines lands on Parry Island near Eniwetok after a naval and air bombardment. The enemy must be cleared out of a network of nearly invisible spider holes, trenches, and bunkers. Japanese soldiers attack marine positions with landmines attached to their legs and waists and are killed.

Seventh Air Force A-24 Banshees and P-40s from Makin Island bomb Mille Atoll. One of the P-40s uses wing-mounted rockets for the first time.

Carrier aircraft from five carriers and seven small carriers in Rear Admiral Marc A. Mitscher's TF 58 bomb Saipan, Tinian, Rota, and Guam, sinking two Japanese transports off Saipan.

U.S. submarine *Gato* torpedoes and sinks a Japanese repair ship off Truk.

U.S. submarine *Tang* attacks a Japanese convoy, sinking a gunboat near Saipan.

NEW BRITAIN: Fifth Air Force sends over 60 B-25 Mitchells and B-24 Liberators to bomb Iboki plantation in support of the marines.

Thirteenth Air Force sends more than 40 B-24 Liberators to bomb Lakunai and Keravat airfields. In another attack, 20 P-40s and navy fighters support over 70 navy SBD Dauntless dive-bombers in an attack on shipping in Keravia Bay.

The B-24 Liberators of the 370th Bombardment Squadron (Heavy), 307th Bombardment Group (Heavy), redeploy from Guadalcanal to Munda.

NEW IRELAND: Captain Arleigh A. Burke's TG 39.4 bombards airstrips, piers, and anchorages at Kavieng. A Japanese minelayer, two cargo ships, and two other vessels are sunk by gunfire off New Ireland. A Japanese auxiliary submarine chaser is sunk by a mine near Kavieng.

Navy SBD Dauntless dive-bombers and TBF Avengers attack shipping at Rabaul, sinking two guardboats, a merchant tanker, and a cargo ship.

NEW GUINEA: Fifth Air Force sends over 30 B-25 Mitchells and P-39 Airacobras to attack the Madang area.

U.S. submarine *Puffer* torpedoes and sinks a Japanese army transport off Borneo.

February 23

CBI: In Burma, Chinese forces capture Yawngbang Ga without meeting any opposition.

MEDITERRANEAN: Fifteenth Air Force sends 102 B-24 Liberators escorted by P-38 Lightnings to attack the Steyr ball bearing factory in Austria. Over 120 German fighters attack the formations and 17 bombers are lost. Aircrews and fighter pilots escorting the mission report at least 30 confirmed kills.

German submarine *U-510* torpedoes and sinks a U.S. tanker in the Gulf of Aden.

ITALY: At Anzio, Major General Lucas is relieved of command of VI Corps and replaced by his deputy commander, Major General Lucian Truscott. General Sir Harold Alexander, commander of the Fifteenth Army Group, is disappointed in Lucas and has General Clark remove him from command.

Twelfth Air Force P-40s attack a gun position near Campoleone and patrol the skies over Anzio.

SOUTHWEST PACIFIC AREA: Reconnaissance by B-25 Mitchells over the Admiralties shows no signs of activity on Los Negros Island or on Momote airfield. Given this information, MacArthur rejects the assessment of his intelligence chief (confirmed from Ultra intercepts) that the Japanese have over 4,000 men on the island and decides to launch an immediate attack. He terms this a reconnaissance in force. If successful, he intends to press the attack; if unsuccessful, he can recall his forces. MacArthur calls his plan "a gamble in which I have everything to win, little to lose."

PACIFIC: U.S. submarine *Plunger* attacks a Japanese convoy and sinks a transport near Chichi Jima. U.S. submarine *Pogy* attacks a Japanese convoy, sinking a cargo ship and damaging a merchant tanker near Okinawa. U.S. submarine *Snook* attacks a Japanese convoy, sinking a transport near Chichi Jima.

CENTRAL PACIFIC: Operation Catchpole. The 22nd Marines report Parry Island is secured. The 3rd Battalion of the 106th Infantry Regiment takes control of the island. American casualties for this operation are 1,096. Japanese losses are 1,000 killed. Brigadier General Thomas E. Watson (USMC), the amphibious commander for the Marshalls operation, is unimpressed by the army's performance, an opinion he is more than willing to share. The rapid and unexpected success of the attack on the Marshalls allows Admiral Nimitz to advance his planning timetable for the scheduled assault on the Mariana Islands by nearly 12 weeks. The formula for success for amphibious assaults has clearly been validated during the Marshalls operation: heavy volumes of concentrated firepower from artillery, air strikes, and naval gunfire followed by an amphibious assault that joins tanks, infantry, demolition, and flamethrower teams working together to destroy Japanese defensive positions and move rapidly inland.

Navy F4F Hellcats, TBF Avengers, and SBD Dauntless dive-bombers from TG 58.2 and TG 58.3 sink a cargo ship off Tinian and another off Saipan. A Japanese gunboat is also sunk. U.S. submarine *Sunfish* and aircraft from the carrier USS *Yorktown* sink a Japanese collier west of Saipan. U.S. submarine *Tang* torpedoes and sinks a Japanese repair ship west of Saipan.

NEW BRITAIN: Thirteenth Air Force B-25 Mitchells, with navy fighter support, bomb Vunakanau and Keravat airfields. P-38 Lightnings, freed from defending bombers against the threat of Japanese aircraft, attack Rabaul for the first time.

NEW GUINEA: Fifth Air Force sends B-24 Liberators and A-20 Havocs to attack the airfield, support facilities, and antiaircraft positions at Wewak.

U.S. submarine *Balao* attacks a Japanese convoy north of Biak and sinks a cargo ship. U.S. submarine *Cod* torpedoes and sinks a Japanese fleet tanker off Halmahera.

February 24

CBI: The U.S. 5307th Composite Unit (Provisional), known as Merrill's Marauders, begins moving from Ningbyen to establish the trail block at Walawbum and conduct raids on Japanese forces in the Hukawng Valley in cooperation with Chinese forces. The unit's total strength is 2,750 men.

In Burma, Tenth Air Force B-24 Liberators bomb the marshaling yard at Mandalay and targets of opportunity at Akyab, Monywa, and Pakokku. P-51 Mustangs, A-36 Intruder (Apache) fighter-bombers, and P-40s attack bridges, radio stations, supply points, and Japanese troops.

Fourteenth Air Force P-40s strafe the airfield at Myitkyina in Burma.

ETO: Eighth Air Force sends 81 B-24 Liberators against V-weapon sites in France. The B-24s are escorted 61 P-47 Thunderbolts and 49 hit the primary targets. Against another V-weapon site, 258 B-17s are sent and 109 hit the primary target. The B-17s are escorted by 81 P-38 Lightnings, 94 P-47 Thunderbolts, and 22 P-51 Mustangs. Pilots report one enemy aircraft destroyed on the ground. One P-38 is damaged. Seven B-17s are lost and 76 bombers are damaged. Aircrew losses are five wounded and 63 missing.

During the night, five B-17s drop leaflets over Amiens, Rennes, Paris, Rouen, and Le Mans.

Ninth Air Force sends 180 B-26 Marauders to attack V-weapon sites in France.

MEDITERRANEAN: The CCS instructs the commander in chief of the Mediterranean Theater to continue operations in Italy, while preparing operational plans to support Overlord with two divisions for an amphibious landing in southern France (Anvil).

Fifteenth Air Force sends 87 B-17s escorted by 87 P-38 Lightnings and 59 P-47 Thunderbolts to attack the aircraft component factory in Steyr, Austria. Over 120 German fighters, some firing rockets, attack the formations. A total of 16 bombers are lost and 18 damaged. Aircrews report nine confirmed kills and seven probables. Three P-38s are lost. Fighter pilots report 26 confirmed kills and five probables.

Navy PBY-5A Catalinas, employing Magnetic Anomaly Detection (MAD) equipment, a PV-1 Patrol Bomber, and a Royal Air Force Catalina bomb German submarine *U-761* in the Straits of Gibraltar. British destroyers rescue 51 survivors. This is the first U-boat detected and destroyed by MAD.

SOUTHWEST PACIFIC AREA: General MacArthur orders Alamo Force to plan for an immediate reconnaissance of Los Negros Island. The 2nd Squadron, 5th Cavalry Regiment, 1st Cavalry Division is tasked with the mission. Brigadier General William Chase is to command the operation, which consists of about a thousand men. MacArthur announces he will personally supervise the landings.

U.S. submarine *Grayback* torpedoes and sinks a Japanese oiler and damages a transport off Formosa.

CENTRAL PACIFIC: U.S. transport planes begin landing on the airfield at Kwajalein.

U.S. submarine *Tang* attacks a Japanese convoy west of Saipan and sinks a cargo ship.

NEW GEORGIA: The B-24 Liberators of the 394th Bombardment Squadron (Heavy), 5th Bombardment Group (Heavy), redeploy from Guadalcanal to Munda.

NEW BRITAIN: Amphibious elements leapfrogging along the northern coast land the 5th Marines near Iboki to locate the Japanese.

On Arawe, the Japanese withdraw, following the order for a general retreat toward Rabaul.

Thirteenth Air Force B-25 Mitchells, with fighter escort, bomb Rabaul. This attack is followed by 12 P-38 Lightnings with bombs, followed by a bombing run by 11 B-24 Liberators. Other B-24s bomb Rapopo.

The P-38 Lightnings of the 80th Fighter Squadron, 8th Fighter Group, redeploy from Dobodura, New Guinea, to Cape Gloucester.

NEW IRELAND: Two U.S. destroyers are damaged by a shore battery on New Ireland.

ADMIRALTIES: Fifth Air Force sends over 50 B-25 Mitchells and B-24 Liberators to bomb Momote airfield on Los Negros Island and Lorengau on Manus Island.

NEW GUINEA: Fifth Air Force B-24 Liberators and A-20 Havocs attack targets around Hansa Bay.

February 25

CBI: The 91st Fighter Squadron, 81st Fighter Group arrives at Karachi, India, from Italy. The squadron will be equipped with P-47D Thunderbolts.

ATLANTIC: President Roosevelt writes to Prime Minister Churchill recommending an all-out attack in upper Burma to build air strength in China that will provide support for the attack against either Formosa or Luzon.

ETO: End of Big Week. Eighth Air Force attacks aircraft production facilities and industrial targets in Germany. Over Augsburg and Stuttgart, 246 of 268 bombers hit the primary targets. Aircrews report eight confirmed kills and four probables. Over Regensburg, 267 of 290 B-17s hit the primary target. Aircrews report 13 confirmed kills and one probable. Over Furth, 172 of 196 B-24 Liberators hit the primary target. Aircrews report two confirmed kills and two probables. The missions are escorted by 73 P-38 Lightnings, 687 Eighth and Ninth Air Force P-47 Thunderbolts, and 139 Eighth and Ninth Air Force P-51 Mustangs. Fighter pilots report 26 confirmed kills and four probables. A P-47 and two P-51s are lost. Eight fighters are damaged. Three pilots are missing. For the final day of Big Week, 31 bombers are lost and 301 are damaged. Aircrew losses are four killed, 26 wounded, and 301 missing.

Ninth Air Force sends 191 B-26 Marauders to bomb Venlo, Saint-Trond, and Cambrai/Epinoy airfields in France as a diversion in support of Big Week bombing missions.

Together the Eighth and Fifteenth Air Force have dropped 10,000 tons of bombs on targets during Big Week. Big Week will have important effects on the preparation for the Normandy landing. First, German fighter squadrons will be forced to redeploy from France to Germany. Second, German fighters will be pulled from the eastern front to protect German cities. Finally, more and more inexperienced German pilots will be forced to fly missions they are not prepared for because of the heavy losses in experienced combat pilots.

The cost for the Americans is high. During the week Eighth Air Force has lost 109 bombers and over 800 are damaged. Crew losses are 83 killed, 103 wounded, and over a thousand missing. A total of 20 fighter pilots are also missing. It is a battle of attrition that the United States Army Air Force is capable of winning.

MEDITERRANEAN: Fifteenth Air Force sends 46 B-17s and 103 B-24 Liberators, escorted by 85 P-38 Lightnings and 40 P-37s, to attack aircraft production facilities at Regensburg, Germany. The Germans respond with over 200 fighters, shooting down 33 bombers and damaging 20 others. Aircrew casualties are three killed, seven wounded, and 110 missing. Aircrews and fighter pilots report 93 confirmed kills and 17 probables.

Other B-17s attack Klagenfurt, Austria, and the docks at Pola, Italy. B-24 Liberators attack Fiume, Italy, and the Graz airfield in Austria, as well as the port area at Zara, Yugoslavia. Over 30 aircraft are lost. Aircrews report 90 confirmed kills.

ITALY: Twelfth Air Force P-40s attack guns and troop concentrations near Campoleone and Carroceto. A-36 Intruder (Apache) fighter-bombers attack Terracina.

SOUTHWEST PACIFIC AREA: U.S. submarine *Hoe* attacks a Japanese convoy, sinking a fleet tanker and damaging another near Davao in the Philippines.

CENTRAL PACIFIC: U.S. submarine *Tang*, continuing its attack on the Japanese convoy engaged previously, sinks a fleet tanker west of Saipan.

NEW BRITAIN: Thirteenth Air Force B-25 Mitchells bomb Rapopo; this attack is followed by 21 B-24 Liberators and 17 P-38 Lightnings attacking the same target.

Destroyer Division 90 (Commander Edmund B. Taylor) bombards Rabaul.

NEW IRELAND: Destroyer Squadron 12 (Captain Rodger W. Simpson) encounters and sinks two cargo ships en route to bombard Kavieng. Two destroyers are damaged by shore batteries during the bombardment.

ADMIRALTIES: Fifth Air Force B-25 Mitchells bomb Lorengau on Manus Island

NEW GUINEA: Fifth Air Force B-25 Mitchells and A-20 Havocs attack targets in the Alexishafen-Madang area.

U.S. submarine *Rasher* torpedoes and sinks two Japanese cargo ships off Bali.

February 26

ALEUTIANS: Eleventh Air Force XI Bomber Command is directed to conduct day and night armed photographic reconnaissance missions in the Kurile Islands whenever weather permits.

CBI: Fourteenth Air Force B-25 Mitchells attack shipping in French Indochina, sinking a Vichy surveying vessel and dredging ship.

ITALY: In the II Corps area, elements of the 88th Infantry Division and French troops relieve units of the 36th Infantry Division at Monte Castellone.

PACIFIC: Japanese aircraft attack U.S. submarine *Grayback* in the East China Sea and cause some damage.

CENTRAL PACIFIC: Seventh Air Force B-25 Mitchells from Tarawa and Abemama Island attack Wotje and Jaluit Atolls. P-40s from Makin Island bomb and strafe targets on Mille Atoll.

The B-24 Liberators of the 27th and 38th Bombardment Squadrons (Heavy), 30th Bombardment Group (Heavy), redeploy from Nanumea Island in the Ellice Islands to Abemama and Makin Islands.

NEW BRITAIN: Thirteenth Air Force P-40s and navy fighters support a navy SBD Dauntless dive-bomber attack on logistics targets at Wunapope. Soon afterward, 22 B-25 Mitchells, with fighter support, attack the same target. This is followed by seven P-38 Lightnings making a follow-on attack.

ADMIRALTIES: Fifth Air Force B-24 Liberators bomb Momote on Los Negros Island.

NEW GUINEA: Fifth Air Force B-24 Liberators bomb Wewak. B-25 Mitchells, along with P-39 Airacobras, attack targets in the Madang-Alexishafen area.

U.S. submarine *Gato* attacks a Japanese convoy and sinks a cargo ship carrying troops northwest of Hollandia.

February 27

CBI: Tenth Air Force P-51 Mustangs and A-36 Intruder (Apache) fighter-bombers and two B-25 Mitchells attack ammunition dumps near the Kamaing-Walawbum road.

In China, Fourteenth Air Force P-40s bomb and heavily damage the railroad bridge at Puchi.

ITALY: The light cruiser USS *Philadelphia* provides naval gunfire support to Allied forces at Anzio.

SOUTHWEST PACIFIC AREA: The Alamo Scouts, an independent reconnaissance unit, land a six-man team on Los Negros to gain firsthand information on Mamote airfield and the status of Japanese forces on the island.

PACIFIC: U.S. submarine *Trout* torpedoes and sinks a Japanese cargo ship east of Formosa, and USS *Grayback* torpedoes and sinks a cargo ship in the East China Sea.

NEW BRITAIN: At Arawe, a company of the 112th Cavalry with two platoons of tanks advances north to locate the enemy and finds the area abandoned.

Thirteenth Air Force sends 21 B-24 Liberators and 24 B-25 Mitchells escorted by 14 P-38 Lightnings to bomb Wunapope. Navy SBD Dauntless dive-bombers, escorted by army P-40s and navy fighters, attack antiaircraft positions at Lakunai.

ADMIRALTIES: Fifth Air Force B-25 Mitchells attack Momote on Los Negros Island and Lorengau on Manus Island.

NEW GUINEA: Fifth Air Force B-24 Liberators escorted by P-40s bomb airfields at Wewak. B-25 Mitchells bomb targets in the Hansa Bay area, and over 30 A-20 Havocs attack Alexishafen.

U.S. submarine *Cod* torpedoes and sinks a Japanese cargo ship near Halmahera.

February 28

CBI: The Marauders arrive at Tanja Ga and are ordered to Walawbum at the southern end of the Hukwang valley to cut the Kamaing road south of Walawbum and threaten the headquarters of the Japanese 18th Army.

Tenth Air Force B-24 Liberators bomb the Mandalay marshaling yard.

Fourteenth Air Force P-40s strafe the Myitkyina airfield.

ETO: Eighth Air Force attacks V-weapon sites in France. Bad weather over the targets minimizes effectiveness. The first target is hit by 49 B-24 Liberators with 61 P-47 Thunderbolts providing escort. One B-24 is damaged. On another raid, B-17s are sent, escorted by 81 P-38 Lightnings, 94 P-47 Thunderbolts, and 22 P-51 Mustangs. Only 109 of the 258 dispatched hit the primary target. Fighter pilots report one probable enemy aircraft destroyed on the ground. Seven B-17s are lost and 75 damaged. Aircrew losses are five wounded and 63 missing.

Ninth Air Force sends 180 B-26 Marauders to attack V-weapon sites, but bad weather also limits the effectiveness of the attack.

PACIFIC: U.S. submarine *Sand Lance* torpedoes and sinks a Japanese transport east of Musashi Wan, off Paramushiru, Kuriles. The submarine later runs aground off Paramushiru.

CENTRAL PACIFIC: Seventh Air Force P-40s from Makin Island bomb the runway and radio installation on Mille Atoll. B-25 Mitchells from Tarawa bomb the airfield on Wotje Atoll.

NEW BRITAIN: Thirteenth Air Force B-25 Mitchells, with fighter escort, bomb Rabaul and P-38 Lightnings make a follow-on attack a few minutes later. Shortly thereafter, 11 B-24 Liberators continue the bombing. P-39 Airacobras attack Monoitu Mission. B-24s also bomb Rapopo, while army P-40s and navy fighters escort SBD Dauntless dive-bombers in an attack on Wunapope.

ADMIRALTIES: Fifth Air Force sends over 50 B-25 Mitchells and B-24 Liberators to bomb Momote airfield on Los Negros Island and Lorengau on Manus Island.

NEW GUINEA: Fifth Air Force B-24 Liberators and A-20 Havocs attacks targets in the Hansa Bay area.

U.S. submarine *Balao* attacks a Japanese convoy and sinks a cargo ship and transport northwest of Manokwari.

February 29

CBI: In China, Fourteenth Air Force sends 23 B-24 Liberators and B-25 Mitchells to attack Yoyang. B-24 aircrews report fires and secondary explosions from supply warehouses. B-25 aircrews report damage to the railroad yards. The bombers are escorted by 16 P-40s.

ETO: Eighth Air Force sends B-17s to attack aircraft production facilities and B-24 Liberators to attack V-weapon sites. Of the 218 B-17s that hit the primary target over Brunswick, Germany, one bomber is lost and 54 are damaged. Aircrew losses are four wounded and 10 missing. Escorting the bombers are 61 P-38 Lightnings, 346 Eighth and Ninth Air Force P-47 Thunderbolts, and 147 Eighth and Ninth Air

Force P-51 Mustangs. The fighter pilots claim only one confirmed kill. Four fighters are lost and two are damaged. The four pilots are reported missing. There are no losses for the 38 B-24 Liberators that hit the primary target. One P-47 from the 79 P-47s escorting the bombers is lost. The pilot is reported as missing.

During the night, five B-17s drop leaflets over Orleans, Lille, Reims, Cambrai, and Chateauroux, France.

Ninth Air Force B-26 Marauders bomb a coastal gun position and the Breck-sur-Mer airfield in France.

ITALY: German forces attack the 3rd Infantry Division's defenses at Anzio in an attempt to crush the center of the Allied line. At Carano, units of the 509th Parachute Infantry, the 30th Infantry, and the 7th Infantry, supported by tanks and artillery, hold the German attack. Allied artillery fires about 66,000 shells during the attack and 247 fighter bombers and 24 light bombers attack German troop and tank concentrations. The 504th Parachute Infantry, the 1st Special Service Force, and the Rangers turn back a diversionary attack on the right flank of the beachhead at the Mussolini Canal.

Twelfth Air Force B-26 Marauders bomb the airfields at Viterbo, while B-25 Mitchells bomb troops and gun positions near Cisterna. P-40s, A-36 Intruder (Apache) fighter-bombers, and A-20 Havocs attack German troop concentrations around the Anzio beachhead. P-40s attack targets at Littoria and a German tank assembly area near Cisterna.

A U.S. LST is damaged by German shore battery fire off Anzio.

PACIFIC: Navy PB4Y-1 Privateers from Apamama, and staging through Kwajalein and Roi, conduct out low-level bombing raid on Wake Island.

During the night U.S. submarine *Rock* makes a surface attack on a three-ship convoy and is damaged by surface gunfire southeast of Okinawa and is forced to terminate her patrol.

CENTRAL PACIFIC: U.S. submarine *Sargo* attacks a Japanese convoy and damages a cargo ship near Palau.

U.S. submarine *Trout* attacks a Japanese convoy headed for Guam, sinking a transport southeast of Okinawa and damaging another transport. USS *Trout* is sunk shortly after the attack.

NEW BRITAIN: Thirteenth Air Force B-25 Mitchells, with navy fighter escort, bomb targets around Rabaul. This attack is followed by P-38 Lightnings attacking the same targets.

Destroyer Division 44 (Commander James R. Pahl) bombards wharf areas and installations at Rabaul.

ADMIRALTIES, LOS NEGROS: Operation Brewer. Rear Admiral William M. Fechteler's Naval Task Group 76.1, with nine destroyers and three high-speed transports, lands the 2nd Squadron 5th Cavalry at Hayne Harbor on Los Negros in the midst of a heavy rainfall and after an air and naval bombardment. Two light cruisers and four destroyers of Task Force 74 bombard Japanese positions on Los Negros and Manus.

The first troops ashore rapidly advance and capture Momote airfield. MacArthur lands on shore, walks up to Lieutenant Marvin J. Henshaw, and pins the Distinguished

Service Cross on him. The Americans pull back off the airfield to a smaller and more defensible perimeter. Later that night the Japanese attack the American positions, threatening to overwhelm the small force.

Fifth Air Force B-24 Liberators and B-25 Mitchells make limited attacks on Japanese positions due to bad weather over the island.

NEW GUINEA: Fifth Air Force B-24 Liberators and A-20 Havocs bomb Wewak and Hollandia.

March 1

ALEUTIANS: Eleventh Air Force's XI Strategic Air Force (Provisional) is activated at Shemya Island. The command's subordinate units are the XI Bomber Command and XI Fighter Command, both located at Near Island.

CBI: One regiment of the Chinese 30th Division leaves Ledo for Shingbwiyang. The 93rd Fighter Squadron, 81st Fighter Group arrives at Karachi, India, from Italy. The squadron will be equipped with P-47D Thunderbolts and will fly its first mission in mid-August. Tenth Air Force P-40s attack the Myitkyina airfield.

In China, Fourteenth Air Force sends 14 B-25 Mitchells and 16 P-40s to attack targets around Nanchang.

ATLANTIC: In the North Atlantic, a U.S. destroyer escort sinks German submarine *U-603* and, in coordination with two destroyers, sinks *U-709* as well.

ETO: The Ninth Air Force's IX Troop Carrier Command establishes a Pathfinder school to provide pre-invasion training to paratroopers in all navigational aids for guiding planes to the drop zones.

The P-47 Thunderbolts of the 390th Fighter Squadron, 366th Fighter Group arrive from the United States. The squadron's first mission will be in mid-March.

ITALY: German attacks against the 7th and 15th Infantry of the 3rd Infantry Division defending the line south of Cisterna at Anzio fail to gain any ground.

Twelfth Air Force P-40s attack gun positions and vehicles.

CENTRAL PACIFIC: Seventh Air Force A-24s and P-40s from Makin Island attack Jaluit and Mille Atolls in the Marshalls. B-25 Mitchells bomb Maloelap Atoll.

BOUGAINVILLE: Thirteenth Air Force B-24 Liberators bomb Kahili and P-39 Airacobras bomb and strafe Monoitu Mission.

ADMIRALTIES, LOS NEGROS: Alamo Force commander Lieutenant General Walter Krueger, anticipating trouble, orders immediate reinforcements from the remainder of the 5th Cavalry to Los Negros.

Fifth Air Force B-24 Liberators and B-25 Mitchells bomb Los Negros Island and Lorengau on Manus Island.

NEW GUINEA: Over 100 army aircraft and Royal Australian Air Force aircraft participate in an attack on Hansa Bay, Madang, Alexishafen, and Wewak.

March 2

CBI: The Chinese 22nd and 38th Divisions attack Japanese forces near Maingkwan. The Marauders begin a flanking movement in an attempt to block the line of retreat at Walawbum. Japanese forces fail to drive the Americans off.

Tenth Air Force P-40s attack a fuel storage area at Myitkyina, artillery at Shingban, and trucks on a road near Walawbum.

ETO: Eighth Air Force sends 327 B-17s and 154 B-24 Liberators against the Frankfurt am Main marshaling yard. The PFF system fails and many of the bombers miss the primary target. A total of 136 bombers hit the primary target. Aircrews report two confirmed kills. Eight B-17s and one B-24 are lost. Aircrew losses are 17 killed, nine wounded, and 91 missing. Fighter escort is provided by 33 P-38 Lightnings, 445 Eighth and Ninth Air Force P-47 Thunderbolts, and 111 P-51 Mustangs. Fighter pilots report 17 confirmed kills and two probables. Three fighters are lost and 10 are damaged. Three pilots are reported as missing.

Over the air depot at Chartres, France, 84 of 106 B-17s hit the primary target, escorted by 89 P-38 Lightnings, 145 Eighth and Ninth Air Force P-47 Thunderbolts, and 47 Ninth Air Force P-51 Mustangs. One bomber is lost and 12 are damaged. Aircrew losses are one wounded and 10 missing. Fighter pilots report two enemy aircraft destroyed on the ground. One P-38 is shot down.

During the night, five B-17s drop leaflets over Caen, Amiens, Rouen, Chartres, and Rennes in France.

Ninth Air Force sends B-26 Marauders to attack V-weapon sites and airfields.

MEDITERRANEAN: Lieutenant General Alexander M. Patch is selected as commander of the Seventh Army, which will conduct Anvil/Dragoon, the invasion of southern France.

The 459th Bombardment Group (Heavy) with B-24 Liberators becomes operational, giving the Fifteenth Air Force 13 heavy bomber groups.

ITALY: Fifteenth Air Force sends 241 B-24 Liberators and 100 B-17s, with 113 P-38 Lightnings and 63 P-47 Thunderbolts, to attack German positions in front of the 3rd Infantry Division at Anzio. The bombing attacks limit the effectiveness of the enemy's attack against the 7th Infantry.

Twelfth Air Force B-26 Marauders attack an assembly area near Carroceto. B-26s and B-25 Mitchells bomb enemy positions near Cisterna. P-40s, A-36 Intruder (Apache) fighter-bombers, and A-20 Havocs attack German troops at Cisterna and Littoria.

SOUTHWEST PACIFIC AREA: U.S. submarine *Narwhal* delivers ammunition and supplies and evacuates personnel on Mindanao in the Philippines.

CENTRAL PACIFIC: Seventh Air Force B-25 Mitchells bomb Maloelap Atoll. B-24s from Makin and Abemama Islands bomb Ponape and Kusaie Islands in the Carolines.

U.S. submarine *Burrfish* attacks a Japanese cargo ship south of Truk, but fails to damage it; the USS *Picuda* follows with a torpedo attack that sinks the cargo ship.

BOUGAINVILLE: Thirteenth Air Force P-39 Airacobras attack Japanese positions at Piano and Monoitu Missions.

The 67th Fighter Squadron, 347th Fighter Group, based in the Russell Islands, redeploys to Bougainville Island. The squadron will transition from P-39 Airacobras to P-38 Lightnings.

NEW BRITAIN: Thirteenth Air Force B-25 Mitchells bomb Rabaul and Rapopo. B-24 Liberators conduct a follow-on attack on Rabaul. Minutes later, 14 P-38 Lightnings follow the bombers with another strike.

NEW IRELAND: Navy SBD Dauntless dive-bombers and TBF Avengers damage a small Japanese cargo vessel near Rabaul.

ADMIRALTIES, LOS NEGROS: The Momote airfield is occupied as 5th Cavalry troopers expand their perimeter. Japanese infiltrators attack during the night. The 40th Seabee Battalion fights as infantry to repel attacks. Additional artillery is also landed.

Fifth Air Force sends more than 60 B-25 Mitchells and A-20 Havocs to attack Japanese positions on the island. The bombers are escorted by P-47 Thunderbolts. The fighter pilots report seven Japanese fighters shot down.

NEW GUINEA: Fifth Air Force B-24 Liberators and P-40s attack targets near Hansa Bay area and around Madang and Alexishafen.

March 3

ALEUTIANS: Eleventh Air Force sends nine B-24 Liberators from Shemya Island to search for enemy shipping and six P-40s search between Shemya and halfway to Attu. Bad weather and dangerous flying conditions limit the missions. Headquarters XI Bomber Command moves from Adak Island to Shemya Island.

CBI: The Marauders block the road to Walawbum. A battalion of troops from the Chinese 65th Regiment attacks Japanese defenses at Maingkwan, supported by tanks of the 1st Provisional Tank Group. Lagang Ga is cleared for a landing strip.

Tenth Air Force P-40s, A-36 Intruder (Apache) fighter-bombers, P-51 Mustangs, and B-25 Mitchells attack logistics and transportation targets.

ATLANTIC: President Roosevelt announces that ships of the Italian fleet will be distributed among the United States, Great Britain, and the Soviet Union.

ETO: Eighth Air Force sends 555 B-17s and 193 B-24 Liberators against industrial targets and aircraft production facilities at Berlin, Erkner, and Oranienburg. Bad weather forces most of the bombers to abort the mission. Eleven bombers are lost. Aircrews report three confirmed kills and one probable. Aircrew losses are five killed, 11 wounded, and 103 missing. The mission is escorted by 89 P-38 Lightnings, 484 Eighth and Ninth Air Force P-47 Thunderbolts, and 130 Eighth and Ninth Air Force P-51 Mustangs. Seven fighters are lost and 15 are damaged. Pilots report eight confirmed kills and one probable. One pilot is wounded and six are reported as missing.

During the night, two B-24s are lost during a Carpetbagger mission.

Ninth Air Force sends 218 B-26 Marauders to bomb airfields and military installations in France.

ITALY: The 3rd Infantry Division begins local counterattacks from the Anzio beachhead. The Germans have lost 3,500 men and 30 tanks in five days of fighting. With its forces used up, the German Fourteenth Army goes on the defensive.

Fifteenth Air Force sends over 200 B-17s and B-24 Liberators with over 50 P-47 Thunderbolts as escort to bomb the marshaling yards at Rome, Littorio, and Tiburtina. B-24s also bomb air facilities at Canino, Viterbo and Fabrica di Roma.

At Anzio, Twelfth Air Force P-40s attack gun positions and A-36 Intruder (Apache) fighter-bombers attack targets between Magliano Romano and Rome.

SOUTHWEST PACIFIC AREA: U.S. submarine *Narwhal* torpedoes and damages a Japanese river gunboat in the Sulu Sea, as it searches for an American submarine.

PACIFIC: Navy Task Force 94, commanded by Rear Admiral Wilder D. Baker, with one light cruiser and eight destroyers, begins a two-day sweep of the Kuriles. Weather conditions force the mission to be cancelled. All TF 94 ships are damaged by heavy weather.

U.S. submarine *Sand Lance* attacks a Japanese convoy and sinks a transport west of Uruppu Island in the Kuriles. The *Sand Lance* later torpedoes and sinks a Soviet cargo ship *Belorussia*, believing it to be a Japanese ship.

CENTRAL PACIFIC: Seventh Air Force B-24 Liberators out of Makin Island bomb Ponape Island. B-25 Mitchells from Tarawa bomb Maloelap Atoll.

NEW BRITAIN: Thirteenth Air Force P-40s and navy fighters support an SBD Dauntless dive-bomber attack on Rabaul. This is followed by 24 B-25 Mitchells and 20 B-24 Liberators attacking the same target.

ADMIRALTIES, LOS NEGROS: The Japanese attack the American perimeter throughout the night. The destroyer U.S. *Mullany* provides point-blank fire support to the infantry. Over 750 Japanese are killed. U.S. casualties are 61 killed.

Fifth Air Force supports the ground forces with 14 A-20 Havocs and B-25 Mitchells attacking enemy positions.

NEW GUINEA: Fifth Air Force B-24 Liberators bomb targets near Hansa Bay and Alexishafen. P-39 Airacobras attack Madang.

U.S. submarine *Rasher* attacks a Japanese convoy in Celebes Sea, sinking an army transport off Halmahera.

March 4

CBI: In Burma, the 3rd and 2nd Battalions of the Marauders complete roadblocks on the Kamaing Road. The Japanese unsuccessfully attack the 3rd Battalion, now in established defensive positions.

In China, Fourteenth Air Force B-25 Mitchells and 23 P-40s (16 of them Chinese) attack Kiungshan airfield. Aircrews report heavy damage. Fighter pilots report 17 Japanese aircraft shot down. Japanese aircraft bomb the airfield at Suichwan and cause major damage. B-25 Mitchells and P-40s attack industrial and transportation targets in French Indochina.

ETO: Eighth Air Force sends over 500 B-17 bombers escorted by 86 P-38 Lightnings, 563 Eighth and Ninth Air Force P-47 Thunderbolts, and 121 Eighth and Ninth Air Force P-51 Mustangs against industrial targets in Berlin. Bad weather prevents about half from hitting the primary targets. Fifteen bombers are lost and 121 damaged. Aircrew losses are three killed, 11 wounded, and 141 missing. Fighter pilots report eight confirmed kills and three probables. U.S. losses are 24 fighters shot down and eight damaged. Two pilots are killed and 22 are missing.

Bad weather aborts a Ninth Air Force mission against airfields in France.

PACIFIC: In the South China Sea, U.S. submarine *Bluefish* attacks a Japanese convoy, sinking an oiler and escaping during a depth-charge attack.

CENTRAL PACIFIC: Seventh Air Force P-40s from Makin Island bomb and strafe runways at Mille Atoll. B-25 Mitchells from Tarawa bomb the airfield at Wotje Atoll.

NEW BRITAIN: Thirteenth Air Force P-40s and navy fighters and dive-bombers attack Rabaul.

ADMIRALTIES, LOS NEGROS: The 2nd Squadron 7th Cavalry arrives on the island after a preparatory bombardment. Fifth Air Force A-20 Havocs and B-25 Mitchells attack Japanese positions.

Navy Task Force 74, commanded by Rear Admiral Victor A. C. Crutchley (RN), with an Australian heavy cruiser, two U.S. light cruisers, and four U.S. destroyers, bombards Japanese shore batteries and positions in the Admiralty Islands.

Sergeant Troy A. McGill leads a squad in G Troop, 5th Cavalry Regiment, 1st Cavalry Division. His men are suddenly attacked near dawn by over 200 Japanese soldiers. McGill, with eight men, holds for only a short time until only one other trooper is still standing. Sergeant McGill orders the man to safety while he continues the fight, firing his rifle until it ceases to function. Without hesitation Sergeant McGill attacks the onrushing Japanese, using his rifle as a club and fighting with great ferocity until he is killed. More than 100 dead enemy soldiers lie around his squad's position. For his heroism and leadership Sergeant McGill will be awarded the Medal of Honor.

NEW GUINEA: Fifth Air Force B-24 Liberators bomb airfields at Wewak. Other B-24s bomb Hollandia and A-20 Havocs bomb targets in the Saidor area.

U.S. submarine *Peto* attacks a Japanese convoy, and sinks a cargo ship off Hollandia. The enemy depth-charge attack is ineffective.

March 5

CBI: The Japanese conduct several unsuccessful attacks on defensive positions of the 2nd Battalion of Merrill's Marauders. To avoid fighting an increasingly stronger enemy force, the 2nd Battalion withdraws to the 3rd Battalion location near the Numpyek River at Wesu Ga.

The Chinese force the Japanese out of Maingkwan, and guerrillas from Detachment 101 ambush Japanese forces as they retreat. Elements of the 1st Provisional Tank Group encounter the headquarters of the Japanese 18th Division.

During the night, Colonel Philip G. Cochran's Air Commando Unit flies Major General Orde C. Wingate's Chindits by glider into an area about 50 miles northeast of Indaw in central Burma to raid Japanese lines of communication. U.S. engineer troops land first to prepare the landing zone, code-named Broadway. Of the 67 gliders launched on the mission, 32 reach Broadway. These gliders land 539 men and nearly 66,000 pounds of supplies.

Tenth Air Force B-25 Mitchells, A-36 Intruder (Apache) fighter-bombers, P-51 Mustangs, and P-40s attack targets in Shingban and Myitkyina.

ETO: Eighth Air Force sends 219 B-24 Liberators, escorted by 34 P-38 Lightnings, 185 P-47 Thunderbolts, and 88 Eighth and Ninth Air Force P-51 Mustangs, to attack a number of airfields in France. Bad weather forces most of the bombers to abort the mission. Aircrews report 14 confirmed kills and two probables. Four B-24s are lost and 23 are damaged. Aircrew losses are one wounded and 35 missing. Fighter pilots report 14 confirmed kills. Five fighters are lost and five are damaged. Two pilots are killed, two are wounded, and five are missing.

During the night, five B-17s drop leaflets over Le Mans, Paris, Orleans, and Reims. A Carpetbagger mission in support of resistance fighters is also flown.

Ninth Air Force sends 217 B-26 Marauders to attack V-weapon sites in France.

ITALY: Twelfth Air Force P-40s attack Pontecorvo and A-36 Intruder (Apache) fighter-bombers attack Formia.

SOUTHWEST PACIFIC AREA: U.S. submarine *Narwhal* delivers cargo and evacuates personnel from the Philippines.

U.S. submarine *Rasher,* continuing its pursuit of a Japanese convoy in the Celebes Sea, torpedoes and damages a cargo ship.

CENTRAL PACIFIC: Seventh Air Force P-40s from Makin Island attack the runways and airfield installations at Mille Atoll. B-25 Mitchells bomb Maloelap and Mille Atolls.

NEW BRITAIN: Thirteenth Air Force sends 22 B-25 Mitchells with navy fighter escort to bomb Simpson Harbor. B-24 Liberators bomb Rabaul and the airfield at Tobera. P-38 Lightnings attack Borpop airfield.

ADMIRALTIES, LOS NEGROS: Major General Innis P. Swift, the 1st Cavalry Division commander, lands on the island to lead the final phase of the operation.

Fifth Air Force sends 30 B-24 Liberators to bomb enemy positions on the island.

March 6

CBI: The Marauders meet elements of the Chinese 38th Division. Over the past three days the Marauders have lost eight killed and 36 wounded. Japanese casualties are estimated at 800 killed. The Japanese abandon Walawbum to defend Kamaing, the major logistics and support base for the Fourteenth Army now fighting at Kohima and Imphal. First Lieutenant James L. Tilly and his section of Kachin Rangers ambushes Japanese supply lines.

Tenth Air Force P-40s attack supply sites near Walawbum.

ETO: Eighth Air Force sends 504 B-17s and 226 B-24 Liberators, escorted by 86 P-38 Lightnings, 615 Eighth and Ninth Air Force P-47 Thunderbolts, and 100 Eighth and Ninth Air Force P-51 Mustangs, to attack industrial facilities in the suburbs of Berlin. The bombers hit mostly secondary targets or targets of opportunity. Bomber losses are the highest yet for a single day: 53 B-17s are lost and 298 damaged; 16 B-24s are lost and 55 damaged. Aircrew losses are 17 killed, 31 wounded, and 686 missing. Fighter pilots report 82 confirmed kills in the air, one on the ground, and eight probables. Eleven fighters are lost and nine damaged. Two pilots are wounded and 11 are missing.

During the night, five B-17s drop leaflets over Nantes, Cambrai, Lille, Chateauroux, and Lorient in France. A Carpetbagger mission in support of the resistance fighters is also flown.

Ninth Air Force sends 260 B-26 Marauders to bomb V-weapon sites and airfields in France.

The 93rd and 94th Troop Carrier Squadrons of the 439th Troop Carrier Group and the 510th and 511th Fighter-Bomber Squadrons, 405th Fighter-Bomber Group with P-47 Thunderbolts, arrive in England from the United States.

MEDITERRANEAN: Convoy UGS 33 (United States to Mediterranean, Slow) headed to Alexandria, Egypt, hits an Allied minefield off Tunis. One U.S. freighter is sunk and another freighter is heavily damaged.

ITALY: Twelfth Air Force P-40s attack German gun positions north of the Anzio beachhead and near Littoria, and bomb Frosinone.

SOUTHWEST PACIFIC AREA: General MacArthur accepts Reno IV, a plan that proposes an offensive along western New Guinea, followed by a strike north to Mindanao in the Philippines. From Mindanao, U.S. forces will be in position to move into the China-Formosa area. A long-range bomber offensive against Japan can be launched from Luzon. With the Reno IV plan, MacArthur is determined not to take a secondary role to the navy and uses the recapture of the Philippines as the focus of the American strategic bombing campaign against Japan rather than the Mariana Islands. He also believes that the recapture of the Philippines is essential to the restoration of American honor.

CENTRAL PACIFIC: Seventh Air Force A-24 Banshees and P-40s from Makin Island attack the airfield on Mille Atoll. B-25 Mitchells from Tarawa bomb the airfield at Wotje Atoll.

U.S. submarine *Nautilus* attacks a Japanese convoy near Saipan and sinks a transport. A Japanese torpedo boat makes an unsuccessful attack on the *Nautilus.*

BOUGAINVILLE: Thirteenth Air Force P-39 Airacobras attack Monoitu Mission.

NEW BRITAIN: The 5th Marines land on the west coast of Willaumez Peninsula and locate a large Japanese force, which is consolidating after the retreat from western New Britain. The 1st and 2nd Battalions of the 5th Marines land and, supported by tanks, move inland. Two tanks are immediately disabled, one by mud and another by mines. Fifth Air Force P-39 Airacobras and P-38 Lightnings from Cape Gloucester airfield strafe and bomb the Cape Hoskins-Talasea area. Japanese mortar attacks on the beachhead kill nine marine artillerymen and wound 39 others.

Thirteenth Air Force B-25 Mitchells with fighter escort bomb Tobera.

NEW IRELAND: Thirteenth Air Force B-24 Liberators and P-38 Lightnings bomb Kavieng and Panapai airfield.

ADMIRALTIES, LOS NEGROS: The 2nd Squadron 7th Cavalry (2/7 Cavalry) attacks north to protect the flank of the 12th Cavalry Regiment, which attacks with artillery, tanks, and engineers attached to capture Salami Plantation and Salami beach. The 12th Cavalry has just landed that morning and is to assist the 2/7 Cavalry in opening Seeadler Harbor to prepare for additional landings.

Fifth Air Force B-25 Mitchells bomb Japanese positions.

A destroyer in TF 74 is damaged by Japanese guns at the mouth of Seeadler Bay.

NEW GUINEA: Fifth Air Force P-39 Airacobras attack Madang,

March 7

CBI: At Walawbum, the Chinese 22nd Division, reinforced by Marauders and supported by tanks from the 1st Provisional Tank Group, breaks the front lines of the Japanese 18th Division. They recapture jeeps, armored cars, and trucks that had been captured from the British at Rangoon in 1942. They also acquire the official seal of the 18th Division. About 2,500 Marauders are still fit for combat.

Tenth Air Force P-51 Mustangs and A-36 Intruder (Apache) fighter-bombers attack targets of opportunity from Walawbum to Shaduzup, and two B-25 Mitchells attack troop concentrations northwest of Shaduzup.

ETO: Ninth Air Force sends 112 B-26 Marauders and 18 A-20 Havocs to attack V-weapon sites, military installations, and targets of opportunity in France.

The headquarters of the 371st Fighter Group and the 404th, 405th, and 406th Fighter Squadrons arrive in England from the United States. The squadrons, equipped with P-47 Thunderbolts, will fly their first mission in mid-April. The headquarters of the 405th Fighter-Bomber Group and 509th Fighter-Bomber Squadron arrive with P-47 Thunderbolts. The squadron's first mission is in mid-April. The headquarters of the 409th Bombardment Group (Light) and the 640th, 641st, and 643rd Bombardment Squadrons (Light) arrive with A-20 Havocs and their first mission will be in mid-April. The Ninth Air Force receives the 422nd Night Fighter Squadron with P-61 Black Widow night fighters. Its first mission is scheduled for early July.

MEDITERRANEAN: Fifteenth Air Force sends B-17s to attack the submarine base at Toulon, France. B-24 Liberators bomb marshaling yards and air depots in Italy. P-47 Thunderbolts and P-38 Lightnings fly escort.

ITALY: Twelfth Air Force P-40s attack enemy positions at Anzio. A-36 Intruder (Apache) fighter-bombers hit transportation targets.

SOUTHWEST PACIFIC AREA: SWPA headquarters notifies Alamo Force to prepare plans to seize Aitape and Hollandia. Aitape is 90 miles west-northwest of Wewak and has an airfield. Hollandia is a major Japanese base located on the coast of north-central New Guinea. General MacArthur is reading the Japanese military codes provided by Ultra. He realizes that Hollandia has few defenses against amphibious attack and the Japanese are anticipating an attack on Madang. In defending against the expected attack on Madang, the Japanese are moving fighter aircraft into Hollandia and preparing to defend Hansa Bay and Wewak. MacArthur plans to bypass these defenses completely and attack the Japanese where they least expect it.

CENTRAL PACIFIC: Seventh Air Force B-24 Liberators from Abemama Island bomb Kusaie Island and Jaluit Atoll. P-40s bomb the airfield at Mille Atoll. B-25 Mitchells bomb antiaircraft positions, storage areas, and barracks on Taroa Island in the Maloelap Atoll.

NEW BRITAIN: The Japanese defend Volupai plantation, especially the trails leading out, as they are the main routes of escape to Rabaul for the Japanese. The 2nd battalion 5th Marines attacks and pushes the enemy back along the trails.

Thirteenth Air Force sends 24 B-25 Mitchells with navy fighters to attack the airfield at Tobera. P-40s bomb and strafe Rabaul.

Fifth Air Force P-38 Lightnings attack targets in the Talasea area.

ADMIRALTIES, LOS NEGROS: The 2nd Squadron 12th Cavalry conducts an amphibious assault from Salami plantation to Papitalai mission. The 5th Cavalry occupies Porlaka.

Fifth Air Force B-24 Liberators and B-25 Mitchells attack Japanese positions.

Task Force 74 continues bombardment of Japanese defensive positions and shore batteries in the Admiralties.

NEW GUINEA: Japanese shore battery sinks a U.S. motor torpedo boat in Hansa Bay, New Guinea.

March 8

CBI: The JCS issues instructions to General Stilwell and Admiral Mountbatten establishing command and control relationships for the B-29 strategic bombing offensive against Japan called Operation Matterhorn. The JCS will be responsible for the direction of the Tenth and Fourteenth Air Forces, determining targets for Matterhorn strikes. Stilwell remains responsible for the defense of the B-29 bases in China, and Admiral Mountbatten for bases in the SEAC area. The targets are Japanese urban industrial areas, shipping, and aircraft production facilities. The oil fields in Sumatra, Netherlands East Indies, are designated as secondary targets.

Tenth Air Force B-24 Liberators mine waters off Thailand in the Gulf of Siam. A cargo ship is sunk.

ETO: Eighth Air Force sends 414 B-17s and 209 B-24 Liberators, escorted by 104 P-38 Lightnings, 613 Eighth and Ninth Air Force P-47 Thunderbolts, and 174 Eighth and Ninth Air Force P-51 Mustangs, to attack a ball bearing plant at Erkner, a suburb of Berlin. Of the 320 B-17s and 150 B-24 Liberators that hit the primary target, 28 B-17s and nine B-24s are lost and one B-17 and two B-24s are damaged. Aircrews report 63 confirmed kills and 17 probables. Aircrew losses are four killed, 14 wounded, and 364 missing. Fighter pilots report 87 confirmed kills and 12 probables in the air as well as eight confirmed kills and four probables on the ground. Eighteen fighters are lost and 23 are damaged. Pilot losses are three killed, two wounded, and 18 missing.

The B-24s of the 786th Bombardment Squadron (Heavy), 466th Bombardment Group (Heavy) arrive in England from the United States. The squadron's first mission is late March.

Ninth Air Force sends over 225 B-26 Marauders to attack Volkel and Soesterberg airfields in the Netherlands. Headquarters 303rd Fighter Wing and the 95th, 97th, and 98th Troop Carrier Squadrons of the 440th Troop Carrier Group arrive in England from the United States. The squadrons are equipped with C-47s.

ITALY: Twelfth Air Force B-25 Mitchells and B-26 Marauders attack transportation targets. P-40 fighter-bombers, A-36 Intruder (Apache) fighter-bombers, and P-47 Thunderbolts attack targets around Rome.

SOUTHWEST PACIFIC AREA: MacArthur submits his Reno IV plan to the JCS. The plan focuses on an attack on Mindanao in November 1944, followed by an attack on Luzon in January 1945.

PACIFIC: In the South China Sea, U.S. submarine *Lapon* attacks a Japanese convoy southeast of Hong Kong and damages a cargo ship.

CENTRAL PACIFIC: Japanese aircraft bomb logistics storage areas on Engebi Island at Eniwetok.

BOUGAINVILLE: A Japanese force of about 19,000 soldiers converges from all over the island to attack the 23,000-yard perimeter of General Oscar W. Griswold's XIV Corps. About 27,000 infantrymen of the American Division, commanded by General John R. Hodge, and 37th Infantry Division, commanded by Major General Robert S. Beightler, have established strong defensive positions with mines, bunkers, trenches, and barbed wire. Artillery, air, and naval gunfire support is also available.

The XIV Corps defensive position is anchored on Hill 700 (defended by the 145th Infantry Regiment, 37th Infantry Division) in the center and Hill 260 (defended by the 182nd Infantry Regiment of the Americal Division) on the east side of the crescent-shaped perimeter. During the night the Japanese attack Hill 700, but are stopped.

NEW BRITAIN: As the 1st Battalion 5th Marines struggles forward through thick jungle and muddy ravines, the 2nd Battalion occupies Bitokara Mission after the Japanese abandon the position. The battalion pushes forward and occupies an abandoned airstrip. Patrols run into heavy resistance near Mount Schleuther.

Thirteenth Air Force B-24 Liberators and B-25 Mitchells, along with P-40s and P-39 Airacobras, attack Rabaul.

ADMIRALTIES, LOS NEGROS: The 2nd Squadron 7th Cavalry eliminates the last Japanese stronghold protecting Seeadler Harbor.

Fifth Air Force B-25 Mitchells conduct several low-level strikes supporting the capture of Lombrun plantation.

March 9

CBI: Tenth Air Force B-24 Liberators, P-51 Mustangs, and P-40s attack Japanese supply sites and the road bridge at Kamaing. P-51s, P-40s, and A-36 Intruder (Apache) fighter-bombers support Chinese ground forces at Walawbum and Shaduzup.

In China, Fourteenth Air Force B-25 Mitchells and 24 Chinese P-40s of the Chinese-American Composite Wing (CACW) attack industrial and transportation targets at Shihhweiyao.

ATLANTIC: German submarine *U-255* torpedoes destroyer escort *Leopold* 650 miles west of Scotland. The ship is badly damaged and later scuttled.

ETO: Eighth Air Force sends 361 B-17s and 165 B-24 Liberators against targets in Berlin, escorted by 83 P-38 Lightnings, 572 Eighth and Ninth Air Force P-47 Thunderbolts, and 153 Eighth and Ninth Air Force P-51 Mustangs. Of the 339 B-17s that hit the target, six are lost and one damaged. Of the 150 B-24s that hit secondary targets, two are lost and one damaged. Aircrew losses are 10 killed, 18 wounded, and 63 missing. One fighter is lost and three are damaged. One pilot is killed, one wounded, and one missing.

The B-24s of the 784th, 785th, and 787th Bombardment Squadrons (Heavy), 466th Bombardment Group (Heavy), arrive in England from the United States. The squadrons will fly their first mission in late March.

ITALY: Fifteenth Air Force receives Headquarters, 463rd Bombardment Group (Heavy), from the United States.

Twelfth Air Force B-25 Mitchells bomb a bridge at Montalto di Castro. A-20 Havocs attack a tank repair depot near Tivoli, and P-40s attack German gun positions near Campoleone.

German submarine *U-450* is sunk by a U.S. destroyer off Anzio.

PACIFIC: In the South China Sea, USS *Lapon* continues its attack on the Japanese convoy it encountered previously, sinking a cargo ship that is towing the cargo ship that *Lapon* damaged the previous day.

CENTRAL PACIFIC: Seventh Air Force B-25 Mitchells based on Abemama Island attack Taroa Island, Maloelap Atoll. B-24 Liberators from Tarawa attack Ponape and Kusaie Islands.

BOUGAINVILLE: The Japanese attack Hill 700 again, seizing a key position and making a small penetration in the defensive line. SBD Dauntless dive-bombers and TBF Avengers from the 1st Marine Air Wing support the defense. Despite heavy artillery fire and repeated counterattacks for two days, the Japanese hold the position.

Thirteenth Air Force B-25 Mitchells bomb Japanese installations on the hills beyond Empress Augusta Bay.

NEW BRITAIN: The 1/5 and 2/5 Marines, advancing to the attack, discover the enemy has abandoned Mount Schleuther.

Thirteenth Air Force sends 24 B-25 Mitchells along with over 40 P-39 Airacobras and P-40s to bomb the docks at Simpson Harbor at Rabaul, followed by 19 B-24 Liberators, which bomb Rabaul and the airfields.

ADMIRALTIES, LOS NEGROS: The 2nd Brigade (7th and 8th Cavalry Regiments), 1st Cavalry Division, commanded by Brigadier General Verne Mudge, arrives at Seeadler Harbor on Los Negros. The brigade is ordered to seize Manus Island.

Fifth Air Force B-25 Mitchells bomb Lorengau and other targets on Manus Island.

March 10

CBI: General Joseph Stilwell's Northern Combat Area Command headquarters approves General Merrill's plan to gain control of the Moguang Valley by making a flanking movement south to cut the Kamaing Road. The movement will be supported by two regiments of the Chinese 38th Division. The 1st Battalion of the Marauders and a Chinese regiment will move to Shaduzup; the 2nd and 3rd Battalions will move south of Shaduzup to Inkangahtawng, followed by another Chinese regiment. Meanwhile, the 22nd and 38th Chinese Divisions and elements of the 1st Provisional Tank Group will attack along the main road toward Kamaing.

Tenth Air Force B-24 Liberators and B-25 Mitchells bomb Kamaing. P-40s, P-51 Mustangs, and P-38 Lightnings hit Japanese near Walawbum.

In China, Fourteenth Air Force sends six B-24 Liberators to bomb the docks at Kowloon.

ETO: During the night five Eighth Air Force B-17s drop leaflets over Brussels, Antwerp, Ghent, and Monceau-sur-Sambre, Belgium.

Ninth Air Force receives the B-26 Marauders of the 585th Bombardment Squadron (Medium), 394th Bombardment Group (Medium), from the United States. The squadron's first mission will be in late March. The 96th Troop Carrier Squadron, 440th Troop Carrier Group, with C-47s arrives in England from the United States.

MEDITERRANEAN: German submarine *U-952* torpedoes and sinks a U.S. freighter off Palermo, Sicily. An Italian destroyer, acting as escort, makes no effort to respond to the attack.

ITALY: Twelfth Air Force B-26 Marauders and B-25 Mitchells bomb rail targets. P-40s and A-36 Intruder (Apache) fighter-bombers attack German positions near Littoria and guns and tanks at Cisterna.

CENTRAL PACIFIC: Seventh Air Force A-24s and P-40s from Makin Island and B-25 Mitchells from Tarawa attack airfields, antiaircraft positions, and radio installations at Mille and Wotje Atolls. B-25 Mitchells, operating out of Engebi Island in Eniwetok Atoll, bomb Kusaie Island.

BOUGAINVILLE: The Japanese make an early morning attack on Hill 260, a strongpoint outside of the Americal Division's main defensive line, occupied by 80 men and divided into two positions, North Knob and South Knob. South Knob is captured in the attack except for six Americans who hold out in a bunker and resist all attempts to finish them off. General Oscar W. Griswold, the XIV Corps commander, orders the 182nd Infantry Regiment,
Americal Division, to hold Hill 260 at all costs. A counterattack fails to drive the Japanese off the hill.

A portion of Hill 260, where the Americal Division's 182nd Infantry Regiment fought for nine days against a Japanese attempt to take this position. Company E of the 182nd won a Distinguished Unit Citation for its heroic defense of this ground.

Thirteenth Air Force B-25 Mitchells bomb Japanese positions and P-39 Airacobras attack targets at Kepiai Plantation.

NEW BRITAIN: Thirteenth Air Force B-24 Liberators bomb Rabaul.

ADMIRALTIES: Fifth Air Force sends 11 B-25 Mitchells to bomb Lorengau and targets of opportunity on Manus Island.

NEW GUINEA: U.S. submarine *Bowfin* attacks a Japanese convoy in the Ceram Sea and damages a cargo ship.

March 11

ETO: Eighth Air Force sends 124 B-17s, escorted by 90 P-47 Thunderbolts and 50 P-51 Mustangs, to attack the marshaling yard at Munster, Germany. Of the 120 bombers that hit the primary target, one is lost and 24 are damaged. Ten crewmen are reported missing. Two P-51s are lost and two P-47s are damaged. Two pilots are reported missing.

Another raid by 51 B-24 Liberators, escorted by 40 P-38 Lightnings and 213 P-47 Thunderbolts, on V-weapon sites in France results in 34 bombers hitting the primary target. One bomber is damaged, two P-47s are lost, and three damaged. One pilot is wounded and two are reported as missing.

Headquarters of the 467th Bombardment Group (Heavy) and the 789th, 790th, and 791st Bombardment Squadrons (Heavy) arrive in England from the United States. The B-24-equipped squadrons will fly their first mission in mid-April.

Ninth Air Force sends 61 B-26 Marauders to bomb V-weapon sites in France.

Headquarters for the 53rd Troop Carrier Wing and Headquarters of the 440th Troop Carrier Group arrive from the United States. Headquarters for the 394th Bombardment Group (Medium) and the 484th, 586th, and 587th Bombardment Squadrons (Medium) arrive in England from the United States. The B-26-equipped squadrons will conduct their first mission in late March.

Over 100 B-17s, escorted by P-47 Thunderbolts, bomb the marshaling yard at Padua. B-24 Liberators bomb the marshaling yards at Pontassieve and Prato and the Iesi airfield.

Fifteenth Air Force sends over 100 B-24 Liberators, escorted by P-38 Lightnings, to bomb the harbor at Toulon, France.

B-17s of the 772nd Bombardment Squadron (Heavy), 463rd Bombardment Group (Heavy), arrive in Italy. The squadron's first mission is scheduled for mid-March.

Allied aircraft sink German submarines *U-380* and *U-410* near Toulon, France.

ITALY: Twelfth Air Force P-40s, A-36 Intruder (Apache) fighter-bombers, and P-47 Thunderbolt fighter-bombers attack a logistics depot, industrial sites, supply trains, and railroad facilities.

CENTRAL PACIFIC: Seventh Air Force B-24 Liberators, operating from Kwajalein Atoll, bomb Wake Island.

BOUGAINVILLE: The 2nd Battalion 148th Infantry Regiment (37th Infantry Division) supported by artillery fire attacks to recapture Hill 700, but fails to gain ground.

The Japanese reinforce Hill 260 and press the American defenders to a perimeter around North Knob. A counterattack by the 182nd Infantry of the Americal Division with flamethrowers allows the six trapped Americans to escape but makes no further progress to capture South Knob on Hill 260.

During the night the Japanese attack the 129th Infantry Regiment of the 37th Infantry Division defending positions west of Hill 700. This position is strongly defended and the Japanese make no gains.

Thirteenth Air Force P-40s and B-24 Liberators bomb Japanese positions.

NEW BRITAIN: As the 3/5 Marines land on the Willaumez Peninsula beachhead, patrols seek to locate the retreating Japanese.

Thirteenth Air Force B-24 Liberators and B-25 Mitchells, supported by P-38 Lightnings, bomb Rabaul.

ADMIRALTIES: The 5th Cavalry attacks Hill 260 on Los Negros Island and fails to capture the position.

Fifth Air Force sends 12 B-25 Mitchells to bomb Lorengau on Manus Island.

NEW GUINEA: A-20 Havocs and P-39 Airacobras attack targets in the Madang area. P-47 Thunderbolts attack targets in the Hansa Bay area.

U.S. submarine *Bowfin* torpedoes and sinks a Japanese cargo ship west of Halmahera Island.

March 12

CBI: The 1st Battalion of the Marauders moves south to cut the main road near Shaduzup as the Chinese 22nd and 38th Divisions advance. The Marauders have the Chinese 113th Regiment attached to them. The 2nd Battalion and 3rd Battalion of the Marauders move toward Inkangahtawng. The rest of the 3rd Battalion moves to block Japanese troop movement over the Chindwin River.

Tenth Air Force P-40s, A-36 Intruder (Apache) fighter-bombers, and P-51 Mustangs attack troops and supply sites near Kamaing and bomb the town of Shaduzup.

ATLANTIC: The JCS issues a directive declaring Formosa-China-Luzon to be the operational objectives in the Pacific for 1944, ordering Admiral Nimitz's staff to begin planning for the invasion of Formosa (Operation Causeway), scheduled for the spring of 1945.

The JCS orders offensive operations against Kavieng, New Ireland, cancelled, but allows seizure of the Mussa Islands or Emirau, north of Kavieng, as a substitute. Offensive operations to seize Hollandia in New Guinea are approved as outlined in MacArthur's Reno IV plan. Truk will be bypassed and the Mariana Islands will be captured by June 15, with the Palau Islands following in September. General MacArthur is to prepare plans for an invasion of Mindanao scheduled for November 15. The JCS sets February 15, 1945 as the date for a decision on whether to continue with the conquest of the Philippines by capturing Luzon, or to conduct operations to capture Formosa. The JCS maintains its two-pronged offensive plan, which was first laid out in May 1943, but does not indicate whether the Philippines will be liberated as the main effort (MacArthur's plan) or bypassed in favor of a main effort directed against Formosa (Nimitz's plan).

ETO: Eighth Air Force sends 52 B-24 Liberators against a V-weapon site in France. Of the 46 bombers that hit the primary target, one is lost and 26 are damaged. Only one crewman is wounded.

Eighth Air Force receives the B-24s of the 788th Bombardment Squadron (Heavy), 467th Bombardment Group (Heavy), from the United States. The squadron will fly its first mission in mid-April.

Ninth Air Force receives Headquarters, 474th Fighter Group, and the 428th, 429th, and 430th Fighter Squadrons. The squadrons, equipped with P-38 Lightnings, will fly their first mission in late April.

ITALY: The light cruisers USS *Philadelphia* and USS *Brooklyn* provide gunfire support at Anzio.

PACIFIC: The JCS instructs Admiral Nimitz to plan for offensive operations to occupy the Palau Islands beginning September 8, 1944. The operation is called Stalemate.

U.S. submarine *Flying Fish* torpedoes and sinks a Japanese cargo ship southeast of the Ryukyu Islands.

BOUGAINVILLE: The 148th Infantry Regiment captures Hill 700 after methodically attacking the captured pillboxes on the hill one at a time with grenades, flame-throwers, and bazookas. Over 300 Japanese soldiers are found dead on the hill.

The 182nd Infantry Regiment supported by infantry companies from the 132nd Infantry attacks again to capture South Knob on Hill 260 but is unable to hold the gains made.

During the night the Japanese make another assault against the 129th Infantry Regiment's defensive line west of Hill 700. One small penetration is stopped and an infantry counterattack supported by tanks restores the original line.

NEW BRITAIN: Thirteenth Air Force sends 22 B-25 Mitchells, with navy fighters, to bomb Simpson harbor at Rabaul. This is followed by 18 B-24 Liberators, with navy fighter cover, attacking the Rabaul customs wharf area. This is followed by 64 P-40s, P-38 Lightnings, and P-39 Airacobras bombing the town of Rabaul.

ADMIRALTIES: The 2nd Squadron, 7th Cavalry, supported by naval gunfire and Australian Air Force P-40 aircraft, lands with one tank to clear Hauwei Island, to secure it as an artillery base in support of the attack on Lorengau on Manus Island.

Fifth Air Force sends 12 B-25 Mitchells to bomb Japanese positions and communication at Lorengau.

NEW GUINEA: Fifth Air Force B-24 Liberators, B-25 Mitchells, and A-20 Havocs bomb Wewak.

U.S. submarine *Gato* torpedoes and sinks a Japanese cargo ship north of Manokwari.

March 13

CBI: The 1st Battalion of the Marauders reaches Makuy Bum.

Tenth Air Force sends B-25 Mitchells, P-40s, A-36 Intruder (Apache) fighter-bombers, and P-51 Mustangs to attack targets of opportunity in the Shaduzup area.

Japanese submarine *I-26* torpedoes, then bombards a U.S. collier off the east coast of India.

ATLANTIC: In the North Atlantic west of Ireland, TBF Avengers from escort carrier USS *Bogue*, British B-17s working with a destroyer, a destroyer escort, and a Canadian armed merchant cruiser sink German submarine *U-575*.

ETO: Eighth Air Force sends 127 B-17s and 144 B-24 Liberators, escorted by 213 P-47 Thunderbolts, to bomb V-weapon sites in France, but the mission is cancelled because of poor weather conditions over the target. Two B-17s are lost and 61 damaged; 14 B-24s are damaged. Aircrew losses are six killed, one wounded, and 20 missing. One P-47 is damaged.

During the night, seven B-17s drop leaflets over Reims, Orleans, Paris, Amiens, Rouen, and Chartres.

Ninth Air Force sends 40 B-26 Marauders to attack a V-weapon site in France.

ITALY: Fifteenth Air Force receives the 775th Bombardment Squadron (Heavy), 463rd Bombardment Group (Heavy) from the United States. The B-17-equipped squadron will fly its first mission in mid-March.

Twelfth Air Force B-26 Marauders and B-25 Mitchells bomb marshaling yards and railroad bridges. P-40s attack logistics targets near Velletri and gun positions.

PACIFIC: U.S. submarine *Sand Lance* attacks a Japanese convoy off Honshu, Japan, sinking a light cruiser and a cargo ship. Japanese escort ships drop 105 depth charges, keeping *Sand Lance* at deep submergence for 18½ hours.

U.S. submarine *Tautog* torpedoes and sinks a Japanese cargo ship and a transport west of Rashuwa Island in the Kuriles.

CENTRAL PACIFIC: Seventh Air Force B-25 Mitchells from Engebi Island, Eniwetok Atoll, bomb Kusaie Island. The B-24 Liberators of the 38th Bombardment Squadron (Heavy), 30th Bombardment Group (Heavy), redeploy from Nanumea in the Ellice Islands to Kwajalein Atoll.

BOUGAINVILLE: The 129th Infantry of the 37th Infantry Division, supported by tanks, drives the Japanese back and regains its original positions. The Japanese abandon Hill 700 and the 1st Battalion of the 132nd Infantry fights the Japanese for control of the South Knob of Hill 260.

NEW GEORGIA: The B-24 Liberators of the 31st Bombardment Squadron (Heavy), 7th Bombardment Group (Heavy), Thirteenth Air Force, redeploy from Munda to Guadalcanal.

NEW BRITAIN: Thirteenth Air Force B-24 Liberators and B-25 Mitchells bomb the Rabaul area. P-39 Airacobras, P-40s, and P-38 Lightnings bomb logistics sites in the Wunapope area.

ADMIRALTIES: The 2nd Squadron of the 7th Cavalry, supported by tanks, clears the last enemy resistance on Hauwei Island. Artillery is landed to support the attack on Manus Island.

NEW GUINEA: Fifth Air Force sends over 160 aircraft (B-24 Liberators, B-25 Mitchells, A-20 Havocs, P-47 Thunderbolts, and P-40s) against the Japanese airbase at Wewak. Aircrews report eight Japanese aircraft shot down.

March 14

CBI: In China, 20 Japanese bombers attack Fourteenth Air Force airfields at Hengyang and Suichwan.

ITALY: Twelfth Air Force B-26 Marauders and B-25 Mitchells bomb marshaling yards. P-40s attack German positions at the Anzio beachhead and bomb logistics targets. A-36 Intruder (Apache) fighter-bombers and P-47 Thunderbolts attack rail targets at Ortia.

CENTRAL PACIFIC: Seventh Air Force B-25 Mitchells from Engebi Island, Eniwetok Atoll, bomb Kusaie Island. B-25 Mitchells from Tarawa bomb Wotje Atoll.

NEW BRITAIN: Thirteenth Air Force P-40s and P-39 Airacobras attack Wunapope. B-24 Liberators, with navy fighter cover, bomb Rabaul near Simpson Harbor while B-25 Mitchells, with navy fighter cover, bomb the town of Rabaul.

NEW IRELAND: The 4th Marine Regiment lands on Emirau Island, between Kavieng and the Admiralties. The island becomes a base for PT boats and aircraft.

ADMIRALTIES: On Los Negros Island, the 5th Cavalry captures Hill 260 with the support of the 12th Cavalry and artillery fire and air bombardment.

NEW GUINEA: Fifth Air Force B-24 Liberators, B-25 Mitchells, and A-20 Havocs, supported by Allied fighters, bomb the Japanese airbase at Wewak.

March 15

ETO: Eighth Air Force sends 187 B-17s and 157 B-24 Liberators, escorted by 121 P-38 Lightnings and 467 Eighth and Ninth Air Force P-47 Thunderbolts, against industrial targets at Brunswick, Germany. One B-17 and two B-24 Liberators are lost and 45 bombers are damaged. Aircrew losses are one killed, four wounded, and 30 missing. Fighter pilots report 39 confirmed kills and three probables. Five fighters are lost and six are damaged. Five pilots are missing.

During the night seven B-17s drop leaflets over Rennes, Lille, Reims, Le Mans, Paris, and Chartres.

Ninth Air Force sends 118 B-26 Marauders to attack marshaling yards and airfields in France.

ITALY: Major General Sir Bernard Freyberg gains the approval of the Mediterranean Theater commander in chief, General Sir Henry Maitland Wilson, to attack the monastery on Monte Cassino—against the recommendation of the Fifth Army commander, Lieutenant General Mark Clark. Freyberg plans to blast Monte Cassino and drive Combat Command B of the 1st Armored Division through on Route 6. Over Monte Cassino, Fifteenth Air Force and Twelfth Air Force bombers attack in waves every 15 minutes. In between the waves, artillery concentrations hit the mountain. A total of 72 B-25 Mitchells, 101 B-26 Marauders, and 262 B-17s and B-24 Liberators drop more than 2,000 bombs equal to nearly 1,200 tons of explosives on Monte Cassino. Nearly 750 Allied artillery pieces fire 200,000 rounds on the target as well. Tragically, a number of bombs and artillery shells land short of their intended target, killing or wounding 142 friendly troops. P-47 Thunderbolts, A-36s, P-40s, and A-20 Havocs follow up with low-level attacks on Cassino. Despite the incredible firepower, there is no appreciable damage to the enemy defenses.

The U.S. 85th Infantry Division, commanded by Major General John B. Coulter, arrives in Italy as part of Fifth Army. This is one of the first all-draftee divisions formed.

The Fifteenth Air Force receives the B-17s of the 773rd Bombardment Squadron (Heavy), 463rd Bombardment Group (Heavy). The squadron's first mission is scheduled for late March. The B-24 Liberators of the 780th Bombardment Squadron (Heavy), 465th Bombardment Group (Heavy) arrive from the United States. The squadron will fly its first mission in early May.

SOUTH PACIFIC: Major General Hubert R. Harmon, commander of Thirteenth Air Force, is designated Commander Air Solomons (COMAIRSOLS).

CENTRAL PACIFIC: Seventh Air Force B-24 Liberators from Kwajalein Atoll bomb Truk Atoll in the Carolines. B-25 Mitchells from Tarawa bomb Maloelap Atoll. The B-24 Liberators of the 27th Bombardment Squadron (Heavy), 30th Bombardment Group (Heavy), redeploy from Nanumea Island to Kwajalein Atoll.

BOUGAINVILLE: After two days of nearly continuous artillery barrages and company-size raids, the Japanese abandon South Knob on Hill 260, leaving behind over 560 dead. The Americal Division's casualties mount to over 700.

The Japanese assault the 129th Infantry Regiment's defensive line, again attacking toward Piva airfield, and break through and advance 100 yards before being turned back by tank and infantry counterattacks.

NEW BRITAIN: Thirteenth Air Force B-25 Mitchells, P-40s, P-39 Airacobras, P-38 Lightnings, and navy fighters attack logistics bases at Wunapope. B-25 Mitchells, with navy fighter cover, bomb Lakunai airfield. B-24 Liberators bomb Rapopo airfield.

ADMIRALTIES: The 2nd Brigade 1st Cavalry lands on Manus Island. The 8th Regiment moves toward Lorengau airfield, supported by the 7th Cavalry, which establishes a beachhead defensive perimeter. Over 200 bunkers are cleared during the advance. Fifth Air Force sends 36 B-25 Mitchells to bomb Tingo village and the Lugos Mission areas.

NEW GUINEA: Fifth Air Force sends over 200 aircraft (B-24 Liberators, B-25 Mitchells, A-20 Havocs, P-38 Lightnings, P-47 Thunderbolts, and P-40s) to attack facilities and the airbase at Wewak. Fighter pilots report 11 confirmed kills.

March 16

ETO: Eighth Air Force sends 501 B-17s and 213 B-24 Liberators, escorted by 125 P-38 Lightnings, 608 Eighth and Ninth Air Force P-47 Thunderbolts, and 135 Eighth and Ninth Air Force P-51 Mustangs, to bomb targets in Germany. Aircrews report 68 confirmed kills and 32 probables. A total of 23 bombers are lost and one B-24 is damaged. Aircrew losses are seven killed, 17 wounded, and 217 missing. Fighter pilots report 78 confirmed kills and seven probables, with one confirmed kill on the ground. Ten fighters are lost and 12 are damaged. Nine pilots are missing.

MEDITERRANEAN: Navy PBY-5A Catalinas, using magnetic anomaly detection (MAD) equipment, detect German submarine *U-392* as it transits the Straits of Gibraltar. The Catalinas bomb the U-boat, and a British frigate and destroyer conduct a depth charge attack, sinking the U-boat.

ITALY: Twelfth Air Force B-26 Marauders, A-20 Havocs, and A-36 Intruder (Apache) fighter-bombers attack German positions around Cassino-Piedimonte area and gun positions along the Anzio battlefront.

PACIFIC: U.S. submarine *Flying Fish* attacks a Japanese convoy in the Ryukyus, sinking a cargo ship but failing to damage a tanker.

U.S. submarine *Tautog* torpedoes and sinks a Japanese destroyer and cargo ship off Hokkaido, Japan. *Tautog* escapes a pursuit by two destroyers.

SOUTHWEST PACIFIC AREA: U.S. submarine *Lapon* attacks but fails to hit a Japanese seaplane tender west of Luzon in the South China Sea.

CENTRAL PACIFIC: Seventh Air Force B-25 Mitchells from Tarawa and Abemama Island bomb Wotje and Mille Atolls.

U.S. submarine *Silversides* attacks a Japanese convoy and sinks a cargo ship in the vicinity of Palau.

BOUGAINVILLE: Thirteenth Air Force B-24 Liberators bomb Monoitu Mission.

NEW BRITAIN: Thirteenth Air Force B-24 Liberators and B-25 Mitchells bomb the Vunakanau airfield and radar site. B-25 Mitchells, P-39 Airacobras, and P-40s attack Wunapope.

NEW GUINEA: Fifth Air Force B-24 Liberators, B-25 Mitchells, and A-20 Havocs attack antiaircraft positions, support facilities, and logistics sites at Wewak.

Navy PBY Catalinas attack a Japanese convoy north of Hollandia, damaging four ships

March 17

CBI: The SEAC commander, Admiral Lord Louis Mountbatten, sends a message to Prime Minister Churchill and President Roosevelt requesting that the two leaders appeal to Generalissimo Chiang Kai-shek to release another Chinese division to Burma.

Tenth Air Force B-25 Mitchells, P-51 Mustangs, and A-36 Intruder (Apache) fighter-bombers attack Japanese positions and supplies around Kamaing. P-40s attack Myitkyina airfield.

ATLANTIC: TBF Avengers from the escort carrier USS *Block Island,* along with a destroyer and destroyer escort, sink German submarine *U-801* west of the Cape Verdes.

ETO: Eighth Air Force sends 135 P-47 Thunderbolts on a low-level strafing run against airfields in France and the Netherlands. Fighter pilots report three confirmed kills and two probables, all on the ground. Two P-47s are lost and the pilots are reported as missing.

Ninth Air Force sends 70 B-26 Marauders to bomb the marshaling yard at Criel-sur-Mer, France.

The headquarters of the 441st Troop Carrier Group and the 99th, 100th, 301st, and 302nd Troop Carrier Squadrons arrive in England from the United States. The squadrons are equipped with C-47s.

MEDITERRANEAN: Fifteenth Air Force sends over 200 B-24 Liberators escorted by P-47 Thunderbolts and P-38 Lightnings to bomb Vienna, Austria. Half of the bombers abort due to bad weather.

German submarine *U-371* attacks a convoy headed for Naples off Bougie, Algeria, and torpedoes a U.S. freighter.

ITALY: Twelfth Air Force B-25 Mitchells bomb marshaling yards. A-20 Havocs attack German troops around Cassino.

CENTRAL PACIFIC: Seventh Air Force redeploys the B-24 Liberators of the 392nd Bombardment Squadron (Heavy), 30th Bombardment Group (Heavy), from Abemama Island to Kwajalein Atoll.

NEW BRITAIN: Thirteenth Air Force B-25 Mitchells bomb logistics sites at Wunapope.

ADMIRALTIES: The 1st Squadron 8th Cavalry Regiment captures Lorengau airfield after heavy air and naval bombardment.

NEW GUINEA: Fifth Air Force sends almost 100 aircraft (B-24 Liberators, B-25 Mitchells, and A-20 Havocs) to attack the Japanese base at Wewak.

March 18

CBI: General Joseph Stilwell orders Merrill's Marauders (the U.S. 5307th Composite Unit (Provisional)) to block the Tanai Valley from the south.

In China, Fourteenth Air Force P-40s attack transports on the Yangtze River. In French Indochina, P-40s damage a bridge north of Haiphong.

ATLANTIC: German submarine *U-311* torpedoes a U.S. tanker in convoy CU 17 (New York to United Kingdom) in the North Atlantic. The tanker is abandoned and scuttled.

ETO: Eighth Air Force sends over 500 B-17s and over 200 B-24 Liberators, escorted by 113 P-38 Lightnings, 598 Eighth and Ninth Air Force P-47 Thunderbolts, and 214 Eighth and Ninth Air Force P-51 Mustangs, against aircraft production facilities, airfields, and air depots in Germany. A total of 43 bombers are lost and 246 damaged. Aircrew losses are 10 killed, 22 wounded, and 436 missing. Fighter pilots report 39 confirmed kills and five probables in the air and three confirmed kills and two probables on the ground. Thirteen fighters are lost and 133 are damaged. Pilot losses are one wounded and 12 missing.

During the night six B-17s drop leaflets over Cambrai, Lille, Paris, Amiens, Rouen, and Caen.

ITALY: Fifteenth Air Force sends nearly 1,000 B-17s and B-24 Liberators to bomb aviation targets, including 406 B-17 and B-24 Liberators escorted by 186 P-38 Lightnings and P-47 Thunderbolts to attack German airfields in northern Italy. A total of 56 German aircraft are destroyed on the ground. Aircrews report 23 confirmed kills and seven probables. Fighter pilots report 33 confirmed kills and three probables. Seven bombers and four fighters are shot down.

The 774th Bombardment Squadron (Heavy), 463rd Bombardment Group (Heavy), brings B-17s to Italy. The squadron's first mission will be in late March.

Twelfth Air Force B-25 Mitchells, B-26 Marauders, and A-20 Havocs bomb marshaling yards and railroad bridges. P-40s, A-36 Intruder (Apache) fighter-bombers, and P-47 Thunderbolts attack gun positions in the Anzio beachhead area and motor transport and logistics support facilities around Cassino.

SOUTHWEST PACIFIC AREA: SWPA headquarters sets a date for the Hollandia invasion named Operation Reckless—April 22. The plan involves an amphibious assault to capture Aitape and the Tadji airfield, followed by two simultaneous amphibious landings at Humboldt Bay and Tanahmerah Bay to seize airfields at Hollandia.

PACIFIC: U.S. submarine *Lapon* attacks a Japanese convoy, sinking a transport near Hong Kong.

CENTRAL PACIFIC: Naval Task Group 50.10—formed around the carrier *Lexington* and battleships USS *Iowa* and *New Jersey,* with a seven-destroyer screen, under the command of Rear Admiral Willis A. Lee—attacks Japanese installations on Mille Island in the Marshalls. The *Iowa* is damaged by fire from a shore battery.

BOUGAINVILLE: Eighteen P-39 Airacobras of Thirteenth Air Force, along with several navy fighter-bombers, attack Japanese shipping.

ADMIRALTIES: Lorengau village is captured. The 7th Cavalry Regiment clears more enemy bunkers and moves to clear Rossum Road.

NEW GUINEA: Fifth Air Force sends B-24 Liberators, B-25 Mitchells, and A-20 Havocs against support facilities and antiaircraft positions at Wewak.

TG 74.5 (Captain Kenmore M. McManes) bombards Japanese installations at Wewak.

U.S. submarine *Rock* is damaged by depth charges off North Borneo but remains on patrol.

March 19

CBI: The 2nd Battalion and a portion of the 3rd Battalion of the Marauders, supported by the Kachin Rangers, establish a road block on the Kamaing Road. The remainder of the 3rd Battalion provides security against a Japanese surprise attack.

The B-25 Mitchells of the 82nd Bombardment Squadron (Medium), 12th Bombardment Group (Medium), arrive at Tezgaon, India, from Italy. The squadron's first mission is scheduled for late April.

In China, Fourteenth Air Force B-25 Mitchells, P-38 Lightnings, and P-51 Mustangs attack vessels on the Yangtze River.

German submarine *U-510* torpedoes and sinks a U.S. freighter off the west coast of India.

ATLANTIC: TBF Avengers from escort carrier USS *Block Island* sink German submarine *U-1059* near the Cape Verde Islands.

ETO: Nearly 200 B-17s of Eighth Air Force, escorted by 82 P-47 Thunderbolts, bomb V-weapon sites in France. One B-17 is lost and 88 are damaged. Two crewmen are wounded and 100 are missing. One P-47 is damaged and the pilot wounded. P-47 Thunderbolts with 500-pound bombs attack Gilze-Rijen airfield in the Netherlands, supported by 39 P-51 Mustangs.

During the night, six B-17s drop leaflets over The Hague, Rotterdam, Leeuwarden, Utrecht, and Amsterdam in the Netherlands.

Ninth Air Force sends 152 B-26 Marauders and 65 A-20 Havocs to bomb V-weapon sites in France.

MEDITERRANEAN: Fifteenth Air Force sends 234 B-17s and B-24 Liberators, escorted by over fighters, to bomb the Klagenfurt, Austria, air depot. B-24s also bomb the Graz air depot and the marshaling yards at Knin and Metkovic in Yugoslavia. Aircrews report 30 confirmed kills. U.S. aircraft losses are 17 bombers and one fighter.

Twelfth Air Force B-26 Marauders and B-25 Mitchells attack roads, bridges, ports, and logistics support facilities. P-40s attack German positions at Anzio.

ITALY: U.S. submarine chaser sinks a German E-boat near Anzio.

CENTRAL PACIFIC: Seventh Air Force B-24 Liberators from Kwajalein Atoll bomb Wake Island. B-25 Mitchells from Abemama Island and Tarawa bomb Maloelap, Jaluit, and Mille Atolls.

NEW BRITAIN: Thirteenth Air Force sends B-25 Mitchells to bomb Wunapope.

NEW GUINEA: Fifth Air Force B-24 Liberators, B-25 Mitchells, A-20 Havocs, and P-38 Lightnings bomb the area around Wewak and destroy a convoy northwest of Wewak, sinking two cargo ships and two escort vessels.

March 20

CBI: The Chinese 38th Division is ordered to trap Japanese forces near Kamaing.

The B-25 Mitchells of the 12th Bombardment Group (Medium) arrive at Tezgaon, India, from Italy. The squadron's first mission will be in mid-April.

ETO: Eighth Air Force sends nearly 500 B-17s and B-24 Liberators, escorted by 44 P-38 Lightnings, 345 P-47 Thunderbolts, and 205 Eighth and Ninth Air Force P-51 Mustangs, to attack targets in Germany, but bad weather causes over 300 bombers to abort the mission. Seven bombers are lost and 166 damaged. Aircrews report two confirmed kills. Aircrew losses are one killed, 11 wounded, and 61 missing. Fighter pilots report four confirmed kills with one additional confirmed kill on the ground. Eight fighters are lost and 13 are damaged. Pilot losses are eight missing.

The Ninth Air Force sends B-26 Marauders and A-20 Havocs to bomb V-weapon sites and airfields in France. The 67th Tactical Reconnaissance Group completes a mission begun on February 23 to photograph 160 miles of French coastline.

ITALY: Fifteenth Air Force receives the headquarters of 464th Bombardment Group (Heavy) and 778th Bombardment Squadron (Heavy) from the United States. The B-24 Liberator-equipped squadron will fly its first mission at the end of April.

Twelfth Air Force B-25 Mitchells bomb marshaling yards, railroad bridges, and ports. A-36 Intruder (Apache) fighter-bombers drop food bundles for ground forces near Cassino.

SOUTHWEST PACIFIC AREA: U.S. submarine *Angler* evacuates 58 people, including women and children, from Panay in the Philippines.

PACIFIC: U.S. submarine *Pollack* torpedoes and sinks a Japanese auxiliary netlayer off Torishima in the Nanpo Islands south of Honshu, Japan. *Pollack* avoids the submarine chaser.

CENTRAL PACIFIC: Headquarters, 30th Bombardment Group (Heavy) moves from Abemama Island to Kwajalein Atoll.

U.S. submarine *Picuda* (SS-382) torpedoes and sinks a Japanese stores ship near Yap in the Carolines.

BOUGAINVILLE: Thirteenth Air Force P-40s and P-39 Airacobras bomb Numa Numa and targets of opportunity along the coast.

NEW BRITAIN: Thirteenth Air Force B-24 Liberators bomb Vunakanau airfield and B-25 Mitchells bomb Lakunai. Fifth Air Force P-40s on armed reconnaissance attack villages and barges.

NEW IRELAND: Rear Admiral Robert M. Griffin's Task Force 37, with four battleships, two escort carriers, and destroyers, bombards Kavieng, New Ireland.

Navy Task Group 31.2 under command of Commodore Lawrence F. Reifsnider lands the 4th Marine Division on undefended Emirau Island, Bismarck Archipelago, completing the strategic encirclement of Rabaul.

ADMIRALTIES: The 868th Bombardment Squadron (Heavy) of the Thirteenth Air Force redeploys from Munda, New Georgia, to Los Negros Island with radar-equipped B-24 Liberators.

NEW GUINEA: Fifth Air Force B-24 Liberators bomb the Aitape airfield. P-39 Airacobras and A-20 Havocs attack a Japanese headquarters on the Bogadjim Road.

March 21

CBI: The 22nd and 38th Chinese Divisions and elements of the 1st Provisional Tank Group continue the attack toward Jambu Bum. A battalion and other elements of the Marauders advance toward Inkangahtawng.

Headquarters, 12th Bombardment Group (Medium), arrives at Tezgaon, India. The B-25 Mitchells of the 83rd and 434th Bombardment Squadrons (Medium) arrive at Kurmitola, India, from Italy. The squadrons will fly their first mission in late April.

ETO: Eighth Air Force sends 65 B-24 Liberators escorted by 48 P-47 Thunderbolts against V-weapon sites in France. Of the 56 bombers that hit the target, seven are damaged. After an attack on the Bordeaux area by 41 P-51 Mustangs, fighter pilots report 12 confirmed kills in the air and another nine confirmed kills on the ground. Seven P-51 Mustangs are lost and two are damaged. Pilot losses are one wounded and seven missing.

During the night, seven B-17s drop leaflets over The Hague, Amsterdam, Leeuwarden, Rotterdam, and Utrecht in the Netherlands.

ITALY: The 34th Infantry Division begins landing at Anzio to relieve the 3rd Infantry Division. The beachhead is far from quiet, even though no major combat has taken place since March 3. German artillery and aircraft attack the Allied troops almost daily. About 3,000 tons of supplies are landed at the beach every day. Raids and artillery fire cost the Allies about 100 casualties per day.

Twelfth Air Force B-26 Marauders attack railroad bridges and viaducts and P-47 Thunderbolts attack railroad bridges. P-40s attack German positions on the Anzio battleline and A-36 Intruder (Apache) fighter-bombers airdrop food to ground troops near Cassino.

CENTRAL PACIFIC: Seventh Air Force B-24 Liberators and B-25 Mitchells from Tarawa bomb Maloelap Atoll.

U.S. submarine *Bashaw* torpedoes and damages a Japanese vessel in the Palau Islands.

NEW BRITAIN: Thirteenth Air Force B-25 Mitchells bomb Lakunai airfield and B-24 Liberators bomb Vunakanau airfield. Fifth Air Force P-40s and A-20 Havocs on armed reconnaissance attack targets of opportunity.

March 22

CBI: The Japanese offensive against India makes significant gains, advancing 30 miles into India toward Imphal.

In French Indochina, Fourteenth Air Force sends four B-25 Mitchells to attack transportation targets. One bomber is lost.

ATLANTIC: In establishing priorities for the Allied air forces, the CCS decides Neptune has priority over Pointblank (attacks on German war production). General Eisenhower, as Supreme Commander, Allied Expeditionary Force, will direct the operations of Allied air forces to attack targets in support of the invasion and to limit the ability of German forces to reinforce Normandy. The road and rail networks of France are to become primary targets.

ETO: Eighth Air Force sends 474 B-17s and 214 B-24 Liberators, escorted by 125 P-38 Lightnings, 496 Eighth and Ninth Air Force P-47 Thunderbolts, and 196 Eighth and Ninth Air Force P-51 Mustangs, to bomb aviation industry plants at Oranienburg and Basdorf, Germany. Cloud cover forces the bombers to attack secondary targets near Berlin and targets of opportunity. The bombers also drop over six million leaflets. Bomber losses are 12 downed and 348 damaged. Aircrew losses are 20 wounded and 135 missing. Fighter pilots report only one confirmed kill on the ground. Twelve fighters are lost and 11 are damaged. Pilot losses are one wounded and 12 missing.

ITALY: Fifteenth Air Force B-17s bomb marshaling yards, supported by P-38 Lightnings and P-47 Thunderbolts. Twelfth Air Force B-26 Marauders and B-25 Mitchells attack railroad bridges. P-40s bomb German positions around Avezzano and Pico.

Pilots of P-40s, flying cover over Anzio and Cassino, report two German fighters shot down.

PACIFIC: U.S. submarine *Growler* makes an unsuccessful attack on a Japanese cargo vessel in the Ryukyus.

CENTRAL PACIFIC: U.S. submarine *Tunny* torpedoes and damages a Japanese tanker west of the Palaus,

BOUGAINVILLE: Thirteenth Air Force B-24 Liberators bomb targets around Buka, Monoitu, Kahili, and Kara.

NEW BRITAIN: Thirteenth Air Force B-25 Mitchells bomb Lakunai airfield and B-24 Liberators bomb Tobera.

NEW GUINEA: Fifth Air Force sends over 130 aircraft (B-24 Liberators, B-25 Mitchells, A-20 Havocs, and P-40s) to attack Wewak.

March 23

ALEUTIANS: Eleventh Air Force sends a detachment of P-40s and P-38 Lightnings of the 11th Fighter Squadron, 343rd Fighter Group, from its man base on Adak Island to Amchitka Island.

CBI: Two battalions of Merrill's Marauders arrive at Inkanghtawng intending to block the Kamaing Road, but the Japanese are in defensive positions.

Tenth Air Force P-40s bomb Japanese logistics sites at Kamaing and other P-40s fly armed reconnaissance over the Mogaung Valley.

In French Indochina, Fourteenth Air Force B-25 Mitchells attack railroad targets and rolling stock and attack bridges between Vinh and Thanh Hoa.

ETO: Eighth Air Force sends 524 B-17s and 244 B-24 Liberators, escorted by 119 P-38 Lightnings, 539 Eighth and Ninth Air Force P-47 Thunderbolts, and 183 Eighth and Ninth Air Force P-51 Mustangs, to bomb airfields and aircraft production facilities in Germany. Due to cloud cover, only 68 B-24 Liberators hit the primary target and 639 bombers hit secondary targets or targets of opportunity. A total of 28 bombers are lost and 323 are damaged. Aircrews report 33 confirmed kills and eight probables. Fighter pilots report 22 confirmed kills and one probable, and two confirmed kills on the ground. Four fighters are lost and three are damaged. Aircrew casualties are five killed, nine wounded, and 278 missing. Four fighter pilots are reported as missing.

During the night five B-17s drop leaflets over Grenoble, Vichy, Lyon, Toulouse, and Limoges in France.

Ninth Air Force sends 220 B-26 Marauders on a morning mission to bomb a marshaling yard and airfields in France. This is followed by an afternoon raid by 146 B-26s on a marshaling yard.

ITALY: Twelfth Air Force B-26 Marauders and B-25 Mitchells bomb marshaling yards and railroad bridges. P-40s and A-36 Intruder (Apache) fighter-bombers attack German positions in the Cassino area.

SOUTHWEST PACIFIC AREA: U.S. submarine *Bowfin* attacks a Japanese convoy off the south coast of Mindanao, sinking a transport and a cargo ship. *Bowfin* escapes a counterattack from an escort vessel.

CENTRAL PACIFIC: Seventh Air Force B-24 Liberators from Kwajalein Atoll bomb Wake Island. B-25 Mitchells from Eniwetok Atoll bomb Ponape Island. B-25s from Tarawa bomb Maloelap and Jaluit Atolls, using the navy's new airfield at Majuro Atoll to refuel and rearm for multiple strikes.

U.S. submarine *Tunny* torpedoes and sinks Japanese submarine *I-42* southwest of Angaur Island in the Palaus.

BOUGAINVILLE: Another Japanese assault begins on the 129th Infantry Regiment's lines. Seven battalions of artillery hit the attackers who still must be stopped by a series of tank and infantry counterattacks. An estimated 5,000 Japanese are killed. U.S. casualties are 263 killed.

NEW BRITAIN: Two destroyers bombard Japanese installations on the Mussau Islands of the St. Matthias Group, Bismarck Archipelago.

NEW GUINEA: The Reckless Task Force is assembled under the I Corps commander, Lieutenant General Robert L. Eichelberger. The Aitape landing force is composed of the 163rd RCT of the 41st Infantry Division. It is commanded by Brigadier General Jens A. Doe and has a combination of 7,000 combat troops and nearly 9,000 service and air force personnel in support. It is to seize the Tadji airfield and make it operational for Allied aircraft to support the Hollandia landings. The Hollandia Task Force is composed of the 24th Infantry Division and the 41st Infantry Division (less the 163rd). The 41st Division, commanded by Major General Horace A. Fuller, will land at Humboldt Bay; the 24th Division, commanded by Major General Frederick A. Irving, will land at Tanahmerah Bay. The divisions will move to capture the several airfields in the area and consolidate forces to defend the established perimeter. Task Force 77, under Rear Admiral Daniel E. Barbey, will support the landing along with Task Force 58 from Fifth Fleet, which will provide carrier air support. The total operation consists of 58,000 men, 13,000 of whom are engineers essential to opening roads through nearly impassable jungle and building the airfields necessary to support offensive operations.

Fifth Air Force B-24 Liberators, B-25 Mitchells, A-20 Havocs, and P-47 Thunderbolts attack numerous targets in Aitape, Wewak, Alexishafen, and Hansa Bay.

March 24

CBI: The Marauders of the 2nd Battalion discover Japanese forces are occupying Inkangahtawng in strength. In the skirmishes that follow, 200 Japanese troops are killed and the Marauders suffer 15 casualties.

ETO: Eighth Air Force sends 230 B-17s to attack Schweinfurt but most bomb the Frankfurt am Main marshaling yard. Three B-17s are lost and 71 damaged. Also, 206 B-24 Liberators are sent against the Metz and Nancy airfields in France. The primary target is cloud covered and most bomb secondary targets. There are no losses, but 24 bombers are damaged. Aircrew casualties for the two missions are 14 killed, four wounded, and 30 missing. The missions are escorted by 84 P-38 Lightnings, 301 Eighth and Ninth Air Force P-47 Thunderbolts, and 55 Eighth and Ninth Air Force P-51 Mustangs. Fighter pilots report one confirmed kill in the air and two on the ground. Five aircraft are lost and four pilots are reported missing.

During the night five B-17s drop leaflets over Tours and Lorient in France, and over Charleroi, Brussels, and Antwerp in Belgium.

ITALY: The Mediterranean Allied Tactical Air Force and Twelfth Air Force under Major General John K. Cannon begins Operation Strangle, large-scale air interdiction operations intended to prevent supplies and reinforcements from reaching southern Italy. The air campaign will last until May 11. Combat Command B of the 1st Armored Division is withdrawn from Cassino to move to Anzio.

Fifteenth Air Force sends over 100 B-24 Liberators to bomb marshaling yards and road bridges. Six bombers are lost and aircrews report 10 German fighters shot down.

Twelfth Air Force B-25 Mitchells attack logistics sites, harbor installations, bridges, and railroads. A-20 Havocs, P-40s, and A-36 Intruder (Apache) fighter-bombers bomb German positions near Cassino.

CENTRAL PACIFIC: Seventh Air Force B-25 Mitchells from Tarawa bomb Jaluit while B-25s flying from Eniwetok Atoll attack Ponape Island and Ant Island in the Carolines.

BOUGAINVILLE: The Japanese again attack the 129th Infantry Regiment, but are halted. This ends the Japanese attempt to break the defensive line of XIV Corps. They have lost over 8,000 casualties and begin to withdraw into the jungle.

NEW BRITAIN: B-25 Mitchells bomb Tobera airfield. P-38 Lightnings, P-39 Airacobras, and P-40s attack Wunapope.

ADMIRALTIES, LOS NEGROS: The 1st Squadron, 5th Cavalry and 2nd Squadron, 12th Cavalry make a coordinated attack and seize the crest of Hill 260. The capture of this position ends organized resistance on the island.

March 25

ALEUTIANS: Eleventh Air Force B-24 Liberators from Shemya Island bomb Kurabu Cape and part of Onnekotan Island.

CBI: The 1st Battalion of Marauders establishes a road block south of Shaduzup. The 2nd Battalion retreats toward Manpin.

Tenth Air Force P-40s bomb the Kamaing area. The Japanese send five medium bombers and 30 fighters to attack Allied airfields in Burma and India.

ETO: Ninth Air Force sends over 140 B-26 Marauders to attack the Hirson marshaling yard in France.

ITALY: Twelfth Air Force B-26 Marauders bomb the dockyard at Leghorn. P-40 fighter-bombers attack German positions along the Anzio battleline.

PACIFIC: JCS approves the reassignment of all SOPAC forces to MacArthur's Southwest Pacific Area command and to Admiral Nimitz's Pacific Oceans Area command. General MacArthur will take operational control of XIV Corps headquarters and the 37th, 25th, 43rd, 93rd, and 40th Infantry Divisions, as well as the Thirteenth Air Force and all navy and marine air units. Nimitz will take operational control of the I Marine Amphibious Corps and the 1st and 3rd Marine Divisions.

U.S. submarine *Pollack* attacks a Japanese convoy and sinks a submarine chaser in the Bonin Islands.

CENTRAL PACIFIC: Headquarters of VII Bomber Command moves from Tarawa to Kwajalein Atoll.

A destroyer escort and a submarine chaser sink Japanese submarine *I-32* south of Wotje Atoll in the Marshalls.

NEW BRITAIN: Fifth Air Force P-40s attack a Japanese headquarters at Cape Hoskins.

ADMIRALTIES: The 7th Cavalry, reinforced by the 8th Cavalry, along with artillery and air support, defeats the last remnant of Japanese defenders on Manus Island. At Los Negros, Seeadler Harbor becomes one of the largest naval bases in the Pacific. Los Negros airfield is established along with hospitals and supply depots. With the Admiralties under Allied control, the Japanese stronghold at Rabaul is isolated, allowing MacArthur's forces to concentrate on western New Guinea. The battle for these key islands has cost the Americans 330 killed and 1,189 wounded.

NEW GUINEA: Fifth Air Force B-24 Liberators, B-25 Mitchells, and A-20 Havocs bomb Wewak. The Japanese move their air headquarters from Wewak to Hollandia.

March 26

CBI: The 2nd Battalion of the Marauders moves to Nhpum Ga where it receives resupply by airdrop. The Marauders are supported by the 1st and 2nd Troop Carrier Squadrons and the 27th and 315th Troop Carrier Squadrons. The C-47s drop 376 tons of supplies to the Marauders during March. L-4 and L-5 light aircraft of the 71st Liaison Squadron provide rapid medical evacuation of casualties from small jungle clearings. The 3rd Battalion arrives and the Marauders establish a hasty defense awaiting an expected flank attack against Shaduzup.

ETO: Eighth Air Force sends over 400 B-17s and B-24 Liberators, escorted by 266 P-47 Thunderbolts, to attack V-weapon sites in France. Five bombers are lost and 117 are damaged. Aircrew losses are two killed, 15 wounded, and 50 missing. Fighter pilots report one confirmed kill and one probable. One fighter is lost and five damaged. One pilot is reported missing.

During the night, six B-17s drop leaflets over Caen, Rennes, Amiens, Paris, and Rouen.

Ninth Air Force sends 338 B-26 Marauders and 35 A-20 Havocs to attack the torpedo-boat pens at Ijmuiden in the Netherlands. Nearly 140 P-47 Thunderbolts and P-51 Mustangs attack the Creil marshaling yard and other military installations in France.

ITALY: Fifteenth Air Force B-17s and B-24 Liberators escorted by P-47 Thunderbolts and P-38 Lightnings attack docks, marshaling yards, and air depots.

Twelfth Air Force B-26 Marauders and B-25 Mitchells attack transportation targets. A-20 Havocs attack German troops near Velletri. P-47 Thunderbolts damage a railway bridge while P-40s attack German positions along the Anzio battleline.

Lieutenant General Willis D. Crittenberger arrives in Italy with his IV Corps headquarters.

CENTRAL PACIFIC: Admiral Nimitz sends a warning order to General William H. Rupertus, commander of the 1st Marine Division, to be prepared to invade Peleliu Island by September 15.

Seventh Air Force B-25 Mitchells fly from Eniwetok Atoll to bomb Ponape Island. B-25s from Tarawa bomb Jaluit Atoll, rearm at Majuro Atoll, and attack Jaluit again en route back to Tarawa.

U.S. submarine *Tullibee* is sunk by a circular run of its own torpedo, north of the Palaus.

NEW BRITAIN: Thirteenth Air Force B-25 Mitchells bomb Vunakanau airfield and make a night raid on Rabaul. Fifth Air Force P-39 Airacobras and P-40s attack Cape Hoskins and troops around Talasea.

BOUGAINVILLE: Thirteenth Air Force B-24 Liberators attack Japanese positions and targets of opportunity on islands at the mouth of the Tekessi River and near Monoitu. Fighters support ground forces who attack supply points and Japanese positions near the mouths of the Tekessi and Maririei Rivers.

NEW GUINEA: Fifth Air Force sends over 220 aircraft (B-24 Liberators, B-25 Mitchells, A-20 Havocs, and fighters) to attack Wewak, Aitape, and the Hansa Bay area.

March 27

CBI: The 2nd and 3rd Battalions of the U.S. 5307th Composite Unit (Provisional), known also as Merrill's Marauders, arrive at Auche.

Tenth Air Force B-24 Liberators hit logistics sites at Kamaing, while about 50 A-36 Intruder (Apache) fighter-bombers and two B-25 Mitchells attack Japanese forces near Myitkyina and support ground forces near Kamaing.

ETO: Eighth Air Force sends nearly 550 B-17s and 168 B-24 Liberators, escorted by 132 P-38 Lightnings, 706 Eighth and Ninth Air Force P-47 Thunderbolts, and 122 Eighth and Ninth Air Force P-51 Mustangs, against airfields in France. Six bombers are lost and 10 are damaged. Aircrew losses are 31 killed, four wounded, and 61 missing. Fighter pilots report eight confirmed kills in the air and 30 on the ground with one probable on the ground. Ten aircraft are lost and seven are damaged. One pilot is wounded and 10 are reported missing.

Ninth Air Force sends 18 B-26 Marauders to attack V-weapon sites in France.

The C-47s of the 303rd, 305th, and 306th Troop Carrier Squadrons, 442nd Troop Carrier Group, arrive from the United States.

ITALY: Twelfth Air Force B-26 Marauders and B-25 Mitchells bomb railroad bridges. P-47 Thunderbolts and P-40s maintain cover over the Cassino and Anzio battlelines.

The destroyer USS *Livermore* provides gunfire support at Anzio.

CENTRAL PACIFIC: Seventh Air Force B-25 Mitchells and B-24 Liberators from Tarawa attack Maloelap, Mille, and Wotje Atolls. B-25s from Eniwetok Atoll bomb Jaluit Atoll.

The 9th Troop Carrier Squadron with C-47s deploys from Hickam Field, Hawaii, to Abemama Island.

BOUGAINVILLE: Japanese forces begin withdrawing from the Empress Augusta Bay area.

NEW BRITAIN: Thirteenth Air Force B-25 Mitchells attack Wunapope with incendiaries, causing heavy damage.

New Guinea: Fifth Air Force sends over 200 aircraft (B-24 Liberators, B-25 Mitchells, A-20 Havocs, P-47 Thunderbolts, P-40s, and P-39 Airacobras) to attack logistics sites, shipping, bridges, and troop concentrations around Wewak, Hansa Bay, and Madang.

Saidor becomes the new base for the P-47 Thunderbolts of the 341st Fighter Squadron, 348th Fighter Group.

U.S. submarine *Hake* torpedoes and sinks a Japanese merchant tanker south of Borneo.

U.S. submarine *Rasher* attacks a Japanese convoy in the Java Sea, sinking a cargo ship.

March 28

Aleutians: Eleventh Air Force deploys the P-38 Lightnings of the 18th Fighter Squadron, 343rd Fighter Group, from Amchitka Island to Attu Island.

CBI: The Japanese make their first attack on the 2nd Battalion's defenses at Nhpum Ga.

The 3rd Battalion now at Hsamshingyang provides artillery support and protects the only available drop zone for resupply and evacuation of casualties in the area. The 1st Battalion, after driving Japanese defenders off, blocks the Kamaing Road below Shaduzup and is reinforced by Chinese forces. The Chinese 38th and 22nd Divisions are now pressuring Japanese forces from two directions.

Headquarters of XX Bomber Command arrives at Kharagpur, India, from the United States.

ETO: Eighth Air Force sends nearly 400 B-17s against airfields in France and 77 B-24 Liberators against the Ijmuiden E-boat pens in the Netherlands. The missions are escorted by 46 P-38 Lightnings, 284 P-47 Thunderbolts, and 123 P-51 Mustangs. The B-24 Liberators abort the mission due to weather conditions over the target. Two B-17s are lost and 120 damaged. Aircrew losses are three killed, two wounded, and 28 missing. Fighter pilots report 30 confirmed kills and one possible, all on the ground. Three fighters are lost and the pilots reported as missing.

Italy: Fifteenth Air Force sends almost 400 B-17s and B-24 Liberators escorted by P-38 Lightnings and P-40s to bomb marshaling yards. Fighter pilots report 12 German fighters shot down. Five U.S. fighters are lost.

The Fifteenth Air Force receives the B-24 Liberators of the 781st Bombardment Squadron (Heavy), 465th Bombardment Group (Heavy), from the United States.

Twelfth Air Force B-25 Mitchells bomb bridges, railway junctions, and marshaling yards. P-40s attack German gun positions on the Anzio battleline and targets of opportunity in the Cassino area.

Pacific: U.S. submarine *Barb* torpedoes and sinks a Japanese cargo ship off Rasa Island.

Central Pacific: Seventh Air Force B-25 Mitchells from Abemama Island and Tarawa bomb Jaluit, Mille, and Maloelap Atolls.

Bougainville: Elements of the 93rd Division arrive at Empress Augusta Bay. American infantrymen find the Japanese have abandoned Hill 260.

Thirteenth Air Force P-40s attack the Numa Numa logistics base.

New Britain: Thirteenth Air Force B-25 Mitchells bomb Tobera airfield.

New Ireland: Destroyers bombard Japanese positions on Kapingamarangi Atoll, north of New Ireland, destroying a radio and meteorological station.

New Guinea: U.S. submarine *Silversides* torpedoes and sinks a Japanese cargo ship off Manokwari.

March 29

CBI: General Stilwell makes a formal request to Generalissimo Chiang Kai-shek for additional Chinese forces to be sent to Burma. Chiang offers two divisions.

In Burma, General Merrill is evacuated and Colonel Charles N. Hunter takes command temporarily as the Japanese make their second attack on Nhpum Ga. Despite the 3rd Battalion's attempts to stall the Japanese with ambushes, the enemy begins surrounding the 2nd Battalion of the Marauders.

The headquarters of the 1st Air Commando Group is activated at Hailakandi, India. The group has a B-25 Mitchell bomber section, a P-51 Mustang fighter section, a light-plane section with L-1 Stinsons and L-5 Sentinels (short take-off and landing light aircraft), a C-47 transport section, a glider section with CG-4As and TG-5s, and a light-cargo section with UC-64s.

In China, Fourteenth Air Force P-40s and P-51 Mustangs attack the railroad station, airfield and bridge near Nanchang.

Japanese submarine *I-26* torpedoes a U.S. freighter of the coast of India. As the ship is abandoned, the *I-26* surfaces and shells the ship, setting it afire. The Japanese gun crew then turns to the lifeboats and rafts, killing one American. The submarine rams and sinks one of the lifeboats, takes four men prisoner, then departs.

ETO: Eighth Air Force sends 236 B-17s, escorted by 50 P-38 Lightnings, 242 P-47 Thunderbolts, and 136 Eighth and Ninth Air Force P-51 Mustangs, against industrial targets in Germany. Nine bombers are lost and 67 damaged. Aircrews report eight confirmed kills and three probables. Aircrew losses are two killed, five wounded, and 90 missing. Fighter pilots report 44 confirmed kills and four probables and another 13 confirmed kills and seven probables on the ground. Twelve fighters are lost and 18 are damaged. Pilot losses are two killed, three wounded, and 10 missing.

Another attack by 77 B-24 Liberators on V-weapon sites in France escorted by 37 P-47 Thunderbolts results in only 30 hitting the primary target due to radar guidance failures. Eight bombers are damaged. Aircrew losses are 18 killed and one wounded.

Ninth Air Force receives the P-47 Thunderbolts of the 48th Fighter Group and 492nd, 493rd, and 494th Fighter Squadrons. The first mission for the squadrons is scheduled for late April. The headquarters of the 442nd Troop Carrier Group and 304th Troop Carrier Squadron arrives from the United States with C-47s.

Mediterranean: Two U.S. destroyers, three submarine chasers, and four British destroyers conduct antisubmarine operations off Sicily and sink German submarine *U-223*.

Italy: Fifteenth Air Force sends nearly 400 B-17s and B-24 Liberators against ball bearing production, marshaling yards, and industrial production. The bombers are escorted by P-47 Thunderbolts and P-38 Lightnings. Aircrews report 13 aircraft destroyed. Six U.S. aircraft are lost.

Twelfth Air Force B-25 Mitchells attack Viterbo airfield. B-26 Marauders bomb Leghorn. P-40s attack logistics sites and tank repair facilities. A-36 Intruder (Apache) fighter-bombers attack Civitavecchia and targets of opportunity. Spitfires, P-40s, and P-47 Thunderbolts patrol the Anzio battlelines.

SOUTHWEST PACIFIC AREA: U.S. submarine *Haddo* torpedoes and damages a Japanese cargo ship in the South China Sea, northwest of Luzon Island.

CENTRAL PACIFIC: Thirteenth Air Force B-24 Liberators from Munda on New Georgia carry out the first daylight raid on Truk Atoll. En route, the bombers arm at Torokina on Bougainville, then fly to Nissan Island in the Solomons for refueling before moving on to Truk. Aircrews report 31 Japanese aircraft destroyed in the air and 50 aircraft on the ground. Two B-24s are lost.

U.S. submarine *Tunny* torpedoes and damages the Japanese battleship *Musashi* off Palau.

NEW GUINEA: Fifth Air Force B-24 Liberators bomb Hollandia; B-25 Mitchells and A-20 Havocs bomb Wewak.

March 30

ETO: Eighth Air Force sends 24 P-47 fighter-bombers escorted by 50 other P-47 Thunderbolts to dive-bomb Eindhoven and Sosterburg airfields in the Netherlands. P-47s strafe Venlo, Deelen, and Twente/Enschede airfields. One fighter is lost and three damaged. The pilot is reported missing. Two German aircraft are reported destroyed.

During the night, six B-17s drop leaflets over Rouen, Rennes, Reims, Paris, and Amiens.

MEDITERRANEAN: Nearly 350 Fifteenth Air Force B-17s and B-24 Liberators bomb marshaling yards at Sofia, Bulgaria, and industrial targets and airfield at Imotski, Yugoslavia. Four bombers are lost. Reports state 13 German fighters are shot down.

The Fifteenth Air Force receives the B-24 Liberators of the 777th Bombardment Squadron (Heavy), 464th Bombardment Group (Heavy), in Italy from the United States.

Twelfth Air Force B-25 Mitchells bomb the harbor at Leghorn. P-40s and A-36 Intruder (Apache) fighter-bombers attack an ammunition storage area near Roccasecca and trucks, bridges, and logistics sites.

ITALY: Destroyer USS *Eberle* provides gunfire support off Anzio.

CENTRAL PACIFIC: Seventh Air Force B-24 Liberators from Kwajalein and Eniwetok Atolls bomb Truk.

Task Force 58 under Admiral Raymond A. Spruance (Commander Fifth Fleet), with the fast carriers USS *Lexington,* USS *Bunker Hill,* and USS *Hornet,* begins attacking airfields, shipping, facilities, and installations at Palau, Yap, Ulithi, and Woleai in the Carolines. For the first time carrier aircraft lay minefields. Carrier aircraft also sink five fleet tankers, a destroyer, 12 smaller support ships, five transports, three tankers, two guardboats, six cargo ships, and a number of other smaller vessels.

While on lifeguard duty off the Palaus the USS *Tunny* is mistaken for a Japanese submarine and attacked by TBF Avengers. The damage forces *Tunny* to terminate her patrol.

U.S. submarine *Picuda* attacks a Japanese convoy and sinks a transport southwest of Guam. U.S. submarine *Stingray* attacks a Japanese convoy and sinks a transport near Saipan.

NEW BRITAIN: Thirteenth Air Force P-38 Lightnings attack Rabaul with incendiaries. B-25 Mitchells bomb Wunapope.

NEW GUINEA: Fifth Air Force sends 60 B-24 Liberators, escorted by 90 P-38 Lightnings and P-47 Thunderbolts, to attack Hollandia to eliminate Japanese air power. At least 199 Japanese aircraft are destroyed on the ground or shot down. B-25 Mitchells, A-20 Havocs, P-47 Thunderbolts, P-40s, and P-39 Airacobras attack Wewak and Madang.

U.S. submarine *Darter* torpedoes and sinks a Japanese cargo ship northwest of Manokwari.

March 31

ALEUTIANS: Eleventh Air Force inactivates the headquarters units of XI Bomber Command and XI Fighter Command.

CBI: The 2nd Battalion of the Marauders is surrounded at Nhpum Ga. The beleaguered troops are resupplied with water and ammunition by airdrops.

ITALY: The Allies complete the shift of forces across the Italian peninsula, giving Eighth Army the Liri valley and the potentially fastest way to Rome. Mark Clark's Fifth Army is to advance on a narrow front to turn the right flank of the German army while holding the southern edge of the Liri valley. The Eighth Army will then break through at Cassino and push up the Liri valley to Valmontone and trap the German Tenth Army with the help of VI Corps from Anzio. Clark has little interest in playing second fiddle to the British. He plans to use the French Expeditionary Corps and the U.S. II Corps to cut the Itri-Pico Road and be in a position to move faster than the Eighth Army on the road to Rome and capture the city first.

PACIFIC: Commander in Chief of the Japanese Combined Fleet, Admiral Koga Mineichi, is killed in a plane crash en route to Davao Island in the Philippines.

CENTRAL PACIFIC: Seventh Air Force B-24 Liberators from Eniwetok Atoll bomb Truk.

The B-24s of the 431st Bombardment Squadron (Heavy), 11th Bombardment Group (Heavy), redeploy from Tarawa to Kwajalein Atoll.

Carrier aircraft from Admiral Raymond A. Spruance's TF 58 sink a Japanese guardboat in the Palau Islands.

NEW BRITAIN: Thirteenth Air Force B-25 Mitchells bomb logistics sites, while P-40s attack Wunapope. P-39 Airacobras and P-38 Lightnings bomb Rabaul with incendiaries.

NEW GUINEA: Fifth Air Force sends 60 B-24 Liberators escorted by P-38 Lightnings to bomb Hollandia, damaging the three airfields and a large number of aircraft on the ground. Reporting shows 14 Japanese aircraft shot down. Over 120 A-20 Havocs and B-25 Mitchells bomb targets around Tadji, Wewak, and Hansa Bay.

April 1

CBI: A combat team of the 3rd Battalion of Marauders attempts to clear Japanese defenders from the trail to Nhpum Ga.

ATLANTIC: General Arnold is designated as the executive agent to the JCS for B-29 deployments, missions, and targets.

ETO: Eighth Air Force sends 245 B-17s and 195 B-24 Liberators, escorted by 280 P-47 Thunderbolts and 195 Eighth and Ninth Air Force P-51 Mustangs, to bomb the chemical production facilities at Ludwigshafen, Germany. The B-17s abort the mission and the B-24s disperse to attack targets of opportunity. Seven B-17s are damaged. Aircrews report one confirmed kill. Twelve B-24s are lost and 45 are damaged. Aircrew losses are nine killed, 12 wounded, and 113 missing. Fighter pilots report 13 confirmed kills on the ground and five in the air with two probables. Four aircraft are lost and 14 are damaged. Four pilots are reported missing.

MEDITERRANEAN: German aircraft using aerial torpedoes attack convoy UGS 36 (United States to Mediterranean, Slow) off Algiers, damaging a freighter. It is later beached and returned to service.

ITALY: Fifteenth Air Force receives the headquarters of the 49th Bombardment Wing (Heavy).

Twelfth Air Force B-25 Mitchells and B-26 Marauders attack bridges and railroads. A-20 Havocs attack ammunition storage area and P-40s attack fuel storage areas and bridges.

PACIFIC: U.S. submarine *Flying Fish* torpedoes and sinks a cargo ship in the Bonin Islands.

CENTRAL PACIFIC: Seventh Air Force B-24 Liberators from Makin Island, the Gilbert Islands, and Kwajalein Atoll, bomb Truk.

BOUGAINVILLE: Thirteenth Air Force P-38 Lightnings bomb the mission at Monoitu and P-40s attack logistics bases at Numa Numa.

NEW BRITAIN: Thirteenth Air Force P-39 Airacobras and P-40s attack the wharf area at Simpson Harbor. Three P-40s conduct a follow-on attack on oil and coal storage areas. During the night B-25 Mitchells bomb Rabaul.

NEW GUINEA: The Japanese effort to reinforce western New Guinea brings their total number of ground troops available to 50,000 men.

Fifth Air Force B-24 Liberators bomb Ceram Island in the Moluccas and B-25 Mitchells attack Penfoei on Timor Island.

April 2

CBI: The Marauders receive 75 millimeter pack howitzers via airdrop at Hsamshingyang. The 3rd Battalion can now provide artillery support to the 2nd Battalion surrounded at Nhpum Ga.

Tenth Air Force P-40s bomb Kamaing.

The first operational B-29 of the XX Bomber Command, piloted by Colonel Leonard F. Harman, lands at Chakulia, India. The headquarters of 40th Bombardment Group (Very Heavy) arrives at Chakulia from the United States.

MEDITERRANEAN: Fifteenth Air Force sends a total of 125 B-17s and over 150 B-24 Liberators against the Steyr, Austria, ball bearing factory and aircraft component production facility. Twenty bombers are lost and 30 damaged. Aircrews report 84 confirmed kills and fighter pilots report 32 confirmed kills. One P-38 is lost.

B17s bomb the marshaling yard at Brod, Yugoslavia. B-24s bomb an air depot at Mostar and a marshaling yard at Bihać in Yugoslavia. Nineteen bombers are lost to enemy fighters. Aircrews report over 150 enemy fighters shot down.

SOUTHWEST PACIFIC AREA: U.S. submarine *Hake* torpedoes and damages a tanker off Singapore.

CENTRAL PACIFIC: Seventh Air Force B-24 Liberators from Eniwetok bomb Truk and B-25 Mitchells bomb Jaluit and Maloelap Atolls. Thirteenth Air Force sends 31 B-24 Liberators on a raid on against Dublon Island, Truk Atoll. Warehouses and the docks are damaged. Aircrews report over 30 enemy fighters shot down. Four B-24s are lost.

U.S. submarine *Greenling* is conducting a month-long reconnaissance of islands in the Marianas. USS *Salmon* is conducting a similar reconnaissance mission in the Carolines, examining Ulithi, Yap, and Woleai Atoll.

NEW BRITAIN: Thirteenth Air Force sends 23 B-25 Mitchells to bomb Lakunai.

NEW GUINEA: Fifth Air Force sends over 120 bombers and fighters against Wewak, Hansa Bay, Madang, and Bogadjim. B-25 Mitchells bomb Dili and Penfoei on Timor Island.

April 3

CBI: President Roosevelt appeals to Generalissimo Chiang Kai-shek to move Y Force against the Japanese holding the Burma Road in Yunnan province. The request is backed up with a threat to divert all supplies to the Fourteenth Air Force. Chiang accepts and orders the Y Force of six armies (16 infantry divisions total) to joint the offensive.

General Stilwell meets with Admiral Louis Mountbatten, commander of SEAC, and General William Slim, British Fourteenth Army commander, to review campaign objectives for Burma. Stilwell is given the task of using the Chinese-American forces under his command to clear the Japanese from the Mogaung Valley to Myitkyina.

ETO: Ninth Air Force IX Bomber Command establishes a new operational leave policy to adjust to conditions that make it nearly impossible for any bomber crew to survive the 50-mission tour of duty limit. Aircrews can take one week leave between the 25th and 30th missions. Aircrews can take two weeks leave between their 40th and 50th missions.

MEDITERRANEAN: Fifteenth Air Force sends over 450 B-17s and B-24 Liberators to bomb targets in Hungary and Yugoslavia. B-17s attack hit an aircraft production facility in Budapest, Hungary, and a marshaling yard at Brod, Yugoslavia. B-24s miss the rendezvous with escorting fighters, but continue the mission against a marshaling yard at Budapest. The 137 fighters that escort the B-17s report 24 confirmed kills.

ITALY: Twelfth Air Force B-25 Mitchells and B-26 Marauders bomb railway bridges and ammunition storage sites. A-36 Intruder (Apache) fighter-bombers attack railroad targets and P-40s attack supply and transportation targets.

PACIFIC: U.S. submarine *Pollack* attack a Japanese convoy, sinking a cargo ship off Honshu, Japan.

CENTRAL PACIFIC: Seventh Air Force B-24 Liberators, staging through Eniwetok, bomb Truk. B-25 Mitchells from Abemama and Tarawa attack Maloelap and Jaluit Atolls.

B-24 Liberators of the 98th Bombardment Squadron (Heavy), 11th Bombardment Group (Heavy), redeploy from Tarawa to Eniwetok Atoll.

NEW BRITAIN: Thirteenth Air Force sends 23 B-25 Mitchells against Rabaul after six B-25 Mitchells bomb Rabaul during the night.

NEW GUINEA: Fifth Air Force sends over 300 B-24 Liberators, B-25 Mitchells, A-20 Havocs, and P-38 Lightnings to attack the airfields at Hollandia. Supported by Ultra intelligence, the Americans are able to destroy several hundred aircraft parked on the ground and 26 are reported to have been destroyed in the air. This attack completely eliminates the Japanese air force over central New Guinea and marks American air dominance for the remainder of the campaign.

P-40s, P-47 Thunderbolts, and P-39 Airacobras attack targets around Wewak, Hansa Bay, Bogia, and Madang.

April 4

CBI: Sergeant Ray Matsumoto, a Marauder with 2nd Battalion on Nhpum Ga, places himself close to the Japanese lines to overhear the officers briefing their soldiers on the next attack. He returns and warns the defenders, who fall back from their main line of defense and establish new positions. When the Japanese do attack, they find the defensive line abandoned. The Japanese are confused by this discovery, but then Matsumoto pretends to be a Japanese officer and begins giving orders to charge. The soldiers respond and move directly into the massed fire of the prepared Marauders. Matsumoto's initiative and resourcefulness by all accounts probably save the battalion from being overrun.

Tenth Air Force sends over 120 fighter-bombers and four B-25 Mitchells against supply sites around Mogaung and support ground forces near Kamaing and Myitkyina.

ATLANTIC: Headquarters of the Twentieth Air Force is activated in Washington, D.C.

ETO: Eighth Air Force receives the B-24 Liberators of the 836th, 837th, 838th, and 839th Bombardment Squadrons (Heavy), 487th Bombardment Group, and the headquarters of the 339th Fighter Group from the United States. The bomber squadrons will fly their first missions in early May.

Ninth Air Force receives the P-47 Thunderbolts of the 410th Fighter Squadron and headquarters of the 373rd Fighter Group. The squadron's first mission is scheduled for early May. Headquarters units of the 404th Fighter-Bomber Group, the 406th Fighter-Bomber Group, and the 410th Bombardment Group (Light) arrive. The A-20 Havocs of the 644th, 645th, 646th, and 647th Bombardment Squadrons (Light) will fly their first missions in early May. P-38 Lightnings of the 393rd and 394th Fighter Squadrons of the 367th Fighter Group will fly their first missions in early May.

MEDITERRANEAN: To assist the Soviet offensive, Fifteenth Air Force bombers attack rail transportation and rail facilities in Romania and Hungary to prevent resupply or reinforcement of German forces in the east. One mission involves 350 B-17s and B-24 Liberators escorted by 119 P-38 Lightnings targeting the marshaling yards at Bucharest, Romania. Only 28 B-24s hit the target as others turn back in heavy weather. The bombers without fighter escort are attacked by 50 German fighters, which shoot down seven bombers. Aircrews report 40 confirmed kills and 13 probables.

CENTRAL PACIFIC: Shore battery fire damages a U.S. destroyer off Wotje Atoll.

BOUGAINVILLE: Thirteenth Air Force P-40s attack barges in Gazelle Harbor. Ten B-25 Mitchells bomb Buka airfield and P-38 Lightnings conduct ground support missions along Empress Augusta Bay.

CENTRAL PACIFIC: Seventh Air Force B-25 Mitchells from Abemama Island and Tarawa attack Ponape Island, and Jaluit and Maloelap Atolls.

NEW GUINEA: Fifth Air Force B-24 Liberators bomb Wewak.

April 5

ETO: Eighth Air Force B-24 Liberators sent to bomb V-weapon sites in France abort the mission due to heavy clouds. An attack by 96 P-38 Lightnings, 236 P-47 Thunderbolts, and 124 P-51 Mustangs against German airfields is also limited by heavy cloud cover. Fighter pilots report 98 confirmed kills and four probables. Nine aircraft are lost and 11 are damaged. Pilot casualties are one killed and eight missing.

One of 17 B-24 Liberators sent to support a Carpetbagger mission is lost over Europe.

Eighth Air Force receives the headquarters of the 487th Bombardment Group (Heavy), the 503rd, 504th, and 505th Fighter-Bomber Squadrons, 339th Fighter-Bomber Group. The P-51 Mustang-equipped squadrons will fly their first missions in late April. The B-24 Liberators of the 832nd, 833rd, 834th, and 835th Bombardment Squadrons (Heavy) of the 486th Bombardment Group (Heavy) will fly their first missions in early May.

Ninth Air Force receives the headquarters, 36th Fighter Group, and the P-47 Thunderbolts of the 22nd Fighter Squadron. The squadron's first mission is scheduled for early May. The headquarters, 50th Fighter Group, and the P-47s of the 10th, 81st, and 313th Fighter Squadrons are scheduled for their first missions in early May. The P-38 Lightnings of the 392nd Fighter Squadron and headquarters, 367th Fighter Group, arrive. The squadron's first mission will be in early May. Headquarters, 397th Bombardment Group (Medium), and the B-26 Marauders of the 596th, 597th, 598th, and 599th Bombardment Squadrons (Medium) will fly their first missions in late April. The P-47s of the 411th and 412th Fighter Squadrons, 373rd Fighter Group, will fly their first missions in early May. The P-47s of the 506th, 507th, and 508th Fighter-Bomber Squadrons, 404th Fighter-Bomber Group, and the 513th Fighter-Bomber Squadron, 406th Fighter-Bomber Group, will also fly their first missions in early May.

MEDITERRANEAN: Fifteenth Air Force sends over 300 B-17s and B-24 Liberators against marshaling yards in Ploeşti, Romania and at Nis and Leskovac in Yugoslavia.

A total of 95 B-17s and 135 B-24 Liberators are sent to bomb the Ploeşti marshaling yards. Aircrews report 41 confirmed kills. Thirteen bombers are lost.

ITALY: Twelfth Air Force P-40s and A-36 Intruder (Apache) fighter-bombers attack transportation and logistics targets.

CENTRAL PACIFIC: Seventh Air Force B-25 Mitchells from Tarawa bomb Maloelap Atoll, then land at Majuro Atoll in the Marshall Islands to rearm and refuel, then bomb Jaluit Atoll en route back to Tarawa.

Headquarters of the 11th Bombardment Group (Heavy) moves from Tarawa to Kwajalein.

Navy PB4Y Privateer sinks a Japanese auxiliary submarine chaser off Moen Island at Truk.

Navy TBM Avengers and FM-2 Wildcat fighters damage Japanese submarine *I-45* operating northeast of the Marshalls.

BOUGAINVILLE: Thirteenth Air Force sends 12 B-25 Mitchells to bomb Kara.

NEW GUINEA: Fifth Air Force B-24 Liberators, B-25 Mitchells, A-20 Havocs, and P-38 Lightnings attack Hollandia and Humboldt Bay. P-47 Thunderbolts and P-40s attack targets around Hansa Bay-Bogia and Wewak. B-24 Liberators bomb Kaimana and Efman Island.

B-25 Mitchells bomb Koepang on Timor Island.

April 6

CBI: Elements of the 1st Provisional Tank Group support the Chinese 22nd Division at Shaduzup.

General Chennault, commander of Fourteenth Air Force, sends General Stilwell an assessment warning of a possible large-scale Japanese offensive in eastern China. To stop the Japanese attack and provide air support for Chinese forces, he requests an additional 8,000 to 10,000 tons of supplies a month be flown over the Hump. Stilwell, pressed to provide logistics support for the B-29 strategic bombing program, fly supplies to British forces, and support the Chinese-American offensive in Burma, is unable to provide any more assistance to Chennault.

ATLANTIC: General Henry H. "Hap" Arnold assumes command of the Twentieth Air Force at Washington, D.C.

ETO: Eighth Air Force Mission sends 12 B-24 Liberators with 27 P-47 Thunderbolts escorting to attack V-weapon sites in France.

Ninth Air Force receives the P-47 Thunderbolts of the 23rd Fighter Squadron, 36th Fighter Group, and the 512th Fighter-Bomber Squadron, 406th Fighter-Bomber Group. The squadrons' first missions are scheduled for early May.

MEDITERRANEAN: Fifteenth Air Force B-24 Liberators bomb the airfield at Zagreb, Yugoslavia. Six bombers are lost. Aircrews report 17 enemy fighters shot down.

ITALY: Twelfth Air Force B-25 Mitchells bomb the airfield at Perugia. B-26 Marauders bomb a bridge near Orvieto. A-36 Intruder (Apache) fighter-bombers attack rail lines and bridges.

CENTRAL PACIFIC: Seventh Air Force B-24 Liberators from Kwajalein bomb Wake Island. B-25 Mitchells from Abemama Island bomb Jaluit Atoll, rearm at Majuro Atoll, and hit Maloelap Atoll en route back to Abemama. Thirteenth Air Force sends 34 B-24 Liberators to attack Dublon Island at Truk.

NEW BRITAIN: Thirteenth Air Force sends 22 B-25 Mitchells to bomb Lakunai airfield.

NEW GUINEA: Fifth Air Force P-39 Airacobras, P-40s, and P-47 Thunderbolts attack targets around Wewak, Aitape, and Madang.

B-25 Mitchells bomb Koepang, Timor Island.

April 7

ALEUTIANS: Eleventh Air Force sends eight B-24 Liberators to attack a Japanese convoy located near Matsuwa Island in the Kuriles, but they turn back due to a variety of engine, navigation, and weather problems.

CARIBBEAN: Sixth Air Force VI Bomber Command redeploys the B-24 Liberators of the 74th and 397th Bombardment Squadrons (Heavy) from Guatemala City, Guatemala, and the Galapagos Islands to Rio Hato, Panama.

CBI: The 3rd Battalion of Marauders makes slow progress against Japanese strongpoints set up around Nhpum Ga. The 1st Battalion makes a forced march to join the rest of the unit at Nhpum Ga.

Tenth Air Force P-51 Mustangs and B-25 Mitchells attack Japanese positions throughout the Mogaung Valley.

In China, Fourteenth Air Force B-24 Liberator aircrews on a sweep from Hong Kong to Formosa report sinking a large riverboat and a small cargo ship and damaging two other cargo ships. One of the two B-24s sent on the mission is lost. In French Indochina, P-40s attack small vessels in Haiphong harbor and report sinking four.

The headquarters of the 462nd Bombardment Group (Very Heavy), XX Bomber Command, arrives at Piardoba, India, from the United States.

ATLANTIC: Destroyer USS *Champlin* rams German submarine *U-856* in mid-Atlantic. *Champlin* and a destroyer escort subsequently sink the U-boat.

ITALY: Fifteenth Air Force sends over 400 B-17s and B-24 Liberators escorted by nearly 100 P-38 Lightnings to attack marshaling yards. Aircrews report 20 confirmed kills.

Twelfth Air Force A-36 Intruder (Apache) fighter-bombers attack gun emplacements and rail targets near Orvieto. P-40s and P-47 Thunderbolts attack logistics sites, bridges, and transportation targets around Rome.

SOUTHWEST PACIFIC AREA: U.S. submarine *Scamp* is damaged by a bomb from a Japanese floatplane off Mindanao and terminates her patrol.

CENTRAL PACIFIC: Seventh Air Force B-25 Mitchells from Tarawa bomb Maloelap Atoll, rearm at Majuro Atoll, and bomb Jaluit Atoll en route back to Tarawa.

U.S. submarine *Pampanito* is damaged by depth charges off the Marianas but remains on patrol.

BOUGAINVILLE: Thirteenth Air Force P-40s attack Japanese pillboxes near the Reini River and B-24 Liberators bomb Monoitu mission.

NEW BRITAIN: Thirteenth Air Force B-25 Mitchells bomb Talili Bay and Vunakanau and Tobera airfields. Another six B-25s conduct a night bombing raid on Rabaul.

The headquarters of the 5th Bombardment Group (Heavy) moves from Munda, New Georgia, to Momote airfield, Los Negros Island, in the Admiralties.

U.S. destroyer *Saufley* sinks Japanese submarine *I-2* off New Hanover in the Bismarck Archipelago.

NEW GUINEA: Fifth Air Force B-24 Liberators bomb Wakde Island. B-25 Mitchells bomb the barracks at Penfoei, on Timor Island.

April 8

CBI: In French Indochina, Fourteenth Air Force sends 11 B-24 Liberators to bomb the railyards in Hanoi. In China, nine B-24 Liberators bomb the airfield on Samah Bay, Hainan Island, while four others lay mines in the bay.

ETO: Eighth Air Force sends 314 B-17s and 350 B-24 Liberators divided into three separate forces, escorted by 136 P-38 Lightnings, 438 Eighth and Ninth Air Force P-47 Thunderbolts, and 206 Eighth and Ninth Air Force P-51 Mustangs, to attack airfields in northwest Germany and aircraft production facilities near Brunswick. Aircrews report 58 confirmed kills and four probables. Thirty-four bombers are lost and 349 damaged. Aircrew casualties are nine killed, 31 wounded, and 340 missing. Fighter pilots report 88 confirmed kills in the air and 49 on the ground with nine probables. A total of 23 fighters are lost and 20 are damaged. All 23 pilots of the downed aircraft are reported missing.

During the night five B-17s drop one million leaflets over Liege, Brussels, Ghent, Antwerp, and Mont-sur-Sombre, Belgium.

Ninth Air Force sends 198 B-26 Marauders to attack the marshaling yard at Hasselt and bomb Coxyde airfield in Belgium. P-47 Thunderbolts bomb targets near Hasselt.

ITALY: Fifteenth Air Force receives the headquarters of the 484th Bombardment Group (Heavy) and the B-24 Liberators of the 824th and 827th Bombardment Squadrons (Heavy) from the United States. The squadrons' first missions will be in late April.

CENTRAL PACIFIC: Seventh Air Force B-24 Liberators flying out of Kwajalein bomb Truk. B-25 Mitchells from Abemama Island bomb Ponape Island and B-25s from Tarawa attack Maloelap Atoll, rearm at Majuro Atoll and bomb Jaluit Atoll en route to Tarawa.

U.S. submarine *Seahorse* attacks a Japanese convoy off Guam, hitting an ammunition ship, which explodes and damages a destroyer. A water tanker is also damaged in another attack. *Seahorse* avoids a depth charge attack.

U.S. submarine *Trigger* is damaged by depth charges off the Marianas but remains on patrol.

BOUGAINVILLE: Thirteenth Air Force B-24 Liberators bomb Monoitu mission.

NEW BRITAIN: Thirteenth Air Force B-25 Mitchells bomb Lakunai airfield.

NEW IRELAND: Thirteenth Air Force B-25 Mitchells bomb Kavieng airfield during the night.

NEW GUINEA: Fifth Air Force P-40s attack targets of opportunity in the Aitape-Wewak area.

April 9

CBI: Japanese abandon their attack on Nhpum Ga as the 3rd Battalion of the Marauders links up with the 2nd Battalion. The 2nd Battalion has held off Japanese forces for seven days. The Japanese withdraw toward Kamaing. U.S. losses are 59 killed, 314 wounded, and 379 evacuated for various diseases. About 400 Japanese are killed. The Marauders have about 1,400 men available to continue the campaign out of the 3,000 who began. The 1st and 3rd Battalions of the Marauders withdraw to Nawbum, while the 2nd Battalion rests and reorganizes at Senjo Ga. The 2nd Battalion is reduced by casualties and sickness to less than half-strength. The Marauders believe that after 90 days in the field they should be relieved, but General Stilwell needs them for the capture of Myitkyina.

Fourteenth Air Force B-25 Mitchells sink a merchant vessel off Hainan Island. **ATLANTIC:** TBM Avengers and FM-2 Wildcat fighters from the escort carrier USS *Guadalcanal* together with four destroyer escorts sink German submarine *U-515* off Madeira Island.

ETO: Eighth Air Force sends 296 B-17s and 246 B-24 Liberators, escorted by 119 P-38 Lightnings, 387 Eighth and Ninth Air Force P-47 Thunderbolts, and 213 Eighth and Ninth Air Force P-51 Mustangs, against aircraft production facilities at Rahmel and Poznan in Poland and Marienburg and Warnemund in Germany. Aircrews report 45 confirmed kills and eight probables. A total of 32 bombers are lost and 117 damaged. Aircrew casualties are 25 killed, 21 wounded, and 320 missing. Fighter pilots report 20 confirmed kills and one probable in the air and 19 confirmed kills on the ground. Ten fighters are lost and 15 are damaged. Pilot losses are three killed, two wounded, and six missing.

During the night, five B-17s drop nearly three million leaflets over Rouen, Paris, Amiens, and Caen. A total of 23 B-24 Liberators support Carpetbagger operations. **ITALY:** Fifteenth Air Force receives the B-17s of the 815th, 816th, and 840th Bombardment Squadrons (Heavy) of the 483rd Bombardment Group (Heavy). The squadrons' first mission is scheduled for mid-April.

Twelfth Air Force P-40 and A-36 fighter-bombers attack railroad targets, motor transport, and gun positions.

Destroyer USS *Hilary P. Jones* provides gunfire support at Anzio. **PACIFIC:** U.S. submarine *Whale* torpedoes and sinks a Japanese cargo ship off the northwestern coast of Kyushu, Japan.

CENTRAL PACIFIC: Seventh Air Force B-25 Mitchells from Abemama Island bomb Jaluit Atoll, rearm at Majuro Atoll, and then attack Maloelap Atoll en route back to Abemama.

U.S. submarine *Seahorse* attacks a Japanese convoy and sinks a transport off Saipan.

U.S. submarine *Trigger* takes on more damage after a second depth charge attack near the Marianas but continues her patrol. **NEW BRITAIN:** Thirteenth Air Force B-25 Mitchells bomb Lakunai. Other B-25s bomb Rabaul during the night. **NEW GUINEA:** Fifth Air Force B-25 Mitchells bomb Aitape. B-24 Liberators and A-20 Havocs bomb Wewak and P-39 Airacobras attack targets in the Madang area.

April 10
CARIBBEAN: Sixth Air Force VI Bomber Command redeploys the B-24 Liberators of the 9th Bombardment Squadron (Heavy) from the Galapagos Islands to Howard Field, Panama Canal Zone.

CBI: In French Indochina, Fourteenth Air Force B-25 Mitchells damage bridges at Phu Dien Chau.

The JCS informally approves Operation Matterhorn, the plan for the strategic bombing of Japan, which had been approved in principle by President Roosevelt on November 10, 1943. The B-29 Superfortresses based in Calcutta, India, and staging through advanced airfields in the area of Chengtu, China, will be assigned to the 58th Bombardment Wing (Very Heavy) of the XX Bomber Command. The XX Bomber Command in turn will be assigned to the newly activated Twentieth Air Force, operating under General Henry H. "Hap" Arnold, who will serve as the executive agent for the JCS in determining missions and targets.

ATLANTIC: TBM Avengers and FM-2 Wildcat fighters from the escort carrier *Guadalcanal* sink German submarine *U-68* off Madeira Island.

ETO: Eighth Air Force sends 486 B-17s and 243 B-24 Liberators against aviation production targets and airfields in Belgium and France, escorted by 51 P-38 Lightnings, 295 P-47 Thunderbolts, and 150 Eighth and Ninth Air Force P-51 Mustangs. Aircrews report six confirmed kills and two probables. Three bombers are lost and 123 damaged. Aircrew losses are five wounded and 30 missing. Fighter pilots report 52 confirmed kills. Two aircraft are lost and five are damaged. Two pilots are reported missing.

P-38 Lightnings and P-47 Thunderbolts are sent against airfields in France. Three aircraft are lost and one damaged. Fighter pilots report two confirmed kills on the ground. Three pilots are reported missing.

During the night five B-17s drop two million leaflets over Lille, Le Mans, Chartres, Reims, and Orleans in France. A total of 23 B-24s fly in support of Carpetbagger operations.

Ninth Air Force sends 258 B-26 Marauders and 41 A-20 Havocs, including 12 aircraft dropping Window (aluminum chaff to eliminate radar tracking), to attack coastal batteries in France. Another 267 B-26 Marauders and A-20 Havocs are sent to bomb a marshaling yard, an airfield, coastal defenses, and V-weapon sites in Belgium. P-47 Thunderbolts attack the Evreux airfield in France.

ITALY: In the III Corps area the 85th Infantry Division begins moving into the Allied line near Minturo.

Fifteenth Air Force receives the B-24 Liberators of the 776th Bombardment Squadron (Heavy) of the 464th Bombardment Group (Heavy) from the United States. The squadron's first missions are scheduled for late April.

Twelfth Air Force B-25 Mitchells and B-26 Marauders attack transportation targets. A-20 Havocs bomb an ammunition storage area.

SOUTHWEST PACIFIC AREA: MacArthur approves Alamo Force's plan for Reckless, the assault on Hollandia. MacArthur's confidence is high. "It should win without question," he notes.

CENTRAL PACIFIC: Seventh Air Force B-24 Liberators, staging through Eniwetok, bomb Truk and B-25 Mitchells attack Ponape from Abemama Island.

NEW BRITAIN: Admiral Nimitz releases the 40th Infantry Division to Southwest Pacific Area command in order to get the 1st Marine Division back under his operational control for future operations in the Central Pacific. Major General Rapp Brush, commander of the 40th, begins preparations to occupy New Britain.

Thirteenth Air Force B-25 Mitchells bomb the Ratawul logistics base.

NEW GUINEA: Fifth Air Force sends 60 B-24 Liberators to work with navy destroyers offshore in attacking antiaircraft positions near the airfields at Hansa Bay.

April 11

CBI: Tenth Air Force P-51 Mustangs, A-36 Intruder (Apache) fighter-bombers, and B-25 Mitchells fly ground support missions near Maungkan and attack Japanese positions in the Mogaung Valley.

The XX Bomber Command receives the headquarters, 444th Bombardment Group (Very Heavy), and 676th Bombardment Squadron (Very Heavy) at Charra, India, with B-29 Superfortresses. The 25th Bombardment Squadron (Very Heavy), 40th Bombardment Group (Very Heavy), arrives at Chakulia, India with B-29 Superfortresses. The squadrons' first missions are scheduled for early June.

ETO: Eighth Air Force sends 643 B-17s and 274 B-24 Liberators escorted by 124 P-38 Lightnings, 454 Eighth and Ninth Air Force P-47 Thunderbolts, and 241 Eighth and Ninth Air Force P-51 Mustangs against aircraft production facilities in northern Germany. The bombers also drop 2.4 million leaflets. Aircrews report 73 confirmed kills and 24 probables. A total of 64 bombers are lost and 411 damaged. Aircrew casualties are 19 killed, 31 wounded, and 652 missing. Fighter pilots report 51 confirmed kills and five probables in the air and 65 confirmed kills on the ground. A total of 16 fighters are lost and 29 are damaged. Pilot losses are 16 missing.

During the night, five B-17s drop two million leaflets over Paris, Rouen, Le Mans, Rennes, Vichy, Lyon, Limoges, and Toulouse.

Ninth Air Force sends 229 B-26 Marauders and 36 A-20 Havocs (including three dropping Window) to attack military installations in Belgium. P-47 Thunderbolts dive-bomb a military installation and an airfield in France.

First Lieutenant Edward S. Michael of the 364th Bomber Squadron, 305th Bomber Group, is piloting a B-17 over Germany when his group is attacked by a number of German fighters. Michael's B-17 receives heavy damage from antiaircraft fire and the fighters, forcing it to fall out of the protective air formation. It becomes the focus of enemy fighter attention. Although seriously wounded, and his copilot unconscious, Michael maintains control of the bomber. When notified that the load of incendiary bombs his plane carries is in danger of catching fire, he orders the crew to bail out. Michael continues to avoid enemy antiaircraft and fighters, seeking a place to land within friendly lines. His own heavily bleeding wounds cause him to lose consciousness even as the copilot takes the controls. Michael regains consciousness and flies the damaged bomber to an airfield on the coast of England, landing safely and saving the members of the crew who remained with the bomber. For his heroic skill and dedication to duty, First Lieutenant Michael will receive the Medal of Honor.

MEDITERRANEAN: German bombers and torpedo bombers attack Convoy UGS 37 (United States to Mediterranean, Slow) east of Algiers. One destroyer escort and one freighter are damaged.

German aircraft begin active aerial mining near Anzio.

ITALY: Twelfth Air Force B-25 Mitchells and B-26 Marauders attack rail targets.

Southwest Pacific Area: General George C. Kenney, commanding general of Allied Air Force, SWPA, creates the Thirteenth Air Task Force (Provisional) from elements of the Thirteenth Air Force and other units.

U.S. submarine *Redfin* torpedoes and sinks a Japanese destroyer in the northern Celebes Sea.

Central Pacific: Seventh Air Force B-25 Mitchells from the Gilbert Islands bomb Ponape Island, rearm at Majuro Atoll, and bomb Jaluit and Maloelap Atolls on the return to the Carolines.

Bougainville: Thirteenth Air Force P-40s and P-39 Airacobras bomb Aitara and pilots report destroying a bridge near Mawareka.

New Britain: Thirteenth Air Force P-40s and P-39 Airacobras attack Rabaul and Talili Bay ammunition storage sites.

New Guinea: Fifth Air Force A-20 Havocs and B-25 Mitchells supported by 30 P-47 Thunderbolts and P-40s, attack antiaircraft positions, logistics bases, and personnel areas at Hollandia. B-24 Liberators and B-25s bomb barges and antiaircraft positions near Hansa Bay.

April 12

CBI: Tenth Air Force B-25 Mitchells, P-40s, A-36 Intruder (Apache) fighter-bombers, and P-51 Mustangs conduct a ground support mission in the Mogaung Valley and attack logistics sites and targets of opportunity in the Mogaung, Myitkyina, Kamaing, Taungni, and Shaduzup areas.

ETO: Eighth Air Force sends 455 B-17s and B-24 Liberators against industrial facilities in Germany, escorted by 124 P-38 Lightnings, 449 Eighth and Ninth Air Force P-47 Thunderbolts, and 193 Eighth and Ninth Air Force P-51 Mustangs. Aircrews report 10 confirmed kills and six probables. Six B-17s are lost and 28 bombers are damaged. Aircrew casualties are 12 killed, 16 wounded, and 56 missing. Fighter pilots report 18 confirmed kills and one probable, with another confirmed kill on the ground. Five fighters are lost and 23 damaged. Pilot losses are five missing.

Ninth Air Force sends 231 B-26 Marauders and 20 A-20 Havocs to attack railroad, shore batteries, radar installations, airfields, and V-weapon sites along the coast of Belgium and France. Over 70 P-47 Thunderbolts conduct dive-bombing attacks on military installations in northern France.

Mediterranean: Fifteenth Air Force sends over 400 B-17s and B-24 Liberators escorted by more than 200 P-38 Lightnings and P-47 Thunderbolts to attack production facilities in Austria and Yugoslavia. One B-17 and six B-24s are lost. Aircrews and fighter pilots report a total of 43 confirmed kills and 13 probables.

The Fifteenth Air Force receives the headquarters of the 465th Bombardment Group (Heavy) and the B-24s of the 783rd Bombardment Squadron (Heavy) from the United States. The squadron's first mission will be in early May.

Italy: Twelfth Air Force B-25 Mitchells and B-26 Marauders attack road and rail bridges. A-36 Intruder (Apache) fighter-bombers, P-40s, and P-47 Thunderbolts attack logistics sites, railroad bridges, and vehicles.

Pacific: U.S. submarine *Halibut* torpedoes and sinks a Japanese army passenger-cargo ship near the Ryukyus.

Central Pacific: Seventh Air Force B-25 Mitchells from Abemama Island, bomb Maloelap Atoll, rearm at Majuro Atoll, and bomb Jaluit Atoll en route back to Abemama.

Bougainville: Thirteenth Air Force P-40s and P-39 Airacobras attack the Numa Numa trail and harbor area.

New Britain: Thirteenth Air Force sends 23 B-25 Mitchells and 11 P-39 Airacobras to attack Rabaul and seven B-25 Mitchells attack the logistics base at Ratawul. P-40s and P-39 Airacobras attack Vunakanau airfield.

Admiralties: The headquarters of Thirteenth Air Force's 5th Bombardment Group (Heavy) is ordered to redeploy from Guadalcanal and New Georgia to Los Negros Island. This headquarters will become the core of the newly created Thirteenth Air Task Force.

New Guinea: Fifth Air Force sends B-24 Liberators, B-25 Mitchells, and A-20 Havocs, with over 60 P-38 Lightnings, to bomb antiaircraft positions, airfields, logistics sites, and shipping construction. B-24 Liberators, B-25 Mitchells, A-20 Havocs, and P-39 Airacobras bomb and strafe targets around Wewak, Madang, and along Hansa Bay.

Fifth Air Force B-24 Liberators, B-25 Mitchells, B-26 Marauders, and P-38 Lightnings bomb Japanese installations in Hollandia, sinking a cargo ship and three fishing vessels. A-20 Havocs sink a cargo ship in Humboldt Bay, Hollandia.

April 13

Aleutians: Eleventh Air Force sends three B-24 Liberators on an armed reconnaissance and bombing mission over the Matsuwa Island airfield and installations on Onnekotan Island.

CBI: Tenth Air Force B-25 Mitchells, P-40s, P-51 Mustangs, and A-36 Intruder (Apache) fighter-bombers fly ground support missions near Kamaing and attack Japanese positions in the Mogaung Valley.

B-29 Superfortresses of the XX Bomber Command arrive in India. The headquarters 468th Bombardment Group (Very Heavy) and the 792nd, 793rd, 794th, and 795th Bombardment Squadrons (Very Heavy) are located at Kharagpur. The 444th Bombardment Group (Very Heavy) and the 677th and 679th Bombardment Squadrons (Very Heavy) are located at Charra. The squadrons' first missions are scheduled for early June.

ETO: Eighth Air Force sends 415 B-17s and 211 B-24 Liberators against industrial production facilities in Germany, escorted by 134 P-38 Lightnings, 504 Eighth and Ninth Air Force P-47 Thunderbolts, and 233 Eighth and Ninth Air Force P-51 Mustangs. A total of 38 bombers are lost and 352 damaged. Aircrew casualties are 15 killed, 19 wounded, and 369 missing. Nine fighters are lost and 13 damaged. Two pilots are wounded and eight are missing.

During the night four B-17s drop leaflets over Amsterdam, The Hague, and Eindhoven in the Netherlands.

Ninth Air Force sends 121 B-26 Marauders and 37 A-20 Havocs to attack a marshaling yard, coastal batteries, airfields and V-weapon sites along the coast of

France and Belgium. Bad weather causes most of the aircraft to abort the mission. P-47 Thunderbolts conduct dive-bombing attacks on V-weapon sites.

MEDITERRANEAN: Fifteenth Air Force sends 535 B-17s and B-24 Liberators against aircraft production facilities in Hungary. Fourteen bombers are lost and aircrews report 40 enemy fighters shot down and over 120 aircraft destroyed on the ground.

The Fifteenth Air Force receives the B-24 Liberators of the 779th Bombardment Squadron (Heavy) of the 464th Bombardment Group (Heavy) from the United States. The squadron's first mission is scheduled for the end of April.

ITALY: Twelfth Air Force B-25 Mitchells and B-26 Marauders attack bridges and a marshaling yard. A-36 Intruder (Apache) fighter-bombers and P-40s attack bridges, rail lines, and vehicles.

CENTRAL PACIFIC: Seventh Air Force B-24 Liberators from Eniwetok bomb Truk. B-25s from Abemama Island bomb Ponape Island. B-25s from Tarawa bomb Jaluit Atoll, rearm at Majuro Atoll, and bomb Maloelap Atoll on their return to Tarawa.

Thirteenth Air Force B-24 Liberators bomb Truk.

U.S. submarine *Harder* torpedoes and sinks a Japanese destroyer near Guam.

NEW BRITAIN: Thirteenth Air Force sends 24 B-25 Mitchells to attack logistics bases at Talili Bay and Ratawul, while P-40s and P-39 Airacobras attack the Rabaul area.

ADMIRALTIES: The B-17s and B-24 Liberators of the 394th Bombardment Group (Heavy), 5th Bombardment Group (Heavy), Thirteenth Air Force redeploy from Guadalcanal to Momote airfield on Los Negros Island.

NEW GUINEA: Fifth Air Force B-24 Liberators and A-20 Havocs attack airfields on the north coast of New Guinea. A-20 Havocs attack Japanese facilities at Aitape. P-39 Airacobras, B-25 Mitchells, and B-24s attack targets around Hansa Bay and Wakde Island.

April 14

CBI: The Chinese agree to support an offensive in Burma with Y Force.

Tenth Air Force P-40s attack Japanese positions in the Mogaung Valley.

ETO: The air plan for Neptune is laid out, consisting of a preparation phase and an assault phase. Air Chief Marshall Trafford Leigh-Mallory is the commander of the tactical air forces. The British Second Tactical Air Force and the U.S. Ninth Air Force are to provide support to the ground forces landing on the beaches. The Second Tactical Air Force targets are rail lines, bridges, airfields, coastal batteries, and radar sites in order to restrict German reinforcements from reaching the beachhead.

General Eisenhower, commander of Supreme Headquarters Allied Expeditionary Forces (SHAEF), takes operational control of strategic air forces from the CCS to support the invasion of Europe. Eisenhower now can direct what targets are to be attacked within the ETO, subject to the approval of the CCS. As a primary mission, the strategic air forces will target industrial and economic targets in Germany and provide direct support to the ground forces as a secondary mission. Strategic forces will attack French and Belgian rail lines to restrict resupply and reinforcement of German forces in Normandy.

ITALY: Twelfth Air Force B-25 Mitchells and B-26 Marauders target rail facilities, viaducts, and bridges. A-36 Intruder (Apache) fighter-bombers and P-40s attack rail lines and bridges as well as logistics sites, gun positions, and production facilities.

CENTRAL PACIFIC: Seventh Air Force B-25s from Eniwetok bomb Ponape Island. B-25s from Abemama Island bomb Jaluit Atoll rearm at Majuro Atoll, and bomb Maloelap Atoll on the return to Tarawa. Thirteenth Air Force sends 19 B-24 Liberators to bomb Truk.

Japanese bombers attack Eniwetok Atoll but cause no significant damage.

BOUGAINVILLE: Thirteenth Air Force P-40s and P-39 Airacobras attack targets in the northeast section of the island.

NEW BRITAIN: Thirteenth Air Force sends 24 B-25 Mitchells and P-40s and P-39 Airacobras to attack the logistics base at Ratawul and hit targets at Wunapope.

April 15

ALEUTIANS: During the night three Eleventh Air Force B-24 Liberators on an armed reconnaissance mission over Matsuwa and Onnekotan Islands attack several targets, including Matsuwa airfield.

Vice Admiral Frank Jack Fletcher takes command of Alaskan Sea Frontier at Adak, Aleutian Islands.

ATLANTIC: The CCS authorizes an increase in naval forces to support the new assessment that increases the number of assault divisions for Neptune from three to five. The total naval force available includes six battleships, 22 cruisers, and 93 destroyers.

ETO: Eighth Air Force sends 132 P-38 Lightnings, 262 P-47 Thunderbolts, and 222 Eighth and Ninth Air Force P-51 Mustangs on a fighter sweep attacking airfields in central and western Germany. Fighter pilots report a total of 57 confirmed kills and one probable. U.S. aircraft losses are 33 downed and 36 damaged. Thirty pilots are reported missing.

MEDITERRANEAN: Fifteenth Air Force sends 448 B-17s and B-24 Liberators with fighter escort to attack marshaling yards in Romania and Yugoslavia.

Army Air Force personnel begin meetings with Josef Broz Tito, leader of the Yugoslav partisans, at his headquarters in Drvar, Yugoslavia. The objective is to enlist Tito's support in assisting downed U.S. air crewmen to escape capture and return to friendly lines.

ITALY: Twelfth Air Force B-25 Mitchells and B-26 Marauders attack the Leghorn marshaling yard. P-47 Thunderbolts, P-40s, and A-36 Intruder (Apache) fighter-bombers attack rail lines, vehicles, tanks, and gun positions.

SOUTHWEST PACIFIC AREA: U.S. submarine *Redfin* attacks a Japanese convoy southwest of Mindanao and damages a cargo ship.

PACIFIC: Japanese cargo ship is sunk off Honshu, Japan, probably by a mine laid by U.S. submarine *Steelhead.*

CENTRAL PACIFIC: Major General Robert W. Douglass, Jr., takes command of the Seventh Air Force.

B-25 Mitchells from Tarawa bomb Maloelap Atoll, rearm at Majuro Atoll, and bomb Mille and Jaluit Atolls on the return to Tarawa.

Abemama Naval Base in the Gilbert Islands is established.

NEW BRITAIN: Thirteenth Air Force sends 24 B-25 Mitchells to bomb an ammunition storage facility on Talili Bay, followed by 11 P-39 Airacobras hitting the same target. P-38 Lightnings attack the logistics base at Wunapope.

ADMIRALTIES: Thirteenth Air Force redeploys the B-24 Liberators of the 72nd Bombardment Squadron (Heavy), 5th Bombardment Group (Heavy), from Munda, New Georgia, to Momote airfield, Los Negros Island.

NEW GUINEA: Fifth Air Force sends over 180 B-24 Liberators, B-25 Mitchells, and A-20 Havocs to attack airfields and Japanese positions near Aitape and along the northern coast. P-39 Airacobras attack Japanese positions, logistics sites, and vehicles between Hansa Bay and the Alexishafen area.

April 16

CBI: Nine P-38 Lightnings from the Tenth Air Force shoot down three Japanese medium bombers at Zayatkwin, near Rangoon.

The XX Bomber Command receives the 768th Bombardment Squadron (Very Heavy), 462nd Bombardment Group (Very Heavy), at Piardoba, India. The B-29 Superfortresses will fly their first missions in early June.

ATLANTIC: The battleship USS *Wisconsin* is commissioned at Philadelphia, Pennsylvania. It is the last battleship built for the U.S. Navy.

German submarine *U-550* torpedoes a tanker in convoy CU 1 (New York to United Kingdom) off the New Jersey coast. The tanker is abandoned. Later, the destroyer escort USS *Gandy* rams *U-550* off Nantucket Shoals and, with other escort ships, sinks the U-boat.

MEDITERRANEAN: Fifteenth Air Force sends 432 B-17s and B-24 Liberators to attack industrial production facilities in Romania and Yugoslavia and marshaling yards in Romania.

The Fifteenth Air Force reports the 31st Fighter Group is operational. The P-51 Mustang-equipped unit had been transferred from Twelfth Air Force earlier in the month.

German submarine *U-407* attacks convoy UGS 37 (United States to Mediterranean, Slow) off Libya and torpedoes two U.S. freighters. One is sunk and the other is beached.

ITALY: Twelfth Air Force B-25 Mitchells bomb railway bridges. A-20 Havocs attack fuel storage areas. P-40s, P-47 Thunderbolts, and A-36 Intruder (Apache) fighter-bombers attack transportation targets, vehicles, and ammunition storage sites.

SOUTHWEST PACIFIC AREA: U.S. submarine *Redfin* makes a second attack on a Japanese convoy southwest of Mindanao, sinking a cargo ship.

CENTRAL PACIFIC: Seventh Air Force B-25 Mitchells, staging through Eniwetok, bomb Truk. B-25s from Abemama Island bomb Maloelap Atoll, rearm at Majuro Atoll, and bomb Mille Atoll en route back to Abemama.

NEW BRITAIN: Thirteenth Air Force sends 24 B-25 Mitchells to attack the logistics base at Ratawul. P-40s and P-39 Airacobras attack Rabaul.

ADMIRALTIES: Thirteenth Air Force redeploys the B-24 Liberators of the 23rd Bombardment Squadron (Heavy), 5th Bombardment Group (Heavy), from Munda, New Georgia, to Momote airfield, Los Negros Island.

NEW GUINEA: Fifth Air Force sends over 170 B-24 Liberators, B-25 Mitchells, and A-20 Havocs to bomb targets around Hollandia. P-38 Lightnings attack targets around Madang. B-24s attack Wakde Island.

B-25s bomb Koepang on Timor Island.

U.S. submarine *Paddle* attacks a Japanese convoy and sinks a transport and a cargo ship in the Ceram Sea.

April 17

CBI: The Japanese *Ichigo* Offensive in China. The Japanese attempt to forestall Allied efforts to establish B-29 bases in China and to secure for themselves an overland supply route stretching from Seoul, Korea, to Saigon, French Indochina. Because of the effectiveness of the U.S. submarine campaign on shipping, the Japanese armies in China require this overland supply route to sustain any offensive operations. The Japanese employ 820,000 men in this offensive, with the initial attack directed against Hunan province. The Chinese are completely unprepared and the Fourteenth Air Force has already warned Stilwell and Chiang Kai-shek that it will be unable to stem the advance. The Japanese forces cross the Yellow River and begin an advance toward the rail line at Hankow.

General Stilwell orders General Chennault to defend the B-29 airbases at Cheng-tu as the Japanese begin an offensive to open a north-south corridor from the Yellow River to Hangkow and south to Changsha and then to Hengyang. The intent is to link with Japanese forces in Indochina. Two Japanese divisions cross the Yellow River with tanks.

Tenth Air Force B-25 Mitchells and P-51 Mustangs support ground forces. P-51s are diverted to intercept Japanese aircraft over Imphal, India. Fighter pilots report three confirmed kills.

ATLANTIC: A minesweeper and submarine chaser sink German submarine *U-986* in the North Atlantic.

ETO: Eighth Air Force sends 15 B-24 Liberators escorted by 33 P-47 Thunderbolts to bomb the V-weapon site at Wizernes, France. During the night five B-17s drop one million leaflets over Rennes, Brest, Nantes, Lorient, and St-Nazaire France.

MEDITERRANEAN: Fifteenth Air Force sends 470 B-17s and B-24 Liberators to attack production facilities in Bulgaria and Yugoslavia; B-17s bomb industrial areas marshaling yards, and an air depot in Yugoslavia and Bulgaria. Over 20 fighters escort the bombers. Aircrews and fighters report 25 confirmed kills.

Two U.S. freighters are damaged when they hit Allied mines off the Isle of Capri.

ITALY: Twelfth Air Force B-25 Mitchells attack bridges and A-20 Havocs attack a fuel storage area. P-40s, P-47 Thunderbolts, and A-36 Intruder (Apache) fighter-bombers attack logistics sites, rail lines, and gun positions.

SOUTHWEST PACIFIC AREA: U.S. submarines *Barb* and *Steelhead* shell the phosphate works on Rasa Island in the southwest Philippines.

PACIFIC: U.S. submarine *Searaven* torpedoes and sinks a Japanese auxiliary minesweeper south of Haha Jima in the Bonin Islands.

CENTRAL PACIFIC: Seventh Air Force B-25 Mitchells based on Tarawa bomb Maloelap Atoll, rearm at Majuro Atoll, and bomb Mille Atoll on the return to Tarawa.

U.S. submarine *Harder* attacks a Japanese convoy and sinks a cargo ship near Woleai Atoll in the Carolines.

NEW BRITAIN: Thirteenth Air Force sends 24 B-25 Mitchells to attack Rapopo airfield. Over 40 P-39 Airacobras and P-40s attack Matupi with incendiaries.

NEW GUINEA: Fifth Air Force sends more than 20 B-24 Liberators to bomb logistics depots and troop concentrations in Kai Island in the Moluccas.

April 18

ALEUTIANS: U.S. freighter hits a mine and sinks off Sanak Island in the Aleutians.

CBI: Tenth Air Force sends 15 B-25 Mitchells and four P-51 Mustangs to bomb Kamaing and attack the Myitkyina-Bhamo road.

ETO: Eighth Air Force sends 501 B-17s and 275 B-24 Liberators, escorted by 119 P-38 Lightnings, 296 P-47 Thunderbolts, and 219 Eighth and Ninth Air Force P-51 Mustangs, against airfields and aircraft production facilities in Germany. Weather conditions force some aircraft to attack targets of opportunity around Berlin. Aircrews and fighter pilots report 33 confirmed kills and five probables. A total of 19 bombers are lost and 204 are damaged. Aircrew casualties are two killed, 17 wounded, and 188 missing. Fighter pilots report five aircraft lost and 31 damaged. Four pilots are reported missing.

B-24 Liberators, escorted by 36 P-47s attack a V-weapon site at Watten, France. One bomber is damaged.

During the night, five B-17s drop over two million leaflets over Stavanger, Oslo, Bergen, and Trondheim, Norway.

Eighth Air Force receives the headquarters of the 492nd Bombardment Group (Heavy) from the United States.

Ninth Air Force sends 277 B-26 Marauders (including 24 dropping Window, strips of aluminum intended to disrupt radar) and 37 A-20 Havocs to bomb gun positions and marshaling yards at Dunkirk, Calais, and Charleroi in France.

ITALY: Fifteenth Air Force P-38 Lightnings and P-47 Thunderbolts strafe airfields.

Twelfth Air Force P-40s and P-47s attack fuel storage areas and a railroad bridge.

PACIFIC: U.S. submarine *Gudgeon* is sunk off Iwo Jima.

U.S. submarine *Tambor* torpedoes and sinks a Japanese guardboat near Wake Island.

A Japanese convoy of four transports and escorts from Pusan, Korea, carrying elements of the 32nd and 35th Divisions to reinforce garrisons in the Halmaheras and in northwestern New Guinea, meets a second convoy from Shanghai.

CENTRAL PACIFIC: Seventh Air Force B-24 Liberators from Eniwetok escort navy PB4Y Privateers on a photographic reconnaissance mission of Saipan, Tinian, and Aguijan Islands. The B-24s bomb Saipan in the Marianas, and two bombers are lost. Other B-24s from Eniwetok attack Truk. B-25 Mitchells from Tarawa bomb Ponape

Island. B-24s from Kwajalein bomb Wake Island. B-25 Mitchells from Abemama Island bomb Jaluit Atoll, rearm at Majuro Atoll, and bomb Maloelap Atoll on the return flight to Abemama.

NEW BRITAIN: Thirteenth Air Force B-25 Mitchells, unable to bomb the primary target at Vunakanau, bomb Tobera airfield. P-39 Airacobras and P-40s attack the logistics base at Wunapope.

ADMIRALTIES: B-24 Liberators of Thirteenth Air Task Force launch from Momote Airfield, Los Negros Island, to bomb Woleai Atoll and Mariaon Island in the Carolines.

NEW GUINEA: Fifth Air Force takes operational control of the new Thirteenth Air Task Force (Provisional) commanded by Major General St. Clair Streett. The unit has elements of the Thirteenth Air Force, some Royal Australian Air Force (RAAF) squadrons, navy air units from Seventh Fleet, and Fifth Air Force units located in the Admiralties and New Britain.

April 19

ATLANTIC: TBF Avengers from escort carrier USS *Tripoli* attack German submarine *U-543* without success.

ETO: Eighth Air Force sends 246 B-17s and 249 B-24 Liberators, escorted by 127 P-38 Lightnings, 439 Eighth and Ninth Air Force P-47 Thunderbolts, and 131 Eighth and Ninth Air Force P-51 Mustangs against airfields in Germany. Aircrews report 17 confirmed enemy aircraft kills and one probable. Five bombers are lost and 33 are damaged. Aircrew casualties are three killed, 11 wounded, and 63 missing. Fighter pilots report 16 confirmed kills and one probable. Two fighters are lost and nine are damaged. Two pilots are reported missing.

Another attack by 27 B-24s escorted by 47 Ninth Air Force P-47 Thunderbolts against V-weapon sites at Watten, France, results in no losses.

Ninth Air Force sends over 350 B-26 Marauders and A-20 Havocs to bomb marshaling yards, city areas, and targets of opportunity in southern Germany.

MEDITERRANEAN: The CCS orders Mediterranean theater commander in chief, General Sir Henry Maitland Wilson, to initiate offensive operations in Italy to support Overlord.

ITALY: Twelfth Air Force B-26 Marauders and B-25 Mitchells bomb marshaling yards, and P-47 Thunderbolts attack rail lines, rail cars, and a marshaling yard.

SOUTHWEST PACIFIC AREA: U.S. submarine *Finback* torpedoes and sinks a Japanese sampan in the Strait of Malacca.

PACIFIC: Headquarters Twentieth Air Force takes operational control of XX Bomber Command. Twentieth Air Force receives the 769th and 770th Bombardment Squadrons (Very Heavy) of the 462nd Bombardment Group (Very Heavy) from the United States. Arriving at Piardoba, India, the B-29 Superfortresses will fly their first missions in early June.

CENTRAL PACIFIC: Seventh Air Force B-24 Liberators from Eniwetok bomb Truk. B-25 Mitchells from the Gilbert Islands bomb Ponape Island.

Thirteenth Air Force sends 21 B-24 Liberators to bomb the airfield on Satawan Atoll in the Carolines, located west of Truk.

New Britain: P-39 Airacobras and P-40s attack logistics sites at Matupi and the airfield at Rapopo.

New Guinea: An Allied naval force initiates Operation Cockpit. Admiral Sir James F. Somerville (RN), commander in chief of the British Eastern Fleet, commands a combined force of British and American ships (the carrier USS *Saratoga* and three destroyers) intended to attack Japanese defenses and shipping in the Netherlands East Indies. This is the first combined offensive operation in the Indian Ocean. Carrier aircraft from the *Saratoga* and HMS *Illustrious* sink a minelayer and two transports.

April 20

CBI: The Chinese 22nd Division finally advances after strong pressure from General Stilwell. Chiang Kai-shek's influence on the division commander has prevented Stilwell's orders from being carried out.

ETO: Eighth Air Force sends 630 B-17s and 212 B-24 Liberators, escorted by 89 P-38 Lightnings, 211 P-47 Thunderbolts, and 88 P-51 Mustangs, to attack 33 V-weapon sites in France. Nine bombers are lost and 348 are damaged. Aircrew casualties are 12 killed, 34 wounded, and 89 missing. Fighter pilots report four confirmed kills in the air and four on the ground. Two fighters are lost and one is damaged. Two pilots are reported missing.

Eighth Fighter Command sends 35 P-51 fighter-bombers and 56 P-38 fighter-bombers to attack airfields in France and Belgium. The P-38s abort the mission.

During the night, five B-17s drop nearly two million leaflets over Nantes, Orleans, Tours, and Paris.

Ninth Air Force sends nearly 400 B-26 Marauders and A-20 Havocs to attack gun positions, the airfield at Poix, and V-weapon sites. In addition, nearly 140 P-47 Thunderbolts bomb marshaling yards in France.

Mediterranean: German torpedo planes attack the 87-ship convoy UGS 38 (United States to Mediterranean, Slow) off the coast of French Morocco. Destroyer USS *Lansdale* is sunk as well as a U.S. freighter carrying ammunition. Another freighter is torpedoed and damaged, but makes it to Algiers.

Italy: Fifteenth Air Force sends over 300 B-17s and B-24 Liberators escorted by over 250 fighters to attack marshaling yards and harbor installations.

Twelfth Air Force B-25s and B-26 Marauders bomb the marshaling yard and fuel storage areas at Leghorn. A-36 Intruder (Apache) fighter-bombers and P-40s attack rail lines, rail cars, and fuel storage areas. Around Cassino fighter-bombers attack gun positions, bridges, trucks, troops, and other targets.

Central Pacific: U.S. submarine *Seahorse* (SS-304) torpedoes and sinks Japanese submarine *RO-45* off the Marianas.

Southern Pacific: Major General Field Harris (USMC) becomes Commander Air Solomons (COMAIRSOLS).

Central Pacific: Seventh Air Force B-25 Mitchells from Tarawa bomb Maloelap, rearm at Majuro Atoll, and bomb Jaluit Atoll on the return to Tarawa. The B-25s of the 396th Bombardment Squadron (Medium), 41st Bombardment Group (Medium), redeploy from Tarawa to Makin Island.

NEW BRITAIN: Thirteenth Air Force B-25 Mitchells attack the logistics base at Matupi and P-39 Airacobras and P-40s attack the Lakunai and Keravat airfields.

ADMIRALTIES: B-24 Liberators of the 31st Bombardment Squadron (Heavy), 5th Bombardment Group (Heavy) redeploy from Guadalcanal to Momote airfield, Los Negros Island.

NEW GUINEA: Fifth Air Force B-24 Liberators bomb the airfields on Noemfoor Island.

B-24s of the Thirteenth Air Task Force of the Fifth Air Force bomb Woleai Atoll in the Carolines.

April 21

CBI: In Burma, Tenth Air Force B-25 Mitchells bomb logistics sites and camps at Kamaing. B-24 Liberators bomb fuel storage sites at Lashio. Fourteenth Air Force P-40s attack construction equipment and troops at Lashio.

ETO: Ninth Air Force sends 236 B-26 Marauders and 34 A-20 Havocs to attack gun positions, coastal defenses, and V-weapon sites in France. Four B-26s are lost. Over 175 P-47 Thunderbolts conduct dive-bombing attacks on marshaling yards in France.

MEDITERRANEAN: Fifteenth Air Force sends over 100 B-24 Liberators to bomb marshaling yards at Bucharest, Romania. Some bombers fail to receive the recall message and hit the primary target. About 40 P-38 Lightnings and P-51 Mustangs accompany the bombers to the target and fight off 30 German fighters. P-51 Mustangs report 17 confirmed kills and seven probables. This is the first combat action for P-51 Mustangs over deep targets. Other fighters returning to base encounter 40 German fighters. Aircrews and fighter pilots report 35 confirmed kills.

ITALY: Twelfth Air Force A-20 Havocs attack an ammunition storage area. P-47 Thunderbolts, along with P-40s and A-36 Intruder (Apache) fighter-bombers, attack rail lines, vehicles, trains, a motor transport concentration, and several gun positions.

CENTRAL PACIFIC: Seventh Air Force B-24 Liberators from Kwajalein bomb Wotje Atoll. B-24 Liberators from Eniwetok stage through Kwajalein and bomb Truk. B-25 Mitchells from Engebi Island, Eniwetok Atoll, bomb Ponape Island. B-25 Mitchells on Abemama Island bomb Maloelap Atoll, rearm at Majuro Atoll, and bomb Jaluit Atoll on their return to Abemama.

U.S. submarine *Stingray* sinks after hitting an underwater obstacle west of the Marianas.

BOUGAINVILLE: Thirteenth Air Force P-39 Airacobras, unable to attack Rabaul due to bad weather over the target, divert to attack targets around Tinputs Harbor.

NEW BRITAIN: Thirteenth Air Force sends 24 B-25 Mitchells to attack the logistics base at Matupi.

ADMIRALTIES: Construction of a new airfield is completed at Mokerang on Manus Island.

Thirteenth Air Force orders Headquarters, 307th Bombardment Group (Heavy), to redeploy from New Georgia and Guadalcanal to the Admiralty Islands, where it will become part of the Thirteenth Air Task Force.

New Guinea: Fifth Air Force sends 21 B-24 Liberators to bomb the airfields on Noemfoor Island. Over 300 B-24 Liberators, B-25 Mitchells, and A-20 Havocs attack targets around Tadji, Wewak, and Madang.

Navy Task Force 58, with five carriers and seven small carriers, commanded by Vice Admiral Marc A. Mitscher, attacks Japanese airfields and defensive positions at Hollandia, Wakde, and Sawar, in preparation for Operations Persecution and Reckless. A Japanese cargo ship is sunk by aircraft off Sarmi and U.S. Navy aircraft sink several small Japanese cargo vessels.

April 22

CBI: Elements of the U.S. 1st Provisional Tank Group support Chinese infantry near Warazup.

In Burma, Tenth Air Force B-25 Mitchells bomb Kamaing. Fourteenth Air Force P-40s report destroying 10 boxcars and a truck near Lashio.

Fourteenth Air Force B-24 Liberators attack a Japanese convoy from Singapore anchored off the coast of French Indochina, near Saigon, and sink a transport, a fleet tanker, a cargo vessel, and a merchant tanker. Another tanker is damaged.

ETO: Eighth Air Force sends 526 B-17s and 277 B-24 Liberators, escorted by 132 P-38 Lightnings, 485 Eighth and Ninth Air Force P-47 Thunderbolts, and 242 Eighth and Ninth Air Force P-51 Mustangs against the marshaling yard at Hamm, Germany. Aircrews report 20 confirmed kills and six probables. A total of 15 bombers are lost and 212 are damaged. Aircrew casualties are seven wounded and 89 missing. Fighter pilots report 40 confirmed kills and two probables. A total of 13 fighters are lost and 23 are damaged. One pilot is wounded and 12 are reported missing.

During the night five B-17s drop more than 1 million leaflets over Orleans, Tours, Rouen, Nantes, Lille, Reims, Chartres, and Paris.

Eighth Air Force receives Headquarters, 398th Bombardment Group (Heavy), and the B-17s of the 600th, 601st, 602nd, and 603rd Bombardment Squadrons (Heavy). The squadrons' first missions are scheduled for early May. The B-24s of the 844th, 845th, 846th, and 847th Bombardment Squadrons (Heavy) of the 489th Bombardment Group (Heavy) arrive from the United States. The squadrons' first missions are scheduled for late May.

Ninth Air Force sends over 400 B-26 Marauders and nearly 90 A-20 Havocs against V-weapon sites in France. About 275 P-47 Thunderbolts and P-51 Mustangs conduct dive-bomb attacks on marshaling yards in Belgium.

Italy: Twelfth Air Force B-25 Mitchells and B-26 Marauders attack bridges and viaducts. A-20 Havocs attack the Valmontone ammunition storage area and P-47 Thunderbolts attack rail lines, trains, and a marshaling yard. P-40s attack gun positions north of the Anzio battle line and attack logistics storage areas and troop positions at Fondi, Terracina, and Formia.

Central Pacific: Seventh Air Force B-24 Liberators from Kwajalein bomb Wotje Atoll on a nighttime raid. B-24s from Kwajalein attack Wotje during the day. B-25 Mitchells from Tarawa bomb Maloelap and Mille Atolls, rearm at Majuro Atoll, and bomb Jaluit Atoll on return to Tarawa. Thirteenth Air Force sends 17 B-24 Liberators to bomb Dublon, Param, and Eten Islands in Truk Atoll.

A Navy PB4Y Privateer sights survivors of USAAF B-24 Liberators damaged over the Marianas and ditched on April 18; a PBY sent to rescue the aviators suffers damage in landing and is unable to take off (see April 23).

NEW BRITAIN: The marines fight the final engagement with elements of Japanese forces in western New Britain. The campaign has cost the Americans 310 killed and 1,083 wounded and has been fought in some of the most forbidding conditions any combat unit will encounter in the Second World War. The Japanese have lost nearly three times the number of American casualties and are now clustered around Rabaul, virtual prisoners and no longer a factor in the war.

Thirteenth Air Force B-25 Mitchells bomb logistics bases at Ratawul and Talili Bay. P-39 Airacobras and P-40s attack Rapopo and Lakunai airfields.

NEW GUINEA: Operation Reckless. Navy Task Force 77 under Rear Admiral Daniel E. Barbey lands troops at Aitape and Tanahmerah Bay in Operation Persecution, and at Humboldt Bay, Hollandia, in Operation Reckless. The landings take place 300 miles behind the main Japanese defensive perimeter. Rear Admiral Barbey also commands Naval Task Group 77.1, which lands the 163rd RCT, 41st Infantry Division (Brigadier General Doe), at Aitape. TG 77.2 under command of Rear Admiral Fechteler lands the 24th Infantry Division (Major General Irving) at Tanahmerah Bay. TG 77.3 (Captain Alfred G. Noble) lands the 41st Infantry Division (Major General Irving) at Humboldt Bay. TF 78 is the escort carrier force under Rear Admiral Ralph E. Davison, which provides air cover for the landings. TF 74 (Rear Admiral Victor A. C. Crutchley, Royal Navy) and TF 75 (Rear Admiral Russell S. Berkey) provide gunfire support. TF 58 with five carriers and seven small carriers under Vice Admiral Marc A. Mitscher also provides air support.

The 24th Infantry Division and 41st Infantry Division land on the beaches near Hollandia after a 45-minute naval and air bombardment and encounter no opposition. Lieutenant General Robert L. Eichelberger, commander of I Corps, along with Lieutenant General Walter Krueger, Alamo Force commander, Rear Admiral Daniel E. Barbey, and General MacArthur accompany the troops. At Tanahmerah Bay, the 19th and 21st RCTs of the 24th Infantry Division encounter a swamp that prevents inland movement. The beach at Humboldt Bay is shallow and supplies begin to pile up along the shore until engineers can open roads into the interior.

Two battalions of the 163rd RCT land at Aitape and encounter no enemy. They move inland and capture Tadji airfield.

Fifth Air Force sends over 20 B-24 Liberators to bomb airfields on Noemfoor Island. Over 80 B-24s and A-20 Havocs attack targets near Wewak. Over 100 B-24s and B-25 Mitchells attack Hansa Bay, Wewak, Bogia, and Madang.

April 23

ALEUTIANS: Eleventh Air Force sends three B-24 Liberators to conduct photographic reconnaissance of Matsuwa Island and operate within 100 miles of the Kurile Islands.

CBI: In China, Fourteenth Air Force sends 14 P-40s to attack artillery at Sienning and cavalry forces at Kuan-Fou-Chiao.

ETO: Eighth Air Force sends 136 P-38s, 166 P-47 Thunderbolts, and 80 P-51 Mustangs to attack airfields and other targets in France, Belgium, and Germany. Fighter pilots report 11 confirmed kills on the ground. Seven aircraft are lost and 25 are damaged. Seven pilots are reported missing.

During the night five B-17s drop nearly two million leaflets over Rennes, Brest, Lorient, St-Nazaire, and Nantes, France. Nine B-24s support Carpetbagger operations.

The Eighth Air Force receives the B-24s of the 4th, 7th, 18th, and 391st Bombardment Squadrons (Heavy) of the 34th Bombardment Group (Heavy). The squadrons' first missions are scheduled for late May.

Ninth Air Force sends 307 B-26 Marauders and 57 A-20 Havocs to attack V-weapon sites, gun positions, and marshaling yards in France and Belgium. About 1,000 P-47 Thunderbolts and P-51 Mustangs conduct dive-bombing attacks on targets throughout France and the Netherlands.

MEDITERRANEAN: Fifteenth Air Force sends 583 B-24 Liberators and 171 B-17s to attack three aircraft production targets near Vienna, Austria. Over 100 German aircraft attack the formations and shoot down two B-17s and 11 B-24s along with three fighters. Aircrews and fighter pilots report a total of 51 confirmed kills and 16 probables.

ITALY: Twelfth Air Force B-25 Mitchells and B-26 Marauders attack bridges, a marshaling yard, and viaducts. P-47 Thunderbolts, A-36 Intruder (Apache) fighter-bombers, and P-40s attack rail lines and bridges.

SOUTHWEST PACIFIC AREA: A Japanese destroyer hits a mine dropped by Fourteenth Air Force aircraft in the Makassar Strait.

PACIFIC: U.S. submarine *Seadragon* attacks a Japanese convoy and sinks a cargo ship off Honshu, Japan.

CENTRAL PACIFIC: Plans for Operation Forager are completed. The naval force is composed of 14 battleships, seven fleet carriers, eight light carriers, and 14 escort carriers, supported by 136 destroyers. Land forces consist of two amphibious corps, composed of three marine and two army divisions and one marine brigade. On June 15, the first landings will begin on Saipan, followed by Tinian and Guam.

Seventh Air Force B-24 Liberators from Kwajalein bomb Truk and Wotje Atolls. B-25 Mitchells from Makin Island bomb Ponape Island and Jaluit and Maloelap Atolls.

In the Marianas, destroyer *Gansevoort* rescues B-24 Liberator crewmen and the crew of a Navy PBY Catalina initially sent to rescue the bomber crew, shot down on April 18.

NEW BRITAIN: Thirteenth Air Force P-39 Airacobras and P-40s attack Tobera and B-25 Mitchells bomb Matupi Island.

NEW GUINEA: Operation Reckless. Elements of the 24th Infantry Division struggle through exceptionally difficult terrain and advance 10 miles from their landing site at Tanahmerah Bay. At Humboldt Bay, a lone Japanese aircraft drops a single bomb that hits the supplies piled all along the beach. Ammunition, gasoline, vehicles, rations, and every other type of supplies are destroyed in a terrific inferno. The heroic efforts of the 2nd Engineer Special Brigade prevent a total disaster, but over 120 Americans are killed or wounded.

The 127th Infantry Regiment of the 32nd Infantry Division lands at Aitape to reinforce the 163rd RCT in case of a Japanese counterattack.

Fifth Air Force B-24 Liberators bomb the airfields on Noemfoor Island. Aircrews report 14 enemy aircraft shot down. B-24s bomb Wewak, Boram, and But airfields; B-24 Liberators, B-25 Mitchells, and A-20 Havocs attack airfields, antiaircraft positions, and troops at Hansa Bay. A-20 Havocs, P-47 Thunderbolts, P-38 Lightnings, and P-39 Airacobras also attack targets along Hansa Bay and around Wewak and also near Uligan harbor.

Thirteenth Air Task Force B-24 Liberators under Fifth Air Force bomb the airfield and logistics bases on Woleai Atoll.

April 24

ALEUTIANS: In the Kurile Islands, an Eleventh Air Force B-24 Liberator flies a photo reconnaissance and bombing run over Matsuwa Island. A second B-24 flies weather and bombing runs over Shasukotan, Yekaruma, Kharimkotan, and Onnekotan Islands.

CBI: Tenth Air Force P-40s, P-51 Mustangs, A-36 Intruder (Apache) fighter-bombers, and B-25 Mitchells bomb logistics storage areas, railroads, and Japanese positions near Kamaing and Myitkyina.

In Thailand, Fourteenth Air Force B-25 Mitchells damage bridges.

Two Twentieth Air Force B-29 Superfortresses are the first to fly the Hump route. They land at Kwanghan, China.

U.S. submarine *Robalo* is damaged by an air attack off the coast of French Indochina but remains on patrol.

ATLANTIC: The zones of occupation for postwar Germany are allocated. The United States will occupy southwest Germany. Berlin, although in the Soviet Zone, will be divided into occupation zones as well.

ETO: Eighth Air Force sends 524 B-17s and 230 B-24 Liberators, escorted by 131 P-38 Lightnings, 490 Eighth and Ninth Air Force P-47 Thunderbolts, and 246 Eighth and Ninth Air Force P-51 Mustangs, against aircraft production facilities, airfields, and targets of opportunity in Germany. A total of 40 bombers are lost and 257 damaged. Aircrew casualties are 11 killed, 27 wounded, and 371 missing. Fighter pilots report 70 confirmed enemy kills and six probables in the air and 57 confirmed kills on the ground. Seventeen fighters are lost and 31 damaged. Seventeen pilots are reported missing.

During the night five B-17s drop over one million leaflets on Amsterdam, Rotterdam, The Hague, and Utrecht in the Netherlands and over Lille and Reims in France. Eight B-24s support Carpetbagger missions.

Ninth Air Force sends 32 P-47 Thunderbolts against the Louvain marshaling yard in Belgium.

MEDITERRANEAN: Fifteenth Air Force sends over 520 B-17s and B-24 Liberators escorted by over 250 fighters against marshaling yards, aircraft production facilities, and rail lines in Romania, Yugoslavia, and Italy.

ITALY: Twelfth Air Force B-26 Marauders attack railroad bridges. A-20 Havocs attack the ammunition storage area at Valmontone. P-40s, P-47 Thunderbolts, and A-36 Intruder (Apache) fighter-bombers attack shipping off Leghorn, marshaling yards, rail lines, vehicles, and targets of opportunity.

Private First Class John C. Squires is the platoon messenger in A Company, 30th Infantry Regiment, 3rd Infantry Division, as it attacks German positions at Spaccasassi Creek near Padiglione. This is his first offensive action, and he reaches the leading platoon, makes a quick assessment of the situation, and makes a recommendation to the platoon leader for an alternate approach. On his own initiative, Private First Class Squires organizes a group of stragglers into an ad hoc squad and leads them forward. At Spaccasassi Creek Squires puts troops in position and brings up reinforcements as his platoon is reduced to only 14 men by enemy fire. On every trip to bring up reinforcements he has to cross a minefield under artillery fire. The Germans make three counterattacks on the platoon's position, and each time Private First Class Squires engages the enemy with a Browning automatic rifle and a captured German machine gun. He also engages 21 German soldiers in a close battle on the flank of the American position, firing a machine gun into their midst and capturing the entire attacking force. He employs additional captured machine guns, instructing the members of his platoon on their operation and function. He continues to hold the position against German attacks. For his dedication to duty and leadership Private First Class Squires will receive the Medal of Honor.

CENTRAL PACIFIC: Seventh Air Force B-25 Mitchells from Engebi Island bomb Ponape Island. B-25s from Makin Island bomb Jaluit and Wotje Atolls.

The headquarters of the 41st Bombardment Group (Medium) moves from Tarawa to Makin Island.

NEW BRITAIN: Thirteenth Air Force P-40s attack the airfield at Tobera.

NEW GUINEA: At Aitape, Tadji airfield is operational. Australian Air Force P-40s arrive to support the American infantry.

Fifth Air Force B-24 Liberators bomb the airfields on Noemfoor Island. B-24s also bomb airfields at Wewak area. B-25 Mitchells and A-20 Havocs attack targets around Hansa Bay, and Uligan harbor and support Allied forces at Madang.

April 25

CBI: Tenth Air Force B-25 Mitchells, P-51 Mustangs, and B-24 Liberators attack Japanese enemy positions, logistics sites, airfields, and headquarters elements.

ETO: Eighth Air Force sends 355 B-17s and 199 B-24 Liberators against marshaling yards and airfields in France and Germany, escorted by 177 P-38 Lightnings, 296 P-47 Thunderbolts, and 246 Eighth and Ninth Air Force P-51 Mustangs. A total of 36 bombers are lost and 59 damaged. Aircrew casualties are two killed, seven wounded, and 69 missing. Fighter pilots report 39 confirmed kills and seven probables in the air and 29 confirmed kills and seven probables on the ground. Two fighters are lost and eight are damaged. One pilot is killed and two are missing.

An attack by 28 B-24s escorted by 40 P-47s to bomb V-weapon sites in France results in no friendly losses.

During the night, six B-17s drop four million leaflets over northeastern France.

Ninth Air Force sends 240 B-26 Marauders and 69 A-20 Havocs to attack V-weapon sites and gun positions in France. Bad weather over the targets causes most of the bombers to abort the mission. Nearly 150 P-47 Thunderbolts conduct dive-bomb attacks on airfields in France and Belgium.

ITALY: Fifteenth Air Force B-24 Liberators bomb an aircraft production facility and marshaling yards in northern Italy.

Fifteenth Air Force receives the B-24s of the 782nd Bombardment Squadron (Heavy), 465th Bombardment Group (Heavy), from the United States. The squadron's first missions are scheduled for early May.

Twelfth Air Force A-20 Havocs, P-40s, and P-47 Thunderbolts attack lines of communication north of Rome, attacking fuel storage areas, marshaling yards, bridges, gun positions, and logistics support sites.

PACIFIC: U.S. submarine *Guavina* torpedoes and sinks a Japanese cargo ship northwest of Chichi Jima in the Bonin Islands.

CENTRAL PACIFIC: Seventh Air Force B-24 Liberators from Kwajalein stage through Eniwetok to conduct a night bombing attack on Guam and Truk. The bombers then fly on to Los Negros Island in the Admiralties. During the day the B-24s bomb Wotje and Maloelap Atolls. B-25 Mitchells from Engebi Island bomb Ponape Island. B-25s from Makin Island bomb Jaluit and Wotje Atolls.

Thirteenth Air Force sends 15 B-24s on a dawn raid on Truk.

BOUGAINVILLE: Thirteenth Air Force P-39 Airacobras cause heavy damage to a logistics base at Baitsi.

NEW BRITAIN: Thirteenth Air Force sends 23 B-25 Mitchells to attack Tobera airfield.

NEW GUINEA: Heavy rains wash out the Tadji airfield at Aitape. Despite several efforts to maintain it, the airfield is eventually abandoned.

Fifth Air Force B-25 Mitchells bomb Japanese troops near Hollandia and attack villages near Tanahmerah.

U.S. submarine *Crevalle* torpedoes and sinks a Japanese cargo ship north of Borneo.

April 26

ALEUTIANS: Destroyer escort USS *Gilmore* sinks Japanese submarine *I-180*, southwest of Cherikof Island, Aleutians.

CBI: Tenth Air Force A-36 Intruder (Apache) fighter-bombers, P-40s, and P-51 Mustangs together with three B-25 Mitchells attack Japanese positions, logistics storage areas, and targets of opportunity at Mogaung, Kamaing, and elsewhere in the Mogaung Valley.

Japanese fighters intercept Twentieth Air Force B-29 Superfortresses as they are flying over the Hump to China. No losses are reported.

ATLANTIC: Four U.S. destroyer escorts sink German submarine *U-488* in mid-Atlantic.

ETO: Eighth Air Force sends 357 B-17s and 238 B-24 Liberators, escorted by 90 P-38 Lightnings, 311 Eighth and Ninth Air Force P-47 Thunderbolts, and 153 Eighth and Ninth Air Force P-51 Mustangs, against industrial production facilities in Germany. No bombers are lost and 141 are damaged. Five fighters are lost and one damaged. LSTs carrying American infantry.

An attack by 33 P-38 Lightnings against Le Mans airfield and 24 P-51 Mustangs against Cormeilles-en-Vexin airfield results in no friendly losses.

During the night five B-17s drop leaflets over Ghent, Antwerp, Brussels, Liege, and Gosselies in Belgium.

Ninth Air Force publishes its tactical air plan to support Operation Neptune.

SOUTHWEST PACIFIC AREA: U.S. submarine *Bonefish* torpedoes and sinks a Japanese transport at the entrance to Davao Gulf in the Philippines.

U.S. submarine *Jack* spots a Japanese convoy carrying the 32nd and 35th Divisions to reinforce garrisons in the Halmaheras and in northwestern New Guinea off the west coast of Luzon. The submarine *Jack* sinks a transport and damages a cargo ship.

PACIFIC: U.S. submarine *Guavina* attacks a Japanese convoy in the Bonin Islands and sinks a transport, but a second attack on a cargo ship is unsuccessful.

U.S. submarine *Sargo* attacks a Japanese convoy and sinks a cargo ship off Honshu, Japan.

CENTRAL PACIFIC: Seventh Air Force B-25 Mitchells from Makin Island bomb Jaluit and Wotje Atolls. B-24 Liberators returning to Kwajalein from Los Negros Island bomb Ponape Island.

BOUGAINVILLE: Thirteenth Air Force P-40s attack Japanese positions near Tabut and Wariki.

NEW BRITAIN: Thirteenth Air Force sends 24 B-25 Mitchells to bomb the Lakunai airfield. P-38 Lightnings and P-39 Airacobras attack Tobera airfield.

NEW GUINEA: Operation Reckless. The 21st Infantry Regiment of the 24th Infantry Division occupies Hollandia airfield. The 186th Infantry Regiment of the 41st Infantry Division captures Cyclops and Sentari airfields.

Fifth Air Force B-25 Mitchells and A-20 Havocs attack airfields at Wewak. P-39 Airacobras and P-47 Thunderbolts attack bridges and targets of opportunity near Madang.

April 27

CBI: General Stilwell meets with Brigadier General Merrill (now recovered and returned to duty) to discuss the capture of Myitkyina, the next mission for the Marauders. Myitkyina is the key to achieving U.S. objectives in Burma. Myitkyina's airfield will allow Tenth Air Force fighters to escort air resupply missions flying the Hump route into China. Control of Myitkyina is an essential requirement allowing the construction of the Ledo Road to China.

To accomplish this mission, the Galahad Task Force is created by combining the battalions of Marauders with Chinese units and irregular forces. K Force is composed of the 3rd Battalion of the Marauders plus the 88th Regiment of the Chinese 30th Division. M Force is composed of 2nd Battalion of the Marauders plus 200–250 Kachin Rangers from Detachment 101. H Force is composed of 3rd Battalion of the Marauders plus the 150th Regiment of the Chinese 50th Division. The Chinese 22nd and 38th Divisions are to capture Kamaing and clear the Hukawng Valley while K Force, leading the way and followed by H Force, heads for Nawbum. The Marauders have to cross the Kumon mountain range, reaching heights of over 9,000 feet.

Tenth Air Force sends P-40s, P-51 Mustangs, A-36 Intruder (Apache) fighter-bombers, and B-25 Mitchells to attack fuel storage areas, gun positions, and troops in the Mogaung valley.

ETO: The Allies conduct the first full-scale rehearsal of the Neptune Plan, an exercise called Tiger near Plymouth, England. This rehearsal involves the Utah assault landing group under Rear Admiral D. P. Moon. German fast-attack boats torpedo eight LSTs (landing ship tank) conducting invasion rehearsals. One LST is sunk and two are heavily damaged. Over 600 soldiers and sailors die in the attack, but the losses are not reported, in order to protect operational security.

Eighth Air Force sends 596 B-17s and B-24 Liberators, with 47 P-38 Lightnings, 262 P-47 Thunderbolts, and 48 P-51 Mustangs flying as escort, to bomb V-weapon sites near Pas-de-Calais and Cherbourg in France. Of the 307 B-17s and 169 B-24s that hit the primary targets, four bombers are lost and 254 are damaged. Aircrew losses are three killed, 16 wounded, and 40 missing. Fighter pilots report two aircraft lost and two pilots missing.

Another attack by 288 B-17s and 198 B-24s, escorted by 106 P-38 Lightnings, 283 P-47 Thunderbolts, and 154 P-51 Mustangs against marshaling yards and airfields in France and Belgium, results in four bombers lost and 86 damaged. Fighter pilots report three confirmed kills in the air and four on the ground. Four aircraft are lost and three damaged.

During the night five B-17s drop five million leaflets over cities in northwestern France. One B-24 is lost out of 21 sent in support of Carpetbagger operations.

P-38 Lightnings, modified to carry a bombardier and a Norden bombsight in place of guns, are called Droopsnoots. The P-38H/Ls can carry a 4,000-pound bomb load (the same as a B-17) and, because of its speed, does not require fighter escort. These Droopsnoot P-38s attack Albert/Meaulte airfield in France. Six bombers are damaged. P-51s conduct a dive-bomb attack on Cormeilles-en-Vexin airfield in France without any friendly losses.

The Eighth Air Force receives the B-24s of the 849th and 850th Bombardment Squadrons (Heavy), of the 490th Bombardment Group (Heavy) from the United States. The squadrons' first missions are scheduled for late May.

Ninth Air Force sends B-26 Marauders and A-20 Havocs with over 275 P-47s and P-51 dive bombers to attack gun emplacements, marshaling yards, and airfields in France and Belgium.

SOUTHWEST PACIFIC AREA: The Japanese convoy carrying the 32nd and 35th Divisions to reinforce garrisons in the Halmaheras and in northwestern New Guinea arrives at Manila.

PACIFIC: U.S. submarine *Halibut* attacks a Japanese convoy and sinks a minelayer and a merchant transport near Okinawa.

U.S. submarine *Seadragon* torpedoes and damages a Japanese cargo ship off Shikoku, Japan.

CENTRAL PACIFIC: Seventh Air Force B-24 Liberators, staging through Eniwetok Atoll, bomb Truk in a night raid. B-25 Mitchells from Eniwetok attack Ponape Island. Other B-25s from Makin Island attack Jaluit, Wotje, and Mille Atolls.

Thirteenth Air Force sends 16 B-24 Liberators to bomb Truk.

The B-25s of the 820th Bombardment Squadron (Medium), 41st Bombardment Group (Medium), redeploy from Tarawa to Makin Island.

U.S. submarine *Bluegill* (SS-242) sinks a Japanese light cruiser west of the Sonsorol Islands.

U.S. submarine *Seahorse* attacks a Japanese convoy and sinks a transport near Saipan. *Seahorse* escapes a depth-charge attack.

U.S. submarine *Trigger* attacks a Japanese convoy north of Palau, and sinks a transport and damages an escort vessel and a cargo ship.

NEW BRITAIN: Thirteenth Air Force B-25 Mitchells and P-39 Airacobras bomb the logistics base at Talili Bay.

NEW GUINEA: Engineers begin construction of airfields at Hollandia.

April 28

CBI: In Burma, Galahad's K Force and H Force begin the overland movement to Myitkyina. The arduous trip takes a heavy toll on men and animals. Many of the men are infected with scrub typhus. Colonel Henry L. Kinnison, leader of K Force, dies of the disease on the march.

Tenth Air Force A-36 Intruder (Apache) fighter-bombers, P-40s, P-51 Mustangs, and one B-25 Mitchell attack targets in the Mogaung Valley.

In China, Fourteenth Air Force sends 26 B-24 Liberators, escorted by 10 P-51 Mustangs, to destroy two bridges over the Yellow River near Chengchow after the Japanese drive Chinese forces from the area. The Japanese continue to make progress, forcing the Chinese-American Composite Wing to guard the B-29 fields at Cheng-tu. The Fourteenth Air Force is to prevent Japanese forces from crossing the Yellow River and attack the rail lines providing supplies to the armies.

U.S. submarine *Flasher* damages a Vichy cargo ship in the South China Sea.

ATLANTIC: Secretary of the Navy Frank Knox dies in Washington, D.C.

Nine German motor torpedo boats attack a convoy of eight LSTs entering Lyme Bay, England, sinking two and damaging another.

ETO: Eighth Air Force sends 117 B-17s against airfields in France escorted by 118 P-47 Thunderbolts and 87 P-51 Mustangs. Two bombers are lost and 38 damaged. Fighter pilots report eight confirmed kills on the ground. Two fighters are lost and two are damaged. Casualties are 20 crewmen and two fighter pilots missing. Another attack on V-weapon sites in France by 106 B-17s escorted by 46 P-47 Thunderbolts results in two bombers lost and 47 damaged. Three air crewmen are wounded and 21 are missing.

Tours and Chateaudun airfields in France are attacked by Droopsnoot P-38 Lightnings. One bomber is lost and two are damaged. Later, 32 P-47 Thunderbolts, with four P-47 escorts, dive-bomb Chateaudun airfield and report one confirmed kill on the ground.

B-24s bomb V-weapon sites in France escorted by 50 P-47 Thunderbolts. Six bombers are damaged and nine crewmen are wounded.

During the night five B-17s drop leaflets over cities in France, Belgium, and the Netherlands. B-24s support Carpetbagger operations.

Eighth Air Force receives the B-24s of the 848th and 851st Bombardment Squadrons (Heavy), 490th Bombardment Group (Heavy), from the United States. The first mission of the 848th is scheduled for early June; the first mission of the 851st is scheduled for late May.

Ninth Air Force sends nearly 250 B-26 Marauders to bomb marshaling yards in France. The bombers are recalled due to bad weather, but 18 B-26s bomb an airfield as a secondary target.

ITALY: Fifteenth Air Force sends over 450 B-17s and B-24 Liberators escorted by P-51 Mustangs and P-47 Thunderbolts to attack port facilities. During the air attack on Toulon, German submarine *U-421* is sunk in the harbor.

Twelfth Air Force B-26s and B-25 Mitchells attack railway bridges and viaducts. A-20 Havocs, P-40s, and P-47 Thunderbolts attack fuel storage areas.

SOUTHWEST PACIFIC AREA: U.S. submarines *Bang, Parche,* and *Tinosa* attack a Japanese convoy off of Luzon. USS *Bang* sinks a cargo ship and damages another.

PACIFIC: U.S. submarine *Halibut* bombards Japanese installations on Kure Jima in the Bonin Islands. U.S. submarine *Pogy* torpedoes and sinks Japanese submarine *I-183* off Shikoku Island, Japan.

CENTRAL PACIFIC: Seventh Air Force B-25 Mitchells from Makin Island attack Jaluit and Mille Atolls, rearming at Majuro Atoll, and then return to Makin.

Vice Admiral Marc A. Mitscher's TF 58 with five carriers and seven small carriers begins a two-day attack on Japanese shipping, oil and ammunition storage sites, aircraft facilities, and other installations at Truk. TBF Avengers with two destroyers sink Japanese submarine *I-174* north of Truk.

BOUGAINVILLE: Thirteenth Air Force P-39 Airacobras attack gun positions near Mamagata and logistics sites in the area.

NEW BRITAIN: The 40th Infantry Division begins the relief of the 1st Marine Division.

Thirteenth Air Force B-25 Mitchells bomb the logistics base at Wunapope and bomb Rapopo airfield. P-40s and P-39 Airacobras attack Vunakanau airfield.

NEW GUINEA: Fifth Air Force B-24 Liberators and B-25 Mitchells bomb the airfields at Wakde and Biak. P-47 Thunderbolts, P-39 Airacobras, A-20 Havocs, and P-70s hit targets along the northern coast.

Thirteenth Air Task Force of the Fifth Air Force sends 21 B-24s to bomb the airfield on Woleai Atoll.

April 29

ETO: Eighth Air Force sends 446 B-17s and 233 B-24 Liberators against targets in Berlin, escorted by 117 P-38 Lightnings, 463 Eighth and Ninth Air Force P-47

Thunderbolts, and 234 Eighth and Ninth Air Force P-51 Mustangs. A total of 63 bombers are lost and 434 damaged. Aircrew casualties are 18 killed, 38 wounded, and 606 missing. Fighter pilots report 13 aircraft lost and 31 damaged. One pilot is wounded and 12 are missing.

During the night four B-17s drop one million leaflets over cities in northern France and the Netherlands. Fourteen B-24s support Carpetbagger operations.

Ninth Air Forces ends 217 B-26 Marauders to attack marshaling yards in France, but the mission is aborted due to heavy cloud cover over the targets.

MEDITERRANEAN: Fifteenth Air Force sends 573 B-17s and B-24 Liberators, with fighter escort, to attack the naval base at Toulon, France.

ITALY: Twelfth Air Force B-25 Mitchells and B-26 Marauders attack bridges, while A-20 Havocs attack a fuel storage area. P-40s and P-47 Thunderbolts attack rail lines, gun positions, vehicles, bridges, logistics sites, and a marshaling yard.

CENTRAL PACIFIC: Seventh Air Force B-24 Liberators, staging through Eniwetok from Kwajalein, bomb Truk and Jaluit Atolls. B-25 Mitchells from Makin Island also bomb Jaluit and Ponape Islands.

BOUGAINVILLE: Thirteenth Air Force P-39 Airacobras bomb and strafe targets on Buka Island and throughout Bougainville, including Kieta and Numa Numa. B-25 Mitchells bomb Kara and Buka airfields.

ADMIRALTIES: The headquarters of the 307th Bombardment Group (Heavy) moves from New Georgia Island to Los Negros Island.

NEW GUINEA: Fifth Air Force sends over 90 B-24 Liberators and B-25 Mitchells to bomb Japanese positions on Wakde Island.

April 30

CBI: Tenth Air Force B-25 Mitchells attack Japanese tanks, bridges, and logistics sites around Kalewa.

H Force, following K Force, begins the attack toward Myitkyina.

Fourteenth Air Force has about 400 operational aircraft out of a total of 500. General Chennault is receiving about 6,000 tons of supplies a month to keep his aircraft operational.

Chiang Kai-shek demands that the stockpile of supplies for the B-29 strategic bombers at Chengtu be diverted to Fourteenth Air Force to stop the Japanese offensive. Stilwell, backed by President Roosevelt, refuses.

ATLANTIC: German submarine *U-711* torpedoes and sinks a U.S. freighter south of Bear Island in the Norwegian Sea.

ETO: Eighth Air Force sends 240 B-17s and 55 B-24 Liberators, escorted by 128 P-38 Lightnings, 268 P-47 Thunderbolts, and 248 Eighth and Ninth Air Force P-51 Mustangs, to attack airfields and V-weapon sites in France. One bomber is lost and 21 are damaged. One crewman is wounded and 10 are missing. Fighter pilots report 20 probable kills. Four aircraft are lost and seven damaged. One pilot is wounded and three are missing.

P-38 Lightnings with Droopsnoot bomb Tours airfield in France. One P-38 is lost and one damaged. Another 22 P-38 Lightnings with Droopsnoot attack

Orleans/Bricy airfield. Two P-38s are damaged. P-47 Thunderbolts bomb the airfield and attack a V-weapon site. P-47 Thunderbolts conduct a dive-bomb attack on Romorantin airfield. The pilots report nine confirmed kills and one probable.

During the night four B-17s drop two million leaflets over cities and towns in Belgium, France, and the Netherlands. Twenty B-24s support Carpetbagger operations.

Ninth Air Force sends over 300 B-26 Marauders and A-20 Havocs to attack marshaling yards and V-weapon site construction in France.

ITALY: Fifteenth Air Force sends 500 B-17s and B-24 Liberators to attack industrial production facilities and marshaling yards. For this month, fighter pilots report 209 confirmed kills, 38 probable kills, and 104 possibles in air combat.

The Fifteenth Air Force receives the headquarters of 485th Bombardment Group (Heavy) and the B-24s of the 828th, 829th, 830th, and 831st Bombardment Squadrons (Heavy). The squadrons' first missions are scheduled for mid-May.

Twelfth Air Force B-25 Mitchells and B-26 Marauders attack railroad bridges. P-40s attack rail lines and P-47 Thunderbolts attack rail lines, rail cars, and other targets.

SOUTHWEST PACIFIC AREA: The Japanese convoy carrying the 32nd and 35th Divisions to reinforce garrisons at Manokwari and Halmahera departs Manila.

U.S. submarine *Bang* again attacks the convoy it had encountered previously, sinking a merchant tanker off the northwest coast of Luzon.

U.S. submarine *Flasher* torpedoes and sinks a French gunboat in the South China Sea.

CENTRAL PACIFIC: Seventh Air Force sends 41 B-24 Liberators from Kwajalein to bomb Wake Island. B-25 Mitchells from Makin Island bomb Jaluit Atoll. B-25s from Engebi Island bomb Ponape Island.

Navy TF 58 continues air attacks on targets in the Carolines and expands toward the Palau Islands as well. A transport and merchant vessel are sunk. A gunboat is damaged at Truk by carrier aircraft.

BOUGAINVILLE: Thirteenth Air Force P-39 Airacobras attack targets on Buka Island and Ivituri mission, the Kieta area, and the Mamagata logistics base at Bougainville.

NEW BRITAIN: Thirteenth Air Force P-40s and P-38 Lightnings bomb Vunakanau airfield and B-25 Mitchells bomb Vunakambi Plantation.

NEW GUINEA: Fifth Air Force P-39 Airacobras and P-47 Thunderbolts attack Japanese troops and logistics sites around Hansa Bay. A-20 Havocs and B-25 Mitchells bomb Wewak. B-24 Liberators bomb Noemfoor Island.

Thirteenth Air Task Force under Fifth Air Force sends 23 B-24s to bomb Woleai Atoll.

May 1

CBI: Tenth Air Force P-40s attack Kamaing; B-24 Liberators bomb Maymyo, the Mandalay marshaling yard, and oil facilities at Yenangyaung.

In China, Fourteenth Air Force P-40s attack the airfield at Yuncheng and B-25 Mitchells along with P-40s bomb Tangyang airfield.

Twentieth Air Force reports the four B-29 airfields in the Cheng-tu area are operational.

ETO: General Eisenhower receives instructions from the JCS to plan for U.S. forces to occupy the Netherlands and northwest Germany once hostilities end in Europe.

Eighth Air Force sends 531 B-17s and B-24 Liberator bombers with 209 fighters as escort to attack 23 V-weapon sites in France. Due to heavy cloud cover, only three of the primary targets are hit. A total of 37 bombers are damaged and five crewmen are killed.

A second attack by 135 B-17s and 151 B-24 Liberators, escorted by 120 P-38 Lightnings, 272 P-47 Thunderbolts, and 166 P-51 Mustangs, targets marshaling yards in France and Belgium. Three bombers are lost and 117 are damaged. Thirty crewmen are missing. Fighter pilots report six confirmed kills. Three fighters are lost and five are damaged.

During the night five B-17s drop one million leaflets over cities and towns in France and the Netherlands. A total of 25 B-24 Liberators support Carpetbagger operations.

Eighth Air Force receives the headquarters of the 489th Bombardment Group (Heavy) from the United States.

Ninth Air Force sends 450 B-26 Marauders and A-20 Havocs to attack marshaling yards and industrial production facilities in France and Belgium.

ITALY: At the planning conference for Operation Diadem, the breakout of the Liri Valley and the drive to Rome, Lieutenant General Mark Clark seeks to get the Fifteenth Army Group commander, General Sir Harold Alexander, to approve Clark's desire for the U.S. forces of the Fifth Army to capture Rome. Although his direct request is denied, Alexander gives enough vague guidance to Clark to allow him to shift forces as necessary. May 11 is set as D-day for the attack.

Twelfth Air Force B-26 Marauders and B-25 Mitchells attack bridges and viaducts and a marshaling yard. P-40s and P-47 Thunderbolts attack rail tracks, bridges, logistics bases, rail cars, and industrial targets.

SOUTHWEST PACIFIC AREA: U.S. submarine *Bluegill* torpedoes and sinks a Japanese cargo ship east of Mindanao in the Philippines.

CENTRAL PACIFIC: Shore-based Air Force Forward Area (Task Force 59) is activated under Major General Willis H. Hale to control all army, navy, and Marine Corps shore-based aircraft in the Central Pacific forward area.

Seventh Air Force B-25 Mitchells from Makin Island bomb Jaluit Atoll.

Naval Task Group 58.7, commanded by Vice Admiral Willis A. Lee, with seven battleships and 14 destroyers, bombards facilities on Ponape Island in the Carolines. Carrier aircraft provide cover.

BOUGAINVILLE: P-39 Airacobras attack a number of targets on the island.

NEW BRITAIN: Thirteenth Air Force B-24 Liberators bomb coastal guns, and P-39 Airacobras, P-40s, and 30 navy SBD Dauntless dive-bombers attack Vunakambi Plantation.

NEW GUINEA: Fifth Air Force sends over 180 B-25 Mitchells, A-20 Havocs, and P-40s to attack Wewak and the Hansa Bay area.

Fifth Air Force receives the headquarters of the 86th Fighter Wing at Finschhafen from the United States.

The Thirteenth Air Task Force under Fifth Air Force sends B-24s against the Woleai and Eauriprik Atolls in the Carolines.

A Navy PB4Y Privateer damages a Japanese cargo vessel off Biak.

May 2

CBI: Fourteenth Air Force B-24 Liberators report sinking two cargo ships in the Formosa Straits. The Japanese commit nearly 75,000 troops to accomplish their offensive objectives in China.

ATLANTIC: The JCS orders General Stilwell to shift his emphasis from supporting the British efforts in Burma and opening the Burma Road to developing air bases in China by February 1945 to support the planned attack on Formosa, the Philippines, the Ryukyus, or the coast of China.

ETO: Eighth Air Force sends 50 B-24 Liberators escorted by 50 P-47 Thunderbolts and 52 P-51 Mustangs to attack V-weapon sites in the Pas-de-Calais area of France.

Ninth Air Force sends over 250 B-26 Marauders and A-20 Havocs to bomb marshaling yards in France. A total of 400 P-47 Thunderbolts and P-51 Mustangs conduct dive-bomb attacks on airfields and marshaling yards in France and the Netherlands.

ITALY: Fifteenth Air Force sends over 250 B-17s and B-24 Liberators against a marshaling yard and railroad bridge. Most of the bombers abort the mission due to bad weather.

Twelfth Air Force B-25 Mitchells and B-26 Marauders attack bridges and marshaling yards. P-40s and P-47 Thunderbolts attack rail lines, gun positions near Anzio, a road bridge, vehicles, and logistics bases.

CENTRAL PACIFIC: During the night Seventh Air Force B-24 Liberators, staging through Eniwetok Atoll from Kwajalein, bomb Truk.

B-25 Mitchells from Makin Island attack Wotje Atoll, rearm at Majuro Atoll, and bomb Jaluit Atoll on the return to Makin. B-25 Mitchells from Engebi Island, Eniwetok, attack Ponape Island.

BOUGAINVILLE: Thirteenth Air Force P-39 Airacobras bomb a village near Kieta, the airfield at Koromira, and Rigu mission. P-40s also attack targets near Kieta.

NEW BRITAIN: P-38 Lightnings, P-39 Airacobras, and P-40s attack Rabaul and Vunakambi Plantation logistics sites, while B-25 Mitchells bomb the Talili area.

NEW GUINEA: Fifth Air Force A-20 Havocs, P-47 Thunderbolts, and P-40s attack Japanese positions and facilities from Wewak to Hansa Bay. B-25 Mitchells bomb airfields at Wewak and Boram and facilities on Wakde Island. B-24 Liberators bomb Biak Island.

May 3

CBI: Tenth Air Force B-25 Mitchells bomb Kohima.

In China, Fourteenth Air Force Chinese-American Composite Wing B-25 Mitchells bomb vehicles and troops. B-25 Mitchells and P-40s from the Chinese-American

Composite Wing (CACW) attack logistics sites at Tangyang airfield and damage a bridge over the Yellow River near Chenghsien, destroying several trucks with troops.

Fourteenth Air Force B-24 Liberators attack a Japanese convoy near Formosa, sinking a cargo ship.

ATLANTIC: German submarine *U-765* torpedoes and damages a destroyer escort near Cape Clear, Ireland.

ETO: Eighth Air Force sends 51 B-24 Liberators escorted by 48 P-47 Thunderbolts and 53 P-51 Mustangs to bomb the V-weapon site at Wizernes, France. Of the 47 bombers that hit the target, 33 are damaged and three airmen are wounded.

During the night, five B-17s drop leaflets on cities and towns in France, Belgium, and the Netherlands. One bomber is damaged. Nine B-24 Liberators support Carpetbagger operations.

MEDITERRANEAN: German submarine *U-371* stalks a convoy moving west toward the Straits of Gibraltar, damaging a destroyer escort off Bougie, Algeria. Although tracked by a group of U.S., French, and British destroyers, destroyer escorts, and a minesweeper *U-371* escapes.

ITALY: Twelfth Air Force B-25 Mitchells and B-26 Marauders attack railway bridges and marshaling yards. A-20 Havocs attack an ammunition storage site. P-40s and P-47 Thunderbolts attack rail lines, bridges, logistics sites, and an observation post near Cassino.

SOUTHWEST PACIFIC AREA: U.S. submarine *Flasher* torpedoes and sinks a Japanese cargo ship in the South China Sea.

U.S. submarine *Tinosa* torpedoes and sinks a Japanese cargo ship in the Luzon Strait.

PACIFIC: U.S. submarine *Tautog* torpedoes and sinks a Japanese cargo ship off Uruppu Island in the Kuriles.

CENTRAL PACIFIC: Seventh Air Force B-25 Mitchells from Kwajalein bomb Wotje Atoll. B-25s from Makin Island bomb Wotje Atoll, rearm at Majuro Atoll, and bomb Jaluit Atoll on the return to Makin.

U.S. submarine *Sand Lance* torpedoes and sinks a Japanese transport off Saipan.

BOUGAINVILLE: Thirteenth Air Force sends P-39 Airacobras to bomb targets of opportunity over the island. P-40s returning from the New Britain Island area bomb Pororan.

NEW BRITAIN: Thirteenth Air Force B-25 Mitchells bomb Kulon Plantation and troops nearby.

NEW GUINEA: Fifth Air Force B-24 Liberators, B-25 Mitchells, and A-20 Havocs attack Wewak and Boram airfields, causing heavy damage. Over 100 A-20 Havocs, B-25s, P-47 Thunderbolts, and P-40s also attack Wewak and Hansa Bay. The P-40s of the 7th and 8th Fighter Squadrons, 49th Fighter Group deploy to Hollandia; C-47s of the 65th Troop Carrier Squadron, 433rd Troop Carrier Group, begin operating from Tadji airfield.

May 4
CBI: In Burma, the Chinese 22nd Division captures Inkangahtawng.

Tenth Air Force sends 24 B-24 Liberators to bomb the marshaling yard and a Japanese barracks at Mandalay.

Chinese forces halt on the road to Kamaing after capturing Inkangahtawng.

Fourteenth Air Force P-40s attack Japanese gun positions in China.

ETO: Eighth Air Force sends 591 B-17s, escorted by 50 P-38 Lightnings, 179 P-47 Thunderbolts, and 287 Eighth and Ninth Air Force P-51 Mustangs, to attack targets in Berlin, Brunswick, and in central Germany. The mission is recalled, but 40 B-17s bomb an airfield in the Netherlands. Sixteen bombers are damaged. Two air crewmen are killed and one wounded. Fighter pilots report nine confirmed kills and two probables. Three aircraft are lost and 14 are damaged. Three pilots are missing and one is wounded.

Ninth Air Force sends over 170 B-26 Marauders and 36 A-20 Havocs to attack gun emplacements and other military targets in France.

MEDITERRANEAN: German submarine *U-371* torpedoes and damages a U.S. destroyer escort and a French destroyer escort off the Algerian coast near Constantine, but is heavily damaged by depth charges from two U.S. destroyer escorts, a French destroyer escort, and a British destroyer escort. Three of the crew are killed and 49 are captured after her crew scuttles the U-boat and abandons her. *U-371* is detected and sunk by air and naval assets using the swamp technique of blanketing an area where a U-boat is known or suspected to be located, forcing the submarine to stay submerged until it has to surface to recharge its batteries to survive. Once on the surface, ships and aircraft will converge and overwhelm (swamp) the submarine.

ITALY: Twelfth Air Force B-25 Mitchells and B-26 Marauders attack bridges, rail lines, and marshaling yards. P-40s and P-47 Thunderbolts attack rail lines, marshaling yards, motor transport, logistics sites, and trucks and personnel on the Fondi-Pico road.

SOUTHWEST PACIFIC AREA: U.S. submarines *Bang, Parche,* and *Tinosa* attack Japanese convoy ships in the Luzon Strait. USS *Bang* sinks a cargo ship, USS *Parche* and *Tinosa* both sink two cargo ships.

U.S. submarine *Pargo* torpedoes and sinks a Japanese auxiliary netlayer east of Mindanao in the Philippines.

PACIFIC: U.S. submarine *Tuna* torpedoes and sinks a Japanese guardboat near Wake Island.

CENTRAL PACIFIC: Seventh Air Force B-24 Liberators from Kwajalein and Eniwetok Atolls bomb Ponape Island. B-25s from Makin Island bomb Wotje Atoll, rearm at Majuro Atoll, and bomb Jaluit Atoll on the return to Makin.

BOUGAINVILLE: Thirteenth Air Force sends 38 P-39 Airacobras to attack buildings at Sovele, Tinputs, the Reboine Bay area, Monoitu, and the area near Taki. P-39s attack targets around Koromira.

NEW BRITAIN: The last elements of the 1st Marine Division leave New Britain.

Thirteenth Air Force sends 24 B-25 Mitchells to bomb the Talili Bay area.

NEW GUINEA: Major General William H. Gill, the 32nd Infantry Division commander, takes control of the Aitape Task Force, relieving the 163rd RCT for the Wakde-Biak operation.

Fifth Air Force send over 60 B-24 Liberators, B-25 Mitchells, A-20 Havocs, and P-47 Thunderbolts to attack airfields and other targets around Wewak. A-20 Havocs attack bridges over the Awar River and targets of opportunity in the Hansa Bay area.

Thirteenth Air Task Force under Fifth Air Force sends 26 B-24 Liberators to bomb Mokmer airfield at Biak Island.

May 5

CBI: Tenth Air Force sends over 80 P-40s, P-51 Mustangs, A-36 Intruder (Apache) fighter-bombers, and B-25 Mitchells to attack Japanese positions, logistics sites, vehicles, and targets of opportunity in the Mogaung Valley. B-24 Liberators lay mines in the harbor off Koh Si Chang Island in Thailand.

Fourteenth Air Force sends 11 B-24 Liberators to bomb docks and shipping at Haiphong, French Indochina. In China, the Chinese-American Composite Wing's B-25 Mitchells and P-40s attack a marshaling yard, a logistics site, and troops and vehicles on the road from Loyang to Juchou.

ETO: Eighth Air Force sends 46 B-24 Liberators escorted by 52 P-51 Mustangs to bomb the V-weapon site at Sottevast, France. Of the 33 that hit the target seven B-24s are damaged; four airmen are killed.

During the night, 21 B-24 Liberators support Carpetbagger operations and one bomber is lost.

MEDITERRANEAN: Fifteenth Air Force sends over 640 B-17s and B-24 Liberators to attack targets in Romania and Yugoslavia. The B-17s bomb marshaling yards at Ploeşti and Brasnov in Romania. The 485 B-24s attack the Ploeşti marshaling yard. Nineteen bombers are lost and 19 German fighters are destroyed over the target. Another 147 B-17s and 126 B-24 Liberators attack aircraft production facilities near Vienna, Austria. A total of 28 bombers are lost and three fighters. Aircrews and fighter pilots report a total of 50 confirmed kills and 22 probables.

Twelfth Air Force A-20 Havocs bomb a logistics base. A-36 Intruder (Apache) fighter-bombers, P-47 Thunderbolts, and P-40s attack rail lines around Rome and gun positions near the Anzio battleline.

German submarine *U-967* torpedoes and sinks a U.S. destroyer escort northwest of Oran, Algeria.

PACIFIC: U.S. submarine *Pogy* attacks a Japanese convoy, sinking a transport off Honshu, Japan.

CENTRAL PACIFIC: Seventh Air Force B-25 Mitchells from Eniwetok Atoll bomb Ponape Island. B-25s from Makin Island bomb Wotje Atoll, rearm at Majuro Atoll, and bomb Jaluit Atoll on the return to Makin. B-24 Liberators from Kwajalein Atoll staging through Eniwetok Atoll bomb Truk Atoll during the night.

BOUGAINVILLE: Thirteenth Air Force sends 24 B-25 Mitchells to bomb gun positions on Buka Island. P-39 Airacobras attack buildings and logistics sites. P-40s bomb buildings at Kieta and at nearby Rigu mission.

U.S. motor torpedo boats blockading the southeastern coast of Bougainville encounter several heavily armed barges. One PT boat is sunk.

NEW GUINEA: Fifth Air Force B-24 Liberators bomb Mokmer airfield at Biak Island and B-25 Mitchells bomb logistics sites at Wakde Island. A-20 Havocs, P-47 Thunderbolts, and P-40s attack targets around Wewak and along the coast of Hansa Bay.

May 6

CBI: After marching 65 miles over a 6,000-foot-high mountain trail, the Marauders reach Ritpong, where patrols encounter Japanese forces.

Tenth Air Force P-40s, P-51 Mustangs, and B-25 Mitchells attack targets in the Mogaung Valley.

Fourteenth Air Force sends 61 P-40s and five B-25 Mitchells attack bridges, rail cars, and vehicles in southern China.

ATLANTIC: Destroyer escort USS *Buckley* rams German submarine *U-66*, which has been damaged by air attack in the mid-Atlantic. The sailors of the *Buckley* fight the German submarine crew at close quarters, using small arms, hand grenades, fists, and even coffee mugs before the stricken U-boat sinks.

ETO: Eighth Air Force sends 90 B-17s and 78 B-24 Liberators, escorted by 57 Ninth Air Force P-38 Lightnings, 47 P-47 Thunderbolts, and 81 P-51 Mustangs, against V-weapon targets in France. The B-17s abort the mission due to heavy cloud cover, but 70 B-24s attack the target. A total of 48 bombers are damaged. No losses are reported.

During the night five B-17s drop over three million leaflets on cities and towns in Belgium and France. One B-17 encounters a night fighter and is damaged in the attack, but the aircrew reports the enemy fighter as a probable kill. A total of 22 B-24s support Carpetbagger missions.

A Ninth Air Force mission to attack coastal defenses in France is aborted due to weather.

MEDITERRANEAN: Fifteenth Air Forces ends 300 B-17s and B-24 Liberators escorted by P-51 Mustangs and P-38 Lightnings against aircraft production facilities and marshaling yards in Romania.

Twelfth Air Force A-20 Havocs attack a logistics base at Itri. A-36 Intruder (Apache) fighter-bombers bomb rail lines. P-40s attack gun positions and rail lines. P-47 Thunderbolts attack a marshaling yard and lines of communication.

SOUTHWEST PACIFIC AREA: U.S. submarine *Gurnard* spots a Japanese convoy from Manila carrying the 32nd and 35th Divisions to reinforce garrisons at Manokwari in the Celebes Sea and sinks three cargo ships.

PACIFIC: U.S. submarine *Spearfish* attacks a Japanese convoy in the East China Sea west of Kyushu, Japan, and sinks a cargo ship and damages a supply ship.

CENTRAL PACIFIC: Seventh Air Force B-25 Mitchells from Makin Island and Kwajalein bomb Wotje and Jaluit Atolls. B-24 Liberators, staging through Eniwetok Atoll, escort Navy aircraft on a photo reconnaissance of Guam and bomb the island's two airfields and proceed to Momote airfield at Los Negros Island, Admiralties. Aircrews report four enemy aircraft shot down.

BOUGAINVILLE: Thirteenth Air Force sends 37 P-39 Airacobras and 19 P-40s to attack targets around Porton.

NEW BRITAIN: Thirteenth Air Force sends 24 B-25 Mitchells and 12 P-39 Airacobras to attack targets around Talili Bay.

NEW GUINEA: The 41st Infantry Division is ordered to Wakde Island to support the attack on the Japanese base at Sarmi.

Fifth Air Force sends over 150 B-25 Mitchells, A-20 Havocs, P-47 Thunderbolts, and P-40s to attack targets from Wewak to Hansa Bay.

Thirteenth Air Task Force B-24 Liberators under Fifth Air Force bomb Woleai Atoll.

U.S. submarine *Crevalle* attacks a Japanese convoy off northern Borneo, sinking a fleet tanker.

May 7

CBI: Tenth Air Force B-24 Liberators lay mines in the Gulf of Siam off Sattahib, Thailand.

In China, Fourteenth Air Force B-25 Mitchells bomb Japanese vehicle concentrations and P-40s attack trucks, tanks, and other vehicles.

ETO: Eighth Air Force sends 600 B-17s and 322 B-24 Liberators, escorted by 153 P-38 Lightnings, 317 P-47 Thunderbolts, and 284 P-51 Mustangs, against targets in Berlin. Nine bombers are lost and 300 are damaged. Aircrew casualties are nine killed, 16 wounded, 89 missing. Fighter pilots report four aircraft lost and 10 damaged. Three pilots are reported missing.

During the night three B-17s drop leaflets over towns in central France. A total of 14 B-24s support Carpetbagger missions.

MEDITERRANEAN: Fifteenth Air Force sends over 400 B-17s and B-24 Liberators escorted by P-51 Mustangs and P-38 Lightnings to bomb marshaling yards in Romania and a railroad bridge in Yugoslavia.

Twelfth Air Force A-20 Havocs, A-36 Intruder (Apache) fighter-bombers, P-51 Mustangs, and P-40s attack logistics sites, motor transport, rail lines, gun positions, bridges, and marshaling yards.

SOUTHWEST PACIFIC AREA: U.S. submarines *Bonefish* and *Flasher* torpedo and damage a Japanese cargo ship in the Sulu Sea.

PACIFIC: U.S. submarine *Burrfish* torpedoes and sinks a German oiler bound for Balikpapan off Honshu, Japan.

CENTRAL PACIFIC: Seventh Air Force B-25 Mitchells from Engebi Island bomb Ponape Island. B-25s from Makin Island bomb Jaluit and Wotje Atolls. B-24 Liberators, staging through Eniwetok, bomb Truk during the night.

BOUGAINVILLE: Thirteenth Air Force P-39 Airacobras, P-38 Lightnings, and P-40s bomb logistics sites, bridges, and huts throughout Buka and Bougainville.

NEW GUINEA: The 163rd RCT is relieved from the Aitape operation to prepare for the attack on Wakde Island.

Fifth Air Force B-24 Liberators, B-25 Mitchells, and P-40s attack Biak Island and the coast from Wakde to Hollandia. A-20 Havocs, B-25 Mitchells, P-38 Lightnings, and P-47 Thunderbolts attack targets of opportunity from Wewak to the Hansa Bay area.

The A-20s of the 90th Bombardment Squadron (Light), 3rd Bombardment Group (Light), deploy to Hollandia.

May 8

CBI: The Chinese 38th Division begins its advance to Kamaing.

Tenth Air Force sends nine B-24 Liberators and nine B-25 Mitchells to bomb Moirang. Aircrews report heavy damage to a road bridge. P-38 Lightnings attack Kangaung airfield.

ETO: Eighth Air Force sends 500 B-17s and 307 B-24 Liberators, escorted by 152 P-38 Lightnings, 295 P-47 Thunderbolts, and 282 P-51 Mustangs, to attack Berlin and Brunswick. Aircrews report 76 confirmed kills and 16 probables. A total of 36 bombers are lost and 205 are damaged. Aircrew casualties are eight killed, 15 wounded, and 373 missing. Fighter pilots report 55 confirmed kills and four probables. Thirteen aircraft are lost and six are damaged. One pilot is wounded and 13 are missing.

A second attack with 101 B-17s and 63 B-24s escorted by 97 P-47 Thunderbolts is directed against V-weapon sites at Glacerie and Sottevast, France. Five bombers are lost and 59 are damaged. Two air crewmen are killed, two are wounded, and 47 are missing.

During the night three B-17s drop a million leaflets over cities and towns in France.

Ninth Air Force sends more than 400 B-26 Marauders and A-20 Havocs to bomb marshaling yards, coastal defenses, bridges, airfields, and V-weapon sites in France and Belgium.

MEDITERRANEAN: German submarine *U-230* torpedoes and sinks a U.S. submarine chaser near Palermo, Sicily.

ITALY: Twelfth Air Force A-20 Havocs and P-40s attack logistics sites, rail cars, and vehicles around Rome and Anzio.

SOUTHWEST PACIFIC AREA: U.S. submarine *Hoe* torpedoes and damages a Japanese escort vessel and a tanker in the South China Sea.

PACIFIC: U.S. submarine *Tautog* attacks a Japanese convoy in Tsugaru Strait, sinking a cargo ship.

CENTRAL PACIFIC: Seventh Air Force B-24 Liberators returning from Los Negros to Eniwetok Atoll bomb Ponape Island. B-25 Mitchells from Engebi Island also bomb Ponape.

B-25s from Makin Island bomb Wotje Atoll, rearm at Majuro Atoll, and bomb Jaluit Atoll on the return to Makin.

BOUGAINVILLE: Thirteenth Air Force P-39 Airacobras and P-40s attack a number of targets around Porton, Tsimba, Tarara, Kieta, and Numa Numa. B-25 Mitchells bomb the coast and the airfield area on Buka Island.

NEW BRITAIN: Thirteenth Air Force P-39 Airacobras and P-40s attack Tobera airfield.

New Guinea: Fifth Air Force B-24 Liberators and P-40s attack Mokmer airfield and shipping at Biak Island. A-20 Havocs, P-47 Thunderbolts, and P-40s attack targets of opportunity along the coast from Wewak to Hansa Bay.

The Japanese convoy carrying elements of the 32nd and 35th Divisions reaches Wasile Bay, Halmahera, with only five of its original nine ships.

May 9

CBI: Galahad's M Force and K Force, along with the Chinese 88th Regiment, clear Ritpong of Japanese forces.

Tenth Air Force B-25 Mitchells, A-36 Intruder (Apache) fighter-bombers, P-51 Mustangs, and P-40s attacks targets in the Mogaung Valley.

ETO: The Eighth Air Force participates with all Allied air components to initiate intensive bombing against airfields to prevent their use prior to D-day. The mission involves 462 B-17s and 361 B-24 Liberators, escorted by 144 P-38 Lightnings, 277 P-47 Thunderbolts, and 247 P-51 Mustangs, attack airfields in France, Luxembourg, and Belgium. Four bombers are lost and 117 are damaged. Aircrew casualties are three killed, two wounded, and 64 missing. Fighter pilots report three confirmed kills in the air and one on the ground. Seven aircraft are lost and two are damaged. Six pilots are missing.

During the night three B-17s drop over a million leaflets on the Netherlands and Belgium. A total of 13 B-24s fly in support of Carpetbagger operations.

Ninth Air Force sends over 40 B-26 Marauders to attack marshaling yards, coastal defense guns, bridges, and V-weapon sites in France.

Italy: Twelfth Air Force B-26 Marauders attack a railroad bridge and viaduct. A-20 Havocs attack fuel storage areas. P-47 Thunderbolts and P-40s attack lines of communication.

Southwest Pacific Area: A planning meeting is held at SWPA headquarters to address the need for additional airfields that can handle bombers. The Hollandia airfields are inadequate and planners look to Wakde, 110 miles west of Hollandia, as a solution.

Central Pacific: B-25s from Makin Island bomb Wotje Atoll, rearm at Majuro Atoll, and bomb Jaluit Atoll on the return to Makin. B-24 Liberators from Kwajalein Atoll staging through Eniwetok Atoll bomb Truk during the night.

Bougainville: Thirteenth Air Force P-39 Airacobras and P-38 Lightnings attack barges and an ammunition storage facility near Aitara Mission, while 10 other P-38 Lightnings and 12 B-25 Mitchells bomb Bonis airfield and targets of opportunity in Buka Passage.

New Britain: Thirteenth Air Force P-39 Airacobras and P-40s bomb the Lakunai airfield.

New Guinea: Fifth Air Force sends over 220 A-20 Havocs, P-47 Thunderbolts, and P-40s to attack targets of opportunity along the coast from Wewak to Hansa Bay.

Thirteenth Air Task Force B-24 Liberators under Fifth Air Force bomb Woleai Atoll.

May 10

CBI: The Chinese 198th Division Y Force, or the Chinese Expeditionary Force, under command of General Wei Li-huang and advised by Brigadier General Frank Dorn, crosses the Salween River to join the offensive to drive the Japanese out of north Burma and open the Burma Road.

Tenth Air Force B-25 Mitchells, A-36 Intruder (Apache) fighter-bombers, P-51 Mustangs, P-40s, and 10 B-24 Liberators attack Japanese barracks and logistics sites around Myitkyina and Mogaung as well as gun positions and bridges at Kamaing.

In China, Fourteenth Air Force P-40s attack Japanese convoys, river traffic, and bridges.

ETO: Ninth Air Force sends nearly 300 B-26 Marauders to attack marshaling yards, airfields, and V-weapon targets in France and Belgium.

MEDITERRANEAN: Fifteenth Air Force sends 400 B-17s and B-24 Liberators to attack aircraft production facilities at Wiener Neustadt, Austria. Most of the bombers abort the mission after encountering bad weather, but 147 B-17s and 126 B-24 Liberators hit the target. A total of 28 bombers are lost and three fighters. Aircrews and fighter pilots report a total of 50 confirmed kills and 22 probables. Twelfth Air Force B-25 Mitchells and B-26 Marauders attack bridges while A-36 fighter-bombers, P-51 Mustangs, and P-40s attack lines of communication north of Rome.

ITALY: Destroyers USS *Charles F. Hughes* and USS *Hilary P. Jones* bombard German logistics storage areas near Anzio.

SOUTHWEST PACIFIC AREA: MacArthur approves the Wakde operation and sets May 17 as the date for the attack. The status of Japanese forces in the area is uncertain. The Japanese army has changed its codes, preventing any Ultra intelligence for at least several weeks until the new codes can be broken. The 163rd RCT is given the mission to seize and secure a beachhead in the area of Toem-Arara and capture Wakde Island. Brigadier General Jens A. Doe of the 41st Infantry Division will command the landing force. The rest of the 41st Infantry Division is scheduled to land on Biak Island, 200 miles west of Wakde, on May 27.

U.S. submarine *Cod* attacks a Japanese convoy off the west coast of Luzon, sinking a destroyer and a transport.

CENTRAL PACIFIC: Seventh Air Force B-25 Mitchells from Engebi Island bomb Ponape Island. B-25s from Makin Island bomb Jaluit and Wotje Atolls. B-24 Liberators from Kwajalein Atoll staging through Eniwetok Atoll bomb Truk during the night.

A naval base is established at Eniwetok.

U.S. submarine *Silversides* attacks a Japanese convoy near Guam, sinking an auxiliary cable ship, a gunboat, and a collier. USS *Silversides* survives depth-charging from several escort vessels.

U.S. submarine *Tambor* encounters a Japanese convoy and torpedoes an aircraft transport near Saipan.

BOUGAINVILLE: Thirteenth Air Force sends four B-25 Mitchells to bomb Majuai mission. P-39 Airacobras and P-40s attack barges, villages, enemy positions, a bridge, and the area around Porton Plantation.

New Britain: Thirteenth Air Force sends 41 P-39 Airacobras and P-40s to attack Tobera airfield.

New Guinea: Fifth Air Force B-24 Liberators, A-20 Havocs, P-47 Thunderbolts, and P-40s, along with Royal Australian Air Force aircraft continue to attack targets of opportunity along the coast from Wewak to the Hansa Bay area. B-24s bomb Mokmer airfield on Biak Island.

Thirteenth Air Task Force under Fifth Air Force sends 45 B-24s to bomb the airfield on Eten Island and logistics base at Dublon Island in Truk Atoll.

May 11

CBI: In Burma, Tenth Air Force B-25 Mitchells, A-36 Intruder (Apache) fighter-bombers, P-51 Mustangs, and P-40s attack Myitkyina, Kamaing, and targets of opportunity along the road from Inkangahtawng to Kamaing. The 24 P-51 Mustangs sent to attack the airfield at Meiktila, Anisakan, and Heho report 13 enemy aircraft shot down. B-25 Mitchells attack the railroad in the Shwebo-Sagaing area and other B-25s destroy bridges.

In China, Fourteenth Air Force P-40s destroy the main bridge north of Mangshih.

ETO: Eighth Air Force sends 364 B-24 Liberators escorted by 147 P-38 Lightnings, 188 P-47 Thunderbolts, and 201 P-51 Mustangs to bomb marshaling yards in France. Eight bombers are lost and 50 are damaged. Aircrew casualties are one killed, eight wounded, and 71 missing. Fighter pilots report eight confirmed kills on the ground, and three in the air. Five fighters are lost and 11 are damaged. Five pilots are missing.

Another attack by 609 B-17s, escorted by 99 P-38 Lightnings, 182 Eighth and Ninth Air Force P-47 Thunderbolts, and 190 Eighth and Ninth Air Force P-51 Mustangs, against marshaling yards in Belgium, France, Germany, and Luxembourg results in eight bombers lost and 173 damaged. Aircrew casualties are two killed, 23 wounded, and 83 missing. Fighter pilots report 11 confirmed kills. Four aircraft are lost and the pilots reported missing.

Four B-24s support Carpetbagger operations.

Ninth Air Force sends over 300 B-26 Marauders to attack airfields in France and Belgium.

Italy: Operation Diadem begins. The goal is to occupy German forces in Italy prior to Overlord and capture Rome by breaking the Gustav Line and then breaking out from the Anzio beachhead. Massed artillery fire precedes the infantry attack. Supported by naval gunfire, the French Expeditionary Corps and II Corps, with the 85th and 88th Infantry Divisions abreast, cross the Garigliano River along the western coastline and meet strong opposition. The two divisions are the first made up of all-draftees and this will be their first major combat action. The 85th Infantry Division is commanded by Major General John B. Coulter and the 88th Infantry Division is commanded by Major General John E. Sloan. The 351st Infantry Regiment of the 88th Division leads the II Corps attack. At the hills surrounding the town of Santa Maria Infante, they are stopped. The 350th Infantry Regiment captures Monte Damiano and holds it against a German counterattack. Lieutenant Colonel Raymond E. Kendall of the 2nd Battalion, 351st Infantry, personally leads an attack on a German strongpoint that is holding up his men and slowing the momentum of the attack. Kendall rushes the enemy position, firing a weapon until it runs out of ammunition, then picks up another weapon and fires it. He is killed as he succeeds in destroying a machine gun position. For his exceptional display of courage, Lieutenant Colonel Kendall will be awarded the Distinguished Service Cross.

Twelfth Air Force B-25 Mitchells and B-26 Marauders bomb bridges and rail lines. A-20 Havocs, P-40s, and P-47 Thunderbolts support Allied ground forces, attacking enemy positions along the Gustav Line.

SOUTHWEST PACIFIC AREA: U.S. submarine *Crevalle* evacuates 28 women and children from Negros Island in the Philippines.

PACIFIC: U.S. submarine *Sturgeon* attacks a Japanese convoy, sinking a cargo ship near Chichi Jima in the Bonin Islands.

CENTRAL PACIFIC: Seventh Air Force B-25 Mitchells from Engebi Island bomb Ponape Island and B-25s from Makin Island bomb Jaluit Atoll.

B-24 Liberators from Kwajalein Atoll staging through Eniwetok Atoll bomb Truk during the night.

U.S. submarine *Sand Lance* attacks a Japanese convoy, sinking a transport off Tinian.

BOUGAINVILLE: Thirteenth Air Force P-39 Airacobras, P-40s, and P-38 Lightnings attack piers at Chabai, Ratsua, and Porton, a bridge at Tokinotu, and the Buka Island airfield.

NEW BRITAIN: Thirteenth Air Force P-38 Lightnings bomb a logistics support area near Tobera. B-25 Mitchells, P-40s, and B-24 Liberators attack Vunakanau airfield.

NEW GUINEA: Fifth Air Force B-24 Liberators and B-25 Mitchells bomb gun emplacements and logistics bases on Wakde Island and Mokmer airfield on Biak Island. P-47 Thunderbolts, P-40s, and A-20 Havocs, along with B-24s and B-25s attack bridges and villages, fuel storage areas, and logistics sites along the coast from Hansa Bay to Wewak.

U.S. submarine *Rasher* attacks a Japanese convoy, sinking an auxiliary vessel in the Molucca Sea.

May 12

CBI: The Marauders' K Force meets strong Japanese resistance at Tingkrukawng. H Force moves toward Myitkyina, stopping at the Detachment 101 base at Arang to evacuate the sick and obtain resupply by air.

Tenth Air Force B-25 Mitchells and P-40s attack gun positions and logistics support sites at Myitkyina. P-51 Mustangs attack airfields, reporting eight Japanese aircraft destroyed.

In China, Fourteenth Air Force B-25 Mitchells and P-40s attack military installations, artillery positions, and tanks near Yoyang.

ETO: Eighth Air Force sends 326 B-17s and 265 B-24 Liberators to bomb oil production facilities in Germany. Another 295 B-17s are sent against targets in Czechoslovakia. Aircrews report seven crewmen killed, 21 wounded, and 430 missing. The mission is escorted by 153 P-38 Lightnings, 201 P-47 Thunderbolts, and 381 P-51 Mustangs. Fighter pilots report 61 confirmed kills in the air and another five on the ground. Seven aircraft are lost and 13 are damaged. Pilots report seven pilots missing.

Later that night, five B-17s drop over one million leaflets on Denmark. One bomber is damaged.

Ninth Air Force B-26 Marauders attack coastal defenses, airfields, bridges, railroads, gun positions, and V-weapon sites in France and Belgium. IX Troop Carrier Command runs Operation Eagle, a full-scale rehearsal of the airborne landing plan for Neptune.

ITALY: Fifteenth Air Force sends 730 B-17s and B-24 Liberators to attack command and control targets, airfields, marshaling yards, and railroad bridges. P-38 Lightnings strafe the airfield at Piacenza.

Twelfth Air Force A-20 Havocs attack command and control targets along the battle line, while B-16s and B-25 Mitchells bomb German defensive positions. P-47 Thunderbolts and P-40s attack command posts, gun positions, bridges, lines of communication, and German troops near Monte Cassino.

Second Lieutenant Charles W. Shea, of F Company, 350th Infantry Regiment, 88th Infantry Division, leads his platoon toward a German position on a hilltop near Monte Damiano. German machine guns fire on the company, inflicting a number of casualties and stopping the attack. Second Lieutenant Shea takes the initiative to eliminate the German machine guns. Despite heavy fire, he is able to crawl to one of the positions and throw hand grenades. The survivors surrender to Shea who then moves to the next position and forces them to surrender as well. As the third machine gun fires at him, Second Lieutenant Shea stands up and rushes the position, killing the enemy with rifle fire. For his great courage under fire and his determination to close with the enemy, Second Lieutenant Shea will receive the Medal of Honor.

PACIFIC: U.S. submarine *Tautog* attacks a Japanese convoy off northeast Honshu, Japan, sinking a collier.

CENTRAL PACIFIC: Seventh Air Force B-25 Mitchells from Makin Island bomb Nauru Island.

NEW BRITAIN: Thirteenth Air Force B-25 Mitchells, P-40s, and P-38 Lightnings attack troops and the airfield at Tobera. Army P-39 Airacobras and navy SBD Dauntless dive-bombers and TBF Avenger torpedo-bombers attack barges at Simpson Harbor and Keravia Bay near Rabaul.

NEW GUINEA: Fifth Air Force B-24 Liberators bomb Mokmer airfield on Biak Island. A-20 Havocs, B-25 Mitchells, and P-39 Airacobras and P-40s attack targets near Wewak and the Hansa Bay area. B-21s attack Ambon, Ceram, and Amboina Islands in the Moluccas as well as Timor Island.

May 13

CBI: Tenth Air Force sends almost 100 P-40s and P-51 Mustangs to attack troops, gun positions, and targets of opportunity in the Mogaung Valley. A-36 Intruder (Apache) fighter-bombers, B-25 Mitchells, and B-24 Liberators attack other targets.

In China, Fourteenth Air Force B-25 Mitchells and P-40s attack logistics sites, lines of communication, and convoys.

Twentieth Air Force receives the B-19 Superfortresses of the 771st Bombardment Squadron (Very Heavy), 462nd Bombardment Squadron (Very Heavy), at Piardoba, India, from the United States. The squadron's first mission is scheduled for early June.

ATLANTIC: In the North Atlantic, south of the Azores, destroyer escort *Francis M. Robinson* sinks Japanese submarine *RO-501,* previously German submarine *U-1224,* on its way to Japan.

ETO: Allied planners solidify the force build-up estimates for Neptune. On D-day, the plan calls for 8 2/3 divisions to be on the beachhead. Staff estimates of casualties on D-day are set at 12,000 killed and wounded. On D+1, 10 1/3 divisions will be available, on D+6, 15 1/3 divisions are to be landed, and on D+12, 26–30 divisions will have arrived. By D+40, planners estimate that sufficient forces will be available to separate the U.S. First Army from the 21st Army Group and create the U.S. 12th Army Group. At that time, the estimated troop strength in France is to be 450,000 men and 92,000 vehicles.

Between D+1 and D+10, planners estimate a logistics requirement of 19,500 long tons of supplies per day. By D+25 to D+40, that number is estimated to increase to 42,000 long tons per day. These planning figures do not include fuel, which is estimated at 1,800 tons a day just for the Americans. By D+330 (330 days after D-day), the Allies plan to reach the German border.

Eighth Air Force sends 289 B-17s to attack oil targets in Poland, 199 B-17s against the Osnabruck marshaling yard, and 261 B-24 Liberators against aircraft production facilities. The mission is escorted by 153 P-38 Lightnings, 238 P-47 Thunderbolts, and 346 P-51 Mustangs. Aircrews report 12 bombers lost and 144 damaged. Aircrew losses are one killed, four wounded, and 108 missing. Fighter pilots report 47 confirmed kills in the air and three probables. Five fighters are shot down and 13 are damaged. One pilot is wounded and five are reported missing.

Ninth Air Force sends over 300 B-26 Marauders and A-20 Havocs to attack airfields, coastal defenses, and V-weapon sites in France and Belgium. P-47 Thunderbolts conduct dive-bombing attacks.

ITALY: The French Expeditionary Corps captures Monte Majo and threatens the left wing of the German defensive line in the Liri Valley. II Corps renews its attack, with the 99th Infantry Division ordered to seize Santa Maria Infante and Spigno in order to control the road that links the Liri Valley with Route 7. The 85th Infantry Division is to support the attack. German aircraft attack the 85th Infantry Division near Minturno. Santa Maria Infante falls quickly.

Fifteenth Air Force sends over 670 B-17s and B-24 Liberators to bomb marshaling yards and rail lines to limit German reinforcements. Four AZON-equipped B-17s attack a viaduct near the Brenner Pass. Out of 21 bombs, four are direct hits. AZON (azimuth only) is a 1,000-pound bomb with a device to control the trajectory of the bomb after release. The bomb has radio-controlled fins and is balanced by a battery-powered gyroscope to stabilize the weapon as it falls. A smoke generator in the tail allows for visual tracking to the target.

Twelfth Air Force B-26 Marauders and B-25 Mitchells with A-20 Havocs and P-40s attack German lines of communication, command and control sites, and defensive positions all along the battlefront.

PACIFIC: U.S. submarine *Pogy* torpedoes and sinks a Japanese cargo ship off Honshu, Japan.

CENTRAL PACIFIC: Seventh Air Force B-24 Liberators attack Truk, staging through Eniwetok Atoll from Kwajalein. B-24s from Kwajalein bomb Maloelap and Jaluit Atolls. B-25 Mitchells from Engebi Island bomb Ponape Island.

Navy F4U Corsairs, F4F Hellcats, and SBD Dauntless dive-bombers, B-24 Liberators, and B-25 Mitchells bomb Japanese facilities on Jaluit Atoll.

BOUGAINVILLE: Thirteenth Air Force B-25 Mitchells, P-39 Airacobras, and P-40s attack piers, logistics sites, and villages.

NEW BRITAIN: Thirteenth Air Force B-25 Mitchells, P-39 Airacobras, P-40s, and P-38 Lightnings attack logistics sites at Talili Bay.

ADMIRALTIES: Thirteenth Air Force deploys the B-24 Liberators of the 370th, 371st, 372nd, and 424th Bombardment Squadrons (Heavy), of the 307th Bombardment Group (Heavy), from New Georgia to Momote airfield at Los Negros Island, Admiralties.

NEW GUINEA: Fifth Air Force B-24 Liberators and B-25 Mitchells bomb the Wakde and Arare airfields. P-39 Airacobras, P-40s, A-20 Havocs, and B-25s attack airfields, fuel storage areas, trucks, bridges, and other targets between Wewak and Hansa Bay.

May 14

CBI: Tenth Air Force P-38 Lightnings and P-40s attack lines of communication. B-25 Mitchells and P-51 Mustangs attack Japanese troops. Fighter pilots report four confirmed kills.

In China, Fourteenth Air Force P-40s and P-51 Mustangs attack road and rail traffic. Six Japanese bombers damage the airfield at Kienow.

ETO: Eighth Air Force receives the 435th Fighter Squadron, 479th Fighter Group, in England from the United States. The squadron, equipped with P-38Js (a variant of the P-38 Lightning with additional fuel tanks and an improved engine), is scheduled to fly its first mission in late May.

MEDITERRANEAN: German submarine *U-616* attacks a convoy off Morocco.

ITALY: The 88th Infantry Division reaches Spigno having suffered 2,000 casualties in three days of fighting.

Fifteenth Air Force sends 700 B-17s and B-24 Liberators to attack a marshaling yard and air depots.

Twelfth Air Force B-26 Marauders and B-25 Mitchells attack lines of communication; A-20 Havocs, P-47 Thunderbolts, and P-40s attack command and control sites, defensive positions, and lines of communication all along the battlefront.

First Lieutenant Robert T. Waugh is a platoon leader in the 339th Infantry Regiment, 85th Infantry Division, attacking six German bunker positions on a hill near

Tremensucli. After personally negotiating a minefield, he leads his platoon forward. Waugh orders the platoon to provide covering fire as he advances alone to engage the bunker positions. Throwing phosphorus grenades into the bunkers and firing on the defenders with his Thompson submachine gun, he clears each position. Several days later First Lieutenant Waugh performs the same heroic act, ordering his platoon to lay down a base of fire as he advances alone to destroy two pillboxes with grenades. As a result of his actions Waugh singlehandedly opens a breach in the Gustav Line, having killed 30 enemy soldiers and captured 25 others. For his gallantry in the face of the enemy beyond the call of duty, First Lieutenant Waugh will be receive the Medal of Honor.

CENTRAL PACIFIC: Seventh Air Force sends 53 B-24 Liberators from Kwajalein and 43 B-25 Mitchells from Makin Island to support navy aircraft in a raid on Jaluit Atoll.

U.S. submarines *Aspro* and *Bowfin* attack a Japanese convoy near Palau and sink a cargo ship.

U.S. submarine *Bonefish* attacks a Japanese convoy east of Borneo and sinks a destroyer.

U.S. submarine *Crevalle* is damaged by depth charges off northern Celebes Island.

U.S. submarine *Sand Lance* sinks a cargo ship near Guam. *Sand Lance* escapes after being depth-charged.

BOUGAINVILLE: Thirteenth Air Force P-39 Airacobras and P-40s bomb targets of opportunity.

NEW BRITAIN: Thirteenth Air Force sends 23 B-25 Mitchells to bomb the airfield at Tobera. P-39 Airacobras and P-40s attack logistics and troop areas at Vunakanau.

NEW GUINEA: Fifth Air Force B-24 Liberators and B-25 Mitchells attack the Wakde area. P-39 Airacobras and P-40s, A-20 Havocs, B-24s and B-25s attack targets between Wewak and Hansa Bay.

May 15

CBI: Tenth Air Force B-25 Mitchells, A-36 Intruder (Apache) fighter-bombers, and P-51 Mustangs attack Myitkyina airfield. B-24 Liberators also bomb Myitkyina, Kalewa, and Mandalay.

Fourteenth Air Force receives the 92nd Fighter Squadron, 81st Fighter Group, from Karachi, India, at Kwanghan, China. The squadron, equipped with P-47 Thunderbolts, is scheduled to fly its first mission in early June. The Japanese offensive opens a corridor along the rail line from the Yellow River to Hangkow.

ETO: The final plans for Neptune are briefed to senior commanders at General Montgomery's 21st Army Group Headquarters in London. Montgomery is the commander of all Allied ground forces for the operation. Prime Minister Churchill attends the briefings.

The 21st Army Group's Neptune plan calls for the British Second Army and the U.S. First Army to make the initial landings. On D-day, the United States will land 2 2/3 divisions and 6,800 vehicles on two beaches. The British and Canadians collectively will land three divisions and 8,900 vehicles on three beaches. The airborne forces will be moved by 1,300 transports and 2,000 gliders to their drop zones. The landings will be covered by 800 medium bombers and 2,500 fighter aircraft.

Eighth Air Force sends 166 B-17s and B-24 Liberators, escorted by 104 P-51 Mustangs, to attack V-weapon sites in France. A total of 13 bombers are damaged and one P-51 is lost.

During the night, three B-17s drop over one million leaflets on towns and cities in Belgium and France; five B-24s support Carpetbagger operations.

Eighth Air Force receives the headquarters, 479th Fighter Group, and the P-38J Lightnings of the 434th and 436th Fighter Squadrons from the United States. The squadrons' first missions will be in late May.

Ninth Air Force sends B-26 Marauders and A-20 Havocs to bomb airfields in France.

MEDITERRANEAN: Navy PBY-5 Catalinas and British escort vessels sink German submarine *U-731* in the western Mediterranean.

ITALY: In the II Corps area, the 337th Infantry Regiment of the 85th Infantry Division captures Castellonorato. The 338th Infantry captures Santa Croce, forcing the Germans to abandon other positions. The 351st Infantry of the 88th Infantry Division captures Spigno and pushes on to Itri to cut Route 82, the road link to the Liri Valley and the key to the German defensive line. The 85th Infantry Division is ordered to clear the coastal road to Monte Campese.

Twelfth Air Force B-25 Mitchells and B-26 Marauders attack lines of communication. A-20 Havocs, P-47 Thunderbolts, and P-40s attack German defensive positions, logistics bases, bridges, and motor transport throughout the battlefront.

CENTRAL PACIFIC: U.S. submarine *Aspro* attacks a Japanese convoy near Palau, sinking a transport.

BOUGAINVILLE: Thirteenth Air Force sends 24 B-25 Mitchells and P-40s, P-38 Lightnings, and P-39 Airacobras, along with Navy TBF Avenger torpedo-bombers and SBD Dauntless dive-bombers, to attack a number of targets throughout the island.

NEW GUINEA: Fifth Air Force B-24 Liberators, A-20 Havocs, P-47 Thunderbolts, and P-40s attack targets between Wewak and Hansa Bay. B-24s and B-25 Mitchells attack targets near Wakde and Sarmi and bomb Biak Island.

Thirteenth Air Task Force B-24s from Los Negros Island bomb troops, antiaircraft positions, and logistics sites on Woleai Atoll.

Hollandia airfields support redeployment for A-20 Havocs of the 89th Bombardment Squadron (Light), 3rd Bombardment Group (Light), and P-38 Lightnings of headquarters, 475th Fighter Group and 431st, 432nd, and 433rd Fighter Squadrons.

May 16

CBI: Tenth Air Force B-25 Mitchells, A-36 Intruder (Apache) fighter-bombers, and P-51 Mustangs attack Myitkyina.

ITALY: In the II Corps area the 338th Infantry Regiment of the 85th Infantry Division reaches Route 7. The 351st Infantry of the 88th Infantry Division continues toward Itri and reaches Monte Sant'Angelo. The Gustav Line is finally broken.

Twelfth Air Force B-25 Mitchells and B-26 Marauders attack railroad bridges and a tunnel. A-20 Havocs, P-47 Thunderbolts, and P-40s attack vehicles and major roads to cut off or delay the retreating German forces.

SOUTH PACIFIC: Two U.S. destroyers sink Japanese submarine *I-176*, off northern Choiseul in the Solomons.

CENTRAL PACIFIC: Seventh Air Force B-24 Liberators from Kwajalein bomb Wake Island. B-25 Mitchells from Makin Island bomb Nauru and Ponape Islands.

BOUGAINVILLE: Thirteenth Air Force P-38 Lightnings and P-40s attack Japanese positions.

NEW BRITAIN: Thirteenth Air Force P-39 Airacobras and P-40s attack targets in the Vunakanau area.

NEW GUINEA: Fifth Air Force B-24 Liberators, P-38 Lightnings, A-20 Havocs, and P-40s attack airfields and logistics sites on Wakde, Noemfoor, and Biak Islands.

The A-20 Havocs of the 8th Bombardment Squadron (Light), 3rd Bombardment Group (Light), and the P-47 Thunderbolts of the 9th Fighter Squadron, 49th Fighter Group, redeploy to Hollandia airfields.

May 17

CBI: The H Force of the Marauders conducts an attack on the Myitkyina airfield and captures it, allowing immediate reinforcement by the 679th Engineer Aviation Battalion, which flies in by glider. Chinese and British antiaircraft units also arrive by glider. The 1st Battalion captures the ferry at Pamati, taking advantage of a feint toward the north by 3rd Battalion. Chinese forces reach the outskirts of the city of Myitkyina.

General Stilwell orders two Chinese battalions to capture the town of Myitkyina. The troops end up shooting each other and disintegrate without ever encountering the enemy. The battalions are withdrawn. In the meantime, the Japanese rush reinforcements to Myitkyina. Only 1,310 Americans of the Galahad Task Force reach the objective. By June 1, the large majority of the remainder will be evacuated because of illness.

Tenth Air Force B-25 Mitchells, A-36 Intruder (Apache) fighter-bombers, and P-51 Mustangs attack targets in the Mogaung Valley, including a bridge at Kamaing and Japanese troops near Myitkyina.

In China, Fourteenth Air Force P-40s support Chinese ground forces.

ETO: General Eisenhower, commander of SHAEF, sets the date of the invasion of Europe for June 5 based on tidal and light conditions necessary for the landings. On this date the tides are low enough to expose beach obstacles and there is enough light for visual aerial and naval bombardment of German defenses.

The naval forces available to support Neptune under command of Sir Bertram H. Ramsay are divided into a Western Task Force and an Eastern Task Force. The Western Task Force, under Rear Admiral A. G. Kirk, is subdivided into assault forces U (Utah beach) and O (Omaha beach). The assault forces, preceded by minesweeping flotillas and naval gunfire, will make the initial landings at 0630 hours. The navy is to provide five artificial anchorages (codenamed Gooseberries), two of which will be developed into artificial harbors (codenamed Mulberries) after the beachheads have been established.

These small, versatile, 75 millimeter pack howitzers prove to be invaluable to Merrill's Marauders during the Burma campaign. Here they are providing fire support at Myitkyina during the siege, probably in late May 1944.

The Neptune ground plan calls for General Omar N. Bradley's First Army, composed of the VII Corps under Major General J. Lawton Collins and V Corps commanded by Major General Leonard T. Gerow, to make the landings to establish a beachhead. On D-day, the VII Corps (4th, 90th, and 9th Infantry Divisions) is to land on the beach codenamed Utah, supported by the landings of the 82nd and 101st Airborne Divisions behind the enemy's beach defenses. The VII Corps is expected to cut off the Cotentin Peninsula and capture the port city of Cherbourg in eight days (D+8). The V Corps (1st, 29th, and 2nd Infantry Divisions) is to land on the beach codenamed Omaha and capture the city of St-Lô in nine days (D+9). By D+20, the two corps will close the gap between the forces and drive forward to Avranches. Lieutenant General George S. Patton, Jr.'s Third Army will be landed and under the operational control of Bradley's First Army until D+30, when the Third Army will be dispatched to clear the Brittany peninsula and capture the coastal ports while the First Army attacks south and east toward the Loire River. By D+90, Allied forces are to be ready to capture Paris and then advance on a broad front, with the main effort in the north under General Bernard L. Montgomery's 21st Army Group.

To support Neptune, the navy will provide seven battleships, 32 cruisers, over 100 destroyers, and nearly 100 minesweepers. In total, the Allies will employ 1,213 warships of all types. The landings will employ 229 LSTs and 3,372 landing craft.

MEDITERRANEAN: Fifteenth Air Force sends nearly 500 B-17s and B-24 Liberators against lines of communication and transportation targets in Italy and Yugoslavia. P-38 Lightnings also attack airfields in Italy.

Eight U.S. destroyers, supported by Royal Air Force Wellington bombers, sink German submarine *U-616* in western Mediterranean. German submarine *U-960* attacks one of the destroyers, but its torpedo fails to hit.

ITALY: In the II Corps area the 338th Infantry Regiment of the 85th Infantry Division moves through Formia. The 337th Infantry is at Maranola, isolating Formia on the coastal road. The 351st Infantry Regiment of the 88th Infantry Division captures Monte Ruazzo, but is stopped by strong defenses near the Itri-Pico road.

Monte Cassino falls to the Polish Corps and British forces.

Twelfth Air Force B-26 Marauders and B-25 Mitchells bomb road bridges and airfields. A-20 Havocs attack a command and control target near Valmontone and drop supplies to French troops on Monte Revole. A-20 Havocs, P-47 Thunderbolts, and P-40s attack German defensive positions, lines of communication, and vehicles as the German defenders continue to regroup.

CENTRAL PACIFIC: Seventh Air Force B-24 Liberators from Kwajalein Atoll bomb Wake Island. B-25 Mitchells from Engebi Island bomb Ponape Island.

U.S. destroyers *Frazier* and *Meade* bombard Japanese defenses at Maloelap Atoll in the Marshalls.

U.S. submarines *Sand Lance* and *Tunny* attack a Japanese convoy carrying troops to reinforce Yap and Palau. USS *Sand Lance* sinks a transport near Saipan and USS *Tunny* sinks a cargo ship west of the Marianas. USS *Sand Lance* torpedoes a cargo ship picking up survivors. Both submarines are attacked with depth charges but escape without damage.

New Britain: Thirteenth Air Force sends 25 B-25 Mitchells to bomb the Tobera airfield. Army P-39 Airacobras, P-38 Lightnings, and P-40s support more than 40 U.S. Navy SBD Dauntless dive-bombers in an attack on targets near Vunakanau.

New Guinea: Operation Straightline. Naval Task Force 77, commanded by Rear Admiral William M. Fechteler and with two heavy cruisers, 10 destroyers, and six destroyer escorts, supports the 163rd RCT as it lands at Arara with an hour-long naval gunfire bombardment. Air strikes and rocket-firing LCIs also support the landing. No enemy forces are found in the area. After establishing a beachhead perimeter to serve as a support base for the attack on Wakde Island, elements of the 163rd move to secure Toem.

Fifth Air Force B-24 Liberators and B-25 Mitchells support the landing with early bombing runs. B-24s, with P-38 Lightnings as escort, bomb Sarmi and Mokmer, as well as Noemfoor Island. P-38 Lightnings, P-47 Thunderbolts, P-40s, A-20 Havocs, and medium bombers attack targets between Wewak and the Hansa Bay area.

British Admiral James F. Somerville's combined task force conducts Operation Transom to coincide with the landings at Wakde. Aircraft from the carrier USS *Saratoga* and the British carrier HMS *Illustrious* bomb Japanese shipping and harbor facilities at Surabaya, Java. A transport is sunk and two cargo ships, a tanker, and two submarine chasers are damaged.

May 18

Aleutians: Eleventh Air Force B-25 Mitchells sink two auxiliary vessels in the Kurile Islands.

CBI: Brigadier General Merrill suffers a heart attack and is relieved of command of the Marauders. Colonel John E. McCammon, Merrill's assistant, takes temporary command. The Myitkyina Task Force is formed and includes two regiments of the Chinese 30th Division, elements of the Chinese 50th Division, and the remainder of the Marauders under command of Colonel Charles N. Hunter.

P-40s from the 88th Fighter Squadron arrive at Myitkyina.

Tenth Air Force sends B-25 Mitchells, A-36 Intruder (Apache) fighter-bombers, and P-51 Mustangs to attack Japanese positions in the Mogaung Valley.

Mediterranean: Fifteenth Air Force sends over 400 B-17s and B-24 Liberators to attack industrial targets and marshaling yards in Romania and Yugoslavia. Bad weather over the targets causes most of the bombers to abort the mission. A total of 206 B-17s attack the Ploești oil refineries in Romania. The bombers are attacked by over 100 German fighters over the target. A total of 14 bombers are lost. Aircrews report 28 confirmed kills and 30 probables.

Italy: In the II Corps area, elements of the 85th Infantry Division advance along Route 7.

Twelfth Air Force B-25 Mitchells and B-26 Marauders attack road and rail communications. A-20 Havocs, P-47 Thunderbolts, and P-40s attack German troops, tanks, vehicles, roads, and logistics sites.

Central Pacific: Seventh Air Force B-25 Mitchells from Makin Island bomb Taroa Island on Maloelap Atoll. After rearming at Majuro Atoll the bombers attack Taroa again en route to Makin.

BOUGAINVILLE: Thirteenth Air Force P-39 Airacobras and P-38 Lightnings attack barges off the coast and a logistics base near Mupuai.

ADMIRALTIES: A naval base and naval air station, Manus Island, Admiralty Islands, are established.

NEW GUINEA: Four infantry companies of the 163rd RCT supported by tanks fight nearly 800 Japanese defending Wakde Island in caves, concrete pill boxes, and log bunkers. After a bloody struggle that lasts all day, in which nearly every foot of ground is contested, the Americans kill all but four of the defenders, suffering 40 killed and 107 wounded.

Fifth Air Force B-25 Mitchells, B-24 Liberators, and A-20 Havocs, along with P-38 Lightnings, P-40s, and P-47 Thunderbolts, attack targets between Wewak and Hansa Bay.

B-24s attack targets of opportunity on Halmahera Island in the Moluccas; B-25s bomb targets in the Celebes Islands and the Moluccas.

U.S. submarine *Puffer* attacks a Japanese convoy in the Java Sea, sinking a cargo ship.

May 19

CBI: The Marauders' K Force captures the Mogaung Road. Chinese units arrive by air to reinforce the Allied forces.

Tenth Air Force B-25 Mitchells, A-36 Intruder (Apache) fighter-bombers, P-40s, and P-51 Mustangs attack Japanese positions around Myitkyina.

In China, Fourteenth Air Force B-24 Liberators cause heavy damage to two cargo ships off Hong Kong. P-40s of the Chinese-American Composite Wing (CACW) attack Japanese vehicles, troops, and trucks.

ATLANTIC: James V. Forrestal, undersecretary of the navy since 1940, is appointed secretary of the navy.

ETO: Eighth Air Force sends 588 B-17s to Berlin and 300 B-24 Liberators to Brunswick, escorted by 155 P-38 Lightnings, 182 P-47 Thunderbolts, and 363 P-51 Mustangs. The primary targets are cloud covered, and bombers with H2X radar use it to guide them to the targets. A total of 28 bombers are lost and 355 are damaged. Aircrew casualties are four killed, 24 wounded, and 256 missing. Fighter pilots report 70 confirmed kills in the air and seven on the ground. Fighter losses are 19 aircraft with another 18 damaged. Seventeen pilots are reported missing.

Ninth Air Force sends nearly 300 B-26 Marauders and A-20 Havocs to bomb coastal defenses, ports, and V-weapon sites in France. Cloud cover prevents most bombers from reaching their targets. P-47 Thunderbolts conduct dive-bombing attacks on a number of targets.

MEDITERRANEAN: U.S. light cruiser *Brooklyn* shells German logistics sites along the Italian coast.

Two U.S. destroyers and British aircraft sink German submarine *U-960* in the western Mediterranean.

ITALY: In the II Corps area the 338th Infantry Regiment of the 85th Infantry Division captures Gaeta after the Germans abandon the city. The 351st Infantry captures

Itri and Monte Grande, opening the way for the II Corps to link up with the VI Corps at Anzio.

Fifteenth Air Force sends over 500 B-17s and B-24 Liberators to attack oil storage facilities, railroad bridges, and ports.

Twelfth Air Force B-25 Mitchells and B-26 Marauders attack road and rail communications. A-20 Havocs, P-47 Thunderbolts, and P-40s attack German troops, tanks, vehicles, roads, and logistics sites.

PACIFIC: U.S. submarine *Skate* torpedoes and sinks a Japanese guardboat in the Bonin Islands.

SOUTH PACIFIC: Guided by intercepted Japanese radio traffic, the destroyer escort USS *England* is able to pinpoint the location of Japanese submarines operating in the Solomons as they attempt a redeployment farther north. Japanese submarine *I-16* is the first kill, sunk off Choiseul Island. Over the next five days, USS *England* will sink another five Japanese submarines.

CENTRAL PACIFIC: Navy aircraft from TG 58.6 (Rear Admiral Alfred E. Montgomery) bomb Marcus Island.

NEW BRITAIN: Thirteenth Air Force sends 16 B-25 Mitchells to attack Japanese gun positions and a logistics base at Talili Bay.

NEW GUINEA: Fifth Air Force B-24 Liberators, A-20 Havocs, and P-38 Lightnings attack targets at Noemfoor Island. Other B-24s bomb Biak Island. Nearly 300 B-25 Mitchells, A-20 Havocs, P-47 Thunderbolts, and P-38 Lightnings attack targets from Wewak to Hansa Bay.

May 20

CBI: Tenth Air Force A-36 Intruder (Apache) fighter-bombers, P-40s, and P-51 Mustangs attack bridges, troop assembly areas, and targets of opportunity near Myitkyina and Kamaing.

In China, Fourteenth Air Force B-24 Liberators bomb a Japanese convoy in the South China Sea south of Hong Kong, sinking a cargo ship and damaging two others. Three bombers are lost. Other B-24s attack Japanese warships, damaging an auxiliary submarine chaser in the South China Sea.

P-40s attack Japanese trucks, tanks, and troops.

ETO: Eighth Air Force sends 190 B-17s to bomb the airfield at Orly and the air depot at Villacoublay in France and 177 B-24 Liberators to bomb the airfield and marshaling yard at Reims. Another 271 B-17s and B-24 Liberators are sent against the marshaling yards at Liege and Brussels in Belgium, but heavy cloud cover forces the bombers to abort. A total of two bombers are lost and 102 are damaged. Aircrew casualties are 37 killed, 22 wounded, and 17 missing. The missions are escorted by 146 P-38 Lightnings, 177 P-47 Thunderbolts, and 334 P-51 Mustangs. Fighter pilots report three confirmed kills. Four fighters are lost and five are damaged. The four pilots are reported missing.

Ninth Air Force sends B-26 Marauders to attack airfields, coastal defenses, and V-weapon sites in France. Bad weather causes most of the bombers to abort the mission. P-47 Thunderbolts conduct dive-bombing attacks on numerous targets.

ITALY: The 91st Reconnaissance Squadron reports Fondi is weakly defended. The 350th Infantry of the 88th Infantry Division captures the town and then advances 10 miles toward Monte Alto.

Twelfth Air Force A-20 Havocs, P-47 Thunderbolts, and P-40s attack targets around Vallecorsa and Terracina.

SOUTHWEST PACIFIC AREA: U.S. submarine *Angler* torpedoes and sinks a Japanese transport off eastern Malaysia. USS *Angler* escapes after surviving a depth-charging attack.

U.S. submarine *Picuda* is damaged by depth charges in the Luzon Strait but remains on patrol.

CENTRAL PACIFIC: Seventh Air Force B-25 Mitchells from Engebi Island bomb Ponape Island.

U.S. submarine *Silversides* torpedoes and sinks a Japanese gunboat off Saipan.

Aircraft from the small carrier *San Jacinto* sink a guardboat near Marcus Island.

BOUGAINVILLE: Thirteenth Air Force B-25 Mitchells, P-39 Airacobras, P-40s, and P-38 Lightnings support over 30 U.S. Navy and Marine Corps aircraft in attacking Japanese logistics bases, antiaircraft positions, and troop assembly areas. P-39 Airacobras attack barges in Matchin Bay and bridges at Kieta.

NEW GUINEA: Fifth Air Force B-24 Liberators, A-20 Havocs, and B-25 Mitchells attack targets at Noemfoor Island. Other B-24s bomb Biak Island. B25s, A-20 Havocs, P-47 Thunderbolts, and P-38 Lightnings attack targets from Wewak to Hansa Bay. P-38 Lightnings land on Wakde airfield.

U.S. submarine *Bluegill* torpedoes and sinks a Japanese cargo ship in the Morotai Strait.

May 21

CBI: A Japanese counterattack is stopped by the 3rd Battalion of the Marauders. The men are so weak from illness that many collapse in the middle of the fighting. About 75 to 100 men of the Marauders are being evacuated every day for sickness.

Tenth Air Force B-25 Mitchells, A-36 Intruder (Apache) fighter-bombers, P-40s, and P-51 Mustangs attack Japanese positions, bridges, and troops near Myitkyina.

ETO: Eighth Air Force sends 40 B-17s and 110 B-24 Liberators escorted by 48 P-47 Thunderbolts against V-weapon sites in France. A total of 14 bombers are damaged. Over 600 P-38 Lightnings, P-51 Mustangs, and P-47 Thunderbolts attack railroad bridges and locomotives in Germany. Fighter pilots report 18 confirmed kills in the air and another 17 confirmed kills on the ground. A total of 19 fighters are lost and four damaged. Eighteen pilots are reported missing.

Ninth Air Force sends 50 B-26 Marauders to bomb airfields in France.

ITALY: In the 88th Infantry Division area, the 349th and 351st Infantry move forward to protect the advance of the 350th Infantry toward Monte Alto. The 337th Infantry of the 85th Infantry Division moves toward Terracina.

Twelfth Air Force A-20 Havocs, P-47 Thunderbolts, and P-40s attack lines of communication and German troops.

SOUTHWEST PACIFIC AREA: U.S. submarine *Cero* attacks a Japanese convoy east of the Philippines and misses its target; *Cero* avoids a counterattack by several escort ships. USS *Narwhal* also unsuccessfully attacks a convoy off the east coast of Mindanao Island.

PACIFIC: A tremendous explosion occurs at West Loch, Pearl Harbor, while ammunition is being loaded on LSTs. The accident destroys seven LSTs, three LCTs (landing craft tank), 17 LVTs (landing vehicles tracked), and eight 155 millimeter guns. Two LSTs are damaged.

CENTRAL PACIFIC: Seventh Air Force sends 53 B-24 Liberators from Kwajalein to bomb Wotje Atoll. B-25 Mitchells from Makin Island conduct a follow-on attack. B-24s staging through Eniwetok Atoll bomb Rota Island in the Marianas, rearming at Momote airfield on Los Negros in the Admiralties.

Navy F4U Corsairs, PV-1 Patrol Bombers, B-24 Liberators, and B-25 Mitchells bomb Japanese positions on Wotje Atoll.

U.S. submarine *Billfish* torpedoes and damages a Japanese cargo ship west of the Marianas. The *Billfish* escapes a counterattack from an escort ship.

BOUGAINVILLE: Thirteenth Air Force P-39 Airacobras, P-38 Lightnings, and P-40s attack and destroy two bridges.

NEW BRITAIN: Thirteenth Air Force B-24 Liberators, P-39 Airacobras, and P-40s support Navy SBD Dauntless dive-bombers in an attack on Vunakanau airfield. P-38 Lightnings and navy aircraft bomb Lakunai airfield.

NEW GUINEA: The 158th RCT under Brigadier General Edwin D. Patrick arrives at Toem to expand American control to Sarmi and clear out any remaining Japanese forces in the area.

Fifth Air Force B-24 Liberators, A-20 Havocs, and P-38 Lightnings attack Noemfoor and Biak Islands. B-25 Mitchells, P-47 Thunderbolts, P-40s, and P-38 Lightnings attack targets from Wewak to Hansa Bay.

A-20 Havocs of the 13th Bombardment Squadron (Light), 3rd Bombardment Group (Light), redeploy to airfields in Hollandia.

Thirteenth Air Task Force B-24 Liberators bomb Truk.

May 22

ALEUTIANS: Eleventh Air Force B-25 Mitchells from Attu Island attack a Japanese picket boat near Paramushiru.

CBI: In China, Fourteenth Air Force B-25 Mitchells attack and damage a large cargo ship near Hong Kong. P-51 Mustangs and P-40s attack bridges and convoys.

U.S. submarine *Picuda* torpedoes and sinks a gunboat and the cargo ship it is towing in the South China Sea. The cargo ship was damaged by Fourteenth Air Force bombers on May 20.

ETO: Eighth Air Force sends 342 B-17s against the port at Kiel, Germany, and sends 94 B-24 Liberators to attack V-weapon sites in France. The missions are escorted by 145 P-38 Lightnings, 95 P-47 Thunderbolts, and 328 P-51 Mustangs. Over Kiel, five bombers are lost and 210 are damaged. Only one of the B-24s is damaged. Aircrew losses are four killed, three wounded, and 78 missing. Fighter pilots report 22 confirmed kills and four probables. Seven fighters are lost and seven are damaged. Six pilots are reported missing.

P-47 Thunderbolts conduct attacks on railroad bridges at Hasselt and Liege in Belgium. One P-47 is lost and one is damaged.

During the night, four B-17s drop 320,000 leaflets on The Hague, Haarlem, Rotterdam, and Utrecht in the Netherlands. A total of 12 B-24s fly in support of Carpetbagger operations.

Ninth Air Force sends over 600 B-26 Marauders, A-20 Havocs, P-47 Thunderbolts, and P-51 Mustangs to attack airfields and marshaling yards around Cherbourg, Calais, and Paris.

ITALY: In the II Corps area, the 337th Infantry Regiment attacks Terracina while the 338th Infantry Regiment (85th Infantry Division) moves to Leano to outflank the defenders.

The 36th Infantry Division lands at Anzio. The VI Corps now has seven divisions available for an attack.

Fifteenth Air Force sends over 500 B-17s and B-24 Liberators against marshaling yards and ports. Fifteenth Air Force receives the P-47 Thunderbolts of the 332nd Fighter Group from the Twelfth Air Force.

Twelfth Air Force A-20 Havocs, P-47 Thunderbolts, and P-40s fly ground support missions and attack roads and bridges throughout the battle area.

SOUTHWEST PACIFIC AREA: U.S. submarine *Ray* attacks the convoy attacked previously by USS *Cero*, sinking a cargo ship off the south coast of Mindanao.

PACIFIC: U.S. submarine *Pollack* attacks a Japanese convoy near the Bonin Islands and sinks a destroyer.

CENTRAL PACIFIC: Seventh Air Force sends eight B-25 Mitchells from Engebi Island to bomb Ponape Island.

U.S. destroyers *Bancroft* and *Edwards* bombard Japanese facilities at Wotje Atoll.

BOUGAINVILLE: Thirteenth Air Force P-39 Airacobras bomb logistics depots at Bonis and attack bridges near Kieta.

NEW BRITAIN: Thirteenth Air Force P-39 Airacobras, P-38 Lightnings, and P-40s attack targets of opportunity along the coast near Talili Bay.

NEW IRELAND: Destroyer escort USS *England* sinks Japanese submarine *RO-106* north of Kavieng, New Ireland.

NEW GUINEA: Fifth Air Force B-24 Liberators and B-25 Mitchells bomb Biak Island. P-40s attack Wakde Island. B-24s, B-25 Mitchells, P-38 Lightnings, P-47 Thunderbolts, and P-40s attack targets between Wewak and Hansa Bay.

Headquarters of the 348th Fighter Group and the P-47s of the 341st and 342nd Fighter Squadrons redeploy from Saidor to Wakde Island.

U.S. submarine *Bluegill* is damaged by an air attack off Halmahera but remains on patrol.

May 23

CBI: Tenth Air Force sends 23 P-40s and four A-36 Intruder (Apache) fighter-bombers to attack Japanese positions and logistics storage areas near Myitkyina.

ETO: Eighth Air Force sends 580 B-17s and 465 B-24 Liberators against airfields and marshaling yards in France, escorted by 96 P-38 Lightnings, 142 P-47 Thunderbolts, and 324 P-51 Mustangs. Ninth Air Force supports the raid with 644 P-47 Thunderbolts and P-38 Lightnings. Three bombers are lost and 86 are damaged. Aircrew losses are 22 killed, four wounded, and 10 missing. Fighter pilots report no enemy aircraft kills and three aircraft damaged. Ninth Air Force pilots report two P-38s and two P-47s are lost.

P-51s conduct dive-bombing attacks on a railroad bridge in Belgium, losing one aircraft.

During the night, four B-17s drop over 900,000 leaflets on towns and cities in Belgium and the Netherlands. A total of seven B-24s fly in support of Carpetbagger operations.

Ninth Air Force B-26 Marauders bomb airfields and coastal batteries in France while P-38 Lightnings attack rail cars.

ITALY: In the II Corps area, the 337th Infantry Regiment of the 85th Infantry Division captures Terracina as the Germans withdraw.

A massive artillery bombardment at Cisterna precedes the Allied breakout from Anzio (called Operation Buffalo). The 1st Special Service Force gains control of Route 7 at Cisterna. The 1st Armored Division, supported by two battalions of the 135th Infantry Regiment of the 34th Infantry Division and two battalions of the 6th Armored Infantry Regiment, attacks toward Cisterna. Initially stopped by large minefields, the engineers use a device called a snake, a line of explosives that clears paths through minefields. Once clear of the mines, the tanks break through the German defenses. The objective is Valmontone along Route 6, to cut off the German forces in the Liri and Sacco valleys. The 3rd Infantry Division makes small gains as it attacks toward Cisterna, suffering heavy casualties. The 45th Infantry Division attacks on the left flank of the beachhead and makes good initial progress. The 1st Special Service Force is stopped by a German counterattack and one company is captured. The 133rd Infantry Regiment from the 34th Infantry Division relieves the 1st SSF on the line.

Fifteenth Air Force sends over 300 B-17s and B-24 Liberators to attack German troops and lines of communications at Avezzano and Valmontone.

Twelfth Air Force A-20 Havocs, P-47 Thunderbolts, and P-40s attack targets in the Liri Valley and German defenses at Anzio, in support of Operation Buffalo.

Light cruiser USS *Brooklyn* and destroyers USS *Kearny* and *Ericsson* shell German positions near Ardea, Italy.

In the midst of an attack against German positions near Carano, Italy, Second Lieutenant Thomas W. Fowler of the 1st Armored Division encounters two infantry platoons stopped before a minefield. Lieutenant Fowler makes his way through the minefield, clearing a path by lifting the mines out of the ground with his hands. He then leads the infantrymen through the minefield and deploys the men in position. He then guides tanks through the minefield to support the infantry. Moving out in front of the infantry, he scouts German positions and leads an attack that succeeds in capturing the positions. He organizes his troops for a counterattack and fights without regard for his personal safety, rescuing wounded tankers and infantrymen in the face of intense enemy fire. Second Lieutenant Fowler's initiative, selflessness, and leadership will win him the Medal of Honor.

Private First Class John W. Dutko of the 3rd Infantry Division takes cover in an abandoned enemy trench near Ponte Rotto, Italy, as German artillery shells rain down around him. Leaving cover, he makes a singlehanded attack on three German machine-gun positions and an 88 millimeter gun. Private First Class Dutko advances to within 30 yards of the first machine gun and knocks out the position with a hand grenade. Wounded by fire from the second machine-gun position, Dutko charges the 88 millimeter gun, firing his Browning automatic rifle (BAR) from the hip and kills the crew. He then turns on the machine-gun position that had wounded him and eliminates it. He is then hit and wounded again by another machine-gun crew. Running the next 20 yards he kills the last of the enemy with a burst of fire from his BAR, then collapses and dies. For his extraordinary gallantry and courage, Private First Class John W. Dutko will receive the Medal of Honor.

Technical Sergeant Van T. Barfoot of the 157th Infantry Regiment, 45th Infantry Division, is participating in an assault against German troops holding entrenchments on dominating terrain near Carano, Italy. As his platoon is halted by enemy fire, Technical Sergeant Barfoot moves off alone to locate the enemy's left flank. He crawls to within hand grenade range of a machine-gun position and eliminates it. Now outflanking the enemy, he moves parallel to the trench line, killing and capturing Germans. Firing his Thompson submachine gun as he goes, he accounts for the capture of 17 prisoners, then consolidates his platoon on the captured position, on which the Germans launch an infantry counterattack supported by three tanks. Taking a bazooka, Technical Sergeant Barfoot places himself directly in the path of the tanks and knocks the first one out with a well-aimed shot. Barfoot uses his submachine gun to kill the tank crew. Barfoot drives off the enemy and is able to destroy a German artillery piece. He then assists in moving two of his wounded soldiers to safety. For his extraordinary acts of heroism, Technical Sergeant Barfoot will receive the Medal of Honor.

Technical Sergeant Ernest H. Dervishian of the 135th Infantry Regiment, 34th Infantry Division, finds himself ahead of his company during an attack against German defenses near Cisterna, Italy. Dervishian, with four other soldiers, approaches a railroad embankment and comes upon German soldiers hiding in dugouts. He then begins moving among the dugouts, forcing the Germans to surrender, and gathers 25 prisoners. Technical Sergeant Dervishian then captures six more enemy soldiers as they attempt to retreat. When another four Americans join Dervishian's group, he sends them to occupy a large vineyard, but when the men come under machine-gun fire he leads an attack into the vineyard. Dervishian uses a hand grenade and his M-1 carbine to force four Germans to surrender. As another machine gun opens up on the Americans, Dervishian leaps into the abandoned enemy position and, taking their machine gun, engages the other position. As German soldiers attempt to flank him, Dervishian engages both threats simultaneously, using a captured machine pistol and the machine gun. Five enemy soldiers signal they want to surrender, and Dervishian moves past them to eliminate all resistance in the vineyard. Locating another machine-gun position, he fires on it and forces six more Germans to surrender to him. For his exemplary courage and combat skill, Technical Sergeant Dervishian will receive the Medal of Honor.

CENTRAL PACIFIC: Seventh Air Force B-25 Mitchells from Makin Island bomb Jaluit Atoll. B-24 Liberators staging from Los Negros Island bomb Ponape Island.

BOUGAINVILLE: Thirteenth Air Force P-39 Airacobras and P-40s attack bridges and barges throughout the island.

NEW BRITAIN: Thirteenth Air Force B-24 Liberators bomb Tobera. B-25 Mitchells, P-39 Airacobras, P-38 Lightnings, and P-40s attack Japanese positions around Rabaul.

NEW IRELAND: Destroyer escort USS *England* sinks Japanese submarine *RO-104* north of Kavieng.

NEW GUINEA: Fifth Air Force B-24 Liberators, A-20 Havocs, and P-38 Lightnings bomb Biak Island. P-40s attack Japanese positions on the Biri River and P-38 Lightnings fly ground support missions near Aitape. B-24s and B-25s, along with A-20 Havocs and P-39 Airacobras, attack targets between Wewak and Hansa Bay.

U.S. submarine *Cero* torpedoes and sinks a Japanese cargo ship. Working with USS *Ray,* an army tanker is successfully torpedoed and damaged off Halmahera Island.

U.S. submarine *Raton* torpedoes and sinks a Japanese merchant vessel west of Borneo.

May 24

CBI: General Joseph Stilwell reinforces Myitkyina with the 209th Engineer Combat Battalion, converting them to infantry.

Tenth Air Force sends over 20 P-40s to attack targets at Myitkyina. Pilots report destroying eight barracks buildings, a railroad bridge, and a defensive position.

ETO: Eighth Air Force sends 616 B-17s and 490 B-24 Liberators against airfields in France and targets near Berlin. The mission is escorted by 144 P-38 Lightnings, 178 P-47 Thunderbolts, and 280 P-51 Mustangs. A total of 33 bombers are lost and 257 are damaged. Aircrew casualties are four killed, 24 wounded, and 482 missing. Fighter pilots report 33 confirmed kills in the air and seven probables. Ten aircraft are lost and seven are damaged. One pilot is wounded and 10 are reported missing.

Nearly 200 P-47s and P-51s attack bridges and airfields in France. Pilots report three confirmed kills in the air and two on the ground. Three P-51s are lost and six are damaged.

During the night four B-17s drop two and one-half million leaflets on towns and cities in France and Belgium. Three B-24 Liberators fly in support of Carpetbagger.

Ninth Air Force sends over 450 B-26 Marauders to attack airfields, coastal defenses, and V-weapon sites in France. P-38 Lightnings and P-47s conduct dive-bombing attacks on airfields.

MEDITERRANEAN: Fifteenth Air Force sends over 600 B-17s and B-24 Liberators to bomb aircraft production facilities and airfields in Austria. Six B-24s are lost over Bad Voslau airfield.

ITALY: In the II Corps area, elements of the 337th Infantry of the 85th Infantry Division capture Terracina, the II Corps objective. Combat Command B of 1st Armored Division advances beyond Route 7. Combat Command A advances and isolates

Cisterna. The 3rd Infantry Division begins an attack on Cisterna supported by artillery, but is slowed by enemy defenses. At Carano, the 180th Infantry Regiment of the 45th Infantry Division stops an enemy counterattack.

Twelfth Air Force B-25 Mitchells and B-26 Marauders bomb roads north of the battle area to block German forces. A-20 Havocs, P-47 Thunderbolts, and P-40s attack convoys and troop movements.

Private James H. Mills of F Company, 15th Infantry Regiment, 3rd Infantry Division, is in his first combat action near Cisterna di Littoria. Moving ahead of his platoon to reach a flanking position on a German strongpoint, Private Mills kills or captures several enemy soldiers. He then charges a German position while firing his rifle from his hip and forces the six soldiers to surrender. He continues to advance, and several more enemy soldiers are killed or captured. Realizing that the strongpoint is heavily defended, Mills volunteers to approach within 100 yards of the strongpoint and draw enemy fire while the rest of the platoon maneuvers. Mills crawls close to the strongpoint and stands up to deliver rifle fire into the position. The Germans react with a heavy volume of machine-gun and rifle fire. Untouched, he ducks into a small draw to reload and continues firing. He repeats this four times until his platoon is able to capture the position in a quick rush, taking 22 Germans prisoners and without American casualties. For his extraordinary courage and skill, Private Mills will receive the Medal of Honor.

Private First Class Henry Schauer, 3rd Infantry Division, is a member of a patrol operating near Cisterna di Littoria. Carrying a Browning automatic rifle, Private First Class Schauer demonstrated exceptional courage and coolness under fire the previous day, engaging enemy troops in several stand-up fights at close range, eliminating snipers and several German machine-gun positions. When a German tank and a machine-gun fire from positions only 100 yards away from the patrol, Private First Class Schauer crawls 20 yards toward the enemy and then stands up. Bringing the Browning automatic rifle to his shoulder as bullets and tank rounds strike all around him, Schauer eliminates the machine gun with a short, accurate burst of fire. For his exceptional courage and skill, Private First Class Schauer will receive the Medal of Honor.

Sergeant Sylvester Antolak of B Company, 15th Infantry Regiment, 3rd Infantry Division, leads his squad near Cisterna di Littoria. Encountering enemy fire from a position nearly 200 yards away, Sergeant Antolak moves forward to engage the Germans. As he advances he is hit several times. Each time he drops, but struggles to his feet and continues to move forward, firing his Thompson submachine gun. As he reaches the German position he kills two Germans and forces 10 others to surrender. Consolidating his squad on the objective, he refuses medical attention and orders his men to follow him on an assault of a second position 100 yards distant. As he advances to close with the enemy he is killed, but his squad continues forward and captures the position in close combat. His superb fighting courage and heroic leadership will win Sergeant Antolak the Medal of Honor.

SOUTHWEST PACIFIC AREA: U.S. submarine *Flying Fish* suffers some damage when one of her torpedoes explodes prematurely. The *Flying Fish* remains on patrol in the Philippine Sea.

U.S. submarine *Gurnard* attacks a Japanese convoy in the Celebes Sea and sinks a fleet tanker off the coast of Mindanao. U.S. submarine *Narwhal* lands men and supplies on Samar Island.

In the South China Sea U.S. submarine *Lapon* torpedoes and sinks two Japanese cargo ships.

U.S. submarine *Perch* attacks a Japanese convoy in the South China Sea, but misses its target.

U.S. submarine *Raton* attacks a Japanese convoy east of Singapore and sinks one escort vessel and damages another.

PACIFIC: Lieutenant General Robert C. Richardson, Jr., is assigned as the overall army commander in the Pacific Ocean Areas including responsibility for the Twentieth Air Force. Lieutenant General Millard F. Harmon is named air commander and deputy commander of the Twentieth Air Force. The assignments will be effective as of August 1.

CENTRAL PACIFIC: Seventh Air Force B-25 Mitchells from Makin Island bomb Wotje Atoll, rearm at Majuro Atoll, and bomb Jaluit Atoll on the return to Makin. B-25s from Engebi Island bomb Ponape Island.

BOUGAINVILLE: Thirteenth Air Force sends 51 P-39 Airacobras, P-40s, and P-38 Lightnings to attack the airfield on Buka Island and the radar station at Cape Lalahan.

NEW BRITAIN: Thirteenth Air Force B-25 Mitchells, P-38 Lightnings, and P-40s attack targets in and around Rabaul.

NEW IRELAND: Destroyer escort USS *England* sinks Japanese submarine *RO-116* north of Kavieng.

NEW GUINEA: Brigadier General Edwin D. Patrick takes command of the Wakde Task Force from Brigadier General Doe, who leaves for Biak. Elements of the 158th RCT cross the Tor River moving toward Sarmi and encounter heavy fire from Japanese in prepared defensive positions at the Tirfoam River.

Fifth Air Force B-25 Mitchells, A-20 Havocs, P-38 Lightnings, P-47 Thunderbolts, and P-39 Airacobras attack targets from Wewak to Hansa Bay.

Lieutenant General Walter Krueger, commander of Alamo Force, moves his headquarters to Hollandia.

May 25

ALEUTIANS: An Eleventh Air Force B-24 Liberator from Shemya Island flies a reconnaissance and bombing mission in the Kurile Islands.

CBI: A Chinese attack against the Japanese defenses at Myitkyina fails. The Marauders are losing 75 to 100 men a day to disease as the siege of Myitkyina continues.

U.S. infantry replacements arrive in India. They are minimally trained and completely unprepared for jungle warfare, but are sent to Myitkyina three days later. Chinese forces capture Kamaing and defeat Japanese counterattacks.

Tenth Air Force sends 28 P-38 Lightnings to attack targets near Mandalay. Pilots report destroying 10 railroad cars near Shwebo. The Chinese Y Force is near Lungling.

ETO: Eighth Air Force sends 600 B-17s and 428 B-24 Liberators against airfields, gun batteries, and marshaling yards in France and Belgium, escorted by 136 P-38 Lightnings, 181 P-47 Thunderbolts, and 287 P-51 Mustangs. Four bombers are lost and 152 are damaged. Aircrew casualties are one killed, six wounded, and 48 missing. Fighter pilots report 13 confirmed kills in the air and three on the ground as well as two probables. A total of 12 aircraft are lost and 15 are damaged. The 12 pilots are reported missing.

Ninth Air Force sends over 200 B-26 Marauders to attack bridges and airfields in Belgium and France. P-47s conduct dive-bombing attacks on a number of targets.

MEDITERRANEAN: Fifteenth Air Force sends B-17s and B-24 Liberators fly against targets in southern France. The B-17s attack the marshaling yard at Lyon, while B-24s attack marshaling yards at Amberieux, Toulon, and Givors.

ITALY: At Anzio, Cisterna falls to the 7th Infantry Regiment of the 3rd Infantry Division and 1,000 German soldiers are taken prisoner. The 1st Armored Division moves into the Velletri Gap, which leads to Valmontone and Route 6—the main highway to Rome. The 91st Reconnaissance Squadron of the II Corps meets engineers from VI Corps at Borgo Grappo.

Lieutenant General Mark Clark informs the VI Corps commander, Major General Lucian Truscott, of his intent to move the direction of the attack toward Rome. The 3rd Infantry Division and the 1st Special Service Force will hold Route 6.

Twelfth Air Force B-25 Mitchells and B-26 Marauders bomb roads north of the battle area to block German forces. A-20 Havocs, P-47 Thunderbolts, and P-40s attack German defensive positions, convoys, and troop movements.

U.S. destroyer *Kendrick* shells German positions in Ardea, Italy.

CENTRAL PACIFIC: Seventh Air Force B-25 Mitchells from Engebi Island bomb Ponape Island.

U.S. submarine *Flying Fish* attacks a Japanese convoy and sinks a guardboat and a cargo ship north of Palau.

BOUGAINVILLE: Thirteenth Air Force sends 15 B-25 Mitchells, with 32 P-39 Airacobras and P-40s, in support of 25 navy SBD Dauntless dive-bombers to attack logistics sites at Porton. P-40s attack Monoitu mission and P-39 Airacobras attack the Cape Lalahan radar station.

NEW BRITAIN: Thirteenth Air Force B-24 Liberators bomb Rabaul, Lakunai, and Rapopo and B-25 Mitchells bomb logistics depots near Talili Bay.

NEW GUINEA: A battalion of the 158th Infantry continues the attack against Japanese defenses, but is stopped before Lone Tree Hill. The hill is actually a number of hills covered by heavy jungle and has been converted into a formidable strongpoint.

The 162nd and 186th Infantry Regiments of the 41st Infantry Division depart Humboldt Bay for Biak Island. Major General Horace H. Fuller commands the division. Task Force 77 under Rear Admiral William M. Fechteler supports the attack with two heavy cruisers, three light cruisers, and 21 destroyers.

Fifth Air Force B-24 Liberators attack targets near Wakde. B-25s, and B-24s along with P-38 Lightnings, P-40s, P-47 Thunderbolts, and A-20 Havocs attack targets near Wewak.

May 26

CBI: Operational control of the 27th Troop Carrier Squadron is transferred from Tenth Air Force to Fourteenth Air Force to fly aerial resupply missions to the Chinese Y Force.

The Japanese begin another offensive in central China, advancing toward Tungling Lake with 70,000 troops.

ETO: Ninth Air Force sends over 400 B-26 Marauders and A-20 Havocs to attack airfields and bridges in France while over 100 P-47 Thunderbolts and P-51 Mustangs also attack other airfields. P-47s and P-38 Lightnings conduct dive-bombing attacks on various targets.

MEDITERRANEAN: Fifteenth Air Force sends nearly 700 bombers against targets in southern France and Yugoslavia. B-17s and B-24 Liberators bomb marshaling yards in France while other B-24s attack assembly areas at Bihać, Yugoslavia.

ITALY: At Anzio, General Clark shifts the attack from the east to the Albano Road. The 1st Armored Division supports the attack from the right while the 3rd Infantry Division continues its advance toward Velletri. The 34th and 45th Infantry Divisions are to drive toward Lanuvio and Campoleone respectively. Clark is unwilling to continue the attack toward Valmontone, although it will gain the most promising result and has the potential to cut off German forces. In that case, the British Eighth Army would have the main route to Rome and the glory of capturing the city. Clark, unwilling to give General Montgomery that opportunity, drives the bulk of his forces westward to the shorter and more direct route to Rome. This leaves the Germans an opening for a general retreat.

Twelfth Air Force B-26 Marauders and B-25 Mitchells attack railroad targets and bomb roads. A-20 Havocs, P-47 Thunderbolts, and P-40s attack convoys on the Rome-Bracciano road as the Germans attempt to reinforce defenses south of Rome.

First Lieutenant Beryl R. Newman leads a platoon of inexperienced infantrymen in the 133rd Infantry Regiment, 34th Infantry Division. Approaching German defenses near Cisterna, he and several scouts are fired upon by two German machine guns on a hill about 100 yards away. Ignoring the fire, First Lieutenant Newman remains standing to locate the enemy. He then gives orders for one squad to maneuver to flank the enemy position while another squad joins him. All the time Newman is returning fire on the German positions. As the maneuvering squad is stopped by enemy fire, First Lieutenant Newman attacks alone, firing his weapon as he advances, and captures the two positions. As he encounters other German soldiers, he kills them and then clears a nearby house and captures 11 heavily armed Germans inside. His leadership, determination, and extraordinary acts of courage in the face of the enemy will win him the Medal of Honor.

CENTRAL PACIFIC: Forty-five Seventh Air Force B-25 Mitchells from Makin Island attack Jaluit Atoll. B-25s from Engebi Island search for a downed B-25 crew around Ponape Island. The bombers locate the crew and a navy destroyer will later rescue them.

Destroyers bombard Japanese shore batteries and installations on Mille Atoll.

Destroyer escort USS *England* sinks Japanese submarine *RO-108* northeast of Manus.

U.S. submarine *Permit* torpedoes and damages Japanese submarine *I-44* near Truk.

U.S. submarine *Tambor* torpedoes and sinks a Japanese stores ship west of the Marianas.

New Britain: Thirteenth Air Force P-39 Airacobras and P-40s attack targets around Rabaul. B-25 Mitchells attack logistics depots at Talili Bay.

New Guinea: Naval gunfire and air strikes on Lone Tree Hill fail to cause any damage to the enemy; follow-on infantry attack falters in the deep undergrowth.

Fifth Air Force B-24 Liberators bomb Biak Island; B-25 Mitchells bomb Lone Tree Hill. B-25s, A-20 Havocs, P-38 Lightnings, P-40s, and P-47 Thunderbolts attack targets from Wewak to Hansa Bay.

The P-47s of the 340th Fighter Squadron, 348th Fighter Group, redeploy from Saidor to Wakde Island.

U.S. submarine *Cabrilla* torpedoes and sinks a Japanese transport off Celebes Island.

May 27

CBI: Fourteenth Air Force P-40s, using rockets, attack targets at Nanchang and Puchi.

ETO: Eighth Air Force sends 653 B-17s and 473 B-24 Liberators against airfields, marshaling yards, and gun positions in France and Germany, escorted by 170 P-38 Lightnings, 238 P-47 Thunderbolts, and 302 P-51 Mustangs. A total of 24 bombers are lost and 207 are damaged. Aircrew casualties are seven killed, 12 wounded, and 234 missing. Fighter pilots report 39 confirmed kills in the air, one probable, and nine confirmed kills on the ground. Seven fighters are lost and 10 are damaged. The seven pilots are reported missing.

During the night, three B-17s drop leaflets over towns and cities in Belgium and France.

Ninth Air Force sends nearly 600 B-26 Marauders against railroad bridges and marshaling yards in France.

Mediterranean: Fifteenth Air Force sends nearly 700 B-17s and B-24 Liberators against marshaling yards in southern France, escorted by P-38 Lightnings and P-51 Mustangs.

Italy: The 6th Armored Infantry of the 1st Armored Division stops a German counterattack near Artena. The 15th Infantry of the 3rd Infantry Division later captures Artena. Elements of the 36th Infantry Division locate a gap in the German lines atop Monte Artemisio, which marks an undefended gap between two German corps. The three regiments of the division occupy the hill and bring up artillery to fire on German positions along Route 6. This makes the German defense of Valmontone no longer possible. The 34th and 45th Infantry Divisions make slow progress toward Lanuvio and Campoleone.

Twelfth Air Force B-26 Marauders and B-25 Mitchells attack lines of communication. A-20 Havocs, P-47 Thunderbolts, and P-40s attack a number of targets throughout the battle area, including bridges, rail lines, enemy defensive positions, and roads.

CENTRAL PACIFIC: Seventh Air Force sends 24 B-24 Liberators from Kwajalein and 52 B-25 Mitchells from Engebi Island to attack Ponape Island.

NEW BRITAIN: Thirteenth Air Force P-39 Airacobras, P-38 Lightnings, and P-40s along with navy and marine aircraft hit targets at Rabaul.

NEW GUINEA: At Sarmi, the 158th RCT attack on Lone Tree Hill makes little progress. The Americans are fighting well trained and disciplined Japanese troops who are experts at camouflage. The American attack collapses into a series of uncoordinated assaults. Two battalions of the 163rd Infantry depart for Biak, leaving one battalion at Toem.

At Aitape, a 5,000-foot runway to accommodate bombers is completed near the abandoned Tadji airfield.

Naval Task Force 77 (Rear Admiral William M. Fechteler) commands the landing on Biak (Operation Horlicks). Heavy and light cruisers and destroyers of TG 77.2 (Rear Admiral Victor A. C. Crutchley, RN) and TG 77.3 (Rear Admiral Russell S. Berkey) provide gunfire support. At Biak, a bombing run by 54 Fifth Air Force B-24 Liberators precedes the landing of the 186th and 162nd Infantry Regiments on the beachhead near Bosnek. On the first day, 12 tanks, 500 trucks, and 2,400 tons of supplies are landed. Japanese bombers attack the beachhead and all are shot down before causing any damage. The Americans meet no resistance as they expand the beachhead.

Fifth Air Force sends B-24s and B-25 Mitchells to attack targets on Biak after the initial bombardment. B-25s, A-20 Havocs, P-38 Lightnings, and P-40s bomb targets near Wewak.

May 28

CBI: The 236th Engineer Combat Battalion arrives at Myitkyina. The collection of American troops who arrive as replacements is integrated into the engineer-Marauder unit and eventually become known as New Galahad.

ATLANTIC: German submarine *U-549* torpedoes and sinks escort carrier USS *Block Island* and damages a destroyer escort northwest of Canary Islands. Two destroyer escorts sink *U-549*.

ETO: Eighth Air Force sends 865 B-17s and 417 B-24 Liberators against oil production facilities in Germany, escorted by 182 P-38 Lightnings, 208 P-47 Thunderbolts, and 307 P-51 Mustangs. Aircrews report 37 confirmed kills and 29 probables. A total of 33 bombers are lost and 211 damaged. Aircrew casualties are seven killed, 19 wounded, and 272 missing. Fighter pilots report 27 confirmed kills and one probable. Nine fighters are lost and 14 are damaged. Nine pilots are reported missing. Ninth Air Force supports the bombing mission with 527 fighters. Pilots report 33 confirmed kills in the air and five on the ground. Five U.S. fighters are lost.

During the night five B-17s drop leaflets over Belgium and Norway. A total of 22 B-24s fly in support of Carpetbagger operations. One bomber is lost.

Ninth Air Force sends over 600 B-26 Marauders and A-20 Havocs to attack marshaling yards, railway bridges, and V-weapon sites in France and Belgium. Eight aircraft are lost. P-47s conduct dive-bombing attacks on targets close by.

MEDITERRANEAN: Fifteenth Air Force B-24 Liberators bomb a marshaling yard and port facilities in Italy and troop assembly areas at Niksic in Yugoslavia.

U.S. motor torpedo boats sink a German corvette in the Ligurian Sea.

ITALY: 1st Armored Division moves to support 45th Infantry Division. The 36th Infantry Division takes 1st Armored Division's place in the line to the right of the 34th Infantry Division. The 34th reaches Lanuvio. II Corps gives operational control of the 88th Infantry Division to IV Corps. General Truscott learns of the gap in the German lines at Monte Artemisio.

Twelfth Air Force B-26 Marauders and B-25 Mitchells attack lines of communication. A-20 Havocs, P-47 Thunderbolts, and P-40s attack a number of targets throughout the battle area, including bridges, rail lines, enemy defensive positions, and roads.

CENTRAL PACIFIC: Seventh Air Force sends 29 B-25 Mitchells staging from Eniwetok to bomb Jaluit Atoll. The bombers continue on and land at Makin Island. B-25s from Engebi Island bomb Mille Atoll in the Marshalls. B-24 Liberators from Eniwetok bomb Saipan and Guam Islands in the Marianas. The B-24s that hit Guam continue to Momote airfield at Los Negros Island to rearm. The B-24s targeting Saipan return to Eniwetok.

U.S. submarine *Silversides* torpedoes and sinks two Japanese transports north of Saipan and escapes counterattacks by aircraft and escorts.

NEW BRITAIN: Thirteenth Air Force B-24 Liberators, B-25 Mitchells, and P-38 Lightnings attack the Lakunai airfield. P-39 Airacobras and P-40s support navy SBD Dauntless dive-bombers attacking Tobera airfield.

NEW IRELAND: Destroyers from Destroyer Squadron 41 bombard Japanese installations on northern coast of New Ireland.

NEW GUINEA: At Sarmi, a third attack on Lone Tree Hill fails to make any progress. The 158th RCT withdraws to the Tirfoam River.

At Biak, the 162nd Infantry Regiment advances toward three airfields, which are the objectives of the operation. These airfields are critical to both the Americans and the Japanese. Japanese control of the Biak airfields is essential to any type of air attack on Nimitz's fleet to the north and to providing air cover for the Japanese fleet. For the Americans, Biak's airfields are essential for further operations in western New Guinea and the Philippines. From Biak, MacArthur's air force can provide cover for Nimitz's upcoming operations in the Palau Islands. The Japanese have put 10,700 troops on Biak, and unlike other garrisons, they intend to reinforce the island.

The leading battalion of the 162nd is hit by a Japanese counterattack using tanks and infantry. Forced to retreat, Major General Fuller requests from Lieutenant General Krueger the 163rd Infantry to reinforce the division.

Fifth Air Force B-24 Liberators and B-25 Mitchells bomb Japanese defenses and gun positions on Biak Island and other targets on Noemfoor Island. B-25s, A-20 Havocs, and P-38 Lightnings attack targets near Wewak. A-20 Havocs conduct tree-top-level airstrikes on Japanese positions on Lone Tree Hill.

Thirteenth Air Task Force B-24s bomb the airfield on Woleai Atoll.

U.S. submarine *Rasher* attacks a Japanese convoy in the eastern Celebes Sea, damaging a gunboat off Halmahera.

Fire from a shore battery on Biak Island damages destroyer *Stockton*.

May 29

ALEUTIANS: Eleventh Air Force B-25 Mitchells bomb Shimushu and attack vessels off the island. Other B-25s escorted by four P-38 Lightnings sink a patrol boat in the Kurile Islands.

CBI: The 209th Engineers and the Marauders attack in an attempt to break the Japanese lines. Although they take their initial objectives, they are forced back after heavy Japanese counterattacks.

Tenth Air Force B-25 Mitchells and P-40s attack Japanese defensive positions at Bhamo and Mohnyin.

ETO: Eighth Air Force sends 50 B-17s and 443 B-24 Liberators, escorted by 184 P-38 Lightnings, 187 P-47 Thunderbolts, and 302 P-51 Mustangs, to attack aircraft and oil production facilities in Germany and Poland. Aircrews report 62 confirmed kills and 37 probables. A total of 34 bombers are lost and 330 are damaged. Aircrew casualties are two killed, 18 wounded, and 318 missing. Fighter pilots report 39 confirmed kills in the air, one probable, and 16 confirmed kills on the ground. Ten aircraft are lost and nine are damaged. Eight pilots are reported missing.

Ninth Air Force supports the mission with 592 fighters. The pilots report one confirmed kills and two U.S. aircraft lost. Ninth Air Force sends over 400 B-26 Marauders and A-20 Havocs to bomb airfields, marshaling yards, railroad bridges, coastal batteries, and V-weapon sites in France and Belgium. P-47 Thunderbolts bomb targets nearby.

MEDITERRANEAN: Fifteenth Air Force sends 829 B-17s and B-24 Liberators against aircraft production facilities in Austria and assembly areas in Yugoslavia. Over 530 B-24 Liberators attack aircraft production facilities near Vienna, Austria. More than 150 German fighters attack the formations and eight bombers are lost. Fighter pilots escorting this mission report 18 confirmed kills in the air and 12 on the ground. For all the targets, a total of 23 bombers are lost and fighter pilots report over 60 confirmed kills.

ITALY: At Anzio, the 45th Infantry Division, with 1st Armored Division in support, reaches Campoleone. The Americans make a two-mile penetration of German lines; strongpoints are bypassed by tanks and are reduced by infantry. The 168th Infantry Regiment of the 34th Infantry Division captures Lanuvio but fails to hold the high ground against German counterattacks. The 36th Infantry Division reaches Velletri, taking the place of the 1st Armored Division.

Twelfth Air Force B-25 Mitchells and B-26 Marauders bomb railroad bridges and transportation targets. A-20 Havocs attack assembly areas and logistics depots. A-20 Havocs, P-47 Thunderbolts, and P-40s attack enemy defensive positions and roads.

Captain William W. Galt, 168th Infantry Regiment, 34th Infantry Division, is a battalion operations officer who volunteers to lead an attack on German positions at Villa Crocetta. He commandeers the only operational tank destroyer and takes the lead, followed by a company of infantry. Captain Galt stands on the turret of the tank destroyer, designating targets with the vehicle's .30-caliber machine gun and tossing hand grenades into the German trenches. As the trench line is cleared, Captain Galt is killed when an anti-tank round hits the American tank destroyer. For his supreme act of courage and leadership, Captain Galt will receive the Medal of Honor.

PACIFIC: Admiral Nimitz's staff issues an order to prepare for an attack on the Palau Islands scheduled for September 8. Major General Geiger, commander of the III Amphibious Corps, is designated as commander of the ground forces, with four divisions divided into two corps. The 1st Marine Division and the army's 81st Infantry Division will make up III Amphibious Corps and will capture the islands of Peleliu and Angaur. XXIV Corps, made up of the 7th and 77th Infantry Divisions, will attack Babelthuap. The 27th Infantry Division in New Caledonia will be the reserve.

SOUTH PACIFIC: Major General James T. Moore (USMC) is appointed Commander, Air Solomons (COMAIRSOLS).

BOUGAINVILLE: Thirteenth Air Force sends 24 P-39 Airacobras and 16 P-40s to attack Japanese positions near Tinputs Harbor and Arigua Plantation.

NEW BRITAIN: Thirteenth Air Force B-25 Mitchells, P-38 Lightnings, P-39 Airacobras, and U.S. Navy aircraft attack antiaircraft positions and logistics sites in the Rabaul area.

NEW GUINEA: At Biak, the 163rd Infantry fights off three Japanese counterattacks at Mokmer village, one of which is led by tanks. The 162nd Infantry is forced to retreat to the beachhead.

B-24 Liberators bomb Japanese positions on Biak. A-20 Havocs, B-25 Mitchells, and P-47 Thunderbolts attack targets in the Wewak area. B-25s and P-40s attack Japanese positions near Sarmi. B-24s of the Thirteenth Air Task Force bomb Woleai Atoll and nearby islands in the Carolines.

May 30

ALEUTIANS: Eleventh Air Force B-25 Mitchells sink a Japanese guardboat northeast of Paramushiro, Kuriles, and damage a guardboat east of the Kuriles.

CBI: General Joseph Stilwell replaces Colonel John E. McCammon with General Haydon L. Boatner to take command of the Myitkyina Task Force.

Tenth Air Force B-25 Mitchells and P-40s attack railroad targets around Mogaung, Myitkyina, Hopin, and Loilaw.

In China, Fourteenth Air Force B-25 Mitchells and P-40s attack strongpoints, supply, and defensive positions at Loyang. Japanese aircraft bomb Hengyang and Liangshan airfields, causing extensive damage to the fuel storage areas and destroying four aircraft on the ground.

ETO: Eighth Air Force sends 518 B-17s and 460 B-24 Liberators, escorted by 186 P-38 Lightnings, 184 P-47 Thunderbolts, and 302 P-51 Mustangs, to attack aircraft production facilities in Germany, marshaling yards in France and Belgium, and V-weapon sites in France. Aircrews report eight confirmed kills and five probables. A total of 12 bombers are lost and 131 damaged. Aircrew losses are five killed, 12 wounded, and 114 missing. Fighter pilots report 50 confirmed kills in the air, three probables, and seven confirmed kills on the ground. Nine aircraft are lost and nine are damaged. Nine pilots are reported missing. Ninth Air Force supports the mission with 637 fighter aircraft. The pilots report eight confirmed kills in the air and three U.S. aircraft lost.

In another mission Eighth Air Force sends 100 P-47s to attack four railroad bridges in France. One Thunderbolt is lost.

Ninth Air Force sends over 300 B-26 Marauders against airfields and highway bridges while about 400 P-47s conduct dive-bombing attacks on targets in France.

MEDITERRANEAN: Fifteenth Air Force sends almost 500 B-17s and B-24 Liberators to bomb marshaling yard in Yugoslavia and aircraft production facilities in Austria. The bombers are escorted by P-38 Lightnings and P-51 Mustangs.

ITALY: The 3rd Infantry Division and the 1st Special Service Force link up with units from II Corps advancing from the west and come under the Corps' operational control for the attack into Valmontone. The 1st Armored Division and the 45th Infantry Division are unable to move beyond Campoleone on the Albano Road. Combat Command A is reinforced with a battalion from the 135th Infantry Regiment of the 34th Infantry Division. Combat Command B is reinforced with an armored infantry battalion of the 6th Armored Infantry Regiment. The tanks and infantry advance about a mile and are halted by enemy fire. The 1st Armored Division loses 23 tanks and the Americans suffer 200 casualties in the failed attack. The rest of the 34th Infantry Division again attacks Lanuvio and again is driven off by heavy fire. The 142nd and 143rd Infantry Regiments of the 36th Infantry Division climb Colli Laziali and are in position to overlook the entire rear of the enemy. The 141st Infantry Regiment of the 36th Infantry Division moves to outflank the German defenses at Velletri. The 85th Infantry Division reaches the Anzio beachhead.

Twelfth Air Force B-26 Marauders and B-25 Mitchells attack bridges and viaducts. A-20 Havocs attack assembly areas and logistics depots. P-47 Thunderbolts and P-40s attack enemy defensive positions and roads.

SOUTHWEST PACIFIC AREA: U.S. submarine *Guitarro* torpedoes and sinks a Japanese cargo ship southeast of Formosa.

PACIFIC: U.S. submarine *Pompon* torpedoes and sinks a Japanese passenger-cargo ship off Kyushu, Japan.

CENTRAL PACIFIC: Seventh Air Force B-24 Liberators from Kwajalein Atoll bomb Truk and Wake Island. B-25 Mitchells from Engebi Island bomb Ponape Island.

BOUGAINVILLE: Thirteenth Air Force P-39 Airacobras and P-40s bomb bridges, roads, the airfield at Buka Island, a barge anchorage, and logistics sites.

NEW BRITAIN: Thirteenth Air Force B-25 Mitchells bomb Tobera and P-38 Lightnings, P-40s, and P-39 Airacobras attack logistics sites.

NEW GUINEA: Fifth Air Force B-25 Mitchells bomb Japanese positions on Biak Island. B-25s bomb and strafe the coastline near Sarmi Point. B-24s, B-25s, and A-20 Havocs bomb Wewak.

U.S. submarine *Rasher* attacks the convoy it had attacked previously, sinking a gunboat in the eastern Celebes Sea.

Fifth Air Force B-25 Mitchells damage a Japanese cargo vessel west of Manokwari.

May 31

CBI: By the end of May at least 5,000 Japanese troops are in defensive positions around the town of Myitkyina as the monsoon rains begin. Even though Allied strength reaches 12,000, the Japanese continue to defend tenaciously. The siege of Myitkyina begins and will last until August.

Tenth Air Force B-25 Mitchells and P-40s attack Japanese positions, rail lines, and logistics sites near Myitkyina, Kamaing, and the Mogaung area. The airfield and town of Bhamo are also attacked.

In China, Fourteenth Air Force P-51 Mustangs and P-40s attack shipping on the Yangtze River. Pilots report five small ships are hit. B-25 Mitchells damage a bridge at Kengluang and B-24 Liberators bomb Lungling.

ETO: Twenty Allied combat divisions are in Britain to support Overlord. The total number of U.S. troops in Britain is 1.5 million, completing the target numbers established for the Bolero plan in early 1942.

Eighth Air Force sends 533 B-17s and 496 B-24 Liberators, escorted by 193 P-38 Lightnings, 180 P-47 Thunderbolts, and 309 P-51 Mustangs against marshaling yards, rail lines, and aircraft production facilities in France, Belgium, the Netherlands, and Germany. One bomber is lost and 111 are damaged. Aircrew casualties are two killed, four wounded, and 10 missing. Fighter pilots report four confirmed kills on the ground. Three fighters are lost and four are damaged. Three pilots are reported missing.

P-47s attack Gutersloh airfield and report five confirmed kills and one probable. One U.S. fighter is damaged. P-38 Lightnings with Droopsnoot attack Rehein/Hopsten airfield. Pilots report five confirmed kills on the ground.

A total of 22 B-24s fly in support of Carpetbagger operations.

Ninth Air Force sends nearly 200 B-26 Marauders to bomb canal locks and highway bridges in France.

MEDITERRANEAN: Fifteenth Air Force sends nearly 500 B-17s and B-24 Liberators to bomb oil refineries at Ploeşti, Romania. A total of 15 bombers are lost to antiaircraft fire or German fighters. U.S. fighter pilots report over 40 confirmed kills.

ITALY: At Anzio, II Corps has operational control of the 3rd Infantry Division, the 85th Infantry Division, the 88th Infantry Division, and the 1st Special Service Force. The 85th Infantry Division attacks at Lariano to protect the 36th Infantry Division's flank and prevent a German counterattack from the enemy position on the Alban Hills.

Twelfth Air Force B-26 Marauders and B-25 Mitchells attack assembly areas and roads. A-20 Havocs, P-47 Thunderbolts, and P-40s attack enemy defensive positions, bridges, roads, and logistics sites.

Private Furman L. Smith of the 135th Infantry Regiment, 34th Infantry Division, is among the lead elements advancing to capture a German strongpoint near Lanuvio. About 80 German soldiers mount a counterattack, inflicting many casualties and forcing the company to retreat. Private Smith refuses to leave his wounded comrades behind. Moving them to relative safety in nearby shell craters, Smith then defends the position, firing his rife on the enemy until killed. Private Smith's courage and dedication to duty at the cost of his own life will win him the Medal of Honor.

PACIFIC: U.S. submarines *Barb* and *Herring* rendezvous in the Sea of Okhotsk to coordinate operations against Japanese shipping. *Herring* attacks a convoy, sinking an escort vessel and a cargo ship west of Matsuwa Island. *Barb* sinks a cargo ship and a transport southwest of Paramushiru.

NEW BRITAIN: Thirteenth Air Force B-25 Mitchells, P-38 Lightnings, P-39 Airacobras, and P-40s bomb logistics depots, vehicle concentrations, and wharves around Rabaul.

NEW IRELAND: Destroyer escort USS *England,* assisted by destroyers USS *McCord* and *Hazelwood* and destroyer escorts USS *George, Raby,* and *Spangler,* sinks Japanese submarine *RO-105* north of Kavieng.

NEW GUINEA: At Biak, the 163rd Infantry Regiment lands at Bosnek, having been ordered to move from Wakde.

Fifth Air Force B-25 Mitchells and A-20 Havocs fly cover over the beachhead on Biak Island. B-25s and P-47 Thunderbolts attack Japanese positions near Sarmi. B-24 Liberators and P-39 Airacobras attack targets near Wewak.

June 1

ALEUTIANS: Eleventh Air Force sends two B-24 Liberators from Shemya Island in the Aleutians to photograph and bomb installations at Buroton Bay in the Kuriles.

CBI: The Japanese 18th Division is withdrawn from the Burma battlefront.

Tenth Air Force B-25 Mitchells bring ammunition into the Imphal area. P-40s attack Japanese positions near Myitkyina.

In China, Fourteenth Air Force redeploys the P-51 Mustangs of the 76th Fighter Squadron, 23rd Fighter Group, to Lingling from Suichwan. P-47 Thunderbolts of the 91st Fighter Squadron, 81st Fighter Group, move from Karachi, India, to Fungwanshan. The P-38 Lightnings of the 449th Fighter Squadron, 51st Fighter Group, will redeploy from Suichwan to Kweilin.

ETO: General Eisenhower and his staff begin meeting daily to work out last-minute details and receive weather updates. On this day in England sit 10 armored divisions and 48 infantry divisions, a total of 1.5 million men and 16 million tons of supplies. There are 4,200 tanks, 13,700 vehicles, and 3,500 artillery pieces assembled and waiting for the order that will send them off to participate in one of the greatest events in history.

Ninth Air Force sends nearly 100 B-26 Marauders to attack airfields and coastal defense batteries from the Belgian border to the Cherbourg Peninsula in France.

ITALY: In the II Corps area, the 85th and the 3rd Infantry Divisions attack to capture Route 6, but the attack is slowed by a German counterattack. The 338th Infantry Regiment of the 85th Infantry Division is stopped near Lariano, and the 337th Infantry Regiment advances toward Monte Castellaccio. The 1st Special Service Force reaches Colle Ferro south of Valmontone, capturing 200 prisoners and opening the way for the French Expeditionary Corps to advance on Route 6 from the east.

In the VI Corps area, the 179th and 180th Infantry Regiments of the 45th Infantry Division attack up the Alban Road, but make no progress. The 34th Infantry Division is stalled by German defenses at Lanuvio. The 36th Infantry Division captures Velletri after the Germans withdraw. American artillery units occupy Monte Artemisio and begin to fire directly on German positions.

Twelfth Air Force B-25 Mitchells and B-26 Marauders support the Fifth Army offensive, attacking German defensive positions, vehicles, and lines of communication. P-40s attack German positions along the east coast of Italy. Destroyers USS *Champlin* and *MacKenzie* shell German strongpoints and shore batteries.

SOUTHWEST PACIFIC AREA: U.S. submarine *Narwhal* lands men and supplies on Mindanao.

PACIFIC: U.S. submarine *Herring* continues attacks against Japanese shipping, sinking a transport and a cargo ship while at anchor near Matsuwa Island, Kuriles. Japanese shore batteries score two direct hits on the submarine's conning tower, and the *Herring* is lost with all hands.

U.S. submarine *Pintado* torpedoes and sinks a Japanese transport and damages another northwest of Saipan.

CENTRAL PACIFIC: Seventh Air Force B-25 Mitchells from Eniwetok bomb Ponape Island.

NEW BRITAIN: Thirteenth Air Force B-25 Mitchells bomb Rabaul and logistics depot near Tobera. P-38 Lightnings and P-40s attack barges and buildings.

ADMIRALTIES: The headquarters of Thirteenth Air Force's XIII Bomber Command redeploys from Guadalcanal to Los Negros Island.

NEW GUINEA: At Biak, the 186th Infantry Regiment advances north to cover the flank of the 162nd Infantry as it advances down the coastal road toward the airfields.

Fifth Air Force B-25 Mitchells and A-20 Havocs attack targets on Noemfoor and Biak Islands. B-25s, A-20 Havocs, and P-39 Airacobras attack targets along the coast from Wakde to Hollandia, and bomb Wewak.

B-24 Liberators bomb Amboina on Ambon Island, Kai Island in the Moluccas, and Boeroe Island in the Sunda Islands.

June 2

ALEUTIANS: Eleventh Air Force B-24 Liberators conduct a photoreconnaissance and bombing run on Matsuwa Island in the Kuriles.

CBI: An attack by Chinese and American forces at Myitkyina gains about 100 yards in the face of strong Japanese resistance.

Tenth Air Force B-25 Mitchells fly ammunition into the Imphal, India, area in support of British forces.

In China, Fourteenth Air Force sends over 80 P-40s and P-51 Mustangs to attack Japanese infantry and vehicles at Tungcheng and Chungyang.

ETO: For the next three days, the Eighth Air Force will attack transportation and airfields in France and attack coastal defenses in the Pas-de-Calais area, to provide a diversion that will focus German attention on the expected invasion area, rather than the actual invasion area in Normandy. An attack against V-weapon sites in the Pas-de-Calais area involves 633 B-17s and 293 B-24 Liberators. Another 242 B-17s bomb rail lines around Paris, while 77 B-24s attack the Bretigny airfield. Seven bombers are lost and 140 are damaged. Aircrew casualties are two killed, five wounded, and 69 missing.

During the evening, five B-17s drop leaflets on towns and cities in Belgium and France. A total of 18 B-24 Liberators fly in support of Carpetbagger operations.

Ninth Air Force sends over 300 B-26 Marauders and A-20 Havocs to bomb V-weapon sites and coastal defense batteries along the English Channel. P-38 Lightnings and P-47 Thunderbolts conduct dive-bombing attacks on V-weapon sites, fuel storage areas, railroad bridges, and rail lines.

MEDITERRANEAN: Under command of Lieutenant General Ira C. Eaker, the Fifteenth Air Force initiates the first Frantic shuttle-bombing mission. The intent of Frantic is to support the Soviet armies by flying bombing missions from the Mediterranean and Britain and landing at three bases opened to the western Allies: Poltava, Mirgorod, and Piryatin. A total of 130 B-17s, escorted by 70 P-51 Mustangs, bomb the marshaling yard at Debreczen, Hungary, and land in Soviet Ukraine at Poltava and Mirgorod. The P-51 Mustangs land at Piryatin. One B-17 is lost. A total of seven Frantic missions will be flown. Pathologically suspicious of the Americans, the Soviets demonstrate a reluctance to cooperate and impose strict controls on Allied aircrews, which limits the effectiveness of the mission.

Nearly 400 B-24 Liberators attack marshaling yards at Szeged, Miskolc, and Szolnok, Hungary, and Simeria in Romania. P-51s and P-38 Lightnings provide escort.

ITALY: Outflanked and pressured from two directions, German forces begin a general retreat toward Rome. In II Corps, the 30th Infantry Regiment of the 3rd Infantry Division captures Valmontone. The 8th Infantry Division cuts Route 6 and the 351st Infantry Regiment occupies San Cesareo. In the VI Corps, the 34th Infantry Division captures Villa Crocetta before Lanuvio. The 142nd and 143rd Infantry Regiments of the 36th Infantry Division advance toward the Alban Hills, while the 141st Infantry moves toward Nemi. Once the German command is aware that this is happening, their entire Fourteenth Army is ordered to retreat.

Twelfth Air Force B-26 Marauders and B-25 Mitchells attack assembly areas and roads. A-20 Havocs, P-47 Thunderbolts, and P-40s attack enemy defensive positions, bridges, roads, and logistics sites.

U.S. destroyer *MacKenzie* bombards German guns near Anzio.

Technical Sergeant Yeiki Kobashigawa's platoon runs into heavy fire from German machine gun positions in the vicinity of Lanuvio, Italy. Technical Sergeant Kobashigawa locates one of the positions and crawls forward with one of his men to throw a grenade. Kobashigawa then stands up and assaults the position, firing his Thompson submachine gun while the other soldier provides covering fire. During the fight one German soldier is killed and two surrender. Another German machine gun fires on Kobashigawa and his comrade. The two men again work together to attack the position, with Kobashigawa throwing grenades and providing covering fire as his fellow soldier charges in to capture four Germans. Technical Sergeant Kobashigawa continues to direct the efforts of his men in eliminating two more machine gun positions. For his extraordinary courage and skill in close combat with the enemy, Technical Sergeant Kobashigawa will receive the Medal of Honor.

Private Shinyei Nakamine of the 100th Infantry Battalion is halted by German fire as he participates in an attack on German defenses near La Torreto, Italy. German machine guns firing from a small knoll 200 yards to the front have forced the soldiers to seek cover. Private Nakamine begins crawling uphill toward the German positions. At about 25 yards, he charges forward and eliminates the position, firing his Thompson submachine gun, killing three enemy soldiers, and capturing two others. As his unit resumes its advance, Private Nakamine attacks another machine gun position and destroys it with hand grenades. Another machine gun position fires on him and, as he leads an automatic rifle team toward the enemy, he is killed. For his extraordinary heroism and devotion to duty Private Nakamine will receive the Medal of Honor.

SOUTHWEST PACIFIC AREA: U.S. submarine *Guitarro* torpedoes a Japanese escort vessel near Formosa.

U.S. submarine *Picuda* attacks a Japanese convoy headed to Singapore, sinking an escort vessel east of Formosa.

U.S. submarine *Shark* attacks a Japanese convoy, sinking a transport west of the Marianas.

CENTRAL PACIFIC: Seventh Air Force B-25 Mitchells from Makin Island bomb Nauru Island.

BOUGAINVILLE: Thirteenth Air Force P-39 Airacobras attack the airfield on Buka Island and bomb logistics depots in the Kara-Kahili area.

NEW BRITAIN: Thirteenth Air Force P-38 Lightnings, P-39 Airacobras, and P-40s attack targets near Vunakanau.

NEW GUINEA: At Biak, Japanese aircraft bomb the Bosnek beachhead. The Americans occupy nearby Owi Island and find it unoccupied.

Fifth Air Force B-24 Liberators bomb Japanese defensive positions above Mokmer airfield. B-24s, P-39 Airacobras, and Royal Australian Air Force (RAAF) fighters attack targets around Wewak.

Thirteenth Air Task Force B-24s bomb Truk Atoll.

June 3

CBI: The CCS instructs Admiral Lord Louis Mountbatten, SEAC commander, to concentrate his efforts on opening an overland route to China, employing all the resources he has currently available in theater.

Tenth Air Force B-25 Mitchells bomb Japanese troops near Imphal, India, while other B-25s fly ammunition resupply missions to British forces. P-40s attack the Mogaung area.

ETO: The weather forecast for June 5, the expected date of the invasion of Europe, is poor. Assault shipping begins moving out into the English Channel in anticipation of the execute order.

Eighth Air Force sends 238 B-17s and 124 B-24 Liberators, escorted by 91 P-38 Lightnings and 129 P-47 Thunderbolts, to attack 22 coastal defenses in the

Pas-de-Calais area. A total of 45 bombers are damaged, but aircrews report no casualties. A second strike on 16 of the original targets by 97 B-17s and 98 B-24 Liberators is escorted by 102 P-38 Lightnings, 34 P-47 Thunderbolts, and 83 P-51 Mustangs. Two B-17s are damaged. One P-51 is lost and one P-38 is damaged. One pilot is reported missing.

During the night 23 B-24 Liberators fly in support of Carpetbagger operations.

Ninth Air Force sends over 250 B-26 Marauders and A-20 Havocs against airfields, highway bridges, and coastal defense batteries in northern France. P-38 Lightnings and P-47s conduct dive-bombing attacks on widespread targets.

ITALY: In the VI Corps area, the 168th Infantry Regiment of the 34th Infantry Division captures Lanuvio as the rest of the division moves to block Route 7. The 45th Infantry Division prepares to move to Albano with the 1st Armored Division to follow and reach Route 7 in order to get to Rome as quickly as possible.

In the II Corps area, the 85th Infantry Division crosses the Alban Hills toward Frascato. The 88th Infantry Division advances on Route 6, occupying Colona after fighting small elements of retreating Germans.

Intercepts from Ultra confirm that the Germans will not fight for Rome.

Twelfth Air Force A-20 Havocs, P-47 Thunderbolts, and P-40s support II Corps south of Rome and attack bridges to cut off the German retreat.

Private Elden H. Johnson, 15th Infantry Regiment, 3rd Infantry Division, faces a German night ambush near Valmontone, Italy. As flares light the kill zone, Private Johnson stands up and signals his patrol leader to withdraw the other 12 men of the patrol. Johnson then advances toward the enemy, firing his Browning automatic rifle from the hip. After killing a machine gun crew, he reloads and continues his assault, firing on enemy soldiers nearest him. Critically wounded by a burst of machine gun fire, Private Johnson refuses to stop fighting as he pulls himself up to a kneeling position to fire a final burst. His extraordinary courage and willingness to sacrifice himself for his comrades will win him the Medal of Honor.

CENTRAL PACIFIC: Seventh Air Force B-24 Liberators staging through Eniwetok Atoll bomb Truk. B-25 Mitchells from Engebi Island bomb Nauru Island.

NEW GUINEA: At Biak, the 162nd Infantry fights Japanese defenders at a strongpoint identified as Parai defile, a large outcropping of coral covered with trees and brush.

Fifth Air Force B-24 Liberators, B-25 Mitchells, and A-20 Havocs attack Japanese positions above Mokmer airfield and attack the airfields themselves. P-38 Lightnings and P-47 Thunderbolts clear Japanese fighters over the island.

Thirteenth Air Task Force B-24s bomb Eten and Dublon Islands at Truk Atoll.

A Japanese dive-bomber hits U.S. destroyer *Reid* north of Biak.

A navy PBY Catalina damages a Japanese torpedo boat northwest of Manokwari. Fifth Air Force A-20 Havocs sink a fishing boat in the same area.

June 4

CBI: Tenth Air Force B-25 Mitchells fly ammunition resupply missions to British forces at Imphal, India. In Burma, P-40s attack Japanese positions near Myitkyina and Kamaing.

ATLANTIC: When Naval Task Group 22.3 (commanded by Captain Daniel V. Gallery and composed of escort carrier USS *Guadalcanal* and destroyer escorts USS *Pillsbury, Pope, Flaherty, Chatelain,* and *Jenks*) forces German submarine *U-505* to surface off the coast of French West Africa, Lieutenant (j.g.) Albert L. David of USS *Pillsbury* leads a boarding party onto the stricken submarine, knowing full well that at any moment scuttling charges can detonate and destroy the U-boat. Without hesitation, he climbs down the conning tower hatch and begins directing the efforts of his men to keep the U-boat seaworthy until additional salvage personnel can arrive and prepare it for movement to the United States. This is the U.S. Navy's first successful boarding and capture of an enemy warship on the high seas since 1815. For his exceptional courage and determination, Lieutenant (j.g.) David will receive the Medal of Honor.

ETO: Receiving current weather reports of heavy overcast and choppy seas, General Eisenhower decides to delay the landings by 24 hours as assault ships are recalled to ports.

Eighth Air Force sends 201 B-17s and 56 B-24 Liberators against seven targets in the Pas-de-Calais area, escorted by 130 P-47 Thunderbolts and 42 P-51 Mustangs. Ten B-17s are damaged and aircrews report no casualties. Fighter pilots report two P-51s lost but no casualties. A second strike sends 222 B-17s and 68 B-24s against eight coastal defense positions also in the Pas-de-Calais area. The bombers use radar Pathfinders to hit their targets. Only 19 bombers are damaged. Aircrews report one killed. A third strike with 263 B-17s and 185 B-24s attacking railroad bridges, airfields, and rail lines is escorted by 135 P-47 Thunderbolts and 277 P-51 Mustangs. A total of 65 bombers are damaged. Aircrews report 10 killed and four wounded. Fighter pilots report one confirmed kill. One P-51 is lost and two are damaged. No casualties are reported. Ninth Air Force sends over 300 B-26 Marauders and A-20 Havocs to attack roads, bridges, and coastal defense batteries. Nearly 200 P-47s and P-51s conduct dive-bomber attacks on rail lines, rail cars, and bridges.

ITALY: Rome Falls. The 3rd Infantry Division arrives at the Aniene River east of Rome and the 30th Infantry Regiment captures the bridges over the river. The first troops to arrive in the city are from the 88th Infantry Division's cavalry reconnaissance troop. Brigadier General Robert T. Frederick enters Rome with the 1st Regiment of the 1st Special Service Force linked up with 3rd Battalion, 13th Armored Regiment, and artillery. Elements of the 338th Infantry Regiment of the 85th Infantry Division enter Rome as the first unit of VI Corps. Elements of the 1st Armored Division and the 36th Infantry Division move in to occupy the city. Ecstatic Italians crowd around the tired troops. Since May 11, the Fifth Army has suffered 17, 931 casualties to reach the city.

Fifteenth Air Force sends more than 500 B-17s and B-24 Liberators against marshaling yards and railroad bridges.

Twelfth Air Force A-20 Havocs, P-47 Thunderbolts, and P-40s attack bridges and convoys.

PACIFIC: U.S. submarine *Flier* torpedoes and sinks a Japanese troopship off the Bonin Islands.

U.S. submarine *Golet* torpedoes and sinks a Japanese guardboat east of Japan.

CENTRAL PACIFIC: Seventh Air Force B-24 Liberators staging through Eniwetok Atoll, bomb Truk during the night. B-25 Mitchells from Engebi Island attack Ponape Island.

USS *Shark, Pilotfish,* and *Pintado* form a coordinated submarine attack group (TG 17.12) to seek out Japanese convoys. *Shark* torpedoes and sinks an army transport northwest of Saipan.

BOUGAINVILLE: Thirteenth Air Force P-39 Airacobras attack a vehicle park near Komai. P-38 Lightnings attack logistics sites and one B-25 bombs Kahili.

NEW GUINEA: Japanese bombers attack Rear Admiral Victor A. C. Crutchley's Allied cruiser and destroyer task forces (TF 74 and TF 75) off Biak. U.S. light cruisers *Nashville* and *Phoenix* are damaged.

Fifth Air Force A-20 Havocs bomb the town and harbor at Manokwari and shipping in Geelvink Bay.

Fifth Air Force B-24 Liberators sink a Japanese landing ship northeast of Morotai Island.

A-20 Havocs bomb Manokwari and Japanese shipping in Geelvink Bay. Pilots report four ships sunk.

June 5

CBI: General Stilwell arrives in Chungking from Burma to meet with Generalissimo Chiang Kai-shek and General Chennault on the situation in China. Although he is very doubtful that Chennault can stop the Japanese, Stilwell agrees to divert an additional 1,500 tons of supplies destined for the B-29s at Chengtu to the Fourteenth Air Force. Tenth Air Force B-25 Mitchells bomb Bhamo and other B-25s fly ammunition resupply missions to support British forces at Imphal. P-40s bomb the Myitkyina area and Mogaung.

The headquarters of the 3rd Combat Cargo Group is activated in India, along with the C-47-equipped 9th, 10th, 11th, and 12th Combat Cargo Squadrons. This will allow the 4th Troop Carrier Squadron, 62nd Troop Carrier Group, and the 16th, 17th, 18th, and 35th Troop Carrier Squadrons of the 64th Troop Carrier Group to return to Italy and Sicily. These units have been supporting the CBI theater since April.

ETO: Weather reports indicate poor weather in the English Channel, but the forecast for the next 24 hours shows improvement over the invasion area. High winds and rough seas are expected for the evening of June 6. At 0400, General Eisenhower makes the decision to go, authorizing the order for the invasion of Europe to proceed on June 6.

Eighth Air Force sends 464 B-17s and 206 B-24 Liberators escorted by 127 P-47 Thunderbolts and 245 P-51 Mustangs to attack coastal defenses in the Normandy area. Six bombers are lost and 77 are damaged. Aircrew casualties are one killed, 10 wounded, and 47 missing. Fighter pilots report one P-47 and one P-51 lost. One fighter is damaged. P-51s attack a truck convoy and the airfield near Lille.

A total of 11 B-24 Liberators fly in support of Carpetbagger operations. One bomber is lost over Belgium.

A U.S. minesweeper hits a mine off Normandy, France, and sinks. An LST is damaged when it also hits a mine nearby.

Ninth Air Force sends over 100 B-26 Marauders to attack coastal defense batteries, while over 100 P-47s conduct dive-bombing attacks against targets in the same area.

During the night 1,662 aircraft and 517 gliders of the IX Troop Carrier Command begin their flight to the Cotentin Peninsula to drop paratroopers of the 82nd and 101st Airborne Divisions and thus initiate the Allied invasion of Europe. The paratroopers are to be dropped near Ste-Mère Eglise and Carentan to capture bridges, road junctions, and beach exits that will allow VII Corps to move inland to capture Cherbourg.

Lieutenant Colonel Leon R. Vance, Jr., of the 489th Bomber Group is in a B-24 as part of an attack against German coastal defensive positions near Wimereaux, France. As the bomber approaches the target, antiaircraft fire causes serious damage to the engines and kills the pilot and wounds several crewmen, including Lieutenant Colonel Vance, whose right foot is nearly severed. Vance continues to lead the formation and releases bombs on target. After applying a tourniquet to his leg, Lieutenant Colonel Vance and the copilot attempt to bring the stricken bomber back to England on one engine. Bringing the bomber over land, the crew is able to bail out safely. When he hears that one of the crewmen is unable to bail out of the bomber, and that a 500-pound bomb is lodged in the bomb bay, Vance decides to ditch in the English Channel as the best means to give the crewman a chance for survival. Vance's nearly severed foot has become trapped behind the copilot's seat, forcing him to lie on the floor using only aileron and elevators for control while watching out from the side window of the cockpit as he brings the plane down to the water. On landing, Vance is trapped in the cockpit but is thrown clear by an explosion. Recovering from the blast, he begins a search to locate the remaining crewman until rescued. For his extraordinary acts of courage and skill in the face of a life-threatening injury Lieutenant Colonel Vance will receive the Medal of Honor.

ITALY: Lieutenant General Mark Clark and his commanders lead a victory parade through the streets of Rome to the city hall. Brigadier General Edgar E. Hume will become the Allied military governor of Rome.

VI Corps continues to move north to capture Civitavecchia, which has a 100,000-barrel oil terminal that is critical to sustainment of the Fifth Army. Another objective is the major airfields at Viterbo, which will provide a base for close air support missions as well as long-range bombing missions to Germany.

Fifteenth Air Force sends over 400 B-17s and B-24 Liberators escorted by P-38 Lightnings and P-51 Mustangs against railroad bridges and marshaling yards.

Twelfth Air Force B-25 Mitchells and B-26 Marauders attack road bridges north of Rome. A-20 Havocs, P-47 Thunderbolts, and P-40s attack convoys, bridges, rail lines, and roads.

SOUTHWEST PACIFIC AREA: U.S. submarine *Nautilus* lands supplies at Mindanao in the Philippines.

U.S. submarine *Puffer* attacks a Japanese convoy in the Sulu Sea and sinks an underway replenishment vessel and oiler and damages a tanker.

PACIFIC: Twentieth Air Force sends 98 B-29 Superfortresses from India on their first combat mission, the railroad shops at Bangkok. Of the 77 that hit the target, five bombers are lost, all due to events unrelated to combat.

CENTRAL PACIFIC: Seventh Air Force B-25 Mitchells from Makin Island bomb Nauru Island. B-25s from Engebi Island bomb Ponape Island. B-24 Liberators from Eniwetok Atoll attack Guam and proceed to Momote airfield on Los Negros Island.

The USS *Shark, Pilotfish,* and *Pintado* submarine attack group (of TG 17.12) pursue the convoy encountered the previous day west of the Marianas. USS *Shark* torpedoes and sinks two transports.

BOUGAINVILLE: Thirteenth Air Force P-39 Airacobras attack vehicles, logistics sites, and the Buka airfield.

NEW BRITAIN: Thirteenth Air Force sends 23 B-25 Mitchells to attack a vehicle park at Rabaul. P-39 Airacobras and P-38 Lightnings attack targets in the Rabaul area.

NEW GUINEA: Japanese aircraft attack Wakde airfield, damaging nearly 100 U.S. aircraft parked on the field.

MacArthur is troubled by the lack of progress on Biak and tells Lieutenant General Krueger to get the 41st Infantry Division moving. MacArthur asks, "Is the advance being pushed with sufficient determination?" This question will drive Krueger to pressure Major General Fuller to achieve decisive results fast.

The P-38 Lightnings of the 7th Fighter Squadron, 49th Fighter Group, move from Hollandia to Biak Island. P-39 Airacobras of the 110th Tactical Reconnaissance Squadron, 71st Tactical Reconnaissance Group, redeploy to Tadji.

June 6

CBI: Tenth Air Force B-25 Mitchells attack Japanese positions around Imphal, while other B-25s fly resupply missions to British forces. A-36 Intruder (Apache) fighter-bombers, P-51 Mustangs, and P-40s attack the areas near Myitkyina and Mogaung.

In China, Fourteenth Air Force B-25 Mitchells, P-40s, and P-51 Mustangs attack Japanese positions near Tayang Chiang. B-25s bomb Pailochi airfield.

U.S. submarine *Raton* attacks a Japanese convoy and sinks a coast defense vessel off the shores of French Indochina near Saigon. Although damaged by depth charges, *Raton* remains on patrol.

ETO: D-day: The Normandy Invasion. At 0115 hours, the 13,000 paratroopers of the 101st and 82nd Airborne Divisions, in 925 C-47s from IX Troop Carrier Command, begin dropping over the Cotentin Peninsula. The drops are scattered due to German antiaircraft fire and misidentified drop zones. About 1,500 of the 6,000 paratroopers from the 101st Airborne Division land outside of their designated drop zones. The 507th and 508th Parachute Infantry Regiments of the 82nd Airborne are dropped far from their intended drop zones. Many drown in flooded fields; others land directly on German positions. Nevertheless, small bands of paratroopers gather and seek a way to accomplish their assigned missions. The 500 gliders with 4,000 additional reinforcements, anti-tank guns, ammunition, medical supplies, and rations will not arrive for another four hours. At 0300 transports in the English Channel begin loading troops into landing craft.

This famous photo by Robert Capa illustrates the confusion and shock of combat. Here soldiers cluster around German landing obstacles at Normandy, June 6, 1944.

At 0430, the 4th and 24th Cavalry Squadrons capture the islands at St. Marcouf to secure them in preparation for the landings. Elements of the 3rd Battalion, 505th Infantry Regiment, 82nd Airborne Division, capture Ste-Mère Eglise, the first town in France to be liberated by Allied forces. The division is missing 4,000 men and more than half of its equipment is lost.

The invasion fleet of thousands of warships, merchantmen, and landing craft is under the command of Admiral Sir Bertram H. Ramsay (RN). Ramsay's command is divided into two task forces: a Western (American) Task Force and an Eastern (British) Task Force. The Western Task Force, commanded by Rear Admiral Alan G. Kirk, is composed of two assault forces—the O Force, under command of Rear Admiral John L. Hall, and the U Force, under command of Rear Admiral Donald P. Moon. O Force is responsible for the Omaha landing beach and U Force is responsible for Utah beach.

U.S. destroyer *Corry* is sunk by a mine off Utah beach as it attempts to avoid fire from German shore batteries.

At 0550 the naval bombardment begins, intending to destroy beach obstacles and German strongpoints, followed by 276 B-26 Marauders from Ninth Air Force.

At 0600, Eighth Air Force bombers begin dropping 2,746 tons of bombs on suspected German positions.

At 0630 on Utah beach, the 2nd Battalion, 8th Infantry Regiment, 4th Infantry Division, of the VII Corps under Major General J. Lawton Collins is the first ashore. The soldiers find themselves far south of their intended landing site as a result of high seas and strong currents. A group of 28 tanks also lands on the beach. The assistant division commander of the 4th Infantry Division has landed with the first wave. Brigadier General Theodore Roosevelt, Jr., makes a quick assessment and decides to assault the beach exit from the division's current position. Moving under enemy fire, he directs troops off the beach and moves them inland. The 22nd and 12th Infantry Regiments clear beach exits 1, 3, and 4 and move off the beach, advancing six miles inland. Casualties have been light: 20 men killed and 200 wounded. Roosevelt's seasoned, precise, calm, and unfaltering leadership is critical in making the beach assault a success. For his courage and inspired leadership under fire, Roosevelt will receive the Medal of Honor. By the end of the day, 20,000 men and 7,000 vehicles have landed on Utah.

Soldiers crowded into a landing craft approach the beach at Normandy, June 6, 1944.

At 0630 on Omaha beach, the 16th and 18th Regimental Combat Teams from the 1st Infantry Division and the 115th and 116th Infantry Regiments of the 29th Infantry Division land and are immediately brought under heavy fire from 12

On Utah beach, the 8th Infantry Regiment of the 4th Infantry Division begins moving inland on the causeways to link up with paratroopers of the 101st Airborne Division.

German strongpoints manned by two regiments of combat-experienced soldiers. The initial wave is nearly annihilated as the troops struggle through three bands of untouched beach obstacles. Mines destroy many landing craft on approach, and heavy seas swamp landing craft and tanks attempting to reach the beach. In the first half-hour of the attack, casualties are approaching 30 percent. The rising tide has trapped landing craft on a sandbar, forcing disembarking troops to wade nearly 100 yards directly into German machine-gun fire. Obstacles and mines on the beach prevent any organized landing effort. Brigadier General Norman D. Cota, the assistant division commander of the 29th Infantry Division, walks along the beach pushing his men forward and ignoring the fire of the German machine guns. Slowly the American soldiers gain a bit of cohesion and begin making small advances through small gaps in the defenses.

About 100 men of the 2nd Ranger Battalion scale the cliffs at Pointe du Hoc, three miles west of Omaha, to destroy a coastal battery position but find it abandoned. The Rangers later locate the guns in the rear of the German lines and destroy them. The Rangers then form a defensive perimeter and must fight for their lives against German counterattacks.

First Lieutenant Jimmie W. Monteith, Jr., of the 16th Infantry Regiment, 1st Infantry Division, lands as part of the first assault wave on Omaha beach. Despite the heavy fire that sweeps the beach, First Lieutenant Monteith gathers the survivors and leads them to a place of relative safety near the cliffs. He returns to the beach to lead two tanks through a minefield to positions where they can begin providing supporting fire. He rejoins his men and leads them in an assault to capture a hill from which he can outflank enemy positions. Defending the position against a number of counterattacks, First Lieutenant Monteith risks his life often to reorganize the defense. Although soon surrounded, he continues to encourage his men until killed. In recognition of First Lieutenant Monteith's courage and determination to accomplish his mission in the face of all odds, he will receive the Medal of Honor.

On the assault on Omaha beach, Technician Fifth Grade John R. Pinder, Jr., of the 6th Infantry Regiment, 1st Infantry Division, finds himself 100 yards offshore under concentrated machine-gun and artillery fire. Carrying a radio, he is attempting to wade ashore when he is seriously wounded. Continuing to struggle ashore, Technician Fifth Grade Pinder ignores his wound and refuses medical assistance. Knowing how critical the communications equipment is to the success of the mission, Pinder makes several trips into the open, fire-swept beach to retrieve equipment. Wounded again, he returns to assemble a radio set and establish communications. Shortly thereafter he is killed by enemy fire. Technician Fifth Grade Pinder's dedication to duty and courage will win him the Medal of Honor.

At 0730 the situation on Omaha beach is critical. Only 16 of 48 tanks reach the beach and the engineer demolition teams are almost entirely eliminated. Those still alive are struggling to survive in the midst of heavy mortar and machine-gun fire. Nevertheless, the soldiers collect in small groups, and anonymous pockets of men begin pushing forward to make the critical 200 yards and reach the five exit corridors in the cliffs facing the beach.

Naval gunfire support for the VII Corps at Utah beach is under the command of Rear Admiral Morton L. Deyo. Admiral Carleton F. Bryant commands the bombardment group supporting the V Corps at Omaha. The groups are evenly balanced, although Bryant's group has received one additional battleship and two additional destroyers. At Omaha beach, American destroyers play a critical role in eliminating German defensive positions and allowing the infantrymen to advance inland. The USS *McCook* moves to within 1,300 yards of the beach, firing over 1,000 five-inch rounds into German positions. USS *Carmick* moves to within 900 yards, firing a total of 1,127 rounds. The USS *Frankford* hits targets on the beach located 400 yards away.

At Pointe-du-Hoc, two destroyers (USS *Satterlee* and HMS *Talybont*) come within 1,000 yards of the shore to put devastating fire on German positions and allow the Rangers to climb the cliffs.

At 0900, American troops are moving inland, encountering German forces defending the access to the roads at Vierville-sur-Mer, Colleville-sur-Mer, and St. Laurent. American casualties for the V Corps on Omaha are assessed at 2,400 killed, wounded, and missing. At the end of the day 13 gaps in the German defensive line have been made. The 116th RCT of the 29th Infantry Division has control of Vierville and St. Laurent and is advancing west to find VII Corps. The 16th RCT of the 1st Infantry Division controls Colleville and is establishing defensive positions to protect the southeastern portion of the beachhead.

At 1300, Lieutenant Colonel Robert G. Cole of the 101st Airborne Division meets elements of the 8th Infantry Regiment of the 4th Infantry Division coming off Utah beach. Elements of the 502nd Parachute Infantry Regiment capture Poppeville, securing the last of the four causeway exits off the beach. The 101st suffers 1,200 casualties during the first day of the invasion. The 82nd Airborne secures the western edge of the beachhead, but is unable to hold the key bridges over the Merderet River.

Eighth Air Force supports the invasion with a dawn attack by 882 B-17s and 543 B-24 Liberators on targets along the coast near the invasion beaches. Bad weather causes most of the bombers to miss their targets or not continue the mission. Most of the bombs are dropped up to three miles inland, leaving the main targets untouched. One B-24 is lost and 16 bombers are damaged. Aircrew casualties are 12 killed, two wounded, and 13 missing. A follow-on mission intended to help seal off the invasion area from German reinforcements also runs into bad weather and all but 37 B-24 Liberators of the 380 B-17s and B-24s sent bomb a secondary target at Argentan. Two B-24s are lost and one B-17 is damaged. Aircrews report no casualties. A third attack on the key city of Caen, which is the main route into the flat, open terrain essential for the Allied breakout, is conducted by 58 B-24s through low-hanging clouds. A fourth attack by over 400 B-17s and 300 B-24s hits key defensive areas that must be controlled by the Germans to keep the Allies contained within the beachhead. Of the 325 B-17s and 125 B-24s that hit the primary targets of St-Lô, Coutances, Falaise, Lisieux, Argentan, and Conde-sur-Noireau, one B-24 is lost and 17 bombers are damaged. Aircrew casualties are 10 killed.

P-47 Thunderbolts and P-51 Mustangs escort bombers and attack bridges, rail lines, marshaling yards, rail cars, and roads. Vehicles, communications sites, troops, buildings, artillery, and trains are attacked directly. Fighter pilots report 26 confirmed kills in the air and four on the ground. A total of 25 fighters are lost.

Ninth Air Force sends over 800 A-20 Havocs and B-26 Marauders against coastal defense positions, rail and road junctions, bridges, and marshaling yards. Over 2,000 P-51s and P-47s conduct close air support and dive-bombing missions.

By nightfall 34,000 troops are ashore on Omaha and 23,000 more are moving inland from Utah. Casualties for the American ground forces are 2,500 at Omaha, 197 on Utah, and another 2,500 among the paratroopers.

During the night, 12 B-17s drop leaflets on cities and towns in France and the Netherlands.

MEDITERRANEAN: The 104 B-17s and 42 P-51 Mustangs from Fifteenth Air Force participating in Frantic attack an airfield at Galati, Romania, and return to bases in the Soviet Ukraine. Fighter pilots report eight confirmed kills and two U.S. P-51s are lost. Lieutenant Cullen J. Hoffman is the first fighter pilot to shoot down a German aircraft during a Frantic combat mission when his P-51 happens upon a German dive-bomber over Poland. From Italy, Fifteenth Air Force sends over 500 B-17s and B-24s against a marshaling yard in Yugoslavia and the Ploeşti oil refineries in Romania.

ITALY: Twelfth Air Force B-26 Marauders and B-25 Mitchells attack lines of communication. A-20 Havocs, P-47 Thunderbolts, and P-40s attack roads and rail lines.

SOUTHWEST PACIFIC AREA: U.S. submarine *Harder* attacks a Japanese convoy in the Celebes Sea and sinks a Japanese destroyer off Borneo. Another Japanese destroyer makes an unsuccessful depth-charge attack on the *Harder.*

CENTRAL PACIFIC: Seventh Air Force B-24 Liberators bomb Ponape Island en route to Eniwetok Atoll from Los Negros Island.

USS *Shark, Pilotfish,* and *Pintado* of submarine attack group TG 17.12 continue to pursue the Japanese convoy previously engaged. USS *Pintado* torpedoes and sinks a cargo ship and army transport west of the Marianas.

BOUGAINVILLE: Thirteenth Air Force P-39 Airacobras and U.S. Navy aircraft attack a number of targets, including buildings and a pier near Kahili.

NEW BRITAIN: Thirteenth Air Force P-38 Lightnings bomb a logistics depot near Nordup.

NEW GUINEA: The Reckless operation is completed. The airfields at Hollandia, the target of the operation, are unsuitable for bombers. Nevertheless, Hollandia becomes an important base for future operations. The capture of Hollandia splits the Japanese defenses in half and forces thousands of Japanese into the forbidding interior of New Guinea in an attempt to reach Sarmi; thousands more are isolated from any supply or support. The Japanese losses are over 1,700 killed and 376 captured. American losses are 152 killed and 1,057 wounded.

The 6th Infantry Division begins landing at Toem in support of the 158th RCT facing the enemy at Lone Tree Hill.

Fifth Air Force A-20 Havocs and B-25 Mitchells hit Namber airfield and Japanese tanks near Mokmer on Biak Island. P-39 Airacobras, A-20 Havocs, and Royal Australian Air Force (RAAF) aircraft attack targets between Wewak and Hansa Bay.

Thirteenth Air Task Force B-24 Liberators bomb Truk.

A-20 Havocs attack Japanese shipping off Manokwari. Three vessels are reported sunk.

June 7

CBI: In China, Fourteenth Air Force sends 10 B-25 Mitchells to bomb Lashio and attack targets of opportunity along the Salween River battle line.

ATLANTIC: The JCS, following President Roosevelt's guidance, instructs General Eisenhower that no U.S. forces will occupy southern or southeastern Europe or southwest Germany at the end of the war. Roosevelt seeks to avoid any potential postwar entanglements, especially in the volatile Balkan region.

ETO: The V Corps clears the exit roads for Omaha beach and reaches the line of the Bayeaux-Carentan Road.

Eighth Air Force bombs outlying areas to limit German reinforcements from threatening the beachhead. The first attack by 182 B-17s and 291 B-24 Liberators is supported by radar-equipped Pathfinder aircraft. A total of 18 bombers are damaged. Aircrew casualties are eight killed and three wounded. A second attack by 487 B-17s and 88 B-24 Liberators targets airfields and bridges. Heavy cloud cover prevents many from hitting assigned targets. Two bombers are lost and 182 are damaged. Aircrew casualties are 21 killed, 12 wounded, and 12 missing.

Over the beachhead, 526 P-38 Lightnings and 294 P-51 Mustangs provide aircover and escort bombers. Fighter pilots report two confirmed kills. Eight P-51 Mustangs are lost. One pilot is reported killed and the others are missing. A total of 505 P-47 Thunderbolts and 148 P-51s conduct strafing missions over German lines and pilots report 29 confirmed kills and one probable in the air and 25 confirmed kills on the ground. Fourteen fighters are lost and three damaged. One pilot is reported killed and the others are missing.

B-17s drop leaflets over France, the Netherlands, and Belgium. A total of 14 B-24 Liberators fly in support of Carpetbagger operations in France.

Ninth Air Force sends over 600 B-26 Marauders to attack transportation targets and lines of communication in France. More than 1,000 P-51s and P-47s conduct dive-bombing attacks against German positions; they also escort the B-26 Marauders. Fighters also escort the more than 400 C-47s, C-53s, and gliders that resupply the airborne divisions.

Construction of Mulberries, artificial harbors and sheltered anchorages, begins off Normandy. Mines sink a minesweeper, two LCTs, a motor torpedo boat, and a transport. A U.S. freighter in a convoy carrying troops headed toward Omaha beach hits a mine and suffers some damage but is able to unload the troops on the beach.

ITALY: The 168th Infantry Regiment of the 34th Infantry Division clears Civitavecchia. General Sir Harold R. L. G. Alexander, the Allied ground forces commander, instructs the Fifth Army to advance to the area defined by Pisa, Lucca, and Pistoia as quickly as possible, but logistics and the mountainous terrain limit the speed of the advance. The Fifth Army is about to give up VI Corps and the French Expeditionary Corps to Anvil. The 3rd Infantry Division remains to garrison Rome.

Fifteenth Air Force sends 340 B-17s and B-24 Liberators against harbor facilities, shipyards, and a marshaling yard. A-20 Havocs, P-47 Thunderbolts, and P-40s attack roads, bridges, rail lines, and vehicles.

PACIFIC: U.S. submarine *Whale* torpedoes and damages two Japanese transports north of the Bonin Islands.

CENTRAL PACIFIC: Seventh Air Force B-25 Mitchells from Makin Island bomb Ponape Island.

Remnants of the Japanese convoy attacked by USS *Shark, Pilotfish,* and *Pintado* of submarine attack group TG 17.12 reach Saipan, but only half of an infantry regiment's soldiers have survived the trip and most of the unit's equipment has been lost. This will have an important effect on the outcome of any future battle for Saipan.

BOUGAINVILLE: Thirteenth Air Force P-39 Airacobras and P-38 Lightnings attack Japanese positions near Monoitu.

NEW GUINEA: At Biak, the 186th Infantry Regiment of the 41st Infantry Division captures Mokmer airfield, but finds itself trapped by heavy Japanese fire coming from the high ridges overlooking the airfield. One battalion of the 162nd Infantry holds the Japanese at Parai defile, while the rest of the regiment joins the 186th at Mokmer airfield.

Fifth Air Force B-25 Mitchells bomb Japanese positions on Biak Island. A-20 Havocs attack shipping near Manokwari.

Thirteenth Air Task Force B-24 Liberators attack Truk.

Naval advanced base at Hollandia, New Guinea is established.

U.S. submarine *Harder* torpedoes and sinks a Japanese destroyer north of Celebes Island.

June 8

CBI: In Burma, Tenth Air Force B-25 Mitchells attack Japanese positions around Imphal, while others fly ammunition resupply missions. B-24 Liberators mine approaches to Bangkok. A-36 Intruder (Apache) fighter-bombers and P-51 Mustangs attack Japanese positions near Mogaung.

ETO: The 29th Infantry Division relieves the Rangers at Pointe du Hoc and advances to capture Grandcampe. V Corps establishes contact with the British 50th Division advancing from Gold beach. Eighth Air Force sends 640 B-17s and 538 B-24 Liberators escorted by 116 P-51 Mustangs to attack lines of communication and airfields outside of the invasion area. Three bombers are lost and 140 are damaged. Aircrew losses are 28 killed, four wounded, and 30 missing. Fighter pilots report three confirmed kills. Two fighters are lost and one is damaged. One pilot is reported killed and one missing.

Over the beachhead, 381 P-38 Lightnings, 24 P-47 Thunderbolts, and 89 P-51 Mustangs fly sweeps and patrols. Another 333 P-47s and 526 P-51s fly fighter-bomber missions against lines of communication. The fighter pilots report 28 confirmed kills in the air and two probables. Another 21 German aircraft are reported as confirmed kills on the ground. A total of 20 aircraft are lost and three are damaged. Twenty pilots are reported missing.

Ninth Air Force sends almost 400 B-26 Marauders to attack lines of communication, assembly areas, and logistics bases around Calais, France. Over 1,000 fighters escort the bombers.

General Carl Spaatz, commander of the U.S. Strategic Air Forces in Europe (USSTAF), directs that Germany's oil production capability will be the primary target for offensive bombing operations.

A U.S. destroyer escort and LST hit mines off the Normandy beaches and sink. Two destroyers are damaged by mines.

Technical Sergeant Frank D. Peregory of K Company, 3rd Battalion, 116th Infantry Regiment, 29th Infantry Division, encounters a German strongpoint overlooking the town of Grandcampe. When neither tank nor artillery fire is effective against the position, Technical Sergeant Peregory makes the decision to attack the enemy alone. Advancing up the hill in the face of heavy fire, he comes upon a trench that leads to the strongpoint. Entering the trench, he finds himself in the midst of a squad of Germans soldiers. Using hand grenades and his bayonet, he kills eight men and captures three others. Advancing through the trench, he captures 32 more Germans, including the machine gunners holding up his unit's advance. Technical Sergeant Peregory's extraordinary courage and determination will win him the Medal of Honor.

MEDITERRANEAN: Fifteenth Air Force sends 52 B-17s, with P-47 Thunderbolts providing escort, to bomb the navy yard and drydocks at Pola, Yugoslavia.

ITALY: An armored task force from Combat Command A of the 1st Armored Division captures Viterbo.

Twelfth Air Force A-20 Havocs, P-47 Thunderbolts, and P-40s attack convoys, bridges, rail lines, and roads.

SOUTHWEST PACIFIC AREA: U.S. submarine *Hake* torpedoes and sinks a Japanese destroyer at Davao Gulf, Mindanao.

U.S. submarine *Rasher* attacks a Japanese convoy in the Celebes Sea, sinking an underway replenishment vessel south of Davao.

PACIFIC: U.S. submarine *Whale* remains on patrol after being damaged by depth charges north of the Bonins.

CENTRAL PACIFIC: Seventh Air Force B-24 Liberators from Eniwetok Atoll conduct a night raid on Truk and Ponape Island. B-25 Mitchells from Makin Island bomb Nauru Island.

BOUGAINVILLE: Thirteenth Air Force sends 32 P-39 Airacobras and six P-38 Lightnings to attack logistics sites and Japanese positions.

NEW BRITAIN: Thirteenth Air Force sends 24 B-25 Mitchells to bomb logistics sites.

ADMIRALTIES: Thirteenth Air Task Force B-24 Liberators staging from the Admiralties bomb Truk.

NEW GUINEA: At Sarmi, Lieutenant General Walter Krueger orders Brigadier General Edwin D. Patrick to halt his attack on Lone Tree Hill and reform at Toem to be prepared to depart and support the planned attack on Noemfoor Island.

At Biak, the Japanese bring reinforcements by ship. During this operation, Task Force 74, commanded by Australian rear admiral Victor Alexander Charles Crutchley, with one heavy cruiser, three light cruisers, and 10 destroyers, engages five Japanese destroyers.

Fifth Air Force B-25 Mitchells, P-38 Lightnings, B-24 Liberators, and A-20 Havocs encounter Japanese fighters over Manokwari during a bombing run against shipping off the town. P-40s attack logistics sites near Sarmi. A-20 Havocs attack targets near Wewak.

Off Manokwari, Fifth Air Force B-25 Mitchells escorted by P-38 Lightnings attack a Japanese convoy of seven destroyers, each towing a large landing barge bringing reinforcements to Biak. Aircrews report two destroyers damaged and three barges sunk. As the convoy approaches Biak, the Allied combined surface forces, TF 74 and TF 75, attack the destroyers. The Japanese ships retreat.

U.S. submarine *Harder* evacuates coast-watchers from the northeast coast of Borneo.

June 9

CBI: American engineers, now a provisional regiment, are joined with the Marauders to form a brigade. The engineers attack Myitkyina and advance toward the town.

Tenth Air Force B-25 Mitchells attack Japanese positions around Imphal, while others fly ammunition resupply missions. A-36 Intruder (Apache) fighter-bombers, P-51 Mustangs, and P-40s attack Japanese positions near Myitkyina and Mogaung.

In China, Fourteenth Air Force B-25 Mitchells, P-40s, and P-51 Mustangs attack river shipping, Japanese troops, and the airfields at Hankow and Wuchang.

ETO: The VII Corps has reached most of its D-day objectives. The 4th Infantry Division is advancing toward Cherbourg but is halted before Varreville. The 82nd Airborne Division has established a bridgehead over the Merderet River beyond Ste-Mère Eglise and links with groups of paratroopers dropped west of the bridges. An eight-mile gap still exists between VII and V Corps on the beachhead. General Bradley orders VII Corps to capture Carentan and V Corps to capture Isigny in order to close the gap. V Corps attacks with three divisions. The 1st Infantry Division makes contact with British forces along the Bayeux Road; elements of the 29th Infantry Division capture Isigny.

V Corps is reinforced by the 2nd Infantry Division and advances south and west to link up with VII Corps. The 1st Infantry Division moves east to link with the British advancing from Gold beach. The 29th Infantry Division captures Isigny.

A U.S. destroyer damaged by a mine the previous day is sunk by German aircraft off the Normandy beaches. German fast torpedo boats attack a convoy in the English Channel, torpedoing and sinking one LST and damaging another. Fire from a German shore battery hits a U.S. freighter as it disembarks troops on the beach.

Private First Class Charles N. DeGlopper is a paratrooper in C Company, 325th Glider Infantry Regiment, 82nd Airborne Division, advancing to secure a bridgehead across the Merderet River at La Fiere, France. After clearing a few enemy positions, the platoon finds itself cut off and takes cover in a shallow roadside ditch. Private DeGlopper volunteers to hold the enemy off as the platoon attempts a withdrawal through a hedgerow. Picking up his Browning automatic rifle (BAR), DeGlopper emerges from the ditch and stands in the road to fire on German troops. Although immediately wounded, DeGlopper continues to fire. Hit again, he falls to his knees and continues to fire on the enemy until killed. His courageous act of sacrifice saves his fellow paratroopers and will win Private First Class DeGlopper the nation's highest award for valor, the Medal of Honor.

MEDITERRANEAN: Fifteenth Air Force sends nearly 500 B-17s and B-24 Liberators to attack production facilities and depots in Munich, Germany. B-24s also bomb oil storage sites at Porto Marghera in Italy. The bombers are escorted by P-47 Thunderbolts, P-38 Lightnings, and P-51 Mustangs. Fighter pilots report more than 30 confirmed kills.

ITALY: The 1st Armored Division and the 85th and 88th Infantry Divisions capture Viterbo. The IV Corps relieves VI Corps. The IV Corps is commanded by Major General Willis D. Crittenberger; it is made up of the 34th and 36th Infantry Divisions and the 1st Armored Division. Two other divisions, the 88th and 91st Infantry Divisions, will be added later in the campaign. The VI Corps is to prepare for Operation Anvil, the invasion of southern France. The 85th and 88th Infantry Divisions are replaced by the 6th South African Armored Division.

Twelfth Air Force B-25 Mitchells and B-26 Marauders attack road bridges north of Rome. A-20 Havocs, P-47 Thunderbolts, and P-40s attack convoys, bridges, rail lines, and roads.

SOUTHWEST PACIFIC AREA: U.S. submarine *Harder* torpedoes and sinks a Japanese destroyer south of Davao Island.

PACIFIC: U.S. submarine *Swordfish* attacks a Japanese convoy east of the Bonins, sinking a destroyer.

CENTRAL PACIFIC: Seventh Air Force B-24 Liberators conduct a night raid on Truk from Eniwetok Atoll.

Fifth Air Force B-24s bomb the airfield on Peleliu in the Palau Islands.

BOUGAINVILLE: Thirteenth Air Force P-39 Airacobras bomb Buka, logistics sites near the Buka airfield, and attack Japanese positions at Arigua Plantation.

NEW BRITAIN: Thirteenth Air Force sends 32 B-25 Mitchells, 20 P-39 Airacobras, and five P-38 Lightnings to attack logistics bases and gun positions around Talili Bay.

NEW IRELAND: U.S. destroyers bombard Japanese repair facilities on New Ireland.

NEW GUINEA: At Biak, engineers land near the Mokmer airfield to begin reconstruction. Elements of the 162nd and 186th Infantry Regiments assault the ridge overlooking the airfield. This begins a three-day battle in intense tropical heat and on nearly impassible ridges of coral.

Fifth Air Force A-20 Havocs bomb shipping in Manokwari harbor. B-24 Liberators, B-25 Mitchells, A-20 Havocs, and P-39 Airacobras, along with Royal Australian Air Force (RAAF) aircraft, bomb targets in Wewak area. The P-47s of the 39th Fighter Squadron, 35th Fighter Group, redeploy to Nadzab. Fifth Air Force A-20 Havocs attack Japanese shipping off Manokwari, sinking six cargo vessels.

Thirteenth Air Task Force B-24s bomb Alet airfield and other targets on Truk.

June 10

CBI: Tenth Air Force B-24 Liberators fly ammunition resupply missions to British forces at Imphal. A-36 Intruder (Apache) fighter-bombers, P-51 Mustangs, and P-40s attack Japanese positions near Myitkyina and Mogaung.

In China, Fourteenth Air Force redeploys P-51s of the 75th Fighter Squadron, 23rd Fighter Group, from Hengyang to Lingling.

ETO: In England, three members of the JCS, General Marshall, General Arnold, and Admiral King, meet informally with the British Chiefs of Staff to discuss future operations in the Mediterranean and the Pacific.

Four Allied corps are ashore at Normandy. The 4th Infantry Division of VII Corps begins to move north against Montebourg on its way to capture Cherbourg. The 90th Infantry Division passes through the 82nd Airborne Division to enlarge the bridgehead over the Merderet River and advances west to cut the Cotentin Peninsula.

Elements of the 101st Airborne Division make contact with the 29th Infantry Division near Carentan, making the initial link between V and VII Corps on the American portion of the Normandy battlefront and forming a cohesive and continuous front line. German forces retreat to the Elle River as V Corps advances. The 2nd Infantry Division of V Corps clears Trévières and Forêt de Cerisy.

Eighth Air Force sends 507 B-17s and 495 B-24 Liberators, escorted by 364 P-51 Mustangs and 405 P-38 Lightnings flying sweep and escort, to attack lines of communication and airfields outside of the invasion area. Cloud cover prevents many bombers from hitting their primary targets. One bomber is lost and 67 are damaged. Aircrew losses are six killed, four wounded, and 10 missing. Fighter pilots report five confirmed kills in the air and two probables, as well as one probable kill on the ground. Seven fighters are lost. The pilots are reported as missing.

Over the beachhead, 506 P-47 Thunderbolts and 213 P-51s fly fighter-bomber missions. The fighter pilots report eight confirmed kills in the air and one on the ground. A total of 17 aircraft are lost and three are damaged. One pilot is reported killed and the others are missing.

During the night 11 B-17s drop leaflets on Norway and France.

Ninth Air Force sends over 500 B-26 Marauders and A-20 Havocs against German assembly areas, bridges, artillery positions, and marshaling yards.

A German shore battery sinks a U.S. destroyer off Normandy. A freighter unloading on Utah beach is damaged by a bomb.

MEDITERRANEAN: Fifteenth Air Force sends 46 P-38 Lightnings all armed with a 1,000-pound bomb and escorted by 48 P-38s to conduct dive-bombing attacks on the oil refinery at Ploeşti, Romania. A total of 22 P-38s are lost and pilots report 20 German fighters shot down.

ITALY: Fifteenth Air Force sends over 500 B-17s and B-24 Liberators against marshaling yards, oil storage facilities, and an oil refinery.

Twelfth Air Force B-25 Mitchells and B-26 Marauders attack road bridges north of Rome. A-20 Havocs, P-47 Thunderbolts, and P-40s attack convoys, bridges, rail lines, and roads.

German aircraft attack U.S. ships off Anzio. A minesweeper, an LST, an LCI, and a cargo ship are damaged.

CENTRAL PACIFIC: Seventh Air Force B-24 Liberators from Eniwetok Atoll conduct a night raid on Truk and Ponape Island. B-25 Mitchells from Makin Island bomb Nauru Island.

Navy PB4Y Privateers cover the movement of Vice Admiral Marc A. Mitscher's Task Force to the Marianas to provide early warning and to intercept and destroy any Japanese aircraft. Sightings of the PB4Y Privateers are commonplace for the Japanese and will not arouse suspicion of a major American fleet movement, which would be the case if other aircraft were suddenly sighted in the area.

Destroyer escort *Bangust* sinks Japanese submarine *RO-42* northeast of Kwajalein.

BOUGAINVILLE: Thirteenth Air Force P-39 Airacobras and navy aircraft attack logistics sites on Buka Island and trucks near Tsirogei on Bougainville.

NEW BRITAIN: Thirteenth Air Force P-38 Lightnings use skip-bombing to hit supply tunnels at Keravia Bay. B-25 Mitchells attack antiaircraft positions, while P-39 Airacobras support navy SBD Dauntless dive-bombers in attacking other antiaircraft positions.

NEW IRELAND: Destroyer USS *Taylor* sinks Japanese submarine *RO-111* north of New Ireland.

NEW GUINEA: The Japanese assemble a task force consisting of two battleships, three heavy cruisers, two light cruisers, and seven destroyers to escort transports with over 800 soldiers to reinforce Biak. As the 41st Infantry Division continues to make little progress, Lieutenant General Krueger notifies Lieutenant General Robert L. Eichelberger of I Corps to be prepared to take control of the battle.

Fifth Air Force B-25 Mitchells, A-20 Havocs, and Royal Australian Air Force (RAAF) aircraft attack targets at Wewak. Fifth Air Force B-25 Mitchells bomb Japanese shipping off Manokwari, sinking one vessel.

The headquarters of the 312th Bombardment Group (Light) and the 387th Bombardment Squadron (Light) redeploy to Hollandia. The 389th Bombardment Squadron (Light) redeploys to Nadzab. Both squadrons are equipped with A-20 Havocs.

June 11

CBI: In Burma, Tenth Air Force sends 30 B-25 Mitchells to fly ammunition resupply missions to the Imphal area in support of British forces. A-36 Intruder (Apache) fighter-bombers, P-51 Mustangs, and P-40s attack targets at Myitkyina and Mogaung.

In China, Fourteenth Air Force P-40s, P-51 Mustangs, and P-38 Lightnings attack Japanese garrisons and river traffic. Aircrews on three B-25 Mitchells report sinking a cargo ship in the South China Sea.

ATLANTIC: Navy TBM Avengers and FM-2 Wildcat fighters from escort carrier USS *Croatan* and its destroyer escorts sink German submarine *U-490* in the North Atlantic west of the Azores.

ETO: Eighth Air Force sends 471 B-17s and 584 B-24 Liberators to attack airfield targets in France, escorted by 87 P-47 Thunderbolts and 144 P-51 Mustangs. Over 400 bombers abort the mission or fail to bomb due to clouds and limited Pathfinder support. Three bombers are lost and 26 bombers are damaged. Aircrew casualties are one killed, three wounded, and 24 missing. Over the beachhead 143 P-38 Lightnings support ground operations. Fighter pilots report two confirmed kills. Seventy-seven P-38 Lightnings, 195 P-47 Thunderbolts, and 268 P-51 Mustangs

The battleship USS *Nevada,* damaged at Pearl Harbor and refitted, fires her 14-inch and five-inch guns at German positions on the Normandy beachhead, June 6, 1944.

fly fighter-bomber missions against gun emplacements, rail and road traffic, and other communication targets in France. Fighter pilots report three confirmed kills and two probables. Eight aircraft are lost and seven of the eight pilots are reported missing.

During the night five B-17s drop leaflets on France and the Netherlands.

Ninth Air Force sends 129 B-26 Marauders and A-20 Havocs to attack rail and road bridges, rail lines, oil tanks, and artillery.

The battleships *Nevada, Texas,* and *Arkansas* provide naval gunfire support to ground forces 10 miles inland at Carentan.

German fast torpedo boats attack Allied shipping near Normandy, sinking an LST and damaging another. A U.S. destroyer is damaged. German aircraft sink an LCI.

Lieutenant Colonel Robert G. Cole commands the 3rd Battalion, 502nd Parachute Infantry Regiment, 101st Airborne Division. As the paratroopers approach the bridges that lead to Carentan, his unit comes under rifle, machine-gun, mortar, and artillery fire from strongpoints 150 yards to its front. Unable to move forward or backward and suffering casualties, Cole decides to take decisive action. He orders a bayonet charge on the enemy positions. He is the first to stand up and, carrying a pistol, he moves forward heedless of the fire directed at him. He picks up an

M-1 rifle with a bayonet and leads his men forward, capturing the strongpoint and securing the bridgehead across the Douve River. For his extraordinary act of courage and decisive leadership in the face of a determined enemy, Lieutenant Colonel Cole will receive the Medal of Honor.

MEDITERRANEAN: From the Soviet Ukraine 126 B-17s and 60 P-51 Mustangs from Fifteenth Air Force supporting Frantic fly back to Italy. En route, 121 B-17s bomb the Focsani airfield in Romania. One B-l7 is lost.

Fifteenth Air Force sends over 500 B-17s and B-24 Liberators against a marshaling yard in Yugoslavia and oil production and storage facilities in Constanta and Giurpiu in Romania. Fighter pilots and aircrews report over 60 confirmed kills.

ITALY: The Fifth Army occupies a position from Viterbo to Tusconia and north to Tarquinia. The IV Corps occupies a 30-mile front. The IV Corps relieves VI Corps and takes operational control of the 36th Infantry Division. The 36th Infantry Division is reinforced with tanks and the newly arrived 361st RCT of the 91st Infantry Division.

Twelfth Air Force A-20 Havocs, P-47 Thunderbolts, and P-40s attack convoys, bridges, and roads.

SOUTHWEST PACIFIC AREA: U.S. submarine *Redfin* torpedoes and sinks a Japanese tanker west of Davao.

PACIFIC: U.S. submarine *Barb* torpedoes and sinks two Japanese merchant fishing vessels in the Sea of Okhotsk.

CENTRAL PACIFIC: Operation Forager. The air and naval bombardment of Saipan in the Mariana Islands begins. Admiral Raymond A. Spruance is overall commander. Admiral Kelly Turner is the amphibious task force commander. Lieutenant General Holland M. Smith, commanding the V Amphibious Corps of two marine divisions and one army division, is the ground force commander. Major General Thomas E. Watson commands the 2nd Marine Division; Major General Harry Schmidt commands the 4th Marine Division; Major General Ralph C. Smith commands the 27th Infantry Division. The ground forces involved in the invasion of Saipan number over 71,000 men.

Task Force 58 sends F4F Hellcats, accompanied by TBF Avengers and SB2C Helldiver dive-bombers, to conduct attacks on airfields in the Marianas. These attacks are a complete surprise, allowing the Americans to gain air superiority. F4F Hellcats on combat air patrol intercept and shoot down Japanese aircraft venturing near TF-58's carriers.

Seventh Air Force B-24 Liberators from Eniwetok Atoll make a night bombing raid on Truk. B-25 Mitchells from Makin Island bomb Ponape Island.

BOUGAINVILLE: Thirteenth Air Force P-39 Airacobras attack Japanese troop positions and antiaircraft guns.

NEW BRITAIN: Thirteenth Air Force sends B-25 Mitchells, P-38 Lightnings, and P-39 Airacobras to support navy SBD dive-bombers attacking antiaircraft positions near Rapopo.

NEW GUINEA: Fifth Air Force B-25 Mitchells, A-20 Havocs, and P-47 Thunderbolts attack targets along the coast between Wewak and Hansa Bay.

Thirteenth Air Task Force B-24 Liberators bomb Dublon Island at Truk and the airfield on Peleliu Island.

A naval base is established at Biak Island.

June 12

ETO: On this day, the Allied beachhead is secured, approximately 2,500 prisoners have been captured, and 16 additional Allied divisions have landed. This translates into a total of 326,547 men, 54,186 vehicles, and 104,428 tons of supplies.

In the VII Corps area, Carentan is captured by Task Force F, composed of the 501st Parachute Infantry Regiment and the 327th Glider Infantry Regiment.

The V corps attacks with the 1st Infantry Division to capture Caumont. The 29th Infantry Division attacks toward St-Lô, the town that occupies a key road intersection that is the only way out of the *bocage* and marshes that hold the American advance to a costly crawl. The *bocage* is a maze of man-made hedgerows on dirt embankments that are often 12 to 14 feet high. Each one has been made into a fortress by German troops and allows a small number of soldiers to create an extensive and formidable defense-in-depth. The sunken roads and trails into the *bocage* have been turned into death traps. The Americans must fight exhausting battles for each and every field. Casualties in the V Corps infantry divisions are high, a total of 5,846 since D-day (1,225 of those are killed in action). The casualties among American divisions will be so high that an infantry unit's entire strength will be replaced about every 90 days.

Carentan is captured by elements of the 101st Airborne Division. German counterattacks fail to dislodge the Americans. In the VII Corps area, the 82nd Airborne and 9th Infantry Divisions advance toward the town of St-Sauveur-le-Victome to cut the base of the Carentan Peninsula. The 4th and 90th Infantry Divisions move north toward Cherbourg.

In the V Corps area, the 1st Infantry Division attacks toward Caumont in support of the British XXX Corps attack and captures the town.

Eighth Air Force sends 769 B-17s and 673 B-24 Liberators against 16 airfields and six railroad bridges in northwest France, escorted by 234 P-38 Lightnings, 80 P-47 Thunderbolts, and 201 P-51 Mustangs. Aircrews report one confirmed kill and one probable. Eight bombers are lost and 243 are damaged. Casualties reported are seven killed, 14 wounded, and 58 missing. Fighter pilots report 20 confirmed kills in the air and one on the ground. Seven aircraft are lost and one is damaged. Six pilots are reported missing.

A separate attack by 93 P-38 Lightnings and 183 P-47 Thunderbolts is conducted against railroad bridges. Pilots report five confirmed kills in the air and one on the ground. Nine fighters are lost and two are damaged. The nine pilots are reported missing.

During the night seven B-17s drop leaflets on France and Belgium. A total of 16 B-24 Liberators fly in support of Carpetbagger operations.

Ninth Air Force sends 509 B-26 Marauders and A-20 Havocs to attack marshaling yards, road and rail junctions, bridges, artillery positions, and troop assembly areas. The bombers are escorted by 45 P-38 Lightnings and 152 P-51 Mustangs of the Eighth Air Force.

Admiral King, General Marshall, and General Arnold visit the Normandy beachhead.

ITALY: The 141st Infantry Regiment of the 36th Infantry Division receives engineers, artillery, the 91st Reconnaissance Squadron, and a battalion of infantry from the 361st Infantry Regiment of the 91st Infantry Division, forming Task Force Ramey, named after its commander, Brigadier General Rufus S. Ramey. Task Force Ramey is ordered to capture Orbetello.

Twelfth Air Force B-25 Mitchells and B-26 Marauders attack bridges, rail lines, and roads.

CENTRAL PACIFIC: Navy F4F Hellcats, accompanied by TBF Avengers and SB2C Helldiver dive-bombers from the 15 fast carriers and escort carriers of Vice Admiral Marc A. Mitscher TF 58, attack airfields and coast defenses on Saipan, Tinian, Guam, Rota, and Pagan Islands in preparation for the landings on Saipan. Carrier aircraft attack a Japanese convoy northwest of Saipan, sinking seven transports, three cargo ships, and several other vessels. A number of minesweepers and auxiliary submarine chasers are damaged.

Destroyer USS *Melvin* sinks Japanese submarine *RO-36* east of Saipan.

Seventh Air Force B-24 Liberators from Eniwetok Atoll attack Truk during the night and follow up with a daylight bombing raid.

BOUGAINVILLE: Thirteenth Air Force sends 20 B-25 Mitchells to attack Malapau village. P-39 Airacobras attack the airfield on Buka Island and attack targets near Komai.

NEW BRITAIN: Thirteenth Air Force B-24 Liberators bomb the runways at Tobera and Rapopo. P-39 Airacobras and 10 P-38 Lightnings support navy aircraft in attacks on logistics depots.

NEW GUINEA: Major General Franklin C. Siebert, commander of the 6th Infantry Division, takes command at Wakde-Sarmi with orders to seize Lone Tree Hill.

Fifth Air Force P-47 Thunderbolts flying cover over the beachhead at Biak engage Japanese fighters. A-20 Havocs bomb troop concentrations and communications between Wewak and Hansa Bay.

Thirteenth Air Task Force B-24 Liberators bomb Truk Atoll and the airfield on Peleliu Island.

June 13

CBI: The American engineer attack on Myitkyina is stopped by a Japanese counterattack, isolating two companies.

In China, Fourteenth Air Force sends 18 B-25 Mitchells and 56 P-51 Mustangs to attack the marshaling yard at Wuchang. B-25 Mitchells and P-51s attack river shipping, troop assembly areas, and airfields in the Tungting Lake region. Changsha, Hankow, Hanyang, and Wuchang are major communication, transport, and logistics areas for the Japanese forces, connecting road, rail, and river traffic in south-central China.

ETO: A German counterattack to prevent V and VII Corps from linking together fails as Combat Command A of the 2nd Armored Division and elements of the 101st Airborne Division defeat the attack.

Eighth Air Force sends 251 B-17s and 408 B-24 Liberators, escorted by 12 P-38 Lightnings, 47 P-47 Thunderbolts, and 174 P-51 Mustangs, against airfields in France. Two bombers are lost and 32 are damaged. Aircrew losses are one killed and 19 missing.

Fighter pilots report four confirmed kills. One fighter is lost and the pilot is reported as missing. The continuous Allied air attacks have destroyed nearly all of the German fuel and ammunition stocks in the battle area. The German Fifteenth Army is still inactive at Pas-de-Calais, as the high command remains convinced that the Normandy landings are a diversion and the main attack is yet to come.

In separate attacks, 97 P-38 Lightnings and 199 P-47s report two confirmed kills and three U.S. aircraft lost and one damaged. The three pilots are reported missing.

During the night eight B-17s drop leaflets on France. Six B-24 Liberators fly in support of Carpetbagger operations in France.

Ninth Air Force sends 397 B-26 Marauders and A-20 Havocs against transportation targets, marshaling yards, and fuel storage sites. The bombers are escorted by 12 P-38 Lightnings and 35 P-47 Thunderbolts from Eighth Air Force.

The first V-1 rocket is launched from Pas-de-Calais against London, initiating a campaign in which over 2,400 V-1s will be launched against England during this month alone. The V-1 is about 17 feet long and carries a 1,875-pound warhead. It is powered by a pulse jet engine and guided by a gyroscope on automatic pilot; it is called a "buzz bomb" for the rapid, sputtering noise the engine makes. The V-1 is intended to change the course of the war by raining destruction on English cities. Although not especially effective, the cumulative impact on the people of London, the main target of the V-1 attacks, worries British leaders. The launch sites of the V-weapons have been priority targets for the British RAF since August 17, 1943, and for the U.S. Eighth Air Force since August 27.

The Germans will launch about 10,000 of these flying bombs at England between June 1944 and March of 1945. Another 10,000 will be launched at targets within Europe during the same period. Only about 3,500 actually hit England. Nearly 4,000 are intercepted and destroyed before reaching their targets and the others never complete the flight. The bombs that do hit cause a total of nearly 24,000 casualties.

MEDITERRANEAN: Fifteenth Air Force sends over 500 B-17s and B-24 Liberators against the aircraft component plants and marshaling yards near Munich, Germany. Aircrews and fighter pilots report more than 30 enemy aircraft shot down. Ten U.S. aircraft are lost and several others are reported missing.

ITALY: Twelfth Air Force B-25 Mitchells and B-26 Marauders attack rail and road traffic and bridges. A-20 Havocs, P-47 Thunderbolts, and P-40s attack convoys, bridges, and roads.

SOUTHWEST PACIFIC AREA: U.S. submarine *Flier* torpedoes and damages a Japanese merchant tanker west of Luzon.

PACIFIC: Cruisers and destroyers of Naval Task Force 94 (Rear Admiral Ernest G. Small) bombard Japanese position on Matsuwa Island in the Kuriles.

U.S. submarine *Barb* torpedoes and sinks a Japanese transport in the Sea of Okhotsk, and escapes a counterattack from a destroyer.

CENTRAL PACIFIC, SAIPAN: Vice Admiral Raymond A. Spruance commands the Fifth Fleet. Vice Admiral Richmond Kelly Turner commands the Joint Expeditionary Force and is responsible for the amphibious landings on Saipan, Tinian, and Guam. Turner also commands the Northern Attack Force responsible for operations at Saipan and Tinian. Rear Admiral Richard L. Conolly commands the Southern Attack Force responsible for operations at Guam. Vice Admiral Marc A. Mitscher's fast carrier task force and Vice Admiral Charles A. Lockwood's submarine force, Pacific Fleet, support the landings. Lieutenant General Holland M. Smith, as V Amphibious Corps commander, controls the ground forces. Smith also will command ground forces on Saipan. Major General Harry Schmidt will command forces on Tinian and Major General Roy S. Geiger will command ground forces on Guam. The ground units consist of three marine divisions (the 2nd, 3rd, and 4th) and two army divisions (27th and 77th Infantry), a separate marine brigade and the army's XXIV Corps Artillery. Lieutenant General Robert C. Richardson commands the army element.

Crewmen of the submarine USS *Barb* display their battle flag, showing Japanese shipping sunk. *(National Archives and Records Administration)*

Carrier aircraft from Task Force 58 continue to attack targets on Saipan. An aircraft transport and a convoy of five cargo vessels are sunk during the air strikes. Vice Admiral Willis A. Lee's TG 58.7 conducts a heavy bombardment of Japanese positions on Saipan and Tinian. Commander William I. Martin is shot down and parachutes into the sea off one of the intended landing beaches on Saipan. After being recovered from the water, he reports that the Japanese have carefully placed markers offshore to guide artillery spotters targeting the incoming American assault waves.

The appearance of Nimitz's naval task force off Saipan leads the Japanese navy to move away from New Guinea and speed northward to seek the climactic naval battle both sides have eagerly sought and planned for decades.

Seventh Air Force B-24 Liberators from Eniwetok Atoll conduct a night raid on Truk and Ponape Island.

NEW BRITAIN: B-25 Mitchells and B-24 Liberators bomb the airfield and antiaircraft positions at Tobera.

NEW GUINEA: U.S. submarine *Narwhal* shells oil tanks at Ceram Island.

Japanese aircraft hit U.S. destroyer *Kalk* off Biak.

June 14

ALEUTIANS: Eleventh Air Force sends four B-24 Liberators on a photoreconnaissance mission over the Kurile Islands. About 20 Japanese fighters intercept the bombers.

CBI: Fourteenth Air Force sends 43 P-40s to attack river shipping and troops near Tungting Lake, Changsha, and Linyang.

U.S. combat air strength in-theater reaches the highest level of the war.

ETO: VII Corps commanded by Major General J. Lawton Collins attacks west toward St-Sauveur-le-Victome with the 9th Infantry Division and the 82nd Airborne Division. The XIX Corps is operational under the command of Major General Charles H. Corlett.

Eighth Air Force sends 853 B-17s and 672 B-24 Liberators against airfields in France, Belgium, and the Netherlands. An oil refinery in Emmerich, Germany, is hit by 61 B-24s. The bombers are escorted by 103 P-47 Thunderbolts. A total of 14 bombers are lost and 605 are damaged. Aircrew casualties are 16 killed, 16 wounded, and 102 missing. Fighter pilots report five probable kills.

Other strikes by 176 P-47 Thunderbolts and 242 P-38 Lightnings attack a German Luftwaffe headquarters at Chantilly, France, and tank columns moving toward the beachhead. Over the beachhead, 200 P-38s and nearly 400 P-47s and P-51 Mustangs fly cover and conduct sweeps in front of the bombers.

During the night three B-17s drop leaflets in France. A total of 20 B-24 Liberators fly in support of Carpetbagger operations.

Ninth Air Force sends over 500 B-26 Marauders and A-20 Havocs to attack road and rail targets, including bridges, marshaling yards, gun positions, and strongpoints. P-47s and P-51s attack troops and vehicle movements around the Cherbourg Peninsula.

German submarine *U-621* torpedoes and sinks an LST off the Normandy beaches.

MEDITERRANEAN: Fifteenth Air Force sends nearly 700 B-17s and B-24 Liberators to attack oil production facilities in Czechoslovakia and Hungary. P-38 Lightnings, P-47 Thunderbolts, and P-51 Mustangs escort the bombers.

ITALY: The 142nd Infantry Regiment of the 36th Infantry Division encounters German forces at Magliano, captures the town, and is replaced by the 361st Infantry Regiment. The 143rd Infantry Regiment moves up the coastal road toward Grosseto.

Twelfth Air Force B-25 Mitchells and B-26 Marauders attack rail and road traffic, ports, and bridges. A-20 Havocs, P-47 Thunderbolts, and P-40s attack bridges and roads.

Staff Sergeant Homer L. Wise of L Company, 142nd Infantry Regiment, 36th Infantry Division, acts to support his platoon's attack at Magliano. After first risking his life to rescue a wounded soldier, Staff Sergeant Wise advances to kill three enemy soldiers with his Thompson submachine gun. Taking a Browning automatic rifle he advances in front of his platoon, destroying a German machine gun with his fire. As enemy fire comes from the flank, Wise approaches a tank and, fully exposed to enemy fire, employs the turret-mounted machine gun, disrupting the enemy and allowing the battalion to capture its objective. For his heroic actions beyond the call of duty, Staff Sergeant Wise will receive the Medal of Honor.

SOUTHWEST PACIFIC AREA: SWPA headquarters instructs Lieutenant General Krueger's Alamo Force to prepare plans for the capture of Noemfoor Island. The island has three airfields and controls the approaches to western New Guinea. More importantly, MacArthur is frustrated that his timetable has been upset by the delay in capturing the airfields at Biak. Unsure when those airfields will be available, he orders an attack to capture other airfields.

U.S. submarine *Rasher* attacks a Japanese convoy in the Celebes Sea, sinking a cargo ship.

PACIFIC: U.S. submarine *Golet* is sunk off northern Honshu, Japan.

CENTRAL PACIFIC: Rear Admiral Jesse B. Oldendorf's TG 52.17 and Rear Admiral Walden L. Ainsworth's TG 52.18 conduct bombardments of Japanese positions on Saipan and Tinian. Fire from a shore battery on Saipan damages the battleship USS *California.* The battleship USS *Tennessee,* heavy cruiser USS *Indianapolis,* a light cruiser, and two destroyers are damaged by enemy fire off Tinian. Destroyer USS *Wadleigh* provides close support for the withdrawal of an underwater demolition team (UDT) after completing a beach reconnaissance mission.

BOUGAINVILLE: Thirteenth Air Force P-39 Airacobras attack targets along the eastern coast of the island from Bonis to Kieta.

NEW BRITAIN: Thirteenth Air Force B-25 Mitchells, P-38 Lightnings, P-39 Airacobras, and U.S. Navy aircraft bomb logistics depots at Wunapope, Ralum, and Keravia Bay.

NEW GUINEA: At Sarmi, the 20th RCT of the 6th Infantry Division replaces the 158th RCT on the Tirfoam River.

At Biak, the 162nd and 186th Infantry Regiments of the 41st Infantry Division attempt a flank attack to drive the Japanese off the ridge overlooking Mokmer airfield. They encounter a position called the West Caves, a major strongpoint and the key to the Japanese defense. A Japanese counterattack with tanks and infantry drives the Americans from the position.

Fifth Air Force B-25 Mitchells, A-20 Havocs, and P-39 Airacobras attack the Wewak area and B-24 Liberators bomb Kamiri airfield on Noemfoor Island.

June 15

CBI: Tenth Air Force sends 30 B-25 Mitchells to fly ammunition resupply missions to British forces at Imphal. A-36 Intruder (Apache) fighter-bombers, P-51 Mustangs, and P-40s attack Mogaung and Myitkyina.

In China, Fourteenth Air Force sends 24 B-24 Liberators to bomb warehouses at Canton. Aircrews report heavy damage to the target.

Twentieth Air Force sends 47 B-29 Superfortresses from Chengtu, China, to bomb the Imperial Iron and Steel Works at Yawata, Japan. This is the first B-29 strike on the Japanese homeland. One B-29 is lost when Japanese fighters catch up with the bomber as it lands with engine trouble at Neihsiang airfield in China.

ATLANTIC: Navy TBF Avengers and FM-2 Wildcats from escort carrier USS *Solomons* sink German submarine *U-860* in the South Atlantic.

ETO: By this day (D+9) 500,000 Allied soldiers have landed on the Normandy beaches. In the VII Corps area, the 82nd Airborne and the 9th Infantry Division attack west of the Meredet River to prevent German forces from threatening the beachhead.

The VIII Corps becomes operational under the command of Major General Troy Middleton. The 101st and 82nd Airborne Divisions and the 90th Infantry Division make up the corps.

Eighth Air Force sends 747 B-17s and 614 B-24 Liberators, escorted by 96 P-38 Lightnings, 202 P-47 Thunderbolts, and 211 P-51 Mustangs, against airfields, V-weapon sites, railroad bridges, and marshaling yards in France and aircraft production facilities and an oil refinery in Germany. Two bombers are lost and 268 are damaged. Aircrew casualties are seven wounded and 18 missing. Fighter pilots report five confirmed kills. Three fighters are lost and the pilots are missing.

P-47s bomb Etaples, France, and one P-47 is lost; P-38 Lightnings fly a fighter sweep in front of the bomber forces.

Ninth Air Force sends over 500 B-26 Marauders and A-20 Havocs to attack fuel and ammunition storage areas, road and rail lines and an armored division headquarters near the Douve River. More than 1,400 P-47s and P-51s fly armed reconnaissance over the Cherbourg Peninsula.

ITALY: The 145th Infantry Regiment of the 36th Infantry Division captures Grosseto after the Germans abandon the town.

Twelfth Air Force B-25 Mitchells and B-26 Marauders attack rail and road traffic and bridges. A-20 Havocs, P-47 Thunderbolts, and P-40s attack convoys, bridges, and roads.

SOUTHWEST PACIFIC AREA: General MacArthur issues Reno V, a revision of earlier plans focused on offensive operations against the Japanese on New Guinea. Reno V lays out the details for an invasion of Mindanao for October 25 and an assault on Leyte in November. With airbases established on these two islands, American forces would have sufficient air cover to attack Luzon and other islands in the Philippines in preparation for an invasion of Formosa. MacArthur believes any operations against Formosa will require the capture of Luzon and the support of the Pacific Fleet. For his part, Admiral Nimitz supports the Leyte invasion, but continues to have doubts on the utility of landing on Luzon.

To support anticipated future operations against the Philippines, the Far Eastern Air Force (FEAF) is formed, combining the Fifth and Thirteenth Air Forces. General George C. Kenney is designated as FEAF commander, and FEAF headquarters is established in Brisbane, Australia. Lieutenant General Ennis C. Whitehead takes command of the Fifth Air Force with headquarters at Nadzab, New Guinea. Thirteenth Air Force headquarters moves from Guadalcanal to Los Negros Island, incorporating the Thirteenth Air Task Force headquarters already operating on the island. Major General St. Clair Streett is designated as the commander of Thirteenth Air Force. The position of Commander Air Solomons (COMAIRSOLS) is redesignated as Commander Air North Solomons (COMAIRNORSOLS). The B-25 Mitchells and fighters, together with other COMAIRSOLS aircraft, will continue to attack targets supporting the neutralization of Rabaul and limiting Japanese actions on Bougainville and Buka islands.

PACIFIC: Carrier-based aircraft from Task Group 58.1 (Rear Admiral Joseph J. Clark) and Task Group 58.4 (Rear Admiral William K. Harrill) attack Japanese positions on Iwo Jima, Chichi Jima, and Haha Jima.

U.S. destroyers sink a crippled Japanese transport damaged by carrier aircraft north of the Bonin Islands. U.S. submarine *Swordfish* attacks a Japanese convoy, sinking a cargo ship north of the Bonin Islands.

CENTRAL PACIFIC, SAIPAN: A false amphibious landing at Tanapag harbor to lure the Japanese away from the actual landing sites on Saipan is unsuccessful. Along with marine amtracs, marines are landed by the army's 708th, 773rd, and 715th Amphibian Tractor Battalions. During the actual landings, the 6th and 8th Marines of the 2nd Marine Division land too far north of the intended beachhead, creating a gap between them and the 23rd and 25th Marines of the 4th Marine Division. Despite a heavy bombardment, the Japanese are well prepared and drop artillery and mortar fire on the marines as they consolidate on the beachhead, causing many casualties. At Afetan Point, the 8th Marines run into strong Japanese resistance, while the 25th Marines begin advancing inland toward Mount Fina Susu. At Agingan Point, elements of the 25th Marines repel a Japanese counterattack. That night the 6th Marines face a Japanese counterattack of nearly 2,000 men supported by tanks. Navy ships fire starshells to illuminate the battlefield while the marines fight a desperate battle to hold their positions. A total of 24 tanks are destroyed. Privates First Class Herbert Dodge and Charlie Merritt, a bazooka team operating on their own, kill seven tanks. They will each be awarded the Navy Cross for gallantry.

Task Force 52, commanded by Vice Admiral Richmond K. Turner, lands marines on Saipan supported by naval gunfire and carrier-based aircraft. Battleship *Tennessee* is damaged by enemy fire.

Task Force 58 TBF Avengers and F4F Hellcat aircraft sink an auxiliary submarine chaser off Rota Island in the Marianas.

NEW BRITAIN: Thirteenth Air Force B-25 Mitchells, P-38 Lightnings, P-39 Airacobras, and P-40s attack Tobera airfield.

NEW GUINEA: At Biak, Lieutenant General Eichelberger arrives with members of his I Corps staff to supervise the battle. The 41st Infantry Division commander, Major General Horace Fuller, immediately submits his resignation to Lieutenant General Krueger, stating that the Sixth Army commander has given his unit too big a mission to be accomplished in such an impossibly short timeline. Eichelberger appoints Brigadier General Jens A. Doe as the new division commander.

FEAF B-24 Liberators, B-25 Mitchells, A-20 Havocs, and P-38 Lightnings attack barges near Manokwari.

June 16

CBI: After several unsuccessful attempts to reach the isolated engineer companies at Myitkyina, survivors are able to withdraw to friendly lines on their own.

Near Lung-ling on the Burma Road, the Y Force is pushed back by a Japanese counterattack.

Tenth Air Force sends 28 A-36 Intruder (Apache) fighter-bombers, P-51 Mustangs, and P-40s against targets near Myitkyina.

ETO: The 82nd Airborne clears St-Sauveur-le-Victome and captures the bridge over the Douve River. This allows for a rapid advance by infantry west toward the coast. The 9th Infantry Division establishes a bridgehead over the Douve River.

A total of 244 V-1 rockets are launched against London.

Eighth Air Force sends 146 B-17s and 224 B-24 Liberators, escorted by 165 P-38 Lightnings, 88 P-47 Thunderbolts, and 172 P-51 Mustangs, to attack airfields and V-weapon sites in France. One bomber is lost and 72 are damaged. Aircrew casualties are five killed, five wounded, and nine missing. Fighter pilots report one confirmed kill and no friendly losses.

70 P-51s performing a sweep against stalled trains drop their external fuel tanks near the rail cars then fire on the tanks to ignite them, setting the rail cars on fire. This improvised maneuver is highly successful. Flying over the front lines, 50 P-38 Lightnings and 75 P-47s attacks German troops, tanks, vehicles, trains, and transportation targets. Three P-38s are reported lost and one is damaged.

During the night 10 B-17s drop leaflets over France.

Ninth Air Force sends over 500 P-47s and P-51s to attack rail lines, bridges, and vehicles on the Cherbourg Peninsula.

Mediterranean: Fifteenth Air Force sends nearly 600 B-17s and B-24 Liberators to attack oil refineries around Vienna, Austria, and industrial production facilities in Czechoslovakia. The bombers are intercepted by about 250 fighters, which shoot down a total of 15 aircraft. Aircrews and fighter pilots report 70 confirmed kills.

Italy: The 143rd Infantry Regiment and the 361st Infantry Regiment cross the Ombrone River east of Grosseto on a bridge erected by engineers. Task Force Ramey enters Triana. In less that a week, IV Corps has advanced 22 miles on a 20-mile front.

Twelfth Air Force B-26 Marauders and B-25 Mitchells attack rail and road bridges, viaducts, and other communication targets. A-20 Havocs bomb ammunition storage areas, while P-47 Thunderbolts and P-40s attack bridges, trucks, and rail lines across the front.

South Pacific: Major General Ralph J. Mitchell (USMC) is designated as Commander Air North Solomons (COMAIRNORSOLS).

Central Pacific: Seventh Air Force B-25 Mitchells form Makin Island bomb Ponape Island.

A task group commanded by Rear Admiral Walden L. Ainsworth with battleships, cruisers, and destroyers bombards Guam.

Two U.S. destroyers sink Japanese submarine *RO-114* west of Tinian.

A U.S. destroyer escort sinks Japanese submarine *RO-44* east of Eniwetok.

Central Pacific, Saipan: The 6th Marines advance toward Mount Tipo Pale, while the 2nd Marines move to Garapan. The 8th Marines struggle through swampy terrain, while the 25th Marines capture Agingan Point. The 165th and 105th Infantry Regiments and the 249th Field Artillery Battalion land on Saipan. The 165th Infantry Regiment is to attack south and west to seize Aslito airfield.

When Gunnery Sergeant Robert H. McCard's tank is hit and damaged by Japanese anti-tank fire and cut off from the rest of his platoon, McCard orders his crew out of the tank while he throws hand grenades to attract enemy fire. Although seriously wounded, McCard remounts his tank and uses a machine gun to engage the enemy. He dies at his position, having saved the lives of his tank crew and killed 16 Japanese soldiers. For his courage under fire and determined effort to continue the fight, Gunnery Sergeant McCard will receive the Medal of Honor.

NEW BRITAIN: FEAF B-24 Liberators bomb Vunakanau airfield at Rabaul. B-25 Mitchells, A-20 Havocs, P-39 Airacobras, and P-40s attack targets from Tobera airfield to Rabaul.

ADMIRALTIES: FEAF B-24 Liberators attack Truk Atoll and the Yap Islands in the Carolines.

NEW GUINEA: FEAF A-20 Havocs, P-39 Airacobras, and P-40s attack targets between Wewak and Hansa Bay.

U.S. submarine *Bluefish* attacks a Japanese convoy, sinking a cargo ship in the Celebes Sea. U.S. submarine *Bream* torpedoes and sinks a Japanese cargo ship and damages another off Halmahera Island.

June 17

ALEUTIANS: Eleventh Air Force supports a naval task force with 12 B-25 Mitchells flying cover for the ships after the task force bombards installations at Kurabu Cape on Paramushiru Island in the Kuriles.

CBI: The Marauders reach the Irrawaddy River north of Myitkyina to stop Japanese reinforcements from arriving.

Tenth Air Force sends 25 B-25 Mitchells to fly ammunition resupply missions to the Imphal area. Eight A-36 Intruder (Apache) fighter-bombers attack Japanese forces at Mogaung.

In China, Fourteenth Air Force B-25 Mitchells and P-51 Mustangs attack troop barges at Changsha. Changsha falls to Japanese forces.

ATLANTIC: Navy TBF Avengers and FM-2 Wildcats from escort carrier USS *Croatan* damage German submarine *U-853*.

ETO: The 9th Infantry Division of the VII Corps reaches the west coast of the Cotentin Peninsula, isolating the remnants of four German divisions.

A total of 174 B-17s and 470 B-24 Liberators attack airfields in France. The B-17s are escorted by 43 P-38 Lightnings, 39 P-47 Thunderbolts, and 90 P-51 Mustangs. Two bombers are lost and 22 are damaged. Aircrew casualties are 22 missing. A total of 470 B-24 Liberators are escorted by 209 P-47 Thunderbolts and 318 P-51s. One bomber is lost and 35 are damaged. Aircrew casualties are 10 missing. Fighter pilots report two confirmed kills in the air and three on the ground.

Nearly 100 P-38s make attacks on railroad bridges. Four P-38s are lost and the pilots are reported missing. A second attack against the same targets is done by 49 P-38s and 39 P-47s, escorted by 47 P-38s. Two additional P-38s are lost.

During the night nine B-17s drop leaflets over French towns and cities.

Ninth Air Force sends 265 B-26 Marauders to attack fuel storage areas, bridges, and rail lines. P-47s and P-51s escort the bombers and attack troop assembly areas, tanks, vehicles, bridges, and gun emplacements.

The 354th Fighter Group (353rd and 356th Fighter Squadrons), the 366th Fighter Group (389th and 391st Fighter Squadrons), and the 371st Fighter Group (405th and 406th Fighter Squadrons) redeploy from England to France. The squadrons all fly P-47s.

MEDITERRANEAN: An Allied naval task force commanded by Rear Admiral Thomas H. Troubridge (RN), including six U.S. destroyers, one destroyer escort, five minesweepers, and a number of other smaller ships and landing craft, puts French troops ashore on the island of Elba.

SOUTHWEST PACIFIC AREA: FEAF B-24 Liberators bomb Truk. MacArthur receives intercepts from Ultra indicating that the Japanese have decided to reinforce the Philippines to stop the anticipated approach of American forces. The Japanese view maintaining the Philippines as essential to the security of their home islands.

U.S. submarine *Hake* attacks a Japanese convoy, sinking a transport southeast of Davao. U.S. submarine *Flounder* attacks the same convoy later in the day and sinks a torpedo recovery ship south of Mindanao. *Flounder* is depth-charged but is not damaged and escapes.

CENTRAL PACIFIC: Seventh Air Force B-24 Liberators from Kwajalein bomb Ponape Island. B-25 Mitchells from Makin Island bomb Nauru Island.

Escort carrier USS *Fanshaw Bay* is damaged east of Saipan by Japanese aircraft. A navy PB4Y-1 Privateer from Eniwetok sinks Japanese submarine *RO-117* north of Truk.

CENTRAL PACIFIC, SAIPAN: The 165th Infantry Regiment of the 27th Infantry Division lands. The 24th and 25th Marines advance toward Aslito airfield, a major objective.

Elements of the 27th Infantry Division arrive on Saipan about June 17, 1944, wading in from offshore LSTs (landing ship tanks).

Admiral Spruance takes his carriers to meet the Japanese fleet approaching Saipan.

NEW BRITAIN: FEAF B-24 Liberators bomb Lakunai airfield. B-25 Mitchells, A-20 Havocs, P-39 Airacobras, and P-38 Lightnings attack targets between Rapopo and Tobera.

NEW GUINEA: Fifth Air Force B-25 Mitchells supported by P-38 Lightnings attack Japanese ships in Sorong harbor on the Vogelkop Peninsula, sinking three cargo ships.

June 18

CBI: The New Galahad Force cuts the Mainga Ferry Road, the main supply route for the Japanese defending Myitkyina.

Tenth Air Force A-36 Intruder (Apache) fighter-bombers, P-51 Mustangs, and P-40s attack targets near Myitkyina and Mogaung.

In China, Japanese forces capture Changsha, at the hub of the major road and rail network. Fourteenth Air Force B-25 Mitchells and P-40s bomb Yoyang. P-40s and P-51 Mustangs attack supply boats at Tungting Lake and strafe cavalry units between Siangyin and Changsha.

ETO: Engineers have cleared the beachheads at Normandy of mines and obstacles and established roads to support the movement of supplies inland. Each infantry division now in Normandy requires about 700 tons of supplies a day to sustain itself in combat.

The 9th Infantry Division captures Barneville, opening a corridor across the Cotentin Peninsula. In the VII Corps area the 4th Infantry Division attacks toward Montebourg, while the 79th and 9th Infantry Divisions attack toward Valogues.

Eighth Air Force sends 890 B-17s against oil refinery targets around Hamburg, Germany. Nearly 500 B-24 Liberators attack V-weapon sites, airfields, and marshaling yards in France. Seven B-17s are lost and 286 damaged. Four B-24s are lost and 53 damaged. Aircrew casualties are one killed, 18 wounded, and 189 missing. The missions are escorted by 198 P-38 Lightnings, 172 P-47 Thunderbolts, and 215 P-51 Mustangs. Fighter pilots report only one P-38 damaged.

Over France, 98 P-38 Lightnings and 87 P-47 Thunderbolts attack railroad bridges; 47 P-51 Mustangs conduct fighter sweeps. Three P-51s are lost and the pilots are reported missing.

A total of nine B-24 Liberators fly in support of Carpetbagger operations in France. One bomber is lost.

Ninth Air Force sends nearly 130 B-26 Marauders and A-20 Havocs against fuel storage areas, marshaling yards, and V-weapon sites. P-47s escort the bombers and attack rail lines, troop assembly areas, and vehicles on the Cherbourg Peninsula.

The 48th Fighter Group (492nd and 493rd Fighter Squadrons) redeploys from England to France and the 354th Fighter Group's 355th Fighter Squadron joins the rest of the group in France. The squadrons all fly P-47s.

SOUTHWEST PACIFIC AREA: In response to a Combined Chiefs of Staff query on the possibility of bypassing the Philippines and the Palaus to attack Formosa or attack the Japanese home island of Kyushu directly, General MacArthur declares these options as unsupportable logistically. He states the Philippines are absolutely necessary as a base of operations for either Formosa or Kyushu. In addition, he repeats his contention on that America has a moral obligation to return to the Philippines.

CENTRAL PACIFIC: Seventh Air Force B-24 Liberators staging from Eniwetok bomb Truk. B-25 Mitchells from Makin Island bomb Nauru Island.

CENTRAL PACIFIC, SAIPAN: The 2nd Battalion of the 165th Infantry Regiment occupies Aslito airfield. The 27th Infantry Division becomes a separate command under Major General Ralph C. Smith.

The 105th Infantry Regiment joins the 165th Infantry Regiment, but has no equipment due to cargo mishandling. Aslito airfield is captured. The 23rd Marines struggle against Japanese defenses near Susupe and suffer heavy casualties. The 8th Marines begin an attack to capture Hill 240. The 24th and 25th Marines reach the east coast of the island on Magicienne Bay and begin the difficult and costly task of blasting Japanese defenders from defensive positions within caves. In the first three days of the attack on the island, the marines have suffered about 5,000 casualties and have not reached the central mountains where the main Japanese defenses are located.

Battleship USS *California* is damaged by friendly fire. Shore battery fire hits a destroyer. Two oilers are damaged by air attacks.

BOUGAINVILLE: FEAF P-39 Airacobras and P-38 Lightnings conduct sweeps over the coastal areas of the island.

NEW BRITAIN: FEAF B-24 Liberators, B-25 Mitchells, P-39 Airacobras, P-38 Lightnings, and P-40s conduct a heavy raid on Rabaul, dropping more than 18 tons of bombs.

NEW GUINEA: At Biak, the 34th Infantry Regiment of the 24th Infantry Division arrives to reinforce the 41st Infantry Division.

FEAF B-25 Mitchells, A-20 Havocs, P-38 Lightnings, P-40s, and P-47 Thunderbolts attack Japanese logistics bases and positions along the coast near Wewak.

June 19

ALEUTIANS: Eleventh Air Force sends two B-24 Liberators to fly an armed photoreconnaissance mission over Paramushiru Island. The bombers then bomb the Suribachi area.

CBI: In Burma, Tenth Air Force sends 30 B-25 Mitchells to fly ammunition resupply missions to Imphal. A-36 Intruder (Apache) fighter-bombers, P-51 Mustangs, and P-40s attack Myitkyina and Mogaung.

In China, Fourteenth Air Force B-25 Mitchells supported by nearly 150 P-40s and P-51 Mustangs attack shipping targets around Tungting Lake. P-40s attack trucks and buildings near the Salween River.

ETO: A storm in the English Channel blows up and lasts for three days. With winds blowing between 25 and 40 miles per hour and waves six-to-eight feet high, the storm is so strong that nearly 1,300 small craft are thrown upon the beaches. The gale wrecks Omaha beach, 300 ships, and the Mulberry dock. As a result, the beach's capacity to offload supplies is reduced by 40 percent. C-47 cargo planes are pressed to deliver supplies of ammunition to Bradley's First Army and VII Corps.

Major General Collins reorganizes units of VII Corps and advances north with the 4th, 79th, and 9th Infantry Divisions, capturing Montebourg in a surprise dawn attack. The 4th Infantry Division clears Montebourg, opening the main road to Cherbourg.

Eighth Air Force sends 464 B-17s to attack airfields in France escorted by 88 P-38 Lightnings and 261 P-51 Mustangs. Seven bombers are lost and 13 damaged. Aircrew casualties are three wounded and 59 missing. Ten fighters are lost and the pilots are reported as missing.

391 B-17s and 312 B-24 Liberators are sent against 35 V-weapon sites in the Pas-de-Calais area, escorted by 196 P-38s, 122 P-47s, and 48 P-51s. One B-24 is lost and 88 bombers are damaged. Aircrew casualties are two wounded and 10 missing. One fighter is damaged.

Ninth Air Force establishes the first operational U.S. airfield in France at Cardonville. Nearly 200 P-47s conduct armed reconnaissance and dive-bombing attacks on six V-weapon sites.

SOUTHWEST PACIFIC AREA: FEAF B-24 Liberators bomb Truk.

CENTRAL PACIFIC: Battle of the Philippine Sea. The Japanese deploy the First Mobile Fleet, commanded by Vice Admiral Jisaburo Ozawa, into three groups to draw the American fleet into a position where both land-based and carrier-based aircraft can converge to destroy the American carriers in a decisive battle. The Japanese fleet is divided into three groups. Vice Admiral Takeo Kurita commands the main battle fleet of four battleships and three light carriers, along with cruisers and destroyers. Vice Admiral Ozawa commands a group of three fleet carriers, supported by cruisers and destroyers. A third group is placed in reserve, consisting of two fleet carriers, one light carrier, a battleship, and cruisers. Admiral Raymond A. Spruance's ships of the Fifth Fleet, consisting of seven fast battleships, 21 cruisers, 69 destroyers, and Mitscher's Task Force 58 with one carrier and 956 aircraft have already been warned of the Japanese approach by U.S. submarines.

Japanese carrier aircraft attack, damaging the battleships USS *South Dakota* and USS *Indiana,* but the Japanese plan has already fallen apart. In the Mariana Islands there are no land-based aircraft left in any condition to assist Vice Admiral Ozawa in overwhelming the Americans. As the Japanese send wave after wave of aircraft to attack Admiral Mitscher's carriers, American fighters rise to meet them and eliminate them with little trouble. At the end of this day pilots and gun crews report 385 of 545 Japanese planes destroyed. One Japanese carrier and two oilers are sunk. Seventeen other Japanese aircraft are destroyed on Guam. U.S. losses are 26 aircraft and 64 crewmen.

In actuality, 330 out of 430 Japanese planes are shot down. Navy pilots call it "The Great Marianas Turkey Shoot."

U.S. submarine *Albacore* torpedoes and sinks the Japanese carrier *Taiho* north of Yap. U.S. submarine *Cavalla* torpedoes and sinks the Japanese carrier *Shokaku* a few miles farther north. Both submarines are heavily depth-charged, but escape unhurt.

Aircraft from escort carrier USS *Suwannee* sink Japanese submarine *I-184* south of Guam.

A Japanese aircraft is shot down in the "Marianas Turkey Shoot."

Seventh Air Force B-24 Liberators staging from Eniwetok bomb Truk. B-24s from Kwajalein and B-25 Mitchells from Makin Island bomb Ponape Island.

CENTRAL PACIFIC, SAIPAN: The 2nd and 4th Marine Divisions consolidate and begin a sweeping movement northward to establish a solid line oriented toward Mount Tapotchau, the dominant terrain feature on the island. The 27th Infantry Division moves to corps reserve and the 2nd Battalion 105th Infantry Regiment is to contain Japanese troops trapped at Nafutan Point on the southern tip of the island. As Lieutenant General Holland Smith reorients the marine divisions toward the north and east, the 105th and 165th Infantry Regiments of the 27th Infantry Division conduct low-level operations to clear the Nafutan Peninsula.

NEW GUINEA: At Sarmi, the 1st Infantry Regiment of the 6th Infantry Division crosses the Tor River in support of the 20th RCT, halted by enemy fire before Lone Tree Hill.

At Biak, the 186th Infantry captures the ridge overlooking Mokmer airfield.

FEAF A-20 Havocs, P-38 Lightnings, P-40s, and P-47 Thunderbolts attack targets along the coast near Wewak. A-20 Havocs bomb airfields at Manokwari on Noemfoor Island.

Fifth Air Force A-20 Havocs attack Manokwari, sinking two Japanese cargo vessels.

June 20

CBI: Vice President Henry Wallace arrives in Chungking, China, as President Roosevelt's personal emissary to assess the situation in China. General Stilwell is in

Burma and unable to meet with Wallace. Chiang Kai-shek and General Chennault, however, are available for meetings and are more than willing to paint the gloomiest possible picture of events. They also press for Stilwell's removal in the interest of preserving Allied unity.

In Burma, Tenth Air Force sends 13 B-25 Mitchells to fly ammunition resupply missions to Imphal. A-36 Intruder (Apache) fighter-bombers and P-40s attack Japanese positions at Myitkyina.

In China, Fourteenth Air Force attacks river shipping and logistics sites along the Yangtze River and at Tungting Lake area with over 100 B-25 Mitchells, P-40s, and P-51 Mustangs. Along the Salween River, B-25s bomb Lungling and P-40s attack Japanese positions.

ETO: The Germans are pushed back to the defenses around Cherbourg, as Major General Collins orders VII Corps (4th, 79th, and 9th Infantry Divisions) to attack toward the city.

Eighth Air Force sends 146 B-24 Liberators against V-weapon sites in the Pas-de-Calais area escorted by 44 P-47 Thunderbolts. Of the 126 that hit the targets, one bomber is lost and 84 are damaged. Aircrew casualties are four killed, eight wounded, and 24 missing. Fighter pilots report three confirmed kills. One P-47 is lost and the pilot is reported as missing.

A total of 341 B-17s and 191 B-24 Liberators are sent against targets in northern Germany. B-17 aircrews report two confirmed kills. Seven bombers are lost and 208 are damaged. Aircrew casualties are four killed, 17 wounded, and 69 missing. The B-24s are escorted by 98 P-38 Lightnings, 86 P-47 Thunderbolts, 38 P-51 Mustangs, and 81 Ninth Air Force P-51 Mustangs. Fighter pilots report 10 confirmed kills in the air and eight on the ground. Three aircraft are lost and two of the pilots are reported missing. Another attack by 512 B-17s against oil refineries in Hamburg, Germany, escorted by 96 P-38 Lightnings and 48 P-47 Thunderbolts, results in seven B-17s lost and 349 damaged. Aircrews report one killed, 13 wounded, and 63 missing. Fighter pilots report no losses.

More than 350 B-24 Liberators attack targets of opportunity in Germany escorted by 50 P-38 Lightnings and 221 P-51 Mustangs. Aircrews report 10 confirmed kills. A total of 34 B-24s are lost and 205 damaged. Aircrew casualties are three killed, six wounded, and 343 missing. Fighter pilots report 28 confirmed kills in the air and five on the ground. Three P-38s are lost and the pilots are reported missing. Over 400 B-17s and B-24s attack ten V-weapon sites in the Pas-de-Calais area, escorted by 72 P-47s and 40 P-51s. One B-24 is lost and 96 are damaged. Ten crewmen are reported missing.

During the night five B-17s drop leaflets over France. A total of 25 B-24 Liberators fly in support of Carpetbagger operations in France.

Ninth Air Force sends over 300 B-26 Marauders and A-20 Havocs to bomb nine V-weapon sites and a coastal defense battery. Over 1,000 P-47s and P-51s attack vehicles, lines of communication, and German troop locations on the Cherbourg Peninsula.

The P-47s of the 390th Fighter Squadron join the other two squadrons of the 366th Fighter Group in France.

ITALY: The Germans establish a defensive line across the rolling hills of the peninsula, called the Trasimeno Line. It protects the ports of Leghorn, Livorno, and Ancona. The IV Corps begins an attack to break the line by advancing up Route 1.

Twelfth Air Force B-25s and B-26 Marauders attack rail lines, while P-47 Thunderbolts and P-40s attack road and rail bridges.

SOUTHWEST PACIFIC AREA: FEAF B-24 Liberators bomb Woleai Atoll, in the Carolines, and Truk.

U.S. submarine *Hake* attacks a Japanese convoy off the south coast of Mindanao, sinking a cargo ship. U.S. submarines *Narwhal* and *Nautilus* land supplies and evacuate personnel from Negros and Panay Islands.

CENTRAL PACIFIC: The Battle of the Philippine Sea. Task Force 58 sends 216 F4F Hellcats, SB2C Helldivers, and TBF Avengers from fleet carriers USS *Hornet, Yorktown, Bunker Hill,* and *Lexington* and from light carriers (carriers built over the incomplete hulls of light cruisers by order of President Roosevelt in 1942) USS *Belleau Wood, Monterey,* and *San Jacinto* to attack the Japanese fleet when it is discovered late in the afternoon. TBF Avengers from USS *Belleau Wood* sink the Japanese carrier *Hiyo* northwest of Yap. The carrier *Zuikaku,* and two small carriers, a battleship, a heavy cruiser, and two destroyers are damaged along with tankers and an oiler. Because the U.S. aircraft were launched at maximum range, Vice Admiral Mitscher orders the ships of the task force to turn on lights to guide the aircraft through the dark night, despite the deadly threat posed by Japanese submarines.

The Battle of the Philippine Sea leaves the Japanese Fleet with only 35 carrier aircraft left. The last of Japan's skilled pilots have been lost and three fleet carriers have been sunk. Another 50 Japanese aircraft on Guam are destroyed, bringing Japanese aircraft losses to a total of 476. American losses are 130 aircraft and 76 pilots and crewmen. Ozawa's fleet retreats toward Okinawa, leaving the Mariana Islands and the sea routes to the Philippines undefended.

Seventh Air Force B-25 Mitchells from Makin Island bomb Ponape Island. B-24 Liberators from Kwajalein bomb Truk.

CENTRAL PACIFIC, SAIPAN: Aslito airfield is serviceable and can support tactical aircraft to support the marine attack northward.

A U.S. destroyer is damaged by a shore battery off Saipan.

NEW BRITAIN: FEAF P-38 Lightnings and some Royal New Zealand Air Force (RNZAF) aircraft attack antiaircraft positions near Rapopo.

NEW GUINEA: At Biak, the 34th RCT of the 24th Infantry Division captures Sorido and Borokoe airfields. The 163rd Infantry captures Hill 320, while the 186th and 162nd Infantry begin an assault on the West Caves, which quickly reveal themselves to be a vast underground complex of tunnels completely invulnerable to air or naval bombardment.

FEAF A-20 Havocs, P-39 Airacobras, and Royal Australian Air Force (RAAF) aircraft attack targets along the coast near Wewak. B-24 Liberators bomb Kamiri airfield on Noemfoor Island.

June 21

CBI: In Burma, Tenth Air Force sends 34 B-25 Mitchells to fly ammunition resupply missions to Imphal. A-36 Intruder (Apache) fighter-bombers and P-40s attack Japanese positions at Myitkyina and Mogaung.

ETO: The XIX and V Corps are ordered to hold positions because of a lack of ammunition availability due to storm damage at the beachhead.

Eighth Air Force sends 163 B-17s in the first Frantic shuttle-bombing mission from Britain. The bombers are escorted by 72 P-38 Lightnings, 38 P-47 Thunderbolts, and 57 P-51 Mustangs. En route to the USSR, 123 of the bombers hit the primary target, the synthetic oil plant at Ruhland, Germany. The 57 P-51s are replaced over Poland by 65 other P-51s. Nearly 30 German fighters attack the bomber formation. Fighter pilots report six enemy aircraft shot down and one P-51 lost. Of the 163 bombers sent on the mission, 144 land at Poltava and Mirgorod. One B-17 is lost. The P-51s land at Piryatin. Total casualties are one killed, five wounded, and 10 missing. During the night 75 German bombers attack the Poltava airfield. The Germans destroy 47 B-17s and heavily damage the rest as well as destroying fuel and ammunition.

A total of 496 B-17s fly on a mission over Berlin escorted by 99 P-38 Lightnings, 95 P-47 Thunderbolts, and 73 P-51 Mustangs. Aircrews report 16 confirmed kills and 20 probables. Sixteen B-17s are lost and 216 damaged. Aircrew casualties are one killed, 10 wounded, and 148 missing. Fighter pilots report four confirmed kills. One fighter is lost and the pilot is reported as missing. Over 360 B-24 Liberators attack targets around Berlin escorted by 148 P-38 Lightnings, 147 P-47 Thunderbolts, and 116 P-51 Mustangs. Aircrews report 13 confirmed kills and three probables. Nineteen B-24s are lost and 152 damaged. Aircrew casualties are 21 killed, 20 wounded, and 182 missing. Fighter pilots report 13 confirmed kills. One fighter is lost and one damaged. One pilot is reported as missing. Another 207 B-17s attack targets in and around Berlin escorted by 108 P-38 Lightnings, 81 P-47 Thunderbolts, and 91 P-51 Mustangs. Nine bombers are lost. Three fighters are lost and one damaged. The pilots are reported missing. Thirty-one B-24s escorted by 99 P-47 Thunderbolts bomb V-weapon sites in France. One B-24 is lost.

During the night five B-17s drop leaflets in France. A total of 21 B-24 Liberators fly in support of Carpetbagger operations in France. Ninth Air Force sends over 250 B-26 Marauders and A-20 Havocs against 13 V-weapon sites in the Pas-de-Calais area of France. P-47 Thunderbolts and P-51 Mustangs bomb bridges and attack lines of communication around Paris.

U.S. destroyer *Davis* is damaged by a mine off the Normandy beaches.

ITALY: Allied forces are presently 110 miles north of Rome. On the front line, Task Force Ramey is relieved by the 1st Armored Division.

Twelfth Air Force B-25 Mitchells and B-26 Marauders attack ships at Leghorn, rail and road traffic, and bridges. A-20 Havocs, P-47 Thunderbolts, and P-40s attack ammunition storage areas, bridges, and roads near the Gothic Line.

SOUTHWEST PACIFIC AREA: U.S. submarine *Bluefish* torpedoes and sinks a Japanese cargo ship near the southern end of the Makassar Strait.

CENTRAL PACIFIC: Seventh Air Force B-24 Liberators from Kwajalein bomb Truk.

U.S. destroyer *Newcomb* and a high-speed minesweeper sink Japanese submarine *I-185,* north of Saipan. TBF Avengers and F4F Wildcats from escort carrier USS *White Plains* sink a Japanese cargo ship off Saipan.

NEW GUINEA: At Biak, Mokmer airfield is open to Allied aircraft.

The Alamo Scouts conduct a reconnaissance of possible landing sites at Noemfoor Island. Lieutenant General Krueger designates the 158th RCT as the Noemfoor Task Force, commanded by Brigadier General Edwin D. Patrick. Over 13,500 men will be involved in the landing. D-day is set for July 2. Krueger designates the 503rd Parachute Infantry Regiment and the 34th Infantry Regiment as the task force reserve. Rear Admiral William M. Fechteler commands Task Force 77, with three cruisers, 23 destroyers, and three rocket-firing LCIs.

FEAF P-39 Airacobras and Royal Australian Air Force (RAAF) aircraft attack targets near Wewak. B-24 Liberators bomb Kamiri airfield on Noemfoor Island and attack shipping at both the Palau Islands and at Truk.

June 22

CBI: Tenth Air Force sends six B-24 Liberators to fly fuel to Kamaing and 40 B-25 Mitchells to supply British forces at Imphal, India, with ammunition. A-36 Intruder (Apache) fighter-bombers, P-51 Mustangs, and P-40s attack Japanese positions at Mogaung and Myitkyina.

In China, Fourteenth Air Force P-40 pilots report damaging a troopship on Tungting Lake. B-24 Liberators bomb dock facilities at Bakli harbor on Hainan Island. Aircrews report one cargo ship sunk.

ATLANTIC: President Roosevelt signs the GI Bill of Rights, authorizing a broad package of benefits for World War II veterans. The bill is intended to smooth demobilization for 16 million discharged American veterans. Veterans will be able to finance their education or purchase a home. It will become among the most important and far-reaching pieces of social legislation ever passed in America and will contribute to the postwar transformation of America.

ETO: The 9th and 79th Infantry Divisions of the VII Corps attack Cherbourg, the heavily defended port that is essential to the success of the Normandy operation. Over 1,000 bombers and fighters also attack the Cherbourg defenses.

As American forces struggle in the *bocage*, Sergeant Curtis G. Cullin, Jr., of the 102nd Cavalry Regiment is credited with discovering a way to turn the tide of battle. He welds scrap steel onto the front of a tank to form a fork-like contraption that allows the tank to bulldoze its way through the hedges, opening a path for the infantry into the open fields behind the hedgerows where they can drive the Germans from their positions.

The Frantic mission B-17s at Mirgorod and P-51 Mustangs at Piryatin are moved east temporarily and will thus avoid a German bomber attack on the two airfields during the night. The bombers and fighters will fly to Italy.

Eighth Air Force sends 108 B-17s and 194 B-24 Liberators escorted by 165 P-47 Thunderbolts and 97 P-51 Mustangs against 12 V-weapon sites near Pas-de-Calais area. One B-17 is lost and 123 bombers are damaged. Aircrew casualties are 10 missing. One P-51 is lost and two P-47s are damaged. One pilot is killed and the other reported missing. Another 216 B-17s are sent to attack the V-weapon site at Nucourt. Only 70 hit the primary target; the rest bomb airfields, bridges, rail lines, and marshaling yards. Four bombers are lost and 188 damaged. Aircrews report one confirmed kill. Aircrew casualties are two killed and 30 missing. One hundred

An infantry squad of the 60th Infantry Regiment, 5th Infantry Division moves into a Belgian town on September 9, 1944, behind the cover of an M4 Sherman tank. The last man in the squad carries a Browning Automatic Rifle; the others are armed with the M-1 Garand rifle. Note that the Sherman tank has a steel rake mounted on its front, used to break through the hedgerows of the Normandy countryside.

and thirteen B-24 Liberators are sent to attack the oil storage facilities near Paris, escorted by P-51 Mustangs. Two bombers are lost and 40 damaged. Aircrew casualties are one killed, two wounded, and 23 missing. Three fighters are lost and the pilots are reported missing.

Another 319 B-17s escorted by 108 P-47 Thunderbolts attack a marshaling yard, an oil depot, airfields, and rail lines in France and Belgium. Three B-17s are lost and 82 are damaged. Aircrew casualties are two killed, five wounded, and 29 missing. Fighter pilots report one confirmed kill. In addition, 149 B-24s escorted by over 200 P-38 Lightnings and P-47s bomb airfields in France. Aircrews report one confirmed kill. A total of 67 B-24 Liberators are damaged. Aircrew losses are one killed and three missing. Fighter pilots report one confirmed kill. Five P-38s are lost and one damaged. The pilots are reported as missing.

During the night nine B-17s drop leaflets over cities and towns in France and the Netherlands. A total of 10 B-24 Liberators fly in support of Carpetbagger operations over France.

Ninth Air Force sends nearly 600 B-26 Marauders and A-20 Havocs supported by more than 1,200 fighters against Cherbourg, supporting the VII Corps attack. B-26s and A-20s also support First Army to reduce several strongpoints. B-26s also attack marshaling yards, fuel supply depots, and a German headquarters. A total of 25 P-47 Thunderbolts are lost.

ITALY: Fifteenth Air Force sends over 600 B-17s and B-24 Liberators against marshaling yards and bridges.

Twelfth Air Force B-25 Mitchells and B-26 Marauders attack rail and road traffic and bridges. A-20 Havocs, P-47 Thunderbolts, and P-40s attack bridges and roads.

SOUTHWEST PACIFIC AREA: U.S. submarine *Flier* torpedoes and sinks a Japanese cargo ship west of Mindoro. U.S. submarine *Narwhal* torpedoes and damages a Japanese tanker in the Sulu Sea.

PACIFIC: U.S. submarine *Batfish* torpedoes and sinks a Japanese cargo ship off Honshu, Japan.

CENTRAL PACIFIC: Seventh Air Force B-24 Liberators from Kwajalein, staging through Eniwetok Atoll, bomb Truk.

CENTRAL PACIFIC, SAIPAN: The 2nd and 4th Marine Divisions begin the assault to seize Mount Tapotchau. The rugged terrain is expertly defended with positions that use every contour of the ground to best advantage. The marines are supported by 18 battalions of artillery, but are able to advance only 1,000 yards. Lieutenant General Holland Smith, bothered by what he believes to be a very slow and cautious movement into Naftuan Peninsula, withdraws the 165th Infantry Regiment and a battalion of the 106th Infantry Regiment of the 27th Infantry Division to support the marine attack.

P-47 Thunderbolts of the 19th Fighter Squadron land at Aslito airfield.

Battleship USS *Maryland* is damaged by an aerial torpedo off Saipan.

NEW GUINEA: The 20th RCT attacks Lone Tree Hill supported by artillery fire and airstrikes from FEAF P-47 Thunderbolts. Advancing up the hill, two battalions are trapped on the slopes and begin a fight for survival after becoming surrounded by Japanese infantry.

FEAF B-25 Mitchells, A-20 Havocs, and P-47 Thunderbolts attack airfields on Noemfoor Island and targets on Manokwari. B-24 Liberators bomb the Yap Islands, Sorol Atoll in the Carolines, and Woleai Atoll.

June 23

CBI: General Joseph Stilwell, concerned about low morale and lack of progress against the Japanese at Myitkyina, replaces Brigadier General Haydon L. Boatner with Brigadier General Theodore F. Wessels as commander of the Myitkyina Task Force.

Tenth Air Force sends 12 B-24 Liberators to fly gasoline to Kamaing and 29 B-25 Mitchells to fly ammunition resupply missions to Imphal, India. A-36 Intruder (Apache) fighter-bombers, P-51 Mustangs, and P-40s attack Japanese positions at Mogaung and Myitkyina.

In China, Fourteenth Air Force sends 20 B-24s to bomb the Hankow docks. Over the Tungting Lake area B-25s, P-40s, and P-51s attack river shipping, bomb a runway at Hengyang, and attack Japanese cavalry troops.

ETO: The 9th Infantry Division captures the German strongpoint at Mont Roc as the battle for Cherbourg continues.

General Eisenhower, SHAEF, responds to the Combined Chiefs of Staff on future operations in the Mediterranean. Eisenhower argues for Anvil, the invasion of southern France in support of Overlord, to go as planned. Overlord is the priority effort for the Allies. A diversion of forces away from France will deny the Allies a major port, which is essential for future operations against Germany, and will prevent a concentration of forces for the decisive battle in the Ruhr.

Eighth Air Force sends 134 B-17s and 106 B-24 Liberators escorted by 161 P-51 Mustangs to attack V-weapon sites. Six of the 12 primary targets are hit. Five bombers are damaged. Fighter pilots report destroying three locomotives, 100 rail cars, and 14 vehicles. One fighter is lost and the pilot is reported missing.

In a later attack, 109 B-17s and 219 B-24 Liberators escorted by 155 P-47 Thunderbolts and 83 P-51 Mustangs attack airfields in France. Most of the B-17s abort the mission due to heavy cloud cover. One B-17 is lost and two are damaged. Aircrew losses are one wounded and 10 missing. Six B-24s are lost and 83 are damaged. Aircrew losses are one killed, three wounded, and 58 missing. Fighter pilots report destroying vehicles, locomotives, and rail cars. P-38 Lightnings fly fighter-bomber missions in the Paris area. Two P-38s are lost and the pilots are reported missing.

A total of 21 B-24s fly in support of Carpetbagger operations.

Ninth Air Force sends nearly 200 A-20 and B-26 Marauders and more than 600 fighters against V-weapon sites in France. The fighters attack road and rail traffic.

The P-47s of the 404th Fighter Squadron, 371st Fighter Group, redeploy from England to France.

MEDITERRANEAN: Fifteenth Air Force sends over 400 B-17s and B-24 Liberators to attack oil facilities and storage depots at Ploeşti and Guirgiu in Romania. The mission, involving 139 B-24 Liberators with P-51 Mustangs as escort against the Ploeşti, Romania, oil refinery, results in six bombers lost. Aircrews and pilots report 24 German aircraft shot down.

Twelfth Air Force A-20 Havocs attack ammunition storage facilities and P-47 Thunderbolts attack rail lines.

Second Lieutenant David R. Kingsley, 97th Bombardment Group, 15th Air Force, is a bombardier of a B-17 approaching Ploeşti, Romania. The bomber takes several hits from antiaircraft fire and is badly damaged, but the pilot is able to bring the B-17 over the target for Kingsley to drop bombs. Losing altitude and straggling behind the formation on the return from Ploeşti, three German fighters attack the B-17. When the tail gunner is badly wounded, Second Lieutenant Kingsley goes to his aid. A few minutes later, the ball turret gunner is wounded and Kingsley treats him as well. When the pilot gives the order for the crew to bail out, Kingsley assists the two wounded crewmen, giving one his parachute. After helping the wounded men to exit the aircraft, he remains in the disintegrating bomber until it crashes. Second Lieutenant Kingsley's heroic and unselfish act saves the life of one of his crew and will win him the Medal of Honor.

PACIFIC: The U.S. submarine *Seawolf* arrives off Peleliu to photograph prospective landing beaches.

CENTRAL PACIFIC: Seventh Air Force B-24 Liberators from Eniwetok bomb Truk. B-25 Mitchells from Engebi Island and B-24s from Kwajalein bomb Ponape Island both day and night.

Aircraft from Rear Admiral Joseph J. Clark's carrier task group (Task Group 58.1) bomb Japanese air facilities and shipping in the Marianas.

CENTRAL PACIFIC, SAIPAN: The 27th Infantry Division is assigned a two-mile front in the center of the battle line. As the 106th and 165th advance to occupy the forward lines, the regiments get entangled and it takes several hours to sort out the confusion. Once the regiments do attack, they encounter heavy Japanese defenses. The 165th makes about 700 yards; the 106th Infantry Regiment about 100 yards. The infantrymen have run into one of the strongest defensive positions on the island. Certain terrain features gain names quickly: "Hell's Pocket," "Purple Heart Ridge," and "Death Valley." By the end of the day only the 2nd Battalion of the 105th Infantry Regiment has been left to guard the Nafutan Peninsula as other battalions are brought to the battle line. The Japanese conduct counterattacks with tanks and infantry on the army positions at night. The 106th Infantry Regiment retreats from its forward position during the night when an ammunition storage site is blown up.

Seventh Air Force P-47 Thunderbolts of the 73rd Fighter Squadron, 318th Fighter Group, are launched from USS *Manila Bay* and land on Saipan Island.

During the night Japanese aircraft conduct high-altitude bombing attacks on amphibious ships off Saipan.

NEW BRITAIN: FEAF B-24 Liberators bomb Tobera airfield and B-25 Mitchells and Allied aircraft attack antiaircraft positions.

NEW GUINEA: At Biak, the main resistance in the West Caves is overwhelmed using tanks, mortars, grenades, TNT charges, and barrels of gasoline. All the airfields on Biak are opened to aircraft. Parai defile also finally is captured, but Japanese infiltrators continue to fight.

FEAF A-20 Havocs, P-39 Airacobras, P-47 Thunderbolts, and Royal Australian Air Force (RAAF) aircraft bomb Wewak. A-20 Havocs and the new A-26 Invader light bomber, intended to replace the A-20s, attack targets off Manokwari. The P-38 Lightnings of the 8th Fighter Squadron, 49th Fighter Group, redeploy from Hollandia to Biak Island.

B-24 Liberators bomb the airfields at Yap and Woleai Atoll. Other B-24s bomb Truk and Peleliu in the Palaus. The A-26 is flown with the 3rd Bombardment Group and aircrews soon determine that the aircraft has insufficient visibility for jungle operations.

June 24

ALEUTIANS: Eleventh Air Force sends three B-24 Liberators on a dawn raid against the airfield at Kurabu Cape on Paramushiru Island.

CBI: Tenth Air Force sends 12 B-24 Liberators to fly gasoline to Kamaing and 29 B-25 Mitchells to fly ammunition resupply missions to Imphal, India. A-36 Intruder (Apache) fighter-bombers, P-51 Mustangs, and P-40s attack Japanese positions at Mogaung and Myitkyina.

In China, Fourteenth Air Force P-40s and P-38 Lightnings attack Japanese cavalry troops near Hengyang.

ATLANTIC: The JCS supports Anvil (the invasion of southern France) because it focuses Allied power on the rapid defeat of Germany. Southern France would provide major ports and allow French forces to assist in liberating their own country.

Navy TBM Avengers from escort carrier USS *Bogue* sink Japanese submarine *I-52* in the Atlantic west of the Azores.

ETO: The VII Corps continues its attack on the forts guarding Cherbourg. Naval gunfire and air bombardment support tanks and infantrymen with bazookas and demolitions.

Eighth Air Force sends 340 B-17s escorted by 185 P-38 Lightnings and 85 P-47 Thunderbolts to attack oil production facilities in Germany. One bomber is lost and 105 are damaged. Aircrew losses are two wounded, and nine missing. Fighter pilots report two confirmed kills on the ground.

In another mission, 407 B-24 Liberators escorted by 45 P-38 Lightnings and 36 P-47 Thunderbolts attack airfields in France. Two bombers are lost and 81 are damaged. Aircrew losses are 20 missing. Fighter pilots report one fighter lost and the pilot missing.

V-weapon sites are the target of 148 B-17s and 227 B-24s throughout the day. Three bombers are lost and 76 bombers are damaged. Aircrew casualties are 20 missing. Another 74 B-17s are sent to attack the Saumur bridge with P-51 Mustangs flying escort. Fighter pilots report four confirmed kills on the ground. More than 200 B-17s and B-24s escorted by 71 P-47s and 50 P-51s attack targets in France. Two bombers are lost. Fighter pilots report 25 confirmed kills on the ground.

During the night five B-17s drop leaflets over France.

Ninth Air Force sends over 400 A-20 and B-26 Marauders and over 400 P-47s against fuel depots, marshaling yards, and rail bridges in France.

The P-47s of the 313th Fighter Squadron, 50th Fighter Group, redeploy from England to France.

MEDITERRANEAN: Fifteenth Air Force sends over 300 B-17s and B-24 Liberators, escorted by P-51 Mustangs, P-47 Thunderbolts, and P-38 Lightnings, to attack rail targets and oil production facilities in Romania. Aircrews report over 20 confirmed kills. Ten U.S. aircraft are lost and others are reported missing.

ITALY: Twelfth Air Force P-47 Thunderbolts attack bridges, rail lines, and German gun positions.

SOUTHWEST PACIFIC AREA: U.S. submarine *Redfin* attacks a Japanese convoy off the southern coast of Leyte, sinking a cargo ship.

PACIFIC: U.S. submarine *Grouper* attacks a Japanese convoy and sinks a cargo ship and merchant tanker south of Yokohama, Honshu, Japan.

U.S. submarine *Tang* (SS-306) attacks a Japanese convoy, sinking three cargo ships and a merchant tanker outside Nagasaki harbor, Kyushu, Japan.

Rear Admiral Joseph J. Clark and Rear Admiral Alfred E. Montgomery's carrier aircraft bomb airfields and facilities on Iwo Jima and Pagan Island in the Marianas.

CENTRAL PACIFIC, SAIPAN: The 106th and 165th Infantry Regiments again make an attack, but it is not effective. The 2nd Marine Division likewise makes little progress. The 4th Marine Division approaches the Kagman Peninsula and encounters civilians and Japanese soldiers in caves. Heat and lack of water have taken a physical toll on the Americans and slow the overall advance.

Unsatisfied with the 27th Infantry Division's lack of progress, Lieutenant General Holland M. Smith, a marine, removes Major General Ralph C. Smith, an army officer, from command and replaces him with Major General Sanderford Jarman, the army officer slated to become the occupation force commander for Saipan. Holland Smith's action creates the greatest interservice furor of the war and is so potentially dangerous to the war effort that the Joint Chiefs of Staff addresses the incident at its meeting in Washington.

P-47 Thunderbolts on Saipan strafe Japanese defensive positions and attack Japanese defenses on Tinian Island.

During the night Japanese aircraft conduct high-altitude bombing attacks on amphibious ships off Saipan.

NEW BRITAIN: FEAF B-24 Liberators, B-25 Mitchells, P-38 Lightnings, P-39 Airacobras, and P-40s supporting other Allied aircraft attack Tobera airfield and other targets.

NEW GUINEA: The 20th RCT continues its fight for survival on Lone Tree Hill. An amphibious assault with an infantry company, the 6th Reconnaissance Troop, and tanks lands at Rocky Point in an attempt to outflank the defenders on the hill. The Japanese effectively prevent any further movement off the narrow beachhead.

FEAF A-20 Havocs, P-39 Airacobras, P-47 Thunderbolts, and Royal Australian Air Force (RAAF) aircraft bomb Wewak. B-25 Mitchells and A-20 Havocs attack Japanese positions within the caves on Biak and the Kamiri airfield on Noemfoor Island.

June 25

ALEUTIANS: Eleventh Air Force sends two B-24 Liberators to bomb the airfield at Kurabu Cape, on Paramushiru Island.

CBI: Tenth Air Force sends 50 B-25 Mitchells to fly ammunition resupply missions to Imphal, India. A-36 Intruder (Apache) fighter-bombers, P-51 Mustangs, and P-40s attack Japanese positions at Mogaung and Myitkyina.

In China, the Fourteenth Air Force reports that its efforts to stall the Japanese ground offensive in the Tungling Lake area since June 17 has resulted in 1,600 Japanese casualties and 377 supply boats destroyed.

Seven B-25 Mitchells of the Chinese-American Composite Wing (CACW) bomb logistics sites near Shayang. B-25 Mitchells and P-40s bomb logistics sites and damage a bridge at Chenghsien. The P-40s of the 75th Fighter Squadron, 23rd Fighter Group, redeploy from Lingling to Kweilin.

ETO: The VII Corps attacks Cherbourg preceded by a heavy naval bombardment by three battleships, four cruisers, and 11 destroyers. The Americans fight their way into the city.

Eighth Air Force sends 263 B-17s, escorted by 46 P-38 Lightnings, 36 P-47 Thunderbolts, and 146 P-51 Mustangs, to attack airfields in France. Five bombers are lost and 115 are damaged. Aircrew losses are 10 killed, five wounded, and 45 missing. Fighter pilots report 10 confirmed kills. One P-51 is lost and the pilot is reported missing. A second mission sends 258 B-24 Liberators escorted by 68 P-47 Thunderbolts and 34 P-51 Mustangs against airfields in France. One bomber is lost and 27 are damaged. Aircrew losses are one killed and two wounded. Another 137 B-24 Liberators escorted by 102 P-38s and 44 P-47s attack airfields. One B-24 is lost and 10 air crewmen are missing. Fighter pilots report eight confirmed kills.

Airfields and bridges in France are attacked with 189 B-17s and 274 B-24 Liberators escorted by 127 P-38s, 35 P-47s, and 181 P-51s. Six bombers are lost and 126 are damaged. Aircrew losses are 11 killed, nine wounded, and 78 missing. Fighter pilots report four confirmed kills. One P-51 is lost and the pilot is reported missing.

A total of 24 B-24s fly in support of Carpetbagger operations.

Ninth Air Force sends over 400 A-20 and B-26 Marauders and over 500 P-47s against fuel storage depots, road, and rail lines in France.

The headquarters of the 50th Fighter Group and the P-47s of the 10th and 81st Fighter Squadrons redeploy from England to France.

Rear Admiral Morton L. Deyo employs gunfire from a battleship, a cruiser, and a destroyer to bombard German shore batteries and coastal defenses at Cherbourg, France. The battleship USS *Texas* and three destroyers are damaged by the gunfire.

First Lieutenant Carlos C. Ogden, commander of K Company, 314th Infantry Regiment, 79th Infantry Division, leads his unit in an attack near Fort de Roule, which guards the approaches to Cherbourg. When First Lieutenant Ogden's company is halted by German fire, Ogden takes an M-1 rifle and rifle grenades and advances toward the enemy alone. Although wounded, he continues to climb the hill and uses the rifle grenades to destroy an 88 millimeter gun position, then uses hand grenades to destroy a machine gun position. Wounded again, First Lieutenant Ogden orders his men forward to take the objective. For his exceptional display of courage and leadership, First Lieutenant Ogden will be awarded the Medal of Honor.

MEDITERRANEAN: In preparation for Anvil, Fifteenth Air Force sends over 600 B-17s and B-24 Liberators to attack marshaling yards, oil storage facilities, and industrial production facilities in southern France and the harbor at Toulon.

ITALY: The 36th Infantry Division is pulled out of the line to prepare for Anvil and is replaced by the 34th Infantry Division.

Twelfth Air Force A-20 Havocs attack ammunition storage facilities. P-40s and P-47 Thunderbolts attack rail lines and bridges.

SOUTHWEST PACIFIC AREA: U.S. submarine *Jack* attacks a Japanese convoy and sinks a merchant tanker off the northwest coast of Luzon.

CENTRAL PACIFIC: Seventh Air Force B-24 Liberators from Kwajalein bomb Truk and Wotje Atolls.

CENTRAL PACIFIC, SAIPAN: The 2nd Battalion of the 105th Infantry Regiment attacks Japanese defenses on the Nafutan Peninsula. Elements of the 8th and 29th Marines reach the heights of Mount Tapotchau. The 165th Infantry Regiment attacks along Purple Heart Ridge into the complex of caves, valleys, and sharp ridgelines. The 106th Infantry Regiment is stopped at Death Valley. Kagman Peninsula is cleared, but at a frightful cost to Japanese civilians, who either refuse to give up or are coerced to stay by Japanese soldiers.

P-47 Thunderbolts on Saipan conduct armed reconnaissance and strafing missions over Saipan and Tinian.

NEW BRITAIN: FEAF B-25 Mitchells, P-38 Lightnings, P-39 Airacobras, and P-40s with Allied aircraft attack antiaircraft positions near Wunapope and plantations at Wide Bay.

NEW GUINEA: The 20th RCT reaches the top of Lone Tree Hill; the tanks at Rocky Point are withdrawn. Although the Americans have gained one position, there are several other strongpoints that must be attacked.

FEAF A-20 Havocs, P-39 Airacobras, P-47 Thunderbolts, and Royal Australian Air Force (RAAF) aircraft bomb Wewak. P-40s and B-24 Liberators attack Kamiri airfield on Noemfoor. B-24s also bomb Yap and Sorol Atoll.

U.S. submarine *Bashaw* attacks a Japanese convoy and sinks a cargo ship northwest of Halmahera Island.

June 26

ALEUTIANS: Eleventh Air Force sends 12 B-25 Mitchells to fly air cover missions for a naval task force after it bombards installations on Paramushiru Island.

CBI: Vice President Henry Wallace sends his report to President Roosevelt from Chungking shortly before departing China. Completely convinced that General Stilwell is the problem, after hours of conversation with Generalissimo Chiang Kai-shek, he recommends that General Stilwell be recalled. He offers General Albert Wedemeyer as a possible replacement.

The Chinese Y Force attacks Tengchung.

Tenth Air Force sends over 30 B-25 Mitchells to fly ammunition resupply missions to Imphal, India. A-36 Intruder (Apache) fighter-bombers, P-51 Mustangs, and P-40s bomb Myitkyina.

In China, Fourteenth Air Force sends 14 B-24 Liberators to attack Hankow. Aircrews report heavy damage. Over the Tungting Lake area more than 180 B-25s, P-51 Mustangs, and P-40s attack river shipping and villages.

Japanese bombers and fighters attack Lingling airfield, damaging the runway and destroying a P-51.

ETO: The 79th Infantry Division captures Fort du Roule, the main stronghold defending Cherbourg. The German garrison of 10,000 men surrenders shortly thereafter. The American victory is lessened by the discovery that the harbor, so critical to the sustainment of American forces in Normandy, is completely wrecked.

Omaha beach is operating at 122 percent above its planned capacity, having landed 268,718 men, 40,191 vehicles, and 125,812 tons of supplies since D-day.

Operation Frantic B-17s leave Poltava and Mirgorod in the Ukraine, USSR, rendezvous with 55 P-51 Mustangs from Piryatin, and proceed to bomb the oil refinery and marshaling yard at Drohobycz, Poland, en route to Italy. Fifteenth Air Force P-51s meet the 71 bombers and escort them to Foggia.

Ninth Air Force loses three P-47 Thunderbolts supporting the attack on Cherbourg. Pilots report three confirmed kills.

MEDITERRANEAN: Fifteenth Air Force sends over 650 B-17s and 36 B-24 Liberators against aircraft production facilities and oil refineries near Vienna, Austria. Nearly 30 bombers and fighters are lost. Aircrews report more than 60 confirmed kills. The 36 B-24 Liberators are attacked by 80 German fighters as they approach the oil refinery. Immediately, 60 more attack as the B-24s begin their bombing run. Ten bombers are lost and aircrews report 34 confirmed kills.

PACIFIC: Cruisers and destroyers, under command of Rear Admiral Ernest G. Small, bombard Japanese positions at Kurabu Zaki, Paramushiro, Kuriles.

CENTRAL PACIFIC: Seventh Air Force B-25 Mitchells from Makin bomb Ponape and Nauru Islands.

CENTRAL PACIFIC, SAIPAN: A force of about 500 Japanese soldiers conducts a breakout from Nafutan Point, slipping past the troops of the 105th Infantry and destroying one P-47 and damaging 20 others at Aslito airfield. As the group moves northward to cross into Japanese lines, they encounter the 25th Marines and are destroyed. Major General Sanderford Jarmin relieves the commander of the 106th Infantry Regiment in an attempt to spur the unit to capture Death Valley. The attack with a new commander is unsuccessful.

P-47 Thunderbolts continue ground support missions on Saipan and attack Japanese positions on Tinian Island. P-61 Black Widow night fighters carry out patrols over Saipan.

NEW BRITAIN: FEAF B-25 Mitchells, P-38 Lightnings, P-39 Airacobras, and P-40s with Allied aircraft attack airfields and antiaircraft positions near Rabaul.

NEW GUINEA: The 1st and 63rd Infantry Regiments of the 6th Infantry Division replace the 20th RCT of the division and launch an attack on the remaining strongpoints at Lone Tree Hill: Hill 225, Mount Saksin, and Hill 265. The two infantry companies isolated on the Rocky Point beachhead finally are able to make contact with the 1st Infantry.

FEAF A-20 Havocs, P-39 Airacobras, P-47 Thunderbolts, and Royal Australian Air Force (RAAF) aircraft bomb Wewak. P-38 Lightnings, P-47 Thunderbolts A-20 Havocs, B-24 Liberators, and B-25 Mitchells attack airfields, shipping, and roads at Noemfoor and Biak Islands and Manokwari, and Japanese defensive positions near Sarmi.

The P-38s of the 9th Fighter Squadron, 49th Fighter Group, redeploy from Hollandia to Biak Island. The 419th Night Fighter Squadron, 18th Fighter Group, Thirteenth Air Force, deploys a detachment of P-61 Black Widow night fighters from its base on Guadalcanal to Nadzab.

Fifth Air Force P-38 Lightnings sink a Japanese cargo ship east of Halmahera Island.

June 27

CBI: Chinese forces and Chindits capture Mogaung, isolating Myitkyina and opening a land route for the Allies to send supplies and reinforcements to Myitkyina.

Tenth Air Force sends eight B-24 Liberators to fly gasoline to Kamaing, Burma, and 52 B-25 Mitchells fly ammunition resupply missions to Imphal, India.

Fourteenth Air Force sends 160 B-25s, P-51 Mustangs, and P-40s over the Tungting Lake area to attack Japanese troop concentrations, logistics sites, and river transportation between Changsha and Hengyang. Aircrews from four B-25s sent against shipping targets in the Formosa Strait report two cargo ships sunk.

ATLANTIC: The JCS rejects the British arguments against Anvil and rejects any further major operations in Italy.

ETO: VII Corps takes the surrender of the last German defenders at Cherbourg. The Germans have destroyed the port so thoroughly that no supplies will be able to move through until July.

Eighth Air Force sends over 250 bombers against V-weapon sites and logistics depots in France, escorted by 149 P-51 Mustangs. Five bombers are lost and 114 are damaged. Aircrew losses are two killed, seven wounded, and 51 missing. Fighter pilots report six confirmed kills during attacks on marshaling yards, bridges, rail lines, and airfields. Two fighters are lost and one is damaged. The two pilots are reported missing.

VII Fighter Command sends 644 P-38 Lightnings, P-47 Thunderbolts, and P-51 Mustangs against airfields and transportation targets. Three P-38s are lost and three are damaged. Three pilots are reported missing and one pilot is wounded. The P-47 pilots report 10 confirmed kills and the P-51 pilots report one confirmed kill.

A total of 16 B-24s fly in support of Carpetbagger operations. During the night four B-17s drop leaflets over France.

Ninth Air Force sends over 700 P-47s against rail facilities, roads, troop concentrations, and artillery positions. The P-47s of the 365th Fighter Group (386th and 387th Fighter Squadrons) redeploy from England to France.

MEDITERRANEAN: Fifteenth Air Force sends nearly 300 B-17 bombers and B-24 Liberators to bomb marshaling yards in Budapest, Hungary, and Brod, Yugoslavia, and bomb oil production facilities in Drohobycz, Poland. About 90 German fighters attack the formations. Three bombers are lost and aircrews report over 30 confirmed kills. P-51s flying a sweep over Budapest report seven confirmed kills.

ITALY: The 34th Infantry Division is stopped by German defenses at the Cecina River, an indication that the Germans have formed a new defensive line.

Twelfth Air Force A-20 Havocs attack ammunition storage facilities. P-40s and P-47 Thunderbolts attack roads, rail lines, and bridges.

SOUTHWEST PACIFIC AREA: U.S. submarine *Seahorse* attacks a Japanese convoy and sinks a merchant tanker off Formosa.

CENTRAL PACIFIC: Seventh Air Force B-24 Liberators staging through Eniwetok bomb Truk.

Aircraft from TF 58 finish off a Japanese water tanker damaged irreparably by USS submarine *Seahorse* off Guam in early April.

CENTRAL PACIFIC, SAIPAN: The 2nd Battalion of the 105th Infantry Regiment clears the last Japanese defenders from Nafutan Peninsula. The 1st Battalion of the 106th Infantry Regiment fights the Japanese for Hell's Pocket and Death Valley. The rest of the 106th Infantry and the 165th Infantry Regiment attack Purple Heart Ridge.

Japanese planes bomb Aslito airfield and Charan Kanoa.

P-47 Thunderbolts strafe Japanese defensive positions and fire rockets on suspected strongpoints on Saipan and attack Japanese positions on Tinian. P-61 Black Widow night fighters fly defensive night patrols.

NEW BRITAIN: Thirteenth Air Force B-25 Mitchells with P-39 Airacobras, P-38 Lightnings, and P-40s attack antiaircraft positions and other targets around Rabaul.

ADMIRALTIES: Thirteenth Air Force's 419th Night Fighter Squadron, 18th Fighter Group, deploys a detachment of P-61 Black Widow night fighters from Guadalcanal to Los Negros Island.

NEW GUINEA: Major General Charles P. Hall, XI Corps commander, takes command of the Aitape Task Force as part of a buildup of forces to conduct a counteroffensive against a major Japanese attack. Ultra intercepts have given the Americans advance warning of enemy plans. The 112th Cavalry RCT reinforces the 32nd Infantry Division along the Driniumor River and supports the defense of the airfield.

FEAF A-20 Havocs, P-39 Airacobras, P-47 Thunderbolts, and Royal Australian Air Force (RAAF) aircraft bomb Wewak. B-24 Liberators, B-25 Mitchells, A-20 Havocs, P-40s, and P-47s attack airfields and gun positions at Manokwari, Biak, and Noemfoor Islands. B-24s bomb the Yap Islands and Sorol Atoll in the Caroline Islands.

June 28

CBI: In China, the Japanese begin offensive operations to capture Henyang, the main city along the axis of advance toward Indochina and the key to the success of the *Ichigo* offensive. About 40 poorly equipped and trained Chinese divisions defend the city. Fourteenth Air Force B-25 Mitchells, P-51 Mustangs, and P-40s conduct attacks on Japanese headquarters, cavalry troops, and lines of communication and supply in the Hengyang area as enemy forces threaten the Fourteenth Air Force's airfield. The B-25s of the 11th Bombardment Squadron (Medium), 341st Bombardment Group (Medium), move from Kweilin to Yang Tong.

Fourteenth Air Force B-24 Liberators attack Japanese convoy off Formosa, sinking a transport.

ATLANTIC: Prime Minister Winston Churchill writes to President Roosevelt with a direct appeal to cancel Anvil, the invasion of southern France in support of Overlord, and divert the resources toward Yugoslavia and northern Italy. Churchill points out that the smaller ports in Normandy are sufficient to supply the Overlord lodgment rather than trying to resupply them from ports in southern France. Instead of southern France, Churchill offers an advance north into the Hungarian plains through the Ljubljana Gap to tie down German divisions that could be used to reinforce the German defenses at Normandy. Finally, Churchill stresses the political-strategic benefits of having Allied forces in the Balkans before the Soviets.

ETO: Eighth Air Force sends 485 B-17s and 378 B-24 Liberators escorted by 188 P-38 Lightnings, 169 P-47 Thunderbolts, and 231 P-51 Mustangs to attack marshaling yards, airfields, bridges, and oil storage facilities in France. Two bombers are lost and 225 damaged. Ten crewmen are wounded and 19 are missing. Fighter pilots report one confirmed kill and three locomotives destroyed. Two fighters are lost and two are damaged. Both pilots are reported missing.

A total of 18 B-24s fly in support of Carpetbagger operations.

Ninth Air Force sends over 200 fighters, all based in France, against bridges, marshaling yards, troop areas, gun emplacements, and ammunition storage sites in France.

The headquarters of the 365th Fighter Group deploys from England to France.
MEDITERRANEAN: The Mediterranean Commander in Chief, General Sir Henry M. Wilson, approves the concept plans for Anvil.

Fifteenth Air Force sends over 200 B-24 Liberators to bomb the marshaling yards and oil refineries at Bucharest, Romania. Another 138 B-24s attack the Karlovo airfield in Bulgaria. Fighter pilots report over 20 confirmed kills over Bucharest.
SOUTHWEST PACIFIC AREA: U.S. submarine *Pargo* attacks a Japanese convoy in Moro Gulf, sinking a cargo ship and damages a smaller vessel about 35 miles east of Zamboanga on Davao Island, Philippines.
PACIFIC: U.S. submarine *Archerfish* sinks a Japanese coast defense vessel southwest of Iwo Jima.

U.S. submarine *Sealion* torpedoes and sinks a Japanese collier in Tsushima Strait.
CENTRAL PACIFIC, SAIPAN: Major General George W. Griner takes command of the 27th Infantry Division from Major General Sanderford Jarmin. Hell's Point is captured.

Seventh Air Force P-47 Thunderbolts attack Japanese defenses on Saipan and Tinian, and P-61 Black Widow night fighters carry out defensive night patrols.
NEW GUINEA: The XI Corps under Major General Charles P. Hall is organized at Aitape. It consists of the 32nd and 43rd Infantry Divisions, along with the 112th Cavalry RCT, corps artillery, and a tank destroyer battalion. Hall is waiting for the Japanese 18th Army, which has been ordered to move west and threaten the American advance and slow down MacArthur's offensive in New Guinea. The Japanese actually have little choice—it is either attack Aitape or die in the jungle.

FEAF A-20 Havocs, P-39 Airacobras, P-47 Thunderbolts, and Royal Australian Air Force (RAAF) aircraft bomb Wewak. B-24 Liberators, B-25 Mitchells, A-20 Havocs, P-40s, and P-47s attack airfields and fuel storage facilities on Noemfoor Island. B-24s bomb the airfield and town on Yap and communications on Sorol and Woleai Atolls.

June 29

CBI: Tenth Air Force sends 16 B-24 Liberators to fly gasoline to Kamaing and 45 B-25 Mitchells to fly ammunition resupply missions to Imphal, India. A-36 Intruder (Apache) fighter-bombers, P-51 Mustangs, and P-38 Lightnings attack Japanese positions at Myitkyina and the Myitnge bridge.

Fourteenth Air Force sends B-25 Mitchells, P-40s, and P-51 Mustangs against Japanese troops and logistics targets in the Tungting Lake area and at Hengyang. Three B-24 Liberators bomb Takao docks in Formosa. P-40s attack rail lines and bridges in French Indochina.
ATLANTIC: President Roosevelt informs Prime Minister Churchill that Anvil is vital to the success of the Normandy invasion. He reminds Churchill of the agreement at Tehran that France is to be the decisive theater in 1944. An advance north in Italy, as the prime minister proposes, followed by offensive operations into Yugoslavia and Hungary would be done in difficult terrain and with limited logistics support. Anvil's advance north in support of the Normandy forces would be slow, but not

as slow as an advance through the Alps, which would contribute little or nothing to the Allied effort in France. For these reasons, Roosevelt stands by the decision that Anvil will go as planned. The president also makes it clear that no U.S. forces will be used in the Balkans and notes that there will be 21 divisions and 5,500 aircraft in the Mediterranean Theater available for offensive operations even after the Anvil forces have been removed. Roosevelt also reminds his fellow politician that the political costs of informing American voters that U.S. forces are being sent somewhere other than France would be catastrophic for him.

ETO: Eighth Air Force sends 179 B-17s to attack the synthetic oil production plant at Bohlen and an aircraft components production facility at Wittenberg. Four bombers are lost and 111 are damaged. Aircrew casualties are two killed, five wounded, and 30 missing. Another mission involves 380 B-17s that attack airfields around Leipzig. Two B-17s are lost and 77 are damaged. Aircrew casualties are two wounded and 21 missing. A separate mission sends 591 B-24 Liberators against airfields and marshaling yards. Nine B-24s are lost and 207 are damaged. Aircrew casualties are two killed, 12 wounded, and 92 missing. The missions are escorted by 203 P-38 Lightnings, 216 P-47 Thunderbolts, and 352 P-51 Mustangs of the Eighth and Ninth Air Forces. Fighter pilots report 34 confirmed kills in the air and 16 on the ground. Three P-51s are lost and the pilots are reported missing.

Ninth Air Force sends almost 200 B-26 Marauders and A-20 Havocs to bomb gun batteries, bridges, and rail lines in France. P-47 and P-38 fighters fly armed reconnaissance and attack enemy aircraft, road and rail junctions, bridges, artillery, and troop concentrations. The P-47s of the 509th and 511th Fighter Squadrons of the 405th Fighter Group redeploy from England to France.

German submarine *U-984* attacks a convoy headed for Omaha Beach, torpedoing and damaging three U.S. freighters.

ITALY: Twelfth Air Force B-25 Mitchells, B-26 Marauders, and A-20 Havocs attack rail and road traffic, ammunition storage sites, and bridges.

SOUTHWEST PACIFIC AREA: U.S. submarine *Bang* torpedoes and damages a Japanese fleet tanker and a merchant tanker west of Luzon.

U.S. submarine *Growler* torpedoes and sinks a Japanese transport in the Luzon Strait.

U.S. submarine *Flasher* attacks a Japanese convoy and sinks a cargo ship and damages an oiler southeast of Singapore.

PACIFIC: U.S. submarine *Sturgeon* attacks a Japanese convoy, sinking a cargo ship off Taira Jima.

CENTRAL PACIFIC: Seventh Air Force B-24 Liberators staging through Eniwetok bomb Truk. B-25 Mitchells from Makin Island bomb Ponape Island.

CENTRAL PACIFIC, SAIPAN: The 27th Infantry Division breaks Japanese resistance at Purple Heart Ridge and Death Valley. The 2nd Marine Division advances toward the town of Garapan. The 6th Marines captures Mount Tipo Pale. The 27th Infantry Division has suffered over 1,800 casualties since landing on Saipan. The 2nd Marine and 4th Marine Divisions have lost about 4,400 men each in 15 days of combat.

Seventh Air Force P-47 Thunderbolts from the airfield on Saipan carry out bombing and strafing missions and attack targets at Tinian.

NEW GUINEA: At Sarmi, the 158th RCT is designated as the Noemfoor Task Force. Elements of 6th Infantry Division reach Maffin airfield past Lone Tree Hill, even as the battle on Lone Tree Hill continues.

As the 34th Infantry attacks Japanese defenses north of the West Caves, Lieutenant General Eichelberger and the I Corps staff depart Biak for Hollandia. Biak, now securely in American hands, protects Hollandia and limits any Japanese movement from their base at Manokwari on the Vogelkop Peninsula in western New Guinea.

FEAF B-24 Liberators, A-20 Havocs, B-25 Mitchells, P-39 Airacobras, P-38 Lightnings, P-40s, and P-47 Thunderbolts attack Japanese positions near Aitape and on Noemfoor Island.

U.S. submarine *Darter* attacks a Japanese convoy off the northern tip of Halmahera Island and sinks a minelayer.

June 30

CBI: Air Transport Command is averaging 46,000 tons of supplies a month delivered to China over the Hump.

Tenth Air Force sends 17 B-24 Liberators to fly gasoline to Kamaing and 47 B-25 Mitchells to fly ammunition resupply missions to Imphal, India. P-38 Lightnings attack the Myitnge bridge.

In China, Fourteenth Air Force B-25 Mitchells P-47 Thunderbolts, and P-40s attack Japanese positions, troop concentrations, and road and river traffic near Tungting Lake.

A P-40 detachment of the 26th Fighter Squadron, 51st Fighter Group, operating from Kweilin returns to Kunming.

ATLANTIC: Guidance from the JCS to Admiral Nimitz maintains the intent for forces in the Pacific Ocean areas to invade Formosa (Operation Causeway), after General MacArthur's Southwest Pacific Area forces have gained control of the central and southern Philippines. The Pacific Ocean Area forces will follow the Formosa operations with operations against the Ryukyu and Bonin Islands in preparation for an assault on the Japanese home islands.

The U.S. Navy has 46,032 vessels of all types currently in active service. The navy has a current strength of 2,981,365. The Marine Corps stands at 472,582. The Coast Guard's personnel strength is 169,258.

ETO: Logisticians on the beachheads at Omaha and Utah achieve nearly impossible results during the last week of June, operating far above planning estimates. An average of 13,500 tons per day has moved across Omaha, and Utah has moved an average of 7,000 tons per day.

Eighth Air Force sends over 150 bombers escorted by more than 160 P-51 Mustangs to attack airfields in France. A total of 27 B-17s are damaged. P-38 Lightnings, P-47s, and P-51s attack bridges and marshaling yards in France. Fighter pilots report three confirmed kills and three probables in the air and one confirmed kill on the ground. One P-38 is lost and one P-47 is damaged. One pilot is reported missing; the other is reported killed.

Ninth Air Force sends over 100 A-20 and B-26 Marauders and more than 600 fighters against fuel storage areas and road junctions. The weather prevents most from making an effective attack. P-47s attack rail lines and marshaling yards.

The headquarters of the 405th Fighter Group and P-47s of the 510th Fighter Squadron redeploy from England to France.

MEDITERRANEAN: Fifteenth Air Force sends 188 B-17s and B-24 Liberators, escorted by 138 P-51 Mustangs and P-38 Lightnings, to bomb an airfield at Zagreb and at Banjaluka in Yugoslavia. The bombers also attack marshaling yards, bridges, and airfields around Budapest, Hungary.

During this month Fifteenth Air Force fighter pilots report a total of 299 confirmed kills, 30 probables, and 87 possibles in the air and 33 confirmed kills and 34 probables on the ground.

ITALY: The 1st Armored Division meets strong resistance on the Cecina River. The 135th and 133rd Infantry Regiments of the 34th Infantry Division in support of the tanks are unable to make a successful attack across the river.

Twelfth Air Force B-25 Mitchells attack the Pietrasanta railway bridge. A-20 Havocs, P-47 Thunderbolts, and P-40s attack convoys, bridges, rail lines, and roads.

SOUTHWEST PACIFIC AREA: SWPA headquarters orders Lieutenant General Krueger's Alamo Force to develop plans to seize, occupy, and defend Cape Sansapor to allow for the uninterrupted movement of Allied naval and air forces. The Vogelkop Peninsula in western New Guinea is the last Japanese stronghold on the island. Controlling Cape Sansapor would put U.S. forces between the Japanese bases of Sorong and Makwari. This achieves two objectives by isolating a large number of Japanese without having to fight them and allows SWPA forces to reach the Netherlands East Indies and the Philippines.

U.S. submarine *Jack* attacks a Japanese convoy west of Manila and sinks two cargo ships.

PACIFIC: U.S. submarine *Plaice* torpedoes and sinks a Japanese gunboat northwest of Chichi Jima.

U.S. submarine *Tang* torpedoes and sinks a Japanese cargo ship in the Yellow Sea off Korea.

CENTRAL PACIFIC, SAIPAN: The 2nd Battalion of the 165th Infantry Regiment captures the last Japanese position on Purple Heart Ridge.

NEW GUINEA: The airfield constructed on Owi Island off Biak is completed.

FEAF B-24 Liberators, A-20 Havocs, B-25 Mitchells, P-40s, and P-47 Thunderbolts attack Noemfoor Island airfields.

The A-20 Havocs of the 389th Bombardment Squadron (Light), 312th Bombardment Group (Light), redeploy from Nadzab to Hollandia.

July 1

ALEUTIANS: Eleventh Air Force sends four B-24 Liberators on a dawn raid on the Kurile Islands. The bombers use radar to bomb Shimushu Island and the Kurabu Cape airfield on Paramushiru Island, through heavy cloud cover.

CBI: General Marshall asks General Stilwell if anything can be done to improve the situation in China. Stilwell's reply is straightforward: He requests command of all Chinese forces. It will take the president to convince Chiang Kai-shek.

In Burma, Tenth Air Force P-40s fly ground support missions near Myitkyina.

In China, Fourteenth Air Force B-25 Mitchells, P-40s, and P-51 Mustangs attack river shipping at the Tungting Lake region. About 300 trucks are strafed and Heng-yang airfield is bombed.

The P-40s of the 76th Fighter Squadron, 23rd Fighter Group redeploy from Lingling to Liuchow.

The B-29 Superfortresses of Twentieth Air Force's 444th Bombardment Group (Very Heavy) and the 676th, 677th, 678th, and 679th Bombardment Squadrons (Very Heavy) redeploy from Charra to Dudhkundi, India.

ATLANTIC: Delegates from 44 countries begin meeting at Bretton Woods, New Hampshire, to deal with anticipated postwar economic disruptions. The International Monetary Fund and the International Bank for Reconstruction and Development (known today as the World Bank) will be established and ready to operate with $10 billion by December 1945. The agreement also provides for a gold exchange standard with only the United States required to convert its currency into gold at a fixed rate. Only central banks of other nations are allowed to redeem U.S. currency for gold.

ETO: The 9th Infantry Division of VII Corps clears final German resistance in the Cotentin Peninsula. U.S. forces have captured 39,000 prisoners. Only Brest remains in German hands. The Allies have landed one million men since D-day, along with 177,000 vehicles. The beachhead is about 70 miles long and 25 miles deep.

Eighth Air Force sends 245 B-24 Liberators and 78 B-17s to bomb V-weapon sites in France. Bad weather forces the recall of all but nine B-24 Liberators, which continue on to their targets. One bomber is lost and several are damaged. Aircrew casualties are one wounded and nine missing. Escorting the bombers are 124 P-51 Mustangs. Fighter pilots report five confirmed kills and one P-51 lost; the pilot is reported missing.

P-38 Lightnings, P-47 Thunderbolts, and P-51s attack rail and road targets in northern France. Pilots report three confirmed kills. One P-47 is lost and two are damaged. Two pilots are reported killed and two are missing.

A total of 18 B-24 Liberators fly in support of Carpetbagger operations over France.

Headquarters of XIX Tactical Air Command redeploys from England to France.

ITALY: In the IV Corps area, Cecina falls to the 34th Infantry Division. The Germans conduct a skilful delaying action, holding the line from Cecina to Ancona with counterattacks, then destroying the bridges as they retreat.

Twelfth Air Force B-25 Mitchells and B-26 Marauders attack docks, rail and road traffic, and bridges. A-20 Havocs, P-47 Thunderbolts, and P-40s attack gun positions, convoys, bridges, and roads.

PACIFIC: U.S. submarine *Tang* torpedoes and sinks a Japanese fleet tanker and a cargo ship off Korea.

CENTRAL PACIFIC: Seventh Air Force B-24 Liberators, staging through Eniwetok Atoll, bomb Truk during the night and follow up with another daylight raid. B-25 Mitchells from Makin Island bomb Ponape Island.

U.S. submarine *Batfish* torpedoes and sinks two Japanese guardboats northwest of the Marianas.

NEW GUINEA: At Owi Island an epidemic of scrub typhus breaks out and spreads to Biak. Before it is stopped, over 1,000 Americans will be stricken and 12 will die of the disease.

FEAF B-24 Liberators, B-25 Mitchells, A-20 Havocs, P-39 Airacobras, P-40s, and P-38 Lightnings attack the airfield, antiaircraft positions, and defensive positions on Noemfoor Island, followed by an attack on the airfield at Manokwari.

B-24s bomb the airfield at Namlea and hit shipping throughout the Molucca Islands.

The C-47s of the 39th Troop Carrier Squadron, 317th Troop Carrier Group, redeploy from Finschhafen to Hollandia.

July 2

CBI: Tenth Air Force P-40s continue support of ground forces near Myitkyina.

In China, Fourteenth Air Force sends 11 B-25 Mitchells and P-40s, P-51 Mustangs, and P-47 Thunderbolts to attack river shipping, assembly areas, and logistics sites in the Tungting Lake region.

Japanese submarine *I-8* torpedoes and damages a U.S. freighter in the Maldives. The ship is abandoned and the submarine surfaces and bombards the ship until it is set afire. The submarine crew picks up survivors and questions them, killing one and beating a number of others. After destroying the lifeboats, the Japanese take three of the American crew below, then leave the rest of the captured Americans to drown. Some are able to return to the stricken freighter and obtain rafts.

ATLANTIC: The Combined Chiefs of Staff issues instructions for the Mediterranean theater commander in chief, General Sir Henry Maitland Wilson, to plan for Anvil, the invasion of southern France in support of Overlord. The execution date is August 15. Three divisions will land initially, with a buildup to a total of 10 divisions. French forces are to capture Toulon and Marseilles. After the cities are captured, Allied forces are to advance north up the Rhône Valley.

Navy TBM Avengers from escort carrier USS *Wake Island* sink German submarine *U-543* southeast of the Azores.

ETO: Eighth Air Force sends 78 B-17s and 272 B-24 Liberators, escorted by 171 P-51 Mustangs, to attack V-weapon sites in France. One B-24 is lost and 34 are damaged. Aircrew losses are four wounded, and nine missing.

In support of Frantic missions, 41 P-51 Mustangs in Italy while en route from the USSR to England join Fifteenth Air Force fighters in escorting Fifteenth bombers against targets in Budapest, Hungary. Fighter pilots report nine confirmed kills. Four fighters are lost and the pilots reported missing.

A total of 37 B-24s fly in support of Carpetbagger operations.

MEDITERRANEAN: Fifteenth Air Force sends over 600 B-17s and B-24 Liberators against oil refineries, rail bridges, airfields, and marshaling yards in Hungary and Yugoslavia.

P-38 Lightnings and P-51 Mustangs sweep over Budapest. Aircrews and fighter pilots report over 50 enemy fighters shot down. About 28 fighters and bombers are lost.

ITALY: Twelfth Air Force B-25 Mitchells and B-26 Marauders attack fuel storage areas, rail and road traffic, and bridges. A-20 Havocs, P-47 Thunderbolts, and P-40s attack bridges and roads.

CENTRAL PACIFIC, SAIPAN: The 2nd Marine Division captures Flame Tree Hill and attacks the town of Garapan.

Seventh Air Force P-47 Thunderbolts on Saipan conduct bombing and strafing attacks on Japanese positions on both Saipan and Tinian.

NEW GUINEA: At Aitape, the 124th Infantry Regiment of the 31st Infantry Division arrives to reinforce XI Corps. General Hall decides to divide his forces between Aitape airfield and the Driniumor River. Although the river appears to be an obstacle to an enemy advance, it is too shallow and too weakly defended to stop a strong attack.

Operation Tabletennis's (Noemfoor Island) Naval Task Force 77, commanded by Rear Admiral William M. Fechteler, lands the 158th Infantry Regiment. Task Force 74 under command of Commodore John A. Collins, Royal Australian Navy, and Task Force 75, commanded by Rear Admiral Russell S. Berkey, provide gunfire support with heavy cruisers, light cruisers, and destroyers. At Noemfoor Island, 33 B-24 Liberators, six B-25 Mitchells, and 15 A-20 Havocs provide air support for the landing. The 158th RCT lands without encountering any opposition near Kamiri airfield, a major objective. Navy demolition teams are forced to blast lanes in the coral reef to get follow-on supplies ashore. Major General Patrick has received information from a captured Japanese soldier that there are 3,000 to 5,000 troops defending the island. Patrick, expecting a tough fight after his experience at Lone Tree Hill, requests reinforcements from the 503rd Parachute Infantry.

Other FEAF B-25s attack barges near Manokwari.

July 3

CBI: Tenth Air Force A-36 Intruder (Apache) fighter-bombers support ground forces near Myitkyina.

In China, Fourteenth Air Force B-24 Liberators bomb Yoyang railroad yards in the Tungting Lake area. B-25 Mitchells drop ammunition to Chinese ground forces at Hengyang. In French Indochina, P-40s damage a bridge.

ITALY: The 135th and the 168th Infantry Regiments of the 34th Infantry Division and the 442nd RCT (a unit made up entirely of Japanese Americans) fight the enemy for control of Rosignato Marittimo and Castellino Marittimo.

ATLANTIC: Destroyer escorts *Frost* and *Inch* sink German submarine *U-154* off the Madeira Islands.

ETO: VII Corps (made up of the 4th, 83rd, 9th, and 30th Infantry Divisions) moves south to support First Army at Carentan. VIII Corps (79th and 90th Infantry Divisions and the 82nd Airborne Division) attacks toward La Haye du Puits, one of the strongest defensive positions in Normandy, with marshes and *bocage* protecting wooded hills that overlook the main roads into the town. The 90th Infantry Division advances toward Mont Castre, but gains only a mile. The 82nd Airborne is held up at La Poterie.

General Omar N. Bradley's 12th Army Group is organized and ready for further combat operations. Since June 6 (D+28), 1 million soldiers, 1 million tons of supplies, and 300,000 vehicles have landed at the Normandy beaches.

Eighth Air Force has 55 B-17s in Italy supporting Frantic operations, joining Fifteenth Air Force bombers in an attack on the marshaling yards at Arad, Romania. The B-17s are escorted by 38 P-51 Mustangs.

Ninth Air Force sends more than 250 P-47 Thunderbolts to attack strongpoints, gun positions, and a fuel storage area, as well as lines of communication in support of the First Army.

The Headquarters of the 358th Fighter Group and the 365th Fighter Squadron with P-47s redeploys from England to France. The P-51 Mustangs of the 382nd Fighter Squadron of the 363rd Fighter Group redeploy from England to France.

MEDITERRANEAN: Fifteenth Air Force sends over 600 B-17s and B-24 Liberators against oil storage facilities, an oil refinery, and a locomotive works at Bucharest, Romania, and transportation targets in Yugoslavia and an oil storage site at Belgrade.

ITALY: Twelfth Air Force B-26 Marauders and A-20 Havocs attack fuel storage sites, and B-25 Mitchells attack bridges, fuel storage tanks, tunnels, and viaducts. A-20 Havocs, P-47 Thunderbolts, and P-40s attack vehicles, ammunition storage areas, and bridges.

PACIFIC: U.S. submarine *Sturgeon* attacks a Japanese convoy, sinking a transport in the Ryukyu Islands. U.S. submarine *Tinosa* attacks a Japanese convoy in the East China Sea, sinking a cargo ship and tanker west of Kyushu, Japan.

CENTRAL PACIFIC: Seventh Air Force B-24 Liberators staging through Eniwetok bomb Truk.

U.S. submarine *Albacore* torpedoes and sinks a Japanese steamer west of Palau.

NEW GUINEA: At Noemfoor, a battalion of the 503rd Parachute Infantry Regiment jumps on the Kamiri airfield as the 158th Infantry extends its perimeter. The jump is poorly conducted and many paratroopers are injured. FEAF P-38 Lightnings and B-25 Mitchells attack Japanese positions and logistics sites near Kamiri and conduct ground support missions. FEAF B-24 Liberators, A-20 Havocs, P-39 Airacobras, P-38 Lightnings, P-40s, and P-47 Thunderbolts attack targets on Manokwari, Biak, and the area around Wewak. B-24s attack airfields, antiaircraft positions, and targets of opportunity on Yap, at Woleai Atoll, and at Peleliu Island.

The C-47s of the 70th Troop Carrier Squadron of the 433rd Troop Carrier Group redeploy from Nadzab to Hollandia.

July 4
CARIBBEAN: German submarine *U-539* torpedoes and damages a U.S. tanker near the Panama Canal Zone.

CBI: Tenth Air Force P-40s support ground forces near Myitkyina. P-47 Thunderbolts and P-51 Mustangs fly an offensive sweep over the Lashio area and patrol the Mogaung area.

In China, Fourteenth Air Force sends 38 B-25 Mitchells, P-40s, P-51 Mustangs, and P-38 Lightnings to attack roads, bridges, artillery, town areas, troop concentrations, and various targets of opportunity throughout the Tungting Lake-Yangtze River area. Hengyang airfield is bombed and supplies are dropped to Chinese troops in the area. Yellow River shipping and airfields and logistics sites and storage facilities in Canton are also attacked.

U.S. submarine *Seahorse* attacks a Japanese convoy in the South China Sea and sinks three cargo ships south of Hong Kong.

ATLANTIC: The Joint Chiefs of Staff presents an assessment of the China crisis to President Roosevelt. The report staunchly defends General Stilwell and questions General Chennault's belief that the Fourteenth Air Force can stem the Japanese offensive only if provided more supplies. The report notes that the diversion of thousands of tons of supplies to the Fourteenth Air Force has had no appreciable effect on the Japanese offensive but is having an effect on the support to Allied forces in the ETO. The JCS recommends a reorganization of the Chinese army and the placement of all forces in China under one commander—General Stilwell.

ETO: VII Corps attacks with two infantry regiments of the 83rd Infantry Division to capture Sainteny. The division is stopped by German positions in the hedgerows, minefields, and marshes, and takes heavy casualties.

Eighth Air Force sends 300 B-17s and 258 B-24 Liberators, escorted by 199 P-38 Lightnings, 189 P-47 Thunderbolts, and 244 P-51 Mustangs, to attack airfields in France. Bad weather over the targets forces most of the bombers to abort the mission. One B-17 is lost, 93 are damaged. Aircrew losses are three wounded, and nine missing. Fighter pilots attack marshaling yards and bridges and report 17 confirmed kills in the air and one on the ground. One P-38 is lost and one is damaged. The pilot is reported missing.

A total of 36 B-24s fly in support of Carpetbagger operations.

Ninth Air Force sends 95 A-20 and B-26 Marauders to bomb a rail bridge and German strongpoints. Over 900 P-47s attack troop concentrations, gun positions, rail lines, marshaling yards, bridges, highways, and a unit headquarters.

The P-47s of the 366th and 367th Fighter Squadrons of the 358th Fighter Group and the 494th Fighter Squadron, 48th Fighter Group, redeploy to France. The P-51s of the 381st Fighter Squadron of the 363rd Fighter Group also arrive in France.

MEDITERRANEAN: The headquarters of Seventh Army moves to Naples, Italy, and continues planning for Anvil. Seventh Army is composed of VI Corps commanded by Major General Lucian K. Truscott, and three divisions, the 3rd Infantry Division, commanded by Major General John W "Iron Mike" O'Daniel, the 36th Infantry Division, commanded by Major General John E. Dahlquist, and the 45th Infantry Division, commanded by Major General William W. Eagles. An airborne task force and two French corps under the command of General Jean de Lattre de Tassigny will be added to the invasion force.

Fifteenth Air Force sends over 250 B-17s and B-24 Liberators against an oil refinery, bridges, and railroad repair works in Romania. P-51 Mustangs and P-38 Lightnings escort the bombers and the pilots report 17 confirmed enemy aircraft kills.

ITALY: Combat Command A of the 1st Armored Division and the 361st Infantry Regiment break enemy defenses near Cecina. The 1st Armored Division is relieved on the line by the 88th Infantry Division.

Twelfth Air Force A-20 Havocs attack ammunition storage facilities and P-40s and P-47 Thunderbolts attack bridges, rail lines, roads, and guns.

PACIFIC: U.S. submarine *Tang* torpedoes and sinks two Japanese cargo ships in the Yellow Sea off the west coast of Korea.

U.S. submarine *S-28* is lost during training exercises off Oahu, Hawaii. No cause is determined.

CENTRAL PACIFIC: B-24 Liberators, staging through Eniwetok Atoll, bomb Truk.

Carrier aircraft and surface ships under Rear Admiral Joseph J. Clark and Rear Admiral Ralph E. Davison attack Japanese installations on Iwo Jima, Chichi Jima, and Haha Jima.

A submarine chaser, landing ships, and a number of other auxiliary vessels are sunk or damaged in the area.

Destroyer *David W. Taylor* and destroyer escort *Riddle* sink Japanese submarine *I-10* northeast of Saipan.

U.S. submarine *Guavina* torpedoes and sinks a Japanese transport near Palau.

NEW GUINEA: At Noemfoor, the 503rd Parachute Infantry Regiment drops another battalion on the Kamiri airfield. This jump is also poorly conducted. In two days the regiment has suffered 126 jump injuries—before encountering the enemy. Kornasoren airfield is captured.

FEAF A-20 Havocs fly ground support missions near Kamiri airfield. P-47 Thunderbolts strafe targets of opportunity on Biak Island.

B-24 Liberators bomb Yap, Woleai, and Sorol Atolls, and Peleliu Island.

The A-20 Havocs of the 388th Bombardment Squadron (Light), 312th Bombardment Group (Light), redeploy from Nadzab to Hollandia.

July 5

CBI: Tenth Air Force P-40s and A-36 Intruder (Apache) fighter-bombers attack targets around Myitkyina.

Fourteenth Air Force B-25 Mitchells with eight P-40s escorting the bombers attack Japanese forces north of Hengyang. Twelve Japanese aircraft intercept the formation; in the fight, three enemy aircraft are shot down and three are damaged. One P-40 is shot down and two are damaged. The downed pilot is captured and one pilot is wounded. P-51s and P-40s and B-25 Mitchells attack logistics sites, gun batteries, bridges, vehicles, ammunition dumps, town areas, and troops throughout the Tungting Lake area.

ATLANTIC: Destroyer escorts *Thomas* and *Baker* sink German minelayer submarine *U-233* off Halifax, Nova Scotia.

ETO: The 313th Infantry Regiment of the 79th Infantry Division, VIII Corps, cuts through *bocage* to attack the left flank of the German position at La Haye du Puits and gain a small foothold on Montgardon Ridge, the key to the German defensive line.

The headquarters element of Lieutenant General George S. Patton, Jr.'s Third Army lands in France to prepare to take command of the right flank of the American line.

Eighth Air Force sends 79 B-17s to attack airfields in the Netherlands and 221 B-24 Liberators against V-weapon sites in France, escorted by P-51 Mustangs. A total of 49 B-24s are damaged. Aircrew losses are one wounded. Fighter pilots report four confirmed kills in the air and one on the ground. Two fighters are lost and the pilots are reported missing. Another 70 B-17s attack the marshaling yard at Béziers escorted by 228 P-47 Thunderbolts and P-51s. Fighter pilots report 18 confirmed kills and one probable in the air and one confirmed kill on the ground. Three fighters are lost and the pilots are reported missing. A raid by 93 P-47s escorted by P-38 Lightnings on bridges and transportation targets in France results in pilots reporting three confirmed kills in the air and one on the ground. Two P-47s and two P-38s are lost. One P-38 is damaged.

A total of eight B-24s fly in support of Carpetbagger operations. During the night eight B-17s drop leaflets over France. One bomber is lost.

Eighth Air Force B-17s, as part of the Frantic operation, bomb a marshaling yard at Béziers, France with Fifteenth Air Force B-24 Liberators while en route to Britain from Italy. P-51 Mustangs escorting the bombers also return to Britain.

The P-51s of the 380th Fighter Squadron, 363rd Fighter Group, move from England to France.

Ninth Air Force sends 180 A-20 and B-26 Marauders and over 600 fighters against transportation targets along the battlefront.

German submarine *U-390* torpedoes and damages a U.S. freighter en route from Utah Beach to Southampton, England. It will be repaired and returned to service.

MEDITERRANEAN: Fifteenth Air Force sends nearly 500 B-17s and B-24 Liberators against the Montpellier and Béziers marshaling yards and the submarine pens and harbor installations at Toulon.

ITALY: Allied Forces Headquarters Mediterranean instructs General Sir Harold R. L. G. Alexander, Allied ground force commander, to give all priority to the preparations for Anvil, the invasion of the southern coast of France.

Twelfth Air Force B-25 Mitchells bomb marshaling yards, a railroad bridge, and fuel supply depots. A-20 Havocs attack logistics storage areas and rail lines. P-47 Thunderbolts and P-40s attack bridges and roads.

Twelfth Air Force B-17s and B-24 Liberators bomb marshaling yards, submarine pens, and harbor installations at Toulon. German submarines *U-586* and *U-642* are sunk in Toulon harbor.

PACIFIC: U.S. submarine *Plaice* sinks Japanese auxiliary netlayer in the Bonin Islands.

U.S. submarine *Sunfish* torpedoes and sinks a Japanese cargo ship off Paramushiru in the Kuriles.

NEW GUINEA: At Noemfoor, a Japanese counterattack against Kamiri airfield is driven back.

FEAF P-38 Lightnings, P-40s, and P-47 Thunderbolts fly ground support missions on Noemfoor Island and attack barges, airfields, and troop concentrations on Biak Island and at Moemi, Manokwari, and in the Wakde area. B-24 Liberators bomb airstrips and antiaircraft guns on Yap Island, Woleai and Sorol Atolls, and Peleliu Island.

Fifth Air Force B-24 Liberators sink a Japanese cargo vessel off western New Guinea.

July 6

CARIBBEAN: German submarine *U-516* torpedoes and sinks a U.S. tanker in the Caribbean north of Venezuela.

CBI: President Roosevelt contacts Generalissimo Chiang, proposing that Stilwell be promoted to full general and given command of all Chinese forces. "I feel that the case of China is so desperate that if radical and properly applied remedies are not immediately effected, our common cause will suffer a disastrous setback." Chiang Kai-shek makes a surprisingly positive response, but ultimately takes no action.

Tenth Air Force sends 12 P-40s to attack a bridge near Myitkyina.

In China, Fourteenth Air Force B-25 Mitchells, P-40s, and P-51 Mustangs attack river shipping, bridges, troop concentrations, and road traffic around Tungting Lake and the Yangtze River. B-25s airdrop supplies to Chinese ground forces on the Salween River front. During the night the bombers attack Tien Ho airfield at Canton.

Brigadier General LaVern G. Saunders becomes the commander of XX Bomber Command, Twentieth Air Force, with headquarters at Kharagpur, India.

CENTRAL PACIFIC: U.S. submarine *Sealion* attacks a Japanese convoy in the East China Sea and sinks a cargo ship off Ningpo, China.

B-24 Liberators staging through Eniwetok Atoll conduct a night raid on Truk and conduct a follow-on attack during the day. B-25 Mitchells from Makin Island bomb Nauru Island.

ETO: The 90th Infantry Division of VIII Corps captures Monte Castre, the main defensive position protecting the right flank of the German defenses at La Haye du Puits.

Major General Collins, the VII Corps commander, employs the 4th Infantry Division to support the 83rd Infantry Division's attempt to capture Sainteny. Entire infantry companies have to be committed to capture just one section of the *bocage*, expertly defended by German infantrymen and tanks.

Eighth Air Force sends 641 B-17s and 159 B-24 Liberators, escorted by 141 P-38 Lightnings and 83 P-51 Mustangs, to attack V-weapon sites in France. One B-17 is damaged. Aircrew losses are two killed and three wounded. Fighter pilots report four confirmed kills. One P-38 is lost. The pilot is reported missing. Another 262 B-24s bomb the dock area at Kiel, Germany, escorted by P-51 Mustangs. Three bombers are lost and 106 damaged. Aircrew losses are eight wounded and 22 missing. One P-51 is lost and the pilot is reported missing. In the late afternoon 73 B-17s and 148 B-24s attack six V-weapon sites, bridges, and an airfield in northern France, escorted by 443 P-38s, P-47s, and P-51s. One P-47 is lost. Over Paris, 212 P-38s and P-47s fly fighter-bomber missions against rail and road targets. Pilots report 11 confirmed kills and one probable. Two P-47s are lost and the pilots are reported missing.

A total of 20 B-24s fly in support of Carpetbagger operations. One bomber is lost.

During the night seven B-17s drop leaflets over Belgium and France.

Ninth Air Force sends 500 A-20 and B-26 Marauders and about 600 fighters against bridges, fuel depots, rail lines, and a V-weapon location in France. The fighters attack rail facilities, roads, troop concentrations, and artillery positions.

The headquarters of the 404th Fighter Group and the P-47s of the 506th, 507th, and 508th Fighter Squadrons redeploy from England to France. The P-47s of the 388th Fighter Squadron, 365th Fighter Group, also redeploy to France.

ITALY: Fifteenth Air Force sends over 500 B-17s and B-24 Liberators, escorted by P-51 Mustangs and P-38 Lightnings, against marshaling yards, railroad bridges, an oil refinery, and fuel storage areas.

Twelfth Air Force A-20 Havocs attack an ammunition ship at La Spezia and also attack fuel storage depots. A-20 Havocs, P-47 Thunderbolts, and P-40s attack rail lines and bridges.

PACIFIC: U.S. submarine *Cobia* torpedoes and sinks a Japanese guardboat east of the Bonin Islands.

U.S. submarine *Tang* torpedoes and sinks a Japanese cargo ship in Chosin Bay, Korea.

CENTRAL PACIFIC: Admiral Nimitz proposes to support General MacArthur's attack on the Philippines by attacking the Palaus, specifically Peleliu, Angaur, Yap, and Ulithi, to establish naval and air bases to support MacArthur's invasion.

Seventh Air Force P-47 Thunderbolts based on Saipan bomb and strafe Japanese positions on Saipan and Tinian.

Carrier aircraft bomb coastal defenses, antiaircraft guns, logistics storage sites, and airfields on Guam and Rota.

NEW GUINEA: At Sarmi, the 63rd Infantry Regiment of the 6th Infantry Division holds Hill 225 and Mount Saksin at Lone Tree Hill. Hill 265 is still in Japanese hands.

At Noemfoor, the 2nd Battalion 158th RCT conducts an amphibious landing at Romboi Bay to capture Number airfield.

FEAF B-25 Mitchells, A-20 Havocs, P-39 Airacobras, P-38 Lightnings, P-40s, and P-47 Thunderbolts attack targets in the Wewak area. B-25s, P-39s, P-38s, P-40s, and P-47s attack along the coast of the Vogelkop Peninsula; the P-38s, P-40s, and P-47s attack targets in the Manokwari area. B-24 Liberators bomb the town and logistics storage areas on Yap and the airfield at Woleai Atoll.

U.S. submarine *Paddle* attacks a Japanese convoy and sinks a destroyer northwest of Halmahera.

July 7

CBI: In China, Fourteenth Air Force B-25 Mitchells and P-51 Mustangs and P-47 Thunderbolts attack bridges, river shipping, troop areas, gun emplacements, and ammunition storage sites in the Tungting Lake area. B-25s and P-51 Mustangs bomb Tien Ho and White Cloud airfields.

During the night Twentieth Air Force sends 14 B-29 Superfortresses from bases at Chengtu, China, to bomb Sasebo, Omura, and Tobata in Japan. Sasebo takes the heaviest hit, while three bombers attack secondary and last resort targets at Laoyao and around Hankow in China.

U.S. submarine *Flasher* torpedoes and sinks a transport off the coast of French Indochina.

ETO: The XIX Corps (the 35th and 29th Infantry Divisions) attacks across the Vire River. The 313th Infantry Regiment of the 79th Infantry Division, VIII Corps, captures Montgardon Ridge at La Haye du Puits and defends it against German tank and infantry counterattacks. The division has suffered 2,000 casualties in five days of combat.

The XIX Corps (30th Infantry Division and 29th Infantry Division) crosses the Vire River north of St-Lô. General Bradley adds the 3rd Armored Division to XIX Corps to use its tanks to exploit a possible breakthrough. The 3rd Armored Division passes one combat command through the bridge-head heading for St-Lô, but the result is chaos as the tanks of the 3rd Armored and the infantry of the 30th Infantry Division are hopelessly entan-gled. Meanwhile, the Germans reinforce St-Lô.

German tanks and vehicles were vulnerable to air attack by the Ninth Air Force throughout July and August of 1944. This group of vehicles was hit near Mortain, France.

Eighth Air Force sends 303 B-17s and 373 B-24 Liberators, escorted by 409 P-38 Lightnings, P-47 Thunderbolts, and P-51 Mus-tangs, to attack oil production facilities and refineries, aircraft production facilities, a marshaling yard, and airfields in Germany. Aircrews report 39 confirmed kills and five probables. Thirty bombers are lost and 239 are damaged. Aircrew losses are three killed, 17 wounded, and 294 missing. Fighter pilots report 55 confirmed kills in the air and three on the ground and one probable in the air. Six fighters are lost. The pilots are reported missing.

In another attack, 453 B-17s, escorted by 247 P-47s and P-51s, bomb oil produc-tion facilities, airfields, and ball bearing plants in Germany. Seven B-17s are lost and 154 are damaged. Aircrew casualties are 15 killed, five wounded, and 50 missing. Fighter pilots report 20 confirmed kills in the air and one on the ground. One P-51 is damaged and the pilot is wounded.

A total of 21 B-24s fly in support of Carpetbagger operations. During the night six B-17s drop leaflets over France and Belgium.

Ninth Air Force sends over 100 A-20 and B-26 Marauders and more than 500 fighters against bridges, railroads, gun emplacements, marshaling yards, ammuni-tion storage sites, rail and road traffic, and also to conduct ground support missions in France.

The headquarters of the 36th Fighter Group redeploys from England to France. The P-47s of the 362nd Fighter Group (377th, 378th, 379th Fighter Squadrons) redeploy to France.

MEDITERRANEAN: Fifteenth Air Force sends over 500 B-17s and B-24 Liberators to attack synthetic oil plants in Germany and an airfield and marshaling yard in Zagreb, Yugoslavia.

Twelfth Air Force A-20 Havocs bomb La Spezia harbor, motor transport, and fuel storage areas. B-26 Marauders and B-25 Mitchells bomb railway bridges. A-20 Havocs, A-36 Intruder (Apache) fighter-bombers, P-51 Mustangs, and P-40s attack rail lines, bridges, ammunition storage areas, and roads.

ITALY: Twelfth Air Force's XII Tactical Air Command with fighters and fighter-bombers redeploys to Corsica to support Anvil/Dragoon.

Southwest Pacific Area: U.S. submarine *Mingo* torpedoes and sinks a Japanese destroyer west of Mindoro Island.

Pacific: Admiral Nimitz redraws plans for the attack on the Palaus, changing the name of the operation from Stalemate to Stalemate II. The target date for the invasion is reset for September 15. Because the battles at Guam and Saipan have involved army and marine forces for far longer than originally planned, the III Amphibious Corps (1st Marine Division and 81st Infantry Division) are tasked with capturing Peleliu and Angaur. To prevent any Japanese interference with the Palau operation, Iwo Jima, Chichi Jima, and Yap are to be attacked to eliminate Japanese air forces.

U.S. submarine *Skate* attacks a Japanese convoy in the south of the Sea of Okhotsk, sinking a destroyer and damaging a cargo ship.

U.S. submarine *Sunfish* attacks a group of Japanese fishing boats in the Kuriles, sinking four of them.

Central Pacific, Saipan: The Japanese make a suicide attack against the 105th Infantry Regiment and break through its defenses, charging through an unnoticed gap between the two forward battalions. The 3rd Battalion, 10th Marine artillery fires its guns point-blank against the waves of attackers. Over 900 soldiers and marines are killed. The Japanese suffer 4,300 casualties. The 106th Infantry Regiment conducts a counterattack.

Seventh Air Force P-47 Thunderbolts on Saipan bomb and strafe Japanese positions on Saipan and Tinian. P-61 Black Widow night fighters carry out interceptor missions over Guam and Saipan.

Between late June and early July, Lieutenant Colonel William J. O'Brien, commander of the 1st Battalion, 105th Infantry Regiment, 27th Infantry Division, leads his unit through some of the most difficult terrain yet encountered in the Pacific, at Saipan. When Japanese fire stops the forward elements of the battalion, Lieutenant Colonel O'Brien mounts a tank and, fully exposed to enemy fire, directs the attack. He later leads a small detachment to maneuver around an enemy position to clear the area and regain the momentum of the attack, capturing machine guns and an artillery piece. On the seventh of July, O'Brien's battalion is one of the targets of the Japanese night counterattack. Faced with thousands of enemy soldiers overrunning his unit, Lieutenant Colonel O'Brien leads his men, carrying two .45-caliber automatic pistols and firing at the enemy. Seriously wounded and out of ammunition, O'Brien takes over a .50-caliber machine gun mounted on a jeep and continues to fight. He dies surrounded by Japanese bodies. For his unsurpassed courage under fire, his dramatic leadership, and his unconquerable spirit, Lieutenant Colonel O'Brien will be awarded the Congressional Medal of Honor.

During the Japanese night assault, Private First Class Harold C. Agerholm of the 4th Battalion, 10th Marines, 2nd Marine Division, volunteers to assist in evacuating the wounded. He drives a litter Jeep back and forth along the American lines in the midst of desperate fighting and personally brings in 45 wounded. He is killed by enemy fire as he attempts to rescue two wounded marines. For his unselfish acts of courage and dedication to duty, Private First Class Agerholm will receive the Medal of Honor.

New Guinea: Hill 265, the last remaining Japanese stronghold on Lone Tree Hill, is attacked in a simultaneous assault from the 63rd and 1st RCTs, which assault the enemy with tanks, flamethrowers, artillery fire, and bazookas. It will take five days to complete the task.

FEAF A-20 Havocs, P-39 Airacobras, P-47 Thunderbolts, and Royal Australian Air Force (RAAF) aircraft bomb Wewak. B-24 Liberators bomb Yap Island, the Sorol Atoll radio station, and the airfield on Woleai Atoll.

U.S. submarine *Bonefish* torpedoes and sinks a Japanese guardboat off Borneo.

July 8

CBI: The Chinese Y Force surrounds Tengchung with eight divisions.

Tenth Air Force sends 12 B-25 Mitchells, A-36 Intruder (Apache) fighter-bombers, and P-40s to attack targets and a bridge at Myitkyina and fly ground support missions.

In China, Fourteenth Air Force sends B-25 Mitchells, P-40s, P-38 Lightnings, and P-47s against river shipping, trucks, bridges, logistics storage areas, troop concentrations, and command posts around Tungting Lake. Twenty Japanese aircraft bomb Kanchou and Suichwan airfields. At Suichwan they cause enough damage to make the airfield unusable for a few days. In French Indochina 10 P-40s attack coastal shipping and five B-25s destroy two bridges at Cam Lo.

ETO: The 82nd Airborne Division is relieved by the 8th Infantry Division in VIII Corps. The 82nd will return to England as a strategic reserve and prepare for another possible airborne landing.

Although over 1,000 bombers are sent against bridges, tunnels, rail lines, and V-weapon sites in France, bad weather allows only about 460 to hit their primary targets.

The bombers are escorted by 266 P-38 Lightnings and P-51 Mustangs and 36 P-47 Thunderbolts. Four bombers are lost and 92 are damaged. Aircrew losses are two killed, seven wounded, and 32 missing. Fighter pilots report 20 confirmed kills on the ground. One fighter is lost and the pilot is reported missing.

In another mission, 264 B-17s and 130 B-24 Liberators, escorted by 286 P-38s, P-47s, and P-51s, attack airfields and rail lines. Eight bombers are lost and 130 are damaged. Aircrew losses are four killed, 16 wounded, and 51 missing.

A total of 17 B-24s fly in support of Carpetbagger operations. During the night four B-17s drop leaflets over France.

Ninth Air Force sends nearly 300 A-20 and B-26 Marauders to bomb V-weapon sites, strongpoints, railroad bridges, ammunition storage areas, and troop assembly areas in France.

Mediterranean: Fifteenth Air Force sends over 500 bombers to attack oil refineries, oil storage areas, airfields, and a marshaling yard near Vienna, Austria. More than 100 German fighters attack the formations. Aircrews and fighter pilots report 50 confirmed kills. A total of 14 fighters and bombers are lost over the target.

Italy: Volterra falls to the 350th Infantry Regiment of the 88th Infantry Division, opening a gap in the German lines and forcing a withdrawal. Major General Paul W. Kendall takes command of the division from Major General John E. Sloan.

Twelfth Air Force B-25 Mitchells and B-26 Marauders attack marshaling yards and rail lines. A-20 Havocs attack fuel storage areas. P-47 Thunderbolts and P-40s attack rail lines, bridges, and roads.

SOUTHWEST PACIFIC AREA: General MacArthur's headquarters submits the Reno V plan, outlining a series of offensive actions from the Vogelkop Peninsula and Morotai in western New Guinea to southern Mindanao in the Philippines for late October, an attack on Leyte in mid-November, and an attack on Luzon in April of 1945. To accomplish his plan, he requires six divisions, including one airborne and one armored division.

PACIFIC: U.S. submarine *Tautog* torpedoes and sinks a Japanese cargo ship off Honshu, Japan.

CENTRAL PACIFIC: During the night Seventh Air Force B-24 Liberators staging through Eniwetok Atoll bomb Truk and conduct a follow-on raid during the day.

Naval Task Group 53.18 under Rear Admiral C. Turner Joy bombards defenses on Guam.

Aircraft sink seven Japanese guardboats off Saipan.

CENTRAL PACIFIC, SAIPAN: The 6th Marines, supported by tanks from Company B, 2nd Tank Battalion, restore the shattered defensive line. Americans witness mass suicides as Japanese civilians jump from cliffs rather than accept defeat. Japanese soldiers commit suicide in large numbers as marines move to occupy Mount Marpi, the last significant defended terrain on the island.

Seventh Air Force P-47 Thunderbolts fly fighter-bomber missions against Japanese defensive positions on Saipan and Tinian.

Sergeant Grant F. Timmerman is a tank commander serving with the 2nd Battalion, 6th Marines. As his tank leads an infantry advance, Sergeant Timmerman maintains a steady fire from the turret-mounted machine gun. Encountering trenches and pillboxes Timmerman begins to fire on the enemy when a grenade lands on top of the turret. To keep it from falling into the open hatch where he stands, Timmerman shouts a warning and covers the grenade with his body. His exceptional valor and dedication to his crew in saving them at the cost of his own life will win him the Medal of Honor.

NEW GUINEA: FEAF B-24 Liberators, A-20 Havocs, P-39 Airacobras, P-47 Thunderbolts, and Royal Australian Air Force (RAAF) aircraft bomb Wewak.

July 9

CBI: Tenth Air Force A-36 Intruder (Apache) fighter-bombers, P-51 Mustangs, P-47 Thunderbolts, and P-40s attack a bridge near the Myitkyina area and strafe Japanese gun positions at Shwebo and targets along the Irrawaddy River.

Fourteenth Air Force B-25 Mitchells bomb a power plant and buildings at Tinh Soc in French Indochina.

ETO: Eighth Air Force sends 150 B-17s escorted by 155 P-47 Thunderbolts and P-51 Mustangs to bomb bridges and airfields in France. Heavy clouds force most to bomb secondary targets. One B-17 is lost and 10 are damaged. Aircrew casualties are nine missing. One P-47 and one P-51 are lost; one pilot is reported missing.

Another mission involves 104 B-24 Liberators and 77 B-17s escorted by 158 P-47s and P-51s attacking V-weapon sites in France. Bad weather conditions limit the bombers and secondary targets are hit. One B-24 is lost and 60 are damaged. Two crewmen are wounded. Fighter pilots report five confirmed kills.

A total of 37 B-24s fly in support of Carpetbagger operations. During the night five B-17s drop leaflets over France.

Ninth Air Force sends over 250 A-20 and B-26 Marauders along with fighters to bomb and strafe rail lines, gun batteries, bridges, fortifications, tanks, ammunition dumps, town areas, and strongpoints in the battle area.

MEDITERRANEAN: Fifteenth Air Force conducts its first Pathfinder-led mission. A total of 222 B-17s and B-24 Liberators, escorted by P-38 Lightnings and P-51 Mustangs, attack oil refineries at Ploeşti, Romania. Aircrews and pilots report 14 confirmed kills. Six fighters and bombers are lost.

First Lieutenant Donald D. Pucket of the 98th Bombardment Group is flying a B-24 Liberator over Ploeşti and has just dropped his bomb load when the aircraft is hit and seriously damaged by antiaircraft fire. With one crewman killed and six others badly wounded, First Lieutenant Pucket turns the controls over to the copilot and begins taking several steps to save the bomber and take care of the wounded. As the crippled bomber continues to lose altitude, First Lieutenant Pucket orders everyone to bail out. Three crewmen refuse to leave the bomber and Pucket decides to stay with the aircraft. As he fights to maintain altitude, the bomber crashes into a mountainside. For his courage, leadership, and dedication to his crew, First Lieutenant Pucket will receive the Medal of Honor.

ITALY: Twelfth Air Force A-20 Havocs attack rail lines and gun positions. P-40s and P-47 Thunderbolts attack rail lines and bridges.

SOUTHWEST PACIFIC AREA: U.S. submarine *Dace* attacks a Japanese cargo vessel in the Celebes Sea but fails to do any damage.

U.S. submarine *Nautilus* lands men and supplies on Pandan Island off the west coast of Mindoro Island.

PACIFIC: U.S. submarine *Sunfish* attacks a Japanese convoy in the Kuriles, sinking a cargo ship.

U.S. submarine *Tautog* torpedoes and sinks a Japanese fishing boat off Hokkaido, Japan.

CENTRAL PACIFIC: B-25 Mitchells from Makin Island bomb Jaluit Atoll.

CENTRAL PACIFIC, SAIPAN: Lieutenant General Holland M. Smith declares Saipan secured, calling it "the decisive battle of the Pacific offensive." Saipan will become an advance base for air attacks on the Japanese home islands. The Americans estimate that 23,811 Japanese soldiers have died on the island and 736 prisoners have been captured. U.S. losses are heavy: 3,225 killed, 13,061 wounded, 326 missing. Army losses are 3,674; marine losses are 10,437.

Just south of Saipan is the island of Tinian. Reconnaissance of beaches for potential landings begins.

Seventh Air Force P-47 Thunderbolts from Saipan attack Japanese forces on Saipan and Tinian. Saipan will become a B-29 Superfortress base for strategic attacks on the Japanese home islands.

New Guinea: FEAF A-20 Havocs and P-47 Thunderbolts attack targets both at Biak and along the coast of Geelvink Bay. B-25 Mitchells, P-39 Airacobras, P-38 Lightnings, and P-40s sink a cargo ship and several barges around Halmahera Island. B-24 Liberators bomb Namlea Airfield and attack Yap and Woleai Atolls.

Fifth Air Force B-25 Mitchells sink Japanese cargo ship near Halmahera Island.

July 10

CBI: Tenth Air Force P-40s and P-51 Mustangs support ground forces at Myitkyina. A-36 Intruder (Apache) fighter-bombers, P-51 Mustangs, P-47 Thunderbolts, and P-40s attack Mogaung.

ETO: First Army staff develops the concept for Operation Cobra, intended to use VII Corps to penetrate German defensive lines west of St-Lô, then exploit the gap with armored and motorized units to reach Coutances.

Six B-17s drop leaflets over France and the Netherlands during the night. A total of 12 B-24 Liberators fly Carpetbagger missions during the night.

Ninth Air Force P-47 Thunderbolts and P-38 Lightnings bomb and strafe gun positions, bridges, troop concentrations, and roads in France. The headquarters of the 71st Fighter Wing redeploys from England to France.

Rear Admiral John Wilkes takes command of U.S. Ports and Bases Command, France, with headquarters at Cherbourg, France.

Italy: Twelfth Air Force B-25 Mitchells and B-26 Marauders attack marshaling yards, railroad bridges, and viaducts. A-20 Havocs, P-47 Thunderbolts, and P-40s attack airfields, rail lines, and roads.

Southwest Pacific Area: USS *Thresher,* part of a U.S. submarine attack group (TG 17.16, commanded by Captain William V. O'Regan), in the South China Sea near Formosa locates and tracks a seven-ship convoy headed for the Philippines.

Pacific: U.S. submarine *Tinosa* torpedoes and sinks a Japanese merchant fishing boat in the East China Sea west of Kyushu.

U.S. submarine *Sealion* torpedoes and sinks two cargo ships in the Yellow Sea off the west coast of Korea.

Central Pacific: Seventh Air Force P-47 Thunderbolts attack Japanese gun positions on Tinian Island. During the night B-24 Liberators stage through Eniwetok Atoll, bomb Truk, and conduct another raid during the day.

New Guinea: Major General Hall orders a battalion of the 128th Infantry and a squadron of the 112th Cavalry to conduct a reconnaissance across the Driniumor River to locate Japanese forces. At the same time over 10,000 Japanese attack XI Corps positions at the river where only an infantry battalion and a cavalry squadron remain to defend the line. The enemy breaks through, isolating the reconnaissance force and other units of the 128th Infantry. Heavy artillery fire slows the Japanese attack.

Lieutenant General Krueger designates 6th Infantry Division as the Sansapor Task Force. Major General Franklin C. Sibert will command 20,500 men in this operation. The 20th RCT of the 6th Infantry Division will serve as the task force reserve at Wakde. D-day is set for July 30. Task Force 77, under Rear Admiral William M. Fechteler, will consist of 24 LSTs, 15 LCIs, five APDs, and 19 destroyers. Task

Force 78, under Rear Admiral Robert S. Berkey, will consist of one heavy cruiser, two light cruisers, and nine destroyers.

July 11

CBI: Tenth Air Force A-36 Intruder (Apache) fighter-bombers, P-51 Mustangs, P-47 Thunderbolts, and P-40s attack a barracks at Myitkyina, bridges at Namkwin and Mohnyin, and the airfield at Lashio.

In China, Fourteenth Air Force sends 28 B-24 Liberators to bomb a logistics storage base at Sinshih. P-40s attack river traffic and the town at Hengyang. B-25 Mitchells bomb the railyards at Sinyang. P-40s and P-47 Thunderbolts support Chinese ground forces between Tengchung and Lungling.

The P-47s of the 93rd Fighter Squadron 81st Fighter Group redeploy from Karachi, India, to Kwanghan.

ETO: A German tank counterattack is stopped by the 9th and 30th Infantry Divisions. The V Corps and the XIX Corps of Bradley's First Army move to capture the town of St-Lô, the key crossroads that leads to the open high ground suitable for large maneuvering forces. St-Lô's formidable defensive terrain is anchored on Hill 192 and Hill 122 and defended by some of the finest quality soldiers in the German Wehrmacht who have made the *bocage* and stone farmhouses into fortresses. Near St-Lô, the 2nd Infantry Division attacks Hill 192 as the 29th Infantry Division fights Germans in the hedgerow defenses and strongpoints. The 38th and 23rd Infantry Regiments of the 2nd Infantry Division attack in a low fog behind an artillery bombardment employing 20,000 artillery rounds with four tank companies. Hill 192 is captured at low cost and secures the flank for the attack of XIX Corps. The 116th and 115th Infantry Regiments of the 29th Infantry Division reach Martinville Ridge and attempt to advance to Hill 122, but are held up by German fire from Hill 122. The 35th Infantry Division of XIX Corps is stopped in the *bocage* after advancing only a mile-and-a-half.

Eighth Air Force sends over 700 B-17s against a marshaling yard and production facilities in Munich, Germany. Over 300 P-38 Lightnings, P-47 Thunderbolts, and P-51s escort the bombers. Four bombers are lost and 133 are damaged. Aircrew casualties are four killed, five wounded, and 40 missing.

Another attack by 435 B-24 Liberators escorted by 324 P-38 Lightnings, P-47 Thunderbolts, and P-51 Mustangs bombs airfields, bridges, and roads in Munich. Sixteen bombers are lost and two are damaged. Aircrew losses are eight killed, 14 wounded, and 149 missing. Fighter pilots report two confirmed kills. One P-47 and two P-51s are lost and one P-51 is damaged. Two pilots are reported missing.

During the night, six B-17s drop leaflets over France. A total of 29 B-24s fly in support of Carpetbagger missions during the night.

Ninth Air Force A-20 Havocs and B-26 Marauders attack fuel storage areas, V-weapon sites, and a rail bridge. P-47s escort the bombers and attack trains, gun positions, and ammunition storage areas.

MEDITERRANEAN: The 1st Airborne Task Force is organized under the command of Major General Robert T. Frederick. The task force is composed of the 2nd Independent British Parachute Brigade, the 509th Parachute Infantry Battalion, the 463rd

Parachute Field Artillery Battalion, the 517th Parachute Regimental Combat Team, the 550th Glider Infantry Battalion, and the 551st Parachute Infantry Brigade. The task force is assigned to Lieutenant General Patch's Seventh Army for Operation Anvil.

Fifteenth Air Force B-24 Liberators bomb the harbor and marshaling yard at Toulon, France.

Twelfth Air Force B-25 Mitchells and B-26 Marauders attack marshaling yards, railroad bridges, and viaducts. A-20 Havocs, A-36 Intruder (Apache) fighter-bombers, P-51 Mustangs, and P-40s attack airfields, fuel storage areas, rail lines, gun positions, and roads.

NEW GUINEA: FEAF B-25 Mitchells bomb airfields at Manokwari during the night. A-20 Havocs, B-25s, P-39 Airacobras, P-38 Lightnings, P-40s, and P-47 Thunderbolts attack Japanese forces in the Sarmi-Sawar area and bomb airfields, shipping, and various installations on Halmahera Island.

July 12

CBI: An attack against Japanese defenses at Myitkyina fails.

Tenth Air Force P-40s support ground forces and 13 B-25 Mitchells attack targets around Myitkyina. The fighters accidentally bomb friendly troops during the attack.

In China, Fourteenth Air Force P-40s attack river shipping at Hengyang.

ATLANTIC: Convoy UGS 46 (United States to Mediterranean, Slow) is attacked off Algiers at dawn by 30 German aircraft. The convoy suffers no damage.

ETO: Before St-Lô at Martinville Ridge, the 29th Infantry Division faces repeated German counterattacks and heavy German artillery fire. Hill 122 remains in German possession and the Americans suffer 2,000 casualties in two days of fighting. German strongpoints and interlocked defensive positions at Hill 101 stop the attack. The 115th Infantry Regiment is stopped at le Cauchais.

Eighth Air Force sends over 1,200 B-17s and B-24 Liberators, escorted by 717 P-38 Lightnings, P-47 Thunderbolts, and P-51 Mustangs, to attack Munich, Germany. A total of 24 bombers are lost and 301 are damaged. Aircrew losses are two killed, seven wounded, and 216 missing. One P-38 is damaged.

During the night six B-17s drop leaflets over France.

Ninth Air Force sends over 300 A-20 and B-26 Marauders to attack fuel storage sites and bridges in France. Escorting P-47s also attack fuel storage sites, rail lines, artillery positions, and troops.

MEDITERRANEAN: Fifteenth Air Force sends over 400 B-24 Liberators to attack marshaling yards, bridges, and rail lines in southern France. Aircrews report 14 confirmed kills. Seven U.S. aircraft are lost.

ITALY: The 362nd and 363rd Infantry Regiments of the 91st Infantry Division attack with elements of the 88th Infantry Division toward the Arno River to capture Pontedera.

Naval units begin mine-clearing operations near Leghorn and at the mouth of the Arno River, raising fears in the German high command that another amphibious landing is being conducted. All landing craft in the Mediterranean at this time is now marked for the Anvil operation. Operation Mallory Major begins as Twelfth Air Force B-26 Marauders and B-25 Mitchells attempt to destroy all the bridges over the Po River. A-20 Havocs attack ammunition storage sites and P-47 Thunderbolts and P-40s attack barges and small boats on the Arno River, as well as roads, vehicle traffic, ammunition storage areas, and gun positions.

SOUTHWEST PACIFIC AREA: Submarine attack group TG 17.16 attacks a Japanese convoy spotted the previous day off the north coast of Luzon. USS *Apogon* makes a torpedo run on a cargo ship, but is damaged by a collision with another cargo ship, forcing *Apogon* to terminate her patrol. USS *Piranha* torpedoes and sinks a cargo ship.

CENTRAL PACIFIC: Seventh Air Force P-47 Thunderbolts from Saipan attack Japanese gun positions on Tinian Island. During the night B-24 Liberators stage through Eniwetok Atoll, bomb Truk and conduct another raid during the day.

NEW GUINEA: A battalion of the 128th Infantry (32nd Infantry Division) stops a Japanese attack toward Aitape. Reconnaissance elements of the 112th Cavalry and the 128th Infantry withdraw westward.

FEAF B-24 Liberators bomb Manokwari airfield and other B-24s bomb Yap. A-20 Havocs, B-25 Mitchells, P-39 Airacobras, P-38 Lightnings, P-40s, and P-47 Thunderbolts attack targets at Wewak.

The A-20 Havocs of the 386th Bombardment Squadron (Light), 312th Bombardment Group (Light), redeploy from Nadzab to Hollandia. The P-38 Lightnings of the 475th Fighter Group redeploy from Hollandia to Biak Island.

July 13

CBI: Tenth Air Force P-40s and P-51 Mustangs conduct ground support missions near Myitkyina. A-36 Intruder (Apache) fighter-bombers, P-51 Mustangs, and P-47 Thunderbolts attack bridges.

Fourteenth Air Force P-40s attack trucks, river shipping, and troop concentrations around Hengyang.

ETO: XIX Corps presses German defenders from the north and east near St-Lô. V Corps (2nd and 5th Infantry Divisions with the 2nd Armored Division and 1st Infantry Division in reserve).

Eighth Air Force sends 677 B-17s escorted by 462 P-38 Lightnings, P-47 Thunderbolts, and P-51 Mustangs to attack rail and industrial facilities at Munich, Germany. Aircrews report 11 confirmed kills and four probables. Nine bombers are lost and 288 are damaged. Aircrew losses are eight killed, 16 wounded, and 86 missing. Fighter pilots report two confirmed kills and one probable. Three fighters are lost and one is damaged.

In another strike, 366 B-24 Liberators escorted by over 80 P-51s are sent against the marshaling yards at Saarbrücken, Germany. One B-24 is lost and 38 are damaged. Aircrew casualties are 23 killed, nine wounded, and 19 missing. One P-51 is lost and one is damaged.

A total of 28 B-24s fly in support of Carpetbagger operations.

Ninth Air Force P-47s and P-38s attack German armor, rail lines, marshaling yards, and bridges in France.

ITALY: Fifteenth Air Force sends 581 B-17s and B-24 Liberators to attack marshaling yards, railroad bridges, and an oil storage facility in northern Italy.

Twelfth Air Force B-25 Mitchells and B-26 Marauders bomb bridges along the Po River valley. A-20 Havocs bomb an ammunition production facility. P-47 Thunderbolts and P-40s attack rail targets.

PACIFIC: U.S. submarine *Cobia* attacks a Japanese convoy, sinking a cargo ship north of the Bonin Islands.

CENTRAL PACIFIC: Seventh Air Force P-47 Thunderbolts from Saipan bomb Japanese positions on Tinian Island. B-24 Liberators from Kwajalein bomb Truk and B-25 Mitchells from Makin Island bomb Nauru Island.

NEW GUINEA: The Americans mount a counterattack to recapture the Driniumor River line. Supported by artillery, the 124th Infantry Regiment (31st Infantry Division), the 112th Cavalry, and the 127th and 128th Infantry Regiments (32nd Infantry Division) advance against the enemy. Fifth Air Force supports the attack with air strikes and aerial resupply of troops in heavy jungle.

Fifth Air Force B-25 Mitchells sink one cargo ship and damage another off Halmahera.

At Noemfoor, the 503rd Parachute Infantry encounters the Japanese at Hill 670.

FEAF P-47 Thunderbolts and P-40s provide ground support along the Driniumor River line. B-24 Liberators bomb Yap and Sorol Atoll.

The B-25s of the 345th Bombardment Group (Medium) redeploy from Nadzab to Biak Island.

July 14

CBI: Tenth Air Force P-40s attack Japanese positions near Myitkyina and 38 P-51 Mustangs and P-47 Thunderbolts attack bridges.

In China, Fourteenth Air Force B-25 Mitchells, P-40s, P-51 Mustangs, and P-47 Thunderbolts attack a Japanese fighter airstrip near Changsha and road and river traffic around Hengyang.

ETO: The 137th Infantry Regiment of the 35th Infantry Division of XIX Corps, supported by tanks, breaks the German line northwest of St-Lô, captures a bridge over the Vire River, and threatens Hill 122, the main German position defending the city. VIII Corps has moved through the *bocage* for 12 straight days and has advanced only eight miles. The 90th Infantry Division has suffered 5,000 casualties.

Eighth Air Force sends 359 B-17s escorted by 465 P-47 Thunderbolts and P-51 Mustangs to drop supplies to French irregular forces in France. Fifteen bombers are damaged. Aircrews report five confirmed kills and two probables. Fighter pilots report four confirmed kills. In another mission, 131 B-24 Liberators escorted by 79 P-38 Lightnings and P-51 Mustangs are sent to attack airfields in France. Nine bombers and one P-38 are damaged. P-38 Lightnings fly fighter-bomber missions against rail targets near Paris. Pilots report two confirmed kills and one P-38 is lost. The pilot is reported missing.

The 55th Fighter Group makes the transition from P-38s to P-51s.

Ninth Air Force sends over 60 A-20 and B-26 Marauders using Oboe (see October 20, 1944 ETO) to bomb rail lines in France. Escorting P-47 Thunderbolts encounter 85 German fighters and report six confirmed kills. Five fighters and their pilots are reported missing. The P-47s attack German defenses along the U.S. First Army front lines and attack rail targets.

MEDITERRANEAN: Fifteenth Air Force sends over 400 B-17s and B-24 Liberators to attack oil refineries at Budapest and at Petfurdo in Hungary. The bombers also hit the marshaling yard at Mantua, Italy.

Twelfth Air Force B-25 Mitchells and B-26 Marauders bomb bridges along the Po River valley. A-20 Havocs bomb an ammunition production facility. P-47 Thunderbolts and P-40s attack gun positions and rail targets.

CENTRAL PACIFIC: Seventh Air Force P-47 Thunderbolts from Saipan attack Japanese defenses on Tinian Island.

Navy PB4Y Privateers bomb Iwo Jima.

Underwater Demolition Team 3 conducts beach reconnaissance at Asan, Guam.

Destroyer escort *William C. Miller* sinks Japanese submarine *RO-48* east of Saipan. Later, the *William C. Miller* will join with high-speed transport *Gilmer* to sink Japanese submarine *I-6* west of Tinian.

NEW GUINEA: FEAF P-47 Thunderbolts, P-38 Lightnings, and P-40s support ground forces along the Driniumor River and bomb Japanese troops near Afua.

P-61 Black Widow night fighters attack airfields on the Vogelkop Peninsula. B-24 Liberators attack Yap. A-20 Havocs attack oil production facilities at Boela on Ceram Island in the Celebes. B-24s and B-25 Mitchells attack barge facilities and gun positions on Timor Island.

The headquarters of the 475th Fighter Group and the P-38s of the 433rd Fighter Squadron move from Hollandia to Biak Island.

U.S. submarine *Sand Lance* attacks a Japanese convoy in the Banda Sea south of Celebes Island and sinks a gunboat.

July 15

CBI: Tenth Air Force P-40s conduct ground support missions against Japanese defenses at Myitkyina. P-47 Thunderbolts and P-51 Mustangs attack bridges. Twenty B-25 Mitchells bomb near Myitkyina area and attack bridges and a logistics site.

Fourteenth Air Force sends 26 P-40s to provide ground support to Chinese forces in the Salween River area. Twelve B-25s bomb Mangshih and Lungling.

ETO: The 134th Infantry Regiment, 35th Infantry Division, of XIX Corps attacks Hill 122 and clears Germans from positions blocking the Isigny–St-Lô road. The infantrymen are supported by 21 tanks, three tank destroyers, and engineers. They advance behind an artillery barrage and airstrikes from P-47 Thunderbolts. The 115th Infantry Regiment attacking toward St-Lô suffers heavy casualties. The 116th and the 175th Infantry of the 29th Infantry Division make advances measured in yards. The 2nd Battalion of the 116th Infantry conducts a night attack and successfully breaks the German defenses, reaching the La Madeleine crossroads on the outskirts of St-Lô. By morning the battalion is isolated from American lines.

Eighth Air Force sends 169 P-38 Lightnings and P-47 Thunderbolts to make fighter-bomber attacks on enemy transport near Paris. Fighter pilots report three fighters lost and 13 damaged. Four pilots are reported missing.

A total of 27 B-24s fly in support of Carpetbagger operations. During the night six B-17s drop leaflets over France.

Ninth Air Force sends P-47s and P-38s to bomb infantry and artillery positions, a marshaling yard, and a bridge in the St-Lô, Argentan, and Falaise areas.

MEDITERRANEAN: Fifteenth Air Force sends over 600 B-17s and B-24 Liberators escorted by P-51 Mustangs and P-38 Lightnings to bomb oil refineries at Ploeşti, Romania.

ITALY: Twelfth Air Force B-25 Mitchells and B-26 Marauders bomb bridges along the Po River valley. A-20 Havocs bomb an ammunition production facility. P-47 Thunderbolts and P-40s attack gun positions, roads, and rail targets.

PACIFIC: U.S. submarine *Skate* torpedoes and sinks a Japanese fishing vessel in the Kuriles.

CENTRAL PACIFIC: Seventh Air Force P-47 Thunderbolts from Saipan bomb and strafe Japanese positions on Tinian Island. B-24 Liberators staging through Eniwetok Atoll bomb Truk.

NEW GUINEA: The 43rd Infantry Division arrives at Aitape, commanded by Major General Leonard T. Wing. High surf and nearly continuous rain delay the landing.

The 34th Infantry Regiment of the 24th Infantry Division leaves Biak Island for Hollandia.

FEAF A-20 Havocs bomb gun emplacements on an island off Manokwari. B-25 Mitchells, P-39 Airacobras, P-38 Lightnings, P-40s, and P-47 Thunderbolts attack targets around Wewak. B-24s bomb the town area, radio station, and barracks buildings on Yap.

The P-38s of the 431st Fighter Squadron 475th Fighter Group redeploy from Hollandia to Biak Island.

July 16

CBI: The Myitkyina Task Force, led by the American combat engineers fighting as infantry, assaults Japanese positions.

Tenth Air Force P-40s conduct ground support missions against Japanese defenses at Myitkyina. P-47 Thunderbolts and P-51 Mustangs attack bridges. Twenty B-25 Mitchells bomb near the Myitkyina area and attack bridges and a logistics site.

In China, Fourteenth Air Force sends 23 B-24 Liberators along with 40 P-51 Mustangs and P-40s to bomb Changsha and targets of opportunity near Hengyang.

The P-38s of the 449th Fighter Squadron 51st Fighter Group redeploy from Kweilin to Chengkung.

ATLANTIC: General Marshall, the army chief of staff, instructs General Jacob L. Devers to form an army group command for Anvil. Devers will be subordinate to General Sir Henry Maitland Wilson until General Eisenhower is ready to take operational control. Devers will have the U.S. Seventh Army under Lieutenant General Alexander M. Patch and the First French Army as his major forces.

ETO: Although the port of Cherbourg has been opened, the Allies can move only about 2,000 tons of supplies a day through the port. Within a month, the tonnage will rise to 12,000 a day, but the amount will still be insufficient to support divisions now requiring a total of up to 26,000 tons of supplies per day.

The 134th Infantry Regiment of the 35th Infantry Division is forced to abandon Hill 122 after a German counterattack, but the infantrymen rally and recapture the hill. A German counterattack on Martinville also fails.

Eighth Air Force sends over 640 B-17s, escorted by 454 P-38 Lightnings, P-47 Thunderbolts, and P-51 Mustangs, to attack Munich and Stuttgart, Germany. Eleven bombers are lost and 160 are damaged. Aircrews report two confirmed kills and three probables. Aircrew losses are two killed, eight wounded, and 91 missing. Two fighters are lost and the pilots are reported missing. Another attack sends over 400 B-24 Liberators escorted by 169 P-38s and P-47s against the marshaling yards at Saarbrücken, Germany. A total of 47 bombers are damaged. Aircrew casualties are one killed, and three wounded. One P-38 is lost and one is damaged.

A U.S. M-10 tank destroyer fires on German positions during the battle for St-Lô, France, in July 1944.

A total of 24 B-24s fly in support of Carpetbagger operations. During the night five B-17s drop leaflets over France.

Ninth Air Force sends 375 A-20 and B-26 Marauders with P-47s and P-38s to attack German strongpoints and defensive positions outside of St-Lô and bridges and fuel storage sites near Rennes.

MEDITERRANEAN: Major General Paul L. Williams, commander of IX Troop Carrier Command, arrives in Italy from England to activate the Provisional Troop Carrier Division to support Anvil.

Fifteenth Air Force sends over 300 bombers escorted by P-51 Mustangs and P-38 Lightnings against oil depots, aircraft production facilities, a marshaling yard, and airfields around Vienna, Austria. Over 100 German fighters attack the formations and shoot down 10 U.S. aircraft. Aircrews and fighter pilots report over 30 enemy fighters shot down.

ITALY: Twelfth Air Force B-25 Mitchells and B-26 Marauders bomb bridges along the Po River valley. A-20 Havocs bomb an ammunition production facility. P-47 Thunderbolts and P-40s attack gun positions, roads, and rail targets.

SOUTHWEST PACIFIC AREA: Submarine attack group TG 17.16 attacks a Japanese convoy off northern Luzon. USS *Piranha* torpedoes and sinks an army transport; USS *Guardfish* torpedoes and sinks a transport and a cargo ship; USS *Thresher* torpedoes and sinks a cargo ship and damages two other cargo ships.

U.S. submarine *Bonefish* torpedoes and sinks a Japanese cargo vessel south of Palawan.

U.S. submarine *Cabrilla* makes an unsuccessful attack on a Japanese convoy off the west coast of Mindanao.

PACIFIC: U.S. submarine *Skate* torpedoes and sinks a Japanese transport east of Sakhalin Island.

CENTRAL PACIFIC: Seventh Air Force P-47 Thunderbolts from Saipan bomb Japanese positions on Tinian Island.

Shore battery fire damages an infantry landing craft supporting the UDT 3 beach reconnaissance operation at Guam.

NEW GUINEA: At Wakde, the 31st Infantry Division under command of Major General John C. Pearsons begins the relief of the 6th Infantry Division. The battle for Wakde-Sarmi and Lone Tree Hill has cost the Americans 114 killed and 284 wounded. There are over 400 non-combat casualties, most of which are classified as neuropsychotic. Over 900 Japanese are dead. Wakde and Maffin Bay will become an important staging base for future operations.

FEAF B-24 Liberators bomb antiaircraft positions at Manokwari. B-24s bomb Yap and Atamboea airfield on Timor Island.

Second Lieutenant Dale E. Christensen of Troop E, 112th Cavalry Regiment, is leading his platoon during one of the many bitter firefights that have occurred on the Driniumor River. A Japanese machine gun is causing casualties among his men and Christensen orders his men to stay in place while he goes forward. Creeping to within range, he eliminates the position with hand grenades. During several subsequent encounter with the enemy, Second Lieutenant Christensen moves ahead alone to locate and destroy enemy positions and leads attacks to throw the Japanese off-balance. On August 4 near Afua, Christensen is killed leading his men in another attack. For his extraordinary and sustained courage and exceptional leadership in a desperate defense against a determined enemy, Second Lieutenant Dale Christensen will be awarded the Medal of Honor.

July 17

CBI: Tenth Air Force P-40s, P-47 Thunderbolts, and P-51 Mustangs attack Japanese positions at Myitkyina in support of Allied ground forces.

In China, Fourteenth Air Force sends 22 B-24 Liberators to bomb Changsha. B-25 Mitchells and P-40s attack the Kaifeng railyards. B-25s and 12 P-40s also attack Tengchung.

ETO: The commander of the 3rd Battalion 116th Infantry Regiment, Major Thomas D. Howie, is killed shortly after telling the division commander "I'll see you in St.-Lô!" The rifle companies in the 29th Infantry Division have been reduced to 30–40 men. Elements of the 116th and 115th Infantry Regiments break German lines using infiltration tactics instead of company formations and relieve the isolated 2nd Battalion of the 116th Infantry. German forces begin the evacuation of St-Lô. Although only a mile from St-Lô, neither battalion is able to advance.

Eighth Air Force sends 331 B-17s and 339 B-24 Liberators, escorted by 433 P-38 Lightnings, P-47 Thunderbolts, and P-51 Mustangs, to attack marshaling yards, roads, bridges, and fuel storage sites in France. One B-17 is lost and 122 are damaged. Aircrew losses are two killed, 10 wounded, and nine missing. Fighter pilots report 18 trucks and 55 rail cars destroyed in strafing attacks. One P-47 is lost and the pilot is reported missing.

During the evening 140 B-17s and B-24 Liberators escorted by over 200 P-51s attack 12 V-weapon sites in the Pas-de-Calais area. A total of 55 bombers are damaged. Aircrew casualties are one killed and five wounded. One P-51 is damaged.

A total of 16 B-24s fly in support of Carpetbagger operations. During the night five B-17s drop leaflets over France and the Netherlands.

Ninth Air Force sends 37 A-20 and 69 B-26 Marauders to attack marshaling yards and a fuel storage site in France. P-47s and P-38s escort the bombers and attack German positions at St-Lô in support of the 29th Infantry Division.

MEDITERRANEAN: Fifteenth Air Force sends 162 B-24 Liberators escorted by P-51 Mustangs and P-38 Lightnings to bomb a marshaling yard and railroad bridges in southern France.

ITALY: The 168th and 133rd Infantry Regiments of the 34th Infantry Division advance toward Leghorn. Major General Vernon E. Pritchard takes command of the 1st Armored Division from Major General Ernest Harmon.

Twelfth Air Force B-25 Mitchells and B-26 Marauders bomb bridges along the Po River valley. A-20 Havocs bomb an ammunition production facility. P-47 Thunderbolts and P-40s attack bridges and rail targets.

SOUTHWEST PACIFIC AREA: U.S. submarine *Cabrilla* again attacks the Japanese convoy, sinking an army transport and damaging another transport off the west coast of Mindanao.

U.S. submarine attack group TG 17.16 locates Japanese ships west of Luzon. USS *Guardfish* torpedoes and sinks a cargo ship; USS *Thresher* torpedoes and sinks a cargo ship near Luzon Strait.

PACIFIC: A cargo ship carrying ammunition explodes at the Port Chicago, California, ammunition depot, destroying a nearby freighter as well. About 5,000 tons of explosives were detonated. The casualties include 250 African-American sailors. Survivors refuse to return to work and 50 are later sent before a court-martial on charges of mutiny.

U.S. submarine *Gabilan* torpedoes and sinks a Japanese minesweeper south of Kyushu, Japan.

CENTRAL PACIFIC: Seventh Air Force P-47 Thunderbolts from Saipan attack Japanese positions at Tinian Island. B-25 Mitchells from Makin Island stage through Engebi Island on Eniwetok Atoll to bomb the airfield and antiaircraft positions on Ponape Island.

Frogmen of UDT 3 begin to use demolitions to clear obstacles off the landing beaches on Guam.

NEW GUINEA: At the Driniumor River, the 112th Cavalry attempts to close the gap to the north with the 124th Infantry Regiment (31st Infantry Division) and to establish a continuous defensive line, but is stopped by a Japanese counterattack.

FEAF B-25 Mitchells, A-20 Havocs, and P-39 Airacobras attack Japanese troops and logistics storage sites between Aitape and Wewak. B-25s bomb Timor Island.

July 18

CBI: Tenth Air Force P-40s and B-25 Mitchells attack Japanese positions at Myitkyina area. P-51 Mustangs support ground forces at Pyindaw.

Fourteenth Air Force P-40s attack river shipping in the Hengyang-Tungting Lake region and bomb the airfield and antiaircraft positions at Hengyang.

ETO: General Norman Cota of the 29th Infantry Division enters St-Lô with the 3rd Battalion of the 116th Infantry, preceded by the body of Major Howie. His soldiers place the body, lying underneath an American flag, in the ruins of St. Croix church;

he becomes known as the "Major of St-Lô." In about two weeks of fighting in the advance to St-Lô, American forces have suffered 40,000 casualties, most of them in infantry units. Since June 6, the fighting in the *bocage* has severely depleted the American infantry divisions. The high casualties have reduced rifle companies to 40 percent strength and only about 30 percent of the officers who landed on the beaches with their soldiers are still with their units. German losses have been estimated at 160,000, including 400 tanks.

The VII Corps reaches the Périers-St-Lô Road, gaining valuable territory in the open fields beyond the *bocage* and an opportunity for maneuver. The 9th and 30th Infantry Divisions from VII Corps cross the Vire River and occupy the high ground.

Bradley's task is to break through west of St-Lô and move to Coutances in order to isolate German forces and attack south to seize Avranches. General Montgomery approves General Bradley's plan for Operation Cobra. Bradley plans to employ over 2,200 aircraft to bomb German positions south of the St-Lô–Périers Road, followed by a 1,000-gun artillery barrage. VII Corps (the 4th, 9th, and 30th Infantry Divisions) will advance through the German lines, followed by an exploitation force of the 2nd and 3rd Armored Divisions and the 1st Infantry Division. Montgomery desires First Army to cut off German defenders in the Périers-Lessay area in the southern section of the Cotentin Peninsula while Lieutenant General Patton's Third Army attacks into Brittany. The Second British Army is to hold German forces in place.

Eighth Air Force sends 644 B-24 Liberators, in conjunction with Ninth Air Force and RAF Bomber Command, to bomb German positions in support of the British Second Army's attack on Caen. One B-24 is lost and 184 are damaged. More than 750 B-17s attack the Kiel port area and the Peenemünde experimental area, which is used for developing V-weapons. Three bombers are lost and 85 are damaged. The bombers are escorted by over 400 P-38 Lightnings and P-51 Mustangs. Over Peenemünde, fighter pilots report 21 confirmed kills. Three P-51s are lost and one damaged. Two pilots are reported missing.

A total of 25 B-24s fly in support of Carpetbagger operations. One bomber is lost.

Ninth Air Force sends over 400 B-26 Marauders and A-20 Havocs to attack German defensive positions in the Caen area.

MEDITERRANEAN: En route to Memminger airfield in Germany 200 B-24 Liberators and B-17s encounter 200 German fighters. In the ensuing air battle, 14 B-17s and 66 German fighters are lost. B-17 aircrews report 66 confirmed kills in the air and 35 aircraft destroyed on the ground. Twenty U.S. aircraft are shot down.

The C-47s of the 439th, 440th, 441st, and 442nd Troop Carrier Commands redeploy from England to Italy as part of the provisional troop carrier division supporting Anvil.

ITALY: The 442nd RCT along with the 133rd and 168th Infantry Regiments of the 34th Infantry Division enter the Arno River Valley to outflank German defenders at Leghorn.

A-20 Havocs and P-47 Thunderbolts make limited attacks on bridges, roads, and rail lines due to bad weather.

SOUTHWEST PACIFIC AREA: U.S. submarine attack group TG 17.3, commanded by Captain Warren D. Wilkin, attacks a Japanese convoy near Luzon Strait. USS *Tilefish* torpedoes a coastal patrol ship, while USS *Sawfish* torpedoes an oiler.

PACIFIC: Tojo Hideki is removed as Japanese premier and war minister, largely as a result of the loss of Saipan, considered an essential part of the outer defensive line protecting Japan.

U.S. submarine *Cobia* torpedoes and sinks a Japanese gunboat and a cargo ship near Chichi Jima.

U.S. submarine *Plaice* attacks a Japanese convoy, sinking a submarine chaser northwest of Chichi Jima.

CENTRAL PACIFIC: Seventh Air Force P-47 Thunderbolts from Saipan attack Japanese positions on Tinian Island. B-24 Liberators from Kwajalein bomb Wotje Atoll. B-24 Liberators staging through Eniwetok Atoll bomb Truk.

NEW GUINEA: American forces establish a continuous defensive line along the Driniumor River, having pushed the Japanese back with concentrated artillery fire and close combat.

FEAF A-20 Havocs and P-47 Thunderbolts attack barges, supply routes, and Japanese troops along the coast from Aitape to Wewak. B-24 Liberators bomb Yap.

U.S. submarine *Lapon* torpedoes and sinks a Japanese auxiliary submarine chaser off Palawan Island and survey ship and auxiliary submarine chaser northwest of Borneo in the Sulu Sea. U.S. submarine *Ray* torpedoes and sinks a Japanese merchant tanker in the Java Sea.

Fifth Air Force B-24 Liberators sink a Japanese transport northwest of Morotai Island.

July 19

CBI: Tenth Air Force B-25 Mitchells, P-40s, and P-51 Mustangs attack Japanese positions at the Myitkyina area and ground force support near Kamaing.

In China, Fourteenth Air Force sends more than 80 P-40s to attack shipping, logistics sites, and Japanese troops in the Tungting Lake area and around Hengyang. The fighters also bomb a radio station, logistics depots, and shipping at Changsha. P-40s also bomb the airfield at Siangtan.

ETO: Eighth Air Force sends over 1,200 B-17s and B-24 Liberators, escorted by over 700 P-38 Lightnings, P-47 Thunderbolts, and P-51 Mustangs, to attack industrial production and transportation targets in Germany. These targets are related to industrial production and transportation. Seventeen bombers and seven fighters are lost. Aircrews report six confirmed kills and four probables. Fighters escorting the bombers also strafe locomotives, rolling stock, and vehicles. Fighter pilots report 17 confirmed kills in the air and 38 on the ground.

A total of five B-24s fly in support of Carpetbagger operations. During the night five B-17s drop leaflets over France and Belgium.

Ninth Air Force sends 262 A-20 and B-26 Marauders against bridges and fuel storage facilities in France. P-47s escorting the bombers attack German positions.

The headquarters of the 373rd Fighter Group redeploys to France. The P-47s of the 513th Fighter Squadron 406th Fighter Group redeploy to France as well.

MEDITERRANEAN: Fifteenth Air Force sends over 400 B-17s and B-24 Liberators escorted by P-51 Mustangs and P-38 Lightnings to conduct follow-on bombing of an ordnance depot, an aircraft production facility, a motor works, and an airfield in the Munich area after Eighth Air Force bombers have hit the targets. A total of 16 U.S. aircraft are lost with others reported missing.

ITALY: Leghorn falls to the 135th and 363rd Infantry Regiments. The Germans have systematically destroyed the port and have sowed the entire city with mines and booby traps.

Twelfth Air Force B-25 Mitchells and B-26 Marauders attack bridges. A-20 Havocs and P-47 Thunderbolts attack rail lines.

SOUTHWEST PACIFIC AREA: U.S. submarine *Flasher* torpedoes and sinks a Japanese light cruiser in the South China Sea. U.S. submarine *Guardfish* attacks a Japanese cargo ship in the South China Sea southwest of Formosa.

PACIFIC: U.S. submarine *Tautog* torpedoes and sinks a Japanese guardboat in the Bonin Islands.

CENTRAL PACIFIC: Seventh Air Force P-47 Thunderbolts attack Japanese positions on Tinian Island.

Destroyer escort USS *Wyman* sinks Japanese submarine *I-5* east of Guam.

NEW GUINEA: FEAF-20 Havocs, P-47 Thunderbolts, P-38 Lightnings, and P-40s attack Japanese troops, logistics sites, gun positions, and targets of opportunity along the Driniumor River and support Allied ground forces around Sarmi and Sawar. B-24 Liberators bomb the airfield on Yap. Some of the bombers miss the primary target and bomb Ngulu and Sorol Atolls in the Carolines.

July 20

CBI: Tenth Air Force P-40s attack targets around Myitkyina.

Fourteenth Air Force B-24 Liberators bomb Changsha. Aircrews report heavy damage. Over 140 P-40s and P-51 Mustangs attack river shipping and road traffic in the Tungting Lake area and attack troop compounds and gun positions near Hengyang.

ATLANTIC: JCS planners reject MacArthur's Reno V plan, indicating that the plan requires more air support than is available in-theater and would require most of the Pacific Fleet. They assess that MacArthur's approach would delay the invasion of Japan by one year.

President Roosevelt is nominated for an unprecedented fourth term of office at the Democratic National Convention in Chicago.

ETO: First Army occupies a line stretching 40 miles from Lessey on the west coast of the Cotentin Peninsula, east along the Pèriers–St-Lô Road to Caumont. Ultra intercepts of German communications indicate that the defenders are nearly at the end of their resources.

The damage to the Normandy beaches from a four-day storm in the English Channel, June 19–22, is repaired. The artificial ports (called Mulberries) are now the main means of moving cargo from ships to shore. During this time the ports handle an average of 6,700 tons of supplies per day.

Eighth Air Force sends 417 B-17s escorted by 253 P-38 Lightnings, P-47 Thunderbolts, and P-51 Mustangs to attack airfields and industrial targets in Germany. Fifteen bombers are lost and 188 are damaged. Aircrew losses are one killed, 10 wounded, and 129 missing. Fighter pilots report five confirmed kills in the air and two on the ground. Four fighters are lost and one P-51 is damaged. Three pilots are reported missing and one pilot is wounded. Another 295 B-17s escorted by 178 P-38 Lightnings, P-47 Thunderbolts, and P-51 Mustangs attack German industrial targets. Two B-17s are lost and 153 are damaged. Aircrew casualties are two wounded and 21 missing. Aircrews report one confirmed kill and one probable in the air and one confirmed kill on the ground. Fighter pilots report one confirmed kill and one probable in the air and one confirmed kill on the ground. One P-51 is lost and one damaged; the pilot is reported missing.

Over 400 B-24 Liberators bomb industrial targets and airfields in Germany escorted by 45 P-47s. One bomber is lost and 31 are damaged. Aircrew casualties are two wounded and nine missing. Fighter pilots report six confirmed kills on the ground. One P-47 is lost. The pilot is reported missing.

A total of 12 B-24s fly in support of Carpetbagger operations.

Ninth Air Force sends 62 A-20 and B-26 Marauders to attack a marshaling yard, and P-47s conduct attacks on rail lines, German troop positions, and bridges.

The C-47 squadrons of the 435th, 436th, and 438th Troop Carrier Groups begin redeployment from England to Italy in preparation for the airborne operation supporting Anvil.

At his secret headquarters in East Prussia, Adolf Hitler survives an assassination attempt when a hidden bomb explodes under a table during a military briefing.

MEDITERRANEAN: Fifteenth Air Force sends over 400 B-17s and B-24 Liberators escorted by P-38 Lightnings and P-51 Mustangs against airfields and aircraft production facilities in Germany. Aircrews and fighter pilots report 19 German fighters shot down.

ITALY: Twelfth Air Force B-25 Mitchells and B-26 Marauders bomb bridges along the Po River valley. A-20 Havocs bomb an ammunition production facility. P-47 Thunderbolts attack rail targets.

PACIFIC: U.S. submarine *Cobia* attacks a three-ship Japanese convoy northwest of Chichi Jima, sinking two auxiliary submarine chasers and damaging a cargo ship. The *Cobia* is rammed during the attack, but the submarine sustains only minor damage.

CENTRAL PACIFIC: Vice Admiral Kelly Turner, commander of the amphibious force, sets a date for the landing on Tinian of July 24. The 2nd and 4th Marine Divisions will make the landings. The 4th Marine Division is commanded by Major General Clifton B. Cates. The previous commander, Major General Harry Schmidt, takes command of V Amphibious Corps, replacing Lieutenant General Holland M. Smith, who is appointed commander, Fleet Marine Forces Pacific.

Seventh Air Force P-47 Thunderbolts from Saipan bomb Tinian Island. B-25 Mitchells from Engebi Island bomb Ponape Island.

NEW GUINEA: At the Driniumor River, the 112th Cavalry and the 127th Infantry Regiments of the 32nd Infantry Division stop a Japanese attack to outflank the American defensive line.

FEAF B-24 Liberators attack the airfield and antiaircraft positions at Manokwari and B-25 Mitchells attack shipping. A-20 Havocs support the American defense at the Driniumor River.

B-24s bomb Yap and targets in the Molucca Islands. B-25 Mitchells attack shipping at Dili on Timor Island.

July 21

CBI: In China Fourteenth Air Force sends 41 P-40s to attack the town, airfield, trucks, river shipping, and troops at Changsha and vehicles, river transportation, and troop positions at Hengyang.

ATLANTIC: The Democratic National Convention in Chicago nominates Senator Harry S. Truman of Missouri to be vice president.

ETO: Eighth Air Force sends 581 B-17s and 529 B-24 Liberators, escorted by over 700 P-38 Lightnings, P-47 Thunderbolts, and P-51 Mustangs, to attack aircraft production facilities and airfields in southern Germany. A total of 31 bombers are lost and 365 are damaged. Aircrews report 10 confirmed kills and two probables. Aircrew casualties are four killed, 11 wounded, and 288 missing. Fighter pilots report six confirmed kills in the air and three on the ground. Eight fighters are lost.

During the night eight B-17s drop leaflets over France. One bomber is damaged.

Ninth Air Force redeploys the headquarters of the 323rd Bombardment Group (Medium) and the B-26 Marauders of the 453rd, 454th, 455th, and 456th Bombardment Squadrons from England to France.

MEDITERRANEAN: Fifteenth Air Force sends 362 B-17s and B-24 Liberators escorted by P-38 Lightnings and P-51 Mustangs to attack a synthetic oil refinery and a marshaling yard in Czechoslovakia. Many bombers are forced to abort the mission due to bad weather en route to the targets.

ITALY: Major General Charles Bolte replaces Major General Charles W. Ryder as commander of the 34th Infantry Division.

Twelfth Air Force A-20 Havocs and P-47 Thunderbolts attack convoys, bridges on the Po River, and roads.

SOUTHWEST PACIFIC AREA: SWPA headquarters orders Lieutenant General Krueger's Alamo Force to prepare plans to seize a section of Morotai Island and establish an airfield there. Morotai Island is 10 miles northeast of Halamahera Island. An airfield at Morotai would isolate the Japanese base at Halamahera Island, holding 30,000 troops. Aircraft from Morotai would also eliminate Japanese air attacks originating from the Netherlands East Indies and the Celebes. More importantly, U.S. aircraft from Morotai can reach Leyte and Mindanao, two key islands in the Philippines, and the ultimate goal of General Douglas MacArthur's efforts since the defeat at Corregidor in 1942.

CENTRAL PACIFIC, GUAM: Operation Stevedore. Landings begin at Guam. The Americans have returned for the first time since the Japanese invasion on December 10, 1941. Admiral Raymond A. Spruance is commander of Fifth Fleet; Naval Task Force 53 is commanded by Rear Admiral Richard L. Conolly. Connolly employs both naval gunfire and aircraft to support the landings. Air cover is provided by 85 fighters, 65 bombers, and 53 torpedo planes from the carrier USS *Wasp.*

The Stars and Stripes is planted on Guam minutes after marines land on the beach, July 20, 1944.

The ground force is the III Marine Amphibious Corps, commanded by Major General Roy S. Geiger. It is composed of the 3rd Marine Division, the 1st Provisional Marine Brigade, and the army's 77th Infantry Division. The 3rd and 21st Marine Regiments of the 3rd Marine Division land between Asan Point and Adelup Point. The 3rd Marines are stopped by heavy fire from steep cliffs facing the beachhead. The 21st Marines find a gap in the Japanese defenses and occupy the ridge above their beachhead. Captain Geary R. Bundschu, commanding A Company of the 1st Battalion 3rd Marines, holds a precarious position on the ridge and is unable to advance in the face of heavy fire. He is killed on the ridge and his marines rename the position Bundschu Ridge. The 22nd Marines take heavy casualties on the beach from artillery fire and mines and advance only about 2,000 yards in the face of enemy fire. The 4th and 22nd Marines make a night attack to seize key high ground and move off the beachhead.

The 1st Provisional Brigade lands between Apaga Point and Bangi Point in Agat Bay. The 77th Infantry Division, commanded by Major General Andrew D. Bruce, lands later in the day, and the 305th Infantry Regiment supports the marines in throwing back a Japanese counterattack that night. The 4th Marines captures Bangi Point and establishes a roadblock. There are 18,500 Japanese troops on the island.

Seventh Air Force P-47 Thunderbolts from Saipan attack Japanese defensive positions on Tinian Island. B-24 Liberators, staging through Eniwetok Atoll, bomb Truk.

Private First Class Luther Skaggs, Jr., becomes the squad leader of a mortar section in a rifle company of 3rd Battalion, 3rd Marines, 3rd Marine Division, after the section takes casualties landing on Asan-Adelup beachhead. Leading the men inland 200 yards he sets up his mortars to provide support for the infantry. During the night, the Japanese conduct several counterattacks. Although sustaining a severe leg wound from a grenade explosion, Private First Class Skaggs applies a tourniquet to his injured leg and, propping himself up in his foxhole, continues to fight. Only after the attack has been stopped by eight hours of continuous fighting does Private First Class Skaggs crawl back to the rear to get medical assistance. For his amazing feat of courage and determination Private First Class Skaggs will be awarded the Medal of Honor.

NEW GUINEA: FEAF B-24 Liberators bomb antiaircraft positions and the airfield at Manokwari. P-39 Airacobras bomb caves and barge locations on Biak Island and support ground forces. B-25 Mitchells attack shipping off the Vogelkop Peninsula. A-20 Havocs, P-39s, and P-47 Thunderbolts attack targets of opportunity.

B-24s attack the airfield at Yap. Aircrews report seven Japanese fighters shot down.

July 22

CBI: Tenth Air Force P-40s attack Japanese positions at Myitkyina.

In China, Fourteenth Air Force sends over 120 P-40s and P-51 Mustangs to attack the town, airfield, railroad yards, and shipping at Hengyang. Over 20 B-24 Liberators bomb Changsha. Aircrews report heavy damage. P-40s sink several large junks off the northeast coast of French Indochina.

ATLANTIC: President Roosevelt departs Washington, D.C., aboard the heavy cruiser USS *Baltimore* to travel to Hawaii and meet with Admiral Nimitz and General MacArthur to discuss the future direction of the Pacific campaign.

ETO: Eighth Air Force sends seven B-17s escorted by 27 P-51 Mustangs to drop leaflets on Bremen, Hamburg, and Kiel in Germany. One B-17 and two P-51s are damaged. One crewman is reported killed.

A total of 44 B-24s fly in support of Carpetbagger operations.

Ninth Air Force redeploys the headquarters of the 367th Fighter Group to France.

MEDITERRANEAN: Fifteenth Air Force sends 76 P-38 Lightnings and 58 P-51 Mustangs on a Frantic mission, attacking airfields at Zilistea and Buzau in Romania en route to airfields in the Soviet Ukraine. Fighter pilots report 56 German aircraft destroyed.

Another mission sends 458 B-17s and B-24 Liberators against the Ploeşti oil refinery in Romania and marshaling yards and a railroad bridge in Yugoslavia.

ITALY: The French Expeditionary Corps is moved out of the front line for the Anvil operation. The British Eighth Army extends its front to fill the gap and link with Fifth Army.

Twelfth Air Force B-25 Mitchells attack bridges. A-20 Havocs and P-47 Thunderbolts attack rail lines, bridges, gun positions, and vehicles.

CENTRAL PACIFIC: Seventh Air Force P-47 Thunderbolts from Saipan use napalm bombs on Japanese positions on Tinian. Napalm is jelled gasoline that creates heavy flames and smoke and is especially effective against Japanese defenses in the caves and deep crevasses that troops have turned into fortresses, often resistant to regular high-explosive bombs.

B-25 Mitchells from Makin Island bomb Ponape Island.

CENTRAL PACIFIC, GUAM: The 21st and 3rd Marine Regiments are held up at Bundschu Ridge by mortar fire and Japanese machine-gun positions placing an effective crossfire across the ridge. The 9th Marines make progress against minimal resistance and occupy Piti on Apra Harbor. That night, elements of the 21st Marines stop a weak Japanese counterattack.

Private First Class Leonard F. Mason of the 2nd Battalion, 3rd Marines, 3rd Marine Division finds himself in a narrow gully when his unit takes fire from two Japanese machine guns concealed only 15 yards away. Mason moves out of the gully to locate the rear of the enemy position and is almost immediately wounded by fire from another enemy position. Although mortally wounded, he destroys the machine guns threatening his platoon and rejoins his unit before being evacuated. Private First Class Mason's extraordinary courage and sacrifice will win him the Medal of Honor.

NEW GUINEA: During the battle along the Driniumor River, Private First Class Donald R. Lobaugh of the 127th Infantry Regiment 32nd Infantry Division finds himself in a precarious situation. He and his platoon have been cut off and surrounded by Japanese troops when his company attempted to withdraw the day before. The platoon has survived the night, but the Japanese have set up a blocking position supported by a machine gun that cuts off their escape route. PFC Lobaugh volunteers to attack the enemy position and leaves the safety of his fighting position to advance across 30 yards of open ground. In full view of the enemy, PFC Lobaugh throws a hand grenade and is wounded. Without pause, he charges the position, firing his weapon. Although hit several times, he continues to fight the enemy until finally killed. PFC Lobaugh's heroic act causes his fellow infantrymen to sweep the enemy position and allows the platoon to reach friendly lines. PFC Lobaugh's extraordinary determination in battle will win him the Medal of Honor.

At Biak, the 163rd Infantry eliminates the last Japanese defensive strongpoint, called the Ibdi pocket. Biak is won but at a cost of 400 dead and 2,000 wounded.

FEAF B-24 Liberators, B-25 Mitchells, A-20 Havocs, P-39 Airacobras, P-38 Lightnings, P-40s, and P-47 Thunderbolts attack shipping targets around the Vogelkop Peninsula and report sinking a Japanese submarine chaser. B-24s attack the airfield at Yap.

July 23

CBI: Under pressure by the Allied attack on Myitkyina, Japanese forces begin to withdraw.

Tenth Air Force B-25 Mitchells and over 100 P-51 Mustangs, A-36 Intruder (Apache) fighter-bombers, P-47 Thunderbolts, and P-40 fighter-bombers hit enemy positions in the Myitkyina area and bomb the Kamaing and Mogaung areas.

In China, Fourteenth Air Force P-40s attack warehouses, trucks, and troops near Changsha and Hengyang. B-25 Mitchells and P-40s attack warehouses and rail lines along the Yellow River. P-40s support Chinese forces along the Salween River. The 449th Fighter Squadron 51st Fighter Group at Chengkung redeploys a detachment of P-38 Lightnings to operate from Yunnani.

ATLANTIC: German submarine *U-861* torpedoes and sinks a U.S. freighter off the Brazilian coast near Rio de Janeiro.

ETO: The headquarters of the 12th Army Group arrives in France. It will become operational on August 1.

Eighth Air Force sends 82 B-17s and 198 B-24 Liberators escorted by 177 P-38 Lightnings and P-51 Mustangs to attack airfields in France. One B-17 is lost and six are damaged; aircrew losses are three killed and three wounded.

A total of 21 B-24s fly in support of Carpetbagger operations.

Ninth Air Force sends over 300 A-20 and B-26 Marauders to attack fuel storage areas and bridges. P-47 Thunderbolts escorting the bombers attack roads, bridges, artillery, strongpoints, troop concentrations, and various targets of opportunity.

MEDITERRANEAN: Fifteenth Air Force sends 42 B-24 Liberators escorted by 15 P-51 Mustangs to bomb the oil refinery at Berat, Albania.

ITALY: The 363rd Infantry Regiment of the 91st Infantry Division occupies Pisa, south of the Arno River. The Fifth Army is halted for rest and resupply.

Twelfth Air Force B-25 Mitchells and B-26 Marauders attack bridges along the Po River valley. A-20 Havocs and P-47 Thunderbolts attack rail lines and roads.

CENTRAL PACIFIC: Seventh Air Force P-47 Thunderbolts on Saipan Island bomb Japanese positions on Tinian Island. The B-25 Mitchells of the 48th Bombardment Squadron (Medium), 41st Bombardment Group (Medium), redeploy from Abemama Island in the Gilbert Islands to Saipan. B-25s from Makin Island attack Nauru Island. B-24 Liberators staging through Eniwetok Atoll, bomb Truk. Other B-24s from Kwajalein bomb Wotje Atoll.

CENTRAL PACIFIC, GUAM: The 3rd and 21st Marine Regiments battle to the top of Bundschu Ridge, but are unable to continue any farther against numerous enemy positions. The Japanese begin marshaling reinforcements near Mount Tenjo.

NEW GUINEA: FEAF B-24 Liberators, A-20 Havocs, B-25 Mitchells, P-39 Airacobras, P-38 Lightnings, P-40s, and P-47 Thunderbolts attack targets on the Vogelkop Peninsula. The headquarters of the 345th Bombardment Group (Medium) and the B-25s of the 500th and 501st Bombardment Squadrons (Medium) redeploy from Nadzab to Biak Island.

B-24s attack the airfield at Yap.

Sergeant Ray E. Eubanks of D Company, 503rd Parachute Infantry Regiment, is attempting to come to the aid of a platoon isolated by the Japanese on Noemfoor Island. When his company takes machine-gun, rifle, and mortar fire from a strong enemy position, Eubanks is ordered to take a squad and lay down a base of fire to suppress the Japanese so that the rest of the company can move forward.

Maneuvering to within 30 yards of the enemy, Sergeant Eubanks halts his men and orders them to continue firing while he moves closer to the enemy position. Taking a Browning Automatic Rifle (BAR) he braves heavy fire to reach a position about 15 yards from the enemy where he is able to deliver accurate fire on the Japanese. Sergeant Eubanks is quickly wounded and his weapon is damaged by a bullet. He nevertheless charges into the enemy position, and using the BAR as a club, eliminates the position before falling mortally wounded. For his great courage in the face of the enemy, Sergeant Eubanks will be awarded the Medal of Honor.

Second Lieutenant George W. G. Boyce, Jr., a platoon leader in the 112th Cavalry Regimental Combat Team, is ordered to attack with his platoon to overcome Japanese defenses near Afua, on the Driniumor River, and open the way for the troop to reach an isolated American unit. As Boyce's platoon moves forward, the Japanese immediately respond with rifle, machine-gun, and mortar fire. As he moves forward with a squad to establish a base of fire, the Japanese throw hand grenades into the midst of the Americans. Second Lieutenant Boyce throws himself on a grenade and saves the lives of several of his men. Boyce's sacrifice will win him the Medal of Honor.

July 24

CBI: Tenth Air Force P-51 Mustangs attack targets near Kamaing and Mogaung and P-40s attack Japanese positions at Myitkyina.

In China, Fourteenth Air Force B-25 Mitchells and P-40s bomb rail facilities at Sienning. P-40s attack Pailochi airfield. Fighter pilots report 30 Japanese aircraft destroyed. P-40s attack river and road transportation and Japanese troop concentrations at Changsha and Hengyang. P-51 Mustangs dive-bomb White Cloud airfield near Canton.

ATLANTIC: German submarine *U-861* attacks convoy JT 99 (Rio de Janeiro to Trinidad) and escapes as aircraft from escort carrier USS *Solomons* close in.

ETO: Operation Cobra. Eighth Air Force sends 909 B-17s and 677 B-24 Liberators, escorted by 478 P-38 Lightnings, P-47 Thunderbolts, and P-51 Mustangs, to attack German defensive positions in front of the U.S. First Army for Operation Cobra, but the mission is cancelled due to heavy cloud cover. One group of bombers, however, continues the mission and flies perpendicular to the intended target, not parallel, as Bradley had desired. The 452 bombers that continue the mission attack German positions and road and rail lines west of St-Lô, but drop 700 tons of bombs short of the intended target, causing 150 American casualties from the 30th Infantry Division.

Three bombers are lost and 144 are damaged. Aircrew casualties are two killed, two wounded, and 21 missing. Fighter pilots report one confirmed kill in the air and one on the ground. Three fighters are lost and two are damaged.

Over Germany 143 P-51 Mustangs fly a sweep over Lechfeld and Leipheim airfields. Pilots report three confirmed kills in the air and 12 on the ground. Two P-51s are lost and seven are damaged. The two pilots are reported missing.

During the night seven B-17s drop leaflets over France. A total of six B-24s fly in support of Carpetbagger operations.

Ninth Air Force sends A-20 and B-26 Marauders to attack bridges and fuel storage sites. P-47s and P-38s attack roads, bridges, and logistics storage sites.

The headquarters of the 370th Fighter Group redeploys to France. Ninth Air Force is now operating from 15 airfields in Normandy.

ITALY: Fifteenth Air Force sends 200 B-17s and B-24 Liberators against a tank repair facility, a ball-bearing production facility, harbor facilities, and airfields in Italy.

Twelfth Air Force B-25 Mitchells and B-26 Marauders attack bridges. A-20 Havocs attack ammunition storage facilities. P-47 Thunderbolts attack bridges, rail lines, and roads.

CENTRAL PACIFIC, TINIAN: Naval Task Force 52, commanded by Rear Admiral Harry W. Hill, lands the 4th Marine Division (Major General Harry Schmidt, USMC) on Tinian. Naval gunfire, carrier aircraft, and land-based aircraft from Saipan support the landing. The 2nd Marine Division conducts a feint off the shore in view of Tinian town, supported by air and naval bombardment and artillery fire from Saipan. The deception becomes a real fight when 6-inch Japanese guns fire on the ships supporting the marines. The battleship *Colorado* is hit 22 times, but is saved by the heroic act of the captain of the destroyer *Norman Scott,* who puts his ship in the line of fire and takes six hits as well. The deception costs 62 men killed and 322 wounded. The Japanese report that the American attempt to land on Tinian has been stopped.

Meanwhile, the 4th Marine Division lands on the northwest corner of the island with minimum resistance. The army's XXIV Corps Artillery supports the landings with fire from Saipan. The 25th Marine Regiment encounters mines, but the 24th Marines reach their objective line. After much confusion and delay, the 23rd Marines land. The 8th Marine Regiment of the 2nd Marine Division, now redeployed north after the deception operation, lands shortly afterward. Within a few hours, 15,600 men are on the island at a cost of 15 killed and 225 wounded. That night, the Japanese counterattack with infantry and tanks, but are driven back by the 24th and 23rd Marines.

Seventh Air Force P-47 Thunderbolts from Saipan attack Japanese positions.

CENTRAL PACIFIC, GUAM: The 77th Infantry Division has completed its landing on Guam and now has responsibility for the southern perimeter of the beachhead.

NEW GUINEA: FEAF B-25 Mitchells of the 499th Bombardment Squadron (Medium), 345th Bombardment Group (Medium), redeploy from Nadzab to Biak Island. The headquarters of the 85th Fighter Wing redeploys to Hollandia.

Fifth Air Force B-24 Liberators sink a Japanese transport in Kau Bay, Halmahera Island.

July 25

CBI: Tenth Air Force P-40s and P-51 Mustangs attack targets around Myitkyina, Kamaing, and Mogaung.

In China, Fourteenth Air Force sends 24 B-24 Liberators to bomb the railyards at Yoyang. P-40 pilots escorting the bombers report six Japanese fighters shot down. P-40s and P-51 Mustangs attack road and river traffic and cavalry units at Changsha and Hengyang. P-47 Thunderbolts and P-51 Mustangs support Chinese ground forces at the Salween River front.

Fourteenth Air Force B-25 Mitchells sink a Japanese salvage vessel east of Hong Kong.

ATLANTIC: German submarine *U-862* torpedoes and sinks a U.S. freighter in the central South Atlantic.

ETO: Operation Cobra. The 21st Army Group begins the breakout from Normandy. Bradley's concept for Cobra is to employ an overwhelming air attack against German positions along a narrow front. Before the enemy can recover, a massed artillery bombardment will follow. The infantry will attack with three divisions of VII Corps followed by three more divisions of VIII Corps to capture Coutances and Granville. The First Army will make the main effort. VII Corps of First Army is to attack on a narrow front along the Périers Road west of St-Lô after heavy air and artillery bombardment and break through the German lines. The 83rd and 9th Infantry Divisions will hold the west side of the breakthrough; the 4th and 30th Infantry Divisions will hold the east side. The 1st Infantry Division, reinforced by a combat command from 3rd Armored Division, will attack to exploit the gap in the German defenses and move toward Coutances. The 2nd Armored Division and the rest of 3rd Armored Division will move into the open country beyond. V Corps and XIX Corps will conduct holding attacks to limit the German response.

Eighth Air Force sends 917 B-17s and 664 B-24 Liberators, escorted by 483 P-38 Lightnings, P-47 Thunderbolts, and P-51 Mustangs, to attack German positions in an area 3,000 yards deep and 7,000 yards wide, saturating it by dropping 4,700 tons of bombs. During the approach to the target, 35 bombers drop their bomb loads early and the 9th and 30th Infantry Divisions are hit. The mistake kills 102 and wounds 380 infantrymen; among those killed is Lieutenant General Lesley J. McNair, the most senior officer in the U.S. Army. Ninth Air Force sends A-20 and B-26 Marauders and P-47 Thunderbolts to strafe and bomb German positions. Three divisions attack on a six-mile front. VII Corps advances two miles. Despite the massive devastation caused by the air attacks and artillery, the Germans are able to recover and mount a defense. The 330th Infantry Regiment of the 83rd Infantry Division makes no progress in the hedgerows. The 9th and the 4th Infantry Divisions stall, and the 30th Infantry Division advances about a mile. The VII Corps commander, Major General J. Lawton Collins, decides to send his exploitation force into the fight, believing that the Germans must not be allowed to recover and regain momentum in the attack.

VII Corps attacks with the 9th, 4th, and 30th Infantry Divisions and, despite the massive destruction of the aerial bombing, make a limited advance.

During Operation Cobra, five bombers are lost and 175 are damaged. Aircrew losses are nine wounded and 46 missing. Fighter pilots report 12 confirmed kills and one probable in the air and two confirmed kills on the ground. Two fighters are lost and five are damaged; two pilots are reported missing.

A total of 17 B-24s fly in support of Carpetbagger operations.

General Eisenhower orders that all American ground forces in France will be reorganized into two armies, designated as the First and the Third, under the 12th Army Group commanded by General Omar Bradley. General Montgomery has operational control over all Allied ground forces until the 12th Army Group is operational.

MEDITERRANEAN: The Anvil Dragoon invasion force begins loading equipment at Naples, Italy. The airborne assault plan is approved. The plan calls for the employment of an airborne division parachuting from 396 C-47s, followed by over 300 gliders. The day after the landings 112 cargo planes will be used for resupply.

Fifteenth Air Force sends 420 B-17s and B-24 Liberators to attack the Hermann Göring tank works in Linz, Austria. P-51 Mustangs and P-38 Lightnings provide escort and encounter nearly 200 German fighters. Aircrews and fighter pilots report over 60 fighters shot down. U.S. aircraft losses total 21.

Operating from airfields in Soviet Ukraine as part of the Frantic missions, 34 P-51s and 33 P-38s attack the airfield and vehicle convoys near Lwow, Poland, and return to the USSR. Pilots report 27 confirmed kills and three probable kills on German dive-bombers.

ITALY: II Corps takes operational control of the 85th, 88th, and 91st Infantry Divisions.

Twelfth Air Force B-25 Mitchells and B-26 Marauders attack bridges. A-20 Havocs attack ammunition storage facilities and rail lines. P-47 Thunderbolts attack bridges, rail lines, and roads.

CENTRAL PACIFIC: Seventh Air Force B-24 Liberators from Kwajalein bomb Truk. The B-24s of the 819th Bombardment Squadron (Heavy), 30th Bombardment Group (Heavy), arrives on Saipan from Hawaii.

Carrier aircraft from Vice Admiral Marc A. Mitscher's TF 58 attack Japanese positions and shipping at Yap, Ulithi, and Palau. F4F Hellcats damage a destroyer north of Babelthuap. Other F4F Hellcats sink a guardboat in the Palaus.

CENTRAL PACIFIC, GUAM: The 3rd and 21st Marine Regiments continue the attack to clear Japanese positions on the ridges. The 9th Marines reach the Sasa River. A Japanese counterattack on the 3rd Marine Division is disorganized, but many enemy attackers are able to reach the beachhead before being killed. The 77th Infantry Division controls the beachhead, allowing the 22nd and 4th Marine Regiments to focus their efforts on the Japanese defenses on the Orote Peninsula.

Captain Louis H. Wilson, Jr., commands a company in the 2nd Battalion, 9th Marines, 3rd Marine Division, and is ordered to attack Fonte Hill. Capturing the position, Captain Wilson organizes a defense and is wounded three times as the Japanese concentrate fire on the marines. He returns from the aid station and reassumes command to defend the position against numerous counterattacks through the night. During one action, he rescues a wounded marine in the face of heavy enemy fire. He battles the Japanese hand-to-hand several times as the marines repel the enemy. In the morning hours, Captain Wilson organizes a patrol to seize a critical position dominating his own position. Despite enemy fire that causes 13 casualties, Captain Wilson and the remaining marines succeed in occupying the position. Captain Wilson's extraordinary dedication to duty and his heroic actions in the face of a superior enemy force will win him the Medal of Honor.

NEW GUINEA: At Noemfoor, after engineers work around the clock for 11 straight days, the Kornasen airfield is made ready for FEAF P-38 Lightnings to land.

July 26

CBI: Tenth Air Force P-40s attack Japanese positions at Myitkyina. P-51 Mustangs attack targets near Mogaung and Kamaing.

In China, Fourteenth Air Force sends B-25 Mitchells and P-40s to attack the town of Tengchung. P-40s and P-38 Lightnings attack targets of opportunity near Tengchung, Lungling, and Mangshih. P-40s bomb Hengyang airfield.

ATLANTIC: President Roosevelt approves the plans for the seizure of Peleliu and the invasion of the Philippines. Both Admiral Nimitz and General MacArthur believe that Peleliu with its airfield must be captured to protect the right flank of MacArthur's Philippine invasion force. The plan for Peleliu is called Operation Stalemate.

ETO: VII Corps commander Major General Collins orders the advance of his armored divisions to exploit the weakened German lines. The 9th, 4th, and 30th Infantry Divisions make steady progress. The 2nd Armored Division advances past St. Gilles and reaches Cauisy. The 3rd Armored Division and the 1st Infantry Division capture Marigny. The V and XIX Corps advance three miles against strong resistance. B-26 Marauders and P-47 Thunderbolts destroy German tank formations attempting to stem the American breakthrough.

Eighth Air Force sends 192 P-47 Thunderbolts to bomb marshaling yards and a fuel storage area in France. One P-47 is lost and 10 are damaged; the pilot is reported missing. A total of nine B-24s fly in support of Carpetbagger operations. During the night seven B-17s drop leaflets over France.

Ninth Air Force sends A-20 Havocs and B-26 Marauders against a fuel storage site. P-47s attack German positions near St-Lô.

MEDITERRANEAN: Operating from airfields in Soviet Ukraine as part of the Frantic missions, 34 P-51s and 33 P-38 Lightnings attack German aircraft near Bucharest and Ploeşti and return to bases in Italy.

More than 300 B-17s and B-24 Liberators attack aircraft production facilities and airfields near Vienna, Austria, an airfield in Hungary, and an oil storage facility at Berat, Albania. Aircrews and fighter pilots report over 70 German fighters shot down.

ITALY: Twelfth Air Force B-25 Mitchells and B-26 Marauders attack bridges. A-20 Havocs bomb roads and vehicles. P-47 Thunderbolts attack gun positions and the airfield at Valence. Pilots report more than 20 aircraft destroyed on the ground.

SOUTHWEST PACIFIC AREA: U.S. submarines carry out a succession of attacks on a Japanese convoy in the South China Sea. USS *Angler* torpedoes and damages a transport; USS *Flasher* torpedoes and sinks a merchant tanker and supports USS *Crevalle* in sinking a cargo ship and transport.

U.S. submarine *Robalo* is sunk by a mine in the Balabac Strait.

U.S. submarine *Sawfish* torpedoes and sinks Japanese submarine *I-29* in Luzon Strait.

PACIFIC: President Roosevelt, aboard the heavy cruiser USS *Baltimore,* arrives at Pearl Harbor. The president and Admiral Leahy will meet with Admiral Nimitz and General MacArthur to discuss future Pacific operations.

CENTRAL PACIFIC: B-25 Mitchells from Engebi Island bomb Ponape Island.

Carrier aircraft from Vice Admiral Marc A. Mitscher's TF 58 attack ground targets and shipping in the western Carolines.

CENTRAL PACIFIC, TINIAN: Seventh Air Force P-47 Thunderbolts and B-25 Mitchells from Saipan attack Japanese positions on Tinian Island. On Tinian, the marines capture Mount Lasso.

CENTRAL PACIFIC, GUAM: A Japanese attack against the marines advancing into the Orote Peninsula is stopped by devastating artillery fire from the 77th Division artillery. Altogether about 26,000 artillery shells are fired. Nevertheless, the advance of the marines into the Orote defenses moves only about 1,500 yards.

NEW GUINEA: FEAF A-20 Havocs and B-25 Mitchells, along with RAAF fighter-bombers, attack Japanese troops, coastal shipping, and other targets of opportunity from Hollandia to Wewak.

B-24 Liberators bomb logistics sites on Woleai Atoll.

July 27

CBI: New Galahad forces capture the northern airfield at Myitkyina.

Tenth Air Force P-51 Mustangs, P-40s, and A-36 Intruder (Apache) fighter-bombers attack Japanese positions around Myitkyina and the area around Kamaing and Mogaung.

ETO: VII Corps captures Périers and Lessay. The 3rd Armored Division and 1st Infantry Division move west to threaten the flank of the German forces at Coutances. VIII Corps captures Avranches, which opens Brittany to American forces. XIX Corps is ordered to capture Vire, a key road junction southeast of St-Lô. The German Seventh Army begins a withdrawal.

Eighth Air Force sends 26 B-17s to bomb coastal batteries in France and Belgium. Another 120 B-24 Liberators attack a command center and industrial targets in Belgium. The bombers are escorted by 154 P-38 Lightnings, P-47 Thunderbolts, and P-51 Mustangs. One B-24 is lost and 32 are damaged. Fighter pilots report one confirmed kill. One P-51 is lost and the pilot is reported missing. Nearly 200 P-38 Lightnings, P-47 Thunderbolts, and P-51 Mustangs fly a fighter-bomber mission against railroad traffic in France. Three fighters are lost and two are damaged. The pilots are reported missing.

During the night seven B-17s drop leaflets over France and the Netherlands.

Ninth Air Force A-20 Havocs and B-26 Marauders bomb Loire and Seine River bridges. P-47s attack German positions near Coutances and St-Lô.

The P-38s of the 393rd and 394th Fighter Squadrons of the 367th Fighter Group and the P-47s of the 512th and 514th Fighter Squadrons of the 406th Fighter Group redeploy to France.

MEDITERRANEAN: Fifteenth Air Force sends 366 B-17s and B-24 Liberators escorted by P-38 Lightnings and P-51 Mustangs to attack an armament plant at Budapest, Hungary.

ITALY: Operation Mallory Major succeeds in cutting the German Fourteenth Army from its supply bases in northern Italy by bombing bridges and roads leading south. However, the benefits are negated because the Allied armies are standing down to rest and refit. Lack of action on the front lines allows the Germans to rebuild and restore their supply lines by August 6, in time for the next Allied offensive. In its advance to the Arno River, the Fifth Army has suffered 18,000 casualties and collected 16,000 German prisoners since the capture of Rome.

Twelfth Air Force A-20 Havocs attack vehicles moving along the Po River valley. B-35s, B-26 Marauders, and P-47 Thunderbolts attack bridges in the Po River valley and aircraft, guns, and rail lines in northwest Italy.

SOUTHWEST PACIFIC AREA: U.S. submarine *Dace* attacks a Japanese convoy and sinks a fleet tanker south of Zamboanga, Philippines.

PACIFIC: The Pearl Harbor Conference. President Roosevelt meets with the Southwest Pacific Area commander, General Douglas MacArthur, and Pacific Ocean Areas commander, Admiral Chester Nimitz, to discuss strategic options in the Pacific. Nimitz lays out his arguments for his Granite plan, directed at Formosa, but leaving open the possibility of capturing Luzon first. MacArthur argues for his Reno V plan, liberating the Philippines prior to invading Japan. He notes that Luzon is a better objective than Formosa. First, the Philippine people will cooperate with Americans, while the population on Formosa may not. The Japanese can also counterattack from China if U.S. forces land on Formosa. MacArthur stresses to Roosevelt the moral obligation of the United States to free the Philippines. In their presentations to the president, MacArthur and Nimitz are in agreement on the basic strategic approach to the defeat of Japan, but differ on the operational objectives that will best achieve this goal.

CENTRAL PACIFIC: Seventh Air Force B-24 Liberators from the Marshall Islands bomb Truk. B-25 Mitchells from Makin Island bomb Jaluit Atoll.

Carrier aircraft from Vice Admiral Marc A. Mitscher's TF 58 attack shipping and ground targets in the western Carolines.

CENTRAL PACIFIC, TINIAN: The 2nd and 4th Marine Divisions advance southward along flat, open terrain, strung out in a single line across the island. Seventh Air Force P-47 Thunderbolts and B-25 Mitchells from Saipan support the advance.

NEW GUINEA: FEAF P-39 Airacobras strafe Japanese troops and small vessels along the west coast of Geelvink Bay. A-20 Havocs, B-25 Mitchells, and P-40s attack Japanese troops, logistics, support facilities, barges, and gun positions along the coast from Aitape to Wewak.

B-25s bomb the airfield on Halmahera Island. B-24 Liberators bomb the airfield on Woleai Atoll and logistics sites on Mariaon and Tagaulap Islands in the Carolines. Other B-24s bomb Dili on Timor Island.

Fifth Air Force B-24 Liberators, B-25 Mitchells, and P-38 Lightnings attack Japanese shipping near Halmahera Island.

July 28

CBI: Tenth Air Force sends over 100 A-36 Intruder (Apache) fighter-bombers, P-40s, and P-51 Mustangs to attack Myitkyina, Kamaing, Mogaung, and Bhamo.

In China, Fourteenth Air Force P-40s and P-51 Mustangs attack Japanese troops, road and river transportation traffic, and targets of opportunity around Tungting Lake. B-25 Mitchells attack the Yoyang railroad yards, a bridge over the Yellow River, and the White Cloud, Tien Ho, and Hankow airfields.

ETO: The 4th Armored Division of VIII Corps establishes contact with the 1st Infantry Division of VII Corps at Coutances, capturing 4,500 prisoners. This is the objective of Operation Cobra. The 2nd and 3rd Armored Divisions attack toward

Granville and Avranches. The 4th Armored Division followed by the 6th Armored Division serves as the spearhead of VIII Corps as it attacks toward the Seine River. XIX Corps reaches Tessy-sur-Vire, while V Corps attacks at Forêt de Cerisy.

Eighth Air Force sends 291 B-24 Liberators escorted by nearly 300 P-47 Thunderbolts and P-51 Mustangs to attack fuel storage sites and V-weapon supply sites in Belgium and France, but the forces are recalled because of cloud cover over the targets. Nine bombers are lost and eight are damaged. Aircrew losses are ten killed. Three fighters are damaged. In another mission 766 B-17s escorted by 386 P-38 Lightnings and P-51 Mustangs attack the synthetic oil plant at Merseburg, Germany. Seven bombers are lost and 217 are damaged. Aircrew losses are one killed, seven wounded, and 67 missing. Fighter pilots report four confirmed kills and one probable. Two fighters are lost and three are damaged. Three pilots are reported missing.

During the night six B-17s drop leaflets over France.

Ninth Air Force sends A-20 Havocs and B-26 Marauders escorted by P-47 Thunderbolts against rail bridges, logistics sites, and ammunition storage areas in France. P-47s and P-38s also provide air cover for U.S. First Army units.

MEDITERRANEAN: Fifteenth Air Force sends 349 B-17s and B-24 Liberators with P-51 Mustangs as escort to attack the Ploeşti, Romania, oil refinery. A total of 20 bombers are lost.

ITALY: Twelfth Air Force A-20 Havocs attack vehicles moving along the Po River valley. B-35s and B-26 Marauders, A-20 Havocs, and P-47 Thunderbolts attack bridges in the Po River valley and aircraft, guns, and rail lines in northwest Italy and vehicles in the Rhône River valley of France.

SOUTHWEST PACIFIC AREA: U.S. submarine *Crevalle* attacks a Japanese convoy off northwestern Luzon, sinking a cargo ship.

CENTRAL PACIFIC, TINIAN: Ushi Point airfield, captured intact by the marines, receives P-47 Thunderbolt fighters. The marines also capture Gurguan airfield without encountering any Japanese.

Seventh Air Force B-25 Mitchells and P-47 Thunderbolts based on Saipan attack suspected Japanese positions.

U.S. Destroyer escorts *Wyman* and *Reynolds* sink Japanese submarine *I-55* east of Tinian.

CENTRAL PACIFIC, GUAM: Fonte Ridge is captured by the 3rd and 21st Marines after days of bitter fighting. The 1st Provisional Marine Brigade captures the Orote airfield after a 45-minute air and naval bombardment; the airfield had been part of the U.S. base on Guam. On December 10, 1941, a Japanese landing force captured the airfield as the marines defending this portion of Guam were forced to surrender.

NEW GUINEA: FEAF P-39 Airacobras strafe Japanese troops and small vessels along the west coast of Geelvink Bay. A-20 Havocs, B-25 Mitchells, and P-40s attack targets along the coast from Aitape to Wewak. B-24 Liberators bomb the airfield on Woleai Atoll. Other B-24s bomb Dili on Timor Island.

The headquarters of the 309th Bombardment Wing (Heavy) redeploys from Saidor to Noemfoor Island.

July 29

ALEUTIANS: Eleventh Air Force sends three B-24 Liberators to fly bombing and reconnaissance missions over Shimushu and Paramushiru Islands.

CBI: Tenth Air Force sends about 100 A-36 Intruder (Apache) fighter-bombers and P-40s to bomb targets at Myitkyina, Kamaing, and Mogaung.

In China, Fourteenth Air Force sends 26 B-24 Liberators to bomb a logistics storage area in Samah Bay on Hainan Island. B-25 Mitchells bomb Hankow airfield, the Kaifeng railroad yards, and the town of Tengchung. P-40s and P-51 Mustangs attack bridges, troops, and river, road, and rail traffic.

Twentieth Air Force sends over 70 B-29 Superfortresses from Chengtu airfield in China to bomb the Showa Steel Works at Anshan and the harbor at Taku. One B-29 is lost to Japanese fighters. It is the first Superfortress to be lost in combat. Another B-29 bombs Chinwangtao and then makes a forced landing at a friendly field near Ankang.

ATLANTIC: The JCS planners reject the idea of an invasion of Luzon as a preliminary operation to the seizure of Formosa, as outlined in MacArthur's Reno V plan. Leyte would serve as the base for the reduction of Japanese air power to prepare for the assault on Formosa. The capture of Formosa is seen as essential in the defeat of Japan, as it would provide air bases for strategic attack on the home islands. The Palau Islands are considered essential to sea and air forces supporting landing in the Philippines. The Bonin Islands will be attacked in April 1945, followed by an invasion of Kyushu in October and a final assault on Tokyo in December.

ETO: Coutances is captured. American air attacks destroy an estimated 137 tanks and 500 other vehicles. VIII and VII Corps attack toward Avranches as German resistance weakens. VIII Corps crosses the Seine River.

Eighth Air Force sends 657 B-17s escorted by 429 P-38 Lightnings, P-47 Thunderbolts, and P-51 Mustangs to attack oil production and storage facilities in Germany and airfields in France. Fifteen bombers are lost and 350 are damaged. Aircrews report 15 confirmed kills and eight probables. Aircrew losses are one killed, 17 wounded, and 138 missing. Fighter pilots report 21 confirmed kills and two probables and three confirmed kills on the ground. At least one of these is the new German Messerschmitt 262 (Me-262), the world's first jet fighter. Seven fighters are lost and seven are damaged; the seven pilots are reported missing.

Another 473 B-24 Liberators escorted by 106 P-51s attack an oil refinery near Bremen, Germany. Two bombers are lost and 96 are damaged. Aircrew losses are three killed, two wounded, and 15 missing. Airfields in France are attacked by 98 B-24s escorted by 142 P-51s. Two bombers are damaged. Aircrew losses are five killed and seven wounded.

A total of 44 B-24s fly in support of Carpetbagger operations. During the night six B-17s drop leaflets over France.

Ninth Air Force P-47 Thunderbolts and P-38 Lightnings provide cover in support of the U.S. First Army.

Eighth Air Force B-17s bomb U-boat facilities in Bremen, destroying German submarines *U-878* and *U-2323*.

Sergeant Hulon B. Whittington, a squad leader with the 41st Armored Infantry Regiment, 2nd Armored Division, faces a German tank and infantry counterattack during the night. Taking charge of the platoon, Whittington reorganizes the defense and takes action to stop a threat by leaping on top of an American tank and directing its fire against oncoming German tanks. In the face of intense fire, Sergeant Whittington then leads a bayonet assault on the stalled enemy column, completely disrupting the German attack. Whittington continues to lead and inspire his men, even providing first aid to the wounded. For his inspiring leadership, devotion to duty, and intrepid acts of courage, Sergeant Whittington will receive the Medal of Honor.

MEDITERRANEAN: The Seventh Army issues the final planning order for Dragoon. The Western Task Force composed of British, French, and American warships under Vice Admiral H. Kent Hewitt will support the landing with five battleships, 20 cruisers, 98 destroyers, and 283 other combat ships. A total of 1,300 landing craft will be employed for the invasion. The XII Tactical Air Force under Brigadier General Gordon P. Saville will have 1,100 aircraft available to fly air cover over the landing beaches. These include British, French, and U.S. squadrons operating from bases in Corsica. Additional air support will be provided by seven British and two U.S. escort carriers with 200 aircraft. VI Corps is to land at three different points on the coast of southern France between Cavalaire-sur-Mer (17 km from St. Tropez) and Saint Raphaël. The divisions of VI Corps are designated as Alpha Force (3rd Infantry Division), Delta Force (45th Infantry Division), and Camel Force (36th Infantry Division). Rear Admiral Spencer S. Lewis will land Camel Force, Rear Admiral Frank J. Lowry will land Delta Force, and Rear Admiral Bertram J. Rodgers will land Alpha Force. The 1st Special Service Force will attack coastal batteries prior to D-day. The 1st Airborne Task Force will land in the vicinity of Le Muy and Le Luc to block German reinforcements from reaching the beachhead. The French Army B, led by General of the Army Jean de Lattre de Tassigny, will follow the 3rd Infantry Division and capture Toulon and Marseilles. D-day is set for August 15.

Frantic operations involve 14 P-38 Lightnings, taking off from bases in Soviet Ukraine to attack targets in Hungary.

ITALY: Twelfth Air Force A-20 Havocs and P-47 Thunderbolts attack airfields, bridges, and rail lines.

SOUTHWEST PACIFIC AREA: U.S. submarine *Perch* torpedoes and sinks a Japanese guardboat in the Philippine Sea, east of Leyte Island.

PACIFIC: President Roosevelt departs Hawaii aboard heavy cruiser *Baltimore* for Adak, Aleutians.

CENTRAL PACIFIC: Seventh Air Force B-24 Liberators from Kwajalein bomb Truk and B-25 Mitchells from Engebi Island bomb Ponape Island.

U.S. submarine *Drum* torpedoes and sinks a Japanese sampan off Palau.

CENTRAL PACIFIC, TINIAN: The 2nd and 4th Marine Divisions continue advancing south and encounter several Japanese strongpoints and repulse weak counterattacks.

Seventh Air Force P-47 Thunderbolts provide ground support to the marines.

CENTRAL PACIFIC, GUAM: The Japanese defenders are driven into a pocket on the Orote Peninsula. The marine barracks is recaptured and the American flag is raised in an emotional ceremony. Major General Roy S. Geiger orders a consolidation to prepare his forces for the second phase of the operation to capture Guam.

NEW GUINEA: FEAF P-39 Airacobras strafe Japanese troops along the west coast of Geelvink Bay. A-20 Havocs, B-25 Mitchells, and P-40s attack Japanese troops, logistics support facilities, barges, and gun positions along the coast from Aitape to Wewak.

B-24 Liberators bomb the airfield on Woleai Atoll and logistics sites on Mariaon and Tagaulap Islands in the Carolines. Other B-24s bomb targets on Timor Island.

July 30

CBI: Tenth Air Force A-36 Intruder (Apache) fighter-bombers and P-40s attack Myitkyina and the Kamaing-Mogaung area.

In China, Fourteenth Air Force sends 11 B-24 Liberators to bomb Wuchang. P-40s and P-51 Mustangs attack bridges, railyards, logistics bases, and road, river, and rail traffic near Tungting Lake. In French Indochina more than 20 P-40s and P-38 Lightnings attack shipping and road traffic around Hanoi.

ETO: The 6th Armored Division captures Avranches. The seizure of Avranches breaks the German defensive line, allowing Third Army to drive across Brittany.

Commander of the Eighth Air Force, Lieutenant General James H. Doolittle, orders that the VIII Air Force Composite Command take operational control of all Carpetbagger, H2X (radar-supported bombing), night leaflet, and weather missions.

Eighth Air Force sends 237 P-47 Thunderbolts and P-51 Mustangs to attack fly fighter sweeps over France seeking German aircraft. Pilots report three confirmed kills in the air and nine on the ground. One fighter is lost and five are damaged. The pilot is reported as missing.

A total of 31 B-24s fly in support of Carpetbagger operations.

Ninth Air Force sends more than 450 A-20 Havocs and B-26 Marauders to attack German defenses in the Chaumont area in support of the U.S. First Army. P-47s escort the bombers and conduct armed reconnaissance in the Orleans-Paris area.

The P-47s of the 410th, 411th, and 412th Fighter Squadrons of the 373rd Fighter Group redeploy from England to France.

MEDITERRANEAN: Fifteenth Air Force sends over 300 B-17s and B-24 Liberators escorted by P-38 Lightnings and P-51 Mustangs to attack marshaling yards in Yugoslavia and an aircraft production facility in Budapest, Hungary.

ITALY: Twelfth Air Force A-20 Havocs and P-47 Thunderbolts attack shipping, rail lines, and bridges.

CENTRAL PACIFIC: Seventh Air Force B-25 Mitchells from Makin Island bomb Jaluit Atoll.

CENTRAL PACIFIC, TINIAN: The 24th Marines attack the town of Tinian supported by artillery and naval gunfire. Flamethrower tanks assist in clearing Japanese defensive positions located in caves. The 25th Marines capture Airfield Number 4. With the capture of the island's main town, the Japanese are squeezed into a four-square-mile area of rocky hills with numerous caves and covered in brush.

Seventh Air Force B-25 Mitchells and P-47 Thunderbolts from Saipan attack Japanese positions.

Private Joseph W. Ozbourn, a Browning Automatic Rifleman with the 1st Battalion, 23rd Marines, 4th Marine Division, is engaged in clearing Japanese troops from dugouts and pillboxes. As he and several other marines approach an enemy position, they are hit by an explosion near a dugout. Private Ozbourn was ready to throw a grenade when the explosion went off. Seeing the live grenade lying on the ground near his comrades, Ozbourn covers it with his body and is killed by the explosion. For his act of self-sacrifice, Private Ozbourn will receive the Medal of Honor.

NEW GUINEA: At the Driniumor River, the 112th Cavalry and the 127th Infantry are almost surrounded during a series of nearly continuous battles that have lasted several days. The Americans, fighting in heavy jungle, are resupplied by airdrops. Over 1,000 men are casualties.

The 6th Infantry Division with 7,300 men lands at Sansapor on Vogelkop, between two Japanese garrisons, one at Manokwari and the other at Sorong airfield. American engineers immediately begin laying out a new airfield.

Operation Globetrotter begins. Naval Task Force 77, commanded by Rear Admiral William M. Fechteler, lands two battalions of the 1st Infantry Regiment of the 6th Infantry Division (Major General Franklin C. Sibert) near Cape Opmari, at the Vogelkop Peninsula. A battalion of the 63rd Infantry lands to support, while other units of the 63rd occupy Middelburg and Amsterdam Islands. The Americans encounter no initial resistance. The engineers begin surveying the area for an airfield. The infantry skirmishes with some Japanese, but the area is secured with the loss of 14 men killed, 29 wounded, and two missing.

FEAF P-39 Airacobras support ground forces on Biak Island and support the landing on the Vogelkop Peninsula. A-20 Havocs, B-25 Mitchells, and P-40s attack Japanese troops, logistics support facilities, barges, and gun positions along the coast from Aitape to Wewak. B-24 Liberators and P-38 Lightnings attack the airfield and oil installations at Boela on Ceram Island in the Moluccas, and other B-24 Liberators hit Morotai Island in the Celebes Islands.

U.S. submarine *Bonefish* torpedoes and sinks a Japanese fleet tanker northeast of Borneo.

Fifth Air Force B-25 Mitchells attack Japanese installations and shipping at Tobele, Halmahera, sinking a small cargo vessel.

July 31

CBI: The Air Transport Command is averaging the delivery of 71,000 tons of supplies a month to China over the Hump.

Tenth Air Force A-36 Intruder (Apache) fighter-bombers and P-40s attack Japanese defenses at Myitkyina and others attack the Kamaing-Mogaung area.

In China, Fourteenth Air Force B-24 Liberators bomb the Wuchang railyards. B-25 Mitchells bomb Hengshan, Siangtan, and Hankow and attack the airfields at Tien Ho, White Cloud, Hengyang, and Wuchang. P-40s and P-51 Mustangs attack bridges, railyards, logistics bases, and road, river, and rail traffic near Changsha and Hengyang.

ETO: Avranches is captured by the 4th Armored Division; the 6th Armored Division advances on Granville. The German flank is completely open. General Eisenhower now attempts to encircle and destroy all German forces in France.

Eighth Air Force sends 705 B-17s escorted by 439 P-47 Thunderbolts and P-51 Mustangs to attack Munich industrial targets and airfields. Ten bombers are lost and 331 are damaged. Aircrew losses are two killed, six wounded, and 82 missing. Fighter pilots report 18 confirmed kills on the ground and one probable in the air. Three fighters are lost and eight are damaged. Three pilots are reported missing.

More than 400 B-24 Liberators escorted by 135 P-38 Lightnings bomb the chemical works at Ludwigshafen and the city of Mannheim. Six bombers are lost and 186 damaged. Aircrew losses are one killed, seven wounded, and 62 missing. One fighter is damaged. Another 104 B-24 Liberators escorted by 38 P-47s and P-51s bomb airfields in France. Four bombers are damaged.

A total of 13 B-24s fly in support of Carpetbagger operations.

Ninth Air Force sends nearly 500 A-20 Havocs and B-26 Marauders to attack bridges and a fuel storage site. P-47s conduct dive-bomb attacks on German positions in support of the U.S. First Army.

The headquarters of the 303rd Fighter Wing and the P-38s of the 392nd Fighter Squadron, 367th Fighter Group, redeploy from England to France.

MEDITERRANEAN: Fifteenth Air Force sends over 350 B-17s and B-24 Liberators to attack oil refineries in Ploeşti, Doicesti, and Targoviste, Romania. At the end of the month Fifteenth Air Force reports 142 German aircraft shot down.

ITALY: Twelfth Air Force A-20 Havocs and P-47 Thunderbolts attack airfields, rail lines, and bridges. Pilots report 50 rail cars destroyed.

SOUTHWEST PACIFIC AREA: The submarine attack group TG 17.15 (Commander Lewis S. Parks) attacks a Japanese convoy northeast of Luzon.

U.S. submarine *Dace* torpedoes and sinks a Japanese cargo vessel south of Davao.

U.S. submarine *Lapon* attacks a Japanese convoy, sinking a merchant tanker off the southern tip of Palawan Island.

Commander Lawson P. "Red" Ramage is commander of the submarine USS *Parche* and is in the Straits of Luzon with two other submarines, searching for convoys headed for Luzon to reinforce Japanese forces. Ramage makes a surface attack on a convoy after evading the protective destroyer screen and proceeds to torpedo a cargo ship and sink one tanker and damage another with successive torpedo hits. As the flaming tankers illuminate the area, Ramage torpedoes a transport ship and orders members of the crew below as he maneuvers to avoid a ramming attack by a fast transport ship. The *Parche* is now caught in a crossfire from Japanese escort ships on all sides and the transport dead ahead. He destroys the ship, firing three torpedoes, and is able to break contact without any harm to the boat. For his valiant fight and calm courage, Commander Ramage will win the Medal of Honor. USS *Steelhead*, supporting *Parche*, sinks one previously damaged cargo ship and sinks another.

CENTRAL PACIFIC: Seventh Air Force B-25 Mitchells from Makin Island bomb Nauru Island. B-24 Liberators from the Marshall Islands bomb Truk.

CENTRAL PACIFIC, TINIAN: The last Japanese defensive position on the island is subjected to an intense air, naval gunfire, and artillery bombardment in preparation for the attack of the 23rd and 24th Marines. The Japanese, in well-concealed positions, are able to survive and battle the marines as they advance. The enemy is overwhelmed and the 8th Marines reach the top of the plateau and defend it against several enemy counterattacks. Seventh Air Force B-25 Mitchells and P-47 Thunderbolts based on Saipan bomb the final defensive positions of the Japanese defenders of Tinian.

CENTRAL PACIFIC, GUAM: The 3rd Marine Division and the 77th Infantry Division attack north to eliminate Japanese defenses. The 1st Provisional Marine Brigade controls the southern half of Guam and the beachhead. The 3rd Marine Regiment captures Agana, the capital of the island. The 307th and 305th Infantry Regiments secure the critical Pago-Agana Road, which allows the forward forces to be resupplied.

NEW GUINEA: The 124th Infantry Regiment, 31st Infantry Division, and a battalion of the 169th Infantry, 43rd Infantry Division, cross the Driniumor River to drive back Japanese troops. The unit is called Ted Force after its commander, Colonel Edwin A. Starr.

FEAF P-39 Airacobras strafe Japanese troops and small vessels along the west coast of Geelvink Bay. A-20 Havocs, B-25 Mitchells, and P-40s attack Japanese troops, logistics support facilities, barges, and gun positions along the coast from Aitape to Wewak.

B-24 Liberators bomb the airfield on Woleai Atoll and logistics sites on Mariaon and Tagaulap Islands in the Carolines. Other B-24s bomb Dili on Timor Island. B-24s bomb the airfield on Halmahera Island.

Operation Globetrotter continues. Naval Task Force 77 (Rear Admiral William M. Fechteler) lands troops on Cape Sansapor, New Guinea.

August 1

CBI: Tenth Air Force A-36 Intruder (Apache) fighter-bombers and P-40s support ground forces at Myitkyina.

In China, Fourteenth Air Force B-25 Mitchells bomb Wuchang airfield. P-40s and P-51 Mustangs attack bridges, railyards, logistics bases, and road, river, and rail traffic near Changsha and Hengyang. The airfield and railyard at Hengyang are also attacked.

ATLANTIC: Anvil, the invasion of southern France in support of Overlord, is officially renamed Dragoon at Prime Minister Churchill's insistence. The new name is rumored to reflect Churchill's opinion of the operation, namely that he was dragooned by the Americans into accepting it.

ETO: The XIX Corps of First Army advances toward Vire after a difficult four-day battle against two German tank divisions.

The 12th Army Group is activated under the command of General Omar N. Bradley with operational control of the First and Third Armies. The First Army is commanded by Lieutenant General Courtney H. Hodges. Hodges has V Corps, XIX Corps, and VII Corps. The Third Army is activated under Lieutenant General George S. Patton, Jr., and has the VIII, XII, XV, and XX Corps: XII Corps under Major General Gilbert R. Cook, the XV Corps under Major General Wade H. Haislip, the XX Corps under Major General Walton H. Walker, and the VIII Corps under

Major General Troy Middleton. VIII Corps has nine of Bradley's 21 divisions. Patton's Third Army is to clear the Brittany Peninsula while First Army attacks south toward Mortain. Middleton is ordered to clear the Brittany Peninsula and open the ports. The 4th and 6th Armored Divisions are to lead the attack. Patton sends two other corps south and southeast. British General Montgomery still has operational control of both the U.S. and British army groups. Realizing far too late that the Pas-de-Calais invasion is a ruse, Hitler finally authorizes the German Fifteenth Army to reinforce the defenders at Normandy.

Eighth Air Force sends 76 B-17s escorted by 51 P-51 Mustangs to attack Tours airfield. One bomber is lost and six are damaged. Aircrew losses are six wounded and 10 missing.

Over 400 B-17s escorted by 138 P-38 Lightnings and P-51 Mustangs bomb airfields and a railway bridge near Paris. Three B-17s are lost and 34 damaged. Aircrew losses are nine killed and 27 missing. Three P-51 Mustangs are damaged and one pilot is killed.

Over 200 B-24s escorted by 127 P-47 Thunderbolts and P-51 Mustangs bomb airfields and bridges near Paris. One bomber is lost and 88 damaged. Aircrew casualties are 20 missing. Fighter pilots report three confirmed kills on the ground. Four fighters are damaged. Another 191 B-24s escorted by 81 P-47s are sent against eight V-weapon sites but bad weather over the targets causes all but 61 to abort the mission. Five bombers are damaged.

Nearly 200 B-17s airdrop nearly 2,300 containers of supplies to French Resistance forces in southeast France in preparation for Dragoon. Five B-17s are damaged.

A total of 21 B-24s fly in support of Carpetbagger operations. During the night six B-17s drop leaflets over France and Belgium.

Ninth Air Force establishes the XIX Tactical Air Command to provide dedicated air support to the U.S. Third Army. The fighter and fighter-bomber groups are divided between the IX and XIX Tactical Air Commands.

A-20 Havocs and B-26 Marauders bomb rail bridges.

Italy: Twelfth Air Force A-20 Havocs attack bridges in the Po River valley and marshaling yards. B-35s, B-26 Marauders, and P-47 Thunderbolts attack airfields, roads, bridges, rail cars, and rail lines.

Pacific: The Army Air Forces, Pacific Ocean Areas (AAPOA) is activated at Hickam Field, Hawaii. Lieutenant General Millard Harmon is named the commander. Harmon's command provides logistics and administration support for Lieutenant General Robert C. Richardson, Jr.'s U.S. Army Forces, Pacific Ocean Areas (USAFPOA), which includes the Seventh Air Force. Harmon is also responsible to Admiral Chester W. Nimitz, commander in chief, Pacific Ocean Areas (CINCPOA), for operations of Army Air Force air units in the Pacific Ocean Areas. But Harmon, as deputy commander of the Twentieth Air Force, answers only to General Henry H. Arnold in all matters relating to the Twentieth's operations in Nimitz's area of responsibility.

Seventh Amphibious Force is organized under the command of Rear Admiral Daniel E. Barbey.

CENTRAL PACIFIC: Seventh Air Force P-47 Thunderbolts and P-61 Black Widow night fighters on Saipan attack on-call targets on Saipan and Tinian, but concentrate their efforts in support of army and marine forces on Guam.

Naval Air Base, Tinian, is established.

CENTRAL PACIFIC, TINIAN: Tinian is declared secure. Marine casualties are 328 killed and 1,571 wounded.

NEW GUINEA: FEAF B-24 Liberators bomb Utagal Island in the Carolines and Namlea airfield on Buru Island in the Moluccas.

U.S. submarine *Puffer* torpedoes and damages a Japanese oiler northeast of Borneo.

A navy PBY Catalina attacks a Japanese convoy, sinking an ammunition ship in Taliaboe Bay, Soela Island, Netherlands East Indies.

August 2

CBI: In Burma, the last Japanese forces (about 600 men) leave Myitkyina. Only about 200 of the original Marauders remain in the field.

In China, Fourteenth Air Force sends 11 B-25 Mitchells and 32 P-40s and P-38 Lightnings to attack targets near Tengchung. P-40s and P-38s attack shipping and logistics storage sites along the Yangtze River.

ATLANTIC: German submarine *U-804* torpedoes and sinks a destroyer escort off Newfoundland.

ETO: The 4th Armored Division reaches Rennes, while the 6th Armored Division reaches Dinan. St-Malo is bypassed.

Hitler orders a strong counterattack from Vire toward Avranches to restore the German defensive line and trap Third Army behind German lines in Brittany.

Eighth Air Force sends 156 B-17s and 163 B-24 Liberators escorted by 132 P-51 Mustangs to attack oil storage facilities, marshaling yards, logistics depots, and bridges around Paris. Two bombers are lost and 71 are damaged. Aircrew losses are one killed, four wounded, and 18 missing. Two fighters are lost and one is damaged. Two pilots are missing and one is killed.

Another mission sends 195 B-17s and 322 B-24s escorted by 236 P-51 Mustangs to attack V-weapon sites. Three bombers are lost and 128 are damaged. Aircrew losses are five killed, one wounded, and 28 missing. Five fighters are lost and one is damaged. Five pilots are reported missing.

Nearly 300 P-38 Lightnings, P-47s, and P-51s fly fighter-bomber missions against rail and road transport from Paris to Brussels. Pilots report one confirmed kill. Two fighters are lost and nine are damaged. Two pilots are reported missing.

A total of 42 B-24s fly in support of Carpetbagger operations.

Ninth Air Force sends 300 A-20 Havocs and B-26 Marauders to attack bridges and ammunition storage sites. P-47s and P-38s fly close support missions and reconnaissance in support of ground forces.

MEDITERRANEAN: Fifteenth Air Force sends over 300 B-17s and B-24 Liberators escorted by P-38 Lightnings and P-51 Mustangs to attack the harbor at Genoa, Italy, and oil storage facilities and rail targets in southern France.

ITALY: Twelfth Air Force B-25 Mitchells and B-26 Marauders attack bridges. A-20 Havocs and P-47 Thunderbolts attack airfields, bridges, and roads.

Pacific: U.S. submarine *Tautog* attacks a Japanese convoy, sinking a cargo ship off Honshu, Japan.

Central Pacific, Tinian: In spite of the official declaration that the island is secure, the 6th Marines turns back a Japanese counterattack.

Central Pacific, Guam: The Japanese stronghold at Mount Barrigada is the objective of the 307th Infantry Regiment, supported by the 706th Tank Battalion.

New Guinea: FEAF A-20 Havocs, P-47 Thunderbolts, P-38 Lightnings, and P-40s attack targets along the coast. B-24 Liberators and B-25 Mitchells bomb airfields on the Moluccas and Lesser Sunda Islands and shipping off Ceram and Amboina Islands. B-24s bomb Timor Island. At Biak, Mokmer airfield is ready to receive bombers.

August 3

Aleutians: President Roosevelt, aboard heavy cruiser USS *Baltimore,* arrives at Adak in the Aleutians.

CBI: The Chinese 50th Division attacks and captures Myitkyina. The Allies capture 179 Japanese soldiers. The capture of Myitkyina airfield ends the threat of Japanese fighters against the southern Hump air route to China. As a result, supply tonnage nearly doubles in the next few months. This victory, combined with the British victories at Imphal and Kohima, seals the fate of the Japanese forces in Burma. The Ledo Road now advances steadily.

During the siege of Myitkyina Chinese forces have lost 972 killed and over 3,200 wounded and sick. U.S. forces have lost 272 killed and over 1,900 wounded and sick. The Americans have far more cases of illness than the Chinese, mostly because the Chinese forces maintain strict discipline in boiling all drinking water. Americans, far less willing to follow this rule, become sick.

In China, Fourteenth Air Force sends B-24 Liberators to bomb the town of Yoyang and B-25 Mitchells to bomb Mangshih. P-40s, P-51 Mustangs, and P-38 Lightnings attack airfields, troops, logistics support sites, and rail, road, and river traffic around Changsha, Hengyang, and Tangyang.

ETO: The 8th Infantry Division occupies Rennes after the 4th Armored Division had initially seized the city. The VII Corps of First Army clears Mortain. General Eisenhower orders Third Army to use minimum force to clear the Brittany Peninsula. He orders Patton to attack east toward Laval-LeMans-Chartres to sweep behind German forces defending at Normandy. The First Army will continue its attack to hold German forces while Patton begins his flanking maneuver with the XV and XX Corps. Air support from the Ninth Air Force has allowed the rapid advance of many units.

Eighth Air Force sends 345 B-17s escorted by 175 P-51 Mustangs to attack the oil refinery at Merkwille, Germany. Six B-17s are lost and 99 are damaged. Aircrews report four confirmed kills and one probable. Aircrew losses are nine killed, nine wounded, and 54 missing. Fighter pilots report six confirmed kills in the air and five on the ground. Six P-51s are lost. The five pilots are reported missing.

Another 155 B-17s, escorted by 96 P-51 Mustangs, attack bridges in France. Eleven B-17s are damaged. Over 170 B-24 Liberators escorted by 47 P-47 Thunderbolts attack airfields and marshaling yards. A total of 51 bombers are damaged. Nearly 250 B-17s and B-24s escorted by P-51s bomb V-weapon sites in the Pas-de-Calais area. One bomber is lost and 26 bombers are damaged. More than 150 B-24s escorted by 90 P-51s also hit V-weapon sites. One B-24 is lost and 41 damaged. Aircrew casualties are four killed, four wounded, and 10 missing. Another 76 B-24s attack airfields in Belgium escorted by P-47s. Fifty B-24s are damaged. The aircrews in the damaged bombers suffer two killed. Over 130 P-38 Lightnings and P-47s fly fighter-bomber missions against rail traffic near Metz, Strasbourg, and Saarbrücken areas. Pilots report one confirmed kill in the air and one on the ground. One P-47 is lost.

Ninth Air Force sends over 180 A-20 Havocs and B-26 Marauders against rail targets and fuel storage areas.

The P-47s of the 22nd and 23rd Fighter Squadrons, 36th Fighter Group, redeploy from England to France.

MEDITERRANEAN: Fifteenth Air Force sends over 600 B-17s and B-24 Liberators escorted by P-38 Lightnings and P-51 Mustangs to attack industrial targets in Germany. B-24s also bomb communications targets in the Brenner Pass. Aircrews and fighter pilots report 18 German aircraft shot down. A total of 11 U.S. bombers and fighters are lost.

ITALY: Twelfth Air Force B-25 Mitchells and B-26 Marauders attack bridges. A-20 Havocs and P-47 Thunderbolts attack airfields, bridges, and roads.

SOUTHWEST PACIFIC AREA: U.S. submarine *Cod* torpedoes and sinks a Japanese auxiliary netlayer west of Halmahera island in the Molucca Sea.

CENTRAL PACIFIC: Seventh Air Force B-24 Liberators from the Marshall Islands bomb Truk.

CENTRAL PACIFIC, GUAM: The 3rd and the 9th Marines attack toward Finegayan.

Private First Class Frank P. Witek of the 1st Battalion, 9th Marines, 3rd Marine Division, takes several bold actions during several encounters with the enemy. Witek courageously exposes himself to enemy fire to destroy well-camouflaged positions at close range. When his platoon withdraws to consolidate positions with the company, Private First Class Witek stays behind to protect a severely wounded comrade, exchanging fire with the Japanese until the marine is evacuated. When his platoon comes under enemy fire, Witek attacks. He throws hand grenades and fires his rifle, until he is within only a few yards of the Japanese position. As he destroys the machine gun position, he is killed. For his heroic actions and extraordinary dedication to duty, Private First Class Witek will receive the Medal of Honor.

NEW GUINEA: The Ted Force (the 124th Infantry Regiment and a battalion of 169th Infantry Regiment) operates independently and attacks Japanese units wherever they are found behind the Driniumor River. They are resupplied by air and battle the enemy in heavy jungle.

FEAF B-25 Mitchells support ground forces on Biak. A-20 Havocs, P-47 Thunderbolts, P-38 Lightnings, and P-40s bomb Japanese troops.

B-24s bomb Yap and Woleai Atoll and targets at Boela on Ceram Island in the Moluccas.

August 4

ALEUTIANS: Eleventh Air Force P-38 Lightnings accompanied by one B-25 fly in support of a naval force near Massacre Bay on Attu Island in the Aleutians.

President Roosevelt departs Adak, Aleutians, on the heavy cruiser *Baltimore*, headed for Kodiak, Alaska.

CBI: Tenth Air Force B-25 Mitchells and P-51 Mustangs attack Japanese positions near Sahmaw in support of Allied ground forces.

In China, Fourteenth Air Force B-25 Mitchells bomb airfields at Lashio and Hsenwi. P-40s attack vehicles and troops at Tengehung. Other P-40s attack troops, logistics sites, river shipping, and vehicles around Tungting Lake and the Yangtze River.

ATLANTIC: JCS planners schedule the assaults on Leyte and Mindanao to begin on December 1, 1944. The attack on Formosa is scheduled for February 15, 1945. From Formosa, an air and sea blockade would be established while a build-up of forces for the invasion of the Japanese home islands is completed.

The British make a last effort to have forces marked for Dragoon remain in Italy.

ETO: Eighth Air Force sends 963 B-17s and 446 B-24 Liberators, escorted by 766 P-47 Thunderbolts, P-38 Lightnings, and P-51 Mustangs, to attack oil refineries, aircraft production facilities, and airfields in northern Germany. Fifteen bombers are lost and 413 are damaged. Aircrews report one confirmed kill and four probables. Aircrew losses are six killed, 12 wounded, and 143 missing. Fighter pilots report 38 confirmed kills, one probable in the air, and 13 confirmed kills on the ground. Fifteen fighters are lost and six are damaged. Two pilots are killed and 14 are reported missing. Another 78 B-24s attack an airfield and an oil refinery without loss.

An attack on marshaling yards and airfields in France involves 59 B-17s and 95 B-24s escorted by 35 P-47s and P-51s. A total of 29 bombers are damaged.

Four radio-controlled unserviceable B-17s are loaded with explosives and launched at V-weapon sites. This operation is called Aphrodite. The bombers are escorted by 16 P-47s and 16 P-51 Mustangs. None of the bombers hits the intended targets.

Nearly 70 P-47s fly a fighter-bomber mission against Plantlunne airfield. Pilots report 30 confirmed kills on the ground. One P-47 is lost and nine are damaged. The pilot is reported missing.

Ninth Air Force sends 62 A-20 Havocs and B-26 Marauders to attack railroad bridges, ammunition storage sites, and troop concentrations. P-47 and P-38 fighters attack German tanks, troops, and conduct dive-bombing attacks on fuel and ammunition storage sites.

MEDITERRANEAN: With the withdrawal of seven divisions for Dragoon, Field Marshal Sir Harold R. L. G. Alexander, commander of the 15th Army Group, currently has two armies, the British Eighth Army under Lieutenant General Sir Oliver Leese and the Fifth Army under Lieutenant General Mark W. Clark. The Fifth Army has IV Corps with three divisions commanded by Lieutenant General Willis D. Crittenberger and II Corps, also with three divisions, commanded by Major General Geoffrey Keyes. General Leese proposes an attack to seize Bologna, the major rail and road junction that supports the German Gothic Line defenses. Fifteenth Air Force supports the Red Army's request for support. A total of 70 P-38 Lightnings and P-51 Mustangs fly from Italy, attack targets near Focsani, Romania, and land at Frantic bases in Soviet Ukraine.

ITALY: The Germans have established defensive positions along the Arno River.

Twelfth Air Force B-25 Mitchells and B-26 Marauders attack bridges. A-20 Havocs and P-47 Thunderbolts attack convoys, bridges, gun positions, airfields, and roads. The harbor at Nice, France is also attacked.

SOUTHWEST PACIFIC AREA: U.S. submarine *Raton* attacks a cargo ship off Luzon. U.S. submarine *Ray* attacks a Japanese convoy in the Celebes Sea, sinking a cargo ship and avoiding a depth charge attack from an escort ship.

CENTRAL PACIFIC: Seventh Air Force B-25s from the Marshalls bomb Ponape Island.

The headquarters of the 30th Bombardment Group (Heavy) and the B-24s of the 27th, 38th, and 392nd Bombardment Squadrons (Heavy) redeploy from Kwajalein in the Marshalls to Saipan. The C-47s of the 9th Troop Carrier Squadron redeploy from Abemama Island in the Gilberts to Saipan.

Aircraft from TG 58.3 (Rear Admiral Alfred E. Montgomery) bomb airfields on Iwo Jima; aircraft from TG 58.1 (Rear Admiral Joseph J. Clark), together with four light cruisers and seven destroyers organized as TU 58.1.6 under Rear Admiral Laurance T. DuBose, attack a Japanese convoy in the Bonin Islands. A destroyer and collier are sunk by surface ships and aircraft sink four transports and damage two other vessels. One cargo ship is sunk by both gunfire and aircraft.

U.S. submarine *Sterlet* torpedoes and sinks two Japanese guardboats northwest of Chichi Jima.

CENTRAL PACIFIC, GUAM: The 307th Infantry Regiment of the 77th Infantry Division captures the crest of Mount Barrigada. The 3rd Marine Division and the 77th Infantry Division prepare to work in concert to clear the last major Japanese defenses. The marines will capture Finegayan, while the army will capture Yigo and Mount Santa Rosa.

Seventh Air Force B-25 Mitchells from Saipan conduct two attacks on Guam.

CENTRAL PACIFIC, TINIAN: Private First Class Robert L. Wilson of the 2nd Battalion, 6th Marines, 2nd Marine Division, is acting as the point for his squad clearing suspected Japanese positions. As he approaches a pile of rocks a Japanese grenade lands nearby. Shouting a warning, Private First Class Wilson covers the grenade with his body, shielding his comrades from the blast. For his heroic sacrifice Private First Class Wilson will receive the Medal of Honor.

NEW GUINEA: FEAF A-20 Havocs, P-47 Thunderbolts, P-38 Lightnings, and P-40s attack Japanese troops, east of the Driniumor River.

B-24s bomb Yap and Woleai Atoll and targets at Boela on Ceram Island in the Moluccas.

August 5
CBI: Tenth Air Force P-47 Thunderbolts attack targets of opportunity around Bhamo.

In China, Fourteenth Air Force B-25 Mitchells bomb Wanling. P-40s attack Tengchung and communications targets, troops, and trucks near Tungting Lake.

ETO: Eighth Air Force sends 215 B-17s escorted by 174 P-38 Lightnings and P-51 Mustangs to attack oil refineries and tank and aircraft production facilities in northern Germany. Three B-17s are lost and 189 are damaged. Aircrews report three confirmed kills and one probable. Aircrew losses are two killed, eight wounded, and 28 missing. Fighter pilots report 19 confirmed kills and one probable in the air and one confirmed kill on the ground. Four fighters are lost and six are damaged. One pilot is killed, one is wounded, and four are reported missing.

A total of 70 B-24 Liberators, escorted by 41 P-47 Thunderbolts, attack airfields. One bomber is lost and seven are damaged. Nine crewmen are reported missing. Fighter pilots report four confirmed kills.

Another attack by 426 B-17s and 452 B-24 Liberators escorted by 356 P-51s is launched on aircraft component production facilities and airfields in Germany. Nine bombers are lost and 280 are damaged. Aircrews report six confirmed kills and three probables. Aircrew losses are two killed, five wounded, and 15 missing. Two fighters are lost and eight are damaged. Two pilots are reported missing.

A total of 19 B-24s fly in support of Carpetbagger operations. During the night six B-17s drop leaflets over the Netherlands and France.

In France, Ninth Air Force establishes a headquarters element close to the 12th Army Group and the advance headquarters of the Allied Expeditionary Air Force (AEAF) to coordinate air operations to support the ground forces. Operational control of the headquarters of the 50th and 53rd Troop Carrier Wings of the IX Troop Carrier Command is passed to the Mediterranean Allied Air Force in preparation for Anvil-Dragoon. Over 300 A-20 Havocs and B-26 Marauders attack fuel storage sites, railroad bridges, and a marshaling yard. P-47 and P-38 fighters fly armed reconnaissance missions.

SOUTHWEST PACIFIC AREA: U.S. submarine *Cero* attacks a Japanese convoy off Mindanao and sinks an oiler in Davao Gulf.

PACIFIC: Fast Carrier Task Force is reorganized into First Fast Carrier Task Force, Pacific Fleet, commanded by Vice Admiral Marc A. Mitscher, and Second Fast Carrier Task Force, Pacific Fleet, commanded by Vice Admiral John S. McCain.

Aircraft from TG 58.1 (Rear Admiral Joseph J. Clark) and TG 58.3 (Rear Admiral Alfred E. Montgomery) and cruisers and destroyers of TU 58.1.6 (Rear Admiral Laurance T. DuBose) continue attacks on Chichi Jima and Haha Jima. Aircraft damage a fast transport off Chichi Jima. U.S. submarine *Barbel* torpedoes and sinks a Japanese cargo ship in the Bonins.

CENTRAL PACIFIC, GUAM: The 305th Infantry Regiment stops a Japanese tank and infantry counterattack.

Seventh Air Force B-25 Mitchells from Saipan make two bombing attacks on Japanese positions at Guam.

NEW GUINEA: FEAF P-39 Airacobras strafe barges around Geelvink Bay. B-24s bomb Yap and targets at Boela on Ceram Island in the Moluccas. B-25 Mitchells bomb targets in the Celebes and Sunda Islands.

Fifth Air Force B-25 Mitchells sink a Japanese cargo ship at the southern end of Celebes Island.

August 6

CBI: P-51 Mustangs and P-47 Thunderbolts attack targets at Mohnyin, Hopin, Bhamo, Myothit, Katha, Indaw, and other points in northern Burma.

In China, Fourteenth Air Force, P-40s attack Tengchung. P-40s and P-51 Mustangs attack trucks, troop assembly areas, and gun positions near Hengyang. Other P-40s attack river and road transportation around Changsha.

ETO: The Brittany Peninsula is cut off, isolating German garrisons in the port cities of Brest, St-Nazaire, St-Malo, and Lorient. Patton's VIII Corps is assigned the mission of reducing these garrisons. The XV Corps is intended as a pincer to surround German forces from the west by capturing Argentan and linking up with the Canadian First Army pressing from the east.

Eighth Air Force sends 568 B-17s and 445 B-24 Liberators, escorted by 472 P-38 Lightnings, P-47 Thunderbolts, and P-51 Mustangs, to attack oil refineries, airfields, aircraft production facilities, and industrial production targets in northern Germany. A total of 24 bombers are lost and 503 are damaged. Aircrews report two probable kills. Aircrew losses are 15 killed, 26 wounded, and 233 missing. Fighter pilots report 24 confirmed kills in the air and two on the ground. Four fighters are lost and four are damaged. One pilot is killed, one is wounded, and four are missing.

More than 70 B-17s escorted by 154 P-51s support Frantic operations, bombing aircraft production facilities in Poland and flying to bases in Soviet Ukraine. Aircrews report two probable kills. A total of 23 B-17s are damaged. Fighter pilots report seven confirmed kills and two probables. Four P-51s are lost and one is damaged. One pilot is killed and five are reported missing.

Another attack on V-weapon sites in the Pas-de-Calais area is conducted by 24 B-24s escorted by 24 P-47s. Nine B-24s are damaged.

A total of 36 B-24s fly in support of Carpetbagger operations. During the night seven B-17s drop leaflets over France.

Ninth Air Force sends A-20 Havocs and B-26 Marauders to attack fuel storage sites, railroad bridges, and ammunition storage areas. P-47 and P-38 fighters support ground forces.

The headquarters of the 474th Fighter Group and the P-38s of the 428th, 429th, and 430th Fighter Squadrons redeploy from England to France.

MEDITERRANEAN: Fifteenth Air Force sends over 700 B-17s and B-24 Liberators escorted by P-38 Lightnings and P-51 Mustangs to attack oil storage areas, railroad bridges in southern France, and a submarine pen at Toulon.

A total of 60 P-38 Lightnings and P-51 Mustangs fly from Frantic bases in the Soviet Ukraine, attack railroad targets in and around Bucharest and Ploeşti in Romania, and land at bases in Italy.

ITALY: Twelfth Air Force B-25 Mitchells and B-26 Marauders attack bridges in the Rhône valley. A-20 Havocs and P-47 Thunderbolts attack shipping near Genoa and La Spezia, as well as convoys, bridges, and roads. Twelfth Air Force B-17s and B-24 Liberators bomb the submarine pens at Toulon, sinking German submarines *U-471*, *U-952*, and *U-969*.

SOUTHWEST PACIFIC AREA: U.S. submarine *Rasher* torpedoes and sinks a Japanese cargo ship west of Luzon.

PACIFIC: U.S. submarine *Pintado* attacks a Japanese convoy, sinking a cargo ship and damaging escort vessel off the southwest coast of Kyushu.

CENTRAL PACIFIC: Seventh Air Force B-25 Mitchells from Saipan fly two bombing missions against Japanese positions on Guam. B-25s from the Marshals bomb Ponape Island and B-25s from the Gilberts attack Nauru Island in the Gilberts. B-24 Liberators from Kwajalein bomb Wotje Atoll.

NEW GUINEA: FEAF B-25 Mitchells, P-47 Thunderbolts, P-38 Lightnings, and P-40s support ground operations near Sarmi. B-24s bomb logistics facilities at Yap.

August 7

CBI: Tenth Air Force B-25 Mitchells destroy two bridges near Bhamo.

In China, Fourteenth Air Force P-40s attack targets at Hengyang, Changsha, and Tengchung.

ETO: On Hitler's orders, elements of five German armor and infantry divisions supported by aircraft begin a major counterattack that intends to split the First and Third Armies. Achieving surprise, the German advance six miles, intending to reach Avranches and stop Third Army by destroying the logistics depots in the rear of the American lines.

Combat Command B of the 3rd Armored Division stops a German attack. The 2nd Battalion of the 120th Infantry Regiment, 30th Infantry Division, at Mortain conducts a heroic defense at Hill 317 against German tanks. Isolated and resupplied by airdrops, the Americans stop every attack against them. The Germans also lose more than 100 tanks to Allied aircraft. The 35th and 4th Infantry Divisions along with the 2nd Armored Division are diverted to meet the attack. The VII Corps pushes from St-Sever.

General George S. Patton, Jr., moves three corps of the Third Army east to encircle the German army. The 6th Armored Division reaches Brest, traveling 200 miles in five days, but the defenses are too strong to conduct an attack. VIII Corps moves into Brittany to capture the port cities. Major General Wade H. Haislip's XV Corps advances toward LeMans, the main logistics base of the German army.

A communications zone headquarters is established in the ETO to organize the logistics bases at Cherbourg and at Omaha and Utah beaches and the lines of supply from those bases. The sustained air attacks prior to D-day have caused widespread destruction of the French railway and highway systems, preventing any efficient movement of supplies to the forward lines.

In response to a Red Army request for air support, 55 B-17s and 29 P-51 Mustangs supporting Frantic operations attack an oil refinery at Trzebina, Poland, and return to bases in Soviet Ukraine.

Eighth Air Force sends 337 B-17s escorted by 309 P-38 Lightnings and P-51s to attack airfields and bridges in France. Heavy cloud cover forces many bombers to abort the mission; 143 B-17s are damaged. Aircrew casualties are three wounded; fighter pilots report one confirmed kill.

More than 380 B-24 Liberators escorted by 94 P-51s and 34 P-47 Thunderbolts attack bridges, airfields, and production facilities in France. One B-24 is lost and 65 are damaged. Aircrew casualties are eight killed, one wounded, and 11 missing.

Nearly 300 P-47s and P-51s fly fighter-bomber missions against marshaling yards and railroads near Paris. Pilots report four confirmed kills on the ground. Three P-47s and two P-51s are lost and 11 fighters are damaged. Five pilots are reported missing.

During the night five B-17s drop leaflets over France.

The headquarters of IX Tactical Air Command supporting U.S. First Army and the headquarters of XIX Tactical Air Command supporting U.S. Third Army create mobile command posts to keep up with the rapid advance into France.

Ninth Air Force commander, Lieutenant General Lewis H. Brereton, is appointed commanding general of the First Allied Airborne Army.

Ninth Air Force sends nearly 400 A-20 Havocs and B-26 Marauders to attack bridges. P-47 and P-38 fighters attack German positions in support of ground forces.

MEDITERRANEAN: Fifteenth Air Force sends over 350 B-17s and B-24 Liberators escorted by P-38 Lightnings and P-51 Mustangs to attack oil facilities and airfields in Yugoslavia. Aircrews and fighters report 30 enemy aircraft shot down.

ITALY: Twelfth Air Force B-25 Mitchells and B-26 Marauders attack bridges in Italy and France. A-20 Havocs attack shipping targets at Genoa. P-47 Thunderbolts attack bridges, marshaling yards, and roads.

SOUTHWEST PACIFIC AREA: U.S. submarine *Bluegill* attacks a Japanese convoy and sinks a transport southwest of Mindanao. U.S. submarine *Guitarro* attacks a Japanese convoy and sinks an escort vessel off Luzon, then evades a depth-charging attack.

U.S. submarine *Puffer* torpedoes and sinks an auxiliary submarine chaser off southern Davao.

U.S. submarine *Sailfish* torpedoes and damages a Japanese cargo ship in Luzon Strait.

U.S. submarine *Seawolf* lands men and supplies at Tawi Tawi, in the Philippines.

PACIFIC: President Roosevelt arrives at Kodiak, Alaska, on the heavy cruiser USS *Baltimore*, then transfers to destroyer USS *Cummings*.

U.S. submarine *Croaker* torpedoes and sinks a Japanese light cruiser off Nagasaki, Kyushu, Japan.

U.S. submarine *Barbel* torpedoes and sinks a Japanese cargo vessel in the Bonins.

CENTRAL PACIFIC, GUAM: The 306th and 307th Infantry Regiments of the 77th Infantry Division attack and capture Yigo, clearing a Japanese roadblock. Shortly thereafter, the 306th Infantry stops a nighttime Japanese tank attack. The 307th Infantry Regiment, supported by naval gunfire, captures Mount Santa Rosa.

Seventh Air Force B-25 Mitchells from Saipan make two separate attacks on Japanese positions on Guam.

NEW GUINEA: FEAF B-24s bomb logistics facilities at Yap and airfields on Halmahera Island. Pilots report between 35 and 50 aircraft are destroyed or damaged. The P-47s of the 39th Fighter Squadron 35th Fighter Group redeploy from Nadzab to Noemfoor Island. The B-25 Mitchells of the 390th Bombardment Squadron (Medium) 42nd Bombardment Group (Medium) redeploy from the Russell Islands in the Solomons to Hollandia.

U.S. submarine *Sand Lance* is damaged by an air attack off north end of Celebes Island.